Schaefer Online Learning Center Website

Visit the Online Learning Center with PowerWeb, a companion website for Sociology, 8/e that offers students and instructors a variety of resources and activities (www.mhhe.com/schaefer8).

MULTIPLE-CHOICE QUIZZES

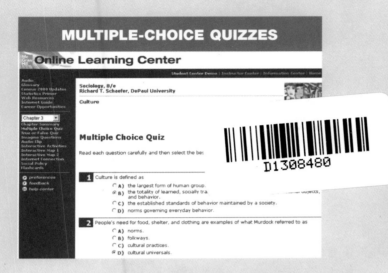

TRUE-FALSE QUIZZES

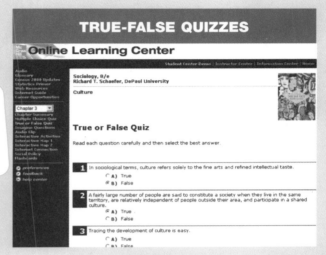

INTERACTIVE ACTIVITIES

The Cultural Time Capsule

In this chapter we have learned about the development of culture around the world. We have also learned that tracing the development of culture is not easy. Your task for this activity is to use your sociological imaginations and make assumptions about three material objects found in a cultural time capsule in the year 2500. These three objects are a CD, a cell phone, and a coin. Imagine that you know nothing about the culture from which these objects came. Using the space below, type out at least ten assumptions you might make about the culture that used these objects.

1.
2.
3.
4.
5.

SOCIAL POLICY EXERCISES

Online Learning Center

Sociology, 8/e
Richard T. Schaefer, DePaul University

Culture

Social Policy: How Americans Feel About Immigrants, Speaking English, and Teaching American Values in the Schools

In this chapter, you have learned about important elements of culture. One of these elements, language, is important because it both describes and shapes culture for us. In the United States today, many languages are spoken, although English is still the dominant one.

A recent survey asked people if they were worried that the United States is no longer an English-speaking nation (meaning that many languages are spoken by the diverse ethnic groups across the United States) and if they felt that immigrants should be required to learn English before they become citizens. To examine the results of this survey, visit http://www.publicagenda.org. From the homepage, select Immigration. Link to Quick Takes, and scroll down the page to Language. Examine each of the three graphs and answer the following questions:

CAREER OPPORTUNITIES

  Career Opportunities

Student Lounge

 Professionals and The Internet

As a student in the social sciences, you will make extensive use of the Internet regardless of the career you choose, and your range of possible careers is very broad. The career path you take will depend a lot on your personality and your values as well as your skills and education.

For some graduates, working with families in direct services is the most satisfying possible job option. Others of you will be most excited by being involved with policy shaping, or program evaluation. Some students will choose the "student career" a bit longer and enter social work or other graduate programs. Some will go directly to work in county or state agencies; while still others will use their education as a background to understand how social institutions such as public education or business organizations interact with individuals and with families. Yet others of you might seek education or training in areas quite different from direct service, such as management or marketing in the health field.

POWERWEB

IMPORTANT:

HERE IS YOUR REGISTRATION CODE TO ACCESS
YOUR PREMIUM McGRAW-HILL ONLINE RESOURCES.

For key premium online resources you need THIS CODE to gain access. Once the code is entered, you will be able to use the Web resources for the length of your course.

If your course is using **WebCT** or **Blackboard**, you'll be able to use this code to access the McGraw-Hill content within your instructor's online course.

Access is provided if you have purchased a new book. If the registration code is missing from this book, the registration screen on our Website, and within your WebCT or Blackboard course, will tell you how to obtain your new code.

Registering for McGraw-Hill Online Resources

To gain access to your McGraw-Hill web resources simply follow the steps below:

1. USE YOUR WEB BROWSER TO GO TO: **http://www.mhhe.com/schaefer8**
2. CLICK ON **FIRST TIME USER**.
3. ENTER THE REGISTRATION CODE* PRINTED ON THE TEAR-OFF BOOKMARK ON THE RIGHT.
4. AFTER YOU HAVE ENTERED YOUR REGISTRATION CODE, CLICK **REGISTER**.
5. FOLLOW THE INSTRUCTIONS TO SET-UP YOUR PERSONAL UserID AND PASSWORD.
6. WRITE YOUR UserID AND PASSWORD DOWN FOR FUTURE REFERENCE. KEEP IT IN A SAFE PLACE.

TO GAIN ACCESS to the McGraw-Hill content in your instructor's **WebCT** or **Blackboard** course simply log in to the course with the UserID and Password provided by your instructor. Enter the registration code exactly as it appears in the box to the right when prompted by the system. You will only need to use the code the first time you click on McGraw-Hill content.

Thank you, and welcome to your McGraw-Hill online Resources!

* YOUR REGISTRATION CODE CAN BE USED ONLY ONCE TO ESTABLISH ACCESS. IT IS NOT TRANSFERABLE.

0-07-248507-8 SCHAEFER: SOCIOLOGY, 8E

REGISTRATION CODE

babbington-58477172

SOCIOLOGY

Sociology Around the World

The countries that are identified on this map are cited in the book, either in the context of research studies or in relevant statistical data. Refer to the subject index for specific page references.

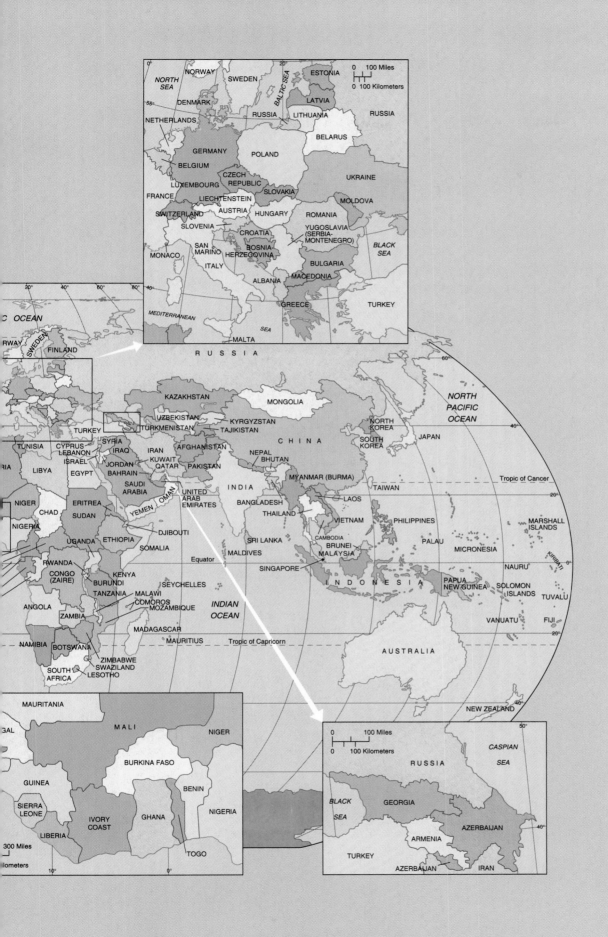

About the Author

Taking Sociology to Work

RICHARD T. SCHAEFER
Professor, DePaul University
B.A. Northwestern University
M.A., Ph.D. University of Chicago

Growing up in Chicago at a time when neighborhoods were going through transitions in ethnic and racial composition, Richard T. Schaefer found himself increasingly intrigued by what was happening, how people were reacting, and how these changes were affecting neighborhoods and people's jobs. His interest in social issues caused him to gravitate to sociology courses at Northwestern University, where he eventually received a B.A. in sociology.

"Originally as an undergraduate I thought I would go on to law school and become a lawyer. But after taking a few sociology courses, I found myself wanting to learn more about what sociologists studied, and fascinated by the kinds of questions they raised." This fascination led him to obtain his M.A. and Ph.D. in sociology from the University of Chicago. Dr. Schaefer's continuing interest in race relations led him to write his master's thesis on the membership of the Ku Klux Klan and his doctoral thesis on racial prejudice and race relations in Great Britain.

Dr. Schaefer went on to become a professor of sociology. He has taught introductory sociology for over 30 years to students in colleges, adult education programs, nursing programs, and even a maximum-security prison. Dr. Schaefer's love of teaching is apparent in his interaction with his students. "I find myself constantly learning from the students who are in my classes and from reading what they write. Their insights into the material we read or current events that we discuss often become part of future course material and sometimes even find their way into my writing."

Dr. Schaefer is author of the eighth edition of *Sociology* (McGraw-Hill, 2003). Dr. Schaefer is also the author of *Racial and Ethnic Groups,* now in its ninth edition, and *Race and Ethnicity in the United States,* second edition. His articles and book reviews have appeared in many journals, including *American Journal of Sociology; Phylon: A Review of Race and Culture; Contemporary Sociology; Sociology and Social Research; Sociological Quarterly;* and *Teaching Sociology.* He served as president of the Midwest Sociological Society in 1994–1995.

Dr. Schaefer's advice to students is to "look at the material and make connections to your own life and experiences. Sociology will make you a more attentive observer of how people in groups interact and function. It will also make you more aware of people's different needs and interests—and perhaps more ready to work for the common good, while still recognizing the individuality of each person."

EIGHTH EDITION

SOCIOLOGY

Richard T. Schaefer

DePaul University

Boston   Burr Ridge, IL   Dubuque, IA   Madison, WI   New York   San Francisco   St. Louis
Bangkok   Bogotá   Caracas   Kuala Lumpur   Lisbon   London   Madrid   Mexico City
Milan   Montreal   New Delhi   Santiago   Seoul   Singapore   Sydney   Taipei   Toronto

Dedication

To my wife, Sandy

McGraw-Hill Higher Education

A Division of The **McGraw-Hill** *Companies*

SOCIOLOGY

Published by McGraw-Hill, a business unit of The McGraw-Hill Companies, Inc., 1221 Avenue of the Americas, New York, NY 10020. Copyright © 2003, 2001, 1998, 1995, 1992, 1989, 1986, 1983, by The McGraw-Hill Companies, Inc. All rights reserved. No part of this publication may be reproduced or distributed in any form or by any means, or stored in a database or retrieval system, without the prior written consent of The McGraw-Hill Companies, Inc., including, but not limited to, in any network or other electronic storage or transmission, or broadcast for distance learning. Some ancillaries, including electronic and print components, may not be available to customers outside the United States.

This book is printed on acid-free paper.

domestic   1 2 3 4 5 6 7 8 9 0 QWV/QWV 0 9 8 7 6 5 4 3
international   1 2 3 4 5 6 7 8 9 0 QWV/QWV 0 9 8 7 6 5 4 3 2

ISBN   0-07-292197-8 (student edition)
ISBN   0-07-248512-4 (annotated instructor's edition)

Publisher : *Phillip A. Butcher*
Senior sponsoring editor: *Sally Constable*
Director of development and media technology: *Rhona Robbin*
Senior marketing manager: *Daniel M. Loch*
Producer, Media technology: *Jessica Bodie*
Project manager: *Diane M. Folliard*
Lead production supervisor: *Lori Koetters*
Freelance design coordinator: *Gino Cieslik*
Supplement producer: *Nathan Perry*
Photo research coordinator: *Judy Kausal*
Photo researcher: *Elyse Rieder*
Cover design: *Gino Cieslik*
Interior design: *Kay Fulton*
Typeface: *10/12 Minion*
Compositor: *GTS Graphics, Inc.*
Printer: *Quebecor World Versailles Inc.*

The cover symbolizes the vibrant, rich, and fascinating diversity of social behavior presented in this book. Professor Schaefer urges readers to become "attentive observers of how people in groups interact and function . . . aware of people's different needs and interests—and perhaps more ready to work for the common good, while still recognizing the individuality of each person."

Library of Congress Cataloging-in-Publication Data

Schaefer, Richard T.
    Sociology / Richard T. Schaefer—8th ed.
        p.   cm.
    Includes bibliographical references and index.
    ISBN 0-07-248507-8 (student ed. : alk. paper) — ISBN 0-07-248512-4 (annotated
    instructor's ed. : alk. paper) — ISBN 0-07-119909-8 (international ed.)
    1. Sociology. 2. Social problems. 3. United States—Social policy. I. Title.
    HM586 .S33 2003
    301—dc21

                                                            2002021908

INTERNATIONAL EDITION ISBN 0-07-119909-8
Copyright © 2003. Exclusive rights by The McGraw-Hill Companies, Inc., for manufacture and export. This book cannot be re-exported from the country to which it is sold by McGraw-Hill. The International Edition is not available in North America.

www.mhhe.com

Contents in Brief

Contents

1 The Sociological Perspective

1 UNDERSTANDING SOCIOLOGY 2

2 SOCIOLOGICAL RESEARCH 30

② Organizing Social Life

③ CULTURE 58

④ SOCIALIZATION 82

⑤ SOCIAL INTERACTION AND SOCIAL STRUCTURE 106

**6 GROUPS AND
ORGANIZATIONS** 132

7 THE MASS MEDIA 156

**8 DEVIANCE AND
SOCIAL CONTROL** 180

③ Social Inequality

12 STRATIFICATION BY GENDER 300

13 STRATIFICATION BY AGE 324

4 Social Institutions

17 GOVERNMENT AND POLITICS 426

18 THE ECONOMY AND WORK 448

19 HEALTH AND MEDICINE 470

23 SOCIAL CHANGE AND TECHNOLOGY 572

List of Boxes

Sociology in the Global Community

Research in Action

Social Inequality

 Taking Sociology to Work

Social Policy Sections

List of Maps

Mapping Life NATIONWIDE

Mapping Life WORLDWIDE

Preface

"What has sociology got to do with me or with my life?" Any student might well ask this question before signing up for a sociology course. Here are some things for that student to consider: Are you influenced by what you see on television? Do you use the Internet? Do you know someone with a tattoo? Did you neglect to vote in the last election? Are you familiar with binge drinking on campus? Do you use alternative medicine? These are just a few of the everyday life situations described in this book that sociology can shed light on, revealing patterns and meanings.

Sociology also looks at large social issues. It seeks to unravel the factors behind the transfer of thousands of jobs from the United States to the developing countries of the Third World. It assesses the ways in which the availability of computer technology and the Internet may increase or reduce inequality. Sociology investigates the social forces that promote prejudice, the persistence of slavery today, the issues surrounding bilingual education, the social networks established by women, the process of growing old in different cultures, and the factors that lead someone to join a social movement and work for social change. In the aftermath of September 11, 2001, sociology has been called on to explain the social consequences of the terrorist attacks—how people coped following the disasters, how they reacted to minority group members, how rumors spread through the mass media. These issues, along with many others, are of great interest to me, but it is the sociological explanations for them that I find especially compelling. The introductory sociology class provides the ideal laboratory in which to confront our society and our global neighbors.

After more than 30 years of teaching sociology to students in colleges, adult education programs, nursing programs, an overseas program based in London, and even a maximum-security prison, I am firmly convinced that the discipline can play a valuable role in teaching critical thinking skills. Sociology can help students to better understand the workings of their own lives as well as of their society and other cultures. The distinctive emphasis on social policy found in this text shows students how to use the sociological imagination in examining such public policy issues as sexual harassment, the AIDS crisis, welfare reform, the death penalty, and privacy and censorship in an electronic age.

My hope is that, through their reading of this book, students will begin to think like sociologists and will be able to use sociological theories and concepts in evaluating human interactions and institutions. From the introduction of the concept of sociological imagination in Chapter 1—which draws on a study that a colleague and I conducted of the food bank system of the United States—this text stresses the distinctive way in which sociologists examine and question even the most familiar patterns of social behavior.

The first seven editions of *Sociology* have been well received; it is currently used in more than 500 colleges and universities. *Sociology,* Eighth Edition, brings the research into the twenty-first century and introduces a number of features designed to appeal to today's students. One thing that remains unchanged, however, is the steady focus on three especially important points:

- **Comprehensive and balanced coverage of theoretical perspectives throughout the text.** Chapter 1 introduces, defines, and contrasts the functionalist, conflict, and interactionist perspectives. We explore their distinctive views of such topics as television (Chapter 1), social institutions (Chapter 5), deviance (Chapter 8), the family (Chapter 14), education (Chapter 16), and health and medicine (Chapter 19).

- **Strong coverage of issues pertaining to gender, age, race, ethnicity, and class in all chapters.** Examples of such coverage include social policy sections on bilingualism (Chapter 3), welfare (Chapter 9), immigration (Chapter 11), and affirmative action (Chapter 18); a chapter opener on the "beauty myth" (Chapter 12); boxes on urban poverty and joblessness (Chapter 9), prejudice against Arab Americans and Muslim Americans (Chapter 11), domestic violence (Chapter 14), the role of grandparents (Chapter 14), and squatter settlements and gated communities (Chapter 20); and sections on the social construction of race (Chapter 11), the treatment of women in education (Chapter 16), and the contingency or temporary workforce (Chapter 18).

- **Use of cross-cultural material throughout the text.** Chapter 10 treats the topic of stratification from a global perspective. This chapter introduces world systems analysis, dependency theory, and modernization theory, and examines multinational corporations and the global economy. Every chapter presents global material and makes use of cross-cultural examples. Among the topics examined are:

Neglect of children in Eastern European orphanages (Chapter 4)

The global "McDonaldization of society" (Chapter 6)

The status of women around the world (Chapter 12)

Issues of aging around the world (Chapter 13)

Transmission of cultural values (Chapter 16)

Affirmative action in South Africa (Chapter 18)

Homelessness worldwide (Chapter 20)

Population policy in China (Chapter 21)

The global disconnect in technology (Chapter 23)

I take great care to introduce the basic concepts and research methods of sociology and to reinforce this material in all chapters. The most recent data are included, making this book more current than all previous editions.

 ## Special Features

Integrated Learning System

The text, its accompanying SocWorld CD-ROM, and the Online Learning Center website work together as an integrated learning system to bring the theories, research findings, and basic concepts of sociology to life for students. Offering a combination of print, multimedia, and web-based materials, this comprehensive system meets the needs of instructors and students with a variety of teaching and learning styles. The material that follows describes the many features of the text, CD-ROM, and Online Learning Center, as well as the supplementary materials that support those resources.

Poster Art

Each chapter opens with a reproduction of a poster or piece of graphic art that illustrates a key theme or concept of the chapter. Accompanying captions help readers to grasp the relevance of the artwork to the chapter.

Chapter Opener

The chapter openers convey the excitement and relevance of sociological inquiry by means of lively excerpts from writings of sociologists and others who explore sociological topics. These openers are designed to expose students to vivid writing on a broad range of topics and to stimulate their sociological imagination. For example, Chapter 3 begins with Horace Miner's classic take on Nacirema culture. Chapter 5 opens with a description of Zimbardo's mock prison study. Cornel West's musings on being a single father introduce Chapter 14. Later, in Chapter 21, Kai Erikson reflects on the value of sociology in understanding the connection between the population and the environment.

Chapter Overview

The opener is followed by a chapter overview that describes the content of the chapter in narrative form.

Key Terms

I have given careful attention to presenting understandable and accurate definitions of each key term. These terms are highlighted in bold italics when they are introduced. A list of key terms and definitions in each chapter—with page references—follows the end of the chapter. In addition, the glossary at the end of the book includes the definitions of the textbook's key terms and the page references for each term.

Research in Action

These sections, which appear in almost every chapter, present sociological findings on topics such as women's social networks, school-related violence, divorce, and why young people don't vote.

Sociology in the Global Community

These sections, which appear in almost every chapter, provide a global perspective on topics such as domestic violence, slavery, racism, and population growth.

Social Inequality

New to this edition, these sections illustrate various types of social stratification. Featured topics include discretionary justice, the Latino middle class, and the "stained glass ceiling" that hovers over female clergy.

Taking Sociology to Work

These sections profile individuals who majored in sociology and use its principles in their work. While these people work in a variety of occupations and professions, they all share a conviction that their background in sociology has been valuable in their careers.

Illustrations

The photographs, cartoons, figures, and tables are closely linked to the themes of the chapters. The maps, titled Mapping Life Nationwide and Mapping Life Worldwide, show the prevalence of social trends. A world map highlighting those countries used as examples in the text appears in the front matter to this book.

Social Policy Sections

The social policy sections that close all but one of the chapters play a critical role in helping students to think like sociologists. They apply sociological principles and theories to important social and political issues being debated by policymakers and the general public. New to this edition are sections on labor unions (Chapter 6), the media and violence (Chapter 7), and world population policy (Chapter 21). All the policy sections now present a global perspective.

Cross Reference Icons

When the text discussion refers to a concept introduced earlier in the book, an icon in the margin points the reader to the exact page.

Chapter Summaries

Each chapter includes a brief numbered summary to aid students in reviewing the important themes.

Critical Thinking Questions

After the summary, each chapter includes critical thinking questions that will help students analyze the social world in which they participate. Critical thinking is an essential element in the sociological imagination.

Additional Readings

An annotated list of books concludes each chapter; these works have been selected as additional readings because of their sociological soundness and their accessibility for introductory students. A list of sociological journals and periodicals is included as well.

Internet Connection Exercises

Exercises in each chapter take students online to analyze social issues relevant to chapter topics. Throughout the text an icon signals where more information and/or updates are available on the book's website.

Endpapers

The front endpaper features a guide to the Online Learning Center website, as well as a description of *SocWorld*, the CD-ROM available with this book. The back endpaper summarizes the applications used in the book to illustrate sociology's major theoretical approaches.

What's New in the Eighth Edition?

The most important changes in this edition include the following (refer as well to the chapter-by-chapter list of changes on pp. xxiv–xxvii and to the *Visual Preview* on pp. xxxi–xxxiv):

Content

- Chapter on the mass media explores their significance for contemporary society.
- "Social Inequality" boxes highlight an important subject of analysis for sociologists today.
- Sections on the feminist perspective provide expanded coverage of this viewpoint.
- Material in several chapters provides a sociological analysis of the events of September 11 and their aftermath (e.g., new material on disaster behavior, new discussion of hate crimes against Muslims and Arab Americans, new material on how U.S. students learned about 9/11, how they responded, and new material on rumors that followed the attacks on the Pentagon and World Trade Center).
- Chapter-opening excerpts drawn from sociological writings convey the excitement and relevance of sociological inquiry (e.g., *Black Picket Fences* by Mary Pattillo-McCoy, *Nickel and Dimed* by Barbara Ehrenreich, and *Sidewalk* by Mitchell Duneier).

Pedagogy

- "Imagine" sections within each chapter pose questions designed to stimulate students' sociological imagination, to enable them to apply major concepts and issues to their own lives.
- "Think About It" captions encourage students to think critically about information presented in maps, graphs, and tables.
- Nine new U.S. and global maps illustrate important trends and developments, bringing the total number of maps in this edition to 24.
- A "Technology Resources" section at the end of each chapter directs students to learning and study tools found on the Online Learning Center website and in the SocWorld CD-ROM that accompanies the new edition.

Supplements

- New Online Learning Center website features interactive quizzes, chapter introductions recorded by the author, social policy exercises, interactive activities, interactive maps, Census 2000 Update links, readings selected by sociologists to correlate with specific chapters, and more!
- SocWorld CD-ROM allows students to instantly explore various topics and concepts through an assortment of video clips (including footage of author Richard T. Schaefer in Singapore), website links, interactive quizzes, and other learning tools.

Also included are audio introductions to each of the book excerpts that open the chapters and additional information about those excerpts and their authors. (SocWorld is packaged free with each new copy of the text.)

- Violence and Terrorism PowerWeb site is accessible through a link on the Online Learning Center for Sociology (described elsewhere in this preface). McGraw-Hill created this unique website in response to the events of September 11 and their aftermath to help instructors and students integrate coverage of terrorism into their courses. This website includes the full texts of more than 60 thought-provoking articles on terrorism, drawn from both the scholarly and the popular press.

- A 90-minute VHS videotape features brief 5–10 minute clips from NBC News that dramatize sociological concepts, serve as lecture launchers, and generate class discussion.

This edition has been thoroughly updated. It includes the most recent data and research findings, many of which were published in the last three years. Recent data from the Census Bureau, Bureau of Labor Statistics, Current Population Reports, the Population Reference Bureau, the World Bank, the United Nations Development Programme, and the Centers for Disease Control have been incorporated.

A more complete, chapter-by-chapter listing of the most significant new material in this edition follows.

● What's New in Each Chapter?

CHAPTER 1 Understanding Sociology

- Addition of feminist view as a major perspective
- Research in Action box: Looking at Sports from Four Theoretical Perspectives
- Expanded section on the sociological imagination, with additional examples and photos
- Material on Ida Wells-Barnett, early Black feminist theorist
- Section on "The Significance of Social Inequality"

CHAPTER 2 Sociological Research

- Research example used throughout chapter: influence of education on income (with new figures)
- Addition of feminist perspective to discussion of ethnographic research
- Discussion of web-based surveys and the limitations of Internet surveying
- Taking Sociology to Work box on chief research officer at Nielsen Media Research

- Expanded discussion of NHSLS study and its implications
- Research in Action box: Framing Survey Questions about Interracial Friendships

CHAPTER 3 Culture

- Example of cultural diffusion (Starbucks in China) and discussion of globalization
- Sociology in the Global Community box: Cultural Sensitivity on the Beat
- Example of terrorist cells in discussion of counterculture

CHAPTER 4 Socialization

- Chapter-opening excerpt from *Black Picket Fences: Privilege and Peril Among the Black Middle Class* by Mary Pattillo-McCoy
- Discussion of face-saving measures taken by the unemployed in Japan
- Expanded discussion of the negative social influences Black families must overcome
- Expanded discussion of the negative influences some parents have on their children
- Expanded discussion of the effects of teenage employment
- Statistics on childcare workers' wages and employee turnover rates
- Statistics on the cost of childcare to families

CHAPTER 5 Social Interaction and Social Structure

- Additional global material on disability as a master status
- Expanded and updated discussion of social networks and technology
- Material on increase in e-mail due to anthrax scare and mobilization of service members overseas
- Updates on AIDS crisis and attempts to lower cost of treatment in developing countries

CHAPTER 6 Groups and Organizations

- Use of TV show *Survivor* as example of coalition building (with photo)
- Sociology in the Global Community box: Management, Russian Style
- Social policy section: The State of the Unions (with map of union membership)

CHAPTER 7 The Mass Media

Note: This is a new chapter, blending entirely new material with material about the media taken from other chapters in the previous edition.

- Chapter-opening excerpt from David Demers' *Global Media: Menace or Messiah?*
- A look at the media from functionalist, conflict, feminist, and interactionist perspectives
- Social Inequality box: The Color of Network TV from Chapter 10 of 7th edition
- Discussion of audience interaction and behavior and composition
- Section examining the media industry, including the effects of media concentration and of the media's global reach
- Extensive discussion of Internet use throughout chapter
- Sociology in the Global Community box, "Good Morning, Bhutan!" about effects of introduction of television in Bhutan
- Social policy section on media violence

CHAPTER 8 Deviance and Social Control

- Chapter-opening excerpt on victimless crime
- Sociology in the Global Community box: Singapore: A Nation of Campaigns
- Research in Action box: Defining Deviancy Down: From Professional Wrestling to the Backyards
- Social Inequality box: Discretionary Justice
- Addition of section on feminist perspective to "Explaining Deviance"
- Taking Sociology to Work box on victim witness specialist
- Material on McVeigh execution in social policy section

CHAPTER 9 Stratification and Social Mobility in the United States

- Chapter-opening excerpt from Barbara Ehrenreich, *Nickel and Dimed: On (Not) Getting By in America*
- Section on the impact of race on social mobility.
- Updated Sociology in the Global Community box on slavery in the twenty-first century
- Updated Social Policy section on welfare in North America and Europe
- Updated statistics on personal income, poverty, and the welfare rolls

CHAPTER 10 Social Inequality Worldwide

- Section on globalization
- Social Inequality box: Stratification in Japan (formerly a Research in Action box)
- Updated and expanded coverage of Wallerstein's world systems analysis

- Coverage of the government campaign to reduce poverty in China
- Coverage of the Pan-Cordillera Women's Network for Peace and Development in the Philippines
- Mapping Life Worldwide: The Borderlands (between the United States and Mexico)
- Coverage of the risks of immigration
- Coverage of the UN-sponsored World Conference Against Racism

CHAPTER 11 Racial and Ethnic Inequality

- Chapter-opening poster on racial profiling
- Chapter-opening excerpt from Helen Zia, *Asian American Dreams: The Emergence of an American People*
- Sociology in the Global Community box: The Empire Strikes Back: Racism in Great Britain
- Social Inequality box: The Latino Middle Class
- Section on Vietnamese Americans
- Discussion of slave reparations debate
- Updated Research in Action box on prejudice against Arab Americans and Muslim Americans
- Updated discussion of marriage patterns among Jewish Americans
- Updated discussion of multiracial ancestry based on 2000 Census statistics
- Discussion of racist fringe groups, with new Mapping Life Nationwide
- Mapping Life Nationwide: Census 2000: The Image of Diversity

CHAPTER 12 Stratification by Gender

- Updated Sociology in the Global Community box on the head scarf and the veil
- Updated Research in Action box on female hockey players and male nurses
- Updated statistics on women in politics, business management, and the labor force
- Updated coverage of abortion law

CHAPTER 13 Stratification by Age

- Chapter-opening excerpt from *Tuesdays with Morrie* by Mitch Albom
- Research in Action box: Crime Against the Elderly
- Discussion of the hospice movement
- Discussion of the ageist portrayal of children by the media
- Updated discussion of bias against aging workers (worsened by the recession)
- Updated discussion of age at retirement, including recent reversal of trend toward early retirement

- Updated discussion of the practice of euthanasia in the Netherlands
- Updated coverage of Oregon's Death with Dignity Act

CHAPTER 14 The Family and Intimate Relationships

- Section on the feminist view of the family
- Research in Action box: The Lingering Impact of Divorce
- Updated Sociology in the Global Community box on domestic violence
- Coverage of the delay in mate selection and marriage, with figure showing percentage of young people who are married in selected countries
- Coverage of changing family patterns among Latinos
- Coverage of grandparents who live with their grandchildren
- Table showing foreign-born adoptees by top ten countries of origin
- Updated and extended figure showing trends in marriage and divorce, 1920–2000
- Coverage of the social and political effects of singlehood
- Coverage of civil union (Vermont)

CHAPTER 15 Religion

- Section on world religions, with summary table
- Sociology in the Global Community box: Jainism in India and the United States
- Social Inequality box: The Stained Glass Ceiling
- Bar graph: Belief in God Worldwide
- Discussion of religious responses to the terrorist attacks of September 11, 2001

CHAPTER 16 Education

- Section on educational testing, with map showing spending on tests by state
- Taking Sociology to Work box on business owner and former regent, Texas State University
- Coverage of foreign students, with table showing countries of origin
- Coverage of gay and lesbian students, with figure showing risks they face
- Figure showing school choice and voucher programs by state

CHAPTER 17 Government and Politics

- Section on political activism on the Internet (converted from media box)
- Social Inequality box: Gender Quotas at the Ballot Box

- Updated Sociology in the Global Community box: Terrorist Violence
- Updated table showing political party preferences in the United States
- Updated Mapping Life Worldwide showing percentage of women in national legislatures

CHAPTER 18 The Economy and Work

- Social Inequality box: Working Women in Nepal
- Updated coverage of private business in China
- Updated coverage of worker alienation: incidence of desk rage
- Coverage of the total number of hours Americans work per year
- Updated coverage of e-commerce and e-lancers
- Updated coverage of Microsoft's temporary workforce
- Updated Sociology in the Global Community box: The Worldwide Jobs-Skills Mismatch
- Updated coverage of affirmative action

CHAPTER 19 Health and Medicine

- Mapping Life Worldwide: Average Life Expectancy
- Research in Action box on an epidemiological study of nuns
- Discussion of study of differential treatment of Black and White Medicare beneficiaries
- Figure on percentage of those without health insurance, by income level and by race and ethnicity
- Discussion of *curanderismo,* Hispanic folk healing practices
- Material on continuing neglect of women by medical establishment
- Mapping Life Nationwide: Availability of Physicians by State
- Discussion of "corporatization" of health care in social policy section

CHAPTER 20 Communities and Urbanization

- Chapter-opening excerpt from Mitchell Duneier, *Sidewalk*
- Section on asset-based community development (ABCD), illustrated by example of relief effort organized in Middletown, NJ, on behalf of families of residents who died in attack on World Trade Center
- Research in Action box on "Store Wars"—the controversy over the effects of superstores on surrounding communities
- Table showing the ten most populous megalopolises in the world, 1970 and 2015 (projected)

- Expanded and updated discussion of urban sprawl
- Graph showing ethnic diversity in the suburbs, 1990 and 2000
- Discussion of the economic effects of prison construction on rural communities

CHAPTER 21 Population and the Environment

- Social Policy section: World Population Policy
- Figure comparing population structure of Afghanistan and the United States
- Mapping Life Nationwide: Where Americans Moved in the 1990s, showing population change by county
- Discussion of the Kyoto Protocol and global warming
- Mapping Life Worldwide: The Impact of Global Warming
- Discussion of the quality of basic water supplies
- Taking Sociology to Work box on research coordinator, Safer Yards
- Updated discussion of the demographic effects of AIDS
- Updated and expanded discussion of U.S. population growth

CHAPTER 22 Collective Behavior and Social Movements

- Case study of disaster behavior following collapse of the World Trade Center
- Discussion of rumors that followed attacks on the Pentagon and World Trade Center
- Expanded discussion of natural versus technological disasters
- Expanded discussion of the bureaucratization of social movements
- Updated discussion of public opinion polls
- Discussion of controversy within the gay and lesbian movement over legalization of homosexual marriages

CHAPTER 23 Social Change and Technology

- Chapter-opening excerpt from Debora L. Spar, *Ruling the Waves: Cycles of Discovery, Chaos, and Wealth from the Compass to the Internet*
- Section on bioterrorism
- Discussion of the preservation of dying languages on the Internet
- Discussion of online gender switching
- Updated discussion of electronic surveillance of the workforce
- Updated discussion of Internet usage by income and racial/ethnic group

Support for Instructors and Students

PRINT RESOURCES

Annotated Instructor's Edition

An annotated instructor's edition (AIE) of the text, prepared by Lynn Newhart of Rockford College in Illinois, offers page-by-page annotations to assist instructors in using textbook material.

Instructor's Resource Manual

This manual, prepared by Richard T. Schaefer and Lynn Newhart, provides sociology instructors with detailed key points, additional lecture ideas (among them alternative social policy issues), class discussion topics, essay questions, topics for student research (along with suggested research materials for each topic), and suggested additional readings (unlike those in the text itself, these are meant for instructors rather than students). Media materials are suggested for each chapter, including videotapes and films.

Two Test Banks

The two test banks that accompany the text were written by Jurgen Hilke of Frederick Community College in Maryland and Clayton Steenberg of Arkansas State University. Multiple-choice and true-false questions are included for each chapter; they will be useful in testing students on basic sociological concepts, application of theoretical perspectives, and recall of important factual information. Correct answers and page references are provided for all questions.

In addition to the printed format, the test banks are available on a CD-ROM for computerized test construction.

Study Guide

The study guide, prepared by Cheryl Johnson of West Virginia University, includes standard features such as detailed key points, definitions of key terms, multiple-choice questions, fill-in questions, and true–false questions. Perhaps the most distinctive feature is the social policy exercise, which is closely tied to the social policy section in the text. All study guide questions are keyed to specific pages in the textbook, and page references are provided for key points and definitions of key terms.

In addition to the questions in the study guide, students can test their mastery of the subject matter by taking the quizzes on the SocWorld CD-ROM and on the Online Learning Center website. Students therefore have three different sets of questions to draw on for review.

Primis Customized Readers

An array of first-rate readings are available to adopters in a customized electronic database. Some are classic articles from the sociological literature; others are provocative pieces written especially for McGraw-Hill by leading sociologists.

McGraw-Hill Dushkin

Any of the Dushkin publications can be packaged with this text at a discount: Annual Editions, Taking Sides, Sources, Global Studies. For more information, please visit the website at **http://www.dushkin.com.**

DIGITAL AND VIDEO RESOURCES

VHS Videotape

A new 90-minute VHS videotape includes brief 5-10 minute excerpts from NBC News that dramatize sociological concepts, serve as lecture launchers, and generate class discussion. It is accompanied by a booklet that offers tips for using the excerpts in the classroom, including suggested discussion questions.

PageOut: The Course Website Development Center

All online content for *Sociology,* Eighth Edition, is supported by WebCT, eCollege.com, Blackboard, and other course management systems. Additionally, McGraw-Hill's PageOut service is available to get you and your course up and running online in a matter of hours, at no cost. PageOut was designed for instructors just beginning to explore web options. Even the novice computer user can create a course website with a template provided by McGraw-Hill (no programming knowledge necessary). To learn more about PageOut, ask your McGraw-Hill representative for details, or fill out the form at **www.mhhe.com/pageout.**

SocWorld CD-ROM

SocWorld, an exciting new CD-ROM, allows students to instantly explore various topics and concepts using an assortment of video clips (among them, footage of author Richard T. Schaefer in Singapore). The accompanying audio introductions include additional information about the book excerpts that open each chapter of *Sociology,* Eighth Edition, and the authors who wrote those excerpts. SocWorld also contains website links, interactive quizzes, and other learning tools. It is packaged free with each new copy of the text.

Online Learning Center Website

The Online Learning Center website that accompanies this text, **www.mhhe.com/schaefer8,** offers a rich array of resources for instructors and students. Here you will find the author's audio introductions to each chapter, as well as interactive quizzes and maps, social policy exercises, PowerPoint slides, Census 2000 updates, chapter glossaries, vocabulary flashcards, PowerWeb, and additional resources. It's also possible to link directly to Internet sites from the Online Learning Center. And you can use any of the material from the Online Learning Center in a course website that you create using PageOut.

PowerWeb

PowerWeb is a resource that is available on the Online Learning Center website. This password-protected site for the introductory sociology course offers instructors and students referenced course-specific web links and articles, student study tools, weekly updates, and additional resources.

In addition to the PowerWeb site for sociology, a special PowerWeb site on violence and terrorism is available from a link on the Online Learning Center. Created in response to the events of September 11 and their aftermath, this unique website helps instructors and students to integrate coverage of terrorism into their courses. Not just another long list of URLs, the site includes the full texts of thought-provoking articles on terrorism from the scholarly and popular press, as well as weekly updates and a 24-hour newsfeed.

Accompanying both the PowerWeb site for sociology and the site for violence and terrorism are correlation guides that link relevant articles to specific chapters in the Eighth Edition of *Sociology,* and provide suggested questions and activities. These correlation guides can be found on the Online Learning Center website. For further information about PowerWeb, visit the following site: **http://mhhe/NewMedia/dushkin/index.html# powerweb.**

PowerPoint Slides

Adopters of *Sociology* can also receive a set of 500 PowerPoint slides developed especially for this edition by Richard T. Schaefer and Thom Holmes. The slides are included on the Instructor's Resource CD-ROM (described below) and in the Instructor's Center of the Online Learning Center website. The set includes bulleted lecture points, graphs, and maps. Instructors are welcome to generate overhead transparencies from the slides if they wish to do so.

Computerized Test Bank CD-ROM

The content of both Test Banks that accompany this text is available on a dual-platform CD-ROM for Windows and Macintosh users.

Instructor's Resource CD-ROM

This CD-ROM includes the contents of the instructor's resource manual, test banks, PowerPoint slides, and more for instructors' convenience in customizing multimedia lectures.

Primis Online

Professors can customize this book by selecting from it only those chapters they want to use in their courses. Primis Online allows users to choose and change the order of chapters, as well as to add readings from McGraw-Hill's vast database of content. Both custom-printed textbooks and electronic eBooks are available. To learn more, contact your McGraw-Hill sales representative, or visit our website at **www.mhhe.com/primis/online**.

⬤ Acknowledgments

Virginia Joyner and Elizabeth Morgan collaborated with me on the eighth edition, bringing fresh insight into presenting the sociological imagination. Robert P. Lamm had been a part of some of the earlier editions of *Sociology*, and his contributions are still apparent.

I deeply appreciate the contributions to this book made by my editors. Rhona Robbin, director of development and media technology, at McGraw-Hill, has continually and successfully challenged me to make each edition better than its predecessor.

I have received strong support and encouragement from Phillip Butcher, publisher; Sally Constable, senior sponsoring editor; and Dan Loch, senior marketing manager. Additional guidance and support were provided by Alyson DeMonte and Amy Shaffer, editorial coordinators; Kim Hooker and Diane Folliard, project managers; Gino Cieslik, designer; Jessica Bodie, media producer; Elyse Rieder, photo editor; and Elsa Peterson and Judy Broder, permissions editors. I would like to express appreciation

to DePaul University students Todd Fuist and Jennifer Michals for their assistance with the preparation of material for this book.

I would also like to acknowledge the contributions of the following individuals: Lynn Newhart of Rockford College in Illinois for her work on the instructor's resource manual and the book's website, for developing the Internet exercises in the text, and for her contributions to the annotated instructor's edition; Clayton Steenberg of Arkansas State University for his work on the first test bank; Jurgen Hilke of Frederick Community College in Maryland for his work on the second test bank; Cheryl Johnson of West Virginia University for her work on the study guide; and Thom Holmes, Anne Sachs, and Ryan Hawkins for their work on the SocWorld CD-ROM.

As is evident from these acknowledgments, the preparation of a textbook is truly a team effort. The most valuable member of this effort continues to be my wife, Sandy. She provides the support so necessary in my creative and scholarly activities.

I have had the good fortune to be able to introduce students to sociology for many years. These students have been enormously helpful in spurring on my own sociological imagination. In ways I can fully appreciate but cannot fully acknowledge, their questions in class and queries in the hallway have found their way into this textbook.

Richard T. Schaefer
schaeferrt@aol.com

Academic Reviewers

This edition continues to reflect many insightful suggestions made by reviewers of the first seven hardcover editions and the four paperback brief editions. The current edition has benefited from constructive and thorough evaluations provided by sociologists from both two-year and four-year institutions.

Cynthia D. Anderson
Iowa State University

Phyllis L. Baker
University of Northern Iowa

Bob Bolin
Arizona State University

Judith Brake
Ozarks Technical Community College

Valerie S. Brown
Cuyahoga Community College

Maria I. Bryant
College of Southern Maryland

Harry F. Dahms
Florida State University

Kay L. Decker
Northwestern Oklahoma State University

Joseph D. Diaz
Southwest State University

Lynda Dickson
University of Colorado, Colorado Springs

Robert Faulkner
University of Massachusetts, Amherst

Jan Fiola
Minnesota State University

Susan Schuller Friedman
California State University–Los Angeles

Robert F. Fulton
Edison Community College

Richard Garnett
Marshall University

Shahin Gerami
Southwest Missouri State University

Christopher Hale
Sacred Heart University

Lillian Holloman
Prince Georges Community College

James R. Hunter
Indiana University–Purdue University at Indianapolis

Cheryl Johnson
West Virginia University

Harold Kerbo
California Polytechnic State University

Diane Levy
University of North Carolina, Wilmington

Stephen C. Light
SUNY–Plattsburgh

Rebecca Matthews
University of Iowa

Carla J. McDaniel
Pulaski Technical College

Dan Monti
Boston University

Hart M. Nelsen
Pennsylvania State University

David Newman
Johnson & Wales University

Kevin R. Ousley
East Carolina University

Timothy J. Owens
Purdue University

Leo W. Pinard II
California Polytechnic State University

Phyllis Puffer
Prestonsburg Community College

Elizabeth Ribet
San Francisco State University

Ferris J. Ritchey
University of Alabama at Birmingham

Robert Rosenwein
Lehigh University

Katherine Rosier
Louisiana State University

Janice M. Schall
Riverside Community College

Richard L. Smith
Oakland Community College

William L. Smith
Georgia Southern University

Sarah A. Soule
University of Arizona

Kenneth L. Stewart
Angelo State University

Professor Steven Swinford
Montana State University

John Tenuto
College of Lake County

Jim Thomas
Northern Illinois University

Anthony C. Trevelino
Camden County College

Jonathan VanGeest
University of Illinois at Chicago

John Robert Warren
University of Washington

Earl Wright
University of Central Florida

The eighth edition of *Sociology* continues its tradition of teaching students how to think critically about society and their own lives from a wide range of classical and contemporary sociological perspectives.

Intriguing Chapter Openers

Chapter openers convey the excitement and relevance of sociological inquiry by means of lively excerpts from writings of sociologists and others who explore sociological topics.

New Distinctive Chapter on the Mass Media

Chapter 7, "The Mass Media" explores the significance of the media for contemporary society, examining topics such as the media's global reach, the lack of diversity on network TV, the growing use of the Internet, and the impact of media violence.

Helpful Chapter Overviews

Chapter overviews provide a bridge between the chapter-opening excerpt and the content of the chapter.

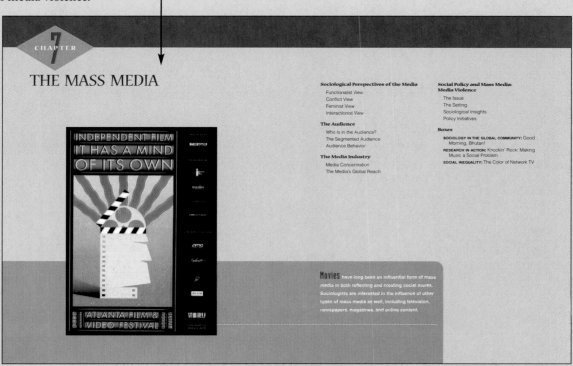

New Thought-Provoking "Social Inequality" Boxes

These boxes on topics such as the Latino middle class, discretionary justice, and stratification in Japan highlight an important area of analysis for sociologists today.

Timely "Sociology in the Global Community" Boxes

These boxes provide a global perspective on topics such as terrorist violence, slavery in the twenty-first century, and racism in Great Britain.

Stimulating "Research in Action" Boxes

These boxes present sociological findings on topics such as prejudice against Arab Americans and Muslim Americans, the lingering impact of divorce, and why young people don't vote.

Social class is a reliable predictor of a person's health. Many of the patients at this public health clinic suffer from chronic illnesses that are directly related to their low incomes, poor diet, and stressful living conditions.

tion highway," and so yet another aspect of social inequality has emerged—the *digital divide*. The poor, minorities, and those who live in rural communities and inner cities are not getting connected at home or at work. A recent government study found that despite falling computer prices, the Internet gap between the haves and have-nots has not narrowed. For example, while 42 percent of all households have a computer, these computers are in about 80 percent of households with family incomes over $75,000 and in fewer than 16 percent in which families make less than $20,000. As wealthier people start to buy high-speed Internet connections, they will be able to take advantage of even more sophisticated interactive services and the digital divide will grow even larger (National Telecommunications Information Administration 1999).

Wealth, status, and power may not ensure happiness, but they certainly provide additional ways of coping with one's problems and disappointments. For this reason, the opportunity for advancement is of special significance to those who are on the bottom of society looking up. These people want the rewards and privileges that are granted to high-ranking members of a culture.

(as well as race) on mortality. Ill health among the poor only serves to increase the likelihood that the poor will remain impoverished (Haywood et al. 2000).

Like disease, crime can be particularly devastating when it attacks the poor. According to the 2000 National Crime Victimization Survey, people in low-income families were more likely to be assaulted, raped, or robbed than were the most affluent people. Furthermore, if accused of a crime, a person with low income and status is likely to be represented by an overworked public defender. Whether innocent or guilty, the accused may sit in jail for months, unable to raise bail (Rennisson 2001).

Even the administration of state lotteries underscores differences in life chances. A lottery participant is six times more likely to be struck by lightning than to win the jackpot, yet states target low-income residents in their lottery promotions. Lottery terminals are more heavily concentrated in poor neighborhoods than in wealthy communities. Lottery advertisements appear most frequently at the beginning of each month, when Social Security and public assistance checks arrive. Based on studies of lottery purchases, state lottery executives view the poor as more likely than the affluent to spend a high portion of their earnings for the very unlikely chance of becoming an instant millionaire (Nibert 2000; Novak and Schmid 1999).

Some people have hoped that the Internet revolution would help level the playing field by making information and markets uniformly available. Unfortunately, however, not everyone is able to get onto the "informa-

Imagine
Imagine a society in which there are no social classes—no differences in people's wealth, income, and life chances. What would such a society be like? Would it be stable, or would its social structure change over time?

Social Mobility

Ronald Reagan's father was a barber, and Jimmy Carter began as a peanut farmer, yet each man eventually achieved the most powerful and prestigious position in our country. The rise of a child from a poor background to the presidency—or to some other position of great prestige, power, or financial reward—is an example of social mobility. The term *social mobility* refers to movement of individuals or groups from one position of a society's stratification system to another. But how significant—how frequent, how dramatic—is mobility in a class society such as the United States?

Figure 11-3
Census 2000: The Image of Diversity

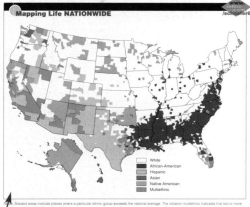

Mapping Life NATIONWIDE

☐ White
■ African-American
☐ Hispanic
☐ Asian
■ Native American
■ Multiethnic

Note: Shaded areas indicate places where a particular ethnic group exceeds the national average. The notation multiethnic indicates that two or more minority groups exceed the national average.
Source: Frey 2001a: 20–21.

Think About It
The United States is a diverse nation. Why, in many parts of the country, can't people see that diversity in their own towns?

the history of slavery in the United States. Whereas many other subordinate groups had little wealth and income, as sociologist W. E. B. Du Bois (1909) and others have noted, enslaved Blacks were in an even more oppressive situation because, by law, they could not own property and could not pass on the benefits of their labor to their children. Today, increasing numbers of

African Americans and sympathetic Whites are calling for *slave reparations* to compensate for the injustices of forced servitude. Reparations could include official expressions of apology from governments such as the United States, ambitious programs to improve African Americans' economic status, or even direct payments to descendants of slaves.

One unmistakable pattern in mate selection is that the process appears to be taking longer today than in the past. A variety of factors, including concerns about financial security and personal independence, has contributed to this delay in marriage. Most people are now well into their 20s before they marry, both in the United States and in other countries (see Figure 14-2).

Aspects of Mate Selection

Many societies have explicit or unstated rules that define potential mates as acceptable or unacceptable. These norms can be distinguished in terms of endogamy and exogamy. *Endogamy* (from the Greek *endon*, "within") specifies the groups within which a spouse must be found

Figure 14-2
Percentage of People Aged 20 to 24 Ever Married, Selected Countries

Country		Men/Women	Percentage
Australia		Men	10.6
		Women	21.6
Canada		Men	10.8
		Women	25.1
Egypt		Men	11.9
		Women	56.1
Finland		Men	5.1
		Women	11.7
Israel		Men	32.4
		Women	39.5
Mexico		Men	38.9
		Women	54.6
Poland		Men	22.9
		Women	52.1
United States		Men	19.3
		Women	33.2

Source: United Nations Population Division 2001.

Think About It
Why is the percentage of young women who are married particularly high in Egypt, Mexico, and Poland? Particularly low in Finland?

and prohibits marriage with others. For example, in the United States, many people are expected to marry within their own racial, ethnic, or religious group and are strongly discouraged or even prohibited from marrying outside the group. Endogamy is intended to reinforce the cohesiveness of the group by suggesting to the young that they should marry someone "of our own kind."

By contrast, *exogamy* (from the Greek *exo*, "outside") requires mate selection outside certain groups, usually one's own family or certain kinfolk. The *incest taboo*, a social norm common to virtually all societies, prohibits sexual relationships between certain culturally specified relatives. For people in the United States, this taboo means that we must marry outside the nuclear family. We cannot marry our siblings, and in most states we cannot marry our first cousins.

Endogamous restrictions may be seen as preferences for one group over another. In the United States, such preferences are most obvious in racial barriers. Until the 1960s, some states outlawed interracial marriage. Nevertheless, the number of marriages between African Americans and Whites in the United States has increased more than six times in recent decades, jumping from 51,000 in 1960 to 307,000 in 1999. Moreover, 25 percent of married Asian American women and 12 percent of married Asian American men are married to a person who is not of Asian descent. Marriage across ethnic lines is even greater among Hispanics; 27 percent of all married Hispanics have a non-Hispanic spouse. While all these examples of racial exogamy are impressive, endogamy is still the social norm in the United States (Bureau of the Census 1998a, 2000a:51).

Interracial unions force a society to reconsider its definitions of race and ethnicity. In Chapter 11, we noted that race is socially constructed in the United States and around the world. But with increasing proportions of children in this country coming from biracial or multiracial backgrounds, traditional definitions of race and ethnicity will become less relevant. Several voluntary associations representing mixed-race children requested that the census offer a new category of "multiracial" or "biracial," so that people would no longer be forced to define themselves as solely "White," "Black," "Asian," or "American Indian." In the end it was decided to let people check off several categories they felt applied to them, but not to provide the "multiracial" or "biracial" classification (Schaefer 2002).

The Love Relationship

Whatever else "love" is, most people would agree it is complicated. Listen to what a Yale University junior has to say on the subject:

New "Imagine" Sections

These sections within each chapter pose questions designed to stimulate students' sociological imagination. They prompt the students to figure out how major concepts and issues apply to their own lives.

Expanded Map Program

Two kinds of maps—"Mapping Life Nationwide" and "Mapping Life Worldwide"—are featured throughout the text. Interactive versions of many of these maps with accompanying questions appear on the book's Online Learning Center website.

New "Think About It" Caption Feature

These captions, which accompany many of the book's maps, graphs, and tables, encourage students to think critically about information presented in illustrative materials.

SOCIAL POLICY AND RELIGION

Religion in the Schools

www.mhhe.com/schaefer8

The Issue

Should public schools be allowed to sponsor organized prayers in the classroom? How about reading Bible verses? Or just a collective moment of silence? Can public school athletes offer up a group prayer in a team huddle? Should students be able to initiate voluntary prayers at school events? Should a school be allowed to post the Ten Commandments in a hallway? Each of these situations has been an object of great dissension among those who see a role for prayer in the schools and those who want to maintain a strict separation of church and state.

Another controversy centers on the teaching of theories about the origin of humans and the universe. Mainstream scientific thinking holds that humans evolved over billions of years from one-celled organisms, and that the universe came into being 15 billion years ago as a result of a "big bang." But these theories are challenged by people who hold to the biblical account of the creation of humans and the universe some 10,000 years ago—a viewpoint known as ***creationism.*** Creationists want their theory taught in the schools as the only one, or at the very least, as an alternative to the theory of evolution.

Who has the right to decide these issues? And what is considered the "right" decision? Religion in the schools constitutes one of the thorniest issues in U.S. public policy today.

The Setting

The issues just described go to the heart of the First Amendment's provisions on religious freedom. On the one hand, the government is required to protect the right to practice one's religion, but on the other hand, it cannot take any measures that would seem to "establish" one religion over another (the church/state separation).

In the key case of *Engle v. Vitale,* the Supreme Court ruled in 1962 that the use of nondenominational prayer in New York schools was "wholly inconsistent" with the First Amendment's prohibition against government establishment of religion. In finding that such organized school prayer violated the Constitution—even when no student was required to participate—the Court argued, in effect, that promoting religious observance was not a legitimate function of government or education. Subsequent Court decisions allow *voluntary* school prayer by students, but forbid school officials to *sponsor* any prayer or religious observance at school events. Despite these rulings, many public schools still regularly lead their students in prayer recitations or Bible reading (Firestone 1999).

The controversy over whether the biblical account of creation should be presented in school curricula recalls the famous "monkey trial" of 1925. In this trial, high school biology teacher John T. Scopes was convicted of violating a Tennessee law making it a crime to teach the scientific theory of evolution in public schools. Creationists today have gone beyond espousing fundamentalist religious doctrine; they attempt to reinforce their position regarding

How, when, and where should prayer be allowed in public schools? These students in Annandale, Virginia, celebrate National Day of Prayer *outside* their high school.

Taking Sociology to Work

STACEY KARP:
President of San Francisco Chapter of NOW (National Organization for Women)

www.mhhe.com/schaefer8

Stacey Karp got involved with NOW when she took a semester off from the University of Wisconsin to work with the San Francisco chapter. After graduating in 1996, she moved to the Bay Area and continued to volunteer for NOW—and soon found herself in the president's position. The work is unpaid for the most part, but Karp feels the experience she is gaining is invaluable.

"My job is to oversee the entire chapter, with its 1,200 members; to set policies; and to be the spokesperson for those policies." In the course of a day, Karp will typically write press releases, attend government hearings, lobby elected officials, talk to constituents, and, if necessary, organize a protest of some sort. One protest Karp participated in was directed against the Promise Keepers, an organization dedicated to having men take responsibility for their families. According to Karp, "in reality the PK is about having men be in *control* of their families—having men make all the decisions and having women be submissive."

Karp chose sociology as her major because she's always been interested in people. "It was a great way to be able to study people, to understand what statistics mean, and to learn how to take action to involve people." A sociology of gender course got Karp interested in women's issues, which then led her to minor in women's studies.

Karp's advice to students: If you are interested in sociology, don't be concerned about what kind of career your degree will lead to. "Pretty much *everything* has to do with sociology. It's all about the study of people and how our society works."

Let's Discuss

1. What would a sociology major bring to the leadership of a political organization such as NOW that a major in political science or management would not?
2. If you held Stacey Karp's position, on which women's issues would you concentrate most? Why?

sexual harassment to pornography to welfare, has fallen out of favor. Both women and men prefer to express their views on these complex issues individually rather than under a convenient umbrella like "feminism." Still, feminism is very much alive in the growing acceptance of women in nontraditional roles and even the basic acknowledgment that a married mother not only can be working outside the home but also perhaps belongs in the labor force. A majority of women say that given the choice, they would prefer to work outside the home rather than stay home and take care of a house and family, and about one-quarter of women prefer Ms. to Miss or Mrs. (Bellafante 1998; Geyh 1998).

The women's movement has undertaken public protests on a wide range of issues. Feminists have endorsed passage of the equal rights amendment, government subsidies for child care (see Chapter 4), affirmative action for women and minorities (see Chapter 18), federal legislation outlawing sex discrimination in education (see Chapter 16), greater representation of women in government (see Chapter 17), and the right to legal abortions (discussed in the social policy section of this chapter). The Taking Sociology to Work box on page 000 describes the efforts of one member of the women's movement, Stacey Karp, president of the San Francisco chapter of NOW.

Minority Women: Double Jeopardy

Many women experience differential treatment not only because of gender but because of race and ethnicity as well. These citizens face a "double jeopardy"—that of subordinate status twice defined. A disproportionate share of this low-status group are also impoverished, so that the double jeopardy effectively becomes a triple jeopardy. The litany of social ills continues for many if we consider old age, ill health, disabilities, and the like.

Feminists have addressed themselves to the particular needs of minority women. The question for African American women, Latinas, Asian American women, and others appears to be whether they should unify with their "brothers" against racism or challenge them for their sexism. One answer is that, in a truly just society, both sexism and racism must be eradicated (C. Epstein 1999).

The discussion of gender roles among African Americans has always provoked controversy. Advocates of Black nationalism contend that feminism only distracts women from full participation in the Black struggle. The existence of feminist groups among Blacks, in their view, simply divides the Black community and thereby serves the dominant White society. By contrast, Black feminists such as Florynce Kennedy argue, in turn, that little is to be gained by adopting or maintaining the gender-role divisions of

Technology Resources

Internet Connection

www.mhhe.com/schaefer8 *Note: While all the URLs listed were current as of the printing of this book, these sites often change. Please check our website* ***(http://www.mhhe.com/schaefer8)*** *for updates and hyperlinks to this exercise and additional exercises.*

1. Zero-Population Growth (ZPG) offers a cyber examination of the issues raised in your chapter. To learn more about the consequences and issues surrounding continued population growth, visit their website (**http://www.zpg.org/**). When you first log on, be sure to take note of the estimated "World Population" and "U.S. Population" figures and track how much time you spend on the site. Imagine that you have to present a report to your class on this organization by examining the following questions.
   (a) Write down the estimated world population and the estimated U.S. population.
   (b) What are the goals of ZPG?
   (c) What kinds of activities or events does ZPG sponsor? How do these events help the organization achieve its goals?
   (d) How does the organization's perspectives compare to those offered by Reverend Thomas Robert Malthus as detailed in your text (see pages 000–000)?
   (e) What new legislation or current technological advances are having an impact on population growth?
   (f) Examine the ZPG fact sheet. Which statistic or other information do you think is important to include in your report to the class? Why?
   (g) Can you identify any nations or parts of the world as being in either the pretransition stage the transition stage, or the posttransition stage?
   (h) Return to the homepage for the site and click on your browser's Refresh or Reload button to bring up the page anew. During the time that you were on the site, how much of an increase was there to the "World Population" and "U.S. Population" figures? What is your reaction to this increase considering what you have learned on the site and in this chapter?
2. Today, environmental activists are working to preserve the environment through organizations such as Greenpeace. Log onto the Greenpeace website and take a virtual tour of this organization's worldwide environmental efforts (**http://www.greenpeace.org/**).
   (a) When did Greenpeace first form?
   (b) What role have the Internet and computers played in the organization?
   (c) What are the overall goals of Greenpeace? What are some of the environmental problems the organization is trying to alleviate and call attention to?
   (d) What "Campaign Events" does the organization sponsor? How do these events help Greenpeace achieve its goals?
   (e) What images and themes do the photographs on the site present?
   (f) Be sure to utilize the "Greenpeace Worldwide" box. Choose at least three different nation-based sites to visit. What common concerns and environmental issues are shared by these three areas of the world? What problems or issues are unique to each area?
   (g) Which environmental problem do you consider to be the most pressing? What can be done to resolve the problem?

Online Learning Center www.mhhe.com/schaefer8

OLC

If you are interested in how Americans feel about the environment, you will want to visit the student center at the Online Learning Center at **www.mhhe.com/schaefer8.** Link to "How Americans Feel About . . ." You will read about three alternative approaches to protecting the environment and view colorful graphs and pie charts showing you whether the Americans surveyed thought the environment would be better, worse, or the same in four years. You can also find out what people your age thought about the long-term future of the environment.

Distinctive Social Policy Sections

These discussions provide a sociological perspective on contemporary social issues such as welfare reform, global immigration, and affirmative action. These sections provide a global view of the issues, are organized around a consistent heading structure to make the material more accessible, and include questions designed to stimulate critical thinking about issues being explored.

Motivational "Taking Sociology to Work" Boxes

"Taking Sociology to Work" boxes profile individuals who majored in sociology and use its principles in their work.

Helpful Technology Resources

One to three Internet Connection exercises at the end of each chapter take students online to analyze social issues relevant to chapter content. Web icons featured throughout the book signal that the related information and exercises can be found on the book's website. Brief descriptions of specific resources on the Online Learning Center website appear after the Internet Connection exercise(s) to encourage readers to visit the book's website.

UNDERSTANDING SOCIOLOGY

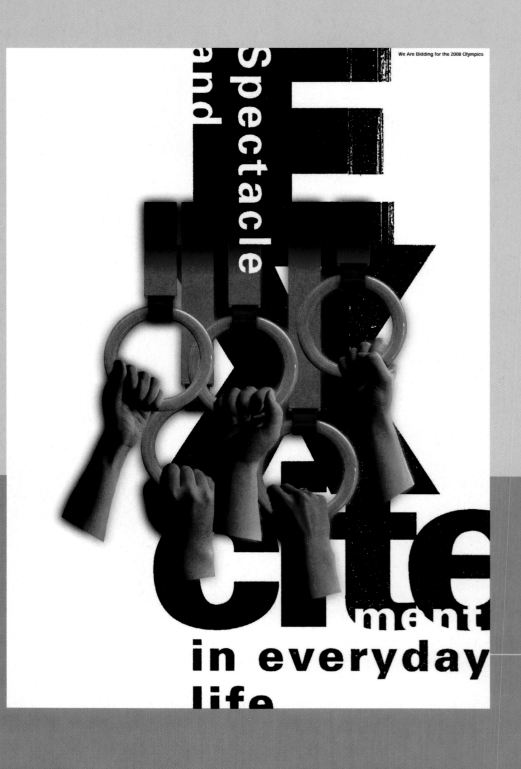

Spectacle and

Excitement

in everyday life

We Are Bidding for the 2008 Olympics

Sociology places us in the context of groups, cultures, and societies. People interact in all three of these settings in the Olympic games. This poster promotes the bid of Osaka, Japan, for the 2008 Summer Olympics.

I first walked into the Blue Mosque in the spring of 1996, when I came to accompany a friend getting her first tattoo. Before entering the clean, comfortable, and friendly shop, I had never thought about getting permanent body art myself. In fact, I had specifically promised my family that I would never become tattooed. After watching my friend go through the experience, I changed my mind and began wondering what forms of body modification I could sport myself. The shop's congenial atmosphere made it easy to return several times while choosing my own piercings and eventually my own tattoo. During my visits, I formed friendships with all the artists, and started dating and eventually married the shop's owner, Lefty. Our home became a stopping ground for tattooists traveling through town and a social center for the shop. . . .

*   *   *

My tattoo recreational life became a research interest after Lefty and I took a vacation to California. Renting a car and roaming the California coastline, we visited a score of tattoo shops, talked about the meaning of tattoos in society, and noted the many changes taking place in the tattoo industry. At the end of one of these conversations, Lefty mentioned that someone should do a study chronicling these changes. As a graduate student in Sociology looking for a dissertation topic, I quickly stepped up to the research task and Lefty willingly assumed the responsibility of key informant. . . .

*   *   *

As a tattooist's wife and a shop regular, I gained a unique view of this social world. Over the two-year participant observation study, I visited the shop between one hundred to two hundred times and was present during thousands of conversations between the tattoo artists at home and at social occasions. . . .

*   *   *

While at home and during social functions, I focused on the social world of professional tattooists while listening to daily conversations regarding their interactions with clients, their hopes, their frustrations, and their goals. The first time tattooees at the Blue Mosque were a unique set made up equally of men and women, ranging in age (18–60) more than heavily tattooed clients of the shop, and were more likely to be middle or upper middle class. My observations reflect the largely conventional, middle class experience of getting a first tattoo. *(Irwin 1999)* ■ 💿

Additional information about this excerpt and about those that open each subsequent chapter can be found on the SocWorld CD-ROM that accompanies this text.

What makes tattooing an appropriate subject for study in sociology? Uniting all sociological studies is their focus on *patterns* of human behavior. Katherine Irwin's tattoo research, for example, tracked the dramatic change in what it meant to get a tattoo in the 1990s, as opposed to earlier periods, when tattooing was primarily associated with fringe groups like biker gangs, punk rockers, and skinheads. First-time tattoo clients of the 1990s, Irwin found, increasingly fit the image of avant-garde or hip individuals, seeking to make a statement about their identities but not to cut themselves off from mainstream society. By continuing to interact with that society, whether as students, or employees, or just members of conventional families, they were in fact making tattooing appear less unconventional. The tattoo has gradually become a badge of trendy social status, instead of a symbol of outcast status (Irwin 2001).

Sociologists are not concerned with what one individual does or does not do, but with what people do as members of a group or interacting with one another, and what that means for the individuals and for society as a whole. Tattooing is, in fact, a subject that sociologists can study in any number of ways. They might examine its history (going back as far as 30,000 years) or its use in different groups and cultures. One study, for example, specifically looks at how the tattoos of prison gang members communicate their status,

rank, and personal accomplishments. Another focuses on the emergence of Christian tattoo parlors, which offer images of Christ or banners that blaze "Born Again" (Gale 1999; Mascia-Lees and Sharpe 1992; Phelan and Hunt 1998).

As a field of study, sociology is extremely broad in scope. You will see throughout this book the range of topics sociologists investigate—from suicide to TV viewing habits, from Amish society to global economic patterns, from peer pressure to pickpocketing techniques. Sociology looks at how others influence our behavior, how major social institutions like the government, religion, and the economy affect us, and how we ourselves affect other individuals, groups, and even organizations.

This chapter will explore the nature of sociology as a field of inquiry and an exercise of the "sociological imagination." How did sociology develop? In what ways does it differ from other social sciences? Why should we use our sociological imagination?

We'll look at the discipline as a science and consider its relationship to other social sciences. We will evaluate the contributions of three pioneering thinkers—Émile Durkheim, Max Weber, and Karl Marx—to the development of sociology. Next we will discuss a number of important theoretical perspectives used by sociologists, and then we'll examine practical applications of the discipline for human behavior and organizations. Finally, we will consider the ways sociology helps us to develop our sociological imagination. ■

● What Is Sociology?

Sociology is the systematic study of social behavior and human groups. It focuses primarily on the influence of social relationships on people's attitudes and behavior and on how societies are established and change. This textbook deals with such varied topics as families, the workplace, street gangs, business firms, political parties, genetic engineering, schools, religions, and labor unions. It is concerned with love, poverty, conformity, discrimination, illness, technology, and community.

The Sociological Imagination

In attempting to understand social behavior, sociologists rely on an unusual type of creative thinking. C. Wright Mills described such thinking as the *sociological imagination*—

an awareness of the relationship between an individual and the wider society. This awareness allows all of us (not just sociologists) to comprehend the links between our immediate, personal social settings and the remote, impersonal social world that surrounds us and helps to shape us (Mills [1959] 2000).

A key element in the sociological imagination is the ability to view one's own society as an outsider would, rather than only from the perspective of personal experiences and cultural biases. Consider something as simple as the practice of eating while walking. In the United States we think nothing of seeing people consuming ice cream cones or sodas or candy bars as they walk along. Sociologists would see this as a pattern of acceptable behavior because others regard it as acceptable. Yet sociologists need to go beyond one culture to place the practice in perspective. This "normal" behavior is quite unacceptable in some other parts of the world. For example, in Japan people do not eat while walking. Streetside sellers and vending machines dispense food everywhere, but the Japanese will stop to eat or drink whatever they buy before they continue on their way. In their eyes, to engage in another activity while eating shows disrespect for the food preparation, even if the food comes out of a vending machine.

The sociological imagination allows us to go beyond personal experiences and observations to understand broader public issues. Unemployment, for example, is unquestionably a personal hardship for a man or woman without a job. However, C. Wright Mills pointed out that when unemployment is a social problem shared by millions of people, it is appropriate to question the way that a society is structured or organized. Similarly, Mills advocated using the sociological imagination to view divorce not simply as the personal problem of a particular man or woman, but rather as a societal problem, since it is the outcome of many marriages. And he was writing this in the 1950s, when the divorce rate was but a fraction of what it is today (Horowitz 1983).

Sociological imagination can bring new understanding to daily life around us. Since 1992, sociologists David Miller and Richard Schaefer (this textbook's author) have studied the food bank system of the United States, which distributes food to hungry individuals and families. On the face of it, food banks seem above reproach. After all, as

Miller and Schaefer learned in their research, more than one out of four children in the United States are hungry. One-third of the nation's homeless people report eating one meal per day or less. What could be wrong with charities redistributing to pantries and shelters food that used to be destined for landfills? In 2000, for example, Second Harvest, a food distribution organization, distributed 1.5 billion pounds of food from hundreds of individual and corporate donors to more than 50,000 food pantries, soup kitchens, and social service agencies.

Many observers would uncritically applaud the distribution of tons of food to 26 million needy Americans. But let's look deeper. While supportive of and personally involved in such efforts, Miller and Schaefer (1993) have drawn on the sociological imagination to offer a more probing view of these activities. They note that powerful forces in our society—such as the federal government, major food retailers, and other large corporations—have joined in charitable food distribution arrangements. Perhaps as a result, the focus of such relief programs is too restricted. The homeless are to be fed, not housed; the unemployed are to be given meals, not jobs. Relief efforts

The sociological imagination allows us to look at everyday life and other cultures in different ways. Take music, for example. Shown here are Miao men in China playing traditional wind instruments and Papua New Guinea drummers in traditional tribal dress. Sociologists, using their sociological imagination, would look at the choices of instruments and expression of tone and rhythm represented by the traditional music of these two cultures. They would ask: What might have influenced these choices? What effect do the different forms of music have on those who hear it? For what purposes is the music used in these societies?

assist hungry individuals and families without challenging the existing social order (for example, by demanding a redistribution of wealth). Of course, without these limited successes in distributing food, starving people might assault patrons of restaurants, loot grocery stores, or literally die of starvation on the steps of city halls and across from the White House. Such critical thinking is typical of sociologists, as they draw on the sociological imagination to study a social issue—in this case, hunger in the United States (Second Harvest 2001; Vladimiroff 1998).

The sociological imagination is an empowering tool. It allows us to look beyond a limited understanding of things to see the world and its people in a new way and through a broader lens than we might otherwise use. It may be as simple as understanding why a roommate from Tennessee prefers country music to hip hop, or it may open up a whole different way of understanding whole populations in the world. For example, in the aftermath of the terrorist attacks on the United States in 2001, many citizens wanted to understand how Muslims throughout the world perceived their country, and why. From time to time this textbook will offer you the chance to exercise your own sociological imagination in a variety of situations. We'll begin with one that may be close to home for you.

Imagine

You attend a rock concert one night and a religious service the next morning. What differences would you see in how the two audiences behaved and in how they responded to the leader? What might account for these differences?

Sociology and the Social Sciences

Is sociology a science? The term **science** refers to the body of knowledge obtained by methods based on systematic observation. Just like other scientific disciplines, sociology engages in organized, systematic study of phenomena (in this case, human behavior) in order to enhance understanding. All scientists, whether studying mushrooms or murderers, attempt to collect precise information through methods of study that are as objective as possible. They rely on careful recording of observations and accumulation of data.

Of course, there is a great difference between sociology and physics, between psychology and astronomy. For this reason, the sciences are commonly divided into natural and social sciences. **Natural science** is the study of the physical features of nature and the ways in which they interact and change. Astronomy, biology, chemistry, geology, and physics are all natural sciences. **Social science** is the study of various aspects of human society. The social sciences include sociology, anthropology, economics, history, psychology, and political science.

These social science disciplines have a common focus on the social behavior of people, yet each has a particular orientation. Anthropologists usually study past cultures and preindustrial societies that continue today, as well as the origins of men and women. Economists explore the ways in which people produce and exchange goods and services, along with money and other resources. Historians are concerned with the peoples and events of the past and their significance for us today. Political scientists study international relations, the workings of government, and the exercise of power and authority. Psychologists investigate personality and individual behavior. So what does *sociology* focus on? It emphasizes the influence that society has on people's attitudes and behavior and the ways in which people shape society. Humans are social animals; therefore, sociologists scientifically examine our social relationships with others.

Let's consider how the different social sciences might approach the hotly debated issue of handgun control. Many people today, concerned about the misuse of firearms in the United States, are calling for restrictions on the purchase and use of handguns. Political scientists studying this issue would look at the impact of political action groups, such as the National Rifle Association (NRA), on lawmakers. Historians would examine how guns were used over time in our country and elsewhere. Anthropologists would focus on the use of weapons in a variety of cultures as means of protection as well as symbols of power. Psychologists would look at individual cases and assess the impact handguns have on their owners as well as on individual victims of gunfire. Economists would be interested in how firearm manufacture and sales affect communities.

And what approach would sociologists take? They might look at the kind of data shown in Table 1-1, which gives an idea of who owns handguns in the United States. They would ask: What explains the significant gender, racial, age, and geographic differences in gun ownership? How would these differences affect the formulation of social policy by city, state, and federal governments? They would examine data from different states to evaluate the effect of gun restrictions on the incidence of firearm accidents or violent crimes involving firearms. They would consider how cultural values and media portrayals influence people's desire to own firearms. Sociologists might also look at data that show how the United States compares to other nations in handgun ownership and use.

Sociologists put their imagination to work in a variety of areas—including aging, criminal justice, the family, human ecology, and religion. Throughout this textbook, you will see how sociologists use their sociological imagination to study and better understand societies. And you

Table 1-1 Gun Ownership in the United States

Sex	
Men	47%
Women	27
Race	
Whites	40%
Non-Whites	19
Age	
18–29	28%
30–49	37
50–64	46
65+	36
Region	
South	46%
Midwest	39
East	29
West	33

Note: Based on a national survey February 1999.

Source: Gallup Poll in Gillespie 1999.

Think About It

What portrait of a typical gun owner can you draw from the data in this table? Why do you think this pattern emerges?

will be encouraged to use it to examine the United States (and other societies) from the viewpoint of a respectful but questioning outsider.

Sociology and Common Sense

Sociology focuses on the study of human behavior. Yet we all have experience with human behavior and at least some knowledge of it. All of us might well have theories about why people get tattoos, for example, or why people become homeless. Our theories and opinions typically come from "common sense"—that is, from our experiences and conversations, from what we read, from what we see on television, and so forth.

In our daily lives, we rely on common sense to get us through many unfamiliar situations. However, this commonsense knowledge, while sometimes accurate, is not always reliable, because it rests on commonly held beliefs rather than on systematic analysis of facts. It was once considered "common sense" to accept that the earth was flat—a view rightly questioned by Pythagoras and

Aristotle. Incorrect commonsense notions are not just a part of the distant past; they remain with us today.

In the United States, "common sense" tells us that an "epidemic" of teen pregnancies accounts for most unwed births today, creating a drag on the welfare system. "Common sense" tells us that people panic when faced with natural disasters, such as floods and earthquakes, or even in the wake of tragedies such as the attacks on New York City and Washington, D. C. in 2001. However, these particular "commonsense" notions—like the notion that the earth is flat—are untrue; neither of them is supported by sociological research. The proportion of unwed mothers in their teens is declining; in fact, women who are *not* in their teens account for most of the unwed mothers, and they make up an estimated 93 percent of women on welfare. (Luker 1996, 1999).

Disasters do not generally produce panic. In the aftermath of disasters and even explosions, greater social organization and structure emerge to deal with a community's problems. In the United States, for example, an emergency "operations group" often coordinates public services and even certain services normally performed by the private sector, such as food distribution. Decision making becomes more centralized in times of disaster.

Like other social scientists, sociologists do not accept something as a fact because "everyone knows it." Instead, each piece of information must be tested and recorded, then analyzed in relationship to other data. Sociology relies on scientific studies in order to describe and understand a social environment. At times, the findings of sociologists may seem like common sense because they deal with facets of everyday life. The difference is that such findings have been *tested* by researchers. Common sense now tells us that the earth is round. But this particular commonsense notion is based on centuries of scientific work upholding the breakthrough made by Pythagoras and Aristotle.

What Is Sociological Theory?

Why do people commit suicide? One traditional commonsense answer is that people inherit the desire to kill themselves. Another view is that sunspots drive people to take their own lives. These explanations may not seem especially convincing to contemporary researchers, but they represent beliefs widely held as recently as 1900.

Sociologists are not particularly interested in why any one individual commits suicide; they are more concerned with identifying the social forces that systematically cause some people to take their own lives. In order to undertake this research, sociologists develop a theory that offers a general explanation of suicidal behavior.

Do disasters produce panic or an organized, structured response? Common sense might tell us the former, but, in fact, disasters bring out a great deal of structure and organization to deal with their aftermath. When the World Trade Center was attacked on September 11, 2001, the command post for emergencies in New York City happened to be in one of the collapsed buildings. Yet by nightfall a new communications and operations center was up and running to guide the rescue and recovery effort.

We can think of theories as attempts to explain events, forces, materials, ideas, or behavior in a comprehensive manner. Within sociology, a ***theory*** is a set of statements that seeks to explain problems, actions, or behavior. An effective theory may have both explanatory and predictive power. That is, it can help us to see the relationships among seemingly isolated phenomena as well as to understand how one type of change in an environment leads to others.

Émile Durkheim ([1897] 1951) looked into suicide data in great detail and developed a highly original theory about the relationship between suicide and social factors. He was primarily concerned not with the personalities of individual suicide victims, but rather with suicide *rates* and how they varied from country to country. As a result, when he looked at the number of reported suicides in France, England, and Denmark in 1869, he also examined the populations of these nations to determine their rates of suicide. He found that whereas England had only 67 reported suicides per million inhabitants, France had 135 per million and Denmark had 277 per million. The question then became: "Why did Denmark have a comparatively high rate of reported suicides?"

Durkheim went much deeper into his investigation of suicide rates, and the result was his landmark work *Suicide,* published in 1897. Durkheim refused to automatically accept unproven explanations regarding suicide, including the beliefs that cosmic forces or inherited tendencies caused such deaths. Instead, he focused on such problems as the cohesiveness or lack of cohesiveness of religious, social, and occupational groups.

Durkheim's research suggested that suicide, while a solitary act, is related to group life. Protestants had much higher suicide rates than Catholics did; the unmarried had much higher rates than married people did; soldiers were more likely to take their lives than civilians were. In addition, there seemed to be higher rates of suicide in times of peace than in times of war and revolution, and in times of economic instability and recession rather than in times of prosperity. Durkheim concluded that the suicide rates of a society reflected the extent to which people were or were not integrated into the group life of the society.

Émile Durkheim, like many other social scientists, developed a theory to explain how individual behavior can be understood within a social context. He pointed out the influence of groups and societal forces on what had always been viewed as a highly personal act. Clearly, Durkheim offered a more *scientific* explanation for the causes of suicide than that of sunspots or inherited tendencies. His theory has predictive power, since it suggests that suicide rates will rise or fall in conjunction with certain social and economic changes.

Of course, a theory—even the best of theories—is not a final statement about human behavior. Durkheim's theory of suicide is no exception; sociologists continue to examine factors that contribute to differences in suicide rates around the world and to a particular society's rate of suicide. For example, although the overall rate of suicide in New Zealand is only marginally higher than in the United States, the suicide rate among young people is 41 percent higher in New Zealand. Sociologists and psychiatrists from that country suggest that their remote, sparsely populated society maintains exaggerated standards of masculinity that are especially difficult for young males. Gay adolescents who fail to conform to their peers' preference for sports are particularly vulnerable to suicide (Shenon 1995; for a critique of Durkheim's work, see Douglas 1967).

Imagine

If you were Durkheim's successor in his research on suicide, how would you proceed to investigate the factors that may explain the increase in suicide rates among young people in the United States today?

The Development of Sociology

People have always been curious about sociological matters—such as how we get along with others, what we do, and whom we select as our leaders. Philosophers and religious authorities of ancient and medieval societies made countless observations about human behavior. They did not test or verify these observations scientifically; nevertheless, these observations often became the foundation for moral codes. Several of the early social philosophers predicted that a systematic study of human behavior would one day emerge. Beginning in the nineteenth century, European theorists made pioneering contributions to the development of a science of human behavior.

Early Thinkers

Auguste Comte

The nineteenth century was an unsettling time in France. The French monarchy had been deposed earlier in the revolution of 1789, and Napoleon had subsequently suffered defeat in his effort to conquer Europe. Amidst this chaos, philosophers considered how society might be improved. Auguste Comte (1798–1857), credited with being the most influential of these philosophers of the early 1800s, believed that a theoretical science of society and systematic investigation of behavior were needed to improve society. He coined the term *sociology* to apply to the science of human behavior.

   Writing in the 1800s, Comte feared that the excesses of the French Revolution had permanently impaired France's stability. Yet he hoped that the study of social behavior in a systematic way would eventually lead to more rational human interactions. In Comte's hierarchy of sciences, sociology was at the top. He called it the "queen" and its practitioners "scientist-priests." This French theorist did not simply give sociology its name; he also presented a rather ambitious challenge to the fledgling discipline.

Harriet Martineau

Scholars were able to learn of Comte's works largely through translations by the English sociologist Harriet Martineau (1802–1876). But Martineau was a path-

Harriet Martineau, an early pioneer of sociology, studied social behavior both in her native England and in the United States.

breaker in her own right as a sociologist. She offered insightful observations of the customs and social practices of both her native Britain and the United States. Martineau's book *Society in America* ([1837] 1962) examines religion, politics, child rearing, and immigration in the young nation. Martineau gives special attention to social class distinctions and to such factors as gender and race.

   Martineau's writings emphasized the impact that the economy, law, trade, and population could have on the social problems of contemporary society. She spoke out in favor of the rights of women, the emancipation of slaves, and religious tolerance. In Martineau's (1896) view, intellectuals and scholars should not simply offer observations of social conditions; they should act on their convictions in a manner that will benefit society. That is why Martineau conducted research on the nature of female employment and pointed to the need for further investigation of this important issue (Lengermann and Niebrugge-Brantley 1998).

Herbert Spencer

Another important contributor to the discipline of sociology was Herbert Spencer (1820–1903). A relatively prosperous Victorian Englishman, Spencer (unlike Martineau) did not feel compelled to correct or improve society; instead, he merely hoped to understand it better. Drawing on Charles Darwin's study *On the Origin of Species,* Spencer applied the concept of evolution of the species to societies in order to explain how they change, or evolve, over time. Similarly, he adapted Darwin's evolutionary view of the "survival of the fittest" by arguing that it is "natural" that some people are rich while others are poor.

Spencer's approach to societal change was extremely popular in his own lifetime. Unlike Comte, Spencer suggested that since societies are bound to change eventually, one need not be highly critical of present social arrangements or work actively for social change. This viewpoint appealed to many influential people in England and the United States who had a vested interest in the status quo and were suspicious of social thinkers who endorsed change.

Émile Durkheim

Émile Durkheim made many pioneering contributions to sociology, including his important theoretical work on suicide. The son of a rabbi, Durkheim (1858–1917) was educated in both France and Germany. He established an impressive academic reputation and was appointed as one of the first professors of sociology in France. Above all, Durkheim will be remembered for his insistence that behavior must be understood within a larger social context, not just in individualistic terms.

As one example of this emphasis, Durkheim ([1912] 1947) developed a fundamental thesis to help understand all forms of society through intensive study of the Arunta, an Australian tribe. He focused on the functions that religion performed for the Arunta and underscored the role that group life plays in defining what we consider religious. Durkheim concluded that, like other forms of group behavior, religion reinforces a group's solidarity.

Another of Durkheim's main interests was the consequences of work in modern societies. In his view, the growing division of labor in industrial societies as workers became much more specialized in their tasks led to what he called *anomie. Anomie* refers to the loss of direction that a society feels when social control of individual behavior has become ineffective. The state of anomie occurs when people have lost their sense of purpose or direction, often during a time of profound social change. In a period of anomie, people are so confused and unable to cope with the new social environment that they may resort to taking their own lives.

Durkheim was concerned about the dangers that alienation, loneliness, and isolation might pose for mod-

ern industrial societies. He shared Comte's belief that sociology should provide direction for social change. As a result, he advocated the creation of new social groups—between the individual's family and the state—which would ideally provide a sense of belonging for members of huge, impersonal societies. Unions would be an example of such a group.

Like many other sociologists, Durkheim did not limit his interests to one aspect of social behavior. Later in this book, we will consider his thinking on crime and punishment, religion, and the workplace. Few sociologists have had such a dramatic impact on so many different areas within the discipline.

Max Weber

Another important early theorist was Max Weber (pronounced "VAY-ber"). Born in Germany in 1864, Weber studied legal and economic history, but he gradually developed an interest in sociology. Eventually, he became a professor at various German universities. Weber taught his students that they should employ *Verstehen,* the German word for "understanding" or "insight," in their intellectual work. He pointed out that we cannot analyze much of our social behavior by the same criteria we use to measure weight or temperature. To fully comprehend behavior, we must learn the subjective meanings people attach to their actions—how they themselves view and explain their behavior.

For example, suppose that a sociologist was studying the social ranking of individuals in a fraternity. Weber would expect the researcher to employ *Verstehen* to determine the significance of the fraternity's social hierarchy for its members. The researcher might examine the effects of athleticism or grades or social skills or seniority on standing within the fraternity. He or she would seek to learn how the fraternity members relate to other members of higher or lower status. While investigating these questions, the researcher would take into account people's emotions, thoughts, beliefs, and attitudes (L. Coser 1977).

We also owe credit to Weber for a key conceptual tool: the ideal type. An *ideal type* is a construct, a made-up model that serves as a measuring rod against which actual cases can be evaluated. In his own works, Weber identified various characteristics of bureaucracy as an ideal type (discussed in detail in Chapter 6). In presenting this model of bureaucracy, Weber was not describing any particular business, nor was he using the term *ideal* in a way that suggested a positive evaluation. Instead, his purpose was to provide a useful standard for measuring how bureaucratic an actual organization is (Gerth and Mills

FIGURE 1-1

Early Social Thinkers

	Émile Durkheim 1858–1917	**Max Weber 1864–1920**	**Karl Marx 1818–1883**
Academic training	Philosophy	Law, economics, history, philosophy	Philosophy, law
Key works	1893—*The Division of Labor in Society* 1897—*Suicide: A Study in Sociology* 1912—*Elementary Forms of Religious Life*	1904–1905—*The Protestant Ethic and the Spirit of Capitalism* 1922—*Wirtschaft und Gesellschaft*	1848—*The Communist Manifesto* 1867—*Das Kapital*

1958). Later in this textbook, we use the concept of ideal type to study the family, religion, authority, and economic systems and to analyze bureaucracy.

Although their professional careers coincided, Émile Durkheim and Max Weber never met and probably were unaware of each other's existence, let alone ideas. This was certainly not true of the work of Karl Marx. Durkheim's thinking about the impact of the division of labor in industrial societies was related to Marx's writings, while Weber's concern for a value-free, objective sociology was a direct response to Marx's deeply held convictions. Thus, it is not surprising that Karl Marx is viewed as a major figure in the development of sociology as well as several other social sciences (see Figure 1-1).

Karl Marx

Karl Marx (1818–1883) shared with Durkheim and Weber a dual interest in abstract philosophical issues and the concrete reality of everyday life. Unlike the others, Marx was so critical of existing institutions that a conventional academic career was impossible, and he spent most of his life in exile from his native Germany.

Marx's personal life was a difficult struggle. When a paper that he had written was suppressed, he fled to France. In Paris, he met Friedrich Engels (1820–1895), with whom he formed a lifelong friendship. They lived at a time when European and North American economic life was increasingly being dominated by the factory rather than the farm.

In 1847, Marx and Engels attended secret meetings in London of an illegal coalition of labor unions, known as the Communist League. The following year, they prepared a platform called *The Communist Manifesto,* in which they argued that the masses of people who have no resources other than their labor (whom they referred to as the *proletariat*) should unite to fight for the overthrow of capitalist societies. In the words of Marx and Engels:

> The history of all hitherto existing society is the history of class struggles. . . . The proletarians have nothing to lose but their chains. They have a world to win. WORKING MEN OF ALL COUNTRIES UNITE! (Feuer 1959:7, 41).

After completing *The Communist Manifesto,* Marx returned to Germany, only to be expelled. He then moved to England, where he continued to write books and essays. Marx lived there in extreme poverty. He pawned most of his possessions, and several of his children died of malnutrition and disease. Marx clearly was an outsider in British society, a fact that may well have affected his view of Western cultures.

In Marx's analysis, society was fundamentally divided between classes that clash in pursuit of their own class interests. When he examined the industrial societies of his time, such as Germany, England, and the United States, he saw the factory as the center of conflict between the exploiters (the owners of the means of production) and the exploited (the workers). Marx viewed these relationships in systematic terms; that is, he believed that an entire system of economic, social, and political relationships maintained the power and dominance of the owners over the workers. Consequently, Marx and Engels argued that the working class needed to *overthrow* the existing class system. Marx's influence on contemporary thinking has been dramatic. His writings inspired those who were later to lead communist revolutions in Russia, China, Cuba, Vietnam, and elsewhere.

Even apart from the political revolutions that his work fostered, Marx's significance is profound. Marx emphasized the *group* identifications and associations that influence an individual's place in society. This area of study is the major focus of contemporary sociology. Throughout this textbook, we will consider how membership in a particular gender classification, age group, racial group, or economic class affects a person's attitudes and behavior. In an important sense, we can trace this way of understanding society back to the pioneering work of Karl Marx.

Modern Developments

Sociology today builds on the firm foundation developed by Émile Durkheim, Max Weber, and Karl Marx. However, the discipline of sociology has certainly not remained stagnant over the last one hundred years. While Europeans have continued to make contributions to the discipline, sociologists from throughout the world and especially the United States have advanced sociological theory and research. Their new insights have helped them to better understand the workings of society.

Charles Horton Cooley

Charles Horton Cooley (1864–1929) was typical of the sociologists who came to prominence in the early 1900s. Cooley was born in Ann Arbor, Michigan, and received his graduate training in economics but later became a sociology professor at the University of Michigan. Like other early sociologists, he had become interested in this "new" discipline while pursuing a related area of study.

Cooley shared the desire of Durkheim, Weber, and Marx to learn more about society. But to do so effectively, Cooley preferred to use the sociological perspective to look first at smaller units—intimate, face-to-face groups such as families, gangs, and friendship networks. He saw these groups as the seedbeds of society in the sense that they shape people's ideals, beliefs, values, and social nature. Cooley's work increased our understanding of groups of relatively small size.

Jane Addams

In the early 1900s, many leading sociologists in the United States saw themselves as social reformers dedicated to systematically studying and then improving a corrupt society. They were genuinely concerned about the lives of immigrants in the nation's growing cities, whether these immigrants came from Europe or from the rural American south. Early female sociologists, in particular, often took active roles in poor urban areas as leaders of community centers known as *settlement houses.* For example, Jane Addams (1860–1935), an active member of the American Sociological Society, cofounded the famous Chicago settlement, Hull House.

Addams and other pioneering female sociologists commonly combined intellectual inquiry, social service work, and political activism—all with the goal of assisting the underprivileged and creating a more egalitarian society. For example, working with the Black journalist and educator Ida Wells-Barnett, Addams successfully prevented racial segregation in the Chicago public schools. Addams' efforts to establish a juvenile court system and a women's trade union also reveal the practical focus of her work (Addams 1910, 1930; Deegan 1991; Lengermann and Niebrugge-Brantley 1998).

By the middle of the twentieth century, however, the focus of the discipline had shifted. Sociologists for the most part restricted themselves to theorizing and gathering information; the aim of transforming society was left to social workers and others. This shift away from social reform was accompanied by a growing commitment to scientific methods of research and to value-free interpretation of data. Not all sociologists were happy with this emphasis. A new organization, the Society for the Study of Social Problems, was created in

A postage stamp honored social reformer Jane Addams, an early pioneer both in sociology and in the settlement house movement.

1950 to deal more directly with social inequality and other social problems.

Robert Merton

Sociologist Robert Merton (1968) made an important contribution to the discipline by successfully combining theory and research. Born in 1910 of Slavic immigrant parents in Philadelphia, Merton subsequently won a scholarship to Temple University. He continued his studies at Harvard, where he acquired his lifelong interest in sociology. Merton's teaching career has been based at Columbia University.

Merton produced a theory that is one of the most frequently cited explanations of deviant behavior. He noted different ways in which people attempt to achieve success in life. In his view, some may deviate from the socially agreed-upon goal of accumulating material goods or the socially accepted means of achieving this goal. For example, in Merton's classification scheme, "innovators" are people who accept the goal of pursuing material wealth but use illegal means to do so, including robbery, burglary, and extortion. Merton bases his explanation of crime on individual behavior—influenced by society's approved goals and means—yet it has wider applications. It helps to account for the high crime rates among the nation's poor, who may see no hope of advancing themselves through traditional roads to success. Chapter 8 discusses Merton's theory in greater detail.

Merton also emphasized that sociology should strive to bring together the "macro-level" and "micro-level" approaches to the study of society. *Macrosociology* concentrates on large-scale phenomena or entire civilizations. Émile Durkheim's cross-cultural study of suicide is an example of macro-level research. More recently, macrosociologists have examined international crime rates (see Chapter 8), the stereotype of Asian Americans as a "model minority" (see Chapter 11), and the population patterns of Islamic countries (see Chapter 15). By contrast, *microsociology* stresses study of small groups and often uses experimental study in laboratories. Sociological research on the microlevel has included studies of how divorced men and women disengage from significant social roles (see Chapter 5); of how conformity can influence the expression of prejudiced attitudes (see Chapter 8); and of how a teacher's expectations can affect a student's academic performance (see Chapter 16).

Today sociology reflects the diverse contributions of earlier theorists. As sociologists approach such topics as divorce, drug addiction, and religious cults, they can draw on the theoretical insights of the discipline's pioneers. A careful reader can hear Comte, Durkheim, Weber, Marx, Cooley, Addams, and many others speaking through the pages of current research. Sociology has also broadened beyond the intellectual confines of North

America and Europe. Contributions to the discipline now come from sociologists studying and researching human behavior in other parts of the world. In describing the work of today's sociologists, it is helpful to examine a number of influential theoretical approaches (also known as *perspectives*).

Major Theoretical Perspectives

Sociologists view society in different ways. Some see the world basically as a stable and ongoing entity. They are impressed with the endurance of the family, organized religion, and other social institutions. Some sociologists see society as composed of many groups in conflict, competing for scarce resources. To other sociologists, the most fascinating aspects of the social world are the everyday, routine interactions among individuals that we sometimes take for granted. These three views, the ones most widely used by sociologists, are the functionalist, conflict, and interactionist perspectives. A more specialized viewpoint that has been influential in recent years is the feminist perspective. Together, these approaches will provide an introductory look at the discipline.

Functionalist Perspective

Think of society as a living organism in which each part of the organism contributes to its survival. This view is the *functionalist perspective,* which emphasizes the way that parts of a society are structured to maintain its stability.

Talcott Parsons (1902–1979), a Harvard University sociologist, was a key figure in the development of functionalist theory. Parsons had been greatly influenced by the work of Émile Durkheim, Max Weber, and other European sociologists. For over four decades, Parsons dominated sociology in the United States with his advocacy of functionalism. He saw any society as a vast network of connected parts, each of which helps to maintain the system as a whole. The functionalist approach holds that if an aspect of social life does not contribute to a society's stability or survival—if it does not serve some identifiably useful function or promote value consensus among members of a society—it will not be passed on from one generation to the next.

Let's examine prostitution as an example of the functionalist perspective. Why is it that a practice so widely condemned continues to display such persistence and vitality? Functionalists suggest that prostitution satisfies needs of patrons that may not be readily met through more socially acceptable forms such as courtship or marriage. The "buyer" receives sex without any responsibility for procreation or sentimental attachment; at the same time, the "seller" makes a living through this exchange.

Such an examination leads us to conclude that prostitution does perform certain functions that society seems to need. However, this is not to suggest that prostitution is a desirable or legitimate form of social behavior. Functionalists do not make such judgments. Rather, advocates of the functionalist perspective hope to explain how an aspect of society that is so frequently attacked can nevertheless manage to survive (K. Davis 1937).

Manifest and Latent Functions

Your college catalog typically states various functions of the institution. It may inform you, for example, that the university intends to "offer each student a broad education in classical and contemporary thought, in the humanities, in the sciences, and in the arts." However, it would be quite a surprise to find a catalog that declared, "This university was founded in 1895 to keep people between the ages of 18 and 22 out of the job market, thus reducing unemployment." No college catalog will declare that this is the purpose of the university. Yet societal institutions serve many functions, some of them quite subtle. The university, in fact, *does* delay people's entry into the job market.

Robert Merton (1968) made an important distinction between manifest and latent functions. *Manifest functions* of institutions are open, stated, conscious functions. They involve the intended, recognized consequences of an aspect of society, such as the university's role in certifying academic competence and excellence. By contrast, *latent functions* are unconscious or unintended functions and may reflect hidden purposes of an institution. One latent function of universities is to hold down unemployment. Another is to serve as a meeting ground for people seeking marital partners.

Dysfunctions

Functionalists acknowledge that not all parts of a society contribute to its stability all the time. A *dysfunction* refers to an element or a process of society that may actually disrupt a social system or lead to a decrease in stability.

We consider many dysfunctional behavior patterns, such as homicide, as undesirable. Yet we should not automatically interpret dysfunctions as negative. The evaluation of a dysfunction depends on one's own values or, as the saying goes, on "where you sit." For example, the official view in prisons in the United States is that inmates' gangs should be eradicated because they are dysfunctional to smooth operations. Yet some guards have actually come to view the presence of prison gangs as functional for their

On the face of it, prison gangs may seem dysfunctional since they pose a threat to security. But prison guards consider these gangs functional for their jobs because they may require overtime, higher pay, and increased staffing.

jobs. The danger posed by gangs creates a "threat to security," requiring increased surveillance and more overtime work for guards as well as requests for special staffing to address prison gang problems (Scott 2001).

Conflict Perspective

In contrast to functionalists' emphasis on stability and consensus, conflict sociologists see the social world in continual struggle. The *conflict perspective* assumes that social behavior is best understood in terms of conflict or tension between competing groups. Such conflict need not be violent; it can take the form of labor negotiations, party politics, competition between religious groups for members, or disputes over the federal budget.

Throughout most of the 1900s, the functionalist perspective had the upper hand in sociology in the United States. However, the conflict approach has become increasingly persuasive since the late 1960s. The widespread social unrest resulting from battles over civil rights, bitter divisions over the war in Vietnam, the rise of the feminist and gay liberation movements, the Watergate scandal, urban riots, and confrontations at abortion clinics offered support for the conflict approach—the view that our social world is characterized by continual struggle between competing groups. Currently, the discipline of sociology accepts conflict theory as one valid way to gain insight into a society.

The Marxist View

As we saw earlier, Karl Marx viewed struggle between social classes as inevitable, given the exploitation of workers under capitalism. Expanding on Marx's work,

The conflict perspective views our social world as a continual struggle between competing groups. This Native American is protesting the use of the word "Indians" by a major league baseball team. By making up other team names that other groups might find offensive, he invites you to put yourself in his shoes.

sociologists and other social scientists have come to see conflict not merely as a class phenomenon but as a part of everyday life in all societies. Thus, in studying any culture, organization, or social group, sociologists want to know who benefits, who suffers, and who dominates at the expense of others. They are concerned with the conflicts between women and men, parents and children, cities and suburbs, and Whites and Blacks, to name only a few. Conflict theorists are interested in how society's institutions—including the family, government, religion, education, and the media—may help to maintain the privileges of some groups and keep others in a subservient position. Their emphasis on social change and redistribution of resources makes conflict theorists more "radical" and "activist" than functionalists (Dahrendorf 1958).

A Racial View: W. E. B. Du Bois

One important contribution of conflict theory is that it has encouraged sociologists to view society through the eyes of those segments of the population that rarely influence decision making. Early Black sociologists such as W. E. B. Du Bois (1868–1963) conducted research that they hoped would assist the struggle for a racially egalitarian society. Du Bois believed that knowledge was essential in combating prejudice and achieving tolerance and justice. Sociology, Du Bois contended, had to draw on scientific principles to study social problems such as those experienced by Blacks in the United States. In addition, Du Bois made a major contribution to sociology through his in-depth studies of urban life—both White and Black.

Du Bois had little patience for theorists such as Herbert Spencer who seemed content with the status quo. He advocated basic research on the lives of Blacks that would separate opinion from fact. In this way he documented their relatively low status in Philadelphia and Atlanta. Du Bois believed that the granting of full political rights to Blacks was essential to their social and economic progress in the United States. Many of his ideas challenging the

The ideas of W. E. B. Du Bois challenged the status quo in both academic and political circles. The first Black person to receive a doctorate from Harvard University, he later helped organize the National Association for the Advancement of Colored People (NAACP).

status quo did not find a receptive audience within either the government or the academic world. As a result, Du Bois became increasingly involved with organizations whose members questioned the established social order, and he helped to found the National Association for the Advancement of Colored People, better known as the NAACP (Lewis 1994, 2000).

The addition of diverse views within sociology in recent years has led to some valuable research, especially for African Americans. For many years, African Americans were understandably wary of participating in medical research studies, because those studies had been used for such purposes as justifying slavery or determining the impact of untreated syphilis. Now, however, African American sociologists and other social scientists are working to involve Blacks in useful ethnic medical research in such areas as diabetes and sickle cell anemia, two disorders that strike Black populations especially hard (St. John 1997).

Interactionist Perspective

Workers interacting on the job, encounters in public places like bus stops and parks, behavior in small groups—these are all aspects of microsociology that catch the attention of interactionists. Whereas functionalist and conflict theorists both analyze large-scale societywide patterns of behavior, the **interactionist perspective** generalizes about everyday forms of social interaction in order to understand society as a whole. In the 1990s, for example, the workings of juries became a subject of public scrutiny. High-profile trials ended in verdicts that left some people shaking their heads. Long before jury members were being interviewed on their front lawns following trials, interactionists tried to better understand behavior in the small-group setting of a jury deliberation room.

Interactionism is a sociological framework for viewing human beings as living in a world of meaningful objects. These "objects" may include material things, actions, other people, relationships, and even symbols.

While functionalist and conflict approaches were initiated in Europe, interactionism developed first in the United States. George Herbert Mead (1863–1931) is widely regarded as the founder of the interactionist perspective. Mead taught at the University of Chicago from 1893 until his death. His sociological analysis, like that of Charles Horton Cooley, often focused on human interactions within one-to-one situations and small groups. Mead was interested in observing the most minute forms of communication—smiles, frowns, nodding of one's head—and in understanding how such individual behavior was influenced by the larger context of a group or

society. Despite his innovative views, Mead only occasionally wrote articles, and never a book. He was an extremely popular teacher, and most of his insights have come to us through edited volumes of lectures that his students published after his death.

The interactionist perspective is sometimes referred to as the *symbolic interactionist perspective*, because interactionists see symbols as an especially important part of human communication. Members of a society share the social meanings of symbols. In the United States, for example, a salute symbolizes respect, while a clenched fist signifies defiance. However, another culture might use different gestures to convey a feeling of respect or defiance.

Consider the different ways various societies portray suicide without the use of words. People in the United States point a finger at the head (shooting); urban Japanese bring a fist against the stomach (stabbing); and the South Fore of Papua, New Guinea, clench a hand at the throat (hanging). These types of symbolic interaction are classified as forms of **nonverbal communication,** which can include many other gestures, facial expressions, and postures.

Since Mead's teachings have become well known, sociologists have expressed greater interest in the interactionist perspective. Many have moved away from what may have been an excessive preoccupation with the large-scale (macro) level of social behavior and have redirected their attention toward behavior that occurs in small groups (microlevel).

Erving Goffman (1922–1982) popularized a particular type of interactionist method known as the **dramaturgical approach.** The dramaturgist compares everyday life to the setting of the theater and stage. Just as actors project certain images, all of us seek to present particular features of our personalities while we hide other qualities. Thus, in a class, we may feel the need to project a serious image; at a party, we want to look relaxed and friendly.

Feminist Perspective

Sociologists began embracing the feminist perspective in the 1970s, although it has a long tradition in many other disciplines. The **feminist perspective** views inequity in gender as central to all behavior and organization. Because it clearly focuses on one aspect of inequality, it is often allied with the conflict perspective. But unlike conflict theorists, those who hold to the feminist perspective tend to focus on the micro-level relationships of everyday life, just as interactionists would. Drawing on the work of Marx and Engels, contemporary feminist theorists often view women's subordination as inherent in capitalist societies. Some radical feminist theorists, however, view the oppression of women as inevitable in *all* male-dominated societies, including those labeled as *capitalist, socialist,* and *communist* (Chafetz 1988, 1999; Tuchman 1992).

An early example of this perspective (long before the label came into use by sociologists) shows up in the life and writings of Ida Wells-Barnett. Following her groundbreaking publications in the 1890s on the practice of lynching Black Americans, she became an advocate in the women's rights campaign, especially the struggle to win the vote for women. Like feminist theorists who succeeded her, Wells-Barnett used her analysis of society as a means of resisting oppression. In her case, she researched what it meant to be African American, a woman in the United States, and a Black woman in the United States (Wells-Barnett 1970).

Feminist scholarship in sociology has broadened our understanding of social behavior by taking it beyond the White male point of view. For example, a family's social standing is no longer defined solely by the husband's position and income. Feminist scholars have not only challenged stereotyping of women; they have argued for a gender-balanced study of society in which women's expe-

Ida Wells-Barnett explored what it meant to be female and Black living in the United States. Her work established her as one of the earliest feminist theorists.

riences and contributions are as visible as those of men (Brewer 1989; Komarovsky 1991; P. England 1999).

The feminist perspective has given sociologists new views of familiar social behavior. For example, past research on crime rarely considered women, and when it did, the studies tended to focus on "traditional" crimes by women like shoplifting. Such a view tended to ignore the role that women play in all types of crime as well as the disproportionate role that they play as *victims* of crime. Research conducted by Meda Chesney-Lind and Noelie Rodriguez (1993) showed that nearly all women in prison had suffered physical and/or sexual abuse when they were young; half had been raped. Contributions by both feminist and minority scholars have enriched all the sociological perspectives.

The Sociological Approach

Which perspective should a sociologist use in studying human behavior? Functionalist? Conflict? Interactionist? How should the feminist view be considered?

Sociology makes use of all these perspectives (see Table 1-2), since each offers unique insights into the same issue. Think about how Katherine Irwin went about studying the tattoo culture in the United States today (described in the chapter opening). She focused on the tattoo's use as a symbol of hip social status (functionalist perspective), and she examined the tensions between a parent and a child who decides to get tattooed, and the disapproval an employer might show toward a tattooed employee (conflict perspective). Research into the actual process of getting tattooed, including the negotiations between the tattoo artist and the tattooee, made use of the interactionist perspective. Using the feminist perspective, Irwin might consider the differences in behavior between men and women who get tattooed, as well as differences in how society may view them. As another example, Box 1-1 shows how sports might look from the different perspectives.

No one approach to a particular issue is "correct." This textbook assumes that we can gain the broadest understanding of our society by drawing on all the major perspectives in the study of human behavior and institutions. These perspectives overlap as their interests coincide but can diverge according to the dictates of each approach and of the issue being studied. A sociologist's theoretical orientation influences his or her approach to a research problem in important ways.

Applied and Clinical Sociology

Many early sociologists—notably, Jane Addams and George Herbert Mead—were strong advocates for social reform. They wanted their theories and findings to be

Table 1-2 Comparing Major Theoretical Perspectives

	Functionalist	Conflict	Interactionist
View of society	Stable, well integrated	Charaterized by tension and struggle between groups	Active in influencing and affecting everyday social interaction
Level of analysis Emphasized	Macro	Macro	Micro analysis as a way of understanding the larger macro phenomena
Key concepts	Manifest functions Latent functions Dysfunction	Inequality Capitalism Stratification	Symbols Nonverbal communication Face-to-face
View of the individual	People are socialized to perform societal functions	People are shaped by power, coercion, and authority	People manipulate symbols and create their social worlds through interaction
View of the social order	Maintained through cooperation and consensus	Maintained through force and coercion	Maintained by shared understanding of everyday behavior
View of social change	Predictable, reinforcing	Change takes place all the time and may have positive consequences	Reflected in people's social positions and their communications with others
Example	Public punishments reinforce the social order	Laws reinforce the positions of those in power	People respect laws or disobey them based on their own past experience
Proponents	Émile Durkheim Talcott Parsons Robert Merton	Karl Marx W. E. B. Du Bois Ida Wells-Barnett	George Herbert Mead Charles Horton Cooley Erving Goffman

relevant to policymakers and to people's lives in general. For instance, Mead was the treasurer of Hull House for many years, where he applied his theory to improving the lives of those who were powerless (especially immigrants). He also served on committees dealing with Chicago's labor problems and public education. Today, **applied sociology** is the use of the discipline of sociology with the specific intent of yielding practical applications for human behavior and organizations.

Often, the goal of such work is to assist in resolving a social problem. For example, in the last 35 years, eight presidents of the United States have established commissions to delve into major societal concerns facing our nation. Sociologists are often asked to apply their expertise to studying such issues as violence, pornography, crime, immigration, and population. In Europe, both academic and governmental research departments are offering increasing financial support for applied studies.

An example of applied sociology is the growing local community research movement. Sociologists at DePaul University in Chicago and their students have been examining the impact of the opening of a Motorola cellular phone plant with 5,000 employees in the small town of Harvard, Illinois. This rural, agriculture-based community has only 6,500 residents and is 80 miles from Chicago (well outside the suburban fringe). Some residents of Harvard view the arrival of Motorola as a great boost to the local economy, but others are fearful of the power of a Fortune 500 company. In studying the social and economic impact of Motorola on Harvard, the DePaul researchers are interested not only in the influence a huge corporation can have on a town but in whether the lifestyle of a rural Illinois community can influence the corporation. Certainly, the

1-1 Looking at Sports from Four Theoretical Perspectives

We generally think of the various perspectives of sociology—functionalist, conflict, interactionist, and feminist—as being applied to "serious" subjects such as the family, health care, and criminal behavior. Yet even sports can be analyzed using these theoretical perspectives.

FUNCTIONALIST VIEW

In examining any aspect of society, functionalists emphasize the contribution it makes to overall social stability. Functionalists regard sports as an almost religious institution that uses ritual and ceremony to reinforce the common values of a society:

- Sports socialize young people into such values as competition and patriotism.
- Sports help to maintain people's physical well-being.
- Sports serve as a safety valve for both participants and spectators, who are allowed to shed tension and aggressive energy in a socially acceptable way.

- Sports "bring together" members of a community (supporting local athletes and teams) or even a nation (as seen during World Cup matches and the Olympics) and promote an overall feeling of unity and social solidarity.

> Despite their differences, functionalists, conflict theorists, interactionists, and feminists would all agree that there is much more to sports than exercise or recreation.

CONFLICT VIEW

Conflict theorists argue that the social order is based on coercion and exploitation. They emphasize that sports reflect and even exacerbate many of the divisions of society:

- Sports are a form of big business in which profits are more important than the health and safety of the workers (athletes).
- Sports perpetuate the false idea that success can be achieved simply through hard work, while failure should be blamed on the individual alone (rather than on injustices in the larger social system). Sports serve as an "opiate" that encourages people to seek a "fix" or temporary "high" rather than focus on personal problems and social issues.
- Sports maintain the subordinate role of Blacks and Latinos, who toil as athletes but are less visible in supervisory positions as coaches, managers, and owners.

INTERACTIONIST VIEW

In studying the social order, interactionists are especially interested in shared under-

Sources: Acosta and Carpenter 2001; Edwards 1973; Eitzen 2001; G. Fine 1987.

---

town has felt the impact of layoffs, with its Motorola workforce down to around 1,100 in 2002. Furthermore, this study shows how a rural community is connected to a global economy. Nationwide in 2001, Motorola cut 40,000 jobs but at the same time poured $3.4 billion into operations in China, making the company the largest foreign investor in that country. This means that sociologists have to consider events in Hunan and Sichuan provinces of China in order to understand what is happening in Illinois (Chandler 2001; *Chicago Tribune* 2002; Kaiser 2001; Koval et al. 1996).

Growing interest in applied sociology has led to such specializations as medical sociology and environmental sociology. The former includes research on how health care professionals and patients deal with disease. As one example, medical sociologists have studied the social impact of the AIDS crisis on families, friends, and communities (see Chapter 5). Environmental sociologists examine the relationship between human societies and the physical environment. One focus of their work is the is-

sue of "environmental justice" (see Chapter 21), which has been raised because researchers and community activists have found that hazardous waste dumps are especially likely to be found in poor and minority neighborhoods (M. Martin 1996).

The growing popularity of applied sociology has led to the rise of the specialty of clinical sociology. Louis Wirth (1931) wrote about clinical sociology more than 60 years ago, but the term itself has become popular only in recent years. While applied sociology may simply evaluate social issues, *clinical sociology* is dedicated to altering social relationships (as in family therapy) or to restructuring social institutions (as in the reorganization of a medical center).

The Sociological Practice Association was founded in 1978 to promote the application of sociological knowledge to intervention for individual and social change. This professional group has developed a procedure for certifying clinical sociologists—much as physical therapists or psychologists are certified. In 1999 a new journal standings of everyday behavior. Interactionists examine sports on the micro level by focusing on how day-to-day social behavior is shaped by the distinctive norms, values, and demands of the world of sports:

- Sports often heighten parent–child involvement; they may lead to parental expectations for participation and (sometimes unrealistically) for success.
- Participation in sports provides friendship networks that can permeate everyday life.
- Despite class, racial, and religious differences, teammates may work together harmoniously and may even abandon previous stereotypes and prejudices.
- Relationships in the sports world are defined by people's social positions as players, coaches, and referees—as well as by the high or low status that individuals hold as a result of their performances and reputations.

FEMINIST VIEW

Feminist theorists point out inequities in gender on both the large scale (in such institutions as the economy, government, and religion) and in everyday social interactions. Since sports on every level of society have traditionally been so dominated by males, feminists find much to be concerned about:

- Sports relegate women to a secondary role as spectators and sexual "prizes" even as they equate masculinity with athleticism in celebrating brute strength and ruthless domination.
- Gender expectations encourage female athletes to be passive and gentle, qualities that do not support the emphasis on competitiveness in sports.
- Efforts to increase and support women's participation in college sports through the federal program Title IX are still viewed as costing

men the privilege of participation rather than expanding the opportunity of women.

Despite their differences, functionalists, conflict theorists, interactionists, and feminists would all agree that there is much more to sports than exercise or recreation. They would also agree that sports and other popular forms of culture are worthy subjects of serious study by sociologists.

Let's Discuss

1. Have you experienced or witnessed discrimination in sports based on gender or race? How did you react? Has Title IX been controversial on your campus? In what ways?
2. Which perspective do you think is most useful in looking at the sociology of sports? Why?

---

was published called *Sociological Practice: A Journal of Clinical and Applied Sociology.*

Applied sociologists generally leave it to others to act on their evaluations. By contrast, clinical sociologists take direct responsibility for implementation and view those with whom they work as their clients. This specialty has become increasingly attractive to sociology graduate students because it offers an opportunity to apply intellectual learning in a practical way. Up to now, a shrinking job market in the academic world has made such alternative career routes appealing.

Applied and clinical sociology can be contrasted with **basic** (or *pure*) **sociology,** which seeks a more profound knowledge of the fundamental aspects of social phenomena. This type of research does not necessarily hope to generate specific applications, although such ideas may result once findings are analyzed. When Durkheim studied suicide rates, he was not primarily interested in discovering a way to eliminate suicide. In this sense, his research was an example of basic rather than applied sociology.

 Imagine

What issues facing your local community would you like to address with applied sociological research?

Developing the Sociological Imagination

In this book, we will be illustrating the sociological imagination in several different ways—by showing theory in practice and research in action; by exploring the significance of social inequality; by speaking across race, gender, and national boundaries; and by highlighting social policy throughout the world.

Theory in Practice

We will illustrate how the major sociological perspectives are helpful in understanding today's issues, whether it be capital punishment or financing health care. Sociologists do not necessarily declare "here I am using functionalism," but their research and approaches do tend to draw on one or more theoretical frameworks, as will become clear in the pages to follow.

Research in Action

Sociologists actively investigate a variety of issues and social behavior. We have already seen that such research might involve the meaning of tattoos and decision making in the jury box. Often the research has direct applications to improving people's lives, as in the case of increasing the participation of African Americans in diabetes testing. Throughout the rest of the book, the research performed by sociologists and other social scientists will shed light on group behavior of all types.

The Significance of Social Inequality

Who holds power? Who doesn't? Who has prestige? Who lacks it? Perhaps the major theme of analysis in sociology today is *social inequaltiy,* a condition in which members of society have differing amounts of wealth, prestige, or power. Whether using the functionalist or feminist perspective, focusing on Arizona or Afghanistan, considering a garden club or the global marketplace, sociologists often see behavior as shaped by social inequality.

Applied sociologists, in particular, seek to understand the effect of inequality and often make the case for social justice. W. E. B. Du Bois (1968:418) noted that the greatest power in the land is not "thought or ethics, but wealth." As we have seen, the contributions of Karl Marx, Jane Addams, and Ida Wells-Barnett also focused on social inequality and social justice. Joe Feagin (2001) echoed this sentiment for the overarching importance of social inequality in his recent presidential address to the American Sociological Association.

Throughout this book you will find the work of sociologists on social inequality highlighted. Many chapters also feature a box with this theme.

Speaking across Race, Gender, and National Boundaries

Sociologists include both men and women, people from a variety of ethnic, national, and religious origins. In their work, sociologists seek to draw conclusions that speak to all people—not just the affluent or powerful. This is not always easy. Insights into how a corporation can increase its profits tend to attract more attention and financial support than do, say, the merits of a needle exchange program for low-income, inner-city residents. Yet sociology today, more than ever, seeks to better understand the experiences of *all* people. In Box 1-2, we take a look at how a woman's role in public places is defined differently from that of a man in different parts of the world.

Social Policy throughout the World

One important way we can use the sociological imagination is to enhance our understanding of current social issues throughout the world. Beginning with Chapter 2, which focuses on research, each chapter will conclude with a discussion of a contemporary social policy issue. In some cases, we will examine a specific issue facing national governments. For example, government funding of child care centers will be discussed in Chapter 4, Socialization; human rights in Chapter 10, Social Inequality Worldwide; and the search for shelters in Chapter 20, Communities and Urbanization. These social policy sections will demonstrate how fundamental sociological concepts can enhance our critical thinking skills and help us to better understand current public policy debates taking place around the world.

In addition, sociology has been used to evaluate the success of programs or the impact of changes brought about by policymakers and political activists. Chapter 9, Stratification and Social Mobility in the United States, includes a discussion of research on the effectiveness of welfare reform experiments. Chapter 19, Health and Medicine, considers the issue of financing health care in the United States and other nations, partly by drawing on studies showing that some people may be vulnerable to a lower quality of medical care than others. These discussions underscore the many practical applications of sociological theory and research.

Sociologists expect the next quarter of a century to be perhaps the most exciting and critical period in the history of the discipline. This is because of a growing recognition—both in the United States and around the world—that current social problems *must* be addressed before their magnitude overwhelms human societies. We can expect sociologists to play an increasing role in the government sector by researching and developing public policy alternatives. It seems only natural for this textbook to focus on the connection between the work of sociologists and the difficult questions confronting the policymakers and people of the United States.

By definition, a public place, such as a sidewalk or a park, is open to all persons. Even some private establishments, such as restaurants, are intended to belong to people as a whole. Yet sociologists and other social scientists have found that societies define access to these places differently for women and men.

In many Middle Eastern societies, women are prohibited from public places and are restricted to certain places in the house. In such societies, the coffeehouse and the market are considered male domains. Some other societies, such as Malagasy, strictly limit the presence of women in "public places" yet allow women to conduct the haggling that is a part of shopping in open-air markets. In

Women in public places—whether in this city in the Ivory Coast or elsewhere in the world—are subject to uninvited and sometimes unwelcome stares.

some West African societies, women actually control the marketplace. In various eastern European countries and Turkey, women appear to be free to move about in public places, but the coffeehouse remains the exclusive preserve of males. Contrast this with coffeehouses in North America, where women and men mingle freely and even engage each other in conversation as total strangers.

While casual observers may view both private and public space in the United States as gender-neutral, private all-male clubs do persist, and even in public spaces

> Women are well aware that a casual helping encounter with a man in a public place can too easily lead to undesired sexual queries or advances.

women experience some inequality. Erving Goffman, an interactionist, conducted classic studies of public spaces, which he found to be settings for routine interactions, such as "helping" encounters when a person is lost and asks for directions. But sociologist Carol Brooks Gardner has offered a feminist critique of Goffman's work: "Rarely does Goffman emphasize the habitual disproportionate fear that women can come to feel in public toward men, much less the routine trepidation that ethnic and racial minorities and the disabled

can experience" (1989:45). Women are well aware that a casual helping encounter with a man in a public place can too easily lead to undesired sexual queries or advances.

Whereas Goffman suggests that street remarks about women occur rarely—and that they generally hold no unpleasant or threatening implications—Gardner (1989:49) counters that "for young women especially, . . . appearing in public places carries with it the constant possibility of evaluation, compliments that are not really so complimentary after all, and harsh or vulgar insults if the woman is found wanting." She adds that these remarks are sometimes accompanied by tweaks, pinches, or even blows, unmasking the latent hostility of many male-to-female street remarks.

According to Gardner, many women have a well-founded fear of the sexual harassment, assault, and rape that can occur in public places. She concludes that "public places are arenas for the enactment of inequality in everyday life for women and for many others" (1989:56).

Let's Discuss

1. How would a coffeehouse in Turkey differ from one in Seattle, Washington? What might account for these differences?
2. Do you know a woman who has encountered sexual harassment in a public place? How did she react? How has her social behavior been changed by the experience?

Sources: Cheng and Liao 1994; Gardner 1989, 1990, 1995; Goffman 1963b, 1971; Rosman and Rubel 1994.

⬤ Chapter Resources

Summary

Sociology is the systematic study of social behavior and human groups. In this chapter, we examine the nature of sociological theory, the founders of the discipline, theoretical perspectives of contemporary sociology, applications of sociology, and ways to exercise the "sociological imagination."

1. An important element in the *sociological imagination*—which is an awareness of the relationship between an individual and the wider society—is the ability to view our own society as an outsider might, rather than from the perspective of our limited experiences and cultural biases.
2. Knowledge that relies on "common sense" is not always reliable. Sociologists must test and analyze each piece of information that they use.
3. In contrast to other *social sciences,* sociology emphasizes the influence that groups can have on people's behavior and attitudes and the ways in which people shape society.
4. Sociologists employ *theories* to examine the relationships between observations or data that may seem completely unrelated.
5. Nineteenth-century thinkers who contributed sociological insights included Auguste Comte, a French philosopher; Harriet Martineau, an English sociologist; and Herbert Spencer, an English scholar.
6. Other important figures in the development of sociology were Émile Durkheim, who pioneered work on suicide; Max Weber, who taught the need for "insight" in intellectual work; and Karl Marx, who emphasized the importance of the economy and of conflict in society.

7. In the twentieth century, the discipline of sociology is indebted to the U.S. sociologists Charles Horton Cooley and Robert Merton.
8. *Macrosociology* concentrates on large-scale phenomena or entire civilizations, whereas *microsociology* stresses study of small groups.
9. The *functionalist perspective* of sociology emphasizes the way that parts of a society are structured to maintain its stability.
10. The *conflict perspective* assumes that social behavior is best understood in terms of conflict or tension between competing groups.
11. The *interactionist perspective* is primarily concerned with fundamental or everyday forms of interaction, including symbols and other types of nonverbal communication.
12. The *feminist perspective* views inequity in gender as central to all behavior and organization.
13. Sociologists make use of all four perspectives, since each offers unique insights into the same issue.
14. *Applied sociology*—the use of the discipline with the specific intent of yielding practical applications for human behavior and organizations—can be contrasted with *basic sociology,* which seeks to gain a more profound knowledge of the fundamental aspects of social phenomena.
15. This textbook makes use of the sociological imagination by showing theory in practice and research in action; by focusing on the significance of social inequality; by speaking across race, gender, and national boundaries; and by highlighting social policy around the world.

Critical Thinking Questions

1. What aspects of the social and work environment in a fast-food restaurant would be of particular interest to a sociologist because of his or her "sociological imagination"?
2. What are the manifest and latent functions of a health club?

3. How might the interactionist perspective be applied to a place where you have been employed or to an organization you joined?

Key Terms

Anomie The loss of direction felt in a society when social control of individual behavior has become ineffective. (page 11)

Applied sociology The use of the discipline of sociology with the specific intent of yielding practical applications for human behavior and organizations. (19)

Basic sociology Sociological inquiry conducted with the objective of gaining a more profound knowledge of the fundamental aspects of social phenomena. Also known as *pure sociology*. (21)

Clinical sociology The use of the discipline of sociology with the specific intent of altering social relationships and facilitating change. (20)

Conflict perspective A sociological approach that assumes that social behavior is best understood in terms of conflict or tension between competing groups. (15)

Dramaturgical approach A view of social interaction that examines people as if they were theatrical performers. (17)

Dysfunction An element or a process of society that may disrupt a social system or lead to a decrease in stability. (15)

Feminist perspective A sociological approach that views inequity in gender as central to all behavior and organization. (17)

Functionalist perspective A sociological approach that emphasizes the way that parts of a society are structured to maintain its stability. (14)

Ideal type A construct or model that serves as a measuring rod against which actual cases can be evaluated. (11)

Interactionist perspective A sociological approach that generalizes about fundamental or everyday forms of social interaction. (17)

Latent functions Unconscious or unintended functions; hidden purposes. (15)

Macrosociology Sociological investigation that concentrates on large-scale phenomena or entire civilizations. (14)

Manifest functions Open, stated, and conscious functions. (15)

Microsociology Sociological investigation that stresses study of small groups and often uses laboratory experimental studies. (14)

Natural science The study of the physical features of nature and the ways in which they interact and change. (7)

Nonverbal communication The sending of messages through the use of posture, facial expressions, and gestures. (17)

Science The body of knowledge obtained by methods based upon systematic observation. (7)

Social inequality A condition in which members of society have differing amounts of wealth, prestige, and power. (22)

Social science The study of various aspects of human society. (7)

Sociological imagination An awareness of the relationship between an individual and the wider society. (5)

Sociology The systematic study of social behavior and human groups. (5)

Theory In sociology, a set of statements that seeks to explain problems, actions, or behavior. (9)

Verstehen The German word for "understanding" or "insight"; used to stress the need for sociologists to take into account people's emotions, thoughts, beliefs, and attitudes. (11)

Additional Readings

Du Bois, W. E. B. 1996. *The Philadelphia Negro: A Social Study.* With a new introduction by Elijah Anderson. Philadelphia: Temple University Press. The reissuing of this classic work, which first appeared in 1899, documents the timelessness of Du Bois' observations a century ago.

Fine, Gary Alan. 1996. *Kitchens: The Culture of Restaurant Work.* Berkeley: University of California Press. A sociological view of the backstage world of contemporary restaurants including the social patterns of dishwashers, servers, cooks, managers, and even restaurant critics.

Fries, Kenny. 1997. *Staring Back: The Disability Experience from the Inside Out.* New York: Penguin. This collection of nonfiction, fiction, and poetry helps us to understand the social significance of being disabled in contemporary society.

Glassner, Barry. 1999. *The Culture of Fear.* New York: Basic Books. Glassner looks at how people's fears of crime, drug use, and other social problems are growing, even though the social reality often does not match the public perceptions.

Ingraham, Chrys. 1999. *White Weddings: Romancing Heterosexuality in Popular Culture.* New York: Routledge. A sociologist considers how weddings today have as much to do with marketing and economics as lasting social relationships.

Lengermann, Patricia Madoo, and Jill Niebrugge-Brantley. 1998. *The Women Founders: Sociology and Social Theory 1830–1930.* New York: McGraw-Hill. A comprehensive examination of the many contributions that women made to early sociological thinking in the United States and Europe.

Levin, Jack. 1999. *Sociological Snapshots 3: Seeing Social Structure and Change in Everyday Life.* Thousand Oaks, CA: Pine Forge Press. The sociological imagination is employed to look at everything from elevator culture and television soap operas to religious cults and the death penalty.

McDonald, Lynn. 1994. *Women Founders of the Social Sciences*. Ottawa, Can.: Carlton University Press. The author examines the important but often overlooked contributions of such pioneers as Mary Wollstonecraft, Harriet Martineau, Beatrice Webb, Jane Addams, and many more.

Tilly, Charles. 1999. *Durable Inequality*. Berkeley: University of California Press. A theoretical look at the persistence of social inequality between Black/White, male/female, and citizen/noncitizen.

Technology Resources

Internet Connection

*Note: While all the URLs listed were current as of the printing of this book, these sites often change. Please check our website (**http://www. mhhe.com/schaefer8**) for updates and hyperlinks to these exercises and additional exercises.*

1. The American Sociological Association (ASA) (**http://www.asanet.org**) is a nonprofit organization with about 13,000 members, including faculty, researchers, practitioners, and students. This site contains some useful information about the field of sociology, society and social life, and careers in sociology. Go to the homepage and link to "Careers in Sociology." Click on "Society and Social Life," and answer the following questions:
   (a) Why is the scope of sociology so broad?
   (b) Why is sociology a rapidly expanding field? Click on your Refresh or Back button. Link to "Sociological Specialties: Many Paths to Understanding the Society."
   (c) Why is the study of racial and ethnic minorities important?
   (d) Why do you think a sociologist would be interested in age discrimination? Click on your Refresh or Back button. Link to one of the "Publications for the Public."
   (e) Which publication did you read? Briefly, what did you learn?

2. Sociologists in the twenty-first century owe a debt of intellectual gratitude to early thinkers and pioneers such as Émile Durkheim, Karl Marx, and Max Weber. To learn about many of the thinkers listed in Chapter 1, visit SocioRealm (**http://www. geocities.com/ College Park/Quad/5889/index. htm**), a site constructed by Jessica Champlin. Choose two of the theorists offered and visit the links associated with them; read some of their original works and biographies. For each theorist, answer the following:
   (a) When did the thinker live? What important historical events were occuring during this time? Did any of these historical events shape

his or her sociological imagination and views on society?
   (b) After reading some of the original works, how would you summarize this person's perspectives? Which of the three main sociological perspectives—functionalism, conflict, or interactionism—would you say this thinker is most associated with? Why?
   (c) What facts did you find most interesting about this person in his or her life story or sociological contributions?
   (d) How do the ideas of this thinker compare and contrast with your other selection? Which of the two thinkers' ideas did you like the most? Why?

3. Sociologists use three main theoretical perspectives when analyzing the social world, including events both historical and current. Log onto Yahoo! (**http://www.yahoo.com**) and choose one of the breaking stories from the "In the News" section. follow the links given, reading articles and viewing pictures from online newspapers and networks on your chosen story. Next, apply functionalist, conflict, and interactionist perspectives to the story (Table 1-2 in your text will be especially helpful).
   (a) How would Karl Marx and conflict thinkers view such an event? Is there tension and struggle between groups? Which groups?
   (b) How would Emile Durkheim and functionalist thinkers examine the story? Can you apply concepts such as manifest functions, latent functions, and dysfunctions?
   (c) What would be the perspective of George Herbert Mead and other interactionists? What symbols are being used to describe the story by the media? Can you apply dramaturgy to the events? Are players in the story trying to project a certain image using symbols?
   (d) Which perspective did you find to be the most interesting? Is one perspective better suited than the others to analyze the story? Why or why not?

SocWorld CD-ROM

This CD, which is packaged free with all new copies of the text, allows you to instantly explore various topics and concepts with an assortment of video clips (including footage of this text's author in Singapore), website links, interactive quizzes, and other learning tools. Also included are audio introductions to each of the book excerpts that open each chapter and additional information about these excerpts and their authors.

Online Learning Center www.mhhe.com/schaefer8

Visit the Online Learning Center, this textbook's specific website, at **www.mhhe.com/schaefer8.** The student center in the Online Learning Center offers a variety of helpful and interesting resources and activities for each chapter. The resources include chapter outlines and summaries, quizzes with feedback, direct links to Internet sites, including those found in the Internet Connection sections at the end of each chapter in your text, and audio clips from the author. The activities include flashcards, crossword puzzles, interactive maps, and interactive exercises. Don't pass up this opportunity to learn more about sociology and to take advantage of resources that will help you master the material in your text and get a better grade in the course!

PowerWeb

Using the password found on the gold and black card that was shrinkwrapped with your book, visit PowerWeb, a website that provides a wealth of resources including quizzes, links to related websites, interactive exercises, time management tips, articles, and a guide to doing research on the web. You will also find daily news on relevant topics. PowerWeb is accessible from a link on the Online Learning Center website. Also accessible from the Online Learning Center is a unique PowerWeb site on violence and terrorism.

SocCity

Explore SocCity, a veritable melting pot of sociology cybersources, information, and Internet activity for students and instructors alike. Whether you are looking for the perfect book for your sociology class, or you are a student looking for some starter sites for your next research paper, SocCity has it.

CAREERS IN SOCIOLOGY

An undergraduate degree in sociology doesn't just serve as excellent preparation for future graduate work in sociology. It also provides a strong liberal arts background for entry-level positions in business, social services, foundations, community organizations, not-for-profit groups, law enforcement, and other types of governmental jobs. Many fields—among them marketing, public relations, and broadcasting—now require investigative skills and an understanding of diverse groups found in today's multiethnic and multinational environment. Moreover, a sociology degree requires accomplishment in oral and written communication, interpersonal skills, problem solving, and critical thinking—all job-related skills that may give sociology graduates an advantage over those who pursue more technical degrees (Benner and Hitchcock 1986; Billson and Huber 1993).

Consequently, while few occupations specifically require an undergraduate degree in sociology, such academic training can be an important asset in entering a wide range of occupations (American Sociological Association, 1993, 1995a). Just to bring this home, a number of chapters highlight a real-life professional who describes how the study of sociology has helped in his or her career. Look for the "Taking Sociology to Work" boxes.

The accompanying figure summarizes sources of employment for those with BA or BS degrees in sociology. It shows that the areas of human services, the not-for-profit sector, business, and government offer major career opportunities for sociology graduates. Undergraduates who know where their career interests lie are well advised to enroll in sociology courses and specialties best suited for those interests. For example, students hoping to become health planners would take a class in medical sociology; students seeking employment as social science research assistants would focus on courses in statistics and methods. Internships, such as placements at city planning agencies and survey research organizations, afford another way for sociology students to prepare for careers. Studies show that students who choose an internship placement have less trouble finding jobs, obtain better jobs, and enjoy greater job satisfaction than students without internship placements (Salem and Grabarek 1986).

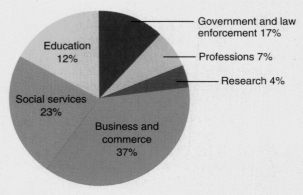

Source: Schaefer. 1998b.

Many college students view social work as the field most closely associated with sociology. Traditionally, social workers received their undergraduate training in sociology and allied fields such as psychology and counseling. After some practical experience, social workers would generally seek a master's degree in social work (MSW) to be considered for supervisory or administrative positions. Today, however, some students choose (where it is available) to pursue an undergraduate degree in social work (BSW). This degree prepares graduates for direct service positions such as caseworker or group worker.

Many students continue their sociological training beyond the bachelor's degree. More than 250 universities in the United States have graduate programs in sociology that offer PhD and/or master's degrees. These programs differ greatly in their areas of specialization, course requirements, costs, and research and teaching opportunities available to graduate student. About 55 percent of the graduates are women (American Sociological Association 2002; Spalter-Roth et al. 2000).

Higher education is an important source of employment for sociologists with graduate degrees. About 83 percent of recent PhD recipients in sociology sought employment in colleges and universities. These sociologists teach not only majors committed to the discipline but also students hoping to become doctors, nurses, lawyers, police officers, and so forth (Spalter-Roth et al. 2000).

Sociology students put in many years and a great deal of work on the way to a PhD. Fortunately, the job market for instructors is looking better than in years past as the size of the college student population steadily grows.

For sociology graduates interested in academic careers, the road to a PhD degree (or doctorate) can be long and difficult. This degree symbolizes competence in original research; each candidate must prepare a book-length study known as a dissertation. Typically, a doctoral student in sociology will engage in four to seven years of intensive work, including the time required to complete the dissertation. Yet even this effort is no guarantee of a job as a sociology professor.

The good news is that over the next 10 years, the demand for instructors is expected to increase because of high rates of retirement among faculty from the baby-boom generation, as well as the anticipated slow but steady growth in the college student population in the United States. Nonetheless, anyone who launches an academic career must be prepared for considerable uncertainty and competition in the college job market (American Sociological Association 1995a; B. Huber 1985).

Of course, not all people working as sociologists teach or hold doctoral degrees. Take government, for example. The Census Bureau relies on people with sociological training to interpret data for other government agencies and the general public. Virtually every agency depends on survey research—a field in which sociology students can specialize—in order to assess everything from community needs to the morale of the agency's own workers. In addition, people with sociological training can put their academic knowledge to effective use in probation and parole, health sciences, community development, and recreational services. Some people working in government or private industry have a master's degree (MA or MS) in sociology; others have a bachelor's degree (a BA or BS).

Currently, about 22 percent of the members of the American Sociological Association use their sociological skills outside the academic world, whether in social service agencies or in marketing positions for business firms. A renewed interest in applied sociology has led to the hiring of an increasing number of sociologists with graduate degrees by businesses, industry, hospitals, and nonprofit organizations. Indeed, studies show that many sociology graduates are making career changes from social service areas to business and commerce. As an undergraduate major, sociology is excellent preparation for employment in many parts of the business world (American Sociological Association 2001).

Whether you take a few courses in sociology or actually complete a degree, you will benefit from the critical thinking skills developed in this discipline. Sociologists emphasize the value of being able to analyze, interpret, and function within a variety of working situations; this is an asset in virtually any career. Moreover, given the rapid technological change evident in the 1990s and the expanding global economy, all of us will need to adapt to substantial social change, even in our own careers. Sociology provides a rich conceptual framework that can serve as a foundation for flexible career development and can assist us in taking advantage of new employment opportunities (American Sociological Association 1995, 1995).

CHAPTER 2

SOCIOLOGICAL RESEARCH

The New Quilt by Herb Kawainui Kane — Courtesy of the artist

Generations Are Counting On You

This Census 2000 poster, developed by the Native Hawaiian and Other Pacific Islanders Census Advisory Subcommittee with assistance from the Bernice Pauahi Bishop Museum, celebrates diversity in America.

USCENSUSBUREAU

United States
**Census
2000**

This is your future.
Don't leave it blank.

Good social research collects data using the established scientific method, as in the census taken by the federal government every 10 years. This poster encouraged all people to respond to census takers from the federal government for the Census 2000. The information collected from such censuses is valuable in sociological studies.

Because public interactions generally matter for only a few crucial seconds, people are conditioned to rapid scrutiny of the looks, speech, public behavior, gender, and color of those sharing the environment. . . . [T]he central strategy in maintaining safety on the streets is to avoid strange black males. . . .

Many blacks perceive whites as tense or hostile to them in public. They pay attention to the amount of eye contact given. In general, black males get far less time in this regard than do white males. Whites tend not to "hold" the eyes of a black person. It is more common for black and white strangers to meet each other's eyes for only a few seconds, and then to avert their gaze abruptly. Such behavior seems to say, "I am aware of your presence," and no more. Women especially feel that eye contact invites unwanted advances, but some white men feel the same and want to be clear about what they intend. This eye work is a way to maintain distance, mainly for safety and social purposes. Consistent with this, some blacks are very surprised to find a white person who holds their eyes longer than is normal according to the rules of the public sphere. As one middle-aged white female resident commented:

Just this morning, I saw a [black] guy when I went over to Mr. Chow's to get some milk at 7:15. You always greet people you see at 7:15, and I looked at him and smiled. And he said "Hello" or "Good morning" or something. I smiled again. It was clear that he saw this as surprising.

*　　　*　　　*

Many people, particularly those who see themselves as more economically privileged than others in the community, are careful not to let their eyes stray, in order to avoid an uncomfortable situation. As they walk down the street they pretend not to see other pedestrians, or they look right at them without speaking, a behavior many blacks find offensive.

*　　　*　　　*

Moreover, whites of the Village often scowl to keep young blacks at a social and physical distance. As they venture out on the streets of the Village and, to a lesser extent, of Northton, they may plant this look on their faces to ward off others who might mean them harm. Scowling by whites may be compared to gritting [looking "tough"] by blacks as a coping strategy. At times members of either group make such faces with little regard for circumstances, as if they were dressing for inclement weather. But on the Village streets it does not always storm, and such overcoats repel the sunshine as well as the rain, frustrating many attempts at spontaneous human communication. *(Anderson 1990: 208, 220–221)* ■ 💿

Additional information about this excerpt and about those that open each subsequent chapter can be found in the SocWorld CD-ROM that accompanies this text.

This study of "eye work" was part of extensive research into life on the street that sociologist Elijah Anderson conducted in two adjacent neighborhoods of Philadelphia—"the Village," a racially mixed area with mixed incomes, and "Northton," mostly Black and low-income. Anderson became intrigued with the nature of social interaction between strangers on the street shortly after moving into the Village community in 1975. Over the next 14 years he undertook a formal study. Using the interactionist perspective, he focused on how such a diverse group of people related to one another in everyday life. In particular, he was interested in their "public behavior," including the way they used eye contact in their daily encounters.

Like any good scientist, Anderson was thorough in his research. He interviewed residents, videotaped street scenes, took extensive notes, photographed settings, and hung out for hours at a time in the local bars, laundromats, and corner stores in the course of his observations. As a Black man, he was also able to draw on his own experiences with the Whites in his neighborhood. Anderson systematically traced how social changes—including gentrification of previously low-income areas, increasing drug use and crime, and declining city services—affected social relations and the ways people negotiated public spaces. Three of his books, *A Place on the Corner* (1978), *Streetwise* (1990), and *Code of the Streets* (1999), came out of this research, and he hopes other researchers will make use of his database for their own studies.

Effective sociological research can be quite thought-provoking. It may suggest many new questions about social interactions that require further study, such as why we make assumptions about people's intentions based merely on their gender or age or race. In some cases, rather than raising additional questions, a study will simply confirm previous beliefs and findings.

This chapter will examine the research process used in conducting sociological studies. How do sociologists go about setting up a research project? And how do they ensure that the results of the research are reliable and accurate? Can they carry out their research without stepping on the rights of those they study?

We will first look at the steps that make up the scientific method in doing research. Then we will take a look at various techniques commonly used in sociological research, such as experiments, observations, and surveys. We will pay particular attention to the ethical challenges sociologists face in studying human behavior and to the debate raised by Max Weber's call for "value neutrality" in social science research. We will also examine the role that technology plays in research today. The social policy section considers the difficulties in researching human sexuality.

Whatever the area of sociological inquiry and whatever the perspective of the sociologist—whether functionalist, conflict, interactionist, or any other—there is one crucial requirement: imaginative, responsible research that meets the highest scientific and ethical standards. ■

What Is the Scientific Method?

Like all of us, sociologists are interested in the central questions of our time. Is the family falling apart? Why is there so much crime in the United States? Is the world lagging behind in its ability to feed the population? Such issues concern most people, whether or not they have academic training. However, unlike the typical citizen, the sociologist has a commitment to the use of the scientific method in studying society. The *scientific method* is a systematic, organized series of steps that ensures maximum objectivity and consistency in researching a problem.

Many of us will never actually conduct scientific research. Why, then, is it important that we understand the scientific method? Because it plays a major role in the workings of our society. Residents of the United States are constantly being bombarded with "facts" or "data." A television news report informs us that "one in every two marriages in this country now ends in divorce," yet Chapter 14 will show that this assertion is based on misleading statistics. Almost daily, advertisers cite supposedly scientific studies to prove that their products are superior. Such claims may be accurate or exaggerated. We can make better evaluations of such information—and will not be fooled so easily—if we are familiar with the standards of scientific research. These standards are quite stringent and demand as strict adherence as possible.

The scientific method requires precise preparation in developing useful research. Otherwise, the research data collected may not prove accurate. Sociologists and other researchers follow five basic steps in the scientific method:

FIGURE 2-1

The Scientific Method

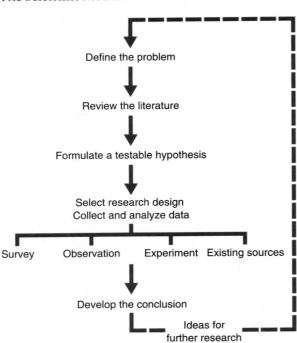

Define the problem

↓

Review the literature

↓

Formulate a testable hypothesis

↓

Select research design
Collect and analyze data

Survey   Observation   Experiment   Existing sources

↓

Develop the conclusion

Ideas for further research

The scientific method allows sociologists to objectively and logically evaluate data they collect. Their findings can prompt further ideas for sociological research.

It seems reasonable to assume that these Columbia University graduates will earn more income than high school graduates. But how would you go about researching this hypothesis?

(1) defining the problem, (2) reviewing the literature, (3) formulating the hypothesis, (4) selecting the research design and then collecting and analyzing data, and (5) developing the conclusion (see Figure 2-1). We'll use an actual example to illustrate the workings of the scientific method.

Defining the Problem

Does it "pay" to go to college? Some people make great sacrifices and work hard to get a college education. Parents borrow money for their children's tuition. Students work part-time jobs or even take full-time positions while attending evening or weekend classes. Does it pay off? Are there monetary returns for getting that degree?

The first step in any research project is to state as clearly as possible what you hope to investigate, that is, *define the problem*. In this instance, we are interested in knowing how schooling relates to income. We want to find out the earnings of people with different levels of formal schooling. Early on, any social science researcher must develop an operational definition of each concept being studied. An *operational definition* is an explanation of an abstract concept that is specific enough to allow a researcher to measure the concept. For example, a sociologist interested in status might use membership in exclusive social clubs as an operational definition of status. Someone studying prejudice might consider a person's unwillingness to hire or work with members of minority groups as an operational definition of prejudice. In our example, we need to develop two operational definitions—education and earnings—in order to study whether it "pays" to get advanced educational degrees.

Initially, we take a functionalist perspective (although we may end up incorporating other approaches). We argue that opportunities for more earning power are related to level of schooling and that schools prepare students for employment.

Reviewing the Literature

By conducting a *review of the literature*—the relevant scholarly studies and information—researchers refine the problem under study, clarify possible techniques to be used in collecting data, and eliminate or reduce avoidable mistakes.

For our example, we would examine information about the salaries for different occupations. We would see if jobs that require more academic training are better rewarded. It would also be appropriate to review other studies on the relationship between education and income.

The review of the literature would soon tell us that many other factors besides years of schooling influence earning potential. For example, we would learn that the children of richer parents are more likely to go to college than those from modest backgrounds, so we might consider the possibility that these parents may also help their children secure better-paying jobs after getting their degrees.

Formulating the Hypothesis

After reviewing earlier research and drawing on the contributions of sociological theorists, the researchers then *formulate the hypothesis.* A **hypothesis** is a speculative statement about the relationship between two or more factors known as *variables.* Income, religion, occupation, and gender can all serve as variables in a study. We can define a **variable** as a measurable trait or characteristic that is subject to change under different conditions.

Researchers who formulate a hypothesis generally must suggest how one aspect of human behavior influences or affects another. The variable hypothesized to cause or influence another is called the **independent variable.** The second variable is termed the **dependent variable** because its action "depends" on the influence of the independent variable.

Our hypothesis is that the higher one's educational degree, the more money a person will earn. The independent variable that is to be measured is the level of educational degree. The variable that is thought to "depend" on it—income—must also be measured.

Identifying independent and dependent variables is a critical step in clarifying cause-and-effect relationships in society. As shown in Figure 2-2, **causal logic** involves the relationship between a condition or variable and a particular consequence, with one event leading to the other. Under causal logic, being less integrated into society may p. 9 be directly related to or produce a greater likelihood of suicide. Similarly, the time students spend reviewing material for a quiz may be directly related to or produce a greater likelihood of getting a high score on the quiz.

A **correlation** exists when a change in one variable coincides with a change in the other. Correlations are an indication that causality *may* be present; they do not necessarily indicate causation. For example, data indicate that working mothers are more likely to have delinquent

Figure 2-2

Causal Logic

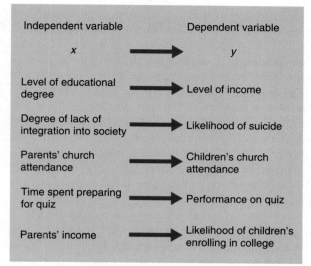

In *causal logic* an independent variable (often designated by the symbol *x*) influences a dependent variable (generally designated as *y*); thus, *x* leads to *y*. For example, parents who attend church regularly (*x*) are more likely to have children who are churchgoers (*y*). Notice that the first two pairs of variables are taken from studies already described in this textbook.

Think About It
Identify two or three variables that might "depend" on this independent variable: number of alcoholic drinks ingested.

children than are mothers who do not work outside the home. But this correlation is actually *caused* by a third variable: family income. Lower-class households are more likely to have a full-time working mother; at the same time, reported rates of delinquency are higher in this class than in other economic levels. Consequently, while having a mother who works outside the home is correlated with delinquency, it does not *cause* delinquency. Sociologists seek to identify the *causal* link between variables; this causal link is generally described by researchers in their hypotheses.

Collecting and Analyzing Data

How do you test a hypothesis to determine if it is supported or refuted? You need to collect information, using one of the research designs described later in the chapter. The research design guides the researcher in collecting and analyzing data.

Selecting the Sample

In most studies, social scientists must carefully select what is known as a *sample*. A **sample** is a selection from a larger population that is statistically representative of that population. There are many kinds of samples, but the one social scientists most frequently use is the random sample. In a **random sample,** every member of an entire population being studied has the same chance of being selected. Thus, if researchers want to examine the opinions of people listed in a city directory (a book that, unlike the telephone directory, lists all households), they might use a computer to randomly select names from the directory. This would constitute a random sample. The advantage of using specialized sampling techniques is that sociologists do not need to question everyone in a population.

Sampling is a complex aspect of research design. In Box 2-1, we consider the approach some researchers took when trying to create an appropriate sample of people in the world's most populous nation—China. We'll also see how they made use of data from the sample.

It is all too easy to confuse the careful scientific techniques used in representative sampling with the many *nonscientific* polls that receive much more media attention. For example, television viewers and radio listeners are encouraged to e-mail their views on today's headlines or on political contests. Such polls reflect nothing more than the views of those who happened to see the television program (or hear the radio broadcast) and took the time, perhaps at some cost, to register their opinions. These data do not necessarily reflect (and indeed may distort) the views of the broader population. Not everyone has access to a television or radio or has the time to watch or listen to a program or has the means and/or inclination to send e-mail. Similar problems are raised by "mail-back" questionnaires found in many magazines and by "mall intercepts" where shoppers are asked about some issue. Even when these techniques include answers from tens of thousands of people, their accuracy will be far less than that of a carefully selected representative sample of 1,500 respondents.

For the purposes of our research example, we will use information collected in the General Social Survey (GSS). Since 1972, the National Opinion Research Center (NORC) has conducted this national survey 23 times, most recently in 2000. A representative sample of the adult population is interviewed on a variety of topics for about one and a half hours. The author of this book examined the responses of the 2,817 people interviewed in 2000 concerning their level of education and income.

"And don't waste your time canvassing the whole building, young man. We think alike."

When conducting a survey, researchers must draw their sample carefully so that it is representative of the general population. (Drawn by Stevenson; ©1980 The New Yorker Magazine, Inc.)

Ensuring Validity and Reliability

The scientific method requires that research results be both valid and reliable. *Validity* refers to the degree to which a measure or scale truly reflects the phenomenon under study. *Reliability* refers to the extent to which a measure produces consistent results. A valid measure of income depends on gathering accurate data. Various studies show that people are reasonably accurate in knowing how much money they earned in the most recent year. One problem of reliability is that some people may not *disclose* accurate information, but most do. In the General Social Survey, only 9 percent of the respondents refused to give their income and another 5 percent said they did not know what their income was. That means 86 percent of the respondents gave their income, which we can assume is reasonably accurate (given their other responses about occupation and years in the labor force).

Developing the Conclusion

Scientific studies, including those conducted by sociologists, do not aim to answer all the questions that can be raised about a particular subject. Therefore, the

Sociology in the Global Community

2-1 "Sent-down" in China

Imagine arriving at school and learning that the entire college was being closed and that, in fact, the government was closing *all* universities. Furthermore, since there was no school for you to attend, you were now being taken to the countryside to work on farms so the country could increase agricultural production.

This is basically what happened to students in China from 1967 to 1978, a period historians refer to as the Cultural Revolution, when China was trying to rid itself of outside influences. During this time, 17 million young urban people—about a third of the youth entering the labor force—were the victims of the government's "send-down" policy. They were forced to live and work in rural areas rather than attend school or work at government jobs they may have held.

Sociologists Xueguang Zhou and Liren Hou of Duke University were interested in what impact these state policies had on the people's lives. To learn more,

the researchers decided to interview those who were "sent-down" as well as comparable people who were not sent to rural areas. They did their representative sampling in several stages: first selecting cities from different geographical areas, then systematically selecting blocks within those cities, and finally randomly selecting and interviewing adults within the blocks. They accumulated a sample of 2,793 people, of whom 855 had been sent-down.

> **17 million young urban people were the victims of the government's "send-down" policy.**

Zhou and Hou found that those who stayed in rural areas more than six years were likely to marry later, have fewer children, and hold poorer jobs than those who spent less time or those who stayed in urban areas. While these differences

may be expected, some findings were surprising. For example, those who were sent-down for only a few years were more likely to graduate from college than those young people who were never sent-down. The researchers argue that many of the youths who left "early" from rural areas were well-connected politically and therefore probably came from more prosperous backgrounds. Also, these young people may have resolved to quickly overcome the adverse effects of the state policy.

Let's Discuss

1. How did the researchers make sure their sample was representative? Do you think selecting names from a phone book would produce the same results? How would you go about selecting a sample population?

2. Describe the independent and dependent variables in this study. (Refer to page 35 if you need to.)

Source: Zhou and Hou 1999.

---

conclusion of a research study represents both an end and a beginning. It terminates a specific phase of the investigation, but it should also generate ideas for future study.

Supporting Hypotheses

In our example, we find that the data support our hypothesis: People with more formal schooling *do* earn more money. As Table 2-1 shows, those with a high school diploma earn more than those who failed to complete high school, but those with an associate's degree earn more than high school graduates. The relationship continues through more advanced levels of schooling, so that those with graduate degrees earn the most.

The relationship is not perfect. Obviously, some people who drop out of high school end up with high incomes, whereas some with advanced degrees have modest incomes, as shown in Figure 2-3. A successful entrepreneur, for example, might not have much formal school-

ing, and a holder of a doctorate degree may choose to work for a low-paying nonprofit institution.

Sociological studies do not always generate data that support the original hypothesis. In many instances, a hypothesis is refuted, and researchers must reformulate their conclusions. Unexpected results may also lead sociologists to reexamine their methodology and make changes in the research design.

Controlling for Other Factors

A **control variable** is a factor held constant to test the relative impact of the independent variable. For example, if researchers wanted to know how adults in the United States feel about restrictions on smoking in public places, they would probably attempt to use a respondent's smoking behavior as a control variable. That is, how do smokers versus nonsmokers feel about smoking in public places? The researchers would compile separate statistics on how smokers and nonsmokers feel about antismoking regulations.

Table 2-1 Education and Income

Income Group	Percentage of Those in Income Group According to Highest Degree Earned				
	Less Than High School Education	High School Diploma	Associate's Degree	BA/BS	Graduate Degree
Under $15,000	56%	31%	22%	19%	11%
$15,000–24,999	23	26	22	15	5
$25,000–34,999	10	19	18	21	10
$35,000–59,999	9	18	30	28	34
$60,000 and over	2	6	8	17	40

Source: Author's analysis of General Social Survey 2000 in Davis and Smith 2001.

Figure 2-3

Impact of College on Income

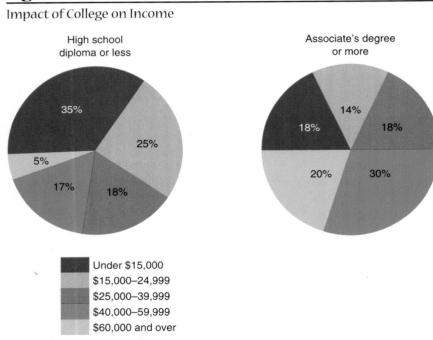

High school diploma or less

Associate's degree or more

Under $15,000
$15,000–24,999
$25,000–39,999
$40,000–59,999
$60,000 and over

Source: Author's analysis of General Social Survey 2000 in Davis and Smith 2001.

Our study of the influence of education on income suggests that not everyone enjoys equal educational opportunities, a disparity that is one of the causes of social inequality. Since education affects a person's income, we may wish to call on the conflict perspective to explore this topic further. What impact does a person's race or gender have? Is a woman with a college degree likely to earn as much as a man with similar schooling? Later in this textbook we will consider these other factors and variables. We will examine the impact that education has on income, while controlling for the variables of gender, race, and other factors.

In Summary: The Scientific Method

Let us briefly summarize the process of the scientific method through a review of the example. We *defined a problem* (the question of whether it pays to get higher educational degrees). We *reviewed the literature* (other studies of the relationship between education and income) and *formulated a hypothesis* (the higher one's educational degree the more money a person will earn). We *collected and analyzed the data*, making sure the data were valid and reliable. Finally, we *developed the conclusion:* The data do support our hypothesis about the influence of education on income.

p. 22

Major Research Designs

An important aspect of sociological research is deciding how to collect the data. A ***research design*** is a detailed plan or method for obtaining data scientifically. Selection of a research design requires creativity and ingenuity. This choice will directly influence both the cost of the project and the amount of time needed to collect the results of the research. Research designs that sociologists regularly use to generate data include surveys, observation, experiments, and existing sources.

Surveys

Almost all of us have responded to surveys of one kind or another. We may have been asked what kind of detergent we use, which presidential candidate we intend to vote for, or what our favorite television program is. A ***survey*** is a study, generally in the form of an interview or questionnaire, that provides researchers with information concerning how people think and act. Among the United States' best-known surveys of opinion are the Gallup poll and the Harris poll. As anyone who watches the news during presidential campaigns knows, these polls have become a staple of political life.

When you think of surveys, you may recall seeing many "person on the street" interviews on local television news shows. While such interviews can be highly entertaining, they are not necessarily an accurate indication of public opinion. First, they reflect the opinions of only those people who happen to be at a certain location. Such a sample can be biased in favor of commuters, middle-class shoppers, or factory workers, depending on which street or area the newspeople select. Second, television interviews tend to attract outgoing people who are willing to appear on the air, while they frighten away others who may feel intimidated by a camera. As we've seen, a survey must be based on precise, representative sampling if it is to genuinely reflect a broad range of the population.

In preparing to conduct a survey, sociologists must not only develop representative samples; they must exercise great care in the wording of questions. An effective survey question must be simple and clear enough for people to understand it. It must also be specific enough so that there are no problems in interpreting the results. Open-ended questions ("What do you think of programming on educational television?") must be carefully phrased to solicit the type of information desired. Box 2-2 illustrates the different results that different phrasing of a question can produce. Surveys can be indispensable sources of information, but only if the sampling is done properly and the questions are worded accurately and without bias.

There are two main forms of surveys: the ***interview,*** in which a researcher obtains information through face-to-face or telephone questioning, and the ***questionnaire,*** which uses a printed or written form to obtain information from a respondent. Each of these has its own advantages. An interviewer can obtain a high response rate because people find it more difficult to turn down a personal request for an interview than

Doonesbury

Think About It
What would constitute a less biased question for a survey on smoking?

Research in Action

2-2 Framing Survey Questions about Interracial Friendships

Do White people really have close Black friends, and vice versa? Many surveys have attempted to gauge the amount of White–Black interaction. But unless the questions are phrased carefully, it is possible to overestimate just how much "racial togetherness" is taking place.

Sociologist Tom Smith, who heads up the respected General Social Survey, no-

> Unless the questions are phrased carefully, it is possible to overestimate just how much "racial togetherness" is taking place.

ticed that a high proportion of Whites and African Americans indicate they have close friends of the other race. But is this, in fact, true? When Smith and his fellow researchers analyzed data from the 1998 General Social Survey they found that response rates varied according to how the question was phrased.

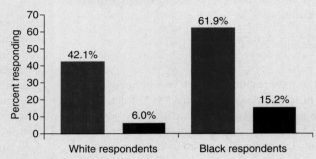

■ Percent who say they have a close friend who is Black or White
■ Percent who name a close friend who is of a different race

Source: Smith 1999.

For example, when asked whether any of their friends that they feel close to was Black, 42.1 percent of Whites said "yes." Yet when asked to give the names of friends they feel close to, only 6 percent of Whites listed a close friend of a different race or ethnicity. The accompanying figure shows the results for both White and Black respondents.

Let's Discuss

1. Why do you think people responded so differently to these two questions? How would you frame a question to get an accurate picture of interracial friendships?
2. Do you have close friends of another race? If asked to list your close friends, would you list someone from a different race?

Source: Smith 1999.

to throw away a written questionnaire. In addition, a skillful interviewer can go beyond written questions and "probe" for a subject's underlying feelings and reasons. On the other hand, questionnaires have the advantage of being cheaper, especially in large samples

Studies have shown that characteristics of the interviewer have an impact on survey data. For example, women interviewers tend to receive more feminist responses from female subjects than do male researchers, and African American interviewers tend to receive more detailed responses about race-related issues from Black subjects than do White interviewers. The possible impact of gender and race only indicates again how much care social research requires (D. Davis 1997; L. Huddy et al. 1997).

Observation

As we saw in the chapter opening, Elijah Anderson gathered his information on street life in Philadelphia through *observing* everyday interaction of the residents. Investigators who collect information through direct participation and/or closely watching a group or community under study are engaged in **observation.** This method allows sociologists to examine certain behaviors and communities that could not be investigated through other research techniques.

Observation research is the most common form of **_qualitative research,_** which relies on what is seen in field or naturalistic settings more than on statistical data. Generally, such studies focus on small groups or communities rather than large groups or whole nations. An increasingly popular form of qualitative research in sociology today is ethnography. *Ethnography* refers to efforts to describe an entire social setting through extended, systematic observation. Anthropologists rely heavily on ethnography. Much as an anthropologist seeks to understand the people of some Polynesian island, the sociologist as an ethnographer seeks to understand and present to us an entire way of life in some setting. Anderson's study involved not just understanding behavior of pedestrians but also understanding all facets of life in two urban neighborhoods.

Quantitative research collects and reports data primarily in numerical form. Most of the survey research discussed so far in this book has been this type of research. While quantitative research can make use of larger samples than qualitative research, it can't look at a topic in as great depth. Neither type of research is necessarily

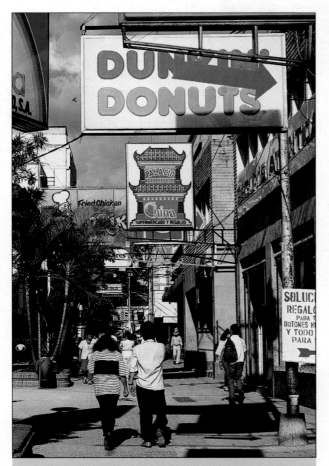

This city in Honduras in Central America provides a rich setting for observation research. An ethnographer would take note of the interplay of cultures in the everyday street life.

better. Usually we are best informed when we rely on studies using a variety of research designs that look at *both* qualitative and quantitative aspects of the same subject.

p.4 In some cases, the sociologist actually "joins" a group for a period of time to get an accurate sense of how it operates. This is called *participant observation*. In the tattoo study described in Chapter 1 as well as in Anderson's study of "eye work," the researcher was a participant observer.

During the late 1930s, in a classic example of participant-observation research, William F. Whyte moved into a low-income Italian neighborhood in Boston. For nearly four years, he was a member of the social circle of "corner boys" that he describes in *Street Corner Society*. Whyte revealed his identity to these men and joined in their conversations, bowling, and other leisure-time activities. His goal was to gain greater insight into the community that these men had established. As Whyte (1981:303) listened to Doc, the leader of the group, he "learned the answers to questions I would not even have had the sense to ask if I had been getting my information solely on an interviewing basis." Whyte's work was especially valuable, since, at the time, the academic world had little direct knowledge of the poor and tended to rely for information on the records of social service agencies, hospitals, and courts (Adler and Johnson 1992).

The initial challenge that Whyte faced—and that every participant observer encounters—was to gain acceptance into an unfamiliar group. It is no simple matter for a college-trained sociologist to win the trust of a religious cult, a youth gang, a poor Appalachian community, or a circle of skid row residents. It requires a great deal of patience and an accepting, nonthreatening type of person on the part of the observer.

Observation research poses other complex challenges for the investigator. Sociologists must be able to fully understand what they are observing. In a sense, then, researchers must learn to see the world as the group sees it in order to fully comprehend the events taking place around them.

This raises a delicate issue. If the research is to be successful, the observer cannot allow the close associations or even friendships that inevitably develop to influence the subjects' behavior or the conclusions of the study. Anson Shupe and David Bromley (1980), two sociologists who have used participant observation, have likened this challenge to that of "walking a tightrope." Even while working hard to gain acceptance from the group being studied, the participant observer *must* maintain some degree of detachment.

The feminist perspective in sociology has drawn attention to a shortcoming in ethnographic research. For most of the history of sociology, studies were conducted

Does arresting someone for domestic assault deter future incidents of violence? An experiment in Miami, Florida, studied this question by making use of control and experimental groups.

on male subjects or about male-led groups and organizations, and the findings were generalized to all people. For example, for many decades studies of urban life focused on street corners, neighborhood taverns, and bowling alleys—places where men typically congregated. Although the insights were valuable, they did not give a true impression of city life because they overlooked the areas where women were likely to gather, such as playgrounds, grocery stores, and front stoops. The feminist perspective focuses on these arenas. Feminist researchers also tend to involve and consult their subjects more than other types of researchers, and they are more oriented to applied sociological research as they seek change or raise consciousness or try to affect policy. In addition, feminist research is particularly open to a multidisciplinary approach, such as making use of historical evidence or legal studies as well as feminist theory (Baker 1999; Lofland 1975; Reinharz 1992).

Experiments

When sociologists want to study a possible cause-and-effect relationship, they may conduct experiments. An *experiment* is an artificially created situation that allows the researcher to manipulate variables.

In the classic method of conducting an experiment, two groups of people are selected and matched for simi-

lar characteristics such as age or education. The researchers then assign the subjects to one of two groups—the experimental or the control group. The *experimental group* is exposed to an independent variable; the *control group* is not. Thus, if scientists were testing a new type of antibiotic drug, they would administer that drug to an experimental group but not to a control group.

Sociologists don't often rely on this classic form of experiment because it generally involves manipulating human behavior in an inappropriate manner, especially in a laboratory setting. However, sociologists do try to recreate experimental conditions in the field. For example, they may compare children's performance in two schools that use different curricula. Another area of investigation that has led to several experimental studies in the field is an examination of police action in domestic assault cases. Emergency calls to a household where domestic violence is occurring account for a significant part of a police officer's work. Sociologists Anthony Pate and Edwin Hamilton (1992) studied cases in Dade County (Miami) Florida in which officers did or did not arrest the violent suspect and then looked at the effect of the arrest or nonarrest on future incidents of assault in the household. In other words, they compared cases where no arrest was made (the control group) with incidents where the suspect was arrested (experimental group). They found that an arrest did have a deterrent effect if the suspect was employed. Pate and Hamilton concluded that while an arrest may be a sobering experience for any individual, the impact of being taken to a police station is greater if a person is employed and is forced to explain what is happening in his or her personal life to a boss.

In some experiments, just as in observation research, the presence of a social scientist or other observer may affect the behavior of people being studied. The recognition of this phenomenon grew out of an experiment conducted during the 1920s and 1930s at the Hawthorne plant of the Western Electric Company. A group of researchers set out to determine how to improve the productivity of workers at the plant. The investigators manipulated such variables as the lighting and working hours to see what impact changes in them had on productivity. To their surprise, they found that *every* step they took seemed to

How do people respond to being observed? Evidently these employees at the Hawthorne plant enjoyed the attention paid them when researchers observed them at work. No matter what variables were changed, the workers increased their productivity every time, including when the level of lighting was *reduced*.

unintended by the initial collectors of information. For example, census data are compiled for specific uses by the federal government but are also valuable for marketing specialists in locating everything from bicycle stores to nursing homes.

Sociologists consider secondary analysis to be *nonreactive,* since it does not influence people's behavior. As an example, Émile Durkheim's statistical analysis of suicide neither increased nor decreased human self-destruction. Researchers, then, can avoid the Hawthorne effect by using secondary analysis.

There is one inherent problem, however: the researcher who relies on data collected by someone else may not find exactly what is needed. Social scientists studying family violence can use statistics from police and social service agencies on *reported* cases of spouse abuse and child abuse. But how many cases are not reported? Government bodies have no precise data on *all* cases of abuse.

Many social scientists find it useful to study cultural, economic, and political documents, including newspapers, periodicals, radio and television tapes, the Internet, scripts, diaries, songs, folklore, and legal papers, to name some examples (see Table 2-2). In examining these sources, researchers employ a technique known as **content analysis,** which is the systematic coding and objective recording of data, guided by some rationale.

Using content analysis, Erving Goffman (1979) conducted a pioneering exploration of how advertisements portrayed women as inferior to men. The ads typically showed women being subordinate to or dependent on others or being instructed by men. They used caressing and touching gestures more than men. Even when presented in leadership-type roles, women were likely to be shown in seductive poses or gazing out into space.

increase productivity. Even measures that seemed likely to have the opposite effect, such as reducing the amount of lighting in the plant, led to higher productivity.

Why did the plant's employees work harder even under less favorable conditions? Their behavior apparently was influenced by the greater attention being paid to them in the course of the research and by the novelty of being subjects in an experiment. Since that time, sociologists have used the term *Hawthorne effect* to refer to subjects of research who deviate from their typical behavior because they realize that they are under observation (S. Jones 1992; Lang 1992; Pelton 1994).

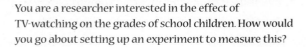

Imagine

You are a researcher interested in the effect of TV-watching on the grades of school children. How would you go about setting up an experiment to measure this?

Use of Existing Sources

Sociologists do not necessarily have to collect new data in order to conduct research and test hypotheses. The term *secondary analysis* refers to a variety of research techniques that make use of previously collected and publicly accessible information and data. Generally, in conducting secondary analysis, researchers utilize data in ways

Researchers today are analyzing the content of films to look at the increase in smoking in motion pictures, despite increased public health concerns. This type of content analysis can have clear social policy implications if it draws the attention of the motion picture industry to the message it may be delivering (especially to young people) that smoking is acceptable, even desirable. For example, a

Table 2-2	Existing Sources Used in Sociological Research

Most Frequently Used Sources

Census data

Crime statistics

Birth, death, marriage, and divorce statistics

Other Sources

Newspapers and periodicals

Personal journals, diaries, e-mail, and letters

Records and archival material of religious organizations, corporations, and other organizations

Transcripts of radio programs

Videotapes of motion pictures and television programs

Webpages

Song lyrics

Scientific records (such as patent applications)

Speeches of public figures (such as politicians)

Votes cast in elections or by elected officials on specific legislative proposals

Attendance records for public events

Videotapes of social protests and rallies

Literature, including folklore

Content analysis of recent films finds this unstated message: smoking is cool. In this still from the 1999 movie *Fight Club,* Brad Pitt is shown enjoying his cigarette. If the movie industry is made aware of the extent of smoking in films and the message that sends to young viewers, perhaps it will try to alter the message.

1999 content analysis found that tobacco use appeared in 89 percent of the 200 most popular movie rentals (Kang 1997; Roberts et al. 1999).

 Ethics of Research

A biochemist cannot inject a drug into a human being unless the drug has been thoroughly tested and the subject agrees to the shot. To do otherwise would be both unethical and illegal. Sociologists must also abide by certain specific standards in conducting research—a ***code of ethics.*** The professional society of the discipline, the American Sociological Association (ASA), first published the *Code of Ethics* in 1971 (most recently revised in 1997), which put forth the following basic principles:

1. Maintain objectivity and integrity in research.
2. Respect the subject's right to privacy and dignity.
3. Protect subjects from personal harm.
4. Preserve confidentiality.
5. Seek informed consent when data are collected from research participants or when behavior occurs in a private context.
6. Acknowledge research collaboration and assistance.
7. Disclose all sources of financial support (American Sociological Association 1997).

These basic principles probably seem clear-cut. How could they lead to any disagreement or controversy? However, many delicate ethical questions cannot be resolved simply by reading the seven points above. For example, should a sociologist engaged in participant-observation research *always* protect the confidentiality of subjects? What if the subjects are members of a religious cult allegedly engaged in unethical and possibly illegal activities? What if the sociologist is interviewing political activists and is questioned by government authorities about the research?

Most sociological research uses *people* as sources of information—as respondents to survey questions, subjects of observation, or participants in experiments. In all cases, sociologists need to be certain that they are not invading the privacy of their subjects. Generally, they handle this by assuring anonymity and by guaranteeing the confidentiality of personal information. However, a study by William Zellner raised important questions about the extent to which sociologists can threaten people's right to privacy.

Accident or Suicide?

An ethical issue—with the right to know posed against the right to privacy—became apparent in research on automobile accidents in which fatalities occur. Sociologist William Zellner (1978) wanted to learn if fatal car crashes are sometimes suicides that have been disguised as accidents in order to protect family and friends (and perhaps to collect otherwise unredeemable insurance benefits). These acts of "autocide" are by nature covert.

In his efforts to assess the frequency of such suicides, Zellner sought to interview the friends, co-workers, and family members of the deceased. He hoped to obtain information that would allow him to ascertain whether the deaths were accidental or deliberate. Zellner told the people approached for interviews that his goal was to contribute to a reduction of future accidents by learning about the emotional characteristics of accident victims. He made no mention of his suspicions of autocide, out of fear that potential respondents would refuse to meet with him.

Zellner eventually concluded that at least 12 percent of all fatal single-occupant crashes are suicides. This information could be valuable for society, particularly since some of the probable suicides actually killed or critically injured innocent bystanders in the process of taking their own lives. Yet the ethical questions still must be faced. Was Zellner's research unethical because he misrepresented the motives of his study and failed to obtain his subjects' informed consent? Or was his deception justified by the social value of his findings?

The answers to these questions are not immediately apparent. Zellner appeared to have admirable motives and took great care in protecting confidentiality. He did not reveal names of suspected suicides to insurance companies, though Zellner did recommend that the insurance industry drop double indemnity (payment of twice the person's life insurance benefits in the event of accidental death) in the future.

Zellner's study raised an additional ethical issue: the possibility of harm to those who were interviewed. Subjects were asked if the deceased had "talked about suicide" and if they had spoken of how "bad or useless" they were.

Are some people who die in single-occupant car crashes actually suicides? One sociological study of possible "autocides" concluded that at least 12 percent of such accident victims have in fact committed suicide. But the study also raised some ethical questions concerning the right to know and the right to privacy.

Could these questions have led people to guess the true intentions of the researcher? Perhaps, but according to Zellner, none of the informants voiced such suspicions. More seriously, might the study have caused the bereaved to *suspect* suicide—when before the survey they had accepted the deaths as accidental? Again, there is no evidence to suggest this, but we cannot be sure.

Given our uncertainty about this last question, was the research justified? Was Zellner taking too big a risk in asking the friends and families if the deceased victims had spoken of suicide before their death? Does the right to know outweigh the right to privacy in this type of situation? And who has the right to make such a judgment? In practice, as in Zellner's study, it is the *researcher,* not the subjects of inquiry, who makes the critical ethical decisions. Therefore, sociologists and other investigators bear the responsibility for establishing clear and sensitive boundaries for ethical scientific investigation.

Preserving Confidentiality

Like journalists, sociologists occasionally find themselves subject to questions from law enforcement authorities because of knowledge they have gained in conducting research. This uncomfortable situation raises profound ethical questions.

In May 1993, Rik Scarce, a doctoral candidate in sociology at Washington State University, was jailed for contempt of court. Scarce had declined to tell a federal grand jury what he knew—or even whether he knew anything—about a 1991 raid on a university research laboratory by animal rights activists. At the time, Scarce was conducting research for a book about environmental protestors and knew at least one suspect in the break-in. Curiously, although chastised by a federal judge, Scarce won respect from fellow prison inmates who regarded him as a man who "wouldn't snitch" (Monaghan 1993:A8).

The American Sociological Association supported Scarce's position when he appealed his sentence. Ultimately, Scarce maintained his silence, the judge ruled that nothing would be gained by further incarceration, and Scarce was released after serving 159 days in jail. In January 1994, the U.S. Supreme Court declined to hear Scarce's case on appeal. The Court's failure to consider his case led Scarce (1994, 1995) to argue that federal legislation is needed to clarify the rights of scholars and members of the press to preserve the confidentiality of research subjects.

Neutrality and Politics in Research

The ethical considerations of sociologists lie not only in the methods they use but also in the way they interpret results. Max Weber ([1904] 1949) recognized that personal values would influence the questions that sociologists select for research. In his view, that was perfectly acceptable, but under no conditions could a researcher allow his or her personal feelings to influence the *interpretation* of data. In Weber's phrase, sociologists must practice **value neutrality** in their research.

As part of this neutrality, investigators have an ethical obligation to accept research findings even when the data run counter to their own personal views, to theoretically based explanations, or to widely accepted beliefs. For example, Émile Durkheim challenged popular con-

 ceptions when he reported that social (rather than supernatural) forces were an important factor in suicide.

Some sociologists believe that neutrality is impossible. At the same time, Weber's insistence on value-free sociology may lead the public to accept sociological conclusions without exploring the biases of the researchers. Furthermore, drawing on the conflict perspective, Alvin Gouldner (1970), among others, has suggested that sociologists may use objectivity as a sacred justification for remaining uncritical of existing institutions and centers of power. These arguments are attacks not so much on Weber himself as on how his goals have been incorrectly interpreted. As we have seen, Weber was quite clear that sociologists may bring values *to* their subject matter. In his view, however, they must not confuse their own values with the social reality under study (Bendix 1968).

Let's consider what might happen when researchers bring their own biases to the investigation. A person investigating the impact of intercollegiate sports on alumni contributions, for example, may focus only on the highly visible revenue-generating sports of football and basketball and neglect the so-called "minor sports" such as tennis or soccer that are more likely to involve women athletes. Despite the early work of W.E.B. Du Bois and Jane Addams, sociologists still need to be reminded that the discipline often fails to adequately consider *all* people's social behavior.

In her book *The Death of White Sociology* (1973) Joyce Ladner called attention to the tendency of mainstream sociology to treat the lives of African Americans as a social problem. More recently, feminist sociologist Shulamit Reinharz (1992) has argued that sociological research should not only be inclusive but also be open to bringing about social change and drawing on relevant research by nonsociologists. Both Reinharz and Ladner maintain that research should always analyze whether women's unequal social status has affected the study in any way. For example, one might broaden the study of the impact of education on income to consider the implications of the unequal pay status of men and women. The issue of value neutrality does not mean you can't have opinions, but it does mean you must work to overcome any biases, however unintentional, that you may bring to your analysis of the research.

Peter Rossi (1987) admits to having liberal inclinations that direct him to fields of study. Yet, in line with Weber's view of value neutrality, Rossi's commitment to rigorous research methods and objective interpretation of data has sometimes led him to controversial findings not necessarily supportive of his own liberal values. For example, his measure of the extent of homelessness in

A homeless woman living in Chicago. Sociologist Peter Rossi came under attack by the Chicago Coalition for the Homeless for finding in a carefully researched study that the city's homeless population was far below the Coalition's estimate. The Coalition accused Rossi of hampering their efforts at social reform.

tive data, such as information obtained in observation research. Numerous software programs such as *Ethnograph* and *NUD*IST* allow the researcher not only to record observations, like a word processing program, but also to identify common behavioral patterns or similar concerns expressed in interviews. For example, after observing students in a college cafeteria over several weeks and putting your observations into the computer, you could then group all your observations related to certain variables, such as "sorority" or "study group."

The Internet affords an excellent opportunity to communicate with fellow researchers as well as to locate useful information on social issues posted on websites. It would be impossible to calculate all the sociological postings on Internet mailing lists or World Wide Web sites. Of course, you need to apply

Chicago in the mid-1980s fell far below the estimates of the Chicago Coalition for the Homeless. Coalition members bitterly attacked Rossi for hampering social reform efforts by minimizing the extent of homelessness. Rossi (1987:79) concludes that "in the short term, good social research will often be greeted as a betrayal of one or another side to a particular controversy."

the same critical scrutiny to Internet material that you would use on any printed resource.

How useful is the Internet for conducting survey research? That's unclear as yet. It is relatively easy to send out or post on an electronic bulletin board a questionnaire and solicit responses. It is an inexpensive way to reach large numbers of potential respondents and get a quick return of responses. However, there are some obvious dilemmas. How do you protect a respondent's anonymity? Second, how do you define the potential audience? Even if you know to whom you sent the questionnaire, the respondents may forward it on to others.

Technology and Sociological Research

Advances in technology have affected all aspects of life, and sociological research is no exception. The increased speed and capacity of computers enable sociologists to handle larger and larger sets of data. In the recent past, only people with grants or major institutional support could easily work with census data. Now anyone with a desktop computer and modem can access census information to learn more about social behavior. Moreover, data from foreign countries concerning crime statistics and health care are sometimes as available as information from the United States.

Researchers usually rely on computers to deal with quantitative data—that is, numerical measures—but electronic technology is also assisting us with qualita-

Web-based surveys are still in their early stages. Even so, the initial results are promising. For example, InterSurvey has created a pool of Internet respondents, initially selected by telephone to be a diverse and representative sample. Using similar methods to locate 50,000 adult respondents in 33 nations, the National Geographic Society conducted an online survey that focused on migration and regional culture. Social scientists are closely monitoring these new approaches to gauge how they might revolutionize one type of research design (W. Bainbridge 1999; R. Morin 2000).

This new technology is exciting, but there is one basic limitation to the methodology: Internet surveying works only with those who are online, who have access to

PAUL DONATO:
Chief Research Officer, Nielsen Media Research

For more than two decades, Paul Donato has been active in media research, both at home and abroad, and in both the print and electronic communication industries. In his current position he oversees research in television ratings, those vital figures that help determine how much advertising should sell for on various television programs. A typical work day takes him from client meetings to administrative work to staff management.

Donato began his study of sociology in the late 1960s and early 1970s, "a particularly interesting time for me from a social policy point of view—for studying what was happening in the streets." His undergraduate sociology degree and his Masters in methodological research, both from State University of New York at Stony Brook, introduced him to conflict theory, systems theory, functional and qualitative analysis, communications and management theory, and critical analysis—all of which he says are relevant in his career. Although Donato acknowledges you can't manage from a book, it helps to at least be informed about issues before you have to face them.

He credits exposure to various ideological perspectives in his sociology courses for his success in the emerging markets abroad, particularly those undergoing political instability. "Most people think we only care about the United States. So anything that you understand about other people's culture, society, ideologies, and politics immediately establishes credibility as you build a business relationship."

Donato's advice for students: "Set objectives for yourself in your study of sociology. Look at the content of your courses and try to figure out the connections with what you think you want to be doing 10 years later."

Let's Discuss

1. Using your sociological imagination, describe what sorts of information a sociologist might find useful from the analysis of TV ratings.
2. Do you know what you want to be doing 10 years from now? If so, what connections, if any, do you see between your career choice and the study of sociology?

the Internet. For some market researchers, such a limitation is acceptable. For example, if you were interested in the willingness of Internet users to order books or make travel reservations online, limiting the sample population to those already online makes sense. However, if you were surveying the general public about plans to buy a computer in the coming year or about their views on a particular candidate, your online research would need to be supplemented by more traditional sampling procedures, such as mailed questionnaires.

Sociological research relies on a number of tools—from observation research and use of existing sources of data to considering how the latest technology can help inform the sociological imagination. We turn now to a research study that used a survey of the general population to learn more about a particular social behavior—human sexuality.

Computers have tremendously extended the range and capability of sociological research, from allowing large amounts of data to be stored and analyzed to facilitating communication with other researchers via websites, newsgroups, and e-mail.

SOCIAL POLICY AND SOCIOLOGICAL RESEARCH

Studying Human Sexuality

The Issue

Here's a scene from the popular TV series *Felicity,* involving an affair between a college student and an older married woman:

> The moment he opens the door to the hotel room, they embrace and begin kissing passionately as he lifts her off of the ground. He removes her blouse, revealing a black lace bra and exposing a tattoo on her lower back. "I like your butterfly tattoo," he says, and she replies, "That's not my only one." They continue to kiss and touch one another as the scene ends. They wake the next morning together in the room. (Kaiser Family Foundation 2001:6)

You can find similar scenes from dozens of TV shows today, and the numbers keep increasing. The Kaiser Family Foundation conducts a study of sexual content on television every two years. The latest report, released in 2001, shows that more than two-thirds of all shows on TV include some sexual content, up from about half of all shows two years earlier (Figure 2-4). Media representations of sexual behavior are important because surveys of teens and young adults tell us that television is a top source of information and ideas about sex for them; it has more influence than schools, parents, or peers (Kunkel et al. 2001).

In this age of devastating sexually transmitted diseases, there is no time more important to increase our scientific understanding of human sexuality. As we will see, however, it is a difficult topic to research because of all the preconceptions, myths, and beliefs we bring to the subject of sexuality. How does one carry out scientific research of such a controversial and personal topic?

The Setting

We have few reliable national data on patterns of sexual behavior in the United States. Until recently, the only comprehensive study of sexual behavior was the famous two-volume Kinsey Report prepared in the 1940s (Kinsey et al. 1948, 1953). Although the Kinsey Report is still widely quoted, the volunteers interviewed for the report were not representative of the nation's adult population. Every two years the general public is interviewed as a part of the federally funded General Social Survey, which

Figure 2-4

Percent of Television Shows that Contain Sexual Content

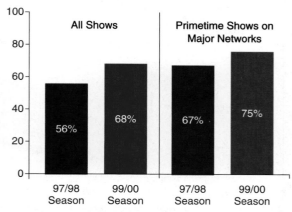

Source: Kaiser Family Foundation 2001:2.

provides some useful information on sexual attitudes. For instance, Figure 2-5 shows how attitudes about premarital sexual behavior have changed since the early 1970s.

In part, we have few reliable data on patterns of sexual behavior because it is difficult for researchers to obtain accurate information about this sensitive subject. Moreover, until AIDS emerged in the 1980s, there was little scientific demand for data on sexual behavior, except for specific areas such as contraception. Finally, even though the AIDS crisis has reached dramatic proportions (as will be discussed in the social policy section of Chapter 5), government funding for studies of sexual behavior is controversial. Because the General Social Survey described above concerns sexual *attitudes* rather than *behavior,* its funding has not been in jeopardy.

Sociological Insights

The controversy surrounding research on human sexual behavior raises the issue of value neutrality. And this becomes especially delicate when one considers the relationship of sociology to the government. The federal government has become the major source of funding for sociological research. Yet Max Weber urged that sociology remain an autonomous discipline and not become unduly influenced by any one segment of society. According to his ideal of value neutrality, sociologists must remain free to reveal information that is embarrassing to government or, for that matter, is supportive

Figure 2-5

Views on Sex before Marriage

Proportion agreeing that it is not wrong at all if a man and a woman have sexual relations before marriage.

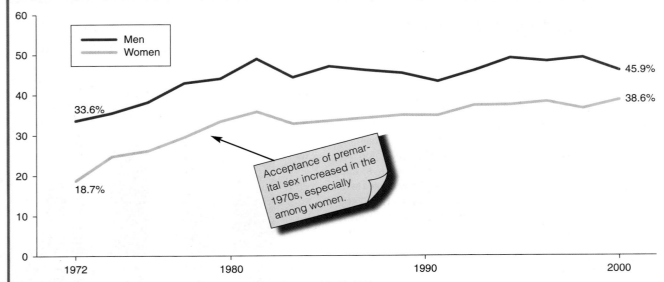

Source: Author's analysis of General Surveys, 1972–2000; see Davis and Smith 2001.

of government institutions. Thus, researchers investigating a prison riot must be ready to examine objectively not only the behavior of inmates but also the conduct of prison officials before and during the outbreak.

Conflict theorists and feminists, among others, are critical of some research that claims to be objective. In turn, their research is occasionally criticized for not sufficiently addressing Weber's concern for value neutrality. In any case, maintaining objectivity may be difficult if sociologists fear that findings critical of government institutions will jeopardize their chances of obtaining federal support for new research projects.

Although the American Sociological Association's *Code of Ethics* expects sociologists to disclose all funding sources, the code does not address the issue of whether sociologists who accept funding from a particular agency may also accept their perspective on what needs to be studied. Lewis Coser (1956:27) has argued that as sociologists in the United States have increasingly turned from basic sociological research to applied research for government agencies and the private sector, "they have relinquished to a large extent the freedom to choose their own problems, substituting the problems of their clients for those which might have interested them on purely theoretical grounds." Viewed in this light, the importance of government funding for sociological studies raises troubling questions for those who cherish Weber's ideal of value neutrality in research. As we'll see in the next section, applied sociological research on human sexuality has run into barriers constructed by government funding agencies.

Policy Initiatives

In 1987 the federal National Institute of Child Health and Human Development sought proposals for a national survey of sexual behavior. Sociologists responded with various proposals that a review panel of scientists approved for funding. However, in 1991, led by Senator Jesse Helms and other conservatives, the U.S. Senate voted 66–34 to forbid funding any survey on adult sexual practices. Helms appealed to popular fears by arguing that such surveys of sexual behavior were intended to "legitimize homosexual lifestyles" and to support "sexual decadence." Two years earlier, a similar debate in Great Britain had led to the denial of government funding for a national sex survey (A. Johnson et al. 1994; Laumann et al. 1994a:36).

Despite the vote by the U.S. Senate, sociologists Edward Laumann, John Gagnon, Stuart Michaels, and Robert Michael developed the National Health and Social Life Survey (NHSLS) to better understand the sexual practices of adults in the United States. The researchers raised $1.6 million of *private* funding to make their study possible (Laumann et al. 1994a, 1994b).

Research into sexual behavior in the United States is complicated by the sensitivity of the subject and the reluctance of government agencies to provide funding. Sociologists had to raise private funds to finance the National Health and Social Life Survey (NHSLS), a nationwide study of the sexual practices of adults.

The researchers made great efforts to ensure privacy during the NHSLS interviews, as well as confidentiality of responses and security in maintaining data files. Perhaps because of this careful effort, the interviewers did not typically experience problems getting responses, even though they were asking people about their sexual behavior. All interviews were conducted in person, although there was also a confidential form that included questions about such sensitive subjects as family income and masturbation. The researchers used several techniques to test the accuracy of subjects' responses, such as asking redundant questions at different times in different ways during the 90-minute interview. These careful procedures helped establish the validity of the NHSLS findings.

Today, research on human sexuality is not the only target of policymakers. Congress began in 1995 considering passage of the Family Privacy Protection Act, which would force all federally funded researchers to obtain written consent from parents before surveying young people on such issues as drug use, antisocial behavior, and emotional difficulties, as well as sexual behavior. Researchers around the country suggest that this legal requirement will make it impossible to survey representative samples of young people. They note that when parents are asked to return consent forms, only about half do so, even though no more than 1 to 2 percent actually object to the survey. Moreover, the additional effort required to get all the forms returned raises research costs by 25-fold (Elias 1996; Levine 2001).

Despite the political battles, the authors of the NHSLS believe that their research was important. These researchers argue that using data from their survey allows us to more easily address such public policy issues as AIDS, sexual harassment, rape, welfare reform, sex discrimination, abortion, teenage pregnancy, and family planning. Moreover, the research findings help to counter some "common-sense" notions. For instance, contrary to the popular belief that women regularly use abortion for birth control and that poor teens are the most likely socioeconomic group to have abortions, the researchers found that three-fourths of all abortions are the *first* for the woman and that well-educated and affluent women are more likely to have abortions than poor teens (K. Sweet 2001).

The NHSLS researchers have lately moved on to other topics. One is studying adolescent behavior in general and another is studying sexuality in China and Chicago, adding health care, jealousy, and violence to the mix of issues. The researchers hope to update the NHSLS data before too much time passes, especially now that the environment for conducting research on human sexuality has improved, and people have proved that they are more comfortable talking about sexual issues. As one of the researchers noted, "People aren't as uptight about sex as their politicians and their funders. That's good news" (K. Sweet 2001:13).

Let's Discuss

1. Why is human sexuality a difficult subject to research? Would you feel comfortable answering questions about your own sex life?
2. How does value neutrality become an important issue in research sponsored by the government?
3. Describe the efforts that the NHSLS researchers made to ensure that their study was confidential and the results were reliable and valid. If you were to conduct a survey in your community of people who engage in premarital sex, how would you set it up?

Appendix I

UNDERSTANDING TABLES AND GRAPHS

Tables allow social scientists to summarize data and make it easier for them to develop conclusions. A *cross-tabulation* is a type of table that illustrates the relationship between two or more characteristics.

During 2000, the National Opinion Research Center interviewed 1,775 people in the United States, ages 18 and over. Each respondent was interviewed and asked: "Do you think the use of marijuana should be made legal or not?" There is no way that, without some type of summary, analysts in the Gallup organization could examine hundreds of individual responses and reach firm conclusions. However, through use of the cross-tabulation presented in the accompanying table, we can quickly see that older people are less likely to favor legalization of marijuana than are younger people.

Graphs, like tables, can be quite useful for sociologists. And illustrations are often easier for the general public to understand, whether they are in newspapers or in Power-Point presentations. Still, as with all data, we need to be careful how they are presented. For example, the two bar graphs on this page present the same data concerning legalization of marijuana as in the table. Yet the differences in attitudes between the age groups seem much more striking in version B than in version A. Both figures are accurate, but because the vertical axis in B uses a different scale, it appears as if virtually no older respondents favored legalization. In reality, about one in five did, compared to a bit more than two of five of the youngest respondents.

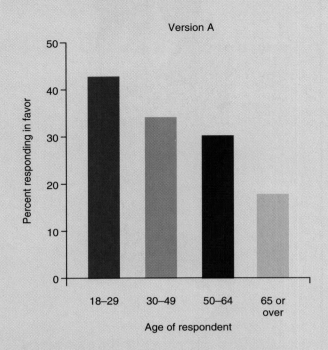

Version A

Attitudes on Legalization of Marijuana		
Age of Respondent	**For**	**Against**
18–29 years	43%	57%
30–49 years	37	58
50–64 years	30	70
65 years and older	19	81

Source: General Social Survey in Davis and Smith 2001.

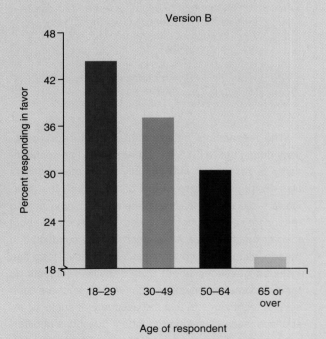

Version B

Source: General Social Survey in Davis and Smith 2001.

Appendix II

WRITING A LIBRARY RESEARCH REPORT

Let's say that you have decided to write a report on cohabitation (unmarried couples living together). How do you go about doing the necessary library research? Students must follow procedures similar to those used by sociologists in conducting original research. First, you must define the problem that you wish to study—perhaps in this case, how much cohabitation occurs and what its impact is on marital happiness later. The next step is to review the literature, which generally requires library research.

The following steps will be helpful in finding information:

1. Check this textbook and other textbooks that you own. Don't forget to begin with the materials closest at hand. At the end of each chapter of this textbook is a listing of books, journals, and electronic sources of information (including CD-ROMs and sites on the Internet and Web).

2. Use the library catalog. Most academic libraries now use computerized systems that access not only the college library's collection but also books and magazines from other libraries available through interlibrary loans. These systems allow you to search for books by author or title. You can use title searches to locate books by subject as well. For example, if you search the title base for the keyword "cohabitation," you will learn where books with that word somewhere in the title are located in the library's book stacks. Near these books will be other works on cohabitation that may not happen to have that word in the title. You may also want to search other related key words, such as "unmarried couples."

3. Investigate using computerized periodical indexes if available in your library. *Sociological Abstracts* online covers most sociological writing since 1974. A recent search found more than 741 articles having to do with cohabitation. Some dealt with laws about cohabitation while others focused on trends in other countries. If you limit your topic to same-sex couples, you would find 33 articles. Other electronic databases cover general-interest periodicals (*Time, Ms., National Review, Atlantic Monthly,* and so forth), reference materials, or newspapers. These electronic systems may be connected to a printer, allowing you to produce your own printout complete with bibliographic information and sometimes even complete copies of articles.

4. Examine government documents. The United States government, states and cities, and the United Nations publish information on virtually every subject of interest to social science researchers. Publications of the Census Bureau, for example, include tables showing the number of unmarried couples living together and some social characteristics of these households. Many university libraries have access to a wide range of government reports. Consult the librarian for assistance in locating such materials.

5. Use newspapers. Major newspapers publish indexes annually or even weekly that are useful in locating information about specific events or issues. Academic Universe News is an electronic index to U.S. and international newspapers.

6. Ask people, organizations, and agencies concerned with the topic for information and assistance. Be as specific as possible in making requests. You might receive very different information on the issue of cohabitation from talking with marriage counselors and with clergy from different religions.

7. If you run into difficulties, consult the instructor, teaching assistant, or librarian.

Once you have completed all research, the task of writing the report can begin. Here are a few tips:

*   Be sure the topic you have chosen is not too broad. You must be able to cover it adequately in a reasonable amount of time and a reasonable number of pages.
*   Develop an outline for your report. You should have an introduction and a conclusion that relate to each other—and the discussion should proceed logically throughout the paper. Use headings within the paper if they will improve clarity and organization.
*   Do not leave all the writing until the last minute. It is best to write a rough draft, let it sit for a few days, and then take a fresh look before beginning revisions.
*   If possible, read your paper *aloud*. Doing so may be helpful in locating sections or phrases that don't make sense.

Remember that you *must* cite all information you have obtained from other sources. If you use an author's exact words, it is essential that they be placed in quotation marks. Even if you reworked someone else's ideas, you must indicate the source of these ideas.

Some professors may require that students use footnotes in research reports. Others will allow students to employ the form of referencing used in this textbook, which follows the format of the American Sociological Association (ASA). If you see "(Merton 1968:27)" listed after a statement or paragraph, it means that the material has been quoted from page 27 of a work published by Merton in 1968 and listed in the reference section at the back of this textbook. (You can also consult the "Preparation checklist for ASA manuscripts" at the ASA website: **www.asanet.org**)

● Chapter Resources

Summary

Sociologists are committed to the use of the scientific method in their research efforts. In this chapter, we examine the basic principles of the scientific method and study various techniques used by sociologists in conducting research.

1. There are five basic steps in the *scientific method:* defining the problem, reviewing the literature, formulating the hypothesis, selecting the research design and then collecting and analyzing data, and developing the conclusion.
2. Whenever researchers wish to study abstract concepts, such as intelligence or prejudice, they must develop workable *operational definitions.*
3. A *hypothesis* usually states a possible relationship between two or more variables.
4. By using a *sample,* sociologists avoid having to test everyone in a population.
5. According to the scientific method, research results must possess both *validity* and *reliability.*
6. The two principal forms of *survey* research are the *interview* and the *questionnaire.*
7. *Observation* allows sociologists to study certain behaviors and communities that cannot be investigated through other research methods.
8. When sociologists wish to study a cause-and-effect relationship, they may conduct an *experiment.*
9. Sociologists also make use of existing sources as in *secondary analysis* and *content analysis.*
10. The *Code of Ethics* of the American Sociological Association calls for objectivity and integrity in research, respect for the subject's privacy, and confidentiality.
11. Max Weber urged sociologists to practice *value neutrality* in their research by ensuring that their personal feelings do not influence the interpretation of data.
12. Technology today plays an important role in sociological research, whether it be a computer database or information from the Internet.
13. Despite failure to obtain government funding, researchers developed the National Health and Social Life Survey (NHSLS) to better understand the sexual practices of adults in the United States.

Critical Thinking Questions

1. Suppose that your sociology instructor has asked you to do a study of homelessness. Which research technique (survey, observation, experiment, existing sources) would you find most useful? How would you use that technique to complete your assignment?
2. How can a sociologist genuinely maintain value neutrality while studying a group that he or she finds repugnant (for example, a White supremacist organization, a satanic cult, or a group of prison inmates convicted of rape)?
3. Why is it important for sociologists to have a code of ethics?

Key Terms

Causal logic The relationship between a condition or variable and a particular consequence, with one event leading to the other. (page 35)

Code of ethics The standards of acceptable behavior developed by and for members of a profession. (44)

Content analysis The systematic coding and objective recording of data, guided by some rationale. (43)

Control group Subjects in an experiment who are not introduced to the independent variable by the researcher. (42)

Control variable A factor held constant to test the relative impact of an independent variable. (37)

Correlation A relationship between two variables whereby a change in one coincides with a change in the other. (35)

Cross-tabulation   A table that shows the relationship between two or more variables. (52)

Dependent variable   The variable in a causal relationship that is subject to the influence of another variable. (35)

Ethnography   The study of an entire social setting through extended systematic observation. (41)

Experiment   An artificially created situation that allows the researcher to manipulate variables. (42)

Experimental group   Subjects in an experiment who are exposed to an independent variable introduced by a researcher. (42)

Hawthorne effect   The unintended influence that observers or experiments can have on their subjects. (43)

Hypothesis   A speculative statement about the relationship between two or more variables. (35)

Independent variable   The variable in a causal relationship that causes or influences a change in a second variable. (35)

Interview   A face-to-face or telephone questioning of a respondent to obtain desired information. (39)

Observation   A research technique in which an investigator collects information through direct participation and/or closely watching a group or community. (40)

Operational definition   An explanation of an abstract concept that is specific enough to allow a researcher to measure the concept. (34)

Qualitative research   Research that relies on what is seen in field or naturalistic settings more than on statistical data. (40)

Quantitative research   Research that collects and reports data primarily in numerical form. (41)

Questionnaire   A printed or written form used to obtain desired information from a respondent. (39)

Random sample   A sample for which every member of the entire population has the same chance of being selected. (36)

Reliability   The extent to which a measure provides consistent results. (36)

Research design   A detailed plan or method for obtaining data scientifically. (39)

Sample   A selection from a larger population that is statistically representative of that population. (36)

Scientific method   A systematic, organized series of steps that ensures maximum objectivity and consistency in researching a problem. (33)

Secondary analysis   A variety of research techniques that make use of previously existing and publicly accessible information and data. (43)

Survey   A study, generally in the form of interviews or questionnaires, that provides researchers with information concerning how people think and act. (39)

Validity   The degree to which a scale or measure truly reflects the phenomenon under study. (36)

Value neutrality   Objectivity of sociologists in the interpretation of data. (46)

Variable   A measurable trait or characteristic that is subject to change under different conditions. (35)

Additional Readings

BOOKS

American Sociological Association. 1997. *Style Guide,* 2d ed. Washington, DC: ASA. This concise handbook (39 pages) provides guidance in writing clearly as well as citation format, including referencing electronic sources such as the Internet.

Best, Joel. 2001. *Damned Lies and Statistics: Untangling Numbers from the Media, Politicians and Activists.* Berkeley: University of California Press. A sociologist demonstrates the value of careful interpretation of data, but also shows how statistics can be used to mislead people about social issues.

Denzin, Norman K., and Yvonna S. Lincoln (eds.). 2000. *Handbook of Qualitative Research,* 2d ed. Thousand Oaks, CA: Sage. The 40 articles in this anthology cover newer techniques used in conducting observation and biographical research, as well as ethical issues facing researchers.

Ericksen, Julia A. 1999. *Kiss and Tell: Surveying Sex in the Twentieth Century.* Cambridge, MA: Harvard University Press. Evaluates the methodology of the hundreds of surveys of human sexuality conducted by sociologists and other social scientists.

Gladwell, Malcolm. 2000. *The Tipping Point.* Boston: Little, Brown. A journalist examines how attaining certain benchmarks or milestones is shown in newsbreaking stories, such as drops in crime, the impact of smoking, and the influence of children's television programming.

Gubrium, Jaber F., and James A. Holstein (eds.). *2001 Handbook of Interview Research: Context and Method.* Thousand Oaks, CA: Sage. Drawing on a variety of disciplines, the editors examine all facets of appropriate interview techniques.

Huff, Darrell. 1954. *How to Lie with Statistics.* New York: Norton. "Figures don't lie, but liars do figure" is an adage that points to the way that statistics can be abused. In this classic book, Huff offers guidance to the reader in how to better understand numbers, graphs, and tables.

Paulos, John Allen. 1988. *Innumeracy.* Harmondsworth, Eng.: Penguin. This brief book considers how important basic mathematics is in everyday life.

JOURNALS

Among the journals that focus on methods of sociological and other social scientific research are the following: *Irb: A Review of Human Subjects Research* (founded in 1979), *Journal of Contemporary Ethnography* (1971), *Qualitative Sociology* (1977), *Social Science Research* (1972), and *Sociological Methods and Research* (1972). Many sociological journals are now available on the Internet, but one specific journal on research is available only online. You can locate *Sociological Research Online* at **http://www.socresonline.org.uk/socresonline/.**

● Technology Resources

Internet Connection

*Note: While all the URLs listed were current as of the printing of this book, these sites often change. Please check our website (**http://www.mhhe.com/schaefer8**) for updates and hyperlinks to this exercise and additional exercises.*

1. As you have learned in this chapter, sampling is an important part of research conducted by sociologists. Fridah Mugo at Cornell University (**http://trochim.human.cornell.edu/mugo/tutorial.htm**) has developed a tutorial explaining the importance of sample size and types of samples, along with much other useful information. Read the tutorial and answer the following questions:
   (a) What is the purpose of sampling?
   (b) Why is the time factor important?
   (c) Why is it important to understand sampling error?
   (d) Explain what "the respondent effect" is, and give your own example of a respondent effect.
   (e) Suppose that your campus wants to know how students feel about co-ed rooms. You have been asked to handle the project. Use two of the sample types discussed to explain how you would go about obtaining this information.

2. The Gallup poll (**http://www.gallup.com**) is one of the best-known national polls in the United States. To learn more about this poll, link to "How Gallup Polls Are Conducted," and answer the following questions:
   (a) What have survey researchers discovered about the confidence of Americans in polls?
   (b) What is the objective of the national Gallup polls?
   (c) What is the difference in the way that the earliest polls selected respondents and the way respondents are selected now to participate in the polls?
   (d) What is one of the oldest question wordings that Gallup has had in its inventory? When was this question first asked?
   (e) Click your Refresh or Back button. Link to the lead story. Briefly, what is it about? What do U.S. citizens think about the issue?

3. One of the most important uses of the scientific method in social science research is to gather and interpret crime statistics. To learn more about how statistics are collected, visit Organized Crime: A Crime Statistics Site offered by Regina Schekall (**http://www.crime.org/**). Here you will find an online tutorial and crime statistics links. Explore the site and answer the following questions:
   (a) What are the steps and process by which researchers and law enforcement agencies obtain and gather crime statistics?
   (b) What is the UCR? Which crime categories are used in the UCR?
   (c) How are victim reports and surveys used to gain a better picture of crime in the United States?
   (d) What are some of the problems and challenges in both gathering and interpreting crime data?
   (e) Link to UCR data online through the site and check the most recent crime rates and statistics for murder-homicide. What statistic or fact surprised you the most and why?
   (f) This site also allows visitors to link to various college and university campus police and safety sites. Try to find your own college or a college near you and link to their data. What kind of crimes are occurring on campus? If rates are reported over time, has there been a change over the last few semesters? What might account for the changes in crime rates, both on the college campus and in society in general?

SocWorld CD-ROM

This CD, which is packaged free with all new copies of the text, allows you to instantly explore various topics and concepts with an assortment of video clips (including footage of this text's author in Singapore), website links, interactive quizzes, and other learning tools. Also included are audio introductions to each of the book excerpts that open each chapter and additional information about these excerpts and their authors.

Online Learning Center   www.mhhe.com/schaefer8

When you visit the student center of the Online Learning Center for this chapter, one of the Internet exercises gives you the opportunity to become a sociological researcher by taking Goffman's research into cyberspace. You will conduct a content analysis of two popular magazines directed toward women and two popular magazines for men. You will be asked to look at the colors, models, clothing, topics, and then analyze them from a sociological viewpoint. After this learning experience, you will never look at magazines the same way again!

PowerWeb

Using the password found on the gold and black card that was shrinkwrapped with your book, visit PowerWeb, a website that provides a wealth of resources including quizzes, links to related websites, interactive exercises, time management tips, articles, and a guide to doing research on the web. You will also find daily news on relevant topics. PowerWeb is accessible from a link on the Online Learning Center website. Also accessible from the Online Learning Center is a unique PowerWeb site on violence and terrorism.

SocCity

Explore SocCity, a veritable melting pot of sociology cybersources, information, and Internet activity for students and instructors alike. Whether you are looking for the perfect book for your sociology class, or you are a student looking for some starter sites for your next research paper, SocCity has it.

CULTURE

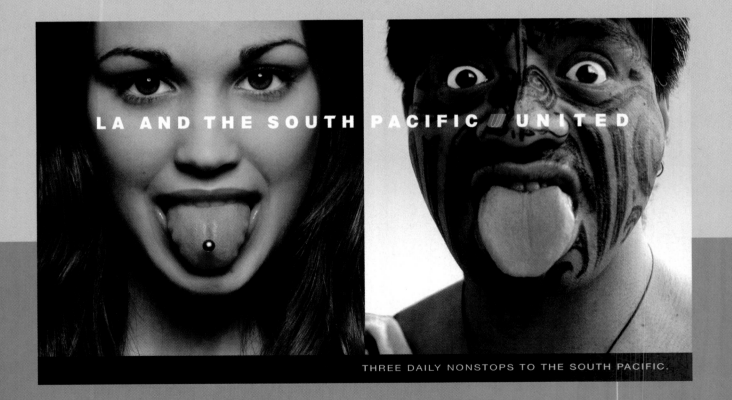

LA AND THE SOUTH PACIFIC / UNITED

THREE DAILY NONSTOPS TO THE SOUTH PACIFIC.

Each culture has its own forms of individual expression, as this billboard for United Airlines illustrates. The young woman from Los Angeles shows off her tongue stud while the South Pacific islander puts on a ceremonial tattooed face.

Nacirema culture is characterized by a highly developed market economy which has evolved in a rich natural habitat. While much of the people's time is devoted to economic pursuits, a large part of the fruits of these labors and a considerable portion of the day are spent in ritual activity. The focus of this activity is the human body, the appearance and health of which loom as a dominant concern in the ethos of the people. While such concern is certainly not unusual, its ceremonial aspects and associated philosophy are unique.

The fundamental belief underlying the whole system appears to be that the human body is ugly and that its natural tendency is to debility and disease. Incarcerated in such a body, man's only hope is to avert these characteristics through the use of the powerful influences of ritual and ceremony. Every household has one or more shrines devoted to this purpose. The more powerful individuals in this society have several shrines in their houses, and, in fact, the opulence of a house is often referred to in terms of the number of such ritual centers it possesses. . . .

While each family has at least one such shrine, the rituals associated with it are not family ceremonies but are private and secret. The rites are normally only discussed with children, and then only during the period when they are being initiated into these mysteries. I was able, however, to establish sufficient rapport with the natives to examine these shrines and to have the rituals described to me.

The focal point of the shrine is a box or chest which is built into the wall. In this chest are kept the many charms and magical potions without which no native believes he could live. These preparations are secured from a variety of specialized practitioners. The most powerful of these are the medicine men, whose assistance must be rewarded with substantial gifts. However, the medicine men do not provide the curative potions for their clients, but decide what the ingredients should be and then write them down in an ancient and secret language. This writing is understood only by the medicine men and by the herbalists who, for another gift, provide the required charm. . . .

The daily body ritual performed by everyone includes a mouth-rite. Despite the fact that these people are so punctilious about care of the mouth, this rite involves a practice which strikes the uninitiated stranger as revolting. It was reported to me that the ritual consists of inserting a small bundle of hog hairs into the mouth, along with certain magical powders, and then moving the bundle in a highly formalized series of gestures. *(Miner 1956: 503–04)* ■ 💿

Additional information about this excerpt and about those that open each subsequent chapter can be found in the SocWorld CD-ROM that accompanies this text.

Anthropologist Horace Miner cast his observant eyes on the intriguing behavior of the Nacirema. If we look a bit closer, however, some aspects of this culture may seem familiar, for what Miner is describing is actually the culture of the United States ("Nacirema" is "American" spelled backward). The "shrine" is the bathroom, and we are correctly informed that in this culture a measure of wealth is often how many bathrooms are in one's house. The bathroom rituals make use of charms and magical potions (beauty products and prescription drugs) obtained from specialized practitioners (such as hair stylists), herbalists (pharmacists), and medicine men (physicians). Using our sociological imagination we could update the Nacirema "shrine" by describing blow-dryers, braided dental floss, Water Piks, and hair gel.

We begin to appreciate how to understand behavior when we step back and examine it thoughtfully, objectively—whether it is our own "Nacirema" culture or another one. Take the case of Fiji, an island in the Pacific. A recent study showed that for the first time eating disorders were showing up among the young people there. This was a society where, traditionally, "you've gained weight" was a compliment and "your legs are skinny" was a major insult. Having a robust, nicely rounded body was the expectation for both men and women. What happened to change this cultural ideal? With the introduction of cable television in 1995, many Fiji islanders, especially girls, have come to want to look like the thin-waisted stars of *Melrose Place* and *Beverly Hills 90210,* not their full-bodied mothers and aunts. By understanding life in Fiji, we can also come to understand our own society much better (Becker 1995; Becker and Burwell 1999).

As aspects of culture become globalized— whether through the media or governmental interaction or economic transaction—how do societies change? How does our society change as we encounter cultures very different from our own? What accounts for cultural variation between and within societies? In this chapter we will see just how basic the study of culture is to sociology. We will examine the meaning of culture and society as well as the development of culture from its roots in the prehistoric human experience to the technological advances of today. The major aspects of culture—including language, norms, sanctions, and values—will be defined and explored. We will see how cultures develop a dominant ideology, and how functionalist and conflict theorists view culture. The discussion will focus both on general cultural practices found in all societies and on the wide variations that can distinguish one society from another. The social policy section will look at the conflicts in cultural values that underlie current debates over bilingualism. ■

● Culture and Society

Culture is the totality of learned, socially transmitted customs, knowledge, material objects, and behavior. It includes the ideas, values, customs, and artifacts (for example, CDs, comic books, and birth control devices) of groups of people. Patriotic attachment to the flag of the United States is an aspect of culture, as is a national passion for the tango in Argentina.

Sometimes people refer to a particular person as "very cultured" or to a city as having "lots of culture." That use of the term *culture* is different from our use in this textbook. In sociological terms, *culture* does not refer solely to the fine arts and refined intellectual taste. It consists of *all* objects and ideas within a society, including ice cream cones, rock music, and slang words. Sociologists consider both a portrait by Rembrandt and a portrait by a billboard painter to be aspects of a culture. A tribe that cultivates soil by hand has just as much of a culture as a people that relies on computer-operated machinery. Each people has a distinctive culture with its own characteristic ways of gathering and preparing food, constructing homes, structuring the family, and promoting standards of right and wrong.

The fact that you share a similar culture with others helps to define the group or society to which you belong. A fairly large number of people are said to constitute a *society* when they live in the same territory, are relatively independent of people outside their area, and participate in a common culture. The city of Los Angeles is more populous than many nations of the world, yet sociologists do not consider it a society in its own right. Rather, it is seen as part of—and dependent on—the larger society of the United States.

A society is the largest form of human group. It consists of people who share a common heritage and culture. Members of the society learn this culture and transmit it from one generation to the next. They even preserve their distinctive culture through literature, art, video recordings, and other means of expression. If it were not for the social transmission of culture, each generation would have to reinvent television, not to mention the wheel.

Having a common culture also simplifies many day-to-day interactions. For example, when you buy an airline ticket, you know you don't have to bring along hundreds of dollars in cash. You can pay with a credit card. When you are part of a society, there are many small (as well as more important) cultural patterns that you take for granted. You assume that theaters will provide seats for the audience, that physicians will not disclose confidential information, and that parents will be careful when crossing the street with young children. All these assumptions reflect basic values, beliefs, and customs of the culture of the United States.

Language is a critical element of culture that sets humans apart from other species. Members of a society generally share a common language, which facilitates day-to-day exchanges with others. When you ask a hardware store clerk for a flashlight, you don't need to draw a picture of the instrument. You share the same cultural term for a small, battery-operated, portable light. However, if you were in England and needed this item, you would have to ask for an "electric torch." Of course, even within the same society, a term can have a number of different meanings. In the United States, *grass* signifies both a plant eaten by grazing animals and an intoxicating drug.

● Development of Culture around the World

We've come a long way from our prehistoric heritage. As we begin a new millennium, we can transmit an entire book around the world via the Internet, we can clone cells, and we can prolong lives through organ transplants. The human species has produced such achievements as the ragtime compositions of Scott Joplin, the poetry of Emily Dickinson, the paintings of Vincent Van Gogh, the novels of Jane Austen, and the films of Akira Kurosawa. We can peer into the outermost reaches of the universe, and we can analyze our innermost feelings. In all these ways, we are remarkably different from other species of the animal kingdom.

Human culture has been evolving for thousands of years. The first archeological evidence of humanlike primates places our ancestors back many millions of years. About 700,000 years ago, people built hearths to harness fire. Archeologists have uncovered tools that date back about 100,000 years. From 35,000 years ago we have evidence of paintings, jewelry, and statues. By that time, elaborate ceremonies were marking marriages, births, and deaths (Harris 1997; Haviland 1999).

Tracing the development of culture is not easy. Archeologists cannot "dig up" weddings, laws, or government, but they are able to locate items that point to the emergence of cultural traditions. Our early ancestors were primates that had characteristics of human beings. These curious and communicative creatures made important advances in the use of tools. Recent studies of chimpanzees in the wild have revealed that they frequently use sticks and other natural objects in ways learned from other members of the group. However, unlike chimpanzees, our ancestors gradually made tools from increasingly durable materials. As a result, the items could be reused and refined into more effective implements.

Cultural Universals

Despite their differences, all societies have developed certain common practices and beliefs, known as *cultural universals.* Many cultural universals are, in fact, adaptations to meet essential human needs, such as people's need for food, shelter, and clothing. Anthropologist George Murdock (1945:124) compiled a list of cultural universals. Some of these include athletic sports, cooking, funeral ceremonies, medicine, and sexual restrictions.

The cultural practices listed by Murdock may be universal, but the manner in which they are expressed varies

Cooking is a cultural universal. Both the Cambodian woman and the Moroccan women in these photos show a preference for food grilled on skewers.

from culture to culture. For example, one society may let its members choose their own marriage partners. Another may encourage marriages arranged by the parents.

Not only does the expression of cultural universals vary from one society to another, it also may change dramatically over time within a society. Each generation, and each year for that matter, most human cultures change and expand through the processes of innovation and diffusion.

Innovation

The process of introducing a new idea or object to a culture is known as *innovation.* Innovation interests sociologists because of the social consequences that introducing something new can have in any society. There are two forms of innovation: discovery and invention. A *discovery* involves making known or sharing the existence of an aspect of reality. The finding of the DNA molecule and the identification of a new moon of Saturn are both acts of discovery. A significant factor in the process of discovery is the sharing of newfound knowledge with others. By contrast, an *invention* results when existing cultural items are combined into a form that did not exist before. The bow and arrow, the automobile, and the television are all examples of inventions, as are Protestantism and democracy.

Globalization, Diffusion, and Technology

The familiar green Starbucks logo leads you into a comfortable coffee shop where you can order decaf latte and a cinnamon ring. What's unusual about that? This Starbucks happens to be located in the heart of Beijing's Forbidden City, just outside the Palace of Heavenly Purity, former residence of Chinese emperors. And it is one of 25 Starbucks stores in China opened in the year 2000 alone. The success of Starbucks in a country in which both coffee drinking and capitalism are novelties has been striking (C. Smith 2000).

The emergence of Starbucks in China represents the rapidly escalating *globalization* of culture today. More and more cultural expressions and practices are crossing national borders and having an effect on the traditions and customs of the societies exposed to them. Sociologists use the term *diffusion* to refer to the process by which a cultural item spreads from group to group or society to society. Diffusion can occur through a variety of means, among them exploration, military conquest, missionary work, the influence of the mass media, tourism, and the Internet.

Sociologist George Ritzer (2000) coined the term "McDonaldization of society" to describe how the principles of fast-food restaurants developed in the United States have come to dominate more and more sectors of societies throughout the world. For example, hair salons and medical

When Shanghai residents meet at Starbucks for coffee, it is in a traditional-style building, but the coffee is the same that you can order in Seattle. The spread of Starbucks to China is an example of cultural diffusion.

clinics now take walk-in appointments. In Hong Kong, sex selection clinics offer a menu of items—from fertility enhancement to methods of increasing the likelihood of producing a child of the desired sex. Religious groups—from evangelical preachers on local stations or websites to priests at the Vatican Television Center—use marketing techniques similar to those that sell "happy meals."

McDonaldization is associated with the melding of cultures, so that we see more and more similarities in cultural expression. In Japan, for example, African entrepreneurs have found a thriving market for hip-hop fashions popularized by teens in the United States. In Austria, the McDonald's organization itself has drawn on the Austrians' love of coffee, cake, and conversation to create the McCafe as part of its fast-food chain. Many critical observers believe that McDonaldization and globalization serve to dilute the distinctive aspects of a society's culture (Alfino et al. 1998; Clark 1994; Rocks 1999).

Some societies try to protect themselves from the invasion of too much culture from other countries, especially the economically dominant United States. The Canadian government, for example, requires that 35 percent of a station's daytime radio programming consist of Canadian songs or artists. In Brazil, a toy manufacturer has eclipsed Barbie's popularity by designing a doll named Susi that looks more like Brazilian girls. Susi has a slightly smaller chest, much wider thighs, and darker skin than Barbie. Her wardrobe includes the skimpy bikinis favored on Brazilian beaches as well as a soccer shirt honoring the Brazilian team. According to the toy company's marketing director, "We wanted Susi to be more Latin, more voluptuous. We Latins appreciate those attributes." Brazilians seem to agree: Five Susi dolls are sold for every two Barbies (DePalma 1999; Downie 2000).

Technology in its many forms has now increased the speed of cultural diffusion and has broadened the distribution of cultural elements. Sociologist Gerhard Lenski has defined **technology** as "information about how to use the material resources of the environment to satisfy human needs and desires" (Nolan and Lenski 1999:41). Today's technological developments no longer have to await publication in journals with limited circulation. Press conferences, often simultaneously carried on the Internet, now trumpet new developments.

Technology not only accelerates the diffusion of scientific innovations but also transmits culture. Later, in Chapter 23, we will discuss the concern in many parts of the world that the English language and North American culture dominate the Internet and World Wide Web. Control, or at least dominance, of technology influences the direction of diffusion of culture. Websites abound with the most superficial aspects of U.S. culture but little information about the pressing issues faced by citizens of other nations. People all over the world find it easier to visit electronic chat rooms about daytime television soaps like *All My Children* than to learn about their own government's policies on day care or infant nutrition programs.

Sociologist William F. Ogburn (1922) made a useful distinction between the elements of material and nonmaterial culture. **Material culture** refers to the physical or technological aspects of our daily lives, including food items, houses, factories, and raw materials. **Nonmaterial culture** refers to ways of using material objects and to customs, beliefs, philosophies, governments, and patterns of communication. Generally, the nonmaterial culture is more resistant to change than the material culture. Consequently, Ogburn introduced the term **culture lag** to refer to the period of maladjustment when the nonmaterial culture is still struggling to adapt to new material conditions. For example, the ethics of using the Internet, particularly issues concerning privacy and censorship, have not yet caught up with the explosion in Internet use and technology (see the social policy section in Chapter 23).

Imagine

If you grew up in your parents' generation—without computers, e-mail, the Internet, pagers, and cell phones—how would your daily life differ from the one you lead today?

Elements of Culture

Each culture considers its own distinctive ways of handling basic societal tasks as "natural." But, in fact, methods of education, marital ceremonies, religious doctrines, and other aspects of culture are learned and transmitted through human interactions within specific societies. Parents in India are accustomed to arranging marriages for their children, whereas parents in the United States leave marital decisions up to their offspring. Lifelong residents of Naples consider it natural to speak Italian, whereas lifelong residents of Buenos Aires feel the same way about Spanish. We'll now take a look at the major aspects of culture that shape the way the members of a society live—language, norms, sanctions, and values.

Language

The English language makes extensive use of words dealing with war. We speak of "conquering" space, "fighting" the "battle" of the budget, "waging a war" on drugs, making a "killing" on the stock market, and "bombing" an examination; something monumental or great is "the bomb." An observer from an entirely different and warless culture could gauge the importance that war and the military have had on our lives simply by recognizing the prominence that militaristic terms have in our language. In the Old West, words such as *gelding, stallion, mare, piebald,* and *sorrel* were all used to describe one animal—the horse. Even if we knew little of this period of history, we could conclude from the list of terms how important horses were in this culture. The Slave Indians of northern Canada, who live in a frigid climate, have 14 terms to describe ice, including 8 for different kinds of "solid ice" and others for "seamed ice," "cracked ice," and "floating ice." Clearly, language reflects the priorities of a culture (Basso 1972; Haviland 1999).

Language is, in fact, the foundation of every culture. **Language** is an abstract system of word meanings and symbols for all aspects of culture. It includes speech, written characters, numerals, symbols, and gestures and expressions of nonverbal communication. Figure 3-1 shows where the major languages of the world are spoken.

While language is a cultural universal, striking differences in the use of language are evident around the world. This is the case even when two countries use the same spoken language. For example, an English-speaking person from the United States who is visiting London

Figure 3-1

Languages of the World

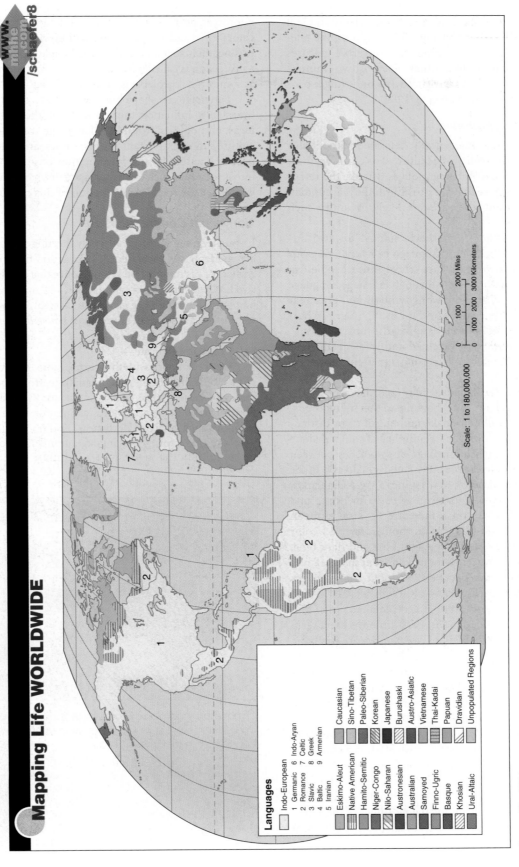

Mapping Life WORLDWIDE

Languages

Indo-European	6 Indo-Aryan
1 Germanic	6 Celtic
2 Romance	7 Greek
3 Slavic	8 Armenian
4 Baltic	9
5 Iranian	

Eskimo-Aleut
Native American
Hamito-Semitic
Niger-Congo
Nilo-Saharan
Austronesian
Australian
Samoyed
Finno-Ugric
Basque
Khosian
Ural-Altaic

Caucasian
Sino-Tibetan
Paleo-Siberian
Korean
Japanese
Burushaski
Austro-Asiatic
Vietnamese
Thai-Kadai
Papuan
Dravidian
Unpopulated Regions

Scale: 1 to 180,000,000

0   1000   2000   3000 Kilometers
0   1000   2000 Miles

Source: Allen 2001.

Think About It
Why do you think people in the United States are much less likely to master more than one language than peoples in other parts of the world?

may be puzzled the first time an English friend says "I'll ring you up." The friend means "I'll call you on the telephone." Similarly, the meanings of nonverbal gestures vary from one culture to another. The positive "thumbs up" gesture used in the United States has only vulgar connotations in Greece (Ekman et al. 1984).

Sapir-Whorf Hypothesis

Language does more than simply describe reality; it also serves to *shape* the reality of a culture. For example, most people in the United States cannot easily make the verbal distinctions about ice that are possible in the Slave Indian culture. As a result, they are less likely to notice such differences.

The *Sapir-Whorf hypothesis,* named for two linguists, describes the role of language in interpreting our world. According to Sapir and Whorf, since people can conceptualize the world only through language, language *precedes* thought. Thus, the word symbols and grammar of a language organize the world for us. The Sapir-Whorf hypothesis also holds that language is not a "given." Rather, it is culturally determined and leads to different interpretations of reality by focusing our attention on certain phenomena.

In a literal sense, language may color how we see the world. Berlin and Kay (1991) have noted that humans possess the physical ability to make millions of color distinctions, yet languages differ in the number of colors that are recognized. The English language distinguishes between yellow and orange, but some other languages do not. In the Dugum Dani language of New Guinea's West Highlands, there are only two basic color terms—*modla* for "white" and *mili* for "black." By contrast, there are 11 basic terms in English. Russian and Hungarian, though, have 12 color terms. Russians have terms for light blue and dark blue, while Hungarians have terms for two different shades of red.

The feminist perspective has noted that gender-related language can reflect—although in itself it will not determine—the traditional acceptance of men and women in certain occupations. Each time we use a term such as *mailman, policeman,* or *fireman,* we are implying (especially to young children) that these occupations can be filled only by males. Yet many women work as *letter carriers, police officers,* and *firefighters*—a fact that is being increasingly recognized and legitimized through the use of such nonsexist language.

Language can also transmit stereotypes related to race. Look up the meanings of the adjective *black* in dictionaries published in the United States. You will find *dismal, gloomy* or *forbidding, destitute of moral light* or *goodness, atrocious, evil, threatening, clouded with anger.* By contrast, dictionaries list *pure* and *innocent* among the meanings of the adjective *white.* Through such patterns of language, our culture

reinforces positive associations with the term (and skin color) *white* and a negative association with *black.* Is it surprising, then, that a list preventing people from working in a profession is called a *blacklist,* while a lie that we think of as somewhat acceptable is called a *white lie?*

Language can shape how we see, taste, smell, feel, and hear. It also influences the way we think about the people, ideas, and objects around us. Language communicates a culture's most important norms, values, and sanctions to people. That's why the introduction of a new language into a society is such a sensitive issue in many parts of the world (see the social policy section of this chapter).

Nonverbal Communication

If you are in the midst of a friendly meeting and one member suddenly sits back, folds his arms, and turns down the corners of his mouth, you know at once that trouble has arrived. When you see a friend in tears, you may give a quick hug. After winning a big game you probably high-five your teammates. These are all examples of *nonverbal communication,* the use of gestures, facial expressions, and other visual images to communicate.

We are not born with these expressions. We learn them, just as we learn other forms of language, from people who share our same culture. This is as true for the basic expressions of happiness and sadness as it is for more complex emotions such as shame or distress (Fridlund et al. 1987).

Like other forms of language, nonverbal communication is not the same in all cultures. For example,

Nonverbal communication can take many forms. A particularly striking example arose out of the horrors of slavery in the United States. People sympathetic to the plight of escaping slaves would hang quilts with patterns similar to this one to indicate a "safe house" or to "point" in the right direction. In this example, the pattern emphasizes the triangles in the upper left corner, pointing in a westerly direction.

sociological research at the microlevel documents that people from various cultures differ in the degree to which they touch others during the course of normal social interaction.

Norms

"Wash your hands before dinner." "Thou shalt not kill." "Respect your elders." All societies have ways of encouraging and enforcing what they view as appropriate behavior while discouraging and punishing what they consider to be improper behavior. *Norms* are established standards of behavior maintained by a society.

In order for a norm to become significant, it must be widely shared and understood. For example, in movie theaters in the United States, we typically expect that people will be quiet while the film is shown. Of course, the application of this norm can vary, depending on the particular film and type of audience. People viewing a serious artistic film will be more likely to insist on the norm of silence than those watching a slapstick comedy or horror movie.

Types of Norms

Sociologists distinguish between norms in two ways. First, norms are classified as either formal or informal. *Formal norms* generally have been written down and specify strict punishments of violators. In the United States, we often formalize norms into laws, which must be very precise in defining proper and improper behavior. Sociologist Donald Black (1995) has termed *law* to be "governmental social control," establishing laws as formal norms enforced by the state. Laws are just one example of formal norms. The requirements for a college major and the rules of a card game are also considered formal norms.

By contrast, *informal norms* are generally understood but they are not precisely recorded. Standards of proper dress are a common example of informal norms. Our society has no specific punishment or sanction for a person who comes to school, say, wearing a monkey suit. Making fun of the nonconforming student is usually the most likely response.

Norms are also classified by their relative importance to society. When classified in this way, they are known as *mores* and *folkways*.

Mores (pronounced "MOR-ays") are norms deemed highly necessary to the welfare of a society, often because they embody the most cherished principles of a people. Each society demands obedience to its mores; violation can lead to severe penalties. Thus, the United States has strong mores against murder, treason, and child abuse, which have been institutionalized into formal norms.

Folkways are norms governing everyday behavior. Folkways play an important role in shaping the daily behavior of members of a culture. Consider, for example, something as simple as footwear. In Japan it is a folkway for youngsters to wear flip-flop sandals while learning to walk. A study of Japanese adults has found that, even barefoot, they walk as if wearing flip-flops—braking their thigh muscles and leaning forward as they step. This folkway may even explain why Japan produces so few competitive runners (Stedman 1998).

Society is less likely to formalize folkways than mores, and their violation raises comparatively little concern. For example, walking up a "down" escalator in a department store challenges our standards of appropriate behavior, but it will not result in a fine or a jail sentence.

In many societies around the world, folkways exist to reinforce patterns of male dominance. Various folkways reveal men's hierarchical position above women within the traditional Buddhist areas of southeast Asia. In the sleeping cars of trains, women do not sleep in upper berths above men. Hospitals that house men on the first floor do not place women patients on the second floor. Even on clotheslines, folkways dictate male dominance: women's attire is hung lower than that of men (Bulle 1987).

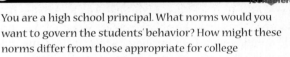

You are a high school principal. What norms would you want to govern the students' behavior? How might these norms differ from those appropriate for college students?

Acceptance of Norms

People do not follow norms, whether mores or folkways, in all situations. In some cases, they can evade a norm because they know it is weakly enforced. It is illegal for U.S. teenagers to drink alcoholic beverages, yet drinking by minors is common throughout the nation. (In fact, teenage alcoholism is a serious social problem.)

In some instances, behavior that appears to violate society's norms may actually represent adherence to the norms of a particular group. Teenage drinkers conform to the standards of a peer group. Conformity to group norms also governed the behavior of the members of a religious cult associated with the Branch Davidians. In 1993, after a deadly gun battle with federal officials, nearly 100 members of the cult defied government orders to abandon their compound near Waco, Texas. After a 51-day standoff, the Department of Justice ordered an assault on the compound and 86 cult members died.

Norms are violated in some instances because one norm conflicts with another. For example, suppose that you live in an apartment building and one night hear the

Cockfighting, anyone? It's legal only in New Mexico, Louisiana, and Oklahoma (shown here) and practiced behind closed doors elsewhere in the nation. What does this situation tell us about social norms?

Sanctions

Suppose that a football coach sends a 12th player onto the field. Or imagine a college graduate showing up in shorts for a job interview at a large bank. Or consider a driver who neglects to put any money into a parking meter. These people have violated widely shared and understood norms. So what happens? In each of these situations, the person will receive sanctions if his or her behavior is detected.

Sanctions are penalties and rewards for conduct concerning a social norm. Note that the concept of *reward* is included in this definition. Conformity to a norm can lead to positive sanctions such as a pay raise, a medal, a word of gratitude, or a pat on the back. Negative sanctions include fines, threats, imprisonment, and stares of contempt.

Table 3-1 summarizes the relationship between norms and sanctions. As you can see, the sanctions that are associated with formal norms (those written down and codified) tend to be formalized as well. If a coach sends too many players onto the field, the team will be penalized 15 yards. The driver who fails to put money in the parking meter will be given a ticket and expected to pay a fine. But sanctions for violations of informal norms

screams of the woman next door, who is being beaten by her husband. If you decide to intervene by ringing their doorbell or calling the police, you are violating the norm of "minding your own business" while, at the same time, following the norm of assisting a victim of violence.

Even when norms do not conflict, there are always exceptions to any norm. The same action, under different circumstances, can cause one to be viewed either as a hero or as a villain. Secretly taping telephone conversations is normally considered illegal and abhorrent. However, it can be done with a court order to obtain valid evidence for a criminal trial. We would heap praise on a government agent who uses such methods to convict an organized crime figure. In our culture, we tolerate killing another human being if it is in self-defense, and we actually reward killing in warfare.

Acceptance of norms is subject to change as the political, economic, and social conditions of a culture are transformed. For example, traditional norms in the United States called for a woman to marry, rear children, and remain at home if her husband could support the family without her assistance. However, these norms have been changing in recent decades, in part as a result of the contemporary feminist movement (see Chapter 12). As support for traditional norms weakens, people feel free to violate them more frequently and openly and are less likely to be punished for doing so.

Table 3-1	**Norms and Sanctions**	
Norms	**Sanctions**	
	Positive	**Negative**
Formal	Salary bonus	Demotion
	Testimonial dinner	Firing from a job
	Medal	Jail sentence
	Diploma	Expulsion
Informal	Smile	Frown
	Compliment	Humiliation
	Cheers	Belittling

can vary. The college graduate who comes to the bank interview in shorts will probably lose any chance of getting the job; on the other hand, he or she might be so brilliant the bank officials will overlook the unconventional attire.

The entire fabric of norms and sanctions in a culture reflects that culture's values and priorities. The most cherished values will be most heavily sanctioned; matters regarded as less critical, on the other hand, will carry light and informal sanctions.

Values

We each have our own personal set of standards—which may include such things as caring or fitness or success in business—but we also share a general set of objectives as members of a society. Cultural *values* are these collective conceptions of what is considered good, desirable, and proper—or bad, undesirable, and improper—in a culture. They indicate what people in a given culture prefer as well as what they find important and morally right (or wrong). Values may be specific, such as honoring one's parents and owning a home, or they may be more general, such as health, love, and democracy. Of course, the members of a society do not uniformly share its values. Angry political debates and billboards promoting conflicting causes tell us that much.

Values influence people's behavior and serve as criteria for evaluating the actions of others. There is often a direct relationship among the values, norms, and sanctions of a culture. For example, if a culture highly values the institution of marriage, it may have norms (and strict sanctions) that prohibit the act of adultery. If a culture views private property as a basic value, it will probably have stiff laws against theft and vandalism.

The values of a culture may change, but most remain relatively stable during any one person's lifetime. Socially shared, intensely felt values are a fundamental part of our lives in the United States. Sociologist Robin Williams (1970) has offered a list of basic values. His list includes achievement, efficiency, material comfort, nationalism, equality, and the supremacy of science and reason over faith. Obviously, not all 290 million people in this country agree on all these values, and we should not look on such a list as anything more than a starting point in defining the national character. Nevertheless, a review of 27 different attempts to describe the "American value system," including the works of anthropologist Margaret Mead and sociologist Talcott Parsons, revealed an overall similarity to the values identified by Williams (Devine 1972).

Each year more than 281,000 entering college students at 421 of the nation's four-year colleges fill out a questionnaire surveying their attitudes. Because this

Figure 3-2

Life Goals of First-year College Students in the United States, 1966–2001

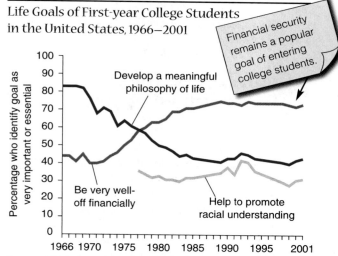

Sources: UCLA Higher Research Institute, as reported in Astin et al. 1994; Sax et al. 2001.

Think About It
Why do you think these values have shifted among college students in the last few decades? Which of these values is important to you? Have your values changed since September 11, 2001?

survey focuses on an array of issues, beliefs, and life goals, it is commonly cited as a barometer of the values of the United States. The respondents are asked what various values are personally important to them. Over the last 33 years, the value of "being very well-off financially" has shown the strongest gain in popularity; the proportion of first-year college students who endorse this value as "essential" or "very important" rose from 44 percent in 1967 to 74 percent in 2001 (see Figure 3-2). By contrast, the value that has shown the most striking decline in endorsement by students is "developing a meaningful philosophy of life." While this value was the most popular in the 1967 survey, endorsed by more than 80 percent of the respondents, it had fallen to sixth place on the list by 2001 and was endorsed by only 43 percent of students entering college.

During the 1980s and 1990s, there was growing support for values having to do with money, power, and status. At the same time, there was a decline in support for certain values having to do with social awareness and altruism, such as "helping others." According to the 2001 nationwide survey, only 38 percent of first-year college students stated that "influencing social values" was an "essential" or a "very important" goal. The proportion of students for whom "helping to promote racial understanding" was an essential or very important goal reached a record high of 42 percent in 1992 but fell to 32 percent in 2001. Like other aspects of culture, such as language and norms, a nation's values are not necessarily fixed.

Culture and the Dominant Ideology

Both functionalist and conflict theorists agree that culture and society are in harmony with each other, but for different reasons. Functionalists maintain that stability requires a consensus and the support of society's members; consequently, there are strong central values and common norms. This view of culture became popular in sociology beginning in the 1950s. It was borrowed from British anthropologists who saw cultural traits as all working toward stabilizing a culture. From a functionalist perspective, a cultural trait or practice will persist if it performs functions that society seems to need or contributes to overall social stability and consensus. This view helps p. 15 ◄ explain why widely condemned social practices such as prostitution continue to survive.

Conflict theorists agree that a common culture may exist, but they argue that it serves to maintain the privileges of certain groups. Moreover, while protecting their own self-interests, powerful groups may keep others in a subservient position. The term ***dominant ideology*** describes the set of cultural beliefs and practices that help to maintain powerful social, economic, and political interests. This concept was first used by Hungarian Marxist Georg Lukacs (1923) and Italian Marxist Antonio Gramsci (1929), but it did not gain an audience in the United States until the early 1970s. In Karl Marx's view, a capitalist society has a dominant ideology that serves the interests of the ruling class.

From a conflict perspective, the dominant ideology has major social significance. Not only do a society's most powerful groups and institutions control wealth and property; even more important, they control the means of producing beliefs about reality through religion, education, and the media. The feminist perspective would also argue that if all of a society's most important institutions tell women that they should be subservient to men, this dominant ideology will help to control women and keep them in a subordinate position (Abercrombie et al. 1980, 1990; R. Robertson 1988).

A growing number of social scientists believe it is not easy to identify a "core culture" in the United States. For support, they point to the lack of consensus on national values, the diffusion of cultural traits, the diversity within our culture, and the changing views of young people (look again at Figure 3-2). Yet there is no way of denying that certain expressions of values have greater influence than others, even in so complex a society as the United States (Abercrombie et al. 1980, 1990; Archer 1988; Wuthnow and Witten 1988). Box 3-1 illustrates that there is a dominant ideology about poverty that derives its strength from the more powerful segments of society and reinforces social inequality.

Cultural Variation

Each culture has a unique character. Inuit tribes in northern Canada—wrapped in furs and dieting on whale blubber—have little in common with farmers in Southeast Asia, who dress for the heat and subsist mainly on the rice they grow in their paddies. Cultures adapt to meet specific sets of circumstances, such as climate, level of technology, population, and geography. This adaptation to different conditions shows up in differences in all elements of culture,

Cultures vary in their taste for films. Europeans and North Americans enjoyed the exotic aspects of *Crouching Tiger, Hidden Dragon* (shown here), but it was not well received in China. Audiences there found it slow-paced, and they were especially annoyed by the clumsy Mandarin spoken by actors more used to Cantonese-speaking roles.

Social Inequality
Dominant Ideology and Poverty

www.
mhhe.
com
/schaefer8

What causes people to be poor? *Individualistic* explanations emphasize personal responsibility: Poor people lack the proper work ethic, lack ability, or are unsuited to the workplace because of problems like drinking or drug abuse. *Structural* explanations, on the other hand, lay the blame for poverty on such external factors as inferior educational opportunities, prejudice, and low wages in some industries. Past research documents that people in the United States generally go along with the individualistic explanation. In short, the dominant ideology holds that people are poor largely because of their own shortcomings.

How pervasive is this view, however? Do the poor and rich alike subscribe to it? In seeking answers, sociologists have conducted studies of how various groups of people view poverty. The research has shown that people with lower incomes are more likely than the wealthy to see the larger socioeconomic system as the cause of poverty. In part this structural view, focusing on the larger job market, relieves them of some personal responsibility for their plight, but it also reflects the social reality that they are close to. On the other

hand, the wealthy tend to embrace the dominant individualistic view because continuation of the socioeconomic status quo is in their best interests. They also prefer to regard their own success as the result of their own accomplishments, with little or no help from external factors.

Sociologist John Morland (1996) surveyed 2,628 people in metropolitan Los Angeles representing a mix of Whites, African Americans, and Latinos. As ex-

> ...the dominant ideology holds that people are poor largely because of their own shortcomings.

pected, he found that members of racial and ethnic minorities are more likely to support structural explanations of poverty than are Whites. He found this is true even among those Blacks and Latinos who are better off economically. Apparently, they are familiar with the historical reality of race-based discrimination, and they can identify with the struggles of fellow group members.

Interestingly, while racial and ethnic minorities tend to support structural explanations more than Whites, they do not reject the individualistic view. This "dual consciousness" among minorities suggests that structural and individualistic explanations need not be considered mutually exclusive.

Is the dominant ideology on poverty widespread? Yes, but it appears that the individualist ideology is dominant in U.S. society not because of a lack of alternatives, but because those who see things differently lack the political influence and status needed to get the ear of the mainstream culture.

Let's Discuss

1. Does support for the dominant ideology about poverty divide along income lines among racial and ethnic minorities? Why or why not?

2. Does your college administration have a "dominant ideology"? How is it manifested? Are there any groups that challenge it? On what basis?

Source: Bobo 1991; Moriand 1996.

---

including norms, sanctions, values, and language. Thus, despite the presence of cultural universals such as courtship and religion, there is still great diversity among the world's many cultures. Moreover, even *within* a single nation, certain segments of the populace develop cultural patterns that differ from the patterns of the dominant society.

Aspects of Cultural Variation

Subcultures

Rodeo cowboys, residents of a retirement community, workers on an offshore oil rig, street gangs—all are examples of what sociologists refer to as *subcultures*. A **subculture** is a segment of society that shares a distinctive pattern of mores, folkways, and values that differs from the pattern of the larger society. In a sense, a subculture can

be thought of as a culture existing within a larger, dominant culture. The existence of many subcultures is characteristic of complex societies such as the United States.

You can get an idea of the impact of subcultures within the United States by considering the variety of seasonal traditions in December. The religious and commercial celebration of the Christmas holiday is an event well-entrenched in the dominant culture of our society. However, the Jewish subculture observes Hanukkah, African Americans have begun to observe the relatively new holiday of Kwanzaa, and some people join in rituals celebrating the winter solstice.

Members of a subculture participate in the dominant culture, while at the same time engaging in unique and distinctive forms of behavior. Frequently, a subculture will develop an **argot,** or specialized language, that distinguishes it

Figure 3-3

The Argot of Pickpockets

Source: Gearty 1996.

from the wider society. For example, if you were to join a band of pickpockets you would need to learn what the dip, dish, and tailpipe are expected to do (see Figure 3-3).

Argot allows "insiders," the members of the subculture, to understand words with special meanings. It also establishes patterns of communication that "outsiders" can't understand. Sociologists associated with the interactionist perspective emphasize that language and symbols offer a powerful way for a subculture to feel cohesive and maintain its identity.

Subcultures develop in a number of ways. Often a subculture emerges because a segment of society faces problems or even privileges unique to its position. Subcultures may be based on common age (teenagers or old people), region (Appalachians), ethnic heritage (Cuban Americans), occupation (firefighters), or beliefs (deaf activists working to preserve deaf culture). Certain subcultures, such as computer hackers, develop because of a shared interest or hobby. In still other subcultures, such as that of prison inmates, members have been excluded from conventional society and are forced to develop alternative ways of living.

Functionalist and conflict theorists agree that variation exists within a culture. Functionalists view subcultures as variations of particular social environments and as evidence that differences can exist within a common culture. However, conflict theorists suggest that variation often reflects the inequality of social arrangements within a society. A conflict perspective would view the challenge to dominant social norms by African American activists, the feminist movement, and the disability rights movement as a reflection of inequity based on race, gender, and disability status. Conflict theorists also argue that subcul-

tures sometimes emerge when the dominant society unsuccessfully tries to suppress a practice, such as the use of illegal drugs.

Countercultures

By the end of the 1960s, an extensive subculture had emerged in the United States composed of young people turned off by a society they believed was too materialistic and technological. This group primarily included political radicals and "hippies" who had "dropped out" of mainstream social institutions. These young men and women rejected the pressure to accumulate more and more cars, larger and larger homes, and an endless array of material goods. Instead, they expressed a desire to live in a culture based on more humanistic values, such as sharing, love, and coexistence with the environment. As a political force, this subculture opposed the United States' involvement in the war in Vietnam and encouraged draft resistance (Flacks 1971; Roszak 1969).

When a subculture conspicuously and deliberately *opposes* certain aspects of the larger culture, it is known as a **counterculture.** Countercultures typically thrive among the young, who have the least investment in the existing culture. In most cases, a 20-year-old can adjust to new cultural standards more easily than someone who has spent 60 years following the patterns of the dominant culture (Zellner 1995).

In the wake of the World Trade Center attack of September 11, 2001, people around the United States learned

"IT'S ENDLESS. WE JOIN A COUNTER-CULTURE; IT BECOMES THE CULTURE. WE JOIN ANOTHER COUNTER-CULTURE; IT BECOMES THE CULTURE..."

Cultures change. Aspects we once regarded as unacceptable—such as men wearing earrings and people wearing jeans in the workplace—and associated with fringe groups (such as men and women with tattoos) are now widely accepted. Countercultural practices are sometimes absorbed by the mainstream culture.

of the existence of terrorist groups operating as a counterculture within their country. This was a situation that generations have lived with in Northern Ireland, Israel, the Palestinian territory, and many other parts of the world. Terrorist cells worldwide are not necessarily fueled only by outsiders. Frequently people become disenchanted with the policies of their own country, and a few take very violent steps.

Culture Shock

Anyone who feels disoriented, uncertain, out of place, even fearful, when immersed in an unfamiliar culture may be experiencing *culture shock.* For example, a resident of the United States who visits certain areas in China and wants local meat for dinner may be stunned to learn that the specialty is dog meat. Similarly, someone from a strict Islamic culture may be shocked upon first seeing the comparatively provocative dress styles and open displays of affection that are common in the United States and various European cultures.

Sometimes culture shock entices tourists. The "long-necked" women and girls of the Kayan tribe have traditionally worn coils of brass weighing up to 12 pounds as a mark of beauty and tribal identity. This costly practice is dying out in their native Myanmar, but as refugees in Northern Thailand, the women find that their long necks attract much-needed income from tourists.

All of us, to some extent, take for granted the cultural practices of our society. As a result, it can be surprising and even disturbing to realize that other cultures do not follow our "way of life." The fact is that customs that seem strange to us are considered normal and proper in other cultures, which may see *our* mores and folkways as odd.

Imagine

You arrive in a developing African country as a Peace Corps volunteer. What aspects of a very different culture do you think would be the hardest to adjust to? What might the citizens of that country find shocking about your culture?

Attitudes toward Cultural Variation

Ethnocentrism

Many everyday statements reflect our attitude that our culture is best. We use terms such as *underdeveloped, backward,* and *primitive* to refer to other societies. What "we" believe is a religion; what "they" believe is superstition and mythology (Spradley and McCurdy 1980).

It is tempting to evaluate the practices of other cultures on the basis of our own perspectives. Sociologist

William Graham Sumner (1906) coined the term *ethnocentrism* to refer to the tendency to assume that one's culture and way of life constitute the norm or are superior to all others. The ethnocentric person sees his or her own group as the center or defining point of culture and views all other cultures as deviations from what is "normal."

Westerners who think cattle are to be used for food might look down on India's Hindu religion and culture, which views the cow as sacred. Or people in one culture may dismiss as unthinkable the mate selection or child-rearing practices of another culture. You might have been tempted to view the Nacirema culture from an ethnocentric point of view—until you learned it is your own culture that Miner describes (see the chapter opening essay).

Conflict theorists point out that ethnocentric value judgments serve to devalue groups and to deny equal opportunities. Psychologist Walter Stephan notes a typical example of ethnocentrism in New Mexico's schools. Both Hispanic and Native American cultures teach children to look down when they are being criticized by adults, yet many "Anglo" (non-Hispanic White) teachers believe that you should look someone in the eye when you are being criticized. "Anglo teachers can feel that these students are being disrespectful," notes Stephan. "That's the kind of misunderstanding that can evolve into stereotype and prejudice" (Goleman 1991:C8).

Sociology in the Global Community

3-2 Cultural Sensitivity on the Beat

www.
mhhe.
com
/schaefer8

The emergency room doctor at a California hospital became concerned when he discovered crimson slashes on a child's back. He summoned police officers to arrest the parents and arranged for a social worker to take the boy. The parents, Chinese immigrants, claimed they were caring for their child with a Chinese folk remedy called coining. It involves treating a fever by lightly running hot coins over the child's body. Chinese-speaking detectives were called in, and they were able to corroborate the parents' story and avert an arrest.

In New York City, a Danish visitor left her child in a stroller outside a café while she had lunch. Concerned diners called the police, who jailed the mother and father for two nights on charges of endangering a child. The child was placed in foster care for four days before being returned to her mother. This incident caused an uproar in Denmark, where it is customary to leave children unattended in strollers outside cafés.

Sikh children in California were removed from their elementary school for wearing daggers. But their religion requires wearing these sacred symbols at all times. They were allowed back to school when they agreed to dull the blade, sew it into its sheath, and secure it in a pouch.

Today 1 out of 10 people in the United States was born abroad, and sometimes the different cultural practices confound law enforcement officers. What can be done to increase cultural sensitivity? California has mandated 24 hours of cultural diversity and discrimination training at all police academies. But many California communities are finding that this is not enough. The Los Angeles Police Department now offers

> Today 1 out of 10 people in the United States was born abroad, and sometimes the different cultural practices confound law enforcement officers.

almost 100 hours of diversity training, and Long Beach requires a three-day course. Los Angeles also established a special Asian Crime Investigation section staffed by officers who are well versed in different Asian cultures.

Training sessions need to be geared toward their audience—police officers. The police department in Phoenix, Arizona, avoids using "touchy-feely" sessions that make veteran officers uncomfortable.

Instead, it focuses on practical issues: how the sensitivity training will help in interviewing suspects, victims, and witnesses; how it will help defuse tense situations; and how it will make the officers themselves feel safer on the streets.

One important result of using sensitivity on the beat is that many would-be arrests can be averted. Once a case enters the legal system, it can be difficult to remove. According to Alison Renteln, an expert in cultural diversity and the law, the police can serve an important role as gatekeepers: "If the police have an understanding of different cultures, they can save everyone—from the defendants to the judges—a lot of problems" (p. A12).

Let's Discuss

1. Do you know anyone who was arrested for doing something that was actually an ethnic custom? How did the case proceed? Were the police trained in cultural diversity?

2. At what point does a cultural practice cross over into a crime? Should coining be considered child abuse, for example? What about female circumcision?

Source: Corwin 2000.

Functionalists, on the other hand, point out that ethnocentrism serves to maintain a sense of solidarity by promoting group pride. Denigrating other nations and cultures can enhance our own patriotic feelings and belief that our way of life is superior. Yet this type of social stability is established at the expense of other peoples. Of course, ethnocentrism is hardly limited to citizens of the United States. Visitors from many African cultures are surprised at the disrespect that children in the United States show their parents. People from India may be repelled by our practice of living in the same household with dogs and cats. Many Islamic fundamentalists in the Arab world and Asia view the United States as corrupt, decadent, and doomed to destruction. All these people may feel comforted by membership in cultures that, in their view, are superior to ours.

Cultural Relativism

While ethnocentrism evaluates foreign cultures using the familiar culture of the observer as a standard of correct behavior, **cultural relativism** views people's behavior from the perspective of their own culture. It places a priority on understanding other cultures, rather than dismissing them as "strange" or "exotic." Unlike ethnocentrism, cultural relativism employs the kind of value neutrality in scientific study that Max Weber saw as so important. Box 3-2 illustrates how police and prosecutors need to be sensitive to different cultural practices in administering criminal justice.

p. 46

Cultural relativism stresses that different social contexts give rise to different norms and values. Thus, we must examine practices such as polygamy, bullfighting, and monarchy within the particular contexts of the cultures in which they are found. While cultural relativism does not suggest that we must unquestionably *accept* every cultural variation, it does require a serious and unbiased effort to evaluate norms, values, and customs in light of their distinctive culture.

There is an interesting extension of cultural relativism, referred to as *xenocentrism*. **Xenocentrism** is the belief that the products, styles, or ideas of one's society are *inferior* to those that originate elsewhere (Wilson et al. 1976). In a sense, it is a reverse ethnocentrism. For example, people in the United States often assume that French fashions or Japanese electronic devices are superior to our own. Are they? Or are people unduly charmed by the lure of goods from exotic places? Such fascination with overseas products can be damaging to competitors in the United States. Some U.S. companies have responded by creating products that *sound* European, such as Häagen-Dazs ice cream (made in Teaneck, New Jersey). Conflict theorists are most likely to consider the economic impact of xenocentrism in the developing world. Consumers in developing nations frequently turn their backs on locally produced goods and instead purchase items imported from Europe or North America.

How one views a culture—whether from an ethnocentric point of view or through the lens of cultural relativism—has important consequences in the area of social policy. A hot issue today is the extent to which a nation should accommodate nonnative language speakers by sponsoring bilingual programs. We'll take a close look at this issue in the next section.

SOCIAL POLICY AND CULTURE

Bilingualism

The Issue

In Sri Lanka, Tamils seek to break away from the Sinhalese-speaking majority. Romanian radio announces that in areas where 20 percent of the people speak Hungarian, bilingual road and government signs will be used. In schools from Miami to Boston to Chicago, school administrators strive to deliver education to their Creole-speaking Haitian students. All over the world, nations are having to face the problem of how to deal with residential minorities who speak a language different from that of the mainstream culture.

Bilingualism refers to the use of two or more languages in a particular setting, such as the workplace or schoolroom, treating each language as equally legitimate. Thus, a program of bilingual education may instruct children in their native language while gradually introducing them to the language of the host society. If the curriculum is also bicultural, it will teach children about the mores and folkways of both the dominant culture and the subculture. To what degree should schools in the United States present the curriculum in a language other than English? This issue has prompted a great deal of debate among educators and policymakers.

The Setting

Languages know no political boundaries. Despite the portrayal of dominant languages in Figure 3-1 (page 65), minority languages are common in many nations. For example, while Hindi is the most widely spoken language in India and English is widely used for official purposes, there are still 18 other languages officially recognized in this nation of about one billion people. According to the Census 2000, 45 million residents of the United States over the age of 5—that's about 18 percent of the population—speak a language other than English as their primary language. Indeed, 50 different languages are each spoken by at least 200,000 residents of this country (Bureau of the Census 2001f).

Schools throughout the world must deal with incoming students speaking many languages. Do bilingual programs in the United States help these children to learn English? It is difficult to reach firm conclusions because bilingual programs in general vary so widely in their approach. They differ in the length of the transition to English and how long they allow students to remain in bilingual classrooms. Moreover, results have been mixed. In the years since California effectively dismantled its bilingual education program, reading and math scores of students with limited English proficiency rose dramatically, especially in the lower grades. Yet a major overview of 11 different studies on bilingual education found that children with limited English who are taught using at least some of their native language perform significantly better on standardized tests than similar children who are taught only in English (J. Steinberg 2000; Greene 1998; see also Pyle 1998).

Sociological Insights

For a long time, people in the United States demanded conformity to a single language. This demand coincides with the functionalist view that language serves to unify members of a society. Immigrant children from Europe and Asia—including young Italians, Jews, Poles, Chinese, and Japanese—were expected to learn English once they entered school. In some cases, immigrant children were actually forbidden to speak their native languages on school grounds. There was little respect granted to immigrants' cultural traditions; a young person would often be teased about his or her "funny" name, accent, or style of dress.

Recent decades have seen challenges to this pattern of forced obedience to our dominant ideology. Beginning in the 1960s, active movements for Black pride and ethnic pride insisted that people regard the traditions of *all* racial and ethnic subcultures as legitimate and important. Conflict theorists explain this development as a case of subordinated language minorities seeking opportunities of self-expression. Partly as a result of these challenges, people began to view bilingualism as an asset. It seemed to provide a sensitive way of assisting millions of non–English-speaking people in the United States to *learn* English in order to function more effectively within the society.

The perspective of conflict theory also helps us understand some of the attacks on bilingual programs. Many of them stem from an ethnocentric point of view, which holds that any deviation from the majority is bad. This attitude tends to be expressed by those who wish to stamp out foreign influence wherever it occurs, especially in our schools. This view does not take into account that success in bilingual education may actually have beneficial results, such as decreasing the number of high school dropouts and increasing the number of Hispanics in colleges and universities.

Policy Initiatives

Bilingualism has policy implications largely in two areas—efforts to maintain language purity and programs to enhance bilingual education. Nations vary dramatically in their tolerance for a variety of languages. China continues to tighten its cultural control over Tibet by extending instruction of Mandarin, a Chinese dialect, from high school into the elementary schools, which will now be bilingual along with Tibetan. Even more forceful is Indonesia, which has a large Chinese-speaking minority; public display of Chinese-language signs or books is totally banned. By contrast, nearby Singapore establishes English as the medium of instruction but allows students to take their mother tongue as a second language, be it Chinese, Malay, or Tamil (Farley 1998).

In many nations, language dominance is a regional issue—for example, in Miami or along the border of Texas, where Spanish speaking is prevalent. A particularly virulent bilingual hot spot is Quebec—the French-speaking province of Canada. The Québécois, as they are known, represent 83 percent of the province's population, but only 25 percent of Canada's total population. A law implemented in 1978 mandated education in French for all Quebec's children except those whose parents or siblings had learned English elsewhere in Canada. While special laws like this one have advanced French in the province, dissatisfied Québécois have moved for secession to form their own separate country. In 1995, the people of Quebec voted to remain united with Canada by only the narrowest of margins (50.5 percent). Language and related cultural areas both unify and divide this nation of 32 million people (Schaefer 2002).

Policymakers in the United States have been somewhat ambivalent in dealing with the issue of bilingualism.

French speakers in Quebec are zealous about protecting the prevalence of their language in the Canadian province. The French Pokémon cards were a response to intense lobbying efforts.

Figure 3-4

States with Official English Laws

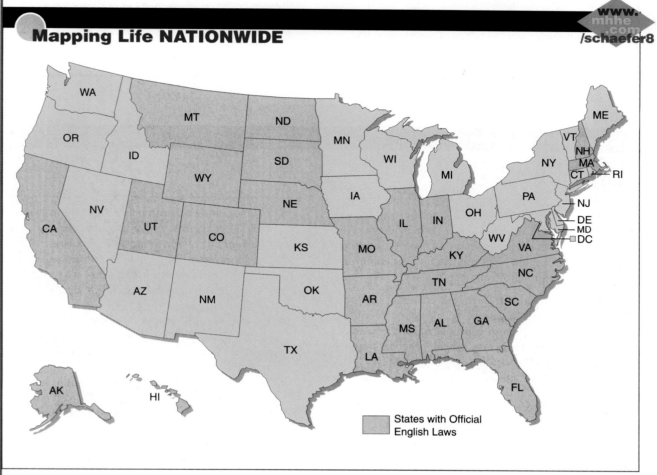

Mapping Life NATIONWIDE

States with Official English Laws

Source: U.S. English 2001.

In 1965, the Elementary and Secondary Education Act (ESEA) provided for bilingual, bicultural education. In the 1970s, the federal government took an active role in establishing the proper form for bilingual programs. However, more recently, federal policy has been less supportive of bilingualism. Local school districts have been forced to provide an increased share of funding for their bilingual programs. Yet bilingual programs are an expense that many communities and states are unwilling to pay and are quick to cut back. In 1998, voters in California approved a proposition that all but eliminated bilingual education: it requires instruction in English for 1.4 million children who are not fluent in the language.

In the United States, there have been repeated efforts to introduce a constitutional amendment to make English the official language of the nation. A major force behind efforts to restrict bilingualism is U.S. English, a nationwide organization founded in 1983 that now claims to have one million members. Its adherents say they feel like strangers in their own neighborhoods, aliens in their own country. By contrast, Hispanic leaders see the U.S. English campaign as a veiled expression of racism.

Despite such challenges, U.S. English seems to be making headway in its efforts to oppose bilingualism. By 2001, 26 states had declared English to be their official language (see Figure 3-4). The actual impact of these measures, beyond their symbolism, is unclear.

Let's Discuss

1. How might someone with an ethnocentric point of view look at bilingualism?
2. Describe how conflict theorists would explain recent developments in bilingual programs in the United States.
3. Have you attended a school with a number of students for whom English is a second language? Did the school set up a special bilingual program? Was it effective? What is your opinion of such programs?

Chapter Resources

Summary

Culture is the totality of learned, socially transmitted customs, knowledge, material objects, and behavior. This chapter examines the basic elements that make up a culture, social practices common to all cultures, and variations that distinguish one culture from another.

1. Sharing a similar culture helps to define the group or society to which we belong.
2. Anthropologist George Murdock has compiled a list of *cultural universals,* general practices found in every culture, including courtship, family, games, language, medicine, religion, and sexual restrictions.
3. Human culture is constantly expanding through *innovation,* including both *discovery* and *invention.*
4. *Diffusion*—the spread of cultural items from one place to another—also changes cultures. But societies resist ideas that seem too foreign as well as those perceived as threatening to their own values and beliefs.
5. *Language,* an important element of culture, includes speech, written characters, numerals, symbols, and gestures and other forms of nonverbal communication. Language both describes culture and shapes it for us.
6. Sociologists distinguish between *norms* in two ways. They are classified as either *formal* or *informal* norms and as *mores* or *folkways.*
7. The more cherished *values* of a culture will receive the heaviest *sanctions;* matters that are regarded as less critical, on the other hand, will carry light and informal sanctions.
8. The *dominant ideology* of a culture describes the set of cultural beliefs and practices that help to maintain powerful social, economic, and political interests.
9. In a sense, a *subculture* can be thought of as a culture existing within a larger, dominant culture. *Countercultures* are subcultures that deliberately oppose aspects of the larger culture.
10. People who measure other cultures by the standard of their own engage in *ethnocentrism*. Using *cultural relativism* allows us to view people from the perspective of their own culture.
11. The social policy of *bilingualism* calls for programs that use two or more languages, treating each as equally legitimate. It is supported by those who want to ease the transition of nonnative language speakers into a host society; it is opposed by those who adhere to a single cultural tradition in language.

Critical Thinking Questions

1. Select three cultural universals from George Murdock's list (see p. 62) and analyze them from a functionalist perspective. Why are these practices found in every culture? What functions do they serve?
2. Drawing on the theories and concepts presented in the chapter, apply sociological analysis to one subculture with which you are familiar. Describe the norms, values, argot, and sanctions evident in that subculture.
3. In what ways is the dominant ideology of the United States evident in the nation's literature, music, movies, theater, television programs, and sporting events?

Key Terms

Argot   Specialized language used by members of a group or subculture. (page 71)

Bilingualism   The use of two or more languages in particular settings, such as workplaces or schoolrooms, treating each language as equally legitimate. (75)

Counterculture   A subculture that deliberately opposes certain aspects of the larger culture. (72)

Cultural relativism   The viewing of people's behavior from the perspective of their own culture. (74)

Cultural universals   General practices found in every culture. (62)

Culture   The totality of learned, socially transmitted customs, knowledge, material objects, and behavior. (61)

Culture lag   A period of maladjustment during which the nonmaterial culture is still struggling to adapt to new material conditions. (64)

Culture shock   The feeling of surprise and disorientation that is experienced when people encounter cultural practices different from their own. (73)

Diffusion   The process by which a cultural item is spread from group to group or society to society. (63)

Discovery   The process of making known or sharing the existence of an aspect of reality. (63)

Dominant ideology   A set of cultural beliefs and practices that helps to maintain powerful social, economic, and political interests. (70)

Ethnocentrism   The tendency to assume that one's own culture and way of life represent the norm or are superior to all others. (73)

Folkways   Norms governing everyday social behavior whose violation raises comparatively little concern. (67)

Formal norms   Norms that generally have been written down and that specify strict rules for punishment of violators. (67)

Informal norms   Norms that generally are understood but are not precisely recorded. (67)

Innovation   The process of introducing new elements into a culture through either discovery or invention. (63)

Invention   The combination of existing cultural items into a form that did not previously exist. (63)

Language   An abstract system of word meanings and symbols for all aspects of culture. It also includes gestures and other nonverbal communication. (64)

Law   Governmental social control. (67)

Material culture   The physical or technological aspects of our daily lives. (64)

Mores   Norms deemed highly necessary to the welfare of a society. (67)

Nonmaterial culture   Ways of using material objects as well as customs, beliefs, philosophies, governments, and patterns of communication. (64)

Norms   Established standards of behavior maintained by a society. (67)

Sanctions   Penalties and rewards for conduct concerning a social norm. (68)

Sapir-Whorf hypothesis   A hypothesis concerning the role of language in shaping cultures. It holds that language is culturally determined and serves to influence our mode of thought. (66)

Society   A fairly large number of people who live in the same territory, are relatively independent of people outside it, and participate in a common culture. (61)

Subculture   A segment of society that shares a distinctive pattern of mores, folkways, and values that differs from the pattern of the larger society. (71)

Technology   Information about how to use the material resources of the environment to satisfy human needs and desires. (64)

Values   Collective conceptions of what is considered good, desirable, and proper—or bad, undesirable, and improper—in a culture. (69)

Xenocentrism   The belief that the products, styles, or ideas of one's society are inferior to those that originate elsewhere. (75)

Additional Readings

BOOKS

Best, Joel (ed.). 2001. *How Claims Spread: Cross-National Diffusion of Social Problems.* Hawthorne, NY: Aldine de Gruyter. Diffusion of culture can also refer to images of social reality, as reflected in this volume.

Cunningham, Michael, and Craig Marberry. 2000. *Crowns: Portraits of Black Women in Church Hats.* New York: Random House. This richly illustrated book makes clear that what we wear conveys the impression we wish to give others.

DeVita, Philip B., and James D. Armstrong, eds. 1998. *Distant Mirrors: America as a Foreign Culture.* 2d ed. Belmont, CA: West/Wadsworth. Nineteen essays by scholars from Europe, Africa, Asia, and Latin America who conduct observation research about U.S. society and culture from the outsider's perspective.

Flores, William V., and Riva Benmayor (eds.). 1997. *Latino Cultural Citizenship: Claiming Identity, Space and Rights*. Boston: Beacon Press. Looks at a variety of Latino communities to learn how Hispanics confront being both Latino and American.

Kraybill, Donald B., and Steven M. Nott. 1995. *Amish Enterprises: From Plows to Profits*. Baltimore: Johns Hopkins University Press. An examination of how the Amish have adapted to capitalism in the United States while maintaining their distinctive values and subculture.

Lakoff, Robin Talmach. 2000. *Language War*. Berkeley: University of California Press. A linguist considers how language shapes a culture and the discussions within a society. Uses case studies of contemporary issues, such as the O. J. Simpson murder trial, the Ebonics controversy, and the Clinton sex scandal.

Lutz, Catherine A., and Jane L. Collins. 1993. *Reading National Geographic*. Chicago: University of Chicago Press. *National Geographic* has been the window to the world, but how has it chosen to present that world? A sociologist and an anthropologist collaborate to answer that question.

Nelson, Alondra, and Thuy Linh N. Tu, with Alicia Headlam Hines (ed.). 2001. *Technicolor: Race, Technology, and Everyday Life*. New York: New York University Press. Analytical look at the intersection of today's technology with race, considering such topics as how ethnic groups are stereotyped about their use of the latest advances.

Zellner, William M. 1995. *Countercultures: A Sociological Analysis*. New York: St. Martin's. An overview of six countercultures found in the United States: the Unification Church, the Church of Scientology, satanists, skinheads, survivalists, and the Ku Klux Klan.

JOURNALS

Among the journals that focus on issues of culture and language are *Academic Questions* (the journal of the National Association of Scholars, founded in 1988), *American Anthropologist* (1988), *Cross-Cultural Research* (1967), *Cultural Studies: Critical Methodologies* (2001), *Cultural Survival Quarterly* (1977), *Ethnology* (1962), *International Journal of the Sociology of Language* (1974), *MultiCultural Social Change* (1979), and *Theory, Culture, and Society* (1982).

Technology Resources

Internet Connection

*Note: While all the URLs listed were current as of the printing of this book, these sites often change. Please check our website (**http://www.mhhe.com/schaefer8**) for updates and hyperlinks to these exercises and additional exercises.*

1. Nonverbal communication is an important element in all cultures. Through gestures and body language, we can express ideas and feelings. As with all elements of culture though, specific forms of nonverbal communication differ among different groups. Visit **http://dir.yahoo.com/Arts/Performing_Arts/Dance/Folk_and_Traditional/** to sample the meanings and forms of dances in differing groups. Choose three of the groups listed on the homepage. Then link to websites dedicated to their folk or traditional forms of dance. For each, answer the following questions:
   (a) Does the name of the dance itself hold any special meaning?
   (b) What purposes/functions does the dance serve for members of the group?
   (c) What is the history or origin of the dance?
   (d) Is the dance still performed today? Is it performed at a specific time of year or under certain conditions?
   (e) What symbolism and gestures do the dancers use? What ideas and feelings do they try to express?
   (f) What similarities and differences among the three groups and dances do you see?
   (g) Why would it be good for a social scientist studying dance forms in different cultures to keep in mind the concepts of cultural relativism, ethnocentrism, and culture shock?
2. Future Culture (**http://www.wcpworld.com/future/culture.htm**) is a website that allows people to explore the concept of culture in more detail and to compare cultural information on a range of areas. Click on the quiz, take it, and answer the following questions:
   (a) Out of the first five questions, how many did you answer correctly?
   (b) How did you score overall?
   Click on your Back button and then click on links. (Note that some of these links cannot be accessed). Then click on "Oceania." Pick two of the countries.

(c)   Where is each country located?

(d)   What is the religion for each country?

(e)   What is the culture like for each country?

Click on your Back button and click on "Central America and the Caribbean." Pick two of the countries listed.

(f)   Where is each country located?

(g)   Give a brief overview of the history of each country.

(h)   What is the culture like for each country?

(i)   How does the culture of these countries compare to the culture of the United States?

3. Museums Around the World (**http:// www.icom. org/vlmp/world.html**) has a list of countries and their museums. This site allows the public to access information about different countries through these museums. Click on "South Africa" and click on the "Robben Island Museum." Explore the site

and be sure to check out the panoramic view of the island. Click on "Brief History."

(a)   What was the primary use of Robben Island?

(b)   Who were some of the people imprisoned on the island?

(c)   What else was Robben Island used for?

Click on your Back button. Then click on "Bulgaria and the National Museum of History." Click on "Virtual Tour" and then on "Hall 9."

(d)   Who were the first settlers in Bulgaria?

(e)   Look at some of the artifacts in this hall. Which ones did you find the most interesting? Why?

Click on "Hall 18."

(f)   What did you learn about the First Bulgarian Kingdom?

(g)   Look at some of the artifacts in this hall. Which ones did you like the most? Why?

Online Learning Center www.mhhe.com/schaefer8

In this chapter, you have learned that language is the foundation of every culture. For a long time, people in the United States demanded conformity to a single language. More recently, however, we have seen challenges to this forced obedience to our dominant ideology. One of the

interactive exercises in the student center of the Online Learning Center (**www.mhhe.com/schaefer8**) will only let you use a "foreign" language to do the activity. You will be taught a simple language called Pig Latin. Give it a try, and see whether or not you feel competent completing the exercise in this "foreign" language.

SOCIALIZATION

Schools can sometimes be stressful arenas of socialization. This poster informs schoolchildren in Japan that they can call a hotline and receive advice concerning stress, bullying by classmates, and corporal punishment from their teachers.

BLACK PICKET FENCES

PRIVILEGE AND PERIL AMONG
THE BLACK MIDDLE CLASS

MARY PATTILLO-McCOY

Charisse . . . is sixteen and lives with her mother and younger sister, Deanne, across the street from St. Mary's Catholic Church and School. Charisse's mother is a personnel assistant at a Chicago university, and is taking classes there to get her bachelor's degree. Mr. Baker is a Chicago firefighter. While her father and mother are separated, Charisse sees her father many times a week at the afterschool basketball hour that he supervises at St. Mary's gym. He and Charisse's mother are on very good terms, and Charisse has a loving relationship with both parents. Mr. Baker is as active as any parent could be, attending the father/daughter dances at Charisse's high school, never missing a big performance, and visiting his daughters often.

Charisse and her sister are being raised by the neighborhood family in addition to their biological parents. "We [are] real close. Like all our neighbors know us because my dad grew up over here. Since the '60s." Charisse is a third-generation Grovelandite just like Neisha Morris. Her grandparents moved into Groveland with Charisse's then-teenage father when the neighborhood first opened to African Americans. . . . Now Charisse is benefiting from the friends her family has made over their years of residence in Groveland, especially the members of St. Mary's church, who play the role of surrogate parents. When Charisse was in elementary school at St. Mary's, her late paternal grandmother was the school secretary, and so the Baker girls were always under the watchful eye of their grandmother as well as the staff, who were their grandmother's friends. And in the evenings Charisse's mother would bring her and her sister to choir practice, where they accumulated an ensemble of mothers and fathers.

After St. Mary's elementary school, Charisse went on to St. Agnes Catholic High School for girls, her father's choice. St. Agnes is located in a suburb of Chicago and is a solid, integrated Catholic school where 100 percent of the girls graduate and over 95 percent go on to college. . . .

Most of Charisse's close friends went to St. Mary's and now go to St. Agnes with her, but her choice of boyfriends shows modest signs of rebellion. . . . Many of Charisse's male interests are older than she, and irregularly employed—although some are in and out of school. She meets many of them hanging out at the mall. One evening, members of the church's youth choir sat around talking about their relationships. Charisse cooed while talking about her present boyfriend, who had just graduated from high school but did not have a job and was uncertain about his future. But in the middle of that thought, Charisse spontaneously changed her attentions to a new young man that she had just met. "Charisse changes boyfriends like she changes her clothes," her sister joked, indicating the impetuous nature of adolescent relationships. *(Pattillo-McCoy 1999:100–102)* ■

Additional information about this excerpt and about those that open each subsequent chapter can be found on the SocWorld CD-ROM that accompanies this text.

This excerpt from *Black Picket Fences: Privilege and Peril among the Black Middle Class* describes the upbringing of a young resident of Groveland, a close-knit African American community in Chicago. The author, sociologist Mary Pattillo-McCoy, became acquainted with Charisse while living in Groveland, where she was doing ethnographic research. Charisse's childhood is similar to that of other youths in many respects. Regardless of race or social class, a young person's development involves a host of influences, from parents, grandparents, and siblings to friends and classmates, teachers and school administrators, neighbors and churchgoers—even youths who frequent the local mall. Yet in some ways, Charisse's development is specifically influenced by her race and social class. Contact with family and community members, for instance, has undoubtedly prepared her to deal with prejudice and the absence of positive images of African Americans in the media.

Sociologists, in general, are interested in the patterns of behavior and attitudes that emerge *throughout* the life course, from infancy to old age. These patterns are part of the process of *socialization,* whereby people learn the attitudes, values, and behaviors appropriate for members of a particular culture. Socialization occurs through human interactions. We learn a great deal from those people most important in our lives—immediate family members, best friends, and teachers. But we also learn from people we see on the street, on television, on the Internet, and in films and magazines.

From a microsociological perspective, socialization helps us to discover how to behave "properly" and what to expect from others if we follow (or challenge) society's norms and values. From a macrosociological perspective, socialization provides for the transmission of a culture from one generation to the next, and thereby for the long-term continuance of a society.

Socialization affects the overall cultural practices of a society, and it also shapes our self-images. For example, in the United States, a person who is viewed as "too heavy" or "too short" does not conform to the ideal cultural standard of physical attractiveness. This kind of unfavorable evaluation can significantly influence the person's self-esteem. In this sense, socialization experiences can help to shape our personalities. In everyday speech, the term **personality** is used to refer to a person's typical patterns of attitudes, needs, characteristics, and behavior.

How much of a person's personality is shaped by culture, as opposed to inborn traits? In what ways does socialization continue into adulthood? Who are the most powerful agents of socialization? In this chapter we will examine the role of socialization in human development. We will begin by analyzing the interaction of heredity and environmental factors. We pay particular attention to how people develop perceptions, feelings, and beliefs about themselves. The chapter will also explore the lifelong nature of the socialization process, as well as important agents of socialization, among them the family, schools, peers, and the media. Finally, the social policy section will focus on the socialization experience of group child care for young children. ∎

The Role of Socialization

What makes us who we are? Is it the genes we are born with? Or the environment in which we grow up? Researchers have traditionally clashed over the relative importance of biological inheritance and environmental factors in human development—a conflict called the *nature versus nurture* (or *heredity versus environment*) debate. Today, most social scientists have moved beyond this debate, acknowledging instead the *interaction* of these variables in shaping human development. However, we can better appreciate how heredity and environmental factors interact and influence the socialization process if we first examine situations in which one factor operates almost entirely without the other (Homans 1979).

Environment: The Impact of Isolation

In the 1994 movie *Nell,* Jodie Foster played a young woman hidden from birth by her mother in a backwoods cabin. Raised without normal human contact, Nell crouches like an animal, screams wildly, and speaks or sings in a language all her own. This movie was drawn from the actual account of an emaciated 16-year-old boy who mysteriously appeared in 1828 in the town square of Nuremberg, Germany (Lipson 1994).

The Case of Isabelle

Some viewers may have found the story of Nell difficult to believe, but the painful childhood of Isabelle was all too real. For the first six years of her life, Isabelle lived in almost total seclusion in a darkened room. She had little

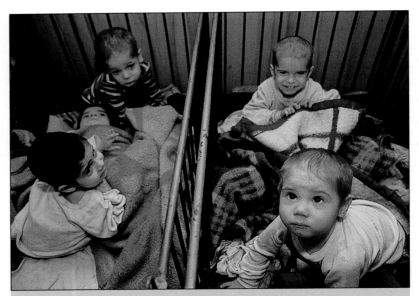

These children in a Romanian orphanage enjoy little adult contact and spend much of their time confined to cribs. This neglect can result in adjustment problems later in life.

contact with other people, with the exception of her mother, who could neither speak nor hear. Isabelle's mother's parents had been so deeply ashamed of Isabelle's illegitimate birth that they kept her hidden away from the world. Ohio authorities finally discovered the child in 1938, when Isabelle's mother escaped from her parents' home, taking her daughter with her.

When she was discovered at age six, Isabelle could not speak. She could merely make various croaking sounds. Her only communications with her mother were simple gestures. Isabelle had been largely deprived of the typical interactions and socialization experiences of childhood. Since she had actually seen few people, she initially showed a strong fear of strangers and reacted almost like a wild animal when confronted with an unfamiliar person. As she became accustomed to seeing certain individuals, her reaction changed to one of extreme apathy. At first, observers believed that Isabelle was deaf, but she soon began to react to nearby sounds. On tests of maturity, she scored at the level of an infant rather than a six-year-old.

Specialists developed a systematic training program to help Isabelle adapt to human relationships and socialization. After a few days of training, she made her first attempt to verbalize. Although she started slowly, Isabelle quickly passed through six years of development. In a little over two months, she was speaking in complete sentences. Nine months later, she could identify both words and sentences. Before Isabelle reached the age of nine, she was ready to attend school with other children. By her 14th year, she was in sixth grade, doing well in school, and emotionally well-adjusted.

Yet, without an opportunity to experience socialization in her first six years, Isabelle had been hardly human in the social sense when she was first discovered. Her inability to communicate at the time of her discovery—despite her physical and cognitive potential to learn—and her remarkable progress over the next few years underscore the impact of socialization on human development (K. Davis 1940, 1947).

Isabelle's experience is important for researchers because it is one of few cases of children reared in total isolation. Unfortunately, however, there are many cases of children raised in extremely neglectful social circumstances. Recently, attention has focused on infants and young children in orphanages in the formerly communist countries of Eastern Europe. For example, in Romanian orphanages, babies lie in their cribs for 18 or 20 hours a day, curled against their feeding bottles and receiving little adult care. Such minimal attention continues for the first five years of their lives. Many of them are fearful of human contact and prone to unpredictable antisocial behavior. This situation came to light as families in North America and Europe began adopting thousands of these children. The adjustment problems for about 20 percent of them were often so dramatic that the adopting families suffered guilty fears of being ill-fit adoptive parents. Many of them have asked for assistance in dealing with the children. Slowly, efforts are being made to introduce the deprived youngsters to feelings of attachment that they never had experienced before (Groza et al. 1999; Talbot 1998).

Increasingly, researchers are emphasizing the importance of early socialization experiences for children who grow up in more normal environments. We now know that it is not enough to care for an infant's physical needs; parents must also concern themselves with children's social development. If, for example, children are discouraged from having friends, they will miss out on social interactions with peers that are critical for emotional growth.

Primate Studies

Studies of animals raised in isolation also support the importance of socialization in development. Harry Harlow (1971), a researcher at the primate laboratory of the University of Wisconsin, conducted tests with rhesus monkeys that had been raised away from their mothers and away from contact with other monkeys. As was the case with Isabelle, the rhesus monkeys raised in isolation were fearful and easily frightened. They did not mate, and the females who were artificially inseminated became abusive mothers. Apparently, isolation had had a damaging effect on the monkeys.

A creative aspect of Harlow's experimentation was his use of "artificial mothers." In one such experiment, Harlow presented monkeys raised in isolation with two substitute mothers—one cloth-covered replica and one covered with wire that had the ability to offer milk. Monkey after monkey went to the wire mother for the life-giving milk, yet spent much more time clinging to the more motherlike cloth model. In this study, the monkeys valued the artificial mothers that provided a comforting physical sensation (conveyed by the terry cloth) more highly than those that provided food. It appears that the infant monkeys developed greater social attachments from their need for warmth, comfort, and intimacy than from their need for milk.

While the isolation studies discussed above may seem to suggest that inheritance can be dismissed as a factor in the social development of humans and animals, studies of twins provide insight into a fascinating interplay between hereditary and environmental factors.

Imagine

What events in your life have had a strong influence on who you are?

The Influence of Heredity

Oskar Stohr and Jack Yufe are identical twins who were separated soon after their birth and raised on different continents in very different cultural settings. Oskar was reared as a strict Catholic by his maternal grandmother in the Sudetenland of Czechoslovakia. As a member of the Hitler Youth movement in Nazi Germany, he learned to hate Jews. By contrast, his brother Jack was reared in Trinidad by the twins' Jewish father. Jack joined an Israeli kibbutz (a collective settlement) at age 17 and later served in the Israeli army. But when they were reunited in middle age, some startling similarities emerged:

> Both were wearing wire-rimmed glasses and mustaches, both sported two pocket shirts with epaulets. They share idiosyncrasies galore: they like spicy foods and sweet liqueurs, are absent-minded, have a habit of falling asleep in front of the television, think it's funny to sneeze in a crowd of strangers, flush the toilet before using it, store rubber bands on their wrists, read magazines from back to front, dip buttered toast in their coffee. (Holden 1980)

The twins also were found to differ in many important respects: Jack is a workaholic; Oskar enjoys leisure-time activities. Whereas Oskar is a traditionalist who is domineering toward women, Jack is a political liberal who is much more accepting of feminism. Finally, Jack is extremely proud of being Jewish, while Oskar never mentions his Jewish heritage (Holden 1987).

Oskar and Jack are prime examples of the interplay of heredity and environment. For a number of years,

researchers at the Minnesota Center for Twin and Adoption Research have been studying pairs of identical twins reared apart to determine what similarities, if any, they show in personality traits, behavior, and intelligence. Thus far, the preliminary results from the available twin studies indicate that both genetic factors and socialization experiences are influential in human development. Certain characteristics, such as temperaments, voice patterns, and nervous habits, appear to be strikingly similar even in twins reared apart, suggesting that these qualities may be linked to hereditary causes. However, identical twins reared apart differ far more in their attitudes, values, types of mates chosen, and even drinking habits; these qualities, it would seem, are influenced by environmental patterns. In examining clusters of personality traits among such twins, researchers have found marked similarities in their tendency toward leadership or dominance, but significant differences in their need for intimacy, comfort, and assistance.

Researchers have also been impressed with the similar scores on intelligence tests of twins reared apart in *roughly similar* social settings. Most of the identical twins register scores even closer than those that would be expected if the same person took a test twice. At the same time, however, identical twins brought up in *dramatically different* social environments score quite differently on intelligence tests—a finding that supports the impact of socialization on human development (McGue and Bouchard 1998).

We need to be cautious when reviewing the studies of twin pairs and other relevant research. Widely broadcast findings have often been based on extremely small samples and preliminary analysis. For example, one study (not involving twin pairs) was frequently cited as confirming genetic links with behavior. Yet the researchers had to retract their conclusions after they increased the sample from 81 to 91 cases and reclassified two of the original 81 cases. After these changes, the initial findings were no longer valid. Critics add that the studies on twin pairs have not provided satisfactory information concerning the extent to which these separated identical twins may have had contact with each other, even though they were "raised apart." Such interactions—especially if they were extensive—could call into question the validity of the twin studies (Kelsoe et al. 1989). As this debate continues, we can certainly anticipate numerous efforts to replicate the research and clarify the interplay between hereditary and environmental factors in human development (Horgan 1993; Leo 1987; Plomin 1989; Wallis 1987).

Sociobiology

Do the *social* traits that human groups display have biological origins? As part of the continuing debate on the relative influences of heredity and the environment, there has been renewed interest in sociobiology in recent years. *Sociobiology* is the systematic study of the biological bases of social behavior. Sociobiologists basically apply naturalist Charles Darwin's principles of natural selection to the study of social behavior. They assume that particular forms of behavior become genetically linked to a species if they contribute to its fitness to survive (van den Berghe 1978). In its extreme form, sociobiology suggests that *all* behavior is the result of genetic or biological factors and that social interactions play no role in shaping people's conduct.

Sociobiology does not seek to describe individual behavior on the level of "Why is Fred more aggressive than Jim?" Rather, sociobiologists focus on how human nature is affected by the genetic composition of a *group* of people who share certain characteristics (such as men or women, or members of isolated tribal bands). In general, sociobiologists have stressed the basic genetic heritage that *all* humans share and have shown little interest in speculating about alleged differences between racial groups or nationalities (Wilson 1975, 1978).

Some researchers insist that intellectual interest in sociobiology will only deflect serious study of the more significant factor influencing human behavior—socialization. Yet Lois Wladis Hoffman (1985), in her presidential address to the Society for the Psychological Study of Social Issues, argued that sociobiology poses a valuable challenge to social scientists to better document their own research. Interactionists, for example, could show how social behavior is not programmed by human biology but instead adjusts continually to the attitudes and responses of others.

Certainly most social scientists would agree that there is a biological basis for social behavior. But there is less support for the most extreme positions taken by certain advocates of sociobiology. Like interactionists, conflict theorists and functionalists believe that people's behavior rather than their genetic structure defines social reality. Conflict theorists fear that the sociobiological approach could be used as an argument against efforts to assist disadvantaged people, such as schoolchildren who are not competing successfully. To resolve the conflict, Edward O. Wilson, a zoologist at Harvard University, has suggested parallel studies of human behavior with a focus on both genetic and social causes (Wilson 2000; see also Guterman 2000; Segerstråle 2000).

The Self and Socialization

We all have various perceptions, feelings, and beliefs about who we are and what we are like. How do we come to develop these? Do they change as we age?

We were not born with these understandings. Building on the work of George Herbert Mead (1964b), sociol-

ogists recognize that we create our own designation: the self. The *self* is a distinct identity that sets us apart from others. It is not a static phenomenon but continues to develop and change throughout our lives.

Sociologists and psychologists alike have expressed interest in how the individual develops and modifies the sense of self as a result of social interaction. The work of p. 17 ◀ sociologists Charles Horton Cooley and George Herbert Mead, pioneers of the interactionist approach, has been especially useful in furthering our understanding of these important issues (Gecas 1982).

Sociological Approaches to the Self

Cooley: Looking-Glass Self

In the early 1900s, Charles Horton Cooley advanced the belief that we learn who we are by interacting with others. Our view of ourselves, then, comes not only from direct contemplation of our personal qualities but also from our impressions of how others perceive us. Cooley used the phrase **looking-glass self** to emphasize that the self is the product of our social interactions with other people.

The process of developing a self-identity or self-concept has three phases. First, we imagine how we present ourselves to others—to relatives, friends, even strangers on the street. Then we imagine how others evaluate us (attractive, intelligent, shy, or strange). Finally, we develop some sort of feeling about ourselves, such as respect or shame, as a result of these impressions (Cooley 1902; Howard 1989).

A subtle but critical aspect of Cooley's looking-glass self is that the self results from an individual's "imagination" of how others view him or her. As a result, we can develop self-identities based on *incorrect* perceptions of how others see us. A student may react strongly to a teacher's criticism and decide (wrongly) that the instructor views the student as stupid. This misperception can easily be converted into a negative self-identity through the following process: (1) the teacher criticized me, (2) the teacher must think that I'm stupid, (3) I *am* stupid. Yet self-identities are also subject to change. If the student receives an "A" at the end of the course, he or she will probably no longer feel stupid.

Mead: Stages of the Self

George Herbert Mead continued Cooley's exploration of interactionist theory. Mead (1934, 1964a) developed a useful model of the process by which the self emerges, defined by three distinct stages: the preparatory stage, the play stage, and the game stage.

The Preparatory Stage. During the *preparatory stage*, children merely imitate the people around them,

"Say cheese!" Children imitate the people around them, especially family members they continually interact with, during the *preparatory stage* described by George Herbert Mead.

especially family members with whom they continually interact. Thus, a small child will bang on a piece of wood while a parent is engaged in carpentry work or will try to throw a ball if an older sibling is doing so nearby.

As they grow older, children become more adept at using symbols to communicate with others. *Symbols* are the gestures, objects, and language that form the basis of human communication. By interacting with relatives and friends, as well as by watching cartoons on television and looking at picture books, children in the preparatory stage begin to understand the use of symbols. Like spoken languages, symbols vary from culture to culture and even between subcultures. Raising one's eyebrows may mean astonishment in North America, but in Peru it means "money" or "pay me," while in the Pacific island nation of Tonga it means "yes" or "I agree" (Axtell 1990).

The Play Stage. Mead was among the first to analyze the relationship of symbols to socialization. As children develop skill in communicating through symbols, they gradually become more aware of social relationships. As a result, during the *play stage*, the child becomes able to pretend to be other people. Just as an actor "becomes" a character, a child becomes a doctor, parent, superhero, or ship captain.

Mead, in fact, noted that an important aspect of the play stage is role playing. ***Role taking*** is the process of mentally assuming the perspective of another, thereby enabling one to respond from that imagined viewpoint. For example, through this process, a young child will gradually learn when it is best to ask a parent for favors. If the parent usually comes home from work in a bad mood, the child will wait until after dinner when the parent is more relaxed and approachable.

The Game Stage. In Mead's third stage, the *game stage,* the child of about eight or nine years old no longer just plays roles but begins to consider several actual tasks and relationships simultaneously. At this point in development, children grasp not only their own social positions, but also those of others around them—just as in a football game the players must understand their own and everyone else's positions. Consider a girl or boy who is part of a scout troop out on a weekend hike in the mountains. The child must understand what he or she is expected to do, but also must recognize the responsibilities of other scouts as well as the leaders. This is the final stage of development under Mead's model; the child can now respond to numerous members of the social environment.

Mead uses the term ***generalized other*** to refer to the attitudes, viewpoints, and expectations of society as a whole that a child takes into account. Simply put, this concept suggests that when an individual acts, he or she takes into account an entire group of people. For example, a child will not act courteously merely to please a particular parent. Rather, the child comes to understand that courtesy is a widespread social value endorsed by parents, teachers, and religious leaders.

At the game stage, children can take a more sophisticated view of people and the social environment. They now understand what specific occupations and social positions are and no longer equate Mr. Williams only with the role of "librarian" or Ms. Franks only with "principal." It has become clear to the child that Mr. Williams can be a librarian, a parent, and a marathon runner at the same time and that Ms. Franks is one of many principals in our society. Thus, the child has reached a new level of sophistication in his or her observations of individuals and institutions.

Mead: Theory of the Self

Mead is best known for his theory of the self. According to Mead (1964b), the self begins as a privileged, central position in a person's world. Young children picture themselves as the focus of everything around them and find it difficult to consider the perspectives of others. For example, when shown a mountain scene and asked to describe what an observer on the opposite side of the mountain sees (such as a lake or hikers), young children describe only objects visible from their own vantage point. This childhood tendency to place ourselves at the center of events never entirely disappears. Many people with a fear of flying automatically assume that if any plane goes down, it will be the one they are on. And who reads the horoscope section in the paper without looking at their own horoscope first? And why else do we buy lottery tickets if we do not imagine ourselves winning?

Nonetheless, as people mature, the self changes and begins to reflect greater concern about the reactions of others. Parents, friends, co-workers, coaches, and teachers are often among those who play a major role in shaping a person's self. Mead used the term *significant others* to refer to those individuals who are most important in the development of the self. Many young people, for example, find themselves drawn to the same kind of work their parents engage in (Schlenker 1985).

In some instances, studies concerning significant others have generated controversy among researchers. For example, some researchers contend that African American adolescents are more "peer-oriented" than their White counterparts because of presumed weaknesses in Black families. However, investigations indicate that these hasty conclusions were based on limited studies focusing on less affluent Blacks. In fact, there appears to be little difference in who African Americans and Whites from similar economic backgrounds regard as their significant others (Giordano et al. 1993; Juhasz 1989).

Imagine

Who have been your significant others? Are you someone else's significant other?

Goffman: Presentation of the Self

How do we manage our "self"? How do we display to others who we are? Erving Goffman, a sociologist associated with the interactionist perspective, suggested that many of our daily activities involve attempts to convey impressions of who we are.

Early in life, the individual learns to slant his or her presentation of the self in order to create distinctive appearances and satisfy particular audiences. Goffman (1959) refers to this altering of the presentation of the self as *impression management.* Box 4-1 describes an everyday example of this concept—the way students behave after receiving their exam grades. In analyzing such everyday social interactions, Goffman makes so many explicit parallels to the theater that his view has been termed the *dramaturgical approach.* According to this perspective, people resemble performers in action. For example, a clerk may try to appear busier than he or she actually is if a supervisor happens to be watching. A customer in a singles' bar may try to look as if he or she is waiting for a particular person to arrive.

Goffman (1959) has also drawn attention to another aspect of the self—*face-work.* How often do you initiate some kind of face-saving behavior when you feel embarrassed or rejected? In response to a rejection at the singles' bar, a person may engage in face-work by saying, "There really isn't an interesting person in this entire crowd." We feel the need to maintain a proper image of the self if we are to continue social interaction.

In some cultures, people engage in elaborate deceptions to avoid losing face. In Japan, for example, where lifetime employment has until recently been the norm, "company men" thrown out of work by a deep

Double Dutch jump roping contests require contestants to carry out several tasks at once and to understand the roles of others—characteristics of the *game stage* outlined by George Herbert Mead.

Research in Action

4-1 Impression Management by Students after Exams

www.
mhhe
.com
/schaefer8

When you get an exam back, you probably react differently with fellow classmates, depending on the grades that you and they earned. This is all part of impression management, as sociologists Daniel Albas and Cheryl Albas demonstrated. They explored the strategies that college students use to create desired appearances after receiving their grades on exams. Albas and Albas divide these encounters into three categories: those between students who have all received high grades (Ace–Ace encounters), those between students who have received high grades and those who have received low or even failing grades (Ace–Bomber encounters), and those between students who have all received low grades (Bomber–Bomber encounters).

Ace–Ace encounters occur in a rather open atmosphere because there is comfort in sharing a high mark with another high achiever. It is even acceptable to violate the norm of modesty and brag when among other Aces since, as one student admitted, "It's much easier to admit a high mark to someone who has done better than you, or at least as well."

Ace–Bomber encounters are often sensitive. Bombers generally attempt to avoid such exchanges because "you . . . emerge looking like the dumb one" or "feel like you are lazy or unreliable." When forced into interactions with Aces, Bombers work to appear gracious and congratulatory. For their part, Aces offer sympathy and support for the dissatisfied Bombers and even rationalize their own "lucky" high scores. To help Bombers save face,

> **When forced into interactions with Aces, Bombers work to appear gracious and congratulatory.**

Aces may emphasize the difficulty and unfairness of the examination.

Bomber–Bomber encounters tend to be closed, reflecting the group effort to wall off the feared disdain of others. Yet, within the safety of these encounters, Bombers openly share their disappointment and engage in expressions of mutual self-pity that they themselves call "pity parties." They devise face-saving excuses for their

poor performances, such as "I wasn't feeling well all week" or "I had four exams and two papers due that week." If the grade distribution in a class includes particularly low scores, Bombers may blame the professor, who will be attacked as a sadist, a slave driver, or simply an incompetent.

As is evident from these descriptions, students' impression management strategies conform to society's informal norms regarding modesty and consideration for less successful peers. In classroom settings, as in the workplace and in other types of human interactions, efforts at impression management are most intense when status differentials are more pronounced, as in encounters between the high-scoring Aces and the low-scoring Bombers.

Let's Discuss

1. How do you react with those who have received higher or lower grades than you? Do you engage in impression management? How would you like others to react to your grade?
2. What social norms govern the students' impression management strategies?

Source: Albas and Albas 1988.

economic recession may feign employment, rising as usual in the morning, donning suit and tie, and heading for the business district. But instead of going to the office, they congregate at places such as Tokyo's Hibiya Library, where they pass the time by reading before returning home at the usual hour. Many of these men are trying to protect family members, who would be shamed if neighbors discovered the family breadwinner was unemployed. Others are deceiving their wives and families as well (French 2000a).

Goffman's work on the self represents a logical progression of the sociological efforts begun by Cooley and Mead on how personality is acquired through socialization and how we manage the presentation of our self to others. Cooley stressed the process by which we come to create a

"YOU NEED TO WORK ON YOUR GAME FACE."

Impression management is important not just in athletics, but in any pursuit that involves other people.

self; Mead focused on how the self develops as we learn to interact with others; Goffman emphasized the ways in which we consciously create images of ourselves for others.

Psychological Approaches to the Self

Psychologists have shared the interest of Cooley, Mead, and other sociologists in the development of the self. Early work in psychology, such as that of Sigmund Freud (1856–1939), stressed the role of inborn drives—among them the drive for sexual gratification—in channeling human behavior. More recently, psychologists such as Jean Piaget have emphasized the stages through which human beings progress as the self develops.

Like Charles Horton Cooley and George Herbert Mead, Freud believed that the self is a social product and that aspects of one's personality are influenced by other people (especially one's parents). However, unlike Cooley and Mead, he suggested that the self has components that work in opposition to each other. According to Freud, our natural impulsive instincts are in constant conflict with societal constraints. Part of us seeks limitless pleasure, while another part seeks out rational behavior. By interacting with others, we learn the expectations of society and then select behavior most appropriate to our own culture. (Of course, as Freud was well aware, we sometimes distort reality and behave irrationally.)

Research on newborn babies by the Swiss child psychologist Jean Piaget (1896–1980) has underscored the importance of social interactions in developing a sense of self. Piaget found that newborns have no self in the sense of a looking-glass image. Ironically, though, they are quite self-centered; they demand that all attention be directed toward them. Newborns have not yet separated themselves from the universe of which they are a part. For these babies, the phrase "you and me" has no meaning; they understand only "me." However, as they mature, children are gradually socialized into social relationships even within their rather self-centered world.

In his well-known *cognitive theory of development*, Piaget (1954) identified four stages in the development of children's thought processes. In the first, or *sensorimotor*, stage, young children use their senses to make discoveries. For example, through touching they discover that their hands are actually a part of themselves. During the second, or *preoperational*, stage, children begin to use words and symbols to distinguish objects and ideas. The milestone in the third, or *concrete operational*, stage is that children engage in more logical thinking. They learn that even when a formless lump of clay is shaped into a snake, it is still the same clay. Finally, in the fourth, or *formal operational*, stage, adolescents are capable of sophisticated abstract thought and can deal with ideas and values in a logical manner.

Piaget has suggested that moral development becomes an important part of socialization as children develop the ability to think more abstractly. When children learn the rules of a game such as checkers or jacks, they are learning to obey societal norms. Those under eight years old display a rather basic level of morality: rules are rules, and there is no concept of "extenuating circumstances." However, as they mature, children become capable of greater autonomy and begin to experience moral dilemmas as to what constitutes proper behavior.

According to Jean Piaget, social interaction is the key to development. As they grow older, children give increasing attention to how other people think and why they act in particular ways. In order to develop a distinct personality, each of us needs opportunities to interact with others. As we saw earlier, Isabelle was deprived of the chance for normal social interactions, and the consequences were severe (Kitchener 1991).

Freshman cadets at the Virginia Military Institute crawl up a muddy hill in the school's gritty rite of passage.

Socialization and the Life Course

The Life Course

Adolescents among the Kota people of the Congo in Africa paint themselves blue, Mexican American girls go on a daylong religious retreat before dancing the night away, Egyptian mothers step over their newborn infants seven times, students at the Naval Academy throw hats in the air. These are all ways of celebrating *rites of passage,* a means of dramatizing and validating changes in a person's status. The Kota rite marks the passage to adulthood. The color blue, viewed as the color of death, symbolizes the death of childhood. Hispanic girls celebrate reaching womanhood with a *quinceañera* ceremony at age 15. In the Cuban American community of Miami, the popularity of the *quinceañera* supports a network of party planners, caterers, dress designers, and the Miss Quinceañera Latina pageant. For thousands of years, Egyptian mothers have welcomed their newborns to the world in the Soboa ceremony by stepping over the seven-day-old infant seven times. The Naval Academy seniors celebrate their graduation from college by hurling their hats skyward (Cohen 1991; Garza 1993; McLane 1995; Quadagno 2002).

These specific ceremonies mark stages of development in the life course. They indicate that the socialization process continues throughout all stages of the human life cycle. Sociologists and other social scientists use the life-course approach in recognition that biological changes mold but do not dictate human behavior from birth until death.

In the culture of the United States, each individual has a "personal biography" that is influenced by events both in the family and in the larger society. While the completion of religious confirmations, school graduations, marriage, and parenthood can all be regarded as rites of passage in our society, people do not necessarily experience them at the same time. The timing of these events depends on such factors as one's gender, economic background, where one lives (central city, suburb, or rural area), and even when one was born.

We encounter some of the most difficult socialization challenges (and rites of passage) in the later years of life. Assessing one's accomplishments, coping with declining physical abilities, experiencing retirement, and facing the inevitability of death may lead to painful adjustments. Old age is further complicated by the negative way that many societies, including the United States, view and treat the elderly. The common stereotypes of the elderly as helpless and dependent may well weaken an older

Body painting is a ritual marking the passage to puberty among young people in Liberia in northern Africa.

person's self-image. However, as we will explore more fully in Chapter 13, many older people continue to lead active, productive, fulfilled lives—whether within the paid labor force or as retirees.

Imagine

What was the last rite of passage you participated in? Was it formal or informal?

Anticipatory Socialization and Resocialization

The development of a social self is literally a lifelong transformation that begins in the crib and continues as one prepares for death. Two types of socialization occur at many points throughout the life course: anticipatory socialization and resocialization.

Anticipatory socialization refers to the processes of socialization in which a person "rehearses" for future positions, occupations, and social relationships. A culture can function more efficiently and smoothly if members become acquainted with the norms, values, and behavior associated with a social position before actually assuming that status. Preparation for many aspects of adult life begins with anticipatory socialization during childhood and adolescence and continues throughout our lives as we prepare for new responsibilities.

You can see the process of anticipatory socialization take place when high school students start to consider what colleges they may attend. Traditionally, this meant looking at publications received in the mail or making campus visits. However, with new technology, more and more students are using the Web to begin their college experience. Colleges are investing more time and money in developing attractive websites where students can take "virtual" campus walks and hear audio clips of everything from the alma mater to a sample zoology lecture.

Occasionally, assuming new social and occupational positions requires us to *unlearn* a previous orientation. **Resocialization** refers to the process of discarding former behavior patterns and accepting new ones as part of a transition in one's life. Often resocialization occurs when there is an explicit effort to transform an individual, as happens in reform schools, therapy groups, prisons, religious conversion settings, and political indoctrination camps. The process of resocialization typically involves considerable stress for the individual, much more so than socialization in general or even anticipatory socialization (Gecas 1992).

Resocialization is particularly effective when it occurs within a total institution. Erving Goffman (1961) coined the term **total institutions** to refer to institutions, such as prisons, the military, mental hospitals, and convents, that regulate all aspects of a person's life under a single authority. Because the total institution is generally cut off from the rest of society, it provides for all the needs of its members. Quite literally, the crew of a merchant vessel at sea becomes part of a total institution. So elaborate are its requirements, and so all-encompassing are its activities, a total institution often represents a miniature society.

Goffman (1961) has identified four common traits of total institutions:

- All aspects of life are conducted in the same place and are under the control of a single authority.
- Any activities within the institution are conducted in the company of others in the same circumstances— for example, novices in a convent or army recruits.
- The authorities devise rules and schedule activities without consulting the participants.
- All aspects of life within a total institution are designed to fulfill the purpose of the organization. Thus, all activities in a monastery might be centered on prayer and communion with God. (Davies 1989; Rose et al. 1979)

People often lose their individuality within total institutions. For example, a person entering prison may experience the humiliation of a **degradation ceremony** as he or she is stripped of clothing, jewelry, and other personal possessions. From this point on, scheduled daily routines allow for little or no personal initiative. The individual becomes secondary and rather invisible in the overbearing social environment (Garfinkel 1956).

Agents of Socialization

As we have seen, the culture of the United States is defined by rather gradual movements from one stage of socialization to the next. The continuing and lifelong socialization process involves many different social forces that influence our lives and alter our self-images.

The family is the most important agent of socialization in the United States, especially for children. We'll also give particular attention in this chapter to five other agents of socialization: the school, the peer group, the mass media, the workplace, and the state. The role of religion in socializing young people into society's norms and values will be explored in Chapter 15.

Family

Children in Amish communities are raised in a highly structured and disciplined manner. But they are not immune to the temptations posed by their peers in the non-Amish world—"rebellious" acts such as dancing, drinking, and riding in cars. Still, Amish families don't get too concerned; they know the strong influence they ultimately exert over their offspring (see Box 4-2). The same is true for the family in general. It is tempting to say that the "peer group" or even the "media" really raise kids these days, especially when the spotlight falls on young people involved in shooting sprees and hate crimes. Almost all available research, however, shows that the role of the family in socializing a child cannot be underestimated (W. Williams 1998; for a different view see Harris 1998).

The lifelong process of learning begins shortly after birth. Since newborns can hear, see, smell, taste, and feel heat, cold, and pain, they are constantly orienting

Sociology in the Global Community

4-2 Raising Amish Children

Jacob is a typical teenager in his Amish community in Lancaster County, Pennsylvania. At 14 he is in his final year of schooling. Over the next few years he will become a full-time worker on the family farm, taking breaks only for three-hour religious services each morning. When he is a bit older, Jacob may bring a date in his family's horse-drawn buggy to a community "singing." But he will be forbidden to date outside his own community and can marry only with the deacon's consent. Jacob is well aware of the rather different way of life of the "English" (the Amish term for non-Amish people). One summer he and his friends hitchhiked late at night to a nearby town to see a movie, breaking several Amish taboos. His parents learned of his adventure, but like most Amish they are confident that their son will choose the Amish way of life. What is this way of life and how can the parents be so sure of its appeal?

Jacob and his family live in a manner very similar to their ancestors, members of the conservative Mennonite church who migrated to North America from Europe in the eighteenth and nineteenth centuries. Schisms in the church after 1850 led to a division between those who wanted to preserve the "old order" and those who favored a "new order" with more progressive methods and organization. Today the old order Amish live in about 50 communities in the United States and Canada. Estimates put their number at about 80,000 with approximately 75 percent living in three states—Ohio, Pennsylvania, and Indiana.

The old order Amish live a "simple" life and reject most aspects of modernization and contemporary technology. That's why they spurn such conveniences as electricity, automobiles, radio, and television. The Amish maintain their own schools and traditions, and they do not want their children socialized into many

> The old order Amish live a "simple" life and reject most aspects of modernization and contemporary technology.

norms and values of the dominant culture of the United States. Those who stray too far from Amish mores may be excommunicated and shunned by all other members of the community—a practice of social control called *Meiding*. Sociologists sometimes use the term "secessionist minorities" to refer to groups like the Amish who reject assimilation and coexist with the rest of society primarily on their own terms.

Life for Amish youth attracts particular attention since their socialization pushes them to forgo movies, radio, television, cosmetics, jewelry, musical instruments of any kind, and motorized vehicles. Yet, like Jacob did, Amish youth often test their subculture's boundaries during a period of discovery called *rumspringe,* a term that literally means "running around." Amish young people attend barn dances where taboos like drinking, smoking, and driving cars are commonly broken. Parents often react by looking the other way, sometimes literally. For example, when they hear radio sounds from a barn or a motorcycle entering the property in the middle of the night, they don't immediately investigate and punish their offspring. Instead, they will pretend not to notice, secure in the comfort that their children almost always return to the traditions of the Amish lifestyle. Research shows that only about 20 percent of Amish youth leave the fold, generally to join a more liberal Mennonite group, and rarely does a baptized adult ever leave. The socialization of Amish youth moves them gently but firmly into becoming Amish adults.

Let's Discuss

1. What makes Amish parents so sure that their children will choose to remain in the Amish community?
2. If you lived in an Amish community, how would your life differ from the way it is now? In your opinion, what advantages and disadvantages would that lifestyle have?

Sources: Zellner 2001; Meyers 1992; Remnick 1998.

themselves to the surrounding world. Human beings, especially family members, constitute an important part of their social environment. People minister to the baby's needs by feeding, cleansing, carrying, and comforting the baby.

As both Charles Horton Cooley and George Herbert Mead noted, the development of the self is a critical aspect of the early years of one's life. However, how children develop this sense of self can vary from one society to another. For example, parents in the United States would never think of sending six-year-olds to school unsupervised. But this is the norm in Japan, where parents push their children to commute to school on their own from an early age. In cities like Tokyo, first-graders must learn to negotiate buses, subways, and long walks. To ensure their safety, parents carefully lay out rules: never talk to strangers; check with a station attendant if you get off at the wrong stop; if you miss your stop stay on to the end of the line, then call; take stairs, not escalators; don't fall asleep. Some parents equip the children with cell phones or pagers. One parent acknowledges that she worries, "but after they are 6, children are supposed to start being independent from the mother. If you're still taking your child to school after the first month, everyone looks at you funny" (Tolbert 2000:17).

While we consider the family's role in socialization, we need to remember that children do not play a passive role. They are active agents, influencing and altering the families, schools, and communities of which they are a part (Corsaro 1997).

In the United States, social development includes exposure to cultural assumptions regarding gender and race. African American parents, for example, have learned that children as young as two years old can absorb negative messages about Blacks in children's books, toys, and television shows—all of which are designed primarily for White consumers. At the same time, African American children are exposed more often than others to the inner-city youth gang culture. Because most Blacks, even those who are middle class, live near very poor neighborhoods, children such as Charisse (see the chapter opening excerpt) are susceptible to these influences, despite their parents' strong family values (Linn and Poussaint 1999; Pattillo-McCoy 1999).

The term **gender roles** refers to expectations regarding the proper behavior, attitudes, and activities of males and females. For example, we traditionally think of "toughness" as masculine—and desirable only in men—while we view "tenderness" as feminine. As we will see in Chapter 12, other cultures do not necessarily assign these qualities to each gender in the way that our culture does.

As the primary agents of childhood socialization, parents play a critical role in guiding children into those gender roles deemed appropriate in a society. Other adults, older siblings, the mass media, and religious and educational institutions also have a noticeable impact on a child's socialization into feminine and masculine norms. A culture or subculture may require that one sex or the other take primary responsibility for socialization of children, economic support of the family, or religious or intellectual leadership.

Interactionists remind us that socialization concerning not only masculinity and femininity, but also marriage and parenthood, begins in childhood as a part of family life. Children observe their parents as they express affection, deal with finances, quarrel, complain about in-laws, and so forth. This represents an informal process of anticipatory socialization. The child develops a tentative model of what being married and being a parent are like. (We will explore socialization for marriage and parenthood more fully in Chapter 14.)

Typically, parents are thought to have a positive effect on their children's socialization. But that is not al-

Entrepreneur Yla Eason poses with the ethnic dolls her company creates and merchandises. Young girls learn about themselves and their social roles by playing with dolls.

ways the case. A survey of nearly 600 teens in New York, Texas, Florida, and California indicated that 20 percent had shared drugs other than alcohol with their parents, and about 5 percent were actually introduced to drugs by their mothers or fathers. Approximately 1.5 million children under the age of 18, or 2 percent of all U.S. youths, have a parent in a state or federal prison at some time during the year. Socialization within the family, whether positive or negative, is a powerful process (Leimward 2000; Mumola 2000).

School

Where did you learn the national anthem? Who taught you about the heroes of the American Revolution? Where were you first tested on your knowledge of your culture? Like the family, schools have an explicit mandate to socialize people in the United States—and especially children—into the norms and values of our culture.

As conflict theorists Samuel Bowles and Herbert Gintis (1976) have observed, schools in this country foster competition through built-in systems of reward and punishment, such as grades and evaluations by teachers. Consequently, a child who is working intently to learn a new skill can sometimes come to feel stupid and unsuccessful. However, as the self matures, children become capable of increasingly realistic assessments of their intellectual, physical, and social abilities.

Functionalists point out that, as agents of socialization, schools fulfill the function of teaching children the values and customs of the larger society. Conflict theorists agree but add that schools can reinforce the divisive aspects of society, especially those of social class. For example, higher education in the United States is quite costly despite the existence of financial aid programs. Students from affluent backgrounds have an advantage in gaining access to universities and professional training. At the same time, less affluent young people may never receive the preparation that would qualify them for the best-paying and most prestigious jobs. The contrast between the functionalist and conflict views of education will be discussed in more detail in Chapter 16.

In teaching students the values and customs of the larger society, schools in the United States have traditionally socialized children into conventional gender roles. Professors of education Myra Sadker and David Sadker (1985:54; 1995) note that "although many believe that classroom sexism disappeared in the early '70s, it hasn't." A report released in 1992 by the American Association of University Women—which summarized 1,331 studies of girls in school—concludes that schools in the United States favor boys over girls.

According to this report, girls show a disturbing pattern of *downward* intellectual mobility compared with boys, because they are treated differently. Teachers praise boys more than girls and offer boys more academic assistance. Boys receive praise for the intellectual content of their work, whereas girls are more likely to be praised for being neat. Teachers reward boys for assertiveness (for example, calling out answers without raising their hands) while reprimanding girls for similar behavior. Finally, girls often are not expected or encouraged to pursue high-level mathematics or science courses. The report concludes that girls are less likely than boys to reach their academic potential and insists that "the system must change" (American Association of University Women 1992:84; Bailey and Campbell 2000).

In other cultures as well, schools serve socialization functions. During the 1980s, for example, Japanese parents and educators were distressed to realize that children were gradually losing the knack of eating with chopsticks. This became a national issue in 1997 when school lunch programs introduced plastic "sporks" (combined fork and spoon, used frequently in the United States). National leaders, responding to the public outcry, banished sporks in favor of *hashi* (chopsticks). On a more serious note, Japanese schools have come under increasing pressure in recent years as working parents have abdicated more and more responsibility to educational institutions. To rectify the imbalance, the Japanese government in 1998 promoted a guide to better parenting, calling on parents to read more with their children, allow for more playtime, limit TV watching, and plan family activities, among other things (Gauette 1998).

Peer Group

Ask 13-year-olds who matters most in their lives and they are likely to answer "friends." As a child grows older, the family becomes somewhat less important in social development. Instead, peer groups increasingly assume the role of Mead's significant others. Within the peer group, young people associate with others who are approximately their own age and who often enjoy a similar social status.

Peer groups can ease the transition to adult responsibilities. At home, parents tend to dominate; at school, the teenager must contend with teachers and administrators.

This Japanese school maintains the Japanese cultural practice of eating with chopsticks. When school lunch programs introduced the "spork" (combined plastic spoon and fork) in the late 1990s, Japanese parents raised a fuss and forced a return to the traditional chopsticks.

But within the peer group, each member can assert himself or herself in a way that may not be possible elsewhere. Nevertheless, almost all adolescents in our culture remain economically dependent on their parents, and most are emotionally dependent as well.

Peers can be the source of harassment as well as support. This problem has received considerable attention in Japan, where bullying in school is a constant fact of life. Groups of students act together to humiliate, disgrace, or torment a specific student, a practice known in Japan as *ijime*. Most students go along with the bullying out of fear that they might be the target some time. In some cases the *ijime* has led to a child's suicide. In 1998, the situation became so desperate that a volunteer association set up a 24-hour telephone hotline in Tokyo just for children (see the chapter opening poster). The success of this effort convinced the government to sponsor a nationwide hotline system (Matsushita 1999; Sugimoto 1997).

Gender differences are noteworthy in the social world of adolescents. Males are more likely to spend time in *groups* of males, whereas females are more likely to interact with a *single* other female. This pattern reflects differences in levels of emotional intimacy; teenage males are less likely to develop strong emotional ties than are females. Instead, males are more inclined to share in group activities. These patterns are evident among adolescents in many societies besides the United States (Dornbusch 1989).

Mass Media and Technology

In the last 80 years, media innovations—radio, motion pictures, recorded music, television, and the Internet—have become important agents of socialization. Television, in particular, is a critical force in the socialization of children in the United States. Remarkably, 32 percent of children in the United States under the age of 7 have their own television, and 53 percent of all children ages 12 to 18 have their own sets. As Figure 4-1 shows, young people in the United States spend 5.5 hours per day with some form of media, mostly television. Little wonder that the American Academy of Pediatrics has urged parents not to allow children under 2 years old to watch television. Parents should also avoid using any kind of media as an electronic baby-sitter and should try to create an "electronic media–free" environment in their children's rooms (Rideout et al. 1999). The impact of the media and related technology on socialization will be covered in detail in Chapter 7.

Television, however, is not always a negative socializing influence. One benefit is that television programs and even commercials can expose young people to unfamiliar lifestyles and cultures. Not only do children in the United States learn about life in "faraway lands," but also inner-city children learn about the lives of farm children and vice versa. The same goes for children living in other countries.

Sociologists and other social scientists have also begun to consider the impact of technology on socialization, especially as it applies to family life. The Silicon Valley Cultures Project studied families in California's Silicon Valley (a technological corridor) for 10 years beginning in 1991. Although these families may not be typical, they probably represent a lifestyle that more and more households will approximate. This study has found that technology in the form of e-mail, webpages, cellular phones, voice mail, digital organizers, and pagers is allowing householders to let outsiders do everything from grocery shopping to soccer pools. The researchers are also finding that families are socialized into multitasking (doing more than one task at a time) as the social norm; devoting one's full attention to one task—even eating or driving—is less and less common on a typical day (Silicon Valley Cultures Project 2001).

Figure 4-1

Children's Media Usage

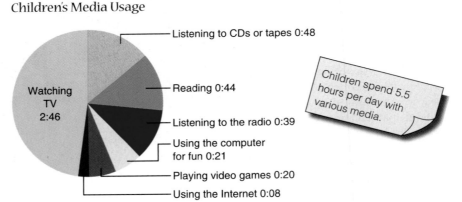

Source: Based on Rideout et al. 1999.

Think About It
How does your use of the media compare to these national averages?

Especially during adolescence, peers are important agents of socialization. Teens learn to assert their independence in the company of their friends, and strengthen their gender identities through stereotypical activities such as video games.

Some observers feel that the increasing number of teenagers who are working earlier in life and for longer hours are now finding the workplace almost as important an agent of socialization as school. In fact, a number of educators complain that student time at work is adversely affecting schoolwork. Figure 4-2 shows data from two international studies. The level of teenage employment in the United States, the highest among industrial countries, may provide one explanation for why U.S. high school students lag behind those in other countries on international achievement tests. A study released in 2001 found that for teenagers, working more than 20 hours a week often leads to lower grades, higher alcohol use, and too little time spent with parents and family members (Cooper 1998; Greenhouse 2001).

Socialization in the workplace becomes different when it involves a more permanent shift from an after-school job to full-time employment. Occupational socialization can be most intense during the transition from

Workplace

Learning to behave appropriately within an occupation is a fundamental aspect of human socialization. In the United States, working full-time confirms adult status; it is an indication to all that one has passed out of adolescence. In a sense, socialization into an occupation can represent both a harsh reality ("I have to work in order to buy food and pay the rent") and the realization of an ambition ("I've always wanted to be an airline pilot") (Moore 1968:862).

It used to be that "going to work" began with the end of our formal schooling, but that is no longer the case, at least not in the United States. More and more young people work today, and not just for a parent or relative. Adolescents generally seek jobs in order to make spending money; 80 percent of high school seniors say little or none of what they earn goes to family expenses. And these teens rarely look on their employment as a means of exploring vocational interests or getting on-the-job training.

This boy's day doesn't end when school lets out. So many teenagers now work after school, the workplace has become another important agent of socialization for that age group.

Figure 4-2

Teenagers on the Job and in School—International Comparisons

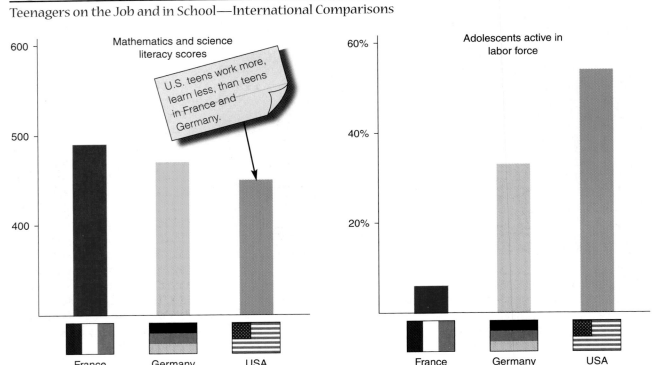

Sources: Commission on Behavioral Social Sciences Education 1998; Third International Mathematics and Science Study 1998.

school to job, but it continues through one's work history. Technological advances may alter the requirements of the position and necessitate some degree of resocialization. Many men and women today change occupations, employers, or places of work many times during their adult years. Therefore, occupational socialization continues throughout a person's years in the labor market.

College students today recognize that occupational socialization is not socialization into one lifetime occupation. They anticipate going through a number of jobs. A survey of college students and recent graduates found that 78 percent plan to stay with their employer for no longer than three years. One out of every four anticipate staying with a first employer only one year (Jobtrak.com 2000a).

The State

Social scientists have increasingly recognized the importance of the state as an agent of socialization because of its growing impact on the life course. Traditionally, family members have served as the primary caregivers in our culture, but in the twentieth century, the family's protective function has steadily been transferred to outside agencies such as hospitals, mental health clinics, and insurance companies. The state runs

many of these agencies or licenses and regulates them (Ogburn and Tibbits 1934).

In the past, heads of households and local groups such as religious organizations influenced the life course most significantly. However, today national interests are increasingly influencing the individual as a citizen and an economic actor. For example, labor unions and political parties serve as intermediaries between the individual and the state.

The state has had a noteworthy impact on the life course by reinstituting the rites of passage that had disappeared in agricultural societies and in periods of early industrialization. For example, government regulations stipulate the ages at which a person may drive a car, drink alcohol, vote in elections, marry without parental permission, work overtime, and retire. These regulations do not constitute strict rites of passage: most 18-year-olds choose not to vote, and most people choose their age of retirement without reference to government dictates. Still, the state shapes the socialization process by regulating the life course to some degree and by influencing our views of appropriate behavior at particular ages (Mayer and Schoepflin 1989).

In the social policy section that follows, we will see that the state is under pressure to become a provider of child care, which would give it a new and direct role in the socialization of infants and young children.

SOCIAL POLICY AND SOCIALIZATION

Child Care around the World

www.
mhhe
.com
/schaefer8

The Issue

The rise in single-parent families, increased job opportunities for women, and the need for additional family income have all propelled an increasing number of mothers of young children into the paid labor force of the United States. In 1999, more than 65 percent of all mothers with children under the age of six were part of the labor force. Who, then, takes care of the children of these women during work hours?

For 35 percent of all preschoolers with employed mothers, the solution has become group child care programs. Day care centers have become the functional equivalent of the nuclear family, performing some of the nurturing and socialization functions previously handled only by family members (Bureau of the Census 2000a: 409; K. Smith 2000). But how does group day care compare to care in the home? And what is the state's responsibility to assure quality care?

The Setting

Few people in the United States, Great Britain, or elsewhere can afford the luxury of having a parent stay at home or of paying for high-quality live-in child care. For millions of mothers and fathers, finding the right kind of child care is a challenge to parenting and to the pocketbook.

Researchers have found that high-quality child care centers do not adversely affect the socialization of children; in fact, good day care benefits children. The value of preschool programs was documented in a series of studies conducted by the National Institute of Child Health and Human Development in the United States. They found no significant differences in infants who had received extensive nonmaternal care as compared with those who had been cared for solely by their mothers. The researchers also reported that more infants in the United States are being placed in child care outside the home and that, overall, the quality of these arrangements is better than had been found in previous studies. It is difficult, however, to generalize about child care since there is so much variability among day care providers, and even among policies from one state to another (Gardner 2001; NICHD 1998).

Sociological Insights

Studies assessing the quality of child care outside of the home reflect the microlevel of analysis and the interest that interactionists have in the impact of face-to-face interaction. They also explore macro-level implications for the functioning of social institutions like the family. But some of the issues surrounding day care have also been of interest from the conflict perspective.

Quality day care in the United States is not equally available to all families. Parents in wealthy neighborhoods have an easier time finding day care than those in poor or working-class communities. *Affordable* child care is also a problem. Viewed from a conflict perspective, child care costs are an especially serious burden for lower-class families. Indeed, the poorest families spend 25 percent of their income for preschool child care, while families who are *not* poor pay only 6 percent or less of their income for day care.

The feminist perspective echoes the concern of conflict theorists that high-quality child care receives little governmental support because it is regarded as "merely a way to let women work." Nearly all child care workers (97 percent) are women; many find themselves in low-status, minimum-wage jobs. Typically, food servers, messengers, and gas station attendants make more than child care workers, 55 percent of whom earn less than $8.50 per hour. Not surprisingly, turnover among employees in child care centers runs as high as 40 percent per year (Bureau of the Census 2000a: 418; Murray 2000; Haynes 2001).

Policy Initiatives

Policies regarding child care outside the home vary throughout the world. Most developing nations do not have the economic base to provide subsidized child care. Working mothers rely largely on relatives or take their children to work. Even those industrial countries with elaborate programs of subsidized child care occasionally fall short of the needs for quality supervised child care.

When policymakers decide that child care is desirable, they must determine the degree to which taxpayers should subsidize it. In Sweden and Denmark, one-third to one-half of children under age three were in government-subsidized child care full-time in 2001. In the United States, where government subsidies are not available, the total cost of

People in Sweden pay higher taxes than do U.S. citizens, but they have access to excellent preschool day care at little or no cost.

options previously open to East German mothers, who had become accustomed to government-supported child care.

Experts in child development view such reports as a vivid reminder of the need for greater governmental and private-sector support for child care. Edward Zigler, director of the Bush Center on Child Development at Yale University, concludes, "It's not just that we're not doing anything. It's that we're perfectly satisfied in this country to every day put children in settings that compromise their growth and development. It's a tragedy, and the cost to this country is going to be immense" (Baker 1994:26).

child care averaged between $3,500 and $6,000 per family per year (Gornick and Meyers 2001).

There is a long way to go in making quality child care more affordable and more accessible, not just in the United States, but throughout the world. In an attempt to reduce government spending, France is considering cutting back the budgets of subsidized nurseries, even though waiting lists already exist and the French public heartily disapproves of any cutbacks (Hank 2001; L. King 1998). In Germany, reunification has reduced the

Let's Discuss

1. Were you ever in a day care program? Do you recall the experience as good or bad? In general, do you think it is desirable to expose young children to the socializing influence of day care?
2. In the view of conflict theorists, why does child care receive little government support?
3. Should the costs of day care programs be paid by government, by the private sector, or entirely by parents?

Chapter Resources

Summary

Socialization is the process whereby people learn the attitudes, values, and actions appropriate for members of a particular culture. This chapter examined the role of socialization in human development; the way in which people develop perceptions, feelings, and beliefs about themselves; the lifelong nature of the socialization process; and the important agents of socialization.

1. Socialization affects the overall cultural practices of a society; it also shapes the images that we hold of ourselves.

2. Heredity and environmental factors interact in influencing the socialization process. *Sociobiology* is the systematic study of the biological bases of social behavior.

3. In the early 1900s, Charles Horton Cooley advanced the belief that we learn who we are by interacting with others, a phenomenon he calls the *looking-glass self.*

4. George Herbert Mead, best known for his theory of the *self,* proposed that as people mature, their selves begin to reflect their concern about reactions

from others—both *generalized others* and *significant others.*

5. Erving Goffman has shown that many of our daily activities involve attempts to convey distinct impressions of who we are, a process called **impression management.**

6. Socialization proceeds throughout the life course. Some societies mark stages of development with formal *rites of passage.* In the culture of the United States, significant events such as marriage and parenthood serve to change a person's status.

7. As the primary agents of socialization, parents play a critical role in guiding children into those **gender roles** deemed appropriate in a society.

8. Like the family, schools in the United States have an explicit mandate to socialize people—and

especially children—into the norms and values of our culture.

9. Peer groups and the mass media, especially television, are important agents of socialization for adolescents.

10. We are most fully exposed to occupational roles through observing the work of our parents, of people whom we meet while they are performing their duties, and of people portrayed in the media.

11. The state shapes the socialization process by regulating the life course and by influencing our views of appropriate behavior at particular ages.

12. As more and more mothers of young children have entered the labor market, the demand for child care has increased dramatically, posing policy questions for many nations around the world.

Critical Thinking Questions

1. Should social research be conducted in areas such as sociobiology, even though many investigators believe that this type of analysis is potentially detrimental to large numbers of people?

2. Drawing on Erving Goffman's dramaturgical approach, discuss how the following groups engage

in impression management: athletes, college instructors, parents, physicians, and politicians.

3. How would functionalists and conflict theorists differ in their analysis of socialization by the mass media?

Key Terms

Anticipatory socialization Processes of socialization in which a person "rehearses" for future positions, occupations, and social relationships. (page 94)

Cognitive theory of development Jean Piaget's theory of how children's thought progresses through four stages. (92)

Degradation ceremony An aspect of the socialization process within total institutions, in which people are subjected to humiliating rituals. (94)

Dramaturgical approach A view of social interaction that examines people as if they were theatrical performers. (90)

Face-work The efforts of people to maintain the proper image and avoid embarrassment in public. (90)

Gender roles Expectations regarding the proper behavior, attitudes, and activities of males and females. (96)

Generalized other The attitudes, viewpoints, and expectations of society as a whole that a child takes into account in his or her behavior. (89)

Impression management The altering of the presentation of the self in order to create distinctive appearances and satisfy particular audiences. (90)

Looking-glass self A concept that emphasizes the self as the product of our social interactions with others. (88)

Personality In everyday speech, a person's typical patterns of attitudes, needs, characteristics, and behavior. (85)

Resocialization The process of discarding former behavior patterns and accepting new ones as part of a transition in one's life. (94)

Rites of passage Rituals marking the symbolic transition from one social position to another. (93)

Role taking The process of mentally assuming the perspective of another, thereby enabling oneself to respond from that imagined viewpoint. (89)

Self A distinct identity that sets us apart from others. (88)

Significant others Those individuals who are most important in the development of the self, such as parents, friends, and teachers. (90)

Socialization The process whereby people learn the attitudes, values, and behaviors appropriate for members of a particular culture. (85)

Sociobiology The systematic study of biological bases of social behavior. (88)

Symbols The gestures, objects, and language that form the basis of human communication. (89)

Total institutions Institutions that regulate all aspects of a person's life under a single authority, such as prisons, the military, mental hospitals, and convents. (94)

Additional Readings

BOOKS

Adler, Patricia A., and Peter Adler. 1998. *Peer Power: Preadolescent Culture and Identity.* New Brunswick, NJ: Rutgers University Press. Using eight years of observation research, sociologists discuss the role of peer groups and family as they relate to popularity, social isolation, bullying, and boy–girl relationships.

Benjamin, Gail R. 1997. *Japanese Lessons.* New York: New York University Press. An American anthropologist recounts her children's year in a Japanese school.

Best, Amy L. 2000. *Prom Night: Youth, Schools, and Popular Culture.* New York: Routledge. An analysis of contemporary high schools using social events as a means of looking at gender and race differences. The chapter "Divided Dance Floor" considers how race in school affects the interaction of students.

Dunbar-Ortiz, Roxanne. 1997. *Red Dirt: Growing Up Okie.* London: Verso. An adult remembers her upbringing in a poor White family in rural Oklahoma.

Goffman, Erving. 1959. *The Presentation of Self in Everyday Life.* New York: Doubleday. Goffman demonstrates his interactionist theory that the self is managed in everyday situations in much the same way that a theatrical performer carries out a stage role.

Hersch, Patricia. 1999. *A Tribe Apart: A Journey into the Heart of American Adolescence.* New York: Ballantine Books. Eight teenagers in Reston, Virginia, struggle with the growing freedom and complexity of adolescence.

Pollack, William. 1998. *Real Boys: Rescuing Our Sons from the Myths of Boyhood.* New York: Henry Holt. A clinical psychologist looks at the disenchantment experienced by so many boys because their true emotions are kept hidden.

Rosier, Katherine Brown. 2000. *Mothering Inner-City Children: The Early School Years.* New Brunswick, NJ: Rutgers University Press. Based on in-depth interviews with low-income mothers, this sociological analysis explains how low-income African American families cope with the daily pressures and responsibilities of child rearing.

Tobin, Joseph J., David Y. H. Wu, and Dana H. Davidson. 1989. *Preschool in Three Cultures: Japan, China, and the United States.* New Haven, CT: Yale University Press. A comparative look at formal early childhood education in three nations, drawing on the views of parents, teachers, and administrators.

JOURNALS

Among the journals that deal with socialization issues are *Adolescence* (founded in 1966), *Childhood: A Global Journal of Child Research* (1993), *Ethology and Sociobiology* (1979), *Journal of Personality and Social Psychology* (1965), and *Young Children* (1945).

Technology Resources

Internet Connection

/schaefer8 *Note: While all the URLs listed were current as of the printing of this book, these sites often change. Please check our website (**www.mhhe.com/schaefer8**) for updates and hyperlinks to this exercise and additional exercises.*

1. Erving Goffman's exploration of total institutions offers a sociological perspective of daily life inside prisons, the military, mental hospitals, and convents. Review the list of four common traits shared by all total institutions on page 94 of your text. Then, log onto the Cybrary of the Holocaust (**http://remember.org**). Spend time learning about the Holocaust in general, and life in concentration camps in particular, utilizing the video, photographs, stories, and research links on the site.

(a) What story or image had the greatest impact on you? Why? What new facts did you learn through your online visit?

(b) Reflecting on Goffman's ideas, identify how Nazi-run concentration camps qualify as total institutions. What occurred during the degradation ceremony that prisoners were exposed to upon entering the camps?

(c) What/who was the authority in the camps under which all aspects of life were conducted?

(d) In what specific ways were the activities of prisoners monitored by others?

(e) What was the daily routine of prisoners? What control, if any, did they have over their own lives?

(f) What were the main purposes of these camps, and how were prisoners forced to fulfill those purposes?

(g) Has looking at the Holocaust through a sociological lens changed the way you view this time in history? How so?

2. The American Academy of Pediatrics has a website that deals with violence and the media (**http://www.aap.org/advocacy/childhealthmonth/media.htm**). Read the site's fact sheet and answer the following questions:

(a) By age 18, how many acts of violence will the average American child have viewed on television?

(b) How does media violence affect children?

(c) How can parents reduce the effect of media violence on their children?

(d) How do you think media violence affects young children?

3. Amish.net (**http://Amish.net/lifestyle.asp**) helps the public to understand the Amish lifestyle. Read the article "The Amish Lifestyle" and answer the following questions:

(a) What is the primary language of the Amish?

(b) How many Amish live in North America?

(c) What are the several groups of Amish?

(d) What is the importance of family to the Amish?

(e) Read Amish Life FAQs. What is the term used for Amish adolescents who "sow their wild oats"?

(f) How do the Amish deal with children who have special needs?

(g) What do Amish children do during the day?

(h) Why do Amish children choose to remain in the Amish community when they reach adulthood?

On-Line Learning Center www.mhhe.com/schaefer8

The development of the social self is literally a lifelong transformation that begins in the crib and continues throughout one's life course. One type of socialization that can occur at some point in the life course is resocialization. *Resocialization* refers to the process of discarding former behavior patterns and accepting new ones as part of a transition in one's life. One of the Internet activities in the student center of the Online Learning Center (**www.mhhe.com/ schaefer8**) gives you a glimpse into the resocialization experienced by those in concentration camps. Spend time learning about the Holocaust in general, and life in concentration camps through the presentation of a video, photographs, and stories.

CHAPTER 5

SOCIAL INTERACTION
AND SOCIAL STRUCTURE

In our social interaction with other cultures it is important to know what social rules apply. In Japan, for example, it is impolite to leave your chopsticks sticking up in the rice bowl—a symbol of death for the Japanese and an insult to their dead ancestors. This poster was created by an advertising agency that promises to steer its clients in the United States clear of such gaffes in the Asian market.

The quiet of a summer Sunday morning in Palo Alto, California, was shattered by a screeching squad car siren as police swept through the city picking up college students in a surprise mass arrest. Each suspect was charged with a felony, warned of his constitutional rights, spread-eagled against the car, searched, handcuffed and carted off in the back seat of the squad car to the police station for booking.

After being fingerprinted and having identification forms prepared for his "jacket" (central information file), each prisoner was left isolated in a detention cell to wonder what he had done to get himself into this mess. After a while, he was blindfolded and transported to the "Stanford County Prison." Here he began the induction process of becoming a prisoner—stripped naked, skin searched, deloused, and issued a uniform, bedding, soap and towel. By late afternoon when nine such arrests had been completed, these youthful "first offenders" sat in dazed silence on the cots in their barren cells.

These men were part of a very unusual kind of prison, an experimental or mock prison, created by social psychologists for the purpose of intensively studying the effects of imprisonment upon volunteer research subjects. When we planned our two-week long simulation of prison life, we were primarily concerned about understanding the process by which people adapt to the novel and alien environment in which those called "prisoners" lose their liberty, civil rights, independence and privacy, while those called "guards" gain social power by accepting the responsibility for controlling and managing the lives of their dependent charges. . . .

Our final sample of participants (10 prisoners and 11 guards) were selected from over 75 volunteers recruited through ads in the city and campus newspapers. . . . Half were randomly assigned to role-play being guards, the others to be prisoners. Thus, there were no measurable differences between the guards and the prisoners at the start of this experiment. . . .

At the end of only six days we had to close down our mock prison because what we saw was frightening. It was no longer apparent to most of the subjects (or to us) where reality ended and their roles began. The majority had indeed become prisoners or guards, no longer able to clearly differentiate between role playing and self. There were dramatic changes in virtually every aspect of their behavior, thinking and feeling. In less than a week the experience of imprisonment undid (temporarily) a lifetime of learning; human values were suspended, self-concepts were challenged and the ugliest, most base, pathological side of human nature surfaced. We were horrified because we saw some boys (guards) treat others as if they were despicable animals, taking pleasure in cruelty, while other boys (prisoners) became servile, dehumanized robots who thought only of escape, of their own individual survival and of their mounting hatred for the guards. *(Zimbardo et al. 1974:61, 62, 63; Zimbardo 1972:4)* ■ 💿

Additional information about this excerpt and about those that open each subsequent chapter can be found on the SocWorld CD-ROM that accompanies this text.

In this a study directed and described by the social psychologist Philip Zimbardo, college students adopted predictable patterns of social interaction (those expected of guards and prisoners) when they were placed in a mock prison. Sociologists use the term *social interaction* to refer to the ways in which people respond to one another, whether face to face or over the telephone or on the computer. In the mock prison, social interactions between guards and prisoners were highly impersonal. The guards addressed the prisoners by number rather than name, and they wore reflector sunglasses that made eye contact impossible.

As in many real-life prisons, the simulated prison at Stanford University had a social structure in which guards held virtually total control over prisoners. The term *social structure* refers to the way in which a society is organized into predictable relationships. The social structure of Zimbardo's mock prison influenced how the guards and prisoners interacted. Zimbardo (1992:576) notes that it was a real prison "in the minds of the jailers and their captives." His simulated prison experiment, first conducted more than 30 years ago, has subsequently been repeated (with similar findings) both in the United States and in other countries. In fact, the British Broadcasting Company (BBC) in 2002 canceled a reality-based television program called "The Experiment" based on the simulated prison experiment because the participants' behavior degenerated significantly in just six days.

The closely linked concepts of social interaction and social structure are central to sociological study. Sociologists scrutinize patterns of behavior to understand and accurately describe the social interactions of a community or society and the social structure in which they take place. Who determines how we should behave with one another? Is it possible to redefine or change that "social reality"? How do we get our social roles, and how do they affect our interactions?

This chapter begins by considering how social interaction shapes the way we view the world around us. We will focus than on the five basic elements of social structure: statuses, social roles, groups, social networks, and social institutions. Groups are important because much of our social interaction occurs in them. Social institutions such as the family, religion, and government are a fundamental aspect of social structure. We will contrast the functionalist, conflict, and interactionist approaches to the study of social institutions. We will also examine the typologies developed by Ferdinand Tönnies and Gerhard Lenski for comparing modern societies with simpler forms of social structure. The social policy section will consider the AIDS crisis and its implications for social institutions throughout the world. ∎

Social Interaction and Reality

When someone shoves you in a crowd, do you automatically push back? Or do you consider the circumstances of the incident and the attitude of the instigator before you react? Chances are you do the latter. According to sociologist Herbert Blumer (1969:79), the distinctive characteristic of social interaction among people is that "human beings interpret or 'define' each other's actions instead of merely reacting to each other's actions." In other words, our response to someone's behavior is based on the *meaning* we attach to his or her actions. Reality is shaped by our perceptions, evaluations, and definitions.

These meanings typically reflect the norms and values of the dominant culture and our socialization experiences within that culture. As interactionists emphasize, the meanings that we attach to people's behavior are shaped by our interactions with them and with the larger society.

Consequently, social reality is literally constructed from our social interactions (Berger and Luckmann 1966).

Defining and Reconstructing Reality

How do we define our social reality? As an example, let us

pp. 4–5 ◀

consider something as simple as how we regard tattoos. Even as recently as a few years ago, most of us in the United States considered tattoos as something "weird" or "kooky." We associated them with fringe countercultural groups, such as punk rockers, bike gangs, and skinheads. A tattoo elicited an automatic negative response among many people. Now, however, there are so many tattooed people, including society's trendsetters and major sports figures, and the ritual of getting a tattoo has become so legitimized, the mainstream culture regards tattoos differently. At this point, as a result of increased social interactions with tattooed people, tattoos look perfectly at home to us in a number of settings.

In challenging the stereotypes of African Americans and Muslim Americans, boxing champion Muhammad Ali helped to redefine their social reality. Today, courageous in the face of degenerative disease, he is reconstructing the social reality of disabled Americans. Ali was honored at the opening of the 1996 Olympic games in Atlanta, where he lit the ceremonial torch.

creation of a White male syndicate, which sponsored his early matches when he was known as Cassius Clay. Soon, however, the young boxer rebelled against those who would keep him or his race down. He broke the old stereotypes of self-effacing Black athletes. He insisted on his own political views (including refusing to serve in the Vietnam War), his own religion (Black Muslim), and his own name (Muhammad Ali). Not only did Ali change the world of sports, he also had a hand in altering the world of race relations (Remnick 1998).

Viewed from a sociological perspective, Ali was redefining social reality by looking much more critically at the racist thinking and terminology that restricted him and other African Americans.

Negotiated Order

As we have just seen, people can reconstruct social reality through a process of internal change, taking a different view of everyday behavior. Yet people also reshape reality by *negotiating* changes in patterns of social interaction. The term **negotiation** refers to the attempt to reach agreement with others concerning some objective. Negotiation does not involve coercion; it goes by many names, including *bargaining, compromising, trading off, mediating, exchanging, "wheeling and dealing,"* and *collusion*. It is through negotiation as a form of social interaction that society creates its social structure (Strauss 1977; see also Fine 1984).

Negotiation occurs in many ways. As interactionists point out, some social situations, such as buying groceries, involve no mediation, while other situations require negotiation. For example, we may negotiate with others regarding time ("When should we arrive?"), space ("Can we have a meeting at your house?"), or even assignment of places while waiting for concert tickets. In traditional societies, impending marriage often leads to negotiations between the families of the husband and wife. For example, anthropologist Ray Abrahams (1968) has described how the Labwor people of Africa arrange for an amount of property to go from the groom's to the bride's family at the time of marriage. In the view of the Labwor, such bargaining over an exchange of cows and sheep culminates not only in a marriage but, more important, in the linking of two clans or families.

The ability to define social reality reflects a group's power within a society. In fact, one of the most crucial aspects of the relationship between dominant and subordinate groups is the ability of the dominant or majority group to define a society's values. Sociologist William I. Thomas (1923), an early critic of theories of racial and gender differences, recognized that the "definition of the situation" could mold the thinking and personality of the individual. Writing from an interactionist perspective, Thomas observed that people respond not only to the objective features of a person or situation but also to the *meaning* that the person or situation has for them. For example, in Philip Zimbardo's mock prison experiment, student "guards" and "prisoners" accepted the definition of the situation (including the traditional roles and behavior associated with being a guard or prisoner) and acted accordingly.

As we have seen throughout the last 40 years—first in the civil rights movement of the 1960s and since then among such groups as women, the elderly, gays and lesbians, and people with disabilities—an important aspect of the process of social change involves *re*defining or *recon*structing social reality. Members of subordinate groups challenge traditional definitions and begin to perceive and experience reality in a new way. For example, the world champion boxer Muhammad Ali began his career as the

While such family-to-family bargaining is common in traditional cultures, negotiation can take much more elaborate forms in modern industrial societies. Consider college financial aid programs. From a sociological perspective, such programs are formal norms (reflected in established practices and procedures for granting aid to college students).Yet the programs undergo revision through negotiated outcomes involving many interests, including foundations, banks, the admissions office, and the faculty. On an individual level, the student applicant will mediate with representatives of the college financial aid office. Changes in the individual situations will occur through such negotiations (Maines 1977, 1982; Thomas 1984).

Negotiations underlie much of our social behavior. Because most elements of social structure are not static, they are subject to change through bargaining and exchanging. Sociologists use the term *negotiated order* to underscore the fact that the social order is continually being constructed and altered through negotiation. **Negotiated order** refers to a social structure that derives its existence from the social interactions through which people define and redefine its character.

We can add negotiation to our list of cultural universals pp. 62–63 ◀ because all societies provide guidelines or norms in which negotiations take place. The recurring role of negotiation in social interaction and social structure will be apparent as we examine the major elements of social structure (Strauss 1977).

● Elements of Social Structure

We can examine predictable social relationships in terms of five elements: statuses, social roles, groups, social networks, and social institutions. These elements make up social structure just as a foundation, walls, and ceilings make up a building's structure. The elements of social structure are developed through the lifelong process of socialization, described in Chapter 4.

Statuses

We normally think of a person's "status" as having to do with influence, wealth, and fame. However, sociologists use **status** to refer to any of the full range of socially defined positions within a large group or society—from the lowest to the highest position. Within our society, a person can occupy the status of president of the United States, fruit picker, son or daughter, violinist, teenager, resident of Minneapolis, dental technician, or neighbor. A person can hold a number of statuses at the same time.

Figure 5-1
Social Statuses

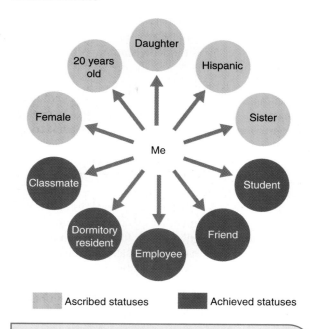

■ Ascribed statuses   ■ Achieved statuses

Think About It
The person in this figure—"me"—occupies many positions in society, each of which involves distinct statuses. How would you define *your* statuses? Which have the most influence in your life?

Ascribed and Achieved Status

Sociologists view some statuses as *ascribed*, while they categorize others as *achieved* (see Figure 5-1). An **ascribed status** is "assigned" to a person by society without regard for the person's unique talents or characteristics. Generally, this assignment takes place at birth; thus, a person's racial background, gender, and age are all considered ascribed statuses. These characteristics are biological in origin but are significant mainly because of the *social* meanings they have in our culture. Conflict theorists are especially interested in ascribed statuses, since these statuses often confer privileges or reflect a person's membership in a subordinate group. The social meanings of race and ethnicity, gender, and age will be analyzed more fully in Chapters 11–13.

In most cases, we can do little to change an ascribed status. But we can attempt to change the traditional constraints associated with such statuses. For example, the Gray Panthers—an activist political group founded in 1971 to work for the rights of older people—have tried to modify society's negative and confining stereotypes of the elderly (see Chapter 13). As a result of their work and that of other groups supporting older citizens, the ascribed status of "senior citizen" is no longer as difficult for millions of older people.

An ascribed status does not necessarily have the same social meaning in every society. In a cross-cultural study, sociologist Gary Huang (1988) confirmed the long-held view that respect for the elderly is an important cultural norm in China. In many cases, the prefix "old" is used respectfully: calling someone "old teacher" or "old person" is like calling a judge in the United States "your honor." Huang points out that positive age-seniority distinctions in language are uncommon in the United States; consequently, we view the term *old man* as more of an insult than a celebration of seniority and wisdom.

Unlike ascribed statuses, an ***achieved status*** comes to us largely through our own efforts. Both "bank president" and "prison guard" are achieved statuses, as are "lawyer," "pianist," "sorority member," "convict," and "social worker." You must do something to acquire an achieved status—go to school, learn a skill, establish a friendship, or invent a new product. As we see in the next section, our ascribed status heavily influences our achieved status. Being male, for example, decreases the likelihood that a person would consider being a child care worker.

Master Status

Each person holds many different and sometimes conflicting statuses; some may connote higher social positions, and some, lower positions. How, then, do others view one's overall social position? According to sociologist Everett Hughes (1945), societies deal with inconsistencies by agreeing that certain statuses are more important than others. A ***master status*** is a status that dominates others and thereby determines a person's general position within society. For example, Arthur Ashe, who died of AIDS in 1993, had a remarkable career as a tennis star; but at the end of his life, his status as a well-known personality with AIDS may have outweighed his statuses as a retired athlete, an author, and a political activist. Throughout the world many people with disabilities find that their status as "disabled" is given undue weight, which overshadows their actual ability to perform successfully in meaningful employment (See Box 5-1).

Our society gives such importance to race and gender that they often dominate our lives. These ascribed statuses often influence achieved status. The African American activist Malcolm X (1925–1965), an eloquent and controversial advocate of Black power and Black pride in the early 1960s, recalled that his feelings and perspectives changed dramatically while in eighth grade. His English teacher, a White man, advised him that his goal of becoming a lawyer was "no realistic goal for a nigger" and encouraged him instead to become a carpenter. Malcolm X (1964:37) found that his position as a Black man (ascribed status) was an obstacle to his dream of becoming a lawyer

(achieved status). In the United States, ascribed statuses of race and gender can function as master statuses that have an important impact on one's potential to achieve a desired professional and social status.

Social Roles

What Are Social Roles?

Throughout our lives, we are acquiring what sociologists call *social roles*. A ***social role*** is a set of expectations for people who occupy a given social position or status. Thus, in the United States, we expect that cab drivers will know how to get around a city, that receptionists will be reliable in handling phone messages, and that police officers will take action if they see a citizen being threatened. With each distinctive social status—whether ascribed or achieved—come particular role expectations. However, actual performance varies from individual to individual. One secretary may assume extensive administrative responsibilities, whereas another may focus on clerical duties. Similarly, in Philip Zimbardo's mock prison experiment, some students were brutal and sadistic guards, but others were not.

Roles are a significant component of social structure. Viewed from a functionalist perspective, roles contribute to a society's stability by enabling members to anticipate the behavior of others and to pattern their own actions accordingly. Yet social roles can also be dysfunctional by restricting people's interactions and relationships. If we view a person *only* as a "police officer" or a "supervisor," it will be difficult to relate to this person as a friend or neighbor.

Role Conflict

Imagine the delicate situation of a woman who has worked for a decade on an assembly line in an electrical

Police officers may face role strain when they try to develop positive community relations but still maintain an authoritative position.

When officials in New Hampshire required a handicap access ramp for a mountain shelter, they were ridiculed for wasting taxpayer money. Who could climb a mountain in a wheelchair, critics asked? In the summer of 2000 that challenge impelled several intrepid climbers, some in wheelchairs, to make a 12-hour trek over rocks and rough trail so that they could enter the shelter in triumph. Stereotypes about the disabled are gradually falling away as a result of such feats. But the status of disabled still carries a stigma.

Throughout history and around the world, people with disabilities have often been subjected to cruel and inhuman treatment. For example, in the early twentieth century, the disabled were frequently viewed as subhuman creatures who were a menace to society. In Japan more than 16,000 women with disabilities were involuntarily sterilized with government approval from 1945 to 1995. Sweden recently apologized for the same action taken against 62,000 of its citizens in the 1970s.

Such blatantly hostile treatment of people with disabilities generally gave way to a *medical model,* which views the disabled as chronic patients. Increasingly, however, people concerned with the rights of the disabled have criticized this model as well. In their view, it is the unnecessary and discriminatory barriers present in the environment—both physical and attitudinal—that stand in the way of people with disabilities more than any biological limitations do. Applying a *civil rights model,* activists emphasize that those with disabilities face widespread prejudice, discrimination, and

segregation. For example, most voting places are inaccessible to wheelchair users and fail to provide ballots that can be used by those unable to read print.

Drawing on the earlier work of Erving Goffman, contemporary sociologists have suggested that society has attached a stigma to many forms of disability and that this stigma leads to prejudicial treatment. Indeed, people with disabilities frequently observe that the nondisabled see them only as blind, wheelchair users, and so forth, rather than as complex human beings with individual strengths and weaknesses, whose blindness or use of a wheelchair is merely one aspect of their

> **In Japan more than 16,000 women with disabilities were involuntarily sterilized with government approval from 1945 to 1995.**

lives. A review of studies of people with disabilities disclosed that most academic research on the subject does not differentiate gender—thereby perpetuating the view that a disability overrides other personal characteristics. Consequently, disability serves as a master status.

Without question, people with disabilities occupy a subordinate position in the United States. By 1970, a strong political movement for disability rights had emerged across the United States. Women and men involved in this movement are working to challenge negative views of disabled people and to modify the social structure by reshaping laws, institutions, and environments so that people with

disabilities can be fully integrated into mainstream society.

The effort to overcome the master status is global in nature. Despite a regulation in China that universities may not reject students because of a physical disability, many universities do just that. In fact, in the last five years, the dozens of universities in Beijing alone have accepted only 236 students with *any* kind of disability, however minor. It appears that bias against the disabled runs deep in China, and many universities use a mandate to nurture physical development as an excuse to keep out the disabled. Kenya's constitution outlaws discrimination on the basis of many characteristics, including race, sex, tribe, place of origin, creed, and religion, but not on the basis of disability. The African nation of Botswana, on the other hand, has plans to assist its disabled, most of whom live in rural areas and need special services for mobility and economic development. In many countries, disability rights activists are targeting issues essential to overcoming master status and to being a full citizen; these issues include employment, housing, education, and access to public buildings.

Let's Discuss

1. Does your campus present barriers to disabled students? If so, what kind of barriers—physical, attitudinal, or both? Describe some of them.
2. Why do you think nondisabled people see disability as the most important characteristic of a disabled person? What can be done to help people see beyond the wheelchair and the seeing-eye dog?

Sources: Albrecht et al. 2001; Goffman 1963a; Murphy 1997; Newsday 1997; Ponczek 1998; Rosenthal 2001; Shapiro 1993; Willet and Deegan 2000.

plant and has recently been named supervisor of the unit she worked in. How is this woman expected to relate to her longtime friends and co-workers? Should she still go out to lunch with them, as she has done almost daily for years? Is it her responsibility to recommend the firing of an old friend who cannot keep up with the demands of the assembly line?

Role conflict occurs when incompatible expectations arise from two or more social positions held by the same person. Fulfillment of the roles associated with one status may directly violate the roles linked to a second status. In the example above, the newly promoted supervisor will most likely experience a sharp conflict between her social and occupational roles.

Imagine you are a journalist walking down this alley as you witness the mugging going on here. What do you do? Try to stop the crime? Or take a picture for your magazine? This was the role conflict that Sarah Leen, a professional photographer, experienced when she stopped to change a lens and take a picture of this scene. At the same time, Leen felt fear for her own safety. People in certain professions—among them, journalism—commonly experience role conflict during disasters, crimes, and other distressing situations.

Role conflicts call for important ethical choices. So, the new supervisor will have to make a difficult decision about how much allegiance she owes her friend and how much she owes her employers who have given her supervisory responsibilities.

Another type of role conflict occurs when individuals move into occupations that are not common among people with their ascribed status. Male preschool teachers and female police officers experience this type of role conflict. In the latter case, female officers must strive to reconcile their workplace role in law enforcement with the societal view of a woman's role, which does not embrace many skills needed in police work. And while female police officers encounter sexual harassment, as women do throughout the labor force, they must also deal with the "code of silence," an informal norm that precludes their implicating fellow officers in wrongdoing (Fletcher 1995; Martin 1994).

Imagine

If you were a male nurse, what aspects of role conflict would you need to consider? Now imagine you are a professional boxer and a woman. What conflicting role expectations might that involve? In both cases, how well do you think you would handle role conflict?

Role Strain

Role conflict describes the situation of a person dealing with the challenge of occupying two social positions simultaneously. However, even a single position can cause problems. Sociologists use the term **role strain** to describe the difficulty that arises when the same social position imposes conflicting demands and expectations.

In the chapter opening example, social psychologist Philip Zimbardo unexpectedly experienced role strain. He initially saw himself merely as a college professor directing an imaginative experiment in which students played the roles of either guard or inmate. However, he soon found that as a professor, he is also expected to look after the welfare of the students or at least not to endanger them. Eventually he resolved the role strain by making the difficult decision to terminate the experiment. Twenty-five years later, in a television interview, he was still reflecting on the challenge of this role strain (CBS News 1998).

Role Exit

Often, when we think of assuming a social role, we focus on the preparation and anticipatory socialization that a person undergoes for that role. This is true if a person is about to become an attorney, a chef, a spouse, or a parent. Yet, until recently, social scientists have given less attention to the adjustments involved in *leaving* social roles.

Sociologist Helen Rose Fuchs Ebaugh (1988) developed the term **role exit** to describe the process of disengagement from a role that is central to one's self-identity and reestablishment of an identity in a new role. Drawing on interviews with 185 people—among them ex-convicts, divorced men and women, recovering alcoholics, ex-nuns, former doctors, retirees, and transsexuals—Ebaugh (herself a former nun) studied the process of voluntarily exiting from significant social roles.

Ebaugh has offered a four-stage model of role exit. The first stage begins with *doubt*. The person experiences frustration, burnout, or simply unhappiness with an

This college student in India decorated his dorm room with photos of beautiful women and fast cars. They may signify his attempt to create a new identity, the final stage in his exit from the role of high school student living at home.

accustomed status and the roles associated with this social position. The second stage involves a *search for alternatives*. A person unhappy with his or her career may take a leave of absence; an unhappily married couple may begin what they see as a temporary separation.

The third stage of role exit is the *action stage* or *departure*. Ebaugh found that the vast majority of her respondents could identify a clear turning point that made them feel it was essential to take final action and leave their job, end their marriage, or engage in another type of role exit. Twenty percent of respondents saw their role exit as a gradual, evolutionary process that had no single turning point.

The last stage of role exit involves the *creation of a new identity*. Many of you participated in a role exit when you made the transition from high school to college. You left behind the role of offspring living at home and took on the role of a somewhat independent college student living with peers in a dorm. Sociologist Ira Silver (1996) has made a study of the central role that material objects play in this transition. The objects that students choose to leave home (like stuffed animals and dolls) are associated with their prior identities. They may remain deeply attached to these objects but do not want them to be seen as part of their new identities at college. The objects they bring with them symbolize how they now see themselves and how they wish to be perceived. CDs and wall posters, for example, are calculated to say, "This is me."

Groups

In sociological terms, a **group** is any number of people with similar norms, values, and expectations who interact with one another on a regular basis. The members of a women's college basketball team, of a hospital's business office, or of a symphony orchestra constitute a group. However, the residents of a suburb would not be considered a group, since they rarely interact with one another at one time.

Every society is composed of many groups in which daily social interaction takes place. We seek out groups to establish friendships, to accomplish certain goals, and to fulfill social roles that we have acquired. We'll explore the various types of groups in which people interact in detail in Chapter 6, where sociological investigations of group behavior will also be examined.

Groups play a vital part in a society's social structure. Much of our social interaction takes place within groups and is influenced by their norms and sanctions. Being a teenager or a retired person takes on special meanings when you interact within groups designed for people with that particular status. The expectations associated with many social roles, including those accompanying the statuses of brother, sister, and student, become more clearly defined in the context of a group.

New technology has broadened the definition of groups to include those who interact electronically—a significant number of Americans. Not all the "people" with whom we converse are real. At some websites, *chatterbots*—fictitious correspondents created by artificial intelligence programs—respond to questions as if a human were replying. While answering product or service-related questions, the chatterbot may begin "chatting" with an online consumer about family or the weather. Ultimately, such conversations may develop into a group that includes other online correspondents, both real and artificial. New groups organized around old interests, such as antique collection or bowling, have already arisen from this type of virtual reality (Van Slambrouck 1999a).

For the human participant, such online exchanges offer a new opportunity to alter one's image—what Goffman (1959) refers to as impression management. How might you present yourself to an online discussion group?

Even though you may not be totally sure whom you are "talking" to online, the Internet has added a massive new dimension to social interaction.

Social Networks and Technology

Groups do not merely serve to define other elements of the social structure, such as roles and statuses; they also are an intermediate link between the individual and the larger society. We are all members of a number of different groups and through our acquaintances make connections with people in different social circles. This connection is known as a ***social network***—that is, a series of social relationships that links a person directly to others and through them indirectly to still more people. Social networks may constrain people by limiting the range of their interactions, yet these networks may also empower people by making available vast resources (Lin 1999).

Involvement in social networks—commonly known as *networking*—is especially valuable in finding employment. Albert Einstein was successful in finding a job only when a classmate's father put him in touch with his future employer. These kinds of contacts, even those that are weak and distant, can be crucial in establishing social networks and facilitating transmission of information.

In the workplace, networking pays off more for men than for women because of the traditional presence of men in leadership positions. A 1997 survey of executives found that 63 percent of men use networking to find new jobs compared to 41 percent of women. Thirty-one percent of

the women use classified advertisements to find jobs, compared to only 13 percent of the men. Still, as we see in Box 5-2, women at all levels of the paid labor force are beginning to make effective use of social networks. A study of women who were leaving the welfare rolls to enter the paid workforce found that networking was an effective tool in their search for employment. Informal networking also helped them to locate child care and better housing—keys to successful employment (Carey and McLean 1997; Henly 1999).

With advances in technology, we can now maintain social networks electronically. We don't need face-to-face contacts for knowledge sharing anymore. It is not uncommon for those looking for employment or for a means of identifying someone with common interests to first turn to the Internet. First impressions now begin on the web. Many high school students get a first look at their future college via a webpage. A survey of college students found that 79 percent consider the quality of an employer's website important in deciding whether or not to apply for a job there (Jobtrak.com 2000b).

Sociologist Manuel Castells (1997, 1998, 2000) views the emerging electronic social networks as fundamental to new organizations and the growth of existing businesses and associations. One emerging electronic network, in particular, is changing the way people interact. "Texting" began first in Asia in 2000 and has now taken off in North America and Europe. It refers to wireless e-mails exchanged over cell phones in the small screens featured in newer models. Initially, texting was popular among young users, who sent shorthand messages such as "WRU" (where are you?) and "CU2NYT" (see you tonight). But now the business world has seen the advantages of transmitting updated business or financial e-mails via cell phones or handheld Palm Pilots. Sociologists, however, caution that such devices create a workday that never ends and that increasingly people are busy checking their digital devices rather than holding conversations with those around them (Rosen 2001).

A study released in 2000 documented a rise in the amount of time people are spending online in their homes. The increase suggests that face-to-face interactions may well be declining, since there are only so many hours in anyone's day. Indeed, a third of the respondents said

Research in Action
5-2 Women's Social Networks

www.mhhe.com/schaefer8

While sociologists have rightly given a good deal of attention to "old boy networks," there has been growing interest in the social networks created by women.

Sociologist Pierrette Hondagneu-Sotelo conducted observation research and interviews among Hispanic women (primarily Mexican immigrants) who live in San Francisco and are employed as domestic workers in middle- and upper-class homes. These women engage in what sociologist Mary Romero has called "job work." That is, the domestic worker has several employers and cleans each home on a weekly or biweekly basis for a flat rate of pay for the work completed (in Spanish, *por el trabajo*) as opposed to being paid an hourly rate (*por la hora*). Job work typically involves low pay, no reimbursement for transportation costs, and no health care benefits.

At first glance, we might expect that women engaged in such job work would be isolated from each other since they work alone. However, Hondagneu-Sotelo found that these Hispanic women have created strong social networks. Through interactions in various social settings—such as picnics, baby showers, church events, and informal gatherings at

women's homes—they share such valuable information as cleaning tips, remedies for work-related physical ailments, tactics for negotiating better pay and gratuities, and advice on how to leave undesirable jobs.

Networking has also been useful for members of the A Team, a social network of 12 to 14 women who are senior health care professionals in the Boston area. The

> The A Team began in 1977 through a series of casual lunches attended by young women beginning their careers in a health care field dominated by middle-aged men.

A Team began in 1977 with a series of casual lunches attended by young women beginning their careers in a health care field dominated by middle-aged men.

By 1984, many members of the A Team had advanced to middle-management or more senior positions in local hospitals or state government. But the group realized that women still did not hold any chief executive officer (CEO)

positions in hospitals in the Boston area. Because members felt that their qualifications matched those of the men being named as CEOs, they joined forces in an all-out effort to help one another make the contacts that could lead to top posts. The A Team networked with head-hunters, hospital trustees, female executives in other industries, and local politicians; held seminars to educate members on such topics as how to analyze financial statements; and continued informal networking efforts (including phoning friends and former associates to recommend colleagues).

The results of this networking were impressive. As of 1995, many women from the A Team hold top executive posts in hospitals and other health care institutions in the Boston area.

Let's Discuss

1. Have you ever participated in a job- or school-related network? If so, did you benefit from the opportunities it offered? In what way?
2. Suppose you want to land a professional job in the field of your choice. What people or organizations might help you to reach your goal? How would you get started?

Sources: Gabor 1995: Hondagneu-Sotelo 2001; Reskin and Padavic 1994; Romero 1998.

they spent more than five hours a week online while at home. Of those heavy users, 8 percent reported attending fewer social events as a result of their online surfing, and 13 percent said they were spending less time with family and friends.

Of course, the Internet can also promote social contacts, especially among those who have few opportunities, such as the disabled and the geographically isolated. The number of retired people who frequent chatrooms created for older users has increased sharply. Participants at websites such as ThirdAge report that they have formed new online friendships to replace old ones formed at the workplace (Galant 2000; Nie and Erbring 2000). In Chap-

ter 23, we will examine further the ways in which computer technology has assisted the formation of larger and even international social networks.

In 2001, the anthrax scare and the mobilization of troops for the Afghanistan conflict combined to increase our reliance on e-mail in unintended ways. Concerns about the delivery of anthrax spores in posted mail led many people and organizations to accept only electronic mail. At the same time, military personnel sent overseas turned increasingly to e-mail to stay in touch with friends and family members at home. Aboard one aircraft carrier, for example, the 5,000 crew members had to sign up a day in advance for a half hour of computer time. All told, they

117

wrote and read about 60,000 e-mails a day. Contrast this with the situation a few years ago, when sailors had to wait as long as a month for a letter from home. As one crew member said, "Without e-mail, I'd be going even crazier than I already am" (Stack 2001:A3).

Imagine

If you were deaf, what impact might Instant Messaging on the Internet have for you?

Social Institutions

The mass media, the government, the economy, the family, and the health care system are all examples of social institutions found in our society. *Social institutions* are organized patterns of beliefs and behavior centered on basic social needs, such as replacing personnel (the family) and preserving order (the government).

A close look at social institutions gives sociologists insight into the structure of a society. Consider religion, for example. The institution of religion adapts to the segment of society that it serves. Church work has very different meanings for ministers who serve a skid row area or a suburban middle-class community. Religious leaders assigned to a skid row mission will focus on tending to the ill and providing food and shelter. By contrast, clergy in affluent suburbs will be occupied with counseling those considering marriage and divorce, arranging youth activities, and overseeing cultural events.

Functionalist View

One way to understand social institutions is to see how they fulfill essential functions. Anthropologist David F. Aberle and his colleagues (1950) and sociologists Raymond Mack and Calvin Bradford (1979) have identified five major tasks, or functional prerequisites, that a society or relatively permanent group must accomplish if it is to survive (see Table 5-1):

1. *Replacing personnel.* Any group or society must replace personnel when they die, leave, or become incapacitated. This is accomplished through such means as immigration, annexation of neighboring groups of people, acquisition of slaves, or normal sexual reproduction of members. The Shakers, a religious sect that came to the United States in 1774, are a conspicuous example of a group that has *failed* to replace personnel. Their religious beliefs commit the Shakers to celibacy; to survive, the group must recruit new members. At first, the Shakers proved quite successful in attracting members and reached a peak of about 6,000 members in the United States during the 1840s. However, as of

Table 5-1	Functions and Institutions
Functional Prerequisite	**Social Institutions**
Replacing personnel	Family Government (immigration)
Teaching new recruits	Family (basic skills) Economy (occupations) Education (schools) Religion (sacred teachings)
Producing and distributing goods and services	Family (food preparation) Economy Government (regulations regarding commerce) Health care system
Preserving order	Family (child rearing, regulation of sexuality) Government Religion (morals)
Providing and maintaining a sense of purpose	Government (patriotism) Religion

2001, the only Shaker community left in this country was a farm in Maine with six members (Associated Press 2001).

2. *Teaching new recruits.* No group or society can survive if many of its members reject the established behavior and responsibilities. Thus, finding or producing new members is not sufficient. The group or society must encourage recruits to learn and accept its values and customs. This learning can take place formally within schools (where learning is a manifest function) or informally through interaction and negotiation in peer groups (where instruction is a latent function).

3. *Producing and distributing goods and services.* Any relatively permanent group or society must provide and distribute desired goods and services for its members. Each society establishes a set of rules for the allocation of financial and other resources. The

accept, the groups to which we belong, and the institutions within which we function. For example, the social roles associated with being a judge occur within the larger context of the criminal justice system. The status of "judge" stands in relation to other statuses, such as attorney, plaintiff, defendant, and witness, as well as to the social institution of government. Although courts and jails have great symbolic importance, the judicial system derives its continued significance from the roles people carry out in social interactions (Berger and Luckmann 1966).

Social Structure in Global Perspective

Modern societies are complex, especially when compared with earlier social arrangements. Sociologists Ferdinand Tönnies and Gerhard Lenski have offered ways to contrast modern societies with simpler forms of social structure.

Tönnies's *Gemeinschaft* and *Gesellschaft*

Ferdinand Tönnies (1855–1936) was appalled by the rise of an industrial city in his native Germany during the late 1800s. In his view, this city marked a dramatic change from the ideal type of a close-knit community, which Tönnies termed *Gemeinschaft,* to that of an impersonal mass society known as *Gesellschaft* (Tönnies [1887] 1988).

The **Gemeinschaft** (pronounced guh-MINE-shoft) community is typical of rural life. It is a small community in which people have similar backgrounds and life experiences. Virtually everyone knows one another, and social interactions are intimate and familiar, almost as one might find among kinfolk. There is a commitment to the larger social group and a sense of togetherness among community members. People relate to others in a personal way, not just as "clerk" or "manager." With this more personal interaction comes less privacy: we know more about everyone.

Social control in the *Gemeinschaft* community is maintained through informal means such as moral persuasion, gossip, and even gestures. These techniques work effectively because people genuinely care about how others feel toward them. Social change is relatively limited in the *Gemeinschaft;* the lives of members of one generation may be quite similar to those of their grandparents.

By contrast, the **Gesellschaft** (pronounced guh-ZELL-shoft) is an ideal type characteristic of modern urban life. Most people are strangers and feel little in common with other community residents. Relationships are governed by social roles that grow out of immediate tasks, such as purchasing a product or arranging a business meeting.

Self-interests dominate, and there is generally little consensus concerning values or commitment to the group. As a result, social control must rely on more formal techniques, such as laws and legally defined punishments. Social change is an important aspect of life in the *Gesellschaft;* it can be strikingly evident even within a single generation.

Table 5-2 summarizes the differences between the *Gemeinschaft* and the *Gesellschaft* as described by Tönnies. Sociologists have used these terms to compare social structures stressing close relationships with those that emphasize less personal ties. It is easy to view *Gemeinschaft* with nostalgia as a far better way of life than the "rat race" of contemporary existence. However, the more intimate relationships of the *Gemeinschaft* come with a price. The prejudice and discrimination found within *Gemeinschaft* can be quite confining; ascribed statuses such as family background often outweigh a person's unique talents and achievements. In addition, *Gemeinschaft* tends to be distrustful of the individual who seeks to be creative or just to be different.

Lenski's Sociocultural Evolution Approach

Sociologist Gerhard Lenski takes a very different view of society and social structure. Rather than distinguishing between two opposite types of societies, as Tönnies had, Lenski sees human societies as undergoing change according to a dominant pattern, known as **sociocultural evolution.** This term refers to the "process of change and development in human societies that results from cumulative growth in their stores of cultural information" (Lenski et al. 1995:75).

"I'd like to think of you as a person, David, but it's my job to think of you as personnel."

In a *Gesellschaft,* people are likely to relate to one another in terms of their roles rather than their individual backgrounds.

Table 5-2 Comparison of *Gemeinschaft* and *Gesellschaft*

Gemeinschaft	*Gesellschaft*
Rural life typifies this form.	Urban life typifies this form.
People share a feeling of community that results from their similar backgrounds and life experiences.	People perceive little sense of commonality. Their differences in background appear more striking than their similarities.
Social interactions, including negotiations, are intimate and familiar.	Social interactions, including negotiations, are more likely to be task-specific.
There is a spirit of cooperation and unity of will.	Self-interests dominate.
Tasks and personal relationships cannot be separated.	The task being performed is paramount; relationships are subordinate.
There is little emphasis on individual privacy.	Privacy is valued.
Informal social control predominates.	Formal social control is evident.
There is less tolerance of deviance.	There is greater tolerance of deviance.
Emphasis is on ascribed statuses.	There is more emphasis on achieved statuses.
Social change is relatively limited.	Social change is very evident—even within a generation.

Think About It
How would you classify the communities with which you are familiar? Are they more *Gemeinschaft* or *Gesellschaft*?

In Lenski's view, a society's level of technology is critical to the way it is organized. He defines **technology** as "information about the ways in which the material resources of the environment may be used to satisfy human needs and desires" (Nolan and Lenski 1999:414). The available technology does not completely define the form that a particular society and its social structure take. Nevertheless, a low level of technology may limit the degree to which it can depend on such things as irrigation or complex machinery. As technology advances, Lenski sees society as evolving from preindustrial to industrial to postindustrial.

Preindustrial Societies

How does a preindustrial society organize its economy? If we know that, it is possible to categorize the society. The first type of preindustrial society to emerge in human history was the **hunting-and-gathering society,** in which people simply rely on whatever foods and fibers are readily available. Technology in such societies is minimal. Or-

ganized in groups, people move constantly in search of food. There is little division of labor into specialized tasks.

Hunting-and-gathering societies are composed of small, widely dispersed groups. Each group consists almost entirely of people related to one another. As a result, kinship ties are the source of authority and influence, and the social institution of the family takes on a particularly important role. Tönnies would certainly view such societies as examples of *Gemeinschaft*.

Since resources are scarce, there is relatively little inequality in terms of material goods. Social differentiation within the hunting-and-gathering society is based on such ascribed statuses as gender, age, and family background. The last hunting-and-gathering societies had virtually disappeared by the close of the twentieth century (Nolan and Lenski 1999).

Horticultural societies, in which people plant seeds and crops rather than subsist merely on available foods, emerged about 10,000 to 12,000 years ago. Members of horticultural societies are much less nomadic than hunters and gatherers. They place greater emphasis on the production of tools and household objects. Yet technology within horticultural societies remains rather limited. They cultivate crops with the aid of digging sticks or hoes (Wilford 1997).

The last stage of preindustrial development is the *agrarian society*, which emerged about 5,000 years ago. As in horticultural societies, members of agrarian societies are primarily engaged in the production of food. However, the introduction of new technological innovations such as the plow allows farmers to dramatically increase their crop yield. They can cultivate the same fields over generations, thereby allowing the emergence of still larger settlements.

The social structure of the agrarian society continues to rely on the physical power of humans and animals (as opposed to mechanical power). Nevertheless, the social structure has more carefully defined roles than in horticultural societies. Individuals focus on specialized tasks, such as repair of fishing nets or work as a blacksmith. As human settlements become more established and stable, social institutions become more elaborate and property rights take on greater importance. The comparative permanence and greater surpluses of agrarian society make it more feasible to create artifacts such as statues, public monuments, and art objects and to pass them on from one generation to the next.

Industrial Societies

Although the industrial revolution did not topple monarchs, it produced changes every bit as significant as those resulting from political revolutions. The industrial revolution, which took place largely in England during the period 1760 to 1830, was a scientific revolution focused on the application of nonanimal (mechanical) sources of power to labor tasks. It brought about changes in the social organization of the workplace, as people left the homestead and began working in central locations such as factories.

As the industrial revolution proceeded, a new form of social structure emerged. An *industrial society* is a society that depends on mechanization to produce its goods and services. Industrial societies rely on new inventions that facilitate agricultural and industrial production and on new sources of energy such as steam. Many societies underwent an irrevocable shift from an agrarian-oriented economy to an industrial base. No longer did an individual or a family typically make an entire product. Instead, specialization of tasks and manufacturing of goods became increasingly common. Workers, generally men but also women and even children, left the home to labor in central factories.

The process of industrialization had distinctive social consequences. Families and communities could not continue to function as self-sufficient units. Individuals, villages, and regions began to exchange goods and services and become interdependent. As people came to rely on the labor of members of other communities, the family lost its unique position as the source of power and authority. The need for specialized knowledge led to more formalized education, and education emerged as a social institution distinct from the family.

Postindustrial and Postmodern Societies

When the sociocultural evolutionary approach first appeared in the 1960s, it paid relatively little attention to how maturing industrialized societies may change with the emergence of even more advanced forms of technology. More recently, in evaluating the increasingly rapid pace of technological and social change, Gerhard Lenski and his collaborators have observed,

> The only things that might conceivably slow the rate of technological innovation in the next several decades are nuclear war, collapse of the world economy, or an environmental catastrophe. Fortunately, none of these appears likely in that time frame. (Lenski et al. 1995: 441)

Lenski and other sociologists have studied the significant changes in the occupational structure of industrial societies as they shift from manufacturing to service economies. Social scientists call these technologically advanced nations *postindustrial societies*. Sociologist Daniel Bell (1999) defines **postindustrial society** as a society whose economic system is engaged primarily in the processing and control of information. The main output of a postindustrial society is services rather than manufactured goods. Large numbers of people become involved in occupations devoted to the teaching, generation, or dissemination of ideas.

Bell views this transition from industrial to postindustrial society as a positive development. He sees a general decline in organized working-class groups and a rise in interest groups concerned with such national issues as health, education, and the environment. Bell's outlook is functionalist because he portrays postindustrial society as basically consensual. Organizations and interest groups will engage in an open and competitive process of decision making. The level of conflict between diverse groups will diminish, leading to much greater social stability.

Conflict theorists take issue with Bell's functionalist analysis of postindustrial society. For example, Michael Harrington (1980), who alerted the nation to the problems of the poor in his book *The Other America,* was critical of the significance that Bell attached to the growing class of white-collar workers. Harrington conceded that scientists, engineers, and economists are involved in important political and economic decisions, but he disagreed with

Bell's claim that they have a free hand in decision making, independent of the interests of the rich. Harrington followed in the tradition of Marx by arguing that conflict between social classes will continue in postindustrial society.

More recently, sociologists have gone beyond discussion of postindustrial societies to the ideal type of postmodern society. A *postmodern society* is a technologically sophisticated society that is preoccupied with consumer goods and media images (Brannigan 1992). Such societies consume goods and information on a mass scale. Postmodern theorists take a global perspective and note the ways that aspects of culture cross national boundaries. For example, residents of the United States may listen to reggae music from Jamaica, eat sushi and other types of Japanese food, and wear clogs from Sweden (Lyotard 1993).

The emphasis of postmodern theorists is on observing and describing newly emerging cultural forms and patterns of social interaction. Within sociology, the postmodern view offers support for integrating the insights of various theoretical perspectives—functionalism, conflict theory, feminist theory, interactionism, and labeling theory—while also incorporating other contemporary approaches. Feminist sociologists argue optimistically that, with its indifference to hierarchies and distinctions, postmodernism will discard traditional values of male dominance in favor of gender equality. Yet others contend that despite new technology, postindustrial and postmodern societies can be expected to experience the problems of inequality that plague industrial societies (Ritzer 1995a; Sale 1996; Smart 1990; Turner 1990; van Vucht Tijssen 1990).

Ferdinand Tönnies and Gerhard Lenski present two visions of society's social structure. While different, both approaches are useful, and this textbook will draw on both. The sociocultural evolutionary approach emphasizes a historical perspective. It does not picture different types of social structures coexisting within the same society. Consequently, according to this approach, one would not expect a single society to include hunters and gatherers along with a postmodern culture. By contrast, sociologists frequently observe that a *Gemeinschaft* and a *Gesellschaft* can be found in the same society. For example, a rural New Hampshire community less than 100 miles from Boston is linked to the metropolitan area by the technology of the modern information age.

The work of Tönnies and Lenski reminds us that a major focus of sociology has been to identify changes in social structure and the consequences for human behavior. At the macrolevel, we see society shifting to more advanced forms of technology. The social structure becomes increasingly complex, and new social institutions emerge to assume some functions previously performed by the family. On the microlevel, these changes affect the nature of social interactions between people. Each individual takes on multiple social roles, and people come to rely more on social networks rather than solely on kinship ties. As the social structure becomes more complex, people's relationships tend to become more impersonal, transient, and fragmented.

In the social policy section we will examine the impact of the AIDS crisis on the social structure and social interaction in the United States and other nations.

SOCIAL POLICY AND SOCIAL STRUCTURE

The AIDS Crisis

/schaefer8

The Issue

In his novel *The Plague,* Albert Camus (1948:34) wrote, "There have been as many plagues as wars in history, yet always plagues and wars take people equally by surprise." Regarded by many as the distinctive plague of the modern era, AIDS certainly caught major social institutions—particularly the government, the health care system, and the economy—by surprise when it initially became noticed by medical practitioners in the 1970s. It has since spread around the world. While there are encouraging new therapies to treat people, there is currently no way to

eradicate AIDS by medical means. Therefore, it is essential to protect people by reducing the transmission of the fatal virus. But how is this to be done? And whose responsibility is it? What role do social institutions have?

The Setting

AIDS is the acronym for *acquired immune deficiency syndrome.* Rather than being a distinct disease, AIDS is actually a predisposition to disease caused by a virus, the human immunodeficiency virus (HIV). This virus gradually destroys the body's immune system, leaving the carrier vulnerable to infections such as pneumonia that those with healthy immune systems can generally resist. Transmission of the virus from one person to another appears to require either intimate sexual contact or exchange of blood or bodily fluids (whether from contaminated hypodermic needles or syringes, transfusions of infected blood, or transmission from an infected mother to her child before or during birth). Health practitioners pay particular attention to methods of transmitting HIV because there is no cure or vaccine for AIDS at this time.

The first cases of AIDS in the United States were reported in 1981. While the numbers of new cases and deaths have recently shown some evidence of decline, there were 335,000 people living with AIDS or HIV by mid-2001, with more than 17,000 dying each year. Women account for a growing proportion of new cases. Racial and ethnic minorities account for 58 percent of all cases. Worldwide, AIDS is on the increase, with an estimated 40 million people infected and 3 million dying annually (see Figure 5-2). AIDS is not evenly distributed, and those ar-

eas least equipped to deal with it—the developing nations of sub-Saharan Africa—face the greatest challenge (Centers for Disease Control 2002; UNAIDS 2001).

Sociological Insights

Dramatic crises like the AIDS epidemic are likely to bring about certain transformations in a society's social structure. From a functionalist perspective, if established social institutions cannot meet a crucial need, new social networks are likely to emerge to fill that function. In the case of AIDS, self-help groups—especially in the gay communities of major cities—have organized to care for the sick, educate the healthy, and lobby for more responsive public policies.

The label of "person with AIDS" or "HIV-positive" often functions as a master status. People with AIDS or infected with the virus actually face a powerful dual stigma. Not only are they associated with a lethal and contagious disease, but they have a disease that disproportionately afflicts already stigmatized groups, such as gay males and intravenous drug

Figure 5-2

The Geography of People Living with HIV/AIDS, 2001

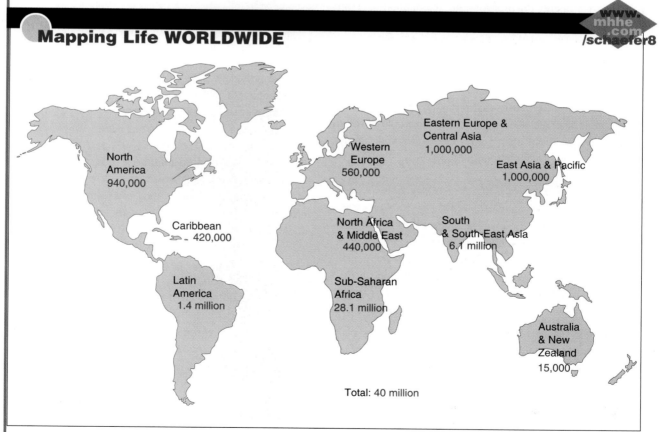

Mapping Life WORLDWIDE

www.mhhe.com /schaefer8

North America 940,000

Western Europe 560,000

Eastern Europe & Central Asia 1,000,000

East Asia & Pacific 1,000,000

Caribbean 420,000

North Africa & Middle East 440,000

South & South-East Asia 6.1 million

Latin America 1.4 million

Sub-Saharan Africa 28.1 million

Australia & New Zealand 15,000

Total: 40 million

Source: UNAIDS 2001:27.

users. This linkage with stigmatized groups delayed recognition of the severity of the AIDS epidemic; the media took little interest in the disease until it seemed to be spreading beyond the gay community. Viewed from a conflict perspective, policymakers were slow to respond to the AIDS crisis because those in high-risk groups—gay men and IV drug users—were comparatively powerless. However, studies in the United States show that people with the virus and with AIDS who receive appropriate medical treatment are living longer than before. This may put additional pressure on policymakers to address the issues raised by the spread of AIDS (Steinhauer 2000).

On the microlevel of social interaction, observers widely forecast that AIDS would lead to a more conservative sexual climate—among both homosexuals and heterosexuals—in which people would be much more cautious about involvement with new partners. Yet it appears that many sexually active people in the United States have not heeded precautions about "safe sex." Data from studies conducted in the early 1990s indicated a growing complacency about AIDS, even among those most vulnerable (*AIDS Alert* 1999).

Another interactionist concern is the tremendous impact that taking the appropriate medication has on one's daily routine. Tens of thousands of AIDS patients are having to reorder their lives around their medical regimens. Even infected patients without the symptoms of AIDS find the concentrated effort that is needed to fight the disease—taking 95 doses of 16 different medications every 24 hours—extremely taxing. Think for a moment about the effect such a regimen would have on your own life, from eating and sleeping to work, study, child care, and recreation (see Figure 5-3).

Policy Initiatives

Given the absence of a medical cure or vaccine, policy initiatives emphasize the need for more information about how AIDS is contracted and spread. In an address before the American Sociological Association, Canadian sociologist Barry Adam (1992) argued that sociologists can make an important contribution to AIDS-related research. He outlined four directions for such sociological research:

- How is information about AIDS produced and distributed? Is the distribution of information about how to have "safer sex" being limited or even censored?
- How does an AIDS "folklore"—false information about remedies and cures—emerge and become

integrated into a community? Why do certain communities and individuals resist or ignore scientific information about the dangers of AIDS?
- How are medical and social services made available to people with AIDS? Why are these services often denied to the poorest patients?
- How is *homophobia* (fear of and prejudice against homosexuality) related to fears concerning AIDS? In what ways does homophobia correlate with other forms of bias?

Adam's questions underscore the impact of the AIDS crisis on social interaction and social structure. Addressing these questions will allow policymakers to better assess such initiatives as sex education programs in schools, needle exchange programs, and policies regarding AIDS testing.

AIDS has struck all societies, but not all nations can respond in the same manner. In some nations, cultural practices may prevent people from dealing with the AIDS epidemic realistically. They are less likely to take the necessary preventive measures, including more open discussion of sexuality, homosexuality, and drug use. Prevention has shown signs of working among target groups, such as drug users, pregnant women, and gay men and lesbians, but these initiatives are few and far between in developing nations. The prescribed treatment for a pregnant woman to reduce mother-to-baby transmission of AIDS costs about $1,000—many times the average annual income in much of the world where risk of AIDS is greatest. Africa, for example, accounts for 80 percent of the world's AIDS deaths. Even more costly is the medication for adult patients with HIV, which costs $71,000 a year (Pear 1997a; Sawyer 2000; Specter 1998b; Sternberg 1999).

The high cost of drug treatment programs has generated intensive worldwide pressure on the major pharmaceutical companies to lower their prices to patients in developing nations of the world, especially sub-Saharan Africa. In 2001, bowing to this pressure, several of the companies agreed to make the combination therapies available at cost (about $600 per person per year). Even this much lower cost will not be easily met by the residents of developing countries so devastated by AIDS. Moreover, the prospect of cheaper medicine is sure to stimulate the demand for care, which, in turn, will create the need for more resources (Brundtland 2001).

Let's Discuss

1. Has information on how to avoid getting AIDS been made available to you? Do you personally know of a

Figure 5-3

Daily Dosing for AIDS

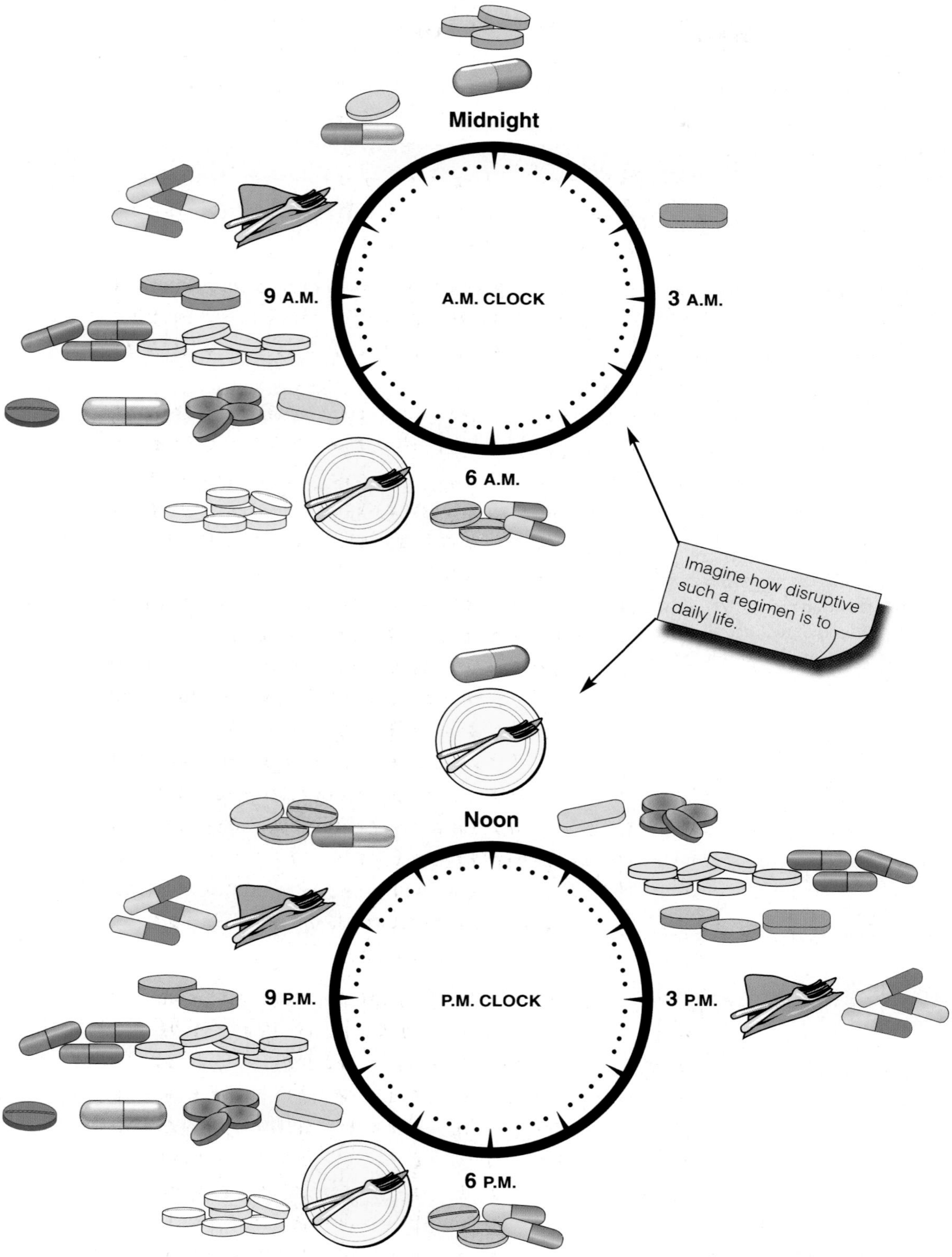

> Imagine how disruptive such a regimen is to daily life.

Note: Regimen may vary due to individual reactions to medications taken together. Shapes and colors of the 16 different prescriptive drugs are symbolic rather than realistic.

Source: Schaefer in consultation with Roxane Laboratories 2000.

case in which such information was withheld from someone or censored? If so, why and by whom?

2. Have you come across AIDS "folklore" (misinformation) on your campus or in your neighborhood? If so, how widespread do you think it is?

3. If you were a sociologist who wanted to understand why some people knowingly ignore the dangers of AIDS, how would you go about studying the problem?

Chapter Resources

Summary

Social interaction refers to the ways in which people respond to one another. *Social structure* refers to the way in which a society is organized into predictable relationships. This chapter examines the basic elements of social structure—statuses, social roles, groups, networks, and institutions.

1. We shape our social reality based on what we learn through our social interactions. Social change comes from redefining or reconstructing social reality. Sometimes change is *negotiated.*

2. An *ascribed status* is generally assigned to a person at birth, whereas an *achieved status* is attained largely through one's own effort.

3. In the United States, ascribed statuses, such as race and gender, can function as *master statuses* that have an important impact on one's potential to achieve a desired professional and social status.

4. With each distinctive status—whether ascribed or achieved—come particular *social roles,* the set of expectations for people who occupy that status.

5. Much of our patterned behavior takes place within *groups* and is influenced by the norms and sanctions established by groups. Groups serve as links to *social networks* and their vast resources.

6. The mass media, the government, the economy, the family, and the health care system are all examples of *social institutions* found in the United States.

7. One way to understand social institutions is to see how they fulfill essential functions, such as replacing personnel, training new recruits, and preserving order.

8. The conflict perspective argues that social institutions help to maintain the privileges of the powerful while contributing to the powerlessness of others.

9. Interactionist theorists emphasize that our social behavior is conditioned by the roles and statuses that we accept, the groups to which we belong, and the institutions within which we function.

10. Ferdinand Tönnies distinguished the close-knit community of *Gemeinschaft* from the impersonal mass society known as *Gesellschaft.*

11. Gerhard Lenski views human societies as changing historically as technology advances, which he calls *sociocultural evolution.*

12. The AIDS crisis affects every social institution, including the family, the schools, the health care system, the economy, and the government, as well as the social interactions of people touched by the epidemic.

Critical Thinking Questions

1. People in certain professions seem particularly susceptible to role conflict. For example, journalists commonly experience role conflict during disasters, crimes, and other distressing situations. Should they offer assistance to the needy or cover breaking news as reporters? Select two other professions and discuss the types of role conflict they might experience.

2. The functionalist, conflict, and interactionist perspectives can all be used in analyzing social institutions. What are the strengths or weaknesses in each perspective's analysis of social institutions?

3. In what ways does HIV serve to underscore issues of race, class, and gender in the United States today?

Key Terms

Achieved status A social position attained by a person largely through his or her own efforts. (page 112)

Agrarian society The most technologically advanced form of preindustrial society. Members are primarily engaged in the production of food but increase their crop yield through such innovations as the plow. (123)

Ascribed status A social position "assigned" to a person by society without regard for the person's unique talents or characteristics. (111)

Gemeinschaft Close-knit communities, often found in rural areas, in which strong personal bonds unite members. (121)

Gesellschaft Communities, often urban, that are large and impersonal, with little commitment to the group or consensus on values. (121)

Group Any number of people with similar norms, values, and expectations who interact with one another on a regular basis. (115)

Homophobia Fear of and prejudice against homosexuality. (126)

Horticultural societies Preindustrial societies in which people plant seeds and crops rather than subsist merely on available foods. (123)

Hunting-and-gathering society A preindustrial society in which people rely on whatever foods and fibers are readily available in order to live. (122)

Industrial society A society that depends on mechanization to produce its goods and services. (123)

Master status A status that dominates others and thereby determines a person's general position within society. (112)

Negotiated order A social structure that derives its existence from the social interactions through which people define and redefine its character. (111)

Negotiation The attempt to reach agreement with others concerning some objective. (110)

Postindustrial society A society whose economic system is primarily engaged in the processing and control of information. (123)

Postmodern society A technologically sophisticated society that is preoccupied with consumer goods and media images. (124)

Role conflict The situation that occurs when incompatible expectations arise from two or more social positions held by the same person. (113)

Role exit The process of disengagement from a role that is central to one's self-identity and reestablishment of an identity in a new role. (114)

Role strain The situation that occurs when the same social position imposes conflicting demands and expectations. (114)

Social institutions Organized patterns of beliefs and behavior centered on basic social needs. (118)

Social interaction The ways in which people respond to one another. (109)

Social network A series of social relationships that links a person directly to others and through them indirectly to still more people. (116)

Social role A set of expectations for people who occupy a given social position or status. (112)

Social structure The way in which a society is organized into predictable relationships. (109)

Sociocultural evolution The process of change and development in human societies that results from cumulative growth in their stores of cultural information. (121)

Status A term used by sociologists to refer to any of the full range of socially defined positions within a large group or society. (111)

Technology Information about the ways in which the material resources of the environment may be used to satisfy human needs and desire. (122)

Additional Readings

BOOKS

Albom, Mitch. 1997. *Tuesdays with Morrie.* New York: Doubleday. Social interaction can take place under unusual circumstances, as chronicled in the relationship between a young man and his ailing former sociology professor, Morrie Schwartz.

Bell, Daniel. 1999. *The Coming of Post-Industrial Society: A Venture in Social Forecasting.* New York: Basic Books. Updated with a new foreword, this book describes the current economic trend away from growing food or making products for a living and toward the provision of services and information as a livelihood.

Ebaugh, Helen Rose Fuchs. 1988. *Becoming an Ex: The Process of Role Exit.* Chicago: University of Chicago Press. Sociologist Ebaugh examines the phenomenon of becoming an "ex"—for example, an ex-convict, an ex-nun, a divorced person, or a mother who has lost custody of her children.

Epstein, Steven. 1996. *Impure Science: AIDS, Activism, and the Politics of Knowledge.* Berkeley, CA: University of

California Press. A sociologist examines AIDS research from the perspective of how it has been influenced by social and political forces.

Kephart, William M., and William M. Zellner. 2001. *Extraordinary Groups: An Examination of Unconventional Lifestyles.* 7th ed. New York: Worth. Among the groups described in this very readable book are the Amish, the Oneida community, the Mormons, Hasidic Jews, Jehovah's Witnesses, and the Romani (commonly known as Gypsies).

Lustig, Myron W., and Jolene Koester. 1999. *Intercultural Competence: Interpersonal Communication Across Cultures.* 3rd ed. New York: Longman. A blend of practical applications and theory concerning the importance of communicating with people from many different cultures.

Putnam, Robert D. 2000. *Bowling Alone: The Collapse and Revival of American Community.* New York: Simon and Schuster. A public policy scholar considers whether what he calls "social capital"—community

activity and group participation—has declined in the last few decades.

Shilts, Randy. 1987. *And the Band Played On: Politics, People, and the AIDS Epidemic.* New York: St. Martin's Press. Shilts, a reporter for the *San Francisco Chronicle,* offers this devastating critique of the nation's medical, political, and media establishments for allowing the AIDS epidemic to reach grave proportions before taking it seriously.

Skolnick, Jerome H., and Elliot Currie (eds.). 2000. *Crisis in American Institutions.* 11th ed. Needham Heights, MA: Allyn and Bacon. A collection of readings focused on the problems facing social institutions in the United States.

JOURNALS

Among the journals that focus on issues of social interaction and social structure are *Journal of Contemporary Ethnography* (formerly *Urban Life,* founded 1971) and *Symbolic Interaction* (1977).

⬤ Technology Resources

/schaefer8

Internet Connection

*Note: While all the URLs listed were current as of the printing of this book, these sites often change. Please check our website (**http://www.mhhe.com/schaefer8**) for updates and hyperlinks to this exercise and additional exercises.*

1. Our lives are both enriched and complicated by the vast array of social roles that we play. The text reveals how the variety of roles makes us susceptible to role conflict and role strain. See how the terms from pages 112–114 can be applied to the social life of a former president of the United States by logging onto The Whitehouse (**http://www.whitehouse.gov/history/presidents/eisenhower-clinton. html**). There you will find biographies and links on presidents from Washington through Bush. Choose a president and explore the material provided to answer the following questions:

   (a) What political, family, educational, and social roles has the president played in his life? What statuses has he held? Which of these are ascribed and which are achieved?

   (b) Has this mix of roles ever led to role conflict or role strain? How so?

   (c) Before becoming the leader of the United States, did the person you selected have a mas-

ter status? Why would the role of "president" be considered a master status?

   (d) Imagine you are a two-term president leaving office. How could you apply Helen Rose Fuchs Ebaugh's role exit model to the process?

   (e) If you were president, what impact would this position have on the other social roles that you currently have? How would family life, friendships, hobbies, and other daily activities be affected?

2. The Centers for Disease Control (CDC) is committed to preventing HIV infections and to reducing the incidence of HIV-related illness and death, in collaboration with community, state, national, and international partners. To learn more about HIV/AIDS, go to this website: **http://cdc.gov/hiv/dhap.htm.** Explore the site and answer the following questions:

   (a) Link to "Basic Statistics" and look at "Areas Reporting Most Cases." Which state or territory had the greatest number of cumulative AIDS cases?

   Click on your Back button. Link to "Slide Sets." Select "Surveillance by Race/Ethnicity." Download the slides (you may find it best to use Adobe Acrobat to do this).

(b) How has the proportional distribution of AIDS cases shifted among racial/ethnic groups in the United States since the beginning of the epidemic?

(c) Of the 733,374 AIDS cases reported to CDC through 1999, Blacks and Hispanics accounted for what percent of children with AIDS?

(d) Scroll through the slides until you come to slide 16: AIDS Cases Reported in 1999 and Estimated 1999 Population, by Race/Ethnicity, United States. Study the slide and read the discussion below it. Why is the distribution of cases among some racial/ethnic groups disproportional to their distribution of the general population? Give examples.

(e) Look at slide 17: Adult/Adolescent AIDS Rates per 100,000 Black Population Reported in 1999. What is the AIDS rate per 100,000 Black population for your home state?

(f) Look at slide 19. What is the adult/adolescent AIDS rate per 100,000 Hispanic population for your home state?

(g) Look at slide 21. What is the adult/adolescent AIDS population per 100,000 White population for your home state?

(h) Click your Back button until you return to the first page. Read at least two responses to hoaxes and rumors. Write a brief summary of one hoax/rumor and the response to it.

(i) One focus of this chapter has been social interaction. Do you know anyone who has AIDS? What do you consider to be the master status of that person? How has the disease affected that person's social interactions?

3. This chapter opens with a discussion of a study conducted by Philip Zimbardo. This study, known as the Stanford prison experiment, provides a revealing glimpse into social interaction and social structure. The Stanford prison experiment website (**http://www. prisonexp.org**) presents a slide show and discussions of the experiment. Explore the site and view the slides; then answer the following questions:

(a) How was reality defined and reconstructed in this experiment?

(b) How did this experiment affect the achieved statuses of the students involved?

(c) Can you apply the concept of master status to anyone involved in the experiment? Explain.

(d) Discuss the social roles of the participants from both a functionalist and a conflict perspective.

(e) Your text discusses how Philip Zimbardo experienced role strain during the experiment. Do you think any of the students experienced role strain? Explain.

(f) The term *role exit* is used to describe the process of disengagement from a role that is central to one's self identity and reestablishment of an identity in a new role. Do you think it was difficult for both the guards and the prisoners to exit their roles and reestablish their identities as students? Explain.

Online Learning Center   www.mhhe.com/schaefer8

Try the crossword puzzle in the student center of the Online Learning Center (**www.mhhe.com/schaefer8**). Working this crossword puzzle is a great way to see how familiar you are with the important terms and concepts related to social interaction and social structure. It's also an enjoyable way to review for exams.

GROUPS AND ORGANIZATIONS

the second annual
insect collector's
convention

december 23 & 24
at the los angeles
county arboretum
(818) 762-3762
for information

Groups come in all sizes and cover a broad array of interests. This poster promotes the annual convention of insect collectors in southern California.

ay Kroc, the genius behind the franchising of McDonald's restaurants, was a man with big ideas and grand ambitions. But even Kroc could not have anticipated the astounding impact of his creation. McDonald's is the basis of one of the most influential developments in contemporary society. Its reverberations extend far beyond its point of origin in the United States and in the fast-food business. It has influenced a wide range of undertakings, indeed the way of life, of a significant portion of the world. And that impact is likely to expand at an accelerating rate.

However, this is not a book about McDonald's, or even about the fast-food business. . . . Rather, McDonald's serves here as the major example, the paradigm, of a wide-ranging process I call *McDonaldization*. . . . As you will see, McDonaldization affects not only the restaurant business but also education, work, health care, travel, leisure, dieting, politics, the family, and virtually every other aspect of society. McDonaldization has shown every sign of being an inexorable process, sweeping through seemingly impervious institutions and regions of the world. . . .

Other types of businesses are increasingly adapting the principles of the fast-food industry to their needs. Said the vice-chairman of Toys 'R' Us, "We want to be thought of as a sort of McDonald's of toys." . . . Other chains with similar ambitions include Jiffy Lube, AAMCO Transmissions, Midas Muffler & Brake Shops, Hair Plus, H&R Block, Pearle Vision Centers. . . .

Other nations have developed their own variants of this American institution. . . . Paris, a city whose love for fine cuisine might lead you to think it would prove immune to fast food, has a large number of fast-food croissanteries; the revered French bread has also been McDonaldized. India has a chain of fast-food restaurants, Nirula's, that sells mutton burgers (about 80% of Indians are Hindus, who eat no beef) as well as local Indian cuisine. Mos Burgers is a Japanese chain with over fifteen hundred restaurants that, in addition to the usual fare, sell Teriyaki chicken burgers, rice burgers, and "Oshiruko with brown rice cake." Russkoye Bistro, a Russian chain, sells traditional Russian fare such as pirogi (meat and vegetable pies), blini (thin pancakes), Cossack apricot curd tart, and, of course, vodka. . . .

McDonald's is such a powerful model that many businesses have acquired nicknames beginning with Mc. Examples include "McDentists" and "McDoctors," meaning drive-in clinics designed to deal quickly and efficiently with minor dental and medical problems; "McChild" care centers, meaning child care centers such as Kinder-Care; "McStables," designating the nationwide race horse-training operation of Wayne Lucas; and "McPaper," designating the newspaper *USA TODAY*. (Ritzer 2000:1–4, 10) ■ ◕

Additional information about this excerpt and about those that open each subsequent chapter can be found on the SocWorld CD-ROM that accompanies this text.

n this excerpt from *The McDonaldization of Society*, sociologist George Ritzer contemplates the enormous influence of a well-known fast-food organization on modern-day culture and social life. Ritzer defines **McDonaldization** as "the process by which the principles of the fast-food restaurant are coming to dominate more and more sectors of American society as well as the rest of the world" (Ritzer 2000:1). In his book, he shows how the business principles on which the fast-food industry is founded—efficiency, calculability, predictability, and control—have changed not only the way Americans do business, but the way they live their lives.

Despite the runaway success of McDonald's and its imitators, and the advantages these enterprises bring to millions of people around the world, Ritzer is critical of their effect on society. The waste and environmental degradation created by billions of disposable containers and the dehumanized work routines of fast-food crews are two of the disadvantages he cites in his critique. Would the modern world be a better one, Ritzer asks, if it were less McDonaldized?

This chapter considers the impact of groups and organizations on social interaction. Do we behave differently in large groups than in small ones? How do we make large organizations manageable? What effect are social changes today having on the structure of groups? The chapter begins by noting the distinctions between various types of groups, with particular attention given to the dynamics of small groups. We will examine how and why formal organizations came into existence and describe Max Weber's model of the modern bureaucracy. We'll also look at organizational change and technology's impact on the organization of the workplace. The social policy section will focus on the status of organized labor unions today. ∎

Understanding Groups

Most of us use the term *group* loosely to describe any collection of individuals, whether three strangers sharing an elevator or hundreds attending a rock concert. However, in sociological terms a **group** is any number of people with similar norms, values, and expectations who interact with one another on a regular basis. College sororities and fraternities, dance companies, tenants' associations, and chess clubs are all considered examples of groups. The important point is that members of a group share some sense of belonging. This characteristic distinguishes groups from mere *aggregates* of people, such as passengers who happen to be together on an airplane flight, or from *categories* of people, those who share a common feature (such as being retired) but otherwise do not act together.

Consider the case of a college *a cappella* singing group. It has agreed-upon values and social norms. All members want to improve their singing skills and schedule lots of performances. In addition, like many groups, the singing ensemble has both a formal and an informal structure. The members meet regularly to rehearse; they choose leaders to run the rehearsals and manage their affairs. At the same time, some group members may take on unofficial leadership roles by coaching new members in singing techniques and performing skills.

The study of groups has become an important part of sociological investigation because they play such a key role in the transmission of culture. As we interact with others, we pass on our ways of thinking and acting—from language and values to ways of dressing and leisure activities.

Types of Groups

Sociologists have made a number of useful distinctions between types of groups—primary and secondary groups, in-groups and out-groups, and reference groups.

Primary and Secondary Groups

Charles Horton Cooley (1902:2357) coined the term **primary group** to refer to a small group characterized by intimate, face-to-face association and cooperation. The members of a street gang constitute a primary group; so do members of a family living in the same household, as well as a group of "sisters" in a college sorority.

Primary groups play a pivotal role both in the socialization process (see Chapter 4) and in the development of roles and statuses (see Chapter 5). Indeed, primary groups can be instrumental in a person's day-to-day existence. When we find ourselves identifying closely with a group, it is probably a primary group.

We also participate in many groups that are not characterized by close bonds of friendship, such as large college classes and business associations. The term **secondary group** refers to a formal, impersonal group in which there is little social intimacy or mutual understanding (see Table 6-1). The distinction between primary and secondary groups is not always clear-cut. Some social clubs may become so large and impersonal that they no longer function as primary groups.

p. 115

Table 6-1	Comparison of Primary and Secondary Groups	
Primary Group	**Secondary Group**
Generally small	Usually large
Relatively long period of interaction	Relatively short duration, often temporary
Intimate, face-to-face association	Little social intimacy or mutual understanding
Some emotional depth in relationships	Relationships generally superficial
Cooperative, friendly	More formal and impersonal

Secondary groups often emerge in the workplace among those who share special understandings about their occupation. Almost all of us have come in contact with people who deliver food, but, using observation research, two sociologists have given us new understanding of the secondary group ties that emerge in this occupation (see Box 6-1).

In-Groups and Out-Groups

A group can hold special meaning for members because of its relationship to other groups. People in one group sometimes feel antagonistic to or threatened by another group, especially if that group is perceived as being different culturally or racially. Sociologists identify these "we" and "they" feelings by using two terms first employed by William Graham Sumner (1906): *in-group* and *out-group*.

An **in-group** can be defined as any group or category to which people feel they belong. Simply put, it comprises everyone who is regarded as "we" or "us." The in-group may be as narrow as a teenage clique or as broad as an entire society. The very existence of an in-group implies that there is an out-group viewed as "they" or "them." An **out-group** is a group or category to which people feel they do *not* belong.

In-group members typically feel distinct and superior, and see themselves as better than people in the out-group. Proper behavior for the in-group is simultaneously viewed as unacceptable behavior for the out-group. This double standard enhances the sense of superiority. Sociologist Robert Merton (1968) describes this process as the conversion of "in-group virtues" into "out-group vices." We can see this differential standard operating in worldwide discussions of terrorism. When a group or a nation

takes aggressive actions, it usually justifies them as necessary, even if civilians are hurt and killed. Opponents are quick to label such actions with the emotion-laden term of "terrorist" and appeal to the world community for condemnation. Yet these same people may themselves retaliate with actions that hurt civilians, which the first group will then condemn.

Conflict between in-groups and out-groups can turn violent on a personal as well as a political level. In 1999 two disaffected students at Columbine High School in Littleton, Colorado, launched an attack on the school that left 15 students and teachers dead, including themselves. The gunmen, members of an out-group that other students referred to as the Trenchcoat Mafia, apparently resented the taunting of an in-group referred to as the Jocks. Similar episodes have occurred in schools across the nation, where rejected adolescents, overwhelmed by personal and family problems, peer group pressure, academic responsibilities, or media images of violence, have struck out against more popular classmates.

In-group members who actively provoke out-group members may have their own problems, including limited time and attention from working parents. Sociologists David Stevenson and Barbara Schneider (1999), who studied 7,000 teenagers, found that despite many opportunities for group membership, young people spend an average of

"So long, Bill. This is my club. You can't come in."

An exclusive social club is an in-group whose members consider themselves superior to others.

Research in Action

6-1 Pizza Delivery Employees as a Secondary Group

We all tend to take pizza delivery for granted. We may not even take note of the person who brings the pizza to our door. But sociologists Patrick Kinkade and Michael Katovich did. Using an interactionist perspective they explored the social relationships that developed among urban pizza delivery drivers as they socialized during work while waiting for orders and after work in bars. In fact, one of the researchers spent 18 months as a pizza delivery person at three locales in Ft. Worth, Texas. What they found was that pizza deliverers form a tight network based on the ordinary transactions and the occasional dangerous interactions of their profession.

Within their culture, the pizza delivery drivers take risks and receive minimal rewards. While attacks on them are usually publicized, they are not documented statistically. But the drivers themselves are well aware of the possible dangers and talk to one another a great deal about them. During the observation period, two drivers were robbed and eight others were "tailed," resulting in four automobile accidents.

The researchers found that the world of this secondary group is "hypermasculine," with racist and sexist overtones. The drivers uniformly characterized the dangers to their safety as coming from members of racial and ethnic communities, even when there was no evidence of this. The drivers also regularly boasted of their sexual prowess and told and retold accounts of sexual favors they received from customers.

Among the 106 drivers studied by the researchers, five types emerged:

- *The comedian.* This individual uses humor to neutralize or trivialize the anxiety of making runs into neighborhoods perceived as high-risk.

> **Within their culture, the pizza delivery drivers take risks and receive minimal rewards.**

- *The adventurer.* The adventurer claims to invite problems and actually looks forward to testing himself in dangerous situations.
- *The denier.* This individual attempts to neutralize anxiety by suggesting a problem does not exist or is exaggerated.
- *The fatalist.* This person recognizes and admits the risk of danger but simply accepts it without making any effort to neutralize it.

- *The pro.* The pro generally has had a long history in the delivery business, having worked for several pizza services, often serving as an assistant manager, if not a manager, at one of the other stores.

In general, the researchers found through observation and interview that urban pizza deliverers derive more satisfaction from their secondary group membership than from monetary rewards. Group membership and identity, therefore, are very important. The study shows how people, especially in urban environments, make use of secondary groups to "carve out a niche" in the larger social world. They accept their identity as a delivery person and assume a particular type that they feel comfortable with.

Let's Discuss

1. Think about a secondary group to which you belong. Can you identify any common role types? If so, describe them.
2. If you were to do research like that of Kinkade and Katovich, what group would you choose to study? What research techniques would you use?

Source: Kinkade and Katovich 1997.

three-and-a-half hours alone every day. While youths may claim they want privacy, they also crave attention, and striking out at members of an in-group or out-group, be they the wrong gender, race, or friendship group, seems to be one way to get it.

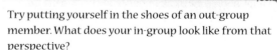

Imagine

Try putting yourself in the shoes of an out-group member. What does your in-group look like from that perspective?

Reference Groups

Both in-groups and primary groups can dramatically influence the way an individual thinks and behaves. Sociologists call any group that individuals use as a standard for evaluating themselves and their own behavior a *reference group*. For example, a high school student who aspires to join a social circle of hip-hop music devotees will pattern his or her behavior after that of the group. The student will begin dressing like these peers, listening to the same tapes and CDs, and hanging out at the same stores and clubs.

Reference groups have two basic purposes. They serve a normative function by setting and enforcing standards of conduct and belief. The high school student who wants the approval of the hip-hop crowd will have to follow the group's dictates to at least some extent. Reference groups also perform a comparison function by serving as a standard against which people can measure themselves and others. An actor will evaluate himself or herself against a reference group composed of others in the acting profession (Merton and Kitt 1950).

Reference groups may help the process of anticipatory socialization. For example, a college student majoring in finance may read *The Wall Street Journal,* study the annual reports of corporations, and listen to midday stock market news on the radio. The student is using financial experts as a reference group to which he or she aspires.

p. 94 ◄—

Often, two or more reference groups influence us at the same time. Our family members, neighbors, and coworkers all shape different aspects of our self-evaluation. In addition, reference group attachments change during the life cycle. A corporate executive who quits the rat race at age 45 to become a social worker will find new reference groups to use as standards for evaluation. We shift reference groups as we take on different statuses during our lives.

Studying Small Groups

Sociological research on the microlevel and research from the interactionist perspective usually focus on the study of small groups. The term **small group** refers to a group small enough for all members to interact simultaneously, that is, to talk with one another or at least be well acquainted. Certain primary groups, such as families, may also be classified as small groups. However, many small groups differ from primary groups in that they do not necessarily offer the intimate personal relationships characteristic of primary groups. For example, a manufacturer may bring together its seven-member regional sales staff twice a year for an intensive sales conference. The salespeople, who live in different cities and rarely see one another, constitute a small secondary group, not a primary group.

We may think of small groups as being informal and unpatterned; yet, as interactionist researchers have revealed, there are distinct and predictable processes at work in the functioning of small groups. A long-term ethnographic study of street gangs in Chicago revealed an elaborate structure resembling that of a family business. A street gang there is composed of several geographically based units called *sets,* each of which possesses a leader, lower-ranking officers, and a rank-and-file membership. Besides staffing the economic network of the drug trade, gang members develop relationships with tenant leaders in public housing projects and participate in nondelinquent social activities important to the maintenance of their authority in the neighborhood (Venkatesh 2000).

Size of a Group

At what point does a collection of people become too large to be called a small group? That is not clear. If there are more than 20 members, it is difficult for individuals to interact regularly in a direct and intimate manner. But even within a range of 2 to 20 people, group size can substantially alter the quality of social relationships. For example, as the number of group participants increases, the most active communicators become even more active relative to others. Therefore, a person who dominates a group of 3 or 4 members will be relatively more dominant in a 15-person group.

Group size also has noticeable social implications for members who do not assume leadership roles. In a larger group, each member has less time to speak, more points of view to absorb, and a more elaborate structure to function in. At the same time, an individual has greater freedom to ignore certain members or viewpoints than he or

Groups come in all types and sizes. The members of this Manchester, Vermont, group belong to a national club of bicycle history buffs called the Wheelmen. They take their Victorian-era bicycles out for rides, often dressed in period costume from the late 1800s, as shown here.

she would in a smaller group. It is harder to disregard someone in a 4-person workforce than in an office with 30 employees or someone in a string quartet than in a college band with 50 members.

German sociologist Georg Simmel (1858–1918) is credited as the first sociologist to emphasize the importance of interaction processes within groups and note how they change as group size changes. The simplest of all social groups or relationships is the *dyad,* or two-member group. A wife and a husband constitute a dyad, as does a business partnership or a singing duo. In a dyad, one is able to achieve a special level of intimacy that cannot be duplicated in larger groups. However, as Simmel ([1917] 1950) noted, a dyad, unlike any other group, can be destroyed by the loss of a single member. Therefore, the threat of termination hangs over a dyadic relationship perhaps more than over any other type.

Obviously, the introduction of one additional person to a dyad dramatically transforms the character of the small group. The dyad now becomes a three-member group, or *triad.* The new member has many ways of interacting with and influencing the dynamics of the group. The new person may play a *unifying* role within a triad. When a married couple has its first child, the baby may serve to bind the group closer together. A newcomer may also play a *mediating* role within a three-person group. If two roommates in an apartment are perpetually sniping at each other, the third roommate may attempt to remain on good terms with both and arrange compromise solutions to problems. Finally, a member of a triad can choose to employ a *divide-and-rule* strategy. This is the case, for example, with a coach who hopes to gain greater control over two assistants by making them rivals (Nixon 1979).

Coalitions

As groups grow to the size of triads or larger, we can expect coalitions to develop. A *coalition* is a temporary or permanent alliance geared toward a common goal. Coalitions can be broad-based or narrow, and can take on many different objectives. Sociologist William Julius Wilson (1999b) has described community-based organizations in Texas that include Whites and Latinos, working class and affluent, who have banded together to work for improved sidewalks, better drainage systems, and comprehensive street paving. Out of this type of coalition building, Wilson hopes, will emerge better interracial understanding.

Some coalitions are intentionally short lived. Short-term coalition building is a key to success in the popular TV program *Survivor.* In *Survivor I,* broadcast in 2000, the four members of the "Tagi alliance" banded together to vote fellow castaways off the island. The political world is also the scene of many temporary coalitions. For example, in 1997 big tobacco companies joined with antismoking

Survivor I's coalition, the "Tagi alliance": Kelly, Rudy, Susan, and Richard (left to right).

groups to draw up a settlement for reimbursing states for tobacco-related medical costs. Soon after the settlement was announced the coalition members returned to their decades-long fight against each other (Pear 1997b).

The effects of group size and coalitions on group dynamics are but two of the many aspects of the small group that sociologists have studied. Another area, conformity and deviance, is examined in Chapter 7. Although it is clear that small-group encounters have a considerable influence on our lives, we are also deeply affected by much larger groupings of people, as we'll see in the next section.

Understanding Organizations

Formal Organizations and Bureaucracies

As contemporary societies have shifted to more advanced forms of technology and their social structures have become more complex, our lives have become increasingly dominated by large secondary groups referred to as *formal organizations.* A *formal organization* is a group designed for a special purpose and structured for maximum efficiency. The United States Postal Service, the McDonald's fast-food Industry, the Boston Pops orchestra, and the college you attend are all examples of formal organizations. Organizations vary in their size, specificity of goals, and degree of efficiency, but they all are structured to facilitate the management of large-scale operations. They also have a bureaucratic form of organization (described in the next section).

In our society, formal organizations fulfill an enormous variety of personal and societal needs and shape the lives of every one of us. In fact, formal organizations have become such a dominant force that we must create organizations to supervise other organizations, such as the Securities and Exchange Commission (SEC) to regulate the brokerage companies. It sounds much more exciting to say that we live in the "computer age" than in the "age of formal organization"; however, the latter is probably a more accurate description of our times (Azumi and Hage 1972; Etzioni 1964).

Ascribed statuses such as gender, race, and ethnicity influence how we see ourselves within formal organizations. For example, a study of women lawyers in the nation's largest law firms found significant differences in these women's self-images. In firms in which fewer than 15 percent of partners were women, the female lawyers were likely to believe that "feminine" traits were strongly devalued and that masculinity was equated with success. As one female attorney put it, "Let's face it: this is a man's environment, and it's sort of Jock City, especially at my firm." Women in firms where female lawyers were better represented in positions of power had a stronger desire for and higher expectations of promotion (Ely 1995:619).

Characteristics of a Bureaucracy

A **bureaucracy** is a component of formal organization that uses rules and hierarchical ranking to achieve efficiency. Rows of desks staffed by seemingly faceless people, endless lines and forms, impossibly complex language, and frustrating encounters with red tape—all these unpleasant images have combined to make *bureaucracy* a dirty word and an easy target in political campaigns. As a result, few people want to identify their occupation as "bureaucrat" despite the fact that all of us perform various bureaucratic tasks. Elements of bureaucracy enter into almost every occupation in an industrial society.

Complaints about bureaucracy are not limited to the business world. During the 1990s, the bureaucratic nature of the United Nations' humanitarian efforts in Somalia came under attack. The five international agencies designated to run relief efforts in Somalia had more than 12,000 employees, of whom only 116 were serving in the impoverished, war-torn African nation. Moreover, like many bureaucracies, the relief apparatus was slow in dealing with a drastic problem. In the words of a former United Nations worker in Somalia, "The average U.N. person takes 15 days to reply to a fax. . . . 3,000 people can die in 15 days" (Longworth 1993:9).

Max Weber ([1922] 1947), first directed researchers to the significance of bureaucratic structure. In an important sociological advance, Weber emphasized the basic similarity of structure and process found in the otherwise dissimilar enterprises of religion, government, education, and business. Weber saw bureaucracy as a form of organization quite different from the family-run business. For analytical purposes, he developed an *ideal type* of bureaucracy that would reflect the most characteristic aspects of all human organizations. By **ideal type** Weber meant a construct or model that could serve as a standard for evaluating specific cases. In actuality, perfect bureaucracies do not exist; no real-world organization corresponds exactly to Weber's ideal type.

p. 11 ◀

Weber proposed that whether the purpose is to run a church, a corporation, or an army, the ideal bureaucracy displays five basic characteristics. A discussion of those characteristics, as well as the dysfunctions (or potential negative consequences) of a bureaucracy, follows. (Table 6-2 summarizes the discussion.)

p. 15 ◀

1. **Division of Labor.**   Specialized experts perform specific tasks. In your college bureaucracy, the admissions officer does not do the job of registrar; the guidance counselor doesn't see to the maintenance of buildings. By working at a specific task, people are more likely to become highly skilled and carry out a job with maximum efficiency. This emphasis on specialization is so basic a part of our lives that we may not realize that it is a fairly recent development in Western culture.

   The downside of division of labor is that the fragmentation of work into smaller and smaller tasks can divide workers and remove any connection they might feel to the overall objective of the bureaucracy. In *The Communist Manifesto* (written in 1848), Karl Marx and Friedrich Engels charged that the capitalist system reduces workers to a mere "appendage of the machine" (Feuer 1959). Such a work arrangement, they wrote, produces extreme

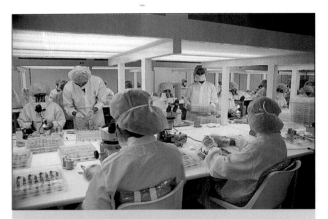

These workers in an electronics factory in India perform specialized tasks, a characteristic of division of labor in an organization.

alienation—a condition of estrangement or dissociation from the surrounding society. (Alienation will be discussed in greater detail in Chapter 18.) According to both Marx and conflict theorists, restricting workers to very small tasks also weakens their job security, since new employees can be easily trained to replace them.

Although division of labor has certainly enhanced the performance of many complex bureaucracies, in some cases it can lead to **trained incapacity;** that is, workers become so specialized that they develop blind spots and fail to notice obvious problems. Even worse, they may not care about what is happening in the next department. Some observers believe that such developments have caused workers in the United States to become less productive on the job.

The explosion of the U.S. space shuttle *Challenger* in 1986, in which seven astronauts died, reveals the negative consequences of a bureaucratic division of labor. While the *Challenger* disaster is remembered primarily as a technical failure, its roots lay in the social organization of the National Aeronautics and Space Administration (NASA), whose officials decided to proceed with the launch despite a potentially serious problem. According to sociologist Diane Vaughan (1996, 1999), the defect that caused the accident was discovered as early as 1977; in 1985 it was labeled a "launch constraint" (reason not to launch). On the day the *Challenger* was scheduled to take off, engineers from a company that manufactured a critical part recommended that NASA cancel the launch, but the 34 people who participated in the final prelaunch teleconference ignored their

The 1986 *Challenger* disaster was not just a technical failure but an example of the negative consequences of the bureaucratic division of labor.

warning. Ultimately, no one was held responsible for the catastrophe. At its worst, a narrow division of labor can allow everyone to avoid responsibility for a critical decision.

2. **Hierarchy of Authority.**   Bureaucracies follow the principle of hierarchy; that is, each position is under the supervision of a higher authority. A president heads a college bureaucracy; he or she selects members of the administration, who in turn hire their own staff. In the Roman Catholic church, the pope is the supreme authority; under him are cardinals, bishops, and so forth.

3. **Written Rules and Regulations.**   What if your sociology professor gave a classmate an A for having such a friendly smile? You might think that wasn't fair—that it was "against the rules."

Rules and regulations, as we all know, are an important characteristic of bureaucracies. Ideally,

Table 6-2 Characteristics of a Bureaucracy

Characteristic	Positive Consequence	Negative Consequence	
		For the Individual	For the Organization
Division of labor	Produces efficiency in large-scale corporation	Produces trained incapacity	Produces a narrow perspective
Hierarchy of authority	Clarifies who is in command	Deprives employees of a voice in decision making	Permits concealment of mistakes
Written rules and regulations	Let workers know what is expected of them	Stifle initiative and imagination	Lead to goal displacement
Impersonality	Reduces bias	Contributes to feelings of alienation	Discourages loyalty to company
Employment based on technical qualifications	Discourages favoritism and reduces petty rivalries	Discourages ambition to improve oneself elsewhere	Allows Peter principle to operate

through such procedures, a bureaucracy ensures uniform performance of every task. This prohibits your classmate from receiving an A for a nice smile, because the rules guarantee that all students will receive essentially the same treatment.

Through written rules and regulations, bureaucracies generally offer employees clear standards for an adequate (or exceptional) performance. In addition, procedures provide a valuable sense of continuity in a bureaucracy. Individual workers will come and go, but the structure and past records give the organization a life of its own that outlives the services of any one bureaucrat.

Of course, rules and regulations can overshadow the larger goals of an organization and become dysfunctional. What if a hospital emergency room physician failed to treat a seriously injured person because he or she had no valid proof of U.S. citizenship? If blindly applied, rules no longer serve as a means to achieving an objective but instead become important (and perhaps too important) in their own right. Robert Merton (1968) has used the term *goal displacement* to refer to overzealous conformity to official regulations.

4. **Impersonality.** Max Weber wrote that in a bureaucracy, work is carried out *sine ira et studio,* "without hatred or passion." Bureaucratic norms dictate that officials perform their duties without the personal consideration of people as individuals.

Although this is intended to guarantee equal treatment for each person, it also contributes to the often cold and uncaring feeling associated with modern organizations. We typically think of big government and big business when we think of impersonal bureaucracies. But today even small firms have telephone systems greeting callers with an electronic menu.

5. **Employment Based on Technical Qualifications.** Within the ideal bureaucracy, hiring is based on technical qualifications rather than on favoritism, and performance is measured against specific standards. Written personnel policies dictate who gets promoted, and people often have a right to appeal if they believe that particular rules have been violated. Such procedures protect bureaucrats against arbitrary dismissal, provide a measure of security, and encourage loyalty to the organization.

In this sense, the "impersonal" bureaucracy can be considered an improvement over nonbureaucratic organizations. College faculty members, for example, are ideally hired and promoted according to their professional qualifications, including degrees earned and research published, and not because of who they know. Once they are granted tenure, their jobs are protected against the whims of a president or dean.

Although any bureaucracy ideally will value technical and professional competence, personnel

Are organizational structures "culture free"? That is, would similar organizations in different cultures exhibit similar characteristics in how they are structured and controlled? That is a popular hypothesis among many social scientists. But a study of organizations in Russia suggests otherwise. Sociologists George Miller and Olga Gubin conducted in-depth interviews with the CEOs of 35 organizations in the greater Moscow area, including banks, hospitals, hotels, trading companies, and manufacturing concerns. On their evidence, organizations in Russia are to some extent "culture bound."

The Russian organizations differ in very basic ways from comparable Western organizations. In industrial societies, studies have generally found that, with increasing size and specialization of tasks, organizations tend to formalize rules and procedures and to *decentralize* control. Not only do lower-level executives have more decision-making power, but the formalized rules provide an impersonal means of ensuring that various organizational tasks get done. In Russia, however, Miller and Gubin found that increased organizational size, specialization, and formalization were all associated with *greater,* not less, centralization of control and decision making.

Why this difference? Miller and Gubin propose several cultural factors. First, Russia has a long history of authoritarian government, from the tsars through the communist revolution. Second, the Soviet system gave a few people tremendous authority. Most of the executives today

> **"If my employees don't like it or disagree with me, I fire them."**

were trained in that system and felt that "the leader is responsible for everything" (p. 83). They have brought their centralized communist managerial techniques to the new market economy. Finally, Miller and Gubin point to the turbulent economic environment in Russia today, which makes falling back on old practices easier than learning new managerial skills. Added to this turbulence is the pervasive influence of the Russian mafia. To protect their organizations from criminal infiltration, many chief executives say they have to rule with a heavy hand.

As new organizational leaders emerge and as Russians gain more experience with capitalist practices, it will be interesting to see if the centralization of authority persists. For now, as one bank president put it, "My organization is extremely centralized it is true. If my employees don't like it or disagree with me, I fire them."

Let's Discuss

1. What advantages and disadvantages does an authoritarian organizational structure have? What are the advantages and disadvantages of a highly decentralized organization?

2. Analyze your campus culture and bureaucracy. How much authority is centralized in the administration? What kinds of decision-making powers do professors and students have? If you could change the bureaucratic structure on campus, what kinds of changes would you make?

Source: Miller and Gubin 2000:83—84.

---

decisions do not always follow this ideal pattern. Dysfunctions within bureaucracy have become well publicized, particularly because of the work of Laurence J. Peter. According to the **Peter principle,** every employee within a hierarchy tends to rise to his or her level of incompetence (Peter and Hull 1969). This hypothesis, which has not been directly or systematically tested, reflects a possible dysfunctional outcome of structuring advancement on the basis of merit. Talented people receive promotion after promotion until, sadly, some of them finally achieve positions that they cannot handle with their usual competence (Blau and Meyer 1987).

The five characteristics of bureaucracy, developed by Max Weber more than 75 years ago, describe an ideal type rather than offer a precise definition of an actual bureaucracy. Not every formal organization will possess all of Weber's characteristics. In fact, there can be wide variation among actual bureaucratic organizations. In Box 6-2, we consider how some bureaucracies function today in Russia and how they differ from those in Western countries.

Bureaucratization as a Process

In a typical citizen's nightmare, you have to speak to 10 or 12 individuals in a corporation or government agency to find out which official has jurisdiction over a particular problem. You get transferred from one department to another until you finally hang up in disgust. Sociologists have used the term **bureaucratization** to refer to the process by which a group, organization, or social movement becomes increasingly bureaucratic.

Normally, we think of bureaucratization in terms of large organizations. But bureaucratization also takes place within small-group settings. Sociologist Jennifer Bickman

Mendez (1998) studied domestic houseworkers employed in central California by a nationwide franchise. She found that housekeeping tasks were minutely defined, to the point that employees had to follow 22 written steps for cleaning a bathroom. Complaints and special requests went not to the workers, but to an office-based manager. The impersonality and efficiency of this bureaucratic system is yet another example of the McDonaldization of the workplace.

Oligarchy: Rule by a Few

Conflict theorists have examined the bureaucratizing influence on social movements. German sociologist Robert Michels (1915) studied socialist parties and labor unions in Europe before World War I and found that such organizations were becoming increasingly bureaucratic. The emerging leaders of these organizations—even some of the most radical—had a vested interest in clinging to power. If they lost their leadership posts, they would have to return to full-time work as manual laborers.

Through his research, Michels originated the idea of the *iron law of oligarchy,* which describes how even a democratic organization will develop into a bureaucracy ruled by a few (the oligarchy). Why do oligarchies emerge? People who achieve leadership roles usually have the skills, knowledge, or charismatic appeal (as Weber noted) to direct, if not control, others. Michels argues that the rank and file of a movement or organization look to leaders for direction and thereby reinforce the process of rule by a few. In addition, members of an oligarchy are strongly motivated to maintain their leadership roles, privileges, and power.

Michels's insights continue to be relevant today. Contemporary labor unions in the United States and Western Europe bear little resemblance to those organized spontaneously by exploited workers. Conflict theorists have pointed to the longevity of union leaders, who are not always responsive to the needs and demands of the membership and seem more concerned with maintaining their own positions and power. (The policy section at the end of this chapter focuses on the status of labor unions today).

At least one study raises questions about Michels's views. Based on her research on "pro-choice" organizations, which endorse the right to legal abortions, sociologist Suzanne Staggenborg (1988) disputes the assertion that formal organizations with professional leaders inevitably become conservative and oligarchical. She notes that many formal organizations in the pro-choice movement appear to be more democratic than informal groups; the routinized procedures that they follow make it more difficult for leaders to grab excessive power (see also E. Scott 1993.)

While the "iron law" may sometimes help us to understand the concentration of formal authority within organizations, sociologists recognize that there are a number of checks on leadership. Groups often compete for power within a formal organization. For example, in an automotive corporation, divisions manufacturing heavy machinery and passenger cars compete against each other for limited research and development funds. Moreover, informal channels of communication and control can undercut the power of top officials of an organization, as we will now see.

Bureaucracy and Organizational Culture

How does bureaucratization affect the average individual who works in an organization? The early theorists of formal organizations tended to neglect this question. Max Weber, for example, focused on management personnel within bureaucracies, but he had little to say about workers in industry or clerks in government agencies.

According to the *classical theory* of formal organizations, also known as the *scientific management approach,* workers are motivated almost entirely by economic rewards. This theory stresses that only the physical constraints of workers limit productivity. Therefore, workers are treated as a resource, much like the machines that began to replace them in the twentieth century. Management attempts to achieve maximum work efficiency through scientific planning, established performance standards, and careful supervision of workers and production. Planning under the scientific management approach involves efficiency studies but not studies of workers' attitudes or feelings of job satisfaction.

It was not until workers organized unions—and forced management to recognize that they were not objects—that theorists of formal organizations began

Organizations have a human face, too. These hospital cooks may follow formal procedures in their jobs, but they also form an informal social network during lunch and breaks throughout the workday.

to revise the classical approach. Along with management and administrators, social scientists became aware that informal groups of workers have an important impact on organizations (Perrow 1986). An alternative way of considering bureaucratic dynamics, the *human relations approach,* emphasizes the role of people, communication, and participation within a bureaucracy. This type of analysis reflects the interest of interactionist theorists in small-group behavior. Unlike planning under the scientific management approach, planning based on the human relations perspective focuses on workers' feelings, frustrations, and emotional need for job satisfaction.

The gradual move away from a sole focus on the physical aspects of getting the job done—and toward the concerns and needs of workers—led advocates of the human relations approach to stress the less formal aspects of bureaucratic structure. Informal groups and social networks within organizations develop partly as a result of people's ability to create more direct forms of communication than under the formal structure. Charles Page (1946) has used the term *bureaucracy's other face* to refer to the unofficial activities and interactions that are such a basic part of daily organizational life.

pp. 42–43 A series of classic studies illustrates the value of the human relations approach. The Hawthorne studies alerted sociologists to the fact that research subjects may alter their behavior to match the experimenter's expectations. The major focus of the Hawthorne studies, however, was the role of social factors in workers' productivity. One aspect of the research investigated the switchboard-bank wiring room, where 14 men were making parts of switches for telephone equipment. The researchers discovered that these men were producing far below their physical capabilities. This was especially surprising because they would earn more money if they produced more parts.

Why was there such an unexpected restriction of output? The men feared that if they produced switch parts at a faster rate, their pay rate might be reduced or some might lose their jobs. As a result, this group of workers established their own (unofficial) norm for a proper day's work. They created informal rules and sanctions to enforce it. Yet management was unaware of such practices and actually believed that the men were working as hard as they could (Roethlisberger and Dickson 1939; for a different perspective, see Vallas 1999).

Voluntary Associations

In the mid-nineteenth century, the French writer Alexis de Tocqueville noted that people in the United States are "forever forming associations." By 2001, there were more than 23,000 voluntary associations. *Voluntary associations* are organizations established on the basis of common interest, whose members volunteer or even pay to participate. The Girl Scouts of America, the American Jewish Congress, the Kiwanis Club, and the League of Women Voters are all considered voluntary associations; so, too, are the American Association of Aardvark Aficionados, the Cats on Stamps Study Group, the Mikes of America, the New York Corset Club, and the William Shatner Fellowship. (Gale Research Group 2001).

The categories of "formal organization" and "voluntary association" are not mutually exclusive. Large voluntary associations such as the Lions Club and the Masons have structures similar to those of profit-making corporations. At the same time, certain formal organizations, such as the Young Men's Christian Association (YMCA) and the Peace Corps, have philanthropic and educational goals usually found in voluntary associations. The Democratic Party and the United Farm Workers union are considered examples of voluntary associations. Even though membership in a political party or union can be a condition of employment and therefore not genuinely voluntary, political parties and labor unions are usually included in discussions of voluntary associations.

The AARP is a voluntary association of people aged 50 and older, both retired and working, that advocates for the needs of older Americans. A huge organization, it has been instrumental in maintaining Social Security benefits to retirees. Here AARP volunteers staff a phone bank in an effort to get out the vote in Des Moines, Iowa.

Participation in voluntary associations is not unique to the United States. This textbook's author attended a carnival in London featuring bungee-jumping, at which participants were expected to jump from a height of 180 feet. Skeptics were given assurances of the attraction's safety by being told that the proprietor belonged to a voluntary association: the British Elastic Rope Sports Association. An analysis of 15 industrial nations, including the United States, showed that *active* memberships in voluntary associations typically increased during the 1980s and 1990s. Only relatively inactive memberships in religious organizations and labor unions have showed a decline. On the whole, then, voluntary associations are fairly healthy (Baer et al. 2000).

Voluntary associations can provide support to people in preindustrial societies. During the post–World War II period, migration from rural areas of Africa to the cities was accompanied by a growth in voluntary associations, including trade unions, occupational societies, and mutual aid organizations developed along old tribal ties. As people moved from the *Gemeinschaft* of the countryside to the *Gesellschaft* of the city, these voluntary associations provided p. 121 immigrants with substitutes for the extended groups of kinfolk that they had had in their villages (Little 1988).

Membership in voluntary associations is not random. The most consistent predictor of participation is socioeconomic status—that is, a person's income, education, and occupation. People of higher socioeconomic status are more likely to belong to and participate actively in such organizations. Partly, this reflects the cost of group memberships, which may exclude people with limited income from joining (Sills 1968; J. Williams et al. 1973).

Voluntary associations in the United States are largely segregated by gender. Half of them are exclusively female, and one-fifth are all-male. The exclusively male associations tend to be larger and more heterogeneous in terms of background of members. As noted in Chapter 5, membership in all-male associations holds more promise for making desirable business contacts than membership in all-female groups. Although participation varies across the population of the United States, most people belong to at least one voluntary association (see Figure 6-1), while more than one-fourth maintain three or more memberships.

Sociologists have applied functionalist analysis to the study of voluntary associations. David Sills (1968) has identified several key functions that these groups serve within our society. First, they mediate between individuals and government. Professional associations such as the American Medical Association mediate between their members and government in such matters as licensing and legislation. Second, voluntary associations give people training in organizational skills that is invaluable for future officeholders—and for better performance within most

Figure 6-1

Membership in Voluntary Associations in the United States

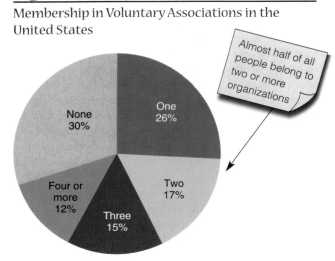

Source: J. Davis and Smith 2001:347.

> **Think About It**
> How many voluntary associations do you belong to? What functions do they serve?

jobs. Third, organizations such as the National Association for the Advancement of Colored People (NAACP), the National Women's Political Caucus, and the American Association of Retired Persons (AARP) help to bring traditionally disadvantaged and underrepresented groups into the political mainstream. In 1993, the National Association of Twentysomethings was established to provide its members (ages 18 through 29) with employment information and counseling, financial planning, and health insurance. Finally, voluntary associations assist in governing. During the influx of Central American refugees and immigrants in the 1990s, religious and charitable groups became deeply involved in helping resettle the new arrivals.

The importance of voluntary associations—and especially of their unpaid workers (or volunteers)—is increasingly being recognized. Traditionally, we have devalued unpaid work, even though the skill levels, experience, and training demands are often comparable with those of wage labor. Viewed from a conflict perspective, the critical difference has been that women perform a substantial amount of volunteer work. Feminists and conflict theorists agree that, like the unpaid child care and household labor of homemakers, the effort of volunteers has been too often ignored by scholars—and awarded too little respect by the larger society—because it is viewed as "women's work." Failure to recognize women's volunteerism obscures a critical contribution women make to a society's social structure (Daniels 1987, 1988).

Organizational Change

Just as individuals and relationships change, so too do organizations, both formal and voluntary. The most obvious changes often involve personnel: a new president of the United States is elected, an executive is fired, a star athlete retires. However, sociologists are most interested in how the organization itself changes.

These changes often relate to other social institutions, particularly the government. Its regulatory statutes, licensing procedures, tax laws, and contracting for goods and services directly influence the structure of formal organizations. For example, government policies relating to affirmative action (see Chapter 18) or disability rights (see Chapter 5) influence the internal decisions of organizations and may even require the hiring of new personnel.

In addition, an organization's goals may change over time along with its leaders and structure. A church starts a basketball league; an oil company purchases a movie studio; a chewing tobacco firm begins to manufacture ballpoint pens. Such actions take place when an organization decides that its traditional goals are no longer adequate. It must then modify its previous objectives or cease to exist.

Goal Multiplication

If an organization concludes that its goals must change, it will typically establish additional goals or expand upon its traditional objectives. For example, in the 1970s many colleges began continuing education programs to meet the needs of potential students holding full-time jobs and wishing to take classes at night. In the 1980s, colleges opened their campuses to the Elder Hostel organization, enabling older people to live and learn along with much younger college students.

Goal multiplication takes place when an organization expands its purposes. Generally, this is the result of changing social or economic conditions that threaten the organization's survival. The YMCA has practiced such goal multiplication. Reflecting its name, the Young Men's Christian Association had a strong evangelistic focus during its beginnings in the United States in the 1850s. Bible study and tent revival meetings were provided by the early YMCAs. However, in the early 1900s, the YMCA began to diversify its appeal. It attempted to interest members by offering gymnasium facilities and residence quarters. Gradually, women, Lutherans, Roman Catholics, Jews, and the "unchurched" were accepted and even recruited as members.

The most recent phase of goal multiplication at the YMCA began in the 1960s. In larger urban areas, the organization became involved in providing employment training and juvenile delinquency programs. As a result, the YMCA received substantial funding from the federal government. This was a dramatic change for an organization whose income had previously come solely from membership fees and charitable contributions. The YMCA's impressive range of activities currently includes social service programs for the disabled, day care centers, fitness classes for office workers, residence dormitories for college students and single adults, "learning for living" classes for adults, and senior citizens' facilities (Schmidt 1990).

These transitions in the YMCA were not always smooth. At times, major contributors and board members withdrew support because of opposition to organizational changes; they preferred the YMCA to remain as it had been. However, the YMCA has survived and grown by expanding its goals from evangelism to general community service (Etzioni 1964; Zald 1970).

The Young Men's Christian Association (YMCA) has experienced goal multiplication in recent decades. Its range of activities currently includes social service programs for people with disabilities, day care centers (shown here), fitness classes for office workers, residence dormitories for college students and single adults, and senior citizens' facilities.

Goal Succession

Unlike goal multiplication, **goal succession** occurs when a group or organization has either realized or been denied its goal. If the group is to continue, it must identify an entirely new objective. Cases of goal succession are rare because most organizations never fully achieve their goals. Those that do, such as a committee supporting a victorious candidate for public office, usually dissolve.

Sociologist Peter Blau (1964), who coined the term *succession of goals,* noted that organizations do not necessarily behave in a rigid manner when their goals are achieved or become irrelevant. Rather, they may shift toward new objectives. A case in point is the Foundation for Infantile Paralysis, organized in 1938. For some time, the foundation's major goals were to support medical research on polio and to provide assistance for victims of the disease. However, in 1955 the Salk vaccine was found to be an effective protection against paralytic polio. This left the foundation, so to speak, "unemployed." A vast network of committed staff members and volunteers was suddenly left without a clear rationale for existence. The group might have disbanded at this point, but instead it selected a new goal—combating arthritis and birth defects—and in 1958 took on the new name of March of Dimes Birth Defects Foundation (Etzioni 1964; Sills 1957).

Technology's Impact on the Workplace

In 1968, Stanley Kubrick's motion picture *2001: A Space Odyssey* dazzled audiences with its futuristic depiction of travel to Jupiter. We have passed 2001, and it is clear that we have not lived up to this target of outer space exploration. However, what about the portrayal of computers? In *2001* a mellow-voiced computer named HAL is very efficient and helpful to the crew, only to try to take over the entire operation and destroy the crew in the process. Computers can now successfully compete against chess champions, but they are as far short of achieving the artificial intelligence of HAL as earthlings are of accomplishing manned travel to Jupiter.

Still, the computer today is a commanding presence in our lives, and in the workplace in particular. It is not just that the computer makes tedious, routine tasks easier, such as electronically correcting the spelling of documents. It has affected the workplace in far more dramatic ways (Liker et al. 1999).

Telecommuting

Increasingly, the workforce is turning into *telecommuters* in many industrial countries. **Telecommuters** are employees who work full-time or part-time at home rather than in an outside office and who are linked to their supervisors and colleagues through computer terminals, phones, and fax machines (see Chapter 18). One national survey showed that next to on-site day care, most office workers want virtual offices that allow them to work off-site. Not surprisingly, the number of telecommuters increased from 8.5 million in 1995 to 23.6 million in 2000 (Carey and Jerding 1999; International Telework Association and Council 2000).

What are the social implications of this shift toward the virtual office? From an interactionist perspective, the workplace is a major source of friendships; restricting face-to-face social opportunities could destroy the trust that is created by face-to-face "handshake agreements." Thus, telecommuting may move society further along the continuum from *Gemeinschaft* to *Gesellschaft*. On a more positive note, telecommuting may be the first social change that pulls fathers and mothers back into the home rather than pushing them out. The trend, if it continues, should also increase autonomy and job satisfaction for many employees (Castells 2001b; Nie 1999).

Telecommuters are linked to their supervisors and colleagues through computer terminals, phones, and fax machines.

Imagine

If your first full-time job after college involved telecommuting, what do you think would be the advantages and disadvantages of working out of a home office? Do you think you would be satisfied as a telecommuter? Why or why not?

Electronic Communication

Electronic communication in the workplace has generated some heat lately. On the one hand, e-mailing is a convenient way to push messages around, especially with the CC (carbon copy) button. It's democratic too—lower-status employees are more likely to participate in e-mail discussion than in face-to-face communications, which gives organizations the benefit of the experiences and views of more of their workforce. But e-mailing is almost too easy to use. At Computer Associates, a software company, people were e-mailing colleagues in the next cubi-

cle. To deal with the electronic chaos, the company's CEO took the unusual step of banning all e-mails from 9:30 to 12 and 1:30 to 4. Other companies have limited the number of CCs that can be sent and banned systemwide messages (Gwynne and Dickerson 1997).

There are other problems with e-mail. It doesn't convey body language, which in face-to-face communication can soften insensitive phrasing and make unpleasant messages (such as a reprimand) easier to take. It also leaves a permanent record, and that can be a problem if messages are written thoughtlessly. In an antitrust case that the federal government brought against Microsoft in 1998, the prosecutors used as evidence e-mail sent to and from Microsoft's CEO Bill Gates. Finally, as will be discussed in detail in Chapter 23, companies can monitor e-mail as a means of "watching" their employees. Dartmouth professor Paul Argenti advises those who use e-mail, "Think before you write. The most important thing to know is what not to write" (Gwynne and Dickerson 1997:90).

SOCIAL POLICY AND ORGANIZATIONS

The State of the Unions

The Issue

How many people do you know who belong to a labor union? Chances are you can name a lot fewer people than someone could 50 years ago. In 1954, unions represented 39 percent of workers in the private sector of the U.S. economy; in 2001, they represented only 14 percent (AFL-CIO 2001). What has happened to diminish the importance of organized labor today? Have unions perhaps outlived their usefulness in a rapidly changing global economy dominated by the service industry?

The Setting

Labor unions consist of organized workers sharing either the same skill (as in electronics) or the same employer (as in the case of postal employees). Unions began to emerge during the Industrial Revolution in England in the 1700s. Groups of workers banded together to extract concessions from employers, as well as to protect their positions. They frequently tried to protect their jobs by limiting entry to their occupation based on gender, race, ethnicity, citizenship, age, and sometimes rather arbitrary measures of skill levels. Today we see less of this protection of special

interests, but individual labor unions are still often the target of charges of discrimination (as are employers) (Form 1992).

The experience of labor unions varies widely in different countries. In some, such as Britain and Mexico, unions play a key role in the foundation of governments. In others, such as Japan and Korea, their role in politics is very limited and even their ability to influence the private sector is relatively weak. Unions in the United States sometimes can have a significant influence on employers and elected officials, but their effect varies dramatically by type of industry and even region of the country (see Figure 6-2 on page 151) (Form 1992).

Few people today would dispute the fact that union membership is declining. What accounts for this decline? Among the reasons offered are the following:

1. **Changes in the type of industry.** Manufacturing jobs, the traditional heart of the labor union, have declined, giving way to postindustrial service jobs.

2. **Growth in part-time jobs.** Between 1982 and 1998, the number of temporary jobs rose 577 percent while total employment increased only 41 percent. It was only in 2000 that laws governing collective bargaining allowed temporary workers to join a union.

3. **The legal system.** The United States has not made it particularly easy for unions to organize and bargain, and some government measures have made it more difficult. A dramatic example was President Ronald Reagan's firing of 11,000 air traffic controllers in 1981 when their union threatened to walk off the job while seeking a new contract.

4. **Globalization.** The threat of jobs leaving the country has undercut the ability of union leaders to organize workers at home. Some say that labor union demands for wage increases and additional benefits have themselves spurred the exodus of jobs to developing nations, where wages are significantly lower and unions virtually nonexistent.

5. **Employer offensive.** Increasingly hostile employers have taken court actions to block efforts by unions to represent their workers.

6. **Union rigidity and bureaucratization.** Labor has been slow to embrace women, minorities, and immigrants. Furthermore, in some unions the election of leadership seems to dominate organization activity (AFL-CIO 2001; Clawson and Clawson 1999; Cornfield 1991; Greenhouse 2000; *Migration News* 2001).

Perhaps as a result of all these factors, confidence in unions is low. Only 1 out of 10 persons in the United States expresses a great deal of confidence in unions, more than for major corporations and government but far less than for educational and religious institutions and the military (Bureau of the Census 2000a:475).

Sociological Insights

Both Marxists and functionalists would view unions as a logical response to the emergence of impersonal, large-scale, formal, and often alienating organizations. This view certainly characterized the growth of unions in major manufacturing industries with a sharp division of labor. However, as manufacturing has declined, unions have had to look elsewhere for growth (Cornfield 1991).

Today labor unions in the United States and Europe bear little resemblance to those early unions organized spontaneously by exploited workers. In line with the oligarchic model developed by Robert Michels (see p. 144), unions have become increasingly bureaucratized under a self-serving leadership. Conflict theorists would point out that the longer union leaders are in office the less responsive they are to the needs and demands of the rank and file and the more concerned they are with maintaining their own positions and power.

Workers who "own" the company as majority stockholders, such as the United Airlines employees shown here, may experience role conflict. What happens, for example, when their salary demands diminish earnings returns?

Yet research shows that under certain circumstances union leadership can change significantly. Smaller unions are vulnerable to changes in leaders, as are unions whose members shift in composition, such as going from being predominantly White to African American or Latino (Cornfield 1991; Form 1992).

Many union employees encounter role conflict. For example, they agree to provide a needed service and then organize a "strike" to withhold it. This role conflict is especially apparent in the so-called helping occupations: teaching, social work, nursing, law enforcement, and firefighting. These workers may feel torn between carrying out their professional responsibilities and enduring working conditions they find unacceptable (Aronowitz and DiFazio 1994).

Sociologists have observed another role conflict: employees who suddenly become "owners" of a business.

Figure 6-2

Union Membership in the United States

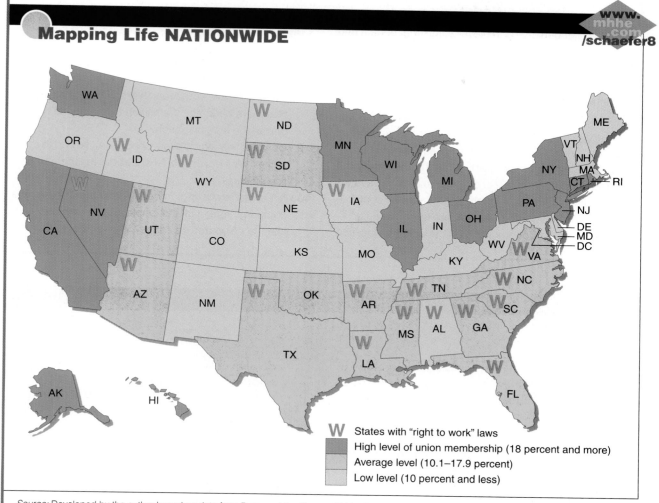

Mapping Life NATIONWIDE

www.mhhe.com/schaefer8

W States with "right to work" laws

High level of union membership (18 percent and more)

Average level (10.1–17.9 percent)

Low level (10 percent and less)

Source: Developed by the author based on data from Bureau of the Census 2000a:446; National Right to Work Legal Defense Foundation 2001a.

Think About It

What is the relationship in the states between union membership and the presence of "right to work" laws?

Take the case of United Airlines (UAL). Since 1994, the employees have owned the majority shares of the company. They may have changed the slogan from "fly the friendly skies" to "fly our friendly skies," but tensions still prevail. Union after union within UAL has threatened to strike or has performed slowdowns, even though the members constitute the major shareholders of the company. Obviously, while everybody agreed to call the workers "owners," the pilots, mechanics, airline attendants, and others did not act like owners, and UAL management did not treat them like owners (L. Zuckerman 2001).

Policy Initiatives

United States law grants workers the right to self-organize via unions. But we are unique among industrial democracies in allowing employers to actively oppose their employees' decision to organize (Comstock and Fox 1994).

A major barrier to union growth exists in the 20 states that have so-called right to work laws (see Figure 6-2). In these states, workers cannot be *required* to join or pay dues or fees to a union. The very term *right to work* reflects the anti-union view that a worker should not be forced to join a union, even if that union may negotiate on his or her behalf and achieve results that benefit that worker. This situation is unlikely to change in either direction. That is, right to work states will remain so; those without the laws typically have a strong union tradition or restrict union activities in other ways (National Right to Work Legal Defense Foundation 2001b).

European labor unions tend to play a major role in political elections. (The ruling party in Great Britain, in fact, is called the Labour party.) Although unions in the United States play a lesser political role, they have recently faced attacks for their large financial contributions to political campaigns. Debate over campaign finance reform in Congress in 2001 raised the question

of whether labor unions should be able to use dues to support a particular candidate or promote a position via "issue ads" that favors one particular party, usually the Democrats. (We will return to the topic of campaign financing in Chapter 17.)

Let's Discuss

1. What kinds of unions are represented on your college campus? Have you been aware of union activity? Has there been any opposition to the unions on the part of the administration?
2. Do you think airline pilots should be allowed to strike? Why or why not? How about teachers or police officers?
3. If a union is working on behalf of all the workers of a company, should all the employees be required to join the union and pay dues? Why or why not?

Chapter Resources

Summary

Social interaction among human beings is necessary to the transmission of culture and the survival of every society. This chapter examines the social behavior of groups, formal organizations, and voluntary associations.

1. When we find ourselves identifying closely with a group, it is probably a *primary group*. A *secondary group* is more formal and impersonal.
2. People tend to see the world in terms of *in-groups* and *out-groups*, a perception often fostered by the very groups to which they belong.
3. *Reference groups* set and enforce standards of conduct and perform a comparison function for people's evaluations of themselves and others.
4. Interactionist researchers have revealed that there are distinct and predictable processes at work in the functioning of *small groups*. The simplest group is a *dyad*, composed of two members. *Triads* and larger groups increase ways of interacting and allow for *coalitions* to form.
5. As societies have become more complex, large *formal organizations* have become more powerful and pervasive.
6. Max Weber argued that, in its ideal form, every *bureaucracy* shares five basic characteristics:

division of labor, hierarchical authority, written rules and regulations, impersonality, and employment based on technical qualifications.
7. Bureaucracy can be understood as a process and as a matter of degree; thus, an organization is more or less bureaucratic than other organizations.
8. When leaders of an organization build up their power, it can lead to oligarchy (rule by a few).
9. The informal structure of an organization can undermine and redefine official bureaucratic policies.
10. People belong to *voluntary associations* for a variety of purposes—for example, to share in joint activities or to get help with personal problems.
11. An organization's goals may change over time, either through the addition of goals (*goal multiplication*) or the replacement of old goals with new ones (*goal succession*).
12. Technology has transformed workplace organizations through telecommuting and electronic communication.
13. *Labor unions* are on the decline because of major shifts in the economy.

Critical Thinking Questions

1. Think about how behavior is shaped by reference groups. What different reference groups at different periods in your life have shaped your outlook and your goals? In what ways have they done so?
2. Within a formal organization, are you likely to find primary groups, secondary groups, in-groups, out-groups, and reference groups? What functions do these groups serve for the formal organization? What dysfunctions might occur as a result of their presence?
3. Max Weber identified five basic characteristics of bureaucracy. Select an actual organization familiar to you (for example, your college, a workplace, a religious institution or civic association you belong to) and apply Weber's analysis to that organization. To what degree does it correspond to Weber's ideal type of bureaucracy?

Key Terms

Alienation   A condition of estrangement or dissociation from the surrounding society. (page 141)

Bureaucracy   A component of formal organization in which rules and hierarchical ranking are used to achieve efficiency. (140)

Bureaucratization   The process by which a group, organization, or social movement becomes increasingly bureaucratic. (143)

Classical theory   An approach to the study of formal organizations that views workers as being motivated almost entirely by economic rewards. (144)

Coalition   A temporary or permanent alliance geared toward a common goal. (139)

Dyad   A two-member group. (139)

Formal organization   A group designed for a special purpose and structured for maximum efficiency. (139)

Goal displacement   Overzealous conformity to official regulations within a bureaucracy. (142)

Goal multiplication   The process through which an organization expands its purpose. (147)

Goal succession   The process through which an organization identifies an entirely new objective because its traditional goals have been either realized or denied. (148)

Group   Any number of people with similar norms, values, and expectations who interact with one another on a regular basis. (135)

Human relations approach   An approach to the study of formal organizations that emphasizes the role of people, communication, and participation within a bureaucracy and tends to focus on the informal structure of the organization. (145)

Ideal type   A construct or model that serves as a standard for evaluating specific cases. (140)

In-group   Any group or category to which people feel they belong. (136)

Iron law of oligarchy   A principle of organizational life under which even democratic organizations will become bureaucracies ruled by a few individuals. (144)

Labor unions   Organized workers who share either the same skill or the same employer. (149)

McDonaldization   The process by which the principles of the fast-food restaurant have come to dominate certain sectors of society, both in the United States and throughout the world. (135)

Out-group   A group or category to which people feel they do not belong. (136)

Peter principle   A principle of organizational life according to which each individual within a hierarchy tends to rise to his or her level of incompetence. (143)

Primary group   A small group characterized by intimate, face-to-face association and cooperation. (135)

Reference group   Any group that individuals use as a standard in evaluating themselves and their own behavior. (137)

Scientific management approach   Another name for the *classical theory* of formal organizations. (144)

Secondary group   A formal, impersonal group in which there is little social intimacy or mutual understanding. (135)

Small group   A group small enough for all members to interact simultaneously, that is, to talk with one another or at least be acquainted. (138)

Telecommuters   Employees who work full-time or part-time at home rather than in an outside office and who are linked to their supervisors and colleagues through computer terminals, phone lines, and fax machines. (148)

Trained incapacity   The tendency of workers in a bureaucracy to become so specialized that they develop blind spots and fail to notice obvious problems. (141)

Triad   A three-member group. (139)

Voluntary associations   Organizations established on the basis of common interest, whose members volunteer or even pay to participate. (145)

Additional Readings

BOOKS

Alfino, Mark, John S. Caputo, and Robin Wynyard. 1998. *McDonaldization Revisited: Critical Essays on Consumer Culture.* Westport, CT: Praeger. A multidisciplinary look at George Ritzer's approach to Max Weber's theory of rationalization and how it has been applied first to McDonald's restaurants and now to institutions worldwide.

Fagenson, Ellen A. 1993. *Women in Management: Trends, Issues, and Challenges in Managerial Diversity.* Newbury Park, CA: Sage. This anthology focuses on the continued underrepresentation of women in managerial positions within formal organizations.

Jaffee, David. 2001. *Organization Theory: Tension and Change.* New York: McGraw-Hill. A political scientist provides a concise analysis of the development and evolution of organizational theories, forms, and practices.

Kincheloe, Joe L. 2002. *The Sign of the Burger: McDonald's and the Culture of Power.* Berkeley, CA: University of California Press. Kincheloe explores the various ways McDonald's affects us, serving as a shorthand for the power of U.S. culture, a symbol of consumerism, and an indicator of the condition of labor in a globalized economy.

Nishiguchi, Toshihiro. 1994. *Strategic Industrial Sourcing: The Japanese Advantage.* New York: Oxford University Press. Drawing on eight years of research and more than 1,000 interviews, Nishiguchi offers insight into how very large industrial corporations have developed in Japan and have come to dominate that nation's economy.

Ritzer, George. 2000. *The McDonaldization of Society.* New Century Edition. Thousand Oaks, CA: Pine Forge Press. The most recent, complete elaboration of the McDonaldization thesis since Ritzer first advanced it in 1993.

Schleuning, Neala J. 1994. *Women, Community, and the Hormel Strike of 1985–1986.* Westport, CT: Greenwood. An in-depth look at the impact that a strike by a labor union had on 1,500 striking families.

Tannock, Stuart. 2001. *Youth at Work: The Unionized Fastfood and Grocery Workplace.* Philadelphia, PA: Temple University Press. Tannock writes from experience about the low-wage world of youth employment. He finds that unionization doesn't do much for young workers in U.S. supermarkets, but the unionized fastfood industry in Canada pays more attention to the concerns of young part-timers.

Vaughan, Diane. 1996. *The Challenger Launch Decision: Risky Technology, Culture, and Deviance at NASA.* Chicago: University of Chicago Press. A detailed look at the work culture of the National Aeronautics and Space Administration (NASA) and its suppliers—and the impact of that work culture on the fatal launch of the U.S. space shuttle *Challenger* in 1986.

Weber, Max. [1921] 1964. *The Theory of Social and Economic Organization.* Translated by A. M. Henderson and Talcott Parsons. Still a very readable account of organization theory, including the characteristics of a bureaucracy.

JOURNALS

Among the journals that focus on the study of groups and organizations are *Academy of Management Journal* (founded in 1958), *Administration and Society* (1969), *Administrative Science Quarterly* (1956), *Clinical Sociology Review* (1981), *Organization: Interdisciplinary Journal of Organization Theory and Society* (1994), *Organizational Studies* (1980), *Small Group Research* (formerly *Small Group Behavior,* 1970), *Social Psychology Review* (1948), and *Work and Occupations* (1974).

Technology Resources

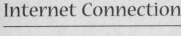

Internet Connection

*Note: While all the URLs listed were current as of the printing of this book, these sites often change. Please check our website (**http://www.mhhe.com/schaefer8**) for updates and hyperlinks to these exercises and additional exercises.*

1. One of Max Weber's most important contributions to sociology has been his examination of bureaucracies. To learn more, log onto The Dead Sociologists' Society, a website by Larry R. Ridener (**http://www2.pfeiffer.edu/~/ridener/DSS/INDEX.**

HTML). (This site is case sensitive.) Click on the picture of Weber and read "The Person," "A Summary of Ideas," and "The Original Work."

(a) What connections can be drawn between Max Weber's life story and his theory? How did childhood, education, work, and personal relationships shape his sociological ideas and research?

(b) What fact did you learn about Weber's life that interested you the most? Why?

(c) What connections can be drawn between Weber's "Types of Authority" and his thinking on bureaucracies? Give your own example of a leader from politics, history, or religion for each of Weber's type of authority.

(d) Do Weber's "Characteristics of a Bureaucracy" (described in Table 6-2 in the book as well as on the website) apply to your place of current or past employment? Why would the place where you work be considered a bureaucracy? Or why would it *not* be considered as such?

(e) Do the ideas from the chapter regarding primary and secondary groups, in- and out-groups, and reference groups also apply to where you work? How so?

2. Max Weber outlined the characteristics of bureaucracies: division of labor, hierarchy of authority, written rules and communications, impersonality, and employment based on technical qualifications. A modern twist on Weber's thinking can be found in the work of George Ritzer. To learn more about Ritzer's ideas regarding the McDonaldization of society, log onto Lycos (**http://www.lycos.com**) and enter the name George Ritzer in the search engine. Visit the sites that deal with McDonaldization and answer the following questions.

(a) What does Ritzer mean by McDonaldization? How are fast-food techniques relevant to the wider culture?

(b) Define the terms *efficiency, calculability, predictability,* and *control.* What examples of each concept does the site offer? Can you think of other examples?

(c) Where else do you see "McDonaldization" in our society?

(d) What does the "irrationality of rationality" mean?

(e) In what ways does Ritzer's work parallel Weber's?

(f) What arguments could be made by those who might disagree with Weber and Ritzer? Is there anything good or beneficial about living in a rationalized society?

3. The Young Men's Christian Association (**http://www.ymca.net/**) is the largest not-for-profit community service organization in America, working to meet the health and social service needs of 17.5 million men, women, and children in 10,000 communities. Click on "About the YMCA Movement" and then click on "History." Read the article and answer the following questions.

(a) Where and when was the YMCA founded?

(b) What did George Williams do?

(c) By the end of the Civil War, how many YMCAs were left?

(d) What did Moody and Mott do?

(e) Return to "History" and click on "YMCA World." Then click on "Facts." What are the three main priorities of the YMCA?

(f) Click on "Around the World." Pick two YMCAs in any two countries and compare and contrast them.

Online Learning Center

The focus of this chapter has been groups and organizations. Everyone is a member of an "in-group" and most people have also been members of an "out-group." Visit the student center in the Online Learning Center (**www.mhhe.com/schaefer8**) and link to the first Interactive Activity called "In-Groups," "Out-Groups," and "Unwords." For this activity, you will be asked to discuss your experiences as a member of an in-group and an out-group. You can also do the word scramble, which contains key words or phrases from your chapter.

CHAPTER 7

THE MASS MEDIA

Movies have long been an influential form of mass media in both reflecting and creating social mores. Sociologists are interested in the influence of other types of mass media as well, including television, newspapers, magazines, and online content.

Without question, Disney enjoys one of the best corporate images in the world. . . . Disney films, goods and services are widely perceived to promote prosocial values, including love, obedience, parental respect, independence, honesty, humility, integrity, courage, sacrifice, compassion, kindness, good citizenship, equality and democracy. . . .

Needless to say, a lot of people believe that if more media companies were like Disney, the world would be a better place. But not everyone shares this imagination.

Global Media as Menace   To many scholars and critics around the world, Disney and other media that exhibit the characteristics of the corporate form of organization are the stuff nightmares are made of. . . .

Global media don't really care about promoting a diversity of ideas, democratic principles or equality, the critics argue. All they care about is profits. . . . News and entertainment programming are trivial and do more to encourage consumerism and materialism than a robust debate about social inequities and injustices. And most Disney children's films, such as _The Lion King_, help reinforce a patriarchal value system that discriminates against women and other groups.

Global media have too much power, the critics argue. They point out that at the beginning of the 20th century most privately owned newspapers, magazines and book publishing companies were small and were owned and operated by individuals or families. . . .

But today . . . just 12 media corporations alone account for more than half of the $250 billion (U.S. dollars) in yearly worldwide revenues generated by the communications industry, which now includes radio, television, cable, satellite and online services. . . .

This power, the critics argue, represents a major threat to good journalism and democratic principles. The assumption underlying most Western political systems is that a diversity of ideas is crucial for good decision-making. But global media, the critics contend, are less likely to publish information that offends powerful groups and elites, because that kind of content could alienate advertisers, news sources or consumers and sink the bottom line. . . .

Global Media as Messiah   Some free-market media economists and media executives tell a different story. Global corporate media like Disney, they argue, are the organizational solution to inefficiencies and poor productivity in the marketplace. Global media emerge because national media are incapable of satisfying the information and entertainment needs of an increasingly complex and interdependent world. . . .

Because global media are products of or are heavily influenced by Western culture, they help spread values like representative democracy, free speech, equality for women and minorities, and the notion that a diversity of ideas is important. . . . And global media have the potential to help integrate disparate countries and cultures into a global village, reducing the potential for war or social conflict. . . . *(Demers 1999:3–6)* ■ ◉

Additional information about this excerpt and about those that open each subsequent chapter can be found on the SocWorld CD-ROM that accompanies this text.

I n his book *Global Media: Menace or Messiah?* Washington State University communications professor David Demers poses the title's question about global media organizations that generate messages for hundreds of millions of people around the world. This is a relatively new question: Until the advent of radio networks a hundred years ago, people had to wait days or weeks to read in newspapers what was occurring just a few hundred miles away. Now we can hardly escape from all news, all the time, as the electronic media keep us up to date with events as they happen throughout the world.

By **mass media** sociologists refer to the print and electronic instruments of communication that carry messages to often widespread audiences. Print media include newspapers, magazines, and books; electronic media include radio, television, motion pictures, and the Internet. Advertising, which falls into both categories, is also a form of mass media.

The pervasiveness of the mass media in society is obvious. Consider a few examples. TV dinners were invented to accommodate the millions of "couch potatoes" who won't miss their favorite television programs. Today *screen time* encompasses not just television viewing but also playing video games and surfing the Internet. Candidates for political office rely on their media consultants to project a winning image both in print and in the electronic media. World leaders use all forms of media for political advantage, whether it is to gain territory or to make a successful bid for the Olympics. AIDS education projects in parts of Africa and Asia owe much of their success to media campaigns.

Few aspects of society are as central as the mass media. Through the media we expand our understanding of people and events beyond what we experience in person. The media inform us about different cultures and lifestyles and about the latest forms of technology. For sociologists, the key question is how the mass media affect our social institutions and how they influence our social behavior. They want to know: Why are the media so influential? Who benefits from media influence, and why? How do we maintain cultural and ethical standards in the face of negative media images?

In this chapter, we will consider the ways sociologists help us to understand the mass media. First, we will take a look at how the various sociological perspectives view the media. Then we will examine just who makes up the media's audience as well as how the media operate, especially in their global reach. In the social policy section we consider whether violence shown in the media breeds violent behavior in their audience. ■

Sociological Perspectives of the Media

The penetration of mass media into people's homes has been dramatic over the last sixty years. As Figure 7-1 shows, the percentage of homes with televisions rose from less than 10 percent in 1950 to close to 100 percent in 2000. In what follows we'll examine the impact of the mass media from the points of view of the various sociological perspectives.

Functionalist View

The most obvious function of mass media is to entertain. Except for clearly stated news or educational programming, we often think the explicit purpose of the mass media is to occupy our leisure time—from comics and crossword puzzles in newspapers to the latest music releases playing on the radio or the Internet. While this is true, we may be overlooking other important functions of the mass media. They also socialize us, enforce social norms, confer status, and keep us informed about our social environment. One important dysfunction of the mass media is that they may act as a narcotic, desensitizing us to events (Lazarsfeld and Merton 1948; Wright 1986).

Agent of Socialization

The media increase social cohesion by presenting a more or less standardized, common view of culture through mass communication. Sociologist Robert Park (1922) studied how newspapers helped immigrants to the United States adjust to their environment by changing their customary habits and teaching them the opinions held by people in their new home country. The mass media unquestionably play a significant role in providing a collective experience for members of a society. Think about how the mass media "bring together" members of a community or even a nation by showing important events and ceremonies (such as inaugurations, press conferences, parades, state funerals, and the Olympics) and through coverage of disasters (such as the 1986

p. 98

Figure 7-1

Rise of the Mass Media

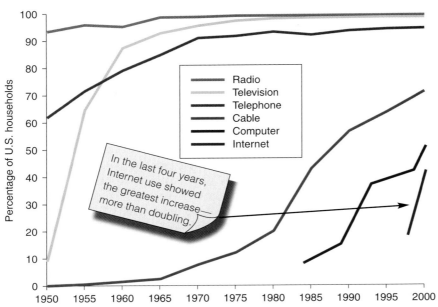

Source: Author's calculations based on Bureau of the Census 1975:43, 783, 796; 2000a:567: Newburger 2001; Television Bureau of Advertisers 2001.

Think About It
Why do you think more households today have a television than a telephone?

Television coverage of the terrorist attacks brought together these Penn State University students on September 11, 2001, to watch the unfolding news events.

Challenger explosion, the 1995 bombing in Oklahoma City, and the terrorist attacks on New York City and Washington, D.C., in 2001).

Which media outlets did people turn to in the aftermath of the 2001 tragedy? Television and the telephone were the primary means by which people in the United States "bonded." But the Internet also played a prominent role. About half of all Internet users—more than 53 million people—received some kind of news about the attacks online. Nearly three-fourths of Internet users communicated via e-mail to show patriotism, to discuss events with family and friends, or to reconnect with friends. More than a third of Internet users read or posted material in online forums. In the first 30 days alone, the Library of Congress collected in one Internet site more than half a million pages having to do with the terrorist attacks. As a Library director noted, "The Internet has become for many the public commons, a place where they can come together and talk" (Miller and Darlington 2002; Mirapaul 2001:E2; Rainie 2001).

The socialization process of the mass media is not universally well regarded. Many people worry about the effect of using television as a baby-sitter or the impact of violent programming on viewer behavior (see the social policy section). Some people adopt a blame-the-media mentality, in which the media is blamed for anything that goes wrong, especially with young people. In Box 7-1, sociologist Deena Weinstein explores why rock music is so often cast as a villain.

Enforcer of Social Norms

The media often reaffirm proper behavior by showing what happens to people who act in a way that violates societal expectations. These messages are conveyed when the

Research in Action

7-1 Knockin' Rock: Making Music a Social Problem

www.
mhhe.
com
/schaefer8

In 1990 rock artist Judas Priest was sued by the parents of two boys who carried out a suicide pact. The parents claimed that the lyrics of Priest's song "Beyond the Realms of Death" encouraged the boys to opt out of life. That case was dismissed, but it symbolizes the antagonism that rock music has aroused in society, creating a cultural divide between generations.

In fact, rock music has come under attack for decades as the source of all sorts of evils—sexual promiscuity, teen pregnancy, drug use, satanism, suicide, abuse of women, and communism, to name just a few. Critics, who generally come from the religious and political right, point to the obscene lyrics of heavy metal, the anger of rap songs, the decadent lifestyles of rock artists, and the explicit movements and gestures of the performers as causes of deviant behavior in the youth generation.

The criticisms have had an impact. The U.S. Senate held hearings about obscene music, and record companies instigated voluntary labeling, to alert buyers to explicit lyrics. Anxious parents today attempt to monitor the music their kids buy, the music videos they watch, and the Internet songs they download. In a word, rock music has been made into a social problem.

But is rock truly a social problem in that it causes undesirable behavior? Sociologist Deena Weinstein thinks not. In her research she found "no sociologically credible evidence that rock caused sexual promiscuity, rape, drug abuse, satanism, and suicide. Indeed, there is clear evidence that it is not the cause of such behaviors" (1999).

That is not to say that rock music has no part to play in these problems. According to Weinstein, rock music functions as a symbolic rebellion. It reflects the values

> Rock music has come under attack for decades as the source of all sorts of evils— sexual promiscuity, teen pregnancy, drug use, satanism, suicide, abuse of women, and communism, to name just a few.

of those who cherish the music, and these may be values that other groups in society want to inhibit. Rock music legitimizes the "disapproved" behaviors by giving them a symbolic form and making them public. Weinstein acknowledges, however, that symbols can have "complex and varied relations to behavior."

Weinstein shows how the symbolic function of rock has changed over succeeding generations, matching the concerns and values of each youth generation—from the early "rock 'n' roll" rebellion of teenagers against a society conforming to respectable middle-class codes in the 1950s to the defiant rap music and satanic appeals of heavy metal symbolizing the alienation of marginalized youth in the 1990s.

In every decade, rock's detractors have tended to be the older generation—generally white, middle class, politically conservative, and religious. Bewildered by rapid social changes and a youth culture resisting adult authority, the older generation makes rock into a convenient scapegoat for all their own fears and failures. The result is that they are more concerned with "killing the messenger" than paying attention to the message embedded in rock's symbolic rebellion. But, as Weinstein (1999) points out, "What could be more gratifying for a young symbolic rebel than to be thought of by the adult world as really important, as really dangerous?"

Let's Discuss

1. Describe how rock and rap music today reflects the values of the youth generation.
2. How would a conflict theorist and a functionalist look at the interplay of rock music and its supporters and detractors?

Sources: Weinstein 1999, 2000.

"bad guy" gets clobbered in cartoons or is thrown in jail on *NYPD Blue*, for example. Yet the media also sometimes glorify disapproved behavior, whether it is physical violence, disrespect to a teacher, or drug use.

The media play a critical role in shaping perceptions about the risks of substance use, although not necessarily in a positive fashion. Increases in substance use among youth during the 1990s were linked to a decline in warning and antidrug messages from the media; the proliferation of pro-use messages from the entertainment industry,

and high levels of tobacco and alcohol product advertising and promotion. Media research using content analysis shows that in the 200 most popular movie rentals in 1996 and 1997, alcohol use appeared in 93 percent, tobacco use in 89 percent, and illicit drug use in 22 percent, with marijuana and cocaine use depicted most often. Analysis of the 1,000 most popular songs during the same period showed that 27 percent referred to either alcohol or illicit drugs. In 1999, 44 percent of entertainment programs aired by the four major television networks

Mass media can serve to reinforce proper behavior. But they can also endorse illicit activity, such as drag racing down city streets, as shown in this still from the 2001 box office hit *The Fast and the Furious*.

portrayed tobacco use in at least one episode (Ericson 2001; Roberts et al. 1999).

In 1997, a federal law required the television networks to provide one free minute for every minute the government bought for a public service announcement with an antidrug message. The networks subsequently made an agreement with the government to drop the free minutes in exchange for embedding aggressive antidrug messages in their programs, such as *ER, The Practice,* and *Sabrina the Teenage Witch*. Some people objected, saying that the networks were evading their legal responsibility in using the public airwaves, but criticism really mounted when word got out that the government agency overseeing drug policy was screening scripts in advance and even working on the story lines of shows. Many critics felt this represented a slippery slope that could open the way for government to plant messages in the media on other topics as well, such as abortion or gun control (Albiniak 2000).

Conferral of Status

The mass media confer status on people, organizations, and public issues. Whether it is an issue such as the homeless or a celebrity such as Jennifer Lopez, the media single out one from thousands of other similarly placed issues or people to become significant. Table 7-1 depicts how certain public figures are prominently featured on weekly magazine covers. Obviously, *People* magazine alone was

not responsible for making Princess Diana into a worldwide figure, but collectively all the media outlets created a notoriety that Princess Victoria of Sweden, for one, did not "enjoy."

Surveillance of the Social Environment

The *surveillance function* refers to the collection and distribution of information concerning events in the social environment. The media collect and distribute facts about a variety of events, including stock market quotations and tomorrow's weather, as well as election campaigns, play openings, sports events, and international conflicts.

But what exactly constitutes a "fact"? Who gets portrayed as a hero, a villain, a patriot, a terrorist? The media generally define these for the audience, using a definition that reflects the values and orientation of the decision makers within media organizations.

Imagine

You are a news junkie. Where would you gather your "facts" or information? Is it more likely to be from newspapers, tabloids, magazines, TV newscasts, or the Internet? Why would you choose that medium?

Dysfunctional Media: The Narcotizing Effect

In addition to the functions previously noted, the media perform a *dysfunction*, as identified by sociologists Paul Lazarsfeld and Robert Merton (1948). They created the term *narcotizing dysfunction* to refer to the phenomenon whereby the media provide such massive amounts of information that the audience becomes numb and generally fails to act on the information, regardless of how compelling the issue. Interested citizens may take in the information, but they may make no decision or take no action.

Consider how often the media initiate a great outpouring of philanthropic support for natural disasters or family crises documented on local news stations. But then what happens? Research shows that as the tragedy is prolonged, viewer fatigue begins. The mass media audience becomes numb, desensitized to the suffering, and even starts to conclude that a solution to the crises has been found (Moeller 1999).

Table 7-1   Status Conferred by Magazines

Rank/Person	Number of Times on Cover of *Time*	Rank/Person	Number of Times on Cover of *People*	Rank/Person	Number of Times on Cover of *Ebony*
1. Richard Nixon	59	1. Princess Diana	52	1. Muhammad Ali	15
2. Ronald Reagan	34	2. Julia Roberts	19	1. Michael Jackson	15
3. Bill Clinton	29	3. Elizabeth Taylor	15	3. Whitney Houston	14
4. Dwight Eisenhower	22	4. Jackie Onassis	13	4. Janet Jackson	12
4. Lyndon Johnson	22	4. Sarah Ferguson	13	5. Diahann Carroll	11
4. Gerald Ford	22	4. Michael Jackson	13	5. Lena Horne	11
7. Jimmy Carter	19	4. Cher	13	5. Sidney Poitier	11
8. George Bush	18	8. Madonna	10	8. Bill Cosby	10
9. Jesus Christ	17	9. John Travolta	9	9. Halle Berry	9
9. Henry Kissinger	17	9. Princess Caroline (Monaco)	9	9. Sammy Davis, Jr.	9
9. John F. Kennedy	17				

Source: Author's content analysis of primary cover subject for full run of the periodicals (*Time* March 3, 1923; *People* March 4, 1974; *Ebony* November 1945) through January 1, 2002.

Think About It

How do the magazines differ in the types of people they feature on their covers? Which type do you think enjoys more status? Why?

The media's narcotizing dysfunction was identified over 50 years ago, when just a few homes had television and well before the advent of electronic media. At that time, sociologists felt this dysfunction was going largely unnoticed, but today it is common to point out the ill effects of addiction to television or the Internet, especially among young people.

Conflict View

Conflict theorists emphasize that the media reflect and even exacerbate many of the divisions of our society and world, including those based on gender, race, ethnicity, and social class. They point in particular to the media's ability to decide what gets transmitted through gatekeeping.

Gatekeeping

What story is placed on page 1 of the morning newspaper? Which motion picture plays three screens at the local Cineplex rather than one? What picture is not released at all? What news makes it onto the evening broadcast? Lurking behind these decisions is usually the presence of powerful figures, such as publishers, editors, and other media moguls.

The mass media constitute a form of big business in which profits are generally more important than the quality of the product (programming). Within the mass media, a relatively small number of people control what eventually reaches the audience, a process known as *gatekeeping.* This term describes how material must travel through a series of checkpoints (or gates) before it reaches the public. A select few decide what images to bring to a broad audience. In many countries the government plays a gatekeeping role. A study for the World Bank found that in 97 countries, 60 percent of the top five TV stations and 72 percent of the largest radio stations are government-owned (World Bank 2001b:183).

Gatekeeping prevails in all kinds of media. In the recording industry, gatekeepers may reject a popular local band because it competes with a group already on their label. Or, even if the band gets recorded, radio station programmers may reject it because it does not fit their station's "sound." Television network programmers may keep a pilot for a new TV series off the air because the gatekeepers believe it does not appeal to their target audience. Similar decisions are made by gatekeepers in the publishing industry (Wilson and Wilson 2001).

Gatekeeping is not as dominant in at least one form of mass media—the Internet. You can send virtually any message you want to electronic bulletin boards. You can create a webpage to advance any argument you might wish, including one that insists the earth is flat. The Internet is a means to quickly disseminate information (or misinformation) without going through any significant gatekeeping process. Nevertheless, the Internet is not totally without restrictions. Laws in many nations try to regulate content on such issues as gambling, pornography, and even political views. Popular Internet service providers will terminate accounts for offensive behavior. After the terrorist attack in 2001, eBay did not allow people to sell parts of the World Trade Center on its online auction. The World Bank study found that 17 countries place significant controls on Internet content (2001b:187).

Critics of the content of mass media argue that the gatekeeping process reflects a desire to maximize profits. Why else, they argue, would movie star Julia Roberts make the cover of *Time* magazine rather than Palestinian leader Yasir Arafat? We will consider later in this chapter the role that corporate structure plays in the content and delivery of mass media. Another criticism of the gatekeeping process is that what content makes it through the gates does not reflect the diversity of the audience, as we will now see.

Dominant Ideology: Constructing Reality

Conflict theorists argue that the mass media serve to maintain the privileges of certain groups. Moreover, while protecting their own interests, powerful groups may limit the representation of others in the media. The term ***dominant ideology*** describes the set of cultural beliefs and practices that help to maintain powerful social, economic, and political interests. The media transmit messages that virtually define what we regard as the real world, even though these images are frequently at wide variance from the larger society.

p. 70

Television programmers have capitalized on the appeal of reality shows (such as *Survivor*) to young viewers. *The Amazing Race* is one that made it through the gatekeeping process. In this show, pairs of contestants roam the world in a global treasure hunt. These contestants are seeking clues in Paris.

When the mass media seek the assistance of the powerful, the influence of the dominant ideology can be especially explicit. Filmmakers who want their motion pictures about the military to look authentic often seek assistance from Pentagon consultants, but sometimes the government refuses to cooperate because it feels the military is portrayed in an unfavorable way. In some cases, the Hollywood film industry actually *changes* the movie in order to gain access to military bases and military equipment.

For example, in the 1986 Paramount release *Top Gun*, the original script called for Tom Cruise's love interest (played by Kelly McGillis) to be an enlisted woman in the Navy. That presented a major problem for the Navy, which forbids fraternization between officers and enlisted persons. So, in the final version, McGillis played an employee of an outside contractor. The Navy was so delighted with the movie it set up recruiting stations in theater lobbies. More recently, the Air Force successfully convinced Warner Brothers to depict the Air National Guard rescuing a sinking boat in the 2000 film *The Perfect Storm*. Although it was the Coast Guard that performed this rescue in the event on which this film was based, Warner Brothers studio heads adjusted the reality on the screen to get the kind of technical assistance they wanted from the Air Force (Robb 2001).

Mass media decision makers are overwhelmingly White, male, and wealthy. It may come as no surprise, then, that the media tend to ignore the lives and ambitions of subordinate groups, among them working-class people, African Americans, Hispanics, gays and lesbians,

Making movies about governmental agencies or the military is a lot easier when the filmmakers can count on the cooperation of the government. *Apollo 13,* which glorified NASA's space program, easily won government approval. But *G. I. Jane,* featuring Demi Moore as a Navy SEAL who bucks high-ranking military and government officials, did not get approved.

people with disabilities, overweight people, and older people. Even worse, the content may create false images or **stereotypes** of these groups that become accepted as accurate portrayals of reality.

Television content is a prime example. How many characters who are overweight can you name? Even though in real life one out of every four women is obese (30 or more pounds over a healthy body weight), only 3 out of 100 TV characters are portrayed as obese. Heavyset men and women on television programs have fewer romances, talk less about sex, eat more often, and are the object of ridicule more often than their thin counterparts.

Minority groups are also stereotyped in TV shows. Almost all the leading roles are cast as White, even in urban-based programs such as *Friends,* which is situated in ethnically diverse New York City. Blacks on television tend to be featured mainly in crime-based dramas, and

Latinos are virtually ignored. Box 7-2 discusses the distorted picture of society presented on prime-time television programs (Hellmich 2001).

Another concern about the media from the conflict perspective is that television distorts the political process. Until the campaign finance system is truly reformed and enforced, candidates with the most money (often backed by powerful lobby groups) are able to buy exposure to voters and saturate the air with commercials attacking their opponents (see Chapter 17).

Dominant Ideology: Whose Culture?

Globalization projects the dominating reach of the U.S. media into the rest of the world. Movies produced in the United States account for 65 percent of the global box office. Magazines as diverse as *Cosmopolitan* and *Reader's Digest* sell two issues abroad for every one they sell in the United States. *The X-Files* airs in 60 coun-

pp. 63—64 ◄

tries. These media cultural exports undermine the distinctive traditions and art forms of other societies and encourage their cultural and economic dependence on the United States. Countries throughout the world decry U.S. exports, from films to language to Bart Simpson. In the opening essay to this chapter, David Demers (1999) posed the relevant question: Are the global media a "menace or messiah?" (Farhi and Rosenfeld 1998).

Nations that feel a loss of identity may try to defend against the cultural invasion from foreign countries, especially the economically dominant United States. As Figure 7-2 shows, even Canada has attempted to monitor and regulate diffusion.

We risk being ethnocentric, however, if we overstress U.S. dominance and assume other nations do not play a role. For example *Survivor, Who Wants to Be a Millionaire,* and *Iron Chef,* immensely popular TV programs in the United States, came from Sweden, Britain, and Japan, respectively. The steamy telenovelas of Mexico and other Spanish-speaking countries owe very little of their origin to soap operas on U.S. television. Still, the money behind media operations based in the United States is a dominating influence worldwide.

Cultural domination goes beyond films, books, magazines, and TV programs. It also applies to what ideas and facts get transmitted. Many developing nations have long argued for a greatly improved two-way flow of news and information between industrialized nations and developing nations. They complain that the news from the Third World is scant, and what news there is reflects unfavorably on the developing nations. For example, what do you know about South America? Most people in the United States will mention the two topics that dominate the news from countries south of the border: revolution and drugs. Most know little else about the whole continent. To

In late spring 1999, as the television networks prepared their schedules for the coming season, an article in the *Los Angeles Times* hit the broadcasting industry like a bombshell. In all 26 new prime-time series, all the leading characters, as well as the vast majority of the supporting casts, would be White. The public response was immediate. The NAACP, alarmed by the "virtual whitewash in programming," threatened a lawsuit.

The following television season, Latino organizations decried the lack of Hispanics on television. Only 2 percent of all prime-time characters are Latino. This virtual absence on network programming prompted comedian Paul Rodriguez to observe "now the Taco Bell Chihuahua dog is probably the most prominent Hispanic actor represented on television" (Bark 2000:30). Media stars such as *West Wing*'s Martin Sheen (born Ramon Estevez) often downplay their Latin heritage.

Despite the underrepresentation of minorities on television shows, network gatekeepers seemed surprised by the news of the all-White season. In the aftermath of the *Times* article, producers, writers, executives, and advertisers blamed one another for the oversight. Television programming was dictated by advertisers, a former executive claimed; if advertisers said they wanted blatantly biased programming, the networks would provide it. Jery Isenberg, chairman of the Caucus for Producers, Writers & Directors, blamed the networks, saying that writers would produce a series about three-headed Martians if the networks told them to.

> Marc Hirshfeld, an NBC executive, claims some White producers have told him they don't know *how* to write for Black characters.

Beyond these excuses, real reasons can be found for the departure from the diversity exhibited in past shows and seasons. In recent years, the rise of more networks, cable TV, and the Internet has fragmented the broadcast entertainment market, siphoning viewers away from the general-audience sitcoms and dramas of the past. Both the UPN and WB networks produce situation comedies and even full nights geared toward African American audiences. With the proliferation of cable channels such as Black Entertainment Television (BET) and the Spanish-language Univision, and websites that cater to every imaginable taste, there no longer seems to be a need for broadly popular series such as *The Cosby Show*, the tone and content of which appealed to Whites as well as Blacks in a way the newer series do not. The result of these sweeping technological changes has been a sharp divergence in viewer preference.

Meanwhile, the mainstream network executives, producers, and writers remain overwhelmingly White. Most of them live far from ethnically and racially diverse inner-city neighborhoods and tend to write and produce stories about people like themselves. Marc Hirshfeld, an NBC executive, claims some White producers have told him they don't know *how* to write for Black characters. Stephen Bochco, producer of *NYPD Blue*, is a rare exception. His series, *City of Angels*, featured a mostly non-White cast, like the people

Sources: Bark 2000; Braxton 1999; Hoffman 1997; Lowry et al. 1999; Poniewozik 2001; Soriano 2001; Wood 2000.

remedy this imbalance, a resolution to monitor the news and content that cross the borders of developing nations was passed by the United Nations Educational, Scientific, and Cultural Organization (UNESCO) in the 1980s. The United States disagreed with this proposal, and it was one factor that prompted the United States to withdraw from UNESCO back in the mid-1980s (Dominick 2002).

Feminist View

Feminists continue the argument advanced by conflict theorists that the mass media stereotype and misrepresent social reality. The media are a powerful influence on how we look at men and women, and, according to this view, their images of the sexes communicate unrealistic, stereotypical, and limiting perceptions. Here are three problems feminists believe arise from media coverage (Wood 1994):

1. Women are underrepresented, which suggests that men are the cultural standard and women are insignificant.
2. Men and women are portrayed in ways that reflect and perpetuate stereotypical views of gender. It is women, for example, who are shown in peril, needing to be rescued by a male, and rarely the reverse.
3. Depictions of male–female relationships emphasize traditional sex roles and normalize violence against women.

Sociologists have long noted the stereotypical depiction of women and men in the mass media. Erving Goffman (1979) in *Gender Advertisements* showed how femininity and masculinity were displayed in photographs used regularly in magazine advertisements. His observations still

Bochco grew up with in an inner-city neighborhood.

In the long run, media observers believe, the major networks will need to integrate the ranks of gatekeepers before they achieve true diversity in programming. Adonis Hoffman, director of the Corporate Policy Institute, has urged network executives to throw open their studios and boardrooms to minorities. Hoffman thinks such a move would empower Black writers and producers to present a true-to-life portrait of African Americans. There are some signs of agreement from the networks. According to Doug Herzog, president of Fox Entertainment, real progress means incorporating diversity from within.

Why should it matter that minority groups aren't visible on major network television, if they are well represented on other channels such as UPN, WB, BET, and Univision? The problem is that Whites as well as minorities see a distorted picture of their society every time they turn on network TV. In Hoffman's words, "African Americans, Latinos and Asians, while portrayed as such, are not merely

walk-ons in our society—they are woven into the fabric of what has made this country great" (Hoffman 1997:M6).

Let's Discuss

1. Do you watch network TV? If so, how well do you think it represents the diversity of U.S. society?

2. Have you seen a movie or TV show recently that portrayed members of a minority group in a sensitive and realistic way—as real people rather than as stereotypes or token walk-ons? If so, describe the show.

---

are relevant today. In the ads, men gaze at women in a manner that suggests superiority. Women are more likely than men to be shown unclothed or in danger or even physically victimized. In her introduction to this classic analysis, feminist Vivian Gornick describes the depiction of women as reflecting "innumerable small murders of the mind and spirit [that] take place daily" (1979:ix).

As in other areas of sociology, feminist researchers caution against assuming that what holds true for men's media behavior is true for everyone. Researchers, for example, have studied the different ways that women and men approach novels, television, and the Internet. According to 2001 data, women's use of the Internet is increasing faster than men's. Women are also more likely to regard e-mail as a means of maintaining contact with friends and relatives. Their use of websites differs in fundamental ways from the way men use them. Women are

more likely to seek health and religious information, research new jobs, and play games online. Men are more likely to use the web to get news, shop, seek financial information, and participate in online auctions (Fox and Rainie 2001; Rainie and Kohut 2000).

Interactionist View

Interactionists are especially interested in shared understandings of everyday behavior. They examine the media on the microlevel to see how they shape day-to-day social behavior. Scholars increasingly point to the mass media as the source of major daily activity; some argue that television serves virtually as a primary group for many individuals who share TV viewing. Other mass-media participation is not necessarily face to face. For example, we usually listen to the radio or read the newspaper as a solitary

167

Figure 7-2

What Is Canadian?

Celine Dion		Lenny Kravitz
Canadian	**Nationality**	Not Canadian
"My Heart Will Go On"	**Song**	"American Woman"
Not Canadian	**Lyricist**	Canadian
Not Canadian	**Composer**	Canadian
1 point*		2 points*

*At least two points are required for music to be considered Canadian.

Source: DePalma 1999.

Canadians try to ward against U.S. influence by controlling what is played on the radio. The government requires that 35 percent of a station's programming in the daytime be Canadian. But what is Canadian? A complicated set of rules gives points based on whether the artist, the composer, the lyricist, or the production is Canadian. A song that earns 2 points meets the government requirements. Canadian Celine Dion singing "My Heart Will Go On" would not be classified as Canadian.

activity, although it is possible to share that event with others (Cerulo et al. 1992; Waite 2000).

Friendship networks can emerge from shared viewing habits or from recollection of a cherished television series from the past. Family members and friends often gather for parties centered on the broadcasting of popular events such as the Super Bowl or the Academy Awards. And, as we've seen, television virtually serves as a baby-sitter or a "playmate" for many children and even infants.

The power of the mass media encourages political leaders and entertainment figures to carefully manipulate their images through public appearances called photo opportunities or "photo ops." By embracing symbols (posing with celebrities or in front of prestigious landmarks), these staged events attempt to convey self-serving definitions of social reality.

The interactionist perspective also helps us to understand more about one important aspect of the entire mass media system—the audience. How do we actively participate in media events? How do we construct with others the meaning of media messages?

● The Audience

One night a few years ago, I was watching "my" Chicago Bulls make yet another bid for the NBA championship. Michael Jordan made a spectacular steal and went on to score a game-winning basket. I shouted, but what I

Fans of the TV show *Star Trek* (known as Trekkies) meet in costume at a convention celebrating the anniversary of the show's concept. Many television series inspire interactions among viewers who like to share the experience.

remember most were the cheers I heard from others in Chicago through the open window. Earlier that year my son was watching *Beverly Hills 90210* in his college dorm room. One of the characters revealed that she was going to attend my son's university. He and his friends screamed when they heard this, and simultaneously they heard cheers all across the campus. In a very unusual way we had both been reminded that we are part of a larger audience.

Who Is in the Audience?

Sociologists distinguish the mass media from other social institutions by the necessary presence of an audience. It can be an identifiable, finite group, such as an audience at a jazz club or a Broadway musical. Or it can be much larger and undefined, such as the viewer audience for VH-1 on television or the people who read the same issue of *USA Today*. The audience may be a secondary group gathered in a large auditorium, or it may be a primary group, such as a mother and her son watching the latest Disney video at home.

We can look at the audience from both the level of *microsociology* and *macrosociology*. At the microlevel, we would consider how the audience members interacting among themselves would respond to the media or, in the case of live performances, would perhaps influence the performers. At the macrolevel, we would examine broader societal consequences of the media, such as early childhood education through programming like *Sesame Street*.

Even if the audience is spread out over a wide geographic area and the members don't know one another, we would still find that the audience is somewhat distinctive in terms of age, gender, income, political party, formal schooling, race, and ethnicity. Table 7-2 presents data collected in 1999 for a study of audiences in a variety of settings in Chicago. Although these results may not be predictable for all audiences, they demonstrate that audiences do vary in their composition. Performers, marketing agents, and advertisers are well aware of this variation and closely study such attendance patterns.

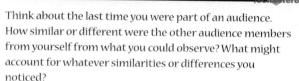

Think about the last time you were part of an audience. How similar or different were the other audience members from yourself from what you could observe? What might account for whatever similarities or differences you noticed?

The Segmented Audience

Once a media outlet, such as a radio station or a magazine, has identified its audience, it targets that group. The media are increasingly marketing themselves to a *particular*

Table 7-2 Who's in the Audience?

Setting	Under Age 35	Men	White	Black	Hispanic Descent*
Art museum	38%	48%	73%	22%	13%
Blues festival	37	48	46	48	8
Comedy club	52	41	82	15	10
Dance/ballet	39	44	86	10	13
Film	41	49	73	21	12
Jazz festival	30	51	37	56	7
Live theater	29	48	83	13	5
Rock concert	56	53	89	7	7
Symphony/opera	34	50	84	11	6

*Persons of Hispanic descent may be of any race.

Source: Caro 2001:5, 7.

When President George W. Bush needed to burnish his environmental image, he traveled to a national park to proclaim his devotion to the environment. In this "photo op" he is announcing a proposal to restore the Everglades in Florida.

mit public messages that reach a sizable, heterogeneous, and scattered audience (Dominick 2002).

Audience Behavior

Sociologists have long researched how audiences interact with one another and then how they share information after the media event is concluded. The role of audience members as opinion leaders particularly intrigues social researchers. An *opinion leader* is someone who, through day-to-day personal contacts and communication, influences the opinions and decisions of others. Sociologist Paul Lazarsfeld and his colleagues (1948) pioneered the study of opinion leaders in their research on voting behavior in the 1940s. They found that opinion leaders encourage their relatives, friends, and coworkers to think positively about a particular candidate, perhaps pushing them to listen to the politician's speeches or read the campaign literature.

Today, film critics often attribute the success of low-budget independent movies to word of mouth. This is another way of stating that the mass media influence opinion leaders who, in turn, influence still others. The

audience. To some degree, this specialization is driven by advertising. Advertising media specialists have sharpened their ability through survey research to identify particular target audiences. As a result, Nike would be much more likely to promote a new line of golf clubs on the Golf Cable Channel, for example, then it would on an episode of *Frasier.* The many more choices that the growing Internet and satellite broadcast channels offer audiences also fosters specialization. Members of these audiences are more likely to *expect* content geared to their own interests.

This specialized targeting of audiences has led some scholars to ponder whether there is still a "mass" in mass media. Are viewing audiences so segmented that there are fewer and fewer large collective audiences? That is not yet clear. Even though we seem to be in an age of *personal* computers and *personal* digital assistants (or PDAs), large formal organizations still do trans-

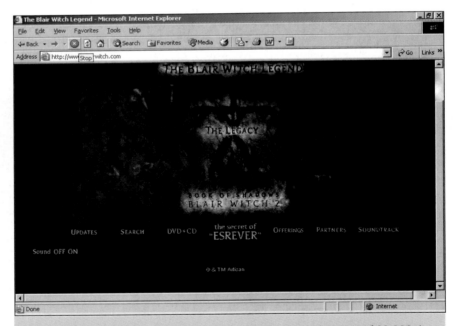

The Blair Witch Project was an independent film made for about $60,000; it grossed $141 million in the United States. The film achieved phenomenal success because opinion leaders passed on word-of-mouth recommendations both in person and on Internet chat rooms. A webpage devoted to the film (shown here) also generated a buzz.

audience, then, is not a passive group of people but is a group of active consumers who often are impelled to interact with others about the media event (Croteau and Hoynes 2000; Wright 1986).

Despite the role of opinion leaders, members of an audience do not all interpret media in the same way. Often their response is influenced by social characteristics such as occupation, race, education, and income. Take the example of the televised news coverage of the riots in Los Angeles in 1992. These riots were an angry response to the acquittal of two White police officers accused of severely beating a Black motorist.

Sociologist Darnell Hunt (1997) was interested in finding out how the social composition of audience members would affect how they interpreted the news coverage. He gathered 15 groups from the Los Angeles area, with group members equally divided among Whites, African Americans, and Latinos. He showed each group a 17-minute film clip from the televised coverage of the riots and asked the group members to discuss how they would describe what they just saw to a 12-year-old. In analyzing the group discussions, Hunt found that although gender and class did not cause respondents to vary their answers by much, race did.

Hunt went beyond noting simple racial differences in perceptions; he also analyzed how the differences were manifested. For example, Black viewers were much more likely than Latinos or Whites to refer to the events in terms of "us" and "them" in the group discussion. Another difference was that Black and Latino viewers were more animated and critical than the White groups as they watched the film segment. White viewers tended to be quiet, still, and unquestioning, suggesting that they were more comfortable with the news coverage than the Blacks or Hispanics. (In Chapter 22 we will consider in greater detail the behavior of mass audiences.)

● The Media Industry

"My Heart Will Go On," the hit song from the movie *Titanic*, was a real crowd pleaser. But how did this song come into being? That requires looking at the music industry from what researchers call the production perspective. It emphasizes the media production process rather than the specific media product. So while music may be the apparent medium, the process requires the contribution of a songwriter, a performer, a movie soundtrack producer, a music video director, advertisers, and promoters, to name just a few participants in the music industry (Croteau and Hoynes 2000).

Media Concentration

Who owns this production process in the media? Ownership is getting more and more centralized. Even though there continue to be thousands of independent media outlets in every state, the clear trend has been toward centralization. We can point to a handful of multinational corporations that dominate the publishing, broadcasting, and film industries (Croteau and Hoynes 2000).

A prime example of this concentration was the merger in 2001 of AOL and Time Warner. Figure 7-3 shows how this new corporation permeates almost every media sector. The AOL network along with its Netscape Internet browser operates the most popular Internet sites

Figure 7-3

The Media Conglomerate: AOL Time Warner
2000 Revenues: $36.2 billion
Number of employees: 81,800

Source: Fortune 2001; AOL Time Warner 2002; Schiesel 2001.

Sociology in the Global Community

7-3 Good Morning, Bhutan!

Bhutan is a country of fewer than 2 million people in the heart of the vast Himalayan mountains. Ruled by a hereditary monarchy, the people are allowed little room to dissent. Neither political parties nor unions are permitted. The police enforce the wearing of traditional dress in public. One of the country's policies puts "gross national happiness" ahead of gross national product. Another policy, "quality not quantity," guards against the unwanted influence of foreigners by strictly limiting tourism. Only 8,000 tourists received visas in 2000, and they each had to pay $200 a day for the privilege of visiting the remote Buddhist kingdom.

Given the geographical isolation and the strictly controlled society, it is little wonder that mass media are limited in Bhutan. Bhutan's neighbor India has 22

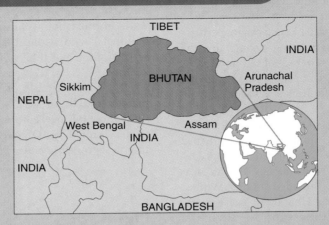

telephone lines per 1,000 households compared to Bhutan's 7, and 120 radios per 1,000 households compared to Bhutan's 17. But most striking of all, Bhutan had *no* television broadcast station in 1997, while India had 562. Except for very small, isolated island nations, no other country in the world had no television.

That all changed in June of 1999. At

that time Bhutan's king announced the arrival of modern communications technology, along with this warning to his subjects: "Use your good sense and judgment. Television and the Internet can be both beneficial and harmful to the individual and society" (Bloom 2001:21). Bhutan's only local broadcast station was supposed to provide the country with content of its own, but a lack of technical experience has limited programming to an hour a day. However, there are 44 other channels with programming from other countries, including Hindi movie channels, CNN, the Indian and U.S. versions of MTV, sports channels, Discovery, the BBC, and a Chinese channel.

The effect of this programming on the small kingdom has been dramatic. Sitcoms and action films have overshadowed the traditional spoken stories that

Source: Bloom 2001; Bureau of the Census 2000a:836; Third World Institute 2001; U.S. Department of State 1997.

and boasts more than 32 million online subscribers worldwide. Time Warner is the largest U.S. magazine publisher based on advertising dollars. AOL Time Warner subsidiaries Warner Brothers and New Line Cinema rank among the top 10 motion picture producers. Warner Music Group artists accounted for 38 of the top 200 best-selling albums and 16 percent of all U.S. album sales in 2000. Time Warner Cable provides many of the most popular cable channels including HBO, TBS, CNN, TNT, and Nickelodeon. WB network broadcasts such successful series as *Sabrina the Teenage Witch* and *Dawson's Creek* (K. Alexander 2001; AOL Time Warner 2002; *New York Times* 2001; Roberts 2001).

And AOL Time Warner is only one media giant. Add to the list Walt Disney (which includes ABC, ESPN, and Lifetime networks), Rupert Murdoch's News Corporation of Australia (which includes Fox Network Television, book publishers, numerous newspapers and magazines including *TV Guide,* and Twentieth Century Fox), SONY of Japan (which includes Columbia Pictures, IMAX, CBS

Records, and Columbia Records), and Viacom (which includes Paramount, MTV, CBS, Simon and Schuster, and Blockbuster). This concentration of media giants fosters considerable cross promotion. For example, the release of the Warner Brothers film *Harry Potter and the Sorcerer's Stone* in 2001 was heavily promoted by both CNN and *Time* magazine. In fact, *Time* managed to devote six pages to the film's release in the midst of the war in Afghanistan and even placed Harry Potter in a conspicuous insert on a cover featuring President George W. Bush.

Some observers think that the government should regulate media concentration. It did so in the 1940s, when the major Hollywood studios were forced to sell off the movie theaters they owned. But today the government takes more of a "hands-off" attitude. Without government intervention, the media giants will continue to grow as long as there are benefits to being large.

Sociologists David Croteau and William Hoynes (2001) question if the public interest is being served by the growing concentration of media. They are concerned transmit social values. Young girls dance the latest steps shown on MTV. Young boys pose with homemade belts honoring their World Wrestling Federation heroes. Nightclub patrons wear halter tops and leather jackets. The violent language heard on television has entered everyday speech.

Kinley Dorji, editor of Bhutan's only newspaper, deplores the modernization

> ## "[W]e've been pried open quite dramatically."

and Westernization introduced by television. "The young people want to dress like their new heroes on television, like their favorite movie stars. A generation gap is emerging with great contrast." He notes that "we've always been this exotic, hidden, mystical land," but as a result of the electronic invasion "we've been pried open quite dramatically" (Bloom 2001:21).

It appears that the effort to limit the influence of foreigners has hit a snag. No trekkers could so thoroughly change a society as the electronic invaders in Bhutan who are marching across the TV screen.

Let's Discuss

1. What are the advantages of bringing modern communications

technology to a previously isolated nation? What are the disadvantages?
2. If you were in charge of programming Bhutan's local TV station, what kinds of programs would you introduce to help maintain the traditional culture and resist the invasive aspects of Western culture?

Television, recently introduced in Bhutan, brings Oprah Winfrey into the living room of this Bhutanese family. It is their first day of owning a TV set.

that innovation and independence will decline as media empires grow. For example, the 1994 motion picture *Forrest Gump* was most widely advertised on VH-1 and UPN networks; Blockbuster video stores later promoted the video, complete with reshowing of *Entertainment Tonight* features on the film. Several books related to the film were published by Simon and Schuster. What might appear to have been a multi-outlet media buzz about a movie was actually centrally controlled. Viacom owns Paramount Studios, the company that released *Forrest Gump,* and also owns VH-1, UPN, Blockbuster, *Entertainment Tonight,* and Simon and Schuster (Farhi 1995).

Similar concerns are raised about the situation in such countries as China, Cuba, Iraq, and North Korea, where the ruling party owns and controls the media. The difference, which is considerable, is that the gatekeeping process in the United States is in the hands of private individuals who desire to maximize profits. In the other countries, the gatekeeping process lies with political leaders who desire to maintain control of the government.

We should note that there is one significant exception to the centralization and concentration of the media—the Internet. Currently the web is fairly accessible through independent outlets, giving access to literally millions of "producers" of media content. Media conglomerates, well aware of the Internet's potential, are already delivering their well-produced, sophisticated material via the web. However, for now, the Internet allows the individual to become a media entrepreneur with a potential audience of millions.

The Media's Global Reach

Has the rise of the electronic media created a "global village"? Canadian linguist Marshall McLuhan predicted this result some 40 years ago. Today, physical distance is no longer a barrier, and instant messaging is possible across the world. The mass media have indeed begun to create a global village in terms of communication. As Figure 7-4 shows, not all countries are equally connected,

Figure 7-4

Media in Selected Countries

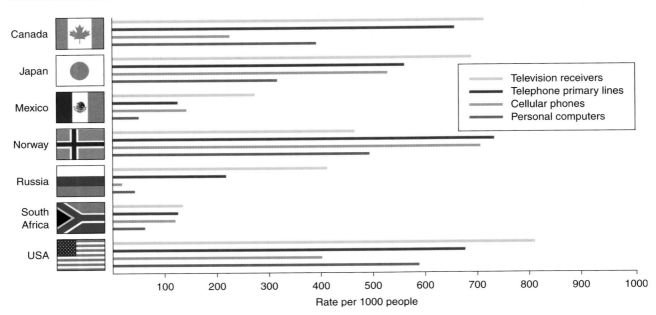

Rate per 1000 people

Source: Bureau of the Census 2001a:858.

but the progress is staggering when we consider that voice transmission was just beginning 100 years ago (McLuhan 1964, McLuhan and Fiore 1967).

The media are not only broad in reach but they permeate all aspects of everyday life. Take advertising for example. Consumer goods are vigorously marketed worldwide, from advertisements on baggage carriers at airports to imprints on the sand of beaches. Little wonder that people around the world develop loyalty to a brand and are as likely to desire sporting a logo of Nike, Coca-Cola, or Harley-Davidson as they are of their favorite soccer or baseball team (Klein 1999).

The key to creating a truly global network that reaches directly into workplaces, schools, and homes is the introduction of the Internet in the mass media. Whereas much of the online global transmission today is limited to print and pictures, the capacity to send audio and video via the Internet will increasingly reach into every part of the world. Social interaction will then truly take place on a global stage.

The Internet also has facilitated other forms of communication. Reference materials and data banks can now be made accessible across national boundaries. Informa-

tion related to international finance, marketing, trade, and manufacturing are literally a keystroke away. We also can see the emergence of truly world news outlets and the promotion of a world music that is not clearly identifiable with any single culture. Even the most future-oriented thinker would find the growth in the reach of the mass media in postindustrial and postmodern societies remarkable (Castells 2000; Croteau and Hoynes 2000).

The lack of one national home for the various forms of mass media points to a potential dilemma for users. People are concerned that unhealthy influences and even crime are taking place in today's electronic global village and that there are few, if any, controls to prevent them. For example, the leaders of Bhutan worry about the impact that newly introduced television programming is having on their culture and their people (see Box 7-3). Similarly, industrial countries, including the United States, are concerned about everything from video poker to pornography to hacking industrial and government agency information databanks on the electronic highways. In the policy section that follows, we consider how violence portrayed in the media can have an unwanted influence on society.

SOCIAL POLICY AND MASS MEDIA

Media Violence

/schaefer8

The Issue

A film depicts the story of 42 ninth-graders abducted to a remote island and forced to play the ultimate game of Survivor: Kill or be killed until only one is left. In gruesome detail, the movie portrays teachers doing away with students, young girls murdering shy admirers, and popular students killing rivals with hatchets and grenades, poison and machine guns. The film, *Battle Royale,* by renowned Japanese director Kinji Fukasaku, shows a Japan that is falling apart in the early 21st century. Millions are out of work, bureaucrats have lost control, and the government is convinced that its deadly game is the only way to teach rampaging juveniles a lesson (Magnier 2001).

What effect does this movie and hundreds of others like it (not to mention TV programs, computer and video games, and Internet sites) have on audiences? Does violence in the media lead people, especially youth, to become more violent? This question has been raised since the early days of comic books when POW! and SPLAT! were accompanied by vivid pictures of fights. Today the mass media show far more violent and gruesome scenes. Table 7-3 gives an idea of how much violence shows up on television and in motion pictures. Content analyses of television programming shows that media have gradually become more violent, even in programs targeted to children (Parents Television Council 2001a, 2001b).

The Setting

We spend a great deal of time with the media. According to a communications industry study, we spend 10 hours every day with television, videotaped movies, computer games, radio, and other media outlets. At the end of a week, the time averages more than 69 hours—far more than a full workweek (Bureau of the Census 2000a:566).

But does this mean that watching hours of mass media with violent images causes one to behave differently? This research question is exceedingly complex since many social factors influence behavior. The most comprehensive analysis of more than 200 studies on media violence and aggressive behavior found that exposure to violence causes short-term increases in the aggressive behavior of youth. Another more recent study found that less television and other media exposure is related to less observed physical aggression. But in such research

Table 7-3 Violence in the Media, 1998–1999

Medium	Acts of Violence	Acts of Serious Violence	Violent Acts per Episode/Movie
Television	3,381	1,754	12 (6 serious)
Broadcast and cable movies	865	485	17 (10 serious)
Theatrical release movies	2,319	1,377	46 (28 serious)

Note: Content analysis of television season covers all major broadcast and cable systems in the 1998–1999 television season. Movie releases refer to the top 50 grossing motion pictures in 1998. Serious violence refers to FBI index offenses.

Source: Lichter et al. 1999.

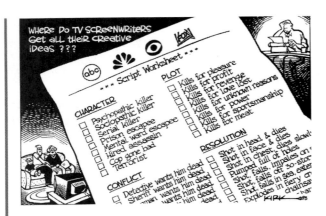

findings it is important to recognize that other factors besides the media are also related to aggressive behavior. Witnessing and experiencing violence within one's own home and encouragement by others have also been shown to be related to violent behavior (Johnson et al. 2002; Paik and Comstock 1994; Robinson et al. 2001; U.S. Surgeon General 2001).

Sociological Insights

The controversy surrounding violence and the media raises basic questions about the function of the media. If some of its functions are to entertain, socialize, and enforce social norms, how can violence be a part of that message, especially when the offender rarely pays any apparent consequences for violent behavior?

Even if a viewer does not necessarily become more violent from watching violent images, there could be a desensitization taking place. Using the premise of the narcotizing dysfunction, one might suggest that extended exposure to violent imagery leads to an increased tolerance and acceptance of violence in others.

Both conflict and feminist theorists are troubled that the victims depicted in violent imagery are often those who are given less respect in real life: women, children, the poor, racial minorities, citizens of foreign countries, and even the physically disabled. The media routinely portray rapes in a way that further devalues women. Many women are cast as prostitutes in even well-regarded motion pictures, from Federico Fellini's *Nights of Cabiria* (1956) to Jodie Foster in *Taxi Driver* (1976) to Julia Roberts in *Pretty Woman* (1990) to Elisabeth Shue in *Leaving Las Vegas* (1995).

Interactionists are especially interested in finding out if violence in media may then become a script for real-life behavior. Aggression is a product of socialization,

and people may model themselves after the violent behavior they see, especially if the situations approximate their lives. Battling dinosaurs in *Jurassic Park* or apes in *Planet of the Apes* is one thing, but what if the violence represents only a slight adjustment to normal behavior? For example, in the 1995 film *The Program,* Touchstone Films ordered the removal of a scene in which high school football players prove their manhood by lying in the middle of a highway at night. This action came after several deaths had occurred when young men tried to prove their own manhood by imitating the scene.

Policy Initiatives

Policymakers have responded to the links between violence depicted in the media and real-life aggression on two levels. In public statements, politicians are quick to call for more family-oriented, less violent content, but on the legislative level, policymakers are reluctant to engage in what could be regarded as censorship. They encourage the media industries to regulate themselves.

The U.S. Surgeon General's 2001 report on youth violence recommended that parents use V-chip technology that screens the television programs able to be watched by their children. Yet despite parental concerns, a 2001 national study showed that only 17 percent of parents use the chip to block programs with sexual or violent content. In general, most observers agree that parents should play more of a role in monitoring their children's media consumption (Kaiser Family Foundation 2001; U.S. Surgeon General 2001).

Often government studies are initiated by violent events we desperately wish to explain. The 2001 Surgeon General's report on youth violence came out of the 1998 Columbine High School shooting in Colorado. Canada launched a serious look at media violence following a 1989 incident at a Montreal university in which 14 young women were shot to death. A senseless beating of a five-year-old girl by three friends in Norway in 1994 led that country to look at violence in the media. In all these cases, initial calls for stiff government regulation eventually gave way to industry self-regulation and greater adult involvement in young people's viewing patterns (Health Canada 1993; Bok 1998).

Much of our knowledge of media violence comes from the study of children who watch traditional television, and some more recent studies have tried to assess the impact of video games. But we should not lose sight of the fact that media outlets are becoming increasingly diverse, especially with the role the Internet now plays in the delivery of media content. Much of this new content holds great promise for broadening educational horizons, but, unfortunately, these new easily obtainable outlets also offer an unending diet of violence (Alexander and Hanson 2001:44).

Let's Discuss

1. Do you know of anyone whose behavior has become more aggressive from exposure to violence in the media? How is this aggression expressed? Do you notice any changes in your own behavior?
2. To what extent should government act as a media censor, especially in regard to violence directed to young people?
3. What role do you think parents should have in monitoring their children's media diet? Will you limit the hours your children can access media outlets? What alternative activities might children be offered?

Chapter Resources

Summary

The *mass media* refer to the print and electronic instruments of communication that carry messages to often widespread audiences. They pervade all areas of society, from entertainment to education to politics. This chapter examines how the mass media affect our social institutions and influence our social behavior.

1. From the functionalist perspective, the media entertain, socialize, enforce social norms, confer status, and keep us informed (the *surveillance function*). They can be dysfunctional to the extent that they desensitize us to events (the *narcotizing dysfunction*).
2. Conflict theorists see the media as reflecting and even deepening divisions in society through *gatekeeping,* controlling the material that reaches the public, and by spreading the *dominant ideology,* which defines reality and overwhelms local cultures.
3. Feminist theorists point out that media images of the sexes communicate unrealistic, stereotypical, and limiting perceptions of women.
4. Interactionists examine the media on the microlevel to see how they shape day-to-day social behavior, such as shared TV viewing and staged public appearances intended to convey self-serving definitions of reality.

5. The mass media require the presence of an audience—whether it is small and defined or large and amorphous. With increasing numbers of media outlets, there has been more and more targeting of segmented (or specialized) audiences. Social researchers have also studied the role of *opinion leaders* in influencing audiences.
6. The media industry is getting more and more concentrated, creating media conglomerates. This concentration raises concerns about how innovative and independent the media can continue to be. In some countries, governments own and control the media. The Internet is the one significant exception to centralization, allowing millions of people to "produce" their own media content.
7. The media have a global reach, thanks to new communication technology, especially via the Internet. Some people are concerned that the electronic global village will spread unhealthy influences to other cultures.
8. Sociologists are studying the ways that depiction of violence in the media may promote aggressive behavior or desensitization in viewers.

Critical Thinking Questions

1. What kind of audience is targeted by the producers of televised wrestling? By the creators of a Disney animated film? By a rap group? What kinds of factors determine who makes up a particular media audience?
2. Trace the production process for a new television situation comedy (sitcom). Who do you imagine are the gatekeepers in this process?
3. Use the functionalist, conflict, and interactionist perspectives to assess the effects of global TV programming on developing countries.

Key Terms

Dominant ideology   A set of cultural beliefs and practices that helps to maintain powerful social, economic, and political interests. (page 164)

Gatekeeping   The process by which a relatively small number of people control what material eventually reaches the audience. (163)

Mass media   Print and electronic instruments of communication that carry messages to often widespread audiences. (159)

Narcotizing dysfunction   The phenomenon whereby the media provide such massive amounts of information that the audience becomes numb and generally fails to act on the information, regardless of how compelling the issue. (162)

Opinion leader   Someone who, through day-to-day personal contacts and communication, influences the opinions and discussions of others. (170)

Stereotypes   Unreliable generalizations about all members of a group that do not recognize individual differences within the group. (165)

Surveillance function   The collection and distribution of information concerning events in the social environment. (162)

Additional Readings

BOOKS

Bayton, Mavis. 1999. *Frock Rock: Women Performing Popular Music.* New York: Oxford University Press. Based on in-depth interviews and participant observation in Great Britain, this book looks at how and why the occupation "rock musician" remains male-dominated.

Croteau, David, and William Hoynes. 2001. *The Business of Media: Corporate Media and the Public Interest.* Thousand Oaks, CA: Pine Forge Press. Two sociologists examine the mass-media industry and the social changes it has undergone.

Dolby, Nadine. 2001. *Constructing Race: Youth, Identity and Popular Culture in South Africa.* Albany, NY: SUNY Press. An examination of how the media and elements of the popular culture affect adolescents in South Africa.

Johnson, Phylis, and Michael C. Keith. 2000. *Queer Airwaves: The Story of Gay and Lesbian Broadcasting.* The first book-length study of the role of gays and lesbians in television and radio.

McChesney, Robert W. 1999. *Rich Media, Poor Democracy: Communication Politics in Dubious Times.* Urbana, IL: University of Illinois Press. A look at the increasing concentration of newspapers, television stations, and radio stations in the hands of a few wealthy corporations, making the information age harmful for public life, according to the author.

Miller, Toby, Nitin Govil, John McMurria, and Richard Maxwell. 2001. *Global Hollywood.* Bloomington, IN: Indiana University Press. Examines how the network of motion picture production companies, distributors, marketing firms, and banks maximize the impact of big-budget film making from Hollywood on the global marketplace.

Pomerance, Mary (ed.). 2001. *Ladies and Gentlemen, Boys and Girls: Gender in Film at the End of the Twentieth Century.* Albany, NY: SUNY Press. An examination of gender as portrayed in film both in the United States and worldwide.

JOURNALS

Among the journals that consider mass media are *Communication Research* (founded in 1974), *Howard Journal of Communications* (1991), *Journal of Consumer Culture* (2001), *Popular Culture* (1967), *Media, Culture and Society* (1979), and *Public Culture* (1989).

● Technology Resources

Internet Connection

*Note: While all the URLs listed were current as of the printing of this book, these sites often change. Please check our website (**http://www.mhhe.com/schaefer8**) for updates and hyperlinks to these exercises and additional exercises.*

1. This chapter notes that many people view the media as glorifying deviant behavior. The Research in Action box discusses rock music as the source of all sorts of evil, such as the Judas Priest incident. In 1990, the parents of two boys who committed suicide sued Judas Priest, claiming that the lyrics to "Beyond the Realms of Death" caused the boys to kill themselves. The following site allows you to read the lyrics: (**http://priest.the-croc.com**). Link to "JP Lyrics" and then to "Beyond the Realms of Death." Read and analyze the lyrics.

   (a) Do you believe that the lyrics to this song could have caused the boys to kill themselves? Explain.

   Judas Priest isn't the only rock artist to be accused of encouraging antisocial behavior. In April 1999, Eric Harris and Dylan Klebold killed 15 people and wounded 23 at Columbine High School. It was reported that the boys were Marilyn Manson fans. Link to **http://www.wickedland.com/manson/lyrics/holywood.html#10** and read the lyrics to Manson's "The Nobodies." This song has references to Columbine.

   (b) Analyze the lyrics to this song. Do you think this song could influence someone to go out and kill?

2. The Sociology in the Global Community box introduces you to the country of Bhutan—the last country in the world to legalize television. Bhutan has only one homegrown television and radio station. Explore the following site to learn more about the country of Bhutan and its mass media: **http:// www.bbs.com.bt/index.htm.** Link to "Bhutan" and then to "Images" to better understand how geographically isolated the country is and why the mass media are limited. You will see a series of minislides depicting both the country and the people who inhabit Bhutan. Next, link to "About BBS." This will allow you to read a brief history of radio and television in Bhutan.

   (a) When did radio broadcasting start in Bhutan, when did it operate, and how long was it on the air when broadcasting? When is FM service expected to cover the whole country?

   Click on "Programmes" and link to "Television Schedule."

   (b) Which kind of programming (news, documentary, etc.) occurred most often during the week?

   (c) Compare the programs offered on BBS to those of a local channel in your community. In what ways are they different or similar?

   Click on "Home" and link to "Thimphu Top Ten." This will connect you to the English Radio Show that plays the latest music in town. Scan the Top 10 list.

   (d) How many of the songs are familiar to you?

   (e) Were you surprised to find that the Top 10 music list contained many songs that are, or were, popular in the United States? Explain.

   (f) The Bhutanese rely heavily on spoken stories to teach cultural values. There is concern that as sitcoms and action films become more popular, this transmission will become more fragile. List at least two racial or ethnic groups living in the United States and explain how their cultural values may be compromised by the mass media in our country.

Online Learning Center

Visit the student center in the Online Learning Center at **www.mhhe.com/schaefer8** and link to "Imagine." You will first be asked to become a news junkie, thinking about where you would gather your "facts" or information. Next, you will be asked to imagine yourself a part of an audience for a ballet performance and to think about the similarities you might share with other audience members. Use your sociological imagination to answer the questions.

DEVIANCE AND SOCIAL CONTROL

Cigarette smoking has become stigmatized in the United States. These two billboards remind smokers that their habit is socially isolating (top) and life threatening (bottom).

VICTIMLESS CRIME?

Prostitution Drugs Homosexuality Abortion

Robert F. Meier · Gilbert Geis

Heidi Fleiss was in her late twenties when she was arrested for operating a call girl service. At the time, her pediatrician father had reacted flippantly, "I guess I didn't do such a good job on Heidi after all." Later, he would be convicted of conspiring to hide profits from his daughter's call girl ring. Fleiss had dropped out of school when she was sixteen and established a liaison with a playboy-financier who gave her a Rolls-Royce for her twenty-first birthday. In her early twenties, Fleiss interned in the world of prostitution by working for Madame Alex (Elizabeth Adams), Hollywood's reigning call girl entrepreneur until her death in 1995. In 1990, backed by television director and pornography filmmaker Ivan Nagy, 24-year-old Fleiss opened her own business. She now refers to her call girl operation as nothing more than a sensible adjunct to many other Hollywood enterprises. One telling anecdote was how she was paid $40,000 a night by a customer to do little more than play Scheherazade, the Sultan's wife in *Arabian Nights.*

On her income tax return, Fleiss reported that her earnings were generated by "personal counseling." SONY officials paid her thousands of dollars for one such counseling session for executives of an overseas branch; SONY's tax report listed the outlay as a "development deal." Government officials estimate that Fleiss earned several hundred thousand dollars during a period in which she reported income of only $33,000 on her tax return.

At Fleiss' trial, business executive Manuel Santos testified that he sent his private jet to pick up some of Fleiss' call girls. One of them alleged that she flew to Paris, Athens, and Las Vegas to have sex with clients, and that she gave 40 percent of what she earned to Fleiss. Fleiss was sentenced to three years in prison and a $1,000 fine after a jury found her guilty of three counts of pandering. She was also convicted in federal court of eight counts of conspiracy, income tax evasion, and laundering money.

In January, 1997, Fleiss received a 37-month prison sentence for the federal crimes. She also was fined $400, ordered to participate in a substance-abuse program and to perform 300 hours of community service.

Earlier, the California District Court of Appeal had thrown out the previous state verdict and ordered a new trial on the grounds that jury members had been confused about their decision. . . . The appellate court decision further determined that jury members had "traded" votes on the different charges in order to avoid a deadlock, an impermissible procedure. . . .

For some, Fleiss' situation aroused passions that have remained persistently prominent in the feminist debate over prostitution. In an op-ed piece, attorneys Gloria Allred and Lisa Bloom asked rhetorically: "Why is it immoral to be paid for an act that is perfectly legal if done for free?" *(Meier and Geis 1997:36–37)* ■ ◉

Additional information about this excerpt and about those that open each subsequent chapter can be found on the SocWorld CD-ROM that accompanies this text.

In this excerpt from their book *Victimless Crime? Prostitution, Drugs, Homosexuality, Abortion,* sociologists Robert F. Meier and Gilbert Geis explore the role of law and social control in four areas commonly thought of as "victimless crimes." In the case of prostitution, as exemplified by Heidi Fleiss, some people argue that laws on the books create a social problem rather than solving one. Because there is so much disagreement about whether prostitution is wrong or to what extent it is deviant, the law is limited in its scope and effectiveness.

As these authors point out, what behaviors should be considered deviant is not always obvious. Take the issue of binge drinking on campus. On the one hand, we can view it as *deviant,* violating a school's standards of conduct and endangering one's health, but on the other hand it can be seen as *conforming,* complying with a peer culture. In the United States, people are socialized to have mixed feelings about both conforming and nonconforming behavior. The term *conformity* can conjure up images of mindless imitation of one's peer group—whether a circle of teenagers wearing "phat pants" or a group of business executives dressed in similar gray suits. Yet the same term can also suggest that an individual is cooperative or a "team player." What about those who do not conform? They may be respected as individualists, leaders, or creative thinkers who break new ground. Or they may be labeled as "troublemakers" and "weirdos" (Aronson 1999).

This chapter examines the relationship between conformity, deviance, and social control. When does conformity verge on deviance? And how does a society manage to control its members and convince them to conform to its rules and laws? What are the consequences of deviance? The chapter begins by distinguishing between conformity and obedience and then looks at two experiments regarding conforming behavior and obedience to authority. The informal and formal mechanisms used by societies to encourage conformity and discourage deviance are analyzed. We give particular attention to the legal order and how it reflects underlying social values.

The second part of the chapter focuses on theoretical explanations for deviance, including the functionalist approach employed by Émile Durkheim and Robert Merton; the interactionist-based theories; labeling theory, which draws upon both the interactionist and the conflict perspectives; and conflict theory.

The third part of the chapter focuses on crime, a specific type of deviant behavior. As a form of deviance subject to official, written norms, crime has been a special concern of policymakers and the public in general. We will take a look at various types of crime found in the United States, the ways crime is measured, and international crime rates. Finally, the social policy section considers the ultimate punishment for deviance in the United States and in the rest the world—the death penalty. ■

Social Control

As we saw in Chapter 3, each culture, subculture, and group has distinctive norms governing what it deems appropriate behavior. Laws, dress codes, bylaws of organizations, course requirements, and rules of sports and games all express social norms.

How does a society bring about acceptance of basic norms? The term **social control** refers to the techniques and strategies for preventing deviant human behavior in any society. Social control occurs on all levels of society. In the family, we are socialized to obey our parents simply because they are our parents. Peer groups introduce us to informal norms, such as dress codes, that govern the behavior of members. Colleges establish standards they expect of their students. In bureaucratic organizations, workers encounter a formal system of rules and regulations. Finally, the government of every society legislates and enforces social norms.

Most of us respect and accept basic social norms and assume that others will do the same. Even without thinking, we obey the instructions of police officers, follow the day-to-day rules at our jobs, and move to the rear of elevators when people enter. Such behavior reflects an effective process of socialization to the dominant standards of a culture. At the same time, we are well aware that individuals, groups, and institutions *expect* us to act "properly." p. 68 ◀ This expectation carries with it **sanctions,** penalties and rewards for conduct concerning a social norm. If we fail to live up to the norm, we may face punishment through informal sanctions such as fear and ridicule, or formal sanctions such as jail sentences or fines.

The challenge to effective social control is that people often receive competing messages about how to behave. While the state or government may clearly define acceptable behavior, friends or fellow employees may encourage quite different behavior patterns. Binge drinking in college is the perfect example. The larger society frowns on

Figure 8-1

College Binge Drinking

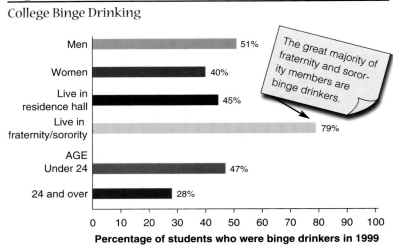

The great majority of fraternity and sorority members are binge drinkers.

Percentage of students who were binge drinkers in 1999

Note: Based on a national survey of more than 14,000 college students in 1999. Binge drinking is defined as one drinking session of at least five drinks for men or four drinks for women during the two weeks prior to the self-administered questionnaire.
Source: Wechsler et al. 2000:203.

Think About It
Why do you think the incidence of binge drinking is so high among fraternity and sorority members?

---

underage drinking and has laws on the books against it. But within the college peer group, drinking is generally accepted, with no sanctions attached to it. Figure 8-1 shows that half the men, 40 percent of the women, and close to 80 percent of fraternity and sorority members engage in binge drinking.

Functionalists contend that people must respect social norms if any group or society is to survive. In their view, societies literally could not function if massive numbers of people defied standards of appropriate conduct. By contrast, conflict theorists maintain that "successful functioning" of a society will consistently benefit the powerful and work to the disadvantage of other groups. They point out, for example, that widespread resistance to social norms was necessary to overturn the institution of slavery in the United States, to win our independence from England, to secure civil rights, to allow women to vote, and to force an end to the war in Vietnam.

Conformity and Obedience

Techniques for social control operate on both the group level and the societal level. People we think of as peers or equals influence us to act in particular ways; the same is true of people who hold authority over us or occupy awe-inspiring positions. Stanley Milgram (1975) made a

useful distinction between these two important levels of social control.

Milgram defined **conformity** as going along with peers—individuals of our own status, who have no special right to direct our behavior. By contrast, **obedience** is defined as compliance with higher authorities in a hierarchical structure. Thus, a recruit entering military service will typically *conform* to the habits and language of other recruits and will *obey* the orders of superior officers. Students will *conform* to the drinking behavior of their peers and will *obey* the requests of campus security officers.

Conformity to Prejudice

We often think of conformity as occurring in rather harmless situations, such as members of an expensive health club who all work out in elaborate and costly sportswear. But researchers have found that people may conform to the attitudes and behavior of their peers even when such conformity means expressing intolerance toward others. Fletcher Blanchard, Teri Lilly, and Leigh Ann Vaughn (1991) conducted an experiment at Smith College and found that statements people overhear others make influence their own expressions of opinion on the issue of racism.

A student who was a confederate (or ally) of the researchers approached 72 White students as each was walking across the campus. She said she was conducting an opinion poll for a class. At the same time, a second White student—actually another confederate working with the researchers—was stopped and asked to participate in the survey. Both students were then asked how Smith College should respond to anonymous racist notes actually sent to four African American students in 1989. The confederate always answered first. In some cases, she condemned the notes; in others, she justified them.

Blanchard and his colleagues (1991:102–103) conclude that "hearing at least one other person express strongly antiracist opinions produced dramatically more strongly antiracist public reactions to racism than hearing others express equivocal opinions or opinions more accepting of racism." When the confederate expressed sentiments justifying racism, subjects were much *less* likely to express antiracist opinions than were those who heard no one else offer opinions. In this experiment, social control (through the process of conformity) influenced people's attitudes, or at least the expression of those attitudes. In the next section, we will see that social control (through the process of obedience) can alter people's behavior.

Obedience to Authority

If ordered to do so, would you comply with an experimenter's instruction to give people increasingly painful electric shocks? Most people would say no; yet, the research of social psychologist Stanley Milgram (1963, 1975) suggests that most of us *will* obey such orders. In Milgram's words (1975:xi), "Behavior that is unthinkable in an individual . . . acting on his own may be executed without hesitation when carried out under orders."

Milgram placed advertisements in New Haven, Connecticut, newspapers to recruit subjects for what was announced as a learning experiment at Yale University. Participants included postal clerks, engineers, high school teachers, and laborers. They were told that the purpose of the research was to investigate the effects of punishment on learning. The experimenter, dressed in a gray technician's coat, explained that in each testing, one subject would be randomly selected as the "learner" while another would function as the "teacher." However, this lottery was rigged so that the "real" subject would always be the teacher while an associate of Milgram's served as the learner.

At this point, the learner's hand was strapped to an electric apparatus. The teacher was taken to an electronic "shock generator" with 30 lever switches. Each switch was labeled with graduated voltage designations from 15 to 450 volts. Before beginning the experiment, subjects were given sample shocks of 45 volts to convince them of the authenticity of the experiment.

The experimenter instructed the teacher to apply shocks of increasing voltage each time the learner gave an incorrect answer on a memory test. Teachers were told that "although the shocks can be extremely painful, they cause no permanent tissue damage." In reality, the learner did not receive any shocks.

The learner deliberately gave incorrect answers and acted out a prearranged script. For example, at 150 volts, the learner would cry out, "Get me out of here!" At 270 volts, the learner would scream in agony. When the shock reached 350 volts, the learner would fall silent. If the teacher wanted to stop the experiment, the experimenter would insist that the teacher continue, using such statements as "The experiment requires that you continue" and "You have no other choice; you *must* go on" (Milgram 1975:19–23).

The results of this unusual experiment stunned and dismayed Milgram and other social scientists. A sample of psychiatrists had predicted that virtually all subjects would refuse to shock innocent victims. In their view, only a "pathological fringe" of less than 2 percent would continue administering shocks up to the maximum level. Yet almost *two-thirds* of participants fell into the category of "obedient subjects."

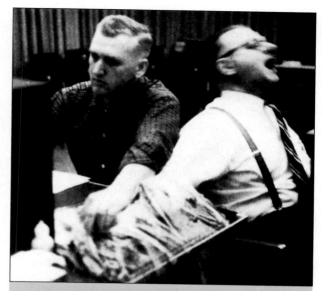

In one of Stanley Milgram's experiments, the "learner" supposedly received an electric shock from a shock plate when he answered a question wrong. At the 150-volt level, the "learner" would demand to be released and would refuse to place his hand on the shock plate. The experimenter would then order the actual subject (the "teacher") to force the hand onto the plate, as shown in the photo. Though 40 percent of the true subjects stopped complying with Milgram at this point, 30 percent did force the "learner's" hand onto the shock plate, despite his pretended agony.

Why did these subjects obey? Why were they willing to inflict seemingly painful shocks on innocent victims who had never done them any harm? There is no evidence that these subjects were unusually sadistic; few seemed to enjoy administering the shocks. Instead, in Milgram's view, the key to obedience was the experimenter's social role as a "scientist" and "seeker of knowledge."

Milgram pointed out that in the modern industrial world, we are accustomed to submitting to impersonal authority figures whose status is indicated by a title (professor, lieutenant, doctor) or by a uniform (the technician's coat). Because we view the authority as larger and more important than the individual, we shift responsibility for our behavior to the authority figure. Milgram's subjects frequently stated, "If it were up to me, I would not have administered shocks." They saw themselves as merely doing their duty (Milgram 1975).

From an interactionist perspective, one important aspect of Milgram's findings is the fact that subjects in follow-up studies were less likely to inflict the supposed shocks as they were moved physically closer to their victims. Moreover, interactionists emphasize the effect of *incrementally* administering additional dosages of 15 volts. In effect, the experimenter negotiated with the teacher and convinced the teacher to continue inflicting higher levels of punishment. It is doubtful that anywhere near the two-thirds rate of obedience would have been reached had the experimenter told the teachers to administer 450 volts immediately to the learners (Allen 1978; Katovich 1987).

Milgram launched his experimental study of obedience to better understand the involvement of Germans in the annihilation of six million Jews and millions of other people during World War II. In an interview conducted long after the publication of his study, he suggested that "if a system of death camps were set up in the United States of the sort we had seen in Nazi Germany, one would be able to find sufficient personnel for those camps in any medium-sized American town" (CBS News 1979:7–8).

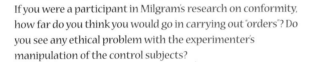
Imagine

If you were a participant in Milgram's research on conformity, how far do you think you would go in carrying out "orders"? Do you see any ethical problem with the experimenter's manipulation of the control subjects?

Informal and Formal Social Control

The sanctions used to encourage conformity and obedience—and to discourage violation of social norms—are carried out through informal and formal social control. As the term implies, people use *informal social control* casually to enforce norms. Examples of informal social control include smiles, laughter, raising an eyebrow, and ridicule.

In the United States and many other cultures, adults often view spanking, slapping, or kicking children as a proper and necessary means of maintaining authority. Child development specialists counter that such corporal punishment is inappropriate because it teaches children to solve problems through violence. They warn that slapping and spanking can escalate into more serious forms of abuse. Yet, despite a 1998 policy statement by the American Academy of Pediatrics that corporal punishment is not effective and can indeed be harmful, 59 percent of pediatricians support the use of corporal punishment, at least in certain situations. Our culture widely accepts this form of informal social control (Wolraich et al. 1998).

Formal social control is carried out by authorized agents, such as police officers, physicians, school administrators, employers, military officers, and managers of movie theaters. It can serve as a last resort when socialization and informal sanctions do not bring about desired behavior. An increasingly significant means of formal

social control in the United States is to imprison people. During the course of a year, 5.7 million adults undergo some form of correctional supervision—jail, prison, probation, or parole. Put another way, almost one out of every 30 adult Americans is subject to this very formal type of social control every year (Beck et al. 2000).

Which behaviors are subject to formal social control and how severe should the sanctions be? Societies vary. In the nation of Singapore, chewing of gum is prohibited, feeding birds can lead to fines of up to $640, and there is even a $95 fine for failing to flush the toilet. Singapore deals with serious crimes especially severely. The death penalty is mandatory for murder, drug trafficking, and crimes committed with firearms. Box 8-1 describes the campaigns launched by Singapore's government to enforce social norms.

How aware are you of governmental social control? Look around and you will see many signs of it. New Jersey protects it schools with a Drug-Free School Zone, and the houseowner in Rockford, Illinois, who piled trash in his front lawn received a code violation notice from his city government.

Sociology in the Global Community

8-1 Singapore: A Nation of Campaigns

"Males with Long Hair Will Be Attended to Last!" "Throwing Litter from Apartments Can Kill!" "No Spitting!" These are some of the posters sponsored by the Singapore government in its effort to enforce social norms in this small nation of some four million people living in a totally urbanized area in southeast Asia.

While Singapore is governed by a democratically elected parliament, one party has dominated the government since its independence in 1965. And it has not hesitated to use its authority to launch a number of campaigns to shape the social behavior of its citizens. In most cases these campaigns are directed against "disagreeable" behavior—littering, spitting, chewing gum, failing to flush public toilets, teenage smoking, and the like. Courtesy is a major concern, with elaborate "Courtesy Month" celebrations scheduled to both entertain and educate the populace.

Some campaigns take on serious issues and are backed by legislation. For example, in the 1970s the government asked its citizens to "Please Stop at Two" in family planning; tax and schooling benefits rewarded those who complied. However, this campaign was so successful that in the 1980s the government began a "Have Three or More If You Can Afford to" campaign. In this case it provided school benefits for larger families. In another attempt at social control, the government has

> **Courtesy is a major concern, with elaborate "Courtesy Month" celebrations scheduled to both entertain and educate the populace.**

launched a "Speak Mandarin" campaign to encourage the multiethnic, multilingual population to accept Mandarin as the dialect of choice.

For the most part, Singaporeans cheerfully accept their government's admonitions and encouragement. They see the results of being clean and courteous:

Singapore is a better place to live. Corporations also go along with the government and even help to sponsor some of the campaigns. As one corporate sponsor noted: "If (people) see Singapore as a clean country, they will view companies here as clean." Political scientist Michael Haas refers to this compliance as "the Singapore puzzle": citizens of Singapore accept strict social control dictates in exchange for continuing prosperity and technological leadership in the world.

Let's Discuss

1. How would you react to an administration-sponsored campaign at your college against drinking? What would be some positive aspects of such a campaign? What would be some negative aspects?

2. Is rudeness in U.S. society considered normal or deviant? Explain your position.

Sources: Dorai 1998; Haas 1999; Third World Institute 2001.

Another controversial example of formal social control is the use of surveillance techniques. Hundreds of cities in Great Britain have installed closed-circuit television systems on "high streets" (the main shopping and business area) in an effort to reduce crime on the street. The use of public surveillance has made its way to the United States as well. Critics of the system believe it is too intrusive, but supporters counter that it will make the public feel more secure. This argument got a boost after the terrorist attacks of September 11, 2001. Broad sectors of society at that time seemed willing to allow for greater social control measures. One proposal called for placing a network of cameras on busy urban street corners. The cameras would then transmit images to computers programmed to recognize faces, a process that is gradually being refined (Barstow 2001; Kasindorf 2001; Schrag 2002; Uttley 1993).

Law and Society

Some norms are so important to a society they are formalized into laws controlling people's behavior. *Law* may be defined as governmental social control (Black 1995). Some laws, such as the prohibition against murder, are directed at all members of society. Others, such as fishing and hunting regulations, primarily affect particular categories of people. Still others govern the behavior of social institutions (corporate law and laws regarding the taxing of nonprofit enterprises).

Sociologists see the creation of laws as a social process. Laws are created in response to perceived needs for formal social control. Sociologists have sought to explain how and why such perceptions arise. In their view, law is not merely a static body of rules handed down from generation to generation. Rather, it reflects continually changing standards of what is right and wrong, of how violations are to be determined, and of what sanctions are to be applied (Schur 1968).

Sociologists representing varying theoretical perspectives agree that the legal order reflects the values of those in a position to exercise authority. Therefore, the creation of criminal law can be a most controversial matter. Should it be against the law to employ illegal immigrants in a factory (see Chapter 11), to have an abortion (see Chapter 12), or to smoke on an airplane? Such issues have been bitterly debated because they require a choice among competing values. Not surprisingly, laws that are unpopular—such as the prohibition of alcohol under the Eighteenth Amendment in 1919 and the widespread establishment of a 55-mile-per-hour speed limit on highways—become difficult to enforce when there is no consensus supporting the norms.

Socialization is actually the primary source of conforming and obedient behavior, including obedience to law. Generally, it is not external pressure from a peer group or authority figure that makes us go along with social norms. Rather, we have internalized such norms as valid and desirable and are committed to observing them. In a profound sense, we want to see ourselves (and to be seen) as loyal, cooperative, responsible, and respectful of others. In the United States and other societies around the world, people are socialized both to want to belong and to fear being viewed as different or deviant.

Control theory suggests that our connection to members of society leads us to systematically conform to society's norms. According to sociologist Travis Hirschi and other control theorists, our bonds to family members, friends, and peers induce us to follow the mores and folkways of our society. We give little conscious thought to whether we will be sanctioned if we fail to conform. Socialization develops our self-control so well that we don't need further pressure to obey social norms. While control theory does not effectively explain the rationale for every conforming act, it nevertheless reminds us that while the media may focus on crime and disorder, most members of most societies conform to and obey basic norms (Gottfredson and Hirschi 1990; Hirschi 1969).

Deviance

What Is Deviance?

For sociologists, the term *deviance* does not mean perversion or depravity. ***Deviance*** is behavior that violates the standards of conduct or expectations of a group or society (Wickman 1991:85). In the United States, alcoholics, compulsive gamblers, and the mentally ill would all be classified as deviants. Being late for class is categorized as a deviant act; the same is true of dressing too casually for a formal wedding. On the basis of the sociological definition, we are all deviant from time to time. Each of us violates common social norms in certain situations.

Is being overweight an example of deviance? In the United States and many other cultures, unrealistic standards of appearance and body image place a huge strain on people—especially on adult women and girls—based on how they look. Journalist Naomi Wolf (1992) has used the term *beauty myth* to refer to an exaggerated ideal of beauty, beyond the reach of all but a few females, which has unfortunate consequences. In order to shed their "deviant" image and conform to (unrealistic) societal norms, many women and girls become consumed with adjusting their appearances. Yet what is deviant in our culture may be celebrated in another. In Nigeria, for example, being fat is a mark of beauty. Part of the coming-of-age ritual calls for young girls to spend a month in a "fattening room." Among the Nigerians, being thin at this point in the life course is deviant (Simmons 1998).

Deviance involves the violation of group norms, which may or may not be formalized into law. It is a comprehensive concept that includes not only criminal behavior but also many actions not subject to prosecution. The public official who takes a bribe has defied social norms, but so has the high school student who refuses to sit in an assigned seat or cuts class. Of course, deviation from norms is not always negative, let alone criminal. A member of an exclusive social club who speaks out against its traditional policy of excluding women, Blacks, and Jews from admittance is deviating from the club's norms. So is a police officer who "blows the whistle" on corruption or brutality within the department.

Standards of deviance vary from one group (or subculture) to another. In the United States, it is generally considered acceptable to sing along at a folk or rock concert, but not at the opera. Just as deviance is defined by place, so too is it relative to time. For instance, drinking alcohol at 6:00 P.M. is a common practice in our society, but engaging in the same behavior at breakfast is viewed as a deviant act and as symptomatic of a drinking problem. Table 8-1 offers additional examples of untimely acts that we regard as deviant in the United States.

From a sociological perspective, deviance is hardly objective or set in stone. Rather, it is subject to social definitions within a particular society at a particular time. For that reason, what is considered deviant can shift from one social era to another, as Box 8-2 shows. In most instances, those individuals and groups with the greatest status and power define what is acceptable and what is deviant. For example, despite serious medical warnings about the dangers of tobacco as far back as 30 years ago, cigarette smoking continued to be accepted—in good

www.
mhhe
.com
/schaefer8

Veronika Vester likes to watch her boyfriend Kidd Krayz compete in backyard wrestling matches, a hot sport among teenagers today. The teenage boys join informal federations that hold free-form matches in neighborhood backyards. The boys sometimes use weapons, such as fire, thumbtacks, and barbed wire, as they body slam and pile drive each other. Videos of the matches are sold on the web. At first, the blood put Veronika off: "I turned around. I couldn't watch it—and then as time goes on, it's just like the normal thing. . . . Now I'm out there yelling, 'Yeah! Hit him!'" (Carpenter 2000: E3).

How did wrestling—a well-respected and even gentlemanly Olympic sport—get to this point? How does swinging a barbed-wire bat at someone's head become a "normal thing"? According to sociologist Brendan Maguire, it is a question of "defining deviancy down"—redefining deviance so that what might have been unacceptable behavior at one time is considered normal today. In his study of professional wrestling in the United States, Maguire found that the sport became increasingly violent and outrageous over the course of a century in an attempt to attract fans.

Professional wrestling started out as a legitimate athletic activity in the late 1800s, but by the early 1900s matches began to be fixed. The public lost interest until the 1950s when wrestling was revived through the use of colorful competitors such as Gorgeous George. A downturn in the 1960s and '70s led to another change—the use of cable television to broadcast weekly matches that featured slick productions, larger and better athletes, good versus evil story lines, and aggressive marketing. But by the 1990s this recipe for success began to stall and another change was in order: no more good guys versus bad guys. This time around *all*

the wrestling stars would engage in lying, cheating, and violation of rules. Violence, heavy metal music, and pyrotechnics were added to the mix.

Maguire documents several categories in which deviancy got "defined down" in wrestling. One is *morality:* No longer is there a clear-cut "good guy" in professional wrestling. Another category is *racism:* Racist imagery and stereotypes are common themes in wrestling today. For instance, one wrestler pretends to be a pimp. Stereotypes also pervade *sexism,* in which women are treated as objects controlled by men. At one match, for example, a woman was tied to a Satanic symbol and hoisted into the air while the wrestler vowed to "sacrifice" her. Many wrestling personalities today use *sex* as a

> **How does swinging a barbed-wire bat at someone's head become a "normal thing"?**

theme, whether portraying themselves as porn stars or showing off their buttocks. Finally, *violence* has been defined down. Today's professional matches feature verbal threats, destruction of property, bodily harm, and use of weapons—from chairs and chains to barbed-wire bats.

The formula seems to work. Professional wrestling today is a billion-dollar industry, with 35 million viewers tuning in each week. And as we have seen, the violence spills over into the backyard wrestling matches. At some point, of course, the behavior might become too repulsive and send professional wrestling lurching in the other direction, as deviance gets defined up. For now, Maguire speculates that we are seeing the results of individuals freeing themselves of a tradi-

Backyard wrestling can be dangerous to your health! In this match in the backyard of a house in Santa Ana, California, one contestant flips the other as the "referee" takes cover. Most combatants wear little, if any, protective gear.

tional ethical structure that had been built up over centuries before colliding with major social forces unleashed in the 1960s that emphasized civil liberties and individual freedoms.

Let's Discuss

1. Some parents maintain that backyard wrestling is better for the kids than hanging out on the streets. Do you agree? What problems, if any, do you see with the sport?
2. Many people see deviancy being "defined down" in the entertainment field. In what ways does this show up? In what other areas of life do you see deviancy being redefined?

Sources: Carpenter 2000; Maguire 2000.

Table 8-1 Untimely Acts

Ringing a doorbell at 2 A.M.

Working on New Year's Eve

Having sex on a first date

Playing a stereo loudly in early morning hours

Having an alcoholic drink with breakfast

An instructor's ending a college class after 15 minutes

Getting married after having been engaged for only a few days

Taking five years or more to complete high school

Source: Reese and Katovich 1989.

Think About It

How might a 20-year-old and a 50-year-old view these "untimely acts" differently?

part because of the power of tobacco farmers and cigarette manufacturers. It was only after a long campaign led by public health and anti-cancer activists that cigarette smoking became more of a deviant activity. Today many state and local laws limit where people can smoke.

While deviance can include relatively minor day-to-day decisions about our personal behavior, in some cases it can become part of a person's identity. This process is called *stigmatization*, as we will now see.

Deviance and Social Stigma

There are many ways a person can acquire a deviant identity. Because of physical or behavioral characteristics, some people are unwillingly cast in negative social roles. Once they have been assigned a deviant role, they have trouble presenting a positive image to others, and may even experience lowered self-esteem. Whole groups of people—for instance, "short people" or "redheads"—may be labeled in this way. The interactionist Erving Goffman coined the term *stigma* to describe the labels society uses to devalue members of certain social groups (Goffman 1963a; Heckert and Best 1997).

p. 90

Prevailing expectations about beauty and body shape may prevent people who are regarded as ugly or obese from advancing as rapidly as their abilities permit. Both overweight and anorexic people are assumed to be weak in character, slaves to their appetites or to media images. Because they do not conform to the beauty myth, they may be viewed as "disfigured" or "strange" in appearance, bearers of what Goffman calls a "spoiled identity." However, what constitutes disfigurement is a matter of interpretation. Of the one million cosmetic procedures done every year in the United States alone, many are performed on women who would be objectively defined as having a normal appearance. And while feminist sociologists have accurately noted that the beauty myth makes many women feel uncomfortable with themselves, men too lack confidence in their appearance. The number of males who choose to undergo cosmetic procedures has risen sharply in recent years; men now account for 9 percent of such surgeries, including liposuction (Kalb 1999; Saukko 1999).

Often people are stigmatized for deviant behaviors they may no longer engage in. The labels "compulsive gambler," "ex-convict," "recovering alcoholic," and "ex-mental patient" can stick to a person for life. Goffman draws a useful distinction between a prestige symbol that draws attention to a positive aspect of one's identity, such as a wedding band or a badge, and a stigma symbol that discredits or debases one's identity, such as a conviction for child molestation. While stigma symbols may not always be obvious, they can become a matter of public knowledge. Starting in 1994 many states required convicted sex offenders to register with local police departments. Some communities publish the names and addresses, and in some instances even the pictures, of convicted sex offenders on the web.

A person need not be guilty of a crime to be stigmatized. Homeless people often have trouble getting a job, because employers are wary of applicants who cannot give a home address. Moreover, hiding one's homelessness is difficult, since agencies generally use the telephone to contact applicants about job openings. If a homeless person has access to a telephone at a shelter, the staff generally answers the phone by announcing the name of the institution—a sure way to discourage prospective employers. Even if a homeless person surmounts these obstacles and manages to get a job, she or he is often fired when the employer learns of the situation.

> Kim had been working as a receptionist in a doctor's office for several weeks when the doctor learned she was living in a shelter and fired her. "If I had known you lived in a shelter," Kim said the doctor told her, "I would never have hired you. Shelters are places of disease." "No," said Kim. "Doctors' offices are places of disease." (Liebow 1993:53–54)

Regardless of a person's positive attributes, employers regard the spoiled identity of homelessness as sufficient reason to dismiss an employee.

While some types of deviance will stigmatize a person, other types do not carry a significant penalty. Some good examples of socially tolerated forms of deviance can be found in the world of high technology.

Deviance and Technology

Technological innovations such as pagers and voice mail can redefine social interactions and the standards of behavior related to them. When the Internet was first made available to the general public, no norms or regulations governed its use. Because online communication offers a high degree of anonymity, uncivil behavior—speaking harshly of others or monopolizing chat room "space"—quickly became common. Online bulletin boards designed to carry items of community interest became littered with commercial advertisements. Such deviant acts are beginning to provoke calls for the establishment of formal rules for online behavior. For example, policymakers have debated whether to regulate the content of websites featuring hate speech and pornography (see the social policy section of Chapter 23).

Some deviant uses of technology are criminal, though not all participants see it that way. Downloading of music, typically protected by copyright, is widely accepted. The pirating of software, motion pictures, and CDs has become a big business (see Figure 8-2). At conventions and swap meets, pirated copies of movies and CDs are sold openly. Some of the products are obviously counterfeit, but many come in sophisticated packaging, complete with warranty cards. When vendors are willing to talk, they say they merely want to be compensated for their time and the cost of materials, or that the software they have copied is in the public domain.

Though most of these black market activities are clearly illegal, many consumers and small-time pirates are proud of their behavior. They may even think themselves smart for figuring out a way to avoid the "unfair" prices charged by "big corporations." Few people see the pirating of a new software program or a first-run movie as a threat to the public good, as they would embezzling from a bank. Similarly, most businesspeople who "borrow" software

Figure 8-2

A New Form of Deviance: Digital Piracy

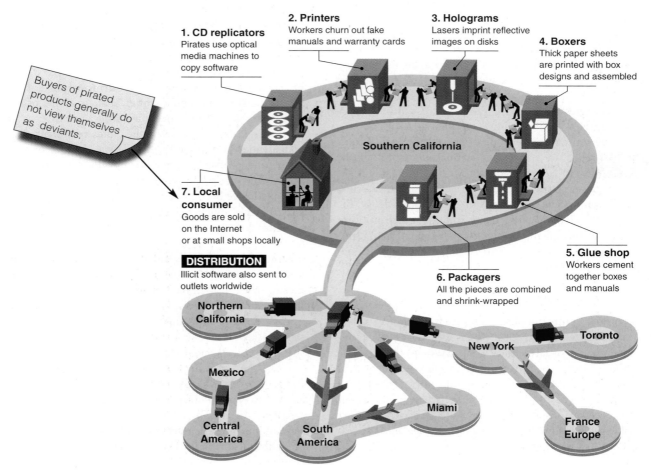

Source: Huffstutter et al. 1999:A29.

from another department, even though they lack a site license, do not think they are doing anything wrong. No social stigma attaches to their illegal behavior.

Deviance, then, is a complex concept. Sometimes it is trivial, sometimes profoundly harmful. Sometimes it is accepted by society and sometimes soundly rejected. What accounts for deviant behavior and people's reaction to it? In the next section we will examine four theoretical explanations for deviance.

Explaining Deviance

Why do people violate social norms? We have seen that deviant acts are subject to both informal and formal sanctions of social control. The nonconforming or disobedient person may face disapproval, loss of friends, fines, or even imprisonment. Why, then, does deviance occur?

Early explanations for deviance identified supernatural causes or genetic factors (such as "bad blood" or evolutionary throwbacks to primitive ancestors). By the 1800s, there were substantial research efforts to identify biological factors that lead to deviance and especially to criminal activity. While such research has been discredited in the twentieth century, contemporary studies, primarily by biochemists, have sought to isolate genetic factors leading to a likelihood of certain personality traits. Although criminality (much less deviance) is hardly a personality characteristic, researchers have focused on traits that might lead to crime, such as aggression. Of course, aggression can also lead to success in the corporate world, professional sports, or other areas of life.

The contemporary study of possible biological roots of criminality is but one aspect of the larger sociobiology debate. In general, sociologists reject any emphasis on genetic roots of crime and deviance. The limitations of current knowledge, the possibility of reinforcing racist and sexist assumptions, and the disturbing implications for rehabilitation of criminals have led sociologists to largely draw on other approaches to explain deviance (Sagarin and Sanchez 1988).

pp. 87–88 ◄

Functionalist Perspective

According to functionalists, deviance is a common part of human existence, with positive (as well as negative) consequences for social stability. Deviance helps to define the limits of proper behavior. Children who see one parent scold the other for belching at the dinner table learn about approved conduct. The same is true of the driver who receives a speeding ticket, the department store cashier who is fired for yelling at a customer, and the college student who is penalized for handing in papers weeks overdue.

Durkheim's Legacy Émile Durkheim ([1895] 1964) focused his sociological investigations mainly on criminal acts, yet his conclusions have implications for all types of deviant behavior. In Durkheim's view, the punishments established within a culture (including both formal and informal mechanisms of social control) help to define acceptable behavior and thus contribute to stability. If improper acts were not sanctioned, people might stretch their standards of what constitutes appropriate conduct. As Box 8-2 illustrated, the gradual intensification of violence in professional wrestling, which has proceeded unsanctioned, has led to much greater tolerance of what was once considered deviant behavior.

Kai Erikson (1966) illustrated the boundary-maintenance function of deviance in his study of the Puritans of seventeenth-century New England. By today's standards, the Puritans placed tremendous emphasis on conventional morals. Their persecution and execution of women as witches represented continuing attempts to define and redefine the boundaries of their community. In effect, their changing social norms created "crime waves," as people whose behavior was previously acceptable suddenly faced punishment for being deviant (Abrahamson 1978; N. Davis 1975).

Durkheim ([1897] 1951) also introduced the term *anomie* into sociological literature to describe a loss of direction felt in a society when social control of individual behavior has become ineffective. Anomie is a state of normlessness that typically occurs during a period of profound social change and disorder, such as a time of economic collapse. People become more aggressive or depressed, and this results in higher rates of violent crime and suicide. Since there is much less agreement on what constitutes proper behavior during times of revolution, sudden prosperity, or economic depression, conformity and obedience become less significant as social forces. It also becomes much more difficult to state exactly what constitutes deviance.

Merton's Theory of Deviance What do a mugger and a teacher have in common? Each is "working" to obtain money that can then be exchanged for desired goods. As this example illustrates, behavior that violates accepted norms (such as mugging) may be performed with the same basic objectives in mind as those of people who pursue more conventional lifestyles.

On the basis of this kind of analysis, sociologist Robert Merton (1968) adapted Durkheim's notion of anomie to explain why people accept or reject the goals of a society, the socially approved means of fulfilling their aspirations, or both. Merton maintained that one important cultural goal in the United States is success, measured largely in terms of money. In addition to providing this goal for people, our society offers specific instructions on how to pursue success—go to school, work hard, do not quit, take advantage of opportunities, and so forth.

What happens to individuals in a society with a heavy emphasis on wealth as a basic symbol of success? Merton reasoned that people adapt in certain ways, either by conforming to or by deviating from such cultural expectations. Consequently, he developed the **anomie theory of deviance,** which posits five basic forms of adaptation (see Table 8-2).

Conformity to social norms, the most common adaptation in Merton's typology, is the opposite of deviance. It involves acceptance of both the overall societal goal ("become affluent") and the approved means ("work hard"). In Merton's view, there must be some consensus regarding accepted cultural goals and legitimate means for attaining them. Without such consensus, societies could exist only as collectives of people—rather than as unified cultures—and might experience continual chaos.

Of course, in a society such as that of the United States, conformity is not universal. For example, the means for realizing objectives are not equally distributed. People in the lower social classes often identify with the same goals as those of more powerful and affluent citizens yet lack equal access to high-quality education and training for skilled work. Even within a society, institutionalized means for realizing objectives vary. For instance, it is legal to gain money through roulette or poker in Nevada, but not in neighboring California.

The other four types of behavior represented in Table 8-2 all involve some departure from conformity. The "innovator" accepts the goals of a society but pursues them with means regarded as improper. For example, Harry King—a professional thief who specialized in safecracking for 40 years—gave a lecture to a sociology class and was asked if he had minded spending time in prison. King responded,

> I didn't exactly like it. But it was one of the necessary things about the life I had chosen. Do you like to come here and teach this class? I bet if the students had their wishes they'd be somewhere else, maybe out stealing, instead of sitting in this dumpy room. But they do it because it gets them something they want. The same with me. If I had to go to prison from time to time, well, that was the price you pay. (Chambliss 1972:x)

Table 8-2   Modes of Individual Adaptation

Mode	Institutionalized Means (Hard Work)	Societal Goal (Acquisition of Wealth)
NONDEVIANT		
Conformity	+	+
DEVIANT		
Innovation	−	+
Ritualism	+	−
Retreatism	−	−
Rebellion	±	±

Note: + indicates acceptance; − indicates rejection; ± indicates replacement with new means and goals.

Source: Merton 1968:1940.

Harry King saw his criminal lifestyle as an adaptation to the goal of material success or "getting something you want." Denied the chance to achieve success through socially approved means, some individuals (like King) turn to illegitimate paths of upward mobility.

In Merton's typology, the "ritualist" has abandoned the goal of material success and become compulsively committed to the institutional means. Work becomes simply a way of life rather than a means to the goal of success. An example is the bureaucratic official who blindly applies rules and regulations without remembering the larger goals of an organization. Certainly this would be true of a welfare caseworker who refuses to assist a homeless family because their last apartment was in another district.

The "retreatist," as described by Merton, has basically withdrawn (or "retreated") from both the goals *and* the means of a society. In the United States, drug addicts and vagrants are typically portrayed as retreatists. There is also growing concern that adolescents addicted to alcohol will become retreatists at an early age.

The final adaptation identified by Merton reflects people's attempts to create a *new* social structure. The "rebel" feels alienated from dominant means and goals and may seek a dramatically different social order. Members of a revolutionary political organization, such as the Irish Republican Army (IRA) or right-wing militia groups, can be categorized as rebels according to Merton's model.

Merton's theory, though popular, has had relatively few applications. Little effort has been made to determine to what extent all acts of deviance can be accounted for by his five modes. Moreover, while Merton's theory is useful in examining certain types of behavior, such as illegal gambling by disadvantaged "innovators," his formulation fails to explain key differences in rates. Why, for example, do some disadvantaged groups have lower rates of reported crime than others? Why is criminal activity not viewed as a viable alternative by many people in adverse circumstances? Merton's theory of deviance does not answer such questions easily (Clinard and Miller 1998).

Still, Merton has made a key contribution to the sociological understanding of deviance by pointing out that deviants (such as innovators and ritualists) share a great deal with conforming people. The convicted felon may hold many of the same aspirations that people with no criminal background have. This helps us understand deviance as socially created behavior, rather than as the result of momentary pathological impulses.

Interactionist Perspective

The functionalist approach to deviance explains why rule violation continues to exist in societies despite pressures to conform and obey. However, functionalists do not indicate how a given person comes to commit a deviant act or why on some occasions crimes do or do not occur. The emphasis on everyday behavior that is the focus of the interactionist perspective is reflected in two explanations of crime—cultural transmission and routine activities theory.

Cultural Transmission White teenagers in suburban Los Angeles attempt to achieve fame within a subculture of "taggers." These young people "tag" (spray graffiti on) poles, utility boxes, bridges, and freeway signs in the San Fernando Valley. While law enforcement officials prefer to view them as "visual terrorists," the taggers gain respect from their peers by being "up the most" on prominent walls and billboards and by displaying the flashiest styles. Even parents may tolerate or endorse such deviant behavior by declaring, "At least my kid's not shooting people. He's still alive" (Wooden 1995:124).

These teenagers demonstrate that humans *learn* how to behave in social situations—whether properly or improperly. There is no natural, innate manner in which people interact with one another. These simple ideas are not disputed today, but this was not the case when sociologist Edwin Sutherland (1883–1950) first advanced the argument that an individual undergoes the same basic socialization process whether learning conforming or deviant acts.

Sutherland's ideas have been the dominating force in criminology. He drew on the *cultural transmission* school, which emphasizes that one learns criminal behavior through interactions with others. Such learning includes not only techniques of lawbreaking (for example, how to break into a car quickly and quietly) but also the motives, drives, and rationalizations of criminals. We can also use the cultural transmission approach to explain the behavior of those who habitually use alcohol or drugs.

Sutherland maintained that through interactions with a primary group and significant others, people acquire definitions of proper and improper behavior. He used the term *differential association* to describe the process through which exposure to attitudes *favorable* to criminal acts leads to violation of rules. Research suggests that this view of differential association also applies to such noncriminal deviant acts as smoking, truancy, and early sexual behavior (Jackson et al. 1986).

To what extent will a given person engage in activity regarded as proper or improper? For each individual, it will depend on the frequency, duration, and importance of two types of social interaction experiences—those that endorse deviant behavior and those that promote acceptance of social norms. People are more likely to engage in norm-defying behavior if they are part of a group or subculture that stresses deviant values, such as a street gang.

Sutherland offers the example of a boy who is sociable, outgoing, and athletic and who lives in an area with a

"Taggers"—teenage graffiti artists—spray paint on a wall in Oakland, California. According to the interactionist Edwin Sutherland, teenagers are socialized into engaging in such deviant acts.

high rate of delinquency. The youth is very likely to come into contact with peers who commit acts of vandalism, fail to attend school, and so forth, and may come to adopt such behavior. However, an introverted boy living in the same neighborhood may stay away from his peers and avoid delinquency. In another community, an outgoing and athletic boy may join a Little League baseball team or a scout troup because of his interactions with peers. Thus, Sutherland views learning improper behavior as the result of the types of groups to which one belongs and the kinds of friendships one has with others (Sutherland and Cressey 1978).

According to its critics, however, the cultural transmission approach may explain the deviant behavior of juvenile delinquents or graffiti artists, but it fails to explain the conduct of the first-time impulsive shoplifter or the impoverished person who steals out of necessity. While not a precise statement of the process through which one becomes a criminal, differential association theory does direct our attention to the paramount role of social interaction in increasing a person's motivation to engage in deviant behavior (Cressey 1960; Jackson et al. 1986; Sutherland and Cressey 1978).

Routine Activities Theory Another, more recent interactionist explanation considers the requisite conditions for a crime or deviant act to occur: there must be at the same time and in the same place a perpetrator, a victim, and/or an object of property. ***Routine activities theory*** contends that criminal victimization is increased when motivated offenders and suitable targets converge. It goes without saying that you cannot have car theft without automobiles, but the greater availability of more valuable automobiles to potential thieves *heightens* the likelihood that such a crime will occur. Campus and airport parking lots, where vehicles may be left in isolated locations for long periods of time, represent a new target for crime unknown just a generation ago. Routine activity of this nature can occur even in the home. If a parent keeps a number of liquor bottles in an easily accessed place, juveniles can siphon off contents without attracting attention to their "crime." The theory derives its name of "routine" from the fact that the elements of a criminal or deviant act come together in normal, legal, and routine activities. It is interactionist because of its emphasis on everyday behavior and microlevel social interaction.

Advocates of this theory see it as a powerful explanation for the rise in crime during the last 50 years. Routine activity has changed to make crime more likely. Homes left vacant during the day or during long vacations are more accessible as targets of crime. The greater presence of consumer goods that are highly portable, such as video equipment and computers, is another

Outdoor ATMs invite trouble: They provide an ideal setting for the convergence of a perpetrator, a victim, and an article of property (cash). According to routine activities theory, crimes are more likely to occur wherever motivated offenders meet vulnerable targets.

aspect making crime more likely (Cohen and Felson 1979; Felson 1998).

Some significant research supports the routine activities explanation. For example, studies of crime in the aftermath of Hurricane Andrew in Florida in 1992 show that certain crimes increased as citizens and their property became more vulnerable. Studies of urban crime have documented the existence of "hot spots" where people are more likely to be victimized because of their routine comings and goings, such as tourist destinations (Cromwell et al. 1995; Sherman et al. 1989).

Perhaps what is most compelling about this theory is that it broadens our effort to understand crime and deviance. Rather than focus just on the criminal, routine activities theory also brings into the picture the behavior of the victim. However, we need to resist the temptation to *expect* the higher victimization of some groups, such as racial and ethnic minorities, much less to consider it their own fault (Akers 1997).

Labeling Theory

The Saints and Roughnecks were two groups of high school males continually engaged in excessive drinking, reckless driving, truancy, petty theft, and vandalism. There the similarity ended. None of the Saints was ever arrested, but every Roughneck was frequently in trouble with police and townspeople. Why the disparity in their treatment? On the basis of his observation research in their high school, sociologist William Chambliss (1973) concluded that social class played an important role in the varying fortunes of the two groups.

The Saints hid behind a facade of respectability. They came from "good families," were active in school organizations, planned on attending college, and received good grades. People generally viewed their delinquent acts as a few isolated cases of "sowing wild oats." By contrast, the Roughnecks had no such aura of respectability. They drove around town in beat-up cars, were generally unsuccessful in school, and aroused suspicion no matter what they did.

We can understand such discrepancies by using an approach to deviance known as **labeling theory.** Unlike Sutherland's work, labeling theory does not focus on why some individuals come to commit deviant acts. Instead, it attempts to explain why certain people (such as the Roughnecks) are *viewed* as deviants, delinquents, "bad kids," "losers," and criminals, while others whose behavior is similar (such as the Saints) are not seen in such harsh terms. Reflecting the contribution of interactionist theorists, labeling theory emphasizes how a person comes to be labeled as deviant or to accept that label. Sociologist Howard Becker (1963:9; 1964), who popularized this approach, summed it up with this statement: "Deviant behavior is behavior that people so label."

Labeling theory is also called the **societal-reaction approach,** reminding us that it is the *response* to an act and not the behavior itself that determines deviance. For example, studies have shown that some school personnel and therapists expand educational programs designed for learning-disabled students to include those with behavioral problems. Consequently, a "troublemaker" can be improperly labeled as learning-disabled, and vice versa.

Traditionally, research on deviance has focused on people who violate social norms. In contrast, labeling theory focuses on police, probation officers, psychiatrists, judges, teachers, employers, school officials, and other regulators of social control. These agents, it is argued, play a significant role in creating the deviant identity by designating certain people (and not others) as "deviant." An important aspect of labeling theory is the recognition that some individuals or groups have the power to *define* labels and apply them to others. This view recalls the conflict perspective's emphasis on the social significance of power.

In recent years the practice of *racial profiling,* in which people are identified as criminal suspects purely on the basis of their race, has come under public scrutiny. Studies confirm the public's suspicions that in some jurisdictions, police officers are much more likely to stop African American males than White males for routine traffic violations, in the expectation of finding drugs or guns in their cars. Civil rights activists refer to these cases sarcastically as DWB violations ("Driving While Black"). Beginning in 2001, profiling took a new turn as people who appeared to be Arab or Muslim came under special scrutiny.

The labeling approach does not fully explain why certain people accept a label and others are able to reject it. In fact, this perspective may exaggerate the ease with which societal judgments can alter our self-images. Labeling theorists do suggest, however, that how much power one has relative to others is important in determining a person's ability to resist an undesirable label. Competing approaches (including that of Sutherland) fail to explain why some deviants continue to be viewed as conformists rather than as violators of rules. According to Howard Becker (1973), labeling theory was not conceived as the *sole* explanation for deviance; its proponents merely hoped to focus more attention on the undeniably important actions of those people officially in charge of defining deviance (N. Davis 1975; compare with Cullen and Cullen 1978).

The popularity of labeling theory is reflected in the emergence of a related perspective, called social constructionism. According to the **social constructionist perspective,** deviance is the product of the culture we live in. Social constructionists focus specifically on the decision-making process that creates the deviant identity. They point out that "missing children," "deadbeat dads," "spree killers," and "date rapists" have always been with us, but at times have become *the* major social concern of the moment because of intensive media coverage (Liska and Messner 1999; Wright et al. 2000).

Imagine

You are a teacher. What kinds of labels freely used in educational circles might be attached to your students?

Conflict Theory

Conflict theorists point out that people with power protect their own interests and define deviance to suit their own needs. Sociologist Richard Quinney (1974, 1979, 1980) is a leading exponent of the view that the criminal justice system serves the interests of the powerful. Crime, according to Quinney (1970), is a definition of conduct created by authorized agents of social control—such as

In the 1930s, the Federal Bureau of Narcotics launched a campaign to portray marijuana as a dangerous drug rather than the pleasure-inducing substance people regarded it as at the time. From a conflict perspective, those in power often use such tactics to coerce others into adopting a different point of view.

The perspective advanced by labeling and conflict theorists forms quite a contrast to the functionalist approach to deviance. Functionalists view standards of deviant behavior as merely reflecting cultural norms, whereas conflict and labeling theorists point out that the most powerful groups in a society can shape laws and standards and determine who is (or is not) prosecuted as a criminal. They would be unlikely to apply the label "deviant" to the corporate executive whose decisions lead to large-scale environmental pollution. In the opinion of conflict theorists, agents of social control and powerful groups can generally impose their own self-serving definitions of deviance on the general public.

Feminist Perspective

For many years any husband who forced his wife to have sexual intercourse—without her consent and against her will—was not legally considered to have committed rape. The laws defined rape as pertaining only to sexual relations between people not married to each other. These laws reflected the overwhelmingly male composition of state legislatures at the time.

It took repeated protests by feminist organizations to finally get changes in the criminal law defining rape. As of 1996, husbands in all 50 states could be prosecuted under most circumstances for the rape of their wives. There remain alarming exceptions: for example, in Tennessee a husband may legally use force or coercion to rape his wife as long as no weapon is present and he has not inflicted "serious bodily harm." Despite such exceptions, the rise of the women's movement has unquestionably led to important changes in societal notions of criminality. For example, judges, legislators, and police officers now view wife battering and other forms of domestic violence as serious crimes (National Center on Women and Family Law 1996).

When it comes to crime and to deviance in general, society tends to treat women in a stereotypical fashion. For example, consider how women who have many and frequent sexual partners are more likely than men who are promiscuous to be viewed with scorn. Cultural views and attitudes toward women influence how they are perceived and labeled. In addition, the feminist perspective emphasizes that deviance, including crime, tends to flow from economic relationships.

Let's look at a couple of these relationships. Traditionally, men have had greater earning power than their wives. This means that wives may be reluctant to report acts of abuse to the authorities and thereby lose what may be their primary or even sole source of income. In the workplace, men have exercised greater power than women in pricing and product control, giving the men greater opportunity to engage in such crimes as embezzlement and

legislators and law enforcement officers—in a politically organized society. He and other conflict theorists argue that lawmaking is often an attempt by the powerful to coerce others into their own morality (see also Spitzer 1975).

This helps to explain why our society has laws against gambling, drug usage, and prostitution, many of which are violated on a massive scale (we will examine these "victimless crimes" later in the chapter). According to the conflict school, criminal law does not represent a consistent application of societal values, but instead reflects competing values and interests. Thus, marijuana is outlawed in the United States because it is alleged to be harmful to users, yet cigarettes and alcohol are sold legally almost everywhere.

Conflict theorists contend that the entire criminal justice system of the United States treats suspects differently on the basis of their racial, ethnic, or social class background (see Box 8-3).

Social Inequality
8-3 Discretionary Justice

www.
mhhe
.com
/schaefer8

Income and race matter when it comes to the criminal justice system. The conflict perspective reminds us that while the basic purpose of law is to maintain stability and order, it can actually perpetuate inequality. Researchers have found that discretionary differences in the way social control is exercised put deprived African Americans and Hispanics at a disadvantage in the justice system both as juveniles and adults. Richard Quinney and other conflict theorists argue that in this way the criminal justice system acts to keep the poor and oppressed in their deprived positions.

How do sociologists determine that suspects and offenders get treated differently based on racial, ethnic, and social class backgrounds? One way is to look at

> **White offenders on average receive shorter sentences than comparable Latino and African American offenders.**

convicted criminals and compare the types of sentences they received for equivalent crimes. This can get complicated because researchers must take into consideration a number of factors that affect sentencing. For example, in their study of federal court data, sociologists Darrell Steffensmeier and Stephen Demuth examined the severity of the crime and the convict's prior arrest record. After taking these and other factors into consideration, they still found that White offenders on average receive shorter sentences than comparable Latino and African American offenders.

Sentencing, moreover, represents only one area of discretion exercised by officials in the criminal justice system. As the accompanying table shows, there are many points where discretion is applied. At each

Discretion within the Criminal Justice System

Criminal Justice Officials	Discretionary Powers
Police	Enforce specific laws Investigate specific crimes Search people, vicinities, buildings Arrest or detain people
Prosecutors	File charges or petitions for judicial decision Seek indictments Drop cases Reduce charges Recommend sentences
Judges or magistrates	Set bail or conditions for release Accept pleas Determine delinquency Dismiss charges Impose sentences Revoke probation
Probation officers	File presentence reports Recommend sentences
Correctional officials	Assign people to type of correctional facility Award privileges Punish for disciplinary infractions
Parole authorities	Determine date and conditions of parole Revoke parole

Source: Adapted from Department of Justice, 1988:59.

of these points lower-income people and members of racial and ethnic minorities are at a distinct disadvantage. Race matters, class matters, income matters.

Let's Discuss

1. Do you know anyone who received a stiff sentence because he or she couldn't afford a good lawyer? Conversely, do you know anyone who was able to avoid a sentence because of an expensive legal defense? What solutions do you see to these inequities in the criminal justice system?

2. Take each criminal justice official in the table and consider how that person's discretionary powers might affect an indigent Black defendant accused of stealing a car.

Sources: Butterfield 2000; Hawkins et al. 2000; Quinney 1974; Steffensmeier and Demuth 2000; Texeira 2000.

fraud. But as women take more active and powerful roles both in the household and in business, the differences between men and women in deviance and crime will undoubtedly narrow.

Feminist scholarship can be expected to grow dramatically in exploring such topics as white-collar crime, drinking behavior (refer back to Table 8-1), drug abuse, differential sentencing rates between the genders, and the whole question of how to define deviance today (Maguire and Radosh 1999).

Crime

Crime is a violation of criminal law for which some governmental authority applies formal penalties. It represents a deviation from formal social norms administered by the state. Laws divide crimes into various categories, depending on the severity of the offense, the age of the offender, the potential punishment that can be levied, and the court that holds jurisdiction over the case.

Over 1.4 million violent crimes were reported in the United States in 2000, including more than 15,500 homicides. The key ingredients in the incidence of street crime appear to be drug use and the widespread presence of firearms. According to the FBI, 18 percent of all reported aggravated assaults, 41 percent of reported robberies, and 66 percent of reported murders involved a firearm. Even with a recent decline in major crime in the United States, current levels exceed the levels experienced in the 1960s (Department of Justice 2001d).

Types of Crime

Rather than relying solely on legal categories, sociologists classify crimes in terms of how they are committed and how society views the offenses. In this section, we will examine four types of crime as differentiated by sociologists: professional crime, organized crime, white-collar crime, and "victimless crimes."

Professional Crime

Although the adage "crime doesn't pay" is familiar, many people do make a career of illegal activities. A *professional criminal* (or career criminal) is a person who pursues crime as a day-to-day occupation, developing skilled techniques and enjoying a certain degree of status among other criminals. Some professional criminals specialize in burglary, safecracking, hijacking of cargo, pickpocketing, and shoplifting. Such people have acquired skills that reduce the likelihood of arrest, conviction, and imprisonment. As a result, they may have long careers in their chosen "professions."

Edwin Sutherland (1937) offered pioneering insights into the behavior of professional criminals by publishing an annotated account written by a professional thief. Unlike the person who engages in crime only once or twice, professional thieves make a business of stealing. They devote their entire working time to planning and executing crimes and sometimes travel across the nation to pursue their "professional duties." Like people in regular occupations, professional thieves consult with their colleagues concerning the demands of work, thus becoming part of a subculture of similarly occupied individuals. They exchange information on possible places to burglarize, on outlets for unloading stolen goods, and on ways of securing bail bonds if arrested.

Organized Crime

A 1978 government report uses three pages to define the term *organized crime.* For our purposes, we will consider **organized crime** to be the work of a group that regulates relations between various criminal enterprises involved in various illegal activities, including the smuggling and sale of drugs, prostitution, and gambling. Organized crime dominates the world of illegal business just as large corporations dominate the conventional business world. It allocates territory, sets prices for goods and services, and acts as an arbitrator in internal disputes.

Organized crime is a secret, conspiratorial activity that generally evades law enforcement. It takes over legitimate businesses, gains influence over labor unions, corrupts public officials, intimidates witnesses in criminal trials, and even "taxes" merchants in exchange for "protection" (National Advisory Commission on Criminal Justice 1976).

Its success has allowed organized crime to serve as a means of upward mobility for groups of people struggling to escape poverty. Sociologist Daniel Bell (1953) used the term *ethnic succession* to describe the sequential process of leadership of organized crime. The leadership of Irish Americans in the early part of the twentieth century gave way to Jewish Americans in the 1920s and then to Italian Americans in the early 1930s. More recently, ethnic succession has become more complex, reflecting the diversity of the nation's latest immigrants. Colombian, Mexican, Russian, Chinese, Pakistani, and Nigerian immigrants are among those who have begun to play a significant role in organized crime activities (Chin 1996; Kleinknecht 1996).

There has always been a global element in organized crime. But law enforcement officials and policymakers now acknowledge the emergence of a new form of organized crime that takes advantage of advances in electronic communications. *Transnational* organized crime includes

Taking Sociology to Work

TIFFANY ZAPATA-MANCILLA:
Victim Witness Specialist, Cook County State's Attorney's Office

Tiffany Zapata-Mancilla's typical day brings her into contact with all manner of crime victims—including those who have survived murder attempts, domestic assault, child abuse, robbery, and other violent crimes—as well as family members who testify on behalf of victims. She works closely with victims who are witness to a crime, since they are invariably called to testify in a trial. "My job is to make the courtroom experience for them as comfortable as possible," she says. That may entail offering these victim witnesses referral for crisis counseling, court escort, court orientation, help with impact statements, assistance with restitution, protection services, transportation, child care, emergency financial assistance, or just a hot lunch. Her caseload of 500 cases come through the four to eight courtrooms to which she is assigned in Chicago's Cook County.

"My sociological background helps me in all situations on a daily basis." In particular, it helps her to recognize the underlying societal issues at play, even in what seem to be horrendous individual acts of crime, and to lead the victims to recognize these issues as well. "I do not judge those who come into the courtroom; I can only judge society." According to Zapata-Mancilla, that doesn't mean that individuals have no personal responsibility for their life choices, but it helps to understand that people are conditioned by the environment and society they live in. One of her cases involved a young man who was to testify as to who killed his younger brother in a gang shootout.

By the time of the trial two years later, he denied knowing anything about the killing and afterward went out to eat with the defendant. It appears he might have been offered a drug job in return for not testifying. Instead of being judgmental, Zapata-Mancilla recognized the situation as one of the need for the young man to survive. Social problems such as poverty dictate to some degree the choices people believe they have to make.

Zapata-Mancilla majored in sociology at DePaul University after being hooked by her introductory course. She went on to earn her master's degree in sociology there in 2001. "I was very interested in societal issues such as poverty, crime, organized crime, and gang involvement, and how they influenced the lifestyles and psychology of individuals. Sociology, for me, offers reasons, not excuses, for why individuals act and react in certain ways." She also thinks that she has gained a greater understanding of herself as a Latina woman through her studies.

Her advice for students: "Keep an open mind and don't be judgmental of others."

Let's Discuss

1. Why do you think victim witnesses need special attention?
2. What aspect of sociological study do you think best prepared Zapata-Mancilla for her job?

---

drug and arms smuggling, money laundering, and trafficking in illegal immigrants and stolen goods, such as automobiles (Office of Justice Programs 1999).

White-Collar and Technology-Based Crime

Income tax evasion, stock manipulation, consumer fraud, bribery and extraction of "kickbacks," embezzlement, and misrepresentation in advertising—these are all examples of **white-collar crime,** illegal acts committed in the course of business activities, often by affluent, "respectable" people. Edwin Sutherland (1949, 1983) likened these crimes to organized crime because they are often perpetrated through occupational roles (Friedrichs 1998).

A new type of white-collar crime has emerged in recent decades: computer crime. The use of high technology allows one to carry out embezzlement or electronic fraud, often leaving few traces, or to gain access to a company's inventory without leaving one's home. An adept programmer can gain access to a firm's computer by tele-

phone and then copy valuable files. It is virtually impossible to track such people unless they are foolish enough to call from the same phone each time. According to a 2000 study by the FBI and the Computer Security Institute, 70 percent of companies relying on computer systems reported theft of electronic information for an estimated loss of $10 billion to all businesses (Piller 2000).

Sutherland (1940) coined the term *white-collar crime* in 1939 to refer to acts by individuals, but the term has been broadened more recently to include offenses by businesses and corporations as well. *Corporate crime,* or any act by a corporation that is punishable by the government, takes many forms and includes individuals, organizations, and institutions among its victims. Corporations may engage in anticompetitive behavior, acts that lead to environmental pollution, tax fraud, stock fraud and manipulation, the production of unsafe goods, bribery and corruption, and worker health and safety violations (Simpson 1993).

"BUT IF WE GO BACK TO SCHOOL AND GET A GOOD EDUCATION, THINK OF ALL THE DOORS IT'LL OPEN TO WHITE-COLLAR CRIME."

Given the economic and social costs of white-collar crime, one might expect the criminal justice system to take this problem quite seriously. Yet white-collar offenders are more likely to receive fines than prison sentences. In federal courts—where most white-collar cases end up—probation is granted to 40 percent of those who have violated antitrust laws, 61 percent of those convicted of fraud, and 70 percent of convicted embezzlers (Gest 1985). Amitai Etzioni's study (1985, 1990) found that in 43 percent of the incidents, either no penalty was imposed or the company was required merely to cease engaging in the illegal practice and to return any funds gained through illegal means (for a different view, see Manson 1986).

Moreover, conviction for such illegal acts does not generally harm a person's reputation and career aspirations nearly so much as conviction for street crime would. Apparently, the label "white-collar criminal" does not carry the stigma of the label "felon convicted of a violent crime." Conflict theorists don't find such differential labeling and treatment surprising. They argue that the criminal justice system largely disregards the white-collar crimes of the affluent, while focusing on crimes often committed by the poor. If an offender holds a position of status and influence, his or her crime is treated as less serious, and the sanction is much more lenient (Maguire 1988).

 www. mhhe. com /schaefer8

Imagine

As a newspaper editor, how might you treat front-page stories on corporate crime differently than those centered on violent crimes?

Victimless Crimes

White-collar and street crimes endanger people's economic or personal well-being against their will (or without their direct knowledge). By contrast, sociologists use the term *victimless crimes* to describe the willing exchange among adults of widely desired, but illegal, goods and services. The opening excerpt for this chapter provided some insights into the world of prostitution, widely regarded as a victimless crime (Schur 1965, 1985).

Some activists are working to decriminalize many of these illegal practices. Supporters of decriminalization are troubled by the attempt to legislate a moral code of

อย่าล่อ

อย่าแต่งอย่างนี้ ให้เสื่อมเสียศักดิ์ศรีจุฬาฯ

Do we victimize victims? In Thailand, female college students are warned that miniskirts can "encourage" sex crimes.

behavior for adults. In their view, it is impossible to prevent prostitution, drug abuse, gambling, and other victimless crimes. The already overburdened criminal justice system should instead devote its resources to "street crimes" and other offenses with obvious victims.

Despite the wide use of the term *victimless crime*, however, many people object to the notion that there is no victim other than the offender in such crimes. Excessive drinking, compulsive gambling, and illegal drug use contribute to an enormous amount of personal and property damage. A person with a drinking problem can become abusive to a spouse or children; a compulsive gambler or drug user may steal to pursue his obsession. And feminist sociologists contend that prostitution, as well as the more disturbing aspects of pornography, reinforce the misconception that women are "toys" who can be treated as objects rather than people. According to critics of decriminalization, society must not give tacit approval to conduct that has such harmful consequences (Flavin 1998; Jolin 1994; National Advisory Commission on Criminal Justice 1976; Schur 1968, 1985).

The controversy over decriminalization reminds us of the important insights of labeling and conflict theories presented earlier. Underlying this debate are two interesting questions: Who has the power to define gambling, prostitution, and public drunkenness as "crimes"? And who has the power to label such behaviors as "victimless"? It is generally the state legislatures and, in some cases, the police and the courts.

Again, we can see that criminal law is not simply a universal standard of behavior agreed on by all members of society. Rather, it reflects the struggle among competing individuals and groups to gain governmental support for their particular moral and social values. For example, such organizations as Mothers Against Drunk Driving (MADD) and Students Against Drunk Driving (SADD) have had success in recent years in modifying public attitudes toward drunkenness. Rather than being viewed as a victimless crime, drunkenness is increasingly being associated with the potential dangers of driving while under the influence of alcohol. As a result, the mass media are giving greater (and more critical) attention to people who are guilty of drunk driving, and many states have instituted more severe fines and jail terms for a wide variety of alcohol-related offenses.

Crime Statistics

Crime statistics are not as accurate as social scientists would like. However, since they deal with an issue of grave concern to the people of the United States, they are frequently cited as if they were completely reliable. Such data do serve as an indicator of police activity, as well as an approximate indication of the level of certain crimes. Yet it would be a mistake to interpret these data as an exact representation of the incidence of crime.

Understanding Crime Statistics

Reported crime is very high in the United States, and the public continues to regard crime as a major social problem. However, there was a significant decline in violent crime nationwide in the United States following many years of increases. A number of explanations have been offered, including:

- A booming economy and falling unemployment rates for most of the 1990s
- Community-oriented policing and crime prevention programs
- New gun control laws
- A massive increase in the prison population, which at least prevents inmates from committing crimes outside the prison population.

It remains to be seen whether this pattern will continue, but even with current declines, reported crimes remain well above those of other nations and exceed the reported rates in the United States of just 20 years earlier. Feminist scholars draw our attention to one significant variation: the proportion of major crimes committed by women has increased. In a recent five-year period (1995–2000), female arrests for major reported crime remained virtually the same, while comparable male arrests declined by 6 percent (Department of Justice 2001d:216).

Sociologists have several ways of measuring crime. Historically, they have relied on police data, but underreporting has always been a problem with such measures. Because members of racial and ethnic minority groups have not always trusted law enforcement agencies, they have often refrained from contacting the police. Feminist sociologists and others have noted that many women do not report rape or spousal abuse out of fear that officials will regard the crime as their fault. Partly because of the deficiencies of official statistics, the National Crime Victimization Survey was initiated in 1972. The Bureau of Justice Statistics, in compiling this report, seeks information from law enforcement agencies but also interviews members of 86,800 households annually and asks if they have been victims of a specific set of crimes during the preceding year. In general, **victimization surveys** question ordinary people, not police officers, to determine whether they have been victims of crime. As shown in Figure 8-3, data from these surveys reveal a fluctuating crime rate with significant declines in both the 1980s and 1990s.

Unfortunately, like other crime data, victimization surveys have particular limitations. They require first that victims understand what has happened to them and also that victims disclose such information to interviewers. Fraud, income tax evasion, and blackmail are examples of crimes that are unlikely to be reported in victimization

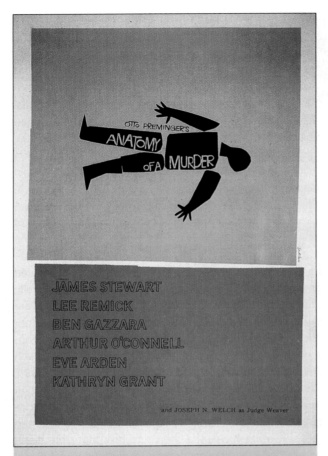

In 1959, when the film *Anatomy of a Murder* was released, there were just over 8,100 homicides in the United States, a rate of 4.6 per 100,000 population. By 2000, more than 15,200 homicides were committed, making a rate of 5.5 per 100,000—an increase of 20 percent.

Figure 8-3

Victimization Rates, 1973–2000

Violent victimizations per 1,000 population age 12 or over

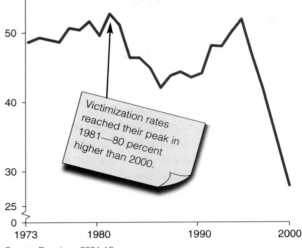

Source: Rennison 2001:12.

studies. Nevertheless, 93 percent of all households have been willing to cooperate with investigators for the National Crime Victimization Survey (Rennison 2001).

International Crime Rates

If it is difficult to develop reliable crime data in the United States, it is even more difficult to make useful cross-national comparisons. Nevertheless, with some care, we can offer preliminary conclusions about how crime rates differ around the world.

During the 1980s and 1990s, violent crimes were much more common in the United States than in western Europe. Murders, rapes, and robberies were reported to the police at much higher rates in the United States. Yet the incidence of certain other types of crime appears to be higher elsewhere. For example, England, Italy, Australia, and New Zealand all have higher rates of car theft than

the United States (International Crime Victim Survey 2001).

Why are rates of violent crime so much higher in the United States? Sociologist Elliot Currie (1985, 1998) has suggested that our society places greater emphasis on individual economic achievement than do other societies. At the same time, many observers have noted that the culture of the United States has long tolerated, if not condoned, many forms of violence. When coupled with sharp disparities between poor and affluent citizens, significant unemployment, and substantial alcohol and drug abuse, all these factors combine to produce a climate conducive to crime.

There are, however, disturbing increases in violent crime evident in other Western societies. For example, crime in Russia has skyrocketed since the overthrow of Communist party rule (with its strict controls on guns and criminals) in 1991. Whereas there were fewer than 260 homicides in Moscow in 1988, there are now more than 1,000 homicides per year. Organized crime has filled a power vacuum in Moscow since the end of communism; one result is that gangland shootouts and premeditated "contract hits" have become more common. Some prominent reformist politicians have been targeted as well. Russia is the only nation in the world that incarcerates a higher proportion of its citizens than the United States. Russia imprisons 580 per 100,000 of its adults on a typical day compared to 550 in the United States, fewer than 100 in Mexico or Britain, and only 16 in Greece (Currie 1998; Shinkai and Zvekic 1999).

SOCIAL POLICY AND SOCIALIZATION

The Death Penalty in the United States and Worldwide

www.mhhe.com/schaefer8

The Issue

On June 11, 2001, Timothy McVeigh, the bomber of a federal building in Oklahoma City that took the lives of hundreds, was executed by the federal government. McVeigh was the first federal death row prisoner to be put to death in nearly four decades. On the state level, more than 700 prisoners have been executed since 1977. These deaths raise many questions from both supporters and critics of capital punishment: How can we prevent the execution of innocent men and women? Is it right to use a punishment that imitates what it seeks to condemn? Is life in prison enough of a punishment for truly heinous crimes? Does capital punishment help deter crime?

Historically, execution has served as a significant form of punishment for deviance from social norms and criminal behavior. For centuries, the death penalty was used in North America for murder, alleged witchcraft, and a few other crimes. Little thought was given to its justification; capital punishment was simply assumed to be morally and religiously justified. In 1834, Pennsylvania became the first state to end its use of executions. Currently, 38 states, the military, and federal statutes continue to provide for execution for selected crimes (Snell 2001).

Execution still raises emotional issues, however. People in the United States and in other nations that have the death penalty criticize capital punishment, especially when it might apply to young people convicted of murders. In 1997, the UN Human Rights Commission called for a moratorium on all capital punishment. It noted, in particular, that only five nations permit the execution of defendants who committed their crimes while younger than 18—the United States, Iran, Pakistan, Saudi Arabia, and Yemen (Turner 1998; UN Human Rights Commission 1997).

The Setting

Death penalties are not unusual anywhere in the world. As Figure 8-4 shows, about half of all nations maintain the death penalty. In 2001, there were 66 executions in the United States. At least 1,625 prisoners were known to be executed in 37 countries in 1998, and another 3,899 defendants were sentenced to death in 78 nations. The countries executing the most people were, in order, China, the Congo, the United States, and Iran. However, since 1996 Chile, Ukraine, and Russia have halted all executions. In the decade of the 1990s, more than 30 nations, including Ireland, Italy, Canada, Great Britain, and Spain, have abolished the death penalty. Only three nations have introduced the death penalty since 1985, and only one of those countries has executed anyone yet. Many nations that permit the death penalty do so only under extraordinary circumstances; Mexico, for example, has not executed anyone since 1937. Yet in some countries the death penalty does remain popular. In Japan, where only 40 people were executed between 1993 and 2001, a national survey conducted in 1999 showed that 80 percent of the public approved of the penalty (Amnesty International 1999; Death Penalty Information Center 2000a; Japan Times Staff 1999; Struck 2001).

For many years, the Supreme Court waffled on the issue of capital punishment. In a landmark 5–4 decision in 1972, *Furman v. Georgia,* the Court held that state death penalty laws, as administered then, were unconstitutional because the states allowed too much discretion to judges and juries in applying the death sentence. Lower courts must consider the circumstances of the crime and the character and previous record of the defendant before imposing the death penalty. In 1976, in *Gregg v. Georgia,* the Court specifically ruled that capital punishment, if administered under the Court's guidelines, was constitutional. Executions can be appropriate so long as they do not involve needless pain or suffering and are not grossly out of proportion to the severity of the crime. Many states then changed their statutes to meet the Court's standards.

Sociological Insights

The debate over the death penalty has traditionally focused on its appropriateness as a form of punishment and its value in deterring criminals. Viewed from the functionalist perspective of Émile Durkheim, sanctioning of deviant acts helps to reinforce the standards of proper behavior within a society. In this light, supporters of capital punishment insist that fear of execution will prevent at least some criminals from committing serious offenses. Moreover, in their view, the death penalty is justified even if it does not

Figure 8-4

Death Penalty Status

Mapping Life WORLDWIDE

EUROPE
1 BELGIUM
2 NETHERLANDS
3 LUXEMBOURG
4 SWITZERLAND
5 GERMANY
6 DENMARK
7 POLAND
8 CZECH REP.
9 SLOVAKIA
10 AUSTRIA
11 HUNGARY
12 ROMANIA
13 BULGARIA
14 GREECE
15 ALBANIA
16 MACEDONIA
17 YUGOSLAVIA
18 BOSNIA & HERZEGOVINA
19 CROATIA
20 SLOVENIA
21 MOLDOVA
22 LITHUANIA
23 LATVIA
24 ESTONIA

AFRICA
1 SENEGAL
2 GAMBIA
3 GUINEA BISSEAU
4 GUINEA
5 SIERRA LEONE
6 LIBERIA
7 CÔTE D'IVOIRE
8 BURKINA FASO
9 GHANA
10 TOGO
11 BENIN

Retains death penalty

Retains death penalty, but has not used it in at least 10 years

Retains death penalty only for exceptional crimes (e.g. treason)

Death penalty abolished for all crimes

No death penalty

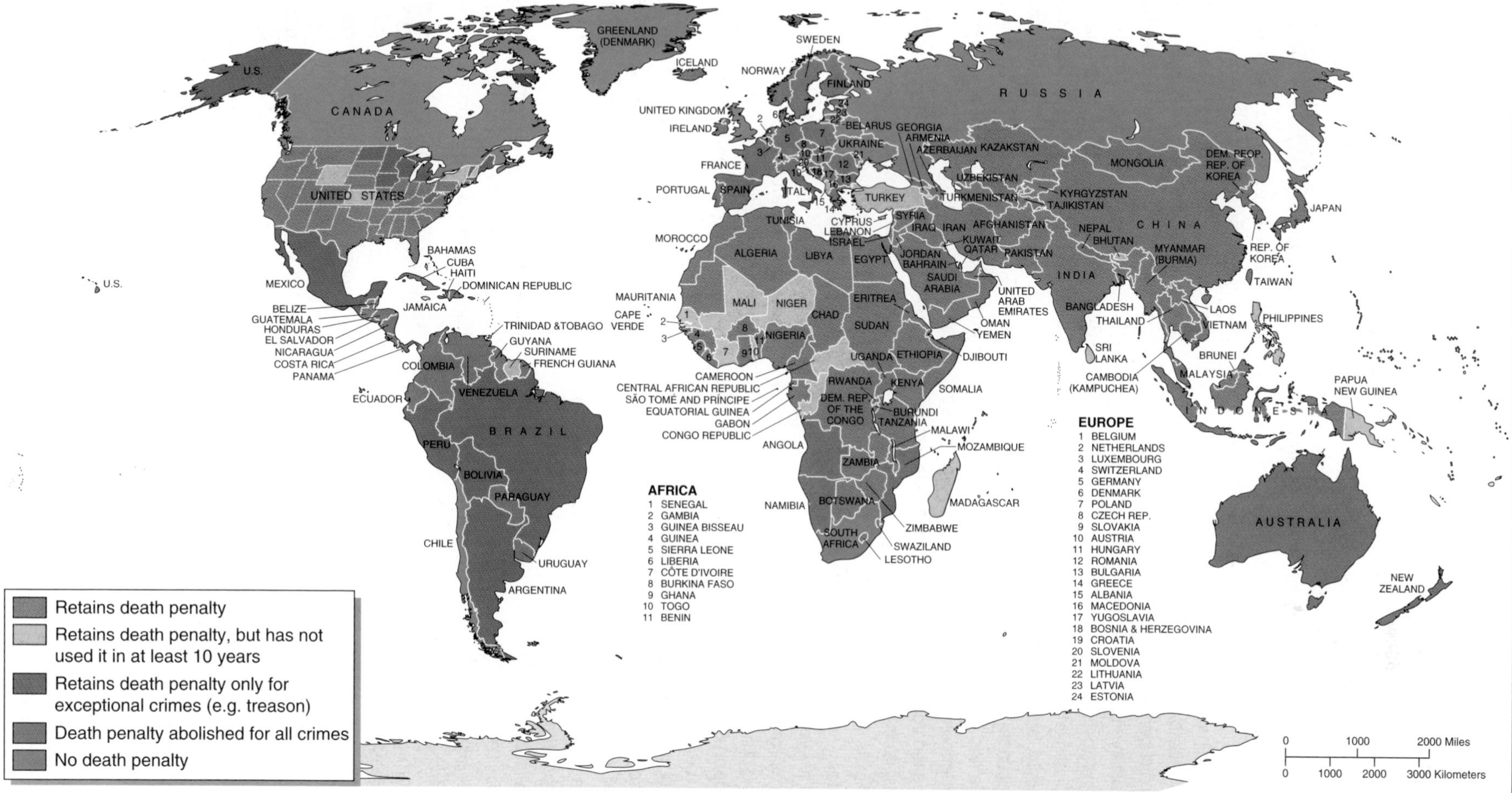

Source: Prepared by author based on Amnesty International 2000 (in conjunction with Death Penalty Information Center).

serve as a deterrent, because such criminals deserve to die for their crimes.

While the functionalist perspective notes the purpose behind the death penalty, there are also dysfunctions. Many citizens are concerned that the alternative to execution, life sentences in prisons, is unnecessarily expensive. However, sentencing a person to death is not cheap. Texas, with hundreds of people on death row, spends an estimated $2.3 million per case, about three times the cost of imprisoning someone in a single cell at the highest security level for 40 years (Death Penalty Information Center 2000a).

The conflict perspective emphasizes the persistence of social inequality in society today. Simply put, poor people cannot afford to hire the best lawyers, but must rely on court-appointed attorneys who are typically overworked and underpaid. With capital punishment in place, this unequal distribution of resources may mean the difference between life and death for poor defendants.

The American Bar Association (1997) has repeatedly expressed concern about the limited defense most defendants facing the death penalty receive. In rural areas of Texas (the state with, by far, the most death row inmates), the maximum compensation to court-appointed lawyers with clients facing the death penalty is $800. In Virginia, the hourly rate for capital defense services works out to about $13. Poorly prepared and poorly supported trial lawyers typically do a poor job. Of the 5,000 death sentences imposed worldwide since 1977, 2,000 have been overturned because the original defense counsel was subsequently deemed incompetent. DNA analysis and other new technologies are exonerating more and more prisoners who were wrongly condemned to die (*The Economist* 1998; Illinois Coalition Against the Death Penalty 2000; McLaughlin 1998).

Another issue of critical concern to conflict theorists and researchers is the possibility of race discrimination. Numerous studies show that defendants are more likely to be sentenced to death if their victims were White rather than Black. About 83 percent of the victims in death penalty cases are White, even though only 50 percent of all murder victims are White. There is also some evidence that Black defendants, who constitute 47 percent of all death row inmates, are more likely to face execution as compared to Whites in the same legal circumstances. There is even evidence that capi-

tal case clients receive poor legal services because of racist attitudes of their own defense counsel. While racism in the criminal justice system is never acceptable, it is particularly devastating when the process results in an execution (Cole 1999; Death Penalty Information Center 2000c).

Policy Initiatives

Many people hesitate to endorse executions, yet when confronted by some blatant horrendous murder in their own country, they feel that the death penalty should be available in some instances. Timothy McVeigh would be an example of such an "appropriate" death penalty case in most people's minds. National surveys conducted since 1936 ask people in the United States whether they favor the death penalty for a person convicted of murder. While support for executions has fluctuated, the majority of people tend to favor the death penalty. In 2001, support was at 67 percent (Death Penalty Information Center 2000b; Paul 2001).

Meanwhile, courts continue to face the issue that only about 250 death sentences are handed out for the more than 18,000 murders that occur annually. How can this be done in a judicially fair manner? Policymakers, however, do not seem concerned with these legal matters. In recent years, federal and state lawmakers have made more crimes punishable by death, curtailed appeals by death row inmates, and paid legal defense costs for far fewer death row lawyers (Bendavid 1998).

International attention has focused on those nations where executions are relatively common (such as China and Iran) as violators of human rights. For nations such as the United States, which usually regards itself as a champion of human rights, the pressure grows from both at home and abroad to abolish capital punishment. However, the death penalty as yet remains popular with both the general public and policymakers in the United States.

Let's Discuss

1. Does the death penalty serve as a deterrent to crime? If so, why are crime rates in the United States comparatively high?
2. What is your position on the death penalty—should it be legal, or should it be abolished? Why?
3. Should youths who have been convicted of violent crimes be subject to the death penalty? Why or why not?

Chapter Resources

Summary

Conformity and deviance are two ways in which people respond to real pressures or to imagined pressures from others. In this chapter, we examine the relationship between conformity, deviance, and mechanisms of social control.

1. A society uses *social control* to bring about acceptance of basic norms.
2. Stanley Milgram defined *conformity* as going along with one's peers; *obedience* is defined as compliance with higher authorities in a hierarchical structure.
3. Some norms are so important to a society they are formalized into *laws.* Socialization is a primary source of conforming and obedient behavior, including obedience to law.
4. Deviant behavior violates social norms. Some forms of deviance carry a negative social *stigma,* while other forms are more or less accepted.
5. From a functionalist point of view, *deviance* and its consequences help to define the limits of proper behavior.
6. Interactionists maintain that we learn criminal behavior from interactions with others *(cultural transmission).* They also stress that for crime to occur, there has to be a convergence of motivated offenders and suitable targets of crime *(routine activities theory).*

7. The theory of *differential association* holds that deviance results from exposure to attitudes favorable to criminal acts.
8. An important aspect of *labeling theory* is the recognition that some people are viewed as deviant while others engaged in the same behavior are not.
9. The conflict perspective views laws and punishments as reflecting the interests of the powerful.
10. The feminist perspective emphasizes that cultural attitudes and differential economic relationships help explain differences in deviance and crime between the genders.
11. *Crime* represents a deviation from formal social norms administered by the state.
12. Sociologists differentiate among professional crime, organized crime, white-collar crime, and victimless crimes (such as drug use and prostitution).
13. Crime statistics are among the least reliable social data, partly because so many crimes are not reported to law enforcement agencies. Rates of violent crime are higher in the United States than in other Western societies, although the difference is lessening.
14. Many nations have the death penalty, but not all of them use it. Sociologists debate the deterrence effect of capital punishment and the social inequality in its use.

Critical Thinking Questions

1. What mechanisms of formal and informal social control are evident in your college classes and in day-to-day life and social interactions at your school?
2. What approach to deviance do you find most persuasive: that of functionalists, conflict theorists, interactionists, or labeling theorists? Why is this

approach more convincing than the other three? What are the main weaknesses of each approach?
3. Rates of violent crime in the United States are higher than in Western Europe, Canada, Australia, or New Zealand. Draw on as many of the theories discussed in the chapter as possible to explain why the United States is such a comparably violent society.

Key Terms

Anomie Durkheim's term for the loss of direction felt in a society when social control of individual behavior has become ineffective. (page 192)

Anomie theory of deviance Robert Merton's theory that explains deviance as an adaptation either of so-

cially prescribed goals or of the means governing their attainment, or both. (193)

Conformity Going along with one's peers, individuals of a person's own status who have no special right to direct that person's behavior. (184)

Control theory A view of conformity and deviance that suggests that our connection to members of society leads us to systematically conform to society's norms. (188)

Crime A violation of criminal law for which some governmental authority applies formal penalties. (199)

Cultural transmission A school of criminology that argues that criminal behavior is learned through social interactions. (194)

Deviance Behavior that violates the standards of conduct or expectations of a group or society. (188)

Differential association A theory of deviance proposed by Edwin Sutherland that holds that violation of rules results from exposure to attitudes favorable to criminal acts. (194)

Formal social control Social control carried out by authorized agents, such as police officers, judges, school administrators, and employers. (186)

Informal social control Social control carried out casually by ordinary people through such means as laughter, smiles, and ridicule. (186)

Labeling theory An approach to deviance that attempts to explain why certain people are viewed as deviants while others engaging in the same behavior are not. (196)

Law Governmental social control. (187)

Obedience Compliance with higher authorities in a hierarchical structure. (184)

Organized crime The work of a group that regulates relations between various criminal enterprises, including the smuggling and sale of drugs, prostitution, and gambling. (199)

Professional criminal A person who pursues crime as a day-to-day occupation, developing skilled techniques and enjoying a certain degree of status among other criminals. (199)

Routine activities theory The notion that criminal victimization increases when there is a convergence of motivated offenders and vulnerable targets. (195)

Sanctions Penalties and rewards for conduct concerning a social norm. (183)

Social constructionist perspective An approach to deviance that emphasizes the role of culture in the creation of the deviant identity. (196)

Social control The techniques and strategies for preventing deviant human behavior in any society. (183)

Societal-reaction approach Another name for *labeling theory.* (196)

Stigma A label used to devalue members of deviant social groups. (190)

Victimization surveys Questionnaires or interviews given to a sample of the population to determine whether people have been victims of crime. (202)

Victimless crime A term used by sociologists to describe the willing exchange among adults of widely desired, but illegal, goods and services. (201)

White-collar crime Crimes committed by affluent individuals or corporations in the course of their daily business activities. (200)

Additional Readings

BOOKS

Best, Joel, ed. 2001. *How Claims Spread: Cross-National Diffusion of Social Problems.* New York: Aldine De Gruyten. Fourteen essays analyze how diverse social issues, such as road rage and gun control, migrate across national boundaries.

Blumstein, Alfred, and Joel Wallman, eds. 2001. *The Crime Drop in America.* New York: Cambridge University Press. A series of essays on the apparent decline in crime, including changes in the drug market in the United States.

Clinard, Marshall B., and Robert F. Miller. 1998. *Sociology of Deviant Behavior,* 10th ed. Fort Worth: Harcourt Brace. An overview of the nature and forms of deviance, including drug use, drunkenness, sexual behavior, and suicide.

Gamson, Joshua. 1998. *Freaks Talk Back: Tabloid Talk Shows and Sexual Nonconformity.* Chicago: University of Chicago Press. A sociologist looks at the presentation of socially dysfunctional or stigmatized behaviors on television talk shows.

McFeely, William S. 2001. *Proximity to Death.* New York: W. W. Norton. An historian looks at the functioning of the Southern Center for Human Rights, which works on behalf of death row inmates.

Miller, Jody. 2001. *One of the Guys: Girls, Gangs, and Gender.* New York: Oxford University Press. A sociological examination of the causes, nature, and meaning of female gang involvement.

Walker, Samuel, Cassia Spohn, and Miram DeLone. 2000. *The Color of Justice: Race, Ethnicity, and Crime in America,* 2d ed. Belmont, CA: Wadsworth/Thomson Learning. Overview of research on racial and ethnic discriminaton in the U.S. criminal justice system.

JOURNALS

Among the journals that focus on issues of social control, deviance, and crime are *Crime and Delinquency* (founded in 1955), *Criminology* (1961), *Deviant Behavior* (1979), *Journal of Research in Crime and Delinquency* (1964), and *Law and Society Review* (1966).

Technology Resources

Internet Connection

Note: While all the URLs listed were current as of the printing of this book, these sites often change. Please check our website (http://www.mhhe.com/schaefer8) for updates and hyperlinks to these exercises and additional exercises.

1. This chapter looks at organized crime, which dominates the world of illegal business. Jerry Capeci's Gangland (**http://www.ganglandnews.com**) is a good site for information about organized crime.
   (a) Choose any two of the button men or wiseguys. List five interesting things you learned about those individuals.
   (b) Read the article about Gregory Scarpa under the daily news column. What are some of the theories about Scarpa's death?
   (c) Read the family history of the Colombo family. Who is the current boss of the family? What are some interesting facts you learned about the family?
   (d) Read the family history of the Gambino family. Who is the current boss of the family? What are some interesting facts you learned about the family?
   (d) Click on the women's page and read about the women who are involved with the crime families. What did you learn?
2. Sociologists and government agencies share a need for timely, accurate, and complete data regarding crime rates. The Federal Bureau of Investigation provides an online examination of crime statistics and a look at the agency itself (**http://www.fbi.gov**) Click on "Most Wanted," "Programs & Initiatives," and "Uniform Crime Reports (UCR)." Then answer the following questions:
   (a) Who are currently the top 10 most-wanted fugitives in the United States according to the FBI? What crimes are they accused of committing?
   (b) According to the data in the UCR section, do overall crime rates appear to be going up or down from 1995 to 2001?
   (c) Choose one crime in particular and track it over the last half-decade. Is the rate going up or down? What might explain this change?
   (d) What is NIBRS and how does it aid in the attempt to acquire more accurate crime data?
   (e) In 2001, how many law enforcement agents were assaulted? How many were killed in the line of duty?
   (f) Which category of persons is most likely to be the victim of a hate crime in terms of race? In terms of religion? In terms of sexual orientation?
   (g) What is NIPC? Why is this an important program of the FBI?
   (h) Why is the collection of crime data so important to social scientists?

Online Learning Center www.mhhe.com/schaefer8

If you are interested in what Americans think about the death penalty, visit the student center of our Online Learning Center at **www.mhhe.com/schaefer8**. Link to "How Americans Feel About . . .". You will find colorful graphs showing you what percent of Americans surveyed favor the death penalty, what percent do not feel it is imposed often enough, and what percent support the death penalty even though they believe innocent people have been executed.

STRATIFICATION AND SOCIAL MOBILITY IN THE UNITED STATES

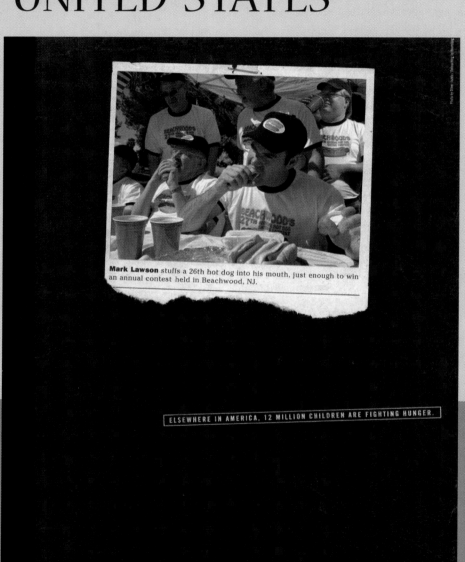

Mark Lawson stuffs a 26th hot dog into his mouth, just enough to win an annual contest held in Beachwood, NJ.

ELSEWHERE IN AMERICA, 12 MILLION CHILDREN ARE FIGHTING HUNGER.

In the United States, some people overindulge while others go hungry, as this public service advertisement reminds us. Social class stratification determines the distribution of resources in our society, from necessities such as food and shelter to relative luxuries such as higher education.

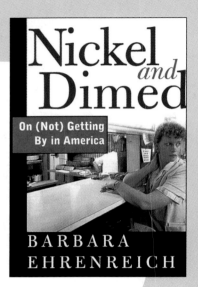

I am, of course, very different from the people who normally fill America's least attractive jobs, and in ways that both helped and limited me. Most obviously, I was only visiting a world that others inhabit full-time, often for most of their lives. With all the real-life assets I've built up in middle age—bank account, IRA, health insurance, multiroom home—waiting indulgently in the background, there was no way I was going to "experience poverty" or find out how it "really feels" to be a long-term low-wage worker. My aim here was much more straightforward and objective—just to see whether I could match income to expenses, as the truly poor attempt to do every day. . . .

In Portland, Maine, I came closest to achieving a decent fit between income and expenses, but only because I worked seven days a week. Between my two jobs, I was earning approximately $300 a week after taxes and paying $480 a month in rent, or a manageable 40 percent of my earnings. It helped, too, that gas and electricity were included in my rent and that I got two or three free meals each weekend at the nursing home. But I was there at the beginning of the off-season. If I had stayed until June 2000 I would have faced the Blue Haven's summer rent of $390 a week, which would of course have been out of the question. So to survive year-round, I would have had to save enough, in the months between August 1999 and May 2000, to accumulate the first month's rent and deposit on an actual apartment. I think I could have done this—saved $800 to $1,000—at least if no car trouble or illness interfered with my budget. I am not sure, however, that I could have maintained the seven-day-a-week regimen month after month or eluded the kinds of injuries that afflicted my fellow workers in the housecleaning business.

In Minneapolis—well, here we are left with a lot of speculation. If I had been able to find an apartment for $400 a month or less, my pay at Wal-Mart—$1,120 a month before taxes—might have been sufficient, although the cost of living in a motel while I searched for such an apartment might have made it impossible for me to save enough for the first month's rent and deposit. A weekend job, such as the one I almost landed at a super-market for about $7.75 an hour, would have helped, but I had no guarantee that I could arrange my schedule at Wal-Mart to reliably exclude weekends. If I had taken the job at Menards and the pay was in fact $10 an hour for eleven hours a day, I would have made about $440 a week after taxes—enough to pay for a motel room and still have some-thing left over to save up for the initial costs of an apartment. But were they really offer-ing $10 an hour? And could I have stayed on my feet eleven hours a day, five days a week? So yes, with some different choices, I probably could have survived in Minneapolis. But I'm not going back for a rematch. *(Ehrenreich 2001:6, 197–198)* ■ ◐

Additional information about this excerpt and about those that open each subsequent chapter can be found on the SocWorld CD-ROM that accompanies this text.

ontrary to popular belief, the majority of poor people in the United States do work; they just don't earn enough to lift themselves out of poverty. In this excerpt from *Nickel and Dimed: On (Not) Getting By in America,* journalist Barbara Ehrenreich describes her attempts to survive as a low-wage worker in two different cities in the United States. Leaving her comfortable home behind, Ehrenreich assumed the identity of a divorced, middle-aged housewife with no college degree and little experience in the paid labor force. She set out to get the best-paying job and the cheapest living quarters she could find, to see whether she could make ends meet. Months later, physically fatigued and demoralized by demeaning work rules—routine drug tests, no talking with coworkers, no bathroom breaks—Ehrenreich confirmed what she had known before she began: getting by in this country as a low-wage worker is a losing proposition.

What puzzled Ehrenreich was why, in an economy in which unemployment was at an all-time low, the people she worked with side by side did not revolt against their low wages and poor working conditions. And why, she wondered, did more prosperous Americans seem oblivious to their plight? The high standard of living in the United States, she knew, depended in part on the low-paid labor of the unskilled workforce she herself had joined.

Ever since people first began to speculate about the nature of human society, their attention has been drawn to the differences between individuals and groups within any society. The term **social inequality** describes a condition in which members of a society have different amounts of wealth, prestige, or power. Some degree of social inequality characterizes every society.

When a system of social inequality is based on a hierarchy of groups, sociologists refer to it as **stratification:**

a structured ranking of entire groups of people that perpetuates unequal economic rewards and power in a society. These unequal rewards are evident not only in the distribution of wealth and income, but even in the distressing mortality rates of impoverished communities. Stratification involves the ways in which one generation passes on social inequalities to the next, thereby producing groups of people arranged in rank order from low to high.

Stratification is a crucial subject of sociological investigation because of its pervasive influence on human interactions and institutions. It inevitably results in social inequality because certain groups of people stand higher in social rankings, control scarce resources, wield power, and receive special treatment. As we will see in this chapter, the consequences of stratification are evident in the unequal distribution of wealth and income within industrial societies. The term **income** refers to salaries and wages. By contrast, **wealth** is an inclusive term encompassing all of a person's material assets, including land, stocks, and other types of property.

Is social inequality an inevitable part of society? How does government policy affect the life chances of the working poor? Is this country still a place where a hardworking person can move up the social ladder? This chapter focuses on the unequal distribution of socially valued rewards and its consequences. We will examine three general systems of stratification, paying particular attention to the theories of Karl Marx and Max Weber, as well as to functionalist and conflict theory. We will see how sociologists define social class and examine the consequences of stratification for people's wealth and income, health, and educational opportunities. And we will confront the question of social mobility, both upward and downward. Finally, in the social policy section, we will address the issue of welfare reform in both North America and Europe. ◼

Understanding Stratification

Systems of Stratification

Look at the three general systems of stratification examined here—slavery, castes, and social classes—as ideal types useful for purposes of analysis. Any stratification system may include elements of more than one type. For example, prior

to the Civil War, you could find in the southern states of the United States social classes dividing Whites as well as the institutionalized enslavement of Blacks.

To understand these systems better, it may be helpful to review the distinction between *achieved status* and *ascribed status*, described in Chapter 5. **Ascribed status** is a social position "assigned" to a person without regard for that person's unique characteristics or talents. By contrast, **achieved status** is a social position attained by a person largely through his or her

pp. 111–112 ◀

own effort. The two are closely linked. The nation's most affluent families generally inherit wealth and status, while many members of racial and ethnic minorities inherit disadvantaged status. Age and gender, as well, are ascribed statuses that influence a person's wealth and social position.

Slavery

The most extreme form of legalized social inequality for individuals or groups is **slavery.** What distinguishes this oppressive system of stratification is that enslaved individuals are *owned* by other people. They treat these human beings as property, just as if they were household pets or appliances.

Slavery has varied in the way it has been practiced. In ancient Greece, the main source of slaves consisted of captives of war and piracy. Although succeeding generations could inherit slave status, it was not necessarily permanent. A person's status might change depending on which city-state happened to triumph in a military conflict. In effect, all citizens had the potential of becoming slaves or of being granted freedom, depending on the circumstances of history. By contrast, in the United States and Latin America, where slavery was an ascribed status, racial and legal barriers prevented the freeing of slaves. As Box 9-1 shows, millions of people still live as slaves around the world.

Castes

Castes are hereditary systems of rank, usually religiously dictated, that tend to be fixed and immobile. The caste system is generally associated with Hinduism in India and other countries. In India there are four major castes, called *varnas.* A fifth category of outcastes, referred to as *untouchables,* is considered to be so lowly and unclean as to have no place within this system of stratification. There are also many minor castes. Caste membership is an ascribed status (at birth, children automatically assume the same position as their parents). Each caste is quite sharply defined, and members are expected to marry within that caste.

Caste membership generally determines one's occupation or role as a religious functionary. An example of a lower caste in India is the *Dons,* whose main work is the undesirable job of cremating bodies. The caste system promotes a remarkable degree of differentiation. Thus, the single caste of chauffeurs has been split into two separate subcastes: drivers of luxury cars have a higher status than drivers of economy cars.

Jacob Lawrence's painting, *Harriet Tubman* Series No. 9, graphically illustrates the torment of slavery as once practiced in the United States. Slavery is the most extreme form of legalized social inequality.

In recent decades, industrialization and urbanization have taken their toll on India's rigid caste system. Many villagers have moved to urban areas where their low-caste status is unknown. Schools, hospitals, factories, and public transportation facilitate contacts between different castes that were previously avoided at all costs. In addition, the government has tried to reform the caste system. India's constitution, adopted in 1950, includes a provision abolishing discrimination against untouchables, who had traditionally been excluded from temples, schools, and most forms of employment. Yet the caste system prevails, and its impact is now evident in electoral politics, as various political parties compete for the support of frustrated untouchable voters who constitute one-third of India's electorate. For the first time, India has someone from an untouchable background serving in the symbolic but high-status position of president. Meanwhile, however, dozens of low-caste people continue to be killed for overstepping their lowly status in life (Dugger 1999; Schmetzer 1999).

Social Classes

A **class system** is a social ranking based primarily on economic position in which achieved characteristics can influence social mobility. In contrast to slavery and caste systems, the boundaries between classes are imprecisely defined, and one can move from one stratum, or level, of society to another. Yet class systems maintain stable stratification hierarchies and patterns of class divisions,

Sociology in the Global Community

9-1 Slavery in the Twenty-first Century

www.
mhhe
.com
/schaefer8

Around the world, at least 27 million people were still enslaved at the beginning of the twenty-first century. And yet the 1948 Universal Declaration of Human Rights, which is supposedly binding on all members of the United Nations, holds that "No one shall be held in slavery or servitude; slavery and the slave trade shall be prohibited in all their forms" (Masland 1992:30, 32).

The United States considers any person a slave who is unable to withdraw his or her labor voluntarily from an employer. In many parts of the world, however, bonded laborers are imprisoned in virtual lifetime employment as they struggle to repay small debts. In other places human beings are owned outright.

The Swiss-based human rights group Christian Solidarity International has focused worldwide attention on the plight of slaves in the West African nation of Sudan. The organization solicits funds and uses them to buy slaves their freedom—at about $50 a slave.

While contemporary slavery may be most obvious in Third World countries, it also afflicts the industrialized nations of the West. Throughout Europe, guest workers and maids are employed by masters who hold their passports, subject them to degrading working conditions, and threaten them with deportation if they protest. Similar tactics are used to

> Around the world, at least 27 million people were still enslaved at the beginning of the twenty-first century.

essentially imprison young women from Eastern Europe who have been brought (through deceptive promises) to work in the sex industries of Belgium, France, Germany, Greece, the Netherlands, and Switzerland.

Within the United States, illegal immigrants have been forced to labor for

years under terrible conditions, either to pay off debts or to avoid being turned over to immigration authorities. But the exposure in the year 2000 of workers toiling under slavelike conditions, together with a shocking government report estimating that 50,000 foreign women had been forced to become sex workers in the United States, have prompted stiffer federal penalties for those who traffic in human beings, and asylum for the victims of such crimes.

Let's Discuss

1. Why are many bonded laborers around the world in the position of slaves?
2. If you were in the position of an illegal immigrant working for what amounts to slave wages, what would you do? Should those who seek the help of the authorities be deported?

Sources: Fisher 1999; France 2000; Jacobs 2001; Richard 2000.

---

and they, too, are marked by unequal distribution of wealth and power.

Income inequality is a basic characteristic of a class system. In 2000, the median household income in the United States was $42,148. In other words, half of all households had higher incomes in that year and half had lower incomes. Yet this fact may not fully convey the income disparities in our society. In 1997, about 144,000 tax returns reported incomes in excess of $1 million. At the same time, about 3 million households reported incomes under $5,000. The people with the highest incomes, generally those heading private companies, earn well above even affluent wage earners. Figure 9-1 shows how much better heads of U.S. corporations are compensated than CEOs (chief executive officers) in other industrial countries. The compensation CEOs receive is not necessarily linked to conventional measures of success. As the U.S. economy worsened in 2001, an analysis showed that the CEOs who received the highest compensation were generally those who authorized the largest layoffs (Andersen

et al. 2001; Bureau of the Census 2000d:vii, 2001a:351; DeNavas-Walt et al. 2001:1, 17).

Sociologist Daniel Rossides (1997) uses a five-class model to describe the class system of the United States: the upper class, the upper-middle class, the lower-middle class, the working class, and the lower class. Although the lines separating social classes in his model are not so sharp as the divisions between castes, he shows that members of the five classes differ significantly in ways other than just income level.

Rossides categorized about 1 to 2 percent of the people of the United States as *upper class,* a group limited to the very wealthy. These people associate in exclusive clubs and social circles. By contrast, the *lower class,* consisting of approximately 20 to 25 percent of the population, disproportionately consists of Blacks, Hispanics, single mothers with dependent children, and people who cannot find regular work or must make do with low-paying work. This class lacks both wealth and income and is too weak politically to exercise significant power.

Figure 9-1

Around the World: What's a CEO Worth?

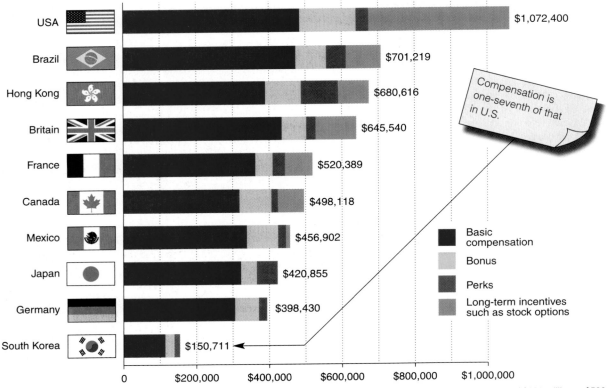

Note: The average annual pay package of the chief executive officer (CEO) of an industrial company with annual revenues of $250 million to $500 million in 10 countries. Figures are from April 1998 and are not weighted to compensate for different costs of living or levels of taxation.

Source: Towers Perrin in A. Bryant 1999:Section 4, p. 1.

Think About It
Why should CEOs in the United States be worth more than those in other countries?

Both of these classes, at opposite ends of the nation's social hierarchy, reflect the importance of ascribed status and achieved status. Ascribed statuses such as race clearly influence a person's wealth and social position. And sociologist Richard Jenkins (1991) has researched how the ascribed status of being disabled marginalizes a person in the labor market of the United States. People with disabilities are particularly vulnerable to unemployment, are often poorly paid, and in many cases are on the lower rung of occupational ladders. Regardless of their actual performance on the job, the disabled are stigmatized as not "earning their keep." Such are the effects of ascribed status.

Sandwiched between the upper and lower classes in Rossides's model are the upper-middle class, the lower-middle class, and the working class. The *upper-middle class,* numbering about 10 to 15 percent of the popula-

tion, is composed of professionals such as doctors, lawyers, and architects. They participate extensively in politics and take leadership roles in voluntary associations. The *lower-middle class,* which accounts for approximately 30 to 35 percent of the population, includes less affluent professionals (such as elementary school teachers and nurses), owners of small businesses, and a sizable number of clerical workers. While not all members of this varied class hold degrees from a college, they share the goal of sending their children there.

Rossides describes the *working class*—about 40 to 45 percent of the population—as people holding regular manual or blue-collar jobs. Certain members of this class, such as electricians, may have higher incomes than people in the lower-middle class. Yet, even if they have achieved some degree of economic security, they tend to identify

Those few Americans who are among the very wealthy form the topmost class in sociologist Daniel Rossides's five-class model of U.S. society. Their expensive lifestyle underscores the unequal distribution of wealth and power in the United States.

with manual workers and their long history of involvement in the labor movement of the United States. Of Rossides's five classes, the working class is noticeably declining in size. In the economy of the United States, service and technical jobs are replacing positions involved in the actual manufacturing or transportation of goods.

Social class is one of the independent or explanatory variables most frequently used by social scientists to shed light on social issues. In later chapters, we will analyze the relationships between social class and divorce patterns (Chapter 14), religious behavior (Chapter 15), and formal schooling (Chapter 16), as well as other relationships in which social class is a variable.

Perspectives on Stratification

Sociologists have engaged in heated debates and reached varying conclusions about stratification and social inequality. No theorist stressed the significance of class for society—and for social change—more strongly than Karl

Marx. Marx viewed class differentiation as the crucial determinant of social, economic, and political inequality. By contrast, Max Weber questioned Marx's emphasis on the overriding importance of the economic sector and argued that stratification should be viewed as having many dimensions.

Karl Marx's View of Class Differentiation

Sociologist Leonard Beeghley (1978:1) aptly noted that "Karl Marx was both a revolutionary and a social scientist." Marx was concerned with stratification in all types of human societies, beginning with primitive agricultural tribes and continuing into feudalism. But his main focus was on the effects of economic inequality on all aspects of nineteenth-century Europe. The plight of the working class made him feel that it was imperative to strive for changes in the class structure of society.

In Marx's view, social relations during any period of history depend on who controls the primary mode of economic production, such as land or factories. Differential access to scarce resources shapes the relationship between groups. Thus, under the feudal estate system, most production was agricultural, and the land was owned by the nobility. Peasants had little choice but to work according to terms dictated by those who owned the land.

Using this type of analysis, Marx examined social relations within *capitalism*—an economic system in which the means of production are largely in private hands and the main incentive for economic activity is the accumulation of profits (Rosenberg 1991). Marx focused on the two classes that began to emerge as the estate system declined—the bourgeoisie and the proletariat. The *bourgeoisie,* or capitalist class, owns the means of production, such as factories and machinery, whereas the *proletariat* is the working class. In capitalist societies, the members of the bourgeoisie maximize profit in competition with other firms. In the process, they exploit workers, who must exchange their labor for subsistence wages. In Marx's view, members of each class share a distinctive culture. He was most interested in the culture of the proletariat, but he also examined the ideology of the bourgeoisie, through which it justifies its dominance over workers.

According to Marx, exploitation of the proletariat will inevitably lead to the destruction of the capitalist system because the workers will revolt. But, first, the working class must develop *class consciousness*—a subjective awareness of common vested interests and the need for collective political action to bring about social change. Workers must often overcome what Marx termed *false consciousness,* or an attitude held by members of a class that does not accurately reflect its objective position. A worker with false consciousness may adopt an individualistic viewpoint toward capitalist exploitation ("*I* am being exploited by *my* boss"). By contrast, the class-conscious worker realizes that *all* workers are being exploited by the bourgeoisie and have a common stake in revolution (Vanneman and Cannon 1987).

For Karl Marx, class consciousness is part of a collective process whereby the proletariat comes to identify the bourgeoisie as the source of its oppression. Revolutionary leaders will guide the working class in its class struggle. Ultimately, the proletariat will overthrow the rule of the bourgeoisie and the government (which Marx saw as representing the interests of capitalists) and will eliminate private ownership of the means of production. In his rather utopian view, classes and oppression will cease to exist in the postrevolutionary workers' state.

How accurate were Marx's predictions? He failed to anticipate the emergence of labor unions, whose power in collective bargaining weakens the stranglehold that capitalists maintain over workers. Moreover, as contemporary conflict theorists note, he did not foresee the extent to which political liberties and relative prosperity could contribute to "false consciousness." Many people have come to view themselves as individuals striving for improvement within "free" societies with substantial mobility—rather than as downtrodden members of social classes facing a collective fate. Finally, Marx did not predict that Communist party rule would be established and later overthrown in the former Soviet Union and throughout Eastern Europe. Still, the Marxist approach to the study of class is useful in stressing the importance of stratification as a determinant of social behavior and the fundamental separation in many societies between two distinct groups, the rich and the poor.

Max Weber's View of Stratification

Unlike Karl Marx, Max Weber insisted that no single characteristic (such as class) totally defines a person's position within the stratification system. Instead, writing in 1916, he identified three analytically distinct components of stratification: class, status, and power (Gerth and Mills 1958).

Weber used the term **class** to refer to people who have a similar level of wealth and income. For example, certain workers in the United States try to support their families through jobs that pay the federal minimum wage. According to Weber's definition, these wage earners constitute a class because they have the same economic position and fate. Although Weber agreed with Marx on the importance of the economic dimension of stratification, he argued that the actions of individuals and groups could not be understood *solely* in economic terms.

Weber used the term **status group** to refer to people who rank the same in prestige or lifestyle. An individual gains status through membership in a desirable group, such as the medical profession. But status is not the same

How does it feel sitting in the chairperson's seat? In the United States a great deal of power resides with corporate boards of directors.

as economic class standing. In our culture, a successful pickpocket may be in the same income class as a college professor. Yet the thief is widely regarded as a member of a low-status group, whereas the professor holds high status.

For Weber, the third major component of stratification reflects a political dimension. **Power** is the ability to exercise one's will over others. In the United States, power stems from membership in particularly influential groups, such as corporate boards of directors, government bodies, and interest groups. Conflict theorists generally agree that two major sources of power—big business and government—are closely interrelated (see Chapters 17 and 18).

In Weber's view, then, each of us has not one rank in society but three. Our position in a stratification system reflects some combination of class, status, and power. Each factor influences the other two, and in fact the rankings on these three dimensions often tend to coincide. John F. Kennedy came from an extremely wealthy family, attended exclusive preparatory schools, graduated from Harvard University, and went on to become president of the United States. Like Kennedy, many people from affluent backgrounds achieve impressive status and power.

At the same time, these dimensions of stratification may operate somewhat independently in determining a person's position. Harry S. Truman was a haberdasher in his native town of Independence, Missouri, but he used a political power base to work his way up to the presidency of the United States in 1945. A widely published poet may achieve high status while earning a relatively modest income. Successful professional athletes have little power but enjoy a relatively high position in terms of class and status. To understand the workings of a culture more fully, sociologists must carefully evaluate the ways in which it distributes its most valued rewards, including wealth and income, status, and power (Duberman 1976; Gerth and Mills 1958).

Is Stratification Universal?

Must some members of society receive greater rewards than others? Do people need to feel socially and economically superior to others? Can social life be organized without structured inequality? These questions have been debated for centuries, especially among political activists. Utopian socialists, religious minorities, and members of recent countercultures have all attempted to establish communities that, to some extent or other, would abolish inequality in social relationships.

Social science research has found that inequality exists in all societies—even the simplest. For example, when anthropologist Gunnar Landtman ([1938] 1968) studied the Kiwai Papuans of New Guinea, he initially noticed little differentiation among them. Every man in the village did the same work and lived in similar housing. However, on closer inspection, Landtman observed that certain Papuans—the men who were warriors, harpooners, and sorcerers—were described as "a little more high" than others. By contrast, villagers who were female, unemployed, or unmarried were considered "down a little bit" and were barred from owning land.

Stratification is universal in that all societies maintain some form of

social inequality among members. Depending on its values, a society may assign people to distinctive ranks based on their religious knowledge, skill in hunting, beauty, trading expertise, or ability to provide health care. But why has such inequality developed in human societies? And how much differentiation among people, if any, is actually essential?

Functionalist and conflict sociologists offer contrasting explanations for the existence and necessity of social stratification. Functionalists maintain that a differential system of rewards and punishments is necessary for the efficient operation of society. Conflict theorists argue that competition for scarce resources results in significant political, economic, and social inequality.

Functionalist View

Would people go to school for many years to become physicians if they could make as much money and gain as much respect working as street cleaners? Functionalists say no, which is partly why they believe that a stratified society is universal.

In the view of Kingsley Davis and Wilbert Moore (1945), society must distribute its members among a variety of social positions. It must not only make sure that these positions are filled but also see that they are staffed by people with the appropriate talents and abilities. Rewards, including money and prestige, are based on the importance of a position and the relative scarcity of qualified

As popular songs and movies suggest, long-haul truck drivers take pride in their low-prestige job. According to the conflict perspective, the cultural beliefs that form a society's dominant ideology, such as the popular image of the truck driver as hero, help the wealthy to maintain their power and control at the expense of the lower classes.

personnel. Yet this assessment often devalues work performed by certain segments of society, such as women's work as homemakers or in occupations traditionally filled by women, or low-status work in fast-food outlets.

Davis and Moore argue that stratification is universal and that social inequality is necessary so that people will be motivated to fill functionally important positions. But, critics say, unequal rewards are not the only means of encouraging people to fill critical positions and occupations. Personal pleasure, intrinsic satisfaction, and value orientations also motivate people to enter particular careers. Functionalists agree but note that society must use some type of reward to motivate people to enter unpleasant or dangerous jobs and jobs that require a long training period. This response does not justify stratification systems in which status is largely inherited, such as slave or caste societies. Similarly, it is difficult to explain the high salaries our society offers to professional athletes or entertainers on the basis of how critical these jobs are to the survival of society (Collins 1975; Kerbo 2000; Tumin 1953, 1985).

Even if stratification is inevitable, the functionalist explanation for differential rewards does not explain the wide disparity between the rich and the poor. Critics of the functionalist approach point out that the richest 10 percent of households account for 20 percent of the nation's income in Sweden, 25 percent in France, and 31 percent in the United States. In their view, the level of income inequality found in contemporary industrial societies cannot be defended—even though these societies have a legitimate need to fill certain key occupations (World Bank 2001a:70–71).

Conflict View

The writings of Karl Marx are at the heart of conflict theory. Marx viewed history as a continuous struggle between the oppressors and the oppressed that would ultimately culminate in an egalitarian, classless society. In terms of stratification, he argued that the dominant class under capitalism—the bourgeoisie—manipulated the economic and political systems in order to maintain control over the exploited proletariat. Marx did not believe that stratification was inevitable, but he did see inequality and oppression as inherent in capitalism (Wright et al. 1982).

pp. 12–13

Like Marx, contemporary conflict theorists believe that human beings are prone to conflict over such scarce resources as wealth, status, and power. However, where Marx focused primarily on class conflict, more recent theorists have extended this analysis to include conflicts based on gender, race, age, and other dimensions. British sociologist Ralf Dahrendorf is one of the most influential contributors to the conflict approach.

Dahrendorf (1959) modified Marx's analysis of capitalist society to apply to *modern* capitalist societies. For Dahrendorf, social classes are groups of people who share common interests resulting from their authority relationships. In identifying the most powerful groups in society, he includes not only the bourgeoisie—the owners of the means of production—but also the managers of industry, legislators, the judiciary, heads of the government bureaucracy, and others. In that respect, Dahrendorf has merged Marx's emphasis on class conflict with Weber's recognition that power is an important element of stratification (Cuff et al. 1990).

Conflict theorists, including Dahrendorf, contend that the powerful of today, like the bourgeoisie of Marx's time, want society to run smoothly so that they can enjoy their privileged positions. Because the status quo suits those with wealth, status, and power, they have a clear interest in preventing, minimizing, or controlling societal conflict.

p. 70

One way for the powerful to maintain the status quo is to define and disseminate the society's dominant ideology. The term **dominant ideology** describes a set of cultural beliefs and practices that helps to maintain powerful social, economic, and political interests. For Karl Marx, the dominant ideology in a capitalist society serves the interests of the ruling class. From a conflict perspective, the social significance of the dominant ideology is that a society's most powerful groups and institutions not only control wealth and property, but, even more important, they control the means of producing beliefs about reality through religion, education, and the media (Abercrombie et al. 1980, 1990; Robertson 1988).

The powerful, such as leaders of government, also use limited social reforms to buy off the oppressed and reduce the danger of challenges to their dominance. For example, minimum wage laws and unemployment compensation unquestionably give some valuable assistance to needy men and women. Yet these reforms also serve to pacify those who might otherwise rebel. Of course, in the view of conflict theorists, such maneuvers can never entirely eliminate conflict, since workers will continue to demand equality, and the powerful will not give up their control of society.

Conflict theorists see stratification as a major source of societal tension and conflict. They do not agree with Davis and Moore that stratification is functional for a society or that it serves as a source of stability. Rather, conflict sociologists argue that stratification will inevitably lead to instability and to social change (Collins 1975; Coser 1977).

Lenski's Viewpoint

Let's return to the question posed earlier—Is stratification universal?—and consider the sociological response. Some form of differentiation is found in every culture, from the most primitive to the most advanced industrial societies of our time. Sociologist Gerhard Lenski, in his sociocultural evolution approach, described how economic systems change as their level of technology becomes more complex, beginning with hunting and gathering and culminating eventually with industrial society. In subsistence-based, hunting-and-gathering societies,

pp. 121–122 ◄

people focus on survival. While some inequality and differentiation are evident, a stratification system based on social class does not emerge because there is no real wealth to be claimed.

As a society advances in technology, it becomes capable of producing a considerable surplus of goods. The emergence of surplus resources greatly expands the possibilities for inequality in status, influence, and power and allows a well-defined, rigid social class system to develop. In order to minimize strikes, slowdowns, and industrial sabotage, the elites may share a portion of the economic surplus with the lower classes, but not enough to reduce their own power and privilege.

As Lenski argued, the allocation of surplus goods and services controlled by those with wealth, status, and power reinforces the social inequality that accompanies stratification systems. While this reward system may once have served the overall purposes of society, as functionalists contend, the same cannot be said for the large disparities separating the haves from the have-nots in current societies. In contemporary industrial society, the degree of social and economic inequality far exceeds the need to provide for goods and services (Lenski 1966; Nolan and Lenski 1999).

● Stratification by Social Class

Measuring Social Class

We continually assess how wealthy people are by looking at the cars they drive, the houses they live in, the clothes they wear, and so on. Yet it is not so easy to locate an individual within our social hierarchies as it would be in slavery or caste systems of stratification. To determine someone's class position, sociologists generally rely on the objective method.

Objective Method

The *objective method* of measuring social class views class largely as a statistical category. Researchers assign individuals to social classes on the basis of criteria such as occupation, education, income, and residence. The key to the objective method is that the *researcher,* rather than the person being classified, identifies an individual's class position.

The first step in using this method is to decide what indicators or causal factors will be measured objectively, whether wealth, income, education, or occupation. The prestige ranking of occupations has proved to be a useful indicator of a person's class position. For one thing, it is much easier to determine accurately than income or wealth. The term *prestige* refers to the respect and admiration that an occupation holds in a society. "My daughter, the physicist" connotes something very different from "my daughter, the waitress." Prestige is independent of the particular individual who occupies a job, a characteristic that distinguishes it from esteem. *Esteem* refers to the reputation that a specific person has earned within an occupation. Therefore, one can say that the position of president of the United States has high prestige, even though it has been occupied by people with varying degrees of esteem. A hairdresser may have the esteem of his clients, but he lacks the prestige of a corporation president.

Table 9-1 ranks the prestige of a number of well-known occupations. In a series of national surveys, sociologists assigned prestige rankings to about 500 occupations, ranging from physician to newspaper vendor. The highest possible prestige score was 100, and the lowest was 0. Physician, lawyer, dentist, and college professor were the most highly regarded occupations. Sociologists have used such data to assign prestige rankings to virtually all jobs and have found a stability in rankings from 1925 to 1991. Similar studies in other countries have also developed useful prestige rankings of occupations (Hodge and Rossi 1964; Lin and Xie 1988; Treiman 1977).

Gender and Occupational Prestige

For many years, studies of social class tended to neglect the occupations and incomes of *women* as determinants of social rank. In an exhaustive study of 589 occupations, sociologists Mary Powers and Joan Holmberg (1978) examined the impact of women's participation in the paid labor force on occupational status. Since women tend to dominate the relatively low-paying occupations, such as bookkeepers and child care workers, their participation in the workforce leads to a general upgrading of the status of most male-dominated occupations. More recent research conducted in both the United States and Europe has assessed the occupations of husbands *and* wives in determining the class positions of families (Sørensen 1994). With more than half of all married women now working outside the home (see Chapter 12), this approach seems long overdue, but it also raises some questions. For example, how is class or status to be judged in dual-career families—by the occupation regarded as having greater prestige, the average, or some other combination of the two occupations?

Table 9-1 Prestige Rankings of Occupations

Occupation	Score	Occupation	Score
Physician	86	Secretary	46
Lawyer	75	Insurance agent	45
Dentist	74	Bank teller	43
College professor	74	Nurse's aide	42
Architect	73	Farmer	40
Clergy	69	Correctional officer	40
Pharmacist	68	Receptionist	39
Registered nurse	66	Barber	36
High school teacher	66	Child care worker	35
Accountant	65	Hotel clerk	32
Airline pilot	60	Bus driver	32
Police officer and detective	60	Truck driver	30
Prekindergarten teacher	55	Salesworker (shoes)	28
Librarian	54	Garbage collector	28
Firefighter	53	Waiter and waitress	28
Social worker	52	Bartender	25
Electrician	51	Farm worker	23
Funeral director	49	Janitor	22
Mail carrier	47	Newspaper vendor	19

Sources: J. Davis and Smith 2001:1401–1409; Nakao and Treas 1990, 1994; NORC 1994.

Sociologists—and, in particular, feminist sociologists in Great Britain—are drawing on new approaches in assessing women's social class standing. One approach is to focus on the individual (rather than the family or household) as the basis of categorizing a woman's class position. Thus, a woman would be classified based on her own occupational status rather than that of her spouse (O'Donnell 1992).

Another feminist effort to measure the contribution of women to the economy reflects a more clearly political agenda. International Women Count Network, a global grassroots feminist organization, has sought to give a monetary value to women's unpaid work. Besides providing symbolic recognition of women's role in labor, this value would also be used to calculate pension programs and benefits that are based on wages received. In 1995 the United Nations placed an $11 trillion price tag on unpaid labor by women, largely in child care, housework, and agriculture. Whatever the figure today, the continued undercounting of many workers' contribution to a family and to an entire economy means virtually all measures of stratification are in need of reform (United Nations Development Programme 1995; Wages for Housework Campaign 1999).

Multiple Measures

Another complication in measuring social class is that advances in statistical methods and computer technology have multiplied the factors used to define class under the objective method. No longer are sociologists limited to annual income and education in evaluating a person's class position. Today, studies use as criteria the value of homes, sources of income, assets, years in present occupations, neighborhoods, and considerations regarding dual careers. Adding these variables will not necessarily paint a different picture of class differentiation in the United States, but it does allow sociologists to measure class in a more complex and multidimensional way.

Whatever the technique used to measure class, the sociologist is interested in real and often dramatic differences in power, privilege, and opportunity in a society. The study of stratification is a study of inequality. Nowhere is this more evident than in the distribution of wealth and income.

Wealth and Income

By all measures, income in the United States is distributed unevenly. Nobel prizewinning economist Paul Samuelson has described the situation in the following words: "If we made an income pyramid out of building blocks, with each layer portraying $500 of income, the peak would be far higher than Mount Everest, but most people would be within a few feet of the ground" (Samuelson and Nordhaus 2001:386).

Recent data support Samuelson's analogy. As Figure 9-2 shows, in 2000, members of the richest fifth (or top 20

Figure 9-2

Comparison of Distribution of Income and Wealth in the United States

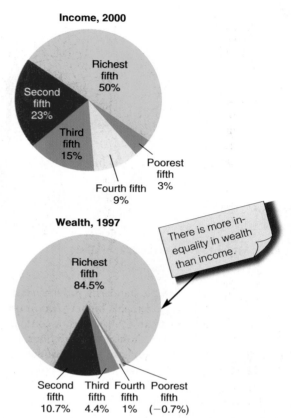

Income, 2000

Richest fifth 50%
Second fifth 23%
Third fifth 15%
Fourth fifth 9%
Poorest fifth 3%

Wealth, 1997

Richest fifth 84.5%
Second fifth 10.7%
Third fifth 4.4%
Fourth fifth 1%
Poorest fifth (−0.7%)

There is more inequality in wealth than income.

Note: Data do not add to 100 percent due to rounding.

Sources: Income data (household) are from Bureau of the Census (DeNavas-Walt et al. 2001:8). Data on wealth are from Wolff 1999.

Figure 9-3

The Growing U. S. Income Gap, 1989–1998

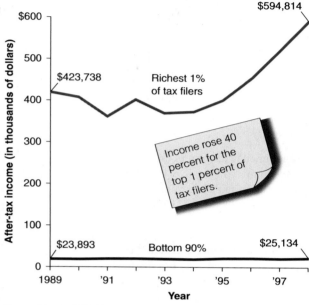

After-tax income (in thousands of dollars)

$594,814
$423,738
Richest 1% of tax filers

Income rose 40 percent for the top 1 percent of tax filers.

$23,893   Bottom 90% $25,134

1989   '91   '93   '95   '97
Year

Source: Shapiro 2001:7.

Think About It
In addition to generous raises and favorable government policies, what else might have accounted for the sharp rise in income for the richest 1 percent of Americans?

percent) of the nation's population earned $141,621 or more, accounting for 50 percent of the nation's total income. In contrast, members of the bottom fifth of the nation's population earned just $10,188 or less, accounting for only 4 percent of the nation's total income.

There has been modest redistribution of income in the United States over the past 70 years. From 1929 through 1970, the government's economic and tax policies shifted income somewhat to the poor. However, in the last three decades—and especially during the 1980s—federal tax policies favored the affluent. Moreover, while the salaries of highly skilled workers and professionals have continued to rise, the wages of less skilled workers have *decreased* when controlled for inflation. As a result, the Census Bureau reports that regardless of the measure used, income inequality rose substantially from 1967 to the end of the century, as Figure 9-3 shows.

Survey data show that only 38 percent of people in the United States believe that government should take steps to reduce the income disparity between the rich and the poor. By contrast, 80 percent of people in Italy, 66 percent in Germany, and 65 percent in Great Britain support governmental efforts to reduce income inequality. It is not surprising, then, that many European countries provide more extensive "safety nets" to assist and protect the disadvantaged. By contrast, the strong cultural value placed on individualism in the United States leads to greater possibilities for both economic success and failure (Lipset 1996).

Wealth in the United States is much more unevenly distributed than income. As Figure 9-2 shows, in 1997, the richest fifth of the population held 85 percent of the nation's wealth. Government data indicate that more than one out of every 100 households had assets over $2.4 million, while one-fifth of all households were in debt and therefore had a negative net worth. Researchers have also found a dramatic disparity in wealth between African Americans and Whites. This disparity is evident even when educational backgrounds are held constant: the households of college-educated Whites have about three times as much wealth as the households of college-educated Blacks (Hurst et al. 1996; Kennickell et al. 2000; Oliver and Shapiro 1995).

Poverty

Approximately one out of every nine people in this country lives below the poverty line established by the federal government. In 2000, 31.1 million people were living in poverty. The economic boom of the 1990s passed these people by. A Bureau of the Census report showed that one in five households had trouble meeting basic needs—everything from paying the utility bills to buying dinner. In this section, we'll consider just how we define "poverty" and who is included in that category (Bauman 1999; Dalaker 2001).

Studying Poverty

The efforts of sociologists and other social scientists to better understand poverty are complicated by the difficulty of defining it. This problem is evident even in government programs that conceive of poverty in either absolute or relative terms. **Absolute poverty** refers to a minimum level of subsistence that no family should be expected to live below. This standard theoretically remains unchanged from year to year. Policies concerning minimum wages, housing standards, or school lunch programs for the poor imply a need to bring citizens up to some predetermined level of existence. For example, in 1997, the federal minimum wage rate was raised to $5.15 an hour. Even so, when one takes inflation into account, this standard is currently *lower* than what workers were guaranteed at any time from 1956 through 1984 (Bureau of the Census 2001a:439).

One commonly used measure of absolute poverty is the federal government's *poverty line,* a money income figure adjusted annually to reflect the consumption requirements of families based on their size and composition. The poverty line serves as an official definition of which people are poor. In 2000, for example, any family of four (2 adults and 2 children) with a combined income of $17,463 or less fell below the poverty line. This definition determines which individuals and families will be eligible for certain government benefits (Dalaker 2001:5).

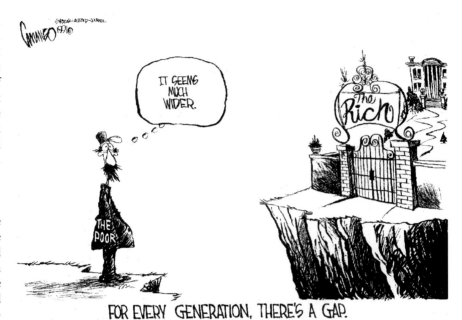

FOR EVERY GENERATION, THERE'S A GAP.

Although by absolute standards, poverty has declined in the United States, it remains higher than in other industrial nations. As Figure 9-4 shows, a comparatively high proportion of U.S. households are poor, meaning that they are unable to purchase basic consumer goods. If anything, this cross-national comparison understates the extent of poverty in the United States, since U.S. residents are likely to pay more for housing, health care, child care, and education than residents of other countries, where such expenses are often subsidized.

By contrast, **relative poverty** is a floating standard of deprivation by which people at the bottom of a society, whatever their lifestyles, are judged to be disadvantaged *in comparison with the nation as a whole.* Therefore, even if the poor of the 1990s are better off in absolute terms than the poor of the 1930s or 1960s, they are still seen as deserving special assistance.

In the 1990s, there was growing debate over the validity of the poverty line as a measure of poverty and a standard for allocating government benefits. Some critics charge that the poverty line is too low; they note that the federal government continues to use 20-year-old nutritional standards in assessing people's level of poverty. If the poverty line is too low, then government data will underestimate the extent of poverty in the United States, and many deserving poor citizens will fail to receive benefits.

Other observers dispute this view. They argue that the poverty line may actually overestimate the number of low-income people because it fails to consider noncash benefits (such as Medicare, Medicaid, food stamps, public

Figure 9-4

Absolute Poverty in Selected Industrial Countries

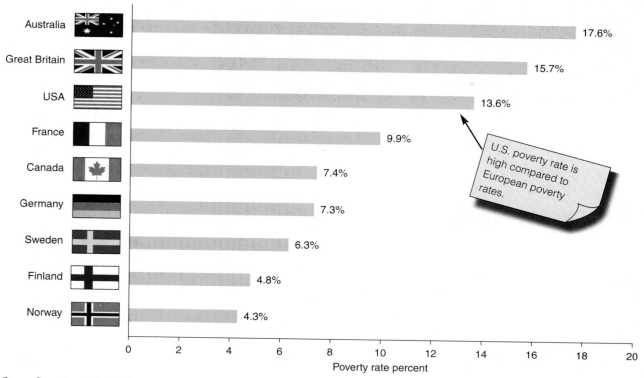

Source: Smeeding et al. 2001:51.

housing, and health care and other fringe benefits provided by some employers). In response, the Bureau of the Census has considered several different definitions of poverty; they showed at most a 1.4 percent lower rate. That is, if the official poverty threshold places 13 percent of the population in the category of the poor, the poverty estimate including *all* these noncash benefits would account for about 11.6 percent of the population (Short et al. 1999; Uchitelle 2001).

Who Are the Poor?

Not only does the category of the poor defy any simple definition; it counters the common stereotypes about "poor people" that Barbara Ehrenreich addressed in her book *Nickel and Dimed*. For example, many people in the United States believe that the vast majority of the poor are able to work but will not. Yet many poor adults do work outside the home, although only a portion work full-time throughout the year. About 54 percent of poor families have at least one full-time worker, compared to 85 percent of all families. Of those poor adults who do not work, most are ill or disabled, or are occupied in maintaining a home (Dalaker 2001:9).

A sizable number of the poor live in urban slums, but a majority live outside these poverty areas. Poverty is no stranger in rural areas, ranging from Appalachia to hard-hit farming regions to Native American reservations. Table 9-2 provides additional statistical information regarding these low-income people in the United States. (The situation of the most destitute poor in the United States and worldwide—the homeless—will be examined in the social policy section of Chapter 20.)

Since World War II, an increasing proportion of the poor people of the United States have been women, many of whom are divorced or never-married mothers. In 1959, female householders accounted for 26 percent of the nation's poor; by 2000, that figure had risen to 50 percent (see Table 9-2). This alarming trend, known as the *feminization of poverty,* is evident not just in the United States but around the world.

About half of all women in the United States living in poverty are "in transition," coping with an economic crisis caused by the departure, disability, or death of a husband. The other half tend to be economically dependent either on the welfare system or on friends and relatives living nearby. A major factor in the feminization

Table 9-2 Who Are the Poor in the United States?

Group	Percentage of the Population of the United States	Percentage of the Poor of the United States
Under 18 years old	26%	37%
18 to 64 years old	61	52
65 years and older	13	11
Whites (non-Hispanic)	83	47
Blacks	12	25
Hispanics	11	23
Asians and Pacific Islanders	4	4
Married couples and families with male householders	82	50
Families with female householders	18	50

Note: Data are for 2000, as reported by the Bureau of the Census in 2001.

Source: Dalaker 2001:2.

of poverty has been the increase in families with women as single heads of the household (see Chapter 14). In 2000, 11.3 percent of all people in the United States lived in poverty, compared to 24.7 percent of households headed by single mothers. Conflict theorists and other observers trace the higher rates of poverty among women to three distinct factors: the diffi- culty in finding affordable child care, sex- ual harassment, and sex discrimination in the labor mar- ket (see Chapter 12) (Dalaker 2001:2).

pp. 101—102

In 2000, 42 percent of poor people in the United States were living in central cities. These highly visible ur- ban residents are the focus of most governmental efforts to alleviate poverty. Yet, according to many observers, the plight of the urban poor is growing worse, owing to the devastating interplay of inadequate education and limited employment prospects. Traditional employment oppor- tunities in the industrial sector are largely closed to the unskilled poor. Past and present discrimination heightens these problems for low-income urban residents who are Black and Hispanic (Dalaker 2001:28).

Sociologist William Julius Wil- son (1980, 1987, 1989, 1996) and other social scientists have used the term **underclass** to describe the long-term poor who lack training and skills. While estimates vary de- pending on the definition, in 1990 the underclass comprised more than 3 million adults in the United States, not including the elderly. In central cities, about 49 percent of the un- derclass are African American, 29 percent are Hispanic, 17 percent are White, and 5 percent are "other" (O'Hare and Curry-White 1992).

Conflict theorists, among oth- ers, have expressed alarm at the por- tion of the nation's population liv- ing on this lower rung of the stratification hierarchy and at soci- ety's reluctance to address the lack of economic opportunities for these people. Often, portraits of the un- derclass seem to "blame the victims" for their own plight while ignoring other factors that push people into poverty. In Box 9-2 we consider Wil- son's latest research into the persis- tence of urban poverty.

Poverty, of course, is not a new phenomenon. Yet the concept of the underclass describes a chilling devel- opment: individuals and families, whether employed or un- employed, who are beyond the reach of any safety net pro- vided by existing social programs. Moreover, membership in the underclass is not an intermittent condition but a long-term attribute. The underclass is understandably alienated from the larger society and engages sporadically in illegal behavior. These illegal acts do little to encourage soci- ety to address the long-term problems of the underclass.

Analyses of the poor reveal that they are not a static social class. The overall composition of the poor changes continually, with some individuals and families moving above the poverty level after a year or two while others slip below it. Still, there are hundreds of thousands of people who remain in poverty for many years at a time. African Americans are more likely than Whites to be "persistently poor." Over a 20-year period, 12 percent of Whites lived be- low the poverty line for 5 or more consecutive years, and 5 percent of Whites lived below the poverty line for 7 or more consecutive years. In this same 20-year period, African Americans were twice as likely as Whites to experience long poverty spells. Two studies in 1998 documented that

Research in Action

9-2 When Jobs Disappear

Woodlawn, an urban neighborhood on Chicago's South Side, used to boast more than 800 commercial and industrial establishments. Today, some 50 years later, there are only about 100 left: mostly barber shops, thrift stores, and small catering businesses. One Woodlawn resident described the changes on returning after many years: "I was just really appalled. . . . those resources are just gone, completely. . . . And . . . everybody has moved, there are vacant lots everywhere" (Wilson 1996:5). Another South Side resident noted, "Jobs were plentiful in the past. You could walk out of the house and get a job. . . . Now, you can't find anything" (p. 36).

More than 35 years have passed since President Lyndon Johnson launched a series of federal programs known as the "war on poverty," yet poverty is still with us. Using surveys, interviews, and census data from 1987 to the present, sociologist and past president of the American Sociology Association William Julius Wilson has undertaken a major study of poverty, the Urban Poverty and Family Life Study (UPFLS). Increasingly, Wilson and his colleagues have noted, the jobless dominate low-income Chicago neighborhoods, some of which have poverty rates of at least 20 percent. The absence of full-time workers is especially noticeable in African American neighborhoods, which have become increasingly marginal to the city's

economic, social, and cultural life. Wilson sees this trend as a movement away from what historian Allan Spear (1967) termed the *institutional ghetto,* where viable social institutions served the minority community, toward a new *jobless ghetto.*

What drives the trend toward increasing poverty in urban areas? According to Wilson, it is primarily the exodus of well-paid jobs, especially in the manufacturing sector. Over the last several decades, U.S. manufacturers have relied more and more on improved technology and skilled workers. They no longer hire many unskilled assembly-line workers,

> **"Jobs were plentiful in the past. You could walk out of the house and get a job."**

who once enjoyed union benefits and some protection from layoffs. A generation ago, the typical ghetto resident might have worked as a machine operator or assembler; today, he is working as a waiter or janitor—if he is working at all.

In Wilson's view, the economy, not the poor, needs to be reformed. He has proposed some initiatives, such as national education standards, to upgrade the skills of youths in poverty-stricken areas. His research also shows a clear need for expanded child care and family support services. And he calls for metropolitan

William Julius Wilson, a sociologist at Harvard University, specializes in the study of urban poverty.

solutions that bridge the central cities with the suburbs. Wilson admits these approaches are not likely to meet with easy acceptance. There is no simple solution to reducing poverty when jobs disappear.

Let's Discuss

1. Have jobs disappeared from a community you live in or near? If so, what changes took place in your neighborhood as a result?
2. Where have the assembly-line jobs that once supported inner-city neighborhoods gone?

Source: Wilson 1996, 1999a.

Hispanics are also displaying chronic or long-term periods of poverty. Both Hispanics and Blacks are less likely than Whites to leave the welfare rolls as a result of welfare reform, discussed in the policy section of this chapter (DeParle 1998; Gottschalk et al. 1994; Naifeh 1998).

Explaining Poverty

Why is it that pervasive poverty continues within a nation of such vast wealth? Sociologist Herbert Gans (1995) has applied functionalist analysis to the existence of poverty and argues that various segments of society

actually *benefit* from the existence of the poor. Gans has identified a number of social, economic, and political functions that the poor perform for society, among them the following:

- The presence of poor people means that society's dirty work—physically dirty or dangerous, dead-end and underpaid, undignified and menial jobs—will be performed at low cost.
- Poverty creates jobs for occupations and professions that "service" the poor. It creates both legal

employment (public health experts, welfare case-workers) and illegal jobs (drug dealers, numbers "runners").

- The identification and punishment of the poor as deviants upholds the legitimacy of conventional social norms and "mainstream values" regarding hard work, thrift, and honesty.

p. 190

- Within a relatively hierarchical society, the existence of poor people guarantees the higher status of the more affluent. As psychologist William Ryan (1976) has noted, affluent people may justify inequality (and gain a measure of satisfaction) by "blaming the victims" of poverty for their disadvantaged condition.

- Because of the lack of political power, the poor often absorb the costs of social change. Under the policy of deinstitutionalization, mental patients released from long-term hospitals have been "dumped" primarily into low-income communities and neighborhoods. Similarly, halfway houses for rehabilitated drug abusers are often rejected by more affluent communities and end up in poorer neighborhoods.

In Gans's view, then, poverty and the poor actually satisfy positive functions for many nonpoor groups in the United States.

Poverty hits women particularly hard throughout the world, a situation known as the "feminization of poverty." Shown here are women and children in India.

Life Chances

Max Weber saw class as closely related to people's *life chances*—that is, their opportunities to provide themselves with material goods, positive living conditions, and favorable life experiences (Gerth and Mills 1958). Life chances are reflected in such measures as housing, education, and health. Occupying a higher position in a society improves your life chances and brings greater access to social rewards. By contrast, people in the lower social classes are forced to devote a larger proportion of their limited resources to the necessities of life.

In times of danger, the affluent and powerful have a better chance of surviving than people of ordinary means. When the supposedly unsinkable British oceanliner *Titanic* hit an iceberg in 1912, it was not carrying enough lifeboats to accommodate all its passengers. Plans had been made to evacuate only first- and second-class passengers. About 62 percent of the first-class passengers survived the disaster. Despite a rule that women and children would go first, about a third of those passengers were male. In contrast, only 25 percent of the passengers in third class survived. The first attempt to alert them to the need to abandon ship came at least 45 minutes after other passengers had been notified (Butler 1998; Crouse 1999; Riding 1998).

Class position also affects health in important ways. In fact, class is increasingly being viewed as an important predictor of health. The affluent avail themselves of improved health services while such advances bypass poor people. The chances of a child's dying during the first year of life are much higher in poor families than among the middle class. This higher infant mortality rate results in part from the inadequate nutrition received by low-income expectant mothers. Even when they survive infancy, the poor are more likely than the affluent to suffer from serious, chronic illnesses such as arthritis, bronchitis, diabetes, and heart disease. In addition, the poor are less likely to be protected from the high costs of illness by private health insurance. They may have jobs without health insurance; may work part-time and not be eligible for employee health benefits; or may simply be unable to afford the premiums (Goode 1999; R. Mills 2000).

All these factors contribute to differences in the death rates of the poor and the affluent. Studies drawing on health data in the United

Social class is a reliable predictor of a person's health. Many of the patients at this public health clinic suffer from chronic illnesses that are directly related to their low incomes, poor diet, and stressful living conditions.

States document the impact of class (as well as race) on mortality. Ill health among the poor only serves to increase the likelihood that the poor will remain impoverished (Haywood et al. 2000).

Like disease, crime can be particularly devastating when it attacks the poor. According to the 2000 National Crime Victimization Survey, people in low-income families were more likely to be assaulted, raped, or robbed than were the most affluent people. Furthermore, if accused of a crime, a person with low income and status is likely to be represented by an overworked public defender. Whether innocent or guilty, the accused may sit in jail for months, unable to raise bail (Rennisson 2001).

Even the administration of state lotteries underscores differences in life chances. A lottery participant is six times more likely to be struck by lightning than to win the jackpot, yet states target low-income residents in their lottery promotions. Lottery terminals are more heavily concentrated in poor neighborhoods than in wealthy communities. Lottery advertisements appear most frequently at the beginning of each month, when Social Security and public assistance checks arrive. Based on studies of lottery purchases, state lottery executives view the poor as more likely than the affluent to spend a high portion of their earnings for the very unlikely chance of becoming an instant millionaire (Nibert 2000; Novak and Schmid 1999).

Some people have hoped that the Internet revolution would help level the playing field by making information and markets uniformly available. Unfortunately, however, not everyone is able to get onto the "information highway," and so yet another aspect of social inequality has emerged—the *digital divide*. The poor, minorities, and those who live in rural communities and inner cities are not getting connected at home or at work. A recent government study found that despite falling computer prices, the Internet gap between the haves and have-nots has not narrowed. For example, while 42 percent of all households have a computer, these computers are in about 80 percent of households with family incomes over $75,000 and in fewer than 16 percent in which families make less than $20,000. As wealthier people start to buy high-speed Internet connections, they will be able to take advantage of even more sophisticated interactive services and the digital divide will grow even larger (National Telecommunications Information Administration 1999).

Wealth, status, and power may not ensure happiness, but they certainly provide additional ways of coping with one's problems and disappointments. For this reason, the opportunity for advancement is of special significance to those who are on the bottom of society looking up. These people want the rewards and privileges that are granted to high-ranking members of a culture.

Imagine

Imagine a society in which there are no social classes—no differences in people's wealth, income, and life chances. What would such a society be like? Would it be stable, or would its social structure change over time?

Social Mobility

Ronald Reagan's father was a barber, and Jimmy Carter began as a peanut farmer, yet each man eventually achieved the most powerful and prestigious position in our country. The rise of a child from a poor background to the presidency—or to some other position of great prestige, power, or financial reward—is an example of social mobility. The term *social mobility* refers to movement of individuals or groups from one position of a society's stratification system to another. But how significant—how frequent, how dramatic—is mobility in a class society such as the United States?

In the movie *Titanic,* the romantic fantasy of a love affair that crossed class lines obscured the real and deadly effects of the social class divide.

Open versus Closed Stratification Systems

Sociologists use the terms *open stratification system* and *closed stratification system* to indicate the amount of social mobility in a society. An **open system** implies that the position of each individual is influenced by the person's *achieved* status. Such a system encourages competition among members of society. The United States is moving toward this ideal type as it attempts to reduce barriers faced by women, racial and ethnic minorities, and people born in lower social classes.

At the other extreme of social mobility is the **closed system,** which allows little or no possibility of moving up. The slavery and caste systems of stratification are examples of closed systems. In such societies, social placement is based on *ascribed* statuses, such as race or family background, which cannot be changed.

Types of Social Mobility

An airline pilot who becomes a police officer moves from one social position to another of the same rank. Each occupation has the same prestige ranking: 60 on a scale ranging from a low of 0 to a high of 100 (see Table 9-1 on page 222). Sociologists call this kind of movement ***horizontal mobility.*** However, if the pilot were to become a lawyer (prestige ranking of 75), he or she would experience ***vertical mobility,*** the movement from one social position to another of a different rank. Vertical mobility can also involve moving *downward* in a society's stratification system, as would be the case if the airline pilot became a bank teller (ranking of 43). Pitirim Sorokin ([1927] 1959) was the first sociologist to distinguish between horizontal and vertical mobility. Most sociological analysis, however, focuses on vertical rather than horizontal mobility.

One way of examining vertical social mobility is to contrast intergenerational and intragenerational mobility. ***Intergenerational mobility*** involves changes in the social position of children relative to their parents. Thus, a plumber whose father was a physician provides an example of downward intergenerational mobility. A film star whose parents were both factory workers illustrates upward intergenerational mobility.

Intragenerational mobility involves changes in social position within a person's adult life. A woman who enters the paid labor force as a teacher's aide and eventually becomes superintendent of the school district experiences upward intragenerational mobility. A man who becomes a taxicab driver after his accounting firm goes bankrupt undergoes downward intragenerational mobility.

Social Mobility in the United States

The belief in upward mobility is an important value in our society. Does this mean that the United States is indeed the land of opportunity? Not unless such ascriptive characteristics as race, gender, and family background have ceased to be significant in determining one's future prospects. We can see the impact of these factors in the occupational structure.

Occupational Mobility

Two sociological studies conducted a decade apart offer insight into the degree of mobility in the nation's occupational structure (Blau and Duncan 1967; Featherman and Hauser 1978). Taken together, these investigations lead to several noteworthy conclusions. First, occupational mobility (both intergenerational and intragenerational) has been common among males. Approximately 60 to 70 percent of sons are employed in higher-ranked occupations than their fathers.

Second, although there is a great deal of mobility in the United States, much of it covers a very "short distance." That is, people who reach an occupational level different from that of their parents usually advance or fall back only one or two out of a possible eight occupational levels. Thus, the child of a laborer may become an artisan or a technician, but he or she is less likely to become a manager or professional. The odds against reaching the top are extremely high unless one begins from a relatively privileged position.

Third, as the later study by Featherman and Hauser (1978) documents, occupational mobility among African Americans remains sharply limited by racial discrimination (see Chapter 11). Even when the researchers compared Black and White males who had similar levels of schooling, parental background, and early career experience, the achievement levels of Blacks were lower than those of Whites. The researchers have also noted that Blacks are more likely than Whites to be downwardly mobile and less likely to be upwardly mobile. Featherman and Hauser offer evidence of a modest decline in the significance of race; yet, we must regard this conclusion with some caution, since they did not consider households with no adult male present or individuals who were not counted in the labor force.

The Impact of Education

Another conclusion of both studies is that education plays a critical role in social mobility. The impact of formal schooling on adult status is even greater than that of family background (although, as we have seen, family background influences the likelihood that one will receive higher education). Furthermore, education represents an important means of intergenerational mobility. Three-fourths of college-educated men achieved some upward mobility, compared with only 12 percent of those who received no schooling (see also J. Davis 1982).

Education's impact on mobility has diminished somewhat in the last decade, however. An undergraduate degree—a B.A. or a B.S.—serves less as a guarantee of upward mobility than it did in the past simply because more and more entrants into the job market now hold such a degree. Moreover, intergenerational mobility is declining, since there is no longer such a stark difference between generations. In earlier decades many high school–educated parents successfully sent their children to college, but today's college students are increasingly likely to have college-educated parents (Hout 1988).

The Impact of Race

Sociologists have long documented the fact that the class system is more rigid for African Americans than it is for members of other racial groups. Black men who have good jobs, for example, are less likely than White men to see their adult children attain the same status. The cumulative disadvantage of discrimination plays a significant role in the disparity between the two groups' experience. Compared to White households, the relatively modest wealth of African American households means that adult Black children are less likely than adult White children to receive financial support from their parents. Indeed, young Black couples are much more likely than young White couples to be assisting their parents—a sacrifice that hampers their social mobility.

The African American middle class has grown over the last few decades, due to economic expansion and the benefits of the civil rights movement of the 1960s. Yet many of these middle-class households have little savings, a fact that puts them in danger during times of crisis. Studies stretching back several decades show that downward mobility is significantly higher for Blacks than it is for Whites (Hout 1984; Wilson 1996; Sernau 2001).

The Impact of Gender

Studies of mobility, even more than those of class, have traditionally ignored the significance of gender, but some research findings are now available that explore the relationship between gender and mobility.

Andrea Jung, President of Avon Corporation, is one of the few women in the United States who have risen to the top of the corporate hierarchy. Despite the passage of equal opportunity laws, occupational barriers still limit women's social mobility.

Women's employment opportunities are much more limited than men's (as Chapter 12 will show). Moreover, according to recent research, women whose skills far exceed the jobs offered them are more likely than men to withdraw entirely from the paid labor force. This withdrawal violates an assumption common to traditional mobility studies: that most people will aspire to upward mobility and seek to make the most of their opportunities.

In contrast to men, women have a rather large range of clerical occupations open to them. But the modest salary ranges and limited prospects for advancement in many of these positions mean there is not much possibility of upward mobility. Moreover, self-employment as shopkeepers, entrepreneurs, independent professionals, and the like—an important road to upward mobility for men—is more difficult for women, who find it harder to secure the necessary financing. Although sons commonly follow in the footsteps of their fathers, women are unlikely to move into their fathers' positions. Consequently, gender remains an important factor in shaping social mobility within the United States. Women in the United States (and in other parts of the world) are especially likely to be trapped in poverty and unable to rise out of their low-income status (P. Smith 1994).

So far in the chapter we have focused on stratification and social mobility within the United States. In the next chapter, we broaden our focus to consider stratification from a global perspective. The social policy section that closes this chapter focuses on the U.S. welfare system, a government program that serves many women and men who are trapped in poverty. The aim of welfare reform has been to encourage these people to find jobs and become self-supporting. We'll also see how other governments have approached welfare reform, and what the results have been.

SOCIAL POLICY AND STRATIFICATION

Rethinking Welfare in North America and Europe

www.
mhhe.
com
/schaefer8

The Issue

- After five years on public assistance, Claudia Melgosa of Glendale, California, is a welfare success story. The 28-year-old mother of two has landed a job at a storage company and moved up to a $9-an-hour customer service position. However, Carlos Sabala of nearby Santa Monica works in a hotel for $7.18 per hour and worries about being edged back into unemployment by the stiff competition for low-wage jobs (Ellis and Ellingwood 1998).

- Hélène Desegrais, a single mother in Paris, France, waited for four months to obtain a place in government-subsidized day care for her daughter. Now she can seek a full-time job, but she is concerned about government threats to curtail such services to keep taxes down (Simons 1997).

- Marcia Missouri of Worcester, Massachusetts, tacks up a handwritten advertisement in the public housing project in which she lives to say that she is available to clean yards and braid hair for a few extra dollars. The sign lists a friend's phone number; she doesn't have a phone of her own (Vobejda and Havenmann 1997).

These are the faces of people living on the edge—often women with children seeking to make a go of it amidst changing social policies. Governments in all parts of the world are searching for the right solution to welfare: How much subsidy should they provide? How much responsibility should fall on the shoulders of the poor?

The Setting

By the 1990s, there was intense debate in the United States over the issue of welfare. Welfare programs were costly, and there was widespread concern (however unfounded) that welfare payments discouraged recipients from seeking jobs. Both Democrats and Republicans vowed to "end welfare as we know it" (Pear 1996:20).

In late 1996, in a historic shift in federal policy, the Personal Responsibility and Work Opportunity Reconciliation Act was passed, ending the long-standing federal guarantee of assistance to every poor family that meets eligibility requirements. It set a lifetime limit of five years of welfare benefits for recipients and required that all able-bodied adults work after two years of benefits (although hardship exceptions are allowed). The federal government would give block grants to the states to use as they wish in assisting poor and needy residents, and it would permit states to experiment with ways to move people off welfare (Wolf 1996).

Other countries vary widely in their commitment to social service programs. But most industrialized nations devote higher proportions of their expenditures to housing, social security, welfare, and unemployment compensation than the United States does. Data available in 2001 indicated that in Ireland, 77 percent of health expenditures were paid for by the government; in Switzerland, 73 percent; in Mexico, 60 percent; but in the United States, only 45 percent (World Bank 2001a:98–100).

Sociological Insights

Many sociologists tend to view the debate over welfare throughout industrialized nations from a conflict perspective: the "haves" in positions of policymaking listen to the interests of other "haves," while the cries of the "have-nots" are drowned out. Critics of so-called welfare reform believe that the nation's economic problems are unfairly being blamed on welfare spending and the poor. From a conflict perspective, this backlash against welfare recipients reflects deep fears and hostility toward the nation's urban and predominantly African American and Hispanic underclass.

Those critical of the backlash note that "welfare scapegoating" conveniently ignores the lucrative federal handouts that go to *affluent* individuals and families. For example, while federal housing aid to the poor was being cut drastically in the 1980s, the amount of tax deductions for mortgage interest and property taxes more than doubled. The National Association of Home Builders, an ardent defender of the mortgage-interest deduction, estimates that it costs the federal government $60 billion a year in lost taxes. This deduction generally benefits affluent taxpayers who own their own homes. According to one study, more than 44 percent of the benefits from this tax break go to the 5 percent of taxpayers with the highest incomes, who together save themselves $22 billion annually (Goodgame 1993; Johnston 1996).

Those who take a conflict perspective also urge policymakers and the general public to look closely at *corporate welfare*—the tax breaks, direct payments, and grants that the government makes to corporations—

rather than to focus on the comparatively small allowances being given to welfare mothers and their children. Any suggestion to curtail such "corporate welfare" brings a strong response from special-interest groups that are much more powerful than any coalition on behalf of the poor. One example of corporate welfare is the airline bailout bill that was passed in the wake of terrorist attacks on the United States in September 2001. Within 11 days the federal government had approved the bailout, whose positive impact was felt largely by airline executives and shareholders. Relatively low-paid airline employees were still laid off, and hundreds of thousands of low-wage workers in airports, hotels, and related industries received little or no assistance. Efforts to broaden unemployment assistance to help these marginally employed workers failed (Hartman and Miller 2001).

Policy Initiatives

The government likes to highlight success stories such as that of Claudia Melgosa (described at the beginning of this section). It is true that people who previously depended on tax dollars are now working and paying taxes themselves. But it is much too soon to see if "workfare" will be successful. The new jobs that were generated by the booming economy of the late 1990s were an unrealistic test of the system. Prospects for the hard-core jobless—those people who are hard to train or are encumbered by drug or alcohol abuse, physical disabilities, or child care needs—have faded as the boom passed and the economy moved into recession.

True, fewer people are now on welfare. By 2001, five years after the welfare reform law was passed, 8.9 million people had left the system, reducing the rolls to 5.4 million people. Yet research showed that most adults who had gone off welfare had taken low-wage jobs that did not offer benefits. As they moved off welfare, their Medicaid coverage ended, leaving them without health insurance. Support has also been lacking for working parents who need high-quality child care. And assistance to immigrants, even those who are legal residents, continues to be limited. As pressure mounts to provide services to these former welfare recipients, the working poor, like Carlos Sabala, complain, "We get nothing" (Bernstein and Greenberg 2001; Boushey et al. 2001; Department of Health and Human Services 2001; Haskins and Blank 2001).

European governments have encountered many of the same citizen demands as found in North America: Keep our taxes low, even if it means reducing services to the poor. However, nations in eastern and central Europe have faced a special challenge since the end of communism. The governments in those nations had traditionally provided an impressive array of social services, but they differed from capitalist systems in several important respects. First, the communist system was premised on full employment, so there was no need to provide unemployment insurance; social services focused on the old and the disabled. Second, subsidies, such as for housing and even utilities, played an important role. With new competi-

tion from the West and tight budgets, some of these countries (as well as Sweden, despite its long history of social welfare programs) are beginning to realize that universal coverage is no longer affordable and must be replaced with targeted programs. Still, only modest cutbacks have been made in European social service programs, leaving them much more generous than those in the United States (Gornick 2001).

Both in North America and Europe, people are beginning to turn to private means to support themselves. For instance, they are investing money for their later years rather than depending on government social security programs. But that solution only works if you have a job and can save money. Increasing proportions of people are seeing the gap between themselves and the affluent growing with fewer government programs aimed to assist them. Solutions are frequently left to the private sector, while government policy initiatives at the national level all but disappear.

Let's Discuss

1. How does the level of spending for social services in the United States compare with that of European countries? What accounts for the differences?
2. Do you think welfare recipients should be required to work? What kind of support should they be given?
3. Has the welfare system that went into effect in the United States in 1996 been successful? Why or why not?

Chapter Resources

Summary

Stratification is the structured ranking of entire groups of people that perpetuates unequal economic rewards and power in a society. In this chapter, we examine three general systems of stratification, the explanations offered by functionalist and conflict theorists for the existence of social inequality, the relationship between stratification and social mobility, and the welfare system in North America and Europe.

1. Some degree of *social inequality* characterizes all cultures.
2. Systems of *stratification* include *slavery, castes,* and social *class.*

3. Karl Marx saw that differences in access to the means of production created social, economic, and political inequality and distinct classes of owners and laborers.
4. Max Weber identified three analytically distinct components of stratification: *class, status group,* and *power.*
5. Functionalists argue that stratification is necessary to motivate people to fill society's important positions; conflict theorists see stratification as a major source of societal tension and conflict.

6. One consequence of social class in the United States is that both *wealth* and *income* are distributed unevenly.
7. The category of the "poor" defies any simple definition, and counters common stereotypes about "poor people." The long-term poor, who lack training and skills, form an *underclass.*
8. Functionalists find that the poor satisfy positive functions for many of the nonpoor in the United States.
9. One's *life chances*—opportunities for obtaining material goods, positive living conditions, and favorable life experiences—are related to one's social class. Occupying a high social position improves a person's life chances.
10. *Social mobility* is more likely to be found in an *open system* that emphasizes achieved status than in a *closed system* that focuses on ascribed characteristics. Race, gender, and family background are important factors in social mobility.
11. Many governments are struggling with how much tax revenue to spend on welfare programs. The trend in the United States is to put welfare recipients to work.

Critical Thinking Questions

1. Sociologist Daniel Rossides has conceptualized the class system of the United States using a five-class model. According to Rossides, the upper-middle class and the lower-middle class together account for about 40 percent of the nation's population. Yet studies suggest that a higher proportion of respondents identify themselves as "middle class." Drawing on the model presented by Rossides, suggest why members of both the upper class and the working class might prefer to identify themselves as "middle class."

2. Sociological study of stratification generally is conducted at the macro level and draws most heavily on the functionalist and conflict perspectives. How might sociologists use the *interactionist* perspective to examine social class inequalities within a college community?

3. Imagine you have the opportunity to do research on changing patterns of social mobility in the United States. What specific question would you want to investigate, and how would you go about it?

Key Terms

Absolute poverty A standard of poverty based on a minimum level of subsistence below which families should not be expected to live. (page 224)

Achieved status A social position attained by a person largely through his or her own efforts. (213)

Ascribed status A social position "assigned" to a person by society without regard for the person's unique talents or characteristics. (213)

Bourgeoisie Karl Marx's term for the capitalist class, comprising the owners of the means of production. (217)

Capitalism An economic system in which the means of production are largely in private hands and the main incentive for economic activity is the accumulation of profits. (217)

Castes Hereditary systems of rank, usually religiously dictated, that tend to be fixed and immobile. (214)

Class A group of people who have a similar level of wealth and income. (218)

Class consciousness In Karl Marx's view, a subjective awareness held by members of a class regarding their common vested interests and need for collective political action to bring about social change. (217)

Class system A social ranking based primarily on economic position in which achieved characteristics can influence social mobility. (214)

Closed system A social system in which there is little or no possibility of individual mobility. (230)

Dominant ideology A set of cultural beliefs and practices that helps to maintain powerful social, economic, and political interests. (220)

Esteem The reputation that a particular individual has earned within an occupation. (221)

False consciousness A term used by Karl Marx to describe an attitude held by members of a class that does not accurately reflect their objective position. (217)

Horizontal mobility The movement of an individual from one social position to another of the same rank. (230)

Income Salaries and wages. (213)

Intergenerational mobility Changes in the social position of children relative to their parents. (230)

Intragenerational mobility Changes in a person's social position within his or her adult life. (230)

Life chances People's opportunities to provide themselves with material goods, positive living conditions, and favorable life experiences. (228)

Objective method   A technique for measuring social class that assigns individuals to classes on the basis of criteria such as occupation, education, income, and place of residence. (221)

Open system   A social system in which the position of each individual is influenced by his or her achieved status. (230)

Power   The ability to exercise one's will over others. (218)

Prestige   The respect and admiration that an occupation holds in a society. (221)

Proletariat   Karl Marx's term for the working class in a capitalist society. (217)

Relative poverty   A floating standard of deprivation by which people at the bottom of a society, whatever their lifestyles, are judged to be disadvantaged in comparison with the nation as a whole. (224)

Slavery   A system of enforced servitude in which people are legally owned by others and in which enslaved status is transferred from parents to children. (214)

Social inequality   A condition in which members of a society have different amounts of wealth, prestige, or power. (213)

Social mobility   Movement of individuals or groups from one position of a society's stratification system to another. (229)

Status group   People who have the same prestige or lifestyle, independent of their class positions. (218)

Stratification   A structured ranking of entire groups of people that perpetuates unequal economic rewards and power in a society. (213)

Underclass   Long-term poor people who lack training and skills. (226)

Vertical mobility   The movement of a person from one social position to another of a different rank. (230)

Wealth   An inclusive term encompassing all of a person's material assets, including land and other types of property. (213)

Additional Readings

BOOKS

Bales, Kevin. 1999. *Disposable People: New Slavery in the Global Economy.* Berkeley: University of California Press. Considers the more than 27 million people around the world who are victims of coerced labor. Offers case studies of Brazil, India, Mauritania, Thailand, the United States, and parts of Europe.

Bluestone, Barry, and Bennett Harrison. 1999. *Growing Prosperity: The Battle for Growth with Equity in the 21st Century.* Boston: Harrison Century Foundation/Houghton Mifflin. A critical look at the impact of the red-hot U.S. economy on the entire population.

Bonacich, Edna, and Richard Appelbaum. 2000. *Behind the Label: Inequality in the Los Angeles Apparel Industry.* Berkeley: University of California Press. Examines the new wave of sweatshops that has made Los Angeles the largest center of clothing production in the United States.

Braun, Denny. 1997. *The Rich Get Richer.* 2d ed. Chicago: Nelson-Hall. A sociologist looks at growing inequality within the United States, as well as throughout the world, with a special focus on the rise of multinational corporations.

Herman, Andrew. 1999. *The "Better Angels" of Capitalism: Rhetoric, Narrative, and Moral Identity among Men of the American Upper Class.* Boulder, CO: Westview Press. An ethnographic study of wealthy men in the United States, which notes how they are able to persuade themselves and others of the legitimacy of their power and privilege.

Oliver, Melvin L., and Thomas M. Shapiro. 1995. *Black Wealth/White Wealth: New Perspectives on Racial Inequality.* New York: Rutledge. A detailed examination of the massive differences in wealth between African Americans and Whites, regardless of education and occupation.

JOURNALS

Among the journals that focus on issues of stratification, social class, and social mobility are *American Journal of Economics and Sociology* (founded in 1941), *Humanity and Society* (1977), *Journal of Poverty* (1997), and *Review of Black Political Economy* (1970). See also the *Current Population Reports* series published by the Bureau of the Census (available at www.census.gov).

Technology Resources

Internet Connection

*Note: While all the URLs listed were current as of the printing of this book, these sites often change. Please check our website (**http://www.mhhe.com/schaefer8**) for updates and hyperlinks to this exercise and additional exercises.*

1. *i*Abolish is a project of the American Anti-Slavery Group (AASG), a grassroots organization founded in 1993 to combat slavery around the world. Go to the project's website (**http://www.iabolish.com**) and answer the following questions:
   (a) What is the mission of *i*Abolish?
   (b) Under "Slavery Today," link to "Special Features" and click on the United States. According to the CIA, how many people are enslaved in the United States today?
   (c) Read the CIA intelligence report. How many women and children are trafficked to the United States each year? Where do they come from?
   (d) What is trafficking?
   (e) What is the purpose of the Victims of Trafficking Protection Act?
   (f) Look at the map. Has a case of slavery been discovered in your state? If not, find a state in which slavery has been discovered and report on the case.

2. In any society, the affluent and powerful have not only more material possessions than others, but significantly more nonmaterial benefits. the motion picture *Titanic* showed that not just passengers' "life chances," but their actual survival of the ship's sinking depended on their social class standing. To learn more about the *Titanic*, go to the website (**http://www.encyclopedia-titanic.org**) and link to "More Articles." Read the first few pages of "The Fateful Journey of Third Class Men on the Titanic" by David Gleicher, and answer the following questions:
   (a) Look at the Passenger Occupancy Table. How many children perished in the after quarters?

   (b) How many single males perished in the forward quarters? Why?
   (c) According to Wilding, how many standard lifeboats were available for the men in third class?
   (d) According to testimony, what kind of rescue efforts were made to save the men in third class?
   (e) If a comparable tragedy were to occur today, do you think third-class passengers would receive the same treatment as others? Why or why not?

3. Dr. John Newmeyer, an epidemiologist at the Haight-Ashbury Free Clinic in San Francisco, has published an essay called "Seven Paths of Upward Social Mobility." Go to his website (**http://www.newmeyer.com/about.html**), link to "Title Index," and select "S to Z." Read the essay entitled "Seven Paths of Upward Mobility" and answer the following questions:
   (a) Do you agree with Dr. Newmeyer that there are only seven paths through which a person can move into a higher social class? Explain.
   (b) The first path listed is Education. Compare what Dr. Newmeyer writes with what your textbook tells you about the impact of education on social mobility.
   (c) Dr. Newmeyer believes that one-third of those born into the lower class in the United States will achieve middle-class status within a generation. Based on what you have learned about stratification in the United States, do you agree with him? Explain, using as examples people you know or have heard of.
   (d) Do you think that for most people, marrying into a higher social class is a realistic means of social class mobility? Why or why not?
   (e) Which of the seven paths do you consider the most effective means of social mobility? Why?

OnLine Learning Center www.mhhe.com/schaefer8

When you visit the student center in the Online Learning Center at **www.mhhe.com/schaefer8,** link to "Audio Clips." Listen to Richard Schaefer, the author of your textbook, talk about some sociology students he taught and their pres- tige rankings of various occupations. These sociology students were all "lifers" in a maximum-security prison. Professor Schaefer defines prestige, then tells you how these students ranked the prestige of police officers, judges, lawyers, and governors.

SOCIAL INEQUALITY
WORLDWIDE

Models courtesy of The LEGO Group.

SPOT THE REFUGEE

There he is. Fourth row, second from the left. The one with the moustache. Obvious really.

Maybe not. The unsavoury-looking character you're looking at is more likely to be your average neighbourhood slob with a grubby vest and a weekend's stubble on his chin.

And the real refugee could just as easily be the clean-cut fellow on his left.

You see, refugees are just like you and me.

Except for one thing.

Everything they once had has been left behind. Home, family, possessions, all gone. They have nothing.

And nothing is all they'll ever have unless we all extend a helping hand.

We know you can't give them back the things that others have taken away.

We're not even asking for money (though every penny certainly helps).

But we are asking that you keep an open mind. And a smile of welcome.

It may not seem much. But to a refugee it can mean everything.

UNHCR is a strictly humanitarian organization funded only by voluntary contributions. Currently it is responsible for more than 23 million refugees around the world.

**UNHCR Public Information
P.O. Box 2500
1211 Geneva 2, Switzerland**

UNHCR

United Nations High Commissioner for Refugees

Though human rights are universal, not everyone in the world enjoys them. Worldwide, millions of people have become refugees from political, ethnic, or religious oppression. This poster, sponsored by the United Nations High Commissioner for Refugees, urges those who are more fortunate to welcome them.

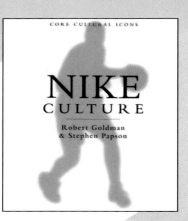

Instantly recognized throughout the world, the *Nike swoosh* sometimes seems to be everywhere—on shirts and caps and pants. The icon is no longer confined to shoes as sponsorship deals have plastered the *swoosh* across jerseys and sporting arenas of all manner, from basketball to football to volleyball to track to soccer to tennis to hockey. *Nike's* growth strategy is based on penetrating new markets in apparel while making acquisitions in sporting goods. The value of the *swoosh* now runs so deep that visitors to remote, rural, and impoverished regions of the Third World report finding peasants sewing crude *swoosh* imitations onto shirts and caps, not for the world market but for local consumption. . . . As the *Nike* symbol has grown ascendant in the marketplace of images, *Nike* has become the sign some people love to love and the sign others love to hate. . . .

Nike is a transnational corporation that links national economies into a complex web of global production arrangement. . . . Almost all production of shoes, apparel and accessories is outsourced to contract suppliers in developing nations while the home office in Beaverton, Oregon designs, develops, and markets the branded goods. . . .

It is very difficult to compete in today's athletic footwear industry without engaging in the outsourcing of labor to relatively unskilled laborers in impoverished nations. Companies in the athletic footwear industry depend on the existence of poor Asian nations where there is a ready surplus of labor force in need of work and wages, even if those wages are below the poverty line. . . .

Nike speaks the language of universal rights, concern for children, transcendence over the categories of age, race, gender, disability or any social stereotype. As moral philosophy, its images speak out against racism, sexism, and ageism. *Nike's* imagery celebrates sport, athletic activity, and play as universally rewarding categories. Playing makes for healthier, more productive citizens, and better self-actualized human beings. However, no matter what its imagery suggests, *Nike,* like any other capitalist firm, must operate within the relationships and constraints of competitive capitalist marketplaces. No matter how many P.L.A.Y. commercials *Nike* runs on TV, there will still be haunting images of production practices in Pakistan, Indonesia, and Vietnam. As the world grows more unified, it becomes increasingly difficult to suppress entirely those gaps between image and practice, between humanism and capitalism, between moral philosophy and the bottom line of corporate profit growth. *(Goldman and Papson 1998:2, 6–8, 184)* ■ 🔴

Additional information about this excerpt and about those that open each subsequent chapter can be found on the SocWorld CD-ROM that accompanies this text.

240

As sociologists Robert Goldman and Stephen Papson note in their book *Nike Culture,* the Nike symbol (the swoosh) and philosophy ("Just do it") have swept the world. People in all parts of the globe pay up to hundreds of dollars for a pair of Air Jordan shoes, and teams in all kinds of sporting arenas wear the Nike logo. Unfortunately, there is another side to Nike's global dominance. Its products are made in harsh sweatshop conditions for very little compensation, mostly in the developing nations. One group critical of Nike's practices claimed in 1996 that the 45 Indonesian workers who participated in making a $70 pair of Air Pegasus shoes shared a total of $1.60. Other stories of Vietnamese and Chinese women who are subject to health and safety hazards, pitifully underpaid, and physically harassed by shop floor managers have also helped to fuel concern about human rights violations.

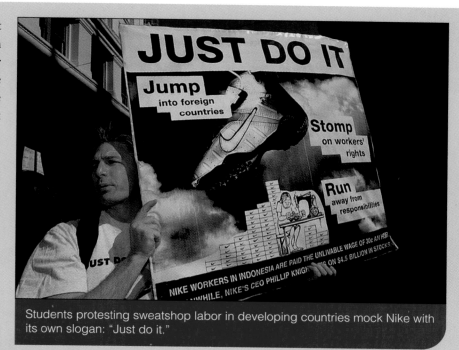

Students protesting sweatshop labor in developing countries mock Nike with its own slogan: "Just do it."

This concern has recently given rise to a nationwide coalition called United Students Against Sweatshops, based on college campuses across the country. Because this is an issue that combines women's rights, immigrant rights, environmental concerns, and human rights, it has linked disparate groups on campus. Nike is not their only target. Many apparel manufacturers contract out their production to take advantage of cheap labor and overhead costs. The student movement—ranging from sit-ins and "knit-ins" to demonstrations and building occupation—has been aimed at ridding campus stores of all products made in sweatshops, both at home and abroad. Pressed by their students, many colleges and universities have agreed to adopt anti-sweatshop codes governing the products they make and stock on campus. And Nike and Reebok, partly in response to student protests, have raised the wages of some 100,000 workers in their Indonesian factories (to about 20 cents an hour—still far below what is needed to raise a family) (Appelbaum and Dreier 1999; Global Alliance for Workers and Communities 2001).

The global corporate culture of the apparel industry focuses our attention on worldwide social stratification—on the enormous gap between wealthy nations and poorer nations. In many respects, the wealth of rich nations depends on the poverty of poor nations. As Figure 10-1 shows, people in industrialized societies benefit when they buy consumer goods made by low-wage workers in developing countries. Yet the low wages workers earn in multinational factories are comparatively high for those countries.

What economic and political conditions explain the divide between rich nations and poor? Within developing nations, how are wealth and income distributed, and how much opportunity does the average worker have to move up the social ladder? How do race and gender affect social mobility in these countries? In this chapter we will focus on stratification around the world, beginning with an examination of who controls the world marketplace. We will consider the impact of colonialism and neocolonialism, of globalization, of the rise of multinational corporations, and of the trend toward modernization. Then we will focus on stratification *within* nations, in terms of the distribution of wealth and income, prestige, and social mobility. In a special case study, we will look closely at social stratification in Mexico, including the social impact of race and gender and the environmental effects of industrialization. The chapter closes with a social policy section on universal human rights. ■

Figure 10-1

The Sweat behind the Shirt

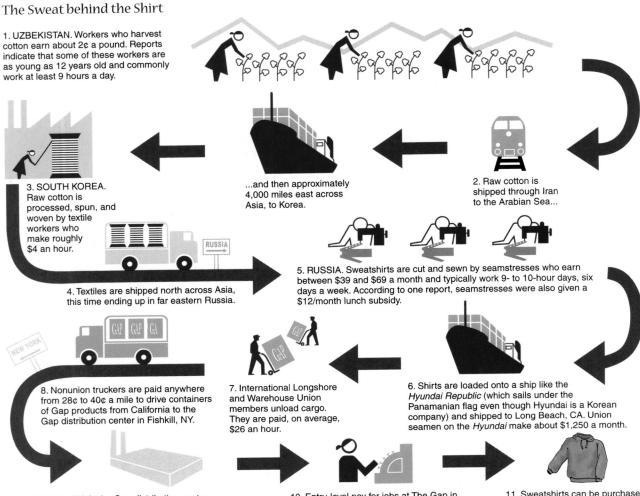

1. UZBEKISTAN. Workers who harvest cotton earn about 2¢ a pound. Reports indicate that some of these workers are as young as 12 years old and commonly work at least 9 hours a day.

3. SOUTH KOREA. Raw cotton is processed, spun, and woven by textile workers who make roughly $4 an hour.

...and then approximately 4,000 miles east across Asia, to Korea.

2. Raw cotton is shipped through Iran to the Arabian Sea...

4. Textiles are shipped north across Asia, this time ending up in far eastern Russia.

5. RUSSIA. Sweatshirts are cut and sewn by seamstresses who earn between $39 and $69 a month and typically work 9- to 10-hour days, six days a week. According to one report, seamstresses were also given a $12/month lunch subsidy.

8. Nonunion truckers are paid anywhere from 28¢ to 40¢ a mile to drive containers of Gap products from California to the Gap distribution center in Fishkill, NY.

7. International Longshore and Warehouse Union members unload cargo. They are paid, on average, $26 an hour.

6. Shirts are loaded onto a ship like the *Hyundai Republic* (which sails under the Panamanian flag even though Hyundai is a Korean company) and shipped to Long Beach, CA. Union seamen on the *Hyundai* make about $1,250 a month.

9. FISHKILL, NY. At the Gap distribution center, nonunion "merchandise handlers" start at $10 an hour.

10. Entry-level pay for jobs at The Gap in midtown Manhattan is $6 an hour (nonunion).

11. Sweatshirts can be purchased for $48, sweat not included.

Source: Gordon, Jesse, and Knickerbocker, *The Nation* 273 (September 3/10, 2001):14.

Think About It
To what extent does the affluence Americans enjoy depend on the labor of workers in less-developed countries?

● Stratification in the World System

Kwabena Afari is a pineapple exporter in Ghana. But for years his customers had to show a great deal of ingenuity to get in touch with him. First a call had to be placed to Accra, the capital city. Someone there would call the post office in Afari's hometown. Then the post office would send a messenger to his home. Afari has recently solved his problem by getting a cellular phone, but his longtime dilemma symbolizes the problems of the roughly 600 million people who live in sub-Saharan Africa and are being left behind by the trade and foreign investment transforming the global economy. One African entrepreneur notes, "It's not that we have been left behind. It's that we haven't even started" (Buckley 1997:8).

It is true that technology, the information highway, and innovations in telecommunications have all made the world a smaller and more unified place. Yet while the world marketplace is gradually shrinking in space and tastes, business profits are not being shared equally. There remains a substantial disparity between the world's "have" and "have-not" nations. For example, in 2001, the average value of goods and services produced per citizen (per capita gross national income) in the industrialized countries of the United States, Japan, Switzerland, Belgium, and Norway was more than $25,000. In seven poorer countries the value was below $700. In fact, the richest 1 percent of the world's population received as much income as the poorest 57 percent. Figure 10-2 illustrates these stark contrasts. Three forces discussed below are particularly responsible for the domination of the world marketplace by a few nations: the legacy of colonialism, the advent of multinational corporations, and modernization (Haub and Cornelius 2001; United Nations Development Programme 2001).

Colonialism, Neocolonialism, and World Systems Analysis

Colonialism is the maintenance of political, social, economic, and cultural domination over a people by a foreign power for an extended period of time (Bell 1981b). In simple terms, it is rule by outsiders. The long reign of the British Empire over much of North America, parts of Africa, and India is an example of colonial domination. The same can be said of French rule over Algeria, Tunisia, and other parts of North Africa. Relations between the colonial nation and colonized people are similar to those between the dominant capitalist class and the proletariat as described by Karl Marx.

By the 1980s, colonialism had largely disappeared. Most of the world's nations that were colonies before World War I had achieved political independence and established their own governments. However, for many of these countries, the transition to genuine self-rule was not yet complete. Colonial domination had established patterns of economic exploitation that continued even after nationhood was achieved—in part because former colonies were unable to develop their own industry and technology. Their dependence on more industrialized nations, including their former colonial masters, for managerial and technical expertise, investment capital, and manufactured goods kept former colonies in a subservient position. Such continuing dependence and foreign domination constitute *neocolonialism.*

The economic and political consequences of colonialism and neocolonialism are readily apparent. Drawing on the conflict perspective, sociologist Immanuel

Wallerstein (1974, 1979, 2000) views the global economic system as divided between nations that control wealth and those from which resources are taken. Neocolonialism allows industrialized societies to accumulate even more capital.

Wallerstein has advanced a *world systems analysis* to describe the unequal economic and political relationships in which certain industrialized nations (among them the United States, Japan, and Germany) and their global corporations dominate the *core* of the system. At the *semiperiphery* of the system are countries with marginal economic status, such as Israel, Ireland, and South Korea. Wallerstein suggests that the poor developing countries of Asia, Africa, and Latin America are on the *periphery* of the world economic system. Core nations and their corporations control and exploit the developing nations' economies, much as the old colonial empires ruled their colonies (Chase-Dunn and Grimes 1995).

The division between core and periphery nations is significant and remarkably stable. A study by the International Monetary Fund (2000) found little change over the course of the *last 100 years* for the 42 economies that were studied. The only changes were Japan's movement up into the group of core nations and China's movement down toward the margins of the semiperiphery nations. Yet Wallerstein (1999) speculates that the world system as we currently understand it may soon undergo unpredictable changes. The world is becoming increasingly urbanized, a trend that is gradually eliminating the large pools of low-cost workers in rural areas. In the future, core nations will have to find other ways to reduce their labor costs. The exhaustion of land and water resources through clear-cutting and other forms of pollution is also driving up the costs of production.

Wallerstein's world systems analysis is the most widely used version of *dependency theory.* According to this theory, even as developing countries make economic advances, they remain weak and subservient to core nations and corporations within an increasingly intertwined global economy. This allows industrialized nations to continue to exploit developing countries for their own gain. In a sense, dependency theory applies the conflict perspective on a global scale.

In the view of world systems analysis and dependency theory, a growing share of the human and natural resources of developing countries is being redistributed to the core industrialized nations. In part, this is because developing countries owe huge sums of money to industrialized nations as a result of foreign aid, loans, and trade deficits. This global debt crisis has intensified the Third World dependency begun under colonialism, neocolonialism, and multinational investment. International financial institutions are pressuring indebted countries to

Figure 10-2

Gross Domestic Product per Capita, 2001

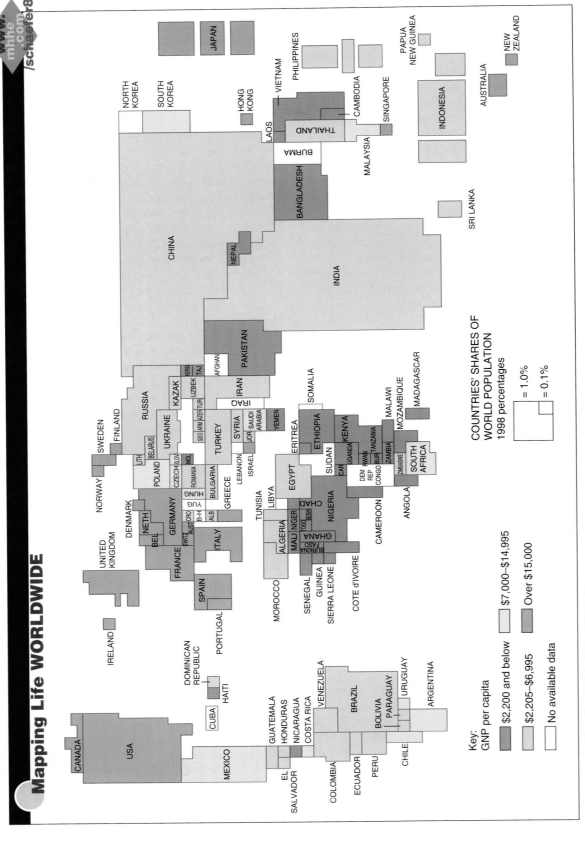

Mapping Life WORLDWIDE

COUNTRIES' SHARES OF WORLD POPULATION
1998 percentages

☐ = 1.0%

☐ = 0.1%

Key:
GNP per capita

☐ $2,200 and below

☐ $7,000–$14,995

☐ $2,205–$6,995

☐ Over $15,000

☐ No available data

Sources: Haub and Cornelius 2001; D. Smith 1999:14–15.

This stylized map reflects the different sizes in population of the world's nations. The color for each country shows the 2001 estimated *gross domestic product* (the total value of goods and services produced by the nation in a given year) per capita. As the map shows, some of the world's most populous countries—such as Nigeria, Bangladesh, and Pakistan—are among the nations with the lowest standard of living, as measured by per capita GDP.

take severe measures to meet their interest payments. The result is that developing nations may be forced to devalue their currencies, freeze workers' wages, increase privatization of industry, and reduce government services and employment.

◉Imagine

You are traveling through a developing country. What evidence do you see of neocolonialism?

Globalization

Closely related to these problems is ***globalization,*** or the worldwide integration of government policies, cultures, social movements, and financial markets through trade and the exchange of ideas. While public discussion of globalization is relatively recent, intellectuals have been pondering its social consequences for a long time. Karl Marx and Frederich Engels warned in the Communist Manifesto (written in 1848) of a world market that would lead to production in distant lands, sweeping away existing working relationships. Today, developments outside a country are as likely to influence people's lives as changes at home. For example, though much of the world was already in recession by September 2001, within weeks the economic repercussions of the terrorist attacks on New York and Washington, D.C., had begun to affect African game wardens and Asian taxi drivers. Some observers see globalization and its effects as the natural result of advances in communications technology, particularly the Internet and satellite transmission of the mass media. Others view it more critically, as a process that allows multinational corporations to expand unchecked. We will examine this issue more fully in the next section (Chase-Dunn et al. 2000; Feketekuty 2001; Feuer 1959; Pearlstein 2001; Third World Institute 2001).

Because world financial markets transcend governance by conventional nation states, international organizations such as the World Bank and the International Monetary Fund have emerged as major players in the global economy. The function of these institutions, which are heavily funded and influenced by countries such as the United States, is to encourage economic trade and development and to ensure the smooth operation of international financial markets. As such they are seen as promoters of globalization and defenders primarily of the interests of core nations. Ever since the meeting of the World Trade Organization (WTO) in Seattle, Washington, in 1999, wherever leaders of the core nations have gathered, protesters have converged to draw attention to a variety of issues, including violations of workers' rights, the destruction of the environment, the loss of cultural identity, and discrimination against minority groups in periphery nations.

Embedded in the concept of globalization is the notion of the cultural domination of periphery nations by the core nations. Simply put, people in the periphery nations lose their traditional values and begin to identify with the culture of the core nations. They may discard or neglect their native language and dress as they attempt to emulate the icons of mass-market entertainment and fashion. Indeed, those who oppose globalization see every consumer product, book, film, or television program exported by core nations as an attack on the traditions and cultural autonomy of other nations. Even *Titanic* or *The X-Files* may be seen as a threat to native cultures, if they dominate the media at the expense of local art forms. As Sembene Ousmane, one of Africa's most prominent writers and filmmakers, noted, "[Today] we are more familiar with European fairy tales than with our own traditional stories" (World Development Forum 1990:4).

p. 63 ◀

In the Italian city of Ponte San Ludovico, a protester demonstrates against globalization with a poster that reads "Another world is possible." This demonstration took place in July 2001, one week before the G8 summit in Genoa.

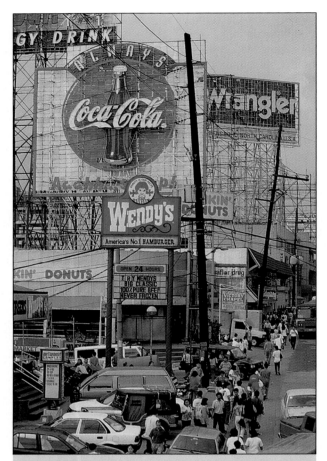

The influence of multinational corporations abroad can be seen in this street scene from Manila, capital of the Philippines.

Multinational Corporations

A key role in neocolonialism today is played by worldwide corporate giants. The term ***multinational corporations*** refers to commercial organizations that are headquartered in one country but do business throughout the world. Such private trade and lending relationships are not new; merchants have conducted business abroad for hundreds of years, trading gems, spices, garments, and other goods. However, today's multinational giants are not merely buying and selling overseas; they are also *producing goods* all over the world, as we saw in the case of Nike (Wallerstein 1974).

Moreover, today's "global factories" (the factories throughout the developing world run by multinational corporations) now have the "global office" alongside them. Multinationals based in core countries are begin-

ning to establish reservations services, centers to process insurance claims, and data processing centers in the periphery nations. As service industries become a more important part of the international marketplace, many companies are concluding that the low costs of overseas operations more than offset the expense of transmitting information around the world.

Do not underestimate the size of these global corporations. Table 10-1 shows that the total revenues of multinational businesses are on a par with the total value of goods and services exchanged in *entire nations*. Foreign sales represent an important source of profit for multinational corporations, a fact that encourages them to expand into other countries (in many cases, the developing nations). The economy of the United States is heavily dependent on foreign commerce, much of which is conducted by multinationals. Almost one out of five manufacturing jobs in the United States has to do with the export of goods to foreign countries (Bureau of the Census 1997a:751).

Functionalist View

Multinational corporations can actually help the developing nations of the world. They bring jobs and industry to areas where subsistence agriculture previously served as the only means of survival. Multinationals promote rapid development through diffusion of inventions and innovations from industrial nations. Viewed from a functionalist perspective, the combination of skilled technology and management provided by multinationals and the relatively cheap labor available in developing nations is ideal for a global enterprise. Multinationals can take maximum advantage of technology while reducing costs and boosting profits.

The international ties of multinational corporations also facilitate the exchange of ideas and technology around the world. They make the nations of the world more interdependent. And these ties may prevent certain disputes from reaching the point of serious conflict. A country cannot afford to sever diplomatic relations, or engage in warfare, with a nation that is the headquarters for its main business suppliers or is a key outlet for exports.

Conflict View

Conflict theorists challenge this favorable evaluation of the impact of multinational corporations. They emphasize that multinationals exploit local workers to maximize profits. Starbucks—the international coffee retailer based in Seattle—gets some of its coffee from farms in Guatemala. But to earn enough money to buy a pound of Starbucks coffee, a Guatemalan farmworker would have

Table 10-1   Multinational Corporations Compared to Nations

Corporation	Revenues ($ millions)	Comparable Nation(s)	Gross Domestic Product ($ millions)
1. *Exxon Mobil (USA)*	$210,392	Austria	$208,200
2. *Wal-Mart (USA)*	193,295	Colombia plus Venezuela	188,800
3. *General Motors (USA)*	184,632	Turkey	185,700
4. *Ford Motor (USA)*	180,598	Denmark	174,300
5. *DaimlerChrysler (Germany)*	150,070	Norway	152,900
8. *General Electric (USA)*	129,853	South Africa	131,100
19. *IBM (USA)*	88,396	Egypt	89,100
21. *Volkswagen (Germany)*	78,852	Malaysia	79,000
30. *SONY (Japan)*	66,100	Chile	67,500
50. *Boeing (USA)*	51,130	Peru	51,900

Notes: Revenues are for 2000. GDP data are for 1999, based on local currencies converted to prevailing U.S. dollar equivalents. Corporations are ranked by their placement on the Fortune 500 list of global corporations.

Sources: For corporate data, *Fortune* 2001a; for GDP data, United Nations Development Programme 2001:178–180.

Think About It

What happens to society when economically, corporations grow bigger than countries and spill across international borders?

to pick 500 pounds of beans, representing five days of work (Entine and Nichols 1996).

The pool of cheap labor in the developing world prompts multinationals to move factories out of core countries. An added bonus for the multinationals is that the developing world discourages strong trade unions. Organized labor in industrialized countries insists on decent wages and humane working conditions, but governments seeking to attract or keep multinationals may develop a "climate for investment" that includes repressive antilabor laws restricting union activity and collective bargaining. If labor's demands in factories run by multinational corporations become threatening, the firm will simply move its plant elsewhere, leaving a trail of unemployment behind. Nike, for example, moved its factories from the United States to Korea to Indonesia to Vietnam, seeking the lowest labor costs. Conflict theorists conclude that, on the whole, multinational corporations have a negative social impact on workers in both industrialized and developing nations.

Workers in the United States and other core countries are beginning to recognize that their own interests are served by helping to organize workers in developing nations. As long as multinationals can exploit cheap labor abroad, they will be in a strong position to reduce wages and benefits in industrialized countries. With this in mind, in the 1990s, labor unions, religious organizations, campus groups, and other activists mounted public campaigns to pressure companies such as Nike, Starbucks, Reebok, the Gap, and Wal-Mart to improve the wages and working conditions in their overseas operations (Applebaum and Dreier, 1999).

Several sociologists who have surveyed the effects of foreign investment conclude that, although it may initially contribute to a host nation's wealth, it eventually increases economic inequality within developing nations. This is true in both income and ownership of land. The upper and middle classes benefit most from economic expansion, whereas the lower classes are less likely to benefit. Multinationals invest in limited areas of an economy

The Laboring American Dream

and in restricted regions of a nation. Although certain sectors of the host nation's economy expand, such as hotels and expensive restaurants, this very expansion appears to retard growth in agriculture and other economic sectors. Moreover, multinational corporations often buy out or force out local entrepreneurs and companies, thereby increasing economic and cultural dependence (Bornschier et al. 1978; Chase-Dunn and Grimes 1995; Evans 1979; Wallerstein 1979).

Modernization

Millions of people around the world are witnessing a revolutionary transformation of their day-to-day life. Contemporary social scientists use the term *modernization* to describe the far-reaching process by which peripheral nations move from traditional or less developed institutions to those characteristic of more developed societies.

Wendell Bell (1981a), whose definition of modernization we are using, notes that modern societies tend to be urban, literate, and industrial. They have sophisticated transportation and media systems. Families tend to be organized within the nuclear family unit rather than the extended-family model (see Chapter 14). Members of societies that have undergone modernization shift allegiance from such traditional sources of authority as parents and priests to newer authorities such as government officials.

Many sociologists are quick to note that terms such as *modernization* and even *development* contain an eth-

nocentric bias. The unstated assumptions behind these terms are that "they" (people living in developing countries) are struggling to become more like "us" (in the core industrialized nations). Viewed from a conflict perspective, these terms perpetuate the dominant ideology of capitalist societies.

There is similar criticism of *modernization theory,* a functionalist approach proposing that modernization and development will gradually improve the lives of people in developing nations. According to this theory, while countries develop at uneven rates, development in peripheral countries will be assisted by the innovations transferred from the industrialized world. Critics of modernization theory, including dependency theorists, counter that any such technology transfer only increases the dominance of core nations over developing countries and facilitates further exploitation.

When we see all the Coca-Cola and IBM signs going up in developing countries, it is easy to assume that globalization and economic change are effecting cultural change. But that is not always the case, researchers note. Distinctive cultural traditions, such as a particular religious orientation or a nationalistic identity, often persist in a developing nation and can soften the impact of modernization. Some contemporary sociologists emphasize that both industrialized and developing countries are "modern." Current researchers are increasingly viewing modernization as movement along a series of social indicators—among them degree of urbanization, energy use, literacy, political democracy, and use of birth control. Clearly, these are often subjective indicators; even in industrialized nations, not everyone would agree that wider use of birth control represents an example of "progress" (Armer and Katsillis 1992; Hedley 1992; Inglehart and Baker 2000).

Current modernization studies generally take a convergence perspective. Using the indicators noted above, researchers focus on how societies are moving closer together despite traditional differences. From a conflict perspective, modernization in developing countries often perpetuates their dependence on and continued exploitation by more industrialized nations. Conflict theorists view such a continuing dependence on foreign powers as an example of contemporary neocolonialism.

Stratification within Nations: A Comparative Perspective

At the same time that the gap between rich and poor nations is widening, so too is the gap between rich and poor citizens *within* nations. As discussed earlier, stratification in developing nations is closely related to their relatively weak and dependent position in the global economy. Local elites work hand in hand with multinational corporations and prosper from such alliances. At the same time, the economic system creates and perpetuates the exploitation of industrial and agricultural workers. That's why foreign investment in developing countries tends to increase economic inequality (Bornschier et al. 1978; Kerbo 2000). As Box 10-1 makes clear, inequality within a society is also evident in industrialized nations such as Japan.

Distribution of Wealth and Income

In at least 18 nations around the world, the most affluent 10 percent of the population receives at least 40 percent of all income: Swaziland (the leader at 50 percent of all income), Bolivia, Brazil, Chile, Colombia, Guatemala, Honduras, Guinea-Bissau, Lesotho, Mali, Mexico, Nicaragua, Nigeria, Papua New Guinea, Paraguay, South Africa, Zambia, and Zimbabwe. Figure 10-3 compares the distribution of income in selected industrialized and developing nations.

Women in developing countries find life especially difficult. Karuna Chanana Ahmed, an anthropologist from India who has studied women in developing nations, calls women the most exploited among oppressed people. Women face sex discrimination beginning at birth. They are commonly fed less than male children, are denied educational opportunities, and are often hospitalized

Figure 10-3

Distribution of Income in Nine Nations

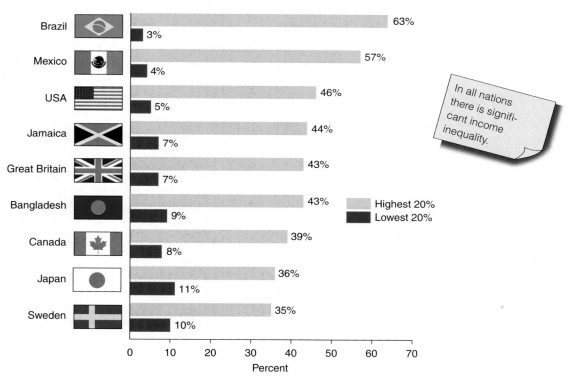

In all nations there is significant income inequality.

- Brazil — Highest 20%: 63%, Lowest 20%: 3%
- Mexico — Highest 20%: 57%, Lowest 20%: 4%
- USA — Highest 20%: 46%, Lowest 20%: 5%
- Jamaica — Highest 20%: 44%, Lowest 20%: 7%
- Great Britain — Highest 20%: 43%, Lowest 20%: 7%
- Bangladesh — Highest 20%: 43%, Lowest 20%: 9%
- Canada — Highest 20%: 39%, Lowest 20%: 8%
- Japan — Highest 20%: 36%, Lowest 20%: 11%
- Sweden — Highest 20%: 35%, Lowest 20%: 10%

Percent

Note: Data are considered comparable although based on statistics covering 1992 to 1997.

Source: United Nations Development Programme 2001:182–184.

Think About It

Why is income inequality higher in the United States than in Canada, Japan, and Sweden?

Social Inequality

Stratification in Japan

A tourist visiting Japan may at first experience a bit of culture shock after noticing the degree to which everything in Japanese life is ranked: corporations, universities, even educational programs. These rankings are widely reported and accepted. Moreover, the ratings shape day-to-day social interactions: Japanese find it difficult to sit, talk, or eat together unless the relative rankings of those present have been established, often through the practice of *meishi* (the exchange of business cards).

The apparent preoccupation with ranking and formality suggests an exceptional degree of stratification. Yet researchers have determined that Japan's level of income inequality is among the *lowest* of major industrial societies (see

While women constitute more than 40 percent of Japan's workforce, they are generally restricted to subordinate positions.

> **Even in developing countries, women are twice as likely to be managers as in Japan.**

Figure 10-3 on page 249). Whereas the pay gap between Japan's top corporate executives and the nation's lowest-paid workers is about 8 to 1, the comparable figure for the United States would be 37 to 1.

One factor that works against inequality is that Japan is rather homogeneous—certainly when compared with the United States—in terms of race, ethnicity, nationality, and language. Japan's population is 98 percent Japanese. But there is discrimination against the nation's Chinese and Korean minorities, and the *Burakumin* constitute a low-status subculture who encounter extensive prejudice.

Perhaps the most pervasive form of inequality in Japan today is gender discrimination. Overall, women earn only about 64 percent of men's wages. Fewer than 10 percent of Japanese managers are female—a ratio that is one of the lowest in the world. Even in developing countries, women are twice as likely to be managers as in Japan.

In 1985, Japan's parliament—at the time, 97 percent male—passed an Equal Employment bill that encourages employers to end sex discrimination in hiring, assignment, and promotion policies. However, feminist organizations were dissatisfied because the law lacked strong sanctions. In a landmark ruling issued in late 1996, a Japanese court for the first time held an employer liable for denying promotions due to sex discrimination. The court ordered a Japanese bank to pay 12 female employees a total of $1.6 mil-

lion and added that 11 of the women must immediately be promoted to management posts.

On the political front, Japanese women have made progress but remain underrepresented. In a study of women in government around the world, Japan ranked near the bottom of the countries studied, with 7 percent of its national legislators female.

Let's Discuss

1. What factors contribute to the relatively low level of income inequality in Japan?

2. Describe the types of gender discrimination found in Japan. Why do you think Japanese women occupy such a subordinate social position?

Sources: Abegglen and Stalk 1985; French 2001a; Inter-Parliamentary Union 2001b; Kerbo and McKinstry 1998; Magnier 1999; Nakane 1970; Sterngold 1992; Strom 2000b.

only when critically ill. Whether inside or outside the home, women's work is devalued. When economies fail, as they did in Asian countries in the late 1990s, women are the first to be laid off from work (Anderson and Moore 1993; Kristof 1998).

Surveys show a significant degree of *female infanticide* (the killing of baby girls) in China and rural areas of India. Only one-third of Pakistan's sexually segregated schools are for women, and one-third of these schools have no buildings. In Kenya and Tanzania, it is illegal for a woman to own a house. In Saudi Arabia, women are prohibited from driving, walking alone in public, and socializing with men outside their families (Murphy 1993). We will explore women's second-class status throughout the world more fully in Chapter 12.

Prestige

Sociologists have recognized that comparative research is essential in determining whether observed patterns of stratification are unique to a single nation, are restricted to a particular type of society (such as industrial or developing nations), or are applicable to a wide range of societies (Kalleberg 1988). We have seen that societies as different as Brazil, Mexico, the United States, and Japan all share a marked inequality in the distribution of income (refer to Figure 10-3). But a person's class position, defined largely in economic terms and reflecting his or her level of wealth and income, is but one component of stratification.

By ranking the prestige of various occupations, sociologists can gain a deeper understanding of another aspect of inequality. But are perceptions in the United States regarding the prestige of occupations comparable to those held in other societies? In an effort to study stratification from a cross-cultural perspective, sociologist Donald Treiman (1977) examined the reputation that certain jobs had in 53 different nations. People were asked to rate occupations and the results were tabulated along a scale ranging from 0 to 100, with higher scores being more prestigious. Treiman found a high degree of correlation or similarity in all contemporary societies, including both industrialized and nonindustrialized nations.

Treiman's pioneering research inspired subsequent efforts to gather and compare data from many societies using the objective method of measuring stratification differences. In one important study, sociologists Nan Lin and Wen Xie (1988) interviewed a random sample of residents of Beijing to study occupational prestige. They found that physicians ranked near the top of the occupational hierarchy, while police officers were near the middle, and garbage collectors were close to the bottom—a finding similar to the results of

p. 222

surveys in the United States. Teachers and professors, however, received much lower prestige ratings in China, reflecting the low wages they receive relative to other occupations. The Chinese respondents gave a much higher prestige rating to textile workers than did respondents in the United States. Textile workers in China evidently fare much better relative to other workers than they do in the United States or Europe.

As one part of their analysis, the researchers compared the prestige rankings of male and female respondents. Although China has officially maintained a national policy of gender equality since 1949, it has not been able to eliminate occupational segregation by gender. Partly as a result, the prestige rankings of Chinese men and women seemed to reflect the structure of occupational opportunity. Males, for example, gave higher ratings than females to such occupations as natural scientist, athlete, driver, and mechanic—all of which are more likely to be held by males. Each gender showed a tendency to rate more highly those occupations most open to it.

Treiman's cross-cultural research reminds us that prestige distinctions are universal; the study of China by Lin and Xie underscores this finding. Even a society that has experienced revolutionary movements and decades of Communist party rule still stratifies itself in its ranking of prestigious occupations.

Social Mobility

Mobility in Industrial Nations

Studies of intergenerational mobility in industrialized nations have found the following patterns:

1. There are substantial similarities in the ways that parents' positions in stratification systems are transmitted to their children.
2. As in the United States, mobility opportunities in other nations have been influenced by structural factors, such as labor market changes that lead to the rise or decline of an occupational group within the social hierarchy.
3. Immigration continues to be a significant factor shaping a society's level of intergenerational mobility (Ganzeboom et al. 1991; Haller et al. 1990; Hauser and Grusky 1988).

Cross-cultural studies suggest that intergenerational mobility has been increasing in recent decades, at least among men. Dutch sociologists Harry Ganzeboom and Ruud Luijkx, joined by sociologist Donald Treiman of the United States (1989), examined surveys of mobility in 35 industrial and developing nations. They found that almost all the countries studied had witnessed increased

Residents of Shanghai stroll along Nanjing Road, China's famed Golden Mile. This thriving coastal city now rivals Tokyo and Hong Kong as a commercial and financial center.

intergenerational mobility between the 1950s and 1980s. In particular, they noted a common pattern of movement away from agriculture-based occupations.

Mobility in Developing Nations

Mobility patterns in industrialized countries are usually associated with intergenerational and intragenerational mobility. However, within developing nations, macro-level social and economic changes often overshadow micro-level movement from one occupation to another. For example, there is typically a substantial wage differential between rural and urban areas, which leads to high levels of migration to the cities. Yet the urban industrial sectors of developing countries generally cannot provide sufficient employment for all those seeking work. When migrants find that they are unable to move upward within the conventional economy, the informal or underground economies described in Box 10-2 become more attractive as a source of employment and financial rewards.

China has made significant although uneven progress in improving the lives of its poor. In 1978, there were an estimated 260 million poor Chinese, but by 1998, their number had dropped to between 40 and 100 million. This sizable reduction resulted in part from a government poverty reduction program targeted at the country's poorest areas. Recent rapid economic growth in the richer coastal provinces has also helped, though poverty reduction efforts have stalled inland, in rural districts. Ironically, the rural agricultural districts are now strained by a skilled labor shortage created by new job opportunities on the coast. And although progress has been notable, the middle class still accounts for just 1 to 2 percent of the population in this nation of 1.3 billion people (Chu 2001; United Nations Development Programme 2000).

A passer-by studies the menu outside the Afghan Kebab House in New York City. Many immigrants take menial jobs as cooks or waiters in exchange for higher wages and the hope of social mobility.

Sociology in the Global Community
10-2   The Informal Economy

www.
mhhe.
com
/schaefer8

Do you know someone who takes in tips and doesn't report the income? Have you traded services with someone—say, a haircut for help with a computer problem? These are aspects of an *informal economy,* the transfer of money, goods, or services that are not reported to the government. Participants in this type of economy avoid taxes, regulations, and minimum wage provisions, as well as expenses incurred for bookkeeping and financial reporting. Anthropologists studying developing nations and preindustrial societies have long acknowledged the existence of informal social networks that make, sell, and trade goods and services. Only recently have these networks been identified as common to all societies.

In industrial societies, the informal economy embraces transactions that are individually quite small but that can be quite significant when taken together. One major segment of this economy involves illegal transactions—such as prostitution, sale of illegal drugs, gambling, and bribery—leading some observers to describe it as an "underground economy." Yet the informal economy also includes unregulated child care services and the unreported income of craftspeople, street vendors, and employees who receive substantial tips. According to estimates, the informal economy may account for as much as 10 to 20 percent of all economic activity in the United States.

Although these informal economic transactions take place in virtually all societies—both capitalist and socialist—the pattern in developing countries differs somewhat from the informal economy of industrialized nations. In the developing world, governments often set up burdensome business regulations that an overworked bureaucracy must administer. When requests for licenses and permits pile up, holding up business projects, legitimate entrepreneurs find they need to "go underground" in order to get anything done. In Latin America, for example, the underground economy is esti-

> When requests for licenses and permits pile up, holding up business projects, legitimate entrepreneurs find they need to go "underground" in order to get anything done.

mated to account for about one-third of the gross domestic product of the area. Informal industrial enterprises, such as textile factories and repair shops, tend to be labor-intensive. Underground entrepreneurs cannot rely on advanced machinery, since a firm's assets can be confiscated for failure to operate within the open economy.

Viewed from a functionalist perspective, the bureaucratic regulations have contributed to the rise of an efficient informal economy in certain countries.

Nevertheless, these regulatory systems are dysfunctional for overall political and economic well-being. Since informal firms typically operate in remote locations to avoid detection, they cannot easily expand even when they become profitable. Given the limited protection for their property and contractual rights, participants in the informal economy are less likely to save and invest their income.

Informal economies have been criticized for promoting highly unfair and dangerous working conditions. A study of the underground economy of Spain found that worker's incomes were low, there was little job security, and safety and health standards were rarely enforced. Both the Spanish government and the nation's trade unions seemed to ignore the exploitation of participants in the informal economy. Still, especially in the developing world, the existence of a substantial underground economy simply reflects the absence of an economic system that is accessible to all residents.

Let's Discuss

1. What conditions contribute to the creation of an informal economy?
2. Describe an informal economy that you have observed or been a part of. Which perspective—functionalist, conflict, or interactionist—do you think best fits the notion of informal economy?

Sources: Ferman et al. 1987; Hershey 1988; Lemkow 1987; Weigard 1992.

Gender Differences and Mobility

Only recently have researchers begun to investigate the impact of gender on the mobility patterns of developing nations. Many aspects of the development process—especially modernization in rural areas and the rural-to-urban migration described above—may result in the modification or abandonment of traditional cultural practices and even marital systems. The effects on women's social standing and mobility are not necessarily positive. As a country develops and modernizes, women's vital role in food production deteriorates, jeopardizing both their autonomy and their material well-being. The movement of families to the cities weakens women's ties to relatives who can provide food, financial assistance, and social support.

In the Philippines, however, women have moved to the forefront of the indigenous peoples' struggle to protect their ancestral land from exploitation by outsiders. Having established their right to its rich minerals and forests, members of indigenous groups had begun to feud among themselves over the way in which the land's resources should be developed. Aided by the United Nations Partners in Development Programme, women volunteers established the Pan-Cordillera Women's Network for Peace and Development, a coalition of women's groups dedicated to resolving local disputes. The women mapped boundaries, prepared development plans, and negotiated more than 2,000 peace pacts among community members. They have also run in elections, campaigned against social problems, and organized residents to work together for the common good (United Nations Development Programme 2000:87).

Studies of the distribution of wealth and income within various countries, comparative studies of prestige, and cross-cultural research on mobility consistently reveal that stratification based on class, gender, and other factors shows up within a wide range of societies. Clearly, a worldwide view of stratification must include not only the sharp contrast between wealthy and impoverished nations but also the layers of hierarchies *within* industrialized societies and developing countries.

Imagine

www.
mhhe
.com
/schaefer8

Imagine that the United States borders a country with a much higher standard of living. In this neighboring country, the salaries of workers with a college degree start at $120,000 a year. What would life in the United States be like?

Stratification in Mexico: A Case Study

Colonialism, neocolonialism, and the domination and exploitation of a peripheral developing country by a core industrialized nation can be clearly seen in the history of Mexico. In this section we will look in some detail at the dynamics of stratification in this country. Since the twentieth century, as we will explore more fully in this case study, there has been a close cultural, economic, and political relationship between Mexico and the United States, but it has clearly been a relationship in which the United States is the dominant party. According to Wallerstein's analysis, the United States is at the core while neighboring Mexico is still on the periphery of the world economic system.

As of 2001, Mexico had more than 100 million residents, making it the eleventh most populous nation in the world. The population is concentrated in the nation's three largest cities: Mexico City (the eighth-largest city in the world), Guadalajara, and Monterrey. For the last half century, growth rates in Mexico City have far outstripped those in U.S. cities. In 1950, Mexico City was 20 percent smaller than Los Angeles, but by 2015, it will be 22 percent larger. Fortunately, for the nation as a whole, population growth seems to be slowing down. Continued rapid population growth would only intensify Mexico's already serious economic and environmental problems (National Intelligence Council 2000; J. Smith 2000).

If we compare Mexico to the United States, the overall differences in the standard of living and in life chances are quite dramatic. The *gross domestic product*—the value of all final goods and services produced within a country—is a commonly used measure of an average resident's economic well-being. In 1999, the gross domestic product per person in the United States came to $31,910; in Mexico, it was a mere $8,070. About 87 percent of adults in the United States have a high school education, compared to only 21 percent of those in Mexico. At birth, people in the United States can expect to live an average of 77 years, whereas life expectancy in Mexico is only 72 years (Bureau of the Census 2000a:826, 830; Haub and Cornelius 2001).

Although Mexico is unquestionably a poor country, the gap between its richest and poorest citizens is one of the widest in the world (refer back to Figure 10-3). In 2001, judged by the standards of the United Nations, 40 percent of the population survived on $2 per day. At the same time, the wealthiest 10 percent of Mexico's people account for 41 percent of the entire nation's income. According to a *Forbes* magazine portrait of the world's wealthiest individuals, Mexico had the fourth-largest number of people on the list—behind only the United States, Germany, and Japan (Castañeda 1995; United Nations Development Programme 2001:9, 183).

Political scientist Jorge Castañeda (1995:71) calls Mexico a "polarized society with enormous gaps between rich and poor, town and country, north and south, white and brown (or *criollos* and *mestizos*)." He adds that the country is also divided along lines of class, race, religion, gender, and age. We will examine stratification within Mexico by focusing on race relations and the plight of Mexican Indians, the status of Mexican women, Mexico's economy and environment, and emigration to the United States and its impact on the U.S.–Mexican "borderlands."

Race Relations in Mexico: The Color Hierarchy

On January 1, 1994, rebels from an armed insurgent group called the Zapatista National Liberation Army seized four towns in the state of Chiapas in southern Mexico. The

Mexican women mourn the 1994 death of a member of the Zapatista National Liberation Army, an insurgent group protesting economic injustices and discrimination against the Indian population in the state of Chiapas.

this hierarchy are the *criollos,* the 10 percent of the population who are typically White, well-educated members of the business and intellectual elites with familial roots in Spain. In the middle is the large, impoverished *mestizo* majority, most of whom have brown skin and a mixed racial lineage as a result of intermarriage. At the bottom of the color hierarchy are the destitute, full-blooded Mexican Indian minority and a small number of Blacks, some descended from 200,000 African slaves brought to Mexico. This color hierarchy is an important part of day-to-day life—enough so that some Mexicans in the cities use hair dyes, skin lighteners, and blue or green contact lenses to appear more White and European. Ironically, however, nearly all Mexicans are considered part Indian because of centuries of intermarriage (Castañeda 1995; DePalma 1995a).

rebels—who named their organization after Emiliano Zapata, a farmer and leader of the 1910 revolution against a corrupt dictatorship—were backed by 2,000 lightly armed Mayan Indians and peasants. Zapatista leaders declared that they had turned to armed insurrection to protest economic injustices and discrimination against the region's Indian population. The Mexican government mobilized the army to crush the revolt, but was forced to retreat as news organizations broadcast pictures of the confrontation around the world. A cease-fire was declared after only 12 days of fighting, but 196 people had already died. Negotiations between the Mexican government and the Zapatista National Liberation Army collapsed in 1996; there has been sporadic violence ever since (J. Smith 2001).

While many factors contributed to the Zapatista revolt, the subordinate status of Mexico's Indian population throughout the country was surely important. Accounting for an estimated 11 percent of Mexico's population, Mexican Indians held no important offices in the central government and only a few of the more than 600 seats in the national assembly. More than 90 percent of the indigenous population lives in houses without sewers, compared with 21 percent of the population as a whole. And whereas just 12 percent of Mexican adults are illiterate, the proportion for Mexican Indians is 48 percent (Darling 2001; J. Smith 2001; Thompson 2001b).

The subordinate status of Mexico's Indians is but one reflection of the nation's color hierarchy, which links social class to the appearance of racial purity. At the top of

Many observers take note of widespread denial of prejudice and discrimination against people of color in Mexico. Schoolchildren are taught that the election of Benito Juárez, a Zapotec Indian, as president of Mexico in the nineteenth century proves that all Mexicans are equal. In addition, Mexico's National Commission of Human Rights has *never* received a complaint alleging racial discrimination and has no process for handling such a complaint. With such denial in mind, there has been a marked growth in the last decade of formal organizations and voluntary associations representing indigenous Indians. The Zapatista revolt in Chiapas was an even more dramatic indication that those at the bottom of Mexico's color hierarchy are weary of inequality and injustice (DePalma 1995a, 1996; Stavenhagen 1994).

The Status of Women in Mexico

In 1975, Mexico City hosted the first international conference on the status of women convened by the United Nations. Much of the focus was on the situation of women in developing countries; in that regard, the situation is mixed. Women now constitute 33 percent of the labor force, an increase in the past 20 years but still behind industrial countries. Unfortunately, Mexican women are even more mired in the lowest-paying jobs than their counterparts in industrial nations. In the political arena, women are rarely seen in top decision-making positions, but they have increased their representation in the

Women account for just a small proportion of elected officials and cabinet ministers in Mexico.

national legislature to 16 percent, ranking Mexico at fortieth among 178 nations worldwide (Inter-Parliamentary Union 2001b; World Bank 2001b:49).

Feminist sociologists emphasize that even when they work outside the home, Mexican women often do not get recognized as active and productive household members, whereas men are typically viewed as the heads of households. As one consequence, women find it difficult to obtain credit and technical assistance in many parts of the country and to inherit land in rural areas. Within manufacturing and service industries, women generally receive little training and tend to work in the least-automated and least-skilled jobs—in good part because there is little expectation that women will pursue career advancement, organize for better working conditions, or become active in labor unions (Kopinak 1995; Martelo 1996; see also Young 1993).

In recent decades, Mexican women have begun to organize to address an array of economic, political, and health issues. Since women continue to serve as the household managers for their families, even when they work outside the home, they are well aware of the consequences

of the inadequate public services in their lower-income urban neighborhoods. As far back as 1973, women in Monterrey—the nation's third-largest city—began protesting the continuing disruptions of the city's water supply. After individual complaints to city officials and the water authority proved fruitless, social networks of female activists began to emerge. These activists sent delegations to confront politicians, organized protest rallies, and blocked traffic as a means of getting media attention. Their efforts brought improvement in Monterrey's water service, but the issue of reliable and safe water remains a concern in Mexico and many developing countries (Bennett 1995).

Mexico's Economy and Environment

Mexico strongly lobbied for acceptance of the North American Free Trade Agreement (NAFTA), ultimately signed in 1993, which provided for the dismantling of almost all trade barriers among the United States, Canada,

Government efforts to control air pollution in Mexico City have had some success, but the number of cars in the city grows each year by 150,000. On the smog-choked day this photo was taken, visibility was just a few blocks.

and Mexico. Mexico hoped its struggling economy would receive a major boost from such a favorable linkage to the world's largest consumer market, the United States. Indeed, in 1995, Mexico recorded its first trade surplus with the United States since 1990. Still, any benefit from NAFTA was dramatically undercut in 1994 by the collapse of the *peso,* Mexico's unit of currency. This collapse reflected a widespread loss of confidence as a result of internal political unrest (the Zapatista revolt, discussed earlier) and the assassination of a leading political figure who had spearheaded economic reform. Although U.S. investment in Mexico has increased since the signing of NAFTA, the implementation of the agreement has meant little in the day-to-day economic struggles of the average Mexican (DePalma 1995b; Robberson 1995). We will examine the impact of NAFTA more fully in Chapter 18.

Adding to the pressures on low-income Mexicans, the nation's Social Security system is in a state of crisis and could soon go bankrupt. During the last 50 years, this system has evolved into a "cradle-to-grave" security blanket covering hospital births, child care, lifetime medical care, retirement pensions, and funeral costs. However, the recent economic crisis has intensified the financial pressures on the system. It is difficult in any case to support a population with more older people than ever before—some of whom need long-term and expensive hospitalization because of heart disease and cancer (DePalma 1995c).

Mexico's recession has also hampered efforts to address the nation's serious environmental problems. Not only was the government reluctant to introduce new measures, but citizens could not afford new cars equipped to improve air quality. At the beginning of the 1990s, air pollutants hit emergency levels in Mexico City half the year. Despite opposition from oil companies, the government gradually introduced stronger controls. For example, the "Today You Can't Drive" program took 20 percent of all vehicles without catalytic converters off the road each weekday. But the situation is still dire; by U.S. standards, Mexico City should be under a smog alert 250 days a year. Furthermore, medical research on the children of Mexico City has found that the majority of them show early signs of lung disease, caused, researchers say, by the air pollution (Goering 2001; Fordham and Calderon-Garcidueana 2001).

The Borderlands

Air and water pollution are but two of the many ways in which the problems of Mexico and the United States intertwine. Growing recognition of the borderlands reflects the increasingly close and complex relationship between these two countries. The term *borderlands* refers to the area of a common culture along the border between Mexico and the United States. Legal and illegal emigration from Mexico to the United States, day laborers crossing the border regularly to go to jobs in the United States, the implementation of the North American Free Trade Agreement, and the exchange of media across the border all make the notion of separate Mexican and U.S. cultures obsolete in the borderlands.

The economic position of the borderlands is rather complicated, as we can see in the emergence of the *maquiladoras* on the Mexican side (see Figure 10-4). These are foreign companies that establish operations in Mexico yet are exempt from Mexican taxes and are not required to provide insurance or benefits for their workers. The *maquiladoras* have attracted manufacturing jobs from other parts of North America to Mexico. As of October 2001 there were one million workers in the *maquiladoras,* where the daily take-home pay for entry-level workers was $4 to $5 a day. Moreover, since many of these firms come from the United States and sell their products to Mexico's vast domestic market, their operations deepen the impact of U.S. consumer culture on Mexico's urban and rural areas (Thompson 2001).

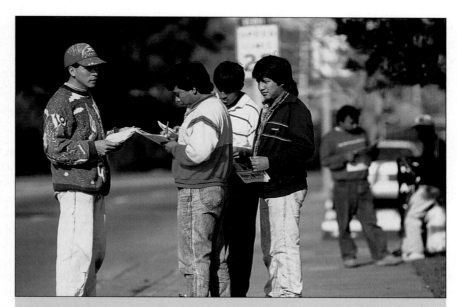

Illegal immigrants from Mexico on a California street, looking for work. The borderlands along the boundary between the United States and Mexico mix the cultures of the two countries.

Figure 10-4

The Borderlands

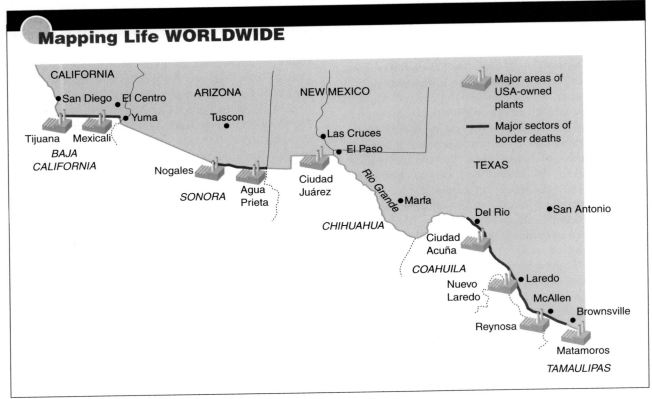

Source: Prepared by the author based on Ellingwood 2001; Thompson 2001a.

Maquiladoras located just south of the U.S.–Mexican border employ uninsured Mexican workers at wages considerably lower than those earned by U.S. workers. In search of higher wages, undocumented Mexicans often attempt to cross the border illegally, risking their lives in the process.

Think About It
How do U.S. consumers benefit from the buildup of factories along the U.S.–Mexican border?

The *maquiladoras* have contributed to Mexico's economic development, but not without some cost. Conflict theorists note that unregulated growth allows the owners to exploit the workers with jobs that lack security, possibilities for advancement, and decent wages. Moreover, many of the U.S.-owned companies require female job applicants to take a urine test to screen out those who are pregnant, a violation of Mexican law as well as the NAFTA agreement and the source of numerous cases of sex discrimination. Social activists also complain that tens of thousands of Mexicans work on *maquiladora* assembly lines for much lower wages, such as $1 an hour, raising again the issue of sweatshop labor noted previously in the chapter (Dillon 1998; Dougherty and Holthouse 1999).

When people in the United States think about the borderlands, they generally think about immigration. As we'll see in the social policy section of Chapter 11, immigration is a controversial political issue in the United States—especially immigration across the Mexican border. For its part, Mexico is concerned about the priorities and policies of its powerful northern neighbor. From Mexico's point of view, the United States too often regards Mexico simply as a reserve pool of easily available cheap labor. The United States encourages Mexicans to cross the border when workers are needed but discourages and "cracks down" on immigrants when they are not. Some people, then, see immigration more as a labor market issue than a law enforcement issue. Viewed from the perspective of Immanuel Wallerstein's world systems analysis and dependency theory, this is yet another example of a core industrialized nation exploiting a peripheral developing country.

The risks of immigration are considerable. When the U.S. government cracks down on illegal immigrants at common entry points along the border, migrants without proper documentation move to more remote and dangerous locations. More than 300 illegal immigrants lose their lives every year while attempting to cross the border, many of them from dehydration in the intense desert heat (Ellingwood 2001).

The social impact of emigration to the United States is felt throughout Mexico. According to sociological research, the earliest emigrants were typically married men of working age who came from the middle of the stratification system. They had enough financial resources to afford the costs and risks of emigration, yet experienced enough financial strain that entering the United States remained attractive. Over time, kinship ties to migrants multiplied and emigration became less class-selective, with entire families making the trek to the United States. More recently, the occupational backgrounds of Mexican emigrants have widened further, reflecting not only changes in U.S. immigration policy but also the continuing crisis in the Mexican economy (Massey 1998).

Many Mexicans who have come to the United States send some part of their earnings back across the border to family members still in Mexico. This substantial flow of money, sometimes referred to as "remittances" or "migradollars," is estimated by the International Monetary Fund at a minimum of $6 to $7 billion annually and accounts for 3 percent of Mexico's gross domestic product. Sociologist Douglas Massey points out that if these funds went solely into the purchase of consumer goods, this would underscore the view of dependency theory that Mexico's economy is little more than an extension of the economy of the United States. In fact, however, some of these "migradollars" are used by Mexicans to establish and maintain small business enterprises, such as handicraft workshops and farms. Consequently, the transfer of "migradollars" does stimulate the local and national economies of Mexico (Durand et al. 1996; *Migration News* 2001b).

We now turn to an examination of how social inequality takes on an especially ugly face in the form of human rights abuse.

Imagine

Imagine a day when the border between the United States and Mexico is completely open. What would the two countries' economies be like? What would their societies be like?

SOCIAL POLICY AND SOCIAL INEQUALITY WORLDWIDE

Universal Human Rights

The Issue

Poised on the third millennium, the world seemed capable of many mighty feats—ranging from explorations of distant solar systems to refinement of tiny genes within human cells. Yet at the same time came constant reminders of how quickly people and their fundamental human rights can be trampled. The end of Soviet dominance of eastern Europe set off bitter and sometimes violent clashes among racial, ethnic, and religious groups in Bosnia, Kosovo, Serbia, and former republics of the Soviet Union itself. In central Africa, Hutus and Tutsis massacred one another in a virulent civil war. Meanwhile, Iraq's mistreated Kurdish minority continued to fight for its rights, as did the Mexican peasants of Indian heritage. A peace agreement between Israel and the Palestinians did not end hostilities or killings in that troubled area.

Human rights refers to universal moral rights belonging to all people because they are human. The most important elaboration of human rights appears in the Universal Declaration of Human Rights, adopted by the United Nations in 1948. This declaration prohibits slavery, torture, and degrading punishment; grants everyone the right to a nationality and its culture; affirms freedom of religion and the right to vote; proclaims the right to seek asylum in other countries to escape persecution; and prohibits arbitrary interference with one's privacy and the arbitrary taking of a person's property. It also emphasizes that mothers and children are entitled to special care and assistance.

What steps, if any, can the world community take to ensure the protection of these rights? And is it even possible to agree on what those rights are?

The Setting

The 1990s tragically brought the term *ethnic cleansing* into the world's vocabulary. Within the former Yugoslavia, Serbs initiated a policy intended to "cleanse" Muslims from parts of Bosnia-Herzegovina and ethnic Albanians from the province of Kosovo. Hundreds of thousands of people have been killed in the fighting in this area, while many others have been uprooted from their homes. Moreover, there have been reports of substantial numbers of rapes of Muslim, Croatian, and Kosovar women by Serbian soldiers. In 1996 a United Nations tribunal indicted eight Bosnian Serb military and police officers for rape, marking the first time that sexual assault was treated as a war crime under international law (Simons 1996c; see also Fein 1995).

Drawing on the principles of the Universal Declaration of Human Rights, in 1995 the United Nations Human Rights Commission condemned Iraq, Iran, and the Sudan for serious human rights violations, including summary executions, cases of torture, and discrimination against women. The commission adopted resolutions expressing concern over human rights abuses in Haiti, Zaire, and Myanmar and only narrowly rejected a resolution to investigate the state of human rights in China (*New York Times* 1995b).

At first, the United States opposed a binding obligation to the Universal Declaration of Human Rights. The government feared that the declaration would cause international scrutiny of the nation's own domestic civil rights controversies (at a time when racial segregation by law was still common). By the early 1960s, however, the United States began to use the declaration to promote democracy abroad (Forsythe 1990).

Sociological Insights

By its very title, the Universal Declaration of Human Rights emphasizes that such rights should be *universal*. Even so, cultural relativism encourages the understanding and respect for the distinctive norms, values, and customs of each culture. In some situations, conflicts arise between human rights standards and local social practices that rest on alternative views of human dignity. For example, is India's caste system an inherent violation of human rights? What about the many cultures of the world that view the subordinate status of women as an essential element in their traditions? Should human rights be interpreted differently in different parts of the world?

In 1993, the United States rejected such a view by insisting that the Universal Declaration of Human Rights set a single standard for acceptable behavior around the world. However, in the late 1990s, certain Asian and African nations were reviving arguments about cultural relativism in an attempt to block sanctions by the United Nations Human Rights Commission (Crossette 1996b; Donnelly 1989; Sciolino 1993).

It is not often that a nation makes a bold statement. Policymakers, including those in the United States, more frequently look at human rights issues from an economic

p. 74

Figure 10-5

Human Rights Index

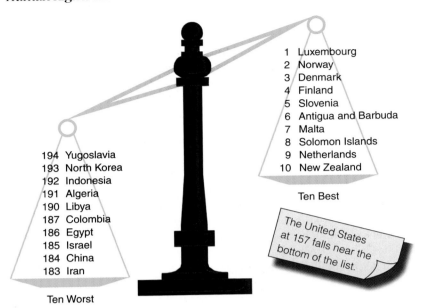

Ten Best

1 Luxembourg
2 Norway
3 Denmark
4 Finland
5 Slovenia
6 Antigua and Barbuda
7 Malta
8 Solomon Islands
9 Netherlands
10 New Zealand

Ten Worst

194 Yugoslavia
193 North Korea
192 Indonesia
191 Algeria
190 Libya
187 Colombia
186 Egypt
185 Israel
184 China
183 Iran

The United States at 157 falls near the bottom of the list.

Notes: Fourteen nations had no abuses. Nations were ranked based on per capita gross domestic product, except for Andorra, Liechtenstein, Monaco, Palau, San Marino, and Tuvalu, for which there were no reliable GDP data.

Sources: The Observer (London) 1999; Haub and Cornelius 2001.

Think About It
What do most of the 10 worst countries have in common? The 10 best countries?

International nongovernmental organizations sometimes step in when governmental and diplomatic initiatives fail to address human rights abuses. This Albanian doctor treating a Serb woman in Kosovo is a member of Médecins sans Frontières, an independent emergency medical aid organization.

perspective. Functionalists would point out how much more quickly we become embroiled in "human rights" concerns when oil is at stake, as in the Middle East, or military alliances come into play, as in Europe. The United States is less likely to want to interfere in an area where its economic concerns are modest (as in Africa) or where it is seeking to advance an economic agenda (as in China).

This intersection of economics and human rights issues has led to the creation of a Human Rights Index (HRI), using a database that weighs measures of human rights violations in a country against its level of economic development. Human rights abuses include such indicators as the denial of minority and women's rights, the presence of political prisoners, and the use of torture. Because poverty and a position at the periphery of the world economic system make equality difficult to achieve, the HRI is adjusted to reflect the level of a nation's development. Figure 10-5 highlights the best nations and worst offenders in this index of 195 nations. On the list, Mexico ranks 178, Russia 153, and the United States 157—much closer to the worst offenders than the best nations, despite the United States' avowed advocacy of human rights.

Perhaps not surprising given its modest ranking on the HRI, the United States sent a very low-level delegation to the UN-sponsored World Conference Against Racism (WCAR) in 2001. Eventually the United States withdrew totally, expressing concern over anti-Israeli sentiment and proposals that former slaveholding countries owed reparations payments to the descendants of slaves. Many other nations at the WCAR balked at any serious consideration of the concerns of minorities within their borders.

Policy Initiatives

Human rights come wrapped up in international diplomacy. For that reason, many national policymakers hesitate to interfere in human rights issues, especially if they conflict with what are regarded as more pressing national concerns. Stepping up to fill the gap are international organizations such as the United Nations and nongovernmental organizations (NGOs) like Médecins sans Frontières and Amnesty International. Most initiatives come from these international bodies.

Médecins sans Frontières (Doctors Without Borders), the world's largest independent emergency medical aid organization, won the 1999 Nobel Peace Prize for its work in countries worldwide. Founded in 1971 and based in Paris, the organization has 5,000 doctors and nurses working in 80 countries. "Our intention is to highlight current upheavals, to bear witness to foreign tragedies and reflect on the principles of humanitarian aid," explains Dr. Rony Brauman, the organization's president (Spielmann 1992:12; also see Daley 1999).

Among the endangered peoples of the world are many indigenous (native or tribal) peoples whose settlement preceded immigration from other countries and colonialism. They include nomadic Bedouins of the Arabic peninsula, the Inuit (Eskimo) of North America, the Sami (or Lapp) of northern Scandinavia, the Ainu of Japan, the Aborigines of Australia, and Brazil's Yanomani Indians. Indigenous peoples are organizing to defend their way of life, assisted by voluntary associations in the core industrialized nations. As one result of this activism, the United Nations has established a working group to draft a Universal Declaration of the Right of Indigenous Peoples (Durning 1993).

Amnesty International monitors human rights violations around the world. Founded in 1961, the organization has chapters in many countries and 400,000 members in the United States alone. It works for the release of men and women detained for their conscientiously held beliefs, their color, ethnic origin, sex, religion, or language—provided they have neither used nor advocated violence. The winner of the 1977 Nobel Prize for Peace, Amnesty International opposes all forms of torture and capital punishment and advocates prompt trials of all political prisoners.

Women's rights got a boost from the 1995 World Conference on Women. The conference delegates agreed on a "platform of action" calling on governments around the world to improve the status of girls, better the economic situation of women, and protect women from increasing levels of violence.

In recent years, there has been growing awareness of lesbian and gay rights as an aspect of universal human rights. In 1994, Amnesty International USA (1994:2) published a pioneering report in which it acknowledged that "homosexuals in many parts of the world live in constant fear of government persecution." The report examined abuses in Brazil, Greece, Mexico, Iran, the United States, and other countries, including cases of torture, imprisonment, and extrajudicial execution. Later in 1994, the United States issued an order that would allow lesbians and gay men to seek political asylum in the United States if they can prove they have suffered government persecution in their home countries solely because of their sexual orientation (Johnston 1994). We'll look at lesbian and gay rights in more detail in Chapter 22.

Ethnic cleansing in the former Yugoslavia; human rights violations in Iraq, Iran, and the Sudan; persecution of the Aborigines of Australia and other indigenous peoples; violence against women inside and outside the family; governmental torture of lesbians and gay men—all these are vivid reminders that social inequality today can have life-and-death consequences. Universal human rights remain an ideal and not a reality.

Let's Discuss

1. Why are there varying definitions of human rights?
2. Does it surprise you that the United States does not rank very high in human rights? Why do you think this is the case?
3. How have feminist groups broadened the debate over universal human rights?

⬤ Chapter Resources

Summary

We can easily see worldwide stratification both in the gap between rich and poor nations and in the inequality *within* countries around the world. This chapter examines stratification within the world economic system, the impact of globalization, modernization, and multinational corporations on developing countries, and the distribution of wealth and income in various nations.

1. As of 1995, the 140 developing nations accounted for 78 percent of the world's population but only 16 percent of all wealth.
2. Former colonized nations are kept in subservient position, subject to foreign domination, through the process of **neocolonialism.**
3. Drawing on the conflict perspective, the **world systems analysis** of sociologist Immanuel

Wallerstein views the global economic system as divided between nations that control wealth (*core nations*) and those from which capital is taken (*periphery nations*).

4. According to **dependency theory,** even as developing countries make economic advances, they remain weak and subservient to core nations and corporations within an increasingly intertwined global economy.
5. **Globalization,** or the worldwide integration of government policies, cultures, social movements, and financial markets through trade and the exchange of ideas, is a controversial trend that critics blame for contributing to the cultural domination of periphery nations by core nations.

6. *Multinational corporations* bring jobs and industry to developing nations, but they also tend to exploit the workers there in order to maximize profits.

7. Many sociologists are quick to note that terms such as *modernization* and even *development* contain an ethnocentric bias.

8. According to *modernization theory,* development in peripheral countries will be assisted by the innovations transferred from the industrialized world.

9. Social mobility is more limited in developing nations than in the core nations.

10. While Mexico is unquestionably a poor country, the gap between its richest and poorest citizens is one of the widest in the world.

11. The subordinate status of Mexico's Indians is but one reflection of the nation's color hierarchy, which links social class to the appearance of racial purity.

12. Growing recognition of the *borderlands* reflects the increasingly close and complex relationship between Mexico and the United States.

13. *Human rights* need to be identified and abuses of those rights corrected in countries throughout the world.

Critical Thinking Questions

1. In what ways is the informal economy evident in your college community and in the city or town where you grew up? Drawing on the functionalist, conflict, and interactionist perspectives, analyze the informal economy as you have seen it in these communities.

2. Imagine that you had the opportunity to spend a year in Mexico studying inequality in that nation. How would you draw on the research designs of sociology (surveys, observation, experiments, existing sources) to better understand and document stratification in Mexico?

3. How active should the U.S. government be in addressing violations of human rights in other countries? At what point, if any, does concern for human rights turn into ethnocentrism by failing to respect the distinctive norms, values, and customs of another culture?

Key Terms

Borderlands The area of a common culture along the border between Mexico and the United States. (page 257)

Colonialism The maintenance of political, social, economic, and cultural dominance over a people by a foreign power for an extended period of time. (243)

Dependency theory An approach that contends that industrialized nations continue to exploit developing countries for their own gain. (243)

Globalization The worldwide integration of government policies, cultures, social movements, and financial markets through trade and the exchange of ideas. (245)

Human rights Universal moral rights belonging to all people because they are human. (259)

Informal economy Transfers of money, goods, or services that are not reported to the government. (253)

Modernization The far-reaching process by which peripheral nations move from traditional or less developed institutions to those characteristic of more developed societies. (248)

Modernization theory A functionalist approach that proposes that modernization and development will gradually improve the lives of people in peripheral nations. (248)

Multinational corporations Commercial organizations that, while headquartered in one country, own or control other corporations and subsidiaries throughout the world. (246)

Neocolonialism Continuing dependence of former colonies on foreign countries. (243)

World systems analysis A view of the global economic system as divided between certain industrialized nations that control wealth and developing countries that are controlled and exploited. (243)

Additional Readings

BOOKS

Adler, William M. 2000. *Mollie's Job: A Story of Life and Work on the Global Assembly Line.* New York: Scribner. A freelance journalist puts a human face on capitalists' worldwide search for cheap labor.

Bonacich, Edna, and Richard Appelbaum. 2000. *Behind the Label: Inequality in the Los Angeles Apparel Industry.* Berkeley: University of California Press. Two sociologists examine the sweatshops that have made Los Angeles the clothing production capital of U.S.

Gereffi, Gary, and Miquel Korenziewicz, eds. 1994. *Commodity Chains and Global Capitalism.* New York: Praeger. The contributors to this volume look at the relationship among a variety of global economy networks that are overtaking the nation-state.

LaFeber, Walter. 1999. *Michael Jordan and the New Global Capitalism.* New York: W. W. Norton. Considers the growing intersection of culture and capital on an international scale.

Levitt, Peggy. 2001. *The Transnational Villagers.* Chicago: University of Chicago Press. A sociologist documents migrants' continued involvement with their countries of origin, even after they have emigrated.

Waring, Marilyn. 1988. *If Women Counted: A New Feminist Economics.* San Francisco: Harper and Row. Waring, a social scientist from New Zealand, considers how women's labor is overlooked in the global economy.

Weigard, Bruce. 1992. *Off the Books: A Theory and Critique of the Underground Economy.* Dix Hills, N.Y.: General-Hall. An examination of the social consequence of people's participation in activities outside the mainstream economy.

The World Bank. *World Development Report.* New York: Oxford University Press. Published annually by the International Bank for Reconstruction and Development (the United Nations agency more commonly referred to as the World Bank), this volume provides a vast array of social and economic indicators regarding world development.

JOURNALS

Among the journals that consider issues of worldwide stratification, uneven development, and universal human rights are *Global Networks* (founded in 2001), *Global Social Policy* (2001), *Holocaust and Genocide Studies* (1987), *Human Rights Quarterly* (1978), *International Journal of Urban and Regional Research* (1976), *International Labor Review* (1921), *Journal of Developing Areas* (1965), *Latin American Research Review* (1956), *Review of Income and Wealth* (1954), and *World Development* (1973).

Technology Resources

Internet Connection

*Note: While all the URLs listed were current as of the printing of this book, these sites often change. Please check our website (**http://www.mhhe.com/schaefer8**) for updates and hyperlinks to this exercise and additional exercises.*

1. As you have learned in this chapter, human rights play an important role in everyday life, just as social inequality does. The Human Rights Web (**http://www.hrweb.org**) is a website dedicated to promoting human rights. Explore the site and then answer the following questions:
   (a) The concept of human rights has existed in Europe under other names since the time of King John of England. What were those names?
   (b) Why was the Magna Carta important?
   (c) Summarize what constitutes a human rights emergency.
   (d) What can you do to promote human rights?
2. Social inequality affects many people worldwide. Inequality.org (**http://www.inequality.org**) provides a great deal of information on social inequality. Go to the website and complete the following exercises:

   (a) Click on "Facts and Figures," then on "Wealth Patterns." How many children were living in poverty in California in 1998?
   (b) In 1995, what percentage of Black households in the United States had no net worth?
   (c) Click on "Income Patterns." How many million U.S. households have an annual income of less than $35,000?
   (d) Click on "Health Patterns." How many U.S. children go hungry regularly?
   (e) What is the life expectancy of a White American? Of an African American?
3. Universal human rights have become a major concern for politicians, sociologists, and activist groups. Direct your web browser to **http://headlines.yahoo.com/Full_Coverage/World/Human_Rights/** and learn about recent events in the area of human rights.
   (a) What news stories dominate the headlines?
   (b) Does it appear that human rights are more or less being respected according to these headlines? What examples can you give to support your answer?

(c)   According to the Universal Declaration of Human Rights, what rights should all persons enjoy? Can you think of any to add to this list?

(d)   Which rights do you feel are the most important? Why?

(e)   What examples from your text or from current events show violation of any of these specific human rights?

(f)   According to the Human Rights Watch World Report 2000, how well does the United States do in respecting universal human rights? What might improve matters in the United States?

(g)   What role might television and the Internet play in improving the observance of human rights?

Online Learning Center www.mhhe.com/schaefer8

This chapter has focused on social inequality worldwide. Test your knowledge about the information presented by visiting the student center in the Online Learning Center at **www.mhhe.com/schaefer8** and take the multiple choice quiz. This quiz will not only test your knowledge, it will give you immediate feedback on the questions that you answered incorrectly.

RACIAL AND ETHNIC INEQUALITY

THE MAN ON THE LEFT IS 75 TIMES MORE LIKELY TO BE STOPPED BY THE POLICE WHILE DRIVING THAN **THE MAN ON THE RIGHT.**

It happens every day on America's highways. Police stop drivers based on their skin color rather than for the way they are driving. For example, in Florida 80% of those stopped and searched were black and Hispanic, while they constituted only 5% of all drivers. These humiliating and illegal searches are violations of the Constitution and must be fought. Help us defend your rights. Support the ACLU.

american civil liberties union
125 Broad Street, 18th Floor, NY, NY 10004 www.aclu.org

Too often, authorities treat individuals differently based solely on their race or ethnicity. This poster dramatizes the injustice of racial profiling, a practice in which the Reverend Martin Luther King, Jr. (left) would be treated with more suspicion than the mass murderer Charles Manson (right).

Ah so. No tickee, no washee. So sorry, so sollee.

Chinkee, Chink. Jap, Nip, zero, kamikaze. Dothead, flat face, flat nose, slant eye, slope. Slit, mamasan, dragon lady. Gook, VC, Flip, Hindoo.

By the time I was ten, I'd heard such words so many times I could feel them coming before they parted lips. I knew they were meant in the unkindest way. Still, we didn't talk about these incidents at home, we just accepted them as part of being in America, something to learn to rise above.

The most common taunting didn't even utilize words but a string of unintelligible gobbledygook that kids—and adults—would spew as they pretended to speak Chinese or some other Asian language. It was a mockery of how they imagined my parents talked to me.

Truth was that Mom and Dad rarely spoke to us in Chinese, except to scold or call us to dinner. Worried that we might develop an accent, my father insisted that we speak English at home. This, he explained, would lessen the hardships we might encounter and make us more acceptable as Americans.

I'll never know if my father's language decision was right. On the one hand, I, like most Asian Americans, have been complimented countless times on my spoken English by people who assumed I was a foreigner. "My, you speak such good English," they'd cluck. "No kidding, I ought to," I would think to myself, then wonder: should I thank them for assuming that English isn't my native language? Or should I correct them on the proper usage of "well" and "good"?

More often than feeling grateful for my American accent, I've wished that I could jump into a heated exchange of rapid-fire Chinese, volume high and spit flying. But with a vocabulary limited to "*Ni hao?*" (How are you?) and "*Ting bu dong*" (I hear but don't understand), meaningful exchanges are woefully impossible. I find myself smiling and nodding like a dashboard ornament. I'm envious of the many people I know who grew up speaking an Asian language yet converse in English beautifully.

Armed with standard English and my flat New Jersey "a," I still couldn't escape the name-calling. I became all too familiar with other names and faces that supposedly matched mine—Fu Manchu, Suzie Wong, Hop Sing, Madame Butterfly, Charlie Chan, Ming the Merciless—the "Asians" produced for mass consumption. Their faces filled me with shame whenever I saw them on TV or in the movies. They defined my face to the rest of the world: a sinister Fu, Suzie the whore, subservient Hop Sing, pathetic Butterfly, cunning Chan, and warlike Ming. Inscrutable Orientals all, real Americans none. (*Zia 2000*) ■ 💿

Additional information about this excerpt and about those that open each subsequent chapter can be found in the SocWorld CD-ROM that accompanies this text.

elen Zia, the journalist and community activist who wrote this reminiscence from her childhood, is the successful daughter of Chinese immigrants to the United States. As her story shows, Zia experienced blatant prejudice against Chinese Americans, even though she spoke flawless English. In fact, all new immigrants and their families have faced stereotyping and hostility, whether they were White or non-White, Asian, African, or East European. In this multicultural society, those who are different from the dominant social group have never been welcome.

Today, millions of African Americans, Asian Americans, Hispanic Americans, and many other racial and ethnic minorities continue to experience the often bitter contrast between the "American dream" and the grim realities of poverty, prejudice, and discrimination. Like class, the social definitions of race and ethnicity still affect people's place and status in a stratification system, not only in this country but

throughout the world. High incomes, a good command of English, and hard-earned professional credentials do not always override racial and ethnic stereotypes or protect those who fit them from the sting of racism.

How do sociologists define race and ethnicity? What is prejudice, and how is it institutionalized in the form of discrimination? In what ways have race and ethnicity affected the experience of immigrants from other countries? What are the fastest growing minority groups in the United States today? In this chapter we will focus on the meaning of race and ethnicity. We will begin by identifying the basic characteristics of a minority group and distinguishing among racial and ethnic groups. Then we will examine the dynamics of prejudice and discrimination. After considering the functionalist, conflict, and interactionist perspectives on race and ethnicity, we'll take a look at patterns of intergroup relations, particularly in the United States. Finally, in the social policy section, we will explore issues related to immigration worldwide. ■

Minority, Racial, and Ethnic Groups

Sociologists frequently distinguish between racial and ethnic groups. The term *racial group* is used to describe a group that is set apart from others because of obvious physical differences. Whites, African Americans, and Asian Americans are all considered racial groups in the United States. While race does turn on physical differences, it is the culture of a particular society that constructs and attaches social significance to these differences, as we will see later. Unlike racial groups, an *ethnic group* is set apart from others primarily because of its national origin or distinctive cultural patterns. In the United States, Puerto Ricans, Jews, and Polish Americans are all categorized as ethnic groups.

Minority Groups

A numerical minority is any group that makes up less than half of some larger population. The population of the United States includes thousands of numerical minorities, including television actors, green-eyed people, tax lawyers, and descendants of the Pilgrims who arrived on the *Mayflower*. However, these numerical minorities are not considered to be minorities in the sociological sense; in fact, the number of people in a group does not necessarily

determine its status as a social minority (or dominant group). When sociologists define a minority group, they are primarily concerned with the economic and political power, or powerlessness, of that group. A *minority group* is a subordinate group whose members have significantly less control or power over their own lives than the members of a dominant or majority group have over theirs.

Sociologists have identified five basic properties of a minority group—unequal treatment, physical or cultural traits, ascribed status, solidarity, and in-group marriage (Wagley and Harris 1958):

1. Members of a minority group experience unequal treatment as compared to members of a dominant group. For example, the management of an apartment complex may refuse to rent to African Americans, Hispanics, or Jews. Social inequality may be created or maintained by prejudice, discrimination, segregation, or even extermination.
2. Members of a minority group share physical or cultural characteristics that distinguish them from the dominant group. Each society arbitrarily decides which characteristics are most important in defining the groups.
3. Membership in a minority (or dominant) group is not voluntary; people are born into the group.

 pp. 111–112 Thus, race and ethnicity are considered *ascribed* statuses.

4. Minority group members have a strong sense of group solidarity. William Graham Sumner, writing in 1906, noted that people make distinctions between members of their own group (the *in-group*)

p. 136 ◀

and everyone else (the *out-group*). When a group is the object of long-term prejudice and discrimination, the feeling of "us versus them" can and often does become extremely intense.

5. Members of a minority generally marry others from the same group. A member of a dominant group is often unwilling to marry into a supposedly inferior minority. In addition, the minority group's sense of solidarity encourages marriages within the group and discourages marriages to outsiders.

Race

The term *racial group* refers to those minorities (and the corresponding dominant groups) set apart from others by obvious physical differences. But what is an "obvious" physical difference? Each society determines which differences are important while ignoring other characteristics that could serve as a basis for social differentiation. In the United States, we see differences in both skin color and hair color. Yet people learn informally that differences in skin color have a dramatic social and political meaning, while differences in hair color do not.

When observing skin color, people in the United States tend to lump others rather casually into such categories as "Black," "White," and "Asian." More subtle differences in skin color often go unnoticed. However, this is not the case in other societies. Many nations of Central America and South America have color gradients distinguishing people on a continuum from light to dark skin color. Brazil has approximately 40 color groupings, while in other countries people may be described as "Mestizo Hondurans," "Mulatto Colombians," or "African Panamanians." What we see as "obvious" differences, then, are subject to each society's social definitions.

The largest racial minorities in the United States are African Americans (or Blacks), Native Americans (or American Indians), and Asian Americans (Japanese Americans, Chinese Americans, and other Asian peoples). Figure 11–1 provides information about the population of racial and ethnic groups in the United States over the past five centuries.

Figure 11-1

Racial and Ethnic Groups in the United States, 1500–2100 (Projected)

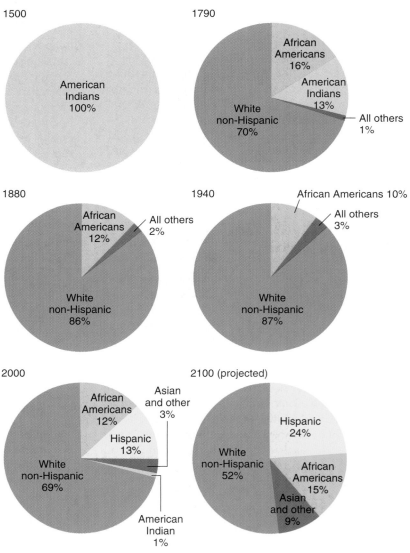

Sources: Author's estimate; Bureau of the Census 1975, 2000c; Grieco and Cassidy 2001; Thornton 1987.

The racial and ethnic composition of what is today the United States has been undergoing change not just for the last 50 years, but for the last 500. Five centuries ago the land was populated only by indigenous Native Americans.

Biological Significance of Race

Viewed from a biological perspective, the term *race* would refer to a genetically isolated group with distinctive gene frequencies. But it is impossible to scientifically define or identify such a group. Contrary to popular belief, there are no "pure races." Nor are there physical traits—whether skin color or baldness—that can be used to describe one group to the exclusion of all others. If scientists examine a smear of human blood under a microscope, they cannot tell whether it came from a Chinese or a Navajo, a Hawaiian or an African American. There is, in fact, more genetic variation *within* races than across them.

Migration, exploration, and invasion have led to intermingling of races. Scientific investigations indicate that the percentage of North American Blacks with White ancestry ranges from 20 percent to as much as 75 percent. Recent DNA findings suggest that some Blacks today can even claim Thomas Jefferson as their ancestor. Such statistics undermine a fundamental assumption of life in the United States: that we can accurately categorize individuals as "Black" or "White" (Herskovits 1930; Roberts 1975).

Some people would like to find biological explanations to help social scientists understand why certain peoples of the world have come to dominate others (see the discussion of sociobiology in Chapter 4). p. 87 Given the absence of pure racial groups, there can be no satisfactory biological answers for such social and political questions.

Social Construction of Race

In the southern part of the United States, it was known as the "one-drop rule." If a person had even a single drop of "Black blood," that person was defined and viewed as Black, even if he or she *appeared* to be White. Clearly, race had social significance in the South, enough so that White legislators established official standards about who was "Black" and "White."

The one-drop rule was a vivid example of the *social construction of race*—the process by which people come to define a group as a race based in part on physical characteristics, but also on historical, cultural, and economic factors. It is an ongoing process subject to some debate, especially in a diverse society such as the United States, where each year increasing numbers of children are born to parents of different racial backgrounds.

In the 2000 census, nearly 7 million people in the United States (or about 2 percent of the population) reported that they were of two or more races. Half the people classified as multiracial were under age 18, suggesting that this segment of the population will grow in the years to come. People who claimed both White and American Indian ancestry were the largest group of multiracial residents (Farley 2001; Grieco and Cassidy 2001).

This statistical finding of millions of multiracial people obscures how individuals handle their identity. The prevailing social construction of race pushes people to choose just one race, even if they acknowledge a broader cultural background. Still, many individuals, especially young adults, struggle against social pressure to choose a single identity, and instead openly embrace multiple heritages. Tiger Woods, the world's best-known professional golfer, considers himself both Asian and African American.

Social construction of race occurs throughout the world, as people in virtually all societies define their position in the social hierarchy in terms of race, ethnicity, and nationality. Given rising immigration rates, not only in the United States but abroad, racial differences frequently erupt in racial conflict (see Box 11-1).

A dominant or majority group has the power not only to define itself legally but to define a society's values. Sociologist William I. Thomas (1923), an early critic of

Not long ago, these children of a White mother and an African American father would automatically have assumed their father's racial identity. Today, however, some children of mixed-race families identify themselves as biracial.

11-1 The Empire Strikes Back: Racism in Great Britain

The British have considerable experience in dealing with people of color. For centuries Great Britain governed imperial colonies in Africa, Asia, and the Caribbean. Yet as recently as 1950, no more than 100,000 non-White people resided in Great Britain, out of a population of 48 million.

This situation began to change in the 1960s, when cheaper transportation and a demand for unskilled labor brought an influx of non-White subjects from the colonies. Quickly, Parliament tightened the nation's immigration laws, which had not been regarded as too lenient when the new arrivals came from overwhelmingly White countries such as Canada or Australia. Today, despite tighter restrictions, the population of Great Britain is much more diverse than in the past. About 3 million British, or 7 percent of the population, are Blacks who hail originally from the Caribbean and Africa, or Asians from India or Pakistan. Most members of these racial minority groups are the children of immigrants, who tend to see England as their native country.

Many of the children of immigrants, now adolescents and young adults, face higher unemployment than their White counterparts. Complaints of police brutality, lack of political representation, and job discrimination are commonplace. In 2001, in the midst of a national election, England's worst race riot in 15 years broke out in the old textile mill town of Oldham. There, after members of the

> **Many of England's cities have "no-go" areas, where Whites or non-Whites fear to enter.**

White supremacist group National Front threw bricks at an Asian family's home, minority youths fought back. Dozens of civilians and police were injured—a shocking statistic in a country unaccustomed to civil violence. Days later, another confrontation broke out in a different city, this time between British Pakistanis and the police.

This outbreak of racial hostility reminded the English of how strongly their color line is drawn. Many of England's

cities have "no-go" areas, where Whites or non-Whites fear to enter. In one year's time, nationally recorded racist incidents had doubled, yet politicians, even in the midst of the national campaign, made virtually no public reference to the violence and its implications. While the three major political parties publicly condemn racial hatred, all seek to reduce immigration from the former colonies.

New immigration restrictions will not solve the problems of people of color who already live in Great Britain, however. Relegated to a subordinate role in the past, these previously quiet minorities are speaking out now, demanding their rights as British subjects.

Let's Discuss

1. Have racial tensions been a problem where you live? If so, what groups are involved? Is immigration an issue?
2. Compare and contrast the racial situation in Great Britain with the racial situation in the United States. What are the similarities between the two countries? The differences?

Sources: Cantle 2001; Lyall 2001; *Migration News* 2002a; Prentice 2001; Schaefer 1993:468–473.

---

theories of racial and gender differences, saw that the "definition of the situation" could mold the personality of the individual. To put it another way, Thomas, writing from the interactionist perspective, observed that people respond not only to the objective features of a situation or person but also to the *meaning* that situation or person has for them. Thus, we can create false images or stereotypes that become real in their consequences. **Stereotypes** are unreliable generalizations about all members of a group that do not recognize individual differences within the group.

In the last 30 years, critics have pointed out the power of the mass media to perpetuate false racial and ethnic stereotypes. Television is a prime example: Almost all the leading dramatic roles are cast as Whites, even in urban-

based programs like *Friends*. Blacks tend to be featured mainly in crime-based dramas.

Imagine

Using a TV remote control, how quickly do you think you could find a television show in which all the characters share your own ethnic background? What about a show in which all the characters share a different ethnic background from your own—how quickly could you find one?

Ethnicity

An ethnic group, unlike a racial group, is set apart from others because of its national origin or distinctive cultural patterns. Among the ethnic groups in the United

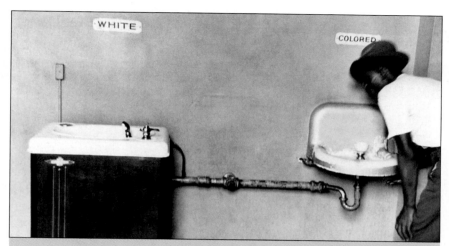

"Whites only" was a common sign in the southern states when "Jim Crow" laws enforced official segregation of the races. In this blatant example of institutional discrimination, Blacks were not allowed to use a new water fountain reserved for Whites, but had to drink from an older fixture nearby.

Prejudice and Discrimination

In recent years, college campuses across the United States have been the scene of bias-related incidents. Student-run newspapers and radio stations have ridiculed racial and ethnic minorities; threatening literature has been stuffed under the doors of minority students; graffiti endorsing the views of White supremacist organizations such as the Ku Klux Klan have been scrawled on university walls. In some cases, there have even been violent clashes between groups of White and Black students (Bunzel 1992; Schaefer 2002).

Prejudice is a negative attitude toward an entire category of people, often an ethnic or racial minority. If you resent your roommate because he or she is sloppy, you are not necessarily guilty of prejudice. However, if you immediately stereotype your roommate on the basis of such characteristics as race, ethnicity, or religion, that is a form of prejudice. Prejudice tends to perpetuate false definitions of individuals and groups.

Sometimes prejudice results from *ethnocentrism*— the tendency to assume that one's culture and way of life represent the norm or are superior to all others. Ethnocentric people judge other cultures by the standards of their own group, which leads quite easily to prejudice against cultures viewed as inferior.

p. 73

One important and widespread form of prejudice is *racism,* the belief that one race is supreme and all others are innately inferior. When racism prevails in a society, members of subordinate groups generally experience prejudice, discrimination, and exploitation. In 1990, as concern mounted about racist attacks in the United States, Congress passed the Hate Crimes Statistics Act. This law directs the Department of Justice to gather data on crimes motivated by the victim's race, religion, ethnicity, or sexual orientation.

Many such crimes are the work of racist fringe groups, which are legion in the United States (see Figure 11-2, left). In 1999 alone, more than 7,800 hate crimes were reported to authorities. Some 56 percent of these crimes against persons involved racial bias, whereas another 10 percent to 17 percent each involved religion, sexual orientation, and ethnic bias. As Figure 11-2, right, shows, laws against such crimes vary from state to state (Department of Justice 2001a).

States are peoples with a Spanish-speaking background, referred to collectively as *Latinos* or *Hispanics,* such as Puerto Ricans, Mexican Americans, Cuban Americans, and other Latin Americans. Other ethnic groups in this country include Jewish, Irish, Italian, and Norwegian Americans. While these groupings are convenient, they serve to obscure differences *within* these ethnic categories (as in the case of Hispanics) as well as to overlook the mixed ancestry of so many ethnic people in the United States.

The distinction between racial and ethnic minorities is not always clear-cut. Some members of racial minorities, such as Asian Americans, may have significant cultural differences from other groups. At the same time, certain ethnic minorities, such as Latinos, may have obvious physical differences that set them apart from other residents of the United States.

Despite categorization problems, sociologists continue to feel that the distinction between racial groups and ethnic groups is socially significant. That is because in most societies, including the United States, physical differences tend to be more visible than ethnic differences. Partly as a result of this fact, stratification along racial lines is more resistant to change than stratification along ethnic lines. Members of an ethnic minority sometimes can become, over time, indistinguishable from the majority—although this process may take generations and may never include all members of the group. By contrast, members of a racial minority find it much more difficult to blend in with the larger society and to gain acceptance from the majority.

Figure 11-2

Racist Fringe Groups and Hate Crime Laws in the United States

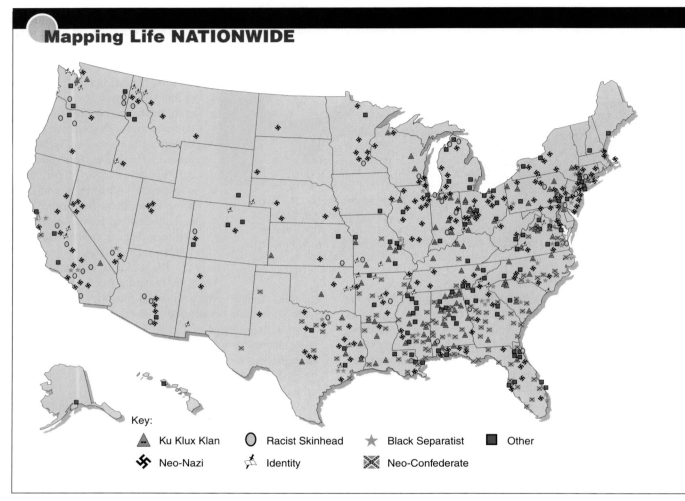

Mapping Life NATIONWIDE

Key:

▲ Ku Klux Klan   ⬭ Racist Skinhead   ★ Black Separatist   ■ Other

卐 Neo-Nazi   ⚐ Identity   ✖ Neo-Confederate

Sources: Anti-Defamation League 2001b; Southern Poverty Law Center 2001.

Think About It

Why do you think state legislators enacted special hate crime laws covering criminal acts that already were illegal?

A particularly horrifying hate crime made the front pages in 1998: In Jasper, Texas, three White men with possible ties to race-hate groups tied up a Black man, beat him with chains, and then dragged him behind their truck until his body was dismembered. Numerous groups in the United States have been victims of hate crimes as well as generalized prejudice. In the wake of the terrorist attacks of September 11, 2001, hate crimes against Asian Americans and Muslim Americans escalated rapidly. Box 11-2 examines prejudice against Arab Americans and Muslims who live in the United States.

The activity of organized hate groups appears to be increasing, both in reality and in virtual reality. Although only a few hundred such groups may exist, there were at least 2,000 websites advocating racial hatred on the Internet in 1999. Particularly troubling were sites disguised as video games for young people, or as "educational sites" about crusaders against prejudice, like Martin Luther King, Jr. The technology of the Internet has allowed race-hate groups to expand far beyond their traditional southern base to reach millions (Sandberg 1999).

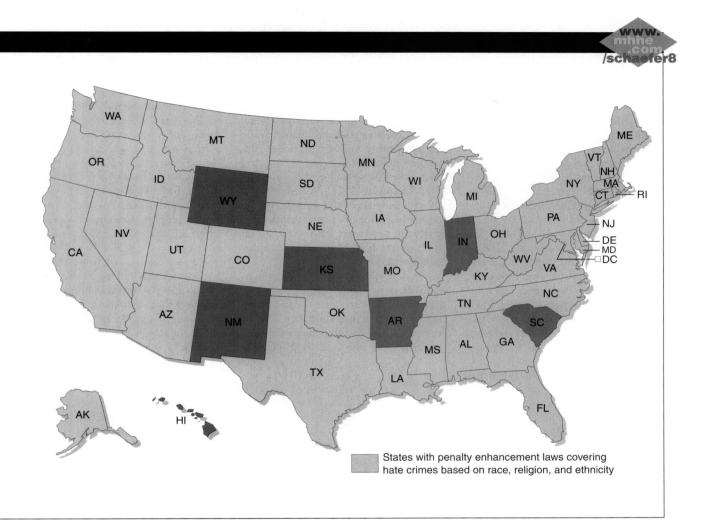

States with penalty enhancement laws covering hate crimes based on race, religion, and ethnicity

Discriminatory Behavior

John and Glenn are alike in almost every way—about the same age, they are both Big Ten college graduates with good jobs. But they find they have different experiences in everyday routines, such as walking into a store. John gets instant attention from the same sales staff that ignores Glenn, even though he has been waiting five minutes. When Glenn is locked out of his car, passersby ignore him, while John receives many offers of help. At an employment agency, Glenn is lectured on laziness and told he will be monitored "real close"; John is encouraged.

What accounts for these differences in the everyday life experiences of two men? Very simply, John is White and Glenn is Black. The two were part of an experiment, conducted by the television newsmagazine *Primetime Live,* to assess the impact of race on the day-to-day lives of residents in a typical U.S. city. Over a three-week period

reporters closely monitored the two men, who had been trained to present themselves in an identical manner. Not once or twice, but "every single day," said program host Diane Sawyer, John and Glenn were treated differently (ABC News 1992).

Prejudice often leads to **discrimination,** the denial of opportunities and equal rights to individuals and groups based on some type of arbitrary bias. Say that a White corporate president with a prejudice against Asian Americans has to fill an executive position. The most qualified candidate for the job is a Vietnamese American. If the president refuses to hire this candidate and instead selects an inferior White candidate, he or she is engaging in an act of racial discrimination.

Prejudiced *attitudes* should not be equated with discriminatory *behavior.* Although the two are generally related, they are not identical, and either condition can be

Research in Action

11-2 Prejudice against Arab Americans and Muslim Americans

www.
mhhe
.com
/schaefer8

As marginal groups with little political power, Arab Americans and Muslim Americans are vulnerable to prejudice and discrimination. In the first five days after the terrorist attack on the World Trade Center in September 2001, these groups filed more than 300 reports of harassment and abuse, including one death. Six years earlier, when the bombing of a federal office building in Oklahoma City was mistakenly attributed to Middle East terrorism, many Arabic and Islamic schoolchildren in the United States were blamed for the attack. One fifth-grade boy was told, "Go back where you came from!" His mother, an attorney and a second-generation Syrian American, asked where her children were supposed to go. One was born in Texas, the other in Oklahoma.

Sociologists have observed two trends in the United States over the last 20 years. First, the numbers of people in the United States who are Arab or who practice the Muslim faith have increased dramatically. Second, the open expression of hostility toward Arab and Muslim people has also increased. Obviously, the coinciding of these two trends has made life unpleasant for many of these people.

Following the attack on the World Trade Center, media representatives recognized how little insight Americans have into Arab cultures and Islamic religious practices. Content analysis of the media has shown that Arabs and Muslims are repeatedly presented as almost cartoonlike figures, whether camel drivers, outrageously wealthy sheiks, or deranged terrorists. Even Disney's 1993 animated film *Aladdin* referred to Arabs as "barbaric." The movie depicted an Arabic guard threatening to cut off a young girl's hand for stealing food, but did not point out

that such punishment would violate Islamic law.

"Profiling" at airports has put some citizens under special surveillance. Fearing terrorists, a number of airlines and law enforcement authorities use appearance and ethnic-sounding names to identify and take aside Arab Americans (or those who match the "profile") and search their belongings. After the terrorist attacks of September 2001, criticism of this practice declined as concern for the public's safety mounted.

Muslim women who choose to don head scarves or *hijbab* in keeping with their tradition to dress modestly encounter harassment from strangers in the street. Many employers insist that the women shed the covering if they wish to get a job or expect

> One fifth-grade boy was told, "Go back where you came from!"

to be promoted. These citizens find it difficult to understand such attitudes in a nation founded on religious freedom.

Many people in the United States inaccurately lump together Arab Americans and Muslims. While these groups overlap, many Arab Americans are Christians (as is true of many Arabs living in the Middle East) and many Muslims (such as African Americans, Iranians, and Pakistanis) are non-Arabs. Currently, there are an estimated 870,000 Arab Americans, and their numbers are rising. Many cling to the culture of their nation of origin, which can vary considerably. For example, Arabs constitute an ethnic group in 22 nations of North Africa and the Middle East, including Morocco, Syria, Iraq, Saudi Arabia, and Somalia.

At present, perhaps as many as 3 million Muslims live in the United States, of whom about 42 percent are African American, 24 percent are South Asian, 12 percent are Arab, and 22 percent are "other." Muslims are followers of Islam, the world's largest faith after Christianity. Islam is based on the teachings found in the Koran (or Al-Qur'an) of the seventh-century prophet Mohammed. Islamic believers are divided into a variety of faiths and sects, such as Sunnis and Shiites, which are sometimes antagonistic toward one another (just as there are religious rivalries among Christians and among Jews).

The first known mosque in the United States was founded in 1929. Today, there are more than 1,200 mosques in this country, of which 80 percent have been established in the last 25 years. The largest group of Muslims in the United States, African Americans, is divided between those who follow mainstream Islamic doctrine and those who follow the teachings of the controversial Nation of Islam (headed by Minister Louis Farrakhan). The Muslim population of the United States is growing significantly, owing to high birthrates, substantial immigration of Muslims, and conversion of non-Muslims.

Let's Discuss

1. Do you know an Arab American or Muslim American who has been the subject of ethnic profiling? If so, explain the circumstances. What was the person's reaction to the experience?

2. What can be done to promote better understanding of Arab and Muslim Americans and counter prejudice and discrimination against them?

Sources: El Badry 1994; Henneberger 1995; Lindner 1998; Power 1998; Shaheen 1999; T. Smith 2001; Weinstein et al. 2001.

present without the other. A prejudiced person does not always act on his or her biases. The White president, for example, might choose—despite his or her stereotypes—to hire the Vietnamese American. This would be prejudice without discrimination. On the other hand, a White corporate president with a completely respectful view of Vietnamese Americans might refuse to hire them for executive posts out of fear that biased clients would take their business elsewhere. In this case, the president's action would constitute discrimination without prejudice.

Discrimination persists even for the most educated and qualified minority group members from the best family backgrounds. Despite their talents and experiences, they sometimes encounter attitudinal or organizational bias that prevents them from reaching their full potential. The term *glass ceiling* refers to an invisible barrier that blocks the promotion of a qualified individual in a work environment because of the individual's gender, race, or ethnicity (Schaefer 2002; Yamagata et al. 1997).

In early 1995, the federal Glass Ceiling Commission issued the first comprehensive study of barriers to promotion in the United States. The commission found that glass ceilings continue to block women and minority group men from top management positions in the nation's industries. While White men constitute about 43 percent of the paid labor force, they hold about 95 of every 100 senior management posts. According to the report, the existence of this glass ceiling results principally from the fears and prejudices of many middle- and upper-level White male managers, who believe that the inclusion of women and minority group men in management circles will threaten their own prospects for advancement (Department of Labor 1995a, 1995b).

The other side of discrimination is the privilege enjoyed by dominant groups. Though most White people rarely think about their "whiteness," taking their status for granted, sociologists and other social scientists are becoming increasingly interested in what it means to be "White." The feminist scholar Peggy McIntosh (1988) has compiled a list of advantages that come with being White, including (1) avoiding having to spend time with people she was trained to mistrust, or who have learned to mistrust her kind; (2) being considered financially

White people tend to underestimate the value of racial privilege, yet without affirmative action programs, employers tend to hire those with backgrounds similar to their own, as this all-White committee meeting suggests.

reliable when using checks, credit cards, or cash; (3) never having to speak for all the people in her racial group; (4) taking a job without having her coworkers suspect she got it because of her race; and (5) being able to worry about racism without being regarded as self-serving. And as we saw in Chapter 7, White people can turn on the television or open up the newspaper and see members of their own race widely represented. Whiteness *does* carry privileges.

Institutional Discrimination

Discrimination is practiced not only by individuals in one-to-one encounters but also by institutions in their daily operations. Social scientists are particularly concerned with the ways in which structural factors such as employment, housing, health care, and government operations maintain the social significance of race and ethnicity. *Institutional discrimination* refers to the denial of opportunities and equal rights to individuals and groups that results from the normal operations of a society. This kind of discrimination consistently affects certain racial and ethnic groups more than others.

The U.S. Commission on Civil Rights (1981:9–10) has identified various forms of institutional discrimination, including:

- Rules requiring that only English be spoken at a place of work, even when it is not a business necessity to restrict the use of other languages.

 **Taking Sociology to Work**

DELORES CLEARY:
Assistant Professor, Central Washington University

Delores Cleary, a Native American woman, left her reservation for Seattle at age 25 with her husband and two children. Shortly after her move, she started taking classes at the local community college. Her first class happened to be an introduction to sociology course. "I just loved sociology and kept taking classes." Her enthusiasm eventually led to a B.A. from Central Washington University in 1989 and a master's and Ph.D. from Washington State in 1994.

She currently teaches three classes a week; conducts research on Native American issues having to do with identity, gambling, and poverty; and is actively involved in community service. Recently she won a large grant to develop an interdisciplinary year-long course on racism. Everything she learned in her academic career applies to what she does now. In the classroom, she emphasizes "the intersection of race, gender, and sexual orientation that impacts people's place in the social structure," to which she brings her own experience. As chair of an Indian parent committee, she finds that her sociology background helps her to negotiate conflict and plan and organize social change.

Cleary claims that the study of sociology "has empowered me to really take control of my life and make change and become a contributing member of society, to benefit humanity." She advises today's students that reading the text and taking the class will help to make changes in their lives, "to understand their place in the world and in American society."

Let's Discuss

1. In what ways has your study of sociology helped you to better understand your place in American society? Were you surprised or upset by any of the things you have learned in this course?

2. Has your study of sociology stimulated your interest in social policy or social action? If so, what issues interest you? How might you and other students become involved in these issues?

- Preferences shown by law and medical schools in the admission of children of wealthy and influential alumni, nearly all of whom are White.
- Restrictive employment-leave policies, coupled with prohibitions on part-time work, that make it difficult for the heads of single-parent families (most of whom are women) to obtain and keep jobs.

Computer technology represents another area of institutional discrimination. As technology increases globally, access to this technology will be crucial in determining who moves ahead and who stays behind. It is apparent in the United States that a racial divide does indeed exist in this area. African Americans are less likely to have a computer in their home than are Whites. As of 2001, 57 percent of White adults had access to the Internet, compared to 47 percent of Hispanics and 43 percent of Blacks. The significance of these differences in access may only increase as better-paying jobs, and even information itself, become increasingly tied to computer technology (Rainie and Packel 2001).

 Imagine

Suddenly, you don't have access to a desktop computer—not at home, at school, or even at work. How will your life change?

In some cases, even ostensibly neutral institutional standards can turn out to have discriminatory effects. African American students at a midwestern state university protested a policy under which fraternities and sororities that wished to use campus facilities for a dance were required to post $150 security deposits to cover possible damages. The Black students complained that this policy had a discriminatory impact on minority student organizations. Campus police countered that the university's policy applied to all student groups interested in using these facilities. However, since overwhelmingly White fraternities and sororities at the school had their own houses that they used for dances, the policy indeed affected only African American and other minority organizations.

There have been attempts to eradicate or compensate for discrimination in the United States. The 1960s saw the passage of many pioneering civil rights laws, including the landmark 1964 Civil Rights Act (which prohibits discrimination in public accommodations and publicly owned facilities on the basis of race, color, creed, national origin, and gender). In two important rulings in 1987, the Supreme Court held that federal prohibitions against racial discrimination protect members of all ethnic minorities—including Hispanics, Jews, and Arab Americans—even though they may be considered White.

For more than 20 years, affirmative action programs have been instituted to overcome past discrimination.

Affirmative action refers to positive efforts to recruit minority members or women for jobs, promotions, and educational opportunities. Many people, however, resent these programs, arguing that advancing one group's cause merely shifts the discrimination to another group. By giving priority to African Americans in school admissions, for example, more qualified White candidates may be overlooked. In many parts of the country and many sectors of the economy, affirmative action is being rolled back, even though it was never fully implemented.

Discriminatory practices continue to pervade nearly all areas of life in the United States today. In part, this is because various individuals and groups actually *benefit* from racial and ethnic discrimination in terms of money, status, and influence. Discrimination permits members of the majority to enhance their wealth, power, and prestige at the expense of others. Less qualified people get jobs and promotions simply because they are members of the dominant group. Such individuals and groups will not surrender these advantages easily. We'll turn now to a closer look at this functionalist analysis, as well as the conflict and interactionist perspectives.

Studying Race and Ethnicity

Relations among racial and ethnic groups lend themselves to analysis from the three major perspectives of sociology. Viewing race from the macro-level, functionalists observe that racial prejudice and discrimination serve positive functions for dominant groups, whereas conflict theorists see the economic structure as a central factor in the exploitation of minorities. The micro-level analysis of interactionist researchers stresses the manner in which everyday contact between people from different racial and ethnic backgrounds contributes to tolerance or leads to hostility.

Functionalist Perspective

What possible use could racial bigotry have for society? Functionalist theorists, while agreeing that racial hostility is hardly to be admired, point out that it indeed serves positive functions for those practicing discrimination.

Anthropologist Manning Nash (1962) has identified three functions that racially prejudiced beliefs have for the dominant group:

A sign in a shop window in Los Angeles advertises the proprietor's prejudice against immigrants. According to the functionalist perspective, open displays of racial and ethnic bigotry are an attempt to maintain the power of the dominant group in society.

1. Such views provide a moral justification for maintaining an unequal society that routinely deprives a minority of its rights and privileges. Southern Whites justified slavery by believing that Africans were physically and spiritually subhuman and devoid of souls (Hoebel 1949).

2. Racist beliefs discourage the subordinate minority from attempting to question its lowly status, which would be to question the very foundations of society.

3. Racial myths encourage support for the existing order by introducing the argument that any major societal change (such as an end to discrimination) would only bring greater poverty to the minority and lower the majority's standard of living. As a result, Nash suggests, racial prejudice grows when a society's value system (for example, one underlying a colonial empire or a regime perpetuating slavery) is being threatened.

Although racial prejudice and discrimination may serve the interests of the powerful, such unequal treatment can also be dysfunctional to a society and even to its dominant group. Sociologist Arnold Rose (1951) outlines four dysfunctions associated with racism:

1. A society that practices discrimination fails to use the resources of all individuals. Discrimination limits the search for talent and leadership to the dominant group.

2. Discrimination aggravates social problems such as poverty, delinquency, and crime and places the financial burden to alleviate these problems on the dominant group.

3. Society must invest a good deal of time and money to defend its barriers to full participation of all members.

4. Racial prejudice and discrimination often undercut goodwill and friendly diplomatic relations between nations.

Conflict Perspective

Conflict theorists would certainly agree with Arnold Rose that racial prejudice and discrimination have many harmful consequences for society. Sociologists such as Oliver Cox (1948), Robert Blauner (1972), and Herbert M. Hunter (2000) have used the **exploitation theory** (or *Marxist class theory*) to explain the basis of racial subordination in the United States. As we saw in Chapter 8, Karl Marx viewed the exploitation of the lower class as a basic part of the capitalist economic system. From a Marxist point of view, racism keeps minorities in low-paying jobs, thereby supplying the capitalist ruling class with a pool of cheap labor. Moreover, by forcing racial minorities to accept low wages, capitalists can restrict the wages of *all* members of the proletariat. Workers from the dominant group who demand higher wages can always be replaced by minorities who have no choice but to accept low-paying jobs.

The conflict view of race relations seems persuasive in a number of instances. Japanese Americans were the object of little prejudice until they began to enter jobs that brought them into competition with Whites. The movement to keep Chinese immigrants out of the United States became most fervent during the latter half of the nineteenth century, when Chinese and Whites fought over dwindling work opportunities. Both the enslavement of Blacks and the extermination and removal westward of Native Americans were, to a significant extent, economically motivated.

However, the exploitation theory is too limited to explain prejudice in its many forms. Not all minority groups have been economically exploited to the same extent. In addition, many groups (such as the Quakers and the Mormons) have been victimized by prejudice for other than economic reasons. Still, as Gordon Allport (1979:210) concludes, the exploitation theory correctly "points a sure finger at one of the factors involved in prejudice, . . . rationalized self-interest of the upper classes."

Interactionist Perspective

A Hispanic woman is transferred from a job on an assembly line to a similar position working next to a White man. At first, the White man is patronizing, assuming that she must be incompetent. She is cold and resentful; even when she needs assistance, she refuses to admit it. After a week, the growing tension between the two leads to a bitter quarrel. Yet, over time, each slowly comes to appreciate the other's strengths and talents. A year after they begin working together, these two workers become respectful friends. This is an example of what interactionists call the *contact hypothesis* in action.

The **contact hypothesis** states that interracial contact between people of equal status in cooperative circumstances will cause them to become less prejudiced and to abandon previous stereotypes. People begin to see one another as individuals and discard the broad generalizations characteristic of stereotyping. Note the factors of *equal status* and *cooperative circumstances*. In the example above, if the two workers had been competing for one vacancy as a supervisor, the racial hostility between them might have worsened (Allport 1979; Schaefer 2002; Sigelman et al. 1996).

As Latinos and other minorities slowly gain access to better-paying and more responsible jobs in the United

States, the contact hypothesis may take on even greater significance. The trend in our society is toward increasing contact between individuals from dominant and subordinate groups. This may be one way of eliminating—or at least reducing—racial and ethnic stereotyping and prejudice. Another may be the establishment of interracial coalitions, an idea suggested by sociologist William Julius Wilson (1999b). To work, such coalitions would obviously need to be built on an equal role for all members.

Contact between individuals occurs on the microlevel. We turn now to a consideration of intergroup relations on a macrolevel.

Patterns of Intergroup Relations

Racial and ethnic groups can relate to one another in a wide variety of ways, ranging from friendships and intermarriages to genocide, from behaviors that require mutual approval to behaviors imposed by the dominant group.

One devastating pattern of intergroup relations is *genocide*—the deliberate, systematic killing of an entire people or nation. This term describes the killing of 1 million Armenians by Turkey beginning in 1915. It is most commonly applied to Nazi Germany's extermination of 6 million European Jews, as well as gays, lesbians, and the Romani people ("Gypsies"), during World War II. The term *genocide* is also appropriate in describing the United States' policies toward Native Americans in the nineteenth century. In 1800, the Native American (or American Indian) population of the United States was about 600,000; by 1850, it had been reduced to 250,000 through warfare with the cavalry, disease, and forced relocation to inhospitable environments.

The *expulsion* of a people is another extreme means of acting out racial or ethnic prejudice. In 1979, Vietnam expelled nearly 1 million ethnic Chinese, partly as a result of centuries of hostility between Vietnam and neighboring China. In a more recent example of expulsion (which had aspects of genocide), Serbian forces began a program of "ethnic cleansing" in 1991 in the newly independent states of Bosnia and Herzegovina. Throughout the former nation of Yugoslavia, the Serbs drove more than 1 million Croats and Muslims from their homes. Some were tortured and killed, others abused and terrorized, in an attempt to "purify" the land for the remaining ethnic Serbs. In 1999, Serbs were again the focus of worldwide condemnation as they sought to "cleanse" the province of Kosovo of ethnic Albanians.

Genocide and expulsion are extreme behaviors. More typical intergroup relations as they occur in North America and throughout the world follow four identifiable pat-

Ethnic Albanian women mourn the death of a man killed by Serbs in the province of Kosovo. Such "ethnic cleansings" have met with worldwide condemnation.

terns: (1) amalgamation, (2) assimilation, (3) segregation, and (4) pluralism. Each pattern defines the dominant group's actions and the minority group's responses. Intergroup relations are rarely restricted to only one of the four patterns, although invariably one does tend to dominate. Therefore, think of these patterns primarily as ideal types.

Amalgamation

Amalgamation happens when a majority group and a minority group combine to form a new group. Through intermarriage over several generations, various groups in the society combine to form a new group. This can be expressed as A + B + C → D, where A, B, and C represent different groups present in a society, and D signifies the end result, a unique cultural-racial group unlike any of the initial groups (Newman 1973).

The belief in the United States as a "melting pot" became very compelling in the first part of the twentieth century, particularly since that image suggested that the nation had an almost divine mission to amalgamate various groups into one people. However, in actuality many residents were not willing to have Native Americans, Jews, African Americans, Asian Americans, and Irish Roman Catholics as a part of the melting pot. Therefore, this pattern does not adequately describe dominant–subordinate relations existing in the United States.

Assimilation

Many Hindus in India complain about Indian citizens who copy the traditions and customs of the British. In Australia, Aborigines who have become part of the dominant society refuse to acknowledge their darker-skinned grandparents on the street. In the United States, some

"Ho, ho, ho" apparently works in any language. As Japanese Americans assimilated the norms and values of mainstream U.S. culture, they created their own "Shogun Santa." This one can be found in the Little Tokyo neighborhood of Los Angeles.

Italian Americans, Polish Americans, Hispanics, and Jews have changed their ethnic-sounding family names to names that are typically found among White, Protestant families.

Assimilation is the process by which a person forsakes his or her own cultural tradition to become part of a different culture. Generally, it is practiced by a minority group member who wants to conform to the standards of the dominant group. Assimilation can be described as an ideology in which $A + B + C \rightarrow A$. The majority A dominates in such a way that members of minorities B and C imitate A and attempt to become indistinguishable from the dominant group (Newman 1973).

Assimilation can strike at the very roots of a person's identity as he or she seeks to blend in with the dominant group. Alphonso D'Abuzzo, for example, changed his name to Alan Alda. This process is not unique to the United States: the British actress Joyce Frankenberg changed her name to Jane Seymour. Name changes, switches in religious affiliation, and dropping of native languages can obscure one's roots and heritage. Moreover, assimilation does not necessarily bring acceptance for the minority group individual. A Chinese American such as Helen Zia (see the chapter-opening excerpt) may speak English fluently, achieve high educational standards, and become a well-respected professional or businessperson and *still* be seen as different, to the extent that other Americans reject her as a business associate, neighbor, or marriage partner.

Imagine

You have immigrated to another country with a very different culture. How might you need to change your behavior?

Segregation

Separate schools, separate seating sections on buses and in restaurants, separate washrooms, even separate drinking fountains—these were all part of the lives of African Americans in the South when segregation ruled early in the twentieth century. ***Segregation*** refers to the physical separation of two groups of people in terms of residence, workplace, and social events. Generally, a dominant group imposes it on a minority group. Segregation is rarely complete, however. Intergroup contact inevitably occurs, even in the most segregated societies.

From 1948 (when it received its independence) to 1990, the Republic of South Africa severely restricted the movement of Blacks and other non-Whites by means of a wide-ranging system of segregation known as ***apartheid.*** Apartheid even included the creation of homelands where Blacks were expected to live. However, decades of local resistance to apartheid, combined with international pressure, led to marked political changes in the 1990s. In 1994, a prominent Black activist, Nelson Mandela, was elected as South Africa's president, the first election in which Blacks (the majority of the nation's population) were allowed to vote. Mandela had spent almost 28 years in South African prisons for his anti-apartheid activities. His election was widely viewed as the final blow to South Africa's oppressive policy of apartheid.

Long-entrenched social patterns are difficult to change, however. In the United States today, despite federal laws that forbid housing discrimination, residential segregation is still the norm, as a recent analysis of living patterns in metropolitan areas shows. Across the nation, neighborhoods remain divided along both racial and ethnic lines. The average White person lives in an area that is at least 83 percent White, while the average African American lives in a neighborhood that is mostly Black. The typical Latino lives in an area that is 42 percent Hispanic. Overall, segregation flourishes at the community and neighborhood level, despite the increasing diversity of the nation as a whole (Lewis Mumford Center 2001).

Whatever the country, residential segregation directly limits people's economic opportunity. Sociologists Douglas Massey and Nancy Denton (1993), in a book aptly titled *American Apartheid,* noted that segregation separates poor people of color from job opportunities and isolates them from successful role models. This pattern repeats itself the world over, from South Central Los Angeles to Oldham, England, and Soweto, South Africa.

Pluralism

In a pluralistic society, a subordinate group does not have to forsake its lifestyle and traditions. *Pluralism* is based on mutual respect among various groups in a society for one another's cultures. It allows a minority group to express its own culture and still to participate without prejudice in the larger society. Earlier, we described amalgamation as A + B + C → D, and assimilation as A + B + C → A. Using this same approach, we can conceive of pluralism as A + B + C → A + B + C. All the groups are able to coexist in the same society (Newman 1973).

In the United States, pluralism is more of an ideal than a reality. There are distinct instances of pluralism: the ethnic neighborhoods in major cities, such as Koreatown, Little Tokyo, Andersonville (Swedish Americans), and Spanish Harlem. Yet there are also limits to such cultural freedom. In order to survive, a society must promote a certain consensus among its members regarding

basic ideals, values, and beliefs. Thus, if a Romanian migrating to the United States wants to move up the occupational ladder, he or she cannot avoid learning the English language.

Switzerland exemplifies a modern pluralistic state. The absence both of a national language and of a dominant religious faith leads to a tolerance for cultural diversity. In addition, various political devices safeguard the interests of ethnic groups in a way that has no parallel in the United States. By contrast, Great Britain has found it difficult to achieve cultural pluralism in a multiracial society. East Indians, Pakistanis, and Blacks from the Caribbean and Africa are experiencing prejudice and discrimination within the dominant White British society. There is pressure to cut off all Asian and Black immigration and a few in Britain even call for expelling those non-Whites currently living there.

Race and Ethnicity in the United States

Few societies have a more diverse population than the United States; the nation is truly a multiracial, multiethnic society. Of course, this has not always been the case. The population of what is now the United States has changed dramatically since the arrival of European settlers in the 1600s, as Figure 11-1 (p. 270) showed. Immigration, colonialism, and in the case of Blacks, slavery determined the racial and ethnic makeup of our present-day society. (See Figure 11-3 for where various racial and ethnic minorities are concentrated in the United States.)

Racial Groups

The largest racial minorities in the United States include African Americans, Native Americans, and Asian Americans.

African Americans

"I am an invisible man," wrote Black author Ralph Ellison in his novel *Invisible Man* (1952:3). "I am a man of substance, of flesh and bone, fiber and liquids—and I might even be said to possess a mind. I am invisible, understand, simply because people refuse to see me."

Over five decades later, many African Americans still feel invisible. Despite their large numbers, they have long been treated as second-class citizens. Currently, by the standards of the federal government, more than 1 out of every 4 Blacks—as opposed to 1 out of every 12 Whites—is poor.

Contemporary institutional discrimination and individual prejudice against African Americans are rooted in

Figure 11-3

Census 2000: The Image of Diversity

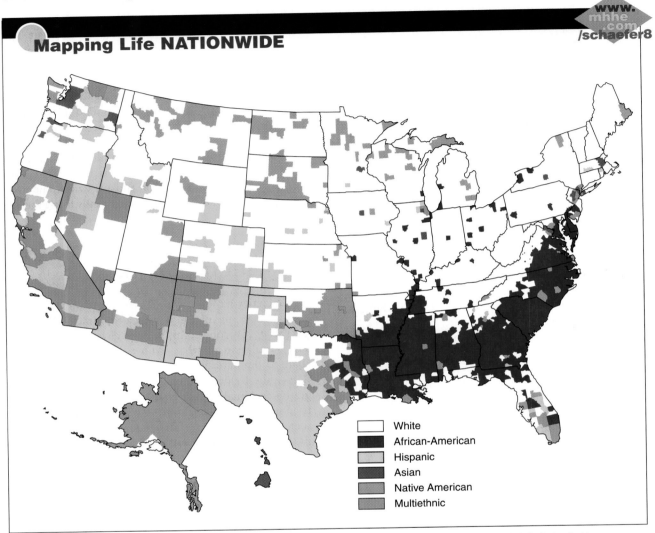

Notes: Shaded areas indicate places where a particular ethnic group exceeds the national average. The notation *multiethnic* indicates that two or more minority groups exceed the national average.

Source: Frey 2001a: 20–21.

Think About It
The United States is a diverse nation. Why, in many parts of the country, can't people see that diversity in their own towns?

the history of slavery in the United States. Whereas many other subordinate groups had little wealth and income, as sociologist W. E. B. Du Bois (1909) and others have noted, enslaved Blacks were in an even more oppressive situation because, by law, they could not own property and could not pass on the benefits of their labor to their children. Today, increasing numbers of

African Americans and sympathetic Whites are calling for *slave reparations* to compensate for the injustices of forced servitude. Reparations could include official expressions of apology from governments such as the United States, ambitious programs to improve African Americans' economic status, or even direct payments to descendants of slaves.

Randall Robinson, leader of the TransAfrica delegation, speaks with reporters on a visit to Haiti. Robinson advocates the payment of reparations to African Americans as compensation for their ancestors' enslavement.

The end of the Civil War did not bring genuine freedom and equality for Blacks. The Southern states passed "Jim Crow" laws to enforce official segregation, and they were upheld as constitutional by the Supreme Court in 1896. In addition, Blacks faced the danger of lynching campaigns, often led by the Ku Klux Klan, during the late nineteenth and early twentieth centuries. From a conflict perspective, Whites maintained their dominance formally through legalized segregation and informally by means of vigilante terror and violence (Franklin and Moss 2000).

A turning point in the struggle for Black equality came in 1954 with the unanimous Supreme Court decision in the case of *Brown v. Board of Education of Topeka, Kansas*. The Court outlawed segregation of public school students, ruling that "separate educational facilities are inherently unequal." In the wake of the *Brown* decision, there was a surge of activism on behalf of Black civil rights, including boycotts of segregated bus companies and sit-ins at restaurants and lunch counters that refused to serve Blacks.

During the decade of the 1960s, a vast civil rights movement emerged, with many competing factions and strategies for change. The Southern Christian Leadership Conference (SCLC), founded by Dr. Martin Luther King, Jr., used nonviolent civil disobedience to oppose segregation. The National Association for the Advancement of Colored People (NAACP) favored use of the courts to press for equality for African Americans. But many younger Black leaders, most notably Malcolm X, turned toward an ideology of Black power. Proponents

of **Black power** rejected the goal of assimilation into White, middle-class society. They defended the beauty and dignity of Black and African cultures and supported the creation of Black-controlled political and economic institutions (Ture and Hamilton 1992).

Despite numerous courageous actions to achieve Black civil rights, Black and White citizens are still separate, still unequal. From birth to death, Blacks suffer in terms of their life chances. Life remains difficult for millions of poor Blacks, who pp. 228–229 must attempt to survive in ghetto areas shattered by high unemployment and abandoned housing. The economic position of Blacks is shown in Table 11-1. At the close of the century, the median household income of Blacks was only 60 percent that of Whites, and the unemployment rate among Blacks was more than twice that of Whites.

There have been economic gains for *some* African Americans—especially middle-class men and women—over the last 50 years. For example, data compiled by the Department of Labor show that the number of African Americans in management areas of the labor market increased nationally from 2.4 percent of the total in 1958 to 8.0 percent in 1999. Yet Blacks still represent only 6 percent or less of all physicians, engineers, scientists, lawyers, judges, and marketing managers. In another area important for developing role models, African Americans and Hispanics together account for less than 8 percent of all editors and reporters in the United States (Bureau of the Census 2000a:416).

In many respects, the civil rights movement of the 1960s left institutionalized discrimination against African Americans untouched. Consequently, in the 1970s and 1980s, Black leaders worked to mobilize African American political power as a force for social change. Between 1970 and 1998, the number of African American elected officials

Table 11-1 Relative Economic Positions of Various Racial and Ethnic Groups, 2000

Characteristic	Whites	African Americans	Native Americans	Asian Americans	Hispanics
Four-year college education, people 25 and over	28.1%	15.5%	9.4%	42.0%	10.6%
Median family income	$49,023	$29,404	$31,799	$52,826	$29,608
Unemployment rate	3.4%	8.0%	———	4.2%	6.8%
People below the poverty line	7.7%	26.1%	25.9%	12.5%	22.8%

Notes: Data on Whites, where available, are for White non-Hispanics. On reservations, estimated median family income for Native American households is $18,063. Income data for Native Americans are for the year 2000; educational data, for the year 1990.

Sources: Bureau of the Census 2000a:43–46; Dalaker 2001:7; DeNavas et al. 2001:5–6; Therrien and Ramirez 2001.

Think About It
Notice how much higher the rate for college education is among Asian Americans than among Whites. Yet the median income for Asian Americans is only slightly higher than it is for Whites. What might explain this disparity?

increased by sixfold. Even so, Blacks remain significantly *underrepresented*. This underrepresentation is especially distressing in view of the fact that sociologist W. E. B. Du Bois observed over 90 years ago that Blacks could not expect to achieve equal social and economic opportunities without first gaining political rights (Bureau of the Census 2000a:288; Green and Driver 1978).

Native Americans

There are 2.5 million Native Americans. They represent a diverse array of cultures, distinguishable by language, family organization, religion, and livelihood. The outsiders who came to the United States—European settlers and their descendants—came to know the native people as "American Indians." By the time the Bureau of Indian Affairs (BIA) was organized as part of the *War* Department in 1824, Indian–White relations had already included three centuries of mutual misunderstanding. Many bloody wars during the nineteenth century wiped out a significant part of the nation's Indian population. By the end of the nineteenth century, schools for Indians operated by the BIA or church missions prohibited the practice of Native American cultures. Yet, at the same time, such schools did little to make the children effective competitors in White society.

Today, life remains difficult for members of the 554 tribal groups in the United States, whether they live in cities or on reservations. For example, one Native American teenager in six has attempted suicide—a rate four

Cabazon men perform a traditional Native American dance during a tribal gathering in California. In recent years, Native Americans have sought to revive customs that Whites once encouraged them to abandon.

times higher than the rate for other teenagers. Traditionally, some Native Americans have chosen to assimilate and abandon all vestiges of their tribal cultures to escape certain forms of prejudice. However, by the 1990s, an increasing number of people in the United States were openly claiming an identity as Native American. Since 1960, the federal government's count of Native Americans has tripled, to an estimated 2.4 million. According to the 2000 census, there was a 26 percent increase in Native Americans during the 1990s. Demographers believe that more and more Native Americans who previously concealed their identity are no longer pretending to be White (Grieco and Cassidy 2001).

The introduction of gambling on Indian reservations threatens to become still another battleground between Native Americans and the dominant White society. About one-third of all tribes operate off-track betting, casino tables for such games as blackjack and roulette, slot machines, high-stakes bingo, sports betting, and video games of chance. The gamblers—who are overwhelmingly *not* Native Americans—typically travel long distances to wager money at the new casinos. While gambling on reservations generates $10 billion annually, the profits are not evenly spread among tribes. Much of Native America is untouched by casino windfalls. According to 1998 estimates, the overall unemployment rate on reservations is over 30 percent, compared to 4 percent for the general population. Some Native Americans oppose gambling on moral grounds and believe that it is being marketed in a manner incompatible with Native American culture. Yet, some reservations have managed profits from gambling well and have invested them in projects for the betterment of the entire reservation. At the same time, established White gambling interests, particularly in Nevada and New Jersey, have pressured Congress to restrict Native American casinos—even though these casinos generate only 5 percent of the nation's overall gambling revenues (Egan 1998; McDowell 2001; Schaefer 2002).

Imagine

www.
mhhe.
com
/schaefer8

You are a Native American whose tribe is about to open a reservation-based casino. Will the casino further the assimilation of your people into mainstream society or encourage pluralism?

Asian Americans

Asian Americans are a diverse group, one of the fastest-growing segments of the U.S. population (up by 69 percent between 1990 and 2000). Among the many groups of Americans of Asian descent are Vietnamese Americans, Chinese Americans, Japanese Americans, and Korean Americans (see Figure 11-4).

Figure 11-4

Major Asian American Groups in the United States, 2000

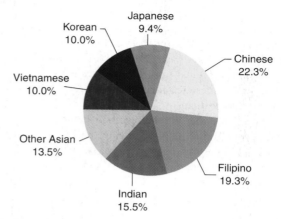

Source: Logan et al. 2001.

Think About It
Do Asian Americans really have a common identity?

Asian Americans are held up as a **model** or **ideal minority** group, supposedly because, despite past suffering from prejudice and discrimination, they have succeeded economically, socially, and educationally without resorting to confrontations with Whites. The existence of a model minority seems to reaffirm the notion that anyone can get ahead in the United States with talent and hard work and implies that those minorities that don't succeed are somehow responsible for their failures. Viewed from a conflict perspective, this becomes yet another instance of "blaming the victims" (Hurh and Kim 1998).

This concept of a model minority ignores the diversity among Asian Americans: There are rich and poor Japanese Americans, rich and poor Filipino Americans, and so forth. In fact, Southeast Asians living in the United States have the highest rate of welfare dependency of any racial or ethnic group. As Table 11-1 shows, Asian Americans have substantially more schooling than other ethnic groups, but their median income is only slightly higher than Whites' income, and their poverty rate is higher. For every Asian American family with an annual income of $75,000 or more, there is another earning less than $35,000 a year. Moreover, even when Asian Americans are clustered at the higher-paying end of the stratification system, the glass ceiling may limit how far up they can go (Bureau of the Census 2000a).

Vietnamese Americans Each Asian American group has its own history and culture. Vietnamese Americans, for instance, came to the United States primarily during and after the Vietnam War—especially after the U.S. withdrawal from the conflict in 1975. Assisted by local agencies, refugees from the communist government in Vietnam settled throughout the United States, tens of thousands of them in small towns. But over time, Vietnamese Americans have gravitated toward the larger urban areas, establishing Vietnamese restaurants and grocery stores in their ethnic enclaves there.

In 1995, the United States resumed normal diplomatic relations with Vietnam. Gradually, the *Viet Kieu,* or Vietnamese living abroad, began to return to their old country to visit, but usually not to take up permanent residence. Today, 30 years after the end of the Vietnam War, sharp differences of opinion remain among Vietnamese Americans, especially the older ones, concerning the war and the present government of Vietnam (Lamb 1997).

Chinese Americans Unlike African slaves and Native Americans, the Chinese were initially encouraged to immigrate to the United States. From 1850 to 1880, thousands of Chinese immigrated to this country, lured by job opportunities created by the discovery of gold. However, as employment possibilities decreased and competition for mining grew, the Chinese became the target of a bitter campaign to limit their numbers and restrict their rights. Chinese laborers were exploited, then discarded.

In 1882, Congress enacted the Chinese Exclusion Act, which prevented Chinese immigration and even forbade Chinese in the United States to send for their families. As a result, the Chinese population steadily declined until after World War II. More recently, the descendants of the nineteenth-century immigrants have been joined by a new influx from Hong Kong and Taiwan. The groups of immigrants sometimes form sharp contrasts in their degree of assimilation, desire to live in Chinatowns, and feelings about this country's relations with the People's Republic of China.

Currently, about 2.7 million Chinese Americans live in the United States. Some Chinese Americans have entered lucrative occupations. Yet many Chinese immigrants struggle to survive under living and working conditions that belie the "model minority" stereotype. New York City's Chinatown district is filled with illegal sweatshops in which recent immigrants—many of them Chinese women—work for minimal wages. Even in "legal" factories in the garment industry, hours are long and rewards are limited. A seamstress typically works 11 hours per day, 6 days a week, and earns about $10,000 a year. Other workers, such as hemmers and cutters, earn only $5,000 per year (Finder 1995; Lum and Kwong 1989).

Japanese Americans There are approximately 1.1 million Japanese Americans in the United States. As a people, they are relatively recent arrivals to this nation. In 1880 only 148 Japanese lived in the United States, but by 1920 there were more than 110,000. Japanese immigrants—called the *Issei,* or first generation—were usually males seeking employment opportunities. Many Whites saw them (along with Chinese immigrants) as a "yellow peril" and subjected them to widespread prejudice and discrimination.

In 1941, the attack on Hawaii's Pearl Harbor by Japan had severe repercussions for Japanese Americans. The federal government decreed that all Japanese Americans on the West Coast must leave their homes and report to "evacuation camps." They became, in effect, scapegoats for the anger that other people in the United States felt concerning Japan's role in World War II. By August 1943, in an unprecedented application of guilt by virtue of ancestry, 113,000 Japanese Americans were forced to live in hastily built camps. In striking contrast, only a few German Americans and Italian Americans were sent to evacuation camps (Hosokawa 1969).

This mass detention was costly for the interned Japanese Americans. The Federal Reserve Board estimates total losses of nearly half a billion dollars. Moreover, the psychological effect on these citizens—including the humiliation of being labeled as "disloyal"—was immeasurable. Eventually, Japanese born in the United States to the *Issei,* called **Nisei,** were allowed to enlist in the Army and serve in a segregated combat unit in Europe. Others resettled in the East and Midwest to work in factories.

In 1983, a federal commission recommended government payments to all surviving Japanese Americans who had been held in detention camps. The commission reported that the detention was motivated by "race prejudice, war hysteria, and a failure of political leadership." It added that "no documented acts of espionage, sabotage, or fifth-column activity were shown to have been committed" by Japanese Americans. In 1988, President Ronald Reagan signed the Civil Liberties Act, which required the federal government to issue individual apologies for all violations of Japanese Americans' constitutional rights and established a $1.25 billion trust fund to pay reparations to the approximately 77,500 surviving Japanese Americans who had been interned (Pear 1983; Takezawa 1995).

Korean Americans At 1.2 million, the population of Korean Americans now exceeds that of Japanese Americans. Yet Korean Americans are often overshadowed by other groups from Asia.

Today's Korean American community is the result of three waves of immigration. The initial wave arrived between 1903 and 1910, when laborers migrated to

Hawaii. The second wave followed the end of the Korean War. Most of these immigrants were wives of U.S. servicemen and war orphans. The third wave, continuing to the present, has reflected the admissions priorities set up in the 1965 Immigration Act. These well-educated immigrants arrive in the United States with professional skills. However, because of language difficulties and discrimination, many must settle at least initially for positions of lower responsibility than those they held in Korea and must suffer through a period of disenchantment. Stress, loneliness, and family strife may accompany the pain of adjustment.

Korean American women commonly participate in the paid labor force, as do many Asian American women. In Korea, the woman is expected to serve as mother and homemaker only. Although these roles carry over to the United States, women are pressed to support their families while their husbands struggle to establish themselves financially. Many Korean American men begin small service and retail businesses and gradually involve their wives in the business. The situation is made more difficult by the hostility that Korean American–run businesses often encounter from their prospective customers (Hurh 1994, 1998; Kim 1999).

In the early 1990s, the apparent friction between Korean Americans and another subordinate racial group, African Americans, attracted nationwide attention. In New York City, Los Angeles, and Chicago, the scene was replayed in which a Korean American merchant confronted a Black person allegedly threatening or robbing a store. The Black neighborhood responded with hostility to what they perceived as the disrespect and arrogance of the Korean American entrepreneur. In South Central Los Angeles, the only shops in which to buy groceries, liquor, or gasoline are owned by Korean immigrants, who have largely replaced the White businesspeople. African Americans were well aware of the dominant role that Korean Americans play in their local retail market. During the 1992 riots in South Central, small businesses owned by Koreans were a particular target. More than 1,800 Korean businesses were looted or burned during the riots; Korean establishments suffered significant damage (Kim 1999).

This type of friction is not new; generations of Jewish, Italian, and Arab merchants encountered similar hostility from what to outsiders seems an unlikely source—another oppressed minority. The contemporary conflict was dramatized in Spike Lee's 1989 movie *Do the Right Thing*, in which African Americans and Korean Americans clashed. The situation stems from Korean Americans' being the latest immigrant group to cater to the needs of inner-city populations abandoned by those who moved up the economic ladder.

Ethnic Groups

Unlike racial minorities, members of subordinate ethnic groups are generally not hindered by physical differences from assimilating into the dominant culture of the United States. However, members of ethnic minority groups still face many forms of prejudice and discrimination. Take the cases of the country's largest ethnic groups—Latinos, Jews, and White ethnics.

Latinos

Together, the various groups included under the general terms *Latinos* and *Hispanics* represent the largest minority in the United States. In 2000, there were more than 35 million Hispanics in this country, including 23 million Mexican Americans, more than 3 million Puerto Ricans, and smaller numbers of Cuban Americans and people of Central and South American origin (see Figure 11-5). This latter group represents the fastest-growing and most diverse segment of the Hispanic community.

According to Census Bureau data, the Latino population now outnumbers the African American population in 6 of the 10 largest cities of the United States: Los Angeles, Houston, Phoenix, San Diego, Dallas, and San Antonio. Hispanics are now the majority of residents in such cities as Miami, Florida; El Paso, Texas; and Santa Ana, California. The rise in the Hispanic population of the United States—fueled by comparatively high birthrates and levels of immigration—could intensify debates over such controversial public policy issues as bilingualism and immigration (Roberts 1994).

Figure 11-5

Major Hispanic Groups in the United States, 2000

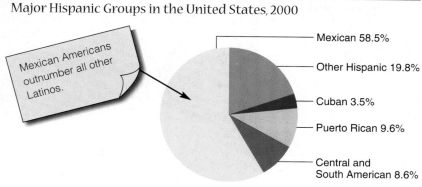

Source: Therrien and Ramirez 2001:1.

The various Latino groups share a heritage of Spanish language and culture, which can cause serious problems for assimilation in the United States. An intelligent student whose first language is Spanish may be presumed slow or even unruly by English-speaking schoolchildren, and frequently by English-speaking teachers as well. The labeling of Latino children as being underachievers, as having learning disabilities, or as suffering from emotional problems can act as a self-fulfilling prophecy for some of the children. Bilingual education in many school districts aims at easing the educational difficulties experienced by Hispanic children and others whose first language is not English.

p. 75

The educational difficulties of Latino students certainly contribute to the generally low economic status of Hispanics. In 1999, about one in four Hispanics earned $35,000 or more, compared to about one in two Whites. By 2000, only 11 percent of Hispanic adults had completed college, compared with 28 percent of non-Hispanic Whites. That same year, 23 percent of all Hispanics in the United States lived below the poverty line (Therrien and Ramirez 2001). Overall, Latinos are not as well off economically as White non-Hispanics, but a middle class is beginning to emerge within the Latino community (see Box 11-3).

Mexican Americans   The largest Latino population comprises Mexican Americans, who can be further subdivided into those descended from the residents of the territories annexed after the Mexican-American War of 1848 and those who have immigrated from Mexico to the United States. The opportunity for a Mexican to earn in one hour what it would take an entire day to earn in Mexico has pushed millions of legal and illegal immigrants north.

Aside from the family, the most important social organization in the Mexican American (or Chicano) community is the church, specifically the Roman Catholic church. The strong identification with the Catholic faith has reinforced the already formidable barriers between Mexican Americans and their predominantly White and Protestant neighbors of the Southwest. At the same time, the Catholic church helps many immigrants develop a sense of identity and assists their assimilation into the norms and values of the dominant culture of the United States. The complexity of the Mexican American community is underscored by the fact that Protestant churches—especially those that endorse expressive, open worship—have gained increasing support among Mexican Americans (Herrmann 1994; Kanellos 1994).

Puerto Ricans   The second-largest segment of Latinos in the United States is composed of Puerto Ricans. Since 1917, residents of Puerto Rico have held the status of American citizens. Many have migrated to New York and other eastern cities. Unfortunately, Puerto Ricans experience serious poverty both in the United States and on the island. Those living in the continental United States have barely half the family income of Whites. As a result, a reverse migration began in the 1970s; more

Members of the Hispanic sorority Sigma Lambda Gamma smile for the camera at Eastern Michigan University. In the United States, about 11 percent of Hispanic adults are college graduates.

No racial or ethnic group belongs to just one social class. Among Latinos, as in society as a whole, there is a social class hierarchy. The recent rapid growth of the Hispanic population, which rose 58 percent in the 1990s, has focused marketers' attention on the burgeoning Latino middle class, which grew 71 percent in the same period. Latino-oriented magazines and advertising, not always published in Spanish, are one sign of this group's growing economic power.

Whereas historically, Latinos have been a disadvantaged ethnic community in the United States, segments of the Mexican American and Cuban American communities have begun to display the typical signs of middle-class status: moderate to high incomes, post-graduate and professional schooling, and substantial assets, including homes in middle- and upper-class neighborhoods. In fact, Mexican Americans were among the first middle-class people in North America. In the 1660s, settlers in San Antonio enjoyed an almost aristocratic status granted by the Spanish crown. Some of these old-line families, as well as Hispanic families in other parts of the Southwest, have been able to retain their elevated status. In the twentieth century, well-trained professionals who fled Cuba following the revolution there created middle-class Hispanic communities in South Florida.

Among other Latinos, social mobility has created an unmistakable middle class. About one in nine Latinos now have college degrees; one in six U.S.-born Latinos is college educated. A growing number of Latinos own their own businesses—more

> **A growing number of Latinos own their own businesses—more than 1.2 million firms nationally.**

than 1.2 million firms nationally. Latino-owned businesses account for about one-quarter of all businesses in metropolitan Los Angeles and San Diego, as well as in the state of New Mexico. Women—that is, *Latinas*—are especially prominent in these businesses, most of which are very small family-owned enterprises.

Will these newly affluent Latinos continue to ally themselves with the concerns of lower-income Hispanics? Although many still favor liberalized immigration laws and bilingual education, some affluent Latinos have begun to back more restrictive immigration policies and to question the wisdom of funding bilingual education.

The assimilated children of the Latino middle class, like all children of immigrants, are caught between two worlds. Over one-quarter of the children of Latino immigrants speak only English at home. One sign that they are blending in with mainstream American culture is that many of these young adults are now studying *Español,* either to boost their careers or to become better acquainted with their roots.

Let's Discuss

1. Have you seen signs of Latino affluence on television or in magazine advertisements? What stores or brand names are pitching their wares directly to Latinos?
2. Why do you think marketers aim their promotional materials at specific racial and ethnic groups?

Sources: Bean et al. 2001; Brischetto 2001; Bureau of the Census 2001b; Campo-Flores 2000; Gonzales 1997; Moore and Pachon 1985; Romney 1998; Therrien and Ramirez 2001.

Puerto Ricans were leaving for the island than were coming to the mainland (Lemann 1991).

Politically, Puerto Ricans in the United States have not been as successful as Mexican Americans in organizing for their rights. For many mainland Puerto Ricans—as for many residents of the island—the paramount political issue is the destiny of Puerto Rico itself. Should it continue in its present commonwealth status, petition for admission to the United States as the 51st state, or attempt to become an independent nation? This question has divided Puerto Rico for decades and remains a central issue in Puerto Rican elections. In a 1998 referendum, voters supported a "none of the above" option, effectively favoring continuing the commonwealth status over statehood, with little support for independence.

Cuban Americans   Cuban immigration into the United States dates back as far as 1831, but it began in earnest following Fidel Castro's assumption of power after the 1959 Cuban revolution. The first wave of 200,000 Cubans included many professionals with relatively high levels of schooling; these men and women were largely welcomed as refugees from communist tyranny. However, more recent waves of immigrants have aroused growing concern, partly because they are less likely to be skilled professionals.

Throughout the various waves of immigration from Cuba since the revolution, Cuban Americans have been encouraged to locate across the United States. Nevertheless, many continue to settle in (or return to) metropolitan Miami, Florida, with its warm climate and proximity to Cuba.

291

The Cuban experience in the United States has been mixed. Some detractors worry about the vehement anticommunism of Cuban Americans and about the apparent growth of a Cuban organized crime syndicate that engages in the drug trade and ganglike violence. Recently, Cuban Americans in Miami have expressed concern over what they view as the indifference of the city's Roman Catholic hierarchy. Like other Hispanics, Cuban Americans are underrepresented in leadership positions within the church. Finally—despite many individual success stories—as a group, Cuban Americans in Miami remain behind "Anglos" (Whites) in their income, rate of employment, and proportion of professionals (Firmat 1994; Llanes 1982).

Jewish Americans

Jews constitute almost 3 percent of the population of the United States. They play a prominent role in the worldwide Jewish community because the United States has the world's largest concentration of Jews. Like the Japanese, many Jewish immigrants came to this country and became white-collar professionals in spite of prejudice and discrimination.

Anti-Semitism—that is, anti-Jewish prejudice—in the United States has often been vicious, although rarely so widespread and never so formalized as in Europe. In many cases, Jews have been used as scapegoats for other people's failures. Not surprisingly, Jews have not achieved equality in the United States. Despite high levels of education and professional training, they are still conspicuously absent from the top management of large corporations (except for the few firms founded by Jews). Until the late 1960s, many prestigious universities maintained restrictive quotas that limited Jewish enrollment. Private social clubs and fraternal groups frequently limit membership to gentiles (non-Jews), a practice upheld by the Supreme Court in the 1964 case of *Bell v. Maryland*.

The Anti-Defamation League (ADL) of B'nai B'rith makes an annual survey of reported anti-Semitic incidents. Although the number has fluctuated, the 1994 tabulation reached the highest level in the 17 years that the ADL has been recording such incidents. The total of reported harassment, threats, episodes of vandalism, and assaults came to 1,547 incidents in 1999. Some incidents were inspired and carried out by neo-Nazi skinheads—groups of young people who champion racist and anti-Semitic ideologies. Such threatening behavior only intensifies the fears of many Jewish Americans, who find it difficult to forget the Holocaust—the extermination of 6 million Jews by the Nazi Third Reich during World War II (Anti-Defamation League 2001a).

As is true for other minorities discussed in this chapter, Jewish Americans face the choice of maintaining ties to their long religious and cultural heritage or becoming as indistinguishable as possible from gentiles. Many Jews have tended to assimilate, as is evident from the rise in marriages between Jews and Christians. A study conducted in 2000 found that more than half of Jews who married chose to marry a non-Jew. Indeed, when asked which was the greater threat to Jewish life in the United States, intermarriage or anti-Semitism, only 41 percent of respondents replied that intermarriage was the greater threat; 50 percent selected anti-Semitism (American Jewish Committee 2001).

White Ethnics

A significant segment of the population of the United States is made up of White ethnics whose ancestors have come from Europe within the last 100 years. The nation's White ethnic population includes about 58 million people who claim at least partial German ancestry, 39 million Irish Americans, 15 million Italian Americans, and 9 million Polish Americans, as well as immigrants from other European nations. Some of these people continue to live

For practicing Jews, the Hebrew language is an important part of religious instruction. This teacher is showing flashcards of Hebrew alphabetic characters to deaf students.

in close-knit ethnic neighborhoods, while others have largely assimilated and left the "old ways" behind (Bureau of the Census 1999a:56).

To what extent are White ethnics found among the nation's elite? Sociologists Richard Alba and Gwen Moore (1982) conducted interviews with 545 people who held important positions in powerful social, economic, and political institutions. They found that White Anglo-Saxon Protestants were overrepresented among the nation's elite, while White ethnics were underrepresented (although not so dramatically as were African Americans, Hispanics, Asian Americans, and Native Americans). Some ethnic minorities appeared to have risen to key positions in particular areas of the elite structure. For example, Irish Catholics were well represented among labor leaders.

White ethnics and racial minorities have often been antagonistic to one another because of economic competition—an interpretation in line with the conflict approach to sociology. As Blacks, Latinos and Native Americans emerge from the lower class, they will initially be competing with working-class Whites for jobs, housing, and educational opportunities. In times of high unemployment or inflation, any such competition can easily generate intense intergroup conflict.

In many respects, the plight of White ethnics raises the same basic issues as that of other subordinate people in the United States. How ethnic can people be—how much can they deviate from an essentially White, Anglo-Saxon, Protestant norm—before society punishes them for a willingness to be different? Our society does seem to reward people for assimilating. Yet, as we have seen, assimilation is no guarantee of equality or freedom from discrimination. In the social policy section that follows, we will focus on immigrants, people who inevitably face the question of whether to strive for assimilation.

SOCIAL POLICY AND RACE AND ETHNICITY

Global Immigration

www.mhhe.com/schaefer8

The Issue

Worldwide immigration is at an all-time high. Each year, 2 to 4 million people move from one country to another. As of the mid-1990s, immigrants totaled about 125 million, representing 2 percent of the global population (Martin and Widgren 1996). Their constantly increasing numbers and the pressure they put on job opportunities and welfare capabilities in the countries they enter raise troubling questions for many of the world's economic powers. Who should be allowed in? At what point should immigration be curtailed?

The Setting

The migration of people is not uniform across time or space. At certain times, wars or famines may precipitate large movements of people either temporarily or permanently. Temporary dislocations occur when people wait until it is safe to return to their home areas. However, more and more migrants who cannot make adequate livings in their home nations are making permanent moves to developed nations. Figure 11-6 shows the destinations of the major migration streams: into North America, the oil-rich areas of the Middle East, and the industrial economies of western Europe and Asia. Currently, seven of the world's wealthiest nations (including Germany, France, the United Kingdom, and the United States) shelter about one-third of the world's migrant population, but less than one-fifth of the total world population. As long as there are disparities in job opportunities among countries, there is little reason to expect this international migration trend to end.

Countries such as the United States that have long been a destination for immigrants have a history of policies to determine who has preference to enter. Often, clear racial and ethnic biases are built into these policies. In the 1920s, U. S. policy gave preference to people from western Europe, while making it difficult for residents of southern and eastern Europe, Asia, and Africa to enter the country. During the late 1930s and early 1940s, the federal government refused to lift or loosen restrictive immigration quotas in order to allow Jewish refugees to escape the terror of the Nazi regime. In line with this policy, the *S.S. St. Louis,* with more than 900 Jewish refugees on board, was denied permission to land in the United States in 1939. This ship was forced to sail back to Europe, where it is estimated that at least a few hundred of its passengers later died at the hands of the Nazis (Morse 1967; Thomas and Witts 1974).

Since the 1960s, policies in the United States have encouraged immigration of people with relatives here as well as of people who have needed skills. This change has significantly altered the pattern of sending nations. Previously,

Figure 11-6

Major Migration Patterns of the 1990s

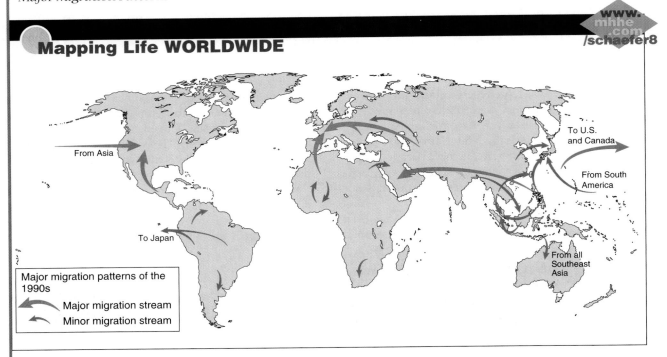

Mapping Life WORLDWIDE

www.mhhe.com /schaefer8

From Asia

To U.S. and Canada

From South America

To Japan

From all Southeast Asia

Major migration patterns of the 1990s

→ Major migration stream
→ Minor migration stream

Source: Martin and Widgren 1996:21

Europeans dominated, but for the last 40 years, immigrants have come primarily from Latin America and Asia (see Figure 11-7). This means that an ever-growing proportion of the United States will be Asian or Hispanic (see Figure 11-8). To a large degree, fear and resentment of this growing racial and ethnic diversity is a key factor in opposition to immigration. In many nations, people are very concerned that the new arrivals do not reflect the cultural and racial heritage of the nation.

Sociological Insights

Despite people's fears about it, immigration provides many valuable functions. For the receiving society, it alleviates labor shortages, such as in the areas of health care and technology in the United States. In 1998, Congress debated not whether individuals with technological skills should be allowed into the country, but just how much to increase the annual number. For the sending nation, migration can relieve economies unable to support large numbers of people. Often overlooked is the large amount of money that immigrants send *back* to their home nations. For example, worldwide immigrants

from Portugal alone send more than $4 billion annually *back* to their home country (World Bank 1995).

There has been considerable research, particularly in the United States, on the impact of immigration on a nation's economy. Studies generally show that it has a positive impact on the economy, although areas experiencing high concentrations of immigrants may find it difficult to meet short-term social service needs. When migrants with skills or educational potential leave developing countries, it can be dysfunctional for those nations. No amount of payments back home can make up for the loss of valuable human resources from poor nations (Martin and Midgley 1999).

Conflict theorists note how much of the debate over immigration is phrased in economic terms. But this debate is intensified when the arrivals are of different racial and ethnic background from the host population. For example, Europeans often refer to "foreigners," but the term does not necessarily mean one of foreign birth. In Germany, "foreigners" refers to people of non-German ancestry, even if they were born in Germany; it does not refer to people of German ancestry born in another country who may choose to come to their "mother country." Fear and dislike of "new" ethnic groups

Figure 11-7

Immigration in the United States, 1820s–1990s

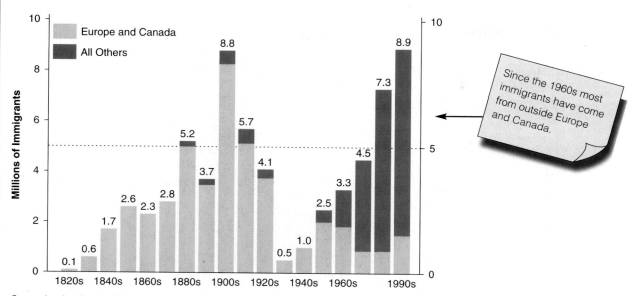

Source: Immigration and Naturalization Service 1999a, 1999b. Projection for the 1990s by the author based on Immigration and Naturalization data.

divide countries throughout the world (see Box 11-1). (Martin and Widgren 1996).

Policy Initiatives

The long border with Mexico provides ample opportunity for illegal immigration into the United States. Throughout the 1980s, there was a growing perception that the United States had lost control of its borders. Feeling public pressure for immigration control, Congress ended a decade of debate by approving the Immigration Reform and Control Act of 1986. The act marked a historic change in immigration policy. For the first time, hiring of illegal aliens was outlawed, and employers caught violating the law became subject to fines and even prison sentences. Just as significant a change was the extension of amnesty and legal status to many illegal immigrants already living in the United States. More than a decade later, however, the 1986 immigration law appears to have had mixed results. Substantial numbers of illegal immigrants continue to enter the country each year, with an estimated 8 to 10 million present at any given time (Deardorff and Blumerman 2001).

In part because the 1986 immigration law failed to end illegal immigration, there has been increasing pressure in several states for further governmental action.

Most dramatically, in November 1994, California's voters overwhelmingly approved Proposition 187, a controversial initiative that (among other provisions) calls for withholding social services and schooling opportunities from illegal immigrants. Constitutional challenges to the law resulted in blocking of all the measure's provisions.

The entire world feels the overwhelming impact of economic globalization on immigration patterns. Europe is also wrestling with policy initiatives. The European Union agreement of 1997 gives the governing commission authority to propose Europewide legislation on immigration beginning in 2002. However, the policies must be accepted unanimously, which seems unlikely. An EU policy that would allow immigrants to live and work in one EU country would allow them to work anywhere. The immigration issue is expected to complicate efforts by the sending nations (such as Turkey) to become members of the EU (Light 1999; Sassen 1999).

The intense debate over immigration reflects deep value conflicts in the culture of many nations. One strand of our culture, for example, has traditionally emphasized egalitarian principles and a desire to help people in their time of need. At the same time, however, hostility to potential immigrants and refugees—whether Chinese in the 1880s, European Jews in the 1930s and 1940s, or

Figure 11-8

Foreign-Born Population of the United States, 1999

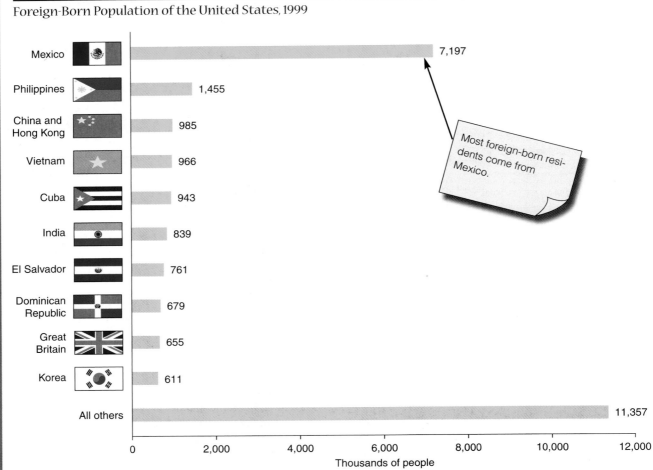

Note: Numbers in thousands.

Source: Bureau of the Census 2000a:48.

Mexicans, Haitians, and Arabs today—reflects not only racial, ethnic, and religious prejudice, but also a desire to maintain the dominant culture of the in-group by keeping out those viewed as outsiders.

Let's Discuss

1. Did you or your parents or grandparents immigrate to the United States from another nation? If so, when and where did your family come from, and why? Did they face discrimination?

2. Do you live, work, or study with recent immigrants to the United States? If so, are they well accepted in your community, or do they face prejudice and discrimination?

3. What is your opinion of the backlash against illegal immigrants in California?

Chapter Resources

Summary

The social dimensions of race and ethnicity are important factors in shaping people's lives in the United States and other countries. In this chapter, we examine the meaning of race and ethnicity and study the major racial and ethnic minorities of the United States.

1. A *racial group* is set apart from others by obvious physical differences, whereas an *ethnic group* is set apart primarily because of national origin or distinctive cultural patterns.
2. When sociologists define a *minority group,* they are primarily concerned with the economic and political power, or powerlessness, of the group.
3. In a biological sense, there are no "pure races" and no physical traits that can be used to describe one group to the exclusion of all others.
4. The meaning that people give to the physical differences between races gives social significance to race, leading to *stereotypes.*
5. *Prejudice* often leads to *discrimination,* but the two are not identical, and each can be present without the other.
6. *Institutional discrimination* results from the normal operations of a society.

7. Functionalists point out that discrimination is both functional and dysfunctional in society. Conflict theorists explain racial subordination by *exploitation theory.* Interactionists focus on the microlevel of race relations, posing *contact hypothesis* as a means of reducing prejudice and discrimination.
8. Four patterns describe typical intergroup relations in North America and elsewhere: *amalgamation, assimilation, segregation,* and *pluralism.*
9. In the United States, the most highly rewarded pattern of intergroup relations is assimilation. Pluralism remains more of an ideal than a reality.
10. Contemporary prejudice and discrimination against African Americans are rooted in the history of slavery in the United States.
11. Asian Americans are commonly viewed as a *model* or *ideal minority,* a stereotype not necessarily beneficial to members of this group.
12. The various groups included under the general term *Latinos* represent the largest ethnic minority in the United States.
13. The increase of immigration worldwide has raised questions in individual nations about how to control the process.

Critical Thinking Questions

1. How is institutional discrimination even more powerful than individual discrimination? How would functionalists, conflict theorists, and interactionists examine institutional discrimination?
2. The text states that "in the United States, pluralism is more of an ideal than a reality." Can the community in which you grew up and the college you attend be viewed as genuine examples of pluralism? Examine the relations between dominant and subordinate racial and ethnic groups in your hometown and your college.
3. What are some of the similarities and differences in the position of African Americans and Hispanics as minorities in the United States? What are some of the similarities and differences in the position of Asian Americans and Jewish Americans?

Key Terms

Affirmative action   Positive efforts to recruit minority group members or women for jobs, promotions, and educational opportunities. (page 279)

Amalgamation   The process by which a majority group and a minority group combine through intermarriage to form a new group. (281)

Anti-Semitism   Anti-Jewish prejudice. (292)

Apartheid   The policy of the South African government designed to maintain the separation of Blacks and other non-Whites from the dominant Whites. (282)

Assimilation   The process by which a person forsakes his or her own cultural tradition to become part of a different culture. (282)

Black power A political philosophy promoted by many younger Blacks in the 1960s that supported the creation of Black-controlled political and economic institutions. (285)

Contact hypothesis An interactionist perspective which states that interracial contact between people of equal status in cooperative circumstances will reduce prejudice. (280)

Discrimination The process of denying opportunities and equal rights to individuals and groups because of prejudice or other arbitrary reasons. (275)

Ethnic group A group that is set apart from others because of its national origin or distinctive cultural patterns. (269)

Ethnocentrism The tendency to assume that one's own culture and way of life represent the norm or are superior to all others. (273)

Exploitation theory A Marxist theory that views racial subordination in the United States as a manifestation of the class system inherent in capitalism. (280)

Genocide The deliberate, systematic killing of an entire people or nation. (281)

Glass ceiling An invisible barrier that blocks the promotion of a qualified individual in a work environment because of the individual's gender, race, or ethnicity. (277)

Institutional discrimination The denial of opportunities and equal rights to individuals and groups that results from the normal operations of a society. (277)

Issei Japanese immigrants to the United States. (288)

Minority group A subordinate group whose members have significantly less control or power over their own lives than the members of a dominant or majority group have over theirs. (269)

Model or ideal minority A group that, despite past prejudice and discrimination, succeeds economically, socially, and educationally without resorting to political or violent confrontations with Whites. (287)

Nisei Japanese born in the United States who were descendants of the Issei. (288)

Pluralism Mutual respect between the various groups in a society for one another's cultures, which allows minorities to express their own cultures without experiencing prejudice. (283)

Prejudice A negative attitude toward an entire category of people, such as a racial or ethnic minority. (273)

Racial group A group that is set apart from others because of obvious physical differences. (269)

Racism The belief that one race is supreme and all others are innately inferior. (273)

Segregation The act of physically separating two groups; often imposed on a minority group by a dominant group. (282)

Stereotypes Unreliable generalizations about all members of a group that do not recognize individual differences within the group. (272)

Additional Readings

BOOKS

Barnes, Annie S. 2000. *Everyday Racism: A Book for All Americans.* Naperville: Sourcebooks. Drawing on her students' experiences, a professor of sociology and anthropology recounts some middle-class African Americans' encounters with racism.

Malcomson, Scott L. 2000. *One Drop of Blood: The American Midsadventure of Race.* New York: Farrar, Straus, and Giroux. A historical account of how race was and is defined in the United States.

Nelson, Alondra, and Thuy Linh N. Tu, with Alicia Headlam Hines (ed.). 2001. *Technicolor: Race, Technology and Everyday Life.* New York: New York University Press. An analytical look at the intersection of technology and race, including stereotyped conceptions about the relationship between ethnicity and computer literacy.

Smith, Tony. 2000. *Foreign Attachments: The Power of Ethnic Groups in the Making of American Foreign Policy.* Cambridge: Harvard University Press. A political scientist considers how ethnic lobbies influence the development of foreign policy.

JOURNALS

Among the journals that focus on issues of race and ethnicity are *Amerasian Journal* (founded in 1971), *The Black Scholar* (1969), *Contemporary Jewry* (1978), *Ethnic and Racial Studies* (1978), *Ethnicities* (2001), *Hispanic Journal of Behavioral Studies* (1979), *Journal of Refugee Studies* (1988), *Multicultural Review* (1992), and *Race and Society* (1997).

● Technology Resources

Internet Connection

*Note: While all the URLs listed were current as of the printing of this book, these sites often change. Please check our website (**http://www.mhhe.com/schaefer8**) for updates and hyperlinks to this exercise and additional exercises.*

1. The Southern Poverty Law Center (**http://www.splcenter.org**) is a nonprofit organization that combats hate, intolerance, and discrimination through education and litigation. Go to the center's website, link to the "Intelligence Project," then "List of Hate Groups," and answer the following questions:
   (a) Scroll down the page and examine the map showing the locations of hate groups in the United States. Are any hate groups located in your home state? If so, which ones are they? If none are listed in your home state, do neighboring states have hate groups? Which ones?
   (b) Link to "Hate Symbols." The drop of blood is one of the Ku Klux Klan's best-known symbols. What does it represent to Klan members?
   (c) What does ZOG stand for? What do these groups believe about the U.S. government?
   (d) What are the 14 words, and what did the Order do?
   (e) Link to "Hate Incidents." How many hate incidents occurred last year in your home state or in the state where you attend school? Briefly describe at least three of those incidents.
   (f) Select three groups from the list of hate groups (for example, Ku Klux Klan, Neo-Confederate, and so on). Type each name into the search

bar for Yahoo or some other search engine and go to the homepage for each group. Briefly summarize your reaction to each group's philosophy.

2. In the mid-nineteenth century, the lure of gold drew people from all over the world to California, turning the sparsely settled territory into a culturally and racially diverse society. At its website, the Oakland Museum of California details how prejudice and discrimination against various racial and ethnic groups intensified during the Gold Rush. To learn more, go to the museum's website (**http://www.museumca.org/goldrush/fever16-di.html**) and read the article titled "Law, Order, and Justice for Some—Discrimination." Then answer the following questions:
   (a) How were Chinese miners treated?
   (b) Who were the Hounds, and what was their main objective?
   (c) Which group of people faced the most prejudice and discrimination? How did most White Americans feel toward that group?
   (d) Ultimately, what efforts were directed toward that group?
   (e) Can you think of any contemporary examples of discrimination that involve either yourself or someone you know?
   (f) Briefly summarize what you consider to be your attitude toward persons of another color, race, or ethnicity. Based on what you have learned in this chapter, are you prejudiced or discriminatory? Explain.

Online Learning Center   www.mhhe.com/schaefer8

The Civil Rights movement has been a defining sociological event in modern U.S. history. To learn more about this movement, go to the Online Learning Center at www.mhhe.com/schaefer8 and visit the student center.

Link to "Internet Exercises," and scroll down to the third exercise. Through the Papers Project, Stanford University has helped preserve the Civil Rights movement. The project is a virtual presentation of the words and life of Dr. Martin Luther King, Jr.

STRATIFICATION BY GENDER

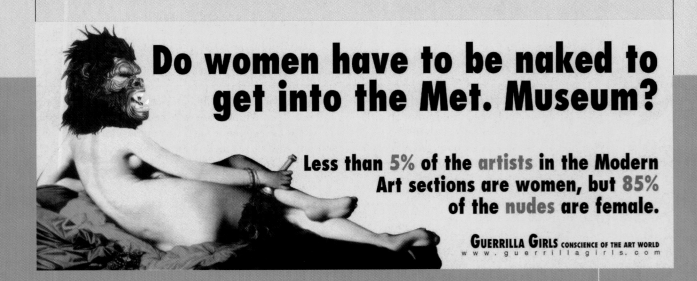

Do women have to be naked to get into the Met. Museum?

Less than **5%** of the **artists** in the Modern Art sections are women, but **85%** of the **nudes** are female.

GUERRILLA GIRLS CONSCIENCE OF THE ART WORLD
w w w . g u e r r i l l a g i r l s . c o m

In 1989 a militant group called the Guerrilla Girls called attention to sexism in the art world with this poster, which protests the underrepresentation of female artists at the world-famous Metropolitan Museum of Art in New York City. This poster and others dealing with sexism in the arts can be viewed at www.guerrillagirls.com.

A t last, after a long silence, women took to the streets. In the two decades of radical action that followed the rebirth of feminism in the early 1970s, Western women gained legal and reproductive rights, pursued higher education, entered the trades and the professions, and overturned ancient and revered beliefs about their social role. A generation on, do women feel free?

The affluent, educated, liberated women of the First World, who can enjoy freedoms unavailable to any women ever before, do not feel as free as they want to. And they can no longer restrict to the subconscious their sense that this lack of freedom has something to do with—with apparently frivolous issues, things that really should not matter. Many are ashamed to admit that such trivial concerns—to do with physical appearance, bodies, faces, hair, clothes—matter so much. But in spite of shame, guilt, and denial, more and more women are wondering if . . . something important is indeed at stake that has to do with the relationship between female liberation and female beauty.

During the past decade, women breached the power structure; meanwhile, eating disorders rose exponentially and cosmetic surgery became the fastest-growing medical specialty. During the past five years, consumer spending doubled, pornography became the main media category, ahead of legitimate films and records combined, and thirty-three thousand American women told researchers that they would rather lose ten to fifteen pounds than achieve any other goal. More women have more money and power and scope and legal recognition than we have ever had before; but in terms of how we feel about ourselves *physically,* we may actually be worse off than our unliberated grandmothers. Recent research consistently shows that inside the majority of the West's controlled, attractive, successful working women, there is a secret "underlife" poisoning our freedom; infused with notions of beauty, it is a dark vein of self-hatred, physical obsessions, terror of aging, and dread of lost control.

It is no accident that so many potentially powerful women feel this way. We are in the midst of a violent backlash against feminism that uses images of female beauty as a political weapon against women's advancement: the beauty myth. . . .

The beauty myth tells a story: The quality called "beauty" objectively and universally exists. Women must want to embody it and men must want to possess women who embody it. This embodiment is an imperative for women and not for men, which situation is necessary and natural because it is biological, sexual, and evolutionary: Strong men battle for beautiful women, and beautiful women are more reproductively successful. Women's beauty must correlate to their fertility, and since this system is based on sexual selection, it is inevitable and changeless.

None of this is true. "Beauty" is a currency system like the gold standard. Like any economy, it is determined by politics, and in the modern age in the West it is the last, best belief system that keeps male dominance intact. *(Wolf 1992:9–10, 12)* ■ ◉

I n this excerpt from Naomi Wolf's book *The Beauty Myth*, a feminist confronts the power of a false ideal of womanhood. In recent decades, American women have broken legal and institutional barriers that once limited their educational opportunities and career advancement. But, Wolf writes, psychologically they are still enslaved by unrealistic standards of appearance. The more freedom women have gained, in fact, the more obsessed they seem to have become with the ideal of the ultra-thin supermodel—an ideal that few women can ever hope to attain without jeopardizing their health or resorting to expensive cosmetic surgery.

Wolf asserts that the Beauty Myth is a societal control mechanism that is meant to keep women in their place—as subordinates to men at home and on the job. But men too are captive to unrealistic expectations regarding their physical appearance. In hopes of attaining a brawny, muscular physique, more and more men are now taking steroids or electing to undergo cosmetic surgery. Today's media bombard men and women with the need to look good in ads hawking everything from nutrition supplements to hair color

formulas to expensive exercise equipment and health club memberships (Thomas and Owens 2000).

The Beauty Myth is but one example of how cultural norms may lead to differentiation based on one's gender. Such differentiation is evident in virtually every human society about which we have information. We saw in Chapters 9 to 11 that most societies establish hierarchies based on social class, race, and ethnicity. This chapter will examine the ways in which societies stratify their members on the basis of gender.

Do gender roles differ from one culture to another? Are women in the United States still oppressed because of their gender, as Naomi Wolf asserts? How does a woman's race affect her social standing? We will begin to answer these and other questions by looking first at how various cultures, including our own, assign women and men to particular social roles. Then we will consider sociological explanations for gender stratification. Next, we will focus on the unique situation of women as an oppressed majority, and on the double jeopardy women of color face. The chapter closes with a social policy section on the intense and continuing controversy over a woman's right to an abortion. ■

Social Construction of Gender

How many air passengers do you think feel a start when the captain's voice from the cockpit belongs to a female? Or what do we make of a father who announces that he will be late for work because his son has a routine medical checkup? Consciously or unconsciously, we are likely to assume that flying a commercial plane is a *man's* job and that most parental duties are, in fact, *maternal* duties. Gender is such a routine part of our everyday activities that we typically take it for granted and only take notice when someone deviates from conventional behavior and expectations.

Although a few people begin life with an unclear sexual identity, the overwhelming majority begin with a definite sex and quickly receive societal messages about how to behave. Many societies have established social distinctions between females and males that do not inevitably result from biological differences between the sexes (such as women's reproductive capabilities).

In studying gender, sociologists are interested in the gender-role socialization that leads females and males to

behave differently. In Chapter 4, **gender roles** were defined as expectations regarding the proper behavior, attitudes, and activities of males and females. The application of traditional gender roles leads to many forms of differentiation between women and men. Both sexes are physically capable of learning to cook and sew, yet most Western societies determine that women should perform these tasks. Both men and women are capable of learning to weld and fly airplanes, but these functions are generally assigned to men.

Gender roles are evident not only in our work and behavior but in how we react to others. We are constantly "doing gender" without realizing it. If the father discussed above sits in the doctor's office with his son in the middle of a workday, he will probably receive approving glances from the receptionist and from other patients. "Isn't he a wonderful father?" runs through their minds. But if the boy's mother leaves *her* job and sits with the son in the doctor's office, she will not receive such silent applause.

We socially construct our behavior so that male–female differences are either created or exaggerated. For example, men and women come in a variety of heights, sizes, and ages. Yet traditional norms regarding marriage and even casual dating tell us that in heterosexual couples, the man should be older, taller, and wiser than the

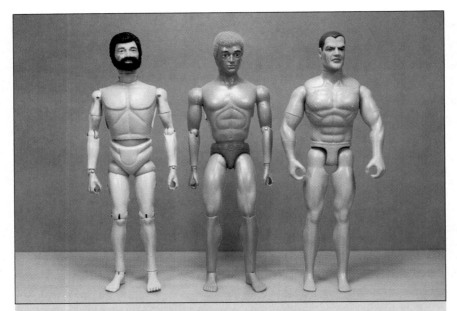

Society often exaggerates male–female differences in appearance and behavior. In 1964, the G.I. Joe doll (left) had a realistic appearance, but by 1992 (middle) it had begun to acquire the exaggerated muscularity characteristic of professional wrestlers (right). The change intensified the contrast with ultra-thin female figures, like the Barbie doll (Angier 1998).

and prejudice against homosexuality. Homophobia contributes significantly to rigid gender-role socialization, since many people stereotypically associate male homosexuality with femininity and lesbianism with masculinity. Consequently, men and women who deviate from traditional expectations about gender roles are often presumed to be gay. Despite the advances made by the gay liberation movement, the continuing stigma attached to homosexuality in our culture places pressure on all males (whether gay or not) to exhibit only narrow "masculine" behavior and on all females (whether lesbian or not) to exhibit only narrow "feminine" behavior (Seidman 1994; see also Lehne 1995).

It is *adults,* of course, who play a critical role in guiding children into those gender roles deemed appropriate in a society. Parents are normally the first and most crucial agents of

woman. As we will see throughout this chapter, such social norms help to reinforce and legitimize patterns of male dominance.

In recent decades, women have increasingly entered occupations and professions previously dominated by men. Yet our society still focuses on "masculine" and "feminine" qualities as if men and women must be evaluated in these terms. Clearly, we continue to "do gender," and this social construction of gender continues to define significantly different expectations for females and males in the United States (Lorber 1994; Rosenbaum 1996; West and Zimmerman 1987).

Gender Roles in the United States

Gender-Role Socialization

Male babies get blue blankets, while females get pink ones. Boys are expected to play with trucks, blocks, and toy soldiers; girls are given dolls and kitchen goods. Boys must be masculine—active, aggressive, tough, daring, and dominant—whereas girls must be feminine—soft, emotional, sweet, and submissive. These traditional gender-role patterns have been influential in the socialization of children in the United States.

An important element in traditional views of proper "masculine" and "feminine" behavior is fear of homosexuality. In Chapter 5, we defined **homophobia** as fear of

When Fannie Barnes first took the controls of a San Francisco cable car, she probably raised a few eyebrows. No female before had ever been a "gripman" in the cable car system.

Table 12-1 An Experiment of Gender Norm Violations by College Students

Norm Violations by Women	Norm Violations by Men
Send men flowers	Wear fingernail polish
Spit in public	Needlepoint in public
Use men's bathroom	Throw Tupperware party
Buy jock strap	Cry in public
Buy/chew tobacco	Have pedicure
Talk knowledgeably about cars	Apply to baby-sit
Open doors for men	Shave body hair

Source: Nielsen et al. 2000:287.

Based on class projects, sociology students were asked to behave in ways that might be regarded as violating gender norms. This is a sample of their actual choices over a seven-year period. Do you agree that these actions test the boundaries of conventional gender behavior?

p. 96 socialization. But other adults, older siblings, the mass media, and religious and educational institutions also exert an important influence on gender-role socialization in the United States and elsewhere.

It is not hard to test how rigid gender-role socialization can be. Just try transgressing some gender norms—say, by smoking a cigar in public if you are female or carrying a purse if you are male. That was exactly the assignment given sociology students at the University of Colorado and Luther College in Iowa. The teachers asked the students to behave in ways that they thought violated norms of how a man or woman should act. The students had no trouble coming up with gender norm "transgressions" (see Table 12-1), and they kept careful notes on how others reacted to their behavior, ranging from amusement to disgust (Nielsen et al. 2000).

Women's Gender Roles

How does a girl come to develop a feminine self-image whereas a boy develops one that is masculine? In part, they do so by identifying with females and males in their families and neighborhoods and in the media. If a young girl regularly sees female characters on television working as defense attorneys and judges, she may believe that she herself can become a lawyer. And it will not hurt if women that she knows—her mother, sister, parents' friends, or neighbors—are lawyers. By contrast, if this young girl sees women portrayed in the media only as models, nurses, and

secretaries, her identification and self-image will be quite different. Even if she does become a professional, she may secretly regret falling short of the media stereotype—a shapely, sexy young woman in a bathing suit.

Television is far from being alone in stereotyping women. Studies of children's books published in the United States in the 1940s, 1950s, and 1960s found that females were significantly underrepresented in central roles and illustrations. Virtually all female characters were portrayed as helpless, passive, incompetent, and in need of a strong male caretaker. By the 1980s, there was somewhat less stereotyping in children's books, with some female characters shown to be active. Nevertheless, boys were still shown engaged in active play three times as often as girls (Kortenhaus and Demarest 1993).

Social research on gender roles reveals some persistent differences between men and women in North America and Europe. Women experience a mandate to both marry and be a mother. Often, marriage is viewed as the true entry into adulthood. And women are expected not only to become mothers but to *want* to be mothers. Obviously, men play a role in these events, but they do not appear to be as critical in identifying the life course for a man. Society defines men's roles by economic success. While women may achieve recognition in the labor force, it is not as important to their identity as it is for men (Doyle and Paludi 1998; Russo 1976).

Traditional gender roles have most severely restricted females. Throughout this chapter, we will see how women have been confined to subordinate roles within the political and economic institutions of the United States. Yet it is also true that gender roles have restricted males.

Men's Gender Roles

> During the game I always played the outfield. Right field. Far right field. And there I would stand in the hot sun wishing I was anyplace else in the world. (Fager et al. 1971)

This is the childhood recollection of a man who, as a boy, disliked sports, dreaded gym classes, and had particular problems with baseball. Obviously, he did not conform to the socially constructed male gender role and no doubt paid the price for it.

Men's roles are socially constructed in much the same way as women's roles are. Family, peers, and the media all influence how a boy or a man comes to view his appropriate role in society. Robert Brannon (1976) and James Doyle (1995) have identified five aspects of the male gender role:

- Antifeminine element—show no "sissy stuff," including any expression of openness or vulnerability.
- Success element—prove one's masculinity at work and sports.
- Aggressive element—use force in dealing with others.
- Sexual element—initiate and control all sexual relations.
- Self-reliant element—keep cool and unflappable.

No systematic research has established all these elements as necessarily common to all males, but specific studies have confirmed individual elements.

Males who do not conform to the socially constructed gender role face constant criticism and even humiliation both from children when they are boys and from adults as men. It can be agonizing to be treated as a "chicken" or a "sissy"—particularly if such remarks come from one's father or brothers. At the same time, boys who successfully adapt to cultural standards of masculinity may grow up to be inexpressive men who cannot share their feelings with others. They remain forceful and tough, but as a result they are also closed and isolated (Faludi 1999; McCreary 1994; Sheehy 1999).

In the last 40 years, inspired in good part by the contemporary feminist movement (examined later in the chapter), increasing numbers of men in the United States have criticized the restrictive aspects of the traditional male gender role. Some men have taken strong public positions in support of women's struggle for full equality and have even organized voluntary associations such as the National Organization for Men Against Sexism (NOMAS), founded in 1975 to support positive changes for men. Nevertheless, the traditional male gender role remains well entrenched as an influential element of our culture (Messner 1997; National Organization for Men Against Sexism 2001).

◯Imagine

You are living in a society in which there are no gender roles. What is your life like?

Cross-Cultural Perspective

To what extent do actual biological differences between the sexes contribute to the cultural differences associated with gender? This question brings us back to the debate

pp. 85–88 ◀ over "nature versus nurture." In assessing the alleged and real differences between men and women, it is useful to examine cross-cultural data.

The research of anthropologist Margaret Mead points to the importance of cultural conditioning—as opposed to biology—in defining the social roles of males and females. In *Sex and Temperament*, Mead ([1935] 2001; 1973) describes typical behaviors of each sex in three different cultures in New Guinea:

> In one [the Arapesh], both men and women act as we expect women to act—in a mild parental responsive way; in the second [the Mundugumor], both act as we expect men to act—in a fierce initiating fashion; and in the third [the Tchambuli], the men act according to our stereotypes for women—are catty, wear curls, and go shopping—while the women are energetic, managerial, unadorned partners. (Preface to 1950 ed.)

Cultural conditioning is important in the development of gender role differences. This sister and brother from Sudest Island in Papua New Guinea expect women to be the honorary heads of the family.

If biology determined all differences between the sexes, then cross-cultural differences, such as those described by Mead, would not exist. Her findings confirm the influential role of culture and socialization in gender-role differentiation. There appears to be no innate or biological reason to designate completely different gender roles for men and women.

In any society, gender stratification requires not only individual socialization into traditional gender roles within the family, but also the promotion and support of these traditional roles by other social institutions such as religion and education. Moreover, even with all major institutions socializing the young into conventional gender roles, every society has women and men who resist and successfully oppose these stereotypes: strong women who become leaders or professionals, gentle men who care for children, and so forth. It seems clear that differences between the sexes are not dictated by biology. Indeed, the maintenance of traditional gender roles requires constant social controls—and these controls are not always effective.

Explaining Stratification by Gender

Cross-cultural studies indicate that societies dominated by men are much more common than those in which women play the decisive role. Sociologists have turned to all the major theoretical perspectives to understand how and why these social distinctions are established. Each approach focuses on culture, rather than biology, as the primary determinant of gender differences. Yet, in other respects, there are wide disagreements between advocates of these sociological perspectives.

The Functionalist View

Functionalists maintain that gender differentiation has contributed to overall social stability. Sociologists Talcott Parsons and Robert Bales (1955) argued that to function most effectively, the family requires adults who will specialize in particular roles. They viewed the traditional arrangement of gender roles as arising out of this need to establish a division of labor between marital partners.

Parsons and Bales contended that women take the expressive, emotionally supportive role and men the instrumental, practical role, with the two complementing each other. *Instrumentality* refers to emphasis on tasks, focus on more distant goals, and a concern for the external relationship between one's family and other social institutions. *Expressiveness* denotes concern for maintenance of harmony and the internal emotional affairs of the family. According to this theory, women's interest in expressive goals frees men for instrumental tasks, and vice

versa. Women become "anchored" in the family as wives, mothers, and household managers; men are anchored in the occupational world outside the home. Of course, Parsons and Bales offered this framework in the 1950s, when many more women were full-time homemakers than is true today. These theorists did not explicitly endorse traditional gender roles, but they implied that dividing tasks between spouses was functional for the family unit.

Given the typical socialization of women and men in the United States, the functionalist view is initially persuasive. However, it would lead us to expect girls and women with no interest in children to become babysitters and mothers. Similarly, males who love spending time with children might be "programmed" into careers in the business world. Such differentiation might harm the individual who does not fit into prescribed roles, while also depriving society of the contributions of many talented people who are confined by gender stereotyping. Moreover, the functionalist approach does not convincingly explain why men should be categorically assigned to the instrumental role and women to the expressive role.

The Conflict Response

Viewed from a conflict perspective, this functionalist approach masks underlying power relations between men and women. Parsons and Bales never explicitly presented the expressive and instrumental tasks as unequally valued by society, yet this inequality is quite evident. Although social institutions may pay lip service to women's expressive skills, it is men's instrumental skills that are most highly rewarded—whether in terms of money or prestige. Consequently, according to feminists and conflict theorists, any division of labor by gender into instrumental and expressive tasks is far from neutral in its impact on women.

Conflict theorists contend that the relationship between females and males has traditionally been one of unequal power, with men in a dominant position over women. Men may originally have become powerful in preindustrial times because their size, physical strength, and freedom from childbearing duties allowed them to dominate women physically. In contemporary societies, such considerations are not so important, yet cultural beliefs about the sexes are long established, as anthropologist Margaret Mead and feminist sociologist Helen Mayer Hacker (1951, 1974) both stressed. Such beliefs support a social structure that places males in controlling positions.

Thus, conflict theorists see gender differences as a reflection of the subjugation of one group (women) by another group (men). If we use an analogy to Marx's analysis of class conflict, we can say that males **pp. 12, 217** are like the bourgeoisie, or capitalists; they control most of the society's wealth, prestige, and power.

Conflict theorists emphasize that men's work is uniformly valued, while women's work (whether unpaid labor in the home or wage labor) is devalued. These women are making tents in a factory in Binghamton, New York.

be labeled "capitalist," "socialist," or "communist" (Feuer 1959; Tuchman 1992).

Feminist sociologists would find little to disagree with in the conflict theorists' perspective but are more likely to embrace a political action agenda. Also, the feminist perspective would argue that the very discussion of women and society, however well meaning, has been distorted by the exclusion of women from academic thought, including sociology. In Chapter 1 we noted the many accomplishments of Jane Addams and Ida Wells-Barnett, but they generally worked outside the discipline. Their work focused on what we would now call applied sociology and social work. At the time, their efforts, while valued as humanitarian, were seen as unrelated to the research and conclusions being reached in academic circles, which, of course, were male academic circles (Andersen 1997; Howard 1999).

Females are like the proletarians, or workers; they can acquire valuable resources only by following the dictates of their "bosses." Men's work is uniformly valued, whereas women's work (whether unpaid labor in the home or wage labor) is devalued.

The Feminist Perspective

A significant component of the conflict approach to gender stratification draws on feminist theory.

pp. 17–18 ◀

Although use of that term is comparatively recent, the critique of women's position in society and culture goes back to some of the earliest works that have influenced sociology. Among the most important are Mary Wollstonecraft's *A Vindication of the Rights of Women* (originally published in 1792), John Stuart Mill's *The Subjection of Women* (originally published in 1869), and Friedrich Engels's *The Origin of Private Property, the Family, and the State* (originally published in 1884).

Engels, a close associate of Karl Marx, argued that women's subjugation coincided with the rise of private property during industrialization. Only when people moved beyond an agrarian economy could males "enjoy" the luxury of leisure and withhold rewards and privileges from women. Drawing on the work of Marx and Engels, contemporary feminist theorists often view women's subordination as part of the overall exploitation and injustice that they see as inherent in capitalist societies. Some radical feminist theorists, however, view the oppression of women as inevitable in *all* male-dominated societies, whether they

Feminist theorists today (including conflict theorists) emphasize that male dominance in the United States goes far beyond the economic sphere. Throughout this textbook, we examine disturbing aspects of men's behavior toward women. The ugly realities of rape, wife battering (see Chapter 14), sexual harassment, and street harassment all illustrate and intensify women's subordinate position. Even if women reach economic parity with men, even if women win equal representation in government, genuine equality between the sexes cannot be achieved if these attacks remain as common as they are today.

Functionalist, conflict, and feminist theorists acknowledge that it is not possible to change gender roles drastically without dramatic revisions in a culture's social structure. Functionalists perceive potential for social disorder, or at least unknown social consequences, if all aspects of traditional gender stratification are disturbed. Yet, for conflict and feminist theorists, no social structure is ultimately desirable if it is maintained by oppressing a majority of its citizens. These theorists argue that gender stratification may be functional for men—who hold power and privilege—but it is hardly in the interests of women.

The Interactionist Approach

While functionalists and conflict theorists studying gender stratification typically focus on macro-level social forces and institutions, interactionist researchers often

Studies show that as many as 96 percent of all interruptions in cross-sex (male–female) conversations are initiated by men.

examine gender stratification on the microlevel of everyday behavior. As an example, studies show that men initiate up to 96 percent of all interruptions in cross-sex (male–female) conversations. Men are more likely than women to change topics of conversation, to ignore topics chosen by members of the opposite sex, to minimize the contributions and ideas of members of the opposite sex, and to validate their own contributions. These patterns reflect the conversational (and, in a sense, political) dominance of males. Moreover, even when women occupy a prestigious position, such as that of physician, they are more likely to be interrupted than their male counterparts are (Ridgeway and Smith-Lovin 1999; Tannen 1990; West and Zimmerman 1983).

In certain studies, all participants are advised in advance of the overall finding that males are more likely than females to interrupt during a cross-sex conversation. After learning this information, men reduce the frequency of their interruptions, yet they continue to verbally dominate conversations with women. At the same time, women reduce their already low frequency of interruption and other conversationally dominant behaviors.

These findings regarding cross-sex conversations have been frequently replicated. They have striking implications when one considers the power dynamics underlying likely cross-sex interactions—employer and job seeker, college professor and student, husband and wife, to name only a few. From an interactionist perspective, these simple, day-to-day exchanges are one more battleground in the struggle for sexual equality—as women try to "get a word in edgewise" in the midst of men's interruptions and verbal dominance (Okamoto and Smith-Lovin 2001; Tannen 1994a, 1994b).

Women: The Oppressed Majority

Many people, both male and female, find it difficult to conceive of women as a subordinate and oppressed group. Yet take a look at the political structure of the United States: Women remain noticeably underrepresented. For example, in 2001, only 5 of the nation's 50 states had a female governor (Arizona, Delaware, Massachusetts, Montana, and New Hampshire). Women have made slow but steady progress in certain political arenas. In 1981, out of 535 members of Congress, there were only

In January 2001, the Congressional Caucus for Women's Issues sat for an official portrait. Representatives Sue Kelly (New York), Judy Biggert (Illinois), Juanita Millender-McDonald (California), and Carolyn Maloney (New York), caucus leaders, occupied the front row (left to right).

21 women: 19 in the House of Representatives and 2 in the Senate. By contrast, the Congress that took office in January 2001 had 86 women: 73 in the House and 13 in the Senate. Yet the leadership of Congress still remains overwhelmingly male (Center for the American Woman and Politics 2001).

In October 1981, Sandra Day O'Connor was sworn in as the nation's first female Supreme Court justice. Still, no woman has ever served as president of the United States, vice president, speaker of the House of Representatives, or chief justice of the Supreme Court. (We will examine women's involvement in politics and government in more detail in Chapter 17.)

Sexism and Sex Discrimination

Just as African Americans are victimized by racism, women suffer from the sexism of our society. *Sexism* is the ideology that one sex is superior to the other. The term is generally used to refer to male prejudice and discrimination against women. In Chapter 11, we noted that Blacks can suffer from both individual acts of racism and institutional discrimination. *Institutional discrimination* was defined as the denial of opportunities and equal rights to individuals or groups that results from the normal operations of a society. In the same sense, women suffer both from individual acts of sexism (such as sexist remarks and acts of violence) and from institutional sexism.

It is not simply that particular men in the United States are biased in their treatment of women. All the major institutions of our society—including the government, armed forces, large corporations, the media, the universities, and the medical establishment—are controlled by men. These institutions, in their "normal," day-to-day operations, often discriminate against women and perpetuate sexism. For example, if the central office of a nationwide bank sets a policy that single women are a bad risk for loans—regardless of their incomes and investments—the institution will discriminate against women in state after state. It will do so even at bank branches in which loan officers hold no personal biases concerning women, but are merely "following orders." We will examine institutional discrimination against women within the educational system in Chapter 16.

Our society is run by male-dominated institutions, yet with the power that flows to men come responsibility and stress. Men have higher reported rates of certain types of mental illness than women do and greater likelihood of death due to heart attack or strokes (see Chapter 19). The pressure on men to succeed, and then to remain on top in a competitive world of work, can be especially intense. This is not to suggest that gender stratification is as damaging to men as it is to women. But it is clear that the power and privilege men enjoy are no guarantee of well-being.

Sexual Harassment

The courts recognize two kinds of sexual harassment. *Sexual harassment* is behavior that occurs when work benefits are made contingent on sexual favors (as a "quid pro quo"), or when touching, lewd comments, or the appearance of pornographic material creates a "hostile environment" in the workplace. In 1998, the Supreme Court ruled that harassment also applied to people of the same sex in the workplace. The "quid pro quo" type of harassment is fairly easy to identify in a court of law. But the issue of hostile environment has become the subject of considerable debate in courts and in the general public (L. Greenhouse 1998a; Lewin 1998a).

Sexual harassment must be understood in the context of continuing prejudice and discrimination against women. Whether it occurs in the federal bureaucracy, in the corporate world, or in universities, sexual harassment generally takes place in organizations in which the hierarchy of authority finds White males at the top and women's work is valued less than men's. One survey in the private sector found that African American women were three times more likely than White women to experience sexual harassment. From a conflict perspective, it is not surprising that women—and especially women of color—are

Sexual harassment can be as subtle as an unwanted hand on the shoulder. Repeated actions of this kind can lead to a "hostile environment."

most likely to become victims of sexual harassment. These groups are typically an organization's most vulnerable employees in terms of job security (J. Jones 1988).

Imagine

How would Naomi Wolf (author of *The Beauty Myth*) interpret the problem of sexual harassment?

The Status of Women Worldwide

The Hindu society of India makes life especially harsh for widows. When Hindu women marry, they join their husband's family. If the husband dies, the widow is the "property" of that family. In many cases, she ends up working as an unpaid servant; in others she is simply abandoned and left penniless. Ancient Hindu scriptures portray widows as "inauspicious" and advise that "a wise man should avoid her blessings like the poison of a snake" (Burns 1998:10). Such attitudes die slowly in the villages, where most Indians live.

Though Westerners tend to view Muslim societies as being similarly harsh toward women, that perception is actually an overgeneralization. Muslim countries are exceedingly varied and complex and do not often fit the stereotypes created by the Western media. For a detailed discussion of the status of Muslim women today, see Box 12-1.

It is estimated that women grow half the world's food, but they rarely own land. They constitute one-third of the world's paid labor force but are generally found in the lowest-paying jobs. Single-parent households headed by women, which appear to be on the increase in many nations, are typically found in the poorest sections of the population. The feminization of poverty has become a global phenomenon. As in the United States, women worldwide are underrepresented politically.

A detailed overview of the status of the world's women, issued by the United Nations in 2000, noted that women and men live in different worlds—worlds that differ in access to education and work opportunities, and in health,

personal security, and human rights. While acknowledging that much has been done to sharpen people's awareness of gender inequities, the report identified a number of areas of continuing concern:

- Despite advances in higher education for women, women still face major barriers when they attempt to use their educational achievements to advance in the workplace. For example, women rarely hold more than 1 to 2 percent of top executive positions.
- Women almost always work in occupations with lower status and pay than men. In both developing and developed countries, many women work as unpaid family laborers. (Figure 12-1 shows the paid labor force participation of women in seven industrialized countries.)
- Despite social norms regarding support and protection, many widows around the world find that they have little concrete support from extended family networks.

Figure 12-1

Percentage of Adult Women in the Paid Labor Force by Country

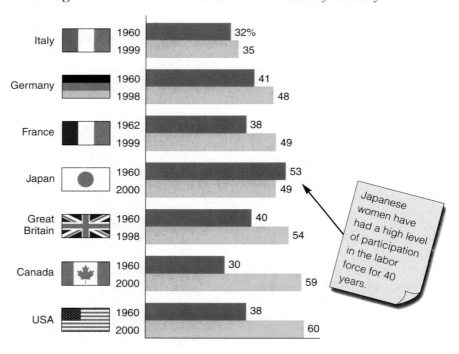

Source: Bureau of Labor Statistics 2001a.

Think About It
In industrialized nations, what appears to be the trend in women's labor force participation?

12-1 The Head Scarf and the Veil: Complex Symbols

The wearing of a veil or head scarf, which is common to many but not all Middle Eastern societies, originated in a verse from the Koran: "Prophet, enjoin your wives, your daughters and the wives of true believers to draw their veils close round them . . . so that they may be recognized and not molested." The injunction to cover one's body in the presence of men to whom one is not closely related is based on a view of women as bearers of the family's honor. To protect their chastity from men's predatory sexual advances, women must keep themselves out of harm's way. Wearing a veil in public is intended to do just that, to signal others that they are not to touch the wearer. A man who ignores that signal does so at his peril, for his action shames not just the woman, but her whole family.

> In effect, the veil represents a rejection of the Beauty Myth, which is so prevalent in Western societies.

The veil is also a way of maintaining a family's social status. Unlike rich families, poor families depend on their wives' and daughters' presence in the fields and markets, where a veil and robe can hamper a woman's ability to work. Thus in some regions of North Africa, Muslim women have never worn the veil. Nor do women veil themselves in small communities, where everyone knows everyone else. Only in cities in a few countries are women required to wear a veil.

In effect, the veil represents a rejection of the Beauty Myth, which is so prevalent in Western societies. While a Muslim woman's beauty is valued, it is not to be seen or exploited by the whole world. By covering themselves almost completely, Muslim women assure themselves and their families that their physical persons will not play a role in their contacts outside the family. Rather, these women will be known only for their faith, their intellect, and their personalities.

In the twentieth century, the veil was politicized by modernization movements that pitted Western cultural values against traditional Islamic values. In Turkey, for instance, the rise to power of President Kemal Atatürk in 1923 sparked a process of sweeping social change, in which government officials attempted to subordinate traditional ethnic and religious influences to their nationalistic goals. They substituted Latin for Arabic in written documents, and purged the spoken language of Persian and Arabic words. Though women weren't forbidden to wear the veil, they were not allowed to veil themselves in public places like schools. Not surprisingly, many Muslims resented these forced social changes. In recent decades, revolutionary movements in countries like Iran and Afghanistan have reinstituted the veil and other Islamic traditions.

In Turkey, however, a modified version of the veil has recently become the symbol of militant feminists. Among educated young women who study at the universities, the new veil signifies an intention to transcend the traditional roles of wife and mother. Women who are professionals, writers, intellectuals, and activists wear it as a public statement of their aspirations.

Two women from South Yemen wear the traditional garb of the Hadramaut region. Restrictions on Muslim women's clothing vary widely from one region to another; in many places, women are not required to cover their faces.

Westerners may think the Turkish feminists' adoption of the veil is strange. Together with some Muslim feminists, people from the West tend to see the veil as a symbol of women's second-class status. But to many Muslim women it makes sense. The veil allows young women to leave their homes in the countryside and mix with strange men in the great universities of the city, without violating Islamic custom. To many Muslim women, the veil is no less than a means of liberation.

Let's Discuss

1. Consider life in a society in which women wear veils. Can you see any advantages, from the woman's point of view? From the man's?
2. Do you find the Western emphasis on physical beauty oppressive? If so, in what ways?

Source: Cancel 1997; Fernea 1998; Gole 1997; Perlman 2000; Read and Bartkowski 1999.

- In many African and a few Asian nations, traditions mandate the cutting of female genitals, typically by practitioners who fail to use sterilized instruments. This can lead to immediate and serious complications from infection or to long-term health problems.
- While males outnumber females as refugees, refugee women have unique needs, such as protection against physical and sexual abuse (United Nations 2000).

Despite these challenges, women are not responding passively; they are mobilizing, individually and collectively. Given the significant underrepresentation of women in government offices and national legislatures, however, the task is difficult, as we shall see in Chapter 17.

What conclusions can we make about women's equality worldwide? First, as anthropologist Laura Nader (1986:383) has observed, even in the relatively more egalitarian nations of the West, women's subordination is "institutionally structured and culturally rationalized, exposing them to conditions of deference, dependency, powerlessness, and poverty." While the situation of women in Sweden and the United States is significantly better than in Saudi Arabia and Bangladesh, women nevertheless remain in a second-class position in the world's most affluent and developed countries.

Second, there is a link between the wealth of industrialized nations and the poverty of the developing countries. Viewed from a conflict perspective or through the lens of Immanuel Wallerstein's world systems analysis, the pp. 241–248 ◀ economies of developing nations are controlled and exploited by industrialized countries and multinational corporations based in those countries. Much of the exploited labor in developing nations, especially in the nonindustrial sector, is performed by women. Women workers typically toil long hours for low pay, but contribute significantly to their families' incomes. The affluence of Western industrialized nations has come, in part, at the expense of women in Third World countries (Jacobson 1993).

Women in the Workforce of the United States

"Does your mother work?" "No, she's just a housewife." This familiar exchange reminds us of women's traditional role in the United States, and it reminds us that women's work has generally been viewed as unimportant. The U.S. Commission on Civil Rights (1976:1) concluded that the passage in the Declaration of Independence proclaiming that "all men are created equal" has been taken too literally for too long. This is especially true with respect to opportunities for employment.

A Statistical Overview

Women's participation in the paid labor force of the United States increased steadily throughout the twentieth century (see Figure 12-2). No longer is the adult woman associated solely with the role of homemaker. Instead, millions of women—married and single, with and without children—are working in the labor force. In 1999, 60 percent of adult women in the United States held jobs outside the home, as compared with 38 percent in 1960. A majority of women are now members of the paid labor force, not full-time homemakers. Among new mothers, 55 percent return to the labor force within a year of giving birth. As recently as 1971, only 31 percent went back to work (Bach and O'Connell 2001; Bureau of Labor Statistics 2001a).

Figure 12-2

Trends in U.S. Women's Participation in the Paid Labor Force, 1890–2000

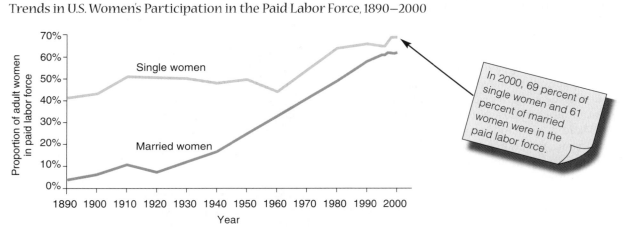

Sources: Bureau of the Census 1975; 2001a:372.

Table 12-2 U.S. Women in Selected Occupations, 2000
Women as Percentage of All Workers in the Occupation

Underrepresented		Overrepresented	
Firefighters	2%	High school teachers	58%
Airline pilots	4	Social workers	73
Engineers	10	Cashiers	78
Police	12	File clerks	80
Clergy	14	Elementary teachers	83
Dentists	19	Librarians	85
Architects	24	Registered nurses	93
Physicians	28	Child care workers	95
Computer systems analysts	29	Receptionists	97
Mail carriers	31	Secretaries	98
College teachers	44	Dental hygienists	99

Source: Bureau of the Census 2001a:380–381.

Yet women entering the job market find their options restricted in important ways. Particularly damaging is occupational segregation, or confinement to sex-typed "women's jobs." For example, in 2000, women accounted for 98 percent of all secretaries, 99 percent of all dental assistants, and 85 percent of all librarians. Entering such sex-typed occupations places women in "service" roles that parallel the traditional gender-role standard under which housewives "serve" their husbands.

Women are *underrepresented* in occupations historically defined as "men's jobs," which often carry much greater financial rewards and prestige than women's jobs. For example, in 1999, women accounted for approximately 60 percent of the paid labor force of the United States. Yet they constituted only 10 percent of all engineers, 19 percent of all dentists, 28 percent of all physicians, and 29 percent of all computer systems analysts (see Table 12-2). In Box 12-2, we consider unique situations that run *against* sex-typing: male nurses and female hockey players.

Women from all groups and men from minority groups sometimes encounter attitudinal or organizational bias that prevents them from reaching their full potential. As we saw in Chapter 11, the term **glass ceiling** refers to an invisible barrier that blocks the promotion of a qualified individual in a work environment because of

the individual's gender, race, or ethnicity. A study of the Fortune 500 largest corporations in the United States showed that only 11.7 percent of the seats on their boards of directors were held by women in 2000 (Strauss and Jones 2000).

One response to the "glass ceiling" and other gender bias in the workplace is to start your own business and work for yourself. This route to success, traditionally taken by men from immigrant and racial minority groups, has become more common among women as they have increasingly sought paid employment outside the home. According to data released in 2001, women own an impressive 5.4 million businesses in the United States. However, many of these operations are very small, self-run firms. Only 16 percent of women-owned businesses have any paid employees (Bureau of the Census 2001c).

The workplace patterns described here have one crucial result: women earn less money than men in the paid labor force. A study done by the General Accounting Office (2002) compared managerial salaries for women and men in the 10 industries that employ 70 percent of women workers, including entertainment, insurance, retailing, public administration, and education. Women managers came closest to matching men's salaries in education, where those who worked full time earned 91 cents for every dollar received by their male counterparts. But on average, women earned only about 78 cents for every dollar earned by men. Particularly troubling was the finding that in most industries, the male-female earnings

When you sit down to watch ice hockey, you expect to watch men playing. When you are being assisted by a nurse, you expect it to be a woman. And in almost every case you would be correct, but not always.

Nationwide, about 7.1 percent of all nurses are male. Sociologist E. Joel Heikes conducted in-depth interviews with male registered nurses employed in hospital settings in Austin, Texas. Heikes reports that male nurses in Austin felt more visible than female nurses, and typically responded by overachieving. Although they did not feel polarized from the female nurses, they did feel socially isolated. Their gender excluded them from informal interactions in which they could have learned more about the day-to-day workings of the hospital.

Stereotyping was also evident. Male nurses were commonly mistaken for physicians—a constant reminder of their deviant position in a traditionally female occupation. When correctly identified as nurses, they faced a much more serious form of stereotyping, the assumption that all male nurses must be gay. Many male nurses told Heikes they felt a need to deny this stigmatized identity.

Sociologist Christine Williams examined the underrepresentation of men in four predominantly female professions: nursing, elementary school teaching, librarianship, and social work. Drawing on in-depth interviews with 99 men and women in these professions in four cities in the United States, Williams found that the experience of tokenism is very different for women and men. While men in these traditionally female professions commonly experience negative stereotyping, they nevertheless benefit from hidden *advantages* stemming from their status as men, such as receiving early and disproportionate encouragement to become administrators. By contrast, women in traditionally male professions often find that their advancement is limited and their token status is hardly an asset.

> Like male nurses, female hockey players are rare specimens, although they have actually been around almost as long as male players.

Like male nurses, female hockey players are rare specimens, although they have actually been around almost as long as male players. A photograph of the daughter of Lord Stanley, founder of the coveted Stanley Cup, shows her playing the sport in 1890. But women were not taken seriously as hockey players until quite recently. Since 1990, the number of female hockey players registered on U.S. hockey teams has increased eightfold; by the end of the 1990s the number of women's teams had risen from 149 to 1,268. In 1998, women made their first appearance on the rink in the Olympics, where the U.S. team took a gold medal.

Still, women are criticized for not being as "tough and strong" as male hockey players. Hockey rules do not allow women to body check, which calls for shoving an opponent hard into the boards on the side of the rink. Sociologist Nancy Theberge found that while players agree that the game is more skill-oriented without checking, they favor including the practice in women's hockey to make it more professional. They reason that if they can make a living at the sport, they should accept the risk of injury that comes with hard play. Ironically, their willingness to accept a more intense level of play comes at a time when many people feel that professional hockey has become too violent; body checking leads to the fights that accompany many men's games.

Even without body checking, Theberge found, injury and pain were routine in the lives of female hockey players. "For these athletes, overcoming injury and pain is a measure of both ability and commitment," she noted. Ironically, as women's involvement in ice hockey grows, the pressure to develop a system that normalizes injury and pain grows.

Let's Discuss

1. Have you ever played a sport or worked in a job that was stereotyped as being more appropriate for the opposite sex? If so, how comfortable were you with your role?

2. Do you think women's hockey rules should be amended to allow body checking? Why or why not? Should men's hockey rules be amended to discourage checking?

Sources: Bureau of the Census 2000a; DeSimone 2000; Elliott 1997; Heikes 1991; Lillard 1998; Theberge 1997; Williams 1992, 1995; Zimmer 1988.

gap had actually widened between 1995 and 2000. The gap remained even after researchers adjusted their findings for variables such as education, age, and marital status. The glass ceiling is very firm.

Women, as we saw in Chapter 9, are also more likely to be poor. Female heads of households and their children account for most of the nation's poor people living in families. Yet not all women are in equal danger of experiencing poverty. Women who are members of racial and ethnic minorities suffer from "double jeopardy"—stratification by race and ethnicity as well as by gender—as we will see later (Bureau of Labor Statistics 2001b).

Figure 12-3

Gender Differences in Child Care and Housework, 1997

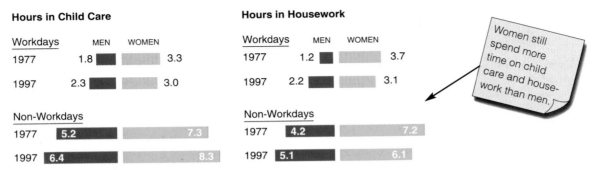

Hours in Child Care

Hours in Child Care

Workdays	MEN	WOMEN
1977	1.8	3.3
1997	2.3	3.0

Non-Workdays		
1977	5.2	7.3
1997	6.4	8.3

Hours in Housework

Workdays	MEN	WOMEN
1977	1.2	3.7
1997	2.2	3.1

Non-Workdays		
1977	4.2	7.2
1997	5.1	6.1

Women still spend more time on child care and housework than men.

Source: Bond et al. 1998:40–41, 44–45.

Social Consequences of Women's Employment

"What a circus we women perform every day of our lives. It puts a trapeze artist to shame." These words by the writer Anne Morrow Lindbergh attest to the lives of women today who try to juggle their work and family lives. This situation has many social consequences. For one thing, it puts pressure on child care facilities and on public financing of day care and even on the fast food industry, which provides many of the meals that women used to prepare during the day. For another, it raises questions about what responsibility male wage earners have in the household.

Who does do the housework when women become productive wage earners? Studies indicate that there continues to be a clear gender gap in the performance of housework, although the differences are narrowing. Still, as shown in Figure 12-3, the most recent study finds women doing more housework and spending more time on child care than men, whether it be on a workday or when off work. Taken together, then, a woman's workday on and off the job is much longer than a man's. A recent development over the last 20 years is women's involvement in elder care. According to a Department of Labor (1998) study, 72 percent of these caregivers are women, typically spending around 18 hours per week caring for a parent.

Sociologist Arlie Hochschild (1989, 1990) has used the phrase "second shift" to describe the double burden—work outside the home followed by child care and housework—that many women face and few men share equitably. On the basis of interviews with and observations of 52 couples over an eight-year period, Hochschild reports that the wives (and not their husbands) drive home from the office while planning domestic schedules and play dates for children—and then begin their second shift. Drawing on national studies, she concludes that women spend 15 fewer hours in leisure activities each week than their husbands do. In a year, these women work an extra month of 24-hour days because of the "second shift"; over a dozen years, they work an extra year of 24-hour days. Hochschild found that the married

Sociologist Arlie Hochschild has used the phrase "second shift" to describe the double burden—work outside the home followed by child care and housework—that many women face and few men share equitably.

couples she studied were fraying at the edges, and so were their careers and their marriages.

With such reports in mind, many feminists have advocated greater governmental and corporate support for child care, more flexible family leave policies, and other pp. 101–102 reforms designed to ease the burden on the nation's families.

Most studies of gender, child care, and housework focus on the time actually spent by women and men performing these duties. However, sociologist Susan Walzer (1996) was interested in whether there are gender differences in the amount of time that parents spend *thinking* about the care of their children. Drawing on interviews with 25 couples, Walzer found that mothers are much more involved than fathers in the invisible, mental labor associated with taking care of a baby. For example, while involved in work outside the home, mothers are more likely to think about their babies and to feel guilty if they become so consumed with the demands of their jobs that they *fail* to think about their babies.

Women: Emergence of a Collective Consciousness

The feminist movement of the United States was born in upstate New York, in a town called Seneca Falls, in the summer of 1848. On July 19, the first women's rights convention began, attended by Elizabeth Cady Stanton, Lucretia Mott, and other pioneers in the struggle for women's rights. This first wave of *feminists,* as they are currently known, battled ridicule and scorn as they fought for legal and political equality for women. They were not afraid to risk controversy on behalf of their cause; in 1872, Susan B. Anthony was arrested for attempting to vote in that year's presidential election.

Ultimately, the early feminists won many victories, among them the passage and ratification of the Nineteenth Amendment to the Constitution, which granted women the right to vote in national elections beginning in 1920. But suffrage did not lead to other reforms in women's social and economic position, and the women's movement became a much less powerful force for social change in the early and middle twentieth century.

The second wave of feminism in the United States emerged in the 1960s and came into full force in the 1970s. In part, the movement was inspired by three pioneering books arguing for women's rights: Simone de Beauvoir's *The Second Sex,* Betty Friedan's *The Feminine Mystique,* and Kate Millett's *Sexual Politics.* In addition, the general political activism of the 1960s led women—many of whom were working for Black civil rights or against the war in Vietnam—to reexamine their own

powerlessness as women. The sexism often found within allegedly progressive and radical political circles made many women decide that they needed to establish their own movement for "women's liberation" (Evans 1980; Firestone 1970; Freeman 1973, 1975).

More and more women became aware of sexist attitudes and practices, including attitudes they themselves had accepted through socialization into traditional gender roles, and began to challenge male dominance. A sense of "sisterhood," much like the class consciousness that Marx hoped would emerge in the proletariat, became evident. Individual women identified their interests with those of the collectivity *women.* No longer were they "happy" in submissive, subordinate roles ("false consciousness" in Marxist terms).

National surveys today, however, show that while women generally endorse feminist positions, they do not necessarily accept the label of "feminist." Close to 40 percent of women considered themselves feminists in 1989; the proportion dropped to about 20 percent in 1998. Feminism as a unified political cause, requiring

Minority women face not only gender bias but racial-ethnic bias in the workplace. Faye Wattleton, former president of Planned Parenthood, broke through both barriers.

STACEY KARP:
President of San Francisco Chapter of NOW (National Organization for Women)

www.
mhhe
.com
/schaefer8

Stacey Karp got involved with NOW when she took a semester off from the University of Wisconsin to work with the San Francisco chapter. After graduating in 1996, she moved to the Bay Area and continued to volunteer for NOW—and soon found herself in the president's position. The work is unpaid for the most part, but Karp feels the experience she is gaining is invaluable.

"My job is to oversee the entire chapter, with its 1,200 members; to set policies; and to be the spokesperson for those policies." In the course of a day, Karp will typically write press releases, attend government hearings, lobby elected officials, talk to constituents, and, if necessary, organize a protest of some sort. One protest Karp participated in was directed against the Promise Keepers, an organization dedicated to having men take responsibility for their families. According to Karp, "in reality the PK is about having men be in *control* of their families—having men make all the decisions and having women be submissive."

Karp chose sociology as her major because she's always been interested in people. "It was a great way to be able to study people, to understand what statistics mean, and to learn how to take action to involve people." A sociology of gender course got Karp interested in women's issues, which then led her to minor in women's studies.

Karp's advice to students: If you are interested in sociology, don't be concerned about what kind of career your degree will lead to. "Pretty much *everything* has to do with sociology. It's all about the study of people and how our society works."

Let's Discuss

1. What would a sociology major bring to the leadership of a political organization such as NOW that a major in political science or management would not?
2. If you held Stacey Karp's position, on which women's issues would you concentrate most? Why?

---

one to accept a similar stance on everything from abortion to sexual harassment to pornography to welfare, has fallen out of favor. Both women and men prefer to express their views on these complex issues individually rather than under a convenient umbrella like "feminism." Still, feminism is very much alive in the growing acceptance of women in nontraditional roles and even the basic acknowledgment that a married mother not only can be working outside the home but also perhaps belongs in the labor force. A majority of women say that given the choice, they would prefer to work outside the home rather than stay home and take care of a house and family, and about one-quarter of women prefer Ms. to Miss or Mrs. (Bellafante 1998; Geyh 1998).

The women's movement has undertaken public protests on a wide range of issues. Feminists have endorsed passage of the equal rights amendment, government subsidies for child care (see Chapter 4), affirmative action for women and minorities (see Chapter 18), federal legislation outlawing sex discrimination in education (see Chapter 16), greater representation of women in government (see Chapter 17), and the right to legal abortions (discussed in the social policy section of this chapter). The Taking Sociology to Work box on this page describes the efforts of one member of the women's movement, Stacey Karp, president of the San Francisco chapter of NOW.

Minority Women: Double Jeopardy

Many women experience differential treatment not only because of gender but because of race and ethnicity as well. These citizens face a "double jeopardy"—that of subordinate status twice defined. A disproportionate share of this low-status group are also impoverished, so that the double jeopardy effectively becomes a triple jeopardy. The litany of social ills continues for many if we consider old age, ill health, disabilities, and the like.

Feminists have addressed themselves to the particular needs of minority women. The question for African American women, Latinas, Asian American women, and others appears to be whether they should unify with their "brothers" against racism or challenge them for their sexism. One answer is that, in a truly just society, both sexism and racism must be eradicated (C. Epstein 1999).

The discussion of gender roles among African Americans has always provoked controversy. Advocates of Black nationalism contend that feminism only distracts women from full participation in the Black struggle. The existence of feminist groups among Blacks, in their view, simply divides the Black community and thereby serves the dominant White society. By contrast, Black feminists such as Florynce Kennedy argue, in turn, that little is to be gained by adopting or maintaining the gender-role divisions of the dominant society. African American journalist Patricia Raybon (1989) has noted that the media commonly portray Black women in a negative light: as illiterate, as welfare mothers, as prostitutes, and so forth. Black feminists emphasize that it is not solely Whites and White-dominated media that focus on these negative images; Black men (most recently, some Black male rap artists) have also been criticized for the way they portray African American women.

The plight of Latinas is usually considered part of either the Latino or the feminist movement, ignoring the distinctive experience of Mexican American, Cuban, Puerto Rican, and Central and South American women. In the past, these women have been excluded from decision making in the two institutions that most directly affect their daily lives: the family and the church. The Hispanic family,

especially in the lower class, feels the pervasive tradition of male domination. The Roman Catholic church relegates women to supportive roles while reserving the leadership positions for men (Browne 1999; De Andra 1996).

We can see that activists among minority women do not agree on whether priority should be granted to fighting for sexual equality or to eliminating inequality among racial and ethnic groups. Neither component of inequality can be ignored. Helen Mayer Hacker (1974:11), who pioneered research on both Blacks and women, stated before the American Sociological Association, "As a partisan observer, it is my fervent hope that in fighting the twin battles of sexism and racism, Black women and Black men will [create] the outlines of the good society for all Americans" (see also Zia 1993).

SOCIAL POLICY AND GENDER STRATIFICATION

The Battle over Abortion from a Global Perspective

www.
mhhe.
com
/schaefer8

The Issue

Few issues seem to stir as much intense conflict as abortion. A critical victory in the struggle for legalized abortion in the United States came in 1973 when the Supreme Court granted women the right to terminate pregnancies. This ruling, known as *Roe v. Wade,* was based on a woman's right to privacy. The Court's decision was generally applauded by pro-choice groups, which believe women have the right to make their own decisions about their bodies and should have access to safe and legal abortion. It was bitterly condemned by those opposed to abortion. For these pro-life groups, abortion is a moral and often a religious issue. In their view, human life actually begins at the moment of conception, and its termination through abortion is viewed essentially as an act of murder.

The Setting

The debate that has followed *Roe v. Wade* revolves around prohibiting abortion altogether or, at the very least, putting limits on it. In 1979, for example, Missouri required parental consent for minors wishing to obtain an abortion, and the Supreme Court upheld this law. Parental notification and parental consent have become especially sensitive issues in the debate over abortion. Pro-life activists argue that the parents of these teenagers should have the right to be notified about— and to permit or prohibit—these abortions. In their view,

parental authority deserves full support at a time when the traditional nuclear family is embattled. However, pro-choice activists counter that many pregnant teenagers come from troubled families where they have been abused. These young women may have good reason to avoid discussing such explosive issues with their parents.

Changing technology has had its impact. "Day-after" pills are available in some nations; these pills can abort the fertilized egg the day after conception. In 2000, the U.S. government allowed for the use of RU-486, an abortion-inducing pill regime that can be used in the first seven weeks of pregnancy. It requires doctor visits but no surgical procedures. In the United States, doctors, guided by ultrasound, can now end a pregnancy as early as eight days after conception. Pro-life activists are concerned that use of this ultrasound technology will allow people to terminate pregnancies of unwanted females in nations where a premium is placed on male offspring.

As of 2002, the people of the United States appeared to support their right to legal abortion, but with reservations. According to a national survey, a little over half of respondents (56 percent) thought that abortion should be legal in certain cases. Twenty-six percent said it should be legal in all cases, and another 17 percent, that it should be illegal in all cases (Gallup 2002a).

Sociological Insights

Sociologists see gender and social class as largely defining the issues surrounding abortion. The intense conflict over abortion reflects broader differences over women's position in society. Sociologist Kristin Luker (1984) has offered a detailed study of activists in the pro-choice and pro-life movements. Luker interviewed 212 activists in California, overwhelmingly women, who spent at least five hours a week working for one of these movements. According to Luker, each group has a consistent, coherent view of the world. Feminists involved in defending abortion rights typically believe that men and women are essentially similar; they support women's full participation in work outside the home and oppose all forms of sex discrimination. By contrast, most antiabortion activists believe that men and women are fundamentally different. In their view, men are best suited for the public world of work, whereas women are best suited for the demanding and crucial task of rearing children. These activists are troubled by women's growing participation in work outside the home, which they view as destructive to the family and ultimately to society as a whole.

Figure 12-4

Restrictions on Public Funding for Abortion

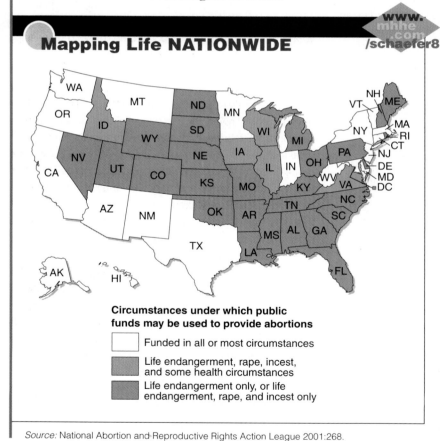

Mapping Life NATIONWIDE

Circumstances under which public funds may be used to provide abortions

☐ Funded in all or most circumstances

◻ Life endangerment, rape, incest, and some health circumstances

◼ Life endangerment only, or life endangerment, rape, and incest only

Source: National Abortion and Reproductive Rights Action League 2001:268.

In terms of social class, the first major restriction on the legal right to terminate a pregnancy affected poor people. In 1976, Congress passed the Hyde Amendment, which banned the use of Medicaid and other federal funds for abortions. The Supreme Court upheld this legislation in 1980. State laws also restrict the use of public funds for abortions (see Figure 12-4). Another obstacle facing the poor is access to abortion providers: In the face of vocal pro-life public sentiment, fewer and fewer hospitals throughout the world are allowing their physicians to perform abortions, except in extreme cases. As of 2001, only about 6 percent of specialists in obstetrics and gynecology were trained and willing to perform abortions under any circumstances, and a majority of those physicians were in their 50s and 60s. To avoid controversy, many medical schools have ceased to offer training in the procedure. Moreover, abortion providers in clinics are intimidated by death threats and actual murders. For poor people in rural areas, this reduction in service makes it more costly to locate and travel to a facility that will accommodate their wishes. Viewed from a conflict perspective, this is one more financial burden that falls especially heavily on low-income women (Edward 2001).

Policy Initiatives

The Supreme Court currently supports the general right to terminate a pregnancy by a narrow 5–4 majority. Although pro-life activists continue to hope for an overruling of *Roe v. Wade,* they have focused in the interim on weakening the decision through such issues as limiting the use of fetal tissue in medical experiments and prohibiting late-term abortions, termed "partial-birth" abortions by pro-life supporters. The Supreme Court continues to hear cases involving such restrictions. In 1998, the Court gave the states the authority (32 have done so) to prohibit abortions at the point where the fetus is viable outside the mother's womb—a definition that continues to be redefined by developments in medical technology (Biskupic 2000).

What is the policy in other countries? As in the United States, many European

Figure 12-5

The Global Divide on Abortion

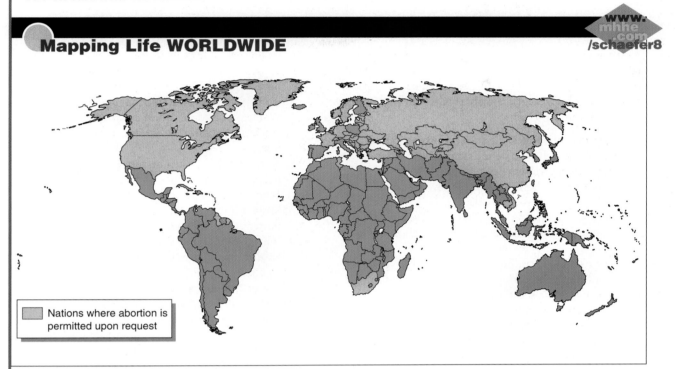

Mapping Life WORLDWIDE

www.mhhe.com
/schaefer8

☐ Nations where abortion is permitted upon request

Note: Data current as of June 2001.

Sources: Developed by the author based on United Nations Population Division 1998b and Gonnot 2001.

nations bowed to public opinion and liberalized abortion laws in the 1970s, although Ireland, Belgium, and Malta continue to prohibit abortion. Austria, Denmark, Greece, the Netherlands, Norway, and Sweden have laws that allow a woman to have an abortion on request. Other countries have much more restrictive legislation, especially concerning abortions in the later stages of pregnancy. Inspired by their counterparts in the United States, antiabortion activists have become more outspoken in Great Britain, France, Spain, Italy, and Germany.

The policies of the United States and developing nations are intertwined. Throughout the 1980s and 1990s, antiabortion members of Congress have often successfully blocked foreign aid to countries that might use the funds to encourage abortion. (We will discuss this political tactic in greater detail in Chapter 21.) And yet these developing nations generally have the most restrictive

abortion laws. As shown in Figure 12-5, it is primarily in Africa, Latin America, and parts of Asia that women are not allowed to terminate a pregnancy upon request. As might be expected, illegal abortions are most common in these nations. According to the World Health Organization (1998), of the 80,000 women's deaths globally that result from abortions, 95 percent are in poor nations, where they occur in defiance of the law.

Let's Discuss

1. Do you know anyone who has undergone an illegal abortion? If so, what were the circumstances? Was the woman's health endangered by the procedure?
2. Do you think teenage girls should have to get their parents' consent before having an abortion? Why?
3. Under what circumstances should abortions be allowed? Explain your reasoning.

⬤ Chapter Resources

Summary

Gender is an ascribed status that provides a basis for social differentiation. This chapter examines the social construction of gender, theories of stratification by gender, women as an oppressed majority group, and the double jeopardy of minority women.

1. In the United States, the social construction of gender continues to define significantly different expectations for females and males.
2. *Gender roles* show up in our work and behavior and in how we react to others.
3. Though females have been more severely restricted than men by traditional gender roles, those roles have also restricted males.
4. The research of anthropologist Margaret Mead points to the importance of cultural conditioning in defining the social roles of males and females.
5. Functionalists maintain that sex differentiation contributes to overall social stability, whereas conflict theorists contend that the relationship between females and males is one of unequal power, with men dominating women. This dominance also shows up in everyday interactions.
6. As one example of their micro-level approach to the study of gender stratification, interactionists have analyzed men's verbal dominance over women through conversational interruptions.
7. Women around the world experience *sexism, institutional discrimination,* and *sexual harassment.*
8. As women have taken on more and more hours of paid employment outside the home, they have been only partially successful in getting their husbands to take a greater role in homemaking duties, including child care.
9. Many women agree with the positions of the feminist movement but reject the label of "feminist."
10. Minority women experience double jeopardy through differential treatment based on both gender and race and ethnicity.
11. The issue of abortion has bitterly divided the United States (as well as other nations) and pitted pro-choice activists against pro-life activists.

Critical Thinking Questions

1. Sociologist Barbara Bovee Polk suggests that women are oppressed because they constitute an alternative subculture that deviates from the prevailing masculine value system. Does it seem valid to view women as an "alternative subculture"? In what ways do women support and deviate from the prevailing masculine value system evident in the United States?
2. In what ways is the social position of White women in the United States similar to that of African
American women, Latinos (Hispanic women), and Asian American women? In what ways is a woman's social position markedly different, given her racial and ethnic status?
3. Imagine that you were asked to study political activism among women. How might you employ surveys, observations, experiments, and existing sources to better understand such activism?

Key Terms

Expressiveness   A term used to refer to concern for maintenance of harmony and the internal emotional affairs of the family. (page 307)

Gender roles   Expectations regarding the proper behavior, attitudes, and activities of males and females. (303)

Glass ceiling   An invisible barrier that blocks the promotion of a qualified individual in a work environment because of the individual's gender, race, or ethnicity. (314)

Homophobia   Fear of and prejudice against homosexuality. (304)

Institutional discrimination   The denial of opportunities and equal rights to individuals and groups that results from the normal operations of a society. (310)

Instrumentality   A term used to refer to emphasis on tasks, focus on more distant goals, and a concern for the external relationship between one's family and other social institutions. (307)

Sexism   The ideology that one sex is superior to the other. (310)

Sexual harassment   Behavior that occurs when work benefits are made contingent on sexual favors (as a quid pro quo), or when touching, lewd comments, or exhibition of pornographic material creates a "hostile environment" in the workplace. (310)

Additional Readings

BOOKS

Backett-Milburn, Kathryn, and Linda McKie (eds.). 2001. *Constructing Gendered Bodies.* New York: Palgrave. A consideration of the ways in which society defines gender, from the occupations and recreational pursuits open to men and women to the different ways in which they approach love, marriage, and disability.

Browne, Irene (ed.). 2001. *Latinas and African American Women at Work: Race, Gender, and Economic Inequality.* New York: Russell Sage Foundation. Thirteen essays on the situation of Black and Hispanic women in the labor force, including their occupations, experiences with segregation and workplace discrimination, and response to social policy.

Kimmel, Michael, and Michael A. Messner. 2001. *Men's Lives.* 5th ed. Needham Heights, MA: Allyn and Bacon. An overview of masculinity, from its development throughout the life course to its place in social relationships, the media, and social movements.

JOURNALS

Among the journals that focus on issues of gender stratification are *Gender and Society* (founded in 1987), *Journal of African American Men* (1995), *Journal of Men's Studies* (1992), *Journeymen* (1991), *Men and Masculinities* (1999), *Sex Roles* (1975), *Signs: Journal of Women in Culture and Society* (1975), *Women: A Cultural Review* (1990), *Women's Review of Books* (1983), *Women's Studies* (1972), and *Women's Studies International Forum* (1978).

● Technology Resources

Internet Connection

*Note: While all the URLs listed were current as of the printing of this book, these sites often change. Please check our website (**http://www.mhhe.com/schaefer8**) for updates and hyperlinks to this exercise and additional exercises.*

1. The Gallup Organization is one of the world's largest management consulting firms, whose core expertise is measuring and understanding human attitudes and behavior. The organization has been publishing the Gallup Poll, the world's leading source of information on public opinion, since 1935. In June 2001, the Gallup News Service reported on a poll of women's attitudes toward both job equity and life satisfaction. Go to **http://www.gallup.com/poll/** and link to "Special Reports." Read "Public Opinion about Abortion—An In-Depth Review," and answer the following questions:

    (a)   What was the key question asked in this poll?

    (b)   What has Gallup found most recently about attitudes toward abortion being legal in all cases? How does this finding compare to past findings?

    (c)   Link to "Gender, Religion, and Other Group Attitudes Toward Abortion." Compare the survey findings for men and women.

    (d)   Do Americans support restrictions on abortion? Is the issue critical to most Americans?

Online Learning Center   www.mhhe.com/schaefer 8

Few issues seem to stir as much intense conflict as abortion. To find out how Americans feel about abortion, visit the student center at our Online Learning Center (**www.mhhe.com/schaefer 8**), and link to "How Americans Feel About . . .". Read an overview of the abortion issue, and then look at the colorful pie charts and graphs. These charts and graphs will show you what percent of Americans surveyed considered themselves pro-choice or pro-life, how they felt about the *Roe v. Wade* decision, and how both men and women felt about the legality of abortion.

STRATIFICATION BY AGE

Society typically expects older people to slow down and "take it easy." This ad for McDonald's in Germany turns that notion on its head. The caption reads: "With the flavor of freedom and adventure."

tuesdays with Morrie

an old man, a young man,

and life's greatest lesson

Mitch Albom

ater that day, we talked about aging. Or maybe I should say the fear of aging—another of the issues on my what's-bugging-my-generation list. On my ride from the Boston airport, I had counted the billboards that featured young and beautiful people. There was a handsome young man in a cowboy hat, smoking a cigarette, two beautiful young women smiling over a shampoo bottle, a sultry-looking teenager with her jeans unsnapped, and a sexy woman in a black velvet dress, next to a man in a tuxedo, the two of them snuggling a glass of scotch.

Not once did I see anyone who would pass for over thirty-five. I told Morrie I was already feeling over the hill, much as I tried desperately to stay on top of it. I worked out constantly. Watched what I ate. Checked my hairline in the mirror. I had gone from being proud to say my age—because of all I had done so young—to not bringing it up, for fear I was getting too close to forty and, therefore, professional oblivion.

Morrie had aging in better perspective.

"All this emphasis on youth—I don't buy it," he said. "Listen, I know what a misery being young can be, so don't tell me it's so great. All these kids who came to me with their struggles, their strife, their feelings of inadequacy, their sense that life was miserable, so bad they wanted to kill themselves . . .

"And, in addition to all the miseries, the young are not wise. They have very little understanding about life. Who wants to live every day when you don't know what's going on? When people are manipulating you, telling you to buy this perfume and you'll be beautiful, or this pair of jeans and you'll be sexy—and you believe them! It's such nonsense."

Weren't you *ever* afraid to grow old, I asked?

"Mitch, I *embrace* aging."

Embrace it?

"It's very simple. As you grow, you learn more. If you stayed at twenty-two, you'd always be as ignorant as you were at twenty-two. Aging is not just decay, you know. It's growth. It's more than the negative that you're going to die, it's also the positive that you *understand* you're going to die, and that you live a better life because of it."

Yes, I said, but if aging were so valuable, why do people always say, "Oh, if I were young again." You never hear people say, "I wish I were sixty-five."

He smiled. "You know what that reflects? Unsatisfied lives. Unfulfilled lives. Lives that haven't found meaning. Because if you've found meaning in your life, you don't want to go back. You want to go forward. You want to see more, do more. You can't wait until sixty-five. . . ." *(Albom 1997:117–118)* ■ 💿

Additional information about this excerpt and about those that open each subsequent chapter can be found in the SocWorld CD-ROM that accompanies this text.

n *Tuesdays with Morrie,* journalist Mitch Albom (1997) recounted his final class with his favorite college professor, the respected Brandeis University sociologist Morrie Schwartz. Albom, who had graduated years before, contacted Schwartz when he learned the professor was dying of amyotrophic lateral sclerosis (ALS), also known as Lou Gehrig's disease. To his surprise, he found that his series of conversations with Morrie, held always on Tuesday, were more about life than death. From this sage man he learned that age has its benefits, and that growing old can also mean growing wise.

Age, like race or gender is socially constructed. It is an ascribed status that dominates people's perceptions of others, obscuring individual differences. Rather than suggesting that a particular elderly person is no longer competent to drive, for instance, we may condemn the entire age group: "Those old codgers shouldn't be allowed on the road." Unless people can begin to look at the life course as a continuum, rather than as a series of finite stages with predictable consequences, such stereotypical attitudes toward age and aging are not likely to change.

What happens in the aging process? How do people's roles change as they age? What are the social implications of the growing number of elderly in the United States? How does ageism affect an older person's employment opportunities? In this chapter we will look at the process of aging throughout the life course. We will examine aging around the world, focusing primarily on older people in the United States. After exploring various theories of the impact of aging, both on the individual and on society, we will discuss the role transitions typical of the major stages in the life course. In the process we will consider the challenges facing the "sandwich generation," middle-aged people who care for both their children and their aging parents. We will pay particular attention to the effects of prejudice and discrimination on older people, and the rise of a political consciousness among the elderly. Finally, in the social policy section, we will discuss the controversial issue of the right to die. ■

● Aging and Society

The Sherpas—a Tibetan-speaking Buddhist people in Nepal—live in a culture that idealizes old age. Almost all elderly members of the Sherpa culture own their homes, and most are in relatively good physical condition. Typically, older Sherpas value their independence and prefer not to live with their children. Among the Fulani of Africa, however, older men and women move to the edge of the family homestead. Since this is where people are buried, the elderly sleep over their own graves, for they are already viewed as socially dead. Like gender stratification, age stratification varies from culture to culture. One society may treat older people with great reverence, while another sees them as unproductive and "difficult" (Goldstein and Beall 1981; Stenning 1958; Tonkinson 1978).

It is understandable that all societies have some system of age stratification and associate certain social roles with distinct periods in one's life. Some of this age differentiation seems inevitable; it would make little sense to send young children off to war or to expect most older citizens to handle physically demanding tasks such as loading goods at shipyards. However, as is the case with stratification by gender, age stratification in the United States goes far beyond the physical constraints of human beings at different ages.

This elderly Sherpa in Nepal is honored for his age. Not all old people are so lucky—in many cultures being old is considered next to dead.

"Being old" is a master status that commonly over-shadows all others in the United States. The insights of labeling theory help us analyze the consequences of aging.

p. 196 Once people are labeled "old," this designation has a major impact on how others perceive them and even on how they view themselves. Negative stereotypes of the elderly contribute to their position as a minority group subject to discrimination, as we'll see later in the chapter.

The model of five basic properties of a minority or subordinate group (introduced in Chapter 11) can be applied to older people in the United States pp. 269–270 to clarify their subordinate status:

1. The elderly experience unequal treatment in employment and may face prejudice and discrimination.
2. The elderly share physical characteristics that distinguish them from younger people. In addition, their cultural preferences and leisure-time activities often differ from those of the rest of society.
3. Membership in this disadvantaged group is involuntary.
4. Older people have a strong sense of group solidarity, as is reflected in the growth of senior citizens' centers, retirement communities, and advocacy organizations.
5. Older people generally are married to others of comparable age.

There is one crucial difference between older people and other subordinate groups, such as racial and ethnic minorities or women: *All* of us who live long enough will eventually assume the ascribed status of being an older person (Barron 1953; Levin and Levin 1980; Wagley and Harris 1958).

Explaining the Aging Process

Aging is one important aspect of socialization—the life-long process through which an individual learns the cultural norms and values of a particular society. There are no clear-cut definitions for different periods of the aging cycle in the United States. *Old age* has typically been regarded as beginning at 65, which corresponds to the retirement age for many workers, but not everyone in the United States accepts this definition. With life expectancy being extended, writers are beginning to refer to people in their 60s as the "young old" to distinguish them from those in their 80s and beyond (the "old old"). Box 13-1 considers some of the consequences of the growth of both these age groups.

The particular problems of the elderly have become the focus for a specialized area of research and inquiry known as gerontology. *Gerontology* is the scientific study of the sociological and psychological aspects of aging and the problems of the aged. It originally developed in the 1930s, as an increasing number of social scientists became aware of the plight of the elderly.

Gerontologists rely heavily on sociological principles and theories to explain the impact of aging on the individual and society. They also draw on the disciplines of psychology, anthropology, physical education, counseling, and medicine in their study of the aging process. Two influential views of aging—disengagement theory and activity theory—can be best understood in terms of the sociological perspectives of functionalism and interactionism, respectively. The conflict perspective also contributes to our sociological understanding of aging.

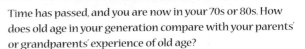

Imagine

Time has passed, and you are now in your 70s or 80s. How does old age in your generation compare with your parents' or grandparents' experience of old age?

Functionalist Approach: Disengagement Theory

Elaine Cumming and William Henry (1961) introduced *disengagement theory* to explain the impact of aging during one's life course. This theory, based on a study of elderly people in good health and relatively comfortable economic circumstances, contends that society and the aging individual mutually sever many of their relationships. In keeping with the functionalist perspective, disengagement theory emphasizes that passing social roles on from one generation to another ensures social stability.

According to this theory, the approach of death forces people to drop most of their social roles—including those of worker, volunteer, spouse, hobby enthusiast, and even reader. Younger members of society then take on these functions. The aging person, it is held, withdraws into an increasing state of inactivity while preparing for death. At the same time, society withdraws from the elderly by segregating them residentially (retirement homes and communities), educationally (programs designed solely for senior citizens), and recreationally (senior citizens' social centers). Implicit in disengagement theory is the view that society should *help* older people to withdraw from their accustomed social roles.

Since it was first outlined more than four decades ago, disengagement theory has generated considerable controversy. Some gerontologists have objected to the implication that older people want to be ignored and "put

An electric water kettle is wired so that people in another location can determine if it has been used in the previous 24 hours. This may seem a zany bit of modern technology, but it symbolizes a change taking place around the globe—the growing needs of an aging population. Welfare Network Ikebukuro Honcho has installed these wired hot pots in Japan so that volunteers can monitor if the elderly have used the devices to prepare their morning tea. An unused pot initiates contacts to see if the older person needs help. This technological monitoring system is an indication of the tremendous growth of Japan's elderly population and, of particular social significance, the increasing numbers who live *alone*.

Around the world, there are more than 425 million people aged 65 or over; they represent about 7 percent of the world's population. In an important sense, the aging of the world's population represents a major success story that has unfolded during the later stages of the twentieth century. Through the efforts of both national governments and international agencies, many societies have drastically reduced the incidence of diseases and their rates of death. Consequently, these nations—especially the industrialized countries of Europe and North America—have increasingly higher proportions of older members.

The overall population of Europe is older than that of any other continent. As the proportion of older people in Europe continues to rise, many governments that have long prided themselves on their

> **An unused pot initiates contacts to see if the older person needs help.**

social welfare programs are examining ways to shift a larger share of the costs of caring for the elderly to the private sector and charities. Germany and France have instituted or are weighing plans to raise the age at which retirees will qualify for pensions.

In most developing countries, people over 60 are likely to be in poorer health than their counterparts in industrialized nations. Yet few of these nations are in a position to offer extensive financial support to the elderly. Ironically, modernization in the developing world, while bringing with it many social and economic advances, has undercut the traditionally high status of the elderly. In many cultures, the earning power of younger adults now exceeds that of older family members.

Worldwide, governments are beginning to pay attention to population aging, and the permanent social transformation it represents. In 1940, of the 227 nations with a population of at least 5,000, only 33 had some form of old-age disability or survivors' program. By 2001 the number stood at 167, or 74 percent of those 227 nations.

Let's Discuss

1. For an older person, how might life in Pakistan differ from life in France?
2. Do you know an aged person who lives alone? What arrangements have been made (or should be made) for care in case of emergency?

Sources: Hani 1998; Haub and Cornelius 2001; Kinsella and Velkoff 2001; Samuelson 2001.

---

away"—and even more to the idea that they should be encouraged to withdraw from meaningful social roles. Critics of disengagement theory insist that society *forces* the elderly into an involuntary and painful withdrawal from the paid labor force and from meaningful social relationships. Rather than voluntarily seeking to disengage, older employees find themselves pushed out of their jobs—in many instances, even before they are entitled to maximum retirement benefits (Boaz 1987).

Although functionalist in its approach, disengagement theory ignores the fact that postretirement employment has been *increasing* in recent decades. In the United States, fewer than half of all employees actually retire from their career jobs. Instead, most move into a "bridge job"—employment that bridges the period between the end of a person's career and his or her retirement. Unfortunately, the elderly can easily be victimized in such "bridge jobs." Psychologist Kathleen Christensen (1990), warning of "bridges over troubled water," emphasizes that older employees do not want to end their working days as minimum-wage jobholders engaged in activities unrelated to their career jobs (Doeringer 1990; Hayward et al. 1987).

Interactionist Approach: Activity Theory

Ask Ruth Vitow if she would like to trade in her New York City custom lampshade business for a condo in Florida, and you will get a quick response: "Deadly! I'd hate it." Vitow is in her nineties and vows to give up her business "when it gives me up." James Russell Wiggins has been working at a weekly newspaper in Maine since 1922. At age 95 he is now the editor. Vitow and Wiggins are among the 9 percent of the men and 3 percent of the women aged 75 years or older who are still participating in the nation's labor force (Himes 2001).

How important is staying actively involved for older people, whether at a job or in other pursuits? A tragic disaster in Chicago in 1995 showed that it can be a matter of life and death. An intense heat wave lasting more than a week—with a heat index exceeding 115 degrees on two consecutive days—resulted in 733 heat-related deaths. About three-fourths of the deceased were 65 and older. Subsequent analysis showed that older people who lived alone had the highest risk of dying, suggesting that support networks for the elderly literally help save lives. Older Hispanics and Asian Americans had lower death rates from the heat wave than did other racial and ethnic groups. Their stronger social networks probably resulted in more regular contact with family members and friends during this critical time (Schaefer 1998a).

These "silver surfers" still enjoy life to the fullest, just as they did when they were young. The lighthouse behind them in Santa Cruz, California, has been converted to a surfing museum.

Often seen as an opposing approach to disengagement theory, ***activity theory*** argues that the elderly person who remains active and socially involved will be best-adjusted. Proponents of this perspective acknowledge that a 70-year-old person may not have the ability or desire to perform various social roles that he or she had at age 40. Yet they contend that old people have essentially the same need for social interaction as any other group.

The improved health of older people—sometimes overlooked by social scientists—has strengthened the arguments of activity theorists. Illness and chronic disease are no longer quite the scourge of the elderly that they once were. The recent emphasis on fitness, the availability of better medical care, greater control of infectious diseases, and the reduction of fatal strokes and heart attacks have combined to mitigate the traumas of growing old. Accumulating medical research also points to the importance of remaining socially involved. Among those who

decline in their mental capacities later in life, deterioration is most rapid in old people who withdraw from social relationships and activities. Fortunately, the aged are finding new ways to remain socially engaged, as evidenced by their increasing use of the Internet, especially to keep in touch with family and friends (Fox 2001; Liao et al. 2000; National Institute on Aging 1999b).

Admittedly, many activities open to the elderly involve unpaid labor, for which younger adults may receive salaries. Such unpaid workers include hospital volunteers (versus aides and orderlies), drivers for charities such as the Red Cross (versus chauffeurs), tutors (as opposed to teachers), and craftspeople for charity bazaars (as opposed to carpenters and dressmakers). However, some companies have recently initiated programs to hire retirees for full-time or part-time work.

Disengagement theory suggests that older people find satisfaction in withdrawal from society. Functionally speaking, they conveniently recede into the background

Taking Sociology to Work

A. DAVID ROBERTS:
Social Worker

Dave Roberts admits to being a "people person," a trait that sociology courses fostered by showing how "everybody has differences; there are little bits of different cultures in all of us." He also had the benefit of "a lot of great teachers" at Florida State University, including Dr. Jill Quadagno in an "Aging" course. It was this class that sparked his interest in aging issues, which led to a certificate in gerontology in addition to a sociology degree in 1998. He realized that there was a good job market in working with the aging baby boom generation.

Volunteer work with the Meals on Wheels program steered him toward working with the elderly. Today Roberts is a social worker in a nursing home, where he is responsible for patients' care plans. In the course of this work, he meets regularly with patients, family members, and medical residents. Roberts finds that the concept of teamwork he learned in group projects in college has helped him in this job. Also, the projects he had to do in school taught him to work on a schedule. Perhaps most importantly, sociology has helped him "to grow as a person to explore different angles, different theories. . . . I'm a better person."

His advice for sociology students: "Just give it a chance; they throw everything into an intro course. Don't get overwhelmed; take it as it comes."

Let's Discuss

1. What other types of employment might be open to a college graduate with a certificate in gerontology?
2. What might be the special rewards of working with the elderly?

---

and allow the next generation to take over. Proponents of activity theory view such withdrawal as harmful to both the elderly and society, however. Activity theorists focus on the potential contributions of older people to the maintenance of society. In their opinion, aging citizens will feel satisfied only when they can be useful and productive in society's terms—primarily by working for wages (Civic Ventures 1999; Dowd 1980; Quadagno 2002).

The Conflict Approach

Conflict theorists have criticized both disengagement theory and activity theory for failing to consider the impact of social structure on patterns of aging. Neither approach, they say, attempts to question why social interaction "must" change or decrease in old age. In addition, these perspectives, in contrast to the conflict perspective, often ignore the impact of social class on the lives of the elderly.

The privileged position of the upper class generally leads to better health and vigor and to less likelihood of dependency in old age. Affluence cannot forestall aging indefinitely, but it can soften the economic hardships faced in later years. Although pension plans, retirement packages, and insurance benefits may be developed to assist older people, those whose wealth allows them access to investment funds can generate the greatest income for their later years.

By contrast, working-class jobs often carry greater hazards to health and a greater risk of disability; aging will be particularly difficult for those who suffer job-related injuries or illnesses. Working-class people also depend more heavily on Social Security benefits and private pension programs. During inflationary times, their relatively fixed incomes from these sources barely keep pace with escalating costs of food, housing, utilities, and other necessities (Atchley 1985).

Conflict theorists have noted that the transition from agricultural economies to industrialization and capitalism has not always been beneficial for the elderly. As a society's production methods change, the traditionally valued role of older people within the economy tends to erode. Their wisdom is no longer relevant.

According to the conflict approach, the treatment of older people in the United States reflects the many divisions in our society. The low status of older people is seen in prejudice and discrimination against them, age segregation, and unfair job practices—none of which are directly addressed by either disengagement or activity theory.

The three perspectives considered here take different views of the elderly. Functionalists portray them as socially isolated with reduced social roles; interactionists see older people as involved in new networks of people in a change of social roles; conflict theorists regard older people as victimized by social structure, with their social roles relatively unchanged but devalued. Table 13-1 summarizes these perspectives.

Table 13-1 Theories of Aging			
Sociological Perspective	View of Aging	Social Roles	Portrayal of Elderly
Functionalist	Disengagement	Reduced	Socially isolated
Interactionist	Activity	Changed	Involved in new networks
Conflict	Competition	Relatively unchanged	Victimized, organized to confront victimization

Role Transitions throughout the Life Course

As we have seen in Chapter 4 and throughout this textbook, socialization is a lifelong process. We simply do not experience things the same way at different points in the life course. For example, one study found that even falling in love differs depending on where we are in the life course. Young unmarried adults tend to treat love as a noncommittal game or else as an obsession characterized by possessiveness and dependency. People over the age of 50 are much more likely to see love as involving commitment, and they tend to take a practical approach to finding a partner who meets a set of rational criteria. The life course, then, affects the manner in which we relate to one another (Montgomery and Sorell 1997).

p. 93

How we move through the life course varies dramatically, depending on the individual. Some people, for instance, start their own households in their early 20s, while others are well into their 30s before beginning a permanent relationship with someone else. Still, it is possible to identify a series of developmental periods, with critical transitions between the various stages, as shown in the model devised by psychologist Daniel Levinson (Figure 13-1).

In the following sections, we will focus on major transitions associated with the later stages of the life course: the sandwich generation, retirement, and death and dying.

The Sandwich Generation

The first transitional period identified by Levinson begins at about age 17 and extends to age 22. It marks the time at which an individual gradually enters the adult world, perhaps by moving out of the parental home, beginning a career, or entering a marriage. The second transitional period, the midlife transition, typically begins at about age 40. Men and women often experience a stressful period of self-evaluation, commonly known as the *midlife crisis,* in which they realize that they have not achieved basic goals and ambitions and have little time left to do so. Thus, Levinson (1978, 1996) found that most adults surveyed experienced tumultuous midlife conflicts within the self and with the external world.

Not all the challenges at this time of life come from career or one's partner. During the late 1990s growing attention focused on the *sandwich generation*—adults who simultaneously try to meet the competing needs of

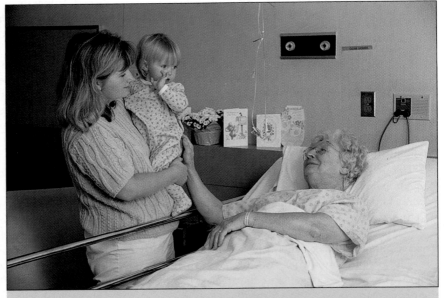

A sandwich-generation mom brings her young child to visit with her bedridden mother. Increasingly, members of the baby boom generation find themselves caring for two generations at once.

Figure 13-1

Developmental and Transitional Periods in Adulthood

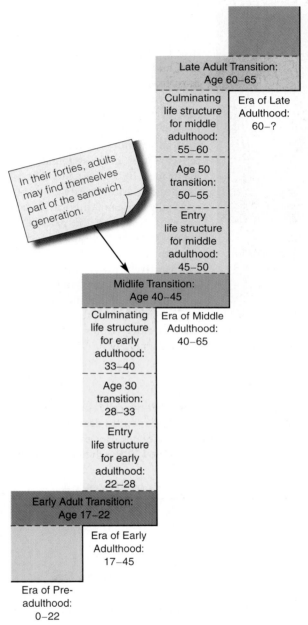

> In their forties, adults may find themselves part of the sandwich generation.

Source: Levinson 1996:18.

Think About It

Which developmental periods do you think you will find the easiest? The hardest?

their parents and of their own children. Caregiving goes in two directions: (1) to children who even as young adults may still require significant direction and (2) to aging parents whose health and economic problems may demand intervention by their adult children. According to a national survey in 1997, almost one-fourth of all households in the United States are providing informal, unpaid care for an older friend or relative. The average caregiver spends 18 hours a week in this assistance. Understandably, this constitutes a significant amount of time for the 40 percent of the caregivers who still have children under 18 (Chatzky 1999; National Alliance for Caregiving 1997; Velkoff and Lawson 1998).

The last major transition identified by Levinson occurs after age 60, and this is a time when dramatic changes take place in people's everyday lives, as we will now see.

Adjusting to Retirement

Retirement is a rite of passage that marks a critical transition from one phase of a person's life to another. Typically, there are symbolic events associated with this rite of passage, such as retirement gifts, a retirement party, and special moments on the "last day on the job." The preretirement period itself can be emotionally charged, especially if the retiree is expected to train his or her successor (Atchley 1976).

From 1950 to the mid-1990s, the average age at retirement in the United States declined, but over the last few years it has reversed direction and begun to climb. In 2000, 12.8 percent of Americans 65 and older were still working—the highest level in more than two decades. A variety of factors explains this reversal: changes in Social Security benefits, an economic shift away from hard manual labor, and workers' concern with maintaining their health insurance and pension benefits. At the same time, longevity has increased, and the quality of people's health has improved with it. According to a study released in 2000, in any given year after age 65, the elderly are now less likely to have a hospital stay or need nursing services than they were in 1993 (Liao et al. 2000; M. Walsh 2001).

Gerontologist Robert Atchley (1976) has identified several phases of the retirement experience:

- *Preretirement,* a period of anticipatory socialization as the person prepares for retirement
- *The near phase,* when the person establishes a specific departure date from his or her job
- *The honeymoon phase,* an often-euphoric period in which the person pursues activities that he or she never had time for before
- *The disenchantment phase,* in which retirees feel a sense of letdown or even depression as they cope with their new lives, which may include illness or poverty

Three generations in this family celebrate their March birthdays together. While we all move through the life course in individual ways, it is possible to identify certain developmental periods with critical transitions between the stages.

- *The reorientation phase,* which involves the development of a more realistic view of retirement alternatives
- *The stability phase,* a period in which the person has learned to deal with life after retirement in a reasonable and comfortable fashion
- *The termination phase,* which begins when the person can no longer engage in basic, day-to-day activities such as self-care and housework

As this analysis demonstrates, retirement is not a single transition but rather a series of adjustments that vary from one person to another. The length and timing of each phase will vary for each individual, depending on such factors as his or her financial and health status. In fact, a person will not necessarily go through all the phases identified by Atchley. For example, people who were forced to retire or who face financial difficulties may never experience a "honeymoon phase." A significant number of retirees continue to be part of the paid labor force of the United States, often taking part-time jobs to supplement their pension income. This is certainly the expectation of baby boomers, as Figure 13-2 shows.

Like other aspects of life in the United States, the experience of retirement varies according to gender, race, and ethnicity. White males are most likely to benefit from a structure of retirement wages as well as to have participated in a formal retirement preparation program. As a result, anticipatory socialization for retirement is most systematic for White men. By contrast, members of racial and ethnic minority groups—especially African Americans—are more likely to exit the paid labor force through disability than through retirement. Because of their comparatively lower incomes and smaller savings, men and women from racial and ethnic minority groups work intermittently after retirement more often than do older Whites (National Institute on Aging 1999a; Quadagno 1999).

Death and Dying

Among the role transitions that typically (but not always) come later in life is death. Until recently, death was viewed as a taboo topic in the United States. However, psychologist Elisabeth Kübler-Ross (1969) through her pioneering

Figure 13-2

Retirement Expectations

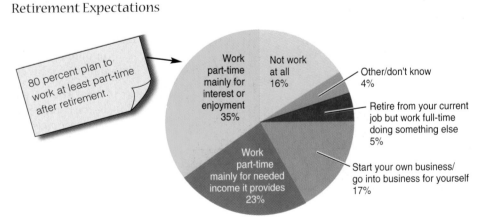

80 percent plan to work at least part-time after retirement.

Work part-time mainly for interest or enjoyment 35%

Not work at all 16%

Other/don't know 4%

Retire from your current job but work full-time doing something else 5%

Start your own business/go into business for yourself 17%

Work part-time mainly for needed income it provides 23%

Note: Survey of the baby boom generation (people born from 1946 to 1964) conducted in 1998.
Source: AARP 1999.

Coffins in Ghana sometimes reflect the way the dead lived their lives. This Methodist burial service is for a woman who died at age 85, leaving behind 11 children, 82 grandchildren, and 60 great-grandchildren. Her coffin, designed as a mother hen, features 11 chicks nestling between the wings (Secretan 1995).

book *On Death and Dying* has greatly encouraged open discussion of the process of dying.

Drawing on her work with 200 cancer patients, Kübler-Ross identified five stages of the experience of dying that a person may undergo:

1. When people finally realize that they are dying, they first *deny* the truth to themselves, their families, and their friends.
2. When denial can no longer be maintained, it is followed by a period of *anger,* which can be directed at almost anyone or anything.
3. In the stage of *bargaining*—often relatively brief—people talk about the unfulfilled goals they will pursue if they somehow recover. In effect, they are hoping to bargain with God for additional time.
4. When people realize that these deals are not realistic, they enter a stage of *depression* and experience a pervasive sense of loss.
5. The final stage, *acceptance,* is not always reached by the dying patient. Those who accept death are not happy about the prospect, but have come to terms with their fate and are ready to die in peace.

As Kübler-Ross (1969:113) notes: "It is as if the pain had gone, the struggle is over, and there comes a time for 'the final rest before the long journey' as one patient phrased it."

Despite its continued popular appeal, the Kübler-Ross five-stage theory of dying has been challenged.

Researchers often can't substantiate these stages. Moreover, this model relies on an assumption that the dying person clearly recognizes that death is nearing. Yet more than 20 percent of people in the United States age 65 and over die in nursing homes; for them and many others, an array of chronic, debilitative, degenerative diseases can mask death. Finally, critics of Kübler-Ross emphasize that even if this five-stage model is accurate for the United States, it does not apply to other cultures that deal with death quite differently (Marshall and Levy 1990; Retsinas 1988).

Functionalists would see those who are dying as fulfilling distinct social functions. Gerontologist Richard Kalish (1985) lists among the tasks of the dying: completing unfinished business, such as settling insurance and legacy matters; restoring harmony to social relationships and saying farewell to friends and family; dealing with medical care needs; and making funeral plans and other arrangements for survivors after death occurs. In accomplishing these tasks, the dying person actively contributes to meeting society's needs for smooth intergenerational transitions, role continuity, compliance with medical procedures, and minimal disruption of the social system despite the loss of one of its members.

This functionalist analysis brings to mind the cherished yet controversial concept of a "good death." One researcher described a good death among the Kaliai, a people of the South Pacific. In that culture, the dying person calls together all his relatives, settles his debts, disposes of his possessions, and then announces that it is time for him to die (Counts 1977). The Kaliai concept of a good death has a parallel in Western societies, where people may speak of a "natural death," an "appropriate death," or "death with dignity." The practice of **hospice care,** introduced in London, England, in the 1960s, is founded on this concept. Hospice workers seek to improve the quality of a dying person's last days by offering comfort and by helping the person to remain at home, or in a homelike setting at a hospital or other special facility, until the end. Currently there are more than 3,100 hospice programs serving over a half million people a year.

Although the Western ideal of the "good death" makes the experience of dying as positive as possible, some critics fear that acceptance of the concept of a good death may direct both individual efforts and social resources away from attempts to extend life. Still others argue that fatally ill

Life begins at 65 for these retirees in Georgetown, Texas, checking out a model of Sun City, a retirement community with full services.

But even at that age, Lenore is no longer unusual in our society. Today, people over 100 constitute, proportionately, the country's fastest-growing age group. They are part of the increasing proportion of the population of the United States composed of older people (Himes 2001; Rimer 1998).

As Figure 13-3 shows, in the year 1900, men and women aged 65 and older constituted only 4.1 percent of the nation's population, but by 2003, this age group will have grown to 12.6 percent. According to current projections, the over-65 segment will continue to increase throughout this century, with the "old old" (people who are 85 and older) increasing in numbers at an ever-faster rate.

In 2003, 14.8 percent of Whites are projected to be older than 65, compared to 8.5 percent of African Americans, 8.2 percent of Asian Americans, and 6.2 percent of Hispanics. These differences reflect the shorter life spans of these latter groups, as well as immigration patterns among Asians and Hispanics, who tend to be young when they enter the country. Yet people of

older people should not just passively accept death, but should forgo further treatment in order to reduce public health care expenditures. As we will see in the social policy section, such issues are at the heart of current debates over the right to die and physician-assisted suicide (Counts 1977; Hospice Foundation of America 2002).

Recent studies in the United States suggest that, in many varied ways, people have broken through the historic taboos about death and are attempting to arrange certain aspects of the idealized "good death." For example, bereavement practices—once highly socially structured—are becoming increasingly varied and therapeutic. More and more people are actively addressing the inevitability of death by making wills, leaving "living wills" (health care proxies that explain their feelings about the use of life-support equipment), donating organs, and providing instructions for family members about funerals, cremations, and burials. Given medical and technological advances and a breakthrough in open discussion and negotiation regarding death and dying, it is more possible than ever that "good deaths" can become a social norm in the United States (La Ganga 1999; Riley 1992).

Age Stratification in the United States

The "Graying of America"

When Lenore Schaefer, a ballroom dancer, tried to get on the *Tonight Show,* she was told she was "too young": she was in her early 90s. When she turned 101, she made it.

Figure 13-3

Actual and Projected Growth of the Elderly Population of the United States

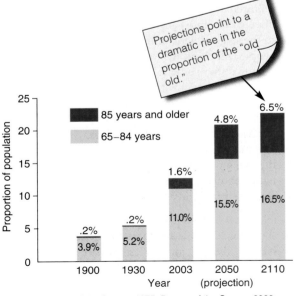

Projections point to a dramatic rise in the proportion of the "old old."

Sources: Bureau of the Census 1975; Bureau of the Census 2000e.

Figure 13-4

Twenty-six Floridas by 2025

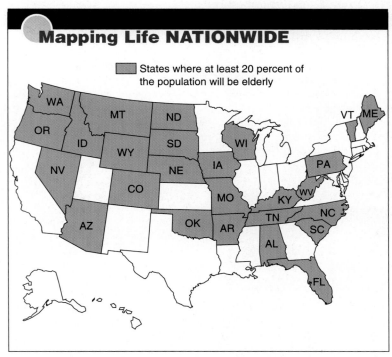

Mapping Life NATIONWIDE

States where at least 20 percent of the population will be elderly

Source: Bureau of the Census in Yax 1999.

color are increasing their presence among the elderly population of the United States (Bureau of the Census 2000e).

The highest proportion of older people are found in Florida, Pennsylvania, Rhode Island, Iowa, West Virginia, and Arkansas. However, many more states are undergoing an aging trend. In 2000, Florida was the state most populated by the elderly, with 17.6 percent of the population over the age of 65. Yet, as Figure 13-4 shows, in about 25 years, more than half of the states will have a greater proportion of elderly than Florida does now (Hetzel and Smith 2001).

While the United States is noticeably graying, the nation's older citizens are in a sense getting younger, owing to improved health and nutrition. Researchers at the National Institute on Aging (1999b) have found a decrease in chronic disability in every age category. From the perspective of activity theory, this welcome change should be encouraged (Horn and Meer 1987).

The graying of the United States is a phenomenon that can no longer be ignored—either by social scientists or by government policymakers. Advocacy groups on behalf of the elderly have emerged and spoken out on a wide range of issues (as we will see later in the chapter). Politicians court the votes of older people, since they are the age group most likely to register and most likely to vote. In fact, in the 2000 presidential race (Bush versus Gore), people 60 or older made up 22 percent of the total vote (Berke 2001).

Wealth and Income

There is significant variation in wealth and poverty among the nation's older people. Some individuals and couples find themselves poor in part because of fixed pensions and skyrocketing health care costs (see Chapter 19). Nevertheless, as a group, older people in the United States are neither homogeneous nor poor. The typical elderly person enjoys a standard of living that is much higher than at any point in the nation's past. Class differences among the elderly remain evident but tend to narrow somewhat: Those older people who enjoyed middle-class incomes while younger tend to remain better off after retirement than those who previously had lower incomes, but the financial gap lessens a bit (Smith and Tillipman 2000).

To some extent, older people owe their overall improved standard of living to a greater accumulation of wealth—in the form of home ownership, private pensions, and other financial assets. But much of the improvement is due to more generous Social Security benefits. While modest when compared with other countries' pension programs, Social Security nevertheless provides 40 percent of all income received by older people in the United States. Currently, about one-tenth of the nation's elderly population lives below the poverty line. At the extreme end of poverty are those groups who were more likely to be poor at earlier points in the life cycle: female-headed households and racial and ethnic minorities. Box 13-2 examines the reasons why members of minority groups have not kept pace with the gains made by other seniors (AARP 2001; Smith and Tillipman 2000).

Viewed from a conflict perspective, it is not surprising that older women experience a double burden; the same is true of elderly members of racial and ethnic minorities. For example, in 2000 the proportion of older Latinos with incomes below the poverty level (18.8 percent) was more than twice as large as the proportion of older non-Hispanic Whites (8.3 percent). Moreover, 10.3 percent of older Americans and 22.3 percent of older African Americans fell below the federal government's poverty line (Dalaker 2001:23–26).

Ageism

Physician Robert Butler (1990) became concerned thirty years ago when he learned a housing development near where he lived in metropolitan D.C. barred the elderly from buying homes. He coined the term *ageism* to refer to

Social Inequality
13-2 Theory of Cumulative Disadvantage

Steve, a White male, grew up in a middle-class family in Pittsburgh. His parents, while not well off, were able to send him through college. Steve worked nights to pay his way through graduate school and obtained a masters in business. He joined a brokerage business and worked his way up the corporate ladder. By the time he retired at 65 as a vice president of the company, Steve had accumulated a nest egg of savings through stock and bond purchases, owned a house in an affluent suburb of Philadelphia, and could look forward to substantial monthly pension payments as well as Social Security.

Contrast Steve's life course with that of James, a Black male from Chicago's South Side. James was raised by a single mother, who generally depended on welfare payments to put food on the table. James actually liked the structure of school but felt pressure to contribute income to the family, so he dropped out of high school to work as an inventory clerk in a warehouse, for little more than minimum wage. When the warehouse closed he bounced around from job to job, with long periods of unemployment. Health

problems also sidelined him. James was never able to save money or to buy a home or an apartment; he felt lucky just to make the rent each month. He never worked anyplace long enough to earn a pension. In his old age James must make do with whatever Social Security income he is entitled to.

James's story illustrates the increasing inequality faced by aging racial and ethnic group members as a result of diminished life chances. While senior citizens as a group have made economic strides, members of racial minorities have not kept pace. Sociologist Angela O'Rand has advanced the notion of *cumulative disadvantage* over the life course to explain what is happening. Two biases work against minority group members: First, they are less likely than Whites to have steady work histories, which would allow

> While senior citizens as a group have made economic strides, members of racial minorities have not kept pace.

them to accumulate wealth (such as a home) that can serve as a valuable nest egg in later years. For example, in 2000 about 47 percent of African Americans owned a home compared to 74 percent of non-Hispanic Whites. The second bias is related to the first. Members of racial minorities are less likely than Whites to be served by pension programs that provide steady income during retirement.

In short, those who are advantaged early in life have more opportunity to receive formal schooling, to obtain a job that leads to advancement up the ladder, to save for retirement, and to have access to dependable retirement savings programs. Their *advantages* accumulate over the life course, while the *disadvantages* suffered by racial and ethnic groups accumulate.

Let's Discuss

1. How did your grandparents' life chances affect the quality of life in their later years?
2. Would a conflict theorist agree with the notion of cumulative disadvantage? Why or why not?

Sources: Bureau of the Census 2001d; Oliver and Shapiro 1995; O'Rand 1996.

---

this differential treatment. Ageism refers to prejudice and discrimination against people because of their age. We may choose to assume someone cannot handle a rigorous job because they are "too old" or we may refuse to give someone a job with authority because they are "too young."

Ageism is especially difficult against the old because at least youthful recipients know that in time they will be "old enough." For many, old age symbolizes disease. With ageism all too common in the United States, it is hardly surprising that older people are barely visible on television. A content analysis of fictional television characters in the early 1990s revealed that only 2 percent were age 65 and over—even though this age group accounted for about 13 percent of the nation's population. A second study found older women particularly underrepresented

on television. But unfair representation based on age is not limited to the elderly. News broadcasts, for example, underrepresent the presence of children in society. By portraying children primarily as victims or as criminals, news reporters exaggerate their role in antisocial behavior. Such treatment of both the young and old are one reason that the media images we receive are detached from social reality (Children Now 2001; Robinson and Skill 1993; Vernon et al. 1990).

Imagine

It is September and you are channel surfing through the new fall TV series. How likely are you to watch a television show that is based on older characters who spend a lot of time together?

This Native American woman carries a *triple* burden: she is female in a society that favors males, elderly in a society that values youth, and a minority member in a society that favors Whites.

Competition in the Labor Force

Participation in paid work is not typical after the age of 65, but it is common. In 2001, 31 percent of the men aged 65 to 69 and 20 percent of the women participated in the paid labor force. While some people view these workers as experienced contributors to the labor force, others see them as "job stealers," a biased judgment similar to that directed against illegal immigrants.

p. 275 ← This mistaken belief not only intensifies age conflict, but leads to age discrimination (Himes 2001).

While firing people simply because they are old violates federal laws, courts have upheld the right to lay off older workers for economic reasons. Critics contend that later the same firms hire young, cheaper workers to replace experienced older workers. As economic growth began to slow in 2001 and companies cut back on their work forces, complaints of age bias grew sharply as older workers began to suspect they were assuming a disproportionate share of the layoffs (Equal Employment Opportunity Commission 2001).

A controlled experiment conducted in 1993 by the AARP confirmed that older people often face discrimination when applying for jobs. Comparable résumés for two applicants—one 57 years old and the other 32 years old—were sent to 775 large firms and employment agencies around the United States. In situations for which positions were actually available, the younger applicant received a favorable response 43 percent of the time. By contrast, the older applicant received favorable responses less than half as often (only 17 percent of the time). One Fortune 500 corporation asked the younger applicant for more information, while it informed the older applicant that no appropriate positions were open (Bendick et al. 1993).

In contrast to the negative stereotypes, researchers have found that older workers can be an *asset* for employers. According to a study issued in 1991, older workers can be retrained in new technologies, have lower rates of absenteeism than younger employees, and are often more effective salespeople. The study focused on two corporations

About 30 percent of older workers choose to remain on the job past the usual retirement age. Research shows they can be retrained in new technologies and are more dependable than younger workers.

Research in Action

13-3 Crime against the Elderly

With regard to crime, the elderly are commonly stereotyped as weak and passive victims, unable to defend themselves. Is there any truth to this preconception?

According to research on victimization of the elderly, older people are actually much less likely than younger ones to become the target of property and violent crimes. People aged 50 to 64 are victimized at less than half the rate of people in their 30s. The rate for people aged 65 or older is even lower: in 2000, about 50 percent of people aged 20 to 24 reported some type of crime against themselves, compared to only 4 percent of those older than 65. In part, different lifestyles may account for these differences between age groups. Compared with crimes involving younger people, most crimes against the elderly occur during daylight hours, in or near their homes.

Whatever the crime, however, older victims tend to suffer greater physical, mental, and financial injury than younger victims. The elderly are less likely than other victims of violent crime to defend

> **People aged 50 to 64 are victimized at less than half the rate of people in their 30s.**

themselves by arguing with or attacking an offender, running away, or calling for help. More than one in five elderly victims sustain injuries in nonlethal violent confrontations. The elderly are also especially vulnerable to consumer fraud: a 1999 study found that 56 percent of those who had suffered telemarketing fraud were aged 50 or older. When they seek assistance from the police, elderly victims of these crimes worry that they will appear incompetent to investigators. They may also fear that family members and friends will react negatively. Crime, then, takes a special toll on the elderly.

Let's Discuss

1. Have any of your elderly relatives or neighbors been victims of crime? If so, what type of crime was involved? Did the person suffer serious harm?
2. Why do you think younger people have much higher rates of victimization than older people? List as many reasons as you can.

Sources: Klaus 2000; Rennison 2001; Department of Justice 2001a, 2001b.

---

based in the United States (the hotel chain Days Inns of America and the holding company Travelers Corporation of Hartford) and a British retail chain—all of which have long-term experience in hiring workers age 50 and over. An official of the private fund that commissioned the study concluded, "We have here the first systematic hard-nosed economic analysis showing older workers are good investments" (Telsch 1991:A16).

Research is slowly beginning to dispel other stereotypes of the elderly, including the idea that they are easily victimized. Box 13-3 discusses the statistics on crimes against the elderly.

The Elderly: Emergence of a Collective Consciousness

During the 1960s, students at colleges and universities across the country, advocating "student power," collectively demanded a role in the governance of educational institutions. In the following decade, the 1970s, many older people became aware that *they* were being treated as second-class citizens and also turned to collective action.

The largest organization representing the nation's elderly is the AARP, founded in 1958 by a retired school principal who was having difficulty getting insurance because of age prejudice. Many of AARP's services involve discounts and insurance for its 33.4 million members (45 percent of Americans aged 50 or older), but the organization also functions as a powerful lobbying group. Recognizing that many elderly are still gainfully employed, it has dropped its full name, American Association of *Retired* Persons.

The potential power of AARP is enormous; it is the third-largest voluntary association in the United States (behind only the Roman Catholic church and the American Automobile Association) and represents one out of every four registered voters in the United States. The AARP has endorsed voter registration campaigns, nursing home reforms, and pension reforms. As an acknowledgment of its difficulties in recruiting members of racial and ethnic minority groups, AARP began a Minority Affairs Initiative. The spokeswoman of this initiative, Margaret Dixon, became AARP's first African American president in 1996 (Holmes 2001; Rosenblatt 2000).

People grow old in many different ways. Not all the elderly face the same challenges or enjoy the same resources. While the AARP lobbies to protect the elderly in general, other groups work in more specific ways. For

Members of SAGE, Senior Action in a Gay Environment, take part in a gay pride demonstration in New York City. This nationwide organization focuses on the special needs of gay seniors.

homosexuals. One such group, Senior Action in a Gay Environment (SAGE), was established in New York City in 1978 and now oversees a nationwide network of local community groups. Like more traditional senior citizens' groups, SAGE sponsors workshops, classes, dances, and food deliveries to the homebound. At the same time, SAGE must deal with special concerns. Many gay couples find that nursing homes won't allow them to share a room. In addition, nearly 90 percent of gay seniors today have no children, and more than two-thirds live alone—twice the percentage of heterosexual seniors. It's not surprising that SAGE has surfaced to deal with these large-scale special needs (Rosenberg 2001; Senior Action in a Gay Environment 1999).

example, the National Committee to Preserve Social Security and Medicare, founded in 1982, successfully lobbied Congress to keep Medicare benefits for the ailing poor elderly. Other large special interest groups represent retired federal employees, retired teachers, and retired union workers (Quadagno 2002).

Still another manifestation of the new awareness of older people is the formation of organizations for elderly

The elderly in the United States are better off today financially and physically than ever before. Many of them have strong financial assets and medical care packages that will take care of most any health need. But, as we have seen, a significant segment is impoverished, faced with the prospect of declining health and mounting medical bills. And some older people may now have to add being aged to a lifetime of discrimination. As in all other stages of the life course, the aged constitute a diverse group in the United States and around the world.

SOCIAL POLICY AND AGE STRATIFICATION

The Right to Die Worldwide

www.mhhe.com
/schaefer8

The Issue

On August 4, 1993, Dr. Jack Kevorkian, a retired pathologist, helped a 30-year-old Michigan man with Lou Gehrig's disease commit suicide in a van. The patient died after inhaling carbon monoxide through a mask designed by Dr. Kevorkian; in doing so, he became the 17th person to commit suicide with Kevorkian's assistance. Kevorkian was openly challenging a Michigan law (aimed at him) that makes it a felony crime—punishable by up to four years in jail—to assist in a suicide. Since then Kevorkian has assisted in numerous other suicides, but it was not until he did it on television in

1998 that charges brought against him resulted in his imprisonment for second-degree murder.

The issue of physician-assisted suicide is but one aspect of the larger debate in the United States and other countries over the ethics of suicide and euthanasia. The term *euthanasia* has been defined as the "act of bringing about the death of a hopelessly ill and suffering person in a relatively quick and painless way for reasons of mercy" (Council on Ethical and Judicial Affairs, American Medical Association 1992:2, 229). This type of mercy killing reminds us of the ideal of "good death" discussed earlier in the chapter. The debate over euthanasia and assisted suicide often focuses on cases involving older people, though it can involve younger adults with terminal and degenerative diseases, or even children.

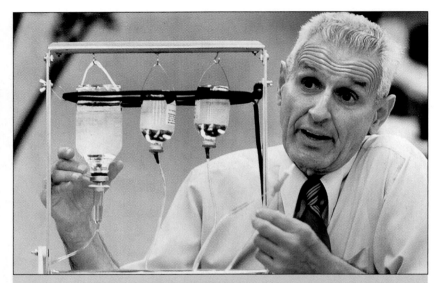

Dr. Jack Kevorkian with the apparatus that administers a lethal injection to those who want assistance in suicide.

The Setting

Many societies are known to have practiced *senilicide*—"killing of the old"—because of extreme difficulties in providing basic necessities such as food and shelter. In a study of the treatment of the elderly in 41 nonindustrialized societies, Anthony Glascock (1990) found that some form of "death-hastening" behavior was present in 21 of them. Killing of the elderly was evident in 14 of these societies, while abandoning of older people was evident in 8 societies. Typically, such death hastening occurs when older people become decrepit and are viewed as "already dead." Death hastening in these nonindustrialized cultures is open and socially approved. Family members generally make decisions, often after open consultation with those about to die.

Currently, public policy in the United States does not permit *active euthanasia* (such as a deliberate injection of lethal drugs to a terminally ill patient) or physician-assisted suicide. Although suicide itself is no longer a crime, assisting suicide is illegal in at least 29 states. There is greater legal tolerance today for *passive euthanasia* (such as disconnecting life-support equipment from a comatose patient).

Sociological Insights

Although formal norms concerning euthanasia may be in flux, informal norms seem to permit mercy killings. According to an estimate by the American Hospital Association, as many as 70 percent of all deaths in the United States are quietly negotiated, with patients, family members, and physicians agreeing not to use life-support technology. In an informal poll of internists, one in five reported that he or she had assisted or helped cause the death of a patient. In a period in which AIDS-related deaths are common, an AIDS underground is known to share information and assistance regarding suicide (Gibbs 1993; Martinez 1993).

p. 124

Conflict theorists ask questions about the values raised by such decisions. By endorsing physician-assisted suicide, are we devaluing the disabled through an acceptance of their premature death? Critics note that we all are only temporarily able-bodied; disease or a speeding automobile can place any one of us among the disabled. By establishing a precedent for ending the lives of selected disabled people, we may unwittingly contribute to negative social views and labeling of all disabled people. Further reflecting the conflict perspective, gerontologist Elizabeth Markson (1992:6) argues that the "powerless, poor or undesirable are at special risk of being 'encouraged' to choose assisted death."

Critics of euthanasia charge that many of its supporters are guilty of ageism and other forms of bias. In a society that commonly discriminates against the elderly and people with disabilities, medical authorities and even family members may decide too quickly that such people should die "for their own good" or (in a view somewhat reminiscent of disengagement theory) "for the good of society." It is also feared that society may use euthanasia to reduce health care costs—rather than striving to make life better for those near the end. Older people may even feel compelled to (prematurely) end their lives to ease the emotional and financial burdens on family members and friends (Glascock 1990:45; *New York Times* 1993b; Richman 1992).

Policy Initiatives

In the industrialized world, euthanasia is widely accepted only in the Netherlands, where physicians perform about 4,000 such procedures a year. According to Dutch law, euthanasia is legal if a patient has voluntarily requested assistance in committing suicide and has received a second medical opinion. National surveys consistently show that 90 percent of the Dutch people, including doctors, accept the practice of euthanasia and physician-assisted suicide (Cloud 2001; Simons 2000).

In the United States, the only state to allow assisted suicide is Oregon, where the Death with Dignity Act became law in 1997. At least 70 terminally ill Oregonians have chosen to end their lives since the law took effect. Similar measures have failed to win support in at least 20 other states, where the issue has encountered sharp opposition. In 2001, President Bush's administration sought to take action against doctors who prescribe lethal drugs for terminally ill patients (Verhovek 2001).

Advances in technology allow us to prolong life in ways that were unimaginable decades ago. But should people be forced or expected to prolong lives that are unbearably painful or that are, in effect, "lifeless"? Unfortunately, medical and technological advances cannot provide answers to complex ethical, legal, and political questions.

Let's Discuss

1. Why do you think "death-hastening" behavior is common in nonindustrialized countries?
2. In what ways are conflict theory and disengagement theory relevant in the debate over the "right to die"?
3. Do you think someone should be allowed to choose to die? Why or why not?

Chapter Resources

Summary

Age, like gender and race, is an ascribed status that forms the basis for social differentiation. This chapter examines theories regarding the aging process, role transitions in the life course, age stratification in the United States, the growing political activism of the nation's elderly population, and the controversy surrounding the right to die.

1. Like other forms of stratification, age stratification varies from culture to culture.
2. In the United States, "being old" is a master status that seems to overshadow all others.
3. The particular problems of the aged have become the focus for a specialized area of research and inquiry known as *gerontology.*
4. *Disengagement theory* implicitly suggests that society should help older people to withdraw from their accustomed social roles, whereas *activity theory* argues that the elderly person who remains active and socially involved will be better adjusted.

5. From a conflict perspective, the low status of older people is reflected in prejudice and discrimination against them and unfair job practices.
6. About 40 percent of those who look after their elderly relatives still have children to care for; these people have been dubbed the *sandwich generation.*
7. As we age, we go through role transitions, including adjustment to retirement and preparation for death.
8. An increasing proportion of the population of the United States is composed of older people.
9. *Ageism* reflects a deep uneasiness on the part of younger people about growing old.
10. The American Association of Retired Persons (AARP) is a powerful lobbying group that backs legislation to benefit senior citizens.
11. The "right to die" often entails physician-assisted suicide, a controversial issue worldwide.

Critical Thinking Questions

1. Are there elderly students at your college or university? How are they treated by younger students and by faculty members? Is there a subculture of older students? How do younger students view faculty members in their fifties and sixties?
2. Is age segregation functional or dysfunctional for older people in the United States? Is it functional or

dysfunctional for society as a whole? What are the manifest functions, the latent functions, and the dysfunctions of age segregation?
3. If you were hired to run a senior center where you live, how would you use what you have learned in this chapter to better the lives of your community's seniors?

Key Terms

Activity theory An interactionist theory of aging that argues that elderly people who remain active and socially involved will be best-adjusted. (page 330)

Ageism Prejudice and discrimination based on a person's age. (337)

Disengagement theory A functionalist theory of aging that contends that society and the aging individual mutually sever many of their relationships. (328)

Euthanasia The act of bringing about the death of a hopelessly ill and suffering person in a relatively quick and painless way for reasons of mercy. (341)

Gerontology The scientific study of the sociological and psychological aspects of aging and the problems of the aged. (328)

Hospice care Treatment of the terminally ill in their own homes, or in special hospital units or other facilities, with the goal of helping them to die easily, without pain. (335)

Midlife crisis A stressful period of self-evaluation that begins about age 40. (332)

Sandwich generation The generation of adults who simultaneously try to meet the competing needs of their parents and their own children. (332)

Senilicide The killing of the aged. (342)

Additional Readings

BOOKS

AARP. 2001. *Beyond 50—A Report to the Nation on Economic Security.* Washington, D.C.: AARP. A detailed report on the social circumstances and trends affecting the 76 million Americans age 50 and over. (This report can be accessed electronically at **www.aarp.org.**)

Best, Amy L. 2000. *Prom Night: Youth, Schools and Popular Culture.* New York: Routledge. A sociologist looks at a significant rite of passage for many adolescents in the United States.

Dychtwald, Ken. 1999. *Age Power: How the 21st Century Will Be Ruled by the New Old.* New York: Putnam. A gerontologist projects social patterns and aging into the future.

Howe, Neil, and Bill Strauss. 1993. *13th Gen: Abort, Retry, Ignore, Fail?* New York: Vintage. A heavily illustrated view of the lifestyles and beliefs of the thirteenth generation in the United States (people born between 1961 and 1981).

Posner, Richard. 1995. *Aging and Old Age.* Chicago: University of Chicago Press. A former law professor and the chief judge of a federal appeals court, Posner analyzes old age in the United States, the voting

patterns of the elderly, ageism, physician-assisted suicide, and social service programs intended to assist older people.

Quadagno, Jill. 2002. *Aging and the Life Course: An Introduction to Social Gerontology,* 2nd ed. New York: McGraw-Hill. A sociological overview not only of the elderly but of the entire process of aging.

Savishinsky, Joel S. 2000. *Breaking the Watch: The Meanings of Retirement in America.* Ithaca, NY: Cornell University Press. A gerontologist considers how workers in the United States approach the end of full-time employment.

JOURNALS

Among the journals that focus on issues of aging and age stratification are *Ageing and Society* (founded in 1981), *Ageing International (1994), Contemporary Gerontology* (1994), *Death Studies* (1976), *Generations* (1976), *The Gerontologist* (1961), *Journal of Aging and Ethnicity* (1996), *Journal of Applied Gerontology* (1982), *Journal of Cross-Cultural Gerontology* (1986), *Journal of Gerontology* (1946), *Research on Aging* (1979), and *Youth and Society* (1968).

Technology Resources

Internet Connection

/schaefer8 *Note: While all the URLs listed were current as of the printing of this book, these sites often change. Please check our website (**http://www. mhhe.com/schaefer8**) for updates and hyperlinks to this exercise and additional exercises.*

1. The Administration on Aging (AoA) offers information of interest to citizens and gerontologists. Go to the AoA's site (**http://www.aoa.gov**), link to "Statistics About Older People," and read "A Profile of Older Americans." Answer the following questions:

(a) In 2000, how many people in the United States were 65 years of age and older? What estimate does the site provide for how many people will be 65 and older in the year 2030?

(b) What percentage of older U.S. men and women were married in 2000? Divorced? Widowed?

(c) What were the current ethnic and racial demographics of older U.S. citizens in 2000?

(d) Find your state in the "Geographic Location" section. How many people 65 and older lived in your state in 2000?

(e) Return to the homepage and link to "Quick Index."

(f) What forms can elder abuse take? About how many people are victims of this form of abuse?

(g) Do you believe that enough attention is given by the media and government to issues of importance to older citizens? Why or why not?

(h) How might the application of the theories presented on pages 328–331 of your textbook be useful in creating policies and programs aimed at alleviating problems faced by older citizens?

2. The Administration on Aging offers many services, one of which is the National Aging Information Center (NAIC). Go to the AoA's website (**http://www.aoa.gov/**) and click on "Quick Index." Select "National Aging Information Center," then "Web Resources." Scroll down the page to "Age Discrimination" and click on "Ageism." Read the section titled "Aging Internet Information Note: Ageism" and answer the following questions:

(a) What is the definition of ageism, according to the NAIC?

(b) What efforts have been made to combat ageism, and by whom?

(c) Read the article titled "Ageism: An Introduction." What is Webster University's definition of ageism?

(d) How does ageism differ from other "isms"?

(e) What are some of the problems that are found in research on ageism?

(f) What are some of the theoretical bases of ageism?

(g) Briefly discuss two studies of ageism.

3. The social policy section in this chapter discusses the right to die, an issue that is hotly debated not just in the United States, but in other countries. Facts on File/News Service, a World Almanac Education Group Company (**http://www.facts. com/icof/i00057.htm**) offers a great deal of information on the controversy surrounding assisted suicide. Explore the site and answer the following questions:

(a) When did the campaign to legalize assisted suicide begin in the United States?

(b) When the state of Oregon passed a law legalizing assisted suicide, how long did the courts block its implementation? What was the Supreme Court's position on the law?

(c) How did Oregonians react to a ballot initiative to repeal the law?

(d) Briefly summarize the arguments of both opponents to and proponents of assisted suicide.

(e) Explain the "slippery slope" debate.

(f) Conflict theorists wonder whether physician-assisted suicide devalues the disabled. Do you think it does? Explain.

(g) Do you think older Oregonians will feel compelled to end their lives prematurely in order to ease the emotional and financial burdens on their family and friends? Explain.

Online Learning Center www.mhhe.com/schaefer8

Aging is a topic that is important to all of us no matter how old we are. The Administration on Aging (AoA) offers online information of interest to people of all ages. To learn about this information, visit the student center of the Online Learning Center at **www.mhhe.com/schaefer8** and link to "Internet Exercises." Scroll down to exercise 3, link to the AoA, and learn about important issues related to aging such as elder abuse and age discrimination.

THE FAMILY AND INTIMATE RELATIONSHIPS

Reproductive technology is changing people's personal lives, raising questions about ethics and social policy in the process. For the first time, mothers can positively identify the fathers of their children, and parents can manipulate their children's genes—a prospect many people find disturbing.

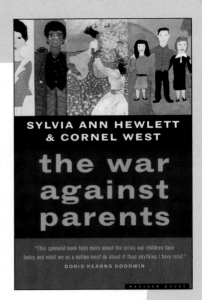

From the time of the breakdown of my marriage to Cliff's mother in 1979 to my marriage to Elleni in 1990, I was forced to deal with a difficult but nonetheless standard set of problems. My ex-wife was awarded custody of two-year-old Cliff and then decided to move to Atlanta. I had no recourse, legal or otherwise. And yet in my struggle to build a close relationship with my son, I now had to cope with an almost impossible set of barriers. Hundreds of miles separated me from Cliff, and I had limited visitation rights—a few specified weekends during the year plus three months in the summer. Besides which, what would I do with my son during our precious time together? My bachelor homes did not provide a supportive context for a four-year-old or a nine-year-old—there were no kids on the block, no basketball hoop in the back yard. But I wrestled with these problems and over time developed a strategy that worked, albeit imperfectly.

I hit upon this great solution for the summers. I would take Cliff back to Sacramento, back to the loving, child-centered home that had been so good to me and my siblings a generation ago. It required a lot of stretching and bending of the rules, but I organized life so that I really could take two and a half months out of the year. It meant postponing book deadlines and taming an almost impossible travel schedule, but it was well worth it. Those summers in Sacramento stand out like jewels in my memory. My parents' home turned out to be a profoundly healing place in which Cliff and I could reach out to one another. It provided the deeply needed (and yet so hard to contrive) rhythms and routines of normal family life. Three meals a day; regular bedtimes; clean clothes; a bevy of cousins—Kahnie, Phillip and Phyllis, Cornel and Erika—just around the corner, on tap for casual play; bicycles and baseball gear in the garage all ready to be put to use whenever a grownup was available. And hovering in the backgrounds, loving, eagle-eyed grandparents. . . . The evening meal was particularly important, as all three generations gathered for a cookout in the back yard. Conversation and laughter flowed, advice was sought and help was freely offered, jokes and stories were traded, and the children, spellbound, hung on the edges, absorbing the spirit and the meaning of family life.

The rest of the year was a struggle. I maintained regular telephone contact with Cliff, calling him several times a week just to hear his voice and shoot the breeze. But in the rushed, tantalizing visits around Thanksgiving, Christmas, and Easter, it was always hard not to lapse into the role of being a "good-time dad," showering gifts on him in an attempt to make up for real time or a deeper agenda. *(Hewlett and West 1998:21–22)* ■

Additional information about this excerpt and about those that open each subsequent chapter can be found in the SocWorld CD-ROM that accompanies this text.

In this excerpt from *The War Against Parents* philosophy scholar Cornel West underscores how deeply family life has been altered by divorce, one of many social factors that have gradually but inevitably turned the traditional nuclear family on its head. The family of today is not what it was a century ago or even a generation ago. New roles, new gender distinctions, new child-rearing patterns have all combined to create new forms of family life. Today, for example, we are seeing more and more women take the breadwinner's role, whether married or as a single parent. Blended families—the result of divorce and remarriage—are almost the norm. And many people are seeking intimate relationships outside marriage, whether it be in gay partnerships or in cohabiting arrangements.

This chapter addresses family and intimate relationships in the United States as well as in other parts of the world. As we will see, family patterns differ from one culture to another and even within the same culture. Despite the differences, however, the family is universal—found in every culture. A *family* can be defined as a set of people related by blood, marriage or some other agreed-upon relationship, or adoption, who share the primary responsibility for reproduction and caring for members of society.

What are families in different parts of the world like? How do people select their mates? When a marriage fails, how does the divorce affect the children? What are the alternatives to the nuclear family, and how prevalent are they? In this chapter we will look at the family and intimate relationships theoretically, from the functionalist, conflict, and interactionist points of view. We'll examine variations in marital patterns and family life, including child rearing, paying particular attention to the increasing numbers of people in dual-income and single-parent families. We'll examine divorce in the United States, and consider diverse lifestyles such as cohabitation, lesbian and gay relationships, and marriage without children. In the social policy section we will confront the controversial issues surrounding new reproductive technologies. ■

● Global View of the Family

Among Tibetans, a woman may be simultaneously married to more than one man, usually brothers. This system allows sons to share the limited amount of good land. A Hopi woman may divorce her husband by placing her belongings outside the door. A Trobriand Island couple signals marriage by sitting in public on a porch eating yams provided by the bride's mother. She continues to provide cooked yams for a year while the groom's family offers in exchange such valuables as stone axes and clay pots (Haviland 1999).

As these examples illustrate, there are many variations in "the family" from culture to culture. Yet the family as a social institution is present in all cultures. Moreover, certain general principles concerning its composition, kinship patterns, and authority patterns are universal.

Composition: What Is the Family?

If we were to take our information on what a family is from what we see on television, we might come up with some very strange scenarios. The media don't always present a realistic view of the family. Moreover, many people still think of the family in very narrow terms—as a married couple and their unmarried children living together, like the family in the old *Cosby Show* or *Family Ties* or even *Dawson's Creek*. However, this is but one type of family, what sociologists refer to as a *nuclear family*. The term *nuclear family* is well chosen, since this type of family serves as the nucleus, or core, upon which larger family groups are built.

Most people in the United States see the nuclear family as the preferred family arrangement. Yet, as Figure 14-1 shows, by 1999 only about a third of the nation's family households fit this model. The proportion of households in the United States composed of married couples with children at home has decreased steadily over the last 30 years, and is expected to continue shrinking. At the same time, the number of single-parent households has increased (see Figure 14-1). Similar trends are evident in other industrialized nations, including Canada, Great Britain, and Japan.

A family in which relatives—such as grandparents, aunts, or uncles—live in the same home as parents and their children is known as an *extended family*. Although not common, such living arrangements do exist in the United States. The structure of the extended family offers certain advantages over that of the nuclear family. Crises such as death, divorce, and illness put less strain on family members, since there are more people who can provide assistance and emotional support. In addition, the extended family constitutes a larger economic unit than the nuclear family. If the family is engaged in a common

In wedding ceremonies in Sumatra, Indonesia, the bride's headdress indicates her village and her social status—the more elaborate the headdress, the higher her status. After she is married, the bride and her husband live with her maternal family, and all property passes from mother to daughter.

Figure 14-1

Types of Family Households in the United States, 1980, 2000, and 2010

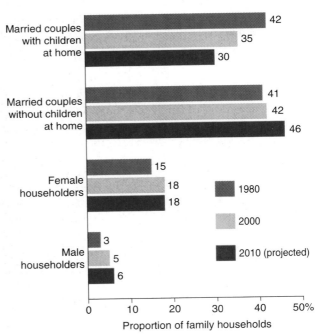

Note: "Children" refers to children under 18. Not included are unrelated people living together with no children present. Because of rounding, numbers may not total 100 percent.

Source: Bureau of the Census 1998c:61,62; 2001a:49.

enterprise—a farm or a small business—the additional family members may represent the difference between prosperity and failure.

In considering these differing family types, we have limited ourselves to the form of marriage that is characteristic of the United States—monogamy. The term *monogamy* describes a form of marriage in which one woman and one man are married only to each other. Some observers, noting the high rate of divorce in the United States, have suggested that "serial monogamy" is a more accurate description of the form that monogamy takes in the United States. Under *serial monogamy,* a person may have several spouses in his or her life but only one spouse at a time.

Some cultures allow an individual to have several husbands or wives simultaneously. This form of marriage is known as *polygamy.* In fact, most societies throughout the world, past and present, have preferred polygamy to monogamy. Anthropologist George Murdock (1949, 1957) sampled 565 societies and found that more than 80 percent had some type of polygamy as their preferred form. While polygamy steadily declined through most of

the twentieth century, in at least five countries in Africa 20 percent of men are still in polygamous marriages (Population Reference Bureau 1996).

There are two basic types of polygamy. According to Murdock, the most common—endorsed by the majority of cultures he sampled—was *polygyny.* Polygyny refers to the marriage of a man to more than one woman at the same time. The various wives are often sisters, who are expected to hold similar values and have already had experience sharing a household. In polygynous societies, relatively few men actually have multiple spouses. Most individuals live in typical monogamous families; having multiple wives is viewed as a mark of status.

The other principal variation of polygamy is *polyandry,* under which a woman can have more than one husband at the same time. This is the case in the culture of the Todas of southern India. Polyandry, however, tends to be exceedingly rare in the world today. It has been accepted by some extremely poor societies that practice female infanticide (the killing of baby girls) and thus have a relatively small number of women. Like many other societies, polyandrous cultures devalue the social worth of women.

Kinship Patterns: To Whom Are We Related?

Many of us can trace our roots by looking at a family tree or listening to elderly family members tell us about their lives—and about the lives of ancestors who died long before we were even born. Yet a person's lineage is more than simply a personal history; it also reflects societal patterns that govern descent. In every culture, children encounter relatives to whom they are expected to show an emotional attachment. The state of being related to others is called **kinship.** Kinship is culturally learned and is not totally determined by biological or marital ties. For example, adoption creates a kinship tie that is legally acknowledged and socially accepted.

The family and the kin group are not necessarily one and the same. Whereas the family is a household unit, kin do not always live together or function as a collective body on a daily basis. Kin groups include aunts, uncles, cousins, in-laws, and so forth. In a society such as the United States, the kinship group may come together only rarely, as for a wedding or funeral. However, kinship ties frequently create obligations and responsibilities. We may feel compelled to assist our kin and feel free to call upon relatives for many types of aid, including loans and baby-sitting.

How do we identify kinship groups? The principle of descent assigns people to kinship groups according to their relationship to an individual's mother or father. There are three primary ways of determining descent. The United States follows the system of **bilateral descent,** which means that both sides of a person's family are regarded as equally important. For example, no higher value is given to the brothers of one's father as opposed to the brothers of one's mother.

Most societies—according to George Murdock, 64 percent—give preference to one side of the family or the other in tracing descent. **Patrilineal** (from Latin *pater,* "father") **descent** indicates that only the father's relatives are important in terms of property, inheritance, and emotional ties. Conversely, in societies that favor **matrilineal** (from Latin *mater,* "mother") **descent,** only the mother's relatives are significant.

New forms of reproductive technology (discussed in the policy section) will force a new way of looking at kinship. Today a combination of biological and social

Smile—it's family reunion time! The state of being related to others is called kinship. Kin groups include aunts, uncles, cousins, and so forth, as shown in this family from Slovakia.

processes can "create" a family member, requiring that more distinctions be made about who is related to whom (Cussins 1998).

Authority Patterns: Who Rules?

Imagine that you have recently married and must begin to make decisions about the future of your new family. You and your spouse face many questions. Where will you live? How will you furnish your home? Who will do the cooking, the shopping, the cleaning? Whose friends will be invited to dinner? Each time a decision must be made, an issue is raised: Who has the power to make the decision? In simple terms, who rules the family? The conflict perspective examines these questions in the context of traditional gender stratification, under which men have held a dominant position over women.

p. 307 ◄

Societies vary in the way that power within the family is distributed. If a society expects males to dominate in all family decision making, it is termed a **patriarchy.** Frequently, in patriarchal societies, such as Iran, the eldest male wields the greatest power, although wives are expected to be treated with respect and kindness. A woman's status in Iran is typically defined by her relationship to a male relative, usually as a wife or daughter. In many patriarchal societies women find it more difficult to obtain a divorce than a man does (Farr 1999). By contrast, in a **matriarchy,** women have greater authority than men. Matriarchies, which are very uncommon, emerged among Native American tribal societies and in nations in which men were absent for long periods of time for warfare or food gathering.

A third type of authority pattern, the *egalitarian family,* is one in which spouses are regarded as equals. This does not mean, however, that each decision is shared in such families. Wives may hold authority in some spheres, husbands in others. Many sociologists believe the egalitarian family has begun to replace the patriarchal family as the social norm in the United States.

Studying the Family

Do we really need the family? A century ago, Friedrich Engels (1884), a colleague of Karl Marx, described the family as the ultimate source of social inequality because of its role in the transfer of power, property, and privilege. More recently, conflict theorists have argued that the family contributes to societal injustice, denies opportunities to women that are extended to men, and limits freedom in sexual expression and selection of a mate. By contrast, the functionalist perspective focuses on the ways in which the family gratifies the needs of its members and contributes to the stability of society. The interactionist view considers more intimate, face-to-face relationships.

Functionalist View

There are six paramount functions performed by the family, first outlined more than 65 years ago by sociologist William F. Ogburn (Ogburn and Tibbits 1934):

1. **Reproduction.** For a society to maintain itself, it must replace dying members. In this sense, the family contributes to human survival through its function of reproduction.
2. **Protection.** Unlike the young of other animal species, human infants need constant care and economic security. The extremely long period of dependency for children places special demands on older family members. In all cultures, it is the family that assumes ultimate responsibility for the protection and upbringing of children.
3. **Socialization.** Parents and other kin monitor a child's behavior and transmit the norms, values, and language of a culture to the child (see Chapters 3 and 4).

   pp. 94–96 ◄

4. **Regulation of sexual behavior.** Sexual norms are subject to change over time (for instance, changes in customs for dating) and across cultures (Islamic Saudi Arabia compared with more permissive Denmark). However, whatever the time period or cultural values in a society, standards of sexual behavior are most clearly defined within the family circle. The structure of society influences these standards. In male-dominated societies, for example, formal and informal norms generally permit men to express and enjoy their sexual desires more freely than women may.
5. **Affection and companionship.** Ideally, the family provides members with warm and intimate relationships and helps them feel satisfied and secure. Of course, a family member may find such rewards outside the family—from peers, in school, at work—and may perceive the home as an unpleasant place. Nevertheless, unlike other institutions, the family is obligated to serve the emotional needs of its members. We *expect* our relatives to understand us, to care for us, and to be there for us when we need them.
6. **Providing of social status.** We inherit a social position because of the "family background" and reputation of our parents and siblings. The family unit presents the newborn child with an ascribed status of race and ethnicity that helps to determine his or her place within a society's stratification system. Moreover, family resources affect children's ability to pursue certain opportunities such as higher education and specialized lessons.

The family has traditionally fulfilled a number of other functions, such as providing religious training, education, and recreational outlets. Ogburn argued that other social institutions have gradually assumed many of these functions. Although the family once played a major role in religious life—Bible reading and hymn singing commonly took place at home—this function has largely shifted to churches, synagogues, and other religious organizations. Similarly, education once took place at the family fireside; now it is the responsibility of professionals working in schools and colleges. Even the family's traditional recreational function has been transferred to outside groups such as Little Leagues, athletic clubs, and Internet chat rooms.

Conflict View

Conflict theorists view the family not as a contributor to social stability, but as a reflection of the inequality in wealth and power found within the larger society. Feminist theorists and conflict theorists note that the family has traditionally legitimized and perpetuated male dominance. Throughout most of human history—and in a very wide range of societies—husbands have exercised overwhelming power and authority within the family. Not until the "first wave" of contemporary feminism in the United States in the mid-1800s was there a substantial challenge to the historic status of wives and children as the legal property of husbands.

While the egalitarian family has become a more common pattern in the United States in recent decades—owing in good part to the activism of feminists beginning in the late 1960s and early 1970s—male dominance within the family has hardly disappeared. Sociologists have found that women are significantly more likely to leave their jobs when their husbands find better employment opportunities than men are when their wives receive desirable job offers (Bielby and Bielby 1992). And unfortunately, many husbands reinforce their power and control over wives and children through acts of domestic violence. (Box 14-1 considers cross-cultural findings about violence within the home.)

Conflict theorists also view the family as an economic unit that contributes to societal injustice. The family is the basis for transferring power, property, and privilege from one generation to the next. The United States is widely viewed as a "land of opportunity," yet social mobility is restricted in important ways. Children "inherit" the privileged or less-than-privileged social and economic status of their parents (and, in some cases, of earlier generations as well). As conflict theorists point out, the social class of their parents significantly influences children's socialization experiences and the protection they receive. This means that the socioeconomic status of a child's family will have a marked influence on his or her nutrition, health care, housing, educational opportunities, and, in many respects, life chances as an adult. For that reason, conflict theorists argue that the family helps to maintain inequality.

Interactionist View

Interactionists focus on the microlevel of family and other intimate relationships. They are interested in how individuals interact with one another, whether they are cohabiting partners or long-time married couples. For example, a study of both Black and White two-parent households found that when fathers are more involved with their children (such as reading, helping with homework, restricting television viewing) children have fewer behavior problems, get along better with others, and are more responsible (Mosley and Thomson 1995).

Another interactionist study might examine the role of the stepparent. The increased number of single parents who remarry has sparked an interest in those who are helping to raise other people's children. While no young girl or boy may dream about one day becoming a stepmom or stepdad, this is hardly an unusual occurrence today. Studies have found that stepmothers are more likely to accept the blame for bad relations with their

stepchildren, whereas stepfathers are less likely to accept responsibility. Interactionists theorize that stepfathers (like most fathers) may simply be unaccustomed to interacting directly with children when the mother isn't there (Bray and Kelly 1999; Furstenberg and Cherlin 1991).

Feminist View

Because "women's work" has traditionally focused on family life, feminist sociologists have taken a strong interest in the family as a social institution. As we saw in Chapter 12, research on gender roles in child care and household chores has been extensive. Sociologists have looked particularly closely at how women's work outside the home impacts their child care and housework—duties Arlie Hochschild (1989, 1990) referred to as the "second shift." Today, researchers recognize that for many women, the second shift includes the care of aging parents as well.

Feminist theorists have urged social scientists and social agencies to rethink the notion that families in which no adult male is present are automatically a cause for concern, or even dysfunctional. They have also contributed to research on single women, single-parent households, and lesbian couples. In the case of single mothers, researchers have focused on the resiliency of many such households, despite economic stress. According to Velma McBride Murray and her colleagues (2001) at the University of Georgia, such studies show that among African Americans, single mothers draw heavily on kinfolk for material resources, parenting advice, and social support. Considering feminist research on the family as a whole, one researcher concluded that the family is the "source of women's strength" (Richardson et al. 2001:297).

Feminists stress the need to broaden family research to include not only gender, race, and social class, but human sexuality and the aging process. They recognize that in any society, the family plays a central role in socializing children. Therefore, the degree to which society manifests sexism is rooted in the family—an institution, ironically, in which women's work is essential. The oppressive way in which most households are organized, then, serves to reinforce societal sexism (Thorne 1992).

Marriage and Family

Currently, close to 90 percent of all men and women in the United States marry at least once during their lifetimes. Historically, the most consistent aspect of family life in this country has been the high rate of marriage. In fact, despite the high rate of divorce, there are indications of a miniboom in marriages in the United States of late, fueled by a strong economy and a return to traditional values (Parker 1998).

Sociology in the Global Community

14-1 Domestic Violence

www.
mhhe
.com
/schaefer8

"It's the same every Saturday night. The husband comes home drunk and beats her." This is how Tania Kucherenko describes her downstairs neighbors in Moscow after turning a deaf ear to the screams of terror and the sounds of furniture being overthrown and glass breaking. "There's nothing we can do. It's best not to interfere." Contempt for women runs deep in Russia, where women who dare to leave their husbands risk losing their legal status, a place to live, and the right to work (Bennett 1997:A1).

Wife battering, child abuse, abuse of the elderly, and other forms of domestic violence are not confined to Russia. Drawing on studies conducted throughout the world, we can make the following generalizations:

- Women are most at risk of violence from the men they know.
- Violence against women is evident in all socioeconomic groups.
- Family violence is at least as dangerous as assaults committed by strangers.
- Though women sometimes exhibit violent behavior toward men, the majority of violent acts that cause injury are perpetrated by men against women.

- Violence within intimate relationships tends to escalate over time.
- Emotional and psychological abuse can be at least as debilitating as physical abuse.
- Use of alcohol exacerbates family violence but does not cause it.

Using the conflict and feminist models, researchers have found that in relationships where the inequality is greater between men and women, the likelihood of assault on wives increases dramatically. This suggests that much of the violence

> **The situation of battered women is so intolerable that it has been compared to that of prison inmates.**

between intimates, even when sexual in nature, is about power rather than sex.

The situation of battered women is so intolerable that it has been compared to that of prison inmates. Criminologist Noga Avni interviewed battered women at a shelter in Israel and found that their day-to-day lives with their husbands or lovers shared many elements of life in an oppressive total institution, as described by Erving Goffman (1961). Physical barriers are imposed

on these women; by threatening further violence, men restrict women to their homes, damaging both their self-esteem and their ability to cope with repeated abuse. Moreover, as in a total institution, these battered p. 94 ◄ women are cut off from external sources of physical and emotional assistance and moral support. In Avni's view, society could more effectively aid victims of domestic violence if it better understood the essential imprisonment of these women.

The family can be a dangerous place not only for women but also for children and the elderly. In 2000, public agencies in the United States received more than 3 million reports of child abuse and/or neglect. That means reports were filed on about 1 out of every 25 children. Another national study found that 1 million violent crimes a year had been committed by current or former spouses, boyfriends, or girlfriends.

Let's Discuss

1. Do you know of a family that experienced domestic violence? Did the victim(s) seek outside help, and was that help effective?
2. How does the degree of equality in a relationship correlate to the likelihood of domestic violence? How might conflict theorists explain this?

NEWS ITEM: 15% of married women suffer physical abuse, and 1-in-3 of them felt it was life-threatening

DOMESTIC VIOLENCE

JAPAN'S DIRTY SECRET

THE JAPAN TIMES 2000 — Rogerdahl@aol.com

Sources: American Bar Association 1999; Avni 1991; Gelles and Cornell 1990; Heise et al. 1999; Rennison and Welchans 2000; Wilson 2000.

When fathers interact regularly with their children, it's a win/win situation. The fathers get close to their offspring and studies show that the children end up with fewer behavior problems.

In this part of the chapter, we will examine various aspects of love, marriage, and parenthood in the United States and contrast them with cross-cultural examples. We're used to thinking of romance and mate selection as strictly a matter of individual preference. Yet, sociological analysis tells us that social institutions and distinctive cultural norms and values also play an important role.

Courtship and Mate Selection

"My rugby mates would roll over in their graves," says Tom Buckley of his online courtship and subsequent marriage to Terri Muir. But Tom and Terri are hardly alone these days in turning to the Internet for matchmaking services. By the end of 1999, more than 2,500 websites were helping people find mates. You could choose from oneandonly.com or 2ofakind.com or cupidnet.com,

among others. One service alone claimed 2 million subscribers. Tom and Terri carried on their romance via e-mail for a year before they met. According to Tom, "E-mail made it easier to communicate because neither one of us was the type to walk up to someone in the gym or a bar and say, 'You're the fuel to my fire' " (Morris 1999:D1).

Internet romance is only the latest courtship practice. In the central Asian nation of Uzbekistan and many other traditional cultures, courtship is defined largely through the interaction of two sets of parents, who arrange spouses for their children. Typically, a young Uzbekistani woman will be socialized to eagerly anticipate her marriage to a man whom she has met only once, when he is presented to her family at the time of the final inspection of her dowry. In the United States, by contrast, courtship is conducted primarily by individuals who may have a romantic interest in each other. In our culture, courtship often requires these individuals to rely heavily on intricate games, gestures, and signals. Despite such differences, courtship—whether in the United States, Uzbekistan, or elsewhere—is influenced by the norms and values of the larger society (Williams 1995).

Interracial unions, which are becoming increasingly common and accepted, are blurring definitions of race. Would the children of this interracial couple be considered Black or White?

One unmistakable pattern in mate selection is that the process appears to be taking longer today than in the past. A variety of factors, including concerns about financial security and personal independence, has contributed to this delay in marriage. Most people are now well into their 20s before they marry, both in the United States and in other countries (see Figure 14-2).

Aspects of Mate Selection

Many societies have explicit or unstated rules that define potential mates as acceptable or unacceptable. These norms can be distinguished in terms of endogamy and exogamy. **Endogamy** (from the Greek *endon,* "within") specifies the groups within which a spouse must be found and prohibits marriage with others. For example, in the

Figure 14-2

Percentage of People Aged 20 to 24 Ever Married, Selected Countries

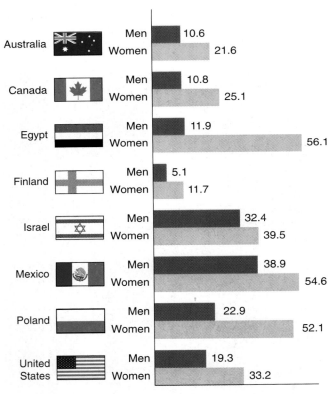

Source: United Nations Population Division 2001.

Think About It
Why is the percentage of young women who are married particularly high in Egypt, Mexico, and Poland? Particularly low in Finland?

United States, many people are expected to marry within their own racial, ethnic, or religious group and are strongly discouraged or even prohibited from marrying outside the group. Endogamy is intended to reinforce the cohesiveness of the group by suggesting to the young that they should marry someone "of our own kind."

By contrast, **exogamy** (from the Greek *exo,* "outside") requires mate selection outside certain groups, usually one's own family or certain kinfolk. The **incest taboo,** a social norm common to virtually all societies, prohibits sexual relationships between certain culturally specified relatives. For people in the United States, this taboo means that we must marry outside the nuclear family. We cannot marry our siblings, and in most states we cannot marry our first cousins.

Endogamous restrictions may be seen as preferences for one group over another. In the United States, such preferences are most obvious in racial barriers. Until the 1960s, some states outlawed interracial marriage. Nevertheless, the number of marriages between African Americans and Whites in the United States has increased more than six times in recent decades, jumping from 51,000 in 1960 to 307,000 in 1999. Moreover, 25 percent of married Asian American women and 12 percent of married Asian American men are married to a person who is not of Asian descent. Marriage across ethnic lines is even greater among Hispanics; 27 percent of all married Hispanics have a non-Hispanic spouse. While all these examples of racial exogamy are impressive, endogamy is still the social norm in the United States (Bureau of the Census 1998a, 2000a:51).

Interracial unions force a society to reconsider its definitions of race and ethnicity. In Chapter 11, we noted that race is socially constructed in the United States and around the world. p. 271 But with increasing proportions of children in this country coming from biracial or multiracial backgrounds, traditional definitions of race and ethnicity will become less relevant. Several voluntary associations representing mixed-race children requested that the census offer a new category of "multiracial" or "biracial," so that people would no longer be forced to define themselves as solely "White," "Black," "Asian," or "American Indian." In the end it was decided to let people check off several categories they felt applied to them, but not to provide the "multiracial" or "biracial" classification (Schaefer 2002).

The Love Relationship

Whatever else "love" is, most people would agree it is complicated. Listen to what a Yale University junior has to say on the subject:

This web page advertises introductions to marriageable young women of Asian descent. Such websites draw many inquiries from American men looking for a submissive wife.

Love isn't in the air these days, at least not in New Haven . . . my peers and I find ourselves in a new world of romance, and we're feeling a little out of our league. We are children of the Age of Divorce, born into the AIDS crisis, reared on Madonna, *Friends,* and *Beverly Hills 90210.* No wonder we're confused. We know we want this thing called love. More than previous generations, though, we're unsure of what love is and how to get it—and we're not so sure that finding it will be worth the trouble (Rodberg 1999:1–2).

Another student claims that "love, like everything else, must be pondered, and we have too many other things to ponder—no matter how much we profess to want love" (quoted in Rodberg 1999:4).

For a variety of reasons, hinted at in these quotations, this generation of college students seems more likely to "hook up" or cruise in large packs than engage in the romantic dating relationships of their parents and grandparents. Still, at some point in their adult lives the great majority of today's students will meet someone they "love" and enter into a long-term relationship that focuses on creating a family.

In the United States, love is important in the courtship process. Living in their own home makes the affectional bond between husband and wife especially important. The couple is expected to develop emotional ties that are free of the demands of other household members for affection. Sociologist William J. Goode (1959) observed that spouses in a nuclear family rely heavily on each other

for the companionship and support that might be provided by other relatives in an extended-family situation.

Parents in the United States tend to value love highly as a rationale for marriage, and they encourage their children to develop intimate relationships based on love and affection. In addition, songs, films, books, magazines, television shows, and even cartoons and comic books reinforce the theme of love. At the same time, our society expects parents and peers to help a person confine his or her search for a mate to "socially acceptable" members of the opposite sex.

Most people in the United States take the importance of falling in love for granted, but love-and-marriage is by no means a cultural universal. Many of the world's cultures give priority in mate selection to factors other than romantic feelings. In societies with *arranged marriages,* often engineered by parents or religious authorities, economic considerations play a significant role. The newly married couple is expected to develop a feeling of love *after* the legal union is formalized, if at all.

Even within the United States, some subcultures carry on the arranged marriage practices of their native cultures. Young people among the Sikhs and Hindus who have immigrated from India, and among Islamic Muslims and Hasidic Jews, allow their parents or designated matchmakers to find spouses within their ethnic community. As one young Sikh declared, "I will definitely marry who my parents wish. They know me better than I know myself." Young people who have emigrated without their families often turn to the Internet to find partners who share their background and goals. Matrimonial ads for the Indian community run on such websites as SuitableMatch.com and INDOLINK.com. One Hasidic Jewish woman noted that the system of arranged marriages "isn't perfect, and it doesn't work for everyone, but this is the system we know and trust, the way we couple, and the way we learn to love. So it works for most of us" (Segall 1998:48, 53).

◉Imagine

Your parents and/or a matchmaker are going to arrange a marriage for you. What kind of mate will they select? Will your chances of having a successful marriage be better or worse than if you selected your own mate?

Variations in Family Life and Intimate Relationships

Within the United States, social class, race, and ethnicity create variations in family life. Understanding these variations will give us a more sophisticated understanding of contemporary family styles in our country.

Social Class Differences

Various studies have documented the differences in family organization among social classes in the United States. The upper class emphasis is on lineage and maintenance of family position. If you are in the upper class, you are not simply a member of a nuclear family but rather a member of a larger family tradition (think of the Rockefellers or the Kennedys). As a result, upper-class families are quite concerned about what they see as "proper training" for children.

Lower-class families do not often have the luxury of worrying about the "family name"; they must first struggle to pay their bills and survive the crises often associated with life in poverty. Such families are more likely to have only one parent in the home, creating special challenges in child care and financial needs. Children in lower-class families typically assume adult responsibilities—including marriage and parenthood—at an earlier age than children of affluent homes. In part, this is because they may lack the money needed to remain in school.

Social class differences in family life are less striking than they once were. In the past, family specialists agreed that there were pronounced contrasts in child-rearing practices. Lower-class families were found to be more authoritarian in rearing children and more inclined to use physical punishment. Middle-class families were more permissive and more restrained in punishing their children. However, these differences may have narrowed as more and more families from all social classes have turned to the same books, magazines, and even television talk shows for advice on rearing children (Kohn 1970; Luster et al. 1989).

Among the poor, women often play a significant role in the economic support of the family. Men may earn low wages, may be unemployed, or may be entirely absent from the family. In 1997, 31.6 percent of all families headed by women with no husband present were below the government poverty line. This compared with only 5.2 percent for married couples (Dalaker and Naifeh 1998:vii).

Many racial and ethnic groups appear to have distinctive family characteristics. However, racial and class factors are often closely related. In examining family life among racial and ethnic minorities, keep in mind that certain patterns may result from class as well as cultural factors.

Racial and Ethnic Differences

The subordinate status of racial and ethnic minorities in the United States profoundly affects their family life. For example, the lower incomes of African Americans, Native Americans, most Hispanic groups, and selected Asian American groups make creating and maintaining successful marital unions a difficult task. The economic restructuring of the last 50 years, described by sociologist William Julius Wilson (1996) and others, has especially affected people living in inner cities and desolate rural areas such as reservations. Further, the immigration policy of the United States has complicated the successful relocation of intact families from Asia and Latin America (Doob 1999).

p. 227

The African American family suffers from many negative and inaccurate stereotypes. It is true that a significantly higher proportion of Black than White families have no husband present in the home (see Figure 14-3). Yet Black single mothers are often part of stable, functioning kin networks, despite the pressures of sexism and racism. Members of these networks—predominantly female kin such as mothers, grandmothers, and aunts—ease financial strains by sharing goods and services. In addition to these strong kinship bonds, Black family life has emphasized deep religious commitment and high aspirations for achievement. The strengths of the Black family were evident during slavery, when Blacks demonstrated a remarkable ability to maintain family ties despite the fact that they had no legal protections and, in fact, were often forced to separate (Morehouse Research Institute and Institute for American Values 1999).

Sociologists have also taken note of differences in family patterns among other racial and ethnic groups. For example, Mexican American men have been described as exhibiting a sense of virility, of personal worth, and of pride in their maleness that is called *machismo.* Mexican Americans are also described as being more familistic than many other subcultures. *Familism* refers to pride in the extended family, expressed through the maintenance of close ties and strong obligations to kinfolk outside the immediate family. Traditionally, Mexican Americans have placed proximity to their extended families above other needs and desires.

These family patterns are changing, however, in response to changes in Latinos' social class standing, educational achievements, and occupations. Like other Americans, career-oriented Latinos in search of a mate but short on spare time are turning to Internet sites such as Latino.com to find romance. When one of these young people meets her heart's desire through a chat room or Web-based service like *Cariño* Connection, she may pull up stakes and move from Cleveland to Miami. As Latinos and other groups assimilate into the dominant culture of

Figure 14-3

Rise of One-Parent Families among Whites, African Americans, Hispanics, and Asians or Pacific Islanders in the United States

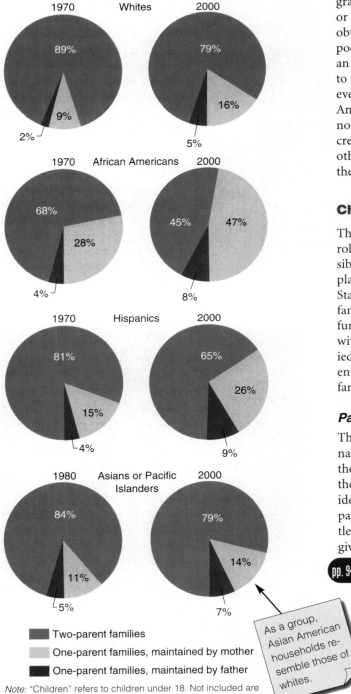

Note: "Children" refers to children under 18. Not included are unrelated people living together with no children present. Early data for Asian Americans are for 1980.

Source: Bureau of the Census 1994:63; Fields 2001:7.

As a group, Asian American households resemble those of whites.

the United States, their family lives take on both the positive and negative characteristics associated with White households (Becerra 1999; Vega 1995).

Within a racial or ethnic minority, family ties can serve as an economic boost. For example, Korean immigrants to the United States generally begin small service or retail businesses involving all adult family members. To obtain the funds needed to begin a business, they often pool their resources through a *kye* (pronounced KAY)—an association (not limited to kinfolk) that grants money to members on a rotating basis so they can gain access to even more additional capital. The *kye* allows Korean Americans to start small businesses long before other minorities in similar economic circumstances. Such rotating credit associations are not unique to Korean Americans; other Asian Americans as well as West Indians living in the United States have used them (Lee 1999).

Child-Rearing Patterns in Family Life

The Nayars of southern India acknowledge the biological role of fathers, but the mother's eldest brother is responsible for her children (Gough 1974). By contrast, uncles play only a peripheral role in child care in the United States. Caring for children is a universal function of the family, yet the ways in which different societies assign this function to family members can vary significantly. Even within the United States, child-rearing patterns are varied. We'll take a look here at parenthood and grandparenthood, adoption, dual-income families, single-parent families, and stepfamilies.

Parenthood and Grandparenthood

The socialization of children is essential to the maintenance of any culture. Consequently, parenthood is one of the most important (and most demanding) social roles in the United States. Sociologist Alice Rossi (1968, 1984) has identified four factors that complicate the transition to parenthood and the role of socialization. First, there is little anticipatory socialization for the social role of caregiver. The normal school curriculum gives scant attention to the subjects most relevant to successful family life—such as child care and home maintenance. Second, only limited learning occurs during the period of pregnancy itself. Third, the transition to parenthood is quite abrupt. Unlike adolescence, it is not prolonged; unlike socialization for work, you cannot gradually take on the duties of caregiving. Finally, in Rossi's view, our society lacks clear and helpful guidelines for successful parenthood. There is little consensus on how parents can produce happy and well-adjusted offspring—or even on what it means to be "well-adjusted." For these

pp. 94—96

Korean family ties often provide a huge economic boost. Not only do family members work together in family businesses such as the husband and wife pictured here; they also contribute financial resources through a rotating credit association known as a kye.

reasons, socialization for parenthood involves difficult challenges for most men and women in the United States.

One recent development in family life in the United States has been the extension of parenthood, as adult children continue to (or return to) live at home. In 1995, more than half of all children ages 18 to 24 and one out of eight of those ages 25 to 34 lived with their parents. Some of these adult children are still pursuing an education, but in many instances, financial difficulties are at the heart of these living arrangements. While rents and real estate prices skyrocketed in the 1990s, salaries for younger workers did not keep pace, and many found themselves unable to afford their own homes. Moreover, with many marriages now ending in divorce—most commonly in the first seven years of marriage—divorced sons and daughters are returning to live with their parents, sometimes with their own children (Bureau of the Census 1997a:58).

Is this living arrangement a positive development for family members? Social scientists have just begun to examine this phenomenon, sometimes called the "boomerang generation" or the "full-nest syndrome" in the popular press. One survey in Virginia seemed to show that neither the parents nor their adult children were happy about continuing to live together. The children often felt resentful and isolated, but the parents also suffered: Learning to live without children in the home is an essential stage of adult life and may even be a significant turning point for a marriage (*Berkeley Wellness Letter* 1990; Mogelonsky 1996).

In some homes, the full nest holds grandchildren. Census data for the year 2000 showed that 5.6 million grandparents lived with their grandchildren, and fully 42 percent were responsible for the youngsters. Special difficulties are inherent in such relationships, including legal custodial concerns, financial issues, and emotional problems for adults and youths alike. Little surprise that support groups such as Grandparents as Parents have emerged to provide assistance (Peterson 2001).

Adoption

In a legal sense, **adoption** is a "process that allows for the transfer of the legal rights, responsibilities, and privileges of parenthood" to a new legal parent or parents (Cole 1985:638). In many cases, these rights are transferred from a biological

The love expressed by this mother and her two children testifies to successful parenting. Even though parenthood is a crucial social role, society generally provides few clear guidelines.

Many people find adoption parties, at which prospective adoptive parents meet children who are waiting to be adopted, disturbing. How would you feel if you were in this girl's shoes, walking a runway at a "fashion show" meant to attract adoptive parents?

parent or parents (often called birth parents) to an adoptive parent or parents.

Viewed from a functionalist perspective, government has a strong interest in encouraging adoption. Policymakers, in fact, have both a humanitarian and a financial stake in the process. In theory, adoption offers a stable family environment for children who otherwise might not receive satisfactory care. Moreover, government data show that unwed mothers who keep their babies tend to be of lower socioeconomic status and often require public assistance to support their children. Government can lower its social welfare expenses if children are transferred to economically self-sufficient families. From a conflict perspective, however, such financial considerations raise the ugly specter of adoption as a means whereby affluent (often infertile) couples "buy" the children of the poor (Bachrach 1986).

Adoption by relatives is still the most common type of adoption in the United States. In most cases, a stepparent adopts the children of a spouse. Adoptions between unrelated persons are growing in number, however. There are two legal methods of adopting an unrelated person: adoptions arranged by licensed agencies and, in some states, private agreements sanctioned by the courts. Children may come from the United States or they may come from abroad. As Table 14-1 shows, more than 16,000 children a year now enter the United States as the adopted children of U.S. citizens.

In some cases the adopters are not married. An important court decision in 1995 in New York held that a couple does not have to be married to adopt a child. Under this ruling, unmarried heterosexual couples, lesbian couples, and gay male couples can all legally adopt children in New York. Writing for the majority, Chief Justice Judith Kaye argued that by expanding the boundaries of who can be legally recognized as parents, the state may be able to assist more children in securing "the best possible home." With this ruling, New York became the third state (after Vermont and Massachusetts) to recognize the right of unmarried couples to adopt children (Dao 1995).

Dual-Income Families

The idea of a family consisting of a wage-earning husband and a wife who stays at home has largely given way to the *dual-income household*. Among married people between the ages of 25 and 34, 96 percent of the men and 72 percent of the women are in the labor force. Why has there been such a rise in the number of dual-income couples? A major factor is economic need. In 1999, the median income for households with both partners employed was 86 percent more than in households in which only one person was working outside the home ($59,699, compared with $31,948). Of course, because of such work-related costs as child care, not all of a family's second wage is genuine additional income. Other factors contributing to the rise of the dual-income model include the nation's declining birthrate (see Chapter 21), the increase in the proportion of women with a college education, the shift in the economy of the United States from manufacturing to service industries, and the impact of the feminist movement in changing women's consciousness (Bureau of the Census 1999a:416; 2000d:6).

Single-Parent Families

In the United States of the late nineteenth century, immigration and urbanization made it increasingly difficult to maintain *Gemeinschaft* communities, where everyone knew one another and shared responsibility for unwed mothers and their children. In 1883, the Florence Crittenton Houses were founded in New York City—and subsequently established around the nation—as refuges for

Table 14-1 Foreign-Born Adoptees by Top Ten Countries of Origin, 1989 and 2000

1989			2000	
Number of Children	Country	Rank	Number of Children	Country
3,544	S. Korea	1	5,053	China
736	Colombia	2	4,269	Russia
648	India	3	1,794	S. Korea
465	Philippines	4	1,518	Guatemala
253	Chile	5	1,122	Romania
252	Paraguay	6	724	Vietnam
222	Peru	7	659	Ukraine
202	Guatemala	8	503	India
201	China	9	402	Cambodia
131	Honduras	10	399	Kazakhstan
Total	6,654		16,443	

Source: Department of State 2001.

Think About It

Why did so many foreign-born adopted children come from these countries in particular? What accounts for the change in countries of origin from 1989 to 2000?

prostitutes (then stigmatized as "fallen women"). Within a few years, the Crittenton homes began accepting unwed mothers as residents. By the early 1900s, sociologist W. E. B. Du Bois (1911) had noted that the institutionalization of unwed mothers was occurring in segregated facilities. At the time that he was writing, there were seven homes of various types nationwide for unwed Black mothers, as well as one Crittenton home reserved for that purpose.

In recent decades, the stigma attached to "unwed mothers" and other single parents has significantly diminished. *Single-parent families,* in which there is only one parent present to care for the children, can hardly be viewed as a rarity in the United States. In 2000, a single

parent headed about 21 percent of White families with children under 18, 35 percent of Hispanic families with children, and 55 percent of African American families with children (see Figure 14-3 on page 359).

The lives of single parents and their children are not inevitably more difficult than life in a traditional nuclear family. It is as inaccurate to assume that a single-parent family is necessarily "deprived" as it is to assume that a two-parent family is always secure and happy. Nevertheless, life in a single-parent family can be extremely stressful, in both economic and emotional terms.

A family headed by a single mother faces especially difficult problems when the mother is a teenager. Drawing

Dad takes breakfast duty while Mom rushes off to work in this "dual-income" family. An increasing proportion of couples in the United States reject the traditional nuclear family model of husband as breadwinner and wife as homemaker.

Although 82 percent of single parents in the United States are mothers, the number of households headed by single fathers has more than quadrupled over the period 1980 to 2000. The stereotypes of single fathers are that they raise only boys or older children. In fact, about 44 percent of children living in such households are girls; almost one-third of single fathers care for preschoolers. Whereas single mothers often develop social networks, single fathers are typically more isolated. In addition, they must deal with schools and social service agencies more accustomed to women as custodial parents (Fields 2001).

What about single fathers who do not head the household? This is typically an understudied group for sociological purposes, but a study of low-income unmarried fathers in Philadelphia came up with some unexpected findings. When asked what their lives would be like without having children, many responded that they would be dead or in jail. This was true even of those fathers who had very little to do with their children. Apparently, the mere fact of fathering children prompts men to get jobs, stay in the community, and stay healthy. Many of these men were upset that they had to hand over money without having a say in how it was spent, or in some cases even having legal access to their offspring (Cohen 1998; Rhodes 2000).

on two decades of social science research, sociologist Kristin Luker (1996:11) observes:

> The short answer to why teenagers get pregnant and especially to why they continue those pregnancies is that a fairly substantial number of them just don't believe what adults tell them, be it about sex, contraception, marriage, or babies. They don't believe in adult conventional wisdom.

Why might low-income teenage women wish to have children and face the obvious financial difficulties of motherhood? Viewed from an interactionist perspective, these women tend to have low self-esteem and limited options; a child may provide a sense of motivation and purpose for a teenager whose economic worth in our society is limited at best. Given the barriers that many young women face because of their gender, race, ethnicity, and class, many teenagers may believe that they have little to lose and much to gain by having a child.

According to a widely held stereotype, "unwed mothers" and "babies having babies" in the United States are predominantly African American. However, this view is not entirely accurate. African Americans account for a disproportionate share of births to unmarried women and to teenagers, but the majority of all babies born to unmarried teenage mothers are born to White adolescents. Moreover, since 1990, birthrates among Black teenagers have declined steadily (Ventura et al. 2001b).

Most households in the United States do not consist of two parents living with their unmarried children.

Stepfamilies

Approximately one-third of all people in the United States will marry, divorce, and then remarry. The rising rates of divorce and remarriage have led to a noticeable increase in stepfamily relationships. In 1980, 9 percent of all family households with children present included a stepparent; by 1990, that figure had almost tripled to 24 percent (Bureau of the Census 1995:64; Cherlin and Furstenberg 1994).

Stepfamilies are an exceedingly complex form of family organization. Here is how one 13-year-old boy described his family.

> Tim and Janet are my stepbrother and sister. Josh is my stepdad. Carin and Don are my real parents, who are divorced. And Don married Anna and together they had Ethan and Ellen, my half-sister and brother. And Carin married Josh and had little Alice, my half-sister (Bernstein 1988).

The exact nature of these blended families has social significance for adults and children alike. Certainly resocialization is required when an adult becomes a stepparent or a child becomes a stepchild and stepsibling. Moreover, an important distinction must be made between first-time stepfamilies and households where there have been repeated divorces, breakups, or changes in custodial arrangements.

In evaluating the rise of stepfamilies, some observers have assumed that children would benefit from remarriage because they would be gaining a second custodial parent and potentially would enjoy greater economic security. However, after reviewing many studies on stepfamilies, sociologist Andrew J. Cherlin (1999:421) concluded that "the well-being of children in stepfamily households is no better, on average, than the well-being of children in divorced, single-parent households." Stepparents can play valuable and unique roles in their stepchildren's lives, but their involvement does not guarantee an improvement. In fact, standards may decline. Some studies conducted by a Princeton economist found that children raised in families with stepmothers are likely to have less health care, education, and money spent on their food than children raised by biological mothers. The measures are also negative for children raised by a stepfather, but only half as negative as in the case of stepmothers. This doesn't mean that stepmothers are "evil"—it may be that the stepmother steps back out of concern for seeming too intrusive, or relies mistakenly

Figure 14-4

Trends in Marriage and Divorce in the United States, 1920–2001

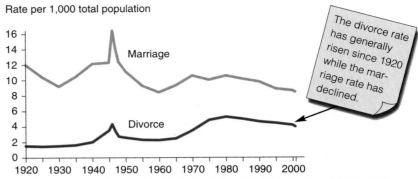

Sources: Bureau of the Census 1975:64, 2000a; *National Vital Statistics Reports* 2001, 2002.

on the biological father to carry out these parental duties (Lewin 2000).

Divorce

"Do you promise to love, honor, and cherish . . . until death do you part?" Every year, people of all social classes and racial and ethnic groups make this legally binding agreement. Yet an increasing number of these promises shatter in divorce. While rates may vary among states, divorce is a nationwide phenomenon.

Statistical Trends in Divorce

Just how common is divorce? Surprisingly, this is not a simple question; divorce statistics are difficult to interpret.

The media frequently report that one out of every two marriages ends in divorce. But this figure is misleading, since many marriages last for decades. It is based on a comparison of all divorces that occur in a single year (regardless of when the couples were married) against the number of new marriages in the same year.

Divorce in the United States, and many other countries, began to increase in the late 1960s, but then started to level off and has even declined since the late 1980s (see Figure 14-4). Partly this is due to the aging of the baby boomer population and the corresponding decline in the proportion of people of marriageable age. But the trend also indicates an increase in marital stability in recent years (National Marriage Project 2001).

Getting divorced obviously does not sour people on marriage. About two-thirds of divorced women and three-fourths of divorced men eventually remarry.

Women are less likely than men to remarry because many retain custody of children after a divorce, which complicates a new adult relationship (Bianchi and Spain 1996).

Some people regard the nation's high rate of remarriage as an endorsement of the institution of marriage, but it does lead to the new challenges of a remarriage kin network composed of current and prior marital relationships. This network can be particularly complex if children are involved or if an ex-spouse remarries.

Factors Associated with Divorce

Perhaps the most important factor in the increase in divorce throughout the twentieth century has been the greater social *acceptance* of divorce. It's no longer considered necessary to endure an unhappy marriage. Most importantly, various religious denominations have relaxed negative attitudes toward divorce, and most religious leaders no longer treat it as a sin. The growing acceptance of divorce is a worldwide phenomenon. In 1998, a few months after a highly publicized divorce by pop superstar Seiko Matsuda, the prime minister of Japan released a survey showing that 54 percent of those polled supported uncontested divorce, compared to 20 percent in 1979 (Kyodo News International 1998a).

A few other factors deserve mention:

- Many states have adopted more liberal divorce laws in the last two decades. No-fault divorce laws, allowing a couple to end their marriage without fault on either side (by specifying adultery, for instance), accounted for an initial surge in the divorce rate after they were introduced in the 1970s, although they appear to have had little effect beyond that.
- Divorce has become a more practical option in newly formed families, since they now tend to have fewer children than in the past.
- A general increase in family incomes, coupled with the availability of free legal aid for some poor people, has meant that more couples can afford costly divorce proceedings.
- As society provides greater opportunities for women, more and more wives are becoming less dependent on their husbands—both economically and emotionally. They may then feel more able to leave if the marriage seems hopeless.

Impact of Divorce on Children

Divorce is traumatic for all involved, as Cornel West made clear in the excerpt that opened this chapter. But it

has special meaning for the more than 1 million children whose parents divorce each year. Of course, for some of these children, divorce signals the welcome end to being witness to a very dysfunctional relationship. A national sample conducted by sociologists Paul R. Amato and Alan Booth (1997) found that in about a third of divorces, the children benefit from parental separation because it lessens their exposure to conflict. But in about 70 percent of all divorces, they found that the parents engaged in a low level of conflict; in these cases, the realities of divorce appeared to be harder for the children to bear than living with the marital unhappiness. Other researchers, using differing definitions of conflict, have found greater unhappiness for children living in homes with marital differences. Still, it would be simplistic to assume that children are automatically better off following the breakup of their parents' marriage. The interests of the parents do not necessarily serve children well.

Divorce can obviously be a painful experience for children, but we should avoid assuming that a *parental* experience is the singular event defining the life of a girl or boy. Large-scale studies in the United States and Great Britain have shown that some of the alleged negative effects of divorce actually result from conditions (such as poverty) that existed *before* the parental separation. Moreover, if divorce does not lower children's access to resources and does not increase stress, its impact on children may be neutral or even positive. Still, recent research suggests that the impact of divorce can extend beyond childhood, affecting a grown person's ability to establish a lasting marital relationship. Scholars disagree on the reason for this lingering effect of divorce (see Box 14-2).

In recent years, concern about the high rate of divorce in the United States and its impact on children has led policymakers to reconsider existing divorce laws. Louisiana's *covenant marriages* have received considerable publicity. Beginning in 1997, couples in that state have had the option of entering a legal union that requires premarital counseling and sets strict limits on divorce; for example, the marriage can be dissolved only after a two-year separation or after documented adultery or abuse. About 3 percent of couples accept the extra restrictions. It is too early to assess the impact of this system on marital longevity. Many states have considered a similar arrangement, but only Arizona and Arkansas have adopted even a modified form of the procedure. Yet even if few states take up Louisiana's initiative, the nation appears willing to enter into a discussion of what educational and parenting programs can reduce marital breakup (Schemo 2001).

Research in Action

14-2 The Lingering Impact of Divorce

What happens to the children of divorce? Early research suggested that the negative effects of divorce on children were confined to the first few years following a breakup. According to these studies, most children eventually adjusted to the change in family structure and went on to live normal lives. But recent studies suggest that the effects of divorce may linger much longer than scholars at first suspected, peaking in the adult years, when grown children are attempting to establish their own marriages and families.

A foremost proponent of this view is psychologist Judith A. Wallerstein, who has been conducting qualitative research on the effects of divorce on children since 1971. Wallerstein has been following the original 131 children in her study for 30 years; her subjects are now aged 28 to 43. She is convinced that these adult children of divorce have had greater difficulty than other adults in forming and maintaining intimate relationships because they have never witnessed the daily give-and-take of a successful marital partnership.

Another researcher, sociologist Paul R. Amato, agrees that divorce can affect children into adulthood, but for a differ-ent reason. Amato, who contributed to a study conducted from 1980 to 1997, thinks that the parents' decision to end their marriage lies at the root of the higher-than-normal divorce rate among their children. In this study, based on telephone interviews, children whose parents had divorced had a 30 percent divorce rate themselves, which is 12 to 13 percent higher than the divorce rate among children whose parents had *not* divorced.

> Recent studies suggest that the effects of divorce may linger much longer than scholars at first suspected.

Significantly, children of parents who did not divorce had roughly the same divorce rate regardless of whether the level of conflict in their parents' marriage was low (17 percent) or high (18 percent). The parental example that a marriage contract can be broken—not the demonstration of poor relationship skills—is what makes an adult child more vulnerable than others to divorce, Amato thinks.

Sociologist Andrew J. Cherlin concedes that divorce can have lingering effects, but thinks the potential for harm has been exaggerated. Cherlin, who has conducted quantitative analyses of the effects of divorce on thousands of children, finds that parental divorce does elevate children's risk of emotional problems, school withdrawal, and teen pregnancy. But most children, he emphasizes, do not develop those problems. Even Wallerstein admits that the ill effects of divorce do not apply across the board. Some children seem to be strengthened by the crisis, she observes, and go on to lead highly successful lives, both personally and professionally.

Let's Discuss

1. Do you know any adult children of divorce who have had difficulty establishing successful marriages? If so, what seems to be the problem, an inability to handle conflict or a lack of commitment to the marriage?
2. What practical conclusions should we draw from the research on children of divorce? Should couples stay together for the sake of their children?

Sources: Amato 2001; Amato and Sobolewski 2001; Bumiller 2000; Cherlin 1999; Wallerstein et al. 2000. For a different view, see Hetherington and Kelly 2002.

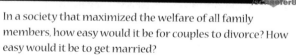

Imagine

In a society that maximized the welfare of all family members, how easy would it be for couples to divorce? How easy would it be to get married?

Diverse Lifestyles

Marriage is no longer the presumed route from adolescence to adulthood. In fact, it has lost much of its social significance as a rite of passage. The nation's marriage rate has dipped by 43 percent since 1960 because people are postponing marriage until later in life and more couples, including same-sex couples, are deciding to form partnerships without marriage (Popenoe and Whitehead 1999).

Cohabitation

Saint Paul once wrote, "It is better to marry than to burn." However, as journalist Tom Ferrell (1979) has suggested, more people than ever "prefer combustible to connubial bliss." One of the most dramatic trends of recent years has been the tremendous increase in male–female couples who choose to live together without marrying, a practice called *cohabitation.*

The number of such households in the United States rose sixfold in the 1960s and increased another 48 percent between 1990 and 1998. According to a 2001 Census Bureau report, at any given time, about 6 percent of opposite-sex couples are unmarried. Half of all people between the ages of 25 and 40 have cohabited. If current trends continue, that will soon be true of half of all people

This young couple in England are cohabiting, an increasingly popular alternative to marriage in many countries today.

in the United States between the ages of 25 and 50 (Bureau of the Census 1999a:60; Clark and Fields 1999; Field 2001).

We can also find increases in cohabitation in Canada, France, Sweden, Denmark, and Australia. Data released in Great Britain indicate that more than 12 percent of people ages 18 to 24 are cohabiting. One report notes that in Sweden it is almost universal for couples to live together before marriage. Demographers in Denmark call the practice of living together *marriage without papers*. In Australia, these couples are known as *de factos* (Blanc 1984; Levinson 1984; O'Donnell 1992; Thomson and Colella 1992).

Some countries have governmental policies that do not encourage marriage. For example, Sweden offers no married-couple allowance for tax purposes, no tax deduction for raising children, and no way for couples to jointly file their income taxes. Not surprisingly, many Swedish couples choose to cohabit rather than to marry. About half of the babies in Sweden are born to unmarried mothers—although there are proportionately many fewer unmarried *teenage* mothers in Sweden than in the United States (*The Economist* 1995).

People commonly associate cohabitation only with college campuses or sexual experimentation. But according to a study in Los Angeles, working couples are almost twice as likely to cohabit as college students are. And census data show that in 2000, 41 percent of unmarried couples had one or more children present in the household. These cohabitants are more like spouses than dating partners. Moreover, in contrast to the common perception that people

who cohabit have never been married, researchers report that about half of all people involved in cohabitation in the United States have been previously married. Cohabitation serves as a temporary or permanent alternative to matrimony for many men and women who have experienced their own divorces or the inability of their parents to remain married (Fields 2001; Popenoe and Whitehead 1999).

Recent research has documented significant increases in cohabitation among older people in the United States. For example, census data indicate that in 1980, there were 340,000 opposite-sex couples who were unmarried, living together, and over the age of 45. By 1998, there were 985,000 such couples—nearly three times as many. Older couples may choose cohabitation rather than marriage for many reasons: because of religious differences, to preserve the full Social Security benefits they receive as single people, out of fear of commitment, to avoid upsetting children from previous marriages, because one partner or both are not legally divorced, or because one or both have lived through a spouse's illness and death and do not want to experience that again. But some older couples simply see no need for marriage and report being happy living together as they are (Bureau of the Census 1999a:60).

Remaining Single

Looking at TV programs today, you would be justified in thinking most households are composed of singles. Although this is not the case, it is true that more and more people in the United States are *postponing* entry into first marriages. As of 2000, one out of every four households in the United States (accounting for over 26 million people) was a single-member household. Even so, fewer than 5 percent of women and men in the United States are likely to remain single throughout their lives (Bureau of the Census 2000a: 103; Simmons and O'Neill 2001).

The trend toward maintaining a single lifestyle for a longer period of time is related to the growing economic independence of young people. This is especially significant for women. Freed from financial needs, women don't necessarily have to marry to enjoy a satisfying life. Divorce, late marriage, and longevity also figure into this trend.

p. 313 ◀

There are many reasons why a person may choose not to marry. (Just ask *Ally McBeal*'s Renee, Richard, Elaine, John, and, of course, Ally.) Singleness is an attractive option for those who do not want to limit their sexual intimacy to one lifetime partner. Also, some men and women do not want to become highly dependent on any one person—and do not want anyone depending heavily on them. In a society that values individuality and self-fulfillment, the single lifestyle can offer certain freedoms that married couples may not enjoy.

Remaining single represents a clear departure from societal expectations; indeed, it has been likened to "being single on Noah's Ark." A single adult must confront the inaccurate view that he or she is always lonely, is a workaholic, and is immature. These stereotypes help support the traditional assumption in the United States and most other societies that to be truly happy and fulfilled, a person must get married and raise a family. To help counter these societal expectations, singles have formed numerous support groups, such as Alternative to Marriage Project (www.unmarried.org).

Singlehood—living without a partner and without children—also has social implications for the broader society. According to Robert Putnam of Harvard University, Americans are now less active both politically and socially than they were in the 1970s, due in part to the fact that more of them are living the single life. Experts worry about a potential decline in support for local schools, as well as a probable rise in the number of elderly people needing home care (Belsie 2001).

Lesbian and Gay Relationships

> We were both raised in middle-class families, where the expectation was we would go to college, we would become educated, we'd get a nice white-collar job, we'd move up and own a nice house in the suburbs. And that's exactly what we've done. (*New York Times* 1998:B2)

Sound like an average family? The only break with traditional expectations in this case is that the "we" described here is a gay couple.

The lifestyles of lesbians and gay men vary greatly. Some live in long-term, monogamous relationships. Some couples live with children from former heterosexual marriages or adopted children. Some live alone, others with roommates. Others remain married and do not publicly acknowledge their homosexuality. In their election exit polls, researchers for the National Health and Social Life Survey and the Voter News Service estimate that 2 to 5 percent of the adult population identify themselves as either gay or lesbian. An analysis of the 2000 Census shows a minimum of at least 600,000 gay households, and a gay and lesbian adult population approaching 10 million (Lauman et al. 1994b:293; Smith and Gates 2001).

The contemporary lesbian and gay rights movement has given an increasing number of lesbians and gay men the support to proclaim their sexual and affectional orientation. Gay activists were distressed in 1986 when a divided Supreme Court ruled, by a 5–4 vote, that the Constitution does not protect homosexual relations between consenting adults, even within the privacy of their own

A national organization called Marriage Equality sponsors advertisements such as this to promote the legal recognition of same-sex marriage.

homes. Nevertheless, as of 2000, 10 states, the District of Columbia, and more than 165 cities and counties in the United States had adopted civil rights laws protecting lesbians and gay men against discrimination in such areas as employment, housing, and public accommodations (American Civil Liberties Union 2000).

Recognition of same-sex partnerships is not uncommon in Europe, including Denmark, Holland, Switzerland, France, Belgium, and parts of Germany, Italy, and Spain. In 2001, the Netherlands converted their "registered same-sex partnerships" into full-fledged marriages, with divorce provisions (Daley 2000).

Gay activist organizations emphasize that despite the passage of state and local laws protecting the civil rights of lesbians and gay men, lesbian couples and gay male couples are prohibited from marrying—and therefore from gaining traditional partnership benefits—in 49 of the 50 states. In 2000, Vermont became the first state to recognize a civil union between two people of the same sex, a marriage in virtually every legal aspect but its name. Many gay couples now go to Vermont to be united, despite the fact that their unions are unlikely to be recognized elsewhere.

As of 2001, 39 municipalities had passed legislation allowing for registration of domestic partnerships, and 110 cities provided employee benefits that extend to domestic partnerships. Under such policies, a **domestic partnership** may be defined as two unrelated adults who reside together, agree to be jointly responsible for their dependents, basic living expenses, and other common necessities, and share a mutually caring relationship. Domestic partnership benefits can apply to such areas as inheritance, parenting, pensions, taxation, housing, immigration, workplace fringe benefits, and health care. Whereas the most passionate support for domestic partnership legislation has come from lesbian and gay male activists, the majority of those eligible for such benefits would be cohabiting heterosexual couples (American Civil Liberties Union 2001).

Domestic partnership legislation, however, faces strong opposition from conservative religious and political groups. In the view of opponents, support for domestic partnership undermines the historic societal preference for the nuclear family. Advocates of domestic partnership counter that such relationships fulfill the same functions for the individuals involved and for society as the traditional family and should enjoy the same legal protections and benefits. The gay couple quoted at the beginning of this section consider themselves a family unit, just like the nuclear family that lives down the street in their West Hartford, Connecticut, suburb. They cannot understand why they have been denied a family membership at their municipal swimming pool (*New York Times* 1998).

In 2000, a national survey showed that only 34 percent of the general public in the United States think gays and lesbians should be allowed to be legally married; 51 percent oppose such an arrangement, and 14 percent are unsure (Associated Press 2000).

Marriage without Children

There has been a modest increase in childlessness in the United States. According to data from the census, about 19 percent of women in 1998 will complete their childbearing years without having borne any children, compared to 10 percent in 1980. As many as 20 percent of women in their 30s expect to remain childless (Bachu 1999).

Childlessness within marriage has generally been viewed as a problem that can be solved through such means as adoption and artificial insemination. More and more couples today, however, choose not to have children and regard themselves as child-free, not childless. They do not believe that having children automatically follows from marriage, nor do they feel that reproduction is the duty of all married couples. Childless couples have formed support groups (with names like "No Kidding") and set up websites on the Internet (Terry 2000).

Economic considerations have contributed to this shift in attitudes; having children has become quite expensive. According to a government estimate in 1999, the average middle-class family will spend $151,590 to feed, clothe, and shelter a child from birth to age 18. If the child attends college, that amount could double, depending on the college chosen. Aware of the financial pressures, some couples are having fewer children than they otherwise might, and others are weighing the advantages of a child-free marriage (Bureau of the Census 2000a:462).

Childless couples are beginning to question current practices in the workplace. While applauding employers'
p. 101
efforts to provide child care and flexible work schedules, some couples nevertheless express concern about tolerance of employees who leave early to take children to doctors, ballgames, or after-school classes. As more dual-career couples enter the paid labor force and struggle to balance career and familial responsibilities, there may be increasing conflicts with employees who have no children (Burkett 2000).

Meanwhile, many childless couples who desperately want children are willing to try any means necessary to get pregnant. The social policy section that follows explores the controversy surrounding recent advances in reproductive technology.

Imagine

What would happen to our society if many more married couples suddenly decided not to have children? How would society change if cohabitation and/or singlehood became the norm?

SOCIAL POLICY AND THE FAMILY

Reproductive Technology

www.
mhhe
.com
/schaefer8

The Issue

The 1997 feature film *Gattaca* told the story of a future United States in which genetic engineering enhanced people's genes. Those who were not "enhanced" in the womb—principally those whose parents could not afford the treatments—suffered discrimination and social hurdles throughout their lives. To borrow a line from the movie, "Your genes are your résumé."

Far-fetched? Perhaps, but today we are witnessing aspects of reproductive technology that were regarded as so much science fiction just a generation ago. "Test tube" babies, frozen embryos, surrogate mothers, sperm and egg donation, and cloning of human cells are raising questions about the ethics of creating and shaping human life. To what extent should social policy encourage or discourage innovative reproductive technology?

The Setting

In an effort to overcome infertility, many couples turn to a recent reproductive advance known as in vitro fertilization (IVF). In this technique, an egg and a sperm are combined in a laboratory dish. If the egg is fertilized, the resulting embryo (the so-called test tube baby) is transferred into the woman's uterus. When combined with drug therapy, IVF increases the likelihood of a successful pregnancy.

The procedure also makes *multiple* births more likely. Between 1980 and 1999, the rate of triplets or larger multiples of babies born to the same mother at the same time increased more than 420 percent. Obviously, this results in substantially larger medical and child care expenses for the parents and presents unique and difficult parenting challenges (Ventura et al. 2001a).

While using technology to enhance the ability to reproduce is a recent phenomenon, the first successful artificial insemination actually took place in 1884 in Philadelphia. However, the ability to preserve sperm, beginning in the 1970s, made the process much simpler, since it eliminated the inconvenience of matching ovulation cycles with sperm donations (Rifkin 1998).

Sociological Insights

Replacing personnel is a functional prerequisite that the family as a social institution performs. Obviously, advances in reproductive technology allow childless couples to fulfill their personal, and societal, goals. The new technology also allows opportunities not previously considered. A small but growing number of same-sex couples are using donated sperm or eggs to have genetically related children and fulfill their desire to have a family (Bruni 1998).

In the future depicted in *Gattaca,* the poor were at a disadvantage in being able to control their lives genetically. The conflict perspective analysts would note that in the world today, the available technologies are often accessible only to the most affluent. Just as techniques were being perfected, insurance companies announced they were terminating coverage of advanced fertility treatments, such as in vitro fertilization. For many infertile couples, cost is a major factor, according to a survey conducted by the Centers for Disease Control and Prevention. In vitro fertilization can cost about $10,000 for each procedure, and there is no guarantee that the procedure will succeed (Stephen 1999).

Conflict theorists further note the irony that while lower-class women have broad access to contraceptive coverage, they have limited access to infertility treatments. Sociologists Leslie King and Madonna Harrington Meyer (1997) conclude that class differences in access to reproductive services lead to a dualistic fertility policy in the United States, one that encourages births among the more affluent and discourages births among the poor, particularly those on Medicaid.

Today it is possible to know the sex of the unborn. Coupled with the ability to legally abort a fetus, this knowledge allows parents to reduce the likelihood of having a baby of an "unwanted sex." This practice has been common in countries with a patriarchal tradition, such as India. Now, however, it is even becoming possible to *preselect* the sex of a baby. Beginning in 1998, at a cost of about $2,500, couples could purchase the expertise that would select the sperm more likely to produce a baby of a desired sex. Feminist theorists are watching these developments closely. They are concerned that in societies where men enjoy a higher status, use of this technology will effectively reduce the presence of women. Initial indications in the United States suggest that couples using this procedure are just as likely to try to engineer a girl as a boy, but this development needs to be monitored in the twenty-first century (Belkin 1999).

Interactionists observe that the quest for information and social support connected with reproductive technology has created new social networks. Like other special-interest groups, couples with infertility problems band together to share information, offer support to one another, and demand better treatment. They develop social networks—sometimes through voluntary associations or Internet support groups—where they share information about new medical techniques, insurance plans, and the merits of particular physicians and hospitals. One Internet self-help group, Mothers of Supertwins, offers supportive services for mothers and lobbies for improved counseling at infertility clinics, to better prepare couples for the demands of many babies at one time (MOST 2001).

Policy Initiatives

In Japan, some infertile couples have caused a controversy by using eggs or sperm donated by siblings for in vitro fertilization. This violates an ethical (though not legal) ban on "extramarital fertilization," the use of genetic material from anyone other than a spouse for conception. While opinion is divided on this issue, most Japanese agree that there should be government guidelines on reproductive technology. Many nations, including England and Australia, bar payments to egg donors, resulting in very few donors in these countries. Even more countries limit how many times a man can donate sperm. Because the United States has no such restrictions, infertile foreigners who can afford the costs view this country as a land of opportunity (Efron 1998; Kolata 1998).

The legal and ethical issues connected with reproductive technology are immense. Many people think we should be preparing for the possibility of a human clone. At this time, however, industrial societies are hard-pressed to deal with present advances in reproductive technology, much less future ones. Already, reputable hospitals are mixing donated sperm and eggs to create embryos that are frozen for future use. This raises the possibility of genetic screening as couples choose what they regard as the most "desirable" embryo—a "de-

The possibility of cloning humans, eerily foreshadowed in Andy Warhol's *The Twenty Marilyns*, poses major ethical dilemmas.

signer baby," in effect. Couples can select (some would say adopt) a frozen embryo that matches their requests in terms of race, sex, height, body type, eye color, intelligence, ethnic and religious background, and even national origin (Begley 1999; Rifkin 1998).

Let's Discuss

1. What are some recent innovations in reproductive technology? What ethical and legal issues do they raise?
2. Do you think the ability to preselect the sex of a baby will result in an imbalance between the sexes? Why or why not?
3. If you were writing legislation to regulate reproductive technology, what guidelines (if any) would you include?

Chapter Resources

Summary

The *family,* in its many varying forms, is present in all human cultures. This chapter examines the state of marriage, the family, and other intimate relationships in the United States and considers alternatives to the traditional nuclear family.

1. There are many variations in the family from culture to culture and even within the same culture.
2. The structure of the *extended family* can offer certain advantages over that of the *nuclear family.*
3. We determine kinship by descent from both parents *(bilateral descent),* from the father *(patrilineal),* or from the mother *(matrilineal).*
4. Sociologists do not agree on whether the *egalitarian family* has replaced the *patriarchal family* as the social norm in the United States.
5. Sociologists have identified six basic functions of the family: reproduction, protection, socialization, regulation of sexual behavior, companionship, and the provision of social status.
6. Conflict theorists argue that the family contributes to societal injustice and denies opportunities to women that are extended to men.
7. Interactionists focus on the microlevel—on how individuals interact in the family and other intimate relationships.
8. Feminists stress the need to broaden research on the family. As do conflict theorists, they see the family's role in socializing children as the primary source of sexism in society.
9. Mates are selected in a variety of ways. Some marriages are arranged. In other societies people choose their own mates. Some societies require a mate to be chosen within a certain group *(endogamy)* or outside certain groups *(exogamy).*
10. In the United States, considerable variation in family life is associated with social class, race, and ethnic differences.
11. Currently, the majority of all married couples in the United States have two partners active in the paid labor force.
12. Among the factors that contribute to the rising divorce rate in the United States are the greater social acceptance of divorce and the liberalization of divorce laws in many states.
13. More and more people are living together without marrying, thereby engaging in what is called *cohabitation.* People are also staying single longer and deciding not to have children within marriage.
14. While many municipalities in the United States have passed *domestic partnership* legislation, such proposals continue to face strong opposition from conservative religious and political groups.
15. Reproductive technology has advanced to such an extent that ethical questions have arisen about the creation and shaping of human life.

Critical Thinking Questions

1. Recent political campaigns have featured extensive discussion of "family values." What does this term mean to you? Why do candidates use it in an election year? Are there ways in which government should act to strengthen family life in the United States? Should government act to promote the nuclear family model, or should it give equal support to all types of families, including single-parent households and families headed by gay and lesbian parents?
2. In an increasing proportion of couples in the United States, both partners work outside the home. What are the advantages and disadvantages of the dual-income model for women, for men, for children, and for society as a whole?
3. Given the high rate of divorce in the United States, is it more appropriate to view divorce as dysfunctional or as a normal part of our marriage system? What are the implications of viewing divorce as normal rather than as dysfunctional?

Key Terms

Adoption In a legal sense, a process that allows for the transfer of the legal rights, responsibilities, and privileges of parenthood to a new legal parent or parents. (page 360)

Bilateral descent   A kinship system in which both sides of a person's family are regarded as equally important. (351)

Cohabitation   The practice of living together as a male–female couple without marrying. (366)

Domestic partnership   Two unrelated adults who have chosen to share one another's lives in a relationship of mutual caring, who reside together, and who agree to be jointly responsible for their dependents, basic living expenses, and other common necessities. (369)

Egalitarian family   An authority pattern in which the adult members of the family are regarded as equals. (352)

Endogamy   The restriction of mate selection to people within the same group. (356)

Exogamy   The requirement that people select mates outside certain groups. (356)

Extended family   A family in which relatives—such as grandparents, aunts, or uncles—live in the same home as parents and their children. (349)

Familism   Pride in the extended family, expressed through the maintenance of close ties and strong obligations to kinfolk. (358)

Family   A set of people related by blood, marriage or some other agreed-upon relationship, or adoption, who share the primary responsibility for reproduction and caring for members of society. (349)

Incest taboo   The prohibition of sexual relationships between certain culturally specified relatives. (356)

Kinship   The state of being related to others. (351)

Machismo   A sense of virility, personal worth, and pride in one's maleness. (358)

Matriarchy   A society in which women dominate in family decision making. (351)

Matrilineal descent   A kinship system that favors the relatives of the mother. (351)

Monogamy   A form of marriage in which one woman and one man are married only to each other. (350)

Nuclear family   A married couple and their unmarried children living together. (349)

Patriarchy   A society in which men dominate family decision making. (351)

Patrilineal descent   A kinship system that favors the relatives of the father. (351)

Polyandry   A form of polygamy in which a woman can have more than one husband at the same time. (350)

Polygamy   A form of marriage in which an individual can have several husbands or wives simultaneously. (350)

Polygyny   A form of polygamy in which a husband can have several wives at the same time. (350)

Serial monogamy   A form of marriage in which a person can have several spouses in his or her lifetime but only one spouse at a time. (350)

Single-parent families   Families in which there is only one parent present to care for children. (362)

Additional Readings

BOOKS

Bianchi, Suzanne M., and Lynne M. Casper. 2000. *American Families* (*Population Bulletin*, December 2000). Washington, DC: Population Reference Bureau. This concise (44-page) publication provides a statistical and social overview of U.S. households at the beginning of the twenty-first century.

Coontz, Stephanie. 1997. *The Way We Really Are: Coming to Terms with America's Changing Families.* New York: Basic Books. A family historian considers how much and how little family organization has changed in the United States.

Hertz, Rosanna, and Nancy L. Marshall, eds. 2001. *Working Families: The Transformation of the American Home.* Berkeley: University of California Press. Two sociologists look at the rise of dual-income families and the social dynamics of work and parenthood.

Hochschild, Arlie Russell. 1997. *Time Bind: When Work Becomes Home and Home Becomes Work.* New York: Metropolitan Books, Henry Holt. The author of *The Second Shift* describes the time crunch working Americans face and its consequences for their families.

Luker, Kristin. 1996. *Dubious Conceptions: The Politics of Teenage Pregnancy.* Cambridge, MA: Harvard University Press. A sociologist analyzes attitudes toward unwed mothers in the United States, including the current "demonization" of these young women.

Mindel, Charles H., Robert W. Habenstein, and Roosevelt Wright, Jr., eds. 1998. *Ethnic Families in America: Patterns and Variations.* 4th ed. Upper Saddle River, NJ: Prentice Hall. This collection of 19 essays covers the family as a social institution in a variety of ethnic contexts, including Cuban American, Asian Indian, Native American, and Amish.

Salinger, Adrienne. 1999. *Living Solo.* Kansas City, MO: Andrews McMeel Publishing. A photojournalist examines the lives of single people, investigating their inner lives, dwelling places, and somewhat eccentric indulgences.

Smith, William L. 1999. *Families and Communes: An Examination of Nontraditional Lifestyles.* Thousand Oaks, CA: Sage. A scholar takes a fresh look at family life within communes, and at communes as substitutes for the nuclear family.

Wallerstein, Judith S., Julia M. Lewis, and Sandra Blaeslee. 2000. *The Unexpected Legacy of Divorce.* New York: Hyperion. A study that tracked children for 25 years after their parents' divorce and examined the impact of the event on their lives.

Zambrana, Ruth E., ed. 1995. *Understanding Latino Families: Scholarship, Policy, and Practice.* Thousand Oaks, CA: Sage. An anthology of 10 specially written articles focusing on family life among Latinos.

JOURNALS

Among the journals focusing on the family are *Family Planning Perspectives* (founded in 1969), *Family Relations* (1951), *International Family Planning Perspectives* (1975), *Journal of Comparative Family Studies* (1970), *Journal of Family Issues* (1980), *Journal of Family Violence* (1986), *Journal of Marriage and the Family* (1938), and *Violence Against Women* (1995).

Technology Resources

Internet Connection

Notes: While all the URLs listed were current as of the printing of this book, these sites often change. Please check our website (http://www.mhhe.com/schaefer8) for updates and hyperlinks to these exercises and additional exercises.

1. The Family Pride Coalition is a group that is dedicated to educating the public about gay, lesbian, bisexual, and transgender families. Visit their website at **http://www.familypride.org,** click on "Issues and News" and then on "Myths and Facts." Answer the following questions:
   (a) How many daughters and sons of gay, lesbian, and bisexual parents does the American Bar Association estimate there are in the United States?
   (b) How many decades have passed since the American Psychological Association removed homosexuality from the *Diagnostic and Statistical Manual* of mental disorders?
   (c) What has research on gay and lesbian parents shown?
   (d) What percentage of child sexual abuse cases involves a heterosexual male perpetrator?
   (e) Of all the myths you read about, which did you find the most interesting?
   (f) Did you believe any of the myths before you read about them on this website?

2. Sociologists who study families examine both the positive and negative aspects of family life. Domestic violence is an example of the dark side of relationships, an issue that, as this chapter demonstrates, is a worldwide problem. To learn more about this social problem, log onto famvi.com, designed by Gary Templeton (**http://www.famvi.com/**). Visit the sections "Other Statistics" and "More Facts" to gain an appreciation of the general issues. Visit the sections on "Comments" and "Writings" to understand how family violence affects the individual.
   (a) Summarize what you learned about children and domestic violence.
   (b) What did you learn about violence and visits to emergency rooms? What does the March of Dimes research tell us?
   (c) Which poems and stories had the greatest impact on you? What lessons did you learn about family violence?
   (d) Describe the logo used by famvi.com. Engage your interactionist skills to discuss what this logo symbolizes. What message does it convey?

3. In 1998, 68.1 percent of children under 18 in the United States lived with two parents, many of whom were stepparents. The Stepfamily Association of America provides information about stepfamilies. Go to their website (**http://www.saafamilies.org**), click on "Facts & FAQs," and answer the following questions:
   (a) What estimated percentage of marriages ends in divorce?
   (b) What percentage of divorced persons eventually remarries?
   (c) Under "Facts & FAQs," click on "Stepfamily Myths." Which myths do you find the most interesting?
   (d) How many of these myths were you already familiar with? How many did you believe?

(e) Under "Facts & FAQs," click on "Research Findings" and read the article "Does Living in a Stepfamily Increase the Risk of Delinquency in Children?" What did the researchers find was the answer to their question?

Online Learning Center www.mhhe.com/schaefer8

When you visit the student center in the Online Learning Center at **www.mhhe. com/schaefer8,** link to "Audio Clips." Richard Schaefer, the author of your text, discusses how chat rooms are playing the role that singles' bars did in the 1980s. Professor Schaefer notes that sociologists want to determine whether the Internet is restructuring dating behavior or merely facilitating it.

CHAPTER 15

RELIGION

In this billboard, Volkswagen of France compares a secular event, the introduction of a new model ("Rejoice, my friends, for a new Golf is born") to a sacred event. While such tongue-in-cheek references to religion may offend believers, they indicate the continuing relevance of religion, even in modern, industrialized societies.

Growing up in a small mixed-blood community of seven hundred on the eastern edge of the Pine Ridge Reservation in South Dakota, I uncritically accepted the idea that the old Dakota religion and Christianity were both "true" and in some mysterious way compatible with each other. There were, to be sure, Christian fundamentalists with their intolerance and the old traditional Indians who kept their practices hidden, but the vast majority of the people in the vicinity more or less assumed that a satisfactory blend had been achieved that guaranteed our happiness.

Although my father was an Episcopal priest with a large number of chapels in a loosely organized Episcopal missionary district known (to Episcopalians) as "Corn Creek," he was far from an orthodox follower of the white man's religion. I always had the feeling that within the large context of "religion," which in a border town meant the Christian milieu, there was a special area in his spiritual life in which the old Dakota beliefs and practices reigned supreme. He knew thirty-three songs; some of them social, some ancient, and several spiritual songs used in a variety of ceremonial contexts. Driving to his chapels to hold Christian services he would open the window of the car and beat the side of the door with his hand for the drum beat and sing song after song. . . .

When I went to college I was exposed to a much larger canvas of human experience upon which various societies had left their religious mark. My first reaction was the belief that most of the religious traditions were simply wrong, that a few of them had come close to describing religious reality, but that it would take some intensive study to determine which religious traditions would best assist human beings in succeeding in the world. It was my good fortune to have as a religion and philosophy professor a Christian mystic who was trying to prove the deepest mysteries of the faith. He also had some intense personal problems which emerged again and again in his beliefs, indicating to me that religion and the specific individual path of life were always intertwined.

Over several years and many profound conversations he was able to demonstrate to me that each religious tradition had developed a unique way to confront some problems and that they had something in common if only the search for truth and the elimination of many false paths. But his solution, after many years, became untenable for me. I saw instead religion simply as a means of organizing a society, articulating some reasonably apparent emotional truths, but ultimately becoming a staid part of social establishments that primarily sought to control human behavior and not fulfill human individual potential. It seemed as if those religions that placed strong emphasis on certain concepts failed precisely in the areas in which they claimed expertise. Thus religions of "love" could point to few examples of their efficacy; religions of "salvation" actually saved very few. The more I learned about world religions, the more respect I had for the old Dakota ways. *(Deloria 1999:273–75)* ■ 💿

Additional information about this excerpt and about those that open each subsequent chapter can be found in the SocWorld CD-ROM that accompanies this text.

In this excerpt from *For This Land,* Vine Deloria—a Standing Rock Sioux—reveals his deep personal ties to the religion of his ancestors, undiluted by the overlays of missionary Christian theology. Even though his father is an Episcopal priest, Deloria is keenly aware of how tribal beliefs intrude and color his father's religious sensibility. He is also aware of the fact that Native American rites and customs have been appropriated by a generation of non-Indians seeking a kind of New Age "magic." For Deloria, Indian spiritual beliefs are an integral part of the Native American culture and help to define that culture. Mixing those beliefs with the beliefs of other religions or systems of thought threatens to undermine the strength of the culture.

Religion plays a major role in people's lives, and religious practices of some sort are evident in every society. That makes religion a *cultural universal,* along with other general practices found in every culture such p. 62 as dancing, food preparation, the family, and personal names. At present, an estimated 4 billion people belong to the world's many religious faiths (see Figure 15-1).

When religion's influence on other social institutions in a society diminishes, the process of *secularization* is said to be underway. During this process, religion will survive in the private sphere of individual and family life (as in the case of many Native American families); it may even thrive on a personal level. But, at the same time, other social institutions—such as the economy, politics, and education—maintain their own sets of norms independent of religious guidance (Stark and Iannaccone 1992).

How do people's religious beliefs and practices differ from one part of the world to the next? What social purposes does religion serve? How do people express their religion, and how do they organize themselves for religious purposes? Has modern communications technology affected religion? In this chapter we will concentrate on religion as it is practiced in modern industrial societies. We will begin with a brief description of the approaches Émile Durkheim introduced, and those later sociologists have used, in studying religion. A brief overview of the world's major religions follows. Next, we will explore religion's role in societal integration, social support, social change, and social control. We'll examine three important dimensions of religious behavior—belief, ritual, and experience—as well as the basic forms of religious organization. We will pay particular attention to the emergence of new religious movements. Finally, the chapter will close with a social policy discussion of the controversy over religion in public schools. ◼

Durkheim and the Sociological Approach to Religion

If a group believes that it is being directed by a "vision from God," sociologists will not attempt to prove or disprove this revelation. Instead, they will assess the effects of the religious experience on the group. What sociologists are interested in is the social impact of religion on individuals and institutions (McGuire 1997).

Émile Durkheim was perhaps the first sociologist to recognize the critical importance of religion in human societies. He saw its appeal for the individual, but—more important—he stressed the *social* impact of religion. In p. 11 Durkheim's view, religion is a collective act and includes many forms of behavior in which people interact with others. As in his work on suicide, Durkheim was not so interested in the personalities of religious believers as he was in understanding religious behavior within a social context.

Durkheim defined *religion* as a "unified system of beliefs and practices relative to sacred things." In his view, religion involves a set of beliefs and practices that are uniquely the property of religion—as opposed to other social institutions and ways of thinking. Durkheim ([1912] 2001) argued that religious faiths distinguish between certain events that transcend the ordinary and the everyday world. He referred to these realms as the *sacred* and the *profane.*

The *sacred* encompasses elements beyond everyday life that inspire awe, respect, and even fear. People become a part of the sacred realm only by completing some ritual, such as prayer or sacrifice. Believers have faith in the sacred; this faith allows them to accept what they cannot understand. By contrast, the *profane* includes the ordinary and commonplace. It can get confusing, however, because the same object can be either sacred or profane depending on how it is viewed. A normal dining room table is profane, but it becomes sacred to Christians if it bears the elements of a communion. A candelabra becomes sacred for Jews when it is a menorah. For Confucians and

Figure 15-1

Religions of the World

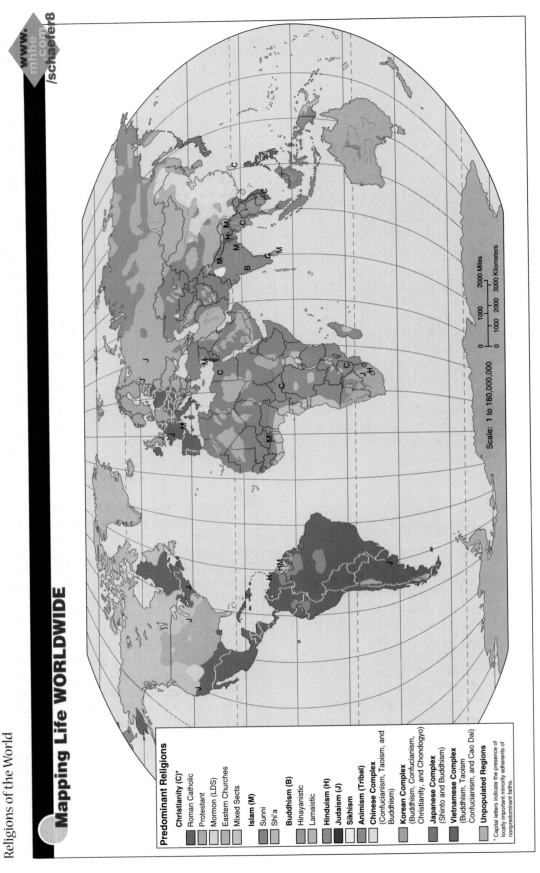

Mapping Life WORLDWIDE

Predominant Religions

Christianity (C)*
- Roman Catholic
- Protestant
- Mormon (LDS)
- Eastern Churches
- Mixed Sects

Islam (M)
- Sunni
- Shi'a

Buddhism (B)
- Hinayanistic
- Lamaistic

Hinduism (H)

Judaism (J)

Sikhism

Animism (Tribal)

Chinese Complex
(Confucianism, Taoism, and Buddhism)

Korean Complex
(Buddhism, Confucianism, Christianity, and Chondogyo)

Japanese Complex
(Shinto and Buddhism)

Vietnamese Complex
(Buddhism, Taoism, Confucianism, and Cao Dai)

Unpopulated Regions

* Capital letters indicate the presence of locally important minority adherents of nonpredominant faiths.

Scale: 1 to 180,000,000

0   1000   2000 Miles
0   1000   2000   3000 Kilometers

Source: Allen 2001:32.

Christmas in Kuwait: A U.S. Marine chaplain conducts a Christmas Eve service in the Kuwaiti desert during a four-day operation against Iraq in December 1998. Chaplains turn secular spaces into sacred spaces, bringing comfort to soldiers serving far from home.

Taoists, incense sticks are not mere decorative items; they are highly valued offerings to the gods in religious ceremonies marking new and full moons.

Following the direction established by Durkheim almost a century ago, contemporary sociologists view religions in two different ways. They study the norms and values of religious faiths through examination of their substantive religious beliefs. For example, it is possible to compare the degree to which Christian faiths literally interpret the Bible, or Muslim groups follow the Qur'an (or Koran), the sacred book of Islam. At the same time, sociologists examine religions in terms of the social functions they fulfill, such as providing social support or reinforcing the social norms. By exploring both the beliefs and the functions of religion, we can better understand its impact on the individual, on groups, and on society as a whole.

World Religions

Tremendous diversity exists in religious beliefs and practices. Overall, about 87 percent of the world's population adheres to some religion; only about 13 percent is nonreligious. Christianity is the largest single faith; the second largest is Islam (see Table 15-1). Although news events often suggest an inherent conflict between Christians and Muslims, the two faiths are similar in many ways. Both are monotheistic (that is, based on a single deity); both

include a belief in prophets, an afterlife, and a judgment day. In fact, Islam recognizes Jesus as a prophet, though not as the son of God. Both faiths impose a moral code on believers, which varies from fairly rigid proscriptions for fundamentalists to relatively relaxed guidelines for liberals.

The followers of Islam, called *Muslims,* believe that Islam's holy scriptures were received from Allah (God) by the prophet Mohammad nearly 1,400 years ago. They see Mohammad as the last in a long line of prophets, preceded by Adam, Abraham, Moses, and Jesus. Islam is more communal in its expression than Christianity, particularly the more individualistic Protestant denominations. Consequently, in countries that are predominantly Muslim, the separation of religion and the state is not considered necessary or even desirable. In fact, Muslim governments often reinforce Islamic practices through their laws. Muslims do vary sharply in their interpretation of several traditions, some of which—such as the wearing of veils by women—are more cultural than religious in origin.

Like Christianity and Islam, Judaism is monotheistic. Jews believe that God's true nature is revealed in the Torah, which Christians know as the first five books of the Old Testament. According to these scriptures, God formed a covenant, or pact, with Abraham and Sarah, the ancestors of the tribes of Israel. Even today, Jews believe, this covenant holds them accountable to God's will. If they follow both the letter and spirit of the Torah, a long-awaited Messiah will one day bring paradise to earth. Although Judaism has a relatively small following compared to other major faiths, it forms the historical foundation for both Christianity and Islam. Consequently, Jews revere many of the same sacred Middle Eastern sites as Christians and Muslims.

Three other faiths developed in a different part of the world, India. The earliest, Hinduism, differs from Judaism, Christianity, and Islam in that it is polytheistic—that is, based on the existence of many deities. It is also distinguished by a belief in reincarnation, or the perpetual rebirth of the soul after death. Unlike Judaism, Christianity, and Islam, which are based largely on sacred texts, Hindu beliefs have been preserved mostly through oral tradition. Box 15-1 describes a second faith, Jainism, that emerged from the Hindu tradition. More so than in other

Table 15-1 Major World Religions

Faith	Current Following, in Millions (and Percent of World Population)	Primary Location of Followers Today	Founder (and Approximate Birth Date)	Important Texts (and Holy Sites)
Buddhism	360 (5.9%)	Southeast Asia, Mongolia, Tibet	Gautama Siddhartha (563 B.C.)	Triptaka (areas in Nepal)
Christianity	2,000 (33%)	Europe, North America, South America	Jesus (6 B.C.)	Bible (Jerusalem, Rome)
Hinduism	811 (13.4%)	India, Indian communities overseas	No specific founder (1500 B.C.)	Sruti and Smrti texts (seven sacred cities, including Vavansi)
Islam	1,190 (19.6%)	Middle East, Central Asia, North Africa, Indonesia	Mohammad (A.D. 570)	Qur'an or Koran (Mecca, Medina, Jerusalem)
Judaism	14 (0.2%)	Israel, United States, France, Russia	Abraham (2000 B.C.)	Torah, Talmud (Jerusalem)

major religions, Hindus and Jains are expected to deny themselves worldly pleasures.

A third religion, Buddhism, developed as a reaction against Hinduism. This faith is founded on the teachings of Siddhartha (later called Buddha, or "the enlightened one"). Through meditation, followers of Buddhism strive to overcome selfish cravings for physical or material pleasures, with the goal of reaching a state of enlightenment, or *nirvana*. Buddhists created the first monastic orders, which are thought to be the models on which monastic orders in other religions, including Christianity, are based. Though Buddhism emerged in India, its followers were eventually pushed out of that country by the Hindus. It is now found primarily in other parts of Asia. (Contemporary adherents of Buddhism in India are relatively recent converts.)

Although the differences among religions are striking, they are exceeded by variations within faiths. Consider the differences within Christianity, from relatively liberal denominations such as Presbyterians or the United Church of Christ to the more conservative Mormons and Greek Orthodox Catholics. Similar divisions exist within Hinduism, Islam, and other world religions (Barrett and Johnson 2001; David Levinson 1996).

The Role of Religion

Since religion is a cultural universal, it is not surprising that it plays a basic role in human societies. In sociological terms, these include both manifest and latent functions. Among its *manifest* (open and stated) functions, religion defines the spiritual world and gives meaning to the divine. Religion provides an explanation for events that seem difficult to understand, such as what lies beyond the grave.

 p. 15

The *latent* functions of religion are unintended, covert, or hidden. Even though the manifest function of church services is to offer a forum for religious worship, they might at the same time fulfill a latent function as a meeting ground for unmarried members.

Functionalists and conflict theorists both evaluate religion's impact as a social institution on human societies. We'll consider a functionalist view of religion's role in integrating society, in social support, and in promoting social change, and then look at religion as a means of social control from the conflict perspective. Note that, for the most part, religion's impact is best understood from a macro-level viewpoint, oriented toward the larger society.

Sociology in the Global Community

15-1 Jainism in India and the United States

www.
mhhe
.com
/schaefer8

In a suburb of Chicago, Shama Khandwala, a young woman of Asian Indian descent, talks about her commitment to nonviolence as she helps her mother cook a vegetarian meal. Like other followers of Jainism (pronounced *Jinism*), Khandwala believes her work should help rather than hurt others, so she has chosen physical therapy as her profession. Jains will not knowingly harm other living beings, including plants and animals, so they do not work in farming or fishing, in the military, or in the manufacture or sale of alcohol or drugs. Unlike adherents of other major religions, in which the concept of the sanctity of life is restricted to human life, Jains shun all meat, fish, and even vegetables whose harvest involves

> Jains shun all meat, fish, and even vegetables whose harvest involves the killing of the entire plant.

the killing of the entire plant, such as carrots and potatoes.

Jainism is a faith with over 4 million followers, most of whom live in India; about 50,000 reside in North America. The religion was founded in India six centuries before the birth of Christ by a young man named Mahavira. Offended by the Hindu caste system, a rigid social hierarchy that reduced some people to the status of outcasts based solely on their birth, and by the numerous Hindu deities, Mahavira left his family and his wealth behind to become a beggar monk. His teachings attracted many followers, and the faith grew and flourished until the Muslim invasions of the twelfth century A.D.

According to the Jain faith, there is no god; each person is responsible for his or her own spiritual well-being. By following a strict code of conduct, Jains believe they can ultimately free their souls from

an endless cycle of death and rebirth and attain *nirvana,* or spiritual bliss. Besides a commitment to nonviolence, the code requires Jains to forswear lying and stealing, practice self-denial and chastity, meditate, and limit their personal wealth. Jains take their faith seriously and are greatly respected for it in India. Though they are a relatively small group, they exercise considerable influence through their business dealings and their charitable contributions.

In the United States, the children of Jain immigrants from India do their best to resist the temptations of mainstream American culture, from hot dogs and leather jackets to the belief in a benevolent and forgiving Supreme Being. But unlike their parents and grandparents, many enjoy onions and garlic, and do not speak *Gujarati,* the traditional language of worship. Like the children of other groups who have immigrated to the United States, they are forging a uniquely American form of their culture and religion.

At a Jain temple in Milpitas, California, a monk sweeps the walk carefully to avoid stepping on insects. Adherents of Jainism revere all forms of life.

Let's Discuss

1. Are you a vegetarian? Will you consider the principle of nonviolence in choosing your occupation? Why or why not?

2. Aside from the obvious differences between Jainism and other major religions with which you may be familiar, such as Christianity, Judaism, and Islam, what are some of the similarities? What aspects of Jainism might Indian immigrants contribute to American society?

Sources: Barrett and Johnson 2001; Caillat 1987; David Levinson 1996; Lieblich 2001.

The social support function is an exception: it is best viewed on the micro-level, directed toward the individual.

The Integrative Function of Religion

Émile Durkheim viewed religion as an integrative power in human society—a perspective reflected in functionalist thought today. Durkheim sought to answer a perplexing question: "How can human societies be held together when they are generally composed of individuals and social groups with diverse interests and aspirations?" In his view, religious bonds often transcend these personal and divisive forces. Durkheim acknowledged that religion is not the only integrative force—nationalism or patriotism may serve the same end.

How does religion provide this "societal glue"? Religion, whether it be Buddhism, Islam, Christianity, or Judaism, offers people meaning and purpose for their lives. It gives them certain ultimate values and ends to hold in common. Although subjective and not always fully accepted, these values and ends help a society to function as an integrated social system. For example, funerals, weddings, bar

Workers install the sculpture *Angel of Harmony* by Wiktor Szostalo on the grounds of the St. Louis Cathedral Basilica. This statue of a black angel sheltering three ethnically diverse children suggests the integrative function of religion.

and bat mitzvahs, and confirmations serve to integrate people into larger communities by providing shared beliefs and values about the ultimate questions of life.

Religion also serves to bind people together in times of crisis and confusion. Immediately after the terrorist attacks of September 11, 2001, on New York City and Washington, D.C., attendance at worship services in the United States increased dramatically. Muslim, Jewish, and Christian clerics made joint appearances to honor the dead and urge citizens not to retaliate against those who looked, dressed, or sounded different from others. The integrative power of religion can be seen, too, in the role that churches, synagogues, and mosques have traditionally played and continue to play for immigrant groups in the United States. For example, Roman Catholic immigrants may settle near a parish church that offers services in their native language, such as Polish or Spanish. Similarly, Korean immigrants may join a Presbyterian church with many Korean American members and with religious practices like those of churches in Korea. Like other religious organizations, these Roman Catholic and Presbyterian churches help to integrate immigrants into their new homeland.

Yet another example of the integrative impact of religion is provided by the Universal Fellowship of Metropolitan Community Churches. It was established in the United States in 1968 to offer a welcoming place of worship for lesbians and gay men. This spiritual community is especially important today, given the many organized religions openly hostile to homosexuality. The Metropolitan Community Church has 44,000 members in its local churches in 15 countries. As part of its effort to support lesbian and gay rights, the Metropolitan Community Church performs same-sex marriages, which it calls "holy union ceremonies" (*Religion Watch* 2001).

In some instances, religious loyalties are *dysfunctional;* they contribute to tension and even conflict between groups or nations. During the Second World War, the German Nazis attempted to exterminate the Jewish people; approximately 6 million European Jews were killed. In modern times, nations such as Lebanon (Muslims versus Christians), Israel (Jews versus Muslims as well as Orthodox versus secular Jews), Northern Ireland (Roman Catholics versus Protestants), and India (Hindus versus Muslims and, more recently, Sikhs) have been torn by clashes that are in large part based on religion.

Religious conflict (though on a less violent level) has been increasingly evident in the United States as well. Sociologist James Davison Hunter (1991) has referred to the "cultural war" taking place in the United States. Christian fundamentalists, conservative Catholics, and Orthodox Jews have joined forces in many communities in a battle against their liberal counterparts for control of the secular culture. The battlefield is an array of familiar

A gay couple attends a special service for gays at Our Lady of Mt. Carmel Church in Chicago. Gay people of faith often feel shut out of congregational life.

social issues, among them multiculturalism, child care (Chapter 4), abortion (Chapter 12), home schooling, gay

pp. 101, 319

rights, and government funding for the arts.

Religion and Social Support

Most of us find it difficult to accept the stressful events of life—death of a loved one, serious injury, bankruptcy, divorce, and so forth. This is especially true when something "senseless" happens. How can family and friends come to terms with the death of a talented college student, not even 20 years old, from a terminal disease?

Through its emphasis on the divine and the supernatural, religion allows us to "do something" about the calamities we face. In some faiths, adherents can offer sacrifices or pray to a deity in the belief that such acts will change their earthly condition. At a more basic level, religion encourages us to view our personal misfortunes as relatively unimportant in the broader perspective of human history—or even as part of an undisclosed divine purpose. Friends and relatives of the deceased college student may see this death as being "God's will" and as having some ultimate benefit that we cannot understand now. This perspective may be much more comforting than the terrifying feeling that any of us can die senselessly at any moment—and that there is no divine "answer" as to why one person lives a long and full life, while another dies tragically at a relatively early age.

Faith-based community organizations have taken on more and more responsibilities in the area of social assistance. In fact, President George W. Bush created the Office of Faith-Based and Community Initiatives to ease regulations that prevent religious groups from competing for government funding. Sociologist William Julius Wilson (1999b) has singled out faith-based organizations in 40 communities from California to Massachusetts as models of social reform. These organizations identify experienced leaders and assemble them into nonsectarian coalitions devoted to community development.

Religion and Social Change

The Weberian Thesis

When someone seems driven to work and succeed we often attribute the "Protestant work ethic" to that person. The term comes from the writings of Max Weber, who carefully examined the connection between religious allegiance and capitalist development. His findings appeared in his pioneering work *The Protestant Ethic and the Spirit of Capitalism* ([1904] 1958a).

Weber noted that in European nations with both Protestant and Catholic citizens, an overwhelming number of business leaders, owners of capital, and skilled workers were Protestant. In his view, this was no mere coincidence. Weber pointed out that the followers of John Calvin (1509–1564), a leader of the Protestant Reformation, emphasized a disciplined work ethic, this-worldly concerns, and a rational orientation to life that have become known as the **Protestant ethic.** One by-product of the Protestant ethic was a drive to accumulate savings that could be used for future investment. This "spirit of capitalism," to use Weber's phrase, contrasted with the moderate work hours, leisurely work habits, and lack of ambition that he saw as typical of the times (Winter 1977; Yinger 1974).

Few books on the sociology of religion have aroused as much commentary and criticism as Weber's work. It has been hailed as one of the most important theoretical works in the field and as an excellent example of macrolevel analysis. Like Durkheim, Weber demonstrated that religion is not solely a matter of intimate personal beliefs. He stressed that the collective nature of religion has social consequences for society as a whole.

Weber provides a convincing description of the origins of European capitalism. But this economic system has subsequently been adopted by non-Calvinists in many parts of the world. Contemporary studies in the United States show little or no difference in achievement orientation between Roman Catholics and Protestants. Apparently, the "spirit of capitalism" has become a generalized cultural trait rather than a specific religious tenet (Greeley 1989).

Conflict theorists caution that Weber's theory—even if it is accepted—should not be regarded as an analysis of mature capitalism as reflected in the rise of multinational corporations that cross national boundaries. p. 246 Marxists would disagree with Max Weber not on the origins of capitalism but on its future. Unlike Marx, Weber believed that capitalism could endure indefinitely as an economic system. He added, however, that the decline of religion as an overriding force in society opened the way for workers to express their discontent more vocally (Collins 1980).

Liberation Theology

Sometimes the clergy can be found in the forefront of social change. Many religious activists, especially in the Roman Catholic church in Latin America, support *liberation theology*—the use of a church in a political effort to eliminate poverty, discrimination, and other forms of injustice evident in a secular society. Advocates of this religious movement sometimes sympathize with Marxism. Many believe that radical change, rather than economic development in itself, is the only acceptable solution to the desperation of the masses in impoverished developing countries. Activists associated with liberation theology believe that organized religion has a moral responsibility to take a strong public stand against the oppression of the poor, racial and ethnic minorities, and women (Smith 1991).

The term *liberation theology* dates back to the 1973 publication of the English translation of *A Theology of Liberation*. This book was written by a Peruvian priest, Gustavo Gutiérrez, who lived in a slum area of Lima during the early 1960s. After years of exposure to the vast poverty around him, Gutiérrez concluded that "in order to serve the poor, one had to move into political action" (Brown 1980:23; Gutiérrez 1990).

Politically committed Latin American theologians came under the influence of social scientists who viewed the domination of capitalism and multinational corporations as central to the hemisphere's problems. One result was a new approach to theology that rejected the models developed in Europe and the United States and instead built on the cultural and religious traditions of Latin America.

While many worshippers support liberation theology, religious leaders in the Roman Catholic church are not happy with the radical movement. The official position of Pope John Paul II and others in the church hierarchy is that clergy should adhere to traditional pastoral duties and keep a distance from radical politics. The Pope specifically came out against church activists in his 1999 visit to Mexico City (Pagani 1999).

Liberation theology may possibly be dysfunctional, however. Some Roman Catholics have come to believe that by focusing on political and governmental injustice, the clergy are no longer addressing their personal and spiritual needs. Partly as a result of such disenchantment, some Catholics in Latin America are converting to mainstream Protestant faiths or to Mormonism.

Religion and Social Control: A Conflict View

Liberation theology is a relatively recent phenomenon and marks a break with the traditional role of churches. It was this traditional role that Karl Marx opposed. In his view, religion *impeded* social change by encouraging

A female minister delivers a benediction, or blessing, by making the sign of the cross over her congregation. Until recent decades, women could not perform religious ceremonies in mainstream Protestant churches.

Social Inequality
15-2 The Stained Glass Ceiling

www. mhhe .com /schaefer8

What is the role of women in organized religion? Most faiths have a long tradition of exclusively male spiritual leadership. Furthermore, most religions are patriarchal, so they tend to reinforce men's dominance in secular as well as spiritual matters. Women do play a vital role as volunteers, staff, and religious educators, but even today, decision making and leadership typically fall to the men. There are exceptions to this rule, such as the Shakers and Christian Scientists, as well as Hinduism with its long goddess heritage, but they are rare.

Nationally, women compose only about 14 percent of U.S. clergy, though they have accounted for at least 20 percent of students enrolled in theological institutions over the last two decades. Women clerics typically have shorter careers than men, often in related fields such as counseling, which do not involve congregational leadership. In faiths that restrict leadership positions to men, women still serve unofficially. For example, about 4 percent of Roman Catholic

> **A stained glass ceiling seems to hover over clergy women, limiting their occupational mobility.**

congregations are led by women who hold nonordained pastoral positions—a necessity in a church that faces a shortage of male priests.

In the United States, congregations headed by women tend to be smaller and poorer than those headed by men. Consequently, women church leaders are much less likely than men to have any paid full-time staff. They are also more likely to begin and end their careers in positions that do not lead to advancement in their denominations. A stained glass ceiling seems to hover over clergy women, limiting their occupational mobility.

Let's Discuss

1. Does a religious community in your town or city have a female leader? If so, was her calling controversial? What do you think her prospects are for career advancement?
2. From society's point of view, what are the pros and cons of admitting women to religious leadership?

Sources: Bureau of the Census 2001a:380; Chang 1997; Konieczny and Chaves 2000.

---

oppressed people to focus on other-worldly concerns rather than on their immediate poverty or exploitation. Marx described religion as an "opiate" particularly harmful to oppressed peoples. He felt that religion often drugged the masses into submission by offering a consolation for their harsh lives on earth: the hope of salvation in an ideal afterlife. For example, during the period of slavery in the United States, White masters forbade Blacks to practice native African religions, while encouraging them to adopt the Christian religion. Christianity taught the slaves that obedience would lead to salvation and eternal happiness in the hereafter. Viewed from a conflict perspective, Christianity may have pacified certain slaves and blunted the rage that often fuels rebellion (McGuire 1997; Yinger 1970).

Marx acknowledged that religion plays an important role in propping up the existing social structure. The values of religion, as already noted, reinforce other social institutions and the social order as a whole. From Marx's perspective, however, religion's promotion of stability within society only helps to perpetuate patterns of social inequality. According to Marx, the dominant religion reinforces the interests of those in power (Harap 1982).

Consider, for example, India's traditional caste system. It defined the social structure of that society, at least among the Hindu majority. The caste system was almost certainly

p. 214 the creation of the priesthood, but it also served the interests of India's political rulers by granting a certain religious legitimacy to social inequality.

Contemporary Christianity, like the Hindu faith, reinforces traditional patterns of behavior that call for the subordination of the less powerful. The role of women in the church is an example of uneven distribution of power. Assumptions about gender roles leave women in a subservient position both within Christian churches and at home. In fact, women find it as difficult to achieve leadership positions in many churches as they do in large corporations. Box 15-2 describes the "stained glass ceiling" that tends to stunt clergywomen's career development even in the most liberal denominations. Like Marx, conflict theorists argue that to whatever extent religion actually does influence social behavior, it reinforces existing patterns of dominance and inequality (Bureau of the Census 1998c:417; Dart 1997).

From a Marxist perspective, religion functions as an "agent of de-politicization" (Wilson 1973). In simpler terms, religion keeps people from seeing their lives and p. 217 societal conditions in political terms—for example, by obscuring the overriding significance of conflicting economic interests. Marxists suggest that by inducing a "false consciousness" among the

387

disadvantaged, religion lessens the possibility of collective political action that can end capitalist oppression and transform society.

Religious Behavior

All religions have certain elements in common, yet these elements are expressed in the distinctive manner of each faith. The patterns of religious behavior, like other patterns of social behavior, are of great interest to sociologists, since they underscore the relationship between religion and society.

Religious beliefs, religious rituals, and religious experience all help to define what is sacred and to differentiate the sacred from the profane. Let us now examine these three dimensions of religious behavior.

Belief

Some people believe in life after death, in supreme beings with unlimited powers, or in supernatural forces. *Religious beliefs* are statements to which members of a particular religion adhere. These views can vary dramatically from religion to religion.

The Adam and Eve account of creation found in Genesis, the first book of the Old Testament, is an example of a religious belief. Many people in the United States strongly adhere to this biblical explanation of creation and even insist that it be taught in public schools. These people, known as *creationists,* are worried by the secularization of society and oppose teaching that directly or indirectly questions biblical scripture. The social policy section at the end of this chapter examines the issue of religion in the schools in depth.

As Figure 15-2 shows, worldwide, the strength of religious beliefs varies dramatically. In general, spirituality is not as strong in industrialized nations as in developing nations. The United States is an exception to this trend toward secularization, in part because the government encourages religious expression (without explicitly supporting it) by allowing religious groups to claim charitable status, and even to receive federal aid for activities such as educational services. And whereas belief in God is relatively weak in formerly communist states such as Russia, surveys show a growth in spirituality in communist countries over the last 10 years.

Ritual

Religious rituals are practices required or expected of members of a faith. Rituals usually honor the divine power (or powers) worshipped by believers; they also remind adherents of their religious duties and responsibilities.

Figure 15-2

Belief in God Worldwide

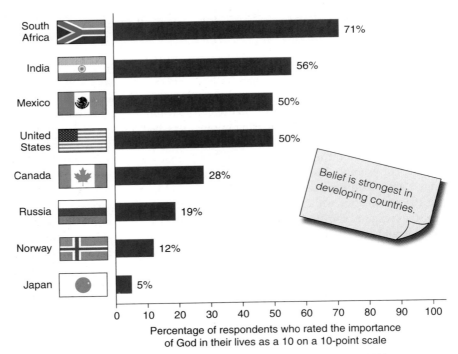

Belief is strongest in developing countries.

Note: Data are from World Values surveys for 1995–1998, except for Canada, 1990–1991.

Source: Inglehart and Baker 2000:47.

Think About It
Canada and the United States are similar in many ways. Why would faith in God be less important to Canadians than to Americans?

Pilgrims on *hajj* to the Grand Mosque in Mecca, Saudi Arabia. Islam requires all Muslims who are able to undertake a pilgrimage to the Holy Land.

Rituals and beliefs can be interdependent; rituals generally involve the affirmation of beliefs, as in a public or private statement confessing a sin (Roberts 1995). Like any social institution, religion develops distinctive normative patterns to structure people's behavior. Moreover, there are sanctions attached to religious rituals, whether rewards (Bar Mitzvah gifts) or penalties (expulsion from a religious institution for violation of norms).

In the United States, rituals may be very simple, such as saying grace at a meal or observing a moment of silence to commemorate someone's death. Yet certain rituals, such as the process of canonizing a saint, are quite elaborate. Most religious rituals in our culture focus on services conducted at houses of worship. Attendance at a service, silent and spoken prayers, and singing of spiritual hymns and chants are common forms of ritual behavior that generally take place in group settings. From an interactionist perspective, these rituals serve as important face-to-face encounters in which people reinforce their religious beliefs and their commitment to their faith (See Box 15-3).

For Muslims, a very important ritual is the *hajj,* a pilgrimage to the Grand Mosque in Mecca, Saudi Arabia.

Every Muslim who is physically and financially able is expected to make this trip at least once. Each year 2 million pilgrims go to Mecca during the one-week period indicated by the Islamic lunar calendar. Muslims from all over the world make the *hajj,* including those in the United States, where many tours are arranged to facilitate this ritual.

Some rituals induce an almost trancelike state. The Plains Indians eat or drink peyote, a cactus containing the powerful hallucinogenic drug mescaline. Similarly, the ancient Greek followers of the god Pan chewed intoxicating leaves of ivy in order to become more ecstatic during their celebrations. Of course, artificial stimulants are not necessary to achieve a religious "high." Devout believers, such as those who practice the pentecostal Christian ritual of "speaking in tongues," can reach a state of ecstasy simply through spiritual passion.

Experience

In sociological study of religion, the term ***religious experience*** refers to the feeling or perception of being in direct contact with the ultimate reality, such as a divine being, or

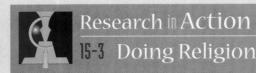

Research in Action

15-3 Doing Religion

www.
mhhe
.com
/schaefer8

More than 100 people in a Black congregation are packed into the living room of an old house. Led by the pastor's wife and four dancing women, the worshippers are singing, dancing, waving their arms. The church is rocking, and the pace doesn't stop for three hours. Across town a White congregation is singing the same hymns, but no one is dancing. The mood is mellow and the drummer looks almost embarrassed to be there. Sharon Bjorkman uncovered these contrasting styles in the course of fieldwork researching forms of worship in churches in the Chicago area. This observation research was part of a nationwide study conducted by the Hartford Institute for Religion Research.

Bjorkman was interested in going beyond the doctrinal background of a particular church and observing the physical actions of the people attending services and those conducting them. As Durkheim noted, defining what is sacred in a religion is a collective act. Using the interactionist perspective, Bjorkman took notes on what happened at services, who participated, and what or who motivated them to do so.

The first thing that she discovered was the disadvantage of being an outsider. For example, not "knowing the ropes," she was unprepared for the strenuous physical activity in the Black church. In the churches she visited she didn't know whether to carry a Bible or what version to use. As Bjorkman notes, you need to be socialized to know what is expected of you in a church service. Depending on the socialization church members receive, usually through example and repri-

> The church is rocking and the pace doesn't stop for three hours.

mand, they will be active or passive, loud or quiet, meditative or demonstrative.

The church leader plays a key role in shaping the congregation's actions. Leaders decide the format of services, including what songs are sung, what instruments are used, and how much to involve the worshippers. In services that call for testimonies from the congregation, the leader would actively solicit certain members and badger them if need be. The

same tactic applied to "altar calls" where congregants would come forward to confess sins or seek blessings.

As important as church leaders are, they would have little influence if the individual members chose not to cooperate. Worship styles, then, are jointly developed by leaders and members. Generally, Bjorkman found, leaders would take small incremental steps to "train" their members to accept a particular style of service.

This study illustrates the crucial part that human relations play within formal organizations. Religious rituals are not just dry formal procedures dictated by a rote program of service. They evolve out of the active participation of leaders and members "doing religion" together.

Let's Discuss

1. Do you attend a church regularly? What style of worship does the church leader set? How does that affect your feelings about your religion?
2. What accounts for differing forms of church rituals, even within the same denomination?

Source: S. Bjorkman 1999; Ammerman et al. 1998.

of being overcome with religious emotion. A religious experience may be rather slight, such as the feeling of exaltation a person receives from hearing a choir sing Handel's "Hallelujah Chorus." But many religious experiences are more profound, such as a Muslim's experience on a *hajj*. In his autobiography, the late African American activist Malcolm X (1964:338) wrote of his *hajj* and how deeply moved he was by the way that Muslims in Mecca came together across lines of race and color. For Malcolm X, the color blindness of the Muslim world "proved to me the power of the One God."

Still another profound religious experience is being "born again"—that is, at a turning point in one's life, making a personal commitment to Jesus. According to a 2001 national survey, 40 percent of people in the United States claimed that they had a born-again Christian experience at some time in their lives. An earlier survey found that

Baptists (61 percent) were the most likely to report such experiences; by contrast, only 18 percent of Catholics and 11 percent of Episcopalians stated that they had been born again. The collective nature of religion, as emphasized by Durkheim, is evident in these statistics. The beliefs and rituals of a particular faith can create an atmosphere either friendly or hostile to this type of religious experience. Thus, a Baptist would be encouraged to come forward and share such experiences with others, whereas an Episcopalian who claimed to have been born again would receive much less support (Princeton Religion Research Center 2000a; 2002).

Imagine

How would your religious beliefs, rituals, and experience differ if you had been raised in a different religious tradition?

The representation of religion can take many forms. This motorcycle club organizes itself as a strong Christian group, even though its attire and lifestyle may be objectionable to many Christians.

Religious Organization

The collective nature of religion has led to many forms of religious association. In modern societies, religion has become increasingly formalized. Specific structures such as churches and synagogues are constructed for religious worship; individuals are trained for occupational roles within various fields. These developments make it possible to distinguish clearly between the sacred and secular parts of one's life—a distinction that could not be made in earlier societies in which religion was largely a family activity carried out in the home.

Sociologists find it useful to distinguish between four basic forms of organization: the ecclesia, the denomination, the sect, and the new religious movement or cult. We can see differences among these types of organizations in such factors as size, power, degree of commitment expected from members, and historical ties to other faiths.

Ecclesiae

An *ecclesia* (plural, *ecclesiae*) is a religious organization that claims to include most or all of the members of a society and is recognized as the national or official religion. Since virtually everyone belongs to the faith, membership is by birth rather than conscious decision. Examples of ecclesiae include Islam in Saudi Arabia and Buddhism in Thailand. However, there can be significant differences even within the category of *ecclesia*. In Saudi Arabia's Islamic regime, leaders of the ecclesia hold vast power over actions of the state. By contrast, the Lutheran church in contemporary Sweden has no such power over the Riksdag (parliament) or the prime minister.

Generally, ecclesiae are conservative in that they do not challenge the leaders of a secular government. In a society with an ecclesia, the political and religious institutions often act in harmony and mutually reinforce each other's power over their relative spheres of influence. Within the modern world, ecclesiae tend to be declining in power.

Denominations

A *denomination* is a large, organized religion not officially linked with the state or government. Like an ecclesia, it tends to have an explicit set of beliefs, a defined system of authority, and a generally respected position in society. Denominations claim as members large segments of a population. Generally, children accept the denomination of their parents and give little thought to membership in other faiths. Denominations also resemble ecclesiae in that generally few demands are made on members. However, there is a critical difference between these two forms of religious organization. Although the denomination is considered respectable and is not viewed as a challenge to the secular government, it lacks the official recognition and power held by an ecclesia (Doress and Porter 1977).

The United States is home to a large number of denominations (see Figure 15-3). In good measure, this is a result of our nation's immigrant heritage. Many settlers in the new world brought with them the religious commitments native to their homelands. Denominations of Christianity found in the United States, such as those of the Roman Catholics, Episcopalians, and Lutherans, were the outgrowth of ecclesiae established in Europe. In addition, new Christian denominations emerged, including the Mormons and Christian Scientists. More recently, immigrants have increased the number of Muslims, Hindus, and Buddhists living in the United States.

Although by far the largest single denomination in the United States is Roman Catholicism, at least 17 other Christian faiths have 1 million or more members. Protestants collectively accounted for about 55 percent of the nation's adult population in 2001, compared with 25

Figure 15-3

Predominant Christian Faiths by Counties of the United States, 1990

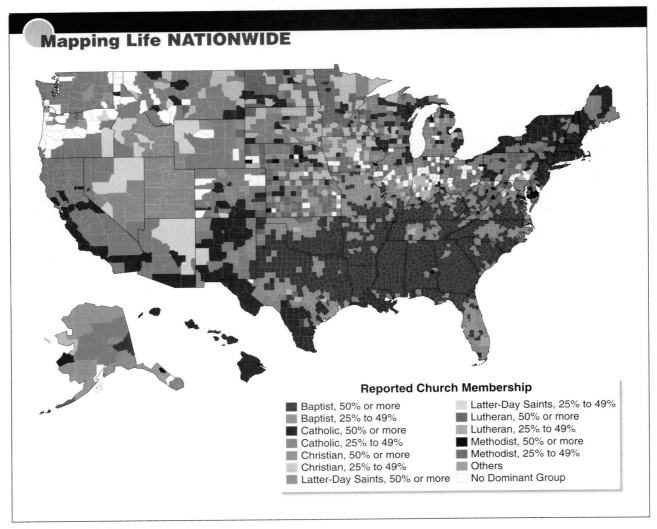

Source: Bradley et al. 1992.

This map, which shows only Christian denominations, nevertheless suggests the large variety of faiths practiced in the United States. In addition, more than 10 million Americans adhere to various non-Christian faiths.

percent for Roman Catholics and 2 percent for Jews. There are also 3 million Muslims in the United States, while large numbers of people adhere to such Eastern faiths as Buddhism (2 million) and Hinduism (1 million) (Lindner 2000; Princeton Religion Research Center 2002).

Sects

A *sect* can be defined as a relatively small religious group that has broken away from some other religious organization to renew what it considers the original vision of the faith. Many sects, such as that led by Martin Luther dur-

ing the Reformation, claim to be the "true church" because they seek to cleanse the established faith of what they regard as extraneous beliefs and rituals (Stark and Bainbridge 1985). Max Weber ([1916] 1958b:114) termed the sect a "believer's church," because affiliation is based on conscious acceptance of a specific religious dogma.

Sects are fundamentally at odds with society and do not seek to become established national religions. Unlike ecclesiae and denominations, sects require intensive commitments and demonstrations of belief by members. Partly owing to their "outsider" status in society, sects frequently exhibit a higher degree of religious fervor and loyalty than more established religious groups do. Recruitment focuses mainly on adults, and acceptance comes through conversion. One current-day sect is called the People of the Church, a movement within the Roman Catholic Church that began in Vienna, Austria. This sect has called for reforms of Catholicism, such as the ordination of women, local election of bishops, and optional celibacy for priests (*Religion Watch* 1995).

Sects are often short-lived. But those that are able to survive may over time become less antagonistic to society and begin to resemble denominations. In a few instances, sects have been able to endure over several generations while remaining fairly separate from society. Sociologist J. Milton Yinger (1970:226–73) uses the term ***established sect*** to describe a religious group that is the outgrowth of a sect, yet remains isolated from society. The Hutterites, Jehovah's Witnesses, Seventh-Day Adventists, and Amish are contemporary examples of established sects in the United States.

New Religious Movements or Cults

In 1997, 38 members of the Heaven's Gate cult were found dead in Southern California after a mass suicide timed to occur with the appearance of the Hale-Bopp comet. They believed the comet hid a spaceship on which they could catch a ride once they had broken free of their "bodily containers."

Partly as a result of the notoriety generated by such groups, the popular media have stigmatized the word *cult* by associating cults with the occult and the use of intense and forceful conversion techniques. The stereotyping of cults as uniformly bizarre and unethical has led sociologists to abandon the term and refer to a cult instead as a *new religious movement (NRM)*. While some NRMs exhibit strange behavior, many do not. They attract new members just like any other religion and often follow teachings similar to established Christian denominations, but with less ritual.

It is difficult to distinguish sects from cults. A ***new religious movement (NRM)*** or ***cult*** is a generally small, secretive religious group that represents either a new religion or a major innovation of an existing faith. NRMs are similar to sects in that they tend to be small and are often viewed as less respectable than more established faiths. However, unlike sects, NRMs normally do not result from schisms or breaks with established ecclesiae or denominations. Some cults, such as those focused on UFO sightings, may be totally unrelated to the existing faiths in a culture. Even when a cult does accept certain fundamental tenets of a dominant faith—such as belief in Jesus as divine or Mohammad as a messenger of God—it will offer new revelations or new insights to justify its claim to be a more advanced religion (Stark and Bainbridge 1979, 1985).

Like sects, NRMs may undergo transformation over time into other types of religious organizations. An example is the Christian Science church, which began as a new religious movement under the leadership of Mary Baker Eddy. Today, this church exhibits the characteristics of a denomination. In fact, most major religions, including Christianity, began as cults. NRMs may be in the early stages of what may develop into a denomination or new religion, or they may just as easily fade away through loss of members or weak leadership (Richardson and van Driel 1997).

The Christian Science Center in Boston, Massachusetts. Christian Scientists believe that all illness can be healed through an understanding of God. The church, which began as a new religious movement, now resembles an established denomination.

Case Study of a Religious Cult: Falun Gong

Cults have a long history; the phenomenon is global in scope. One cult, the Falun Gong in China, is currently attracting worldwide attention. To the casual observer, the followers of Falun Gong (literally, "the Law of the Wheel Breathing Exercise") simply perform slow-motion exercises to music from a tape recorder. But the Falun Gong (pronounced *fah-luhn gung*) is essentially a religious

Practitioners of Falun Gong combine meditation with martial arts exercises, borrowing from Buddhist and Taoist philosophies. Falun Gong's phenomenal growth in China has raised alarms among the Communist leadership, who want no competition for the control of the masses.

movement that borrows heavily from Buddhist and Taoist philosophies and styles itself as a school of qigong (pronounced *chee-gong*), a traditional Chinese practice that uses meditation and martial arts exercises to channel unseen forces and improve health. Founded in 1992 by Li Hongzhi, its adherents—primarily middle-aged women, retirees, and students—number in the tens of millions today.

The group's strong appeal and rapid growth to perhaps 6 million in 2001 have worried the Communist Chinese leadership. The Communist party mistrusts any group whose value system it cannot control. In addition, since Marxism is basically the state "religion," the Chinese authorities might be seeing Falun Gong as a form of liberation theology, meant to rouse the masses. These fears seemed confirmed when 10,000 members of Falun Gong suddenly materialized in Beijing in April of 1999 to demand official recognition from the government. Several months later the government banned the group, put its exiled leader on the most wanted list, and began arresting, detaining, or dispersing thousands of people caught practicing Falun Gong. Apparently, all traces of the organized movement are to be stamped out (Pomfret and Pan 2001).

In the wake of this crackdown, Falun Gong followers turned to the Internet to express their beliefs. Websites such as clearwisdom.net, maintained outside China's borders, offer the faithful another way to learn about the cult's teachings. Yet there is a risk even to this type of activity, as the Chinese Public Security Bureau regularly attempts to trace links between such sites and the home computers of Chinese residents (C. Smith 2001).

Comparing Forms of Religious Organization

How can we determine whether a particular religious group falls into the sociological category of ecclesia, denomination, sect, or NRM? As we have seen, these types of religious organizations have somewhat different relationships to society. Ecclesiae are recognized as national churches; denominations, although not officially approved by the state, are generally widely respected. By contrast, sects as well as NRMs are much more likely to be at odds with the larger culture.

Still, ecclesiae, denominations, and sects are best viewed as types along a continuum rather than as mutually exclusive categories. Table 15-1 summarizes some of the primary characteristics of these ideal types. Since the United States has no ecclesia, sociologists studying this country's religions have naturally focused on the denomination and the sect. These religious forms have been pictured on either end of a continuum, with denominations accommodating to the secular world and sects protesting against established religions. While NRMs have been included in Table 15-2, they are outside the continuum, because they generally define themselves in terms of a new view of life rather than in terms of existing religious faiths (Chalfant et al. 1994).

Advances in electronic communications have led to still another form of religious organization: the electronic church. Facilitated by cable television and satellite transmissions, *televangelists* (as they are called) direct their messages to more people—especially in the United States—than are served by all but the largest denominations. While some televangelists are affiliated with religious denominations, most give viewers the impression that they are disassociated from established faiths.

At the close of the 1990s, the electronic church had taken on yet another dimension: the Internet. In one study, researchers estimated that on a typical day in 2000, as many as 2 million people used the Internet for religious purposes (Larsen 2000). Much of the spiritual content on the Internet is tied to organized denominations. People use cyberspace to learn more about their faith or even just the activities of their own place of worship.

Table 15-2   Characteristics of Ecclesiae, Denominations, Sects, and New Religious Movements

Characteristic	Ecclesia	Denomination	Sect	New Religious Movement (or Cult)
Size	Very large	Large	Small	Small
Wealth	Extensive	Extensive	Limited	Variable
Religious Services	Formal, little participation	Formal, little participation	Informal, emotional	Variable
Doctrines	Specific, but interpretation may be tolerated	Specific, but interpretation may be tolerated	Specific, purity of doctrine emphasized	Innovative, pathbreaking
Clergy	Well-trained, full-time	Well-trained, full-time	Trained to some degree	Unspecialized
Membership	By virtue of being a member of society	By acceptance of doctrine	By acceptance of doctrine	By an emotional commitment
Relationship to the State	Recognized, closely aligned	Tolerated	Not encouraged	Ignored or challenged

Source: Adapted from Vernon 1962; see also Chalfant et al. 1994.

But as more and more people are discovering, the "church" we locate on the World Wide Web exists only in *virtual* reality. For some purposes, virtual religious experience simply will not do. For example, a minyan, a set quorum for Jewish prayers, requires 10 Jews gathered in one space; cyberspace doesn't count at this point. And while Muslims can view the Kabbah, or the Holy Shrine, in Mecca on the Net, they cannot fulfill their religious obligations except by actual pilgrimage there. The Internet, then, isn't suitable for some forms of religious and spiritual expression, but it certainly has added a new dimension to religious behavior (G. Zelizer 1999).

An orthodox Jew slips a magnetic disk containing e-mailed peace prayers into a crevice in the Western Wall of Jerusalem's old city. Although the virtual world of the Internet cannot substitute for traditional forms of organized religion, it does offer religious followers new ways to stay in touch with one another.

Religion in the Schools

The Issue

Should public schools be allowed to sponsor organized prayers in the classroom? How about reading Bible verses? Or just a collective moment of silence? Can public school athletes offer up a group prayer in a team huddle? Should students be able to initiate voluntary prayers at school events? Should a school be allowed to post the Ten Commandments in a hallway? Each of these situations has been an object of great dissension among those who see a role for prayer in the schools and those who want to maintain a strict separation of church and state.

Another controversy centers on the teaching of theories about the origin of humans and the universe. Mainstream scientific thinking holds that humans evolved over billions of years from one-celled organisms, and that the universe came into being 15 billion years ago as a result of a "big bang." But these theories are challenged by people who hold to the biblical account of the creation of humans and the universe some 10,000 years ago—a viewpoint known as **creationism.** Creationists want their theory taught in the schools as the only one, or at the very least, as an alternative to the theory of evolution.

Who has the right to decide these issues? And what is considered the "right" decision? Religion in the schools constitutes one of the thorniest issues in U.S. public policy today.

The Setting

The issues just described go to the heart of the First Amendment's provisions on religious freedom. On the one hand, the government is required to protect the right to practice one's religion, but on the other hand, it cannot take any measures that would seem to "establish" one religion over another (the church/state separation).

In the key case of *Engle v. Vitale,* the Supreme Court ruled in 1962 that the use of nondenominational prayer in New York schools was "wholly inconsistent" with the First Amendment's prohibition against government establishment of religion. In finding that such organized school prayer violated the Constitution—even when no student was required to participate—the Court argued, in effect, that promoting religious observance was not a legitimate function of government or education. Subsequent Court decisions allow *voluntary* school prayer by students, but forbid school officials to *sponsor* any prayer or religious observance at school events. Despite these rulings, many public schools still regularly lead their students in prayer recitations or Bible reading (Firestone 1999).

The controversy over whether the biblical account of creation should be presented in school curricula recalls the famous "monkey trial" of 1925. In this trial, high school biology teacher John T. Scopes was convicted of violating a Tennessee law making it a crime to teach the scientific theory of evolution in public schools. Creationists today have gone beyond espousing fundamentalist religious doctrine; they attempt to reinforce their position regarding

How, when, and where should prayer be allowed in public schools? These students in Annandale, Virginia, celebrate National Day of Prayer *outside* their high school.

the origins of humanity and the universe with quasi-scientific data.

In 1987, the Supreme Court ruled that states could not compel the teaching of creationism in public schools if the primary purpose was to promote a religious viewpoint. For a while, this ruling gave priority to the theory of evolution in most public school districts, but creationists, especially in the South and Midwest, have been persistently chipping away at the dominance of evolutionary theory in the classroom. Many school districts now require that teachers entertain alternative theories to evolution and to the creation of the universe, and some discount evolution altogether.

Sociological Insights

Supporters of school prayer and of creationism feel that strict Court rulings force too great a separation between what Émile Durkheim called the *sacred* and the *profane.* They insist that use of nondenominational prayer can in no way lead to the establishment of an ecclesia in the United States. Moreover, they believe that school prayer—and the teaching of creationism—can provide the spiritual guidance and socialization that many children today do not receive from parents or regular church attendance. Many communities also believe that schools should transmit the dominant culture of the United States by encouraging prayer.

Opponents of school prayer and creationism argue that a religious majority in a community might impose religious viewpoints specific to its faith at the expense of religious minorities. These critics question whether school prayer can remain truly voluntary. Drawing on the interactionist perspective and small-group research, they suggest that children will face enormous social pressure to conform to the beliefs and practices of a religious majority.

Policy Initiatives

School education is fundamentally a local issue, so most initiatives and lobbying have taken place at the local or state level. Religious fundamentalists have had some success in pushing their agenda by getting their own candidates elected to state and local school boards. In 1999, the Kansas Board of Education caused a stir when it voted to delete from the state's science curriculum virtually any mention of evolution and to remove from standardized tests questions having to do with the theory of evolution or the "big bang" theory of the creation of the universe. Later, when the composition of the board changed, the controversial decision was overturned (Glanz 2001).

The activism of religious fundamentalists in the nation's public school system raises a more general question: Whose ideas and values deserve a hearing in classrooms? Critics see this campaign as one step toward sectarian religious control of public education. They worry that at some point in the future, teachers may not be able to use books or make statements that conflict with fundamentalist interpretations of the Bible. For advocates of a liberal education who are deeply committed to intellectual (and religious) diversity, this is a genuinely frightening prospect.

Let's Discuss

1. Was there any organized prayer in the school you attended? Was creationism part of the curriculum?
2. Do you think promoting religious observance is a legitimate function of education?
3. How might a conflict theorist view the issue of organized school prayer?

Chapter Resources

Summary

Religion is a cultural universal, found throughout the world in various forms. This chapter examines the major world religions, the functions and dimensions of religion, and the four basic types of religious organization.

1. Émile Durkheim stressed the social impact of religion in an attempt to understand individual religious behavior within the context of the larger society.

2. Eighty-seven percent of the world's population adheres to some form of religion. Tremendous diversity exists in religious beliefs and practices, which may be heavily influenced by culture.
3. Religion helps to integrate a diverse society and provides social support in time of need.
4. Max Weber saw a connection between religious allegiance and capitalistic behavior in a religious orientation he termed the **Protestant ethic.**

5. In *liberation theology,* the teachings of Christianity become the basis for political efforts to alleviate poverty and social injustice.

6. From a Marxist point of view, religion serves to reinforce the social control of those in power. It discourages collective political action, which could end capitalist oppression and transform society.

7. Religious behavior is expressed through *beliefs, rituals,* and *religious experience.*

8. Sociologists have identified four basic types of religious organization: the *ecclesia,* the *denomination,* the *sect,* and the *new religious movement (NRM),* or *cult.*

9. Advances in communication have led to a new type of church organization, the electronic church. *Televangelists* now preach to more people than belong to many denominations, and roughly 2 million people a day use the Internet for religious purposes.

10. Today, the question of how much religion, if any, should be permitted in the public schools is a matter of intense debate.

Critical Thinking Questions

1. From a conflict point of view, explain how religion could be used to bring about social change. Can you think of an example?

2. What role do new religious movements (or cults) play in the organization of religion? Why are they so often controversial?

3. Do politics and religion mix? Explain your reasoning.

Key Terms

Creationism A literal interpretation of the Bible regarding the creation of humanity and the universe used to argue that evolution should not be presented as established scientific fact. (page 396)

Cultural universal General practices found in every culture. (379)

Denomination A large, organized religion not officially linked with the state or government. (391)

Ecclesia A religious organization that claims to include most or all of the members of a society and is recognized as the national or official religion. (391)

Established sect A religious group that is the outgrowth of a sect, yet remains isolated from society. (393)

Liberation theology Use of a church, primarily Roman Catholicism, in a political effort to eliminate poverty, discrimination, and other forms of injustice evident in a secular society. (386)

New religious movement (NRM) or **cult** A generally small, secretive religious group that represents either a new religion or a major innovation of an existing faith. (393)

Profane The ordinary and commonplace elements of life, as distinguished from the sacred. (379)

Protestant ethic Max Weber's term for the disciplined work ethic, this-worldly concerns, and rational orientation to life emphasized by John Calvin and his followers. (385)

Religion A unified system of beliefs and practices relative to sacred things. (379)

Religious beliefs Statements to which members of a particular religion adhere. (388)

Religious experience The feeling or perception of being in direct contact with the ultimate reality, such as a divine being, or of being overcome with religious emotion. (389)

Religious rituals Practices required or expected of members of a faith. (388)

Sacred Elements beyond everyday life that inspire awe, respect, and even fear. (379)

Sect A relatively small religious group that has broken away from some other religious organization to renew what it views as the original vision of the faith. (392)

Secularization The process through which religion's influence on other social institutions diminishes. (379)

Additional Readings

BOOKS

Demerath III, N. J. 2001. *Crossing the Gods: World Religions and World Politics.* New Brunswick, NJ: Rutgers University Press. A comparative study of church–state relations in 14 countries.

Lee, Martha F. 1996. *The Nation of Islam: An American Millenarium Movement.* Syracuse, NY: Syracuse University Press. A political scientist examines the origins of the organized religion commonly known as the "Black Muslims" and changes in this faith over the last half-century.

Lindner, Eileen W., ed. 2001. *Yearbook of American and Canadian Churches 2001.* Nashville: Abingdon Press. Prepared annually by the National Council of the Churches of Christ, this compendium provides the latest statistical data plus topical articles.

Orfield, Gary, and Holly J. Lebowitz, eds. 2001. *Religion, Race, and Justice in a Changing America.* New York: The Twentieth Century Fund. The changing nature of civil rights and its relationship to organized religion.

JOURNALS

The sociological study of religion is reflected in the *Journal for the Scientific Study of Religion* (founded in 1961), *Religion Watch* (monthly newsletter, 1986), *Review of Religious Research* (1958), *Social Compass* (1954), and *Sociology of Religion* (previously *Sociological Analysis,* 1940).

Technology Resources

Internet Connection

*Note: While all the URLs listed were current as of the printing of this book, these sites often change. Please check our website (**http://www.mhhe.com/schaefer8**) for updates and hyperlinks to these exercises and additional exercises.*

1. In the United States and throughout the world, people follow many different religions. To access statistics about religion worldwide, visit the adherents.com website (**http://www.adherents.com**) and answer the following questions:
   (a) What are the 10 largest denominational families in the United States?
   (b) What are the 10 largest religious bodies in the United States?
   (c) What are the major religions of the world?
   (d) Select "Religion by Location" and pick two countries outside North America. What is the major religion in each?
   (e) Select "Religion by Name" and pick two religions with which you are not familiar. What are they, and where are they most prominent?

2. The emergence of new religious movements has been the subject of public scrutiny recently. Visit **http://religiousmovements.lib.virginia.edu/cultsect/cultsect.htm,** a site which examines cult group controversies. Read the report and answer the following questions:
   (a) When did the concept of brainwashing first come to the public's attention, and why?
   (b) What is the difference between a cult and a sect?
   (c) What is the counter-cult movement? The anti-cult movement?
   (d) Look at some of the webpages for the anti-cult movement. Which impresses you the most?
   (e) Look at some of the webpages for the counter-cult movement. What do you think of them?

Online Learning Center   www.mhhe.com/schaefer8

Do you know the difference between a cult and a sect or between the mundane and the sacred? Test your knowledge by selecting the crossword puzzle at the student center in the Online Learning Center at **www.mhhe.com/schaefer8.** This crossword puzzle is not only challenging; it is also a valuable learning aide.

CHAPTER 16

EDUCATION

DURHAM COUNTY LITERACY COUNCIL

MY MOM IS
A TERRIFIC STUDENT.
SHE'S LEARNING TO READ.

The need for education isn't limited to school-age youths. This poster recognizes adults who strive to learn a skill most of us take for granted: reading. Nationwide, some 10 million adult Americans cannot read English. Some are immigrants from other countries; others suffer from learning disabilities or a disadvantaged upbringing.

In order to find Public School 261 in District 10, a visitor is told to look for a mortician's office. The funeral home, which faces Jerome Avenue in the North Bronx, is easy to identify by its green awning. The school is next door, in a former roller-skating rink. No sign identifies the building as a school. A metal awning frame without an awning supports a flagpole, but there is no flag. . . .

Textbooks are scarce and children have to share their social studies books. The principal says there is one full-time pupil counselor and another who is here two days a week: a ratio of 930 children to one counselor. The carpets are patched and sometimes taped together to conceal an open space. "I could use some new rugs," she observes. . . .

Two first grade classes share a single room without a window, divided only by a blackboard. Four kindergartens and a sixth grade class of Spanish-speaking children have been packed into a single room in which, again, there is no window. A second grade bilingual class of 37 children has its own room but again there is no window.

The library is a tiny, windowless and claustrophobic room. I count approximately 700 books. Seeing no reference books, I ask a teacher if encyclopedias and other reference books are kept in classrooms.

"We don't have encyclopedias in classrooms," she replies. "That is for the suburbs."

The school, I am told, has 26 computers for its 1,300 children. There is one small gym and children get one period, and sometimes two, each week. Recess, however, is not possible because there is no playground. . . .

The school, I am told, is 90 percent black and Hispanic; the other 10 percent are Asian, white or Middle Eastern.

In a sixth grade social studies class the walls are bare of words or decorations. There seems to be no ventilation system, or, if one exists, it isn't working.

On the top floor of the school, a sixth grade of 30 children shares a room with 29 bilingual second graders. Because of the high class size there is an assistant with each teacher. This means that 59 children and four grown-ups—63 in all—must share a room that, in a suburban school, would hold no more than 20 children and one teacher. There are, at least, some outside windows in this room—it is the only room with windows in the school—and the room has a high ceiling. It is a relief to see some daylight. . . .

As I leave the school, a sixth grade teacher stops to talk. . . .

I ask her, "Do the children ever comment on the building?"

"They don't say," she answers, "but they know."

I ask her if they see it as a racial message.

"All these children see TV," she says. "They know what suburban schools are like. Then they look around them at their school. This was a roller-rink, you know. . . . They don't comment on it but you see it in their eyes. They understand." *(Kozol 1991:85, 86, 87, 88)* ■ 💿

Ⅰn the prosperous 1980s, Jonathan Kozol, the author of this passage from *Savage Inequalities*, toured public schools throughout the United States. He found that whereas white students in affluent suburban towns enjoyed state-of-the-art science labs, superb music and art programs, and elaborate athletic facilities, inner-city children were crowded into antiquated, decrepit buildings, deprived of even the most basic requirements—textbooks, classrooms, computers, and counselors. An educator, Kozol challenged his readers to confront the social implications of this stark contrast in educational resources.

Education, like the family and religion, is a *cultural universal.* As such it is an important aspect of socialization—the lifelong process of learning the attitudes, values, and behavior considered appropriate to members of a particular culture. As we saw in Chapter 4, socialization can occur in the classroom or at home, through interactions with parents, teachers, friends, and even strangers. Exposure to books, films, television, and other forms of communication also promotes socialization. When learning is explicit and formalized—when some people consciously teach, while others adopt the role of learner—the process of socialization is called *education.* But students learn far more about their society at school than what is included in the curriculum.

This chapter focuses in particular on the formal systems of education that characterize modern industrial societies. Do public schools offer everyone a way up the socioeconomic ladder, or do they reinforce existing divisions among social classes? What is the "hidden curriculum" in U.S. schools? And what have sociologists learned about the latest trends in education, such as competency testing? We will begin with a discussion of three theoretical perspectives on education: functionalist, conflict, and interactionist. An examination of schools as formal organizations—as bureaucracies and subcultures of teachers and students—follows. Three contemporary educational trends, testing, adult education, and home schooling, merit special mention. The chapter closes with a social policy discussion of controversial school choice programs. ■

Sociological Perspectives on Education

Education is now a major industry in the United States. In the last few decades, an increasing proportion of people have obtained high school diplomas, college degrees, and advanced professional degrees. For example, the proportion of people 25 years of age or over with a high school diploma increased from 41 percent in 1960 to more than 84 percent in 2000. Those with a college degree rose from 8 percent in 1960 to about 27 percent in 1998 (see Figure 16-1 for international comparisons).

Education has become a vast and complex social institution throughout the world. It prepares citizens for the

Figure 16-1

Percentage of Adults 25 to 64 Who Have Completed Higher Education, 1998

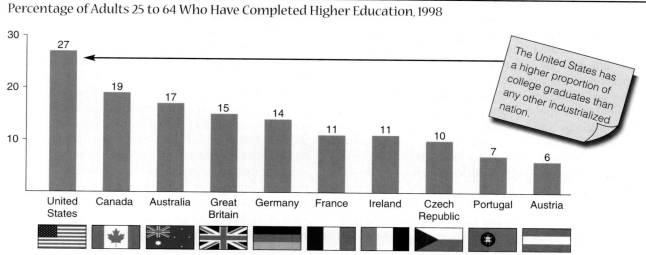

Source: Bureau of the Census 2001a:839.

various roles demanded by other social institutions, such as the family, government, and the economy. The functionalist, conflict, and interactionist perspectives offer distinctive ways of examining education as a social institution.

Functionalist View

Like other social institutions, education has both manifest (open, stated) and latent (hidden) functions. The most basic *manifest* function of education is the transmission of knowledge. Schools teach students how to read, speak foreign languages, and repair automobiles. Education has another important manifest function: bestowing status. Because many believe this function is performed inequitably, it will be considered later, in the section on the conflict view of education.

In addition to these manifest functions, schools perform a number of *latent* functions: transmitting culture, promoting social and political integration, maintaining social control, and serving as agents of change.

Transmitting Culture

As a social institution, education performs a rather conservative function—transmitting the dominant culture. Schooling exposes each generation of young people to the existing beliefs, norms, and values of their culture. In our society, we learn respect for social control and reverence for established institutions, such as religion, the family, and the presidency. Of course, this is true in many other cultures as well. While schoolchildren in the United States are hearing about the accomplishments of George Washington and Abraham Lincoln, British children are hearing about the distinctive contributions of Queen Elizabeth I and Winston Churchill.

In Great Britain, the transmission of the dominant culture in schools goes far beyond learning about monarchs and prime ministers. In 1996, the government's chief curriculum adviser—noting the need to fill a void left by the diminishing authority of the Church of England—proposed that British schools socialize students into a set of core values. These include honesty, respect for others, politeness, a sense of fair play, forgiveness, punctuality, nonviolent behavior, patience, faithfulness, and self-discipline (Charter and Sherman 1996).

Sometimes nations need to reassess their ways of transmitting culture. When an economic crisis hit Asian countries in 1997 and 1998, many Asian students who had been studying abroad could no longer afford to do so. South Korea, for example, had sent 42,000 college students to the United States alone in 1998. Now it had to figure out how to accommodate thousands more students pursuing higher education at home. South Koreans also began to question the content of the curriculum. Their

First-graders in a bilingual class at Acoma Pueblo, New Mexico. These Native American children are holding onto their heritage while learning the English skills they will need to function in mainstream American society.

schools traditionally teach Confucian values with a focus on rote memorization. This leads to an emphasis on accumulating facts as opposed to using reasoning. Entrance to college turns on a highly competitive exam that tests knowledge of facts. Once in college, a student has virtually no opportunity to change his or her program, and the classes continue to rely on memorization. The combination of an economic crisis and growing complaints about the educational process has caused government officials to reevaluate the educational structure. Moreover, growth in juvenile crime, although low by our standards, has led the government to introduce a new civic education program emphasizing honesty and discipline (Institute of International Education 1998; Woodard 1998).

On the college level in the United States, there has been growing controversy over the general education or

Table 16-1 Foreign Students by Country of Origin or Destination

Foreign Students in U.S.		Country of Origin or Destination	U.S. Students Abroad	
Number of Students	Rank of Country of Origin		Number of Students	Rank of Country of Destination
25,279	6	Canada	1,275	17
59,939	1	China	2,949	11
7,273	15	France	11,924	4
10,128	11	Germany	4,744	7
8,139	13	Great Britain	29,289	1
54,664	2	India	811	25
3,490	29	Italy	12,930	3
46,497	3	Japan	2,679	12
45,685	4	Korea	444	36
10,670	10	Mexico	7,374	5
4,156	25	Spain	13,974	2
Total Students 547,867			143,590	

Note: Data for foreign students are from 2000–2001; for U.S. students abroad, from 1999–2000.

Source: Institute of International Education, 2001.

Think About It
Why are sending nations ranked so differently from receiving nations?

basic curriculum requirements. Critics charge that standard academic curricula have failed to represent the important contributions of women and people of color to history, literature, and other fields of study. The underlying questions raised by this debate, still to be resolved, are: Which ideas and values are essential for instruction? Which culture should be transmitted by the schools and colleges of the United States?

Cultural transmission also occurs when students receive their formal schooling in another nation. The United States is a popular destination for college students from abroad: each year, over half a million foreign students enroll at U.S. institutions of higher learning. Typically, only a fourth as many U.S. students choose to study abroad. Of those countries where foreign students originate, Mexico alone receives about as many U.S. students as it sends to the United States, as Table 16-1 shows.

Promoting Social and Political Integration

Yale University requires its freshmen and sophomores to live together on campus in order to foster a sense of community among diverse groups. Many other universities have the same requirement. Education serves the latent function of promoting social and political integration by

Taking Sociology to Work

RAY ZAPATA:
Business Owner and Former Regent, Texas State University

Ray Zapata, investor, community activist, and restaurant owner, thinks his degree in sociology was the best preparation he could have received for a life in business and politics. A graduate of Angelo State University in Texas, Zapata finds that his understanding of society and social diversity has given him perspective on his community and helped him to cooperate with others from different backgrounds. "I think that I can pretty much fit anywhere, whether I'm in New York, London, or South Africa, and I think that's very, very important," he remarks.

Zapata was the second Hispanic to be appointed to the Board of Regents of the Texas State University system. As a regent, he was charged with overseeing both the financial and educational management of the system, which includes working with the state legislature to gain funding for new programs and facilities. During his term he presided over a half-billion-dollar construction program, including a major expansion at his alma mater, Angelo State.

More than the buildings that went up during his term, though, Zapata prides himself on the open admissions policy the Board instituted during his tenure. "If you put education out of reach of the working class or poor people in our society, then I think you lose an opportunity for great minds," he says. One of the most wonderful moments for this regent came when he watched a Hispanic woman who had worked as a janitor at Southwest State University graduate at the top of her class. Zapata wants to see more students like her, including senior citizens, on Texas State campuses. "Education will never hurt you at any age," he says.

Let's Discuss

1. How does an open admissions policy benefit society?
2. In what ways do the elderly benefit from education?

---

transforming a population composed of diverse racial, ethnic, and religious groups into a society whose members share—to some extent—a common identity. Schools in the United States have historically played an important role in socializing the children of immigrants into the norms, values, and beliefs of the dominant culture. From a functionalist perspective, the common identity and social integration fostered by education contribute to societal stability and consensus (Touraine 1974).

In the past, the integrative function of education was most obvious through its emphasis on promoting a common language. Immigrant children were expected to learn English. In some instances, they were even forbidden to speak their native languages on school grounds. More recently, bilingualism has been defended both for its

p. 75 educational value and as a means of encouraging cultural diversity. However, critics argue that bilingualism undermines the social and political integration that education has traditionally promoted.

Maintaining Social Control

In performing the manifest function of transmitting knowledge, schools go far beyond teaching such skills as reading, writing, and mathematics. Like other social institutions, such as the family and religion, education prepares young people to lead productive and orderly lives as

adults by introducing them to the norms, values, and sanctions of the larger society.

Through the exercise of social control, schools teach students various skills and values essential to their future positions within the labor force. They learn punctuality, discipline, scheduling, and responsible work habits, as well as how to negotiate their way through the complexities of a bureaucratic organization. As a social institution, education reflects the interests of the family and in turn prepares young people for their participation in yet another social institution—the economy. Students are being trained for what is ahead, whether it be the assembly line or a physician's office. In effect, then, schools serve as a transitional agent of social control—between parents and employers in the life cycle of most individuals (Bowles and Gintis 1976; Cole 1988).

Schools direct and even restrict students' aspirations in a manner that reflects societal values and prejudices. School administrators may allocate funds for athletic programs while giving much less support to music, art, and dance. Teachers and guidance counselors may encourage male students to pursue careers in the sciences but steer equally talented female students into careers as early childhood teachers. Such socialization into traditional

p. 97 gender roles can be viewed as a form of social control.

Serving as an Agent of Change

So far, we have focused on conservative functions of education—on its role in transmitting the existing culture, promoting social and political integration, and maintaining social control. Yet education can also stimulate or bring about desired social change. Sex education classes were introduced in public schools in response to the soaring pregnancy rate among teenagers. Affirmative action in admissions—giving priority to females or minorities—has been endorsed as a means of countering racial and sexual discrimination. Project Head Start, an early childhood program serving more than 790,000 children annually, has sought to compensate for the disadvantages in school readiness experienced by children from low-income families (Bureau of the Census 1999a:402).

p. 279

Education also promotes social change by serving as a meeting ground where distinctive beliefs and traditions can be shared. In 2000, there were 548,000 foreign students in the United States, of whom 72 percent were from developing nations. Cross-cultural exchanges between these visitors and citizens of the United States ultimately broaden the perspective of both the hosts and their guests. The same is certainly true when students from the United States attend schools in Europe, Latin America, Africa, or the Far East.

Numerous sociological studies have revealed that increased years of formal schooling are associated with openness to new ideas and more liberal social and political viewpoints. Sociologist Robin Williams points out that better-educated people tend to have greater access to factual information, more diverse opinions, and the ability to make subtle distinctions in analysis. Formal education stresses both the importance of qualifying statements (in place of broad generalizations) and the need at least to question (rather than simply accept) established truths and practices. As we saw in Chapter 2, the scientific method relies on *testing* hypotheses and reflects the questioning spirit that characterizes modern education (Williams et al. 1964).

Conflict View

Sociologist Christopher J. Hurn (1985) has compared the functionalist and conflict views of schooling. According to Hurn, the functionalist perspective portrays contemporary education as basically benign. For example, it argues that schools rationally sort and select students for future high-status positions, thereby meeting society's need for talented and expert personnel. By contrast, the conflict perspective views education as an instrument of elite domination. Schools convince subordinate groups of their inferiority, reinforce existing social class inequality, and discourage alternative and more democratic visions of society.

Criticizing the functionalist view, conflict theorists argue that the educational system socializes students into values dictated by the powerful, that schools stifle individualism and creativity in the name of maintaining order, and that the level of change promoted by education is relatively insignificant. From a conflict perspective, the inhibiting effects of education are particularly apparent in the "hidden curriculum" as well as in the differential way in which status is bestowed.

The Hidden Curriculum

Schools are highly bureaucratic organizations (as we will see later). Many teachers rely on the rules and regulations of schools to maintain order. Unfortunately, the need for control and discipline can take precedence over the learning process. Teachers may focus on obedience to the rules as an end in itself. If this occurs, students and teachers alike become victims of what Philip Jackson (1968) has called the *hidden curriculum* (see also Freire 1970; Margolis 2001).

In response to a rising pregnancy rate among adolescent girls, many schools have begun to offer sex education courses that promote abstinence. When schools attempt to remedy negative social trends, they are serving as an agent of social change.

The term *hidden curriculum* refers to standards of behavior that are deemed proper by society and are taught subtly in schools. According to this curriculum, children must not speak until the teacher calls on them and must regulate their activities according to the clock or bells. In addition, they are expected to concentrate on their own work rather than assist other students who learn more slowly. A hidden curriculum is evident in schools around the world. For example, Japanese schools offer guidance sessions during lunch that seek to improve the classroom experience but also to develop healthy living skills. In effect, these sessions instill values and encourage behavior useful for the Japanese business world, such as self-discipline and openness to group problem solving and decision making (Okano and Tsuchiya 1999).

In a classroom overly focused on obedience, value is placed on pleasing the teacher and remaining quiet—rather than on creative thought and academic learning (E. B. Leacock 1969). Habitual obedience to authority p. 185 may result in the type of distressing behavior documented by Stanley Milgram in his classic obedience studies.

Credentialism

Fifty years ago, a high school diploma was a minimum requirement for entry into the paid labor force of the United States; today, a college diploma is virtually the bare minimum. This change reflects the process of *credentialism*—a term used to describe the increase in the lowest level of education needed to enter a field.

In recent decades, the number of occupations viewed as professions has risen. Credentialism is one symptom of this trend. Employers and occupational associations typically contend that such changes are a logical response to the increasing complexity of many jobs. However, in many cases, employers raise degree requirements for a position simply because all applicants have achieved the existing minimum credential (Collins 1979; Dore 1976; Hurn 1985).

Conflict theorists observe that credentialism may reinforce social inequality. Applicants from poor and minority backgrounds are especially likely to suffer from the escalation of qualifications, since they lack the financial resources needed to obtain degree after degree. In addition, upgrading credentials serves the self-interest of the two groups most responsible for this trend. Educational institutions profit from prolonging the investment of time and money that people make by staying in school. Moreover, as C. J. Hurn (1985) has suggested, current jobholders have a stake in raising occupational requirements. Credentialism can increase the status of an occupation and is crucial to demands for higher pay. Max Weber anticipated such possibilities as far back as 1916, concluding that the "universal clamor for the creation of educational certificates in all fields makes for the formation of a privileged stratum in businesses and in offices" (Gerth and Mills 1958:240–241).

Imagine

How would you react if the job you have or plan to pursue suddenly required a higher-level degree? If suddenly the requirements were lowered?

Bestowal of Status

Both functionalist and conflict theorists agree that education performs the important function of bestowing status. As noted earlier, an increasing proportion of people in the United States are obtaining high school diplomas, college degrees, and advanced professional degrees. From a functionalist perspective, this widening bestowal of sta- p. 219 tus is beneficial not only to particular recipients but to society as a whole. In the view of Kingsley Davis and Wilbert E. Moore (1945) society must

In Tokyo's public schools, students learn adult responsibilities early on. In this classroom, classmates take turns serving the lunch.

Private schools such as Phillips Andover Academy in Massachusetts bestow a special status on their students, most of whom come from affluent White families. Conflict theorists charge that the U.S. educational system tends to reinforce social class inequalities.

distribute its members among a variety of social positions. Education can contribute to this process by sorting people into appropriate levels and courses of study that will prepare them for appropriate positions within the labor force.

Conflict sociologists are far more critical of the *differential* way education bestows status. They stress that schools sort pupils according to social class background. Although the educational system helps certain poor children to move into middle-class professional positions, it denies most disadvantaged children the same educational opportunities afforded children of the affluent. In this way, schools tend to preserve social class inequalities in each new generation (Giroux 1988; Labaree 1986; Mingle 1987).

Even a single school can reinforce class differences by putting students in tracks. The term *tracking* refers to the practice of placing students in specific curriculum groups on the basis of test scores and other criteria. Tracking begins very early in the classroom, often in reading groups during first grade. Most recent research on such ability groupings raises questions about its effectiveness, especially for low-ability students. Tracks can reinforce the disadvantages that children from less affluent families may face if they haven't been exposed to reading materials and computers and other forms of educational stimulation in their homes during early childhood years. It is estimated that about 60 percent of elementary schools in the United States and about 80 percent of secondary schools use some form of tracking (Sadker and Sadker 2000; Strum 1993).

Tracking and differential access to higher education are evident in many nations around the world. Japan's educational system mandates equality in school funding and insists that all schools use the same textbooks. Nevertheless, only the more affluent Japanese families can afford to send their children to *juku,* or cram schools. These afternoon schools prepare high school students for examinations that determine admission into prestigious colleges (Efron 1997).

According to a study of teachers' attitudes toward students in the "outback" in rural Australia—an area where sheep vastly outnumber people—students are being prepared to stay in the "bush." Only a small minority seek out electives geared toward preparation for college. However, beginning in the 1980s, parents questioned this agriculture-oriented curriculum in view of rural Australia's declining employment base (Henry 1989).

Conflict theorists hold that the educational inequalities resulting from tracking are designed to meet the needs of modern capitalist societies. Samuel Bowles and Herbert Gintis (1976) argue that capitalism requires a skilled, disciplined labor force and that the educational system of the United States is structured with this objective in mind. Citing numerous studies, they offer support for what they call the *correspondence principle.*

Studies conducted since 1987 suggest that the funding inequities between richer and poorer school districts have actually widened in recent years.

According to this approach, schools with students from different social classes promote the values expected of individuals in each class and perpetuate social class divisions from one generation to the next. Thus, working-class children, assumed to be destined for subordinate positions, are more likely to be placed in high school vocational and general tracks, which emphasize close supervision and compliance with authority. By contrast, young people from more affluent families are largely directed to college preparatory tracks, which stress leadership and decision-making skills—corresponding to their likely futures. While the correspondence principle continues to be persuasive, researchers have noted that the impact of race and gender on students' educational experiences may even overshadow that of class (Cole 1988). In many countries from South Africa to the United States, Black children receive less education than White children, in large part because of an unequal distribution of educational resources. And in many places, such as China, girls still receive less education than boys.

Treatment of Women in Education

The educational system of the United States, like many other social institutions, has long been characterized by discriminatory treatment of women. In 1833, Oberlin College became the first institution of higher learning to admit female students—some 200 years after the first men's college was established. But Oberlin believed that women should aspire to become wives and mothers, not lawyers and intellectuals. In addition to attending classes, female students washed men's clothing, cared for their rooms, and served them at meals. In the 1840s, Lucy Stone, then an Oberlin undergraduate and later one of the nation's most outspoken feminist leaders, refused to write a commencement address because it would have been read to the audience by a male student (Fletcher 1943; Flexner 1972).

In the twentieth century, sexism in education showed up in many ways—in textbooks with negative stereotypes of women, counselors' pressure on female students to prepare for "women's work," and unequal funding for women's and men's athletic programs. But perhaps nowhere was educational discrimination more evident than in the employment of teachers. The positions of university professor and college administrator, which hold relatively high status in the United States, generally are filled by men. Public school teachers, who earn much lower salaries, are largely female.

Women have made great strides in one area: the proportion of women continuing their schooling. As was detailed in Chapter 12, women's access to graduate education and to medical, dental, and law schools has increased dramatically in the last few decades. Pressure from the feminist movement played a major role in opening the doors of these institutions.

In cultures where traditional gender roles remain as social norms, women's education suffers appreciably. For example, in rural China, a school with several hundred students often has only a handful of girls. Although the central government is attempting to address such inequality, the typical five- or six-year-old girl in Chinese villages is engaged in farmwork rather than schoolwork. In 1995, China's State Education Commission estimated that the nation had nearly 10 million school dropouts, most of them girls (Tyler 1995b).

The same gender disparities can be seen in many other countries. Worldwide, illiteracy is generally below 30 percent of the adult population, except in Africa, the Middle East, and South Asia. Yet women account for 70 percent or more of illiterate adults not only in China but in Jordan, Syria, Russia, and South Korea (Smith 1999; Tyler 1995b).

Interactionist View

In George Bernard Shaw's play *Pygmalion,* later adapted into the hit Broadway musical *My Fair Lady,* flower girl Eliza Doolittle is transformed into a "lady" by Professor Henry Higgins. He changes her manner of speech and teaches her the etiquette of "high society." When she is introduced into society as an aristocrat, she is readily accepted. People treat her as a "lady" and she responds as one.

p. 196 The labeling approach suggests that if we treat people in particular ways, they may fulfill our expectations. Children labeled as "troublemakers" may come to view themselves as delinquents. Similarly, a dominant group's stereotyping of racial minorities may limit their opportunities to break away from expected roles.

Can this labeling process operate in the classroom? Because of their focus on micro-level classroom dynamics, interactionist researchers have been particularly interested in this question. Howard S. Becker (1952) studied public schools in low-income and more affluent areas of Chicago. He noticed that administrators expected less of students from poor neighborhoods, and he wondered if teachers were accepting this view. Subsequently, in *Pygmalion in the Classroom,* psychologist Robert Rosenthal and school principal Lenore Jacobson (1968) documented what they referred to as a **teacher-expectancy effect**—the impact that a teacher's expectations about a student's performance may have on the student's actual achievements. This appears to be especially true in lower grades (through grade three) (Brint 1998).

Between 1965 and 1966, children in a San Francisco elementary school were administered a verbal and

Children study in a rudimentary outdoor classroom at a school in northern India. Throughout the developing world, high birth rates and a shortage of educational resources contribute to illiteracy.

reasoning pretest. Rosenthal and Jacobson then *randomly* selected 20 percent of the sample and designated them as "spurters"—children of whom teachers could expect superior performance. On a later verbal and reasoning test, the spurters were found to score significantly higher than before. Moreover, teachers evaluated them as more interesting, more curious, and better-adjusted than their classmates. These results were striking. Apparently, teachers' perceptions that these students were exceptional led to noticeable improvements in performance.

Studies in the United States have revealed that teachers wait longer for an answer from a student believed to be a high achiever and are more likely to give such children

Although the Chinese government is attempting to address educational inequalities, girls continue to receive less education than boys—especially in rural areas.

a second chance. In one experiment, teachers' expectations were even shown to have an impact on students' athletic achievements. Teachers obtained better athletic performance—as measured in the number of sit-ups or push-ups performed—from those students of whom they *expected* higher numbers (Rosenthal and Babad 1985).

Despite these findings, some researchers continue to question the accuracy of the teacher-expectancy effect because of the difficulties in defining and measuring teacher expectancy. Further studies are needed to clarify the relationship between teacher expectations and actual student performance. Nevertheless, interactionists emphasize that ability alone may be less predictive of academic success than one might think (Brint 1998).

Schools as Formal Organizations

Nineteenth-century educators would be amazed at the scale of schools in the United States as we head into the twenty-first century. For example, California's public school system, the largest in the nation, currently enrolls as many children as there were in the entire country's secondary schools in 1950 (Bureau of the Census 1975:368; 2001a:148).

In many respects, today's schools, when viewed as an example of a formal organization, are similar to factories, hospitals, and business firms. Like these organizations, schools do not operate autonomously; they are influenced by the market of potential students. This is especially true of private schools, but could have broader impact if acceptance of voucher plans and other types of school choice programs increases. The parallels between schools and other types of formal organizations will become more apparent as we examine the bureaucratic nature of schools, teaching as an occupational role, and the student subculture (Dougherty and Hammack 1992).

Bureaucratization of Schools

It is simply not possible for a single teacher to transmit culture and skills to children of varying ages who will enter many diverse occupations. The growing number of students being served by individual schools and school systems as well as the greater degree of specialization required within a technologically complex society have combined to bureaucratize schools.

Max Weber noted five basic characteristics of bureaucracy, all of which are evident in the vast majority of schools, whether at the elementary, secondary, or even college level.

pp. 140–142

1. **Division of labor.** Specialized experts teach particular age levels of students and specific subjects. Public elementary and secondary schools now employ instructors whose sole responsibility is to work with children with learning disabilities or physical impairments. In a college sociology department, one professor may specialize in sociology of religion, another in marriage and the family, and a third in industrial sociology.

2. **Hierarchy of authority.** Each employee of a school system is responsible to a higher authority. Teachers must report to principals and assistant principals and may also be supervised by department heads. Principals are answerable to a superintendent of schools, and the superintendent is hired and fired by a board of education. Even the students are hierarchically organized by grade and within clubs and organizations.

3. **Written rules and regulations.** Teachers and administrators must conform to numerous rules and regulations in the performance of their duties. This bureaucratic trait can become dysfunctional; the time invested in completing required forms could instead be spent in preparing lessons or conferring with students.

4. **Impersonality.** As was noted in Chapter 6, the university has been portrayed as a giant, faceless bureaucracy that cares little for the uniqueness of the individual. As class sizes have swelled at schools and universities, it has become more difficult for teachers to give personal attention to each student. In fact, bureaucratic norms may actually encourage teachers to treat all students in the same way despite the fact that students have distinctive personalities and learning needs.

5. **Employment based on technical qualifications.** At least in theory, the hiring of teachers and college professors is based on professional competence and expertise. Promotions are normally dictated by written personnel policies; people who excel may be granted lifelong job security through tenure. Teachers have achieved these protections partly because of the bargaining power of unions (Borman and Spring 1984; Tyler 1985).

Functionalists take a generally positive view of the bureaucratization of education. Teachers can master the skills needed to work with a specialized clientele, since they no longer are expected to cover a broad range of instruction. The chain of command within schools is clear. Students are presumably treated in an unbiased fashion because of uniformly applied rules. Finally, security of position protects teachers from unjustified dismissal. In general, then, functionalists observe that bureaucratization of education increases the likelihood that students,

For many people in the United States, Vietnam is still a painful memory, a distant place devastated by civil war and a long and destructive bombing campaign. Yet this country, unified following the withdrawal of U.S. troops in the 1970s, is now a peaceful and independent nation determined to rebuild its society. Like neighboring countries, Vietnam is struggling to provide its citizens basic services, including formal education. The government of Vietnam spends less than 3 percent of the gross national product on education—about half the proportion spent by industrial countries like the United States and Great Britain. Only about 41 percent of all high school–age children in Vietnam attend school (compared to over 95 percent in the United States), and girls make up just a quarter of high school enrollments there (compared to half in the United States).

Despite these differences, Vietnamese parents' concerns are similar to those of North American parents. According to the World Bank, surveys of Vietnamese households show that parents of school-age children are significantly less satisfied with the quality of the education their children are receiving than are school administrators and local government officials. Parents, analysts suspect, may be more concerned with the outcome of their children's schooling than are school administrators, who may focus more on the quality of the services they deliver. Similar differences of opinion regarding the quality of education can be heard at school board meetings in communities across the United States.

> Only about 41 percent of all high school–age children in Vietnam attend school (compared to over 95 percent in the United States), and girls make up just a quarter of high school enrollments there.

In Vietnam as in the United States, school administration tends to be centralized. In such systems, parents are often frustrated in their efforts to influence educators and hold them accountable for their children's learning. Under extreme conditions, students may learn very little of the prescribed curriculum. For example, in Ghana and Kenya, testing showed that a significant percentage of grade school pupils could score little better than if they had guessed on measures of their learning. Together with parental disenchantment, such results have prompted a search for alternatives to centralized educational systems.

One response has been a move toward community-managed schools. In Nicaragua, school reform has given parents, teachers, and principals greater power over decisions regarding the staffing and educational methods used in local schools. While the results have been mixed, in general student achievement has improved. In El Salvador, a similar program has brought noticeable improvements in the quality of schooling. Parental monitoring of community-managed schools, for example, has halved the rate of teacher absenteeism there.

Let's Discuss

1. Has the quality of the public schools in your community become a subject of debate? If so, what are parents complaining about at school board meetings and other public forums?

2. Do parents in your community have any control over the kind of education their children receive? If so, how do they exercise that control?

Sources: Knowles et al. 1998; World Bank 1999a, 1999b; World Desk Reference 2001.

teachers, and administrators will be dealt with fairly—that is, on the basis of rational and equitable criteria.

By contrast, conflict theorists argue that the trend toward more centralized education has harmful consequences for disadvantaged people. The standardization of educational curricula, including textbooks, will generally reflect the values, interests, and lifestyles of the most powerful groups in our society and may ignore those of racial and ethnic minorities. In addition, the disadvantaged, more so than the affluent, will find it difficult to sort through complex educational bureaucracies and to organize effective lobbying groups. Therefore, in the view of conflict theorists, low-income and minority parents will have even less influence over citywide and statewide educational administrators than they have over local school officials (Bowles and Gintis 1976; Katz 1971). The experiences of parents in many developing countries seem to support this view of centralized education (see Box 16-1).

Sometimes schools can seem overwhelmingly bureaucratic, with the effect of stifling rather than nourishing intellectual curiosity in students. This concern has led many parents and policymakers to push for school choice programs—allowing parents to choose the school that suits their children's needs and forcing schools to compete for their "customers."

In the United States, another significant countertrend to the bureaucratization of schools is the availability of education over the Internet. Increasingly, colleges and universities are reaching out via the Web, offering entire courses and even majors to students in the comfort of their homes. Online curricula provide flexibility for working students and others who may have difficulty attending conventional classes because of distance or disability. Research on this type of learning is just beginning, so the question of whether teacher–student contact can thrive online remains to be settled. Computer-mediated instruction may also have an impact on instructors' status as employees, which we will discuss next, as well as on alternative forms of education like adult education and home schooling.

What would your school be like if it were less bureaucratic?

Teachers: Employees and Instructors

Whether they serve as instructors of preschoolers or graduate students, teachers are employees of formal organizations with bureaucratic structures. There is an inherent conflict in serving as a professional within a bureaucracy. The organization follows the principles of hierarchy and expects adherence to its rules, but professionalism demands the individual responsibility of the practitioner. This conflict is very real for teachers, who experience all the positive and negative consequences of working in bureaucracies (see Table 6-2 on page 142).

A teacher undergoes many perplexing stresses every day. While teachers' academic assignments have become more specialized, the demands on their time remain diverse and contradictory. There are conflicts inherent in serving as an instructor, a disciplinarian, and an employee of a school district at the same time. Burnout is one result of these stresses: 20 percent of new teachers quit the profession within three years (*Education Week* 2000). Order is needed to establish an environment in which students can actually learn. Many observers sense that the nation's schools have been the scene of increasingly violent misbehavior in recent years, although these concerns may be overblown (see Box 16-2).

Given these difficulties, does teaching remain an attractive profession in the United States? In 2001, 5.5 percent of first-year college students indicated that they were interested in becoming elementary school teachers and 4.3 percent, high school teachers. Although these figures reflect a modest upturn in the appeal of teaching in recent years, they are dramatically lower than the 13 percent of first-year male students and 38 percent of first-year female students who had such occupational aspirations in 1968 (Astin et al. 1994; Sax et al. 2001).

Undoubtedly, economic considerations enter into students' feelings about the attractiveness of teaching. In 2000, the average salary for all public elementary and secondary school teachers in the United States was $41,820. This salary places teachers somewhere near the average of all wage earners in the nation. (In private industry, workers with professional responsibilities and educational qualifications comparable with teachers earn salaries ranging from $38,000 to $90,000.) In most other industrial countries, as Figure 16-2 shows, teachers' salaries are higher in relation to the general standard of living (American Federation of Teachers 2001).

The status of any job reflects several factors, including the level of education required, financial compensation, and the respect given the occupation within society. The teaching profession (see Table 9-1, page 222) is feeling pressure in all three of these areas. First, the amount of formal schooling required for teaching remains high, and now the public has begun to call for new competency examinations for teachers. Second, the statistics cited above

Figure 16-2

Teacher Salaries in Selected Countries

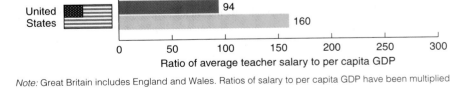

Note: Great Britain includes England and Wales. Ratios of salary to per capita GDP have been multiplied by 100.

Source: National Center for Educational Statistics 1996.

Research in Action

16-2 Violence in the Schools

www.
mhhe
.com
/schaefer8

Littleton, Colorado; Jonesboro, Arkansas; West Paducah, Kentucky; Pearl, Mississippi; Edinboro, Pennsylvania; Springfield, Oregon—these are now more than just the names of small and medium-size cities. They resonate with the sound of gunshots, of kids killing kids on school grounds. As a result, people no longer perceive schools as safe havens. But how accurate is that impression?

Studies of school violence put the recent spate of school killings in perspective:

- A child has less than one in a million chance of being killed at school.
- The number of people killed in school in the 1998–1999 school year was 38 (including adults), about average over the last six years.
- According to the Center for Disease Control, 99 percent of violent deaths of school-aged children in 1992–1994 occurred *outside* school grounds.
- Fewer students are now being found with guns in school.
- With the exception of 1999, school-associated violent deaths declined every year from 1992 through 2000.
- Twenty-three times more children are killed in gun *accidents* than in school killings.

Schools, then, are safer than neighborhoods, but people still are unnerved by the perception of an alarming rise in schoolyard violence that has been generated by heavy media coverage of the recent incidents. Some conflict theorists object to the huge outcry about recent violence in schools. After all, they note, violence in and around inner-city schools has a long history. It seems that only when middle-class White children are the victims does school violence become a plank on the national policy agenda. When violence hits the middle class, the problem is viewed not as an extension of delinquency, but as a structural issue in need of legislative remedies, such as gun control.

Meanwhile, feminists observe that virtually all the offenders are male and, in some instances, such as in the case of Jonesboro, the victims are disproportion-

> A child has less than one in a million chance of being killed at school.

ately female. The precipitating factor for violence is often a broken-off dating relationship—yet another example of violence of men against women (or, in this case, boys against girls).

Increasingly, efforts to prevent school violence are focusing on the ways in which the socialization of young people in the United States contributes to violence. For example, the *Journal of the American Medical Association* published a study of Second Step, a violence prevention curriculum for elementary school students that teaches social skills related to anger management, impulse control, and empathy. The study evaluated the impact of the program on urban and suburban elementary school students and found that it appeared to lead to a moderate decrease in physically aggressive behavior and an increase in neutral and prosocial behavior in school. However, one can never undertake such efforts early enough. The "peaceful play" program in Illinois shows *preschoolers* how to resolve their disputes in a nonviolent fashion. Other approaches to preventing violence include stiffer regulations of gun sales and gun ownership, longer school days, and afterschool programs (to keep young people occupied during unsupervised hours).

Some people believe that a key ingredient to prevention of violence, in or out of school, is greater parental supervision and responsibility for their children. In her book *A Tribe Apart*, Patricia Hersch (1998) documents the lives of eight teens growing up in a Virginia suburb over a three-year period. Her conclusion: Children need meaningful adult relationships in their lives. Former Secretary of Education Richard Riley cites studies showing that youths who feel connected to their parents and schools are less likely to engage in high-risk behavior.

Let's Discuss

1. Has a shooting or other violent episode ever occurred at your school? If so, how did students react? Do you feel safer at school than at home, as experts say you are?

2. What steps have administrators at your school taken to prevent violence? Have they been effective, or should other steps be taken?

Sources: Bowles 1999; Chaddock 1998; Department of Education 1999; Donohue et al. 1998; Grossman et al. 1997; Henry 2000; Hersch 1998; Kaufman et al. 2001; National Center for Education Statistics 1998; Schaefer 1996.

demonstrate that teachers' salaries are significantly lower than those of many professionals and skilled workers. Finally, as we have seen, the overall prestige of the teaching profession has declined in the last decade. Many teachers have become disappointed and frustrated and have left the educational world for careers in other professions.

Student Subcultures

An important latent function of education relates directly to student life: Schools provide for students' social and recreational needs. Education helps toddlers and young children develop interpersonal skills that are essential during adolescence and adulthood. During high school and college years, students may meet future husbands and wives and may establish lifelong friendships.

When people observe high schools, community colleges, or universities from the outside, students appear to constitute a cohesive, uniform group. However, the student subculture is actually much more complex and diverse. High school cliques and social groups may crop up based on race, social class, physical attractiveness, placement in courses, athletic ability, and leadership roles in the school and community. In his classic community study of "Elmtown," August B. Hollingshead (1975) found some 259 distinct cliques in a single high school. These cliques, whose average size was five, were centered on the school itself, on recreational activities, and on religious and community groups.

Amid these close-knit and often rigidly segregated cliques, gay and lesbian students are particularly vulnerable. Peer group pressure to conform is intense at this age. Although coming to terms with one's sexuality is difficult for all adolescents, for those whose sexual orientation does not conform to societal expectations it can be downright dangerous. According to a study by the Massachusetts Department of Education (2000), students who describe themselves as gay, lesbian, or bisexual are significantly more likely than others to attempt suicide, miss classes, and be threatened or injured by other students (see Figure 16-3).

Teachers and administrators are becoming more sensitized to these issues. Perhaps more important, some schools are creating gay–straight alliances (GSAs), school-sponsored support groups that bring gay teens together with sympathetic straight peers. Begun in Los Angeles in 1984, these programs numbered 750 nationwide in 2001; most were founded after the murder of Matthew Shepard, a gay college student, in 1998. While in some districts parents have objected to these organizations, the same court rulings that protect the right of conservative Bible groups to meet on school grounds also protect GSAs (Platt 2001).

We can find a similar diversity at the college level. Burton Clark and Martin Trow (1966) and, more recently, Helen Lefkowitz Horowitz (1987) have identified distinctive subcultures among college students. Here are four ideal types of subcultures that come out of their analyses:

1. The *collegiate* subculture focuses on having fun and socializing. These students define what constitutes a

Figure 16-3

Students at Risk: Gay, Lesbian, and Bisexual

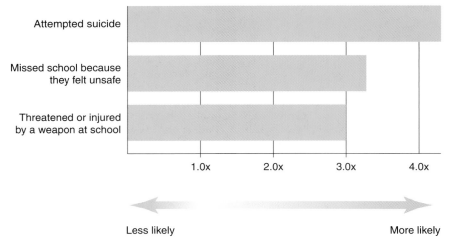

Source: Massachusetts Department of Education 2000.

Students who describe themselves as gay, lesbian, or bisexual are significantly more likely than their straight peers to attempt suicide, miss school, or be threatened or injured.

"reasonable" amount of academic work (and what amount of work is "excessive" and leads to being labeled as a "grind"). Members of the collegiate subculture have little commitment to academic pursuits.

2. By contrast, the *academic* subculture identifies with the intellectual concerns of the faculty and values knowledge for its own sake.

High school students gather in Boston for a Gay/Straight Youth Pride march. An annual event, the march is sponsored by the Governor's Commission on Gay and Lesbian Youth and the Massachusetts Department of Education.

Today the student subculture of many schools in the United States includes young people with disabilities. Federal legislation that took effect in 1980 promotes *mainstreaming,* maximum integration of disabled children with nondisabled children.

3. The *vocational* subculture is primarily interested in career prospects and views college as a means of obtaining degrees that are essential for advancement.
4. Finally, the *nonconformist* subculture is hostile to the college environment and seeks out ideas that may or may not relate to studies. It may find outlets through campus publications or issue-oriented groups.

Each college student is eventually exposed to these competing subcultures and must determine which (if any) seems most in line with his or her feelings and interests.

The typology used by these researchers reminds us that school is a complex social organization—almost like a community with different neighborhoods. Of course, these four subcultures are not the only ones evident on college campuses in the United States. For example, one might find subcultures of Vietnam veterans or former full-time homemakers at community colleges and four-year commuter institutions.

Sociologist Joe R. Feagin has studied a distinctive collegiate subculture: Black students at predominantly White universities. These students must function academically and socially within universities where there are few Black faculty members or Black administrators, where harassment of Blacks by campus police is common, and where the curricula place little emphasis on Black contributions. Feagin (1989:11) suggests that "for minority students life at a predominantly White college or university means long-term encounters with *pervasive whiteness.*" In Feagin's view, African American students at such institutions experience both blatant and subtle racial discrimination, which has a cumulative impact that can seriously damage the students' confidence (see also Feagin et al. 1996).

● Trends in Contemporary Education

While schools are formal organizations that tend to perpetuate their own cultures, they are also subject to broad-based political and social trends that may run counter to their curricula. In this section we will look at three trends that are reshaping education in the United States: the movement toward basic competency testing; increasing interest in adult education; and a small but growing movement toward schooling children at home.

Testing

Few educational issues receive more attention than testing. From preschool screening through entry-level professional examinations, the practice is always under discussion. On the most basic level, testing raises questions about reliability and validity. *Validity* refers to the degree to which a measure or scale truly reflects the phenomenon under study. Does an admissions test really measure the likelihood of future academic success, for instance? *Reliability* refers to the extent to which a measure provides consistent results. If colleges use an essay exam to measure readiness to enter a first-year composition class, for instance, the process of evaluating the essays should produce consistent results, even if different people grade the essays.

p. 36 ◀ Reliability and validity are major issues in constructing any test; rarely are they totally resolved. Scholars who design standardized tests are constantly "tweaking" the questions to improve them. Testing is also expensive—up to $20 or more per student per year (see Figure 16-4). Yet the trend nationwide is toward more testing, not less. Vowing to leave no child behind,

Figure 16-4

Spending on Tests by State

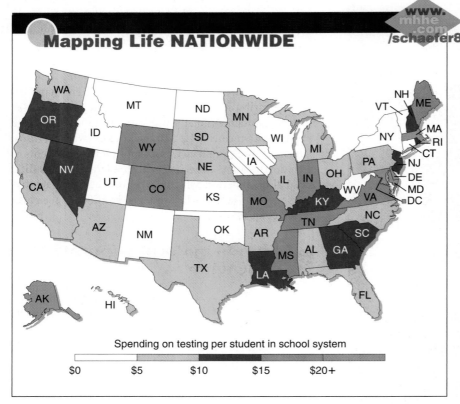

Mapping Life NATIONWIDE

www.mhhe.com /schaefer8

Spending on testing per student in school system

$0 $5 $10 $15 $20+

Notes: Data for Vermont and North Dakota are from fiscal year 2000; all other data are from 2001. No data were available for Iowa, where testing is funded directly by school districts.

Source: Education Commission of the States 2001.

politicians and educators are using the results to measure the achievement of entire classrooms, schools, districts, or even states. And the news media regularly rank public schools by the results of standardized tests taken by third graders (Education Commission of the States 2001; Lemann 1999; Wilgoren 2001).

One danger of putting too much emphasis on testing is that teachers may concentrate too much on what students need to know for an upcoming test. Because the hidden curriculum includes satisfying parents' expectations about their children's test performance, the formal curriculum may narrow to include only the content and skills that are being tested. In the 1990s, the improvement of Texas schoolchildren on the Texas Assessment of Academic Skills (TAAS) received much public attention. Yet their results on the TAAS were not matched by their performance on other standardized exams. The disparity in scores on the different measures raised questions about the validity and reliability of both the TAAS and the other examinations students took (Cuban 2001; Gardner 2001).

Even when test scores are shared only with teachers, students, and parents, they can be difficult to accept. One danger is that a child may be labeled a low achiever, both by teachers and parents. Yet test results are increasingly being reported publicly, by race and ethnicity, gender, English-language proficiency, disability, and socioeconomic status. When properly used, such results can be employed to identify the best educational practices. Improperly used, they may serve only to stigmatize large groups of young people (Education Commission of the States 2001).

Adult Education

Picture a "college student." Most likely, you will imagine someone under 25 years of age. This reflects the belief that education is something experienced and completed during the first two or three decades of life and rarely supplemented after that. However, many colleges and universities have witnessed a dramatic increase in the number of older students pursuing two-year, four-year, and graduate degrees. These older students are more likely to be female—and are more likely to be Black or Hispanic—than is the typical 19- or 20-year-old college student. Viewed from a conflict perspective, it is not surprising that women and minorities are overrepresented among older students; members of these groups are the most likely to miss out on higher education the first time around (Best and Eberhard 1990).

In 1970, only one-quarter of all students taking credit courses in colleges in the United States were 25 years old or older. However, by the mid-1990s, this figure had risen to more than 40 percent (see Figure 16-5). Obviously, sociological models of the collegiate subculture will have to be revised significantly in light of such changes. Moreover, as the age of the "typical" college student has increased, the pp. 101–102 need for on-campus child care has grown. This is especially true in community colleges, where the median age of students is already 31.

One reason for the adult education boom is that the business world is changing rapidly in an age of technological innovation. Business firms have come to accept the view of education as lifelong and may encourage (or require) employees to learn job-related skills. Thus, office assistants are sent to special schools to be trained to use the latest computer software. Realtors attend classes to learn about alternative forms of financing for home buyers. In occupation after occupation, longtime workers and professionals are going back to school to adapt to the new demands of their jobs.

Not all adult education is at the college level. Each year thousands of young adults drop out of high school, sometimes because of family obligations and sometimes out of a desire to enter the workforce or the informal economy. Later these adults may recognize the desirability of a high school diploma and decide to pursue a GED (General Educational Development) diploma, which usually involves taking preparatory classes followed by a series of exams. In recent years the proportion of students who take this alternative route to finishing high school has grown steadily. During the 1990s, the percentage of high school degrees awarded to students aged 18 to 24 years who attended GED programs increased from less than 5 percent to over 10 percent. Thus far, researchers have found conflicting evidence on the effect of a GED versus a traditional degree on employment status and earnings; additional research needs to be done on this topic (Population Reference Bureau 2000).

⬤Imagine

Legislators have passed a law guaranteeing a government-paid college education to all qualified high school graduates. How will your life and the lives of others you know change? How will society change?

Home Schooling

When most people think of school, they think of bricks and mortar and the teachers, administrators, and other employees who staff school buildings. But for an increasing number of students in the United States, home is the classroom and the teacher is a parent. More than 1.5 million students are now being educated at home. That is about 4 percent of the K–12 school population (Garrison 2001).

In the past, families that taught their children at home lived in isolated environments or held strict religious views at odds with the secular environment of public schools. But today, home schooling is attracting a broader range of families not necessarily tied to organized religion. Poor academic quality, peer pressure, and school violence are motivating many parents to teach their children at home. The recent publicity given to school

Many adults return to school in later life to obtain further education, advance their careers, or change their line of work. These adults are studying microbiology.

Figure 16-5

Age Distribution of College Students in the United States, 1970–2010

Since 1970, more and more older students have been enrolling in college.

College enrollment (in millions)

Year	Students under age 25	Students ages 25 and over
1970	6.2	2.4
1998	8.6	5.9
2010 (projected)	10.7	6.8

■ Students under age 25   ■ Students ages 25 and over

Source: National Center for Education Statistics 2001: Table 175.

shooting sprees seems to have accelerated the move toward home schooling.

Whereas supporters of home schooling believe children can do just as well or better in home schools as in public schools, critics counter that because home-schooled children are isolated from the larger community, they lose an important chance to improve their socialization skills. But proponents of home schooling claim their children benefit from contact with others besides their own age group. They also see home schools as a good alternative for children who suffer from attention deficit disorder (ADD) and learning disorders (LDs). Such children often do better in smaller classes, which present fewer distractions to disturb their concentration (National Homeschool Association 1999).

At a home school in Brunswick, Maine, a mother educates her three children. An estimated 3,500 families home-schooled their children in Maine in 1998.

Quality control is an issue in home schooling. While home schooling is legal in all 50 states, only 37 states regulate home schools; 29 monitor students' progress through tests or evaluations. Despite the lack of uniform standards, a national study funded by the Home School Legal Defense Association reports that home-schooled students score higher than others on standardized tests, in every subject and every grade. Almost 25 percent of the students who participated in the study were working above grade level for their age. The top three winners of the 2000 national spelling bee were all schooled at home. Home schooling works, particularly for those who have made a commitment to it (Calhoun 2000; Matthews 1999; Paulson 2000).

Who are the people who are running home schools? In general, they tend to have higher-than-average incomes and educational levels. Most are two-parent families, and their children watch less television than average—both factors that are likely to support superior educational performance. The same students, with the same types of family and the same support from their parents, would probably do just as well in the public schools. As research has repeatedly shown, small classes are better than big classes, and strong parental and community involvement is key (Schnaiberg 1999).

In the next section we will look at another alternative to the public schools, school choice programs.

SOCIAL POLICY AND EDUCATION

School Choice Programs

www.mhhe.com /schaefer8

The Issue

Imagine a school where every child in kindergarten reads, where third graders read *The Iliad,* where children beg to do second drafts of their writing, where classes are small, and where teachers are chosen by the school, not assigned to it. This was the vision dangled before inner-city parents in Jersey City, New Jersey, one evening in 1998 by a private company that runs publicly financed charter schools. That night, hundreds of parents signed their children up, even though the school didn't have a location yet and was run by a company with a short track record (Winerip 1998:44).

Charter schools in New Jersey, like this one in Newark, have become so popular that some of them must use a lottery to select students. While parents are happy with the educational results of these schools, critics are concerned that the most motivated students are being lured away from the regular public schools.

The Setting

This is the world of the school choice movement, which is increasingly pitting parents against public school proponents. The term **school choice programs** refers to various types of educational experiments under which parents can choose where to send their children. In the 1970s, school choice took the form of *magnet schools,* usually centralized public schools that offered special enrichment programs to entice children from their local schools. At first, they were part of an attempt to improve racial balance in the schools, but soon they became known primarily as laboratories for experiments in education. Another form of school choice is **school voucher programs,** which provide for the transfer of public funds to the public or private school of the parents' choice. Because the funds follow the child, the intent is that voucher plans will stimulate local schools to perform better and keep their students. The most recent form of school choice is the *charter school movement,* a nationwide effort that allows parents and private educators (or anyone with an idea for a school) to create and control a school that is chartered by the state and funded by public money.

Proponents of school choice often rely on the work of economists for support (Tucker 1993). The use of school vouchers, for example, was first advanced by Milton Friedman in his book *Capitalism and Freedom* (1962). The idea is to set up a sort of free-market system of education: Parents shop for the school they want, which receives that child's portion of the school budget ($7,000 in New Jersey, for example). The schools that are most popular thrive; those that are not must improve to compete or else close their doors (Tashman 1992). Support for school choice comes from a diverse sampling of the "consumers of education": liberals who oppose compulsory school assignments for their children and seek more freedom of choice; nonpolitical parents disillusioned by schools that have become too impersonal and bureaucratized; and Christian fundamentalists, who view religious education as a means of combating growing secularization.

Sociological Insights

The analogy to business competition within a free-market economy seems deceptive to some observers. While a successful business such as Coca-Cola can expand into new markets across the United States and the world, they argue, an elementary school has a limited potential for expanding its customer base. Rather than expanding, an outstanding school will become ever more selective, as parents compete to enroll their children. Most charter schools in New Jersey are so oversubscribed they use a lottery to select their students. There is concern, too, about the state of public schools, whose most motivated students often end up in school choice programs.

Critics of choice programs are also troubled by the divisive religious issue underlying the voucher policy. About two-thirds of private school students in the United States attend institutions with religious affiliations; among parents who send their children to private schools, as many as 95 percent identify religion as the number-one criterion in choosing a school. For opponents of vouchers and tuition tax credits, any government aid to parochial education—whether direct or indirect—violates the nation's historic

Figure 16-6

School Choice and Voucher Programs by State

Green Pins: City-Wide or Statewide Privately-Funded Voucher Programs
Red Pins: City-Wide Tax-Funded Voucher Programs
Orange States: School Choice Tax Credit Statewide Programs
Yellow States: Statewide Tax-Funded Voucher Programs

Note: Data were current as of July 2001.

Source: Children First CEO America 2001.

Think About It

Why are school choice programs clustered in the eastern half of the United States?

and those with highly educated parents are especially likely to take advantage of these experiments, in part because vouchers and tax credits may not cover the full cost of private school. Despite opposition by many Black civil rights groups, public opinion surveys show strong support for school vouchers among African American parents, who tend to see a voucher program, however flawed, as a welcome alternative to the public schools (Holmes 1999).

Research has just begun on the impact of school choice programs. Thus far, the results are inconclusive: some students do better; others do not. Parents do seem satisfied with the decisions they have made, however. Studies are complicated by the fact that participants in these programs are not necessarily motivated by educational goals. Some parents enroll children in school choice or voucher programs for the sake of convenience—to decrease the distance between the child's school and the parents' workplace or to optimize the parents' work schedules. Clearly, much more research is necessary before a definitive verdict can be made on these programs (General Accounting Office 2001; Gill et al. 2001).

separation of church and state. Moreover, drawing on the functionalist perspective, critics of school choice point out that education in the United States has traditionally promoted social and political integration. Such integration is undermined when students attend private and parochial schools and do not interact with peers across class, racial, ethnic, and religious lines (Bracey 1993; Lines 1985; Martinez et al. 1994).

Viewed from a conflict perspective, the social class and religious implications of school choice programs are a matter of concern—especially when such programs provide financial support for families to send children to private and parochial schools. Studies of existing choice programs suggest that the more affluent households

Policy Initiatives

As interest in school voucher programs grows, the controversy that surrounds them grows as well. Legal challenges have been mounted against several voucher programs, including those affiliated with religious groups. Plaintiffs charged that these programs violated the tradition of separation of church and state. As we saw in the last chapter, the meaning of that fundamental concept is being redefined, and the case of vouchers is no exception. Ultimately, a

pp. 396—397

Supreme Court decision will be necessary to resolve the issue (Goldstein 2001).

So far, school choice policy decisions have been made only at the local and state levels. As Figure 16-6 shows, relatively few parts of the country have true tax-supported voucher programs. On the federal level, legislation calling for government subsidy of tuition vouchers for low-income families failed to come to a vote in 2001, despite support from President George W. Bush (Alvarez 2001).

Interest in school choice is not unique to the United States. In Great Britain, New Zealand, and Sweden, policymakers have given parents a measure of freedom in selecting their children's schools, and government financing of schools is based on enrollment figures. In Australia, Denmark, and the Netherlands, there has been increasing governmental financial support for private schools (*The Economist* 1994; Ladner and McTigue 2001).

Let's Discuss

1. Would you send your child to a private or charter school if the government offered you a tuition voucher? Why or why not?

2. What do you think of the idea that public schools should be able to compete with private schools? What difficulties might they face that private schools do not?

3. Which is more important, maintaining the separation of church and state or fostering educational choice by allowing students to attend religious schools at public expense? Justify your position.

⬤ Chapter Resources

Summary

Education is a cultural universal, found throughout the world, although in varied forms. This chapter examines sociological views of education and analyzes schools as an example of formal organizations.

1. Transmission of knowledge and bestowal of status are manifest functions of education. Among its latent functions are transmitting culture, promoting social and political integration, maintaining social control, and serving as an agent of social change.

2. In the view of conflict theorists, education serves as an instrument of elite domination by creating standards for entry into occupations, bestowing status unequally, and subordinating the role of women in education.

3. Teacher expectations about a student's performance can sometimes have an impact on the student's actual achievements.

4. Today, most schools in the United States are organized in a bureaucratic fashion. Weber's five basic characteristics of bureaucracy are all evident in schools.

5. Nationwide, the trend toward increased testing of public school students has become controversial. Some people question the **reliability** and **validity** of the tests; others fear the practice may narrow the curriculum or encourage negative labeling of whole groups of students.

6. Since 1970, the proportion of older adults enrolled in U.S. colleges and universities has been rising steadily, in part because of sweeping changes in business, industry, and technology. For many Americans, education has become a lifelong pursuit.

7. Home schooling has become a viable alternative to traditional public and private schools. An estimated million or more American children are now educated at home.

8. **School choice** and **school voucher programs** are having a direct effect on public education, forcing some schools to compete or go out of business.

Critical Thinking Questions

1. What are the functions and dysfunctions of tracking in schools? Viewed from an interactionist perspective, how would tracking of high school students influence the interactions between students and teachers? In what ways might tracking have positive and negative impacts on the self-concepts of various students?

2. Are the student subcultures identified in this text evident on your campus? What other student subcultures are present? Which subcultures have the highest (and the lowest) social status? How might functionalists, conflict theorists, and interactionists view the existence of student subcultures on a college campus?

Key Terms

Correspondence principle The tendency of schools to promote the values expected of individuals in each social class and to prepare students for the types of jobs typically held by members of their class. (page 409)

Credentialism An increase in the lowest level of education required to enter a field. (408)

Cultural universals General practices found in every culture. (403)

Education A formal process of learning in which some people consciously teach while others adopt the social role of learner. (403)

Hidden curriculum Standards of behavior that are deemed proper by society and are taught subtly in schools. (408)

Reliability The extent to which a test provides consistent results. (417)

School choice program An educational experiment under which parents can choose where to send their children to school. (421)

School voucher program A form of school choice program in which public funds are transferred to the public or private school of the parents' choice. (421)

Teacher-expectancy effect The impact that a teacher's expectations about a student's performance may have on the student's actual achievements. (410)

Tracking The practice of placing students in specific curriculum groups on the basis of test scores and other criteria. (409)

Validity The degree to which a test truly reflects the phenomenon under study. (417)

Additional Readings

BOOKS

Bowen, William G., and Derek Bok. 1998. *The Shape of the River.* Princeton, NJ: Princeton University Press. Two respected researchers look at the history and social consequences of the consideration of race in college admissions.

Margolis, Eric, ed. 2001. *The Hidden Curriculum in Higher Education.* New York: Routledge. Eleven essays on the ways in which higher education reproduces race, class, and gender hierarchies.

Ravitch, Diane. 2000. *Left Back: A Century of Failed School Reforms.* New York: Simon and Schuster. A respected scholar considers the failure of several massive efforts to improve public schools in the United States.

Sadker, Myra, and David Sadker. 1995. *Failing at Fairness: How America's Schools Cheat Girls.* New York: Touchstone. The authors present a history of women's education in the United States and then critically examine the contemporary treatment of females from elementary school through graduate school.

JOURNALS

The sociology of education is reflected in *Educational Record* (founded in 1920), *Education and Urban Society* (1968), *Education Week* (1981), the *Harvard Educational Review* (1974), *Intercultural Education* (1989), *Journal of Contemporary Education* (1984), *Journal of Educational Finance* (1975), *Phi Delta Kappan* (1915), *Race Ethnicity and Education* (1998), and *Sociology of Education* (1927).

Internet Connection

*Note: While all the URLs listed were current as of the printing of this book, these sites often change. Please check our website (**http://www.mhhe.com/schaefer8**) for updates and hyperlinks to these exercises and additional exercises.*

1. The National Center for Education Statistics (**http://www.nces.ed.gov/**) provides the public with statistical information on education. Click on "Fast Facts." Choose "Postsecondary Education," and answer the following questions:
   (a) What are the three most common majors? Is your major one of them?
   (b) What are the trends in the cost of a college education? Is your college tuition comparable with national trends?
   (c) What percentage of the degrees conferred in 1997–1998 were awarded to White students? To minority students?
   (d) In 1999, what percentage of females earned bachelor's degrees?
   (e) Look at the table of associate degrees. How many women received associate degrees in 1999–2000?
   (f) Look at the table of bachelor's degrees. How many women and men were awarded bachelor's degrees in 1999–2000?

   (g) Look at the table showing the distribution of degrees by racial and ethnic groups. Which group received the most bachelor's degrees? The most master's degrees? The most doctoral degrees?

2. Read the interview with Jonathan Kozol, author of *Savage Inequalities*, that is posted at **http://www.ascd.org.** Link to "Reading Room" and type "Savage Inequalities" in the search bar. Read "On Savage Inequalities: A Conversation with Jonathan Kozol," and answer the following questions:
   (a) What conditions did Kozol find in the public schools in East St. Louis?
   (b) According to Kozol, why do such poor conditions exist in public schools? Do you agree with him?
   (c) What is Kozol's opinion of voucher systems? Do you agree or disagree with him? Explain.
   (d) What are the three significant changes Kozol thinks would make a difference for at-risk students?
   (e) What is Kozol's opinion of tracking? Do you agree? Explain.
   (f) What do you think of the title of Kozol's book *Savage Inequalities?* Is it appropriate?

Online Learning Center www.mhhe.com/schaefer8

The formation of student subcultures is one of the latent functions of education. You can conduct your own "Cyber Student Organization Fair" by visiting the Online Learning Center at **www.mhhe.com/schaefer8,** and linking to the student center. While you are in the student center, link to "Internet Exercises." The third exercise will direct you to links where you can learn about organizations found on university and college campuses.

GOVERNMENT AND POLITICS

Voter apathy is costly, in that it subverts the ideal of a truly representative government. This public service advertisement encourages citizens to take part in shaping their government and society by voting.

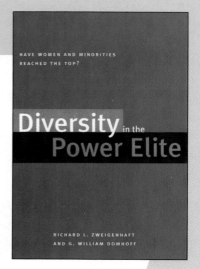

HAVE WOMEN AND MINORITIES
REACHED THE TOP?

Diversity in the
Power Elite

RICHARD L. ZWEIGENHAFT
AND G. WILLIAM DOMHOFF

The power elite and Congress are more diverse than they were before the social movements that emerged in the 1960s brought pressure to bear on corporations, politicians, and government. Although the power elite is still composed primarily of Christian white men, there are now Jews, women, blacks, Latinos, and Asian Americans on the boards of the country's largest corporations; presidential cabinets are far more diverse than was the case forty years ago; and the highest ranks of the military are no longer filled solely by white men. In the case of elected officials in Congress, the trend toward diversity is even greater for women and all of the minority groups that we have studied. . . .

Ultimately we suggest that the increase in diversity at the top contains several ironies, the most important of which is related to what is perhaps the major unresolved tension in American life, between liberal individualism and the class structure. The diversification of the power elite has been celebrated, but this celebration ignores the continuing importance of the class structure. The movements that led to diversity in the power elite have succeeded to some extent, especially for women and minorities from privileged social backgrounds, but there has been no effect on the way the power elite functions or on the class structure itself. . . .

The power elite has been strengthened because diversity has been achieved primarily by the selection of women and minorities who share the prevailing perspectives and values of those already in power. The power elite is not "multicultural" in any full sense of the concept, but only in terms of ethnic or racial origins. This process has been helped along by those who have called for the inclusion of women and minorities without any consideration of criteria other than sex, race, or ethnicity. Because the demand was strictly for a woman on the Supreme Court, President Reagan could comply by choosing a conservative upper-class corporate lawyer, Sandra Day O'Connor. When pressure mounted to have more black justices, President Bush could respond by appointing Clarence Thomas, a conservative black Republican with a law degree from Yale University. It is yet another irony that appointments like these served to undercut the liberal social movements that caused them to happen. . . .

We therefore have to conclude on the basis of our findings that the diversification of the power elite did not generate any changes in an underlying class system. . . . The values of liberal individualism embedded in the Declaration of Independence, the Bill of Rights, and the civic culture were renewed by vigorous and courageous activists, but despite their efforts the class structure remains a major obstacle to individual fulfillment for the overwhelming majority of Americans. This fact is more than an irony. It is a dilemma. It combines with the dilemma of race to create a nation that celebrates equal opportunity but is, in reality, a bastion of class privilege and conservatism. *(Zweigenhaft and Domhoff 1998:176–77, 192, 194)* ■ 💿

Additional information about this excerpt and about those that open each subsequent chapter can be found in the SocWorld CD-ROM that accompanies this text.

Half a century ago C. Wright Mills (1959), the originator of the phrase *the sociological imagination,* studied the political process in the United States and articulated the concept of the power elite. In doing so, Mills stimulated a discussion about how society's most important decisions are made. Mills made a point of stating that the power elite was composed of men. That was no accident; at the time Mills wrote, no women made life-and-death decisions on society's behalf.

Four decades after Mills opened discussion of the subject, psychologist Richard L. Zweigenhaft and sociologist G. William Domhoff returned to the question of who rules America. As the opening excerpt from their book *Diversity in the Power Elite* (1998) shows, they found only modest changes in the nation's power structure. Today, a few privileged women occupy positions in the power elite, but the majority of the nation's decision makers are still men, and virtually all of them are White.

The power elite operates within the framework of the existing political system, be it local, state, national, or international. By *political system,* sociologists mean the social institution that is founded on a recognized set of procedures for implementing and achieving society's goals, such as the allocation of valued resources. Like religion and the family, the political system is a cultural universal: It is found in every society. In the United States, the political system holds the ultimate responsibility for addressing the social policy issues examined in this textbook: child care, the AIDS crisis, sexual harassment, welfare reform, and so forth.

How does the power elite maintain its power? How do other groups attempt to exert theirs? Does our campaign finance system put some groups at a disadvantage, and if so, should it be changed? In this chapter we will analyze the impact of government on people's lives from a sociological point of view. We will begin with a macro-level analysis of the sources of power in a political system, and the three major types of authority. We will see how politics works in the United States, with particular attention to political socialization, citizens' participation in politics, the changing role of women in politics, and the influence of interest groups on political decision making. We'll also look at two models of power in the United States: the elite and the pluralist models. Finally, the social policy section will explore the controversy over campaign financing, an issue that vividly illustrates the close relationship between government and the moneyed interest groups that seek to influence the political process. ■

Power and Authority

A society does not exist in a vacuum. Someone or some group makes important decisions about how to use resources and how to allocate goods, whether it be a tribal chief or a parliament or a dictator. A cultural universal common to all societies, then, is the exercise of power and authority. The struggle for power and authority inevitably involves *politics,* which political scientist Harold Lasswell (1936) tersely defined as "who gets what, when, and how." In their study of politics and government, sociologists are concerned with social interactions among individuals and groups and their impact on the larger political and economic order.

Power

p. 218 Power is at the heart of a political system. According to Max Weber, *power* is the ability to exercise one's will over others. To put it another way, whoever can control the behavior of others is exercising power. Power relations can involve large organizations, small groups, or even people in an intimate association.

There are three basic sources of power within any political system—force, influence, and authority. *Force* is the actual or threatened use of coercion to impose one's will on others. When leaders imprison or even execute political dissidents, they are applying force; so, too, are terrorists when they seize or bomb an embassy or assassinate a political leader (see Box 17-1). *Influence,* on the other hand, refers to the exercise of power through a process of persuasion. A citizen may change his or her position regarding a Supreme Court nominee because of a newspaper editorial, the expert testimony of a law school dean before the Senate Judiciary Committee, or a stirring speech at a rally by a political activist. In each case, sociologists would view such efforts to persuade people as examples of influence. Now let's take a look at the third source of power, *authority.*

Types of Authority

The term *authority* refers to power that has been institutionalized and is recognized by the people over whom it is exercised. Sociologists commonly use the term in connection with those who hold legitimate power

Sociology in the Global Community

17-1 Terrorist Violence

www. mhhe .com /schaefer8

For Americans, the moment that a hijacked commercial airliner slammed into the World Trade Center on the morning of September 11, 2001, terrorism became a frightening reality—something that no longer took place only in foreign countries. It was, of course, not the first terrorist attack on the United States, or even on the World Trade Center. Just six years earlier, the U.S. federal building in Oklahoma City had been truck-bombed by terrorist Timothy McVeigh, who was born and raised in the United States; 168 people died in the blast. And in 1993, terrorists had succeeded in destroying the lower levels of the World Trade Center. But the collapse of the two towers and the loss of nearly 3,000 lives seared the nation's psyche in a way the earlier attacks had not. When letters purporting to contain anthrax spores began arriving at abortion clinics shortly after the attacks and a U.S. citizen was taken into custody by the FBI for sending them, Americans could no longer escape the fact that terrorism had become a home-grown as well as an imported phenomenon.

Such acts of terror, whether perpetrated by a few or by many people, can also be a powerful political force. Formally defined, **terrorism** is the use or threat of violence against random or symbolic targets in pursuit of political aims. An essential aspect of contemporary terrorism involves use of the media. Terrorists may wish to keep secret their individual identities, but they want their political messages and goals to receive as much publicity as possible. Drawing upon Erving Goffman's dramaturgical approach, sociologist Alfred McClung Lee has likened terrorism to the theater, where certain scenes are played out in a predictable fashion. Whether through calls to the media, anonymous manifestos, or other

> An essential aspect of contemporary terrorism involves use of the media.

means, terrorists typically admit responsibility for and defend their violent acts.

For terrorists, the end justifies the means. The status quo is viewed as oppressive; desperate measures are believed essential to end the suffering of the deprived. Convinced that working through the formal political process will not effect desired political change, terrorists insist that illegal actions—often directed against innocent people—are needed. In a sense, terrorists hope to intimidate society and thereby bring about a new political order.

Some political commentators have argued that terrorism defies definition because one person's "terrorist" is another person's "freedom fighter." To many people around the world, for example, Osama bin Laden and the terrorists who destroyed the World Trade Center were heroes. In this view of terrorism, we carry our biases into our evaluation of terrorist incidents and criticize only those perpetrated by groups who do not share our political goals. Sociologists reject this critique, countering that even in warfare there are accepted rules outlawing the use of certain tactics. For example, civilian noncombatants are supposedly immune from deliberate attack and are not to be taken prisoner. If we are to set objective standards regarding terrorism, then we should condemn *any and all people* who are guilty of certain actions, no matter how understandable or even admirable some of their goals may be.

Let's Discuss

1. Have you ever lived in a place where the threat of terrorism was a part of daily life, or known someone who did? What was it like?
2. Can any goal, no matter how noble, justify terrorist activity?

Sources: Eisler 2000; Herman and O'Sullivan 1990; Lee 1983; Lewin 2001; McCoy and Cauchon 2001; R. Miller 1988.

through elected or publicly acknowledged positions. A person's authority is limited by the constraints of a particular social position. Thus, a referee has the authority to decide whether a penalty should be called during a football game but has no authority over the price of tickets to the game.

Max Weber ([1913] 1947) developed a classification system regarding authority that has become one of the most useful and frequently cited contributions of early sociology. He identified three ideal types of authority: traditional, legal-rational, and charismatic. Weber did not insist that only one type applies to a given society or organization. All can be present, but their relative impor-

tance will vary. Sociologists have found Weber's typology valuable in understanding different manifestations of legitimate power within a society.

Traditional Authority

Until the middle of the last century, Japan was ruled by a revered emperor, whose power was absolute and passed down from generation to generation. In a political system based on **traditional authority,** legitimate power is conferred by custom and accepted practice. A king or queen is accepted as ruler of a nation simply by virtue of inheriting the crown; a tribal chief rules because that is the accepted practice. The ruler may be loved or hated,

King Bhumibol Adulyadoj of Thailand reviews the Royal Honor Guard during a ceremony honoring his birthday. In a political system based on traditional authority, power is conferred according to accepted custom—in this case, on the basis of royal birth.

competent or destructive; in terms of legitimacy, that does not matter. For the traditional leader, authority rests in custom, not in personal characteristics, technical competence, or even written law. People accept this authority because "this is how things have always been done." Traditional authority is absolute when the ruler has the ability to determine laws and policies.

Legal-Rational Authority

The U.S. Constitution gives Congress and our president the authority to make and enforce laws and policies. Power made legitimate by law is known as *legal-rational authority.* Leaders derive their legal-rational authority from the written rules and regulations of political systems, such as a constitution. Generally, in societies based on legal-rational authority, leaders are thought to have specific areas of competence and authority, but are not thought to be endowed with divine inspiration, as in certain

societies with traditional forms of authority.

Charismatic Authority

Joan of Arc was a simple peasant girl in medieval France, yet she was able to rally the French people and lead them in major battles against English invaders. How was this possible? As Weber observed, power can be legitimized by the *charisma* of an individual. The term **charismatic authority** refers to power made legitimate by a leader's exceptional personal or emotional appeal to his or her followers. Charisma lets a person lead or inspire without relying on set rules or traditions. In fact, charismatic authority is derived more from the beliefs of followers than from the actual qualities of leaders. So long as people *perceive* a leader as having qualities setting him or her apart from ordinary citizens, that leader's authority will remain secure and often unquestioned.

A young Tony Blair works the crowd outside 10 Downing Street in London shortly after his election as Great Britain's prime minister. Blair's power is an example of charismatic authority.

Unlike traditional rulers, charismatic leaders often become well known by breaking with established institutions and advocating dramatic changes in the social structure and the economic system. Their strong hold over their followers makes it easier to build protest movements that challenge the dominant norms and values of a society. Thus, charismatic leaders such as Jesus, Joan of Arc, Mahatma Gandhi, Malcolm X, and Martin Luther King all used their power to press for changes in accepted social behavior. But so did Adolf Hitler, whose charismatic appeal turned people toward violent and destructive ends in Nazi Germany.

Observing from an interactionist perspective, sociologist Carl Couch (1996) points out that the growth of the electronic media has facilitated the development of charismatic authority. During the 1930s and 1940s, the heads of state of the United States, Great Britain, and Germany all used radio to issue direct appeals to citizens. In recent decades, television has allowed leaders to "visit" people's homes and communicate with them. Time and again, Saddam Hussein has rallied the Iraqi people through shrewd use of television appearances. In both Taiwan and South Korea in 1996, troubled political leaders facing reelection campaigns spoke frequently to national audiences and exaggerated military threats from neighboring China and North Korea, respectively.

As was noted earlier, Weber used traditional, legal-rational, and charismatic authority as ideal types. In reality, particular leaders and political systems combine elements of two or more of these forms. Presidents Franklin D. Roosevelt, John F. Kennedy, and Ronald Reagan wielded power largely through the legal-rational basis of their authority. At the same time, they were unusually charismatic leaders who commanded the personal loyalty of large numbers of citizens.

Imagine

What would our government be like if it were founded on traditional rather than legal-rational authority? What difference would it make to the average citizen?

Political Behavior in the United States

Citizens of the United States take for granted many aspects of their political system. They are accustomed to living in a nation with a Bill of Rights, two major political parties, voting by secret ballot, an elected president, state and local governments distinct from the national government, and so forth. Yet, of course, each society has its own ways of governing itself and making decisions. Just as U.S. residents expect Democratic and Republican candidates

to compete for public offices, residents of the People's Republic of China and Cuba are accustomed to one-party rule by the Communist party. In this section, we will examine a number of important aspects of political behavior within the United States.

Political Socialization

Do your political views coincide with those of your parents? Did you vote in the last election? Did you register to vote, or do you plan to do so? The process by which you acquire political attitudes and develop patterns of political behavior is known as ***political socialization.*** This involves not only learning the prevailing beliefs of a society but also coming to accept the political system, whatever its limitations and problems.

Chapter 6 identified five functional prerequisites that a society must fulfill to survive. One of these was the need to teach recruits to accept the values and customs of the group. In a political sense, this function is crucial; each succeeding generation must be encouraged to accept a society's basic political values and its particular methods of decision making. The principal institutions of political socialization are those that also socialize us to other cultural norms: the family, schools, and the media.

Many observers see the family as playing a particularly significant role in the process. Parents pass on their political attitudes and evaluations to their sons and daughters through discussions at the dinner table and also through the example of their political involvement or apathy. Early socialization does not always determine a person's political orientation; there are changes over time and between generations. Yet research on political socialization continues to show that parents' views have an important impact on their children's outlook (Jennings and Niemi 1981).

Schools provide young people with information and analysis of the political world. Unlike the family and peer groups, schools are easily susceptible to centralized and uniform control. That is why totalitarian societies commonly use educational institutions to indoctrinate the students in certain political beliefs. Even in democracies, where local schools are not under the pervasive control of the national government, political education will generally reflect the norms and values of the prevailing political order.

In the view of conflict theorists, students in the United States learn much more than factual information about their political and economic way of life. They are socialized to view capitalism and representative democracy as the "normal" and most desirable ways of organizing a nation, a form of dominant ideology. At the same time, schools often present competing values and forms of government in a negative fashion or simply ignore them. From a conflict perspective, this

In 1996, anti-tobacco protesters rallied near the site of the Republican National Convention in San Diego. Mass protests are one way public interest groups seek to exert their power.

process in many ways, such as by joining a political club supporting candidates for public office or working to change the party's position on controversial issues. If, however, people do not take an interest in the decisions of major political parties, public officials in a "representative" democracy will be chosen from two unrepresentative lists of candidates.

By the 1980s, it became clear that many people in the United States were beginning to be turned off by political parties, politicians, and big government. The most dramatic indication of this growing alienation comes from voting statistics. Voters of all ages and races appear to be less enthusiastic than ever about elections, even presidential contests. For example, almost 80 percent of eligible voters in the United States went to the polls in the

type of political education serves the interests of the powerful and ignores the significance of the social divisions found within the United States.

Participation and Apathy

In theory, a representative democracy will function most effectively and fairly if an informed and active electorate communicates its views to government leaders. Unfortunately, this is hardly the case in the United States. Virtually all citizens are familiar with the basics of the political process, and most tend to identify to some extent with a political party (see Table 17-1), but only a small minority (often members of the higher social classes) actually participate in political organizations on a local or national level. Studies reveal that only 8 percent of the people in the United States belong to a political club or organization. Not more than one in five has *ever* contacted an official of national, state, or local government about a political issue or problem (Orum 2001).

The failure of most citizens to become involved in political parties diminishes the democratic process. Within the political system of the United States, the political party serves as an intermediary between people and government. Through competition in regularly scheduled elections, the two major parties provide for challenges to public policies and for an orderly transfer of power. An individual dissatisfied with the state of the nation or a local community can become involved in the political party

Table 17-1   Political Preferences in the United States

Party Identification	Percentage of Population
Strong Democrat	15
Not very strong Democrat	18
Independent, close to Democrat	12
Independent	21
Independent, close to Republican	10
Not very strong Republican	15
Strong Republican	10

Note: Data are for 2000. Numbers do not add to 100 percent due to rounding.

Source: Davis and Smith 2001:88.

Think About It
Why do so many U.S. voters identify themselves as independents?

Judge Charles Burton, chairman of the Palm Beach County, Florida, canvassing board, inspects a contested punch card for signs of the voter's intentions during the manual recount that followed the 2000 presidential election. The public perception that many votes were miscounted may have undermined some Americans' faith in their electoral system, strengthening their suspicions that their votes don't count.

presidential election of 1896. Yet by the 2000 election, turnout had fallen to less than 51 percent of all eligible voters. Obviously, even modestly higher voter turnout could dramatically change election outcomes, as we saw in the razor-thin margin in the 2000 presidential election.

While a few nations still command high voter turnout, it is increasingly common to hear national leaders of other countries complain of voter apathy. Japan typically enjoyed 70 percent turnout in its Upper House elections in the 1950s through mid-1980s, but by 1998 turnout was closer to 58 percent. In 2001, only 59 percent of British voters participated in the general elections. The same year, just 55 percent of Swiss voters went to the polls to decide a highly controversial referendum on membership in the European Union (*Facts on File Weekly Digest* 2001a, 2001b; Masaki 1998).

Political participation makes government accountable to the voters. If participation declines, government can operate with less of a sense of accountability to society. This issue is most serious for the least powerful individuals and groups within the United States. Voter turnout has been particularly low among members of racial and ethnic minorities. In post-election surveys, fewer African Americans and Hispanics than Whites report that they actually voted. Many more potential voters fail to register to vote. The poor—whose focus understandably is on survival—are traditionally underrepresented among voters as well. The low turnout found among these groups is explained, at least in part, by their common feeling of powerlessness. Yet these low statistics encourage political power brokers to continue to ignore the interests of the less affluent and the nation's minorities. The segment of the voting population that has shown the *most* voter apathy is the young (see Box 17-2) (Casper and Bass 1998).

Women in Politics

Women continue to be dramatically underrepresented in the halls of government. As of early 2002, there were only 73 women in Congress. They accounted for 60 of the 435 members of the House of Representatives and 13 of the 100 members of the Senate. Only five states had female governors: Arizona, Delaware, Massachusetts, Montana, and New Hampshire (Center for American Women and Politics 2001).

p. 310

Sexism has been the most serious barrier to women interested in holding office. Women were not even allowed to vote in national elections until 1920, and subsequent female candidates have had to overcome the prejudices of both men and women regarding women's fitness for leadership. Not until 1955 did a majority of people state that they would vote for a qualified woman for president. Moreover, women often encounter prejudice, discrimination, and abuse after they are elected. Despite these problems, more women are being elected to political office, and more of them are identifying themselves as feminists.

But while women politicians may be enjoying more electoral success now than in the past, there is evidence that the media cover them differently from men. A content analysis of newspaper coverage of recent gubernatorial races showed that reporters wrote more often about a female candidate's personal life, appearance, or personality than a male candidate's, and less often about her political positions and voting record. Furthermore, when political issues were raised in newspaper articles, reporters were more likely to illustrate them with statements made by male candidates than by female candidates (Devitt 1999).

Research in Action

17-2 Why Don't Young People Vote?

In 1971, there was great optimism. All through the 1960s, young people in the United States had actively participated in a range of political issues—from pushing civil rights to protesting the Vietnam War. They were especially disturbed by the fact that young men were barred from voting but were being drafted to serve in the military and dying for their country. In response to these concerns, the 26th Amendment to the Constitution was ratified in 1971, lowering the voting age from 21 to 18 in federal, state, and local elections.

Now, 40 years later, we can consider the available research and see what happened. Frankly, what is remarkable is what did *not* happen. First, young voters (those between 18 and 21) have not united in any particular political sentiment. We can see in how the young vote the same divisions of race, ethnicity, and gender that are apparent among older age groups.

Second, while the momentum for lowering the voting age came from college campuses, the majority of young voters are not students at all. Many are already part of the workforce and either live with their parents or have established their own households.

Third, and particularly troubling, is their low voter turnout. In the highly competitive 2000 presidential election, only 32 percent of young people cast a vote. Compared to the figure of 50 percent in the 1972 election—the first in which 18-year-olds could vote—this turnout was extremely unfavorable.

What is behind this voter apathy among the young? The popular explanation is that people, especially young people, are alienated from the political system, turned off by the shallowness and negativity of candidates and campaigns. True, studies document that young voters are susceptible to cynicism and distrust, but these are not necessarily associated with voter apathy. Numerous studies show the relationship between how people perceive the candidates and issues and their likelihood of voting is a very com-

plex one. Young people do vote as they age. Any disaffection with the voting booth is certainly not permanent.

Other explanations for the lower turnout among the young seem more plausible. First, the United States is virtually alone in requiring citizens to, in effect, vote twice. They must first *register* to vote, often at a time when issues are not on the front burner and candidates haven't even declared. Then they must vote on election day. Young people, who tend to be mobile and to lead hectic lives, find it difficult to track voting requirements (which vary by state) and be present where they are legally

> While the momentum for lowering the voting age came from college campuses, the majority of young voters are not students at all.

eligible to vote. Time constraints are the single biggest reason that voters gave for not voting in the 1996 election. In 1995, the motor-voter law went into effect, allowing people to register when they applied for or renewed driver's licenses, but this attempt to simplify the registration process has done little to change voting apathy.

Second, while citizens in the United States generally tend to be more active than their counterparts in other countries in politics on the community level, young people often feel unmoved by such local issues as public school financing and land use. Many national issues, such as Social Security and Medicare, also seem very far removed from their immediate concerns. Sometimes issues such as landlord policies or student–police relations surface in college towns, mobilizing the youth vote, but this activism often declines as the issue fades from view.

Research does not point to easy solutions for reversing the three-decade pattern of low turnout among the newest

"Rock the Vote" was the theme of this celebrity get-out-the-vote rally during the 2000 presidential election campaign. But neither Sting (at the microphone) nor the other celebrities were very successful in getting out the vote among young people.

voters. Facilitating the registration and voting process, identifying local issues of interest, grass-roots campaigning, and more careful evaluation of media campaigning may all help. We also need to continue to research potential reasons why more than 7 million people between the ages of 18 and 21 fail to even register to vote and why another million who take that step fail to vote.

Let's Discuss

1. How often do you vote? If you do not vote, what accounts for your apathy? Are you too busy to register? Are community issues uninteresting to you?

2. Do you think voter apathy is a serious social problem? What might be done to increase voter participation in your age group and community?

Sources: Austin and Pinkleton 1995; Casper and Bass 1998; Clymer 2000; Cook 1991; Landers 1988; Leon 1996; Morin 2002; Shogan 1998.

Figure 17-1

Women in National Legislatures

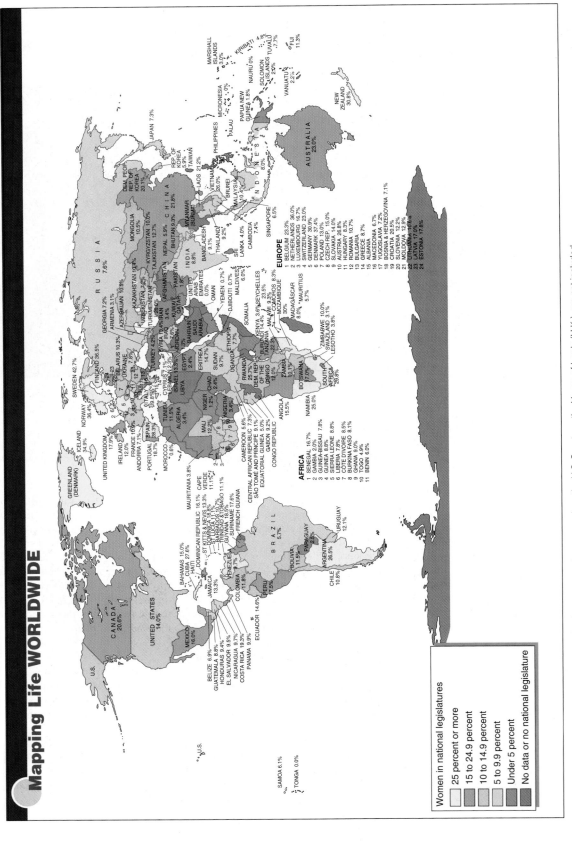

Note: Data are for lower legislative houses only; data on upper houses, such as the U.S. Senate or the House of Lords (U.K.), are not included.

Source: Inter-Parliamentary Union 2001b.

The color key shows the percentage of women in national legislatures as of July 2001. Despite their numbers, women held fewer than half the seats in every national legislature in the world.

Social Inequality

17-3   Gender Quotas at the Ballot Box

www.
mhhe.
com
/schaefer8

Worldwide, women are underrepresented in government. In national legislatures, they make up only 14 percent of the total membership—far below their 49 percent share of the world's population. Only 25 out of 243 legislative bodies, a little more than 10 percent, were headed by women in 2001. The percentage of female cabinet members was even lower in 1996, just under 7 percent.

To remedy this situation, many countries have adopted quotas for female representatives. In some, the government sets aside a certain percentage of seats for women, usually from 10 to 30 percent. In others, political parties have decided that 20 to 40 percent of their candidates should be women. Thirty-two countries now have some kind of female quota system.

In sheer numbers, India has seen the biggest gains in female representation. After a third of all village council seats were set aside for women, almost a million Indian women won election to local office. In South Africa, another country with quotas, women now hold 30 percent

or more of the seats in both houses of Parliament. Compared with South Africa, the United States, which does not have quotas, has not done nearly as well: Women hold only 14 percent of seats in the House of Representatives and 13 percent of seats in the Senate.

In Africa, quotas have been particularly popular in countries where women contributed to independence movements.

> **Thirty-two countries now have some kind of female quota system.**

South African women fought hard against apartheid and received constitutional guarantees against discrimination in return. Ugandan women fought in the National Resistance Army in the 1980s, earning new respect—and new political power—from men. Women now comprise almost 20 percent of Uganda's parliament and form a minimum required percentage of all elected bodies in that country.

With support from President Yoweri Museveni, who appointed a woman, Wandira Kazibwe, as vice president in 1994, Ugandan women have used their newfound power to enact new privileges for themselves. Married women can now share property ownership with their husbands, and widows can retain property after their husbands' death. Women legislators have also increased educational opportunities for girls in an effort to reduce the harsh poverty in their country. In President Museveni's opinion, the presence of women in government has helped to stabilize politics in Uganda. And in a country where women produce much of the wealth, he notes, they deserve to be empowered.

Let's Discuss

1. Why do you think the United States has so few women in government compared to many other nations?
2. Should the United States adopt a quota system? Why or why not?

Sources: Inter-Parliamentary Union 2001a, 2001b; Simmons and Wright 2000.

Figure 17-1 shows the representation of women in national legislatures throughout the world. While the proportion of women has increased in the United States and many other nations, women still do not account for half the members of the national legislature in any country. Sweden ranks the highest, with 42.7 percent. Overall, the United States in 2000 ranked 47th among 170 nations in the proportion of women serving as national legislators (Inter-Parliamentary Union 2001b). To remedy this situation, many countries—including the world's largest democracy, India—have reserved a minimum number of legislative seats for women (see Box 17-3).

A new dimension of women and politics emerged beginning in the 1980s. Surveys detected a growing "gender gap" in the political preferences and activities of males and females. Specifically, women were more likely to register as Democrats than as Republicans. According to political analysts, the Democratic party's support for the right to choose a legal abortion, for family and medical leave legislation, and for governmental action to require

insurers to cover a minimum two-day hospital stay for new mothers has attracted women voters.

The gender gap was still evident in the 2000 presidential election. Data from exit polls revealed that Democrat Al Gore received 54 percent of women's votes, compared to 42 percent of men's votes. The 12 percent gap between the sexes indicates that turnout of female voters is a key to Democratic victories. When women did not turn out in the 1994 congressional elections, solid support from White male voters was an important factor in Republican success (Voter News Service 2000).

Interest Groups

Common needs or common frustrations may lead people to band together in social movements to have an effect in the political arena. Examples include the civil rights movement of the 1960s and the anti–nuclear power movement of the 1980s. We will consider social movements in more detail in Chapter 22. People can also influence the political process through membership in interest groups (some of which, in fact, may be part of larger social movements).

An *interest group* is a voluntary association of citizens who attempt to influence public policy. The National Organization for Women (NOW) is considered an interest group; so, too, are the Juvenile Diabetes Foundation and the National Rifle Association (NRA). Such groups are a vital part of the political process of the United States. Many interest groups (often known as *lobbies*) are national in scope and address a wide array of social, economic, and political issues. Although interest groups represent a wide variety of people, from ultra conservative to the very liberal, those with large amounts of money tend to wield a disproportionate degree of influence over legislators.

One way in which interest groups influence the political process is through their political action committees. A *political action committee* (or *PAC*) is a political committee established by an interest group—say, a national bank, corporation, trade association, or cooperative or membership association—to solicit contributions for particular candidates or political parties. Political action committees distribute substantial funds to candidates, raising concerns that they might have too much influence on those who win electoral contests and take office.

The potential power of PACs emerged in an analysis of two crucial votes taken in the U.S. Senate in 1998. In one, senators defeated a measure that would have increased the tax on a pack of cigarettes; in another, they approved a legal settlement requiring tobacco companies to reimburse states for the increased medical costs caused by tobacco use. Both measures were strongly opposed by tobacco companies. As Figure 17-2 shows, the larger the campaign contributions senators had received from tobacco-interest PACs, the more likely they were to vote against the bills.

As new concerns arise, new lobby groups emerge. In 1999, for example, Yahoo opened a Washington office. Shortly thereafter NetCoalition was created to represent a variety of Internet-based companies, including America Online. Millions of dollars go to lobbying Congress on such issues as allowing more highly skilled workers to enter the United States and limiting restrictions on the Internet. For instance, NetCoalition opposed government efforts to prevent Napster from facilitating the downloading of music over the web (NetCoalition.com 2001; Shiver 2000).

Imagine

Imagine a world in which women, not men, held the majority of elective offices. What kind of world would it be?

Models of Power Structure in the United States

Who really holds power in the United States? Do "we the people" genuinely run the country through elected representatives? Or is it true that, behind the scenes, a small elite controls both the government and the economic system? It is difficult to determine the location of power in a society as complex as the United States. In exploring this critical question, social scientists have developed two basic views of our nation's power structure: the power elite and the pluralist models.

Power Elite Models

Karl Marx essentially believed that nineteenth-century representative democracy was a sham. He argued that industrial societies were dominated by relatively small numbers of people who owned factories and controlled natural resources. In Marx's view, government officials and military leaders were essentially servants of this capitalist class and followed their wishes. Therefore, any key decisions made by politicians inevitably reflected the interests of the dominant bourgeoisie. Like others who hold an *elite model* of power relations, Marx believed that society is ruled by a small group of individuals who share a common set of political and economic interests.

Figure 17-2

Anti-Tobacco Vote and Campaign Contributions

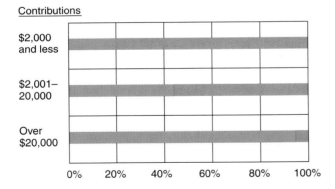

Contributions

Source: Author's analysis of data from the Center for Responsive Politics, Federal Election Commission, and *USA Today* as cited in *USA Today* 1998, p. 16A.

The greater the campaign contribution from tobacco interest groups, the more likely senators were to vote against anti-tobacco laws.

Figure 17-3

Power Elite Models

THE POWER ELITE

a. C. Wright Mills's model, 1956

Source: Domhoff 2001, p. 96.

b. William Domhoff's model, 1998

Mills's Model

Sociologist C. Wright Mills took this model a step further in his pioneering work *The Power Elite* ([1956] 2000b), referred to at the beginning of this chapter. Mills described a small ruling elite of military, industrial, and governmental leaders who controlled the fate of the United States. Power rested in the hands of a few, both inside and outside government—the **power elite.**

A pyramid illustrates the power structure of the United States in Mills's model (see Figure 17-3a). At the top are the corporate rich, leaders of the executive branch of government, and heads of the military (whom Mills called the "warlords"). Directly below are local opinion leaders, members of the legislative branch of government, and leaders of special-interest groups. Mills contended that such individuals and groups would basically follow the wishes of the dominant power elite. At the bottom of the pyramid are the unorganized, exploited masses.

This power elite model is, in many respects, similar to the work of Karl Marx. The most striking difference is that Mills believed that the economically powerful coordinate their maneuvers with the military and political establishments to serve their common interests. Yet, reminiscent of Marx, Mills argued that the corporate rich were perhaps the most powerful element of the power elite (first among "equals"). And, of course, there is a further dramatic parallel between the work of these conflict theo-

rists. The powerless masses at the bottom of Mills's power elite model certainly bring to mind Marx's portrait of the oppressed workers of the world, who have "nothing to lose but their chains."

A fundamental element in Mills's thesis is that the power elite not only includes relatively few members but also operates as a self-conscious, cohesive unit. Although not necessarily diabolical or ruthless, the elite comprises similar types of people who regularly interact with one another and have essentially the same political and economic interests. Mills's power elite is not a conspiracy but rather a community of interest and sentiment among a small number of influential people (Hacker 1964).

Admittedly, Mills failed to clarify when the elite opposes protests and when it tolerates them; he also failed to provide detailed case studies that would substantiate the interrelationship between members of the power elite. Nevertheless, his challenging theories forced scholars to look more critically at the democratic political system of the United States.

Domhoff's Model

More recently, sociologist G. William Domhoff (2001), coauthor of the chapter-opening excerpt from *Diversity in the Power Elite,* has agreed with Mills that a powerful elite runs the United States. He finds that it is still largely White, male, and upper class, as he wrote in his book with

Richard L. Zweigenhaft (1998). But Domhoff stresses the role played both by elites of the corporate community and by the leaders of policy-formation organizations such as chambers of commerce and labor unions. Many of the people in both groups are also members of the social upper class.

While these groups overlap, as Figure 17-3b shows, they do not necessarily agree on specific policies. Domhoff notes that in the electoral arena two different coalitions have exercised influence. A *corporate-conservative coalition* has played a large role in both political parties and has generated support for particular candidates through direct-mail appeals. But there is also a *liberal-labor coalition* based in unions, local environmental organizations, a segment of the minority group community, liberal churches, and the university and arts communities (Zweigenhaft and Domhoff 1998).

Sociologists have come to accept the notion that a limited number of people exercise a vast amount of power. While the elite groups can be identified, their composition changes over time, as does the influence of particular groups. In the 1950s during the military build-up in the Cold War between communist countries and Western democracies, the military was appropriately included in Mills's model as a major player. Fifty years later, the military is no longer so influential, but interest groups play a bigger role, as reflected in Domhoff's model.

Pluralist Model

Several social scientists insist that power in the United States is more widely shared than the elite models indicate. In their view, a pluralist model more accurately describes the nation's political system. According to the **pluralist model,** many conflicting groups within the community have access to government, so that no single group is dominant.

The pluralist model suggests that a variety of groups play a significant role in decision making. Typically, pluralists make use of intensive case studies or community studies based on observation research. One of the most famous—an investigation of decision making in New Haven, Connecticut—was reported by Robert Dahl in his book *Who Governs?* (1961). Dahl found that although the number of people involved in any important decision was rather small, community power was nonetheless diffuse. Few political actors exercised decision-making power on all issues. One individual or group might be influential in a battle over urban renewal but at the same time have little impact over educational policy. Several other studies of local politics, in such communities as Chicago and Oberlin, Ohio, further document that monolithic power structures do not operate on the level of local government.

The pluralist model, however, has not escaped serious questioning. Domhoff (1978, 2001) reexamined Dahl's study of decision making in New Haven and argued that Dahl and other pluralists had failed to trace how local elites prominent in decision making were part of a larger national ruling class. In addition, studies of community power, such as Dahl's work in New Haven, can examine decision making only on issues that become part of the political agenda. This focus fails to address the possible power of elites to keep certain matters that threaten their dominance entirely *out* of the realm of government debate.

Dianne Pinderhughes (1987) has criticized the pluralist model for failing to account for the exclusion of African Americans from the political process. Drawing on her studies of Chicago politics, Pinderhughes points out that the residential and occupational segregation of Blacks and their long political disenfranchisement violated the logic of pluralism—which would hold that such a substantial minority should always have been influential in community decision making. This critique applies to many cities across the United States where other large racial and ethnic minorities, among them Asian Americans, Puerto Ricans, and Mexican Americans, are relatively powerless (Watts 1990).

Historically, pluralists have stressed ways in which large numbers of people could participate in or influence governmental decision making. As we will see in the next section, new communications technologies like the Internet are increasing the opportunity to be heard, not just in countries such as the United States but in developing countries the world over. One common point of the elite and pluralist perspectives stands out, however: Power in the political system of the United States is unequally distributed. All citizens may be equal in theory, yet those high in the nation's power structure are "more equal." New communications technology may or may not change that distribution of power.

Political Activism on the Internet

About one in six people in the United States went online to get the latest vote count during the 2000 presidential election. Not only is the Internet affecting the way people get their news; it is changing the way they think about politics. In one survey, 43 percent of Internet users said the information they received online affected their vote. Modern technology may not eliminate voter apathy, but it is one more way to motivate people to get involved in politics (Pew Research Center for the People and the Press 2001).

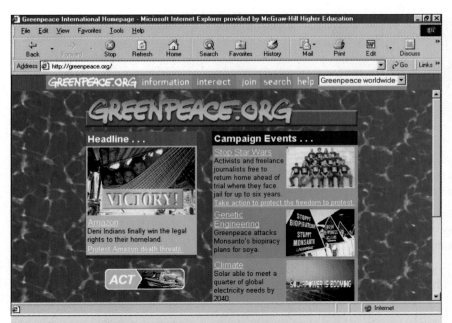

The website for Greenpeace, an international organization of environmental activists, encourages interested citizens to get involved in public affairs.

ficials have decided to advance information technology despite the challenges it poses to government control, according to Elizabeth Economy of the Council on Foreign Relations. The technology is simply too important to China's economic modernization for the government to suppress it. From a conflict theory perspective, then, the Internet seems to have the potential to level the playing field for opposition groups— or at least to minimize the ruling party's clout (Crossette 1999; MacFarquhar 1999; Owens and Palmer 2000; Piller 2001).

Also growing in importance are borderless organizations that unite people of like mind from around the world. These are very tightly knit communities, notes Professor Juan Enriquez of Harvard University. Labor groups and environmental organizations such as Greenpeace have become particularly adept at using e-mail to mobilize activists quickly, wherever they are needed. The result: a completely new kind of power structure, compared to the more familiar face-to-face approach of Washington lobbyists. "The new people with power are those with credibility and an e-mail list," says political consultant Jennifer Laszlo. "You have no idea who they are, where they are, what color they are" (Engardio 1999:145).

The Internet serves grass-roots organizers at the local level, too. In California, proponents of local control of schools established a website dubbed www.localchoice2000.com. Their purpose was not just to publicize an upcoming ballot initiative, but to involve citizens— several million of them—in drafting the document. The group also sought permission to gather the signatures they needed to put the initiative on the ballot electronically, using special PIN numbers. Supporters of these pluralist techniques argued that electronic petitions would save time and money, broaden citizen participation in government, and improve the wording of ballot initiatives (Van Slambrouck 1998).

On the Internet, political activity is not limited to traditional party politics, and certainly not to domestic politics. In far-flung places including China, Mexico, Indonesia, Kosovo, and Malaysia, citizens are making themselves heard through *cyberactivism*—the use of the Internet for political purposes. In China, 10,000 members of the fast-growing Falun Gong religious sect surprised government officials with a mass rally organized on the web. (A similar incident took place in the United States in 1999, when thousands of protesters converged on a meeting of the World Trade Organization in Seattle—11 months after the start of an e-mail campaign.) In Kosovo, the staff of *Koha Ditore,* a dissident newspaper, took to the web after Serbian soldiers closed their office. And in Mexico, the revolutionary *Zapatista* movement gained support from an online campaign for self-rule in the state of Chiapas.

As these incidents illustrate, organizers find the web especially useful in circumventing the restrictive controls of authoritarian regimes. In fact, groups branded as terrorists in a variety of states have used the web to their advantage. Websites can be established outside a country's borders, beyond the control of government officials yet still accessible to the country's citizens. What is more, government officials who would like to clamp down on such activities are constrained by their desire to reap the commercial benefits of the web. For example, Chinese of-

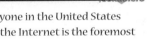

Imagine

Imagine a future in which everyone in the United States has access to the Internet, and the Internet is the foremost political medium. How would government in that society differ from government today?

The Issue

November 23, 1999

Question: How do you reconcile your position on campaign finance reform with all their money you are spending on television advertisements?

Hillary Rodham Clinton: "I believe we ought to have you know, more public financing of campaigns. We don't have it yet, does that mean I shouldn't raise money?"

(Washington Transcript Service 1999:17).

In her successful bid for election to the U.S. Senate, Hillary Rodham Clinton was not the first politician to criticize campaign financing methods while at the same time raising millions of dollars to pay her expenses. Over the last few decades, many seasoned representatives have left office bemoaning the amount of time they had to spend raising money. Nor, as we shall see, are attempts to regulate campaign financing new.

The Setting

Regulation of campaign contributions has a long history, beginning with efforts to bar the requirement that government employees contribute to their bosses' campaign funds. More recently, the focus on both the state and national levels has been on remedying the shortcomings of the Federal Campaign Act of 1974, passed in the wake of the Watergate scandal. In that infamous fiasco, campaign contributions actually financed a break-in at the Democratic National Committee offices, and the obstruction of the ensuing criminal investigation. The Campaign Act of 1974 placed restrictions on so-called *hard money,* or donations made to specific candidates for national office. Hard money is now limited to $10,000 per organiza-

tion or $2,000 per individual donor per election cycle (the primary and election being separate cycles). These limits were intended to keep national candidates or elected officials from being "bought" by the wealthy or by powerful special interest groups.

But soon after passage of the act, contributors and potential recipients—that is, politicians—found loopholes in the new law. In 2002, Congress passed the Bipartisan Campaign Reform Act (BCRA) to address some of those shortcomings. For the first time, limitations were placed on contributions of *soft money*—donations to the major political parties, leadership committees, and political action committees by corporations and special interest groups. Now, no soft money is permitted in federal elections, and its use in state and local elections is limited.

Under the BCRA, major political parties are still allowed to spend hard money freely on *independent expenditures,* or purchases made on behalf of a political position rather than an individual candidate. This *issue advocacy money,* as it has been called, has become an important way of supporting a particular candidate while escaping contribution limits. To support a pro-environment or "green" candidate, for example, donors would purchase television ads expressing concern about the environment and pollution.

THE WHEELS OF GOVERNMENT

For many years, so-called soft money was an important way of funding political campaigns. In 2002, Congress finally agreed to outlaw the practice in federal elections, beginning in 2003.

Eighty-nine-year-old Doris Haddock pauses for a publicity shot on her cross-country walk to Washington in support of campaign finance reform. In the United States, special interest groups have gained a disproportionate amount of power through their financial contributions to political campaigns.

Soon after the BCRA was passed, political pundits began to speculate on how politicians might still amass huge campaign warchests, regardless of the new restrictions. Some speculated that the law would encourage political parties and political interest groups to rely more on direct mail, phone banks, voter mobilization drives, and other unregulated activities. Few thought that the massive amounts that had once been raised as soft money would disappear from politics. In 1992, the Democratic and Republican parties each raised about $50 million in soft money. In 2000, each raised about $250 million—half a billion dollars in total. Undoubtedly, new ways will be found to channel such huge amounts of money in a way that conforms to the BCRA. And predictably, these new innovations in spending will be followed by fresh cries for reform (Malbin et al. 2002).

Sociological Insights

Functionalists would say that political contributions keep the public involved in the democratic process and connected to the candidates. Issue advocacy money also offers voters a way to express their views on issues directly, rather than through the candidates. But conflict theorists would counter that since money brings influence, this use of material wealth allows donors to influence government policymakers in ways that tend to preserve their own wealth. For example, in 1998 congressional debate over the deregulation of

banking services spurred $154 million in contributions from finance, insurance, and real estate interests. How does that type of activity promote democracy? In extreme cases, candidates like the multimillionaires Ross Perot and Steve Forbes have used their own private fortunes to finance their campaigns—an approach that allows them to sidestep public disclosure requirements.

Criticism of campaign financing methods tends to be selective, focusing on the motives of specific donors. In the late 1990s, Chinese American businesspeople made significant financial contributions to the Democratic National Committee, in response to personal efforts by then Vice President Al Gore. Some of the donations turned out to have been funneled from China, which had significant trade interests in the United States. Publicity about the illegal donations, which raised questions about possible corruption and violation of national security interests, stigmatized the entire Asian American community. Ironically, Chinese Americans are relatively powerless politically, compared to other ethnic groups in the United States (Lee 1998).

Interactionists would point out the symbolic significance of the public perception that big money drives elections in the United States. Accurate or not, this impression encourages voter apathy, which is reflected in low turnout at the polls. What good does participating in politics do, voters may wonder, when special interests can spend millions to counteract their efforts?

Policy Initiatives

Surveys have regularly shown that the majority of U.S. voters want campaign finance reform, but are unsure how to achieve it (Simon 1999). One proposal that has been advanced at the state level is to require that the names of donors be made public through posting on the Internet. Another is to place restrictions on how much money anyone can give to any organization for political purposes. While these reform proposals have gained much public sympathy, however, the courts have generally ruled that Internet posting may invade donors' privacy, discouraging them from making campaign contributions. Financial limits may also restrict people's freedom to participate in the political process (McDermott 1999; Simon 1999).

On the national level, traditional reform groups—Common Cause, the League of Women Voters, and Ralph

Nader's organization Public Citizen—continue to call for tighter limits on contributions by both individuals and organizations. But other interest groups, including the American Civil Liberties Union and the Cato Institute, claim that limiting anyone's involvement in the political process is unfair. The BCRA addresses citizens' complaints that politicians are routinely "bought" by wealthy special interests. Yet it also raises the specter of limits on citizens' freedom to support the candidates of their choice. With voter apathy on the rise, such limits may be too high a price to pay for campaign finance reform.

Let's Discuss

1. Did you vote in the most recent election? Does your vote count, or do special interest groups wield more power than voters like you?
2. Do you work for or contribute to political candidates? What about groups that promote special issues, like school prayer, gun control, and free trade? Which is more important to you, the candidate or the issue?
3. Would strict across-the-board spending limits on all candidates for public office help to make the political process more democratic? What about limits on political contributions of all kinds?

Chapter Resources

Summary

1. Every society must have a *political system* in order to have recognized procedures for the allocation of valued resources.
2. There are three basic sources of *power* within any political system: *force, influence,* and *authority.*
3. Max Weber identified three ideal types of authority: *traditional, legal-rational,* and *charismatic.*
4. The principal institutions of *political socialization* in the United States are the family, schools, and the media.
5. Political participation makes government accountable to its citizens, but there is a great deal of apathy in both the United States and other countries.
6. Women are still underrepresented in office but are becoming more successful at winning election to public office.
7. Sometimes people band together in *interest groups* to influence public policy.
8. Advocates of the *elite model* of the power structure of the United States see the nation as being ruled by a small group of individuals who share common political and economic interests (a *power elite*), whereas advocates of a *pluralist model* believe that power is more widely shared among conflicting groups.
9. Around the world, the Internet has become a potent political arena, one that dissident groups can use to oppose the power of authoritarian regimes.
10. Despite legislative efforts to reform campaign financing methods, wealthy donors and special interest groups wield enormous power in U.S. government through their contributions to candidates, political parties, and issue advocacy.

Critical Thinking Questions

1. In many places in the world, the United States is considered a model political system. Drawing on material presented in earlier chapters of this textbook, discuss the values and beliefs on which this political system is founded. Have those values and beliefs changed over time? Has the system itself changed?
2. Who really holds power in the college or university you attend? Describe the distribution of power at your school, drawing on the elite and pluralist models where they are relevant.
3. Imagine that you have joined your state representative's legislative staff as a summer intern. She has assigned you to a committee that is working on solutions to the problem of school violence, particularly school shootings. How could you use what you have learned about sociology to conceptualize the problem? What type of research would you suggest the committee undertake? What legislative solutions might you recommend?

Key Terms

Authority   Power that has been institutionalized and is recognized by the people over whom it is exercised. (page 429)

Charismatic authority   Power made legitimate by a leader's exceptional personal or emotional appeal to his or her followers. (431)

Elite model   A view of society as ruled by a small group of individuals who share a common set of political and economic interests. (438)

Force   The actual or threatened use of coercion to impose one's will on others. (429)

Influence   The exercise of power through a process of persuasion. (429)

Interest group   A voluntary association of citizens who attempt to influence public policy. (438)

Legal-rational authority   Power made legitimate by law. (431)

Pluralist model   A view of society in which many competing groups within the community have access to government, so that no single group is dominant. (440)

Political action committee (PAC)   A political committee established by an interest group—say, a national bank, corporation, trade association, or cooperative or membership association—to solicit contributions for candidates or political parties. (438)

Political socialization   The process by which individuals acquire political attitudes and develop patterns of political behavior. (432)

Political system   The social institution that relies on a recognized set of procedures for implementing and achieving the goals of a group. (429)

Politics   In Harold D. Lasswell's words, "who gets what, when, and how." (429)

Power   The ability to exercise one's will over others. (429)

Power elite   A small group of military, industrial, and government leaders who control the fate of the United States. (439)

Terrorism   The use or threat of violence against random or symbolic targets in pursuit of political aims. (430)

Traditional authority   Legitimate power conferred by custom and accepted practice. (430)

Additional Readings

BOOKS

Doppelt, Jack C., and Ellen Shearer. 1999. *Nonvoters: America's No-Shows.* Thousand Oaks, CA: Sage. Two professors of journalism profile the characteristics of the nearly 100 million U.S. citizens who fail to vote in presidential elections.

Enloe, Cynthia. 1990. *Bananas, Beaches, and Bases: Making Feminist Sense of International Politics.* Berkeley: University of California Press. Enloe studied the lives of women on military bases and of diplomatic wives as part of her examination of the male-dominated agenda of international politics.

Kurtz, Lester R., ed. 1999. *Encyclopedia of Violence, Peace and Conflict.* San Diego, CA: Academic Press. This three-volume set includes interdisciplinary articles on topics like conflict theory, colonialism, mass media, indigenous peoples, and military culture.

Orum, Anthony M. 2001. *Introduction to Political Sociology,* 4th ed. Upper Saddle River, NJ: Prentice Hall. Drawing on both classical thinking and contemporary writing, this book explores the way sociologists see political institutions.

Redish, Martin H. 2001. *Money Talks: Speech, Economic Power, and the Values of Democracy.* New York: NYU Press. A professor of law looks at campaign financing, government funding of the arts, and commercial advertising, arguing against government restrictions.

Zweigenhaft, Richard L., and G. William Domhoff. 1998. *Diversity in the Power Elite.* New Haven: Yale University Press. A psychologist and a sociologist team up to consider why, although women and minorities have made inroads, the overwhelming majority of the elite of the nation continues to be White and male.

JOURNALS

Among the journals that focus on issues of government are the *American Political Science Review* (founded in 1906), *Congressional Digest* (1921), *Congressional Quarterly Weekly Report* (1943), *Insurgent Sociologist* (1969), *Politics and Society* (1973), *Social Policy* (1970), and *Terrorism* (1988).

Internet Connection

*Note: While all the URLs listed were current as of the printing of this book, these sites often change. Please check our website (**http://www.mhhe.com/schaefer8**) for updates and hyperlinks to these exercises and additional exercises.*

1. Rock the Vote (**http://www.rockthevote.org**) is among a growing list of organizations trying to involve youths in the political and voting process. Review the material in Box 17-2, then explore the Rock the Vote website to learn more. On the site, visitors can read information, view pictures, and participate in online polls, as well as discover how to register to vote.

   (a) When and why did Rock the Vote form?

   (b) Choose one of the "Issues" detailed on the site. What recent events are occurring in terms of this issue? How do various politicians stand on this issue? What statistics does the site provide? Why is this issue important?

   (c) What are musicians, actors, and politicians doing about the issue that you chose?

   (d) Take some of the "Interactive Polls." How do your opinions compare to others'?

   (e) What do you think can be done to increase the involvement of young voters in the political process?

2. The Gallup poll is a public opinion survey in which people are asked for their thoughts on various issues, including the president's job performance. Go to Gallup's homepage (**http://www.gallup.com/poll/topics**). Link to "Politics and Elections" and answer the following questions:

   (a) What did you learn about President Bush's most recent quarterly approval ratings?

   (b) What is the president's average job approval rating?

   (c) How do President Bush's job approval ratings compare to those of other presidents, such as John F. Kennedy and Bill Clinton?

   (d) How does the public rate the president's performance on terrorism and defense issues?

   (e) What percentage of respondents approve of the way President Bush is handling the nation's economy?

3. The Center for American Women and Politics (**http://www.rci.rutgers.edu/~cawp/**) is devoted to promoting greater understanding of women's participation in politics. Click on "2002 Fact Sheets," then on "2002 Fact Sheet Summary" and answer the following questions:

   (a) How many state senate seats did women hold in 2002?

   (b) How many state house seats did women hold in 2002?

   (c) By how much has the number of women serving in state legislatures increased since 1969?

   (d) Across the country, how many women held statewide elective office? How many of those women were Democrats? How many were Republicans?

   (e) List the 10 states with the highest percentage of female state legislators. Was your state one of them?

   (f) How many of the women serving in statewide elective office were non-White Hispanics?

   (g) How many of the women serving in the 106th U.S. Congress were non-White Hispanics?

SocWorld CD-ROM

This CD, which is packaged free with all new copies of the text, allows you to instantly explore various topics and concepts with an assortment of video clips (including footage of this text's author in Singapore), website links, interactive quizzes, and other learning tools. Also included are audio introductions to each of the book excerpts that open each chapter and additional information about these excerpts and their authors.

Online Learning Center www.mhhe.com/schaefer8

When you visit the student center in the Online Learning Center at **www.mhhe. com/schaefer8,** link to the flashcards. There is a flashcard for every key term in your text. The flashcards also have definitions for each term. Flashcards are a valuable study tool: They give you the opportunity to see how familiar you are with important terms in the chapter.

PowerWeb

Using the password found on the gold and black card that was shrinkwrapped with your book, visit PowerWeb, a website that provides a wealth of resources including quizzes, links to related websites, interactive exercises, time management tips, articles, and a guide to doing research on the web. You will also find daily news on relevant topics. PowerWeb is accessible from a link on the Online Learning Center website. Also accessible from the Online Learning Center is a unique PowerWeb site on violence and terrorism.

SocCity

Explore SocCity, a veritable melting pot of sociology cybersources, information, and Internet activity for students and instructors alike. Whether you are looking for the perfect book for your sociology class, or you are a student looking for some starter sites for your next research paper, SocCity has it.

THE ECONOMY AND WORK

Around the world, globalization and the advent of e-commerce are transforming the economy, creating new jobs that workers may not be prepared to perform. Lack of educational opportunities, and of the means to afford new technologies, often prevents people in developing countries from taking advantage of economic change.

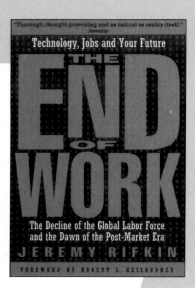

Percy Barnevik is the chief executive officer of Asea Brown Boveri, a 29-billion-dollar-a-year Swiss-Swedish builder of electric generators and transportation systems, and one of the largest engineering firms in the world. Like other global companies, ABB has recently re-engineered its operations, cutting nearly 50,000 workers from the payroll, while increasing turnover 60 percent in the same time period. Barnevik asks, "Where will all these [unemployed] people go?" He predicts that the proportion of Europe's labor force employed in manufacturing and business services will decline from 35 percent today to 25 percent in ten years from now, with a further decline to 15 percent twenty years down the road. Barnevik is deeply pessimistic about Europe's future: "If anybody tells me, wait two or three years and there will be a hell of a demand for labor, I say, tell me where? What jobs? In what cities? Which companies? When I add it all together, I find a clear risk that the 10% unemployed or underemployed today could easily become 20 to 25%." . . .

For some, particularly the scientists, engineers, and employers, a world without work will signal the beginning of a new era in history in which human beings are liberated, at long last, from a life of back-breaking toil and mindless repetitive tasks. For others, the workerless society conjures up the notion of a grim future of mass unemployment and global destitution, punctuated by increasing social unrest and upheaval. On one point virtually all of the contending parties agree. We are, indeed, entering into a new period in history—one in which machines increasingly replace human beings in the process of making and moving goods and providing services. . . .

Most workers feel completely unprepared to cope with the enormity of the transition taking place. The rash of current technological breakthroughs and economic restructuring initiatives seem to have descended on us with little warning. Suddenly, all over the world, men and women are asking if there is a role for them in the new future unfolding across the global economy. Workers with years of education, skills, and experience face the very real prospect of being made redundant by the new forces of automation and information. What just a few short years ago was a rather esoteric debate among intellectuals and a small number of social writers around the role of technology in society is now the topic of heated conversation among millions of working people. They wonder if they will be the next to be replaced by the new thinking machines. . . .

The new high-technology revolution could mean fewer hours of work and greater benefits for millions. For the first time in modern history, large numbers of human beings could be liberated from long hours of labor in the formal marketplace, to be free to pursue leisure-time activities. The same technological forces could, however, as easily lead to growing unemployment and a global depression. *(Rifkin 1995a:11–13)* ■ 💿

Additional information about this excerpt and about those that open each subsequent chapter can be found in the SocWorld CD-ROM that accompanies this text.

n his book *The End of Work*, social activist Jeremy Rifkin takes a look at what the economic world will look like after automation and high technology make human labor more and more obsolete. Economic forces have a huge impact on our lives—from something as basic as whether we can put food on the table to more soul-searching concerns such as "How can I be productive?" Rifkin's view is that we must be prepared to deal with the inevitable dysfunctions and dislocations that accompany a major transformation of the global economic system.

The term ***economic system*** refers to the social institution through which goods and services are produced, distributed, and consumed. As with social institutions such as the family, religion, and government, the economic system shapes other aspects of the social order and is, in turn, influenced by them. Throughout this textbook, you have been reminded of the economy's impact on social behavior—for example, individual and group behavior in factories and offices. You

p. 12 have studied the work of Karl Marx and Friedrich Engels, who emphasized that the economic system of a society can promote social inequality. And you have learned that foreign investment p. 247 in developing countries can intensify inequality among residents.

This chapter will present a sociological analysis of the impact of the economy on people's lives. What makes work satisfying? How has the trend toward deindustrialization changed the work people do? What will the workforce of the twenty-first century look like? We will begin to answer these questions with a macrolevel analysis of two ideal types of economic system, capitalism and socialism. Next, we will examine various aspects of work, including the occupations and professions open to people today, worker alienation and its causes, and worker satisfaction. Then we will take a look at the ways in which the economy is changing at the beginning of the twenty-first century. Finally, in the social policy section we will explore the controversy over affirmative action, an important issue in the workplace. ■

Economic Systems

The sociocultural evolution approach developed by Gerhard Lenski categorizes preindustrial societies p. 122 according to the way in which the economy is organized. The principal types of preindustrial societies, as you recall, are hunting-and-gathering societies, horticultural societies, and agrarian societies.

As noted in Chapter 5, the *industrial revolution*—which took place largely in England during the p. 123 period 1760 to 1830—brought about changes in the social organization of the workplace. People left their homesteads and began working in central locations such as factories. As the industrial revolution proceeded, a new form of social structure emerged: the ***industrial society,*** a society that depends on mechanization to produce its goods and services.

Two basic types of economic systems distinguish contemporary industrial societies: capitalism and socialism. As described in the following sections, capitalism and socialism serve as ideal types of economic systems. No nation precisely fits either model. Instead, the economy of each individual state represents a mixture of capitalism and socialism, although one type or the other is generally useful in describing a society's economic structure. China's economy, for example, has been primarily socialistic, whereas the U.S. economy is much more capitalistic.

Capitalism

In preindustrial societies, land functioned as the source of virtually all wealth. The industrial revolution changed all that. It required that certain individuals and institutions be willing to take substantial risks in order to finance new inventions, machinery, and business enterprises. Eventually, bankers, industrialists, and other holders of large sums of money replaced landowners as the most powerful economic force. These people invested their funds in the hope of realizing even greater profits and thereby became owners of property and business firms.

The transition to private ownership of business was accompanied by the emergence of the capitalist economic system. ***Capitalism*** is an economic system in which the means p. 217 of production are largely in private hands and the main incentive for economic activity is the accumulation of profits. In practice, capitalist systems vary in the degree to which the government regulates private ownership and economic activity (Rosenberg 1991).

Immediately following the industrial revolution, the prevailing form of capitalism was what is termed ***laissez-faire*** ("let them do"). Under the principle of laissez-faire, as expounded and endorsed by British economist Adam Smith (1723–1790), people could compete freely with minimal government intervention in the economy. Business retained the right to regulate itself and essentially operated without fear of government regulation (Smelser 1963).

In the movie *Wall Street* (1987), actors Charlie Sheen and Michael Douglas played greedy speculators engaged in insider trading and stock price manipulation. Popular culture often presents capitalists as selfish people who profit unfairly from the labor of others.

Two centuries later, capitalism has taken on a somewhat different form. Private ownership and maximization of profits still remain the most significant characteristics of capitalist economic systems. However, in contrast to the era of laissez-faire, capitalism today features extensive government regulation of economic relations. Without restrictions, business firms can mislead consumers, endanger the safety of their workers, and even defraud the companies' investors—all in the pursuit of greater profits. That is why the government of a capitalist nation often monitors prices, sets safety standards for industries, protects the rights of consumers, and regulates collective bargaining between labor unions and management. Yet, under capitalism as an ideal type, government rarely takes over ownership of an entire industry.

Contemporary capitalism also differs from laissez-faire in another important respect. Capitalism tolerates monopolistic practices. A ***monopoly*** exists when a single business firm controls the market. Domination of an industry allows the firm to effectively control a commodity by dictating pricing, standards of quality, and availability. Buyers have little choice but to yield to the firm's decisions; there is no other place to purchase the product or service. Monopolistic practices violate the ideal of free competition cherished by Adam Smith and other supporters of laissez-faire capitalism.

Some capitalistic nations, such as the United States, outlaw monopolies through antitrust legislation. Such laws prevent any business from taking over so much of the competition in an industry that it gains control of the market. The U.S. federal government allows monopolies to exist only in certain exceptional cases, such as the utility and transportation industries. Even then, regulatory agencies scrutinize these officially approved monopolies and protect the public. The protracted legal battle between the Justice Department and Microsoft, owner of the dominant operating system for personal computers, illustrates the uneasy relationship between government and private monopolies in capitalistic countries (see Chapter 17).

Conflict theorists point out that although *pure* monopolies are not a basic element of the economy of the United States, competition is much more restricted than one might expect in what is called a *free enterprise system.* In numerous industries, a few companies largely dominate the field and keep new enterprises from entering the marketplace.

Socialism

p. 12 Socialist theory was refined in the writings of Karl Marx and Friedrich Engels. These European radicals were disturbed by the exploitation of the working class as it emerged during the industrial revolution. In their view, capitalism forced large numbers of people to exchange their labor for low wages. The owners of an industry profit from the labor of their workers, primarily because they pay workers less than the value of the goods produced. p. 217

As an ideal type, a socialist economic system attempts to eliminate such economic exploitation. Under ***socialism,*** the means of production and distribution in a society are collectively rather than privately owned. The basic objective of the economic system is to meet people's needs rather than to maximize profits. Socialists reject the laissez-faire philosophy that free competition benefits the general public. Instead, they believe that the central government, acting as the representative of the people, should make basic economic decisions. Therefore, government ownership of all major industries—including steel production, automobile manufacturing, and agriculture—is a major feature of socialism as an ideal type.

In practice, socialist economic systems vary in the extent to which they tolerate private ownership. For example, in Great Britain, a nation with some aspects of both a socialist and a capitalist economy, passenger airline service is concentrated in the government-owned corporation British Airways. Yet private airline companies are allowed to compete with it.

Socialist societies differ from capitalist nations in their commitment to social service programs. For example, the U. S. government provides health care and health insurance for the elderly and poor through the Medicare and Medicaid programs. By contrast, socialist countries typically offer government-financed medical care for *all* citizens. In theory, the wealth of the people as a collectivity is used to provide health care, housing, education, and other key services for each individual and family.

Marx believed that each socialist state would eventually "wither away" and evolve into a *communist* society. As an ideal type, **communism** refers to an economic system under which all property is communally owned and no social distinctions are made on the basis of people's ability to produce. In recent decades, the Soviet Union, the People's Republic of China, Vietnam, Cuba, and nations in Eastern Europe were popularly thought of as examples of communist economic systems. However, this represents an incorrect usage of a term with sensitive political connotations. All nations known as communist in the twentieth century have actually fallen far short of the ideal type.

By the early 1990s, Communist parties were no longer ruling the nations of Eastern Europe. The first major challenge to Communist rule came in 1980 when Poland's Solidarity movement—led by Lech Walesa and backed by many workers—questioned the injustices of that society. While martial law initially forced Solidarity underground, it eventually negotiated the end of Communist party rule in 1989. Over the next two years, dominant Communist parties were overthrown after popular uprisings in the Soviet Union and throughout Eastern Europe. The former Soviet Union, Czechoslovakia, and Yugoslavia were then subdivided to accommodate the ethnic, linguistic, and religious differences within these areas.

As of 2001, China, Cuba, and Vietnam remained socialist societies ruled by Communist parties. Even in these countries, however, capitalism was making inroads. In that year, fully 25 percent of China's production originated in the private business sector. Indeed, at the Chinese Communist party's eightieth anniversary celebration in 2001, President Jiang Zemin asked the party to formally welcome private business owners as members (Wolf 2001).

Cuba, in particular, is adjusting to a dual economy. Although the Communist government leader Fidel Castro remains firmly committed to Marxism, the centrally controlled economy has been in ruins following the end of Soviet aid and the continued trade embargo by the

Soon after the U.S. government lifted its trade embargo against Vietnam in 1994, Coca-Cola and Pepsi rushed in to corner the market. Coca-Cola made its "biggest" statement on the steps of the Opera House in Hanoi.

United States. Reluctantly, Castro has allowed small-scale family-managed businesses, such as restaurants and craft shops, to operate and accept dollars rather than the heavily devalued Cuban peso. This leads to an ironic situation in which government-employed teachers and doctors earn less than the small business operators, taxi drivers, and hotel workers who have access to foreign currency. This situation underscores how difficult it is to understand any nation's economy without considering its position in the global economy (McKinley 1999).

As we have seen, capitalism and socialism serve as ideal types of economic systems. In reality, the economy of each industrial society—including the United States, the European Union, and Japan—includes certain elements of both capitalism and socialism. Whatever the differences, whether they more closely fit the ideal type of capitalism or socialism, all industrial societies rely chiefly on mechanization in the production of goods and services.

◯Imagine

The U.S. economy has become predominantly socialistic rather than capitalistic. What do you as a worker have now that you did not have before? What do you lack?

Aspects of Work

As indicated in the chapter opening, the workplace has undergone tremendous changes in the last few decades, primarily because of automation and the applications of high technology. These changes have affected the types of occupations people enter and their satisfaction (or lack of it) with their jobs. In this section we will examine both these aspects of work.

One aspect of work that has existed for generations is employment in the informal economy—transfers of money, goods, or services that are not reported to the government (see Box 10-2, "The Informal Economy," on page 253). In developing nations, the informal economy represents a significant and often unmeasured part of total economic activity. Yet because this sector of the economy depends to a large extent on the labor of women, work in the informal economy is undervalued or even unrecognized the world over (see Box 18-1).

Occupations and Professions

Whatever we call it—*job, work, occupation, gig, stint, position, duty,* or *vocation*—it is what we do for pay. Our paid labor relates to our social behavior in a number of ways. Preparation for work is a critical aspect of the socializa-

p. 99 ◀
tion process. In addition, our work influences our social identities or what Charles Horton Cooley termed the *looking-glass self*. A person who asks, "What do you do?" expects you to indicate your occupation. We tend to define ourselves by our work. Of course, work has more than a symbolic significance. Our occupations also determine in large part our positions in the stratification system.

In the United States and other contemporary societies, the majority of the paid labor force is involved in providing services, such as health care, education, selling of goods, banking, and government. Along with the shift toward service industries, there has been a rise in the number of occupations viewed as professions. In popular usage, the term *professional* is frequently used to convey a positive evaluation of work ("She's a real professional") or to denote full-time paid performance in a vocation (as in "professional golfer").

Sociologists use the term **profession** to describe an occupation requiring extensive knowledge that is governed by a code of ethics. Professionals tend to have a great degree of autonomy. They are not responsible to a supervisor for every action, nor do they have to respond to the whims of a customer. In general, professionals are their own authority in determining what is best for their clients. Table 18-1 summarizes some of the characteristics used by sociologists to distinguish professions from other occupations.

Table 18-1 Occupations and Professions Compared

Characteristic	Occupation	Profession
Systematic body of theory or abstract knowledge	No	Yes
Training	Relatively short; usually informal	Extensive and formalized
Degree of specialization	Little	Extensive
Autonomy	Little	Extensive
Self-regulatory associations	No	Yes
Relationship to public	"Customer is always right"	Client is viewed as somewhat subordinate
Formal certification	Not necessarily	Yes
Sense of community with similar jobholders	Low	High
Code of ethics	Informal	Highly developed; usually formalized

Sources: Author based on Greenwood 1957; Leicht and Fennell 1997; Lively 2001; Pavalko 1972, 1988.

Nepal, a small and mountainous Asian country of about 24 million people, has a per capita gross national income (GDP) of just $1,280 per year. (The comparable figure in the United States is $31,910.) But gross national income seriously understates the true production level in Nepal, for several reasons. Among the most important is that many Nepalese women work in the informal economy, whose activities are not included in gross national income.

Because women's work is undervalued in this traditional society, it is also

> **Because women's work is undervalued in this traditional society, it is also underreported and underestimated.**

underreported and underestimated. Official figures state that women account for 27 percent of GDP and form 40 percent of the labor force. But Nepalese women are responsible for 60 percent of additional nonmarket production, that is, work done in the informal economy, and 93 percent of the housework (see Figure 18-1).

Most women workers are employed in cultivating corn, rice, and wheat on the family farm, where they spend hours on time-intensive tasks such as fetching water and feeding livestock. Because much of the food they raise is consumed at home, however, it is considered to be

Figure 18-1

Gender Contributions to GDP and Household Maintenance in Nepal

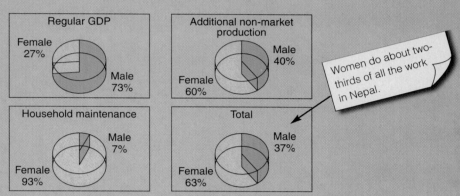

Source: Survey by S. Acharya as cited in Mahbub ul Haq Human Development Centre 2000:54.

nonmarket production. At home, women concentrate on food processing and preparation, care giving, and other household tasks, such as clothes making. Childbearing and rearing and elder care are particularly crucial activities. Yet none of these chores are considered part of GDP; instead, they are dismissed as "women's work," both by economists and by the women themselves.

The figures on housework and non-market production in Nepal come from an independent economic study. To compile them, researchers had to adapt the conventional accounting system by adding a special account dedicated to household maintenance activities. When they did so, women's "invisible work" suddenly became visible and valuable.

Not just in Nepal but in every country, economists need to expand their definitions of work and the labor force to account for the tremendous contributions women make to the world economy.

Let's Discuss

1. In your own family, is "women's work" taken for granted? Have you ever tried to figure out what it would cost your family to pay for all the unpaid work women do?

2. Why is recognizing women's work important? How might life for both men and women change if the true economic value of women's work were recognized?

Sources: Acharya 2000; Haub and Cornelius 2001; Mahbub ul Haq Human Development Centre 2000:54–57.

It is widely agreed that medicine and law are professions, whereas driving a taxi is an occupation. But how do you categorize a paralegal, funeral director, firefighter, or pharmacist? In these cases it's not clear where "occupation" ends and "profession" begins. To some extent, as occupations have become more skill-based and professions tied more and more to large bureaucracies (such as doc-

tors in an HMO), the two ideal types have converged. Moreover, a growing number of occupational groups have claimed and even demanded professional status—often in an attempt to gain greater prestige and financial rewards. In certain instances, existing professions may object to the efforts of a related vocation to achieve designation as a profession. They may fear a loss in business or

Taking Sociology to Work

BINTI HARVEY:
CBS Online Reporter

Binti Harvey writes for the Online Business News Service, a financial news network that is accessed by the web. She covers technology stocks in the two columns she writes daily. In the course of her work, she often talks with the chief financial officers of multinational technology firms.

Harvey finds that her sociology degree, earned at UCLA in 1996, has been of tremendous value in her job. The first aspect is in "writing, writing, writing! Sociology gave me a really strong grasp of the fundamentals of writing. It has helped me with deadlines and to put together a comprehensive yet concise story quickly." Sociology has also helped her to take a broader look at issues and make connections. Finally, and perhaps most importantly, it has played a big role in helping her to understand others. "I'm in a lot of situations with businesspeople who aren't comfortable with a young Black female. My sociological background has helped me understand where they're coming from, their perspective. It has helped

me to help them to see me as a reporter." In Harvey's view, sociology allows people who would normally not have power to empower themselves.

Her advice to sociology students is to learn the terms but put more emphasis on learning the concepts and how to apply them to everyday life. "It's one of the few subjects that you'll encounter in college that you can apply to your daily life."

Let's Discuss

1. Have you learned anything in your sociology course that has helped you in your daily life? If so, explain how.
2. What might you learn from a business report written by a sociology major that you wouldn't learn from a similar report written by a business major? Why would that information be important to an investor? To an employee? To a CEO?

---

clientele or a downgrade in the status of their profession as still more occupations are included. The hostility of the medical profession toward midwifery is an example of such a conflict between an established profession and an occupation that has aspired to professional status.

Work and Alienation: Marx's View

"A moron could learn this job, it's so easy," says one Burger King worker in George Ritzer's study of the fast-food industry (2000:137). Doing repetitive tasks that take minimal skills can be demoralizing and lead to a sense of alienation and isolation in the workplace. Jeremy Rifkin, as we saw in the chapter opening, took this concern a step further: As work becomes more and more automated, human skills become obsolete and workers lose their jobs altogether or are forced into the low-skills service jobs (Rifkin 1996).

All the pioneers of sociological thought were concerned about the negative impact on workers as a result of the changes in the workplace brought about by the industrial revolution. Émile Durkheim ([1893] 1933) argued that as labor becomes more and more differentiated, individuals experience *anomie,* or loss of direction. Workers can't feel the same fulfillment from performing one specialized task in a factory as they did when they were totally responsible for creating a product. It is clear that the im-

personality of bureaucratic organizations can result in a cold and uncaring workplace. But the most penetrating analysis of the dehumanizing aspects of industrialization was offered by Karl Marx.

Marx believed that as the process of industrialization advanced within capitalist societies, workers were robbed of any meaningful relationship with their work. In today's terms, consider the telemarketer making a "cold call" to sell someone a credit card. Does that person feel a part of the financial institution? For Marx, the emphasis on specialization of tasks contributed to a growing sense of alienation among industrial workers. The term *alienation* refers to the situation of being estranged or disassociated from the surrounding society. But it wasn't just the monotonous repetition of the same tasks that concerned Marx. In his view, an even deeper cause of alienation is the *powerlessness* of workers in a capitalist economic system. Workers have no control over their occupational tasks, the products of their labor, or the distribution of profits. Moreover, they are constantly producing property that is owned by others (the members of the capitalist class) (Erikson 1986).

The solution to the problem of workers' alienation, according to Marx, is to give workers greater control over the workplace and the products of their labor. He didn't focus on limited reforms of factory life; rather he envisioned a revolutionary overthrow of capitalist oppression.

After a transition to collective ownership of the means of production (socialism) the ideal of communism would be achieved eventually. Yet the trend in capitalist societies has been toward concentration of ownership by giant corporations. Currently about 48 percent of the paid U.S. labor force is employed in business firms with more than 500 workers. Through mergers and acquisitions, such corporations become even larger, and individual workers find themselves the employees of firms with overwhelming size and power (Bureau of the Census 1999a:557).

When Karl Marx wrote about work and alienation in 1844, the physical conditions of labor were much harsher than they are today. Yet his writings inspired research into alienated labor that persists today, even as workers enjoy safer and more comfortable surroundings. In fact, the growth of the size of businesses, the emergence of huge franchise chains, and the dominance of multinational corporations have only increased the isolation of laborers. Large business organizations report an escalation in episodes of "desk rage," in which employees or angry ex-employees act out their frustrations violently, disrupting the workplace and often raising other workers' alienation in the process (Hodson and Sullivan 1995; Hymowitz and Silverman 2001).

Already by the 1980s the term *burnout* was increasingly being used to describe the stress experienced by a wide range of workers, including professionals, self-employed persons, and even unpaid volunteers. Marx had focused on alienation among the proletarians, whom he viewed as powerless to effect change within capitalist institutions. However, the broader concept of work-related anxiety now covers alienation even among more affluent workers who have a greater degree of control over their working conditions. From a conflict perspective, we have masked the fact that alienation falls most heavily on the lower and working classes by making it appear endemic from the boardroom to the shop floor.

Worker Satisfaction

Most studies of alienation have focused on how structural changes in the economy serve to increase or decrease worker satisfaction. In general, people with greater responsibility for a finished product (such as white-collar professionals and managers) experience more satisfaction than those with little responsibility.

For both women and men working in blue-collar jobs, the repetitive nature of work can be particularly unsatisfying. The automobile assembly line is commonly cited as an extreme example of monotonous work. Studs Terkel (1974:159), in his book *Working,* gives a first-person account of a spot welder's labor:

Stocking shelves may help pay the bills but is unlikely to provide high job satisfaction, especially in a large supermarket where workers have less responsibility and more anonymity.

I stand in one spot, about two- or three-feet area, all night. The only time a person stops is when the line stops. We do about thirty-two jobs per car, per unit, forty-eight units per hour, eight hours a day. Thirty-two times forty-eight times eight. Figure it out, that's how many times I push that button.

Robert Blauner's (1964) classic research study revealed that printers—who often work in small shops and supervise apprentices—were more satisfied with their work than laborers on automobile assembly lines who performed repetitive tasks.

Factors in Job Satisfaction

A number of general factors can reduce the level of dissatisfaction of contemporary industrial workers. Higher wages give workers a sense of accomplishment apart from the task before them. A shorter workweek is supposed to increase the amount of time people can devote to recreation and leisure, thereby reducing some of the discontent stemming from the workplace. But the number of hours Americans work actually *increased* in the 1990s, by the equivalent of about one workweek. Short staffing because of low unemployment rates may have accounted for part of the increase in hours worked; however, many Americans took a second job during this period, just to make ends meet. At the same time, paid absences rose, and the reasons workers gave for their absenteeism indicated low satisfaction. In 1995, 45 percent of absent workers cited personal illness as a reason, but by 1998, only 22 percent gave that reason. Instead, 16 percent cited stress and another 16 percent indicated a sense of entitlement (Stone 1999; Webb 2001).

Numerous studies have shown that positive relationships with coworkers can make a boring job tolerable or even enjoyable. In his often cited "banana time" study, sociologist Donald Roy (1959) examined worker satisfaction by means of a two-month participant observation within a small group of factory machine operators. Drawing on the interactionist perspective, Roy carefully recorded the social interactions among members of his work group, including many structured "times" and "themes" designed to break up long days of simple, repetitive work. For example, the workers divided their food breaks into coffee time, peach time, banana time, fish time, Coke time, and lunch time—each of which occurred daily and involved distinctive responsibilities, jokes, and insults. Roy (1959:166) concludes that his observations "seem to support the generally accepted notion that one key source of job satisfaction lies in the informal interaction shared by members of a work group." The patterned conversation and horseplay of these workers reduced the monotony of their workdays.

Sociologist George Ritzer (1977) has suggested that the relatively positive impression many workers present is misleading. In his view, manual workers are so deeply alienated that they come to expect little from their jobs. Their satisfaction comes from nonwork tasks, and any job-related gratification results from receiving wages. Ritzer's interpretation explains why manual workers—although they say they are satisfied with their occupations—would not choose the same line of work if they could begin their lives over.

Job Satisfaction in Japan

One of the major economic developments of the 1980s was the emergence of Japan as an industrial giant. In earlier decades, many people attributed Japan's economic accomplishments to low wages combined with production of inexpensive goods. However, Japanese salaries in the 1980s were comparable to those of other industrial nations. A more likely explanation of Japan's remarkable

In Seoul in 2001, protesting employees of the dot-com industry took to the streets to demand job security and better working conditions. The year before, South Korean workers logged longer hours than those in 199 other countries (Webb 2001).

success at that time focused instead on the unusual pride that Japanese workers felt in their products. In Japanese plants and factories, workers are expected to assume the role of quality-control inspector. Although actually involved in specialized tasks of production, employees can still identify with the finished product.

For a long time, the collectivist orientation of Japanese culture heavily influenced its capitalist economic system. An individual was perceived as an extension of his or her family, business, or community and as bound together with others in a common purpose. In contrast to U.S. firms, most Japanese companies maintained an ideal of "lifetime employment" for some of their employees. They made substantial investments in training of workers and so were reluctant to lay off employees during a business slump. The employer–employee relationship was paramount. Companies even operated reception halls, gymnasiums and swimming pools, mortgage-lending institutions, and cultural programs for the benefit of their workers.

When job layoffs hit Japan in the 1990s, they caused a stir because the Japanese were accustomed to the idea of lifetime employment with one firm. In this demonstration at Nissan headquarters in Tokyo in 1999, labor activists are protesting auto plant shutdowns and a 14 percent cut in the workforce. The banners on the bus read: "How can you call the mass dismissal of workers Renaissance? Stop the closure of five plants in the Nissan-Renault's large-sized restructuring."

p. 246 ◄
ones. For example, there were 3,882 mergers in 1998 alone, involving $1.4 trillion in business. The nature of the U.S. economy is changing in important ways, in part because the nation's economy is increasingly intertwined with and dependent upon the global economy. In 1998, foreign companies acquired 483 U.S. firms valued together at $232 billion (Bureau of the Census 2001a:493).

In the following sections, we will examine developments in the global economy that have interested sociologists: the changing face of the workforce, deindustrialization, the emergence of e-commerce, and the rise of a contingency (or temporary) workforce. As these trends show, any change in the economy inevitably has social and political implications and soon becomes a concern of policymakers.

The Face of the Workforce

The workforce in the United States is constantly changing. During World War II, when men were mobilized to fight abroad, women entered the workforce in large numbers. And with the rise of the civil rights movement, minorities found numerous job opportunities opening to them. The active recruitment of women and minorities into the workplace, known as *affirmative action,* is the subject of this chapter's social policy section.

While predictions are not always reliable, sociologists and labor specialists foresee a workforce increasingly composed of women and racial and ethnic minorities. In 1960 there were twice as many men in the labor force as women. During the period from 1998 to 2008, the same number of men and women are expected to enter the labor force. It's possible that by 2015 the total numbers of male and female workers may be the same.

The dynamics for race and ethnicity in the workforce are even more dramatic. The number of Black, Latino, and Asian American workers continues to increase at a rate faster than the number of White workers. From 1998 to 2008, it is projected that while 25 million Whites will enter the labor force, 17.4 million Blacks, Latinos, and Asian Americans will also enter. Figure 18-2 shows these patterns from 1986 to a projected 2008 (Fullerton 1997, 1999).

By the close of the 1990s this situation had changed. A severe economic recession hit Japan, resulting in record unemployment. While still low compared to European countries, it meant that almost twice as many people were looking for jobs as there were job openings. Companies facing the impact of a lingering recession and increased competition from abroad for their products set aside the notion of lifetime employment. Interactionists observed that Japanese men—accustomed to job security—were so embarrassed over losing a job that they would keep it a secret from their families for days if not weeks (see Chapter 4). Men in their 50s were now looking for work along with recent college graduates. As a result of this restructuring, the bonds that linked worker and employer are currently weakening. The feelings of worker isolation that Marx and Ritzer wrote about in Europe and North America are becoming increasingly evident in Japan (Barr 1999; Kerbo and McKinstry 1998; Strom 1999).

● The Changing Economy

As advocates of the power elite model point out, the trend in capitalist societies has been toward concentration of ownership by giant corporations, especially multinational

This photo of a street scene in Columbus, Ohio, could have been taken in almost any American city. The U.S. workforce is becoming increasingly diverse in terms of race, ethnicity, and gender.

A more diverse workforce means that relationships between workers are more likely to cross gender, racial, and ethnic lines. Interactionists note that people will find themselves supervising and being supervised by people very different from themselves. In response to these changes, 75 percent of businesses have instituted some type of cultural diversity training programs as of 2000 (Melia 2000).

p. 251

Deindustrialization

What happens when a company decides it is more profitable to move its operations out of a long-established community to another part of the country or out of the country altogether? People lose jobs; stores lose customers; the local government's tax base declines and it cuts services. This devastating process has occurred again and again in the last decade or so.

The term *deindustrialization* refers to the systematic, widespread withdrawal of investment in basic aspects of productivity such as factories and plants. Giant corporations that deindustrialize are not necessarily refusing to invest in new economic opportunities. Rather, the targets and locations of investment change, and the need for labor decreases as technology continues to automate production. First, there may be a relocation of plants from the nation's central cities to the suburbs. The next step may be relocation from suburban areas of the Northeast and Midwest to southern states, where labor laws place more restrictions on unions. Finally, a corporation may simply relocate *outside* the United States to a country with a lower rate of prevailing wages. General Motors, for example, decided to build a multibillion-dollar plant in Spain rather than in Kansas City (Bluestone and Harrison 1982; Rifkin 1995a).

Although deindustrialization often involves relocation, in some instances it takes the form of corporate restructuring, as companies seek to

The workforce more and more reflects the diversity of the population as ethnic minorities enter the labor force and immigrants and their children move from marginal jobs or employment in the informal economy to positions of greater visibility and responsibility. The impact of this changing labor force is not merely statistical.

Figure 18-2

Racial and Ethnic Composition of the U.S. Labor Force, 1986 and 2008 (projection)

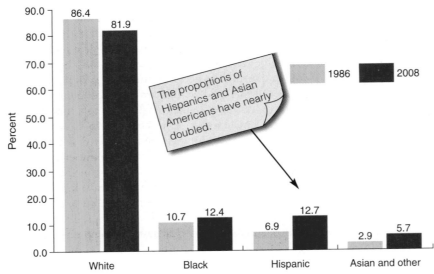

Source: Fullerton 1997:24, 1999:20.

When U.S. plants deindustrialize at home, they often move their investment in manufacturing outside the country to take advantage of low wages. Shown here is an AT&T telephone repair plant located across the border in Nuevo Laredo, Mexico.

reduce costs in the face of growing worldwide competition. When such restructuring occurs, the impact on the bureaucratic hierarchy of formal organizations can be significant. A large corporation may choose to sell off or entirely abandon less productive divisions and eliminate layers of management viewed as unnecessary. Wages and salaries may be frozen and fringe benefits cut—all in the name of "restructuring." Increasing reliance on automation also spells the end of work as we have known it.

The term *downsizing* was introduced in 1987 to refer to reductions in a company's workforce. According to the Department of Labor, about 75 percent of "downsized" employees find new jobs, while 14 percent are forced into retirement and 11 percent do not find new jobs. Among workers laid off from their jobs, 19 percent of Hispanics and 18 percent of African Americans were still unemployed two years later, compared with 11 percent of Whites.

Viewed from a conflict perspective, the unprecedented attention given to downsizing in the mid-1990s reflected the continuing importance of social class in the United States. Conflict theorists note that job loss, affecting factory workers in particular, has long been a feature of deindustrialization. (The social policy section in Chapter 6 describes how trade unions have dealt with job loss and downsizing.) But when large numbers of middle-class managers and other white-collar employees with substantial incomes began to be laid off, suddenly there was great concern in the media over downsizing. By mid-

2000, downsizing was even being applied to dot-com companies, the sector of the economy that flew high in the 1990s (Richtel 2000; Safire 1996; Samuelson 1996a, 1996b).

The social costs of deindustrialization and downsizing cannot be minimized. Plant closings lead to substantial unemployment in a community, which can have a devastating impact on both the micro- and macrolevel. On the microlevel, the unemployed person and his or her family must adjust to a loss of spending power. Both marital happiness and family cohesion may suffer as a result. Although many dismissed workers eventually reenter the paid labor force, they often must accept less desirable positions with lower salaries and fewer benefits. Unemployment and underemployment are tied into many of the social problems discussed throughout this textbook, among them the need for child care, the controversy over welfare, and the issue of health care reform (which will be discussed in Chapter 19).

pp. 101, 232 ←

On the societal, or macro, level, the impact of a plant closing on a community can be as difficult as it is for an individual worker and his or her family. As noted earlier, the community will experience a significant loss of tax revenues, thereby straining its ability to support police and fire protection, schools, parks, and other public services. Moreover, rising unemployment in a community leads to a reduced demand for goods and services. Sales by retail firms and other businesses fall off, and this can lead to further layoffs.

The impact of deindustrialization is evident not only in the United States but also in Asia and western Europe. In an effort to remain competitive within a global economy, many European companies have laid off workers. French sociologist Loïc Wacquant (1993) has studied urban rioting in the United States and Europe and suggests that most communities that are the scene of riots share a common sociological profile. They typically are former working-class communities that were sustained by factories that formed the heart of a manufacturing economy. As their countries' economies shifted to the service- and information-based economy of postindustrial society, the factories closed, leaving these working-class communities jobless. Another social consequence of the shifts in the worldwide economy has been a mismatch of jobs and skills (see Box 18-2).

Sociology in the Global Community

18-2 The Worldwide Jobs–Skills Mismatch

The want ads go on forever, but even in the best of times, millions are seeking work and even more want a better job. Rich countries still have millions of people living in poverty. What is wrong with these pictures? We are seeing a mismatch between the skills that people have and the jobs that are available.

The growth of the service and high-tech information-based economy at the expense of manufacturing translates directly into shifts in employment. Economist Jeremy Rifkin has written of the emergence of a *knowledge class* that is responsible for keeping the worldwide high-tech economy going. This kind of expertise calls for workers with high skills—skills that are difficult to come by among the ranks of the unemployed, whether in Massachusetts or Madagascar. At the same time, many unemployed, especially those who have been downsized, are overqualified for low-paying, service economy jobs, which call for few skills.

The most visible illustration of this mismatch between jobs available and skills needed can be seen among those who immigrate from developing nations to the cities of industrial countries, where the abilities of the knowledge class are most valued. These new arrivals are attracted by higher standards of living, but their lack of technological skills relegates them to poor-paying service sector jobs,

such as food service, custodial work, and support services in hotels and retail establishments.

Foreign labor plays a significant role in many industrial countries—constituting 10 percent or more of the total labor force in the United States, Germany, and Austria and more than 20 percent in Canada, Australia, and Switzerland. Because they send money back home to their families, these foreign workers are an important source of revenue for their homeland, but their generally unskilled jobs make them more vulnerable to un-

> A high school education is now considered insufficient for most highly skilled jobs.

employment in economic downturns than native-born workers.

The jobs–skills mismatch is spreading to the developing nations. For example, the pattern of deindustrialization associated with northern industrial cities in the United States is now beginning to take root in Mexico. The relatively new factories, considered state-of-the-art at the time they were built in the early 1990s to serve multinational corporations, are already downsizing as they become even more automated. Machines are replacing workers in every developing country,

and, increasingly, the remaining jobs require the skills associated with the knowledge class. Economic planners in high-tech–oriented Singapore worry that many older workers there will soon face unemployment because of outdated skills.

In the United States, 84 percent of the population has attained at least a high school degree, but a high school education is now considered insufficient for most highly skilled jobs. Outside Europe, North America, and a few Asian countries, 40 to 60 percent at most have attained that level of education. At the same time that the level of education required for skilled workers worldwide is increasing, there has been little progress to match those needs. Shifting skill requirements and ineffective educational systems have combined to marginalize many immigrant groups around the world as well as native-born peoples left behind by the information and technology boom and the escalation of skills required.

Let's Discuss

1. What is causing the jobs–skills mismatch? Why is this mismatch spreading to developing nations?
2. Do you know someone with skills who was forced to take a low-paying job? What caused this situation?

Sources: Bureau of the Census 2001a:140; Divyanathan 2000; Kasarda 1990; Rifkin 1995b; World Bank 2001a.

E-Commerce

Another development following close on the heels of deindustrialization is the emergence of e-commerce, as online businesses compete with bricks-and-mortar establishments. **E-commerce** refers to the numerous ways that people with access to the Internet can do business from their computers. Amazon.com, for example, began in 1995 as a supplier of book titles but soon became the prototype for online businesses, branching into selling a variety of merchandise, including toys and hardware equipment. By 2001, Amazon.com boasted 29 million

customers in 160 countries. The growth of e-commerce means jobs in a new line of industry as well as growth for related industries, such as warehousing, packing, and shipping. However, the industry is volatile, and many e-commerce companies have yet to turn a profit. In 2000, the speculative dot-com bubble burst, hundreds of companies failed and thousands of unsuspecting employees lost their jobs.

Although e-commerce will not immediately overwhelm traditional businesses, it has brought new social dynamics to the retail trade. Consider the impact on

The New Economy

HEY. I CAN DELETE 10,000 EMPLOYEES WITH A SINGLE MOUSE CLICK.

CUTTING EDGE —

Both unemployed workers and entrants to the paid labor force accept positions as temporary or part-time workers. Some do so for flexibility and control over their work time, but others accept these jobs because they are the only ones available. Young people are especially likely to fill temporary positions. A growing portion of this contingency workforce includes free-lancers who work at home via the Internet: "e-lancers." Employers find it attractive and functional to shift toward a contingency workforce because it allows them to respond more quickly to workforce demands—as well as to hire employees without having to offer the fringe benefits that full-time employees enjoy. All around the United States, large firms have come to rely on part-time or temporary workers, most of whom work part-time involuntarily. Many of these workers feel the effects of deindustrialization and shifts in the global economy. They lost their full-time jobs when companies moved operations to developing nations (Reich 2001).

It is difficult to estimate the size of the contingency workforce of the United States. Heidi Hartmann of the Institute for Women's Policy Research notes that there is no agreement among social scientists as to how to define a "contingent worker" or how many there are. According to one estimate, however, contingent workers constitute about one-fourth of the nation's paid labor force. In 1998, for example, about 28 percent of Microsoft's workforce was temporary. This included a large number of long-term temporaries (those who work more than one year), who have come to refer to their awkward status as "permatemps." In fact, nearly 12,000 long-term temporary workers banded together to sue Microsoft, accusing the company of using their temporary status to deny them benefits. They eventually won a $97 million settlement. Nonetheless, as of the end of 2000, 10 percent of Microsoft workers worldwide were still temps (Greenhouse 2000).

During the 1970s and 1980s, temporary workers typically held low-skill positions at fast-food restaurants, telemarketing firms, and other service industries. Today, the contingent workforce is evident at virtually *all* skill levels and in *all* industries. Clerical "temps" handle word processing and filing duties, managers are hired on a short-term basis to reorganize departments, freelance

traditional retail outlets and on face-to-face interaction with local store owners. Even established companies such as Nike, Timex, Levi's, and Mattel are establishing their own online "stores," bypassing the retail outlets that they have courted for years to directly reach customers with their merchandise. Megamalls once replaced personal ties to stores for many shoppers; the growth of e-commerce with its "cybermalls" is just the latest change in the economy.

Some observers note that e-commerce offers more opportunities to consumers in rural areas (assuming they have the necessary high-tech infrastructure) and those with disabilities. To its critics, however, e-commerce signals more social isolation, more alienation, and greater disconnect for the poor and disadvantaged who are not a part of the new information technology (Amazon.com 2001; Drucker 1999; Stoughton and Walker 1999).

The Contingency Workforce

In the past, the term *temp* typically conjured up images of a replacement receptionist or a worker covering for someone on vacation. However, in association with the deindustrialization and downsizing described above, a "contingency workforce," in which workers are hired only for as long as they are needed, has emerged in the United States, and we have witnessed what has been called the "temping of America."

writers prepare speeches for corporate executives, and blue-collar workers are employed for a few months when a factory receives an unusually high number of orders. A significant minority of temporary employees are contract workers who are being "rented" for specific periods of time by the companies that previously downsized them—and are now working at lower salary levels without benefits or job security (Kirk 1995; Uchitelle 1996).

Workers in the United States generally blame forces outside their control—indeed, outside the nation—for the problems they experience as a result of deindustrialization and the rise of a contingency workforce. The relocation of factories to other countries has unquestionably contributed to job loss in the United States. But there are growing indications that automation is substantially reducing the need for human labor in both manufacturing and service industries. By the year 2020, it is projected that less than 2 percent of the entire global labor force will be engaged in factory work. In Chapter 16, we will look at the role of technology in promoting social and economic change (Rifkin 1996).

In the struggles of part-time workers and the unemployed to make ends meet, we find government and the economy intertwined, as the government steps in with assistance, whether it be unemployment compensation, government-funded child care, or welfare. In the social

An accountant studies a ledger in an office. Increasing numbers of educated, white-collar professionals (such as accountants) have joined low-level "temp" workers in the contingency workforce.

policy section that follows, we examine affirmative action, a controversial issue that provides another example of the link between government and the economy.

Imagine

What will the U.S. workforce look like in 2020? Consider workers' age, gender, race, and ethnicity. How much education will workers need? Will they work full or part time? What will be the most common occupations?

SOCIAL POLICY AND THE ECONOMY

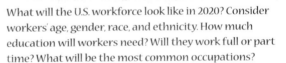

Affirmative Action

/schaefer8

The Issue

Jessie Sherrod began picking cotton in the fields of Mississippi when she was eight years old, earning $1.67 each time she worked a 12-hour day. Today, at 45, she is a Harvard-educated pediatrician who specializes in infectious diseases. But the road from the cotton fields to the medical profession was hardly an easy one. "You can't make up for 400 years of slavery and mistreatment and unequal opportunity in 20 years," she says angrily.

"We had to ride the school bus for five miles . . . and pass by a white school to get to our black elementary school. Our books were used books. Our instructors were not as good. We didn't have the proper equipment. How do you make up for that?" (Stolberg 1995:A14). Some people think it should be done through affirmative action programs.

The term *affirmative action* first appeared in an executive order issued by President John F. Kennedy in 1961. That order called for contractors to "take affirmative action to ensure that applicants are employed, and that employees are treated during employment, without regard to their race, creed, color, or national origin." In 1967, the order was amended by President Lyndon Johnson to also prohibit discrimination on the basis of sex, but affirmative action remained a vague concept. Currently, **affirmative action** refers to positive efforts to recruit minority group members or women for jobs, promotions, and educational opportunities. But many people think that affirmative action programs constitute reverse discrimination against qualified Whites and males. Does government have a responsibility to make up for past discrimination? If so, how far should it go?

The Setting

A variety of court decisions and executive branch statements have outlawed certain forms of job discrimination based on race, sex, or both, including (1) word-of-mouth recruitment among all-White or all-male workforces, (2) recruitment exclusively in schools or colleges that are limited to one sex or are predominantly White, (3) discrimination against married women or forced retirement of pregnant women, (4) advertising in male and female "help wanted" columns when gender is not a legitimate occupational qualification, and (5) job qualifications and tests that are not substantially related to the job. Also, the lack of minority (African American, Asian, Native American, or Hispanic) or female employees may in itself represent evidence of unlawful exclusion (Commission on Civil Rights 1981).

In the late 1970s, a number of bitterly debated cases on affirmative action reached the Supreme Court. In 1978, in the *Bakke* case, by a narrow 5–4 vote, the Supreme Court ordered the medical school of the University of California at Davis to admit Allen Bakke, a White engineer who originally had been denied admission. The justices ruled that the school had violated Bakke's constitutional rights by establishing a fixed quota system for minority students. The Court added, however, that it was constitutional for universities to adopt flexible admissions programs that use race as one factor in decision making.

Figure 18-3

U.S. Median Income by Race, Ethnicity, and Gender, 2000

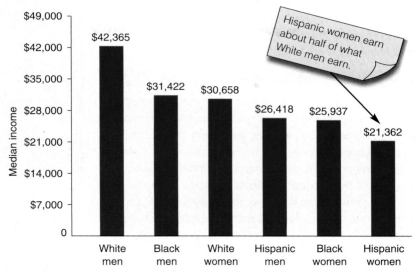

Note: Median income includes all financial sources and is limited to year-round, full-time workers over 15 years of age. "White" refers to non-Hispanic.

Source: Bureau of the Census 2001g.

Sociological Insights

Sociologists—and especially conflict theorists—view affirmative action as a legislative attempt to reduce the inequality embedded in the social structure by increasing the opportunities of groups that have been deprived in the past, such as women and African Americans. The gap in earning power between White males and other groups (see Figure 18-3) is one indication of the inequality that needs to be addressed. But even if they acknowledge the disparity in earnings between White males and others, many people in the United States doubt that everything done in the name of affirmative action is desirable. In a 2001 national survey, 58 percent of respondents said they thought the approach had been good for the nation. But in response to another question, 35 percent said that affirmative action programs should be cut back; only 24 percent supported expanding them (Gallup 2001).

Much less documented than economic inequality are the social consequences of affirmative action policies on everyday life. Interactionists focus on situations in which some women and minorities in underrepresented professions and schools are often mistakenly viewed as products of affirmative action. Fellow students and workers may stereotype them as less qualified and see them as beneficiaries of preference over more qualified White males. Obviously, this is not necessarily the case, but such labeling may well affect social relationships. Sociologist Orlando Patterson (1998) has noted that workplace isolation experienced by minority workers inhibits their advancement up the corporate ladder; yet if efforts to increase their representation are scaled back, these problems in advancement will persist.

Policy Initiatives

By the early 1990s, affirmative action had emerged as an increasingly important issue in state and national political campaigns. Generally, discussion focused on the use of quotas (or the "Q word," as it came to be known) in hiring practices. Supporters of affirmative action argue that hiring goals (or targets) establish floors for minority inclusion but do not exclude truly qualified candidates from any group. Opponents insist that these "targets" are, in fact, quotas that lead to reverse discrimination. However, affirmative action has caused very few claims of reverse discrimination by White people. Fewer than 100 of the more than 3,000 discrimination opinions in federal courts from 1990 to 1994 even raised the issue of reverse discrimination, and reverse discrimination was actually established in only six cases (*New York Times* 1995).

In the 1996 elections, California's voters approved by a 54 to 46 percent margin the California Civil Rights Initiative, also known as Proposition 209. This measure amends the state constitution to *prohibit* any program that gives preference to women and minorities in college admissions, hiring, promotion, or government contracts. In other words, it aims to abolish affirmative action programs. The courts have since upheld the measure. In 1998, voters in Washington state passed a similar anti-affirmative action measure.

The United States is not alone in its struggle to find acceptable ways of compensating for generations of inequality between racial groups. After dismantling the system of apartheid that favored Whites economically and socially, the Republic of South Africa is now trying to level the playing field. Inequality is stark: 88 percent of

the nation's population is non-White, yet this group accounts for only 4 percent of the managerial ranks. The South African government has chosen the term *affirmative action* for its policy to encourage the hiring of Blacks in management positions where none existed before. Because the gaps are much greater than in the United States, there has been a virtual hiring frenzy in the limited pool of black South African managers and professionals. The subject of affirmative action in this nation almost always splits along racial lines: Blacks are infuriated that there is so much injustice to make up for, while Whites are reluctant to embrace the program meant to redress inequality. The specifics may be different from the United States, but the concerns and impatience seen in South Africa are familiar (Daley 1997).

Let's Discuss

1. Would a conflict theorist support the policy of affirmative action? Why or why not?
2. Do you think claims of reverse discrimination have any validity? What should be done about them?
3. If you were to draft legislation either supporting or abolishing affirmative action, what provisions would it include?

● Chapter Resources

Summary

The *economic system* of a society has an important influence on social behavior and on other social institutions.

1. As the industrial revolution proceeded, a new form of social structure emerged: the *industrial society.*
2. Economic systems of *capitalism* vary in the degree to which the government regulates private ownership and economic activity, but all emphasize the profit motive.
3. The basic objective of a *socialist* economic system is to eliminate economic exploitation and meet people's needs.
4. Marx believed that *communism* would naturally evolve out of the socialism stage.
5. In most societies today the trend is toward an increase in jobs providing services and a rise in the number of occupations that aspire to be a *profession.*
6. Industrial jobs can lead to a sense of *alienation* in the workplace. Karl Marx expected that powerless workers would eventually overthrow the capitalist system.
7. The nature of the U.S. economy is changing. Sociologists are interested in the changing face of the workforce, the effects of *deindustrialization,* increased use of a contingency workforce, and the emergence of e-commerce.
8. Despite numerous recent *affirmative action* programs, White males continue to hold the overwhelming majority of prestigious and high-paying jobs in the United States.

Critical Thinking Questions

1. The United States has long been put forward as the model of a capitalist society. Drawing on material in earlier chapters of the textbook, discuss the values and beliefs that have led people in the United States to cherish a laissez-faire, capitalist economy. To what degree have these values and beliefs changed during the past hundred years? What aspects of socialism are now evident in the nation's economy? Have there been basic changes in our values and beliefs to support certain principles traditionally associated with socialist societies?
2. Describe some of the service workers in the college or university that you attend. Are there any issues that point toward alienation in the workplace? Does your school make much use of a contingent workforce, especially among students?
3. Imagine that you have been assigned to study possible changes in the economy of the nearest city. How could you use surveys, observation research, experiments, and existing sources to complete this task?

Key Terms

Affirmative action   Positive efforts to recruit minority group members or women for jobs, promotions, and educational opportunities. (page 465)

Alienation   The situation of being estranged or disassociated from the surrounding society. (456)

Capitalism   An economic system in which the means of production are largely in private hands, and the main incentive for economic activity is the accumulation of profits. (451)

Communism   As an ideal type, an economic system under which all property is communally owned and no social distinctions are made on the basis of people's ability to produce. (453)

Deindustrialization   The systematic, widespread withdrawal of investment in basic aspects of productivity such as factories and plants. (460)

Downsizing   Reductions taken in a company's workforce as part of deindustrialization. (461)

E-commerce   Numerous ways that people with access to the Internet can do business from their computers. (462)

Economic system   The social institution through which goods and services are produced, distributed, and consumed. (451)

Industrial society   A society that depends on mechanization to produce its goods and services. (451)

Laissez-faire   A form of capitalism under which people compete freely, with minimal government intervention in the economy. (451)

Monopoly   Control of a market by a single business firm. (452)

Profession   An occupation requiring extensive knowledge that is governed by a code of ethics. (454)

Socialism   An economic system under which the means of production and distribution are collectively owned. (452)

Additional Readings

BOOKS

Bell, Ella Edmondson, and Stella M. Nkomo. 2001. *Our Separate Ways: Black and White Women and the Struggle for Professional Identity*. Cambridge, MA: Harvard Business School Press. A sociological analysis of the different ways in which African American and White women handle corporate pressure.

Fraser, Jill Andresley. 2001. *White-Collar Sweatshop*. New York: W. W. Norton. An explanation of why, amidst the tremendous corporate profits of the 1990s, American workers' real incomes stagnated and their workweek grew longer.

Gleick, James. 1999. *Faster: The Acceleration of Just About Everything*. New York: Pantheon Books. A journalistic look at the ever-increasing pace of life in the workplace and throughout the lives of people in industrial nations.

Manning, Marable. 2000. *Capitalism Underdeveloped Black America*, updated ed. Cambridge, MA: South End Press. A critical look at capitalism in the United States, with special emphasis on the role of the African American elite.

Moore, Thomas S. 1996. *The Disposable Work Force: Worker Displacement and Employment Instability in America*. New York: Aldine de Gruyter. Drawing on a case study of a plant closing in Wisconsin, Moore examines the displacement of workers in the United States.

Moss, Phillip, and Chris Tilly. 2001. *Stories Employers Tell: Race, Skill, and Hiring in America*. New York: Russell Sage Foundation. A survey of employers in four cities—Atlanta, Boston, Detroit, and Los Angeles—illustrates the role of discrimination in jobs requiring few skills.

Tannock, Stuart. 2001. *Youth at Work: The Unionized Fast Food and Grocery Workplace*. Philadelphia: Temple University Press. A study of young North Americans who work in low-wage positions and the impact of the unionization of their jobs in Canada.

JOURNALS

Among the journals focusing on the economy are *Industrial and Labor Relations Review* (founded in 1947), *Insurgent Sociologist* (1969), *Journal of Consumer Culture* (2001), *Work and Occupations* (1974), and *Work, Employment and Society* (1987).

Technology Resources

Internet Connection

*Note: While all the URLs listed were current as of the printing of this book, these sites often change. Please check our website (**http://www.mhhe.com/schaefer8**) for updates and hyperlinks to these exercises and additional exercises.*

1. Over the years, worker satisfaction has become an important topic for sociological study and analysis. Sociologists frequently conduct surveys in which workers are asked whether or not they are satisfied with their jobs. This exercise allows you to read the results of one such survey, the Annual Food Engineering Job Satisfaction and Salary Survey, conducted by Business News Publishing Company. Go to the web address (**http://www.foodengineering. org/articles/2000/1200/0012survey.htm**) and explore the site. After examining the pie charts, answer the following questions:

   (a) What percentage of workers said they were satisfied with their positions, even though their workload had increased over the last year?

   (b) In which income bracket did workers feel most secure in their jobs? What would the sociologist George Ritzer have said about this finding?

   (c) Do the results of this survey suggest that job satisfaction is related to job security? Explain your answer by giving an example.

(d) The study suggests that employees are satisfied with their experiences on work teams. Compare this finding to those of Donald Roy's study (1959), discussed on page 458.

(e) What did survey respondents think should be changed or improved to increase their job satisfaction?

2. The workforce in any country changes constantly, reflecting the diversity of its population. Aboriginal peoples make up one of the fastest-growing segments of the Canadian population, yet their labor force participation is lower, and their unemployment rate higher, than those of other Canadians. The Aboriginal Workforce Participation Initiative (AWPI) is a partnership initiative of the Canadian government that is committed to increasing Aboriginals' participation in the labor market. To read about the initiative, go to **http://www.ainc-inac.gc.ca/ai/awpi/index_e.html.** Browse through the site and answer the following questions:

(a) Link to "Put the Skills of Aboriginal Peoples to Work for You." What is the population growth of the Aboriginal peoples, compared to the national average?

(b) By what percentage is the population growth of the Aboriginal peoples estimated to increase in the next 25 years?

(c) How do the Aboriginal peoples' educational levels compare to those of other Canadians? What impedes the Aboriginals' full participation in the labor market?

(d) Click your Refresh or Back button and link to "Facts and Figures." Look at the pie chart shown on that page. How many people of Aboriginal ancestry are estimated to live in Canada?

(e) Of those Aboriginal peoples who live on reservations, what percentage lack year-round road access to the nearest service station? How would this statistic affect their labor force participation?

(f) For 2001, what is the forecasted percentage increase in labor force participation for Aboriginal peoples?

(g) What demographic characteristic will have the greatest impact on labor force participation among the Aboriginal peoples?

3. The Bureau of Labor Statistics (**http://www.bls.gov/**) compiles many informative statistics on the U.S. labor force, including employment, unemployment, and earnings data. Study the site and answer the following questions:

(a) What is the current unemployment rate in the United States?

(b) Link to "Economy at a Glance," where you will see a map of the United States. Click on your home state and look at the most current unemployment rate. Has it increased or decreased since December 2000? Does it seem to be following a trend, and if so, what is it?

(c) Click your Refresh or Back button and select a state in another part of the country. What is the current unemployment rate in that state? How does it compare to that of your home state? Compare the trends in the unemployment rate in the two states.

(d) How might you explain the differences (if any) in the unemployment rates and trends in the two states?

(e) Return to the homepage by clicking on your Refresh or Back button. Link to "Wages by Area and Occupation," and select "State." Next, click on "By State," which will produce a map of the United States. Click on either your home state or a state where you would like to live when you finish college. On the list of occupations, click on the one that most closely resembles your major field. What are the current median hourly wages for this occupation? What is the mean annual wage?

(f) Considering your chosen field, the state of the economy, and the effects of downsizing, do you think the mean annual wage will increase, decrease, or remain the same by the time you graduate? Explain your reasoning.

Online Learning Center www.mhhe.com/schaefer8

This chapter has focused on the economic system and the important influences it has on social behavior and on other social institutions. Visit the student center in the Online Learning Center at **www.mhhe.com/schaefer8** and link to "Imagine." You will be asked to imagine what your life might be like if the United States had a predominantly socialistic economy. You will also be asked to imagine what the U.S. workforce will look like in 2020 in terms of age, gender, race, and ethnicity. Read the questions, think about them, and use your *sociological imagination* to answer them.

HEALTH AND MEDICINE

WELCOME TO AMERICA

the only industrialized country besides South Africa without national healthcare

This billboard protests the lack of a national health care program in the United States. The reference to South Africa was especially pointed when the poster first appeared in 1989, because of the racist apartheid regime that held sway there.

THE SCALPEL
AND THE
SILVER BEAR

The First Navajo
Woman Surgeon
Combines
Western Medicine
and
Traditional Healing

LORI ARVISO ALVORD, M.D.
AND
ELIZABETH COHEN VAN PELT

knew that Navajo people mistrusted Western medicine, and that Navajo customs and beliefs, even Navajo ways of interacting with others, often stood in direct opposition to the way I was trained at Stanford to deliver medical care. I wanted to make a difference in the lives of my people, not only by providing surgery to heal them but also by making it easier for them to understand, relate to, and accept Western medicine. By speaking some Navajo with them, by showing respect for their ways, and by being one of them, I could help them. I watched my patients. I listened to them. Slowly I began to develop better ways to heal them, ways that respected their culture and beliefs. I desired to incorporate these traditional beliefs and customs into my practice. . . .

Navajo patients simply didn't respond well to the brusque and distanced style of Western doctors. To them it is not acceptable to walk into a room, quickly open someone's shirt and listen to their heart with a stethoscope, or stick something in their mouth or ear. Nor is it acceptable to ask probing and personal questions. As I adapted my practice to my culture, my patients relaxed in situations that could otherwise have been highly stressful to them. As they became more comfortable and at ease, something even more remarkable—astonishing, even—happened. When patients were trusting and accepting before surgery, their operations seemed to be more successful. If they were anxious, distrustful, and did not understand, or had resisted treatment, they seemed to have more operative or postoperative complications. Could this be happening? The more I watched, the more I saw it was indeed true. Incorporating Navajo philosophies of balance and symmetry, respect and connectedness into my practice, benefited my patients and allowed everything in my two worlds to make sense.

Navajos believe in *hózhǫ́* or *hózhǫ́ni*—"Walking in Beauty"—a worldview in which everything in life is connected and influences everything else. A stone thrown into a pond can influence the life of a deer in the forest, a human voice and a spoken word can influence events around the world, and all things possess spirit and power. So Navajos make every effort to live in harmony and balance with everyone and everything else. Their belief system sees sickness as a result of things falling out of balance, of losing one's way on the path of beauty. In this belief system, religion and medicine are one and the same. . . .

As I have modified my Western techniques with elements of Navajo culture and philosophy, I have seen the wisdom and truth of Navajo medicine too, and how Navajo patients can benefit from it. In this way I am pulling the strands of my life even closer together. The results have been dazzling—*hózhǫ́ni.* It has been beautiful. *(Alvord and Van Pelt 1999:13–15)* ■ 💿

Additional information about this excerpt and about those that open each subsequent chapter can be found in the SocWorld CD-ROM that accompanies this text.

n this excerpt from *The Scalpel and the Silver Bear,* Dr. Lori Arviso Alvord, the first Navajo woman to become a surgeon, describes her effort to bridge the cultural gap between Western medicine and traditional Native American healing. Dropping the impersonal clinical manner she had learned in medical school; Alvord reached out to her Navajo patients; acknowledging their faith in holistic healing practices. Her account communicates the wonder she felt as she watched their health improve. By walking in beauty, Dr. Alvord had become a healer as well as a surgeon.

Alvord's account illustrates the powerful effect of culture on both health and medicine. Culture affects the way people interact with doctors and healers, the way they relate to their families when they are sick, and even the way they think about health. In this chapter, we will consider first the relationship between culture and health. Then we will present a sociological overview of health, illness, health care, and medicine as a social institution. Are some health problems peculiar to certain cultures? Who defines what illness is? How does health care vary from one social class to another and from one nation to another?

We will begin by examining how functionalists, conflict theorists, interactionists, and labeling theorists look at health-related issues. Then we will study the distribution of diseases in a society by gender, social class, race and ethnicity, and age. We'll also look at the evolution of the health care system of the United States. Sociologists are interested in the roles that people play within the health care system and the organizations that deal with issues of health and sickness. Therefore, we will analyze the interactions among doctors, nurses, and patients; alternatives to traditional health care; and the role of government in providing health services to the needy. The chapter continues with an examination of mental illness in which we contrast the medical and labeling approaches to mental disorders. Finally, the social policy section will explore the issue of how to finance health care worldwide. ■

Culture and Health

Culture contributes to differences in medical care as well as in how health is defined. In Japan, for instance, organ transplants are rare. The Japanese do not generally favor harvesting organs from brain-dead donors. Researchers have even shown that diseases themselves are rooted in the shared meanings of particular cultures. The term ***culture-bound syndrome*** refers to a disease or illness that cannot be understood apart from its specific social context (Cassidy 1982:326; Osborne 2001).

In the United States, a culture-bound syndrome known as anorexia nervosa has received increasing attention over the last few decades. First described in England in the 1860s, this condition is characterized by an intense fear of becoming obese and a distorted image of one's body. Those suffering from anorexia nervosa (primarily young women in their teenage years or twenties) drastically lose weight through self-induced semistarvation and self-induced vomiting. Anorexia nervosa is best understood in the context of Western culture, which typically views the slim, youthful body as healthy and beautiful, whereas the fat person is viewed as ugly and lacking in self-discipline.

Culture can also influence the relative incidence of a disease or disorder. In *The Scalpel and the Silver Bear,* Dr. Lori Arviso Alvord writes of the depression and alcoholism that attended life on the reservation. These diseases, she says, are born out of "historical grief": "Navajo children are told of the capture and murder of their forefathers and mothers, and then they too must share in the legacy. . . ." Not just for the Navajo, Alvord writes, but for Black Americans as well, the weight of centuries of suffering, injustice, and loss too often manifests itself in despair and addiction. The rate of alcoholism mortality among Native Americans served by the Indian Health Service is five times that of the general population of the United States (Alvord and Van Pelt 1999:12; Utter 1993:190).

Sociological Perspectives on Health and Illness

If social factors contribute to the evaluation of a person as "healthy" or "sick," how can we define health? We can imagine a continuum with health on one end and death on the other. In the preamble to its 1946 constitution, the World Health Organization defined ***health*** as a "state of complete physical, mental, and social well-being, and not merely the absence of disease and infirmity" (Leavell and Clark 1965:14).

In this definition, the "healthy" end of our continuum represents an ideal rather than a precise condition. Along the continuum, people define themselves as

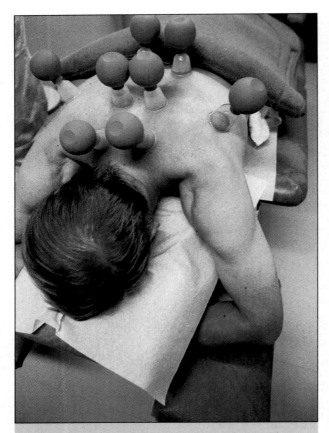

Health care takes many forms around the world. Cupping—a traditional practice used in ancient China, India, Egypt, and Greece—survives in modern Finland (left). Physiotherapists there use suction cups to draw out blood in order to lower patients' blood pressure, improve their circulation, and relieve muscular pain. In the western Pacific (right), the Malaitan people of Laulasi Island, one of the Solomon Islands, believe that a leaf called *raralu* has medicinal properties that reduce swelling. This boy has squeezed a *raralu* leaf to release its juices and used it to bandage his broken finger.

"healthy" or "sick" on the basis of criteria established by each individual, relatives, friends, coworkers, and medical practitioners. Because health is relative, we can view it in a social context and consider how it varies in different situations or cultures (Twaddle 1974; Wolinsky 1980).

Why is it that you may consider yourself sick or well when others do not agree? Who controls definitions of health and illness in our society, and for what ends? What are the consequences of viewing yourself (or being viewed) as ill or disabled? Drawing on four sociological perspectives—functionalism, conflict theory, interactionism, and labeling theory—we can gain greater insight into the social context shaping definitions of health and treatment of illness.

Functionalist Approach

Illness entails breaks in our social interactions both at work and at home. From a functionalist perspective, then, "being sick" must be controlled so that not too many people are released from their societal responsibilities at any one time. Functionalists contend that an overly broad definition of illness would disrupt the workings of a society.

"Sickness" requires that one take on a social role, even if temporarily. The *sick role* refers to societal expectations about the attitudes and behavior of a person viewed as being ill. Sociologist Talcott Parsons (1951, 1972, 1975), well known for his contributions to functionalist theory, has outlined the behavior required of people considered "sick." They are exempted from their normal, day-to-day responsibilities and generally do not suffer blame for their condition. Yet they are obligated to try to get well, and this may include seeking competent professional care. Attempting to get well is particularly important in the world's developing countries. Modern

p. 14

automated industrial societies can absorb a greater degree of illness or disability than horticultural or agrarian societies, where the availability of workers is far more critical (Conrad 1997).

According to Parsons's theory, physicians function as "gatekeepers" for the sick role. They either verify a patient's condition as "illness" or designate the patient as "recovered." The ill person becomes dependent on the doctor because the latter can control valued rewards (not only treatment of illness but also excused absences from work and school). Parsons suggests that the doctor–patient relationship is somewhat like that between parent and child. Like a parent, the physician helps the patient to enter society as a full and functioning adult (Segall 1976).

The concept of the sick role is not without criticism. First, patients' judgments regarding their own state of health may be related to their gender, age, social class, and ethnic group. For example, younger people may fail to detect warning signs of a dangerous illness while the elderly may focus too much on the slightest physical malady. Second, the sick role may be more applicable to people experiencing short-term illnesses than to those with recurring, long-term illnesses. Finally, even simple factors, such as whether a person is employed or not, seem to affect willingness to assume the sick role—as does the impact of socialization into a particular occupation or activity. For example, beginning in childhood, athletes learn to define certain ailments as "sports injuries" and therefore do not regard themselves as "sick." Nonetheless, sociologists continue to rely on Parsons's model for functionalist analysis of the relationship between illness and societal expectations for the sick (Curry 1993).

Conflict Approach

Conflict theorists observe that the medical profession has assumed a preeminence that extends well beyond whether to excuse a student from school or an employee from work. Sociologist Eliot Freidson (1970:5) has likened the position of medicine today to that of state religions yesterday—it has an officially approved monopoly of the right to define health and illness and to treat illness. Conflict theorists use the term *medicalization of society* to refer to the growing role of medicine as a major institution of social control (Conrad and Schneider 1992; McKinlay and McKinlay 1977; Zola 1972, 1983).

The Medicalization of Society

Social control involves techniques and strategies for regulating behavior in order to enforce the distinctive norms p. 183 and values of a culture. Typically, we think of informal social control as occurring within families and peer groups, and formal social control as carried out by authorized agents such as police officers,

judges, school administrators, and employers. However, viewed from a conflict perspective, medicine is not simply a "healing profession"; it is a regulating mechanism as well.

How does it manifest its social control? First, medicine has greatly expanded its domain of expertise in recent decades. Physicians now examine a wide range of issues, among them sexuality (including homosexuality), old age, anxiety, obesity, child development, alcoholism, and drug addiction. Society tolerates such expansion of the boundaries of medicine because we hope that these experts can bring new "miracle cures" to complex human problems as they have to the control of certain infectious diseases.

The social significance of this expanding medicalization is that once a problem is viewed using a *medical model*—once medical experts become influential in proposing and assessing relevant public policies—it becomes more difficult for "common people" to join the discussion and exert influence on decision making. It also becomes more difficult to view these issues as being shaped by social, cultural, or psychological factors, rather than simply by physical or medical factors (Caplan 1989; Conrad and Schneider 1992; Starr 1982).

Second, medicine serves as an agent of social control by retaining absolute jurisdiction over many health care procedures. It has even attempted to guard its jurisdiction by placing health care professionals such as chiropractors and nurse-midwives outside the realm of acceptable medicine. Despite the fact that midwives first brought professionalism to child delivery, they have been portrayed as having invaded the "legitimate" field of obstetrics both in the United States and Mexico. Nurse-midwives have sought

A midwife hands a newborn baby to its mother. Despite the fact that midwives first brought professionalism to child delivery, physicians insist on treating midwifery as a subordinate occupation.

licensing as a way to achieve professional respectability, but physicians continue to exert power to ensure that midwifery remains a subordinate occupation (Friedland 2000).

Inequities in Health Care

The medicalization of society is but one concern of conflict theorists as they assess the workings of health care institutions. As we have seen throughout this textbook, when analyzing any issue, conflict theorists seek to determine who benefits, who suffers, and who dominates at the expense of others. Viewed from a conflict perspective, there are glaring inequities in health care delivery within the United States. For example, poor and rural areas tend to be underserved because medical services concentrate where people are numerous and/or wealthy.

Similarly, from a global perspective, there are obvious inequities in health care delivery. Today, the United States has about 25 physicians per 1,000 people, while African nations have fewer than 1 per 1,000. This situation is only worsened by the "brain drain"—the immigration to the United States and other industrialized nations of skilled workers, professionals, and technicians who are desperately needed by their home countries. As part of this brain drain, physicians and other health care professionals have come to the United States from developing countries such as India, Pakistan, and various African states. Conflict theorists view such emigration out of the Third World as yet another way in which the world's core industrialized nations enhance their quality of life at the expense of developing countries. One way these countries suffer is in lower life expectancy, as Figure 19-1 vividly demonstrates. Life expectancy in Africa and much of Latin America and Asia is far lower than in industrialized nations (World Bank 2000b:190–91).

In another example of global inequities in health care, multinational corporations based in industrialized countries have reaped significant profits by "dumping" unapproved drugs on unsuspecting Third World consumers.

Figure 19-1

Average Life Expectancy at Birth

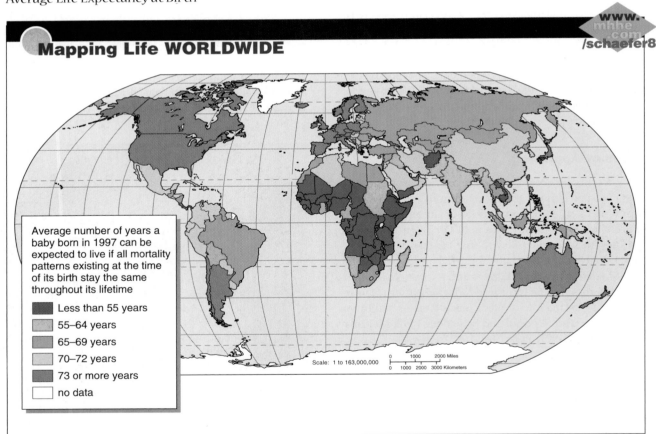

Source: Allen 2001:39.

In some cases, fraudulent capsules and tablets are manufactured and marketed as established products in developing countries. These "medications" contain useless ingredients or perhaps one-tenth of the needed dosage of a genuine medication. Even when the drugs dumped on developing countries are legitimate, the information available to physicians and patients is less likely to include warnings of health hazards and more likely to include undocumented testimonials than in industrialized nations (Silverman et al. 1992).

Conflict theorists emphasize that inequities in health care resources have clear life-and-death consequences. For example, in 2001, the infant mortality rate in the African nation of Sierra Leone ranged as high as 157 infant deaths per 1,000 live births. By contrast, Japan's infant mortality rate was only 3.4 deaths per 1,000 live births and Iceland's was only 2.4. From a conflict perspective, the dramatic differences in infant mortality rates around the world (see Figure 19-2) reflect, at least in part, unequal distribution of health care resources based on the wealth or poverty of various communities and nations.

In 2001, the United States had a rate of 7 infant deaths per 1,000 live births, although it is estimated that the rate in some poor, inner-city neighborhoods in this country exceeds 30 deaths per 1,000 live births. Despite the wealth of the United States, at least 32 nations have *lower* infant mortality rates, among them Canada, Great Britain, and Japan. Conflict theorists point out that, unlike the United States, these countries offer some form of government-supported health care for all citizens, which typically leads to greater availability and greater use of prenatal care. (We will examine government's role in health care in greater detail in the social policy section of this chapter.)

Interactionist Approach

Patients are not simply passive but often actively seek the services of a health care practitioner. This is the interactionist point of view. In examining health, illness, and medicine as a social institution, interactionists generally focus on micro-level study of the roles played by health care professionals and patients (Alonzo 1989; Zola 1983).

Sometimes patients play an active role in health care by *failing* to follow a physician's advice. For example, some patients stop taking medications long before they should, some take an incorrect dosage on purpose, and others never even fill their prescriptions. Such noncompliance results in part from the prevalence of self-medication in our society; many people are accustomed to self-diagnosis and self-treatment. On the other hand, patients' active involvement in their health care can sometimes have very *positive* conse-

Figure 19-2

Infant Mortality Rates, 2001

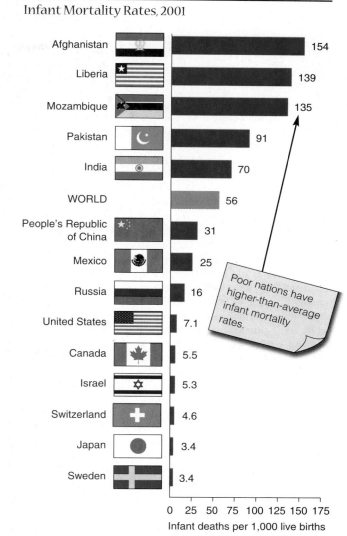

Poor nations have higher-than-average infant mortality rates.

Infant deaths per 1,000 live births

Source: Haub and Cornelius 2001.

quences. Some patients read books about preventive health care techniques, attempt to maintain healthful and nutritious diets, carefully monitor any side effects of medication, and adjust dosage based on such perceived side effects.

The interactionist perspective has been especially helpful in unraveling cultural differences that affect health care in a multicultural society such as that of the United States (see Box 19-1). For example, when Community Action for Women's Health began surveying Native Americans in Los Angeles in 1994 concerning their health care needs, the researchers found that the respondents regarded the surveys as too intrusive and offered little cooperation. Subsequently, the researchers posed questions orally and wrote responses on forms with the image of a traditional

www.
mhhe
.com
/schaefer8

Research in Action

19-1   To Inform or Not to Inform? How Race and Ethnicity Affect Views of Patient Autonomy

Should patients be told the seriousness of their illness? Should they be included in the decisions about what medical care they receive? In the last 25 years, the principle of patient autonomy has become a fundamental ideal of medical care in the United States. According to this principle, "people have the right to make informed decisions about their medical care; consequently, they need the truth about their diagnosis, their prognosis, and the risks and benefits of possible treatments." While the ideal of patient autonomy has won wide acceptance from physicians, policymakers, and the general public, some critics argue that the current focus on patient autonomy reflects an ethnocentric cultural bias by ignoring other values, such as family integrity and physician responsibility.

The question of how race and ethnicity influence attitudes toward patient autonomy was studied by a team of researchers, including an internal medicine specialist and ethicist, anthropologists, translators, a statistician, and a law professor. The researchers administered questionnaires to 800 people age 65 or over in 31 senior citizen centers in Los Angeles County. An equal number came from European American, African American, Korean American, and Mexican American backgrounds.

The major finding of the study was that there are marked differences by race and ethnicity in attitudes toward patient autonomy. While 88 percent of African Americans and 87 percent of European Americans believe that a patient should

be informed of a diagnosis of cancer, the same is true of only 65 percent of Mexican Americans and 47 percent of Korean Americans. Moreover, 69 percent of European Americans and 63 percent of African Americans believe that a patient should be informed of a terminal prognosis, as compared with 48 percent of Mexican Americans and 35 percent of Korean Americans.

> Navajos believe that physicians and other healers should never offer a terminal diagnosis or use any negative language that could trouble or hurt a patient.

One reason why Korean Americans are especially opposed to hearing a terminal prognosis is their belief in the unity of mind and body. Anthropologist Kyeyoung Park, a consultant on the study, noted that this kind of truth-telling is like a death sentence to traditional Koreans because of their view that the body will react to ominous news received by the mind. Many Korean Americans believe that doctors should always be optimistic and positive in their communications with patients.

Similarly, a separate study of residents of a Navajo Indian reservation in Arizona revealed that Navajo culture places a high value on thinking and speaking in a positive way. For Navajos, language can shape

reality. Consequently, Navajos believe that physicians and other healers should never offer a terminal diagnosis or use any negative language that could trouble or hurt a patient. One highly regarded medicine man noted that the mention of death to a patient "is sharper than any needle" (Carrese and Rhodes 1995:828).

In the Los Angeles study, Korean Americans and Mexican Americans were especially likely to believe that the family (and not the patient) should be told of a terminal diagnosis and should make any decisions about the use of life-supporting technology. In the view of Dr. Leslie Blackhall, the director of the study, physicians trained in the United States "may have lost sight of the fact that, for many cultures, the family unit is more important than the individual in decision-making" (Blackhall et al. 1995:825).

The authors of the study conclude that physicians should ask patients if they wish to be informed about their illness and involved in decisions about their care—or if they prefer that family members be given such information and responsibility.

Let's Discuss

1. How has terminal illness been handled in your family? Have relatives who were dying been told the truth about their condition, or has it been withheld from them? Do you think your family's cultural background influenced the decision?
2. Which is more important, the patient's right to know or the patient's faith in the chance of recovery?

Sources: Blackhall et al. 1995; Carrese and Rhodes 1995: Monmaney 1995.

---

medicine wheel printed on them. The researchers then received much greater cooperation, presumably because the respondents felt that the medical team understood their cultural beliefs (*Los Angeles Times* 1995).

Labeling Approach

Labeling theory helps us to understand why certain people are *viewed* as deviants, "bad kids," or criminals whereas others whose behavior is similar

p. 196

are not. Labeling theorists also suggest that the designation "healthy" or "ill" generally involves social definition by others. Just as police officers, judges, and other regulators of social control have the power to define certain people as criminals, health care professionals (especially physicians) have the power to define certain people as "sick." Moreover, like labels that suggest nonconformity or criminality, labels associated with illness commonly reshape how others treat us and how we see ourselves. Our society attaches serious consequences to labels that suggest less-than-perfect physical or mental health (Becker 1963; C. Clark 1983; H. Schwartz 1987).

A historical example illustrates perhaps the ultimate extreme in labeling social behavior as a sickness. As enslavement of Africans in the United States came under increasing attack in the nineteenth century, medical authorities provided new rationalizations for this oppressive practice. Noted physicians published articles stating that the skin color of Africans deviated from "healthy" white skin coloring because Africans suffered from congenital leprosy. Moreover, the continuing efforts of enslaved Africans to escape from their White masters were classified as an example of the "disease" of drapetomania (or "crazy runaways"). The prestigious *New Orleans Medical and Surgical Journal* suggested that the remedy for this "disease" was to treat slaves kindly as one might treat children. Apparently, these medical authorities would not entertain the view that it was healthy and sane to flee slavery or join in a slave revolt (Szasz 1971).

By the late 1980s, the power of a label—"person with AIDS"—had become quite evident. As we saw in our discussion of the late Arthur Ashe, this label often p. 112 functions as a master status that overshadows all other aspects of a person's life. Once someone is told that he or she has tested positive for HIV, the virus associated with AIDS, that person is forced to confront immediate and difficult questions: Should I tell my family members, my sexual partner(s), my friends, my coworkers, my employer? How will these people respond? People's intense fear of this disease has led to prejudice and discrimination—even social ostracism—against those who have (or are suspected of having) AIDS. A person who has AIDS must deal with not only the serious med-

In 1994, former Olympic diving champion Greg Louganis revealed that he had AIDS. The label "person with AIDS" often functions as a master status, overshadowing all other aspects of a person's life.

p. 125 ical consequences of the disease, but also the distressing social consequences associated with the label.

According to labeling theorists, we can view a variety of life experiences as illnesses or not. Recently, premenstrual syndrome, posttraumatic disorders, and hyperactivity have been "labeled" medically recognized disorders. In addition, disagreements continue in the medical community over whether chronic fatigue syndrome constitutes a medical illness.

Probably the most noteworthy medical example of labeling is the case of homosexuality. For years, psychiatrists classified being gay or lesbian not as a lifestyle but as a mental disorder subject to treatment. This official sanction by the psychiatry profession became an early target of the growing gay and lesbian rights movement in the United States. In 1974, members of the American Psychiatric Association voted to drop homosexuality from the standard manual on mental disorders (Adam 1995; Charmaz and Paterniti 1999; Monteiro 1998).

The four sociological approaches described above share certain common themes. First, any person's health or illness is more than an organic condition, since it is subject to the interpretation of others. The impact of culture, family and friends, and the medical profession mean that health and illness are not purely biological occurrences but are sociological occurrences as well. Second, since members of a society (especially industrial societies) share the same health delivery system, health is a group and societal concern. Although health may be defined as the complete well-being of an individual, it is also the result of his or her social environment, as the next section will show (Cockerham 1998).

Social Epidemiology and Health

Social epidemiology is the study of the distribution of disease, impairment, and general health status across a population. Epidemiology initially concentrated on the scientific study of epidemics, focusing on how they started and spread. Contemporary social epidemiology is much broader in scope, concerned not only with epidemics but also with nonepidemic diseases, injuries, drug addiction and alcoholism, suicide, and mental illness. Epidemiology draws on the work of a wide variety of scientists and researchers, among them physicians, sociologists, public health officials, biologists, veterinarians, demographers, anthropologists, psychologists, and meteorologists. Box 19-2 examines a recent epidemiological study of the diseases associated with aging.

Recently, the federal government's Centers for Disease Control and Prevention took on the new role of tracking bioterrorism. Epidemiologists mobilized in 2001 to trace the anthrax outbreak and to prepare for any terrorist use of smallpox or other lethal microbes that could lead to an epidemic.

Researchers in social epidemiology commonly use two concepts: incidence and prevalence. *Incidence* refers to the number of *new* cases of a specific disorder occurring within a given population during a stated period of time, usually a year. For example, the incidence of AIDS in the United States in 1997 was 58,492 cases. By contrast, *prevalence* refers to the total number of cases of a specific disorder that exist at a given time. The prevalence of AIDS in the United States in January 2000 was about 270,000 cases (Centers for Disease Control and Prevention 2000b).

When incidence figures are presented as rates, or as the number of reports per 100,000 people, they are called *morbidity rates.* (The term *mortality rate,* you will recall, refers to the incidence of *death* in a given population.) Sociologists find morbidity rates useful because they reveal that a specific disease occurs more frequently among one segment of a population than another. As we shall see, social class, race, ethnicity, gender, and age can all affect a population's morbidity rates. In 1999, the U.S. Department of Health and Human Services, recognizing the inequality inherent in U.S. morbidity and mortality rates, launched the Campaign for 100% Access and Zero Health Disparities, an ambitious undertaking (Bureau of Primary Health Care 1999).

Social Class

Social class is clearly associated with differences in morbidity and mortality rates. Studies in the United States and other countries have consistently shown that people in the lower classes have higher rates of mortality and disability (see Figure 19-3). A study published in 1998 documents the impact of class on mortality. The authors concluded that Americans whose family incomes were less than $10,000 could expect to die seven years sooner than those with incomes of at least $25,000 (Pamuk et al. 1998:5).

Why is class linked to health? Crowded living conditions, substandard housing, poor diet, and stress all contribute to the ill health of many low-income people in the United States. In certain instances, poor education may lead to a lack of awareness of measures necessary to maintain good health. Financial strains are certainly a major factor in the health problems of less affluent people in the United States.

Another reason for the link of class to health is that the poor—many of whom belong to racial and ethnic minorities—are less able to afford quality medical care. As Figure 19-4 shows, the affluent are more likely to have health insurance, either because they can afford it or because they have jobs that provide it. We will explore the high costs of medical care more fully later in this chapter.

Figure 19-3

Days of Disability by Family Income

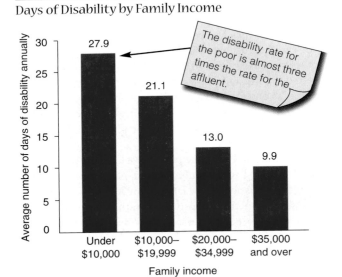

The disability rate for the poor is almost three times the rate for the affluent.

Source: Bureau of the Census 2000a:135.

> **Think About It**
> What factors might account for the higher disability rate among the poor?

At age 93, Sister Nicolette reads, crochets, plays cards, and, until a recent fall, walked several miles a day. Her younger sibling, Sister Mary Ursula, is confined to a wheelchair and can barely lift her head or hands: She is a victim of Alzheimer's disease. Both these real-life sisters had a similar family background and both lived for most of their lives in the same Roman Catholic convent under the same conditions. Why is one so robust and the other so afflicted?

This is one question that Dr. David Snowdon, a scientist at the University of Kentucky, hopes to answer from his long-term study of an order of nuns living in Mankato, Minnesota. He is particularly interested in detecting causes of Alzheimer's disease and in finding ways to delay or prevent its onset. Snowdon started studying the lives of the 678 nuns in 1986, when the sisters ranged in age from 75 to 103. As of 2001, 295 were alive, all were over 85, and some were suffering from Alzheimer's and other diseases of the brain while others were entirely free.

The order of nuns presents an ideal research group for an epidemiological study because the participants lead such similar lives. They eat the same meals, they receive the same health care, none smoke, they drink very little alcohol, none of them have experienced physical changes associated with pregnancy, and most of them were teachers. These similarities allow the researchers to discount some factors that often contribute to illness, such as diet deficiency or smoking. It is also significant that the entire group is made up of aging women. In the past, most medical research of this type had concentrated on White middle-aged men, despite the fact that women constitute the great majority of the elderly population.

Snowdon examines the nuns each year, taking blood samples and testing cognitive ability to trace the course of their health. He also persuaded the nuns to donate their brains after they died because a brain autopsy is the only sure way to diagnose Alzheimer's disease. Although all this information was helpful to Snowdon, he still had to rely on the nuns' memories to establish facts of their background *before* they entered the order, and memories in the elderly can be unreliable, especially among those afflicted with brain disease. Then he ran across a treasure

> The order of nuns presents an ideal research group for an epidemiological study because the participants lead such similar lives.

trove of data—archives in the convent documenting the births, parentage, and socioeconomic backgrounds of the nuns. These data helped to establish the health risk factors for each nun earlier in her life.

Perhaps the most valuable research tools in the archives were autobiographies written by the applicants to the convent when they were in their twenties. From examining these writings and looking at the current health status of the nuns, Snowdon concluded that an active intellectual life, an ability to express oneself with complex ideas, and a positive outlook all correlated with healthy aging and a long life. Sister Nicolette's autobi-

ography, for example, written when she was 20, included this sentence: "After I finished the eighth grade in 1921 I desired to become an aspirant at Mankato but I myself did not have the courage to ask the permission of my parents so Sister Agreda did it in my stead and they readily gave their consent." Contrast this complex thought with a sentence from another nun's autobiographical statement: "After I left school, I worked in the post office." This nun, now in her 90s, has performed steadily worse on her memory tests (Belluck 2001).

Snowdon has found other factors associated with healthy aging, including a good diet and avoiding stroke-causing behavior, and he does not discount the value of spiritual and communal living. But he hopes other studies will back up his findings about the importance of early language ability and a positive emotional outlook in preventive health care.

Let's Discuss

1. What are the advantages of using an order of nuns as participants in an epidemiological study? What other groups might provide the same kind of advantages? Do you think a similar study should be conducted with men? Why or why not?

2. Are you close to anyone suffering from Alzheimer's disease? What do you know about that person's background that might have contributed to the disease? Conversely, among those you know who are healthy in their old age, what in their background has kept them healthy, in your opinion?

Sources: Belluck 2001; Lemonick and Mankato 2001; Nun Study 2001; Snowdon 2001.

Another factor in the link between class and health is evident at the workplace: The occupations of people in the working and lower classes of the United States tend to be more dangerous than those of more affluent citizens. Miners, for example, risk injury or death from explosions and cave-ins; they are also vulnerable to respiratory diseases such as black lung. Workers in textile mills exposed to toxic substances may contract a variety of illnesses, including one disease commonly known as *brown lung disease*. In recent years, the nation has learned of the perils

Figure 19-4

Percentage of People without Health Insurance, 2000

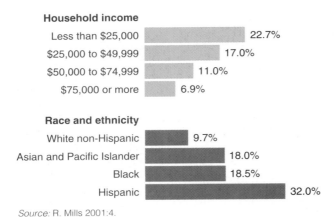

Household income

Less than $25,000   22.7%
$25,000 to $49,999   17.0%
$50,000 to $74,999   11.0%
$75,000 or more   6.9%

Race and ethnicity

White non-Hispanic   9.7%
Asian and Pacific Islander   18.0%
Black   18.5%
Hispanic   32.0%

Source: R. Mills 2001:4.

of asbestos poisoning, a particular worry for construction workers (Hall 1982).

In the view of Karl Marx and contemporary conflict theorists, capitalist societies such as the United States care more about maximizing profits than they do about the health and safety of industrial workers. As a result, government agencies do not take forceful action to regulate conditions in the workplace, and workers suffer many preventable, job-related injuries and illnesses. Research also shows that the lower classes are more vulnerable to environmental pollution than the affluent, not only where they work but also where they live. (See Chapter 21 for a discussion of environmental justice.)

Race and Ethnicity

Health profiles of many racial and ethnic minorities reflect the social inequality evident in the United States. The poor economic and environmental conditions of groups such as African Americans, Hispanics, and Native Americans are manifested in high morbidity and mortality rates for these groups. So dramatic are these differences that the federal government in 1998 launched an initiative to end long-standing racial and ethnic health disparities by the year 2010. It is true that some afflictions, such as sickle-cell anemia among Blacks, have a clear genetic basis. But in most instances, environmental factors contribute to the differential rates of disease and death.

In many respects, the mortality rates for African Americans are distressing. Compared with Whites, Blacks have higher death rates from diseases of the heart, pneumonia, diabetes, and cancer. The death rate from strokes is twice as high among African Americans. Such epidemiological findings reflect in part the fact that a higher proportion of Blacks are found among the nation's lower classes. According to the National Center for Health Statistics (2001), Whites can expect to live 77.2 years. By contrast, life expectancy for Blacks is 71.1 years.

As noted earlier, infant mortality is regarded as a primary indicator of health care, but there is a significant gap in the United States between the infant mortality rates of African Americans and Whites. Generally, the rate of infant deaths is more than twice as high among Blacks. African Americans account for 15 percent of all live births in the nation but 31 percent of infant deaths. Hispanics and Native Americans have infant mortality rates lower than African Americans but higher than Whites (National Center for Health Statistics 2001).

Medical treatment is not exempt from racism. The media often focus on obvious forms of racism such as hate crimes, and overlook the more insidious forms in social institutions like the medical establishment. One study of differential treatment analyzed records of about 40,000 Medicare beneficiaries. Comparing White and Black patients of the *same* social class and experiencing *similar* medical conditions, the study found that White patients were 40 percent more likely to undergo a lifesaving procedure known as cardiac catherization (Chen et al. 2001).

Drawing on the conflict perspective, sociologist Howard Waitzkin (1986) suggests that racial tensions contribute to the medical problems of Blacks. In his view, the stress resulting from racial prejudice and discrimination helps to explain the higher rates of hypertension found among African Americans (and Hispanics) compared with Whites. Hypertension—twice as common in Blacks as in Whites—is believed to be a critical factor in Blacks' high mortality rates from heart disease, kidney disease, and stroke (Morehouse Medical Treatment Effectiveness Center 1999).

Some Mexican Americans as well as many other Latinos adhere to cultural beliefs that make them less likely to use the established medical system. They may interpret their illnesses according to traditional Latino folk practices, or **curanderismo**—a form of holistic health care and healing. Curanderismo influences how one approaches health care and even how one defines illness. Most Hispanics probably use folk healers, or *curanderos*, infrequently, but perhaps 20 percent rely on home remedies. Some illnesses are defined according to folk beliefs, such as *susto* (fright sickness) and *atague* (or fighting attack). Because these complaints often have biological bases, sensitive medical practitioners need to deal with them carefully and diagnose and treat illnesses accurately (Council on Scientific Affairs 1991; Trotter and Chavira 1997).

A Mexican folk healer administers remedies for lethargy, including herbs, flowers, and an egg. About 20 percent of Hispanics rely on home remedies such as these for their ailments.

Gender

A large body of research indicates that, in comparison with men, women experience a higher prevalence of many illnesses, though they tend to live longer. There are variations—for example, men are more likely to have parasitic diseases whereas women are more likely to become diabetic—but, as a group, women appear to be in poorer health than men.

The apparent inconsistency between the ill health of women and their greater longevity deserves an explanation, and researchers have advanced a theory. Women's lower rate of cigarette smoking (reducing their risk of heart disease, lung cancer, and emphysema), lower consumption of alcohol (reducing the risk of auto accidents and cirrhosis of the liver), and lower rates of employment in dangerous occupations explain about one-third of their greater longevity than men. Moreover, some clinical studies suggest that the differences in morbidity may actually be less pronounced than the data show. Researchers argue that women are much more likely than men to seek treatment, to be diagnosed as having diseases, and thus to have their illnesses reflected in data examined by epidemiologists.

From a conflict perspective, women have been particularly vulnerable to the medicalization of society, with everything from birth to beauty treated in an increasingly medical context. Such medicalization may contribute to women's higher morbidity rates as compared with those of men. Ironically, even though women have been especially affected by medicalization, medical researchers have often excluded women from clinical studies. Female physicians and researchers charge that sexism is at the heart of such research practices and insist that there is a desperate need for studies with female subjects. That is one reason for the significance of the long-term nun study, described in Box 19-2.

In 1992, the National Institutes of Health (NIH) established an Office of Research on Women. Its task is to ensure that adequate numbers of women serve both as researchers and as participants in taxpayer-supported studies. Recent studies, however, confirm that women still are sometimes neglected by the medical establishment. Even federally funded clinical research ignores the requirement since 1993 that their data be analyzed to see if women and men respond differently. Similarly, a content analysis of medical journals in the 1990s found that the published research focused primarily on men: no studies excluded men, 20 percent excluded women, and another 30 percent failed to report the findings from female participants (Bates 1999; General Accounting Office 2000; McDonald 1999; Vidaver et al. 2000).

Age

Health is the overriding concern of the elderly. Most older people in the United States report having at least one chronic illness, but only some of these conditions are potentially life threatening or require medical care. At the same time, health problems can affect the quality of life of older people in important ways. Almost half of older people in the United States are troubled by arthritis, and many have visual or hearing impairments that can interfere with the performance of everyday tasks.

Older people are also especially vulnerable to certain types of mental health problems. Alzheimer's disease, the leading cause of dementia in the United States, afflicts an estimated 4 million older people (see Box 19-2). While some individuals with Alzheimer's exhibit only mild symptoms, the risk of severe problems resulting from this disease rises substantially with age. Only 10 percent of people age 65 or over have symptoms of Alzheimer's, but that figure rises to 48 percent of people age 85 and over (Alzheimer's Association 1999).

Not surprisingly, older people in the United States use health services more often than younger people. In 1997, younger people age 15 to 24 visited physicians an average of less than two times a year, compared to more than six annual visits for those 75 and over. Similar

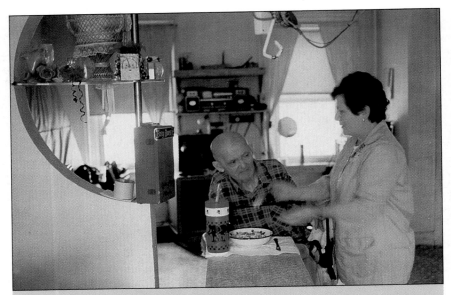

Health problems afflicting the aging population in the United States put pressure on the health care system, including providing enough home health care managers such as the one pictured here in a Pennsylvania household.

the trillion-dollar threshold—more than four times the 1980 figure (see Figure 19-6). In 2000, the amount we spent on health care equaled that spent on education, defense, prisons, farm subsidies, food stamps, and foreign aid combined. By the year 2010, total expenditures for health care in the United States are expected to exceed $2.6 trillion.

The rising costs of medical care are especially burdensome in the event of catastrophic illnesses or confinement in a nursing home. Bills of tens of thousands of dollars are not unusual in the treatment of cancer, Alzheimer's disease, and other chronic illnesses requiring custodial care. As of 2000, drugs used in the United States to combat the HIV virus associated with AIDS could easily cost about $65,000 per patient per year. Health costs in the United States have escalated in part because of the increasing use of expensive technology. For example, the CAT scanner, a direct descendant of the X-ray machine, uses a computer to integrate pictures shot from various angles into a single, multidimensional image of a skull (Sawyer 2000).

The health care system of the United States has moved far beyond the days when general practitioners living in a neighborhood or community typically made house calls and charged modest fees for their services. How did health care become big business involving nationwide hospital chains and marketing campaigns? How have these changes reshaped typical interactions between doctors, nurses, and patients? We will address these questions in the next section of the chapter.

discrepancies show up in rates of hospitalization. Twenty-three percent of people hospitalized in the United States were age 75 and over, while people age 15 to 24 accounted for only 9 percent of those hospitalized. The disproportionate use of the health care system in the United States by older people is a critical factor in all discussions about the cost of health care and possible reforms of the health care system (Bureau of the Census 1999a:134, 138).

In sum, to achieve the goal of 100 percent access and zero health disparities, federal health officials must overcome inequities that are rooted not just in age, but in social class, race and ethnicity, and gender. If that were not enough, they must also deal with a geographical disparity in health care resources. Figure 19-5 shows the differences in the presence of physicians from one state to another. Dramatic differences in the availability of physicians, hospitals, and nursing homes also exist between urban and rural areas within the same state. In the next section we will look more closely at issues surrounding the delivery of health care in the United States.

● Health Care in the United States

As the entire nation is well aware, the costs of health care have skyrocketed in the last 35 years. In 1997, total expenditures for health care in the United States crossed

A Historical View

Today, state licensing and medical degrees confer an authority on medical professionals, which is maintained from one generation to the next. However, health care in the United States has not always followed this model. The "popular health movement" of the 1830s and 1840s emphasized preventive care and what is termed "self-help." There was strong criticism of "doctoring" as a paid occupation. New medical philosophies or sects established their own medical schools and challenged the authority and methods of more traditional doctors. By the 1840s, most states had repealed medical licensing laws. However, through the leadership of the American Medical Association

Figure 19-5

Availability of Physicians by State

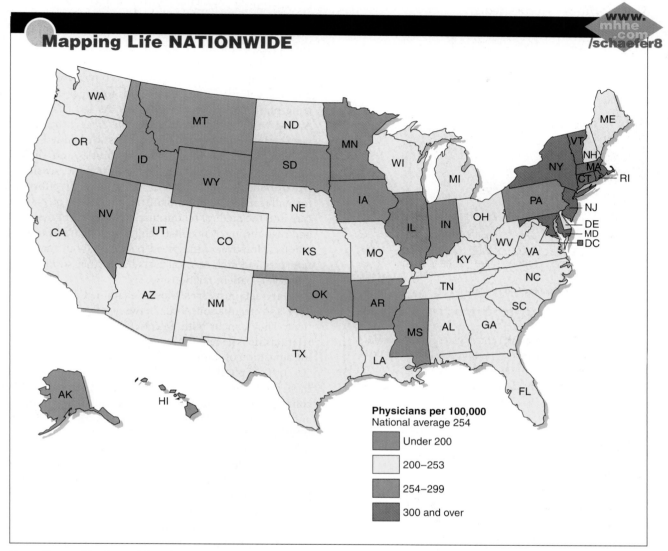

Mapping Life NATIONWIDE

Physicians per 100,000
National average 254

- Under 200
- 200–253
- 254–299
- 300 and over

Source: Bureau of the Census 2001a:106.

(AMA), founded in 1848, "regular" doctors attacked lay practitioners, sectarian doctors, and female physicians in general. (For a different view, see Navarro 1984.)

Once authority was institutionalized through standardized programs of education and licensing, it was conferred upon all who successfully completed these programs. The authority of the physician no longer depended on lay attitudes or the person occupying the sick role; it was increasingly built into the structure of the medical profession and the health care system. As the institutionalization of health care proceeded, the medical profession gained control over both the market for its services and the various organizational hierarchies that govern medical practice, financing, and policymaking. By the 1920s, physicians controlled hospital technology, the division of labor of health personnel, and, indirectly, other professional practices such as nursing and pharmacy (Coser 1984).

Physicians, Nurses, and Patients

Physicians traditionally have a position of dominance in their dealings with both patients and nurses. The functionalist and interactionist perspectives combine to offer a framework for understanding the professional socialization

Figure 19-6

Total Health Care Expenditures in the United States, 1970–2010 (projected)

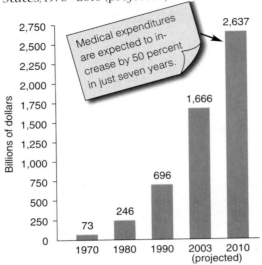

Medical expenditures are expected to increase by 50 percent in just seven years.

Source: Health Care Financing Administration 2001.

Think About It

What social changes in the United States might account for the rise in health care costs from $73 billion in 1970 to more than $1.5 trillion in 2003?

of physicians as it relates to patient care. Functionalists suggest that established physicians and medical school professors serve as mentors or role models who transmit knowledge, skills, and values to the passive learner—the medical student. Interactionists emphasize that students are molded by the medical school environment as they interact with their classmates.

Both approaches argue that the typical training of physicians in the United States leads to rather dehumanizing physician–patient encounters. As Dr. Lori Arviso Alvord writes in *The Scalpel and the Silver Bear,* "I had been trained by a group of physicians who placed much more emphasis on their technical abilities and clinical skills than on their abilities to be caring and sensitive" (Alvord and Van Pelt 1999:13). Despite many efforts to formally introduce a humanistic dimension of patient care into the medical school curriculum, patient overload and cost-cutting by hospitals tend to undercut positive relations. Moreover, widespread publicity about malpractice suits and high medical costs has further strained the physician–patient relationship.

Interactionists have closely examined how compliance and negotiation occur between physician and patient. They concur with Talcott Parsons's view that the relationship is generally asymmetrical, with doctors holding a position of dominance and control of rewards.

Just as physicians have maintained dominance in their interactions with patients, doctors have similarly controlled interactions with nurses. Despite their training and professional status, nurses commonly take orders p. 315 from physicians. Traditionally, the relationship between doctors and nurses has paralleled the male dominance of the United States: Most physicians have been male, whereas virtually all nurses have been female.

Like other women in subordinate roles, nurses have been expected to perform their duties without challenging the authority of men. Psychiatrist Leonard Stein (1967) refers to this process as the *doctor–nurse game.* According to the rules of this "game," the nurse must never disagree openly with the physician. When she has recommendations concerning a patient's care, she must communicate them indirectly in a deferential tone. For example, if asked by a hospital's medical resident, "What sleeping medication has been helpful to Mrs. Brown in the past?" (an indirect request for a recommendation), the nurse will respond with a disguised recommendation statement, such as "Pentobarbital mg 100 was quite effective night before last." Her careful response allows the physician to authoritatively restate the same prescription as if it were *his* idea.

Like nurses, female physicians have traditionally found themselves in a subordinate position because of gender. According to 2000 data, while 44 percent of all medical school graduates in the United States were female, 73 percent of all medical school faculty members were male (Association of American Medical Colleges 2000a, 2000b).

A study of male and female medical residents suggests that the increasing number of women physicians may alter the traditional doctor–patient relationship. Male residents were found to be more focused on the intellectual challenges of medicine and the prestige associated with certain medical specialties. By contrast, female residents were more likely to express a commitment to caring for patients and devoting time to them. In terms of the functionalist analysis of gender stratification offered by sociologists Talcott Parsons and Robert Bales, male residents took the *instrumental,* achievement-oriented role, while female residents took the *expressive,* interpersonal-oriented role. As women continue to enter and move higher in the hierarchies of the medical profession, there will surely be sociological studies to see if these apparent gender differences persist (Geckler 1995).

Patients have traditionally relied on medical personnel to inform them of health care issues, but increasingly they are now turning to the media for health care information. Recognizing this change, pharmaceutical firms are advertising their prescription drugs directly to potential customers through television and magazine advertisements. The Internet is also a growing source for patient information.

Medical professionals are understandably suspicious of these new sources of information. A study published in the *Journal of the American Medical Association* in 2001 found health information on the Internet often incomplete and inaccurate, even on the best sites. Nevertheless, there is little doubt that web research is transforming an increasing proportion of patient–physician encounters, as patients arrive for their doctor's appointments armed with the latest printout from the Internet (Berland 2001).

Imagine
www.mhhe.com/schaefer8

If you were a patient, would you put yourself entirely in the physician's hands? Or would you do some research about your illness on your own? If you were a doctor, would you want your patient checking medical information on Internet sites? Explain your positions.

Alternatives to Traditional Health Care

In traditional forms of health care, people rely on physicians and hospitals for treatment of illness. Yet at least one out of every three adults in the United States attempts to maintain good health or respond to illness through use of alternative health care techniques. For example, in recent decades there has been growing interest in *holistic* (this term is also spelled *wholistic*) medical principles first developed in China. **Holistic medicine** refers to therapies in which the health care practitioner considers the person's physical, mental, emotional, and spiritual characteristics. The individual is regarded as a totality, rather than as a collection of interrelated organ systems. Treatment methodologies include massage, chiropractic medicine, acupuncture (which involves the insertion of fine needles into surface points), respiratory exercises, and the use of herbs as remedies. Nutrition, exercise, and visualization may also be used to treat ailments generally treated through medication or hospitalization (Sharma and Bodeker 1998).

The Navajo concept of *hózhó* (Walking in Beauty) is another example of a holistic approach to health (see the chapter introduction, page 472). Practitioners of holistic medicine do not necessarily function totally outside the traditional health care system. Some, like Dr. Lori Arviso Alvord, have medical degrees and rely on X-rays and EKG machines for diagnostic assistance. Other holistic clinics, often referred to as *wellness clinics,* reject the use of medical technology. The recent resurgence of holistic medicine comes amidst a widespread recognition of the value of nutrition and the dangers of overreliance on prescription drugs (especially those used to reduce stress, such as Valium).

The medical establishment—professional organizations, research hospitals, and medical schools—has generally served as a stern protector of traditionally accepted health care techniques. However, a major breakthrough occurred in 1992 when the federal government's National Institutes of Health—the nation's major funding source for biomedical research—opened an Office of Alternative Medicine, empowered to accept grant requests. Possible areas of study include herbal medicine, mind–body control techniques, and the use of electromagnetism to heal bones. A national study published in *The Journal of the American Medical Association* indicates that 46 percent of the general public uses alternative medicine. Most of it is not covered by insurance. In fact, out-of-pocket expenses for alternative medicine match all out-of-pocket expenses for traditional physician services (Eisenberg et al. 1998; Stolberg 2000).

In some cases, movements for political change have generated health care alternatives. For example, as part of the larger feminist movement beginning in the 1960s, women voiced their dissatisfaction with the traditional health care system. The appearance of the book *Our Bodies, Ourselves* (Boston Women's Health Book Collective 1969, 1992) marked the emergence of the contemporary women's health movement. Women realized that they are by far the most frequent users of health services for

p. 307

Taking Sociology to Work

ERIKA MILES:
Director, Health Programs, CVS.com

"Health care has always fascinated me, and I was lucky enough to discover medical sociology," says Erika Miles. Right after graduating from Colgate University in 1992, Miles worked three years for the Robert Wood Johnson Foundation as a quantitative research assistant, doing studies on physician behavior and underserved populations. Just as Miles was starting graduate school, she discovered the Internet and was hooked. She dropped her graduate studies, taught herself web design, and started doing Internet marketing for various pharmaceutical companies. At CVS.com, an online pharmacy in Seattle, she develops corporate strategies for working with pharmaceutical companies, health care providers, and other Internet companies.

Developing websites in health care has a lot to do with sociology, according to Miles. "Much of the work is really thinking about how people work, act, and react to their surroundings, their families, and their work environments—and how all that relates to their health." She also does "a ton of qualitative and quantitative research," and credits her undergraduate sociology courses with helping her with that aspect of her work.

Miles basically just fell into being a sociology major after starting out with a 200-level course on peace and social change movements, which she loved. "Sociology just made sense, which is more than I can say for a lot of other classes I took." Miles believes that a sociology degree has great potential because it can apply to many different fields. "It is a degree that really helps you learn how to think about the people around you."

Miles's advice to students is to take research classes and write a thesis, whether they are required to or not. "That is really where you get to apply what you've learned."

Let's Discuss

1. What sociological skills might Erika Miles use in developing websites in health care?
2. Are you planning on taking any research classes and/or writing a thesis? How might they be valuable to you in the career of your choosing?

---

themselves, their children, and other dependent family members. Activists agree that women should assume more responsibility for decisions concerning their health. The movement therefore has taken many forms, including organizations working for changes in the health care system, women's clinics, and "self-help" groups.

The goals of the women's health movement are ambitious, but the health care system has proved to be fairly resistant to change. Conflict theorists point out that physicians, medical schools, hospitals, and drug companies all have a vested interest in keeping women in a rather dependent and uninformed position as health care consumers. Despite an increase in female doctors, women remain underrepresented in all key positions in the health care system of the United States.

The Role of Government

It was not until the twentieth century that health care received federal aid. The first significant involvement was the 1946 Hill-Burton Act, which provided subsidies for building and improving hospitals, especially in rural areas. A far more important change came with the enactment in 1965 of two wide-ranging government assistance programs: Medicare, which is essentially a compulsory health insurance plan for the elderly; and Medicaid,

which is a noncontributory federal and state insurance plan for the poor. These programs greatly expanded federal involvement in health care financing for needy men, women, and children. In addition, more than 1,000 government-subsidized community health centers are located in low-income, medically underserved communities (Blendon 1986).

Given rates of illness and disability among elderly people, Medicare has had a huge impact on the health care system. Initially, Medicare simply reimbursed health care providers such as physicians and hospitals for the billed costs of their services. However, as the overall costs of Medicare increased dramatically, the federal government introduced a price-control system in 1983. All illnesses were classified into diagnostic-related groups (DRGs); a reimbursement rate was set for each condition and remained fixed regardless of the individual needs of any patient. In effect, the federal government told hospitals and doctors that it would no longer be concerned with their costs in treating Medicare patients; it would reimburse them only to a designated level (Wynia et al. 2000).

The DRG system of reimbursement has contributed to the controversial practice of "dumping." Under this system, private hospitals transfer patients whose treatment may be unprofitable to public facilities. Many private hospitals in the United States have begun to conduct "wallet biopsies" to investigate the financial status of potential patients. Those judged as undesirable are then refused admission or are dumped. A federal law passed in 1987 made it illegal for any hospital receiving Medicare funds to dump patients, but the practice continues. We will look further into the government's role in health care in the social policy section of this chapter (Feinglass 1987; Sherrill 1995).

Mental Illness in the United States

The words *mental illness* and *insanity* evoke dramatic and often inaccurate images of emotional problems. The media routinely emphasize the most violent behavior of those with disturbances, but mental health and mental illness can more appropriately be viewed as a continuum of behavior that we ourselves move along. Using a less sensational definition, we can consider a person to have a mental disorder "if he or she is so disturbed that coping with routine, everyday life is difficult or impossible." The term **mental illness** should be reserved for a disorder of the brain that disrupts a person's thinking, feeling, and ability to interact with others (Coleman and Cressey 1980: 315; National Alliance for the Mentally Ill 2000).

How prevalent is mental illness? The World Bank finds that in industrial economies, mental disorders account for 4 of the 10 leading causes of disability. In the United States, the Surgeon General estimates that every year, one out of every five Americans suffers from some form of mental illness. The most common disorders include depression, anxiety disorders, and obsessive-compulsive disorders (National Institute of Mental Health 1999).

People in the United States have traditionally maintained a negative and suspicious view of those with mental disorders. Holding the status of "mental patient" or even "former mental patient" can have unfortunate and undeserved consequences. For example, during the 1972 election campaign, the Democratic vice presidential nominee, Senator Thomas Eagleton of Missouri, admitted to having once received treatment for depression. Public reaction was so strong that presidential nominee George McGovern was forced to drop Eagleton from the Democratic ticket.

Politics is not the only arena where people viewed as mentally ill experience second-class treatment. Voting rights are denied in some instances, acceptance for jury duty is problematic, and past emotional problems are an issue in divorce and custody cases. Moreover, content analysis of network television programs and films shows

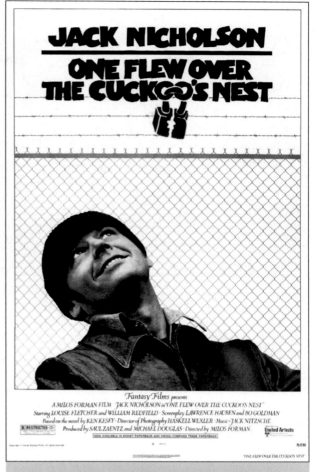

Media emphasis on extreme mental disorders contributes to the stigmatization of mental health issues. This 1975 film featured severe forms of mental illness and portrayed medical practitioners as able to offer little assistance.

mentally ill characters uniformly portrayed in a demeaning and derogatory fashion; many are labeled as "criminally insane," "wackos," or "psychos." From an interactionist perspective, a key social institution is shaping social behavior by manipulating symbols and thereby intensifying people's fears about the mentally ill (Burton 1990; DeFleur and Dennis 1981; Link 1987).

Theoretical Models of Mental Disorders

In studying mental illness, we can draw on both a medical model and a more sociological approach derived from labeling theory. Each model offers distinctive assumptions regarding treatment of people with mental disorders.

According to the *medical model*, mental illness is rooted in biological causes that can be treated through

Social factors such as war can be hazardous to your mental health. Many people who once lived in war zones, like these Rwandans fleeing the horrors of genocide, later suffer from symptoms of severe mental trauma, including depression, nightmares, and flashbacks to violent events.

medical intervention. Problems in brain structure or in the biochemical balance in the brain, sometimes due to injury and sometimes to genetic inheritance, are thought to be at the bottom of these disorders. The Surgeon General of the United States (1999) released an exhaustive report on mental health in which he declared that the accumulated weight of scientific evidence leaves no doubt about the physical origins of mental illness.

That is not to say that social factors do not contribute to mental illness. Just as culture affects the incidence and prevalence of illness in general, its treatment, and the expression of certain culture-bound syndromes, so too it can affect mental illness. In fact, the very definition of mental illness differs from one culture to the next. Mainstream United States culture, for instance, considers hallucinations highly abnormal. But many traditional cultures view them as evidence of divine favor and confer a special status on those who experience them. As we have noted throughout this textbook, a given behavior may be viewed as normal in one society, disapproved of but tolerated in a second, and labeled as "sick" and heavily sanctioned in a third.

In contrast to the medical model, *labeling theory* suggests that mental illness is not really an "illness," since the individual's problems arise from living in society and not from physical maladies. For example, the Surgeon General's report (1999:5) notes that "bereavement symptoms" of less than two months' duration do not qualify as a

mental disorder, but beyond that they may be redefined. Sociologists would see this approach to bereavement as labeling by those with the power to affix labels rather than as an acknowledgment of a biological condition.

Psychiatrist Thomas Szasz (1974), in his book *The Myth of Mental Illness,* which first appeared in 1961, advanced the view that numerous personality disorders are not "diseases," but simply patterns of conduct labeled as disorders by significant others. The response to Szasz's challenging thesis was sharp: The commissioner of the New York State Department of Hygiene demanded his dismissal from his university position because Szasz did not "believe" in mental illness. But many sociologists embraced his model as a logical extension of examining individual behavior in a social context.

Although labeling will not typically "make sane people insane," it undoubtedly causes mentally ill patients to feel devalued by the larger society. And the more they believe they are being negatively labeled, the more difficult they will find it to interact with others. Some mentally ill people may keep their problems and treatment a secret and may withdraw from social contacts. Such coping strategies to deal with labeling can cause problems at work, with family and friends, and in one's own self-esteem (Cockerham 1998; for a different view, see Gove 1980; Link et al. 1989).

The medical model is persuasive because it pinpoints causes of mental illness and treatment for disorders. Yet proponents of the labeling perspective maintain that mental illness is a distinctively social process, whatever other processes are involved. From a sociological perspective, the ideal approach to mental illness integrates the insights of labeling theory with those of the medical approach (Scheff 1999).

Patterns of Care

For most of human history, those suffering from mental disorders were deemed the responsibility of their families. Yet mental illness has been a matter of governmental concern much longer than physical illness has. This is because severe emotional disorders threaten stable social relationships and entail prolonged incapacitation. As early as the 1600s, European cities began to confine the insane in public facilities along with the poor and criminals. Prisoners, indignant at being forced to live with "lunatics," resisted this approach. The isolation of the mentally ill from others in the same facility and from the larger society soon made physicians the central and ultimate authority for their welfare.

In the United States, the period of the 1840s and 1850s was the "age of the asylum." Before 1810, only a few states had institutions for the mentally ill, but by 1860, 28 of the nation's 33 states had such public facilities. At the time, the asylum was touted as a humanitarian and even utopian institution that would rehabilitate the suffering and serve as a model facility for the rest of society. Its social structure emphasized discipline, neatness, fixed schedules, and work assignments for patients. Existing relationships were deemphasized; families were discouraged from visiting with patients because they would disrupt hospital routines (Perrucci 1974; Rothman 1971).

At a community mental health center, outpatients create a newsletter for their day program. In the 1980s, community-based mental health care replaced hospitalization as the typical form of treatment for people with serious mental illnesses.

The residential mental hospital is an example of a total institution in which people are removed from the larger society for an appreciable period of time. Drawing on the work of Erving Goffman, Harold Garfinkel (1956) revealed that people in total institutions undergo "degradation ceremonies" that strip them of their identities, destroy personal dignity, and often lead to confusion and distress. From a functionalist perspective, the crowding and depersonalization inherent in mental hospitals are dysfunctional to the resolution of emotional problems.

p. 94

A major policy development in caring for those with mental disorders came with the passage of the 1963 Community Mental Health Centers Act. The CMHC program, as it is known, not only increased federal government involvement in the treatment of the mentally ill. It also established community-based mental health centers to treat clients on an *outpatient* basis, thereby allowing them to continue working and living at home. The program showed that outpatient treatment could be more effective than the institutionalized programs of state and county mental hospitals.

The expansion of the federally funded CMHC program decreased inpatient care. By the 1980s, community-based mental health care had replaced hospitalization as the typical form of treatment. The deinstitutionalization of the mentally ill reached dramatic proportions across the United States. Whereas state mental hospitals had held almost 560,000 long-term patients in 1955, by 1998 they held fewer than 63,000 patients. Deinstitutionalization was often defended as a social reform that would effectively reintegrate the mentally ill into the outside world. This authentic humanitarian concern behind deinstitutionalization proved to be convenient for politicians whose goal was simply cost cutting (Bureau of the Census 2000a:134; Grob 1995).

In a marked shift from public policy over the last three decades, several states have recently made it easier to commit mental patients involuntarily to hospitals. These changes have come in part because community groups and individual residents have voiced increasing fear and anger about the growing number of mentally ill homeless people living in their midst (and often on the streets). All too often, the severely mentally ill end up in jail or prison after committing crimes that lead to their prosecution. Ironically, family members of these mentally ill men and women complain that they cannot get adequate treatment for their loved ones *until* they have committed violent acts. Nevertheless, civil liberties advocates and voluntary associations consisting of mentally ill people worry about the risks of denying people their constitutional rights and cite horror stories about the abuses people experience during institutionalization (Marquis and Morain 1999; Shogren 1994).

The Issue

Cindy Martin died in 1990 at age 26, after four months of surgery and intensive care at Presbyterian Hospital in Pittsburgh. In the aftermath of her death, her husband's insurance company received a bill for $1.25 million. While accountants attempted to untangle the costs of seven surgical procedures performed on Cindy Martin—including heart, liver, and kidney transplants—this case underscored troubling issues regarding the high cost of health care. Who should pay for the expensive medical procedures? What role, if any, should government play in providing medical care and health insurance for its citizens? (Freudenheim 1990)

In many developing nations of the world, health care issues center on very basic needs of primary care. The goals established at the UN's World Health Assembly in 1981 were modest by North American standards: safe water in the home or within 15 minutes' walking distance; immunization against major infectious diseases; availability of essential drugs within an hour's walk or travel; and the presence of trained personnel for pregnancy and childbirth. While some areas have made significant progress, many developing countries have seen little improvement; in some places, health care has deteriorated (World Bank 1997b).

The focus of this social policy section, however, is on those industrialized (or developed) nations where the *availability* of health care is really not an issue. The question is more one of accessibility and affordability. What steps are being taken to make the available services reachable and affordable?

The Setting

The United States is now the only Western industrial democracy that does not treat health care as a basic right. According to the Bureau of the Census in 2000, some 43 million people in the United States had no health insurance the entire year. The uninsured typically include self-employed people with limited incomes, illegal immigrants, and single and divorced mothers who are the sole providers for their families. As we saw in Figure 19-4 earlier, African Americans, Asian Americans, and Hispanics are less likely than Whites to carry private health insurance. Although people with lower incomes are least likely to be covered, substantial numbers of households at all income levels go without coverage for some or most of any given year (Mills 2000).

National health insurance is a general term for legislative proposals that focus on ways to provide the entire population with health care services. First discussed by government officials in the United States in the 1930s, it has come to mean many different things, ranging from narrow health insurance coverage with minimal federal subsidies to broad coverage with large-scale federal funding.

Opponents of national health insurance insist that it would be extremely costly and would lead to significant tax increases. Defenders counter, however, that other countries have maintained broad governmental health coverage for decades:

- Great Britain's National Health Service is almost totally tax-supported, and health care services are free to all citizens.
- Under Sweden's national health system, medical care is delivered primarily by publicly funded hospitals and clinics, while a national health insurance

system sets fees for health care services and reimburses providers of health care.

- Although Canadians rely on private physicians and hospitals for day-to-day treatment, health care is guaranteed as a right for all citizens. Income taxes finance public medical insurance, medical fees are set by the government, and private health insurance is prohibited.

Ironically, while these countries offer extensive health coverage for all citizens, the United States has higher health care costs than any other nation: an average annual cost of $4,108 per person, compared with $1,824 in Canada and only $1,597 in Great Britain. As Figure 19-7 shows, most industrial nations finance a substantially larger share of health care costs through public expenditures than does the United States (World Bank 2001a:98–100).

Sociological Insights

As conflict theorists suggest, the health care system, like other social institutions, resists basic change. In general, those who receive substantial wealth and power through the workings of an existing institution will have a strong incentive to keep things as they are. In this case, private insurance companies are benefiting financially from the current system and have a clear interest in opposing certain forms of national health insurance. In addition, the American Medical Association (AMA), one of Washing-

ton's most powerful lobbying groups, has been successfully fighting national health insurance since the 1930s. Overall, more than 200 political action committees (PACs) represent the medical, pharmaceutical, and insurance industries. These PACs have contributed millions of dollars each year to members of Congress and used their influence to block any legislation that would threaten their interests (Dolbeare 1982; Kemper and Novak 1991).

The health system is unquestionably undergoing "corporatization," as for-profit health care companies (often linking insurers, hospitals, and groups of physicians) are achieving increasing dominance. Conflict theorists have long argued that an underlying and disturbing aspect of capitalism in the United States is that illness may be exploited for profit. Critics of the corporatization of health care worry that the growing pressures on physicians and other health care providers to make cost-effective decisions may lead to inadequate and even life-threatening patient care (Sherrill 1995).

Policy Initiatives

Early in the 1990s, the U.S. Congress dismissed the idea of any sort of national health insurance. Although virtually everyone agreed that the existing fee-for-service system was too costly, a major move to centralize financing, and hence control, of health care was deemed unacceptable. Yet, even without legislative reform, major changes have been occurring in the United States.

Figure 19-7

Government Expenditure for Health Care

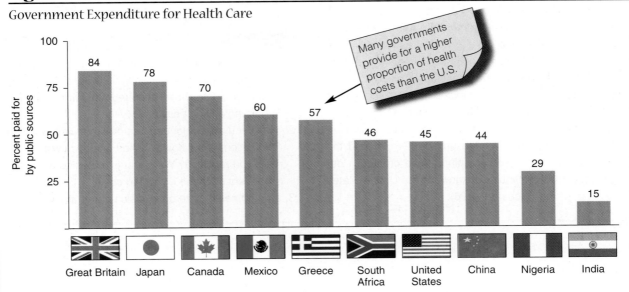

Many governments provide for a higher proportion of health costs than the U.S.

Source: World Bank 2001a:98–100.

As of 1997, managed care plans (as opposed to traditional health insurance) enrolled 85 percent of all workers, up from 52 percent just since 1993. These managed care plans limit one's choice of physicians and treatment but cover most medical costs. **Health maintenance organizations (HMOs),** which provide comprehensive medical services for a preestablished fee, are playing a prominent role in managed care. The number of people in the United States enrolled in HMOs has risen from 6 million in 1980 to 164 million in 1997 (American Association of Health Plans 1998a; Eckholm 1994; Findlay 1998; Kelly and Levy 1995).

There are growing concerns about the quality of care people receive through managed care plans such as HMOs, especially the elderly and minorities, who are less likely to be able to afford private insurance plans. According to a national survey, people in managed care feel they spend less time with physicians, find it more difficult to see specialists, and generally sense that the overall quality of health care has deteriorated (Appleby 1999).

Many industrial countries are paying greater attention to unequal health care delivery. Addressing this problem, however, often creates difficulties. Great Britain, for example, closed facilities in London and other metropolitan areas in an attempt to reassign medical staff to underserved rural areas. In addition to concerns about quality and availability of medical care, Britain's National Health Service remains underfunded (Christie 2001).

Medical services have in the past been delivered according to the ability to pay for services and the availability of facilities and personnel. As governments throughout the world take greater responsibility for health care and as care becomes increasingly expensive, governments can be expected to give more and more attention to controlling expenditures. Although the U.S. federal government has not been as heavily involved as other nations, the introduction of payment according to diagnostic-related groups (DRGs) and the institution of managed care plans have created a degree of control previously unknown in the United States (Mechanic and Rochefort 1996).

The great majority of Americans who have medical insurance now belong to managed care plans. Many have questioned the quality of managed care, complaining that they see the doctor less often under such plans than in the past.

Let's Discuss

1. Are you and your family covered by a health insurance plan? If not, why aren't you covered? Has anyone in your family ever required a medical procedure he or she couldn't pay for?
2. Have you ever belonged to a health maintenance organization? If so, how satisfied were you with the care you received? Were you ever denied a specific treatment because it was too costly?
3. Should health care be a basic right of all Americans?

Chapter Resources

Summary

The meanings of **health,** sickness, and disease are shaped by social definitions of behavior. This chapter considers the relationship between culture and health, several sociological perspectives on health and illness, the distribution of diseases in a society, the evolution of the U.S. health care system, and the sociological dimension of mental health and mental illness. It closes with a discussion of how health care is financed worldwide.

1. The effect of culture on health can be seen in the existence of **culture-bound syndromes,** as well as in cultural differences in medical care and the **incidence** and **prevalence** of certain diseases.

2. According to Talcott Parsons's functionalist perspective, physicians function as "gatekeepers" for the **sick role,** either verifying a person's condition as "ill" or designating the person as "recovered."

3. Conflict theorists use the term *medicalization of society* to refer to medicine's growing role as a major institution of social control.

4. Labeling theorists suggest that the designation of a person as "healthy" or "ill" generally involves social definition by others. These definitions affect how others see us and how we view ourselves.

5. Contemporary **social epidemiology** is concerned not only with epidemics but also with nonepidemic diseases, injuries, drug addition and alcoholism, suicide, and mental illness.

6. Studies have consistently shown that people in the lower classes have higher rates of mortality and disability.

7. Racial and ethnic minorities have higher rates of morbidity and mortality than do Whites. Women tend to be in poorer health than men but live longer. Older people are especially vulnerable to mental health problems, such as Alzheimer's disease.

8. The preeminent role of physicians within the health care system of the United States has given them a position of dominance in their dealings with nurses and patients.

9. Many people seek alternative health care techniques, such as **holistic medicine** and self-help groups.

10. Mental disorders may be viewed from two different perspectives, the medical model and the sociological model, which is based on labeling theory. In the United States, society has traditionally taken a negative, suspicious attitude toward people with mental disorders.

11. In the developed world, an aging population and technological breakthroughs have made health care both more extensive and more costly. At the same time, developing nations struggle to provide primary care for a burgeoning population. Throughout the world, an important issue is who is to pay for this care.

Critical Thinking Questions

1. Sociologist Talcott Parsons has argued that the doctor–patient relationship is somewhat like that between parent and child. Does this view seem accurate? Should the doctor–patient relationship become more egalitarian? How might functionalist and conflict theorists differ in their views of the power of physicians within the health care system of the United States?

2. How would the process of classifying a person as mentally ill differ under the medical model and the sociological model? Draw on Erving Goffman's concept of stigmatization (see Chapter 5).

3. Relate what you have learned about social epidemiology to the question of universal health care coverage. If the United States were to adopt a system of universal coverage, what might be the effect on the incidence and prevalence of disease among Americans of all classes, races and ethnicities, genders, and ages? What might be the ultimate effect of such changes on health care costs?

Key Terms

Culture-bound syndrome A disease or illness that cannot be understood apart from its specific social context. (page 473)

Curanderismo Latino folk medicine using holistic health care and healing. (482)

Health As defined by the World Health Organization, a state of complete physical, mental, and social well-being, and not merely the absence of disease and infirmity. (473)

Health maintenance organization (HMO) An organization that provides comprehensive medical services for a preestablished fee. (494)

Holistic medicine A means of health maintenance using therapies in which the health care practitioner considers the person's physical, mental, emotional, and spiritual characteristics. (487)

Incidence The number of new cases of a specific disorder occurring within a given population during a stated period of time. (480)

Mental illness A disorder of the brain that disrupts a person's thinking, feeling, and ability to interact with others. (489)

Morbidity rates The incidence of diseases in a given population. (480)

Mortality rate The incidence of death in a given population. (480)

Prevalence The total number of cases of a specific disorder that exist at a given time. (480)

Sick role Societal expectations about the attitudes and behavior of a person viewed as being ill. (474)

Social epidemiology The study of the distribution of disease, impairment, and general health status across a population. (480)

Additional Readings

BOOKS

Bosk, Charles L. 1992. *All God's Mistakes: Genetic Counseling in a Pediatric Hospital.* Chicago: University of Chicago Press. Drawing on observation research, Bosk provides an inside look at how a genetic counseling team interacts with parents and with one another.

Cockerham, William C. 1999. *Health and Social Change in Russia and Eastern Europe.* New York: Routledge. An examination of the sociological causes of the decline in life expectancy—unusual in an industrialized society—that began in the 1960s in the countries of the former Soviet Union.

CQ Researcher 2001. *Issues in Health Policy.* Washington, DC: CQ Press. *Congressional Quarterly* researchers have compiled a fine selection covering issues such as vaccine controversies, patients' rights, medical mistakes, and embryo research.

Guillemin, Jeanne. 1999. *Anthrax: The Investigation of a Deadly Outbreak.* Berkeley: University of California Press. A sociologist describes her social-epidemiological investigation into the mystery-shrouded outbreak of anthrax in the Soviet Union in 1979.

Lassey, Marie L., William R. Lassey, and Martin J. Jinks. 1997. *Health Care Systems around the World: Characteristics, Issues, Reforms.* Upper Saddle River, NJ: Prentice Hall. A comparative look at health care delivery in 13 countries, including Canada, China, Japan, Mexico, Russia, and Sweden.

Leavitt, Judith Walzer. 1996. *Typhoid Mary: Captive in the Public's Health.* Boston: Beacon. A professor of the history of medicine and women's studies examines how scientists discovered that a healthy body could carry typhoid, using a notorious case study from the early 1900s.

Riska, Elianne. 2001. *Medical Careers and Feminist Agendas: American, Scandinavian, and Russian Women Physicians.* Hawthorne, NY: Aldine De Gruyter. A cross-cultural comparison of female physicians in three nations.

JOURNALS

Among the journals dealing with issues of health, illness, and health care are *Health: An Interdisciplinary Journal for the Social Study of Health, Illness, and Medicine* (founded in 1997), *Journal of Gender, Culture, and Health* (1996), *Journal of Health and Social Behavior* (1965), *Millbank Memorial Quarterly* (1923), and *Social Science and Medicine* (1967).

Technology Resources

Internet Connection

*Note: While all the URLs listed were current as of the printing of this book, these sites often change. Please check our website (**http://www.mhhe.com/schaefer8**) for updates and hyperlinks to these exercises and additional exercises.*

1. The National Center for Health Statistics (**http://www.cdc.gov/nchs/**) is the federal government's principal vital and health statistics agency. It is also a part of the Centers for Disease Control and Prevention. Link to "News Releases." Click on "2001." Read "Teen Pregnancy Rate Reaches a Record Low in 1997," and answer the following questions:
   (a) When was the all-time high? How much did the teen pregnancy rate fall from that all-time high?
   (b) Which racial/ethnic group had the steepest decline in teen pregnancy rates? What factors appear to account for the declines?
   (c) Summarize the trends in birth, abortion, and fetal loss over the past 20 years.
   (d) Link to "Healthy People" and then to "About Healthy People 2010." What is the purpose of Healthy People 2010?
   (e) Link to "FASTSTATS A TO Z." Select any three diseases. List each disease, and then answer the following question: How many Americans have this disease or die from this disease annually?

2. The Netherlands is the only country in the world that legalizes and openly practices euthanasia. To learn more about this practice, go to the following web address: (**http://www.euthanasia.org/dutch. html**). Explore the site and answer the following questions:
   (a) In the Netherlands, who is involved in the process of euthanasia, and how is the process carried out?
   (b) How does one qualify to die in this manner?

Type in (**http://www.euthanasia.com**) and then click on "Euthanasia—Frequently Asked Questions (FAQs)," and answer the following questions:
   (c) What state in the United States permits assisted suicide?
   (d) According to this site, what are the problems with the definition of "terminal"?
   (e) Do you favor legalizing euthanasia? Briefly state your position.

3. The Substance Abuse and Mental Health Services Administration (**http://www.samhsa.gov/**) is an agency of the U.S. Department of Health and Human Services. First, link to "Mental Health Services," then to "Mental Health Statistics," and finally to "State Mental Health Statistics, Resources, and Services." You will see a map of the United States. Click on your state, and answer the following questions:
   (a) How many adults in your state had a serious mental illness in 1990?
   (b) How many children and adolescents had serious emotional disturbances in 1995?
   Click your Refresh or Back button and return to the map. Link to "Search" and type in *bulimia*. Link to "Eating Disorders," view the slides, and answer the following questions:
   (c) How is anorexia nervosa diagnosed?
   (d) What is the ratio of males to females for this disorder?
   (e) What is the relationship of anorexia nervosa to depression?
   (f) Do you know anyone who is bulimic or anorexic? Would you recommend this website to that person? Why or why not?

Online Learning Center www.mhhe.com/schaefer8

When you visit the student center in the Online Learning Center at **www.mhhe.com/schaefer8,** link to "Flashcards." There is a flashcard for every key term in your text, with a definition for each term. Flashcards are a valuable study tool—they give you the opportunity to see how familiar you are with important terms in the chapter.

COMMUNITIES
AND URBANIZATION

Homelessness has become a major social problem in U.S. cities, as this appeal from the Chicago Coalition for the Homeless suggests. Of all the homeless people living in shelters or on the streets in Chicago, half are family members; the average age of a homeless person is just seven years.

It is not hard to understand why Hakim Hasan came to see himself as a public character. Early one July morning, a deliveryman pulled his truck up to the curb behind Hakim's vending table on Greenwich Avenue off the corner of Sixth Avenue [in lower Manhattan] and carried a large box of flowers over to him.

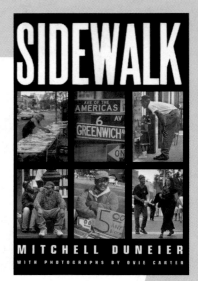

"Can you hold these until the flower shop opens up?" the deliveryman asked.

"No problem," responded Hakim as he continued to set up the books on his table. "Put them right under there."

When the store opened for business, he brought them inside and gave them to the owner.

"Why did that man trust you with the flowers?" I later asked.

"People like me are the eyes and ears of this street," he explained, echoing [sociologist] Jane Jacobs again. "Yes, I could take those flowers and sell them for a few hundred dollars. But that deliveryman sees me here every day. I'm as dependable as any store-owner." . . .

Another day, I was present at the table when a traffic officer walked by to give out parking tickets.

"Are any of these your cars?" she asked Hakim.

"Yes, that one, and that one," said Hakim, pointing.

"What is that all about?" I asked.

"The day I met her, we got into an argument," he explained. "She was getting ready to give the guy across the street a ticket. I say, 'You can't do this!' She said, 'Why not?' I say, ''Cause I'm getting ready to put a quarter in.' She said, 'You can't do that.' I guess that, because of the way I made my argument, she didn't give out the ticket, and from that point onward we became friends. And when she comes on the block, she asks me, for every car on the block that has a violation sign, 'Is that your car?' Meaning, 'Is it someone you know?' And depending on whether I say yes or no, that's it—they get a ticket." . . .

"Are these things part of your job description as a vendor?" I asked him once.

"Let me put it to you this way, Mitch," he replied. "I kind of see what I loosely call my work on the sidewalk as going far, far beyond just trying to make a living selling books. That sometimes even seems secondary. Over time, when people see you on the sidewalk, there is a kind of trust that starts. They've seen you so long that they walk up to you. There have been occasions when I've had to have directions translated out of Spanish into French to get somebody to go someplace!"

It is not only directions and assistance that I have seen Hakim give out. He also tells people a great deal about books—so much so that he once told me he was thinking of charging tuition to the people who stand in his space on the sidewalk. *(Duneier 1999:17–18)* ■

This excerpt from *Sidewalk,* by the sociologist Mitchell Duneier, describes the social position of Hakim Hasan, a sidewalk book vendor in New York City's Greenwich Village. The author, who for two years lived just around the corner from Hasan's table, was so fascinated by street life in the Village that he decided to do observation research on it. As Duneier explains in his book, street vendors like Hasan are just as much a part of the neighborhood as the shopkeepers who occupy the storefronts behind them—even if they don't have a mailing address. In fact, their presence on the street, day in and day out, contributes to the neighborhood's safety and stability (Duneier 1999).

Sociologist Mitchell Duneier (*right*) did participant observation as he worked the tables of sidewalk vendors in Greenwich Village.

This chapter explores communities of all sorts, from rural towns to inner-city neighborhoods and the suburbs that surround them. In sociological terms, a **community** may be defined as a spatial or political unit of social organization that gives people a sense of belonging. That sense of belonging can be based either on shared residence in a particular city or neighborhood, such as Greenwich Village, or on a common identity, such as that of street vendors, homeless people, or gays and lesbians. Whatever the members have in common, communities give people the feeling that they are part of something larger than themselves (Dotson 1991; see also Hillery 1955).

The anthropologist George Murdock (1949) has observed that the community is one of only two truly universal units of social organization (the other being the family). How did communities originate? Why have large cities grown at the expense of small villages in many areas of the world today? And why, even in nations like the United States, are many residents of large and prosperous communities homeless? In this chapter we will begin to answer these questions by tracing the development of communities from their ancient origins to the birth of the modern city and its growth through technological change. In particular, we will examine the rapid and dramatic urbanization that occurred around the world during the twentieth century. Then we will study two different sociological views of urbanization, one stressing its functions and the other its dysfunctions. And we'll compare rural, suburban, and urban communities in the United States today. Finally, in the social policy section, we'll analyze the disturbing phenomenon of homelessness, an all-too-familiar feature of community life. ■

● How Did Communities Originate?

Early Communities

For most of human history, people used very basic tools and knowledge to survive. They satisfied their need for an adequate food supply through hunting, foraging for fruits or vegetables, fishing, and herding. In comparison with later industrial societies, early civilizations were much

p. 122 ◄

more dependent on the physical environment and much less able to alter that environment to their advantage. The emergence of horticultural societies, in which people actually cultivated food rather than merely gathering fruits and vegetables, led to many dramatic changes in human social organization.

It was no longer necessary to move from place to place in search of food. Because people had to remain in specific locations to cultivate crops, more stable and enduring communities began to develop. As agricultural techniques became more and more sophisticated, a cooperative division of labor involving both family members and others developed. It gradually became possible for people to produce more food than they actually needed

This painting shows twelfth-century traders in a port city on the Mediterranean Sea. Such early settlements represented one type of preindustrial city.

for themselves. They could give food, perhaps as part of an exchange, to others who might be involved in nonagricultural labor. This transition from subsistence to surplus represented a critical step in the emergence of cities.

Eventually, people produced enough goods to cover both their own needs and those of people not engaged in agricultural tasks. Initially, the surplus was limited to agricultural products, but it gradually evolved to include all types of goods and services. Residents of a city came to rely on community members who provided craft products and means of transportation, gathered information, and so forth (Nolan and Lenski 1999).

With these social changes came an even more elaborate division of labor, as well as a greater opportunity for differential rewards and privileges. So long as everyone was engaged in the same tasks, stratification was limited to such factors as gender, age, and perhaps the ability to perform the task (a skillful hunter could win unusual respect from the community). However, the surplus allowed for expansion of goods and services, leading to greater differentiation, a hierarchy of occupations, and social inequality. Therefore, surplus was a precondition not only for the establishment of cities but also for the division of members of a community into social classes (see Chapter 9). The ability to produce goods for other communities marked a fundamental shift in human social organization.

Preindustrial Cities

It is estimated that, beginning about 10,000 B.C., permanent settlements free from dependence on crop cultivation emerged. Yet, by today's standards of population, these early communities would barely qualify as cities. The *preindustrial city,* as it is termed, generally had only a few thousand people living within its borders and was characterized by a relatively closed class system and limited mobility. Status in these early cities was usually based on ascribed characteristics such as family background, and education was limited to members of the elite. All the residents relied on perhaps 100,000 farmers and their own part-time farming to provide them with the needed agricultural surplus. The Mesopotamian city of Ur had a population of about 10,000 and was limited to roughly 220 acres of land, including the canals, the temple, and the harbor.

Why were these early cities so small and relatively few in number? Several key factors restricted urbanization:

Reliance on animal power (both humans and beasts of burden) as a source of energy for economic production. This limited the ability of humans to make use of and alter the physical environment.

Modest levels of surplus produced by the agricultural sector. Between 50 and 90 farmers may have been required to support one city resident (Davis [1949] 1995).

Problems in transportation and storage of food and other goods. Even an excellent crop could easily be lost as a result of such difficulties.

Hardships of migration to the city. For many peasants, migration was both physically and economically impossible. A few weeks of travel was out of the question without more sophisticated techniques of food storage.

Dangers of city life. Concentrating a society's population in a small area left it open to attack from outsiders, as well as more susceptible to extreme damage from plagues and fires.

Gideon Sjoberg (1960) examined the available information on early urban settlements of medieval Europe, India, and China. He identified three preconditions of city life: advanced technology in both agricultural and nonagricultural areas, a favorable physical environment, and a well-developed social organization.

For Sjoberg, the criteria for defining a "favorable" physical environment are variable. Proximity to coal and iron helps only if a society knows how to *use* these natural resources. Similarly, proximity to a river is particularly beneficial only if a culture has the means to transport water efficiently to the fields for irrigation and to the cities for consumption.

A sophisticated social organization is also an essential precondition for urban existence. Specialized social roles bring people together in new ways through the exchange of goods and services. A well-developed social organization ensures that these relationships are clearly defined and generally acceptable to all parties. Admittedly, Sjoberg's view of city life is an ideal type, since inequality did not vanish with the emergence of urban communities.

Industrial and Postindustrial Cities

Imagine how life could change by harnessing the energy of air, water, and other natural resources to power society's tasks. Advances in agricultural technology led to dramatic changes in community life, but so did the process of industrialization. The *industrial revolution,* which began in the middle of the eighteenth century, focused on the application of nonanimal sources of power to labor tasks. Industrialization had a wide range of effects on people's lifestyles as well as on the structure of communities. Emerging urban settlements became centers not only of industry but also of banking, finance, and industrial management.

p. 123

The factory system that developed during the industrial revolution led to a much more refined division of labor than was evident in early preindustrial cities. The many new occupations that were created produced a complex set of relationships among workers. Thus, the *industrial city* was not merely more populous than its preindustrial predecessors; it was also based on very different principles of social organization. Sjoberg outlined the contrasts between preindustrial and industrial cities, as summarized in Table 20-1.

In comparison with preindustrial cities, industrial cities have a more open class system and more mobility. After initiatives in industrial cities by women's rights groups, labor unions, and other political activists, formal education gradually became available to many children from poor and working-class families. While ascribed characteristics such as gender, race, and ethnicity remained important, a talented or skilled individual had a greater opportunity to better his or her social position. In these and other respects, the industrial city is genuinely a "different world" from the preindustrial urban community.

Table 20-1 Comparing Types of Cities

Preindustrial Cities (through 18th century)	Industrial Cities (18th through mid-20th century)	Postindustrial Cities (beginning late 20th century)
Closed class system—pervasive influence of social class at birth	Open class system—mobility based on achieved characteristics	Wealth based on ability to obtain and use information
Economic realm controlled by guilds and a few families	Relatively open competition	Corporate power dominates
Beginnings of division of labor in creation of goods	Elaborate specialization in manufacturing of goods	Sense of place fades, transitional networks emerge
Pervasive influence of religion on social norms	Influence of religion limited to certain areas as society becomes more secularized	Religion becomes more fragmented; greater openness to new religious faiths
Little standardization of prices, weights, and measures	Standardization enforced by custom and law	Conflicting views of prevailing standards
Population largely illiterate, communication by word of mouth	Emergence of communication through posters, bulletins, and newspapers	Emergence of extended electronic networks
Schools limited to elites and designed to perpetuate their privileged status	Formal schooling open to the masses and viewed as a means of advancing the social order	Professional, scientific, and technical personnel are increasingly important

Sources: Based on Sjoberg 1960:323–328; Phillips 1996:132–135.

In the latter part of the twentieth century, a new type of urban community emerged. The ***postindustrial city*** is a city in which global finance and the electronic flow of information dominate the economy. Production is decentralized and often takes place outside of urban centers, but control is centralized in multinational corporations whose influence transcends urban and even national boundaries. Social change is a constant feature of the postindustrial city. Economic and spatial restructuring seems to occur each decade if not more frequently. In the postindustrial world, cities are forced into increasing competition for economic opportunities, which deepens the plight of the urban poor (Phillips 1996; Smith and Timberlake 1993).

p. 123

Sociologist Louis Wirth (1928, 1938) argued that a relatively large and permanent settlement leads to distinctive patterns of behavior, which he called ***urbanism.*** He identified three critical factors contributing to urbanism: the size of the population, population density, and the heterogeneity (variety) of the population. A frequent result of urbanism, according to Wirth, is that we become insensitive to events around us and restrict our attention to primary groups to which we are emotionally attached.

Table 20-2	The 10 Most Populous Cities in the World, 1970 and 2015 (in millions)		
1970		**2015 (Projected)**	
1. Tokyo	16.5	1. Bombay (India)	28.2
2. New York	16.2	2. Tokyo	26.4
3. Shanghai (China)	11.2	3. Lagos (Nigeria)	23.2
4. Osaka (Japan)	9.4	4. Dhaka (Bangladesh)	23.0
5. Mexico City	9.1	5. São Paulo (Brazil)	20.4
6. London	8.6	6. Karachi (Pakistan)	19.8
7. Paris	8.5	7. Mexico City	19.2
8. Buenos Aires	8.4	8. Delhi (India)	17.8
9. Los Angeles	8.4	9. New York	17.4
10. Beijing	8.1	10. Jakarta (Indonesia)	17.3

Source: United Nations, quoted in Brockerhoff 2000:10.

Think About It
What trend does this table suggest?

Imagine

What would the ideal city of the future look like? Describe its architecture, public transportation, neighborhoods, schools, and workplaces. What kinds of people would live and work there?

Urbanization

The 1990 census was the first to demonstrate that more than half the population of the United States lives in urban areas of 1 million or more residents. In only three states (Mississippi, Vermont, and West Virginia) do more than half the residents live in rural areas. Clearly, urbanization has become a central aspect of life in the United States (Bureau of the Census 1991b).

Urbanization can be seen throughout the rest of the world, too. In 1900, only 10 percent of the world's people lived in urban areas, but by 2000, that proportion had risen to around 50 percent. By the year 2025, the number of city dwellers could reach 5 billion (Koolhaas et al. 2001:3).

During the nineteenth and early twentieth centuries, rapid urbanization occurred primarily in European and North American cities. Since World War II, however, there has been an urban "explosion" in the world's developing countries (see Figure 20-1). Such rapid growth is evident in the rising number of "squatter settlements," areas occupied by the very poor on the fringe of cities, described in Box 20-1.

Some metropolitan areas have spread so far that they have connected with other urban centers. Such a densely populated area, containing two or more cities and their suburbs, has become known as a ***megalopolis.*** An example is the 500-mile corridor stretching from Boston south to Washington, D.C. It includes New York City, Philadelphia, and Baltimore and accounts for one-sixth of the total population of the United States. Even when it is divided into autonomous political jurisdictions, the megalopolis can be viewed as a single economic entity. The megalopolis is also evident in Great Britain, Germany, Italy, Egypt, India, Japan, and China. Table 20-2 compares the 10 largest megalopolises in the world in 1970 with the projected 10 largest in 2015.

Figure 20-1

Urbanization around the World, 2000

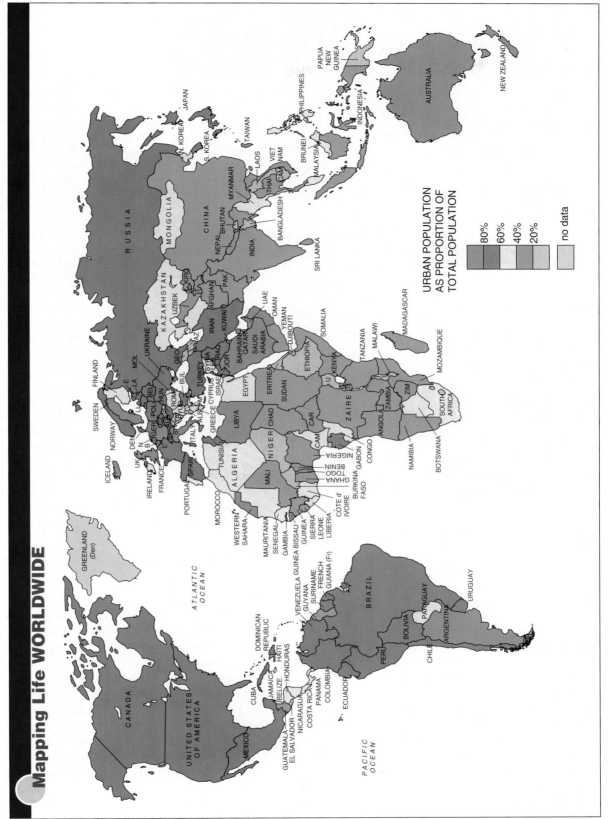

Mapping Life WORLDWIDE

URBAN POPULATION
AS PROPORTION OF
TOTAL POPULATION

80%
60%
40%
20%
no data

Source: Based on data in Haub and Cornelius 2001.

Sociology in the Global Community

20-1 Squatter Settlements

www.
mhhe.
.com
/schaefer8

Bariadas, *favelas, bustees, kampungs,* and *bidonvilles:* The terms vary depending on the nation and language, but the meaning is the same—"squatter settlements." In *squatter settlements,* areas occupied by the very poor on the fringe of cities, housing is constructed by the settlers themselves from discarded material, including crates from loading docks and loose lumber from building projects. While the term "squatter settlement" has wide use, many observers prefer to use a less pejorative term, such as "autonomous settlements."

This type of settlement is very typical of cities in the world's developing nations. In such countries, new housing has not kept pace with the combined urban population growth resulting from births and migration from rural areas. In addition, squatter settlements swell when city dwellers are forced out of housing by astronomical jumps in rent. By definition, squatters living on vacant land are trespassers and can be legally evicted. However, given the large number of poor people who live in such settlements (by UN estimates, 40 or 50 percent of inhabitants of cities in many developing nations), governments generally look the other way.

Obviously squatters live in substandard housing, yet this is only one of the many problems they face. Residents do not receive most public services, since their presence cannot be legally recognized. Police and fire protection, paved streets, and sanitary sewers are virtually nonexistent. In some countries, squatters may have trouble voting or enrolling their children in public schools.

Despite such conditions, squatter settlements are not always as bleak as they

> Squatter settlements are not always as bleak as they may appear from the outside.

may appear from the outside. You can often find a well-developed social organization rather than disorganized collections of people. A thriving "informal economy" typically develops: residents establish small, home-based businesses such as grocery stores, jewelry shops, and the like.

Local churches, men's clubs, and women's clubs are often established in specific neighborhoods within the settlements. In addition, certain areas may form governing councils or membership

associations. These governing bodies may face the usual problems of municipal governments, including charges of corruption and factional splits.

Squatter settlements remind us that respected theoretical models of social science in the United States may not directly apply to other cultures. The various ecological models of urban growth, for example, would not explain metropolitan expansion that locates the poorest people on the urban fringes. Furthermore, solutions that are logical for a highly industrialized nation may not be relevant in the developing nations. Planners in developing nations, rather than focusing on large-scale solutions to urban problems, must think in terms of basic amenities, such as providing water taps or electrical power lines to the ever-expanding squatter settlements.

Let's Discuss

1. Do you know of any "squatters" in your own community? If so, describe them and the place where they live.
2. Given the number of homeless people in the United States, why aren't there more squatters?

Sources: Castells 1983, Patton 1988; Perlman 2001; Yap 1998.

Functionalist View: Urban Ecology

Human ecology is concerned with the interrelationships between people and their spatial setting and physical environment. Human ecologists have long been interested in how the physical environment shapes people's lives (for example, rivers can serve as a barrier to residential expansion) and also how people influence the surrounding environment (air-conditioning has accelerated growth of major metropolitan areas in the Southwest). *Urban ecology* focuses on such relationships as they emerge in urban areas. Although the urban ecological approach examines social change in cities, it is nevertheless functionalist in its orientation because it emphasizes that different elements in urban areas contribute to stability.

Early urban ecologists such as Robert Park (1916, 1936) and Ernest Burgess (1925) concentrated on city life but drew on the approaches used by ecologists in studying plant and animal communities. With few exceptions, urban ecologists trace their work back to the *concentric-zone theory* devised in the 1920s by Burgess (see Figure 20-2a). Using Chicago as an example, Burgess proposed a theory for describing land use in industrial cities. At the center, or nucleus, of such a city is the central business district. Large department stores, hotels, theaters, and financial institutions occupy this highly valued land. Surrounding this urban center are succeeding zones that contain other types of land use and that illustrate the growth of the urban area over time.

Figure 20-2

Comparison of Ecological Theories of Urban Growth

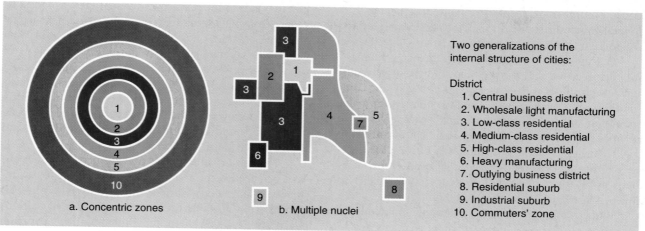

Two generalizations of the internal structure of cities:

District
1. Central business district
2. Wholesale light manufacturing
3. Low-class residential
4. Medium-class residential
5. High-class residential
6. Heavy manufacturing
7. Outlying business district
8. Residential suburb
9. Industrial suburb
10. Commuters' zone

a. Concentric zones   b. Multiple nuclei

Source: Harris and Ullmann 1945:13.

Note that the creation of zones is a *social* process, not the result of nature alone. Families and business firms compete for the most valuable land; those possessing the most wealth and power are generally the winners. The concentric-zone theory proposed by Burgess also represented a dynamic model of urban growth. As urban growth proceeded, each zone would move even farther from the central business district.

Because of its functionalist orientation and its emphasis on stability, the concentric-zone theory tended to understate or ignore certain tensions apparent in metropolitan areas. For example, the growing use by the afflu-

ent of land in a city's peripheral areas was uncritically approved, while the arrival of African Americans in White neighborhoods in the 1930s was described by some sociologists in terms such as "invasion" and "succession." Moreover, the urban ecological perspective gave little thought to gender inequities, such as the establishment of men's softball and golf leagues in city parks without any programs for women's sports. Consequently, the urban ecological approach has been criticized for its failure to address issues of gender, race, and class.

By the middle of the twentieth century, urban populations had spilled beyond the traditional city limits. No longer could urban ecologists focus exclusively on *growth* in the central city, for large numbers of urban residents were abandoning the cities to live in suburban areas. As a response to the emergence of more than one focal point in some metropolitan areas, Chauncy D. Harris and Edward Ullman (1945) presented the *multiple-nuclei theory* (see Figure 20-2b). In their view, all urban growth does not radiate outward from a central business district. Instead, a metropolitan area may have many centers of development, each of which reflects a particular urban need or activity. Thus, a city may have a financial district, a manufacturing zone, a waterfront area, an entertainment center, and so forth. Certain types of business firms and certain types of housing will naturally cluster around each distinctive nucleus (Schwab 1993).

The rise of suburban shopping malls is a vivid example of the phenomenon of multiple nuclei within metropolitan areas. Initially, all major retailing in cities was located in the central business district. Each residential neighborhood had its own grocers, bakers, and butchers, but people traveled to the center of the city to make major purchases at department stores. However, as major metropolitan areas expanded and the suburbs became more populous, an increasing number of people began to shop nearer their homes. Today, the suburban mall is a significant retailing and social center for communities across the United States.

In a refinement of multiple-nuclei theory, contemporary urban ecologists have begun to study what journalist Joel Garreau (1991) has called "edge cities." These communities, which have grown up on the outskirts of major metropolitan areas, are economic and social centers with identities of their own. By any standard of measurement—height of buildings, amount of office space, presence of medical facilities, presence of leisure-time facilities, or, of course, population—edge cities qualify as independent cities rather than large suburbs.

Whether they include edge cities or multiple nuclei, more and more metropolitan areas are characterized by spread-out development and unchecked growth. The metropolitan area of Atlanta, which contains 4.1 million people according to the 2000 census, covers no fewer than 20 counties—an area nearly the size of Hawaii. Overall, 8 out of every 10 U.S. cities extended over a much greater geographical area in 2000 than they did in 1990. Today's cities are very different from the preindustrial cities of a thousand years ago (El Nasser and Overberg 2001; Glanton 2001).

Conflict View: New Urban Sociology

Contemporary sociologists point out that metropolitan growth is not governed by waterways and rail lines, as a purely ecological interpretation might suggest. From a conflict perspective, communities are human creations that reflect people's needs, choices, and decisions—but some people have more influence over these decisions than others. Drawing on conflict theory, an approach that has come to be called the **new urban sociology** considers the interplay of local, national, and worldwide forces and their effect on local space, with special emphasis on the impact of global economic activity (Gottdiener and Hutchison 2000).

New urban sociologists note that ecological approaches typically have avoided examining the social forces, largely economic in nature, that have guided urban growth. For

example, central business districts may be upgraded or abandoned, depending on whether urban policymakers grant substantial tax exemptions to developers. The suburban boom in the post–World War II era was fueled by federal housing policies that channeled investment capital into the construction of single-family homes rather than to affordable rental housing in the cities. Similarly, while some observers suggest that the growth of sun-belt cities is due to a "good business climate," new urban sociologists counter that this term is actually a euphemism for hefty state and local government subsidies and antilabor policies intended to draw manufacturers (Gottdiener and Feagin 1988; Smith 1988).

The new urban sociology draws generally on the conflict perspective and more specifically on sociologist Immanuel Wallerstein's **world systems analysis.** Wallerstein argues that certain industrialized nations p. 243 ← (among them, the United States, Japan, and Germany) hold a dominant position at the *core* of the global economic system. At the same time, the poor developing countries of Asia, Africa, and Latin America are on the *periphery* of the global economy, where they are controlled and exploited by core industrialized nations. Through use of world systems analysis, new urban sociologists consider urbanization from a global perspective. They view cities not as independent and autonomous

Though the African country of Kenya is mostly rural, Nairobi, a city with almost a million residents, is a modern urban area with international business connections. According to world systems analysis, the cities of developing nations exist on the periphery of the global economy, controlled and exploited by the more powerful industrialized nations.

Table 20-3 Comparing Approaches to Urbanization

	Urban Ecology	New Urban Sociology
Theoretical perspective	Functionalist	Conflict
Primary focus	Relationship of urban areas to their spatial setting and physical environment	Relationship of urban areas to global, national, and local forces
Key source of change	Technological innovations such as new methods of transportation	Economic competition and monopolization of power
Initiator of actions	Individuals, neighborhoods, communities	Real estate developers, banks and other financial institutions, multinational corporations
Allied disciplines	Geography, architecture	Political science, economics

entities but rather as the outcome of decision-making processes directed or influenced by a society's dominant classes and by core industrialized nations. New urban sociologists note that the rapidly growing cities of the world's developing countries have been shaped first by colonialism and then by a global economy controlled by core nations and multinational corporations (Gottdiener and Feagin 1988; Smith 1995).

The urban ecologists of the 1920s and 1930s were not ignorant of the role that the larger economy played in urbanization, but their theories emphasized the impact of local rather than national or global forces. By contrast, through a broad, global emphasis on social inequality and conflict, new urban sociologists are pp. 226, 246, 460 ◀ interested in such topics as the existence of an underclass, the power of multinational corporations, and deindustrialization, as well as issues to be examined later in this chapter, such as urban fiscal crises, residential segregation, and homelessness.

Developers, builders, and investment bankers are not especially interested in urban growth when it means providing housing for middle- or low-income people. This lack of interest contributes to the problem of homelessness, which will be discussed in the social policy section at the end of the chapter. These urban elites counter that the nation's housing shortage and the plight of the homeless are not their fault—and insist that they do not have the capital needed to construct and support such housing. But affluent people *are* interested in growth and *can* somehow find capital to build new shopping centers, office towers, and ballparks.

Why, then, can't they provide the capital for affordable housing, ask new urban sociologists? Part of the answer is that developers, bankers, and other powerful real estate interests view housing in quite a different manner from tenants and most homeowners. For a tenant, an apartment is shelter, housing, a home. But for developers and investors—many of them large (and sometimes multinational) corporations—an apartment is simply a housing investment. These financiers and owners are primarily concerned with maximizing profit, not with solving social problems (Feagin 1983; Gottdiener and Hutchison 2000).

As we have seen throughout this textbook—in studying such varied issues as deviance, race and ethnicity, and aging—no single theoretical approach necessarily offers sociologists the only valuable perspective. As is shown in Table 20-3, urban ecology and new urban sociology offer significantly different ways of viewing urbanization that enrich our understanding of this complex phenomenon.

● Types of Communities

Communities vary substantially in the degree to which their members feel connected and share a common identity. Ferdinand Tönnies ([1887]1988) used the p. 121 ◀ term *Gemeinschaft* to describe a close-knit community where social interaction among people is intimate and familiar. It is the kind of place where people in a coffee shop will stop talking when anyone enters, because they are sure to know whoever walks through the door. A shopper at the small grocery store in this town would expect to know every employee, and probably every other customer as well. By contrast, the ideal type of *Gesellschaft* describes modern urban life, in which people feel little in common with others and often form social relationships as a result of interactions focused on immediate tasks, such as purchasing a product. Contemporary city life in the United States generally resembles a *Gesellschaft*.

The following sections will examine different types of communities found in the United States, focusing on the distinctive characteristics and problems of central cities, suburbs, and rural communities.

Central Cities

In terms of both land and population, the United States is the fourth-largest nation in the world. Yet three-quarters of the population is concentrated in a mere 1.5 percent of the nation's land area. In 2000 some 226 million people—accounting for 80 percent of the nation's population—lived in metropolitan areas. Even those who live outside central cities, such as residents of suburban and rural communities, find that urban centers heavily influence their lifestyles (Bureau of the Census 2001a:30).

Urban Dwellers

Many urban residents are the descendants of European immigrants—Irish, Italians, Jews, Poles, and others—who came to the United States in the nineteenth and early twentieth centuries. The cities socialized these newcomers to the norms, values, and language of their new homeland and gave them an opportunity to work their way up the economic ladder. In addition, a substantial number of low-income African Americans and Whites came to the cities from rural areas in the period following World War II.

Even today, cities in the United States are the destinations of immigrants from around the world—including Mexico, Ireland, Cuba, Vietnam, and Haiti—as well as migrants from the United States commonwealth of p. 293 ◄ Puerto Rico. Yet, unlike those who came to this country 100 years ago, current immigrants are arriving at a time of growing urban decay. This makes it more difficult for them to find employment and decent housing.

Urban life is noteworthy for its diversity, so it would be a serious mistake to see all city residents as being alike. Sociologist Herbert J. Gans (1991) has distinguished between five types of people found in our cities:

Indian American residents of Chicago enjoy an outdoor ethnic festival. Many subordinate racial and ethnic groups in the United States live in close-knit urban neighborhoods.

1. *Cosmopolites.* These residents remain in cities to take advantage of unique cultural and intellectual benefits. Writers, artists, and scholars fall into this category.
2. *Unmarried and childless people.* Such people choose to live in cities because of the active nightlife and varied recreational opportunities.
3. *Ethnic villagers.* These urban residents prefer to live in their own tight-knit communities. Typically, immigrant groups isolate themselves in such neighborhoods to avoid resentment from well-established urban dwellers.
4. *The deprived.* Very poor people and families have little choice but to live in low-rent, and often run-down, urban neighborhoods.
5. *The trapped.* Some city residents wish to leave urban centers but cannot because of their limited economic resources and prospects. Gans includes the "downward mobiles" in this category—people who once held higher social positions but who are forced to live in less prestigious neighborhoods owing to loss of a job, death of a wage earner, or old age. Both elderly individuals living alone and families may feel "trapped" in part because they resent changes in their communities. Their desire to live elsewhere may reflect their uneasiness with unfamiliar immigrant groups who have become their neighbors.

These categories remind us that the city represents a choice (even a dream) for certain people and a nightmare for others. Gans's work underscores the importance of neighborhoods in contemporary urban life. Ernest Burgess, in his study of life in Chicago in the 1920s, gave special attention to the ethnic neighborhoods of that city. Many decades later, residents in such districts as Chinatowns or Greektowns continue to feel attached to their own ethnic communities rather than to the larger unit of a city. Even outside ethnic enclaves, a special sense of belonging can take hold in a neighborhood.

In a more recent study in Chicago, Gerald Suttles (1972) coined the term **defended neighborhood** to refer to people's definitions of their community boundaries. Neighborhoods acquire unique identities because residents view them as geographically separate—and socially different—from adjacent areas. The defended neighborhood, in effect, becomes a sentimental union of similar people. Neighborhood phone directories, community newspapers, school and parish boundaries, and business advertisements all serve to define an area and distinguish it from nearby communities.

In some cases, a neighborhood must literally defend itself. Plans for urban renewal or a superhighway may threaten to destroy an area's unique character and sense of attachment. In resisting such changes, a neighborhood may use the strategies and tactics of community organization developed by pioneering organizer Saul Alinsky (1909–1972). Like many conflict sociologists, Alinsky was concerned with the ways in which society's most powerful institutions protect the privileges of certain groups (such as real estate developers) while keeping other groups (such as slum dwellers) in a subservient position. Alinsky (1946) emphasized the need for community residents to fight for power in their localities. In his view, it was only through the achievement and constructive use of power that people could better themselves (Horwitt 1989).

Issues Facing Cities

People and neighborhoods vary greatly within any city in the United States. Yet all residents of a central city—regardless of social class, racial, and ethnic differences—face certain common problems. Crime, air pollution, noise, unemployment, overcrowded schools, inadequate public transportation—these unpleasant realities and many more are an increasing feature of contemporary urban life.

Perhaps the single most dramatic reflection of the nation's urban ills has been the apparent "death" of entire neighborhoods. In some urban districts, business activity seems virtually nonexistent. You can walk for blocks and find little more than a devastating array of deteriorating, boarded-up, abandoned, and burned-out buildings. Such urban devastation has greatly contributed to the growing problem of homelessness, discussed in the social policy section.

Residential segregation has also been a persistent problem in cities across the United States. The segregation has resulted from the policies of financial institutions, the business practices of real estate agents, the actions of home sellers, and even urban planning initiatives (for example, in decisions about where to locate public housing). Sociologists Douglas Massey and Nancy Denton (1993) have used the term *American apartheid* to refer to the residential patterns of the nation. In their view, we no longer perceive segregation as a problem but rather accept it as a feature of the urban landscape. For subordinate minority groups, segregation means not only limited housing opportunities but also less access to employment, retail outlets, and medical services.

Another critical problem for the cities has been mass transportation. Since 1950, the number of cars in the United States has multiplied twice as fast as the number of people. Growing traffic congestion in metropolitan areas has led many cities to recognize a need for safe, efficient, and inexpensive mass transit systems. However, the federal government has traditionally given much more assistance to highway programs than to public transportation. Conflict theorists note that such a bias favors the relatively affluent (automobile owners) as well as corporations such as auto manufacturers, tire makers, and oil companies. Meanwhile, low-income residents of metropolitan areas, who are much less likely to own cars than members of the middle and upper classes, face higher fares on public transit along with deteriorating service (Mason 1998).

In 1968, Dr. Martin Luther King, Jr., observed that "urban transit systems in most American cities have become a genuine civil rights issue." An overcrowded public bus system in Los Angeles County carries 94 percent of the county's passengers—80 percent of whom are African American, Hispanic, Asian American, or Native American—yet receives less than one-third of the county's mass transit expenditures. At the same time, a lavish commuter rail system that already connects or will connect predominantly White suburbs to the downtown business district of Los Angeles carries only 6 percent of the county's passengers yet receives 71 percent of mass transit funding. Similar inequities in funding for public transportation have been challenged in New York City (Kelley 1996:18).

Asset-Based Community Development

For many people, the words *South Bronx, South Central Los Angeles*, or even *public housing* call forth a variety of negative stereotypes and stigmas. How do communities—whether neighborhoods or cities—that have been labeled as ghettos address the challenges they face? Typically, policymakers have identified an area's problems, needs, or deficiencies and then tried to find solutions. But in the last decade, community leaders, policymakers, and applied sociologists have begun to advocate an approach called **asset-based community development (ABCD)**, in which they first identify a community's strengths and then seek to mobilize those assets.

In a distressed community, the ABCD approach helps people to recognize human resources they might otherwise overlook. A community's assets may include its residents' skills; the power of local associations; its institutional resources, whether public, private, or nonprofit; and any physical and economic resources it has. By identifying these assets, planners can help to counter negative images and rebuild even the most devastated communities. The anticipated result is to strengthen the community's capacity to help itself and diminish its need to rely on outside organizations or providers. In fact, one consequence of this approach is to direct assistance to agencies within the community rather than to outside service providers (Asset-Based Community Development Institute 2001; Kretzmann and McKnight 1993; McKnight and Kretzmann 1996).

Tragically, the events of September 11, 2001, have caused many communities both large and small to recognize the ways in which neighbors can depend on one another. Middletown, New Jersey, a suburban community that lost 36 residents in the terrorist attack on the World Trade Center, is one example. In response to the catastrophe, a group of townspeople founded FAVOR (Friends Assisting Victims of Terror) and began canvassing every homeowner and business in the community on behalf of the bereaved families, most of whom had lost a breadwinner. By early November, the group had collected $38,000, along with donations of goods and services ranging from plumbing, car repair, and tree removal to haircuts, karate lessons, and chiropractor's appointments. The town also set up a scholarship fund for the three dozen children who had lost their fathers or mothers. In taking care of their own, the people of Middletown discovered the richness and variety of their resources (Jacobs 2001a, 2001b).

Suburbs

The term *suburb* derives from the Latin *sub urbe*, meaning "under the city." Until recent times, most suburbs were just that—tiny communities totally dependent on urban centers for jobs, recreation, and even water.

Today, the term **suburb** defies any simple definition. The term generally refers to any community near a large city—or, as the Census Bureau would say, any territory within a metropolitan area that is not included in the central city. By that definition, more than 138 million people, or about 51 percent of the population of the United States, live in the suburbs (Kleniewski 2002).

A teacher helps a young student with his homework at a church-based after-school program in Philadelphia. Residents' skills, and the contributions of nonprofit religious organizations, are two of the many resources that form the foundation of asset-based community development.

Three social factors differentiate suburbs from cities. First, suburbs are generally less dense than cities; in the newest suburbs, there are often no more than two dwellings on an acre of land. Second, the suburbs consist almost exclusively of private space. Private ornamental lawns replace common park areas for the most part. Third, suburbs have more exacting building design codes than cities, and these codes have become increasingly precise in the last decade. While the suburbs may be diverse in population, such design standards give the impression of uniformity.

It can also be difficult to distinguish between suburbs and rural areas. Certain criteria generally define suburbs: Most people work at urban (as opposed to rural) jobs, and local governments provide services such as water supply, sewage disposal, and fire protection. In rural areas, these services are less common, and a greater proportion of residents is employed in farming and related activities.

Suburban Expansion

Whatever the precise definition of a suburb, it is clear that suburbs have expanded. In fact, suburbanization has been the most dramatic population trend in the United States throughout the twentieth century. Suburban areas grew at first along railroad lines, then at the termini of streetcar tracks, and by the 1950s along the nation's growing systems of freeways and expressways. The suburban boom has been especially evident since World War II.

Suburbanization is not necessarily prompted by expansion of transportation services to the fringe of a city. The 1923 earthquake that devastated Tokyo encouraged decentralization of the city. Until the 1970s, dwellings were limited to a height of 102 feet. Initially, the poor were relegated to areas outside municipal boundaries in their search for housing; many chose to live in squatter-type settlements. With the advent of a rail network and rising land costs in the central city, middle-class Japanese began moving to the suburbs after World War II (Hall 1977).

Proponents of the new urban sociology contend that factories were initially moved from central cities to suburbs as a means of reducing the power of labor unions. Subsequently, many suburban communities induced businesses to relocate there by offering them subsidies and tax incentives. As sociologist William Julius Wilson (1996) has observed, federal housing policies contributed to the suburban boom by withholding mortgage capital from inner-city neighborhoods, by offering favorable mortgages to military veterans, and by assisting the rapid development of massive amounts of affordable tract housing in the suburbs. Moreover, federal highway and transportation policies provided substantial funding for expressway systems (which made commuting to the cities much easier), while undermining urban communities by building freeway networks through the heart of cities.

All these factors contributed to the movement of the (predominantly White) middle class out of the central cities and, as we shall see, also out of the suburbs. From the perspective of new urban sociology, suburban expansion is far from a natural ecological process; rather, it reflects the distinct priorities of powerful economic and political interests.

Diversity in the Suburbs

In the United States, race and ethnicity remain the most important factors distinguishing cities from suburbs. Nevertheless, the common assumption that suburbia includes only prosperous Whites is far from correct. The last 20 years have witnessed the diversification of suburbs in terms of race and ethnicity. For example, by 2000, 34 percent of Blacks in the United States, 46 percent of Latinos, and 53 percent of Asians lived in the suburbs. Like the rest of the nation, members of racial and ethnic minorities are becoming suburban dwellers, as Figure 20-3 shows (El Nasser 2001; Frey 2001b).

But are the suburban areas recreating the racial segregation of the central cities? A definite pattern of clustering if not outright segregation is emerging. A study of suburban residential patterns in 11 metropolitan areas found that Asian Americans and Hispanics tend to reside in equivalent socioeconomic areas with Whites—that is, affluent Hispanics live alongside affluent Whites, poor Asians near poor Whites, and so on. However, the case for African Americans is quite distinct. Suburban Blacks live in poorer suburbs than Whites, even after taking into account differences in individuals' income, education, and homeownership.

The motion picture *American Beauty* (1999) portrayed the suburbs as all-White non-Hispanic communities. Although such communities have not vanished, they are much less typical now than they were in the past.

Figure 20-3

Ethnic Diversity in U.S. Suburbs, 1990 and 2000

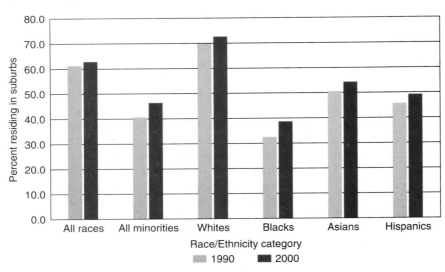

Source: Frey 2001b:7.

Note: Data are for the 102 most populous metropolitan areas (those with populations over 500,000) in the United States in 2000.

Think About It

In addition to the fact that people of all ethnic groups have been moving to the suburbs, what does this graph suggest?

Again, in contrast to prevailing stereotypes, the suburbs include a significant number of low-income people from all backgrounds—White, Black, and Hispanic. Poverty is not conventionally associated with the suburbs, partly because the suburban poor tend to be scattered among more affluent people. In some instances, suburban communities intentionally hide social problems so they can maintain a "respectable image." Soaring housing costs have contributed to suburban poverty, which is expected to rise at a faster rate than city poverty through 2010 (El Nasser 1999).

Sociologist Ivan Fahs, who studied homelessness in suburban Chicago, found that the lead community in finding shelter for the homeless was the suburban county seat. Neighboring communities were reluctant even to acknowledge the homeless in their midst, much less assist in easing the housing problem. Indeed, public officials who live in the suburbs find it difficult to accept the diverse population in their communities (Fahs et al. 1997; Mayor's Task Force on Homelessness 1997). (For a more detailed discussion of homelessness, see the social policy section at the end of this chapter.)

Communities enact *zoning laws,* in theory, to ensure that certain standards of housing construction are satis-fied; these laws generally stipulate land use and architectural design standards. Zoning laws can also separate industrial and commercial enterprises from residential areas. Thus, a suburb might wish to prevent a factory from moving to a quiet residential neighborhood. However, some zoning laws serve as thinly veiled efforts to keep low-income people out of a suburb and have been attacked as "snob statutes." By requiring that a person own a certain number of square feet of land before he or she can build a home—or by prohibiting prefabricated or modular housing—a community can effectively prevent the construction of any homes that lower-class families might be able to afford. The courts have generally let such exclusionary zoning laws stand, even when charges have been made that their enactment was designed to keep out racial minorities and new immigrants with large families (Salins 1996).

Some urban and suburban residents are moving to communities even more remote from the central city or to rural areas altogether. Initial evidence suggests that this move to rural areas is only furthering the racial disparities in our metropolitan areas (Bureau of the Census 1997b; Holmes 1997).

Rural Communities

As we have seen, the people of the United States live mainly in urban areas. Yet one-fourth of the population lives in towns of 2,500 people or less that are not adjacent to a city. As is true of the suburbs, it would be a mistake to view rural communities as fitting into one set image. Turkey farms, coal mining towns, cattle ranches, and gas stations along interstate highways are all part of the rural landscape in the United States.

The historic stereotype of the farmer is a White male. Yet African Americans and women have long played a significant role in agriculture, both in the United States and throughout the world. Women participate actively in agriculture—on large and small farms and in profitable and failing family businesses. Farming women are almost always married and generally have large families. Segregation by gender is typical of farm labor: Men are more likely to be engaged in field work, while women serve their farms as accountants, personnel and equipment managers, and purchasing agents. Many studies have documented the high degree of stress that farming women experience as they attempt to fulfill many demanding social roles (Keating and Munro 1988).

Whereas women are involved in farming in all regions of the United States, 90 percent of African American farmers work in the South. Their farms tend to be small—an average of about 100 acres compared with the national average of 4,400 acres. Moreover, Black farmers are concentrated in areas of the country with severe economic difficulties, including limited job opportunities and few supportive services for residents. In 1950, 10 percent of people running farms in the United States were African American, but by 1997 this figure had fallen to less than 1 percent. In good part, this was not a voluntary withdrawal from farming; farm displacement and loss of land among African Americans occurs at a rate 212 times higher than the rate among White farmers (Jones 1999; Parker 2000).

The postindustrial revolution has been far from kind to the rural communities of the United States. Despite media images, agriculture accounts for only 9 percent of employment in nonurban counties. Indeed, in 1993, the Bureau of the Census calculated that farm residents accounted for only 2 percent of the nation's population—compared with 95 percent in 1790. At the same time that farming has been in decline, so have mining and logging—the two nonagricultural staples of the rural economy. When these jobs disappear, the rural poor who want to be economically self-sufficient face problems. Low-wage jobs are few, distances to services and better-paying jobs are long, and child care options are scarce. In desperation, residents of depressed rural areas have begun to encourage prison construction, which they once discouraged, to bring in badly needed economic development. Ironically, in regions where the prison population has declined, communities have been hurt yet again by their dependence on a single industry (Kilborn 2001).

The construction of large businesses can create its own problems, as small communities that have experienced the arrival of large discount stores, such as Wal-Mart,

Target, Home Depot, or Costco, have discovered. Although many residents welcome the new employment opportunities and the convenience of one-stop shopping, local merchants see their longtime family businesses endangered by formidable 200,000-square-foot competitors with a national reputation. Even when such discount stores provide a boost to a town's economy (and they do not always do so), they can undermine the town's sense of community and identity. Box 20-2 chronicles the "store wars" that often ensue.

Rural communities that do survive may feel threatened by other changes intended to provide jobs, income, and financial security. For example, the town of Postville, Iowa—with a population of only 1,478—was dying in 1987 when an entrepreneur from New York City bought a run-down meat processing plant. The plant was subsequently transformed into a kosher slaughtering house, and today 150 Postville residents are devout Hasidic Jews from the Lubavitcher sect. The new residents occupy key managerial positions in the slaughtering house, while Lubavitcher rabbis supervise the kosher processing of the meat to ensure that it is acceptable under Jewish dietary laws. Initially, there was distrust between longtime residents of Postville and their new neighbors, but gradually each group came to realize that it needed the other (Bloom 2000; Simon 2001).

On a more positive note, advances in electronic communication have allowed some people in the United

Rabbis pray in the locker room at a kosher meat processing plant near Postville, Iowa. When the plant first opened, the rural Christians hired to work there were unfamiliar with Jewish culture and faith, but members of the two groups soon learned to work together.

No organization exists in a vacuum, especially not a corporate giant. Executives of Wal-Mart know that. The epitome of the superstore, Wal-Mart has become the center of controversy in towns and cities across the United States, despite the familiar smiley-face logo and its red, white, and blue corporate image. The reason: a new Wal-Mart can have powerfully negative effects on the surrounding community.

Wal-Mart was founded in 1962 by Sam Walton, whose strategy was to locate new stores in rural communities, where competition from other retailers was weak and unions were not organized. Over the years, as the enormously successful discount chain expanded, Wal-Mart began to move into the fringes of metropolitan areas as well. But the residents of the communities Wal-Mart moved into did not always welcome their new neighbor. In Ashland, Virginia, a community of 7,200 people, residents worried that Wal-Mart would destroy the small-town atmosphere they treasured. Would their cozy grocery store, known for its personal service, survive the discount giant's competition? Would their quaint and charming Main Street fall into decline? Would full-time jobs with full benefits give way to part-time employment? (Studies have shown that superstores ultimately reduce employment.) Ashland's grassroots opposition to Wal-Mart, chronicled in the PBS documentary *Store Wars*, ultimately lost their battle because of Wal-Mart's prom-

ised low prices and increased tax revenues. But citizens in many other communities have won, at least temporarily.

On the urban fringes, too, residents have mobilized to stop new superstores. In Bangor, Maine, environmentalists raised an alarm over a proposed Wal-Mart superstore, to be located next to a marsh that sheltered endangered wildlife. Activists in Riverside, California, also challenged Wal-Mart, again on environmental grounds. But the issue is more complicated in these areas, because communities on the urban fringe are hardly

> In Ashland, Virginia, residents worried that Wal-Mart would destroy the small-town atmosphere they treasured.

untouched by economic development. Wal-Mart's proposed site in Bangor, for instance, is not far from the Bangor mall. And the huge new houses that dot the suburbs surrounding new stores, built on lots carved out of farmland or forest, have had an environmental impact themselves. In fact, the trend toward the superstore seems to parallel the emergence of the megalopolis, whose boundaries push further and further outward, eating up open space in the process. Recognizing the drawbacks of urban sprawl, some planners are beginning to advocate "smart

growth"—restoring the central city and its older suburbs rather than abandoning them for the outer rings.

Not all communities reject superstores. In fact, in Canada, some economically depressed rural communities are actively recruiting new Wal-Marts, seeking the jobs and increased traffic they need to reinvigorate themselves. Across Canada, public reaction to the U.S. chain's arrival has been almost universally positive. Canadian shoppers appreciate Wal-Mart's selection and low prices, and Canadian manufacturers have found a huge new outlet for their wares.

Wal-Mart executives are unapologetic about the chain's rapid expansion. They argue that their aggressive competition has lowered prices and raised working people's standard of living. And they say they have given back to the communities where their stores are located by donating money to educational institutions and local agencies.

Let's Discuss

1. Is there a Wal-Mart, Home Depot, or some other superstore near you? If so, was its opening a matter of controversy in your community?
2. What do you think of the "smart growth" movement? Should communities attempt to redirect business and residential development, or should developers be free to build wherever and whatever they choose?

Sources: D. Ibata 2001; L. Kaufman 2000; *Maine Times* 2001; PBS 2001; B. Simon 2001; Smart Growth 2001; Wal-Mart 2001; Wal-Mart Watch 2000.

States to work wherever they wish. For those who are concerned about quality-of-life issues, working at home in a rural area that has access to the latest high-tech services is the perfect arrangement. No matter where people make their homes—whether in the city, the suburbs, or a country village—economic and technological change will have an impact on their quality of life.

Imagine

You have fast-forwarded to a future in which there are no central cities—just sprawling suburbs and isolated rural communities. What are the economic and social effects of the disappearance of the downtown area?

Seeking Shelter Worldwide

The Issue

A chance meeting brought two old classmates together. In late 1997, Prince Charles encountered Clive Harold during a tour of the offices of a magazine sold by the homeless in London. But while Prince Charles can call several palaces home, Harold is homeless. This modern-day version of the *The Prince and the Pauper* intrigued many people with its message that "it can happen to anyone." Harold had been a successful author and journalist until his marriage fell apart and alcohol turned his life inside out (*Chicago Tribune* 1997b).

The issue of inadequate shelter manifests itself in many ways, for all housing problems can be considered relative. For a middle-class family in the United States, it may mean a somewhat smaller house than they need because that is all they can afford. For a single working adult in Tokyo, it may mean having to commute two hours to a full-time job. For many people worldwide, however, the housing problem consists of merely finding shelter of any kind that they can afford, in a place where anyone would reasonably wish to live. Prince Charles of Buckingham Palace and Clive Harold, homeless person, are extreme examples of a continuum present in all communities in all societies. What can be done to ensure adequate shelter for those who can't afford it?

The Setting

Homelessness is evident in both industrialized and developing countries. According to estimates, the number of homeless persons in the United States numbered at least 750,000 on any given night in 2001, and as many as 3.5 million Americans may experience homelessness for some period each year. Given the limited

In a story the press dubbed "The Prince and the Pauper," Prince Charles was surprised to run into an old classmate while visiting the office of a magazine sold by the homeless—and was even more surprised to learn that the fellow was himself homeless.

amount of space in public shelters, at a minimum, hundreds of thousands of people in the United States are homeless and without shelter (National Alliance to End Homelessness 2001).

In Japan, the problem of homelessness is just as serious. The Japanese usually hide such misfortune, thinking it shameful. But in the past decade, a severe economic downturn has victimized many formerly prosperous citizens, swelling the numbers of the homeless. A chronic space shortage in the heavily populated island nation, together with opposition to the establishment of homeless shelters in residential neighborhoods, has compounded the problem. In 2001, only two homeless shelters served 6,000 to 10,000 homeless people in Tokyo (French 2001b; Prusher 2001).

In Third World countries, rapid population growth has outpaced the expansion of housing by a wide margin, leading to a rise in homelessness. For example, estimates of homelessness in Mexico City range from 10,000 to 100,000, and these estimates do not include the many people living in caves or squatter settlements (see Box 20-1). By 1998, in urban areas alone, 600 million people around the world were either homeless or inadequately housed (Goldstein 1998; Ross 1996).

Sociological Insights

Both in the United States and around the world, being homeless functions as a master status that largely defines a person's position within society. In this case, pp. 112, 190 homelessness tends to mean that in many important respects, the individual is *outside* society. Without a home address and telephone, it is difficult to look for work or even apply for public assistance. Moreover, the master status of being homeless carries a serious stigma and can lead to prejudice and discrimination. Poor treatment of people suspected of being homeless is common in stores and restaurants, and many communities have reported acts of random violence against homeless people.

The profile of homelessness has changed significantly during the last 30 years. In the past, homeless people were primarily older White males living as alcoholics in skid-row areas. However, today's homeless are comparatively younger—with an average age in the low 30s. Overall, an estimated 60 percent of homeless people in the United States are from racial and ethnic mi-

nority groups. Moreover, a 27-city survey done in 2001 found that the homeless population is growing faster than the increase in emergency food and shelter space (Burt et al. 2001; U.S. Conference of Mayors 2001).

Changing economic and residential patterns account for much of this increase in homelessness. In recent decades, the process of urban renewal has included a noticeable boom in *gentrification.* This term refers to the resettlement of low-income city neighborhoods by prosperous families and business firms. In some instances, city governments have promoted gentrification by granting lucrative tax breaks to developers who convert low-cost rental units into luxury apartments and condominiums. Conflict theorists note that although the affluent may derive both financial and emotional benefits from gentrification and redevelopment, the poor often end up being thrown out on the street.

There is an undeniable connection between the nation's growing shortage of affordable housing and the rise in homelessness. Yet sociologist Peter Rossi (1989, 1990) cautions against focusing too narrowly on housing shortages while ignoring structural factors, such as the decline in the demand for manual labor in cities and the increasing prevalence of chronically unemployed young men among the homeless. Rossi contends that structural changes have put everyone in extreme poverty at higher risk of becoming homeless—especially poor people with an accumulation of disabilities (such as drug abuse, bad health, unemployment, and criminal records). Being disabled in this manner forces the individual to rely on family and

This biting cartoon from the *Japan Times* acknowledges the plight of the homeless. As of 2001, the city of Tokyo had only two homeless shelters.

friends for support, often for a prolonged period. If the strain on this support network is so great that it collapses, homelessness may result. While many researchers accept Rossi's theory, the general public often prefers to "blame the victim" for becoming homeless (Elliot and Krivo 1991; Lee 1992; Twombly et al. 2001).

Homeless women often have additional problems that distinguish them from homeless men. Homeless women report more recent injuries or acute illnesses, as well as more chronic health problems, than homeless men. Moreover, these women have experienced more disruption in their families and social networks than homeless men (Liebow 1993).

Sociologists attribute homelessness in developing nations not only to income inequality but also to population growth and an influx of people from rural areas and areas experiencing natural disaster, famine, or warfare. A major barrier to constructing decent, legal, and affordable housing in the urban areas of these developing nations is the political power of large-scale landowners and small-scale land speculators—anyone buying a few lots as investment. In the view of conflict theorists, these groups conspire to enhance their own financial investment by making the supply of legally buildable land scarce. In many cases, residents who can afford building materials have no choice but to become squatters. Those who can't are likely to become homeless.

Policy Initiatives

Thus far, policymakers have often been content to steer the homeless toward large, overcrowded, unhealthy shelters. Many neighborhoods and communities have resisted plans to open large shelters or even smaller residences for the homeless, often raising the familiar cry of "Not in my backyard!" The major federal program intended to assist the homeless is the McKinney Homeless Assistance Act, passed in 1987. This act authorizes federal aid for emergency food, shelter, physical and mental health care, job training, and education for homeless children and adults. Approximately $600 to $800 million in funds are distributed annually to about 100 community-based service organizations (Housing and Urban Development 1999).

According to a report by the National Law Center on Homelessness and Poverty (1996), there was a growing trend in the 1990s toward the adoption of anti-homeless public policies and the "criminalization" of homeless people. In 1995 alone, at least 29 cities enacted curbs on panhandling, sitting on sidewalks, standing near banks at automated teller machines, and other behavior sometimes evident among the homeless. At the same time, more and more policymakers—especially conservative officials—have advocated cutbacks in government funding for the homeless and argued that voluntary associations and religious organizations should assume a more important role in addressing the problem of homelessness (Morse 1999).

By 2001, the availability of low-rent housing had reached the lowest levels since surveys began in 1970. Despite the booming economy during much of the 1990s and occasional media spotlights on the homeless, affordable housing has become harder to find. Nearly 5 million low-income households receive no housing allowance, and most spend a disproportionately large share of their income to maintain their shelter. Research shows that this worsening of affordable housing stems from a substantial drop in the number of unsubsidized low-cost rental housing units in the private market and a growing number of low-income renter households. Meanwhile, federally funded rental assistance has failed to keep pace with the need (Housing and Urban Development 2001).

Developing nations have special problems. They have understandably given highest priority to economic productivity as measured by jobs with living wages. Unfortunately, even the most ambitious economic and social programs may be overwhelmed by minor currency fluctuations, a drop in the value of a nation's major export, or an influx of refugees from a neighboring country. Some of the reforms implemented have included promoting private (as opposed to government-controlled) housing markets, allowing dwellings to be places of business as well, and loosening restrictions on building materials.

All three of these short-term solutions have shortcomings. Private housing markets invite exploitation; mixed residential/commercial use may only cause good housing to deteriorate faster; and the use of marginal building materials leaves low-income residential areas more vulnerable to calamities such as floods, fires, and earthquakes. Large-scale rental housing under government supervision, the typical solution in North America and Europe, has been successful only in economically advanced city-states such as Hong Kong and Singapore (Strassman 1998).

In sum, homeless people both in the United States and abroad are not getting the shelter they need, and they lack the political clout to corral the attention of policymakers.

Let's Discuss

1. Have you ever worked as a volunteer in a shelter or soup kitchen? If so, were you surprised by the type of

people who lived or ate there? Has anyone you know ever had to move into a shelter?

2. Is gentrification of low-income housing a problem where you live? Have you ever had difficulty finding an affordable place to live?

3. What kind of assistance is available to homeless people in the community where you live? Does the help come from the government, from private charities, or both? What about housing assistance for people with low incomes, such as rent subsidies—is it available?

Chapter Resources

Summary

A *community* is a spatial or political unit of social organization that gives people a sense of belonging. This chapter explains how communities originated and analyzes the process of urbanization from both the functionalist and conflict perspectives. It describes various types of communities, including the central cities, the suburbs, and rural communities.

1. Stable communities began to develop when people stayed in one place to cultivate crops; surplus production enabled cities to emerge.

2. Gideon Sjoberg identified three preconditions of city life: advanced technology in both agricultural and nonagricultural areas, a favorable physical environment, and a well-developed social organization.

3. There are important differences between the *preindustrial city,* the *industrial city,* and the *postindustrial city.*

4. Urbanization is evident not only in the United States but throughout the world; by 2000, 45 percent of the world's population lived in urban areas.

5. The *urban ecological* approach is functionalist because it emphasizes that different elements in urban areas contribute to stability.

6. Drawing on conflict theory, *new urban sociology* considers the interplay of a community's political and economic interests as well as the impact of the

global economy on communities in the United States and other countries.

7. Many urban residents are immigrants from other nations and tend to live in ethnic neighborhoods.

8. In the last three decades, cities have confronted an overwhelming array of economic and social problems, including crime, unemployment, and the deterioration of schools and public transit systems.

9. *Asset-based community development (ABCD)* is a new approach to the revitalization of distressed neighborhoods in which planners first identify an area's resources and then mobilize them, channeling assistance to local agencies based in the community.

10. Suburbanization was the most dramatic population trend in the United States throughout the twentieth century. In recent decades, suburbs have witnessed increasing diversity in race and ethnicity.

11. Farming, mining, and logging have all been in decline in the rural communities of the United States.

12. Soaring housing costs, unemployment, cutbacks in public assistance, and rapid population growth have all contributed to rising homelessness around the world. Most social policy is directed toward sending the homeless to large shelters.

Critical Thinking Questions

1. How can the functionalist and conflict perspectives be used in examining the growing interest among policymakers in privatizing public services that are presently offered by cities and other communities?

2. How has your home community (your city, town, or neighborhood) changed over the years you have lived there? Have there been significant changes in the community's economic base and in its racial

and ethnic profile? Have the community's social problems intensified or lessened over time? Is unemployment currently a major problem? What are the community's future prospects?

3. Imagine that you have been asked to study the issue of homelessness in the largest city in your state. How might you draw on surveys, observation research, experiments, and existing sources to help you study this issue?

Key Terms

Asset-based community development (ABCD) An approach to community development in which planners first identify a community's strengths and then seek to mobilize those assets. (page 512)

Community A spatial or political unit of social organization that gives people a sense of belonging, based either on shared residence in a particular place or on a common identity. (501)

Concentric-zone theory A theory of urban growth devised by Ernest Burgess that sees growth in terms of a series of rings radiating from the central business district. (506)

Defended neighborhood A neighborhood that residents identify through defined community borders and a perception that adjacent areas are geographically separate and socially different. (511)

Gentrification The resettlement of low-income city neighborhoods by prosperous families and business firms. (518)

Human ecology An area of study concerned with the interrelationships between people and their spatial setting and physical environment. (506)

Industrial city A city characterized by relatively large size, open competition, an open class system, and elaborate specialization in the manufacturing of goods. (503)

Megalopolis A densely populated area containing two or more cities and their surrounding suburbs. (504)

Multiple-nuclei theory A theory of urban growth developed by Harris and Ullman that views growth as emerging from many centers of development, each of which may reflect a particular urban need or activity. (507)

New urban sociology An approach to urbanization that considers the interplay of local, national, and worldwide forces and their effect on local space, with special emphasis on the impact of global economic activity. (508)

Postindustrial city A city in which global finance and the electronic flow of information dominate the economy. (504)

Preindustrial city A city with only a few thousand people living within its borders and characterized by a relatively closed class system and limited mobility. (502)

Squatter settlements Areas occupied by the very poor on the fringes of cities, in which housing is often constructed by the settlers themselves from discarded material. (506)

Suburb According to the Census Bureau, any territory within a metropolitan area that is not included in the central city. (512)

Urban ecology An area of study that focuses on the interrelationships between people and their environment in urban areas. (506)

Urbanism A term used by Wirth to describe distinctive patterns of social behavior evident among city residents. (504)

World systems analysis A view of the global economic system that sees it as divided between certain industrialized nations and the developing countries that they control and exploit. (508)

Zoning laws Legal provisions stipulating land use and architectural design of housing, often employed as a means of keeping racial minorities and low-income people out of suburban areas. (514)

Additional Readings

BOOKS

Calthorpe, Peter, and William Fulton. 2001. *The Regional City: Planning for the End of Sprawl.* Washington, D.C.: Island Press. Using San Francisco as a case study, two sociologists rethink the notion that the central cities are all declining and the suburbs are all flourishing.

Duany, Andres, Elizabeth Plater-Zyberk, and Jeff Speck. 2000. *Suburban Nation: The Rise of Sprawl and the Decline of the American Dream.* New York: North Point Press. A critical look at most post–World War II suburban development, both residential and commercial.

Fitzpatrick, Kevin, and Mark LaGory. 2000. *Unhealthy Places: The Ecology of Risk in the Urban Landscape.* New York: Routledge. Two urban planners take a spatial view of urban ecology and raise the concept of the "urban health penalty"—the effect of place on an individual's access to health resources.

Hurley, Andrew. 2001. *Diners, Bowling Alleys and Trailer Parks: Chasing the American Dream in the Postwar Consumer Culture.* New York: Basic Books. An examination of how suburban institutions foster a sense of connectedness while reinforcing social class distinctions.

Koolhaas, Rem, et al. 2001. *Mutations*. Barcelona, Spain: Actar. This heavily illustrated book offers a variety of essays on the manufactured landscape of urban areas.

Mitchell, William J. 1999. *E-topia*. Cambridge: MIT Press. A futuristic view of what the world's cities might look like in an age of cybernetics. Written by a dean of architecture, the book predicts a variety of cityscapes based on different cultural traditions, all unified by a global digital network. Visit the author's website at (**http://mitpress.mit.edu/e-books/City_of_Bits/**) for his companion book *City of Bits* (Cambridge: MIT Press, 1996).

Moore, Robert M. III. 2001. *The Hidden America: Social Problems in Rural America for the Twenty-First Century*. Selingsgrove, PA: Susquehanna University Press. This anthology includes essays on topics such as substance abuse, immigration, and homelessness among rural Americans.

Phillips, E. Barbara. 1996. *City Lights: Urban-Suburban Life in the Global Society*. New York: Oxford University Press. Drawing upon all the social sciences, a sociologist looks at the urban–global network of the twentieth century and at alternative urban–suburban futures.

Sassen, Saskia. 2001. *The Global City*, 2nd ed. New Brunswick, NJ: Princeton University Press. A sociologist explains how the transition to a global economy has caused massive social change in New York, London, and Tokyo.

Solnit, Rebecca. 2001. *Hollow City: Gentrification and the Eviction of Urban Culture*. London: Verso. A highly critical work that sees in gentrification the uprooting of bohemian enclaves by the privileged.

Van Vliet, Willem, ed. 1998. *The Encyclopedia of Housing*. Thousand Oaks, CA: Sage Publications. This reference book has more than 500 entries arranged alphabetically from "abandonment" to "zoning."

Waldinger, Roger, ed. 2001. *Strangers at the Gates: New Immigrants in Urban America*. Berkeley: University of California Press. Nine essays on the social impact of immigration on native-born Americans.

JOURNALS

Among the journals that focus on community issues are *European Journal of Housing Policy* (founded in 2001), *Journal of Urban Affairs* (1979), *Rural Sociology* (1936), *Urban Affairs Review* (formerly *Urban Affairs Quarterly*, 1965), *Urban Anthropology* (1972), and *Urban Studies* (1964).

Technology Resources

Internet Connection

*Note: While all the URLs listed were current as of the printing of this book, these sites often change. Please check our website (**http://www.mhhe.com/schaefer8**) for updates and hyperlinks to these exercises and additional exercises.*

1. The National Law Center on Homelessness and Poverty (**http://www.nlchp.org**) is dedicated to providing the public with information on the homeless. Click on "Homelessness and Poverty in America." Read the article and answer the following questions:

   (a) How many men, women, and children are homeless in the United States?

   (b) What percentage of the homeless are families with children? What percentage are veterans? What percentage are mentally disabled?

   (c) Use your Refresh or Back button to return to "Homelessness and Poverty in America." Click on "The Causes." What are the four causes of homelessness?

   (d) Use your Refresh or Back button to return to "Homelessness and Poverty in America." Click on "The Solutions." What are the four suggested solutions to homelessness?

   (e) How would you feel if you suddenly became homeless? How do you think you would survive?

2. Chicago represents one of the largest urban areas in the United States. Don Brown's Chicago Daily Picture Page presents interesting photographs of life in "the Windy City." Direct your web browser to (**http://www.chicagopictures.com/**) and reflect on the images presented. If you prefer, you may substitute photographs from your own or a nearby city discovered through a search engine such as Yahoo! (**http://www.yahoo.com**).

   (a) How would you describe the architecture and use of space as shown in the pictures? How does city architecture differ from rural constructions?

   (b) Based on the images presented, can you see any examples of Herbert J. Gans's urban dweller types (cosmopolites, unmarried/childless people, ethnic villagers, the deprived and/or the trapped) or places where these types might live?

(c) Do the pictures reflect any of the issues currently facing cities as described in this chapter? How so?

(d) What positive features of urban life do the pictures display?

(e) How do the images and themes of the pictures of Chicago or your own city compare to the images and themes presented in the Kentucky Photo File, which features photographs taken by John Perkins (**http://members.iglou.com/perkins/newkpf/file.htm**)?

(f) How do these urban and rural photographs connect to the ideas in this chapter and to the discussion in Chapter 5 of *Gemeinshaft* and *Gesellschaft*?

3. Have you ever wondered what causes homelessness—what social forces and life circumstances separate those who have shelter from those who don't? Hobson's Choice (**http://www.realchangenews.org/hobson_intro.html**) is an online game that helps people understand this complex issue better. Link to "Current Issue" and then click on "Play Hobson's Choice—the game you can't leave." At the start of the game, players find themselves in a particular economic situation and are asked to make choices, each of which leads to a new situation or problem. Log on to the site and play the game four times.

(a) In how many games were you able to escape homelessness? In how many did you find yourself on the street, without shelter?

(b) Reflect on the choices you made. Was there a pattern to them? Which situations seemed to lead toward homelessness and which away from it?

(c) Did you feel frustrated by the results of any of your choices? What choices would you have made differently, and why?

(d) What is a Hobson's choice, and why is it applicable to the issue of homelessness?

(e) What do you think are the most important social causes of homelessness? What can be done, in practical terms, to alleviate the worldwide need for shelter?

Online Learning Center www.mhhe.com/schaefer8

Chicago is one of the largest urban areas in the United States. Learn more about Chicago by visiting the student center in the Online Learning Center at **www.mhhe.com/schaefer8,** and link to "Internet Exercises." Exercise 2 links you to Don Brown's Chicago Daily Picture Page, which presents interesting photos of life in the Windy City. For contrast, link to the Kentucky Photo File.

POPULATION AND
THE ENVIRONMENT

In India, a nation of over a billion people, pollution is becoming a controversial political issue. This billboard graphically suggests the harmful effect of pollution on public health.

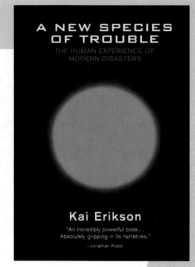

A NEW SPECIES OF TROUBLE

THE HUMAN EXPERIENCE OF MODERN DISASTERS

Kai Erikson

"An incredibly powerful book....
Absolutely gripping in its narratives."
—Jonathan Kozol

Over the past twenty years, research errands of one kind or another have taken me to a number of communities still stunned by the effects of a recent disaster. These include a valley in West Virginia known as Buffalo Creek, devastated by a fearsome flood; an Ojibwa Indian reserve in Canada called Grassy Narrows, plagued by contamination of the waterways along which members of the band had lived for centuries; a town in South Florida named Immokalee, where three hundred migrant farm workers were robbed of the only money most of them had ever saved; a group of houses in Colorado known as East Swallow, threatened by vapors from silent pools of gasoline that had gathered in the ground below; and the neighborhoods surrounding Three Mile Island.

In one respect, at least, these events were altogether different. A flood. An act of larceny. A toxic poisoning. A gasoline spill. A nuclear accident. My assignment in each of those cases was to learn enough about the people who thought they had been damaged by the blow to appear on their behalf in a court of law, so each was a separate research effort, and each resulted in a separate research report.

In another respect, though, it was clear from the beginning that those scenes of trouble had much in common. I was asked to visit them in the first place, obviously, because the persons who issued the invitations thought they could see resemblances there. And just as obviously, I was drawn to them because they touched a corresponding set of curiosities and preoccupations in me. Moreover, common themes seemed to come into focus as I moved from one place to another, so that those separate happenings (and the separate stories told of them) began to fuse into a more inclusive whole. One of the excitements of sociological work in general is to watch general patterns—dim and shapeless at first—emerge from a wash of seemingly unconnected details. . . .

In particular: Soon after the black wall of water and debris ground its way down Buffalo Creek, attorneys for the coal company involved called the disaster "an act of God." . . . However people elsewhere may look upon that . . . reasoning, the residents of Buffalo Creek understood it to be blasphemy. They knew that one does not blame God lightly for the wrongdoings of humankind, . . . and they knew, too, that the phrase itself reflected a degree of indifference bordering on contempt. On both of those counts they reacted with fury.

I thought then that the sharpness of the reaction had a lot to do with cultural particulars: the immediacy of Appalachian spirituality, the paternalism of Appalachian coal camps, the communality of Appalachian society. I would suggest now, though, that the people of the valley were drawing on local languages and sensibilities to express feelings that are far more general, for people elsewhere seem to respect a profound difference between those disasters that can be understood as the work of nature and those that need to be understood as the work of humankind. *(Erikson 1994:11–12, 19)* ■

Additional information about this excerpt and about those that open each subsequent chapter can be found in the SocWorld CD-ROM that accompanies this text.

In this passage from *A New Species of Trouble,* Kai Erikson explains how he brought his sociological imagination to bear on five seemingly unrelated disasters. Each, he realized, had been caused not by natural forces, but by human disregard for the natural world or for other human beings. But while ignorance or negligence is often thought to be at the bottom of such catastrophes, Erikson saw a larger, more sweeping process at work. Consumerism and rapid increases in population, he thought, lay at the bottom of these calamities. Economically, people and their ever-increasing wants and needs had begun to outstrip the capacity of the environment to tolerate their encroachments. Through overpopulation, overconsumption, overbuilding, and overgrazing, people were beginning to overwhelm their physical environment.

What is the relationship between population and the environment? Are humans in danger of overpopulating the world, causing an environmental catastrophe in the process? How does rapid population growth contribute to the movement of large groups of people from one part of the world to another? What do sociologists have to say about population policy and environmental issues? In this chapter, because we cannot begin to understand the deterioration of our physical environment without grasping the effects of human behavior, we will take a sociological overview of world population and some related environmental issues. We will begin with Thomas Robert Malthus's controversial analysis of population trends and Karl Marx's critical response to it. A brief overview of world population history follows. We'll pay particular attention to the current problem of overpopulation, and the prospects for and potential consequences of stable population growth in the United States. We'll see, too, how population growth fuels the migration of large numbers of people from one area of the world to another.

Later in the chapter, we will examine the environmental problems facing the world as we enter the twenty-first century, and will draw on the functionalist and conflict perspectives to better understand environmental issues. It is important not to oversimplify the relationship between population and the environment. Rising population, in itself, does not necessarily destroy the environment, while stable population growth alone is no guarantee of healthful air, water, or land. Nevertheless, as will be evident in the second half of the chapter and in the social policy section on world population policy, increases in population can strain our environmental resources and present difficult choices for policymakers. ■

Demography: The Study of Population

The study of population issues engages the attention of both natural and social scientists. The biologist explores the nature of reproduction and casts light on factors that affect *fertility,* the level of reproduction in a society. The medical pathologist examines and analyzes trends in the causes of death. Geographers, historians, and psychologists also have distinctive contributions to make to our understanding of population. Sociologists, more than these other researchers, focus on the *social* factors that influence population rates and trends.

In their study of population issues, sociologists are keenly aware that various elements of population—such as fertility and *mortality* (the amount of death)—are profoundly affected by the norms, values, and social patterns of a society. Fertility is influenced by people's age of entry into sexual unions and by their use of contraception—both of which, in turn, reflect the social and religious values that guide a particular culture. Mortality is shaped by a nation's level of nutrition, acceptance of immunization, and provisions for sanitation, as well as its general commitment to health care and health education. Migration from one country to another can depend on marital and kinship ties, the relative degree of racial and religious tolerance in various societies, and people's evaluations of employment opportunities.

Demography is the scientific study of population. It draws on several components of population, including size, composition, and territorial distribution, to understand the social consequences of population change (see Figure 21-1). Demographers study geographical variations and historical trends in their effort to develop population forecasts. They also analyze the structure of a population—the age, gender, race, and ethnicity of its members. A key figure in this type of analysis was Thomas Malthus.

Malthus's Thesis and Marx's Response

The Reverend Thomas Robert Malthus (1766–1834) was educated at Cambridge University and spent his life teaching history and political economy. He strongly criticized

Figure 21-1

World Population, 2001

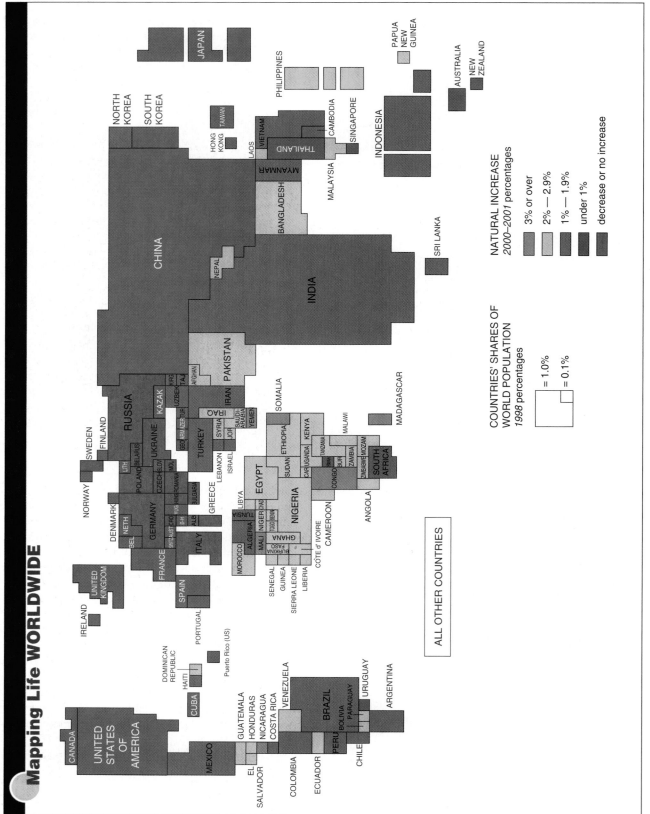

Mapping Life WORLDWIDE

COUNTRIES' SHARES OF WORLD POPULATION
1998 percentages

☐ = 1.0%

▫ = 0.1%

NATURAL INCREASE
2000–2001 percentages

3% or over

2% — 2.9%

1% — 1.9%

under 1%

decrease or no increase

ALL OTHER COUNTRIES

Sources: Haub and Cornelius 2001.

Based on an estimate of population data for 2001, this map of the world has been redrawn so that the size of each country is shown as proportional to its population rather than its geographic area. For example, note how India and China are represented on this map.

two major institutions of his time—the church and slavery—yet his most significant legacy for contemporary scholars is his still-controversial *Essays on the Principle of Population,* published in 1798.

Essentially, Malthus held that the world's population was growing more rapidly than the available food supply. Malthus argued that food supply increases in an arithmetic progression (1, 2, 3, 4, and so on), whereas population expands by a geometric progression (1, 2, 4, 8, and so on). According to his analysis, the gap between food supply and population will continue to grow over time. Even though the food supply will increase, it will not increase nearly enough to meet the needs of an expanding world population.

Malthus advocated population control to close the gap between rising population and food supply, yet he explicitly denounced artificial means of birth control because they were not sanctioned by religion. For Malthus, one appropriate way to control population was to postpone marriage. He argued that couples must take responsibility for the number of children they choose to bear; without such restraint, the world would face widespread hunger, poverty, and misery (Malthus et al. [1824] 1960; Petersen 1979).

Karl Marx strongly criticized Malthus's views on population. Marx pointed to the nature of economic relations in Europe's industrial societies as the central problem. He could not accept the Malthusian notion that rising world population, rather than capitalism, was the cause of social ills. In Marx's opinion, there was no special relationship between world population figures and the supply of resources (including food). If society were well ordered, increases in population should lead to greater wealth, not to hunger and misery.

Of course, Marx did not believe that capitalism operated under these ideal conditions. He maintained that capitalism devoted its resources to the financing of buildings and tools rather than to more equitable distribution of food, housing, and other necessities of life. Marx's work is important to the study of population because he linked overpopulation to the unequal distribution of resources—a topic that will be taken up again later in this chapter. His concern with the writings of Malthus also testifies to the importance of population in political and economic affairs.

The insights of Malthus and Marx regarding population issues have come together in what is termed the *neo-Malthusian view.* Best exemplified by the work of Paul Ehrlich (1968; Ehrlich and Ehrlich 1990), author of *The Population Bomb,* neo-Malthusians agree with Malthus that world population growth is outstretching natural resources. However, in contrast to the British theorist, they insist that birth control measures are needed to regulate

The Reverend Thomas Robert Malthus suggested that the world's population was growing more rapidly than the available food supply.

population increases. Neo-Malthusians have a Marxist flavor in their condemnation of developed nations that, despite their low birthrates, consume a disproportionately large share of world resources. While rather pessimistic about the future, these theorists stress that birth control and sensible use of resources are essential responses to rising world population (Tierney 1990; Weeks 1999; for a critique, see Commoner 1971).

Studying Population Today

The relative balance of births and deaths is no less important today than it was during the lifetime of Malthus and Marx. The suffering that Malthus spoke of is certainly a reality for many people of the world who are hungry and poor. Malnutrition remains the largest contributing factor to illness and death among children in the developing countries. Almost 18 percent of these children will die before age five—a rate over 11 times higher than in developed nations. Warfare and large-scale migration intensify problems of population and food supply. For example, strife in Bosnia, Iraq, and Sudan caused very uneven distribution of food supplies, leading to regional concerns about malnutrition and even starvation. Combating world hunger may require reducing human births, dramatically increasing the world's food supply, or perhaps both at the same time. The study of population-related issues seems to be essential today (World Bank 2000c:277).

In the United States and most other countries, the census is the primary mechanism for collecting population information. A *census* is an enumeration or counting of a population. The Constitution of the United States requires that a census be held every 10 years to determine congressional representation. This periodic investigation is supplemented by *vital statistics;* these records of births, deaths, marriages, and divorces are gathered through a registration system maintained by governmental units. In addition, other governmental surveys provide up-to-date information on commercial developments, educational trends, industrial expansion, agricultural practices, and the status of such groups as children, the elderly, racial minorities, and single parents.

In administering a nationwide census and conducting other types of research, demographers employ many of the skills and techniques described in Chapter 2, including questionnaires, interviews, and sampling. The precision of population projections depends on the accuracy of a series of estimates that demographers must make. First, they must determine past population trends and establish a base population as of the date for which the forecast began. Next, birthrates and death rates must be established, along with estimates of future fluctuations. In making projections for a nation's population trends, demographers must consider migration as well, since a significant number of individuals may enter and leave a country.

Elements of Demography

Demographers communicate population facts with a language derived from the basic elements of human life—birth and death. The *birthrate* (or, more specifically, the *crude birthrate*) is the number of live births per 1,000 population in a given year. In 2001, for example, there were 15 live births per 1,000 people in the United States. The birthrate provides information on the actual reproductive patterns of a society.

One way demography can project future growth in a society is to make use of the *total fertility rate (TFR).* The TFR is the average number of children born alive to any woman, assuming that she conforms to current fertility rates. The TFR reported for the United States in 2001 was 2.1 live births per woman, as compared with over 7.5 births per woman in a developing country such as Niger.

Mortality, like fertility, is measured in several different ways. The *death rate* (also known as the *crude death rate*) is the number of deaths per 1,000 population in a given year. In 2001, the United States had a death rate of 9.0 per 1,000 population. The *infant mortality rate* is the number of deaths of infants under one year of age per 1,000 live births in a given year. This particular measure serves as an important indicator of a society's level of health care; it reflects prenatal nutrition, delivery procedures, and infant screening measures. The infant mortality rate also functions as a useful indicator of future population growth, since those infants who survive to adulthood will contribute to further population increases.

Nations vary widely in the rate of death of newborn children. In 2000, the infant mortality rate for the United States was 7 deaths per 1,000 live births, whereas for the world as a whole it was an estimated 57 deaths per 1,000 live births. At the same time, at least 32 nations have lower rates of infant mortality than the United States, including Great Britain, Canada, and Sweden (see Figure 19-2 on page 477).

A general measure of health used by demographers is *life expectancy,* the median number of years a person can be expected to live under current mortality conditions. Usually the figure is reported as life expectancy *at birth*. At present, Japan reports a life expectancy at birth of 81 years, slightly higher than the United States' figure of 77 years. By contrast, life expectancy at birth is less than 45 in several developing nations, including Zambia.

The *growth rate* of a society is the difference between births and deaths, plus the difference between *immigrants* (those who enter a country to establish permanent residence) and *emigrants* (those who leave a country permanently) per 1,000 population. For the world as a whole, the growth rate is simply the difference between births and deaths per 1,000 population, since worldwide immigration and emigration must of necessity be equal. In 2001, the United States had a growth rate of 0.6 percent, compared with an estimated 1.3 percent for the entire world (Haub and Cornelius 2001).

● World Population Patterns

One important aspect of demographic work involves study of the history of population. But how is this possible? After all, official national censuses were relatively rare before 1850. Researchers interested in early population must turn to archeological remains of settlements, burial sites, baptismal and tax records, and oral history sources.

On October 13, 1999, in a maternity clinic in Sarajevo, Bosnia-Herzegovina, Helac Fatina gave birth to a son, who has been designated as the six billionth person on this planet. Yet until modern times, there were relatively few humans living in the world. One estimate

Table 21-1	Estimated Time for Each Successive Increase of 1 Billion People in World Population	
Population Level	**Time Taken to Reach New Population Level**	**Year of Attainment**
First billion	Human history before 1800	1804
Second billion	123 years	1927
Third billion	33 years	1960
Fourth billion	14 years	1974
Fifth billion	13 years	1987
Sixth billion	12 years	1999
Seventh billion	13 years	2012
Eighth billion	14 years	2026
Ninth billion	16 years	2042

Note: Data for 2012 through 2054 are based on medium projection variant.

Source: United Nations Population Division 2001.

and death rates. This concept, which was introduced in the 1920s, is now widely used in the study of population trends.

As illustrated in Figure 21-2, demographic transition is typically viewed as a three-stage process:

1. *Pretransition stage:* high birthrates and death rates with little population growth.
2. *Transition stage:* declining death rates, primarily the result of reductions in infant deaths, along with high to medium fertility—resulting in significant population growth.
3. *Posttransition stage:* low birthrates and death rates with little population growth.

Demographic transition should be regarded not as a "law of population growth" but rather as a

placed the world population of a million years ago at only 125,000 people. As Table 21-1 indicates, the population has exploded in the last 200 years, and continues to accelerate rapidly (WHO 2000:3; for a different view, see Eberstadt 2001).

Demographic Transition

The phenomenal growth of world population in recent times can be accounted for by changing patterns of births and deaths. Beginning in the late 1700s—and continuing until the middle 1900s— there was a gradual reduction in death rates in northern and western Europe. People were able to live longer because of advances in food production, sanitation, nutrition, and public health care. While death rates fell, birthrates remained high; as a result, there was unprecedented population growth during this period of European history. However, by the late 1800s, the birthrates of many European countries began to decline, and the rate of population growth also decreased (O'Neill and Balk 2001).

The changes in birthrates and death rates in nineteenth century Europe serve as an example of demographic transition. Demographers use this term to describe an observed pattern in changing vital statistics. Specifically, **demographic transition** is the change from high birthrates and death rates to relatively low birthrates

Figure 21-2

Demographic Transition

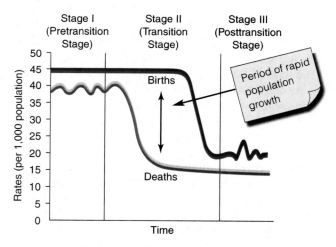

Demographers use the concept of *demographic transition* to describe changes in birthrates and death rates during stages of a nation's development. This graph shows the pattern that took place in presently developed nations. In the first stage, both birthrates and death rates were high, so that there was little population growth. In the second stage, the birthrate remained high while the death rate declined sharply, which led to rapid population growth. By the last stage, which many developing countries have yet to enter, the birthrate also declined, and there was again little population growth.

Sociology in the Global Community

21-1 Population Policy in China

In a residential district in Shanghai, a member of the local family planning committee knocks on the door of a childless couple. Why, she inquires, have they not started a family?

Such a question would have been unthinkable a generation earlier, when family planning officials, in an attempt to avoid a looming population explosion, sometimes resorted to sterilization to enforce the government rule of one child per family. Since then, Shanghai's birthrate has fallen so far it is now lower than the death rate—a situation that has left the city short of workers.

To remedy the shortage, the government has quietly begun to grant exceptions to the one-child policy to adults who are only children themselves. But the new leniency hasn't reversed the decline

in the birthrate, as officials were hoping, for government propaganda stressing the economic benefits of fewer children seems to have changed the public's attitude toward childbearing. Stopping Chinese couples from having babies may be difficult, muses Jin Zuegong, a member of

> Shanghai's birthrate has fallen so far it is now lower than the death rate.

the Municipal Planning Commission in Shanghai, but persuading them to have babies may be even more difficult.

Chinese families are beset, too, by the unforeseen results of their attempts to circumvent the one-child policy. In the past, in an effort to ensure that their one

child would be a male capable of perpetuating the family line, many couples chose to abort female fetuses, or quietly allowed female infants to die of neglect. As a result, China's sex ratio at birth (the ratio of male newborns to female newborns) is now about 117 to 100—well above the normal rate of 105 or 106 to 100. This difference in birthrates translates into 1.7 million fewer female births per year than normal—and down the line, to many fewer childbearers than normal. In 1993 the Chinese government, alarmed by the long-term implications of sex-selected abortion and infanticide, outlawed gender screening of unborn children except when medically necessary.

Chinese women have borne the brunt not just of the government's population

Sources: Beech 2001; Pomfret 2001; Riley 1996; Rosenthal 1999a.

generalization of the population history of industrial nations. This concept helps us understand the growth problems faced by the world in the 1990s. About two-thirds of the world's nations have yet to pass fully through the second stage of demographic transition. Even if such nations make dramatic advances in fertility control, their populations will nevertheless increase greatly because of the large base of people already at prime childbearing age.

The pattern of demographic transition varies from nation to nation. One particularly useful distinction is the contrast between the transition now occurring in developing nations—which include about two-thirds of the world's population—and that which occurred over almost a century in more industrialized countries. Demographic transition in developing nations has involved a rapid decline in death rates without adjustments in birthrates.

Specifically, in the post–World War II period, the death rates of developing nations began a sharp decline. This revolution in "death control" was triggered by antibiotics, immunization, insecticides (such as DDT, used to strike at malaria-bearing mosquitoes), and largely successful campaigns against such fatal diseases as smallpox. Substantial medical and public health technology was imported almost overnight from more developed nations.

As a result, the drop in death rates that had taken a century in Europe was telescoped into two decades in many developing countries.

Birthrates scarcely had time to adjust. Cultural beliefs about the proper size of families could not possibly change as quickly as the falling death rates. For centuries, couples had given birth to as many as eight or more children, knowing that perhaps only two or three would survive to adulthood. Consequently, whereas Europeans had had several generations to restrict their birthrates, peoples of developing nations needed to do the same in less than a lifetime. Many did not, as is evident from the astronomical "population explosion" that was already under way by the middle 1900s. Families were more willing to accept technological advances that prolonged life than to abandon fertility patterns that reflected centuries of tradition and religious training (Crenshaw et al. 2000; McFalls 1998).

The Population Explosion

Apart from war, rapid population growth has been perhaps the dominant international social problem of the past 40 years. Often this issue is referred to in emotional terms as the "population bomb" or the "population

This Chinese billboard advocates the one-child family. Note that the single, happy child is a daughter—an attempt to counter the traditional preference for male children.

policy, but of the economic disloca- tion caused by re- cent market reforms and the redistribu- tion of rural farm- land. In privatized government facto- ries, their need for maternity benefits and child care now limits their employ- ment opportunities; on rural farms, they struggle to cope in their husbands' ab- sence. The female suicide rate in rural China is now the highest in the world.

Experts think this alarming statistic re- flects a fundamental lack of self-esteem among rural Chinese women. The social patterns of centuries, unlike birthrates, cannot be changed in a generation.

Let's Discuss

1. Does any government, no matter how overpopulated a country is, have a right to sterilize people who do not voluntarily limit the size of their families? Why or why not?
2. The Chinese government's one-child policy seems to have back- fired. What other policies might have worked better? Explain why.

explosion." Such striking language is not surprising, given the staggering increases in world population during the twentieth century (refer to Table 21-1). The population of our planet rose from 1 billion around the year 1800 to 6.1 billion by 2001 (Ehrlich and Ellison 2002; Haub and Cornelius 2001).

By the middle 1970s, demographers had observed a slight decline in the growth rate of many developing nations. These countries were still experiencing population increases, yet their *rates* of in- crease had declined as death rates could not go much lower and birthrates began to fall. It appears that family planning ef- forts have been instrumental in this de- mographic change. Beginning in the 1960s, governments in certain develop- ing nations sponsored or supported cam- paigns to encourage family planning. For example, in good part as the result of government-sponsored birth control campaigns, Thailand's total fertility rate fell from 6.1 births per woman in 1970 to

only 1.0 in 2001. And China's strict one-child policy re- sulted in a negative growth rate in some urban areas (see Box 21-1).

AIDS has had a dramatic impact on the death rates in many developing countries, particularly in Africa.

533

Even if family planning efforts are successful in reducing fertility rates, the momentum toward growing world population is well established. The developing nations face the prospect of continued population growth, since a substantial proportion of their population is approaching the childbearing years (see the top of Figure 21-3). The social policy section at the end of this chapter takes a closer look at the challenges policymakers face in developing nations.

A **population pyramid** is a special type of bar chart that distributes the population by gender and age; it is generally used to illustrate the population structure of a society. As Figure 21-3 shows, a substantial portion of the population of Afghanistan consists of children under the age of 15, whose childbearing years are still to come. Thus, the built-in momentum for population growth is much greater in Afghanistan (and in many other developing countries in other parts of the world) than in western Europe or the United States.

Consider, also, population data for India, which in 2000 surpassed 1 billion in population. Sometime between the years 2040 and 2050 India's population will surpass China's. The substantial momentum for growth built into India's age structure means that the nation will face a staggering increase in population in the coming decades—even if its birthrate declines sharply (Dugger 2001).

Population growth is not a problem in all nations. Today, a handful of countries are even adopting policies that *encourage* growth. One such country is Japan, where the total fertility rate has fallen sharply. Nevertheless, a global perspective underscores the serious consequences that could result from overall continued population growth.

pp. 124–128 ◄ A tragic new factor has emerged in the last 15 years that will restrict worldwide population growth: the spread of AIDS. As of 2001, 45 countries were severely affected by the disease. About 88 percent of all AIDS cases are concentrated in those 45 coun-

tries, most of which are located in sub-Saharan Africa—though Cambodia, India, Thailand, Brazil, the Dominican Republic, and Haiti also are significantly affected. In Botswana, the country with the highest prevalence of HIV, one out of every three adults is HIV positive, and life expectancy has dropped from 60 in 1990 to a projected 36 in 2005 (United Nations Population Division 2001).

Imagine

You are living in a country that is so heavily populated, basic resources such as food, water, and living space are running short. What will you do? How will you respond to the crisis if you are a government social planner? A politician?

Figure 21-3

Population Structure of Afghanistan and the United States, 2000

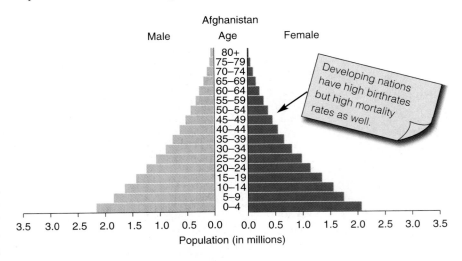

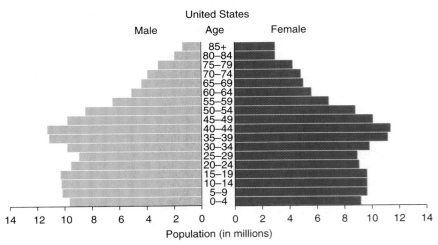

Source: Bureau of the Census 2000d.

Developing nations have high birthrates but high mortality rates as well.

Fertility Patterns in the United States

During the last four decades, the United States and other industrial nations have passed through two different patterns of population growth—the first marked by high fertility and rapid growth (stage II in the theory of demographic transition), the second marked by declining fertility and little growth (stage III). Sociologists are keenly aware of the social impact of these fertility patterns.

The Baby Boom

The most recent period of high fertility in the United States has often been referred to as the *baby boom*. During World War II, large numbers of military personnel were separated from their spouses, but when they returned, the annual number of births began to rise dramatically. Still, the baby boom was not a return to the large families common in the 1800s. In fact, there was only a slight increase in the proportion of couples having three or more children. The boom resulted from a striking decrease in the number of childless marriages and one-child families. Although a peak was reached in 1957, the nation maintained a relatively high birthrate of over 20 live births per 1,000 population until 1964. In 2001, by contrast, the birthrate was 15 live births per 1,000 population—or 30 percent lower than in 1964 (Bureau of the Census 1975; Haub and Cornelius 2001).

It would be a mistake to attribute the baby boom solely to the return home of large numbers of soldiers. High wages and general prosperity during the postwar period encouraged many married couples to have children and purchase homes. In addition, several sociologists—as well as feminist author Betty Friedan (1963)—have noted that there were pervasive pressures on women during the 1950s to marry and become mothers and homemakers (Bouvier 1980).

Stable Population Growth

Although the total fertility rate of the United States has remained low over the last two decades, the nation continues to grow in size because of two factors: the momentum built into our age structure by the post-war population boom and the continued high rates of immigration. Because of the upsurge of births beginning in the 1950s, there are now many more people in their childbearing years than in older age groups (where most deaths occur). This growth of population represents a "demographic echo" of the baby boom generation, many of whom are now parents. Consequently, the number of people born

each year in the United States continues to exceed the number who die. In addition, the nation allows a large number of immigrants to enter each year; these immigrants currently account for between one-fourth and one-third of annual growth.

Despite these trends, in the 1980s and early 1990s, some analysts projected that there would be relatively low fertility levels and moderate net migration over the coming decades. As a result, it seemed possible that the United States might reach *zero population growth (ZPG)*. ZPG is the state of a population in which the number of births plus immigrants equals the number of deaths plus emigrants. Sixty-five countries, 40 of them in Europe, are now at or approaching ZPG. In the recent past, although some nations have achieved ZPG, it has been relatively short-lived (Haub and Cornelius 2001).

What would a society with stable population growth be like? In demographic terms, it would be quite different from the United States of the 1990s. There would be relatively equal numbers of people in each age group, and the median age of the population might perhaps be as high as 38 in 2050 (compared with 35 in 2000). As a result, the population pyramid of the United States (as shown in Figure 21-3) would look more like a rectangle (Bureau of the Census 2001a:13).

There would also be a much larger proportion of older people, especially age 75 and over. They would place a greater demand on the nation's social service programs and health care institutions. On a more positive note, the economy would be less volatile under ZPG, since the number of entrants into the paid labor force would remain stable. ZPG would also lead to changes in family life. With fertility rates declining, women would devote fewer years to child rearing and to the social roles of motherhood; the proportion of married women entering the labor force would continue to rise (Spengler 1978; Weeks 2002).

According to the latest Census Bureau projections, however, the United States is *not* moving toward ZPG. Instead, the nation's population is growing faster than was expected. Previous projections indicated that the U.S. population would stabilize between 290 and 300 million by the middle of the century; however, demographers now believe that by 2050, the population of the United States will reach 404 million. This trend toward growth is unique among industrialized nations. By 2050, the United States will be the only developed nation among the 20 most populous nations in the world.

Why the new projections? The Bureau of the Census has revised its assumptions about the three basic components of a nation's population: fertility, net immigration, and mortality. Overall, U.S. fertility is on the rise because of the fertility rates among African Americans, Hispanics, and Asian Americans. Even though the fertility rates among these racial and ethnic minorities are expected to moderate, their proportion of the national population is increasing. Second, immigration rates are expected to remain high (see the social policy section in Chapter 11). Today, about one-third of the nation's population growth results from net immigration (that is, the number of immigrants entering the United States minus the number of emigrants leaving). By the year 2050, 43 percent of overall population growth will be due to immigration. Finally, despite the impact of the AIDS crisis, the nation's mortality rate is expected to decline, while life expectancy will increase from the current figure of 77 years to 79 years by 2010 (Bureau of the Census 2001a:13; Crossette 2001).

Population and Migration

Along with births and deaths, migration is one of the three factors affecting population growth or decline. The term *migration* refers to relatively permanent movement of people with the purpose of changing their place of residence (Prehn 1991). Migration usually describes movement over a sizable distance, rather than from one side of a city to another.

As a social phenomenon, migration is fairly complex and results from a variety of factors. The most important tend to be economic—financial failure in the "old country" and a perception of greater economic opportunities and prosperity in the new homeland. Other factors that contribute to migration include racial and religious bigotry, dislike for prevailing political regimes, and desire to reunite one's family. All these forces combine to *push* some individuals out of their homelands and to *pull* them to areas believed to be more attractive.

International Migration

International migration—changes of residence across national boundaries—has been a significant force in redistributing the world's population during certain periods of history. For example, the composition of the United States has been significantly altered by immigrants who came here in the nineteenth and twentieth centuries. pp. 293–296 Their entry was encouraged or restricted by various immigration policies.

As noted earlier, immigration into a country can become a significant factor in its population growth.

In recent years, immigration has accounted for 20 to 30 percent of growth in the United States, which has led those troubled by population increases to join those opposed to an influx of foreigners in calling for serious restrictions on immigration. By contrast, however, many other countries are currently receiving a much higher proportion of immigrants. Over the last 10 years, more than 80 percent of population growth in Greece and Austria, and more than 40 percent in Canada and Australia, came from immigration (Bouvier and Grant 1994; Martin and Widgren 1996; Massey 1999).

In the last decade, immigration has become a controversial issue throughout much of Europe. Western Europe, in particular, has become a desirable destination for many individuals and families from former colonies or former communist-bloc countries who are fleeing the poverty, persecution, and warfare of their native lands. Currently, there are 20 million legal immigrants in western Europe, along with an estimated 2 million illegal immigrants. With the number of immigrants and refugees increasing at a time of widespread unemployment and housing shortages, there has been a striking rise in antiforeign (and often openly racist) sentiment in Germany, France, and other countries. Right-wing forces in Germany (including members of the skinhead counterculture examined in Chapter 3) have mounted more than 3,500 attacks on foreigners in recent years. Immigrants from eastern Europe and Asia are often the targets, and there have been attacks as well on Germany's small Jewish community.

Within days of the terrorist attack on the World Trade Center in New York, thousands of Afghan refugees had fled to Pakistan in anticipation of U.S. retaliation. Catastrophic conflicts such as war and terrorist attacks often trigger massive international migrations.

Developing countries in Asia and Africa are also encountering difficulties as thousands of displaced people seek assistance and asylum. For example, at the end of 2000, an estimated 14.5 million people worldwide were refugees or asylum seekers—a number that is equivalent to the population of Michigan or the Netherlands. Half of these people came from two areas, Palestine and Afghanistan. Needless to say, the political and economic problems of developing nations (see Chapter 10) are only intensified by such massive migration under desperate conditions (U.S. Committee for Refugees 2001).

Internal Migration

Migratory movements within societies can vary in important ways. In traditional societies, migration often represents a way of life, as people move to accommodate the changing availability of fertile soil and wild game. In industrial societies, people may relocate as a result of job transfers or because they believe that a particular region has better employment opportunities or a more desirable climate.

Although nations typically have laws and policies governing movement across their borders, the same is not true of internal movement. Generally, residents of a country are legally free to migrate from one locality to another. Of course, this is not the case in all nations; the Republic of South Africa historically restricted the movement of Blacks and other non-Whites through the system of segregation known as *apartheid* (refer back to Chapter 11).

We can identify three distinctive trends of recent internal migration within the United States:

1. *Suburbanization.* During the period 1980–1990, suburban counties grew in population by 14 percent while the total population of the United States rose by 10 percent. The proportion of the population living in central cities stayed constant at about one-third since 1950. Meanwhile, the share of the population living in nonmetropolitan areas declined from 44 percent in 1950 to 20 percent in 1994 (Bureau of the Census 1996b:38).
2. *"Sunning of America."* There has been significant internal migration from the "snow belt" of the north central and northeastern states to the "sun belt" in the South and West. Since 1970, the sun belt has absorbed almost two-thirds of the population growth of the United States. Individuals and families move to the sun belt because of its expanding economy and desirable climate. Businesses are attracted by the comparatively inexpensive energy supplies, increased availability of labor, and relative weakness of labor unions. Since 1990, however, while internal migration to the South has remained

high, migration to the West has lessened as the job boom in that region ended (see Figure 21-4).
3. *Rural life rebound.* In the early 1990s, nonmetropolitan counties gained in population, though the trend began to level off in 1998. This migration to rural areas, which reversed a long-standing trend toward urbanization, reflected concerns about the quality of life in the cities and suburbs. It has since dropped off, as the outskirts of metropolitan areas spread out and many downtown areas experienced a rebirth (K. Johnson 1999; Schachter 2001).

◖Imagine

What would happen if present patterns of migration, both internal and international, reversed themselves? How would your home town change? What would be the effect on the nation's economy? Would your own life change?

● The Environment

Quality of life, whether in the cities, the suburbs, or rural areas, is closely related to the environment. As we saw in Chapter 20, urban sprawl has been encroaching on the fields and forests that surround U.S. cities, replacing them with residential developments and malls. The new construction disturbs wildlife and threatens the water supply, and the cars residents drive to work every day choke the highways, contributing to air pollution and global warming.

Like suburban residents, business owners are reluctant to acknowledge the effects of their activities on the environment, particularly their contribution to global warming. The gradual warming of the world's temperature, many scientists believe, is caused by "greenhouse gases" like carbon monoxide, which are produced by the fuel-burning factories and vehicles on which a developed economy depends. As Figure 21-5 shows, the United States, home to just 5 percent of the world's population, produces a staggering 25 percent of the world's greenhouse gases (Andrews 2001).

In 1997, at an international environmental conference in Kyoto, Japan, the United States signed the Kyoto protocol, an agreement that calls for a worldwide reduction in greenhouse gases. But in March 2001, the United States withdrew support for the protocol, indicating that it was not in the nation's best interest. The decision reflected the complexity of global environmental concerns. Unlike many developing nations, the United States had already taken several measures designed to improve the energy efficiency of cars and factories and reduce their noxious emissions. Further reductions in greenhouse gases, U.S. officials had begun to realize, would mean restricting output at the nation's factories. With an economic

Figure 21-4

Where Americans Moved in the 1990s

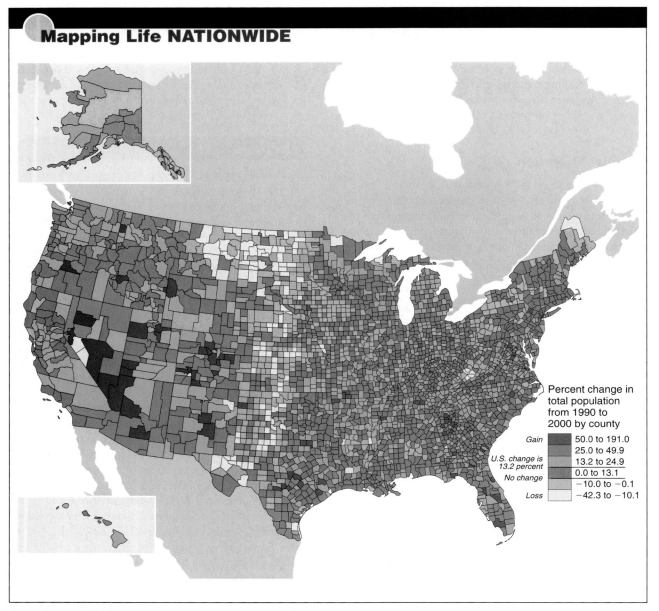

Source: Brewer and Suchan 2001:10.

recession looming in the United States, President George W. Bush backed away from the nation's commitment to improve the global environment.

World leaders were swift to condemn the United States for walking away from the protocol, but U.S. business interests applauded the action. Furthermore, although U.S. citizens saw global warming as a serious problem, in 2001, only 48 percent of them said they would be willing to pay 25 cents more per gallon of gaso-

line to address the issue. Faced with the cost of environmental protection—lower production and higher prices—Americans shrank back from their support of the protocol (Gelbspan 2002; Paul 2001a).

Despite public unwillingness to confront the cost, environmental problems are real. With each passing year, we learn more about the environmental damage caused by burgeoning population levels and consumption patterns. Though disasters like the ones sociologist Kai Erikson

Figure 21-5

The Impact of Global Warming

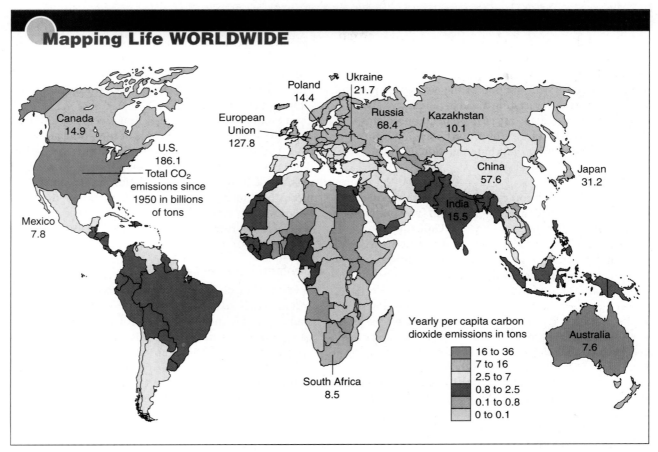

Mapping Life WORLDWIDE

Poland
14.4

Ukraine
21.7

Russia
68.4

Kazakhstan
10.1

European
Union
127.8

Canada
14.9

U.S.
186.1

Total CO$_2$
emissions since
1950 in billions
of tons

China
57.6

Japan
31.2

India
15.5

Mexico
7.8

Yearly per capita carbon
dioxide emissions in tons

Australia
7.6

South Africa
8.5

16 to 36
7 to 16
2.5 to 7
0.8 to 2.5
0.1 to 0.8
0 to 0.1

Source: J. Kluger 2001:30-31.

Think About It

Combine the facts in this map with the information in Table 21-1. Do you think that greenhouse gas emissions will increase as rapidly as the world's population over the next four decades? Why or why not?

investigated (see chapter opening) are still comparatively rare, we can see the superficial signs of despoliation almost everywhere. Our air, our water, and our land are being polluted, whether we live in St. Louis, Mexico City, or Lagos, Nigeria. In the sections that follow, we will survey these problems and see what sociologists have to say about them.

Environmental Problems: An Overview

In recent decades, the world has witnessed serious environmental disasters. For example, Love Canal, near Niagara Falls in New York State, was declared a disaster area in 1978 because of chemical contamination. In the 1940s and 1950s, a chemical company had disposed of waste products on the site where a housing development and a school were subsequently built. The metal drums that held the chemical wastes eventually rusted out, and toxic chemicals with noxious odors began seeping into the residents' yards and basements. Subsequent investigations revealed that the chemical company knew as early as 1958 that toxic chemicals were seeping into homes and a school playground. After repeated protests in the late 1970s, 239 families living in Love Canal had to be relocated.

In 1986, a series of explosions set off a catastrophic nuclear reactor accident at Chernobyl, a part of Ukraine (in what was then the Soviet Union). This accident killed at least 32,000 people. Some 300,000 residents had to be evacuated, and the area became uninhabitable for 19 miles in any direction. High levels of radiation were found as far as 30 miles from the reactor site, and radioactivity levels were well above normal as far away as Sweden and Japan. According to one estimate, the Chernobyl accident and the resulting nuclear fallout may ultimately result in 100,000 excess cases of cancer worldwide (Shcherbak 1996).

While Love Canal, Chernobyl, and other environmental disasters understandably grab headlines, it is the silent, day-to-day deterioration of the environment that ultimately poses a devastating threat to humanity. It is impossible to examine all our environmental problems in detail, but three broad areas of concern stand out: air pollution, water pollution, and contamination of land.

Air Pollution

More than 1 billion people on the planet are exposed to potentially health-damaging levels of air pollution (World Resources Institute 1998). Unfortunately, in cities around the world, residents have come to accept smog and polluted air as "normal." Air pollution in urban areas is caused primarily by emissions from automobiles and secondarily by emissions from electric power plants and heavy industries. Urban smog not only limits visibility; it can lead to health problems as uncomfortable as eye irritation and as deadly as lung cancer. Such problems are especially severe in developing countries. The World Health Organization estimates that up to 700,000 premature deaths *per year* could be prevented if pollutants were brought down to safer levels (Carty 1999).

People are capable of changing their behavior, but they are also unwilling to make such changes permanent. For example, during the 1984 Olympics in Los Angeles, residents were asked to carpool and stagger work hours to relieve traffic congestion and improve the quality of air the athletes would breathe. These changes resulted in a remarkable 12 percent drop in ozone levels. However, when the Olympians left, people reverted to their normal behavior and the ozone levels climbed back up (Nussbaum 1998).

Water Pollution

Throughout the United States, dumping of waste materials by both industries and local governments has polluted streams, rivers, and lakes. Consequently, many bodies of water have become unsafe for drinking,

fishing, and swimming. Around the world, the pollution of the oceans is an issue of growing concern. Such pollution results regularly from waste dumping and is made worse by fuel leaks from shipping and occasional oil spills. In a dramatic accident in 1989, the oil tanker *Exxon Valdez* ran aground in Prince William Sound, Alaska. The tanker's cargo of 11 million gallons of crude oil spilled into the sound and washed onto the shore, contaminating 1,285 miles of shoreline. About 11,000 people joined in a cleanup effort that cost over $2 billion.

Less dramatic than large-scale accidents or disasters, but more common in many parts of the world, are problems with the basic water supply. Worldwide, over a billion people lack safe and adequate drinking water, and nearly half of the world's population has no acceptable means of sanitation—a problem that further threatens the quality of water supplies. The health costs of unsafe water are enormous (World Health Organization and UNICEF 2000).

Contamination of Land

Love Canal made it clear that industrial dumping of hazardous wastes and chemicals also seriously contaminates land. In another noteworthy case of contamination, unpaved roads in Times Beach, Missouri, were sprayed to control dust in 1971 with an oil that contained dioxin. This highly toxic chemical is a by-product of the manufacture of herbicides and other chemicals. After the health dangers of dioxin became evident, the entire community

Rusty barrels leak chemicals into a lake near a city east of Moscow. Throughout the world, industrial pollutants have rendered many water bodies unsafe for fishing, drinking, or swimming.

of 2,800 people was relocated (at a cost of $33 million) and the town of Times Beach was shut down in 1985.

A significant part of land contamination comes from the tremendous demand for landfills to handle the nation's waste. Recycling programs aimed at reducing the need for landfills are perhaps the most visible aspect of environmentalism. How successful have such programs been? In 1980, about 10 percent of urban waste was recycled; the proportion increased steadily throughout the 1980s, but started to level off at about 29 percent in 1998. Experts are beginning to revise their goals for recycling campaigns, which now appear overambitious. Still, a new way to be green has developed: the Internet. For example, over-the-Net commercial transactions allow the downloading of new software, reducing the need for wasteful packaging and shipping materials, including fuel for delivery trucks. And the availability of e-mail and electronic networking encourages people to work at home rather than contribute to the pollution caused by commuting (Belsie 2000; Booth 2000).

What are the basic causes of our growing environmental problems? Neo-Malthusians such as Paul Ehrlich and Anne Erhlich see world population growth as the central factor in environmental deterioration. They argue that population control is essential in preventing widespread starvation and environmental decay. Barry Commoner, a biologist, counters that the primary cause of environmental ills is the increasing use of technological innovations that are destructive to the world's environment—among them plastics, detergents, synthetic fibers, pesticides, herbicides, and chemical fertilizers. In the following sections, we will contrast the functionalist and conflict approaches to the study of environmental issues (Commoner 1971, 1990; Ehrlich 1968; Ehrlich and Ehrlich 1990; Ehrlich and Ellison 2002).

Functionalism and Human Ecology

Earlier, we noted that human ecology is concerned with interrelationships between people and their environment. Environmentalist Barry Commoner (1971:39) has stated that "everything is connected to everything else." Human ecologists, as we've seen, focus on how the physical environment shapes people's lives and also on how people influence the surrounding environment.

In an application of the human ecological perspective, sociologist Riley Dunlap suggests that the natural environment serves three basic functions for humans, as it does for the many animal species (Dunlap 1993; Dunlap and Catton 1983):

1. *The environment provides the resources essential for life.* These include air, water, and materials used to create shelter, transportation, and needed products. If human societies exhaust these resources—for example, by polluting the water supply or cutting down rain forests—the consequences can be dire.

2. *The environment serves as a waste repository.* More so than other living species, humans produce a huge quantity and variety of waste products—bottles, boxes, papers, sewage, garbage, to name just a few. Various types of pollution have become more common because human societies are generating more wastes than the environment can safely absorb.

3. *The environment "houses" our species.* It is our home, our living space, the place where we reside, work, and play. At times we take this for granted, but not when day-to-day living conditions become unpleasant and difficult. If our air is "heavy," if our tap water turns brown, if toxic chemicals seep into our neighborhood, we remember why it is vital to live in a healthful environment.

Dunlap (1993) points out that these three functions of the environment actually compete with one another. Human use of the environment for one of these functions will often strain its ability to fulfill the other two. For example, with world population continuing to rise, we have an increasing need to raze forests or farmland and build housing developments. But each time we do so, we are reducing the amount of land providing food, lumber, or habitat for wildlife.

The tension between the three essential functions of the environment brings us back to the human ecologists' view that "everything is connected to everything else." In facing the environmental challenges of the twenty-first century, government policymakers and environmentalists must determine how they can fulfill human societies' pressing needs (for example, for food, clothing, and shelter) while at the same time preserving the environment as a source of resources, a waste repository, and our home.

Conflict View of Environmental Issues

In Chapter 10, we drew on world systems analysis to show how a growing share of the human and natural resources of the developing countries is being redistributed to the core industrialized nations. This process only intensifies the destruction of natural resources in poorer regions of the world. From a conflict perspective, less affluent nations are being forced to exploit their mineral deposits, forests, and fisheries in order to meet their debt obligations. The poor turn to the only means of survival available to them: They plow mountain slopes, burn plots in tropical forests, and overgraze grasslands (Livernash and Rodenburg 1998).

Taking Sociology to Work

PETER SCHAEFER:
Research Coordinator, Safer Yards

When Peter Schaefer first entered Northwestern University, he didn't expect to major in sociology. But in his sophomore year, an interest in social problems prompted him to sign up for his first course in the discipline. Now, looking back, Schaefer can see that his favorite course, Sociological Theory, dramatically shaped his worldview. "Before that course, I had little to no understanding of how structures such as the political economy affect everyone in profound ways," he says.

Schaefer, who graduated in 1996, is a research coordinator for a Chicago-area lead abatement project called Safer Yards, sponsored by the U.S. Department of Housing and Urban Development (HUD). The main purpose of the project is to decrease the soil contamination children are exposed to while playing in their yards in a low-income inner-city neighborhood. Schaefer's work on the project brings him into contact with a wide range of people of varying social and racial backgrounds, from community members to lead inspectors, data analysts, and research scientists. He is convinced that his degree in sociology helps him to understand and appreciate their differences.

For Schaefer, there is no such thing as a typical workweek. As part of his duties, he has helped to design research and manipu-

late research data, videotaped children playing in their yards, and acted as a translator for Spanish-speaking community members. Though his duties are varied, hardly a day goes by when he does not draw on what he learned in his urban sociology course. "When I encounter signs of gentrification in the Safer Yards target area, I understand what that could mean and how that might affect the members of the community," he explains.

One of the aspects of his work that Schaefer appreciates most is the positive impact the project is having on the community and its children. "This grant has been a wonderful blessing for many families without the economic resources to abate soil lead hazards," he notes. "It's been great to work with a community, and to see a public works project in action."

Let's Discuss

1. Do you know of anyone who suffered from lead exposure as a child? If so, what were the personal consequences? What are the consequences to society?
2. Lead hazards abatement is an expensive process. Who should pay for such services?

In Inez, Kentucky, the president of a coal mining corporation talks with a homeowner about the cleanup of sludge his company spilled into Coldwater Creek. Conflict theorists charge that energy-hungry industrialized nations like the United States are responsible for a disproportionate amount of environmental pollution.

Brazil exemplifies this interplay between economic troubles and environmental destruction. Each year more than 11,000 square miles of the Amazon rain forest are cleared for crops and livestock through burning. The elimination of the rain forest affects worldwide weather patterns, heightening the gradual warming of the earth.

These socioeconomic patterns, with harmful environmental consequences, are evident not only in Latin America but also in many regions of Africa and Asia. Conflict theorists are well aware of the environmental implications of land use policies in the Third World, but they contend that such a focus on the developing countries can contain an element of ethnocentrism. Who, they ask, is more to blame for environmental deterioration: the poverty-stricken and "food-hungry" populations of the world or the "energy-hungry" industrialized nations (Miller 1972:117)?

Conflict theorists point out that Western industrialized nations account for only 25 percent of the world's population but are responsible for 85 percent of worldwide consumption. Take the United States alone: A mere 5 percent of the world's people consume more than half the world's nonrenewable resources and more than one-third of all the raw materials produced. Such data lead conflict theorists to charge that the most serious threat to the environment comes from "affluent megaconsumers and megapolluters" (Bharadwaj 1992; Miller 1972).

Allan Schnaiberg (1994) further refines this analysis by criticizing the focus on affluent consumers as the cause of environmental troubles. In his view, a capitalist system has a "treadmill of production" because of its inherent need to build ever-expanding profits. This treadmill necessitates creating an increasing demand for products, obtaining natural resources at minimal cost, and manufacturing products as quickly and cheaply as possible—no matter what the long-term environmental consequences of this approach.

Environmental Justice

Kennedy Heights, a new subdivision of Houston, attracted buyers in the late 1960s with its tidy brick façade homes and bucolic street names. But what the mostly Black buyers were not told was that the developers had constructed these homes on oil pits abandoned by Gulf Oil decades earlier. After experiencing periodic contaminated water supplies and a variety of illnesses, including large numbers of cancer and lupus, Kennedy Heights residents filed a class-action suit against Chevron, the company that acquired Gulf Oil. This case of environmental pollution is compounded by charges of "environmental racism," based on Gulf Oil documents in 1967 that targeted the area "for Negro residential and commercial development" (Verhovek 1997).

While the Kennedy Heights residents' case is still making its tortuous way through the courts, there are signs that some headway is being made in establishing ***environmental justice,*** a legal strategy based on claims that racial minorities are subjected disproportionately to environmental hazards. In 1998, Shintech, a chemical company, dropped plans to build a plastics plant in an impoverished Black community in Mississippi. Opponents of the plant had filed a civil rights complaint with the Environmental Protection Agency (EPA). EPA administrator Carol Browner praised Shintech's decision: "The principles applied to achieve this solution should be incorporated into any blueprint for dealing with environmental justice issues in communities across the nation" (Associated Press 1998:18).

Following reports from the EPA and other organizations documenting discriminatory locating of hazardous waste sites, President Bill Clinton issued an Executive Order in 1994 that requires all federal agencies to ensure that low-income and minority communities have access to better information about their environment and have an opportunity to participate in shaping government policies that affect their communities' health. Initial efforts to implement the policy have aroused widespread opposition because of the delays it imposes in establishing new industrial sites. Some observers question the wisdom of an order that slows economic development coming to areas in dire need of employment opportunities. On the other hand, there are those who point out that such businesses employ few unskilled or less skilled workers and only make the environment less livable for those left behind (Cushman 1998a; Goldman and Fitton 1994; Pakovic 2001).

 Imagine

Place yourself in Kai Erikson's shoes, then fast-forward a century. Is the "new species of trouble" Erikson wrote about still new? What kinds of human-made disasters do people ask you to deal with? Do people still fight for environmental justice?

SOCIAL POLICY AND POPULATION

World Population Policy

 /schaefer8

The Issue

Six billion and counting: The world's population is growing as you read, threatening the earth's ability to sustain it. Social planners who have grappled with this problem have suggested a policy that provides for a reasonable amount of population growth. But just what is reasonable growth, and how can it be implemented? Social policies that address population growth touch on the most sensitive aspects of people's lives: sexuality, childbearing, and family relationships. For this reason, reaching a global consensus on population issues has been difficult.

The Setting

Beginning in the 1950s, delegates to international conferences sponsored by the United Nations became concerned about the negative consequences of rapid population growth. As we saw earlier (see page 532), the introduction of modern medicine in developing countries had caused a rapid fall in death rates, but birth rates remained high. To reduce the birth rates, planners devised programs aimed at encouraging family planning and limiting the number of children couples had through contraception.

But such programs were controversial. In many developing countries, the traditional culture placed great value on large families. Children were seen as a source of support for their aging parents. To compensate for high infant mortality rates, couples generally had more children than they expected to survive to adulthood. Some government officials, reluctant to deny poor people their means of support in old age, hoped instead that rising living standards would eventually allow people to limit the size of their families.

Population planning programs also came under fire in the United States, from antiabortion activists in particular. Public financial aid, they charged, should not be used to support family planning clinics that provided abortion counseling or services. In 1984, under President Ronald Reagan, U.S. delegates to the World Population Conference in Mexico City announced that the United States would no longer support international population planning programs that provided abortion services (Ashford 2001:8; Rayman-Read 2001).

A nurse in Zambia, Africa, instructs a client in how to use birth control pills. Family planning clinics have helped to slow the population growth rate in developing nations.

Sociological Insights

Functionalists would note that the best course of action for a community might differ from the best course of action for a society. In developing nations, parents see children as potential laborers, and ultimately, as a means of broadening the family's economic base through the children's marriage. Under such conditions, having fewer children may not appear to be a rational choice. Yet for a country that is struggling to provide clean water, food, and shelter to its people, high population growth *is* dysfunctional. Even so, officials of a developing nation may resent powerful industrial nations that attempt to influence (and may appear to dictate) their population policy.

Because the burden of implementing population policy falls particularly on women, sociologists who take the feminist perspective have focused considerable attention on population policy. Early on, feminists charged that workers in government-funded population control programs were distributing contraceptives without sufficient concern for their health risks. In such programs, they added, women were often pressured to adopt certain contraceptive methods not for their own needs, but so the clinics could meet government quotas. Too often, feminist critics complained, population control workers ignored sociocultural influences on sexuality and childbearing—influences that often ran counter to the contraceptives they were distributing (Ashford 2001).

Critics who take the conflict perspective have questioned why the United States and other industrialized nations are so enthusiastic about controlling the population of developing countries. In line with Marx's response to Malthus, they argue that neither large families nor population growth is the cause of hunger and misery. Rather, the unjust economic domination of the world by developed states results in an unequal distribution of the world's resources and in widespread poverty in developing nations (Fornos 1997).

Policy Initiatives

The Mexico City policy established during Ronald Reagan's presidency was overturned during President Clinton's administration. However, in 2001, President George W. Bush reinstated it. Today, the Bush administration requires health workers who receive U.S. government funding to refrain from discussing abortion, either publicly or with their patients. To the extent that international family planning services depend on U.S. government funding, they are clearly hampered by this gag rule, which has politicized otherwise nonpartisan public health programs (Bruni and Lacey 2001; Ehrlich and Ellison 2002; Seims 2001).

Setting aside restrictions such as the Mexico City policy, more funding is needed in those countries where government resources are overtaxed. In sub-Saharan Africa, less than 10 percent of women of childbearing age use contraceptives, compared to 80 percent in China. Family planning is still sparse in poverty-stricken rural areas the world over (Ashford 2001).

Let's Discuss

1. What are the social and cultural attitudes toward family planning in your community? Do people tend to have large families or small ones? What are the reasons they give for their choices?
2. Which perspective on population policy—functionalist, feminist, or conflict—makes the most sense to you? Why?
3. Do you think the U.S. government has a right to dictate abortion policy to other countries? Explain.

Chapter Resources

Summary

The size, composition, and distribution of the U.S. population have an important influence on many of the policy issues presented in this book. This chapter examines various elements of population, the current problem of overpopulation, the possibility of *zero population growth,* and the environmental problems facing our planet.

1. Thomas Robert Malthus suggested that the world's population was growing more rapidly than the available food supply, and that the gap would increase over time. However, Karl Marx saw capitalism, rather than rising world population, as the cause of social ills.
2. The primary mechanism for obtaining population information in the United States and most other countries is the *census.*
3. Roughly two-thirds of the world's nations have yet to pass fully through the second stage of *demographic transition.* Thus they continue to experience significant population growth.
4. Developing nations face the prospect of continued population growth, since a substantial portion of their population is approaching the childbearing years. Some developed nations, however, have begun to stabilize population growth.

5. The most important factors in *migration* tend to be economic—financial failure in the "old country" and a perception of greater economic opportunities elsewhere.
6. Three broad areas of environmental concern are air and water pollution and land contamination.
7. Using the human ecological perspective, sociologist Riley Dunlap suggests that the natural environment serves three basic functions: It provides essential resources, it serves as a waste repository, and it "houses" our species.
8. Conflict theorists charge that the most serious threat to the environment comes from Western industrialized nations.
9. *Environmental justice* concerns the disproportionate subjection of minorities to environmental hazards.
10. World population policy is controversial both in developing countries, where planners' attempts to limit population growth may run counter to traditional cultural values, and in developed countries such as the United States, where funding of international population programs has been politicized.

Critical Thinking Questions

1. Select one of the social policy issues examined in this textbook and analyze in detail how the size, composition, and distribution of the population of the United States have an important influence on that issue.

2. Some European nations are now experiencing population declines. Their death rates are low and their birthrates are even lower than in stage III of the demographic transition model. Does this pattern suggest that there is now a fourth stage in

the demographic transition? Even more important, what are the implications of negative population growth for an industrialized nation in the twenty-first century?

3. Imagine that you have been asked to study the issue of air pollution in the largest city in your state. How might you draw on surveys, observation research, experiments, and existing sources to help you study this issue?

Key Terms

Birthrate The number of live births per 1,000 population in a given year. Also known as the *crude birthrate*. (page 530)

Census An enumeration, or counting, of a population. (530)

Death rate The number of deaths per 1,000 population in a given year. Also known as the *crude death rate*. (530)

Demographic transition A term used to describe the change from high birthrates and death rates to relatively low birthrates and death rates. (531)

Demography The scientific study of population. (527)

Environmental justice A legal strategy based on claims that racial minorities are subjected disproportionately to environmental hazards. (543)

Fertility The level of reproduction in a society. (527)

Growth rate The difference between births and deaths, plus the differences between immigrants and emigrants, per 1,000 population. (530)

Infant mortality rate The number of deaths of infants under one year of age per 1,000 live births in a given year. (530)

Life expectancy The median number of years a person can be expected to live under current mortality conditions. (530)

Migration Relatively permanent movement of people with the purpose of changing their place of residence. (536)

Population pyramid A special type of bar chart that shows the distribution of population by gender and age. (534)

Total fertility rate (TFR) The average number of children born alive to a woman, assuming that she conforms to current fertility rates. (530)

Vital statistics Records of births, deaths, marriages, and divorces gathered through a registration system maintained by government units. (530)

Zero population growth (ZPG) The state of a population with a growth rate of zero, achieved when the number of births plus immigrants is equal to the number of deaths plus emigrants. (535)

Additional Readings

BOOKS

Davis, Michael. 1998. *Ecology of Fear: Los Angeles and the Imagination of Disaster*. New York: Metropolitan Books/Henry Holt and Co. A geographer looks at the nation's second-largest metropolitan area and predicts that the future holds extreme events and abrupt changes.

Fitzpatrick, Kevin, and Mark LaGory. 2000. *Unhealthy Places: The Ecology of Risk in the Urban Landscape*. New York: Routledge. Two sociologists take a spatial view of urban ecology, developing the concept of an "urban health penalty," which is the effect of place on an individual's access to health resources.

French, Hillary. 2000. *Vanishing Borders: Protecting the Planet in the Age of Globalization*. New York: W. W. Norton. An argument for integrating ecological considerations into existing international agreements and the developing rules of global commerce.

Lomborg, Bjorn. 2001. *The Skeptical Environmentalist: Measuring the Real State of the World*. Cambridge, Eng.: Cambridge University Press. A Danish political scientist makes a strong argument for protecting the environment, but cautions that its state may not be as desperate as environmentalists claim.

JOURNALS

The Population Reference Bureau (1875 Connecticut Avenue, N.W., Suite 520, Washington, D.C. 20009-5728) publishes *Population Bulletin* (quarterly), *Population Today* (11 times annually), *Interchange* (quarterly), and occasionally *Teaching Modules*. These publications provide up-to-date information on population and environmental trends. The Bureau of the Census issues *Current Population Reports*, which are helpful to researchers. Other journals focusing on demographic issues include *American Demographics* (founded in 1979), *Demography* (1964), and *International Migration Review* (1964).

Technology Resources

Internet Connection

Note: While all the URLs listed were current as of the printing of this book, these sites often change. Please check our website (http://www.mhhe.com/schaefer8) for updates and hyperlinks to these exercises and additional exercises.

1. Zero-Population Growth (ZPG) offers a cyber examination of the issues raised in your chapter. To learn more about the consequences and issues surrounding continued population growth, visit their website (**http://www.zpg.org/**). When you first log on, be sure to take note of the estimated "World Population" and "U.S. Population" figures and track how much time you spend on the site. Imagine that you have to present a report to your class on this organization by examining the following questions.
   (a) Write down the estimated world population and the estimated U.S. population.
   (b) What are the goals of ZPG?
   (c) What kinds of activities or events does ZPG sponsor? How do these events help the organization achieve its goals?
   (d) How does the organization's perspectives compare to those offered by the Reverend Thomas Robert Malthus, as detailed in your text (see pages 527 and 529)?
   (e) What new legislation or current technological advances are having an impact on population growth?
   (f) Examine the ZPG fact sheet. Which statistic or other information do you think is important to include in your report to the class? Why?
   (g) Can you identify any nations or parts of the world as being in either the pretransition stage, the transition stage, or the posttransition stage?

   (h) Return to the homepage for the site and click on your browser's Refresh or Reload button to bring up the page anew. During the time that you were on the site, how much of an increase was there in the "World Population" and "U.S. Population" figures? What is your reaction to this increase, considering what you have learned on the site and in this chapter?

2. Today, environmental activists are working to preserve the environment through organizations such as Greenpeace. Log onto the Greenpeace website and take a virtual tour of this organization's worldwide environmental efforts (**http://www.greenpeace.org/**).
   (a) When did Greenpeace first form?
   (b) What role have the Internet and computers played in the organization?
   (c) What are the overall goals of Greenpeace? What are some of the environmental problems the organization is trying to alleviate and call attention to?
   (d) What "Campaign Events" does the organization sponsor? How do these events help Greenpeace achieve its goals?
   (e) What images and themes do the photographs on the site present?
   (f) Be sure to utilize the "Greenpeace Worldwide" box. Choose at least three different nation-based sites to visit. What common concerns and environmental issues are shared by these three areas of the world? What problems or issues are unique to each area?
   (g) Which environmental problem do you consider to be the most pressing? What can be done to resolve the problem?

Online Learning Center www.mhhe.com/schaefer8

If you are interested in how Americans feel about the environment, you will want to visit the student center at the Online Learning Center at **www.mhhe.com/schaefer8.** Link to "How Americans Feel About. . . ." You will read about three alternative approaches to protecting the environment and view colorful graphs and pie charts showing whether the Americans surveyed thought the environment would be better, worse, or the same in four years. You can also find out what people your age thought about the long-term future of the environment.

CHAPTER 22

COLLECTIVE BEHAVIOR AND SOCIAL MOVEMENTS

This award-winning poster, created in 1984, garnered international attention for the fledgling animal rights movement. Activists in a wide range of social movements have become adept at using communications technology in their campaigns to change collective behavior.

If somebody at Bowling Green State University of Ohio had talked to somebody at the University of San Diego in California in October of 1998, both schools could have avoided a lot of unnecessary panic. Based on the stories sweeping their respective campuses at the time, a conversation between our imaginary students might have gone something like this:

Bowling Green Student: You're never going to believe what's happening here! People are freaking out.

San Diego Student: You think you're freaking out there, you should see what's going on here! . . . There's this psychic guy—he's supposed to be the most famous psychic in the world, he predicted the Oklahoma City bombing—and he went on Oprah Winfrey's show and predicted there was going to be a mass murder on Halloween at an H-shaped residence hall, and guess what, *we* have an H-shaped residence hall at USD. . . .

(There's a long pause.)

SD: What's the matter?

BG: I don't know what you're talking about, because the psychic who was on *Oprah* didn't say anything about an H-shaped building. He said the massacre was going to take place at a state college in the Midwest and he even mentioned Bowling Green as one of the possibilities, and that's why people are freaking out here!

SD: I don't get it. Did you see the show when the guy was on?

BG: Um, no. Did you?

SD: No, I didn't see it either. What's going on here?

The reason neither of our mythological students saw the psychic's appearance is that there has never been such a segment of *Oprah*. . . .

Nevertheless, the feelings of fear on the campuses of the University of San Diego and Bowling Green State University in the fall of 1998 were very palpable. A story published on Oct. 31 in the *San Diego Union-Tribune* said that "most residents [of the H-shaped hall] were looking for somewhere else to spend the weekend" due to the spreading of a "classic urban legend." . . .

Meanwhile, similar rumors circulated through the University of Michigan, Kent State University, the University of Iowa, and the University of Illinois. Patient spokespeople for Oprah's show explained again that nothing even remotely resembling such an incident had ever happened. . . .

Students at San Diego, Bowling Green, et al., soon realized the scare was borne of pure fiction, but that certainly won't stop the class of '00 or later from going through the whole thing again. The psychic-on-the-talk-show story has been around for years. *(Roeper 1999:91–94)* ■ ◕

Additional information about this excerpt and about those that open each subsequent chapter can be found in the SocWorld CD-ROM that accompanies this text.

P ractically everyone has a tale to tell of an outlandish rumor or prank that they read about or saw on TV or learned of in an e-mail. Richard Roeper, a journalist, has collected many such stories in his book *Urban Legends*. Rumors (such as "the psychic on the talk show") and public opinion (for example, the reaction in the press and on the college campuses) are two forms of collective behavior. Practically all behavior can be thought of as collective behavior, but sociologists have given distinct meaning to the term. Neil Smelser (1981:431), a sociologist who specializes in this field of study, has defined **collective behavior** as the "relatively spontaneous and unstructured behavior of a group of people who are reacting to a common influence in an ambiguous situation."

What guides and governs *collective behavior?* Why do people participate in fads, and what causes mass panics? How do new social movements spread their message to others? In this chapter we will examine a number of sociological theories of collective behavior, including the emergent-norm, value-added, and assembling perspectives. We will give particular attention to certain types of collective behavior, among them crowd behavior, disaster behavior, fads and fashions, panics and crazes, rumors, public opinion, and social movements. We will also look at the role communications technology plays in collective behavior. Sociologists study collective behavior because it incorporates activities that we all engage in on a regular basis. Moreover, they acknowledge the crucial role that social movements can play in mobilizing discontented members of a society and initiating social change. In the social policy section, we will focus on the role that the social movement for lesbian and gay rights plays in promoting change. ■

Theories of Collective Behavior

In 1979, 11 rock fans died of suffocation after a crowd outside Cincinnati's Riverfront Stadium pushed to gain entrance to a concert by The Who. In 1989, when thousands of soccer fans forced their way into a stadium to see the semifinals of the English Cup, more than 90 people were trampled to death or smothered. In 2000, fans surged forward at a Pearl Jam concert in Denmark, killing eight men (DeBarros 2000; D. L. Miller 2000).

Collective behavior is usually unstructured and spontaneous. This fluidity makes it more difficult for sociologists to generalize about people's behavior in such situations. Nevertheless, sociologists have developed various theoretical perspectives that can help us to study—and deal with in a constructive manner—crowds, riots, fads, and other types of collective behavior.

Emergent-Norm Perspective

The early writings on collective behavior imply that crowds are basically ungovernable. However, this is not always the case. In many situations, crowds are effectively governed by norms and procedures, including queuing, or waiting in line. We routinely encounter queues when we await service, as in a fast-food restaurant or bank; or when we wish to enter or exit, as in a movie theater or football stadium. Normally, physical barriers, such as guardrails and checkout counters, help to regulate queu-

ing. When massive crowds are involved, ushers or security personnel may also be present to assist in the orderly movement of the crowd. Nevertheless, there are times when such measures prove inadequate, as the examples just given and the one below demonstrate.

On December 28, 1991, people began gathering outside the City College gymnasium in New York City to see a heavily promoted charity basketball game featuring rap stars and other celebrities. By late afternoon, more than 5,000 people had gathered for the 6:00 P.M. game, even though the gym could accommodate only 2,730 spectators. Although the crowd was divided into separate lines for ticket holders and those wishing to buy tickets at the door, restlessness and discontent swept through both lines and sporadic fights broke out. The arrival of celebrities only added to the commotion and the crowd's tension.

Doors to the gymnasium were finally opened one hour before game time, but only 50 people were admitted to the lobby at a time. Once their tickets had been taken, spectators proceeded down two flights of stairs, through a single unlocked entrance, and into the gym. Those further back in the crowd experienced the disconcerting feeling of moving forward, then stopping for a period of time, then repeating this process again and again. Well past the publicized starting time, huge crowds were still outside, pressing to gain entrance to the building.

Finally, with the arena more than full, the doors to the gym were closed. As rumors spread outside the

Police arrive at a Pearl Jam concert in Roskilde, Denmark, where eight people died when the crowd surged suddenly toward the outdoor stage.

building that the game was beginning, more than 1,000 frustrated fans, many with valid tickets, poured through the glass doors into the building and headed for the stairs. Soon the stairwell became a horrifying mass of people surging against locked metal doors to the gym and crushed against concrete walls. The result was a tragedy: 9 young men and women eventually died, and 29 were injured through the sheer pressure of bodies against one another and against walls and doors (Mollen 1992).

Sociologists Ralph Turner and Lewis Killian (1987) have offered a view of collective behavior that is helpful in assessing a tragic event like this one. It begins with the assumption that a large crowd, such as a group of rock or soccer fans, is governed by expectations of proper behavior just as much as four people playing doubles tennis. But during the episode of collective behavior a definition of what behavior is appropriate or not emerges from the crowd. Turner and Killian call this the **emergent-norm perspective.** Like other social norms, the emergent norm

p. 68

reflects shared convictions held by members of the group and is enforced through sanctions. These new norms of proper behavior may arise in what seem at first to be ambiguous situations. There is latitude for a wide range of acts, yet within a general framework established by the emergent norms (for a critique of this perspective, see McPhail 1991).

Using the emergent-norm perspective, we can see that fans outside the charity basketball game at City Col-

lege found themselves in an ambiguous situation. Normal procedures of crowd control, such as orderly queues, were rapidly dissolving. A new norm was simultaneously emerging: It is acceptable to push forward, even if people in front protest. Some members of the crowd—especially those with valid tickets—may have felt that this push forward was justified as a way of ensuring that they would get to see the game. Others pushed forward simply to relieve the physical pressure of those pushing behind them. Even individuals who rejected the emergent norm may have felt afraid to oppose it, fearing ridicule or injury. Thus, conforming behavior, which we usually associate with highly structured situations, was evident in this rather chaotic crowd, as it had been at

p. 184

the concerts by The Who and Pearl Jam and at the soccer game in England. It would be misleading to assume that these fans acted simply as a united, collective unit in creating a dangerous situation.

Value-Added Perspective

Neil Smelser (1962) proposed still another sociological explanation for collective behavior. He used the **value-added model** to explain how broad social conditions are transformed in a definite pattern into some form of collective behavior. This model outlines six important determinants of collective behavior: structural conduciveness, structural strain, generalized belief, a precipitating factor, mobilization for action, and the exercise of social control.

Initially, in Smelser's view, certain elements must be present for an incident of collective behavior to take place. He uses the term *structural conduciveness* to indicate that the organization of society can facilitate the emergence of conflicting interests. Structural conduciveness was evident in the former East Germany in 1989, just a year before the collapse of the ruling Communist party and the reunification of Germany. The government was extremely unpopular, and there was growing freedom to publicly express and be exposed to new and challenging viewpoints. Such structural conduciveness makes collective behavior possible, though not inevitable.

The second determinant of collective behavior, *structural strain,* occurs when the conduciveness of the social structure to potential conflict gives way to a perception that conflicting interests do, in fact, exist. The intense desire of many East Germans to travel to or emigrate to western European countries placed great strain on the social control exercised by the Communist party. Such structural strain contributes to what Smelser calls a *generalized belief*—a shared view of reality that redefines social action and serves to guide behavior. The overthrow of Communist rule in East Germany and other Soviet-bloc nations occurred in part as a result of a generalized belief that the Communist regimes were oppressive and that popular resistance *could* lead to social change.

Smelser suggests that a specific event or incident, known as a *precipitating factor,* triggers collective behavior. The event may grow out of the social structure, but whatever its origins, it contributes to the strains and beliefs shared by a group or community. For example, studies of race riots have found that interracial fights or arrests and searches of minority individuals by police officers often precede disturbances. The 1992 riots in South Central Los Angeles, which claimed 58 lives, were sparked by the acquittal of four White police officers charged after the videotaped beating of Rodney King, a Black construction worker.

According to Smelser, the four determinants identified above are necessary for collective behavior to occur. However, in addition to these factors, the group must be *mobilized for action.* An extended thundershower or severe snowstorm may preclude such a mobilization. People are also more likely to come together on weekends than on weekdays, in the evening rather than during the daytime.

The manner in which *social control is exercised*—both formally and informally—can be significant in determining whether the preceding factors will end in collective behavior. Stated simply, social control may prevent, delay, or interrupt a collective outburst. In some instances, those using social control may be guilty of misjudgments that intensify the severity of an outbreak. Many observers believe that the Los Angeles police did not respond fast enough when the initial rioting began in 1992, thereby creating a vacuum that allowed the level of violence to escalate.

Sociologists have questioned the validity of both the emergent-norm and value-added perspectives because of their imprecise definitions and the difficulty of testing them empirically. For example, they have criticized the emergent-norm perspective for being too vague in defining what constitutes a norm and have challenged the value-added model for its lack of specificity in defining generalized belief and structural strain. Of these two theories, the emergent-norm perspective appears to offer a more useful explanation of societywide episodes of collective behavior, such as crazes and fashions, than the value-added approach (Brown and Goldin 1973; Quarantelli and Hundley 1975; Tierney 1980).

Smelser's value-added model, however, represents an advance over earlier theories that treated crowd behavior as dominated by irrational, extreme impulses. The value-added approach firmly relates episodes of collective behavior to the overall social structure of a society (for a critique, see McPhail 1994).

Assembling Perspective

A series of football victory celebrations at the University of Texas that spilled over into the main streets of Austin came under the scrutiny of sociologists (Snow et al. 1981). Some participants actively tried to recruit passersby for the celebrations by thrusting out open palms "to get five" or by yelling at drivers to honk their horns. In fact, encouraging still further assembling became a preoccupation of the celebrators. Whenever spectators were absent, those celebrating were relatively quiet. As we have seen, a key determinant of collective behavior is mobilization for action. How do people come together to undertake collective action?

Clark McPhail, perhaps the most prolific researcher of collective behavior in the last three decades, sees people and organizations consciously responding to one another's actions. Building on the interactionist approach, McPhail and Miller (1973) introduced the concept of the assembling process. The *assembling perspective* sought for the first time to examine how and why people move from different points in space to a common location.

A basic distinction has been made between two types of assemblies. *Periodic assemblies* include recurring, relatively routine gatherings of people such as work groups, college classes, and season ticket holders of an athletic series. These assemblies are characterized by advance scheduling and recurring attendance of the majority of participants. For example, members of an introductory sociology class may gather together for lectures every Monday, Wednesday, and Friday morning at 10 A.M. By contrast, *nonperiodic assemblies* include demonstrations, parades, and gatherings at the scene of fires, accidents, and arrests. Such assemblies result from casually transmitted information and are generally less formal than periodic assemblies. One example is the organized rally at Gallaudet University in 1988 backing a deaf

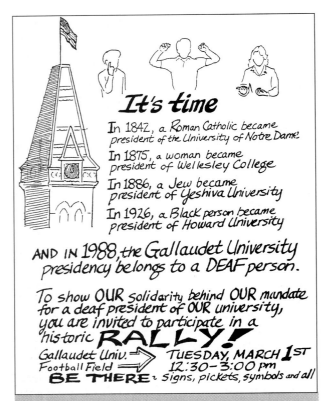

It's time

In 1842, a Roman Catholic became president of the University of Notre Dame.

In 1875, a woman became president of Wellesley College

In 1886, a Jew became president of Yeshiva University

In 1926, a Black person became president of Howard University

AND IN 1988, the Gallaudet University presidency belongs to a DEAF person.

To show OUR solidarity behind OUR mandate for a deaf president of OUR university, you are invited to participate in a historic **RALLY!**

Gallaudet Univ. ➡ TUESDAY, MARCH 1ST
Football Field ➡ 12:30 – 3:00 pm
BE THERE - signs, pickets, symbols and all

Gallaudet University in Washington, D.C., is the only four-year liberal arts college for deaf students in the United States. The leaflet shown here was distributed in 1988 as part of an ultimately successful effort by students, faculty, and alumni to force the board of trustees to appoint the university's first deaf president. Political demonstrations, such as the Gallaudet rally, are examples of nonperiodic assemblies (Christiansen and Barnartt 1995).

person for president of the school for deaf students (see the photo of the campaign leaflet above).

These three approaches to collective behavior give us deeper insight into relatively spontaneous and unstructured situations. Although episodes of collective behavior may seem irrational to outsiders, norms emerge among the participants and organized efforts are made to assemble at a certain time and place.

● Forms of Collective Behavior

Do you remember Cabbage Patch kids? Did you collect pet rocks or *Star Wars* toys when you were young? Any grunge clothes or tube tops lurking in your closet? These are all fads and fashions that depend on collective behav-

ior. Using the emergent-norm, value-added, and assembling perspectives along with other aspects of sociological examination, sociologists have looked at many forms of collective behavior—not only fads and fashions but also crowds, disaster behavior, panics and crazes, rumors, public opinion, and social movements.

Crowds

Crowds are temporary groupings of people in close proximity who share a common focus or interest. Spectators at a baseball game, participants at a pep rally, and rioters are all examples of crowds. Sociologists have been interested in what characteristics are common to crowds. Of course, it can be difficult to generalize, since the nature of crowds varies dramatically. Think about how hostages on a hijacked airplane might feel as opposed to participants in a religious revival.

Like other forms of collective behavior, crowds are not totally lacking in structure. Even during riots, participants are governed by identifiable social norms and exhibit definite patterns of behavior. Sociologists Richard Berk and Howard Aldrich (1972) analyzed patterns of vandalism in 15 cities in the United States during the riots of the 1960s. They found that stores of merchants perceived as exploitative were likely to be attacked, while private homes and public agencies with positive reputations were more likely to be spared. Apparently, looters had reached a collective agreement as to what constituted a "proper" or "improper" target for destruction.

The emergent-norm perspective suggests that during urban rioting a new social norm is accepted (at least temporarily) that basically condones looting. The norms of respect for private property—as well as norms involving obedience to the law—are replaced by a concept of all goods as community property. All desirable items, including those behind locked doors, can be used for the "general welfare." In effect, the emergent norm allows looters to take what they regard as properly theirs (Quarantelli and Dynes 1970; see also McPhail 1991).

Disaster Behavior

Newspapers, television reports, and even rumors bring us word of many disasters around the world. The term **disaster** refers to a sudden or disruptive event or set of events that overtaxes a community's resources so that outside aid is necessary. Traditionally, disasters have been catastrophes related to nature, such as earthquakes, floods, and fires. Yet, in an industrial age, natural disasters have now been joined by such "technological disasters" as airplane crashes, industrial explosions, nuclear meltdowns, and

An aerial photo of the Headwaters Forest in Eureka, California, shows the effects of clear-cutting on the mountainous landscape. Clear-cutting of forests contributes to the unchecked runoff of rainwater, which can erode soil, causing massive landslides.

massive chemical poisonings. The distinction between the two types of disaster is not clear-cut, however. As environmentalists have observed, many human practices either contribute to or trigger natural disasters. Building in flood plains, clear-cutting forests, and erecting rigid structures in earthquake zones all create the potential for disaster (Abramovitz 2001a, 2001b).

Disaster Research

Sociologists have made enormous strides in disaster research, despite the problems inherent in this type of investigation. The work of the Disaster Research Center at the University of Delaware has been especially important. The center has teams of trained researchers prepared to leave for the site of any disaster on four hours' notice. Their field kits include identification material, recording

equipment, and general interview guidelines for use in various types of disasters. En route to the scene, these researchers try to get informed about the conditions they may encounter. Upon arrival, the team establishes a communication post to coordinate fieldwork and maintain contact with the center's headquarters.

Since its founding in 1963, the Disaster Research Center has conducted about 600 field studies of natural and technological disasters in the United States, as well as in other nations. Its research has been used to develop effective planning in such areas as delivery of emergency health care, establishment and operation of rumor-control centers, coordination of mental health services after disasters, and implementation of disaster-preparedness and emergency-response programs. The center has provided training and field research for graduate students. These students maintain a professional commitment to disaster research and often go on to work for disaster service organizations such as the Red Cross and civil defense agencies (Disaster Research Center 2001a; D. L. Miller 2000; Quarantelli 1992).

Case Study: Collapse of the World Trade Center

The September 11, 2001, terrorist attacks on the Pentagon and New York City's World Trade Center caused the largest civilian death toll of any single day in U.S. history, along with billions of dollars worth of property damage. As striking as these losses were, however, the public response to the disaster was equally dramatic. The evacuation from the buildings was remarkably orderly, saving thousands of lives. In fact, many of the lifesaving steps that were taken immediately after the terrorist attacks were the outcome of research done after the explosion of a car bomb at the World Trade Center in 1993 (Murphy and Levy 2001).

Researchers have found that disasters are often followed by the creation of an emergency operations group, which coordinates both public services and some private-sector services, such as food distribution. Decision making becomes more centralized during these periods than it is in normal times. Such was the case on September 11, 2001. New York City's well-designed Emergency Management Center, located in the World Trade Center, was destroyed when the building collapsed and all power at nearby City Hall was cut off. Yet within hours, both an incident command post and a new emergency operations center had been established to direct the search and recovery effort at the 16-acre disaster site. Shortly thereafter came a victims' center, information kiosks, and an office for issuing death certificates, staffed around the clock by counselors, as well as facilities for serving meals to rescue workers. To identify potential hazards to rescuers and survey what had become a gigantic crime

When a terrorist attack destroyed New York City's emergency command center, officials quickly set up a new one to direct the search and recovery effort. Even in times of unimaginable disaster, people respond in predictable ways.

scene, police and public safety officials turned to computer maps and aerial photographs. They also designated places where victims could be identified, human resource functions relocated, and charitable contributions collected (Disaster Research Center 2001b; Dynes 1978; Greenman 2001).

Disaster research has shown that even in natural calamities, maintaining and restoring communications is vital not just to directing relief efforts, but to reducing survivors' anxiety. On September 11, most cell phones in Manhattan were rendered useless by the destruction of communications towers and relay stations. To contact loved ones or to plan their escape from a city clogged with emergency vehicles, people stood in line at pay phones. In the days to follow, families seeking information about their loved ones posted fliers at makeshift information centers. Even in the aftermath of an unimaginable disaster, people and organizations responded in predictable ways (Gibbs 2001).

Fads and Fashions

An almost endless list of objects and behavior patterns seems temporarily to catch the fancy of adults and children. Think about silly putty, hula hoops, the Rubik cube, break dancing, *The Simpsons* T-shirts, Nintendo games, and mosh pits. Fads and fashions are sudden movements toward the acceptance of some lifestyle or particular taste in clothing, music, or recreation (Aguirre et al. 1988; R. Johnson 1985).

Fads are temporary patterns of behavior involving large numbers of people; they spring up independently of preceding trends and do not give rise to successors. By contrast, *fashions* are pleasurable mass involvements that feature a certain amount of acceptance by society and have a line of historical continuity (Lofland 1981, 1985). Thus, punk haircuts would be considered a fashion, part of the constantly changing standards of hair length and style, whereas dancing to the Macarena would be considered a fad of the mid-1990s.

Typically, when people think of *fashions,* they think of clothing, particularly women's clothing. In reality, fads and fashions enter every aspect of life where choices are not dictated by sheer necessity—vehicles, sports, music, drama, beverages, art, and even selection of pets. Any area of our lives that is subject to continuing change is open to fads and fashions. There is a clear commercial motive behind these norms of collective behavior. For example, in about seven months of 1955, over $100 million of Davy Crockett items were sold (worth over $700 million in 2002 dollars), including coonskin caps, toy rifles, knives, camping gear, cameras, and jigsaw puzzles. This was dwarfed by the well over $5 billion Nintendo took in from the 1999 Pokémon fad, ranging from virtual pets to compact discs (Javna 1986; King 1999).

Fads and fashions allow people to identify with something different from the dominant institutions and symbols of a culture. Members of a subculture can break with tradition while remaining "in" with a significant reference group of peers. Fads are generally short-lived and tend to be viewed with amusement or lack of interest by most nonparticipants. Fashions, by contrast, often have wider implications because they can reflect (or give the impression of) wealth and status.

Panics and Crazes

Panics and crazes both represent responses to some generalized belief. A *craze* is an exciting mass involvement that lasts for a relatively long period of time (Lofland 1981, 1985). For example, in late 1973, a press release from a Wisconsin congressman described how the federal bureaucracy had failed to contract for enough toilet paper for government buildings. Then, on December 19, as part of his nightly monologue, *Tonight Show* host Johnny Carson suggested that it would not be strange if the entire nation experienced a shortage of toilet paper. Millions of people took his humorous comment seriously and immediately began stockpiling this item out of fear that it would soon be unavailable. Shortly thereafter, as a consequence of this craze, a shortage of toilet paper actually resulted. Its effects were felt into 1974 (Malcolm 1974; *Money* 1987).

By contrast, a *panic* is a fearful arousal or collective flight based on a generalized belief that may or may not be accurate. In a panic, people commonly think there is insufficient time or inadequate means to avoid injury. Panics often occur on battlefields, in overcrowded burning buildings, or during stock market crashes. The key distinction between panics and crazes is that panics are flights *from* something whereas crazes are movements *to* something.

One of the most famous cases of panic in the United States was touched off by a media event: the 1938 Halloween eve radio dramatization of H. G. Wells's science fiction novel *The War of the Worlds.* This CBS broadcast realistically told of an invasion from Mars, with interplanetary visitors landing in northern New Jersey and taking over New York City 15 minutes later. The announcer indicated at the beginning of the broadcast that the account was fictional, but about 80 percent of the listeners tuned in late.

Many listeners became frightened by what they assumed to be a news report. However, some accounts have exaggerated the extent of people's reactions to *The War of the Worlds.* One report concluded that "people all over the United States were praying, crying, fleeing frantically to escape death from the Martians." In contrast, a CBS national survey of listeners found that only 20 percent were genuinely scared by the broadcast. Although perhaps a million people *reacted* to this program, many reacted by switching to other stations to see if the "news" was being carried elsewhere. This "invasion from outer space" set off a limited panic, rather than mass hysteria (Brown 1954; Cantril 1940; Houseman 1972).

It is often believed that people engaged in panics or crazes are unaware of their actions, but this is certainly not the case. As the emergent-norm perspective suggests, people take cues from one another as to how to act during such forms of collective behavior. Even in the midst of an escape from a life-threatening situation, such as a fire in a crowded theater, people do not tend to run in a headlong stampede. Rather, they adjust their behavior on the basis of the perceived circumstances and the conduct of others who are assembling in a given location. To outside observers studying the events, people's decisions may seem foolish (pushing against a locked door) or suicidal (jumping from a balcony). Yet, for that individual at that moment, the action may genuinely seem appropriate—or the only desperate choice available (Quarantelli 1957).

Rumors

The e-mail carried the subject line "Travelers Beware!" Its message was to warn those planning on going to Mardi Gras in New Orleans in 1997 that a highly organized crime ring there was drugging tourists, removing organs from their bodies, and selling them on the black market. The rumor circulated the country via e-mail and fax, causing an avalanche of calls to the New Orleans Police Department. Of course, an investigation turned up absolutely no evidence of an organ-snatching ring. The department finally set up a website to squash the rumors.

New Orleans wasn't the first city to be struck with this rumor. Similar stories targeted visitors to Houston and Las Vegas. It was said that a visitor to Las Vegas woke up one morning in a bathtub full of ice and minus one kidney. Some version of the organ-snatching tale has swept through numerous countries, repeated by thousands of people. And there has never been one person to verify the story or to offer proof of its truth (Emery 1997).

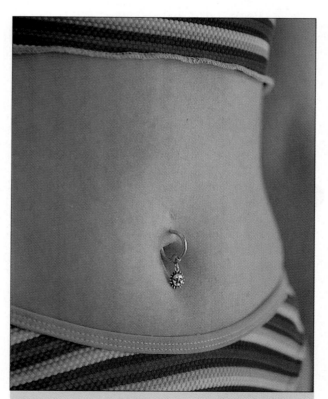

Navel rings can be thought of as a fashion, a new form of body adornment.

Not all rumors we hear are as astonishing as the kidney snatchers or the college dormitory Halloween massacre (see the chapter opening). But none of us is immune from hearing or starting rumors. A *rumor* is a piece of information gathered informally that is used to interpret an ambiguous situation. Rumors serve a function by providing a group with a shared belief. As a group strives for consensus, members eliminate those rumors that are least useful or credible. Sociologist Tamotsu Shibutani (1966) sees this as something akin to the survival of the "fittest" or strongest rumor. Rumors are also a means of adapting to change. If a business is about to be taken over by another firm, rumors usually abound as to the significance that the move will have for personnel. Gradually, such rumors are either verified or discarded, but the very exchange of rumors allows people to cope with changes over which they have little control. Scary rumors probably spread the fastest because fear induces stress and stress is reduced by sharing the fear with others. Moreover, some people enjoy provoking fear in others (Berk 1974; Emery 1997; Rosnow and Fine 1976).

Although some people may start rumors with specific intent to spread a falsehood, Jean-Noël Kapferer (1992:53), a professor of communication in France, suggests that rumors are typically "spontaneous social products, devoid of ulterior motives and underlying strategies." Kapferer argues that the existence and spreading of rumors reflect natural processes within groups. In his view, it is misleading to project the responsibility for a rumor outside the group that hears the rumor, finds it meaningful, and mobilizes to pass it on.

The attack on the Pentagon and the World Trade Center produced a flurry of rumors. According to one false account, a police officer "surfed" a steel beam down 86 floors as one of the towers collapsed. Given the role of the media in covering the event, many rumors centered on them. For example, one rumor suggested that a CNN film of Palestinians dancing in the streets after the attack was actually file footage photographed during the Gulf War. In Pakistan, rumors spread that the vivid photos of the hijacked planes crashing into the World Trade Center had actually been staged. Like these examples, rumors often reinforce people's ideologies and their suspicion of the mass media.

Business firms find that rumors can be damaging, especially ill-founded charges of contamination. In the late 1970s, it was rumored that General Foods' Pop Rocks and Cosmic Candy would explode in children's mouths with tragic results, yet no such explosions took place. Another popular theme of rumors in the marketplace focuses on the charge that a company is using its profits for evil purposes. For example, throughout the 1980s, Procter and Gamble had to counter persistent and unfounded rumors that the company was engaged in satanic activities and that its distinctive corporate trademark was a symbol of Satanism. Businesses can also be hurt by rumors about alleged involvement in controversial practices. In 2000, KFC, formerly known as Kentucky Fried Chicken, had to defend itself against rumors that the company changed its name because its stores were no longer selling the meat of real chickens, but of genetically modified birds with no beaks, feathers, or feet (Collier 2000; Koenig 1985).

Publics and Public Opinion

The least organized and most individualized form of collective behavior is represented by publics. The term *public* refers to a dispersed group of people, not necessarily in contact with one another, who share interest in an issue. As the term is used in the study of collective behavior, the public does not include everyone. Rather, it is a collective of people who focus on some issue, engage in discussion, agree or disagree, and sometimes dissolve when the issue has been decided (Blumer 1955, 1969; Turner and Killian 1987).

The term *public opinion* refers to expressions of attitudes on matters of public policy that are communicated to decision makers. The last part of this definition is particularly important. Theorists of collective behavior see no public opinion without both a public and a decision maker. In studying public opinion, we are not concerned with the formation of an *individual's* attitudes on social and political issues. Instead, we focus on the ways in which a public's attitudes get communicated to decision makers and on the ultimate outcome of the public's attempts to influence policymaking (Turner and Killian 1987).

Polls and surveys play a major role in assessing public opinion. Using the same techniques for developing reliable questionnaire and interview schedules, survey specialists conduct studies of public opinion for business firms (market analyses), the government, the mass media (ratings of programs), and, of course, politicians. Survey data have become extremely influential not only in preselecting the products we buy but in determining which political candidates are likely to win election and even which possible Supreme Court nominees should be selected (Brower 1988).

The earliest political polls were not always reliable. In a famous example of unscientific and misleading polling, the magazine *Literary Digest* sent 18 million postcard ballots across the United States to assess voters' opinions on the 1936 presidential election. The 2 million replies indicated that Republican candidate Alf Landon would defeat Democratic incumbent Franklin D. Roosevelt. *Literary*

Digest predicted a Landon victory, yet Roosevelt was re-elected in a landslide.

Today we would regard this method of polling as completely unreliable. The magazine took its original sample from automobile registration lists and telephone books. Yet, in 1936, in the midst of the Depression, those people with enough money to own a car or a private telephone were hardly a representative cross-section of the nation's voters. Instead, those polled tended to be prosperous citizens who might be likely to support Republican candidates (Squire 1988).

Current political polls are more precise and use representative sampling techniques. As a result, their projections of presidential elections often fall within a few percentage points of the actual vote. The "too close to call" projection in the 2000 Bush–Gore–Nader presidential race was quite correct, as the Florida recount proved. In 1996, all eight national polling services accurately predicted that Bill Clinton would win 49 percent of the popular vote, and the Reuters/Zogby poll was exactly on the mark in its prediction of the vote for Clinton, Republican challenger Bob Dole, and independent candidate Ross Perot (Kagay 1996; Mitofsky 1998; Norman 1996).

While political polling has improved dramatically since the *Literary Digest*'s 1936 fiasco, misleading surveys are still with us. Telephone companies have marketed call-in "polls" using 1-900 area code numbers. Television viewers or newspaper readers are asked to call one number to register an opinion on an issue, or a second number to register an alternative opinion. There are many problems inherent in this type of "polling." The sample that **p. 36** emerges is hardly representative since it includes only those people who happened to see the commercial or advertisement for the poll and who feel strongly enough about the issue to spend the typical charge of $1 for a 900 call.

By the 1990s, surveys of public opinion had become a global phenomenon. With coordinated polling, the opinions of people in countries around the world can be compared. While surveys of public opinion have become more common in many diverse countries, social scientists and polling professionals are well aware that sophisticated sampling techniques are not always used. Exit polling—surveying voters as they leave the polls—has been a fact of political life in the United States and other Western democracies for more than a decade. While it has been successfully conducted in certain developing countries, notably Mexico, use of exit polls in recent elections in Russia has served as a reminder that poor sampling procedures lead to unreliable data (Corning 1993; Specter 1996b).

Social Movements

Social movements are the most all-encompassing type of collective behavior, because they may include aspects of other types such as crowds, rumors, publics, and public opinion. Although such factors as physical environment, population, technology, and social inequality serve as sources of change, it is the *collective* effort of individuals organized in social movements that ultimately leads to change.

Sociologists use the term **social movements** to refer to organized collective activities to bring about or resist fundamental change in an existing group or society (Benford 1992). Herbert Blumer (1955:19) recognized the special importance of social movements when he defined them as "collective enterprises to establish a new order of life."

In many nations, including the United States, social movements have had a dramatic impact on the course of history and the evolution of social structure. Consider the actions of abolitionists, suffragists, civil rights workers, and activists opposed to the war in Vietnam. Members of each social movement stepped outside traditional channels for bringing about social change and yet had a noticeable influence on public policy. Equally dramatic collective efforts in Eastern Europe helped to topple Communist regimes in a largely peaceful manner, in nations that many observers had felt were "immune" to such social change (Ramet 1991).

Social movements imply the existence of conflict, but we can also analyze their activities from a functionalist perspective. Even when unsuccessful, social movements contribute to the formation of public opinion. Initially, the ideas of Margaret Sanger and other early advocates of birth control were viewed as "radical," yet contraceptives are now widely available in the United States. Moreover, functionalists view social movements as training grounds for leaders of the political establishment. Such heads of state as Cuba's Fidel Castro and South Africa's Nelson Mandela came to power after serving as leaders of revolutionary movements. More recently, Poland's Lech Walesa, Russia's Boris Yeltsin, and Czech playwright Vaclav Havel led protest movements against Communist rule and subsequently became leaders of their countries' governments.

How and why do social movements emerge? Obviously, people are often discontented with the way things are. But what causes them to organize at a particular moment in a collective effort to work for change? Sociologists rely on two explanations for why people mobilize: the relative-deprivation and resource-mobilization approaches.

Two views on abortion among social movements in France: In the top photo, members of the pro-choice movement take to the streets. One sign states, "A child if I want it, when I want it." In the bottom photo, a member of the pro-life movement wears a T-shirt that states, "To abort is to kill."

Relative Deprivation

Those members of a society who feel most frustrated and disgruntled by the social and economic conditions of their lives are not necessarily "worst off" in an objective sense. Social scientists have long recognized that what is most significant is how people *perceive* their situation. Karl Marx pointed out that although the misery of the workers was important in reflecting their oppressed state, so was their position *relative* to the capitalist ruling class (Marx and Engels [1847] 1955).

The term *relative deprivation* is defined as the conscious feeling of a negative discrepancy between legitimate expectations and present actualities (Wilson 1973). In other words, things aren't as good as you hoped they would be. Such a state p. 224 may be characterized by scarcity rather than complete lack of necessities (as we saw in the distinction between absolute and relative poverty in Chapter 9). A relatively deprived person is dissatisfied because he or she feels downtrodden relative to some appropriate reference group. Thus, blue-collar workers who live in two-family houses with little lawn space—though hardly at the bottom of the economic ladder—may nevertheless feel deprived in comparison with corporate managers and professionals who live in lavish and exclusive suburbs.

In addition to the feeling of relative deprivation, two other elements must be present before discontent will be channeled into a social movement. People must feel that they have a *right* to their goals, that they deserve better than what p. 243 they have. For example, the struggle against European colonialism in Africa intensified when growing numbers of Africans decided that it was legitimate for them to have political and economic independence. At the same time, the disadvantaged group must perceive that it cannot attain its goals through conventional means. This belief may or may not be correct. Whichever is the case, the group will not mobilize into a social movement unless there is a shared perception that it can end its relative deprivation only through collective action (Morrison 1971).

Critics of this approach have noted that an increase in feelings of deprivation is not always necessary before people are moved to act. In addition, this approach fails to explain why certain feelings of deprivation are transformed into social movements, whereas in other similar situations, there is no collective effort to reshape society. Consequently, in recent years, sociologists have given increasing attention to the forces needed to bring about the emergence of social movements (Alain 1985; Finkel and Rule 1987; Orum 1989).

Resource Mobilization

It takes more than desire to start a social movement. It helps to have money, political influence, access to the media, and workers. The term **resource mobilization** refers to the ways in which a social movement utilizes such resources. The success of a movement for change will depend in good part on what resources it has and how effectively it mobilizes them (see also Gamson 1989; Staggenborg 1989a, 1989b).

Sociologist Anthony Oberschall (1973:199) has argued that to sustain social protest or resistance, there must be an "organizational base and continuity of leadership." As people become part of a social movement, norms develop to guide their behavior. Members of the movement may be expected to attend regular meetings of organizations, pay dues, recruit new adherents, and boycott "enemy" products or speakers. An emerging social movement may give rise to special language or new words for familiar terms. In recent years, social movements have been responsible for such new terms of self-reference as *Blacks* and *African Americans* (used to replace *Negroes*), *senior citizens* (used to replace *old folks*), *gays* (used to replace *homosexuals*), and *people with disabilities* (used to replace *the handicapped*).

Leadership is a central factor in the mobilization of the discontented into social movements. Often, a movement will be led by a charismatic figure, such as Dr. Martin Luther King, Jr. As Max Weber described it in 1904, **p. 431** *charisma* is that quality of an individual that sets him or her apart from ordinary people. Of course, charisma can fade abruptly; this helps account for the fragility of certain social movements (Morris 2000).

Yet many social movements do persist over long periods of time because their leadership is frequently well organized and ongoing. Ironically, as Robert Michels (1915) **p. 143** noted, political movements fighting for social change eventually take on bureaucratic forms of organization. Leaders tend to dominate the decision-making process without directly consulting followers. The bureaucratization of social movements is not inevitable, however. More radical movements that advocate major structural change in society and embrace mass actions tend not to be hierarchical or bureaucratic (Fitzgerald and Rodgers 2000).

Why do certain individuals join a social movement whereas others who are in similar situations do not? **p. 217** Some of them are recruited to join. Karl Marx recognized the importance of recruitment when he called on workers to become *aware* of their oppressed status and develop a class consciousness. In

agreement with the contemporary resource-mobilization approach, Marx held that a social movement (specifically, the revolt of the proletariat) would require leaders to sharpen the awareness of the oppressed. They must help workers to overcome feelings of **false consciousness,** or attitudes that do not reflect workers' objective position, in order to organize a revolutionary movement. Similarly, one of the challenges faced by women's liberation activists of the late 1960s and early 1970s was to convince women that they were being deprived of their rights and of socially valued resources.

Unlike the relative-deprivation approach, the resource-mobilization perspective focuses on strategic difficulties facing social movements. Any movement for fundamental change will almost certainly arouse opposition; effective mobilization will depend in part on how the movement deals with resistance to its activities.

Spillover Effects

Can one social movement grow from another? In the early 1980s, after a period of inactivity, a peace movement reemerged in the United States in a more vibrant form, one that bore many resemblances to the ongoing feminist movement. In fact, noting these similarities, political scientist David Meyer and sociologist Nancy Whittier suggest that social movements have "spillover effects" on other social protest movements. In their view, social movements "grow from and give birth to other movements, work in coalition with other movements, and influence each other indirectly through their effects on the larger cultural and political environment" (1994:277).

Meyer and Whittier argue that the form and content of the U.S. peace movement in the early 1980s reflected the far-reaching impact of the "second wave" of feminism. Indeed, coalitions between feminist and peace organizations became increasingly common in the early 1980s as a response to what both groups viewed as a hostile political climate.

The influence of the women's movement was evident in four distinct areas:

- *Ideological messages.* Peace activists successfully linked traditional themes about war and peace (the dangers of militarism contrasted with women's special caring for life) with feminist themes (analysis of the arms race as a reflection of the larger evils of men's patriarchal rule over women).
- *Tactics.* The activism of women's peace groups drew on feminist traditions of protest, such as sewing and coordinating quilts for large "peace ribbons."
- *Leadership.* Many women active in the peace movement of the 1980s brought their skills and insights directly from years of feminist activism.

22-1 A New Social Movement in Rural India

In the mid-1980s, 5,000 striking textile workers came home from Bombay to mobilize support in their rural villages and to gather food for strikers in the city. As the strike persisted, some strikers stayed in their villages and sought employment on governmental drought-relief projects. However, there were not even enough jobs for rural residents, much less for these new migrants from Bombay.

This was the origin of a new social movement in rural India. With unemployment now confronting an expanded population in rural areas, activists formed a movement that came to be called *Shoshit, Shetkari, Kashtakari, Kamgar, Mukti Sangharsh (SSKKMS)*, which means "exploited peasants, toilers, workers liberation struggle." The initial goal of the movement was to provide drought relief for villagers, but the deeper goal was to bring more power to the rural areas.

> The initial goal of the movement was to provide drought relief for villagers, but the deeper goal was to bring more power to the rural areas.

The SSKKMS movement was unusual when compared to other social movements in India; about half of its partici-pants and many of its leaders were women. This was no accident, for the movement also sought to address gender inequities in the nation. For example, at a meeting seeking support in 1986, Indutai Patankar—a pioneer in the rural women's movement—declared:

> We have gathered here to discuss our problems as women and a rural poor. . . . Not only do we work twice as hard as men but we also do not get equal wages, no child care. . . . We have to organize as women with the other oppressed toilers in urban and rural areas (Desai 1996:214).

Women and men from the movement were equally involved in many forms of

• *Organizational structure.* Drawing on the ideals and values of "feminist process," various organizations of the peace movement established decentralized organizational structures that emphasized egalitarian participation by all members, consensus decision making, and rotation of key roles among members. There was often an aversion to hierarchy and a strong attachment to "local self-determination."

Meyer and Whittier conclude that a social movement can go beyond its expressly articulated goals to influence the larger sector of social movements. Consequently, the "spillover effects" of a particular social movement can persist over time, even in the face of policy defeats and the demise of movement organizations.

Gender and Social Movements

Sociologists point out that gender is an important element in understanding social movement development. In our male-dominated society, women find it more difficult to assume leadership positions in social movement organizations. And while women often disproportionately serve as volunteers in these movements, their work is not always recognized nor are their voices as easily heard as men's. Moreover, gender bias causes the real extent of women's influence to be overlooked. Traditional examination of the sociopolitical system tends to focus on such male-dominated corridors of power as legislatures and corporate

boardrooms to the neglect of more female-dominated domains, such as households, community-based groups, or faith-based networks. But efforts to influence family values, child rearing, relationships between parents and schools, and spiritual values are clearly significant to a culture and society (Ferree and Merrill 2000; Noonan 1995).

Scholars of social movements now realize that gender can affect even the way we view organized efforts to bring about or resist change. For example, an emphasis on using rationality and cold logic to achieve goals helps to obscure the importance of passion and emotion in successful social movements. Calls for a more serious study of the role of emotion are frequently seen as applying only to the women's movement, because emotion is traditionally thought of as feminine. Yet it would be difficult to find any movement from labor battles to voting rights to animal rights where passion was not part of the consensus-building force (Ferree and Merrill 2000; Taylor 1995).

New Social Movements

Beginning in the late 1960s, European social scientists observed that there was a change in both the composition and the targets of emerging social movements. Previously, traditional social movements had focused on economic issues, often led by people who share the same occupation or by labor unions. However, many social movements that have become active in recent decades—including the contemporary women's movement, the political activism, including such direct-action tactics as blocking roads with carts and people until more government projects were approved.

In addition to addressing issues of gender stratification, the SSKKMS movement openly confronted the pervasive inequities associated with *dalit*. This term refers to oppressed people from lower castes (previously called "untouchables"). Movement activists insisted that both women and landless peasants (most of whom are *dalits*) should have equal access to water once dams were completed. This is a critical issue in the lives of rural Indian women, who typically must spend many hours a day in search of good drinking water.

In her analysis of the SSKKMS movement, sociologist Manisha Desai (1996) emphasizes that the movement does not have a single focus, but is committed to multiple struggles for social and economic justice. Desai views the SSKKMS as an example of a new social movement because it incorporates concrete, material targets as well as broad ideological goals.

As with any social movement, there are contradictions in the SSKKMS movement. A middle-class leadership core generally articulates goals for the many exploited villagers in the mass movement. While in one rural area all local assemblies must be at least 30 percent female—a goal rarely achieved in the

United States—rural women sometimes simply serve as fronts for the hidden agendas of their male relatives. Nevertheless, Desai's study of the SSKKMS movement underscores the fact that social movements in general, and new social movements in particular, are found *throughout* the world and not solely in industrialized nations.

Let's Discuss

1. Why do you think so many women participated in the SSKKMS movement? Describe their goals.
2. What would happen if "powerless" people in the United States formed a similar movement? Would it succeed? Why or why not?

peace movement, and the environmental movement—did not have the social class roots typical of the labor protests in the United States and Europe over the preceding 100 years (Tilly 1993).

The term ***new social movements*** was introduced to refer to organized collective activities that promote autonomy and self-determination as well as improvements in the quality of life. These movements may be involved in developing collective identities, have complex agendas that go beyond a single issue, and often cross national boundaries. Educated, middle-class people are significantly represented in some of these new social movements, such as the women's movement and the movement for lesbian and gay rights. However, marginalized people are also involved in new social movements; as one example, some homeless people create communities of squatters who take over abandoned buildings and fight efforts to evict them (Buechler 1995). Box 22-1 describes a new social movement that arose among exploited textile workers in India.

New social movements generally do not view government as their ally in the struggle for a better society. While they typically do not seek to overthrow the government, they may criticize, protest, or harass public officials. Researchers have found that members of new social movements show little inclination to accept established authority, even scientific or technical authority. This is especially evident in the environmental and anti–nuclear power

movements, where movement activists present their own experts to counter those of government or big business (Garner 1996; Scott 1990).

The environmental social movement is one of many new movements that have adopted a worldwide focus. In their efforts to reduce air and water pollution, curtail global warming, and protect endangered animal species, environmental activists have realized that strong regulatory measures within a single country are not sufficient. Similarly, labor union leaders and human rights advocates cannot adequately address exploitative sweatshop conditions in a developing country if a multinational corporation can simply move the factory to another country where it pays workers even less. Whereas traditional views of social movements tended to emphasize resource mobilization on a local level, new social movement theory offers a broader, global perspective on social and political activism. Moreover, today's technology provides new ways to unite groups of people across distances and publicize their concerns. A social movement can even be "virtual," as we will see in the next section.

Imagine

Try to imagine a society without collective behavior—no fads or fashions, panics or crazes, rumors or social movements. Under what conditions could such a society exist? Would you want to live in it?

Research in Action

22-2 Virtual Social Movements

We are accustomed to think of social movements in terms of protest marches and door-to-door petition drives. But the World Wide Web allows for alternative ways to organize people and either bring about fundamental change or resist it. The Internet itself has often been referred to as a "virtual community," and as in any community there are people who seek to persuade others to their point of view. Furthermore, the Internet serves to "bring people together"—say, by transforming the cause of the Mexican Zapatistas into an international lobbying effort, by linking environmentalists on every continent through Greenpeace International, or by e-mailing information and news from abroad to dissidents in China.

Sociologists have begun to call such electronic enhancements of social movements *computer-mediated communication (CMC)*. Electronic communication strengthens a group's solidarity, allowing the fledgling social movement to grow and develop faster than it might otherwise. Thus, face-to-face contact, which was once critical to a social movement, is no longer necessary. Moreover, people can engage in their own virtual community with little impact on their everyday lives. On the Internet, for example, one can mount a petition drive to free a death row inmate without taking days and weekends away from one's job and family. Dissidents can communicate with one another using computers in Internet cafes, with little concern for being traced or monitored by the government.

> The Internet itself has often been referred to as a "virtual community," and as in any community there are people who seek to persuade others to their point of view.

Two studies by Matthew Zook and research by sociologist Roberta Garner examined how many websites express ideological points of view that are contentious or hostile to existing institutions. Garner looked at 542 websites that could be regarded as "ideological postings"; some reflect the interests of a particular group or organization and some are only the opinions of isolated individuals. Among the sites were postings that reflected extreme patriotic views, White racism, attachment to cults, regional separatism and new forms of nationalism, and expression of militant environmentalism.

While the Garner sample was not random and therefore may not be representative of all ideological postings, the hundreds of sites did show some consistencies, many of them also noted by Zook:

- Like conventional social movements, these sites serve as an alternative source of information, bypassing mainstream sources of opinion found in newspaper editorials.
- These nonmainstream movements enjoy legitimacy because no gatekeeper keeps them off the web. By virtue of being on a website, even an unsophisticated one, the information has the appearance of being legitimate.
- The sites rely heavily on written documents, in the form of either manifestos or established documents such as the Constitution or the Bible.

Sources: Calhoun 1998; Castells 1996; Diani 2000; Garner 1999; Rosenthal 2000; Van Slambrouck 1999b; Zook 1996.

Communications Technology and Collective Behavior

Many of the examples that we have used to illustrate collective behavior reflect the impact of communications technology—from radio broadcasts proclaiming that Martians have landed to the Internet as a vehicle for spreading rumors. The World Wide Web is only the latest in a wave of new communications technology that has transformed collective behavior.

How might some of the theoretical perspectives we examined earlier in the chapter evaluate technology's role in collective behavior? Although Neil Smelser's value-added perspective did not explicitly refer to communications technology, his emphasis on people needing to be mobilized for action takes on new meaning today with fax machines and the Internet. With relatively little effort and

Workers, many of them children, are shown in a makeshift cigarette factory in Bangladesh. New social movement theory offers a broad, global perspective on social and political activism, including dealing with exploitation of child labor in developing nations.

Written testimonials (such as "How I Became a Conservative") also proliferate on these websites.

- The presentations are still fairly unsophisticated. While there are glossy animated websites, most sites look like a printed page.

- Unlike conventional social movements, these virtual sites are generally not geared for action. Despite expressions of concern or foreboding (such as the site "Are You Ready for Catastrophic Natural Disasters?"), there are few calls to do anything. Sites such as "Glory to the Cuban Revolution" seek to inform visitors, serve as a resource, and, perhaps, bring people around to their point of view.

Zook as well as Garner and her student researchers found that these sites often seem to define themselves by their choice of links on the web. In other words, with whom do they wish to be associated? This is particularly true of well-established social movements that have expanded to use the Internet. For example, both the leading abortion rights groups and anti-abortion organizations feature links to other groups, but only to those that are like-minded.

The entire process of "links" is very important in the Internet network. How one defines one's ideology determines how a site may be located and who makes links. For example, the website of a female national socialist from Sweden boldly encourages visitors to establish a link from their website to hers as long as they are a part of the "white aryan movement on the Net." Using the term "militia" as opposed to "patriotic" would bring different people to one's site. The terms one uses are important since webpages act as recruiting tools to attract new members to a movement and may, in fact, be the only realistic way that some groups will attract followers.

People in conventional social movements commonly try to infiltrate other groups holding opposing views to learn their strategy or even disrupt their ability to function. There is a parallel to that emerging on the Internet. The term *hactivists* (a merging of "hackers" with "activists") refers to people who invade computer systems electronically, placing embarrassing information on their enemies' webpages or, at the very least, defacing them. During the height of the 1999 NATO attacks on Yugoslavia, movements opposed to the military action bombarded the official NATO website with requests meant to overload it and paralyze its operation.

Research into virtual social movements is still exploratory. Social movement researchers such as Garner and Zook are interested in establishing the relationship between ideological websites and "real" organizations. Do these sites merely reflect a single posting? Or are they the visible manifestation of a broader consensus? And sociologists will be interested in examining a more representative sample of such sites to determine how often they explicitly call for social change.

Let's Discuss

1. What are some of the advantages of having a virtual social movement on the Internet? What might be some disadvantages?

2. If you were to create a webpage designed to attract followers to a social movement, what would it be like?

expense, we can now reach a large number of people in a short period of time. Looking at the new technology from the assembling perspective, we could consider the Internet's listservs and chatrooms as examples of nonperiodic assemblies. Without face-to-face contact or even simultaneous interaction, people can develop an identity with a large collective of like-minded people via the Internet (Calhoun 1998).

Sociology is only beginning to consider the impact of the latest technology on various forms of collective behavior. Technology clearly plays a role in disaster research; moreover, a large number of disasters today are technological in origin. A content analysis of the coverage of disasters by *Time* magazine showed that about 40 percent were technological and 60 percent natural during the 1990s (Bernhardt 1997). (We will consider technological accidents in greater detail in the next chapter.)

We have seen that rumors fly on the Internet. One click of the Send button can forward messages to every person in one's address book. Multiply this by the millions of e-mail account holders to get an idea of the reach of the Internet in distributing rumors. We have seen, too, how Internet rumors can stir panics. In the same way, people can be exposed almost instantly to the latest crazes, fads, and fashions. And people are constantly being encouraged to call a telephone number or log on to a website to register their public opinion on some policy issue.

Can one be part of a "crowd" via the new communications technology? Television and the Internet, as contrasted with books and newspapers, often convey a false sense of intimacy reinforced by immediacy. We seem to be personally hurt by the death of Princess Diana or moved by the troubles of the Kennedy family. Therefore, the latest technology brings us together in an electronic global village to act and to react. Box 22-2 shows how virtual social movements can develop on the Web (Garner 1999).

The new communications technology is also able to create enclaves of similarly minded people. Websites are not just autonomous and independent; they are interconnected through a global electronic network. One website, in turn, lists a variety of other sites that serve as "links." For example, seeking out information on domestic partnerships may lead you to an electronic enclave on the Internet supportive of cohabitation be-

tween men and women or alternatively to an enclave that is supportive of gay and lesbian couples. Developments in communications technology have clearly broadened the way we interact with one another today (Calhoun 1998).

SOCIAL POLICY AND SOCIAL MOVEMENTS

Lesbian and Gay Rights

The Issue

Despite the large numbers of lesbians and gay men in the United States and around the world, homosexuality continues to function in many societies as a master status that carries a stigma. Amnesty International (1994) published a pioneering report documenting that lesbians and gay men suffer from governmental persecution in many parts of the world. In response to such discrimination, a social movement for lesbian and gay rights has emerged across the United States and in many diverse nations. This movement is putting pressure on policymakers to pass legislation establishing and protecting gay and lesbian rights.

The Setting

The first social movement to advance the civil rights of lesbians and gay men was founded in Germany in 1897 by physician Magnus Hirschfeld and others. The Scientific-Humanitarian Committee fought to abolish legal penalties against homosexual behavior and to educate people about gay rights and women's rights. The committee was eventually crushed by the Nazis in 1933; subsequently, at least 10,000 to 20,000 people identified as homosexuals died in Nazi concentration camps. As a result, one cherished symbol of contemporary gay activists—worn on buttons and patches—is a pink triangle, the very emblem gay prisoners were forced to wear by the Nazis (Lauritsen and Thorstad 1974; Plant 1986).

In the United States, the first homosexual organization was founded in Chicago in 1924, and a number of gay and lesbian groups came into existence in the 1950s. Experiences in early gay rights groups gave activists greater organizing ability—an important component of resource mobilization. In addition, there were spillover effects through involvement in other social movements of the 1950s and 1960s, such as those working for civil rights for Blacks, against the war in Vietnam,

and for women's liberation. Many lesbians and gay men were forced to reflect more directly on their own oppression stemming from their sexual orientation (Katz 1992).

Building on earlier homosexual activism and on the growth of lesbian and gay male subcultures in major cities, the contemporary gay movement publicly began in New York City on June 28, 1969. Police raided the Stonewall Inn, an after-hours gay bar, and forced patrons onto the street. But, instead of dispersing, the patrons locked police inside the bar and rioted until official reinforcements arrived. For the next three nights, lesbians and gay men marched through the streets of New York, protesting police raids and other forms of discrimination. Within months, gay liberation groups had appeared in cities and campuses throughout the United States; within two years, similar organizations were evident in Canada, Great Britain, various western European countries, and Australia (Adam 1995; Adam et al. 1999; Garner 1996).

While many voluntary associations supporting lesbian and gay rights are primarily local in their focus, a growing number of national organizations address gay issues. Among these are the National Lesbian and Gay Task Force, which fights for gay rights on a national level while engaging in "grass-roots" organizing; the Human Rights Campaign, which lobbies Congress on gay issues and provides financial support for lesbian and gay male candidates; the Gay and Lesbian Alliance Against Defamation, which promotes fair and accurate representation of lesbians and gay men in the media and protests antigay stereotyping; and Parents, Families, and Friends of Lesbians and Gays, whose chapters in more than 460 U.S. cities and abroad provide support for lesbians, gay men, and their families (GLAAD 2001; Human Rights Campaign 2001; NGLTF 2001; PFLAG 2001).

In response to the AIDS crisis, self-help groups—especially in the gay communities of major cities—have been es-tablished to care for the sick, educate the healthy, and lobby for more responsive public policies. The most outspoken AIDS activist group has been ACT-UP, which has conducted controversial protests and sit-ins in the halls of government and at scientific conferences. In the view of sociologist Barry Adam (1995), while the rise of such self-help and AIDS activist groups has siphoned away many leaders and participants from gay rights organizations, the broad reach of the AIDS crisis has mobilized new constituencies of gay men and their friends and relatives into AIDS and gay activism. Indeed, the militant and dramatic tactics of ACT-UP—which includes lesbian, gay male, and heterosexual members—contributed to the formation in the 1990s of new direct-action groups such as Queer Nation (which attempts to combat homophobia and celebrate sexual diversity) and the Lesbian Avengers (which focuses on issues vital to lesbian survival and visibility) (Cunningham 1992; Kaplan 1990; Trebay 1990).

In the private sector, progress in alleviating discrimination has been uneven. As of 2001, more than 4,285 employers offered benefits to domestic partners (see Chapter 14). However, the many corporate mergers in recent years have sometimes hurt the gay community. For example, when Exxon and Mobil merged, the new entity announced it would end domestic partnership benefits that Mobil had previously provided (Armour 2000; Herrschaft and Mills 2001).

Sociological Insights

Despite the effort of the lesbian and gay rights movement, in 1986 the U.S. Supreme Court ruled, by a narrow 5–4 vote, that the Constitution does not protect homosexual relations between consenting adults, even in the privacy of their own homes. This decision underscored the fact that heterosexuality remains the socially approved form of sexual relations in the United States; the dominant ideology of our society promotes exclusive heterosexual norms. Sociologist Steven Seidman (1994:583) notes, "From secondary school books to public images in advertisements, movies, television shows, magazines, and newspapers, heterosexuality is presented as natural and normal." Viewed from a conflict perspective, the dominant ideology encourages antigay prejudice

and discrimination by excluding positive images of lesbians and gay men while emphasizing narrow stereotypes.

By the 1990s, lesbian and gay male activists had recognized that encouraging people to "come out" could help illustrate the diversity of gay life and assist resource mobilization. Many lesbians and gay men had long felt the need to conceal their identities (remain "in the closet") out of fear that they might lose their jobs, be cut off from their families, or fall victim to hate crimes (see Chapter 11). However, the gay movement has given many individuals the support and strength to "come out" and assert their identities publicly and proudly—as new social movements frequently do for those who are challenging dominant social norms.

Among the many lesbian, gay, and bisexual organizations in the United States and Canada, there are gay sports leagues and singing groups; professional associations, such as those of gay doctors and teachers; campus lesbian and gay male organizations; and groups of African American, Asian American, and Latino gays, some of whom have challenged White domination of the lesbian and gay movement (Brelin 1996:34; T. Lee 2000).

Like all social movements, the movement on behalf of gay and lesbian rights is not unified. Many within the movement see the emphasis on legalizing homosexual marriages as assimilationist. The ideal of sexual fidelity, these critics contend, mimics the heterosexual ideal of monogamy, which is widely violated. According to this view, the recognition of gay rights regardless of one's lifestyle is the

Lesbian and gay activism is not confined to large cities like New York and San Francisco. It shows up in diverse communities across the nation, as indicated by the outreach effort of these members of the University of South Dakota's Gay, Lesbian, and Bisexual Alliance.

movement's only worthy goal (Hequembourg and Arditi 1999; Werum and Winders 2001).

Policy Initiatives

Beginning in the 1990s, opponents of lesbian and gay rights focused on statewide ballot initiatives as a key tactic. In most cases, gay rights supporters have won narrow victories. As of 2001, 11 states and more than 150 cities had passed laws that protect lesbians and gay men against workplace discrimination (ACLU 2001).

Resistance to lesbian and gay rights has also been evident in the battle over possible legalization of same-sex marriages and in the continuing controversy over gays in the military. In 1993, President Bill Clinton considered issuing an executive order against antigay discrimination within the military, but was forced to back down because of heated opposition from military leaders and powerful members of Congress. Under a compromise devised in 1994—known as "Don't Ask, Don't Tell"—lesbians and gay men can continue to serve in the military as long as they keep their homosexuality a secret, while commanders are prohibited from asking about a person's sexual orientation. But commanders *can* investigate and dismiss military personnel if there is evidence that they have committed homosexual acts.

According to a 2000 report, the military is discharging 73 percent *more* gay and lesbian troops today than before the new policy was enacted (Vistica 2000).

A common stereotype has been that lesbian and gay organizations are found only in Western industrialized nations. However, the International Lesbian and Gay Association now has about 300 member organizations in 70 countries. In 1995, Japan held its second annual gay pride march, and gay groups were founded in Bolivia, Kenya, Pakistan, South Korea, and Sri Lanka. There are more than 50 gay and lesbian groups in South Africa, more than a dozen in Mexico, and at least 7 lesbian organizations in Brazil. The spread of the Internet has assisted the creation of many pioneering lesbian and gay organizations. In China, where organizing in public is difficult, gays rely heavily on the Internet to maintain a collective identity (Adam et al. 1999; Dillon 1997; *The Economist* 1996; Friess 2001).

Let's Discuss

1. Viewed from a conflict perspective, how does the dominant ideology of our society encourage antigay prejudice and discrimination?
2. How has the AIDS crisis affected the movement for lesbian and gay rights?
3. In what ways is the social position of lesbians different from that of gay men?

⬤ Chapter Resources

Summary

Collective behavior is the relatively spontaneous and unstructured behavior of a group that is reacting to a common influence in an ambiguous situation. This chapter examines sociological theories used to understand collective behavior and forms of collective behavior, with particular attention to *social movements* and their important role in promoting social change.

1. Turner and Killian's *emergent-norm perspective* suggests that new forms of proper behavior may emerge from a crowd during an episode of collective behavior.
2. Smelser's *value-added model* of collective behavior outlines six important determinants of such behavior: structural conduciveness, structural strain, generalized belief, precipitating factor, mobilization of participants for action, and operation of social control.

3. The *assembling perspective* introduced by McPhail and Miller sought for the first time to examine how and why people move from different points in space to a common location.
4. In *crowds* people are in relatively close contact and interaction for a period of time and are focused on something of common interest.
5. Researchers are interested in how groups interact in times of *disaster*.
6. *Fads* are temporary patterns of behavior involving large numbers of people; *fashions* have more historical continuity.
7. The key distinction between a *panic* and a *craze* is that a panic is a flight *from* something whereas a craze is a mass movement *to* something.
8. A *rumor* is a piece of information used to interpret an ambiguous situation. It serves a social function by providing a group with a shared belief.

9. *Publics* represent the most individualized and least organized form of collective behavior. *Public opinion* is the expression of attitudes on public policy communicated to decision makers.

10. *Social movements* are more structured than other forms of collective behavior and persist over longer periods of time.

11. A group will not mobilize into a social movement unless there is a shared perception that its *relative deprivation* can be ended only through collective action.

12. The success of a social movement will depend in good part on how effectively it mobilizes its resources.

13. *New social movements* tend to focus on more than just economic issues and often cross national boundaries.

14. Advances in communications technology—especially the Internet—have had a major impact on the various forms of collective behavior.

15. A growing number of organizations address national and even international concerns of lesbians and gay men.

Critical Thinking Questions

1. Are the emergent-norm, value-added, and assembling perspectives aligned with or reminiscent of functionalism, conflict theory, or interactionism? What aspects of each of these theories of collective behavior (if any) seem linked to the broader theoretical perspectives of sociology?

2. Without using any of the examples given in the textbook, list at least two examples of each of the following types of collective behavior: crowds, disasters, fads, fashions, panics, crazes, rumors, publics, and social movements. Explain why each example belongs in its assigned category. Distinguish among the types of collective behavior based on the types and degrees of social structure and interaction connected with them.

3. Select one social movement that is currently working for change in the United States. Analyze that movement, drawing on the concepts of relative deprivation, resource mobilization, and false consciousness.

Key Terms

Assembling perspective   A theory of collective behavior introduced by McPhail and Miller that seeks to examine how and why people move from different points in space to a common location. (page 553)

Collective behavior   In the view of sociologist Neil Smelser, the relatively spontaneous and unstructured behavior of a group of people who are reacting to a common influence in an ambiguous situation. (551)

Craze   An exciting mass involvement that lasts for a relatively long period of time. (557)

Crowd   A temporary gathering of people in close proximity who share a common focus or interest. (554)

Disaster   A sudden or disruptive event or set of events that overtaxes a community's resources so that outside aid is necessary. (554)

Emergent-norm perspective   A theory of collective behavior proposed by Turner and Killian that holds that a collective definition of appropriate and inappropriate behavior emerges during episodes of collective behavior. (552)

Fad   A temporary movement toward the acceptance of some particular taste or lifestyle that involves large numbers of people and is independent of preceding trends. (556)

False consciousness   A term used by Karl Marx to describe an attitude held by members of a class that does not accurately reflect its objective position. (561)

Fashion   A pleasurable mass involvement in some particular taste or lifestyle that has a line of historical continuity. (556)

New social movement   An organized collective activity that promotes autonomy and self-determination as well as improvements in the quality of life. (563)

Nonperiodic assembly   A nonrecurring gathering of people that often results from word-of-mouth information. (553)

Panic   A fearful arousal or collective flight based on a generalized belief that may or may not be accurate. (557)

Periodic assembly   A recurring, relatively routine gathering of people, such as a college class. (553)

Public   A dispersed group of people, not necessarily in contact with one another, who share an interest in an issue. (558)

Public opinion   Expressions of attitudes on matters of public policy that are communicated to decision makers. (558)

Relative deprivation   The conscious feeling of a negative discrepancy between legitimate expectations and present actualities. (560)

Resource mobilization   The ways in which a social movement utilizes such resources as money, political influence, access to the media, and personnel. (561)

Rumor   A piece of information gathered informally that is used to interpret an ambiguous situation. (558)

Social movement   An organized collective activity to promote or resist change in an existing group or society. (559)

Value-added model   A theory of collective behavior proposed by Neil Smelser to explain how broad social conditions are transformed in a definite pattern into some form of collective behavior. (552)

Additional Readings

BOOKS

Adam, Barry D., Jan Willem Duyvendak, and André Krouwel, eds. 1999. *The Global Emergence of Gay and Lesbian Politics: National Imprints of a Worldwide Movement.* Philadelphia: Temple University Press. The editors offer portraits of gay and lesbian organizing in 16 nations, including Australia, Brazil, France, Great Britain, Japan, Romania, and Spain.

Fine, Gary Alan, and Patricia A. Turner. 2001. *Whispers on the Color Line: Rumor and Race in America.* Berkeley: University of California Press. Two sociologists consider how and why certain rumors take root in the African American community.

Horowitz, Donald L. 2000. *Mob Rule: The Deadly Ethnic Riot.* Berkeley: University of California Press. A cross-cultural look at racial, ethnic, and religious riots throughout history.

Jasper, James. 1997. *The Art of Moral Protest: Culture, Biography, and Creativity in Social Movements.* Chicago: University of Chicago Press. An analysis of how social movements, ranging from nineteenth-century boycotts to contemporary antinuclear, animal rights, and environmental movements, develop and the impact they have on participants and society as a whole.

Lofland, John. 1996. *Social Movement Organizations: Guide to Research on Insurgent Realities.* New York: Aldine de Gruyter. A noted sociologist offers a handbook on studying social movement organizations.

Miller, David L. 2000. *Introduction to Collective Behavior and Collective Actions.* 2nd ed. Prospect Heights, IL: Waveland. The author, associated with the assembling perspective, covers all the major theoretical approaches of the field. He examines rumors, riots, social movements, immigration, and other forms of collective behavior.

Regan, Tom. 2000. *Defending Animal Rights.* Urbana: University of Illinois Press. A philosopher and participant in the animal rights movement reflects on the movement and compares it to other protests.

Warner, Michael. 1999. *The Trouble with Normal: Sex, Politics, and the Ethics of Queer Life.* New York: The Free Press. A critical examination of the contemporary gay rights movement and its emphasis on the recognition of gay marriages.

JOURNALS

Among those journals that focus on collective behavior and social movements are the *International Journal of Mass Emergencies and Disasters* (founded in 1983), the *Journal of Gay, Lesbian, and Bisexual Identity* (1996), the *Journal of Popular Culture* (1967), *Mobilization* (1996), and *Public Opinion Quarterly* (1937).

● Technology Resources

www.mhhe.com /schaefer8   Internet Connection

Note: While all the URLs listed were current as of the printing of this book, these sites often change. Please check our website (http://www. mhhe.com/schaefer8) for updates and hyperlinks to these exercises and additional exercises.

1. RESULTS (**http://action.org**) is a grassroots citizens' lobby working to create the political will to end hunger and the worst aspects of poverty. Link to "Issues," then click on "Success in 2000" and answer the following questions:

(a) What impact will the Hunger Relief Act have on working families who receive food stamps?

(b) What impact will the Child Care and Development Block Grant (CCDBG) have on children who are eligible for Head Start?

(c) Link to "Global Health." What are three of the infectious diseases responsible for two-thirds of the deaths among children and young adults in Africa and Southeast Asia?

(d) Congress has agreed to provide $60 million for global tuberculosis control. What is the expected impact of this amount?

(e) Link to "Take Action" and select either "Global" or "Domestic." What is the issue being discussed? What action does RESULTS suggest you take?

(f) Do you think RESULTS meets the criteria for a new social movement? Why or why not?

2. Your textbook notes that riots are a form of collective behavior in which participants are governed by identifiable social norms and exhibit definite patterns of behavior. The following website links to information about six riots involving African Americans (**http://afroamhistory.about.com/cs/ raceriots**). Select any three riots, read about them, and answer the following questions:

(a) What social norms were violated during each riot?

(b) What definite patterns of behavior did both African Americans and Whites exhibit during each riot?

(c) What illegal behaviors occurred during each riot?

(d) Was any legislation passed as a result of the riots?

3. You can find links of interest to those studying gay and lesbian rights at **http://fullcoverage.yahoo. com/Full_Coverage/World/Gay_and_Lesbian_ News/.** Log on to the site and examine the following link: "ACLU: Gay and Lesbian Rights." Also, visit PBS: Out of the Past (**http://www.pbs.org/ outofthepast).**

(a) What current legislation and court cases impacting gay and lesbian rights are in the news? Do the outcomes of these legal cases seem to favor or limit civil rights? How so?

(b) Explore the timeline and facts presented on the PBS site. What role did the Stonewall Inn Riots play in the gay rights movement? What were the most surprising facts you learned about the experiences of homosexuals in world or U.S. history?

(c) According to the ACLU site, what are the most important civil liberty issues facing gays and lesbians today?

(d) Has your state decriminalized homosexual sexual encounters?

(e) Does your state or city recognize domestic partnership registration?

(f) Why are domestic partnership registrations important, according to the site?

(g) After reading the "Model Domestic Partnerships" section, how would you summarize the ACLU's definition and requirements of domestic partnerships? What would you add or subtract from this description, and why?

(h) What is ENDA?

(i) Do you believe that equal rights for gay and lesbian citizens are improving or worsening in the United States? Why?

Online Learning Center www.mhhe.com/schaefer8

If you need to review for a test, visit the student center in the Online Learning Center at **www.mhhe.com/schaefer8,** and link to the True/False Quiz. The quiz will test your knowledge and give you immediate feedback on incorrect answers.

SOCIAL CHANGE
AND TECHNOLOGY

(Artificial Intelligence)

Electronic listening music from Warp

Social change and new technology often go hand in hand, as this whimsical cover for an electronic music catalog suggests. Although innovations in technology and the arts are not likely to spawn a new race of robots, they do change the way people live, altering cultural and social patterns in the process.

Chuck D is an unlikely hero of the digital age. With hit albums such as *Yo! Bum Rush the Show* and *Fear of a Black Planet,* the founder of the rap group Public Enemy would seem to inhabit a world far removed from the more conspicuous pioneers of cyberspace, from the Netscapes and Yahoos! and AOLs. In 1998, however, Chuck D stormed into cyberspace. Rather than giving his latest songs to Def Jam, the label that had produced his music for over a decade, the rap artist instead released his music directly onto the Internet, at www.public-enemy.com. It shouldn't have been such a big deal, really: one artist, a handful of songs, and a funky distribution method that probably reached several thousand fans. But in the music business this was very big news. For Chuck D had taken one of the industry's most sacred practices and thrown it, quite literally, into space. With just a couple of songs, he challenged how music was sold and, even more fundamentally, how it was owned. "This is the beginning," proclaimed the rapper, "of the end of domination."

As far as Chuck D was concerned, putting music online was a matter of power, of using new technologies to right old wrongs and give recording artists the influence and money that was rightfully theirs. To the recording industry, however, it was heresy. . . .

Had Chuck D been an isolated case, the studios most likely could have looked the other way. They could have dismissed Chuck D as a simple renegade, a rapper gone bad, and forgotten him and his web site. But the problem was that Chuck D, potentially, was everywhere. In cyberspace, any recording artist could distribute his or her music online; any musician could become a mini-studio, circumventing the record labels and their complex, clunky rules. . . .

Matters reached a head in 1999, when a nineteen-year-old college dropout named Shawn Fanning joined Chuck D in storming the frontier. Backed by his uncle in Boston, Fanning created Napster, a revolutionary system that allowed thousands—even millions—of users to trade their music online. Within months of its release, Napster had become a social phenomenon and a massive commercial threat. Universities complained that Napster was suddenly consuming huge chunks of their Internet bandwidth, and the music industry condemned it as piracy of the most blatant sort: "STEALING," as one music lawyer described it, "in big letters." Ironic foes such as Prince and the rock band Metallica joined the labels in pursuit of these new pirates, while prophets predicted the death of the recorded music industry. "A revolution has occurred in the way music is distributed," wrote one observer, "and the big record companies are in a state of panic." *(Spar 2001: 327–329)* ■ 💿

Additional information about this excerpt and about those that open each subsequent chapter can be found in the SocWorld CD-ROM that accompanies this text.

In this selection from *Ruling the Waves: Cycles of Discovery, Chaos, and Wealth from the Compass to the Internet,* political scientist Debora L. Spar describes the economic repercussions of a recent change in the way popular music is distributed. To students, the advent of Napster meant that suddenly, free music was available to them over the Internet. But to recording artists and record companies, Napster was a revolutionary new technology with the potential to shift the balance of power from the corporate giants that produced popular music to the artists who created and performed it. The distribution of digitized music via the Internet, then, changed both the way people behaved—how they selected, obtained, and listened to music—and the cultural institution that is the music business.

The invention of the personal computer and its integration into people's day-to-day lives is another example of the social change that often follows the introduction of a new technology. *Social change* has been defined as significant alteration over time in behavior patterns and culture (Moore 1967). But what constitutes a "significant" alteration? Certainly the dramatic rise in formal education documented in Chapter 16 represents a change that has had profound social consequences. Other social changes that have had long-term and important consequences include the emergence of slavery as a system of stratification (see Chapter 9), the industrial revolution (Chapters 5 and 20), the increased participation of women in the paid labor forces of the United States and Europe (Chapter 12), and the worldwide population explosion (Chapter 21). In many instances, the social movements studied in Chapter 22 have played an important role in promoting social change.

How does social change happen? Is the process unpredictable, or can we make certain generalizations about it? Why do some people resist social change? What changes are likely to follow the technologies of the future? And what have been the negative effects of the sweeping technological changes of the last century? In this chapter we will examine the process of social change, with special emphasis on the impact of technological advances. Efforts to explain long-term social changes have led to the development of theories of change; we will consider the evolutionary, functionalist, and conflict approaches to change. We will see how vested interests attempt to block changes that they see as threatening. We'll also look at various aspects of our technological future, such as telecommuting, the Internet, biotechnology, and technological accidents. We will examine the effects of technological advances on culture and social interaction, social control, and social stratification and inequality. Taken together, the impact of these technological changes may be approaching a level of magnitude comparable to that of the industrial revolution. Finally, in the social policy section we will discuss the ways in which technological advances have intensified concerns over privacy and censorship. ■

Theories of Social Change

A new millennium provides the occasion to offer explanations of social change, but this is clearly a challenge in the diverse and complex world we inhabit today. Nevertheless, theorists from several disciplines have sought to analyze social change. In some instances, they have examined historical events to arrive at a better understanding of contemporary changes. We will review three theoretical approaches to change—evolutionary, functionalist, and conflict theory—and then take a look at global change today.

Evolutionary Theory

Charles Darwin's (1809–1882) pioneering work in biological evolution contributed to nineteenth-century theories of social change. According to his approach, there has been a continuing progression of successive life forms. For example, since human beings came at a later stage of evolution than reptiles, we represent a more complex form of life. Social theorists sought an analogy to this biological model and originated *evolutionary theory,* which views society as moving in a definite direction. Early evolutionary theorists generally agreed that society was inevitably progressing to a higher state. As might be expected, they concluded in ethnocentric fashion that their own behavior and culture were more advanced than those of earlier civilizations.

p. 10 August Comte (1798–1857), a founder of sociology, was an evolutionary theorist of change. He saw human societies as moving forward in their thinking from mythology to the scientific method. Similarly, Émile Durkheim ([1893]1933) maintained that society progressed from simple to more complex forms of social organization.

The writings of Comte and Durkheim are examples of **unilinear evolutionary theory.** This approach contends that all societies pass pp. 10–11 through the same successive stages of evolution and inevitably reach the same end. English sociologist Herbert Spencer (1820–1903) used a similar approach: Spencer likened society to a living body with interrelated parts that were moving toward a common destiny. However, contemporary evolutionary theorists such as Gerhard Lenski are more likely to picture social change as multilinear than to rely on the more limited unilinear perspective. **Multilinear evolutionary theory** holds that change p. 532 can occur in several ways and that it does not inevitably lead in the same direction (Haines 1988; Turner 1985).

Multilinear theorists recognize that human culture has evolved along a number of lines. For example, the theory of demographic transition graphically demonstrates that population change in developing nations has not necessarily followed the model evident in industrialized nations. Sociologists today hold that events do not necessarily follow in a single or several straight lines but instead are subject to disruptions—a topic we will consider later in the discussion of global social change.

African Americans are now accepted in many exclusive golf clubs that were previously restricted, illustrating the process of *inclusion* described by Talcott Parsons. The phenomenal success of pro golfer Tiger Woods has helped the process along.

Functionalist Theory

Functionalist sociologists focus on what *maintains* a system, not on what changes it. This might seem to suggest that functionalists can offer little of value to the study of social change. Yet, as the work of sociologist Talcott Parsons demonstrates, functionalists have made a distinctive contribution to this area of sociological investigation.

Parsons (1902–1979), a leading proponent of functionalist theory, viewed society as naturally being in a state of equilibrium. By "equilibrium," he meant that p. 14 society tends toward a state of stability or balance. Parsons would view even prolonged labor strikes or civilian riots as temporary disruptions in the status quo rather than as significant alterations in social structure. Therefore, according to his **equilibrium model,** as changes occur in one part of society, there must be adjustments in other parts. If this does not take place, the society's equilibrium will be threatened and strains will occur.

Reflecting an evolutionary approach, Parsons (1966) maintained that four processes of social change are inevitable. The first, *differentiation,* refers to the increasing complexity of social organization. A change from "medicine man" to physician, nurse, and pharmacist is an illustration of differentiation in the field of health. This process is accompanied by *adaptive upgrading,* whereby social institutions become more specialized in their purposes. The division of labor among physicians into obstetricians, internists, surgeons, and so forth is an example of adaptive upgrading.

The third process identified by Parsons is the *inclusion* of groups into society that were previously excluded because of such factors as gender, race, and social class background. Medical schools have practiced inclusion by admitting increasing numbers of women and African Americans. Finally, Parsons contends that societies experience *value generalization,* the development of new values that tolerate and legitimate a greater range of activities. The acceptance of preventive and alternative medicine is an example of value generalization; our society has broadened its view of health care. All four processes identified by Parsons stress consensus—societal agreement on the nature of social organization and values (Johnson 1975; Wallace and Wolf 1980).

Parsons's approach explicitly incorporates the evolutionary notion of continuing progress. However, the dominant theme in his model is balance and stability. Society may change, but it remains stable through new forms of integration. For example, in place of the kinship ties that provided social cohesion in the past, there are laws, judicial processes, and new values and belief systems.

Functionalists assume that social institutions will not persist unless they continue to contribute to the overall society. This leads functionalists to conclude that altering institutions will threaten societal equilibrium. Critics note that the functionalist approach virtually disregards the use of coercion by the powerful to maintain the illusion of a stable, well-integrated society (Gouldner 1960).

Conflict Theory

The functionalist perspective minimizes change. It emphasizes the persistence of social life and sees change as a means of maintaining the equilibrium (or balance) of a society. By contrast, conflict theorists contend that social institutions and practices persist because powerful groups have the ability to maintain the status quo. Change has crucial significance, since it is needed to correct social injustices and inequalities.

Karl Marx accepted the evolutionary argument that societies develop along a particular path. However, unlike Comte and Spencer, he did not view each successive stage as an inevitable improvement over the previous one. History, according to Marx, proceeds through a series of stages, each of which exploits a class of people. Ancient society exploited slaves; the estate system of feudalism exploited serfs; modern capitalist society exploits the working class. Ultimately, through a socialist revolution led by the proletariat, human society will move toward the final stage of development: a classless communist society, or "community of free individuals" as Marx described it in *Das Kapital* in 1867 (see Bottomore and Rubel 1956:250).

As we have seen, Karl Marx had an important influence on the development of sociology. His pp. 12–13 thinking offered insights into such institutions as the economy, the family, religion, and government. The Marxist view of social change is appealing because it does not restrict people to a passive role in responding to inevitable cycles or changes in material culture. Rather, Marxist theory offers a tool for those who wish to seize control of the historical process and gain their freedom from injustice. In contrast to functionalists' emphasis on stability, Marx argues that conflict is a normal and desirable aspect of social change. In fact, change must be encouraged as a means of eliminating social inequality (Lauer 1982).

One conflict sociologist, Ralf Dahrendorf (1959), has noted that the contrast between the functionalist perspective's emphasis on stability and the conflict perspective's focus on change reflects the contradictory nature of society. Human societies are stable and long-lasting, yet they also experience serious conflict. Dahrendorf found that the functionalist approach and the conflict approach were ultimately compatible despite their many areas of disagreement. Indeed, Parsons spoke of new functions that result from social change, and Marx recognized the need for change so that societies could function more equitably.

Global Social Change

We are at a truly dramatic time in history to consider global social change. Maureen Hallinan (1997), in her presidential address to the American Sociological Association, asked those present to consider just a few of the recent political events: the collapse of communism; terrorism in various parts of the world, including the United States; the dismantling of the welfare system in the United States; revolution and famine in Africa and Eastern Europe; the spread of AIDS; and the computer revolution. Just a few months after her remarks came the first verification of the cloning of a complex animal, Dolly the sheep.

In this era of massive social, political, and economic change on a global scale, is it possible to predict change? Some technological changes seem obvious, but the collapse of communist governments in the former Soviet Union and Eastern Europe took people by surprise. However, prior to the Soviet collapse, sociologist Randall Collins (1986, 1995), a conflict theorist, had observed a crucial sequence of events that most observers had missed. In seminars as far back as 1980, and in a book published in 1986, Collins had argued that Soviet expansionism had resulted in an overextension of resources, including disproportionate spending on military forces. Such an overextension will strain a regime's stability. Moreover, geopolitical theory suggests that nations in the middle of a geographic region, such as the Soviet Union, tend to fragment into smaller units over time. Collins predicted that the coincidence of social crises on several frontiers would precipitate the collapse of the Soviet Union.

And that is just what happened. In 1979, the success of the Iranian revolution had led to an upsurge of Islamic fundamentalism in nearby Afghanistan, as well as in the Soviet republics with substantial Muslim populations. At the same time, resistance to Communist rule was growing both throughout Eastern Europe and within the Soviet Union itself. Collins had predicted that the rise of a dissident form of communism within the Soviet Union might facilitate the breakdown of the regime. Beginning in the late 1980s, Soviet leader Mikhail Gorbachev chose not to use military power and other types of repression to crush dissidents in Eastern Europe, offered plans for democratization and social reform of Soviet society, and seemed willing to reshape the Soviet Union into a loose federation of somewhat autonomous states. But, in 1991, six republics

As recently as 10 years ago, South Africa, a nation of 43 million people, was accurately described as a country where race was the sole determinant of power. Regardless of occupation, education, or family background, White South Africans enjoyed legal rights and privileges that were denied to all people of color. Ever since 1948, when it received its independence from Great Britain, South Africa had maintained this rigid segregationist policy, known as *apartheid*.

p. 282

During the 1980s, South Africa felt increasing worldwide economic pressure. At the same time, Black South Africans were more and more vocal about their second-class citizenship. They engaged in many forms of nonviolent and violent protest, including economic boycotts, labor strikes, political demonstrations, and occasional acts of sabotage.

In a dramatic turn of events in 1990, South African prime minister F. W. de Klerk legalized 60 banned Black organizations and freed Nelson Mandela, the leader of the long-outlawed African National Congress (ANC), after 27 years of imprisonment. The following year, de Klerk and Black leaders signed a National Peace Accord, pledging themselves to the establishment of a multiparty democracy.

In 1994, South Africa held its first universal election. Nelson Mandela's ANC received 62 percent of the vote, giving him a five-year term as president. Mandela and

his political party were then faced with a difficult challenge: making the transition from a liberation movement fighting for revolution to a governing party that needed to achieve political compromises. Moreover, an end to the racist policy of apartheid—while applauded around the world—was not in itself a solution to all of South Africa's serious problems. At best, one-fifth of the country's Blacks could compete in the nation's economy, while the balance formed a huge underclass.

> An end to the racist policy of apartheid—while applauded around the world—was not in itself a solution to all of South Africa's serious problems.

Some of the controversial issues facing the government are very familiar to residents of the United States:

- **Affirmative action.** Race-based employment goals and other preference programs have been proposed, yet critics insist that such efforts constitute reverse apartheid.
- **Illegal immigration.** An estimated 2 to 20 percent of South African residents are illegal immigrants, many of whom wish to escape the poverty and political turmoil of neighboring African states.

- **Medical care.** South Africa is confronting the inequities of private health care for the affluent (usually White) and government-subsidized care for others (usually people of color).
- **School integration and upgrading.** Multiracial schools are replacing the segregated school system. As of 1998, 82 percent had no media equipment (televisions or computers), and 57 percent had no electricity.

Perhaps the most difficult issue facing the government is land reform. Between 1960 and 1990, the all-White government forced 3.5 million Black South Africans from their land and frequently allowed Whites to settle on it. By 2001, the government was attempting to resettle 70,000 Black farmers. Though compensation will be offered to current landowners, bitter disputes seem inevitable.

Let's Discuss

1. How would a conflict theorist explain the relatively peaceful revolution in South Africa? What explanation might a functionalist offer?
2. Do you think other nations should use economic pressure to force social change in a country? Why or why not?

Sources: Adam 2000; Daley 1996, 1998; Duke 1998; Schaefer 2002; Sidiropoulos et al. 1996; South African Institute of Race Relations 2001a, 2001b.

---

on the western periphery declared their independence, and within months the entire Soviet Union had formally disintegrated into Russia and a number of other independent nations. (Social change does not always follow this pattern; sometimes it is precipitated by outside pressures, as Box 23-1, on the end of apartheid in South Africa, indicates.)

In her address, Hallinan (1997) cautioned that we need to move beyond the restrictive models of social change—the linear view of evolutionary theory and the

assumptions about equilibrium within functionalist theory. She and other sociologists have looked to "chaos theory" advanced by mathematicians to consider erratic events as a part of change. Hallinan noted that upheavals and major chaotic shifts do occur and that sociologists must learn to predict their occurrence, as Collins did with the Soviet Union. Imagine the dramatic nonlinear social change that will result from major innovations in the areas of communications and biotechnology, a topic we will discuss later in the chapter.

Resistance to Social Change

Efforts to promote social change are likely to meet with resistance. In the midst of rapid scientific and technological innovations, many people are frightened by the demands of an ever-changing society. Moreover, certain individuals and groups have a stake in maintaining the existing state of affairs.

Social economist Thorstein Veblen (1857–1929) coined the term ***vested interests*** to refer to those people or groups who will suffer in the event of social change. For example, the American Medical Association (AMA) has taken strong stands against national health insurance and the professionalization of midwifery. National p. 475 health insurance could lead to limits on the income of physicians, and a rise in the status of midwives could threaten the preeminent position of doctors as the nation's deliverers of babies. In general, those with a disproportionate share of society's wealth, status, and power, such as members of the American Medical Association, have a vested interest in preserving the status quo (Starr 1982; Veblen 1919).

Economic and Cultural Factors

Economic factors play an important role in resistance to social change. For example, it can be expensive for manufacturers to meet high standards for the safety of products and workers. Conflict theorists argue that, in a capitalist economic system, many firms are not willing to pay the price of meeting strict safety standards. They may resist social change by cutting corners within their plants or by pressuring the government to ease regulations.

Communities, too, protect their vested interests, often in the name of "protecting property values." The abbreviation "NIMBY" stands for "not in my backyard," a cry often heard when people protest landfills, prisons, nuclear power facilities, and even bike trails and group homes for people with developmental disabilities. The targeted community may not challenge the need for the facility but may simply insist that it be located elsewhere. The "not in my backyard" attitude has become so common that it is almost impossible

for policymakers to find acceptable locations for such facilities as dump sites for hazardous wastes (Jasper 1997).

Like economic factors, cultural factors frequently shape resistance to change. William F. Ogburn (1922) distinguished between material and nonmaterial aspects of culture. *Material culture* includes inventions, artifacts, and technology; *nonmaterial culture* encompasses ideas, norms, communications, and sop. 64cial organization. Ogburn pointed out that one cannot devise methods for controlling and utilizing new technology before the introduction of a technique. Thus, nonmaterial culture typically must respond to changes in material culture. Ogburn introduced the term ***culture lag*** to refer to the period of maladjustment during which the nonmaterial culture is still adapting to new material conditions. One example is the Internet. Its rapid uncontrolled growth raises questions about whether to regulate it and, if so, how much (see the social policy section in this chapter).

In certain cases, changes in material culture can add strain to the relationships between social institutions. For example, new means of birth control have been developed in recent decades. Large families are no longer economically necessary, nor are they commonly endorsed by social norms. But certain religious faiths, among them Roman Catholicism, continue to extol large families and to disapprove methods of limiting family size such as contraception

"Not in my backyard!" say these demonstrators, objecting to the placement of a new incinerator in a Hartford, Connecticut, neighborhood. The phenomenon of NIMBY has become so common that it is almost impossible for policymakers to find acceptable locations for incinerators, landfills, and dump sites for hazardous wastes.

and abortion. This represents a lag between aspects of material culture (technology) and nonmaterial culture (religious beliefs). Conflicts may emerge between religion and other social institutions, such as government and the educational system, over the dissemination of birth control and family-planning information (Riley et al. 1994a, 1994b).

Resistance to Technology

Technological innovations are examples of changes in material culture that have often provoked resistance. The *industrial revolution*, which took place largely in England **p. 123** during the period 1760 to 1830, was a scientific revolution focused on the application of nonanimal sources of power to labor tasks. As this revolution proceeded, societies relied on new inventions that facilitated agricultural and industrial production and on new sources of energy such as steam. In some industries, the introduction of power-driven machinery reduced the need for factory workers and made it easier to cut wages.

Strong resistance to the industrial revolution emerged in some countries. In England, beginning in 1811, masked craft workers took extreme measures: They conducted nighttime raids on factories and destroyed some of the new machinery. The government hunted these rebels, known as **Luddites**, and ultimately banished some while hanging others. In a similar effort in France, some angry workers threw their wooden shoes (*sabots*) into factory machinery to destroy it, thereby giving rise to the term *sabotage*. While the resistance of the Luddites and the French workers was short-lived and unsuccessful, they have come to symbolize resistance to technology over the last two centuries.

Are we now in the midst of a second industrial revolution, with a contemporary group of Luddites engaged in resistance? Many sociologists believe that we are now **p. 123** living in a *postindustrial society*. It is difficult to pinpoint exactly when this era began. Generally, it is viewed as having begun in the 1950s, when for the first time the majority of workers in industrial societies became involved in services rather than in the actual manufacturing of goods (Bell 1999; Fiala 1992).

Just as the Luddites resisted the industrial revolution, people in many countries have resisted postindustrial technological changes. The term *neo-Luddites* refers to those who are wary of technological innovations and who question the incessant expansion of industrialization, the increasing destruction of the natural and agrarian world, and the "throw it away" mentality of contemporary capitalism with its resulting pollution of the environment. Neo-Luddites insist that whatever the presumed benefits of industrial and postindustrial technology, such technology has distinctive social costs and may represent a danger to the future of the human species and our planet (Bauerlein 1996; Rifkin 1995b; Sale 1996; Snyder 1996).

Such concerns are worth remembering as we turn now to examine aspects of our technological future and their possible impact on social change.

Imagine

You are a neo-Luddite who wants to destroy the Internet. How will you do it? Are your motives the same as or different from those of the Luddites?

Technology and the Future

Technology is information about how to use the material **p. 123** resources of the environment to satisfy human needs and desires. Technological advances— the airplane, the automobile, the television, the atomic bomb, and, more recently, the computer, the fax machine, and the cellular phone—have brought striking changes in our cultures, our patterns of socialization, our social institutions, and our day-to-day social interactions. Technological innovations are, in fact, emerging and being accepted with remarkable speed. For example, scientists at Monsanto estimated in 1998 that the amount of genetic information used in practical applications will double every year. Part of the reason for this explosion in using new technology is that it is becoming cheaper. In 1974, it cost $2.5 million to determine the chemical structure of a single gene; less than 25 years later that cost was $150 (Belsie 1998).

The technological knowledge with which we work today represents only a tiny portion of the knowledge that will be available in the year 2050. We are witnessing an information explosion as well: The number of volumes in major libraries in the United States doubles every 14 years. Individuals, institutions, and societies will face unprecedented challenges in adjusting to the technological advances still to come (Cetron and Davies 1991; Wurman 1989).

In the following sections, we will examine various aspects of our technological future and consider their overall impact on social change, including the strains they will bring. We will focus in particular on recent developments in computer technology and biotechnology.

Computer Technology

The last decade has witnessed an explosion of computer technology in the United States and around the world. We will now examine two aspects of the technological and social changes related to computers: telecommuting and the Internet.

Taking Sociology to Work

LAUREL MILLER:
Executive Producer, Media Technology, McGraw-Hill Companies

When Laurel Miller got her degree from the State University of New York, Albany, in 1972, it was a time of great social change, which she admits influenced her decision to major in sociology. "I was interested in how groups of people worked, how institutions became what they are." She recalls being stimulated by writing papers on a variety of topics, such as the evolution of tennis, ballet, and a specific religious movement.

In her job at McGraw-Hill, Miller develops new media products, such as CD-ROMs and websites, for the humanities and social sciences lists, which of course, include sociology texts. She has to keep up with the changes in technology that have come fast and furious in the last few years. She's been excited to see "the increased acceptance of technology by professors, sales representatives, and editorial staff" to the point that it is now considered the normal way of doing things in the publishing world.

Miller credits her background in sociology with giving her "a broad perspective on events and circumstances that I've been involved in." It also taught her not to jump to conclusions or to form stereotypes. She recommends that sociology students "always remain interested in what is going on around you."

Let's Discuss

1. Do you use CD-ROMs and web research in connection with your sociology class? In what ways, if any, does this technology enhance your studies?
2. How do you think a major in sociology would prepare you for a job like Laurel Miller's? What other field(s) of study would be useful in addition to sociology courses?

Telecommuting

As the industrial revolution proceeded, the factory and the office replaced the home as the typical workplace. But the postindustrial revolution has brought people home again. In 1999, at least 14 million telecommuters in the United States worked at home at least once a month. *Telecommuters* are employees who work full-time or part-time at home rather than in an outside office. They are linked to their supervisors and colleagues through computer terminals, phone lines, and fax machines. As part of a shift toward postindustrial societies linked within a global economy, telecommuting can even cross national boundaries, oceans, and continents (Hall 1999).

Telecommuting clearly facilitates communication between a company's employees who work in different locations, including those who work at home. Telecommuting also reduces time spent on transportation and can be helpful in a family's child care arrangements. At the same time, working at home can be isolating and stressful—and even more stressful if a parent must attempt to combine working at home and caring for children. Moreover, companies still need to encourage face-to-face communication in staff meetings and social settings. Overall, while telecommuting unquestionably offers distinct advantages for many employees and companies, it also presents new challenges (Marklein 1996).

p. 113 The rise of telecommuting is especially beneficial for one subordinate group in the United States: people with disabilities. Computer terminals lend themselves to ancillary devices that make them adaptable to most types of physical impairments. For example, people who are blind can work at home using

In our postindustrial society, computers are in use almost everywhere imaginable.

Students in colleges in North America expect to be able to use the Internet or leave messages through voice mail. They complain when the computer is "slow" or the electronic mailbox is "full." Despite their complaints, they take these services for granted and generally do not even pay directly for them. But in much of the world, it is very different.

The United Nations has tried for years to assist the nation of Madagascar to upgrade its telephone system to be able to handle a 300 baud communication device—the slowest speed available. At this glacial rate, it would take about two minutes to transmit this page without the color and without the graphics. By comparison, in the United States, most people are *discarding* systems 50 times faster and turning to devices that transmit information 180 times faster. The irony is that it costs more per minute to use a telephone in Madagascar and much of Africa than in the United States, so we have a continent paying more per minute to transmit information much more slowly.

This is but one example of the haves and have-nots in the information age. As Figure 23-1 shows, the Internet is virtually monopolized by North America and Europe and a few other industrial nations. They have the most *Internet hosts,* computers directly connected to the worldwide network of interconnected computer systems. In contrast, in 2001, three countries had no Internet service provider at all: Guyana in South America, Guinea-Bissau in Africa, and North Korea.

> In Madagascar, there are 3 telephone lines per 1,000 people, and for all low-income nations the average is 16.

This inequality is not new. We also find dramatic differences in the presence of newspapers, telephones, televisions, and even radios throughout the world. For example, in Madagascar, there are 3 telephone lines per 1,000 people, and for all low-income nations the average is 16. In the United States, there are 644 lines per 1,000 people; for all high-income nations the average is 552. Often in developing nations, and especially their rural areas, radio and television transmission is sporadic, and the programming may be dominated by recycled information from the United States.

The consequences of the global disconnect for developing nations are far more serious than not being able to "surf the Net." Today we have the true emergence of what sociologist Manuel Castells refers to as a "global economy" because the world has the capacity to work as a single unit in real time. However, if large numbers of people and, indeed, entire nations are disconnected from the informational economy, their slow economic growth will continue, with all the negative consequences it has for people. The educated and skilled will immigrate to labor markets that are a part of this global economy, deepening the impoverishment of the nations on the periphery.

Let's Discuss

1. What factors might make it difficult to remedy the global disconnect in developing nations?
2. What are some of the social and economic consequences for nations that are not "connected"?

Sources: Castells 1996, 2000; Matrix.Net 2000; World Bank 2000a; Wresch 1996.

word processors that read messages in a computer voice, or that translate the messages into Braille text (Nelson 1995).

The Internet

The Internet is the world's largest computer network. By 2003, it is estimated to reach some 369 million computer users—ten times the number in 1998 (Global Reach 2000).

The Internet actually evolved from a computer system built in 1962 by the U.S. Defense Department to enable scholars and military researchers to continue to do government work even if part of the nation's communications system was destroyed by a nuclear attack. Until recently, it was difficult to gain access to the Internet without holding a position at a university or a government research laboratory. Today, however, virtually anyone can reach the Internet with a phone line, a computer, and a modem. And it is possible to buy and sell cars, trade stocks, auction off items, research new medical remedies, vote, track down long-lost friends—to mention just a few of the thousands of online possibilities (Reddick and King 2000).

While the rise of the Internet facilitates telecommuting and the spread of a home-based economy, much of the focus of the Internet has been on new forms of communication and social interaction. Early users established a subculture with specific norms and values. These pioneers generally resent formal rules for Internet communication, believe that access to information should be free

Figure 23-1

Geographical Distribution of Internet Hosts, January 2000

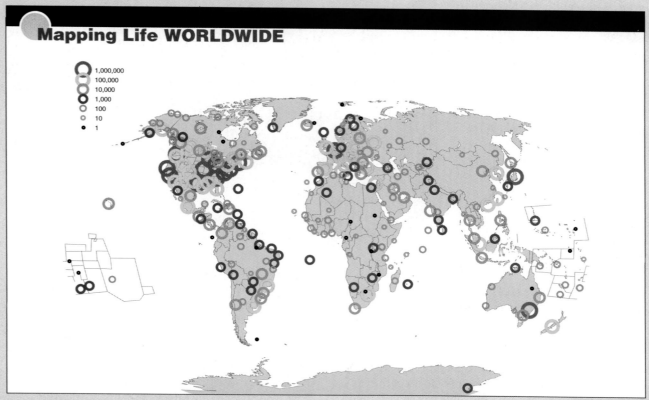

Source: Matrix Information and Directory Services (Matrix.Net 2000).

and unlimited, and distrust efforts to centralize control of the Internet. The subculture of early Internet users also developed argot terms, such as "flaming" (hurling abuse online), "chat rooms" (bulletin boards for people with common interests), and "hacking" (using one's personal computer to break into others' electronic files).

One troubling issue has been raised about day-to-day "life" on the Internet. What, if anything, should be done about use of the Internet by neo-Nazis and other extremist groups who exchange messages of hatred and even bomb-making recipes? What, if anything, should be done about the issue of sexual expression on the Internet? Should there be censorship of "hot chat" and X-rated film clips? Or should there be *complete* freedom of expression? The impact of technological change on issues of privacy

and censorship will be examined in the social policy section at the end of this chapter.

While many people in the United States embrace the Internet, we should note that information is not evenly distributed throughout the population. The same people, by and large, who experience poor health and have few job opportunities also have been left off the information highway. Moreover, this pattern of inequality is global. p. 243 ◄ The core nations that Immanuel Wallerstein describes in his *world systems analysis* have a virtual monopoly on information technology while the developing nations of Asia, Africa, and Latin America are on the periphery, depending on the industrial giants for both the technology and the information it provides. Box 23-2 explores this "global disconnect."

Biotechnology

Sex selection of fetuses, genetically engineered organisms, cloning of sheep and cows—these have been among the significant and yet controversial scientific advances in the field of biotechnology in recent years. George Ritzer's concept of McDonaldization applies to the entire area of biotechnology. Just as the fast-food concept has permeated society, it seems there is now no phase of life exempt from therapeutic or medical intervention. Biotechnology holds itself out as totally beneficial to human beings, but ultimately it reveals itself as in constant need of monitoring and adjustment. As we will see in the following sections, biotechnological advances have raised many difficult ethical and political decisions (Weinstein and Weinstein 1999).

p. 63 ←

Greenpeace activists dressed in mock safety suits demonstrate against the sale of genetically modified corn flour at a supermarket in Mexico City. The potential health effects of genetic engineering have become the subject of much fear and controversy.

Sex Selection

Advances in reproductive and screening technology have brought us closer to effective techniques for sex selection. In the United States, the prenatal test of amniocentesis has been used for more than 25 years to ascertain the presence of certain defects that require medical procedures prior to birth. However, such tests also identify the sex of the fetus, as can ultrasound scans. This outcome has had profound social implications.

In many societies, young couples planning to have only one child will want to ensure that this child is a boy because their culture places a premium on a male heir. In such instances, advances in fetal testing may lead to abortion if the fetus is found to be female. Kuckreja Sohoni, a social scientist from India, notes that many parents in India are "mortally afraid" of having baby girls. Well aware of the pressure on Indian women to produce sons, Sohoni (1994:96), the mother of three teenage girls, admits, "had ultrasound been available when I was having children, I shudder to think how easily I would have been persuaded to plan a sex-selected family."

Fetal testing clinics in Canada currently advertise that they can tell parents the sex of a fetus. Such advertising is particularly targeted at Asian Indian communities in both Canada and the United States. But, in the United States, the preference for a male child is hardly limited to people from India. In one study, when asked what sex they would prefer for an only child, 86 percent of men and 59 percent of women wanted a boy. Moreover, fetal testing to determine the sex of a child is becoming more accepted in the United States (Hall 1993; Sohoni 1994).

From a functionalist perspective, we can view sex selection as an adaptation of the basic family function of regulating reproduction. However, conflict theorists emphasize that sex selection may intensify the male dominance of our society and undermine the advances women have made in entering careers formerly restricted to men.

Genetic Engineering

Even more grandiose than sex selection—but not necessarily improbable—is altering human behavior through genetic engineering. Fish and plant genes have already been mixed to create frost-resistant potato and tomato crops; more recently, human genes have been implanted in pigs to provide humanlike kidneys for organ transplants.

One of the latest developments in genetic engineering is gene therapy. Geneticists in Japan have managed to disable genes in a mouse fetus that carry an undesirable trait and replace them with genes carrying a desirable trait. Such advances raise staggering possibilities for altering animal and human life forms, but gene therapy remains highly experimental and must be assessed as a long, long shot (Kolata 1999).

The debate on genetic engineering escalated in 1997 when scientists in Scotland announced that they had cloned a sheep. After many unsuccessful attempts, scientists finally were able to replace the genetic material of a sheep's egg with DNA from an adult sheep and thereby create a lamb that was a clone of the adult. The very next year, Japanese researchers successfully cloned cows. These developments raised the possibility that, in the near future, we may be able to clone human beings.

In 1997, President Bill Clinton banned any federal support for human cloning and urged private laboratories to abide by a voluntary moratorium until the ethical issues could be carefully considered. William F. Ogburn probably could not have anticipated such scientific developments when he wrote of culture lag 70 years earlier; however, the successful cloning of sheep illustrates again how quickly material culture can change and how nonmaterial culture moves more slowly in absorbing such changes (Morrow 1997; Sale 1997; Wilmut et al. 1997).

While cloning grabs the headlines, there is a growing controversy concerning food that has been genetically modified (GM). This controversy began in Europe but has since spread to other parts of the world, including the United States. The idea behind the technology is to increase food production and make agriculture more economical. Critics use the term *Frankenfood* (as in "Frankenstein") to refer to everything from breakfast cereals using genetically engineered grains to "fresh" tomatoes in the produce department. They object to tampering with nature and are concerned about the possible health effects of GM food. Supporters of the genetically modified food include not just the biotech companies but also those who see the technology as a way to help feed burgeoning populations in Africa and Asia (Golden 1999).

Bioterrorism

Because biotechnology has generally been seen as a benefit to society, critics have been concerned mostly with the possibility of unintended negative consequences. Yet scientists have long recognized that chemical and biological agents can be used intentionally as weapons of mass destruction. Mustard gas was first introduced by combatants in World War I, and nerve gas was used shortly after. Today as many as 26 nations appear to have stockpiled chemical weapons, and another 10 have developed biological weapons programs.

More disturbing still is the prospect that terrorists might develop their own biological or chemical weapons, which are not difficult or expensive to make. The deaths that occurred as a result of anthrax contamination of the U.S. mails in 2001, shortly after the attack on the Pentagon and World Trade Center, underscored the relative ease with which biotechnology can be used for hostile purposes. In fact, between 1975 and August 2000, terrorists created 342 incidents involving biological or chemical agents. Only about a third of those events involved real attacks, and most caused few injuries and even fewer deaths. Yet because chemical and biological weapons are easy to use, these agents, which have come to be known as

A Hazmat worker bags dust samples taken from the Associated Press mailroom in October 2001, after letters containing deadly anthrax bacteria were sent to newsrooms in Florida and New York. The threat of bioterrorism has become a matter of increasing concern to governments and organizations throughout the world.

the poor person's nuclear bomb, are a source of increasing concern to governments the world over (J. Miller et al. 2001; Henry L. Stimson Center 2001; Henry L. Stimson Center in Mullins 2001; White 2002).

Technological Accidents

A carpenter who single-handedly makes a ladder has quite a different investment in the quality of the product than does a technician who develops a small part for a space shuttle. Our increasing reliance on technology has led to a growing separation between people and the outcomes of their actions.

Sociologist Charles Perrow (1999) introduced the term *normal accidents* to refer to failures that are inevitable given the manner in which human and technological systems are organized. Whether in a hospital or an aerospace program, catastrophes are often caused not by massive errors but rather by what appear to be (when considered in isolation) almost incidental human misjudgments and minor technical flaws. In studying normal accidents, engineers focus on the system design, the physical environment, and the possibility of mechanical failure; social scientists evaluate possible *human* error. Generally, 60 to 80 percent of normal accidents are attributed to human factors (Erikson 1994). The chapter-opening excerpt from Kai Erikson's *A New Species of Trouble* in Chapter 21 (see page 526) mentioned several massive accidents that were attributed to human error.

As technology continues to advance at a rapid pace, there are always new possibilities for accidents. For example, the disastrous 1986 launch of the U.S. space shuttle *Challenger* ended in the deaths of seven astronauts. More recently, it became apparent that electronic communication devices are vulnerable to failure. In 1998, the Galaxy IV communications satellite malfunctioned, knocking out the paging systems used by 90 percent of people in the United States. Hospitals could not page their doctors, so old-fashioned "phone trees" were established during the week of no service. The malfunction also took several broadcasters off the air, including National Public Radio. Although the foul-up was ultimately corrected, this incident does underscore the possibilities for chaos in an ever-expanding electronic system (Swanson and Kirk 1998; Vaughan 1996).

System accidents are uncommon, even rare. But, like the death of any individual, which occurs only once, this infrequency is not all that reassuring. Given the serious consequences of a systems failure, we can anticipate that social scientists will work even more closely with engineers to explore how better equipment, training, and organization can reduce the likelihood of normal accidents (Perrow 1999; see also Clarke 1999; D. Miller 2000).

These are but a few vignettes of technological change, viewed from the vantage point of the turn of the century, that raise questions about the future. Sociologists are not fortune-tellers; the focus of the discipline is to examine the society around us, rather than to project decades ahead. But sociologists have no problem in asserting that social change (and technological change) is a given in our world. And so, they remind us, is resistance to change. We cannot know what is ahead. But the sociological imagination—with its probing and theorizing, with its careful empirical studies—can assist us in understanding the past and present and anticipating and adjusting to the future.

Imagine

Try to imagine the world 100 years from now. On balance, is it a world in which technology contributes to or threatens people's well-being? In what ways?

Technology and Society

An ATM machine that identifies a person by his or her facial structure, a small device that sorts through hundreds of odors to ensure the safety of a chemical plant, a cell phone that recognizes its owner's voice. These are real-life examples of technology that were so much science fiction a few short decades ago. Today's computer chip cannot only think but can see, smell, and hear, too (Salkever 1999).

Technological advances can dramatically transform the material culture. Word processing on computers, the pocket calculator, the photocopying machine, and the compact disc player have largely eliminated use of the typewriter, the adding machine, the mimeograph machine, and the turntable—all of which were themselves technological advances.

Technological change also can reshape *nonmaterial* culture. In the following sections, we will examine the effects of technological advances on culture and social interaction, social control, and stratification and inequality.

Culture and Social Interaction

In Chapter 3, we emphasized that language is the foundation of every culture. From a functionalist perspective, language can bring together members of a society and promote cultural integration. However, from a conflict perspective, the use of language can intensify divisions between groups and societies—just look at the battles over language in the United States, Canada, and other societies.

The Internet has often been lauded as a democratizing force that will make huge quantities of information available to great numbers of people around the world. However, while the Internet and its World Wide Web open up access to most societies, close to half of the material is transmitted in English (see Figure 23-2). Without special computer programs, documents in languages such as Chinese and Japanese cannot be transmitted in readable fashion (Colker 1996; Schaefer 1995).

On the other hand, the technology is helping to preserve dying languages that would otherwise be lost to posterity. Various websites are maintaining the vocabularies, grammars, and audio samples of hundreds of languages that have virtually disappeared from the real world. Among those preserved in virtual reality are rare

Figure 23-2

Projected Language Use on the Internet, 2003

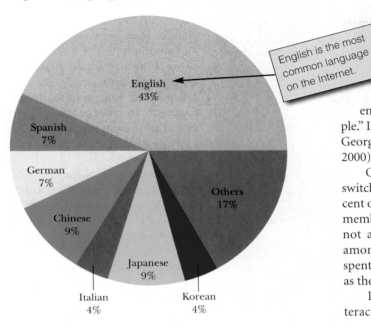

English is the most common language on the Internet.

English 43%

Spanish 7%

German 7%

Chinese 9%

Japanese 9%

Italian 4%

Korean 4%

Others 17%

Source: Global Reach 2001.

Aboriginal Australian dialects with no living native speakers (Pollak 2001).

The domination of the Internet by the English language is not surprising. English has largely become the international language of commerce and communication. Nevertheless, members of other cultures resent the way in which English is the accepted standard on the Internet. In Russia, for example, it is easier for someone to download the works of Tolstoy translated into English than it is to get Tolstoy's work as originally written in Russian (Specter 1996a).

How will social interaction *within* a culture be transformed by the growing availability of electronic forms of communication? Will people turn to e-mail, websites, and faxes rather than telephone conversations and face-to-face meetings? Certainly, the technological shift to telephones reduced the use of letter writing as a means of maintaining kinship and friendship ties. For this reason, some people worry that computers and other forms of electronic communication may be socially isolating. Sociologist Sherry Turkle (1999) has warned that some individuals may become so gratified by their online lives that they lose touch with their families, friends, and work responsibilities.

Yet Turkle (1995, 1999) has found positive effects of Internet usage as well. Over a 10-year period, she made anonymous visits to chat rooms and multiuser domains (MUDs), which allow people to assume new identities in

role-playing games. She also conducted face-to-face interviews with more than 1,000 people who communicate by electronic mail and participate actively in MUDs. Distinguishing between users' on-screen personae and their real identities, Turkle concluded that many MUD users' lives were enhanced by the opportunity to engage in role playing and "become someone else." A new sense of self had emerged, she wrote, that was "decentered and multiple." In making this observation, Turkle was expanding on George Herbert Mead's notion of self (Nass and Moon 2000).

One obvious form of online role playing is gender switching. In a 1999 study, researchers found that 40 percent of their subjects had presented themselves online as a member of the opposite sex. Yet gender switching does not appear to dominate online communication. Even among the gender-switched, the majority of subjects spent only about 10 percent of their time online disguised as the opposite sex (Roberts and Parks 1999).

If electronic communication can facilitate social interaction within a community—if it can create ties among people in different communities or even countries who "meet" in chat rooms or MUDs—then is there genuinely a new interactive world known as "cyberspace"? The term *cyberspace* was introduced in 1984 by William Gibson, a Canadian science fiction writer. He came up with this term after he walked by a video arcade and noticed the intensity of the players hunched over their screens. Gibson felt that these video game enthusiasts "develop a belief that there's some kind of actual space behind the screen. Some place that you can't see but you know is there" (Elmer-DeWitt 1995:4; see also Shields 1996; Wellman et al. 1996).

The emergence of cyberspace can be viewed as yet another step away from Ferdinand Tönnies's concept of the familiar, intimate *Gemeinschaft* to the comparatively impersonal *Gesellschaft*, and as yet another way p. 121 ◀ in which social cohesion is being eroded in contemporary society. Critics of electronic communication question whether nonverbal communication, voice inflections, and other forms of interpersonal interaction will be lost as people turn to e-mail and chat rooms (Schaefer 1995; Schellenberg 1996).

But whereas some conclude that by opening up the world to interaction, we may have reduced face-to-face interaction, others have reached different conclusions. One study surveyed more than 2,000 households nationwide to assess the impact of the Internet on the everyday lives of its users. It found that parents report that they often surf the web together with their children, and that the Internet has had little effect on their children's interactions

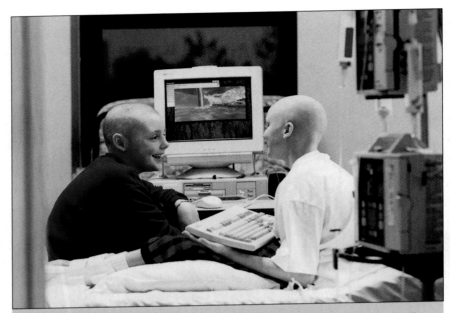

Two young patients at a New York City hospital communicate electronically with peers at a hospital in California. Electronic communication has proved useful in promoting social interaction among children who are seriously ill. The new technology, known as Starbright World, was developed with the assistance of director Steven Spielberg.

with friends. This study concludes that about two-thirds of the population in the United States are using the Internet more than ever and without sacrificing their social lives (Cha 2000; Howard et al. 2001; Nie 2001).

Social Control

A data entry employee pauses to say hello to a colleague. A checker at the supermarket takes a moment to banter with a customer. A customer service telephone representative takes too much time helping callers. Each of these situations is subject to computer surveillance. Given the absence of strong protective legislation, employees in the United States are subject to increasing and pervasive supervision by computers. Supervisors have always scrutinized the performance of their workers, but with so much work now being handled electronically, the possibilities for surveillance have risen dramatically. According to a 2001 study, one-third of the online workforce is under continuous electronic surveillance. With Big Brother watching and listening in more and more, there is a danger that electronic monitoring will become a substitute for effective management or lead to perceptions of unfairness and intrusiveness (Lee 2001; Schulman 2001).

In recent years, a new type of corporate surveillance has emerged. A number of Internet sites are highly critical of the operations of various corporations. On

McSpotlight, one could find attacks on nutritional practices at McDonald's; on Up Against the Wal, one could study advice on how to fight plans to open new Wal-Mart stores in a community. The Internet sites of such "anticorporate vigilantes" are generally protected by the First Amendment, but powerful corporations are carefully monitoring the sites in an attempt to counteract the activities of their critics (Neuborne 1996).

p. 200 Technological advances have also created the possibility for a new type of white-collar crime: computer crime. It is now possible to gain access to a computer's inventory without leaving home and to carry out embezzlement or electronic fraud without leaving a trace. One report released in 2000 put cybercrime losses by big businesses at $10 billion in the United States alone. Typically, discussions of computer crime focus on computer theft and on problems caused by computer "hackers," but widespread use of computers has facilitated many new ways of participating in deviant behavior. Consequently, greatly expanded police resources may be needed to deal with online child molesters, prostitution rings, software pirates, con artists, and other types of computer criminals. There is now a Computer Crime and Intellectual Property section of the Justice Department. The consensus of the heads of the section is that these cases are increasing and becoming more difficult (Piller 2000).

Not all the technological advances relevant to social control have been electronic in nature. DNA data banks have given police a powerful weapon in solving crimes; they have also opened the way to free wrongfully convicted citizens. A 1996 Department of Justice report noted that 28 men convicted of rape had been freed from U.S. prisons after DNA testing established their innocence. From 1996 through 1999, five death row inmates were released on the basis of DNA evidence. Efforts are under way to make such testing and other forms of DNA evidence as easily available as fingerprinting. As of mid-1996, 26 states had begun to develop DNA data banks that eventually will be linked in a nationwide network by the Federal Bureau of Investigation (FBI). While appropriate safeguards must be devised, the expansion of such DNA data banks has the potential to revolutionize law

"Keystroke! ... Keystroke! ... Keystroke!"

enforcement in the United States—especially in the area of sex crimes, where biological evidence is telling (Butterfield 1996; DPIC 2000c).

Another connection between technology and social control is the use of computer databases and electronic verification of documents to reduce illegal immigration into the United States. While concerned about the issue of illegal entry, many Hispanics and Asian Americans nevertheless believe that *their* privacy, rather than that of

Whites, is most likely to be infringed by government authorities (Brandon 1995). The next section of the chapter looks more fully at how technological changes can intensify stratification and inequality based on race, ethnicity, and other factors.

Stratification and Inequality

"Today we stand at the brink of becoming two societies, one largely white and plugged in and the other black and unplugged." This is how Black historian Henry Lewis Gates, Jr., starkly describes today's "digital divide" (Gates 1999: A15). An important continuing theme in sociology is stratification among people. Thus far, there is little evidence to suggest that technology will reduce inequality; in fact, it may only intensify it. Technology is costly, and it is generally impossible to introduce advances to everyone simultaneously. So who gets this access first? Conflict theorists contend that as we travel further and further along the electronic frontier through advances such as telecommuting and the Internet, the disenfranchised poor may be isolated from mainstream society in an "information ghetto," just as racial and ethnic minorities have traditionally been subjected to residential segregation (Ouellette 1993).

Available data show clear differences in use of computers based on class, race, and ethnicity. A national study released in 2001 estimated that only 14 percent of households earning less than $15,000 have access to the Internet, compared to 79 percent of those with incomes of $75,000 or more. Moreover, 56 percent of Asian American households and 46 percent of White households used the Internet, compared with 24 percent of Hispanic and African American households (see Figure 23-3).

This issue goes beyond individual interest or lack of interest in computers. Accessibility is a major concern. According to a study by the Consumer Federation of America and the NAACP (National Association for the Advancement of Colored People), accessibility to computer networks through fiber-optic corridors (the "information superhighway") may bypass poor neighborhoods and minority populations. The researchers concluded that regional telephone companies' plans for these advanced communications networks target affluent areas and may lead to an exclusionary "electronic redlining"

Figure 23-3

Internet Access in the United States, 2000

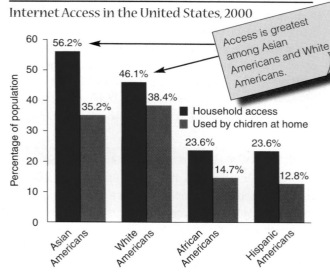

Access is greatest among Asian Americans and White Americans.

Source: Newburger 2001:3–4.

similar to discrimination in fields such as banking, real estate, and insurance. Industry executives counter that they have repeatedly stated their intention to deploy the information superhighway to *all* areas. Congress has proposed regulatory legislation to ensure equal access to the information superhighway by mandating the wiring of schools, libraries, and hospitals. Several communities, such as Manchester, New Hampshire, and Oakland, California, have recently arranged for computer hookups in publicly built low-income housing (Lieberman 1999; Lohr 1994).

The issue of technology and inequality is especially sensitive when viewed in a cross-cultural perspective. Although industrialization has dramatically improved the standard of living of many workers, it has allowed elites to amass untold wealth. Moreover, the activities of multinational corporations have increased the inequality between industrialized core nations (such as the United States, Germany, and Japan) and the periphery of developing countries.

Imagine

One hundred years from now, how might society have changed? Will people be as free as they are today? Will the differences among social classes be more or less pronounced than they are now? What about the differences among nations, races, religions, and ethnic groups?

SOCIAL POLICY AND TECHNOLOGY

Privacy and Censorship in a Global Village

www.mhhe.com/schaefer8

The Issue

In 1992, a huge explosion in a Texaco refinery in Wilmington, California, spread fire and caused panic in a nearby Hispanic community. Soon afterward, the Texaco Corporation was hit by close to 5,000 property damage claims and 14,000 claims of personal injury. Texaco promptly hired a private investigator, but not to probe the cause of the explosion. His task was to unearth compromising information about the claimants and their lawyers, whose class action suits could cost Texaco millions of dollars.

One of the claimants was 23-year-old Rossana Rivera. The private investigator didn't just learn her Social Security number, date of birth, every address where she had lived, names and numbers of present and past neighbors, the number of bedrooms in her house, her welfare history, and the employment background of her children's fathers. He also dredged up two delinquent traffic tickets, which he used to threaten her with arrest if she did not come up with damaging information about the lawyers in her case.

How did he arrive at all this information? For the most part, by buying or uncovering data in commercial databases (which most citizens are unaware of) and searching law enforcement computer files (supposedly off-limits to civilians). The Texaco investigator's actions are not at all unusual these days. According to a deputy U.S. attorney in New Jersey, "The buying and selling of information is just a huge business" (Bernstein 1997: A20).

The biggest customers are companies involved in litigation or business conflicts or just screening applicants. The suppliers in the information network include investigators, underground information brokers, online databases, governments that sell public records, former law enforcement personnel, even former cold war spies. The means of getting information range from simple payments to computer hacking to electronic surveillance to deception in all forms.

At this point in the United States, privacy laws have so many loopholes and are so patchy that it is often difficult to distinguish between data that are obtained legally and data that are gathered illicitly. The other side of the coin is the fear that government will restrict the flow of electronic information too much, stepping over the border into censorship. Some observers, however, feel the government is fully justified in restricting pornographic information. The whole issue of privacy and censorship in this technological age is another case of culture lag, in which the material culture (the technology) is changing faster than the nonmaterial culture (norms controlling the technology).

p. 64

The Setting

The typical consumer in the United States is included in dozens of marketing databases. These lists may seem innocent enough at first. Does it really matter if companies can buy lists for marketing with our names, addresses, and telephone numbers? Part of the problem is that computer technology has made it increasingly easy for any individual, business firm, or government agency to retrieve more

Harry Caul is
an invader of privacy.
The best in the business.
He can record
any conversation
between two people
anywhere.

So far,
three people are dead
because of him.

The Directors Company presents

GENE HACKMAN

"THE CONVERSATION"

Co-starring JOHN CAZALE · ALLEN GARFIELD · CINDY WILLIAMS · FREDERIC FORREST
Music scored by   Co-producer   Written, Produced and Directed by
DAVID SHIRE · FRED ROOS · FRANCIS FORD COPPOLA
Color by TECHNICOLOR® A Paramount Pictures Release

"THE CONVERSATION"

The 1974 motion picture *The Conversation,* in which Gene Hackman eavesdropped on other characters' conversations in their homes and in the park, raised an alarm among viewers concerned about their privacy. A generation later, citizens wonder how much of their electronic communication is monitored, and for what purposes.

and more information about any of us. For decades, information from motor vehicle offices, voter registration lists, and credit bureaus has been electronically stored, yet the incompatibility of different computer systems used to prevent access from one system to another. Today, having some information about a person has made it much easier to get other and perhaps more sensitive information.

The question of how much free expression should be permitted on the Internet relates to the issue of censorship. Pornography websites have proliferated, especially since the Supreme Court struck down federal legislation to regulate "indecent" words and images in 1997 (as we will see later in this section). Some of the X-rated material is perfectly legal, if inappropriate for children who use the Net. Some of the sites are clearly illegal, such as those that serve the needs of pedophiles who prey on young children. Some are morally and legally elusive, such as the "upskirt" sites that post images taken by video cameras aimed under the skirts of unsuspecting women in public places. This is another area in which we can see the results of culture lag.

Sociological Insights

Functionalists can point to the manifest function of the Internet in its ability to facilitate communications. They also can identify the latent function of providing a forum for groups with few resources to communicate with literally tens of millions of people. Poorly financed groups can range from hate organizations to special interest groups vying against powerful wealthy interests. Thus, the functionalist perspective would see many aspects of technology fostering communication. The issue of censorship depends on how one views the content of the message, and the issue of privacy hinges on how information is used.

Even if computers and other forms of modern technology are peering deeper and deeper into our daily lives, some observers insist that we *benefit* from such innovations and can exist quite well with a bit less privacy. Sociologist Amitai Etzioni (1996:14A) bluntly states, "The genie is out of the bottle. We must either return to the Stone Age (pay cash, use carrier pigeons, and forget insurance) or learn to live with shrunken privacy." Etzioni adds that there are many instances in which preservation of the common good requires giving up some part of our privacy. Amnesty International, the global human rights advocacy group, has applauded the expansion of the Internet. This group sees it as a means to reach a wider audience and, in the case of specific cases of torture or repression, to speedily disseminate information worldwide so that appropriate steps can be taken to end unjust situations (Perry 1998a).

Viewed from a conflict perspective, however, there is the ever-present danger that a society's most powerful groups will use technological advances to invade the privacy of the less powerful and thereby maintain or intensify various forms of inequality and injustice. For example, in 1989, the People's Republic of China used various types of technology to identify protestors who had participated in pro-democracy demonstrations at Tiananmen Square and elsewhere. Some protestors identified in this manner received long prison terms because of their activism. During the same period, the Chinese government intercepted the news reports, telephone calls, and facsimile messages of foreign journalists covering the demonstrations. While

encouraging e-commerce, the government began in 2000 to undertake a "security certification" of all Internet content and service providers in China. Conflict theorists argue that control of technology in almost any form remains in the hands of those who already wield the most power, usually at the expense of the powerless and poor (Pomfret 2000).

Interactionists view the privacy and censorship debate as one that parallels concerns people have in any social interaction. Just as we may disapprove of some associations that relatives or friends have with other people, we also express concern over controversial websites and attempt to monitor people's social interactions. Obviously, the Internet facilitates interactions with a broad range of people, with minimal likelihood of detection compared to face-to-face interactions. Moreover, one can easily move a website from one country to another, avoiding not only detection but also prosecution.

Policy Initiatives

In 1986, the federal government passed the Electronic Communications Privacy Act. Wire communications—defined as use of the human voice in telephone and cordless calls—are highly protected. They cannot be subjected to surveillance unless a prosecutor obtains authorization from both the U.S. attorney general and a federal judge. By contrast, telegrams, faxes, and e-mail can be monitored simply with the approval of a judge (Eckenwiler 1995).

In 1996, the Communications Decency Act made it a federal crime to transmit "indecent" or "patently offensive"

material over the Internet without maintaining safeguards to ensure that children cannot see it. Private e-mail and online chat room communications with anyone under the age of 18 were subjected to the same standard. Violations of the law could lead to up to two years in prison and a $250,000 fine (Fernández 1996; Lappin 1996).

Civil liberties advocates insisted that such governmental action infringed on private communications between consenting adults and inevitably limited freedom of speech. They noted that at one point America Online even banned use of the term *breast,* thereby preventing any meaningful discussion of breast cancer or breast examinations. Lawsuits challenging the constitutionality of the Communications Decency Act were supported by such organizations as the American Civil Liberties Union (ACLU), the American Library Association, the American Society of Newspaper Editors, and the National Writers Union. In 1997, the Supreme Court declared that major parts of the act were unconstitutional. The Court called government attempts to regulate content on the Internet an attack on the First Amendment guarantee of freedom of speech (Fernández 1996; Harmon 1998).

Censorship and privacy are also issues globally. In Myanmar (or Burma), the government has ruled that fax machines and computer modems are illegal. In Saudi Arabia, access to the Internet was banned until 1999. Now all Internet connections are routed through a government hub where computers block access to thousands of sites cataloged on a rapidly expanding censorship list—for example, all gambling sites, all free-wheeling chat rooms, and all sites critical of the ruling Saudi family. By contrast, the openness of the Internet in other parts of the Middle East allows scattered Palestinian refugees to communicate with one another and establish websites that provide a history of Palestinian settlements. While China encourages expansion of the Internet, it has been wary of facilitating communication that it regards as disruptive. The government has p. 393 blocked all websites related to the Falun Gong spiritual group, and in 2000 it announced that "state secrets" (very vaguely defined) were banned from the Internet. Meanwhile, the British government is constructing an Internet spy center that is geared to watch all online activity in Great Britain. It will be able to track every website a person visits (Africa News Service 1998; Jehl 1999; MacLeod 2000; Rosenthal 1999b, 2000; Wilkinson 1999).

While some people chastise government efforts to curb technology, others decry their *failure* to limit certain aspects of technology. The United States is developing an international reputation of being opposed to efforts to protect people's privacy. For example, the Center for Public Integrity, a nonpartisan research organization, issued a report in 1998 that critiques the U.S. government for failing to approve legislation protecting the confidentiality of medical records. In another case, America Online revealed to a U.S. Navy investigator the identity of a sailor who had described his marital status online as gay. In 1998, both the Navy and America Online were forced to reach settlements for violating the privacy of the sailor. At the same time, the United States has been vocal in opposing efforts by the 15 European Union countries to implement a tough law designed to protect citizens from computer-age invasions of privacy. The U.S. technology industry does not want to have access to information blocked, since information is vital to global commerce. While a compromise is likely, this case illustrates the fine line between safeguarding privacy and stifling the electronic flow of information (Center for Public Integrity 1998; Perry 1998b; Shenon 1998).

The conflict over privacy and censorship is far from over. As technology continues to advance in the twenty-first century, there are sure to be new battlegrounds.

Let's Discuss

1. What are some of the ways that people can obtain information about us? Are you aware of any databases that contain information about your personal life?
2. Do you think corporations and employers have a right to monitor employees' e-mail and phone calls? Why or why not?
3. Are you more concerned about government censorship of electronic communication or about unauthorized invasion of your privacy? As a policymaker, how would you balance these concerns?

Chapter Resources

Summary

Social change is significant alteration over time in behavior patterns and culture, including norms and values. *Technology* is information about how to use the material resources of the environment to satisfy human needs and desires. This chapter examines sociological theories of social change, resistance to change, and the impact of technology on society's future and on social change.

1. Early advocates of the *evolutionary theory* of social change believed that society was progressing inevitably toward a higher state.
2. Talcott Parsons, a leading advocate of functionalist theory, viewed society as being in a natural state of equilibrium or balance.
3. Conflict theorists see change as having crucial significance, since it is needed to correct social injustices and inequalities.
4. In general, those with a disproportionate share of society's wealth, status, and power have a *vested interest* in preserving the status quo, and will resist change.
5. The period of maladjustment when a nonmaterial culture is still adapting to new material conditions is known as *culture lag.*

6. In the computer age, *telecommuters* are linked to their supervisors and colleagues through computer terminals, phone lines, and fax machines.
7. Early users of the Internet, the world's largest computer network, established a subculture with specific norms and values and a distinctive argot.
8. Advances in biotechnology have raised difficult ethical questions about the sex selection of fetuses and genetic engineering.
9. Social scientists focus on human error in the *normal accidents* associated with increasing reliance on technology.
10. That English has become the dominant language of the Internet and the international language of commerce and communication.
11. Computer and video technology have facilitated supervision, control, and even domination of workers and citizens by employers and the government.
12. Conflict theorists fear that the disenfranchised poor may be isolated from mainstream society in an "information ghetto," just as racial and ethnic minorities have been subjected to residential segregation.

13. Computer technology has made it increasingly easy for any individual, business firm, or government agency to retrieve more and more information about any of us, thereby infringing on our privacy. How much government should restrict access to electronic information is an important policy issue.

Critical Thinking Questions

1. In the last few years we have witnessed phenomenal growth in the use of cellular phones in all parts of the world. Analyze this example of material culture from the point of view of culture lag. Consider how usage, government regulation, and privacy issues are being worked out to keep up with the new technology.
2. Consider one of the technological advances discussed in the section on technology and the future. Analyze this aspect of technology, focusing on whether it is likely to increase or reduce inequality in the coming decades. Whenever possible, address issues of gender, race, ethnicity, and class, as well as inequality between nations.
3. In what ways has social interaction in your college community been affected by the kinds of technological advances examined in this chapter? Are there particular subcultures that are more likely or less likely to employ new forms of electronic communication?

Key Terms

Apartheid The former policy of the South African government, designed to maintain the separation of Blacks and other non-Whites from the dominant Whites. (page 578)

Culture lag A period of maladjustment during which the nonmaterial culture is still adapting to new material conditions. (579)

Equilibrium model The functionalist view that society tends toward a state of stability or balance. (576)

Evolutionary theory A theory of social change that holds that society is moving in a definite direction. (575)

Luddites Rebellious craft workers in nineteenth-century England who destroyed new factory machinery as part of their resistance to the industrial revolution. (580)

Multilinear evolutionary theory A theory of social change that holds that change can occur in several ways, and does not inevitably lead in the same direction. (576)

Normal accidents Failures that are inevitable given the manner in which human and technological systems are organized. (586)

Social change Significant alteration over time in behavior patterns and culture, including norms and values. (575)

Technology Information about how to use the material resources of the environment to satisfy human needs and desires. (580)

Telecommuters Employees of business firms or government agencies who work full-time or part-time at home rather than in an outside office, and who are linked to their supervisors and colleagues through computer terminals, phone lines, and fax machines. (581)

Unilinear evolutionary theory A theory of social change that holds that all societies pass through the same successive stages of evolution and inevitably reach the same end. (576)

Vested interests Those people or groups who will suffer in the event of social change, and who have a stake in maintaining the status quo. (579)

Additional Readings

BOOKS

Castells, Manuel. 2001. *The Internet Galaxy: Reflections on the Internet, Business, and Society.* New York: Oxford University Press. Sociologist Castells explains how the Internet came into being, and shows how it is affecting every aspect of our lives—from politics and the media to our work and social relations.

Garfinkel, Simon, and Deborah Russell. 2000. *Database Nation: The Death of Privacy in the 21st Century.* Sebastapol, CA: O'Reilly and Associates. A critical look at the invasion of people's privacy in cyberspace.

Levinson, Paul. 1999. *Digital McLuhan: A Guide to the Information Millennium.* London: Routledge. An appraisal and application of Marshall McLuhan's theories to the latest technology and mass media.

Lewis, Michael. 2001. *Next: The Future Just Happened.* New York: W. W. Norton. A journalist's optimistic look at the Internet's impact on social change and e-commerce.

McChesney, Robert W. 1999. *Rich Media, Poor Democracy: Communication Politics in Dubious Times.* Urbana, IL: University of Illinois Press. A look at the increasing concentration of newspapers, television stations, and radio stations in the hands of a few wealthy corporations, making the information age harmful for public life, according to the author.

Rifkin, Jeremy. 1998. *The Biotech Century: Harnessing the Gene and Remaking the World.* New York: Jeremy P. Tarcher/Putnam. A provocative examination of fundamental changes in our lives following the advent of computer technology.

Turkle, Sherry. 1995. *Life on the Screen: Identity in the Age of the Internet.* New York: Simon and Schuster. A sociologist examines the possible long-term implications of millions of people interacting electronically.

JOURNALS

Among those journals that focus on issues of social change and technology are *The Futurist* (founded in 1967), *Information, Communication and Society* (1998), *Internet Underground* (1996), *Issues in Science and Technology* (1984), *Privacy and American Business* (1993), *Sociological Theory* (1983), *Technological Forecasting and Social Change* (1969), and *Technology Review* (1899).

Technology Resources

Internet Connection

*Note: While all the URLs listed were current as of the printing of this book, these sites often change. Please check our website (**http://www.mhhe.com/schaefer8**) for updates and hyperlinks to these exercises and additional exercises.*

1. The field of biotechnology has brought us many scientific advances, some of which, like the sex selection of fetuses, are highly publicized and controversial. But were you aware of the intensifying debate over genetically modified (GM) food crops? In "Harvest of Fear," PBS correspondents for *Frontline* and *Nova* explore the issues surrounding the debate. Link to the PBS website (**http://www.pbs.org/wgbh/harvest/**), read the program's Synopsis, and answer the following questions:

   (a) What are the two main reasons for promoting GM technology?

   (b) Why are organizations such as Greenpeace and Friends of the Earth opposed to GM technology?

   (c) What genetically modified crops have been part of the U.S. food supply since 1996?

   (d) What acts have "ecoterrorist" organizations such as the Earth Liberation Front committed in an attempt to deter the use of GM technology?

   (e) How has the secretary of the USDA responded to ecoterrorism?

   (f) How do you personally feel about eating genetically modified foods?

2. The Internet Economy Indicators website (**http://www.internetindicators.com/facts.html**) provides basic information about the history and usage of the Internet. Read the facts given there and answer the following questions:

   (a) How many webpages are on the Net?

   (b) How many adults go online every month?

   (c) What percentage of college graduates looked for careers online in the summer of 2001?

   (d) In which two countries do one in six people use the Internet?

   (e) How many women use the Internet?

   (f) What percentage of companies sells products or services online?

   (g) How often do you use the Internet?

Online Learning Center   www.mhhe.com/schaefer8

Are we alone? Visit the student center in the Online Learning Center at **www.mhhe.com/schaefer8,** and link to "Audio Clips." Listen to Richard Schaefer, the author of your text, discuss how the advent of one new technology has led to our loss of privacy. Professor Schaefer talks about a study of public video cameras conducted by the American Civil Liberties Union in New York City. Is Big Brother watching? Listen to the audio clip; then you decide.

Glossary

Numbers following the definitions indicate pages where the terms were identified. Consult the index for further page references.

A

Absolute poverty   A standard of poverty based on a minimum level of subsistence below which families should not be expected to exist. (224)

Achieved status   A social position attained by a person largely through his or her own efforts (112, 213)

Activity theory   An interactionist theory of aging that argues that elderly people who remain active will be best-adjusted. (330)

Adoption   In a legal sense, a process that allows for the transfer of the legal rights, responsibilities, and privileges of parenthood to a new legal parent or parents. (360)

Affirmative action   Positive efforts to recruit minority group members or women for jobs, promotions, and educational opportunities. (279, 465)

Ageism   A term coined by Robert N. Butler to refer to prejudice and discrimination against the elderly. (337)

Agrarian society   The most technologically advanced form of preindustrial society. Members are primarily engaged in the production of food but increase their crop yield through such innovations as the plow. (123)

Alienation   The condition of being estranged or disassociated from the surrounding society. (141, 456)

Amalgamation   The process by which a majority group and a minority group combine through intermarriage to form a new group. (281)

Anomie   Durkheim's term for the loss of direction felt in a society when social control of individual behavior has become ineffective. (11, 192)

Anomie theory of deviance   A theory developed by Robert Merton that explains deviance as an adaptation either of socially prescribed goals or of the norms governing their attainment, or both. (193)

Anticipatory socialization   Processes of socialization in which a person "rehearses" for future positions, occupations, and social relationships. (94)

Anti-Semitism   Anti-Jewish prejudice. (292)

Apartheid   The former policy of the South African government designed to maintain the separation of Blacks and other non-Whites from the dominant Whites. (282, 578)

Applied sociology   The use of the discipline of sociology with the specific intent of yielding practical applications for human behavior and organizations. (19)

Argot   Specialized language used by members of a group or subculture. (71)

Ascribed status   A social position "assigned" to a person by society without regard for the person's unique talents or characteristics. (111, 213)

Assembling perspective   A theory of collective behavior introduced by McPhail and Miller that seeks to examine how and why people move from different points in space to a common location. (553)

Asset-based community development (ABCD)   An approach to community development in which planners first identify a community's strengths and then seek to mobilize those assets. (512)

Assimilation   The process by which a person forsakes his or her own cultural tradition to become part of a different culture. (282)

Authority   Power that has been institutionalized and is recognized by the people over whom it is exercised. (429)

B

Basic sociology   Sociological inquiry conducted with the objective of gaining a more profound knowledge of the fundamental aspects of social phenomena. Also known as pure sociology. (21)

Bilateral descent   A kinship system in which both sides of a person's family are regarded as equally important. (351)

Bilingualism   The use of two or more languages in particular settings, such as workplaces or educational facilities, treating each language as equally legitimate. (75)

Birthrate   The number of live births per 1,000 population in a given year. Also known as the *crude birthrate*. (530)

Black power   A political philosophy promoted by many younger Blacks in the 1960s that supported the creation of Black-controlled political and economic institutions. (285)

Borderlands   The area of a common culture along the border between Mexico and the United States. (257)

Bourgeoisie   Karl Marx's term for the capitalist class, comprising the owners of the means of production. (217)

Bureaucracy   A component of formal organization in which rules and hierarchical ranking are used to achieve efficiency. (140)

Bureaucratization   The process by which a group, organization, or social movement becomes increasingly bureaucratic. (143)

C

Capitalism   An economic system in which the means of production are largely in private hands and the main incentive for economic activity is the accumulation of profits. (217, 451)

Castes   Hereditary systems of rank, usually religiously dictated, that tend to be fixed and immobile. (214)

Causal logic   The relationship between a condition or variable and a particular consequence, with one event leading to the other. (35)

Census   An enumeration, or counting, of a population. (530)

Charismatic authority   Max Weber's term for power made legitimate by a leader's exceptional personal or emotional appeal to his or her followers. (431)

Class   A term used by Max Weber to refer to a group of people who have a similar level of wealth and income. (218)

Class consciousness   In Karl Marx's view, a subjective awareness held by members of a class regarding their common vested interests and need for collective political action to bring about social change. (217)

Classical theory   An approach to the study of formal organizations that views workers as being motivated almost entirely by economic rewards. (144)

Class system   A social ranking based primarily on economic position in which achieved characteristics can influence mobility. (214)

Clinical sociology   The use of the discipline of sociology with the specific intent of altering social relationships and facilitating change. (20)

Closed system   A social system in which there is little or no possibility of individual mobility. (230)

Coalition   A temporary or permanent alliance geared toward a common goal. (139)

Code of ethics The standards of acceptable behavior developed by and for members of a profession. (44)

Cognitive theory of development Jean Piaget's theory explaining how children's thought progresses through four stages. (92)

Cohabitation The practice of living together as a male–female couple without marrying. (366)

Collective behavior In the view of sociologist Neil Smelser, the relatively spontaneous and unstructured behavior of a group of people who are reacting to a common influence in an ambiguous situation. (551)

Colonialism The maintenance of political, social, economic, and cultural dominance over a people by a foreign power for an extended period of time. (243)

Communism As an ideal type, an economic system under which all property is communally owned and no social distinctions are made on the basis of people's ability to produce. (453)

Community A spatial or political unit of social organization that gives people a sense of belonging, based either on shared residence in a particular place or on a common identity. (501)

Concentric-zone theory A theory of urban growth devised by Ernest Burgess that sees growth in terms of a series of rings radiating from the central business district. (506)

Conflict perspective A sociological approach that assumes that social behavior is best understood in terms of conflict or tension between competing groups. (15)

Conformity Going along with one's peers, individuals of a person's own status, who have no special right to direct that person's behavior. (184)

Contact hypothesis An interactionist perspective that states that interracial contact between people of equal status in cooperative circumstances will reduce prejudice. (280)

Content analysis The systematic coding and objective recording of data, guided by some rationale. (43)

Control group Subjects in an experiment who are not introduced to the independent variable by the researcher. (42)

Control theory A view of conformity and deviance that suggests that our connection to members of society leads us to systematically conform to society's norms. (42)

Control variable A factor held constant to test the relative impact of an independent variable. (37)

Correlation A relationship between two variables whereby a change in one coincides with a change in the other. (35)

Correspondence principle A term used by Bowles and Gintis to refer to the tendency of schools to promote the values expected of individuals in each social class and to prepare students for the types of jobs typically held by members of their class. (409)

Counterculture A subculture that deliberately opposes certain aspects of the larger culture. (72)

Craze An exciting mass involvement that lasts for a relatively long period of time. (557)

Creationism A literal interpretation of the Bible regarding the creation of man and the universe used to argue that evolution should not be presented as established scientific fact. (396)

Credentialism An increase in the lowest level of education required to enter a field. (408)

Crime A violation of criminal law for which formal penalties are applied by some governmental authority. (199)

Cross-tabulation A table that shows the relationship between two or more variables. (52)

Crowds Temporary gatherings of people in close proximity who share a common focus or interest. (52, 554)

Cult Due to the stereotyping, this term has been abandoned by sociologists in favor of *new religious movements*. (379)

Cultural relativism The viewing of people's behavior from the perspective of their own culture. (74)

Cultural transmission A school of criminology that argues that criminal behavior is learned through social interactions. (194)

Cultural universals General practices found in every culture. (62, 379, 403)

Culture The totality of learned, socially transmitted behavior. (61)

Culture-bound syndrome A disease or illness that cannot be understood apart from its specific social context. (473)

Culture lag Ogburn's term for a period of maladjustment during which the nonmaterial culture is still adapting to new material conditions. (64, 579)

Culture shock The feeling of surprise and disorientation that is experienced when people witness cultural practices different from their own. (73)

Curanderismo Traditional Latino or Hispanic folk practices for holistic health care and healing. (482)

D

Death rate The number of deaths per 1,000 population in a given year. Also known as the *crude death rate*. (530)

Defended neighborhood A neighborhood that residents identify through defined community borders and through a perception that adjacent areas are geographically separate and socially different. (511)

Degradation ceremony An aspect of the socialization process within total institutions, in which people are subjected to humiliating rituals. (94)

Deindustrialization The systematic, widespread withdrawal of investment in basic aspects of productivity such as factories and plants. (460)

Demographic transition A term used to describe the change from high birthrates and death rates to relatively low birthrates and death rates. (531)

Demography The scientific study of population. (527)

Denomination A large, organized religion not officially linked with the state or government. (391)

Dependency theory An approach that contends that industrialized nations continue to exploit developing countries for their own gain. (243)

Dependent variable The variable in a causal relationship that is subject to the influence of another variable. (35)

Deviance Behavior that violates the standards of conduct or expectations of a group or society. (188)

Differential association A theory of deviance proposed by Edwin Sutherland that holds that violation of rules results from exposure to attitudes favorable to criminal acts. (194)

Diffusion The process by which a cultural item is spread from group to group or society to society. (63)

Disaster A sudden or disruptive event or set of events that overtaxes a community's resources so that outside aid is necessary. (554)

Discovery The process of making known or sharing the existence of an aspect of reality. (63)

Discrimination The process of denying opportunities and equal rights to individuals and groups because of prejudice or other arbitrary reasons. (275)

Disengagement theory A functionalist theory of aging introduced by Cumming and Henry that contends that society and the aging individual mutually sever many of their relationships. (328)

Domestic partnership Two unrelated adults who have chosen to share one another's lives in a relationship of mutual caring, who reside together, and who agree to be jointly responsible for their dependents, basic living expenses, and other common necessities. (369)

Dominant ideology A set of cultural beliefs

and practices that helps to maintain powerful social, economic, and political interests. (70, 164, 220)

Downsizing Reductions taken in a company's workforce as part of deindustrialization. (461)

Dramaturgical approach A view of social interaction, popularized by Erving Goffman, under which people are examined as if they were theatrical performers. (17, 90)

Dyad A two-member group. (139)

Dysfunction An element or a process of society that may disrupt a social system or lead to a decrease in stability. (15)

E

Ecclesia A religious organization that claims to include most or all of the members of a society and is recognized as the national or official religion. (391)

E-commerce Numerous ways that people with access to the Internet can do business from their computers. (462)

Economic system The social institution through which goods and services are produced, distributed, and consumed. (451)

Education A formal process of learning in which some people consciously teach while others adopt the social role of learner. (403)

Egalitarian family An authority pattern in which the adult members of the family are regarded as equals. (352)

Elite model A view of society as ruled by a small group of individuals who share a common set of political and economic interests. (438)

Emergent-norm perspective A theory of collective behavior proposed by Turner and Killian that holds that a collective definition of appropriate and inappropriate behavior emerges during episodes of collective behavior. (552)

Endogamy The restriction of mate selection to people within the same group. (356)

Environmental justice A legal strategy based on claims that racial minorities are subjected disproportionately to environmental hazards. (543)

Equilibrium model Talcott Parsons's functionalist view of society as tending toward a state of stability or balance. (576)

Established sect J. Milton Yinger's term for a religious group that is the outgrowth of a sect, yet remains isolated from society. (393)

Esteem The reputation that a particular individual has earned within an occupation. (221)

Ethnic group A group that is set apart from others because of its national origin or

distinctive cultural patterns. (269)

Ethnocentrism The tendency to assume that one's culture and way of life represent the norm or are superior to all others. (73, 273)

Ethnography The study of an entire social setting through extended systematic observation. (41)

Euthanasia The act of bringing about the death of a hopelessly ill and suffering person in a relatively quick and painless way for reasons of mercy. (341)

Evolutionary theory A theory of social change that holds that society is moving in a definite direction. (575)

Exogamy The requirement that people select mates outside certain groups. (356)

Experiment An artificially created situation that allows the researcher to manipulate variables. (42)

Experimental group Subjects in an experiment who are exposed to an independent variable introduced by a researcher. (42)

Exploitation theory A Marxist theory that views racial subordination in the United States as a manifestation of the class system inherent in capitalism. (280)

Expressiveness Concern for maintenance of harmony and the internal emotional affairs of family. (307)

Extended family A family in which relatives—such as grandparents, aunts, or uncles—live in the same home as parents and their children. (349)

F

Face-work A term used by Erving Goffman to refer to the efforts of people to maintain the proper image and avoid embarrassment in public. (90)

Fads Temporary movements toward the acceptance of some particular taste or lifestyle that involve large numbers of people and are independent of preceding trends. (556)

False consciousness A term used by Karl Marx to describe an attitude held by members of a class that does not accurately reflect its objective position. (217, 561)

Familism Pride in the extended family, expressed through the maintenance of close ties and strong obligations to kinfolk. (358)

Family A set of people related by blood, marriage (or some other agreed-upon relationship), or adoption who share the primary responsibility for reproduction and caring for members of society. (349)

Fashions Pleasurable mass involvements in some particular taste or lifestyle that have a line of historical continuity. (556)

Feminist perspective A sociological approach that views inequity in gender as cen-

tral to all behavior and organization. (17)

Fertility The amount of reproduction among women of childbearing age. (527)

Folkways Norms governing everyday social behavior whose violation raises comparatively little concern. (67)

Force The actual or threatened use of coercion to impose one's will on others. (429)

Formal norms Norms that generally have been written down and that specify strict rules for punishment of violators. (67)

Formal organization A special-purpose group designed and structured for maximum efficiency. (139)

Formal social control Carried out by authorized agents, such as police officers, physicians, school administrators, employers, military officers, and managers of movie theaters. (186)

Functionalist perspective A sociological approach that emphasizes the way that parts of a society are structured to maintain its stability. (14)

G

Gatekeeping The process by which a relatively small number of people control what material eventually reaches the audience. (163)

Gemeinschaft A term used by Ferdinand Tönnies to describe close-knit communities, often found in rural areas, in which strong personal bonds unite members. (121)

Gender roles Expectations regarding the proper behavior, attitudes, and activities of males and females. (96, 303)

Generalized others A term used by George Herbert Mead to refer to the child's awareness of the attitudes, viewpoints, and expectations of society as a whole that a child takes into account in his or her behavior. (89)

Genocide The deliberate, systematic killing of an entire people or nation. (281)

Gentrification The resettlement of low-income city neighborhoods by prosperous families and business firms. (518)

Gerontology The scientific study of the sociological and psychological aspects of aging and the problems of the aged. (328)

Gesellschaft A term used by Ferdinand Tönnies to describe communities, often urban, that are large and impersonal with little commitment to the group or consensus on values. (121)

Glass ceiling An invisible barrier that blocks the promotion of a qualified individual in a work environment because of the individual's gender, race, or ethnicity. (277, 314)

Globalization The worldwide integration of government policies, cultures, social movements, and financial markets through trade and the exchange of ideas. (245)

Goal displacement Overzealous conformity to official regulations within a bureaucracy. (142)

Goal multiplication The process through which an organization expands its purpose. (147)

Goal succession The process through which an organization identifies an entirely new objective because its traditional goals have been either realized or denied. (148)

Group Any number of people with similar norms, values, and expectations who regularly and consciously interact. (115, 135)

Growth rate The difference between births and deaths, plus the difference between immigrants and emigrants, per 1,000 population. (530)

H

Hawthorne effect The unintended influence that observers or experiments can have on their subjects. (43)

Health As defined by the World Health Organization, a state of complete physical, mental, and social well-being, and not merely the absence of disease and infirmity. (473)

Health maintenance organization (HMO) An organization that provides comprehensive medical services for a preestablished fee. (494)

Hidden curriculum Standards of behavior that are deemed proper by society and are taught subtly in schools. (408)

Holistic medicine A means of health maintenance using therapies in which the health care practitioner considers the person's physical, mental, emotional, and spiritual characteristics. (487)

Homophobia Fear of and prejudice against homosexuality. (126, 304)

Horizontal mobility The movement of an individual from one social position to another of the same rank. (230)

Horticultural societies Preindustrial societies in which people plant seeds and crops rather than subsist merely on available foods. (123)

Hospice care An attempt to improve the quality of a dying person's last days. (335)

Human ecology An area of study concerned with the interrelationships between people and their spatial setting and physical environment. (506)

Human relations approach An approach to the study of formal organizations that emphasizes the role of people, communication, and participation within a bureaucracy and tends to focus on the informal structure of the organization. (145)

Human rights Universal moral rights belonging to all people because they are human. (259)

Hunting-and-gathering society A preindustrial society in which people rely on whatever foods and fibers are really available in order to live. (122)

Hypothesis A speculative statement about the relationship between two or more variables. (35)

I

Ideal type A construct or model that serves as a measuring rod against which specific cases can be evaluated. (11, 140)

Impression management A term used by Erving Goffman to refer to the altering of the presentation of the self in order to create distinctive appearances and satisfy particular audiences. (90)

Incest taboo The prohibition of sexual relationships between certain culturally specified relatives. (356)

Incidence The number of new cases of a specific disorder occurring within a given population during a stated period of time. (480)

Income Salaries and wages. (213)

Independent variable The variable in a causal relationship that, when altered, causes or influences a change in a second variable. (35)

Industrial city A city characterized by relatively large size, open competition, an open class system, and elaborate specialization in the manufacturing of goods. (503)

Industrial society A society that depends on mechanization to produce its economic goods and services. (123, 451, 503)

Infant mortality rate The number of deaths of infants under one year of age per 1,000 live births in a given year. (530)

Influence The exercise of power through a process of persuasion. (429)

Informal economy Transfers of money, goods, or services that are not reported to the government. (253)

Informal norms Norms that generally are understood but are not precisely recorded. (67)

Informal social control Used casually by people to enforce norms. (186)

In-group Any group or category to which people feel they belong. (136)

Innovation The process of introducing new elements into a culture through either discovery or invention. (63)

Institutional discrimination The denial of opportunities and equal rights to individuals and groups that results from the normal operations of a society. (277, 310)

Instrumentality Emphasis on tasks, focus on more distant goals, and a concern for

the external relationship between one's family and other social institutions. (307)

Interactionist perspective A sociological approach that generalizes about fundamental or everyday forms of social interaction. (17)

Interest group A voluntary association of citizens who attempt to influence public policy. (438)

Intergenerational mobility Changes in the social position of children relative to their parents. (230)

Interview A face-to-face or telephone questioning of a respondent to obtain desired information. (39)

Intragenerational mobility Changes in a person's social position within his or her adult life. (230)

Invention The combination of existing cultural items into a form that did not previously exist. (63)

Iron law of oligarchy A principle of organizational life developed by Robert Michels under which even democratic organizations will become bureaucracies ruled by a few individuals. (144)

Issei The early Japanese immigrants to the United States. (288)

K

Kinship The state of being related to others. (351)

L

Labeling theory Attempts to explain why certain people are viewed as deviants. (196)

Labor unions Organized workers who share either the same skill or the same employer. (149)

Laissez-faire A form of capitalism under which people compete freely, with minimal government intervention in the economy. (451)

Language An abstract system of word meanings and symbols for all aspects of culture. It also includes gestures and other nonverbal communication. (64)

Latent functions Unconscious or unintended functions; hidden purposes. (15)

Law Governmental social control. (67)

Legal-rational authority Max Weber's term for power made legitimate by law. (431)

Liberation theology Use of a church, primarily Roman Catholicism, in a political effort to eliminate poverty, discrimination, and other forms of injustice evident in a secular society. (386)

Life chances Max Weber's term for people's opportunities to provide themselves with material goods, positive living conditions, and favorable life experiences. (228)

Life expectancy The average number of years a person can be expected to live under current mortality conditions. (530)

Looking-glass self A concept used by Charles Horton Cooley that emphasizes the self as the product of our social interactions with others. (88)

Luddites Rebellious craft workers in nineteenth-century England who destroyed new factory machinery as part of their resistance to the industrial revolution. (580)

M

Machismo A sense of virility, personal worth, and pride in one's maleness. (358)

Macrosociology Sociological investigation that concentrates on large-scale phenomena or entire civilizations. (14)

Manifest functions Open, stated, and conscious functions. (15)

Mass media Print and electronic instruments of communication that carry messages to often widespread audiences. (159)

Master status A status that dominates others and thereby determines a person's general position within society. (112)

Material culture The physical or technological aspects of our daily lives. (64)

Matriarchy A society in which women dominate in family decision making. (351)

Matrilineal descent A kinship system that favors the relatives of the mother. (351)

McDonaldization The process by which the principles of the fast-food restaurant have come to dominate certain sectors of society, both in the United States and throughout the world. (135)

Megalopolis A densely populated area containing two or more cities and their surrounding suburbs. (504)

Mental illness A disorder of the brain that disrupts a person's thinking, feeling, and ability to interact with others. (489)

Microsociology Sociological investigation that stresses study of small groups and often uses laboratory experimental studies. (14)

Midlife crisis A stressful period of self-evaluation that begins at about age 40. (332)

Migration Relatively permanent movement of people with the purpose of changing their place of residence. (536)

Minority group A subordinate group whose members have significantly less control or power over their own lives than the members of a dominant or majority group have over theirs. (269)

Model or ideal minority A group that, despite past prejudice and discrimination, succeeds economically, socially, and educationally without resorting to political or violent confrontation with Whites. (287)

Modernization The far-reaching process by which a society moves from traditional or less developed institutions to those characteristic of more developed societies. (248)

Modernization theory A functionalist approach that proposes that modernization and development will gradually improve the lives of people in peripheral nations. (248)

Monogamy A form of marriage in which one woman and one man are married only to each other. (350)

Monopoly Control of a market by a single business firm. (452)

Morbidity rates The incidence of diseases in a given population. (480)

Mores Norms deemed highly necessary to the welfare of a society. (67)

Mortality rate The incidence of death in a given population. (480)

Multilinear evolutionary theory A theory of social change that holds that change can occur in several ways and does not inevitably lead in the same direction. (576)

Multinational corporations Commercial organizations that are headquartered in one country but do business throughout the world. (246)

Multiple-nuclei theory A theory of urban growth developed by Harris and Ullman that views growth as emerging from many centers of development, each of which may reflect a particular urban need or activity. (507)

N

Narcotizing dysfunction The effect of providing massive amounts of information to a passive audience that largely fails to act. (162)

Natural science The study of the physical features of nature and the ways in which they interact and change. (7)

Negotiated order A social structure that derives its existence from the social interactions through which people define and redefine its character. (111)

Negotiation The attempt to reach agreement with others concerning some objective. (110)

Neocolonialism Continuing dependence of former colonies on foreign countries. (243)

New religious movement (NRM) or cult A generally small, secretive religious group that represents either a new religion or a major innovation of an existing faith. (393)

New social movements Organized collective activities that promote autonomy and self-determination as well as improvements in the quality of life. (563)

New urban sociology An approach to urbanization that considers the interplay of local, national, and worldwide forces and their effect on local space, with special emphasis on the impact of global economic activity. (508)

Nisei Japanese born in the United States who were descendants of the Issei. (288)

Nonmaterial culture Cultural adjustments to material conditions, such as customs, beliefs, patterns of communication, and ways of using material objects. (64)

Nonperiodic assemblies Nonrecurring gatherings of people that often result from word-of-mouth information. (553)

Nonverbal communication The sending of messages through the use of posture, facial expressions, and gestures. (17)

Normal accidents Failures that are inevitable, given the manner in which human and technological systems are organized. (586)

Norms Established standards of behavior maintained by a society. (67)

Nuclear family A married couple and their unmarried children living together. (349)

O

Obedience Compliance with higher authorities in a hierarchical structure. (184)

Objective method A technique for measuring social class that assigns individuals to classes on the basis of criteria such as occupation, education, income, and place of residence. (221)

Observation A research technique in which an investigator collects information through direct participation in and/or observation of a group, tribe, or community. (40)

Open system A social system in which the position of each individual is influenced by his or her achieved status. (230)

Operational definition An explanation of an abstract concept that is specific enough to allow a researcher to measure the concept. (34)

Opinion leader Someone who through day-to-day personal contacts and communication influences the opinions and discussions of others. (172)

Organized crime The work of a group that regulates relations between various criminal enterprises involved in various illegal activities. (199)

Out-group A group or category to which people feel they do not belong. (136)

P

Panic A fearful arousal or collective flight based on a generalized belief that may or may not be accurate. (557)

Patriarchy A society in which men dominate family decision making. (351)

Patrilineal descent A kinship system that favors the relatives of the father. (351)

Periodic assemblies Recurring, relatively

routine gatherings of people, such as college assemblies. (553)

Personality In everyday speech, a person's typical patterns of attitudes, needs, characteristics, and behavior. (85)

Peter principle A principle of organizational life, originated by Laurence J. Peter, according to which each individual within a hierarchy tends to rise to his or her level of incompetence. (143)

Pluralism Mutual respect between the various groups in a society for one another's cultures, which allows minorities to express their own cultures without experiencing prejudice. (283)

Pluralist model A view of society in which many competing groups within the community have access to governmental officials so that no single group is dominant. (440)

Political action committee (PAC) A political committee established by an interest group—say, a national bank, corporation, trade association, or cooperative or membership association—to solicit contributions for candidates or political parties. (438)

Political socialization The process by which individuals acquire political attitudes and develop patterns of political behavior. (432)

Political system The social institution that relies on a recognized set of procedures for implementing and achieving the goals of a group. (429)

Politics In Harold D. Lasswell's words, "who gets what, when, and how." (429)

Polyandry A form of polygamy in which a woman can have several husbands at the same time. (350)

Polygamy A form of marriage in which an individual can have several husbands or wives simultaneously. (350)

Polygyny A form of polygamy in which a husband can have several wives at the same time. (350)

Population pyramid A special type of bar chart that shows the distribution of the population by gender and age. (534)

Postindustrial city A city in which global finance and the electronic flow of information dominate the economy. (504)

Postindustrial society A society whose economic system is primarily engaged in the processing and control of information. (123)

Postmodern society A technologically sophisticated society that is preoccupied with consumer goods and media images. (124)

Power The ability to exercise one's will over others. (218, 429)

Power elite A term used by C. Wright Mills for a small group of military, industrial, and government leaders who control the fate of the United States. (439)

Preindustrial city A city with only a few thousand people living within its borders and characterized by a relatively closed class system and limited mobility. (502)

Prejudice A negative attitude toward an entire category of people, such as a racial or ethnic minority. (273)

Prestige The respect and admiration that an occupation holds in a society. (221)

Prevalence The total number of cases of a specific disorder that exist at a given time. (480)

Primary group A small group characterized by intimate, face-to-face association and cooperation. (135)

Profane The ordinary and commonplace elements of life, as distinguished from the sacred. (379)

Profession An occupation requiring extensive knowledge that is governed by a code of ethics. (454)

Professional criminal A person who pursues crime as a day-to-day occupation. (199)

Proletariat Karl Marx's term for the working class in a capitalist society. (217)

Protestant ethic Max Weber's term for the disciplined work ethic, this-worldly concerns, and rational orientation to life emphasized by John Calvin and his followers. (385)

Public A dispersed group of people, not necessarily in contact with one another, who share an interest in an issue. (558)

Public opinion Expressions of attitudes on matters of public policy that are communicated to decision makers. (558)

Q

Qualitative research Research that relies on what is seen in the field or naturalistic settings more than on statistical data. (40)

Quantitative research Research that collects and reports data primarily in numerical form. (41)

Questionnaire A printed research instrument employed to obtain desired information from a respondent. (39)

R

Racial group A group that is set apart from others because of obvious physical differences. (269)

Racism The belief that one race is supreme and all others are innately inferior. (273)

Random sample A sample for which every member of the entire population has the same chance of being selected. (36)

Reference group Any group that individuals use as a standard in evaluating themselves and their own behavior. (137)

Relative deprivation The conscious feeling of a negative discrepancy between legitimate expectations and present actualities. (560)

Relative poverty A floating standard of deprivation by which people at the bottom of a society, whatever their lifestyles, are judged to be disadvantaged in comparison with the nation as a whole. (224)

Reliability The extent to which a measure provides consistent results. (36, 417)

Religion According to Émile Durkheim, a unified system of beliefs and practices relative to sacred things. (379)

Religious beliefs Statements to which members of a particular religion adhere. (388)

Religious experience The feeling or perception of being in direct contact with the ultimate reality, such as a divine being, or of being overcome with religious emotion. (389)

Religious rituals Practices required or expected of members of a faith. (388)

Research design A detailed plan or method for obtaining data scientifically. (39)

Resocialization The process of discarding former behavior patterns and accepting new ones as part of a transition in one's life. (94)

Resource mobilization The ways in which a social movement utilizes such resources as money, political influence, access to the media, and personnel. (561)

Rites of passage Rituals marking the symbolic transition from one social position to another. (93)

Role conflict The situation that occurs when incompatible expectations arise from two or more social positions held by the same person. (114)

Role exit The process of disengagement from a role that is central to one's self-identity and reestablishment of an identity in a new role. (114)

Role strain The situation that occurs when the same social position imposes conflicting demands and expectations. (114)

Role taking The process of mentally assuming the perspective of another, thereby enabling one to respond from that imagined viewpoint. (89)

Routine activities theory Contends that criminal victimization is increased when motivated offenders and suitable targets converge. (195)

Rumor A piece of information gathered informally that is used to interpret an ambiguous situation. (558)

S

Sacred Elements beyond everyday life that inspire awe, respect, and even fear. (379)

Sample A selection from a larger population that is statistically found to be representative of that population. (36)

Sanctions Penalties and rewards for conduct concerning a social norm. (68, 183)

Sandwich generation The generation of

adults who simultaneously try to meet the competing needs of their parents and their own children. (332)

Sapir-Whorf hypothesis A hypothesis concerning the role of language in shaping cultures. It holds that language is culturally determined and serves to influence our mode of thought. (66)

School choice program An educational experiment under which parents can choose where to send their children to school. (421)

School voucher program A form of school choice program in which public funds are transferred to the public or private school of the parents' choice. (421)

Science The body of knowledge obtained by methods based upon systematic observation. (7)

Scientific management approach Another name for the *classical theory* of formal organizations. (144)

Scientific method A systematic, organized series of steps that ensures maximum objectivity and consistency in researching a problem. (33)

Secondary analysis A variety of research techniques that make use of publicly accessible information and data. (43)

Secondary group A formal, impersonal group in which there is little social intimacy or mutual understanding. (135)

Sect A relatively small religious group that has broken away from some other religious organization to renew what it views as the original vision of the faith. (392)

Secularization The process through which religion's influence on other social institutions diminishes. (379)

Segregation The act of physically separating two groups; often imposed on a minority group by a dominant group. (280)

Self According to George Herbert Mead, the sum total of people's conscious perceptions of their own identity as distinct from others. (88)

Senilicide The killing of the aged. (342)

Serial monogamy A form of marriage in which a person can have several spouses in his or her lifetime but only one spouse at a time. (350)

Sexism The ideology that one sex is superior to the other. (310)

Sexual harassment Behavior that occurs when work benefits are made contingent on sexual favors. (310)

Sick role Societal expectations about the attitudes and behavior of a person viewed as being ill. (474)

Significant others A term used by George Herbert Mead to refer to those individuals who are most important in the development of the self, such as parents, friends, and teachers. (90)

Single-parent families Families in which there is only one parent present to care for children. (362)

Slavery A system of enforced servitude in which people are legally owned by others and in which enslaved status is transferred from parents to children. (214)

Small group A group small enough for all members to interact simultaneously, that is, to talk with one another or at least be acquainted. (138)

Social change Significant alteration over time in behavior patterns and culture, including norms and values. (575)

Social constructionist perspective An approach to deviance that emphasizes the role of culture in the creation of the deviant identity. (196)

Social control Techniques and strategies for preventing deviant behavior in any society. (183)

Social epidemiology The study of the distribution of disease, impairment, and general health status across a population. (480)

Social inequality A condition in which members of a society have different amounts of wealth, prestige, or power. (22, 213)

Social institutions Organized patterns of beliefs and behavior centered on basic social needs. (118)

Social interaction The ways in which people respond to one another. (109)

Socialism An economic system under which the means of production and distribution are collectively owned. (452)

Socialization The process whereby people learn the attitudes, values, and actions appropriate for individuals as members of a particular culture. (85)

Social mobility Movement of individuals or groups from one position of a society's stratification system to another. (229)

Social movements Organized collective activities to bring about or resist fundamental change in an existing group or society. (559)

Social network A series of social relationships that links a person directly to others and through them indirectly to still more people. (116)

Social role A set of expectations for people who occupy a given social position or status. (112)

Social science The study of various aspects of human society. (7)

Social structure The way in which a society is organized into predictable relationships. (109)

Societal-reaction approach Another name for *labeling theory*. (196)

Society A fairly large number of people who live in the same territory, are relatively independent of people outside it, and participate in a common culture. (61)

Sociobiology The systematic study of the biological bases of social behavior. (88)

Sociocultural evolution The process of change and development in human societies that results from cumulative growth in their stores of cultural information. (121)

Sociological imagination An awareness of the relationship between an individual and the wider society. (5)

Sociology The systematic study of social behavior and human groups. (5)

Squatter settlements Areas occupied by the very poor on the fringes of cities, in which housing is often constructed by the settlers themselves from discarded material. (506)

Status A term used by sociologists to refer to any of the full range of socially defined positions within a large group or society. (111)

Status group A term used by Max Weber to refer to people who have the same prestige or lifestyle, independent of their class positions. (218)

Stereotypes Unreliable generalizations about all members of a group that do not recognize individual differences within the group. (165, 272)

Stigma The labels society uses to devalue members of certain social groups. (190)

Stratification A structured ranking of entire groups of people that perpetuates unequal economic rewards and power in a society. (213)

Subculture A segment of society that shares a distinctive pattern of mores, folkways, and values that differs from the pattern of the larger society. (71)

Suburb According to the Census Bureau, any territory within a metropolitan area that is not included in the central city. (512)

Surveillance function The collection and distribution of information concerning events in the social environment. (62)

Survey A study, generally in the form of interviews or questionnaires, that provides sociologists and other researchers with information concerning how people think and act. (39)

Symbols The gestures, objects, and language that form the basis of human communication. (89)

T

Teacher-expectancy effect The impact that a teacher's expectations about a student's performance may have on the student's actual achievements. (410)

Technology Information about how to use the material resources of the environment to satisfy human needs and desires. (64, 122, 580)

Telecommuters Employees of business

firms or government agencies who work full-time or part-time at home rather than in an outside office and who are linked to their supervisors and colleagues through computer terminals, phone lines, and fax machines. (148, 581)

Terrorism The use or threat of violence against random or symbolic targets in pursuit of political aims. (430)

Theory In sociology, a set of statements that seeks to explain problems, actions, or behavior. (9)

Total fertility rate (TFR) The average number of children born alive to a woman, assuming that she conforms to current fertility rates. (530)

Total institutions A term coined by Erving Goffman to refer to institutions that regulate all aspects of a person's life under a single authority, such as prisons, the military, mental hospitals, and convents. (94)

Tracking The practice of placing students in specific curriculum groups on the basis of test scores and other criteria. (409)

Traditional authority Legitimate power conferred by custom and accepted practice. (430)

Trained incapacity The tendency of workers in a bureaucracy to become so specialized that they develop blind spots and fail to notice obvious problems. (141)

Triad A three-member group. (139)

U

Underclass Long-term poor people who lack training and skills. (226)

Unilinear evolutionary theory A theory of social change that holds that all societies pass through the same successive stages of evolution and inevitably reach the same end. (576)

Urban ecology An area of study that focuses on the interrelationships between people and their environment. (506)

Urbanism A term used by Wirth to describe distinctive patterns of social behavior evident among city residents. (504)

V

Validity The degree to which a scale or measure truly reflects the phenomenon under study. (36, 417)

Value-added model A theory of collective behavior proposed by Neil Smelser to explain how broad social conditions are transformed in a definite pattern into some form of collective behavior. (552)

Value neutrality Max Weber's term for objectivity of sociologists in the interpretation of data. (46)

Values Collective conceptions of what is considered good, desirable, and proper—or bad, undesirable, and improper—in a culture. (69)

Variable A measurable trait or characteristic that is subject to change under different conditions. (35)

Verstehen The German word for "understanding" or "insight"; used by Max Weber to stress the need for sociologists to take into account people's emotions, thoughts, beliefs, and attitudes. (11)

Vertical mobility The movement of a person from one social position to another of a different rank. (230)

Vested interests Veblen's term for those people or groups who will suffer in the event of social change and who have a stake in maintaining the status quo. (579)

Victimization surveys Questioning ordinary people, not police officers, to determine whether they have been victims of crime. (202)

Victimless crimes The willing exchange among adults of widely desired, but illegal, goods and services. (201)

Vital statistics Records of births, deaths, marriages, and divorces gathered through a registration system maintained by governmental units. (530)

Voluntary associations Organizations established on the basis of common interest, whose members volunteer or even pay to participate. (145)

W

Wealth An inclusive term encompassing all of a person's material assets, including land and other types of property. (213)

White-collar crimes Crimes committed by affluent individuals or corporations in the course of their daily business activities. (200)

World systems analysis Immanuel Wallerstein's view of the global economic system as divided between certain industrialized nations that control wealth and developing countries that are controlled and exploited. (243, 508)

X

Xenocentrism The belief that the products, styles, or ideas of one's society are inferior to those that originate elsewhere. (75)

Z

Zero population growth (ZPG) The state of a population with a growth rate of zero, achieved when the number of births plus immigrants is equal to the number of deaths plus emigrants. (535)

Zoning laws Legal provisions stipulating land use and architectural design of housing and often employed as a means of keeping racial minorities and low-income people out of suburban areas. (514)

References

A

AARP. 1999. "New AARP Study Finds Boomers Vary in Their Views of the Future and Their Retirement Years." AARP News Release, June 1. Washington, DC.

AARP. 2001. *Beyond 50—A Report to the Nation on Economic Security.* Washington, DC: AARP.

ABC News. 1992. *Primetime Live: True Colors.* Transcript of November 26 episode.

Abegglen, James C., and George Stalk, Jr. 1985. *Kassha: The Japanese Corporation.* New York: Basic Books.

Abercrombie, Nicholas, Bryan S. Turner, and Stephen Hill, eds. 1990. *Dominant Ideologies.* Cambridge, MA: Unwin Hyman.

———, Stephen Hill, and Bryan S. Turner. 1980. *The Dominant Ideology Thesis.* London: George Allen and Unwin.

Aberle, David E., A. K. Cohen, A. K. Davis, M. J. Leng, Jr., and F. N. Sutton. 1950. "The Functional Prerequisites of a Society." *Ethics* 60 (January):100–111.

Abrahams, Ray G. 1968. "Reaching an Agreement over Bridewealth in Labwor, Northern Uganda: A Case Study." Pp. 202–215 in *Councils in Action,* edited by Audrey Richards and Adam Kuer. Cambridge: Cambridge University Press.

Abramovitz, Janet N. 2001. "Averting Unnatural Disasters." Pp. 123–142 in *State of the World 2001,* edited by Lester R. Brown, Christopher Flavin, and Hilary French. New York: Norton.

———. 2001a. *Unnatural Disasters.* Washington D.C.: Worldwatch Institute.

Acharya, Menna. 2000. *Labor Market Developments and Poverty: With Focus on Economic Opportunities for Women.* Kathmandu, Nepal: Tanka Prasad Acharya Foundation/ FES.

ACLU. 2001. *Lesbian and Gay Rights.* Accessed October 14 (www.aclu.org/issues/gay).

Acosta, R. Vivian, and Linda Jean Carpenter. 2001. "Women in Intercollegiate Sport: A Longitudinal Study: 1977–1998." Pp. 302–308 in *Sport in Contemporary Society: An Anthology.* 6th ed., edited by D. Stanley Eitzen. New York: Worth.

Adam, Barry D. 1992. "Sociology and People Living with AIDS." Pp. 3–18 in *The Social Context of AIDS,* edited by Joan Huber and Beth E. Schneider. Newbury Park, CA: Sage.

———. 1995. The Rise of a Gay and Lesbian Movement. Rev. ed. New York: Twayne.

Adam, Barry P., Jan Willem Duyvendak, and André Krouwei, eds. 1999. *The Global Emergence of Gay and Lesbian Politics: National Impact of a Worldwide Movement.* Philadelphia: Temple University Press.

Adam, Kanya. 2000. "Affirmative Action and Popular Perceptions: The Case of South Africa." *Society* 37 (February):48–55.

Addams, Jane. 1910. *Twenty Years at Hull-House.* New York: Macmillan.

———. 1930. *The Second Twenty Years at Hull-House.* New York: Macmillan.

———, and John M. Johnson. 1992. "Street Corner Society Revisited." *Journal of Contemporary Ethnography* 21 (April):3–10.

Adler, William M. 2000. *Mollie's Job: A Story of Life and Work on the Global Assembly Line.* New York: Scribner.

AFL-CIO. 2001. *More Workers Are Choosing a Voice at Work.* Accessed April 18 (http://www.aflcio.org/voiceatwork/ morejoin/htm).

Africa News Service. 1998 "CPJ's 10 Enemies of the Press." Accessed October 8 (www.elibrary.com/getdoc.cgi?id=113_rydo cid= 435731@library_F+type=O~&dinst=).

Aguirre, Benigno E., E. L. Quarantelli, and Jorge L. Mendoza. 1988. "The Collective Behavior of Fads: The Characteristics, Effects, and Career of Streaking." *American Sociological Review* 53 (August):569–584.

AIDS Alert. 1999. "AIDS Complacency Leads Back to Risk Behavior." November 14, Pp. 127–128.

Akers, Ronald L. 1997. *Criminological Theories: Introduction and Evaluation.* 2d ed. Los Angeles: Roxbury.

Alain, Michel. 1985. "An Empirical Validation of Relative Deprivation." *Human Relations* 38(8):739–749.

Alba, Richard D., and Gwen Moore. 1982. "Ethnicity in the American Elite." *American Sociological Review* 47 (June):373–383.

Albas, Daniel, and Cheryl Albas. 1988. "Aces and Bombers: The Post-Exam Impression Management Strategies of Students." *Symbolic Interaction* 11 (Fall):289–302.

Albiniak, P. 2000. "TV's Drug Deal." *Broadcasting and Cable,* January 17, Pp. 3, 148.

Albom, Mitch. 1997. *Tuesdays with Morrie.* New York: Doubleday.

Albrecht, Gary L., Katerine D. Steelman, and Michael Bury. 2001. *Handbook of Disabilities Study.* Thousand Oaks, CA: Sage.

Alexander, Alison, and Janice Hanson, eds. 2001. *Taking Sides: Mass Media and Society.* 6th ed. New York: McGraw-Hill/Dushkin.

Alexander, Keith L. 2001. "Merged Media Titan's Competitors Gird for Expected Battle." *USA Today,* January 12, Pp. 3B.

Alfino, Mark, John S. Caputo, and Robin Wynyard. 1998. *McDonaldization Revisited: Critical Essays on Consumer Culture.* Westport, CT: Praeger.

Alfino, Mark, John S. Carpeto, and Robin Wyngard. 1998. *McDonaldization Revisited: Critical Essays on Consumer Culture.* Westport, CT: Praeger.

Alinsky, Saul. 1946. *Reveille for Radicals.* Chicago: University of Chicago Press.

Allen, Bern P. 1978. *Social Behavior: Fact and Falsehood.* Chicago: Nelson-Hall.

Allen, John L. 2001. *Student Atlas of World Geography.* 2d ed. Chicago: McGraw-Hill/ Dushkin.

Allport, Gordon W. 1979. *The Nature of Prejudice.* 25th anniversary ed. Reading, MA: Addison-Wesley.

Alonzo, Angelo A. 1989. "Health and Illness and the Definition of the Situation: An Interactionist Perspective." Presented at the annual meeting of the Society for the Study of Social Problems, Berkeley, CA.

Alter, Jonathon. 2000. "The Death Penalty on Trial." *Newsweek,* June 12, pp. 24–32, 34.

Alvarez, Lizette. 2001. "Senate Rejects Tuition and a Key to Bush Education Plan." *New York Times,* June 15, p. A28.

Alvord, Lori Arviso, and Elizabeth Cohen Van Pelt. 1999. *The Scalpel and the Silver Bear.* New York: Bantam.

Alzheimer's Association. 1999. "Statistics/ Prevalence." Accessed January 10, 2000 (http://www.alz.org/facts/stats.htm).

Amato, Paul, and Alan Booth. 1997. *A Generation at Risk.* Cambridge, MA: Harvard University Press.

Amato, Paul R. 2001. "What Children Learn From Divorce." *Population Today,* January, Pp. 1, 4.

———, and Juliana M. Sobolewski. 2001. "The Effects of Divorce and Marital Discord on Adult Children's Psychological Well-Being." *American Sociological Review* 66 (December): 900–921.

Amazon.com. 2001. "About Amazon.com." Accessed September 20 (http://www.amazon.com).

American Association of Health Plans. 1998. "Number of People in HMOs, 1976-96." Accessed August 11, 1998 (http://www.aahp.org/menus/index.cfm?cfid=64953% cfloken=32374).

American Association of University Women. 1992. *How Schools Shortchange Girls.* Washington, DC: American Association of University Women.

American Bar Association. 1997. *Section of Individual Rights and Responsibilities. Section of Litigation (Capital Punishment).* (February). Chicago: Division for Policy Administration, ABA.

———. 1999. "Commission on Domestic Violence." Accessed July 20, 1999 (http://www.abanet.org/domviol/stats.html).

American Civil Liberties Union. 2000. "State and Local Laws Protecting Lesbians and Gay Men Against Workplace Discrimination." Accessed January 19 (http://www.aclu.org/issues/gay/ gaylaws.html).

———. 2001. "Domestic Partnerships: List of Cities, States, and Countries." Accessed August 1 (http://aclu.org/issues/gay/dpstate.html).

American Federation of Teachers. 2001. "Teacher Salaries Fail to Keep Up with Inflation," press release, May 17. Accessed May 18 (http://www.aft.org/press/index.html).

American Jewish Committee. 2001. *2000 Annual Survey of American Jewish Opinion.* Accessed October 25 (http://www.ajc.org/pre/survey2000.htm).

American Sociological Association. 1997. *Code of Ethics.* Washington, DC: American Sociological Association. Available (http://www.asanet.org/members/ecoderev.html).

———. 1999. *Careers in Sociology.* 5th ed. Washington, DC: American Sociological Association.

———. 2001. *Data Brief: Profile of ASA Membership.* Washington, DC: American Sociological Association.

———. 2002. *Guide to Graduate Departments of Sociology, 2002.* Washington, DC: American Sociological Association.

Ammerman, Nancy T., Jackson W. Carroll, Carl S. Dudley, and William McKinney, ed. 1998. *Studying Congregations: A New Handbook.* Nashville, TN: Abingdon Press.

Amnesty International USA. 1994. *Breaking the Silence: Human Rights Violations Based on Sexual Orientation.* New York: Amnesty International.

Amnesty International. 1999. "Facts and Figures on the Death Penalty." Accessed August 4 (http://www.amnesty.excite.com/abolish/act500299.html).

———. 2000. "The Death Penalty: List of Abolitionist and Retentionist Countries." April. Accessed August 7 (http://www.amnesty.org/alib/aipub/2000/ACT/ A5000500.htm).

Andersen, Margaret. 1997. *Thinking About Women: Sociological Perspectives on Sex and Gender.* 4th ed. Boston: Allyn and Bacon.

Anderson, Elijah. 1978. *A Place on the Corner.* Chicago: University of Chicago Press.

———. 1990. *Streetwise: Race, Class, and Change in an Urban Community.* Chicago: University of Chicago Press.

———. 1999. *Code of the Streets.* New York: Norton.

———, and Molly Moore. 1993. "The Burden of Womanhood." *Washington Post National Weekly Edition* 10 (March 22–28):6–7.

Anderson, Sarah, John Cavanagh, Chris Hartman, and Betsy Leondar-Wright. 2001. *Executive Excess 2001: Layoffs, Tax Rebates, The Gender Gap.* Washington DC: United for a Fair Economy.

Andrews, Edmund L. 2001. "Frustrated Europeans Set to Battle U.S. on Climate." *New York Times,* July 16, Pp. A3.

Anti-Defamation League. 2001a. *Audit of Anti-Semitic Incidents.* New York: ADL.

———. 2001b. *Map of State Statutes.* Accessed June 11 (http://www.adl.org/99hatecrime/map_statutes.html).

AOL Time Warner. 2002. *About Us.* Accessed January 2, 2001 at (www.aoltimewarner. com).

Appelbaum, Richard, and Peter Dreier. 1999. "The Campus Anti-Sweatshops Movement." *The American Prospect* (September/October), Pp. 71–78.

Appleby, Julie. 1999. "Rethinking Managed Care." *USA Today,* October 7, Pp. A1–A2.

Archer, Margaret. 1988. *Culture and Agency: The Place of Culture in Social Theory.* Cambridge: Cambridge University Press.

Armer, J. Michael, and John Katsillis. 1992. "Modernization Theory." Pp. 1299–1304 in *Encyclopedia of Sociology,* Vol. 4, edited by Edgar F. Borgatta and Marie L. Borgatta. New York: Macmillan.

Armour, Stephanie. 2000. "Companies Work to Be More Gay-Friendly." *USA Today,* February, Pp. B1.

Aronowitz, Stanley, and William Di Fazio. 1994. *The Jobless Future: Sci-Tech and Dogma of Work.* Minneapolis: University of Minneapolis.

Ashford, Lori S. 2001. "New Population Policies: Advancing Women's Health and Rights." *Population Bulletin* 56 (March).

Asset-Based Community Development Institute. 2001. *Our Mission.* Accessed September 21 (www.northwestern.edu/IPR/abcd. html).

Associated Press. 1998. "Environmental Test Case Averted." *Christian Science Monitor,* September 21, p. 18.

———. 2000. "Opinions on Gay Relationships." *Los Angeles Times,* June 1, p. A31.

Association of American Medical Colleges. 2000. *2000 Medical School Graduate Report: All Schools Report.* Washington, DC: AAMC.

Astin, Alexander, Sarah A. Parrott, William S. Korn, and Linda J. Sax. 1994. *The American Freshman: Thirty Year Trends.* Los Angeles: Higher Education Research Institute.

Atchley, Robert C. 1976. *The Sociology of Retirement.* New York: Wiley.

Atchley, Robert C. 1985. The Social Forces in Later Life: An Introduction to Social Gerontology. 4th ed. Belmont, CA: Wadsworth.

Austin, Erica Weintraub, and Bruce E. Pinkleton. 1995. "Positive and Negative Effects of Political Disaffection on the Less Experienced Voter." *Journal of Broadcasting and Electronic Media* 39 (Spring):215–235.

Axtell, Roger E. 1990. *Do's and Taboos around the World.* 2d ed. New York: John Wiley and Sons.

Azius, Diana A. Terry. 2000. "Latinos are Searching for—and Finding—Love in Cyberspace." *Hispanic,* November, Pp. 51–52.

Azumi, Koya, and Jerald Hage. 1972. *Organizational Systems.* Lexington, MA: Heath.

B

Bachrach, Christine A. 1986. "Adoption Plans, Adopted Children, and Adoptive Mothers." *Journal of Marriage and the Family* 48 (May):243–253.

Bachu, Amara, and Martin O'Connell. 2001. "Fertility of American Women: June 2000." *Current Population Reports,* Ser. p. 20, No. 543. Washington, DC: U.S. Government Printing Office.

Bachu, Amara. 1999. "Is Childlessness Among American Women on the Rise?" Working Paper No. 37, Population Division, U.S. Bureau of Census, Washington, DC.

Backett-Milburn, Kathryn, and Linda McKie, ed. 2001. *Constructing Gendered Bodies.* New York: Palgrave.

Baer, Douglas, James Curtis, and Edward Grabb. 2000. *Has Voluntary Association Activity Declined? A Cross-National Perspective.* Paper

presented at the annual meeting of the American Sociological Association, Washington, DC.

Bailey, Susan McGee, and Patricia B. Campbell. 2000. "The Gender Wars in Education." *Wellesley Centers for Women Research Report* 20 (Fall/Winter):20.

Bainbridge, William Sims. 1999. "Cyberspace: Sociology's Natural Domain." *Contemporary Sociology* 28 (November):664–667.

Baker, Linda. 1994. "Day-Care Disgrace." *The Progressive* 58 (June):26–27.

Baker, Therese L. 1999. *Doing Social Research.* 3d ed. New York: McGraw-Hill.

Bark, Ed. 2000. "La Raza Decries the Lack of 'Color' TV." *Chicago Tribune,* June 17, p. 30.

Barnes, Annie S. 2000. *Everyday Racism: A Book for All Americans.* Naperville, IL: Sourcebooks.

Barr, Cameron W. 1999. "Get Used to It: Japanese Steel Themselves for Downsizing." *Christian Science Monitor,* November 12, Pp. 7–8.

Barrett, David B., and Todd M. Johnson. 2001. "Worldwide Adherents of Selected Religions by Six Continental Areas, Mid-2000." In *Britannica Book of the Year 2001,* p. 302. Chicago: Encyclopedia Britannica.

Barron, Milton L. 1953. "Minority Group Characteristics of the Aged in American Society." *Journal of Gerontology* 8:477–482.

Barstow, David. 2001. "Envisioning an Expensive Future in the Brave New World of Fortress New York." *New York Times,* September 16, p. 16.

Basso, Keith H. 1972. "Ice and Travel among the Fort Norman Slave: Folk Taxonomies and Cultural Rules." *Language in Society* 1 (March):31–49.

Bates, Colleen Dunn. 1999. "Medicine's Gender Gap." *Shape,* October.

Bauerlein, Monika. 1996. "The Luddites Are Back." *Utne Reader* (March/April):24, 26.

Bauman, Kurt J. 1999. "Extended Measures of Well-Being: Meeting Basic Needs." *Current Population Reports,* Ser. p. 70, No. 67. Washington, DC: U.S. Government Printing Office.

Bayton, Mavis. 1999. *Frock Rock: Women Performing Popular Music.* New York: Oxford University Press.

Bean, Frank, Steven Trejo, Randy Capps, and Michael Tyler. 2001. *The Latino Middle Class: Myth, Reality and Potential.* Claremont, CA: The Thomás Rivera Policy Institute.

Becerra, Rosina M. 1999. "The Mexican-American Family." Pp. 153–171 in *Ethnic Families in America: Patterns and Variations,* 4th ed., edited by Charles H. Mindel, Robert W. Habenstein, and Roosevelt Wright, Jr. Upper Saddle River, NJ: Prentice Hall.

Beck, Allen J. et al. 2000. *Correctional Populations in the United States, 1997.* Washington, DC: Bureau of Justice Statistics.

Becker, Anne E. 1995. *Body, Self, and Society: The View from Fiji.* Philadelphia: University of Pennsylvania Press.

———, and R. A. Burwell. 1999. *Acculturation and Disordered Eating in Fiji.* Presented at the annual meeting of the American Psychiatric Association.

Becker, Howard S. 1952. "Social Class Variations in the Teacher-Pupil Relationship." *Journal of Educational Sociology* 25 (April): 451–465.

———. 1963. *The Outsiders: Studies in the Sociology of Deviance.* New York: Free Press.

———, ed. 1964. *The Other Side: Perspectives on Deviance.* New York: Free Press.

———. 1973. *The Outsiders: Studies in the Sociology of Deviance.* Rev. ed. New York: Free Press.

Beech, Hannah. 2001. "China's Lifestyle Choice." *Time* 158 (August 6):32.

Beeghley, Leonard. 1978. *Social Stratification in America: A Critical Analysis of Theory and Research.* Santa Monica, CA: Goodyear Publishing.

Begley, Sharon. 1999. "Designer Babies." *Newsweek* 132 (November 9):61–62.

Belkin, Lisa. 1999. "Getting the Girl." *New York Times Magazine,* July 25, pp. 26–31, 38, 54–55.

Bell, Daniel. 1953. "Crime as an American Way of Life." *Antioch Review* 13 (Summer):131–154.

———. 1999. *The Coming of Post-Industrial Society: A Venture in Social Forecasting.* With new foreword. New York: Basic Books.

Bell, Ella Edmundson, and Stella M. Nkomo. 2001. *Our Separate Ways: Black and White Women and the Struggle for Professional Identity.* Cambridge, MA: Harvard Business School Press.

Bell, Wendell. 1981a. "Modernization." Pp. 186–187 in *Encyclopedia of Sociology.* Guilford, CT: DPG Publishing.

———. 1981b. "Neocolonialism." p. 193 in *Encyclopedia of Sociology.* Guilford, CT: DPG Publishing.

Bellafante, Ginia. 1998. "Feminism: It's All About Me!" *Time* 151 (June 20):54–62.

Belluck, Pam. 2001. "Nuns Offer Clues to Alzheimer's and Aging." *New York Times,* May 7, p. A1.

Belsie, Laurent. 2000. "Strange Webfellows." *Christian Science Monitor,* March 2, Pp. 15–16.

———. 1998. "Genetic Research Data Will Double Annually." *Christian Science Monitor,* July 30, p. B4.

Belsie, Laurent. 2001. "Rise of 'Home Alone' Crowd May Alter US Civic Life." *Christian Science Monitor,* May 24, Pp. 1, 2.

Bendavid, Naftali. 1998. "Surge in Executions Just the Beginning." *Chicago Tribune,* January 4, Pp. 1, 14.

Bendick, Marc, Jr., Charles W. Jackson, and J. Horacio Romero. 1993. *Employment Discrimination against Older Workers: An Experimental Study of Hiring Practices.* Washington, DC: Fair Employment Council of Greater Washington.

Benford, Robert D. 1992. "Social Movements." Pp. 1880–1887 in *Encyclopedia of Sociology,* Vol. 4, edited by Edgar F. Borgatta and Marie Borgatta. New York: Macmillan.

Benjamin, Gail R. 1997. *Japanese Lessons.* New York: New York University Press.

Benner, Richard S., and Susan Tyler Hitchcock. 1986. *Life after Liberal Arts.* Charlottesville: Office of Career Planning and Placement, University of Virginia.

Bennett, Vanora. 1997. "Russia's Ugly Little Secret: Misogyny." *Los Angeles Times,* December 6, Pp. A1, A9, A10.

Berger, Arthur Asa. 2000. *Ads, Foods, and Consumer Culture.* Lanham, MD: Rowan and Littlefield.

Berger, Peter, and Thomas Luckmann. 1966. *The Social Construction of Reality.* New York: Doubleday.

Berk, Richard A. 1974. *Collective Behavior.* Dubuque, IA: Brown.

———, and Howard E. Aldrich. 1972. "Patterns of Vandalism during Civil Disorders as an Indicator of Selection of Targets." *American Sociological Review* 37 (October): 533–547.

Berke, Richard L. 2001. "An Older Electorate, Potent and Unpredictable." *New York Times,* March 21, p. D8.

Berkeley Wellness Letter. 1990. "The Nest Refilled." 6 (February):1–2.

Berland, Gretchen K. 2001. "Health Information on the Internet: Accessibility, Quality, and Readability in English and Spanish." *Journal of American Medical Association* 285 (March 23):2612–2621.

Berlin, Brent, and Paul Kay. 1991. *Basic Color Terms: Their Universality and Evolution.* Berkeley, CA: University of California Press.

Bernhardt, Todd. 1997. "Disaster Mythology: A Contest Analysis from 1985 to 1995." Presented at the annual meeting of the Midwest Sociological Society, April, Des Moines, IA.

Bernstein, Anne C. 1988. "Unraveling the Tangles: Children's Understanding of Stepfamily Kinship." Pp. 83–111 in *Relative Strangers: Studies of Step-Family Press,* edited by W. R. Beer, Totowa, NJ: Rowan and Littlefield.

Bernstein, Jared, and Mark Greenberg. 2001. "Reforming Welfare Reform." *American Prospect.* January 16, Pp. 10–16.

Bernstein, Nina. 1997. "On Line, High-Tech Sleuths Find Private Facts." *New York Times,* September 15, Pp. A1, A20.

Best, Amy L. 2000. *Prom Night: Youths, Schools and Popular Culture.* New York: Routledge.

Best, Fred, and Ray Eberhard. 1990. "Education for the 'Era of the Adult.'" *The Futurist* 21 (May/June):23–28.

Best, Joel, ed. 2001a. *How Claims Spread: Cross-National Diffusion of Social Problems.* Hawthorne, NY: Addine de Gruyter.

———. 2001b. *Damned Lies and Statistics: Untangling Numbers from the Media, Politicians and Activists.* Berkeley, CA: University of California Press.

Bharadwaj, Lakshmik. 1992. "Human Ecology." Pp. 848–867 in *Encyclopedia of Sociology,* Vol. 2, edited by Edgar E. Borgatta and Marie L. Borgatta. New York: Macmillan.

Bianchi, Suzanne M., and Daphne Spain. 1996. "Women, Work, and Family in America." *Population Bulletin* 51 (December).

Bianchi, Suzanne M., and Lynne M. Casper. 2000. "American Families." *Population Bulletin* (December).

Bielby, William T., and Denise D. Bielby. 1992. "I Will Follow Him: Family Ties, Gender-Role Beliefs, and Reluctance to Relocate for a Better Job." *American Journal of Sociology* 97 (March):1241–1267.

Billson, Janet Mancini, and Bettina J. Huber. 1993. *Embarking upon a Career with an Undergraduate Degree in Sociology.* 2d ed. Washington, DC: American Sociological Association.

Biskupic, Joan. 2000. "Abortion Debate Will Continue to Rage." *USA Today,* June 29, p. 9A.

Bjorkman, Sharon. 1999. "Doing Church: The Active Creation of Worship Style." Presented at the Conference of Sociological Ethnography, February 27.

Black, Donald. 1995. "The Epistemology of Pure Sociology." *Law and Social Inquiry* 20 (Summer):829-870.

Blackhall, Leslie J. et al. [5 authors]. 1995. "Ethnicity and Attitudes toward Patient Autonomy." *Journal of the American Medical Association* 274 (September 13): 820–825.

Blanc, Ann Klimas. 1984. "Nonmarital Cohabitation and Fertility in the United States and Western Europe." *Population Research and Policy Review* 3:181–193.

Blanchard, Fletcher A., Teri Lilly, and Leigh Ann Vaughan. 1991. "Reducing the Expression of Racial Prejudice." *Psychological Science* 2 (March):101–105.

Blau, Peter M. 1964. *Exchange and Power in Social Life.* New York: Wiley.

———, and Otis Dudley Duncan. 1967. *The American Occupational Structure.* New York: Wiley.

———, and Marshall W. Meyer. 1987. *Bureaucracy in Modern Society.* 3d ed. New York: Random House.

Blauner, Robert. 1964. *Alienation and Freedom.* Chicago: University of Chicago Press.

———. 1972. *Racial Oppression in America.* New York: Harper and Row.

Blendon, Robert J. 1986. "The Problem of Cost, Access and Distribution of Medical Care." *Daedalus* 115 (Spring):119–135.

Bloom, Alexis. 2001. "Seeing Television with Innocent, and Eager, Eyes." *New York Times,* May 31, Pp. 21; 26.

Bloom, Stephen G. 2000. *Postville: A Clash of Cultures in Heartland America.* San Diego, CA: Harcourt Brace.

Bluestone, Barry, and Bennett Harrison. 1982. *The Deindustrialization of America.* New York: Basic Books.

Blumer, Herbert. 1955. "Collective Behavior." Pp. 165–198 in *Principles of Sociology,* 2d ed., edited by Alfred McClung Lee. New York: Barnes and Noble.

———. 1969. *Symbolic Interactionism: Perspective and Method.* Englewood Cliffs, NJ: Prentice Hall.

Blumstein, Alfred, and Joel Wallman, eds. 2001. *The Crime Drop in America.* New York: Cambridge University Press.

Boaz, Rachel Floersheim. 1987. "Early Withdrawal from the Labor Force." *Research on Aging* 9 (December):530–547.

Bobo, Lawrence. 1991. "Social Responsibility, Individualism, and Redistribution Policies." *Sociological Forum* 6:71-92.

Bogle, Donald. 2001. *Prime Time Blues.* New York: Favor, Straus and Giroux.

Bok, Sissela. 1998. *Mayhem: Violence as Public Entertainment.* Reading, MA: Addison-Wesley.

Booth, William. 2000. "Has Our Can-Do Attitude Peaked?" *Washington Post National Weekly Edition* 17 (February 7):29.

Borman, Kathryn M., and Joel H. Spring. 1984. *Schools in Central Cities: Structure and Process.* New York: Longman.

Bornschier, Volker, Christopher Chase-Dunn, and Richard Rubinson. 1978. "Cross-National Evidence of the Effects of Foreign Investment and Aid on Economic Growth and Inequality: A Survey of Findings and a Reanalysis." *American Journal of Sociology* 84 (November):651–683.

Bosk, Charles L. 1992. *All God's Mistakes: Genetic Counseling in a Pediatric Hospital.* Chicago: University of Chicago Press.

Boston Women's Health Book Collective. 1969. *Our Bodies, Ourselves.* Boston: New England Free Press.

———. 1992. *The New Our Bodies, Ourselves.* New York: Touchstone.

Bottomore, Tom, and Maximilien Rubel, ed. 1956. *Karl Marx: Selected Writings in Sociology and Social Philosophy.* New York: McGraw-Hill.

Boushey, Heather, Chauna Brocht, Bethney Gundersen, and Jared Bernstein. 2001. *Hardships in America: The Real Story of Working Families.* Washington, DC: Economic Policy Institute.

Bouvier, Leon F. 1980. "America's Baby Boom Generation: The Fateful Bulge." *Population Bulletin* 35 (April).

———, and Lindsey Grant. 1994. *How Many Americans? Population, Immigration, and the Environment.* San Francisco: Sierra Club.

Bowles, Samuel, and Herbert Gintis. 1976. *Schooling in Capitalistic America: Educational Reforms and the Contradictions of Economic Life.* New York: Basic Books.

Bowles, Scott. 1999. "Fewer Violent Fatalities in Schools." *USA Today,* April 28, p. 4A.

Bowman, Karlyn. 2001. "Crime Stats: Better But Not Good." *The American Enterprise* 12 (June):60.

Bracey, Gerald W. 1993. "No Magic Bullet." *Phi Delta Kappan* 74 (February):495–496.

Bradley, Martin B. et al. [5 authors]. 1992. *Churches and Church Membership in the United States 1990.* Atlanta, GA: Glenmary Research Center.

Brandon, Karen. 1995. "Computer Scrutiny Adds to Furor over Immigrants." *Chicago Tribune,* December 5, Pp. 1, 16.

Brannigan, Augustine. 1992. "Postmodernism." Pp. 1522–1525 in *Encyclopedia of Sociology,* Vol. 3, edited by Edgar F. Borgatta and Marie L. Borgatta. New York: Macmillan.

Brannon, Robert. 1976. "Ideology, Myth, and Reality: Sex Equality in Israel." *Sex Roles* 6:403–419.

Braun, Denny. 1997. *The Rich Get Richer.* 2d ed. Chicago: Nelson Hall.

Braxton, Greg. 1999. "A Mad Dash for Diversity." *Los Angeles Times,* August 9, Pp. F1-10.

Bray, James H., and John Kelly. 1999. *Stepfamilies: Love, Marriage, and Parenting in the First Decade.* New York: Broadway Books.

Brelin, Christa, ed. 1996. *Strength in Numbers: A Lesbian, Gay, and Bisexual Resource.* Detroit: Visible Ink.

Brewer, Cynthia A., and Trudy A. Suchan. 2001. *Mapping Census 2000: The Geography of U.S. Diversity.* Washington, DC: U.S. Government Printing Office.

Brewer, Rose M. 1989. "Black Women and Feminist Sociology: The Emerging Perspective." *American Sociologist* 20 (Spring):57–70.

Brint, Steven. 1998. *Schools and Societies.* Thousand Oaks, CA: Pine Forge Press.

Brischetto, Robert R. 2001. "The Hispanic Middle Class Comes of Age." *Hispanic Business* 23 (December):21–22, 26.

Brockerhoff, Martin P. 2000. "An Urbanizing World." *Population Bulletin* 55 (September).

Brower, Brock. 1988. "The Pernicious Power of the Polls." *Money,* March 17, Pp. 144–163.

Brown, Michael, and Amy Goldin. 1973. *Collective Behavior: A Review and Reinterpretation of the Literature.* Pacific Palisades, CA: Goodyear.

Brown, Robert McAfee. 1980. *Gustavo Gutierrez.* Atlanta: John Knox.

Brown, Roger W. 1954. "Mass Phenomena." Pp. 833–873 in *Handbook of Social Psychology,* Vol. 2, edited by Gardner Lindzey. Reading, MA: Addison-Wesley.

Browne, Irene. 2001. *Latinas and African Women at Work: Race, Gender and Economic Inequality.* New York: Russell Sage Foundation.

Brownstein, Ronald. 2001. "Jack Valenti's Last Stand." *Premiere* 14 (August):28, 30–31, 33–38.

Brundtland, Gro Harlem. 2001. "Affordable Aids Drugs Are Within Reach." *International Herald Tribune.* Accessed March 1 (http://www.who.int/inf-pr-2001/en/note2001-02.html).

Bruni, Frank. 1998. "A Small-But-Growing Sorority Is Giving Birth to Children for Gay Men." *New York Times,* June 25, p. A12.

———, and Marc Lacey. 2001. "Bush Acts to Deny Money Overseas Tied to Abortion." *New York Times,* January 23, Pp. A1, A14.

Bryant, Adam. 1999. "American Pay Rattles Foreign Partners." *New York Times,* January 17, Sec. 6, Pp. 1, 4.

Buckley, Stephen. 1997. "Left Behind Prosperity's Door." *Washington Post National Weekly Edition,* March 24, Pp. 8–9.

Buechler, Steven M. 1995. "New Social Movement Theories." *Sociological Quarterly* 36 (3):441–464.

Bulle, Wolfgang F. 1987. Crossing Cultures? *Southeast Asian Mainland.* Atlanta: Centers for Disease Control.

Bumiller, Elisabeth. 2000. "Resolute Adversary of Divorce." *New York Times,* December 16, Pp. A17, A19.

Bunzel, John H. 1992. *Race Relations on Campus: Stanford Students Speak.* Stanford, CA: Portable Stanford.

Bureau of Labor Statistics. 2001a. *Comparative Civilian Labor Force Statistics Ten Countries 1959-2000.* Washington, DC: U.S. Department of Labor, Office of Productivity and Technology.

Bureau of Labor Statistics. 2001b. *Highlights of Women's Earnings in 2000 Report* Washington, DC: U.S. Government Printing Office.

Bureau of Primary Health Care. 1999. Home page. Accessed January 18, 2000 (http://www.bphc.hrsa.gov/bphcfactsheet.htm).

Bureau of the Census. 1975. *Historical Statistics of the United States, Colonial Times to 1970.* Washington, DC: U.S. Government Printing Office.

———. 1991. "Half of the Nation's Population Lives in Large Metropolitan Areas." Press release, February 21.

———. 1994. *Statistical Abstract of the United States, 1994.* Washington, DC: U.S. Government Printing Office.

———. 1995. *Statistical Abstract of the United States, 1995.* Washington, DC: U.S. Government Printing Office.

———. 1996. *Statistical Abstract of the United States, 1996.* Washington, DC: U.S. Government Printing Office.

———. 1997b. "Geographical Mobility: March 1995 to March 1996." *Current Population Reports,* Ser. p. 20, No. 497. Washington, DC: U.S. Government Printing Office.

———. 1998a. "Race of Wife by Race of Husband." Internet release of June 10.

———. 1998c. *Statistical Abstract of the United States, 1998.* Washington, DC: U.S. Government Printing Office.

———. 1998f. Voting and Registration: November 1996. Internet release of October 17, 1997. Accessed July 17 (http://www.census.gov/population/socdemo/voting/history/vot0l.txt).

———. 2000a. *Statistical Abstract of the United States, 2000.* Washington, DC: U.S. Government Printing Office.

———. 2000c. "National Population Projections." Internet release of January 13. Accessed May 11 (http://www.census.gov/population/www/projection/natsum-T3html).

———. 2000d. "Money Income in the United States 1999." *Current Population Reports,* Ser. p. 60, No. 209. Washington, DC: U.S. Government Printing Office.

———. 2000e. (NP-D1-A) *Projections of the Resident Population by Age, Sex, Race, and Hispanic Origin: 1999 to 2100.* Washington, DC: U.S. Government Printing Office.

———. 2001a. *Statistical Abstract of the United States, 2001.* Washington, DC: U.S. Government Printing Office.

———. 2001b. *Hispanic 1997 Economic Census Survey of Minority-Owned Enterprises.* Series BC97CS-4. Washington, DC: U.S. Government Printing Office.

———. 2001c. *1997 Revenues for Women-Owned Businesses Show Continued Growth.* News Release of April 4. Washington, DC: U.S. Government Printing Office.

———. 2001d. *International Data Base* Accessed December 14 (http://www.census.gov/1pc/www/idbsvm.html).

———. 2001e. *Hispanic Owned Business:* 1997 Census Brief CENBR/01–4. Washington, DC: U.S. Government Printing Office.

———. 2001f. *Housing Vacancies and Homeownership, Annual Statistics: 2000.* Accessed December 7 (www.census.gov/hhes/www/housing/hvs/annual00/ann00ind.html).

———. 2001g. *March 2001 Current Population Survey.* From Table PINC-03. Accessed February 1, 2002 (www.census.gov/hhes/www/income.html).

———. 2001h. Facts for Features: American/Alaskan Indian Heritage Month: November 2001. CB01-FF.15. Accessed October 22 (www.census.gov).

———. 2001j QT-02. Profile of Selected Social Characteristics. Accessed February 5, 2000 at Factfinder.census.gov.

Burgess, Ernest W. 1925. "The Growth of the City." Pp. 47–62 in *The City,* edited by Robert E. Park, Ernest W. Burgess, and Roderick D. McKenzie. Chicago: University of Chicago Press.

Burkett, Elinor. 2000. *The Baby Boom: How Family Friendly America Cheats the Childless.* New York: Free Press.

Burns, John R. 1998. "Once Widowed in India, Twice Scorned." *New York Times,* March 29, p. A1.

Burt, Maritha B. 2001. *What Will It Take To End Homelessness?* Washington, D.C.: Urban Institute.

Burton, Velmer S., Jr. 1990. "The Consequences of Official Labels: A Research Note on Rights Lost by the Mentally Ill, Mentally Incompetent, and Convicted Felons." *Community Mental Health Journal* 26 (June): 267–276.

Butler, Daniel Allen. 1998. *"Unsinkable:" The Full Story.* Mechanicsburg, PA: Stackpole Books.

Butler, Robert N. 1990. "A Disease Called Ageism." *Journal of American Geriatrics Society* 38 (February):178–180.

Butterfield, Fox. 1996. "U.S. Has Plan to Broaden Availability of DNA Testing." *New York Times,* June 14, p. A8.

Butterfield, Fox. 2000. "Racial Disparities Seen as Pervasive in Juvenile Justice." *New York Times,* April 26, Pp. A1, A18.

C

Caillat, Colette. 1987. "Jainism." p. 507 in *The Encyclopedia of Religion,* Vol. 7, edited by Mircea Eliade. New York: Macmillan.

Calhoun, Craig. 1998. "Community Without Propinquity Revisited." *Sociological Inquiry* 68 (Summer):373–397.

Callas, Steven P. 1999. "Rethinking Post-Fordism: The Meaning of Workplace Flexibility." *Sociological Theory* 17 (March): 68–101.

Calthorpe, Peter, and William Fulton. 2001. *The Regional City: Planning for the End of Sprawl.* Washington, DC: Island Press.

Campo-Flores, Arian. 2000. "Brown Against Brown." *Newsweek* 136 (September 18): 49–51.

Camus, Albert. 1948. *The Plague.* New York: Random House.

Cancel, Cecil Marie. 1997. "The Veil." Assessed October 10, 1999 (http://about.com).

Cantle, Ted. 2001. *Community Cohesion: A Report of the Independent Review Team.* London: Home Office.

Cantril, Hadley. 1940. *The Invasion from Mars: A Study in the Psychology of Panic.* Princeton, NJ: Princeton University Press.

Caplan, Ronald L. 1989. "The Commodification of American Health Care." *Social Science and Medicine* 28 (11):1139–1148.

Carey, Anne R., and Elys A. McLean. 1997. "Heard It Through the Grapevine?" *USA Today,* September 15, p. B1.

Caro, Mark. 2001. "Who Are They?" *Chicago Tribune,* October 15, Pp. 5, 7.

Carpenter, Susan. 2000. "Full of Fight." *Los Angeles Times,* November 29, Pp. E1, E3.

Carrese, Joseph A., and Lorna A. Rhodes. 1995. "Western Bioethics on the Navaho Reservation: Benefit or Harm?" *Journal of the American Medical Association* 274 (September 13):826–829.

Carty, Win. 1999. "Greater Dependence on Cars Leads to More Pollution in World's Cities." *Population Today* 27 (December): 1–2.

Casper, Lynne M., and Loretta E. Bass. 1998. "Voting and Registration in the Election of

November 1996." *Current Population Reports,* Ser. p. 20, No. 504. Washington, DC: U.S. Government Printing Office.

Cassidy, Claire Monod. 1982. "Protein-Energy Malnutrition as a Culture-Bound Syndrome." *Culture, Medicine, and Psychiatry* 6:325–345.

Castañeda, Jorge G. 1995. "Ferocious Differences." *Atlantic Monthly* 276 (July):68–69, 71–76.

Castells, Manuel. 1983. *The City and the Grass Roots.* Berkeley: University of California Press.

———. 1996. *The Information Age: Economy, Society and Culture.* Vol. 1 of *The Rise of the Network Society.* London: Blackwell.

———. 1997. *The Power of Identity.* Vol. 1 of *The Information Age: Economy, Society and Culture.* London: Blackwell.

———. 1998. *End of Millennium.* Vol. 3 of *The Information Age: Economy, Society and Culture.* London: Blackwell.

———. 2000. *The Information Age: Economy, Society and Culture* (3 vols.). 2d. ed. Oxford and Malden, MA: Blackwell.

———. 2001a. "The Information Age: Economy, Society and Culture," Vol. 1. *The Rise of the Network Society.* 2d ed. London: Blackwell.

———. 2001b. *The Internet Galaxy: Reflections on the Internet, Business, and Society.* New York: Oxford University Press.

CBS News. 1979. Transcript of *Sixty Minutes* segment, "I Was Only Following Orders." March 31, Pp. 2–8.

———. 1998. "Experimental Prison." *Sixty Minutes.* June 30.

Center for American Women and Politics. 2001. *Women in the U.S. Congress 2001. Statewide Elective Executive Women 2001.* New Brunswick, NJ: CAWP.

Center for Public Integrity. 1998. *Nothing Sacred: The Politics of Privacy.* Washington, DC: CPI.

Centers for Disease Control and Prevention. 2002. HIV/AIDS Basic Statistics. Accessed on April 10, 2002 at www.cdc.gov/hiv/stats.htm.

Centers for Disease Control. 2000. *HIV/AIDS Surveillance Report.* Mid-year 2000 edition. Accessed April 16, 2001 (http://www.cdc.gov/hiv/stats).

Cerulo, Karen A., Janet M. Ruane, and Mary Chagko. 1992. "Technological Ties that Bind: Media Generated Primary Groups." *Communication Research* 19:109–129.

Cetron, Marvin J., and Owen Davies. 1991. "Trends Shaping the World." *Futurist* 20 (September-October):11–21.

Cha, Ariena Eunjung. 2000. "Painting a Portrait of Dot-Camaraderie." *The Washington Post,* October 26, Pp. E1, E10.

Chaddock, Gail Russell. 1998. "The Challenge for Schools: Connecting Adults with Kids." *Christian Science Monitor,* August 4, p. B7.

Chafetz, Janet Saltzman. 1988. *Feminist Sociology: An Overview of Contemporary Theories.* Itasca, IL: F. E. Peacock.

———, ed. 1999. *Handbook of the Sociology of Gender.* New York: Kluwer Academic Publications.

Chalfant, H. Paul, Robert E. Beckley, and C. Eddie Palmer. 1994. *Religion in Contemporary Society.* 3d ed. Itasca, IL: F. E. Peacock.

Chambliss, Wilham. 1972. "Introduction." Pp. ix–xi in Harry King, *Box Man.* New York: Harper and Row.

———. 1973. "The Saints and the Roughnecks." *Society* 11 (November/December): 24–31.

Chandler, Clay. 2001. "Workers of the World." *Washington Post National Weekly Edition* 19 (December 10):17.

Chang, Patricia M. Y. 1997. "Female Clergy in the Contemporary Protestant Church: A Current Assessment." *Journal for the Scientific Study of Religion* 36 (December): 564–573.

Charmaz, Kathy, and Debora A. Paterniti, eds. 1999. *Health, Illness, and Healing: Society, Social Context, and Self.* Los Angeles, CA: Roxbury.

Charter, David, and Jill Sherman. 1996. "Schools Must Teach New Code of Values." *London Times,* January 15, p. 1.

Chase-Dunn, Christopher, and Peter Grimes. 1995. "World-Systems Analysis." Pp. 387–417 in *Annual Review of Sociology, 1995,* edited by John Hagan. Palo Alto, CA: Annual Reviews.

Chase-Dunn, Christopher, Yukio Kawano, and Benjamin D. Brewer. 2000. "Trade Globalization Since 1795: Waves of Integration in the World System." *American Sociological Review* 65 (February):77–95.

Chatzky, Jean Sherman. 1999. "The Big Squeeze." *Money* 28 (October):129, 131–134, 136–138.

Chen, Jersey, et al. 2001. "Racial Differences in the Use of Cardiac Catheterization After Acute Myocardial Infarction." *New England Journal of Medicine* 344 (May 10).

Cheng, Wei-yuan, and Lung-li Liao. 1994. "Women Managers in Taiwan." Pp. 143–159 in *Competitive Frontiers: Women Managers in a Global Economy,* edited by Nancy J. Adler and Dafna N. Izraeli. Cambridge, MA: Blackwell Business.

Cherlin, Andrew J. 1999. *Public and Private Families: An Introduction.* 2d ed. New York: McGraw-Hill.

———, and Frank Furstenberg. 1994. "Stepfamilies in the United States: A Reconsideration." Pp. 359–381 in *Annual Review of Sociology, 1994,* edited by John Hagan. Palo Alto, CA: Annual Reviews.

Chesney-Lind, Meda, and Noelie Rodriguez. 1993. "Women under Lock and Key." *Prison Journal* 63:47–65.

Chicago Tribune. 1997. "In London, Prince Meets a Pauper, an Ex-Classmate." December 5, p. 19.

———. 2002. Motorola: 400 More Lose Jobs at Harvard Facility (January 10), sect. 2, p. 2.

Children First CEO America. 2001.

Children Now. 2001. *The Local Television News Media's Picture of Children.* Oakland, CA: Children Now.

Chin, Ko-lin. 1996. *Chinatown Gangs: Extortion, Enterprise, and Ethnicity.* New York: Oxford University Press.

Christiansen, John B., and Sharon N. Barnartt. 1995. *Deaf President Now: The 1988 Revolution at Gallaudet University.* Washington, DC: Gallaudet University Press.

Christiansen, Kathleen. 1990. "Bridges over Troubled Water: How Older Workers View the Labor Market." Pp. 175–207 in *Bridges to Retirement,* edited by Peter B. Doeringer. Ithaca, NY: IRL Press.

Christie, Brigan. 2001. "Sociological Medicine's Aches and Pains." Pp. 222–223 in *Encyclopedia*

Britannica Yearbook 2001. Chicago: Encyclopedia Britannica.

Chu, Henry. 2001. "Middle Kingdom's Middle Class." *Los Angeles Times,* June 18, Pp. A1, A7.

Civic Ventures. 1999. *The New Face of Retirement: Older Americans, Civic Engagement, and the Longevity Revolution.* Washington, DC: Peter D. Hart Research Associates.

Clark, Burton, and Martin Trow. 1966. "The Organizational Context." Pp. 17–70 in *The Study of College Peer Groups,* edited by Theodore M. Newcomb and Everett K. Wilson. Chicago: Aldine.

Clark, Candace. 1983. "Sickness and Social Control." Pp. 346–365 in *Social Interaction: Readings in Sociology,* 2d. ed., edited by Howard Robboy and Candace Clark. New York: St. Martin's.

Clark, Charles, and Jason M. Fields. 1999. "First Glance: Preliminary Analysis of Relationship, Marital Status, and Grandparents Items on the Census 2000 Dress Rehearsal." Presented at the annual meeting of the American Sociological Association, August, Chicago.

Clark, Thomas. 1994. "Culture and Objectivity." *The Humanist* 54 (August):38–39.

Clarke, Lee. 1999. *Mission Improbable: Using Fantasy Documents to Tame Disaster.* Chicago: University of Chicago Press.

Clawson, Dan, and Mary Ann Clawson. 1999. "What Has Happened to the U.S. Labor Movement? Union Decline and Renewal." Pp. 95–119 in *Annual Review of Sociology 1999,* edited by Karen S. Cook and John Hagan. Palo Alto, CA: Annual Reviews.

Clinard, Marshall B., and Robert F. Miller. 1998. *Sociology of Deviant Behavior.* 10th ed. Fort Worth: Harcourt Brace.

Cloud, John. 2001. "A License to Kill?" *Time* 157 (August 23):66.

Clymer, Adam. 2000. "College Students Not Drawn to Voting or Politics, Poll Shows. *New York Times.* January 2, p. A14.

Cockerham, William C. 1998. Medical Sociology. 7th ed. Upper Saddle River, NJ: Prentice Hall.

Cohen, David, ed. 1991. *The Circle of Life: Ritual from the Human Family Album.* San Francisco: Harper.

Cohen, Joel E. 1995. *How Many People Can the Earth Support?* New York: Norton.

Cohen, Lawrence E., and Marcus Felson. 1979. "Social Change and Crime Rate Trends: A Routine Activities Approach." *American Sociological Review* 44:588–608.

Cohen, Patricia. 1998. "Daddy Dearest: Do You Really Matter?" *New York Times,* July 11, p. B7.

Cole, David. 1999. *No Equal Justice: Race and Class in the American Criminal Justice System.* New York: The New Press.

Cole, Elizabeth S. 1985. "Adoption, History, Policy, and Program." Pp. 638–666 in *A Handbook of Child Welfare,* edited by John Laird and Ann Hartman. New York: Free Press.

Cole, Mike. 1988. *Bowles and Gintis Revisited: Correspondence and Contradiction in Educational Theory.* Philadelphia: Falmer.

Coleman, James William, and Donald R. Cressey. 1980. *Social Problems.* New York: Harper and Row.

Colker, David. 1996. "Putting the Accent On World Wide Access." *Los Angeles Times,* May 21, p. E3.

Collier, Lorna. 2000. "They're Shocking! They're Scary! And They Hardly Ever Die!" *Chicago Tribune,* April 18, Sect. 5, Pp. 1–2.

Collins, Patricia Hill. 1991. *Black Feminist Thought: Knowledge Consciousness and the Politics of Empowerment.* New York: Routledge.

Collins, Randall. 1975. *Conflict Sociology: Toward an Explanatory Sociology.* New York: Academic.

———. 1980. "Weber's Last Theory of Capitalism: A Systematization." *American Sociological Review* 45 (December):925–942.

———. 1986. *Weberian Sociological Theory.* New York: Cambridge University Press.

———. 1995. "Prediction in Macrosociology: The Case of the Soviet Collapse." *American Journal of Sociology* l00 (May):1552–1593.

Collins, Randall. 1979. *The Credential Society: An Historical Sociology of Education and Stratification.* New York: Academic.

Commission on Behavioral and Social Sciences Education. 1998. *Protecting Youth at Work.* Washington, DC: National Academy Press.

Commission on Civil Rights. 1976. *A Guide to Federal Laws and Regulations Prohibiting Sex Discrimination.* Washington, DC: U.S. Government Printing Office.

———. 1981. *Affirmative Action in the 1980s: Dismantling the Process of Discrimination.* Washington DC: U.S. Government Printing Office.

Commoner, Barry. 1971. *The Closing Circle.* New York: Knopf.

———. 1990. *Making Peace with the Planet.* New York: Pantheon.

Comstock, P., and M. B. Fox. 1994. "Employer Tactics and Labor Law Reform." Pp. 90–109 in *Restoring the Promise of American Labor Law,* edited by S. Friedman, R. W. Hurd, R. A. Oswald, and R. L. Seeber. Ithaca, NY: ILR Press.

Conklin, Mike. 2002. Tuning out Motorola. *Chicago Tribune* (February 21); Section 5, Pp. 1, 4.

Conrad, Peter, and Joseph W. Schneider. 1992. *Deviance and Medicalization: From Badness to Sickness.* Expanded ed. Philadelphia: Temple University Press.

Conrad, Peter, ed. 1997. *The Sociology of Health and Illness: Critical Perspectives.* 5th ed. New York: St. Martin's.

———, and Joseph W. Schneider. 1992. *Deviance and Medicalization: From Badness to Sickness.* Expanded ed. Philadelphia: Temple University Press.

Cook, Rhodes. 1991. "The Crosscurrents of the Youth Vote." *Congressional Quarterly Weekly Report* 49 (June 29):1802.

Cooley, Charles. H. 1902. *Human Nature and the Social Order.* New York: Scribner.

Cooper, Richard T. 1998. "Jobs Outside High School Can Be Costly, Report Finds." *Los Angeles Times,* November 6, p. A1.

Cornfield, Daniel B. 1989. *Becoming a Minority Voice: Conflict and Change in the United Furniture Workers of America.* New York: Russell Sage Foundation.

Corning, Amy. 1993. "The Russian Referendum: An Analysis of Exit Poll Results." *RFE/RL Research Report* 2 (May 7):6–9.

Corwin, Miles. 2000. "Cultural Sensitivity on the Beat." *Los Angeles Times,* January 10, Pp. A1, A12.

Corsaro, William A. 1997. *The Sociology of Childhood.* Thousand Oaks, CA: Pine Forge Press.

Coser, Lewis A. 1956. *The Functions of Social Conflict.* New York: Free Press.

———. 1977. *Masters of Sociological Thought: Ideas in Historical and Social Context.* 2d ed. New York: Harcourt, Brace and Jovanovich.

Coser, Rose Laub. 1984. "American Medicine's Ambiguous Progress." *Contemporary Sociology* 13 (January):9–13.

Couch, Carl. 1996. *Information Technologies and Social Orders.* Edited with an introduction by David R. Maines and Shing-Ling Chien. New York: Aldine de Gruyter.

Council on Ethical and Judicial Affairs, American Medical Association. 1992. "Decisions Near the End of Life." *Journal of the American Medical Association* 267 (April 22–29): 2229–2333.

Council on Scientific Affairs. 1999. "Hispanic Health in the United States." *Journal of the American Medical Association* 265 (January 9): 248–252.

Counts, D.A. 1977. "The Good Death in Kaliai: Preparation For Death in Western New Britain." *Omega.* 7:367–372.

Cox, Oliver C. 1948. *Caste Class and Race: A Study in Social Dynamics.* Detroit: Wayne State University Press.

CQ Researcher. 2001. *Issues in Health Policy.* Washington, DC: CQ Press.

Crenshaw, Edward M., Matthew Christenson, and Doyle Ray Oakey. 2000. "Demographic Transition in Ecological Focus." *American Sociologica1 Review* 65 (June):371–391.

Cressey, Donald R. 1960. "Epidemiology and Individual Contact: A Case from Criminology." *Pacific Sociological Review* 3 (Fall): 47–58.

Cromwell, Paul F., James N. Olson, and D'Aunn Wester Avarey. 1995. *Breaking and Entering: An Ethnographic Analysis of Burglary.* Newbury Park, CA: Sage.

Crossette, Barbara. 1996. "Snubbing Human Rights," *New York Times,* April 28, p. E3.

———. 1999. "The Internet Changes Dictatorship's Rules." *New York Times,* August 1, Sec. 4, p. l.

———. 2001. "Against a Trend, U.S. Population Will Bloom, U.N. Says." *New York Times,* February 28, p. A6.

Croteau, David, and William Hoynes. 2000. *Media/Society: Industries, Images, and Audiences.* 2d ed. Thousand Oaks, CA: Pine Forge.

———. 2001. *The Business of the Media: Corporate Media and the Public Interest.* Thousand Oaks, CA: Pine Forge.

Crouse, Kelly. 1999. "Sociology of the Titanic." *Teaching Sociology Listserv.* May 24.

Cuban, Larry. 2001. "Why Bad Reforms Won't Give Us Good Schools." *American Prospect* 29 (January 1):46–48.

Cuff, E. C., W. W. Sharrock, and D. W. Francis, eds. 1990. *Perspectives in Sociology.* 3d ed. Boston: Unwin Hyman.

Cuklanz, Lisa M. 2000. *Rape on Prime Time: Television, Masculinity, and Sexual Violence.* Philadelphia, PA: University of Pennsylvania Press.

Cullen, Francis T., Jr., and John B. Cullen. 1978. *Toward a Paradigm of Labeling Theory,* Ser. 58. Lincoln: University of Nebraska Studies.

Cumming, Elaine, and William E. Henry. 1961. *Growing Old: The Process of Disengagement.* New York: Basic Books.

Cunningham, Michael Marberry. 2000. *Crowns: Portraits of Black Women in Church Hats.* New York: Random House.

Cunningham, Michael. 1992. "If You're Queer and You're Not Angry in 1992, You're Not Paying Attention." *Mother Jones* 17 (May/June): 60–66, 68.

Current Population Reports, Ser. p. 20, No. 543. Washington, DC: U.S. Government Printing Office.

Currie, Elliot. 1985. *Confronting Crime: An American Challenge.* New York: Pantheon.

———. 1998. *Crime and Punishment in America.* New York: Metropolitan Books.

Curry, Timothy Jon. 1993. "A Little Pain Never Hurt Anyone: Athletic Career Socialization and the Normalization of Sports Injury." *Symbolic Interaction* 26 (Fall):273–290.

Cushman, John H., Jr. 1998. "Pollution Policy Is Unfair Burden, States Tell E.P.A." *New York Times,* May 10, Pp. 1, 20.

Cussins, Choris M. 1998. In *Cyborg Babies: From Techno-Sex to Techno-Tots,* edited by Robbie Davis-Floyd and Joseph Dumit. New York: Routledge.

D

Dahl, Robert A. 1961. *Who Governs?* New Haven, CT: Yale University Press.

Dahrendorf, Ralf. 1959. *Class and Class Conflict in Industrial Sociology.* Stanford, CA: Stanford University Press.

Dalaker, Joseph. 2001. "Poverty in the United States: 2000." *Current Population Reports,* Ser. p. 60, No. 214. Washington, DC: U.S. Government Printing Office.

———, and Mary Naifeh. 1998. "Poverty in the United States: 1997." *Current Population Reports,* Ser. p. 60, No. 201. Washington, DC: U.S. Government Printing Office.

Daley, Suzanne. 1996. "Apartheid's Dispossessed Seek Restitution." *New York Times,* June 25, p. A3.

———. 1997. "Reversing Roles in a South African Dilemma." *New York Times,* October 26, Sec. WE, p. 5.

———. 1998. "A Post-Apartheid Agony: AIDS on the March," *New York Times,* July 23, Pp. A1, A10.

———. 1999. "Doctors' Group of Volunteers Awarded Nobel." *New York Times,* October 16, Pp. A1, A6.

———. 2000. "French Couples Take Plunge that Falls Short of Marriage." *New York Times,* April 18, Pp. A1, A4.

Daniels, Arlene Kaplan. 1987. "Invisible Work." *Social Problems* 34 (December): 403–415.

———. 1988. *Invisible Careers.* Chicago: University of Chicago Press.

Dao, James. 1995. "New York's Highest Court Rules Unmarried Couples Can Adopt." *New York Times,* November 3, Pp. A1, B2.

Darling, Juanity. 2001. "Mexico's Indigenous People Look to Fox's Promise They'll Be Heard." *Los Angeles Times,* July 20, p. A15.

Dart, John. 1997. "Lutheran Women Wait Longer for Pastor Jobs, Survey Finds." *Los Angeles Times,* May 3, Pp. B1, B5.

Davies, Christie. 1989. "Goffman's Concept of the Total Institution: Criticisms and Revisions." *Human Studies* 12 (June):77–95.

Davis, Darren W. 1997. "The Direction of Race of Interviewer Effects Among African-Americans: Donning the Black Mask." *American Journal of Political Science* 41 (January): 309–322.

Davis, James Allen, and Tom W. Smith. 2001. *General Social Surveys, 1972–2000.* Storrs, CT: The Roper Center.

Davis, James. 1982. "Up and Down Opportunity's Ladder." *Public Opinion* 5 (June/July):11–15, 48–51.

Davis, Kingsley. 1937. "The Sociology of Prostitution." *American Sociological Review* 2 (October):744–755.

———. 1940. "Extreme Social Isolation of a Child." *American Journal of Sociology* 45 (January):554–565.

———. 1947. "A Final Note on a Case of Extreme Isolation." *American Journal of Sociology* 52 (March):432–437.

———. [1949] 1995. *Human Society.* Reprint, New York: Macmillan.

———, and Wilbert E. Moore. 1945. "Some Principles of Stratification." *American Sociological Review* 10 (April):242–249.

Davis, Nanette J. 1975. *Sociological Constructions of Deviance: Perspectives and Issues in the Field.* Dubuque, IA: Wm. C. Brown.

De Andra, Roberto M. 1996. *Chicanas and Chicanos in Contemporary Society.* Boston: Allyn and Bacon.

Deardurff, Kevin E. and Lisa M. Blumerman. 2001. "Evaluation Components of International Migration: Estimates of the Foreign-Born Population by Migrant States in 2000." *Working Paper Series* No. 58. Accessed January 8, 2002 (http://www. census.gov/population/www/documentation/twps0058.html).

Death Penalty Information Center. 2000a. "The Death Penalty in 1999: Year End Report." Accessed February 13 (http://www.essential. org/dpic/yrendrpt99.html).

———. 2000b. "History of the Death Penalty. Part II." Accessed February 13 (http://www. essential.org/dpic/history3.html#Innocence).

———. 2000c. "Innocence: Freed from Death Row." Accessed March 20 (http://www. essential.org/dpic/Innocent/ist.html).

———. 2001. *Chile Abolishes the Death Penalty.* Accessed June 12 (http://www. deathpenalty-info.org/dpicintl.html# interexec).

DeBarros, Anthony. 2000. "Concertgoers Push Injuries to High Levels." *USA Today,* August 8, Pp. D1–D2.

Deegan, Mary Jo, ed. 1991. *Women in Sociology: A Bio-Biographical Sourcebook.* Westport, CT: Greenwood.

DeFleur, Melvin L., and Everette E. Dennis. 1981. *Understanding Mass Communication.* Boston: Houghton Mifflin.

Deloria, Jr., Vine. 1999. *For This Land: Writings on Religion in America.* New York: Routledge.

Demerath III, R. J. 2001. *Crossing the Gods: World Religions and Worldly Politics.* New Brunswick. NJ: Rutgers University Press.

Demers, David. 1999. *Global Media: Menace or Messiah.* Cresskill, NJ: Hampton Press.

DeNavas-Walt, Carmen, Robert W. Cleveland, and Marc L. Raemer. 2001. *Money Income in the United States: 2000.* Washington, DC: U.S. Government Printing Office.

DePalma, Anthony. 1995a. "Racism? Mexico's in Denial." *New York Times,* June 11, p. E4.

———. 1995b. "For Mexico, NAFTA's Promise of Jobs Is Still Just a Promise." *New York Times,* October 10, Pp. A1, A10.

———. 1995c. "Insecurity Rocks Mexico's Cradle-to-Coffin System." *New York Times,* November 13, p. A4.

———. 1996. "For Mexico Indians, New Voice but Few Gains." *New York Times,* January 13, Pp. B1, B2.

———. 1999. "Rules to Protect a Culture Make for Confusion." *New York Times,* July 14, Pp. B1, B2.

DeParle, Jason. 1998. "Shrinking Welfare Rolls Leave Record High Share of Minorities." *New York Times,* July 27, Pp. Al, A12.

Department of Education. 1999. *Report on State Implementation of the Gun-Free Schools Act. School Year 1997–98.* Rockville, MD: Westat.

Department of Health and Human Services. 2002. "Change in TANF: Total Number of Recipients." Accessed January 19, 2002 (http://www.acf.dhhs.gov/news/stats/recipients.htm).

Department of Justice. 1988. *Report to the Nation on Crime and Justice.* 2d ed. Washington, DC: U.S. Government Printing Office.

———. 2001a. *Hate Crime Statistics, 1999.* Accessed June 21 (http://www.fbi.gov/).

———. 2001b. *Elderly Victims.* Accessed June 27 (http://www.ojp.usdoj.gov/ovc/publications/inFores/FirsTrep/eldvic.html).

———. 2001c. *Chapter 14 Supplement Victimization of the Elderly.* Accessed June 27 (http://www.ojp.usdoj.gov/ovc/assist/nvaa2000/academy/N-14-ELD.htm).

Department of Justice. 2001d. *Crime in the United States 2000. Uniform Crime Reports.* Washington, DC: U.S. Government Printing Office.

Department of Labor. 1995a. *Good for Business: Making Full Use of the Nation's Capital.* Washington, DC: U.S. Government Printing Office.

———. 1995b. *A Solid Investment: Making Full Use of the Nation's Human Capital.* Washington, DC: U.S. Government Printing Office.

———. 1998. "Work and Elder Care: Facts for Caregivers and Their Employers." Accessed November 20 (http://www.dol.gov/dol/wb/public/wb_pubs/elderc.htm).

Department of State. 2001. *Immigrant Visas Issued to Orphans Coming to the U.S."* Accessed August 1 (http://travel.state.gove/orphan_numbers.html).

Desai, Manisha. 1996. "If Peasants Build Their Own Dams, What Would the State Have Left to Do?" Pp. 209–224 in *Research in Social Movements, Conflicts and Change,* Vol. 19, edited by Michael Dobkowski and Isidor Wallimann. Greenwich, CT: JAI Press.

DeSimone, Bonnie. 2000. "Gold Tendency." *Chicago Tribune Magazine,* February 20, Pp. 9–19.

Devine, Don. 1972. *Political Culture of the United States: The Influence of Member Values on Regime Maintenance.* Boston: Little, Brown.

Devitt, James. 1999. *Framing Gender on the Campaign Trail: Women's Executive Leadership and the Press.* New York: Women's Leadership Conference.

Diani, Marie. 2000. "Social Movement Networks: Virtual and Real." *Information, Communication and Society.* Accessed October 14, 2001 (www.infosoc.co.uk).

Dillon, Sam. 1997. "Gay Rights, Prejudice and Politics in Mexico." *New York Times,* January 4, p. 4.

———. 1998. "Sex Bias at Border Plants in Mexico Reported by U.S." *New York Times,* January 13, p. A6.

Disaster Research Center. 2001a. *The Disaster Research Center.* Accessed October 14 (www.udel.edu/DRC/mission).

———. 2001b. "Teams From Disaster Research Center Study New York's 'Ground Zero.'" Accessed December 27, 2001 (www.udel.edu/PR/NewsReleases/2002/uct/10-22/drc.html).

Divyanathan, Denesh. 2000. "Jobs and Skills Mismatch Widens." *The Straits Times* (Singapore), May 20, p. 97.

Doeringer, Peter B., ed. 1990. *Bridges to Retirement: Older Workers in a Changing Labor Market.* Ithaca, NY: ILR Press.

Dolbeare, Kenneth M. 1982. *American Public Policy: A Citizen's Guide.* New York: McGraw-Hill.

Dolby, Nadine E. 2001. *Constructing Race: Youth Identity and Popular Culture in South Africa.* Albany, NY: State University of New York Press.

Domhoff, G. William. 1978. *Who Really Rules? New Haven and Community Power Reexamined.* New Brunswick, NJ: Transaction.

———. 2001. *Who Rules America?* 4th ed. New York: McGraw-Hill.

Dominick, Joseph R. 2002. *The Dynamics of Mass Communication: Media in the Digital Age.* 7th ed. New York: McGraw-Hill.

Donnelly, Jack. 1989. *Universal Human Rights in Theory and Practice.* New York: Cornell University Press.

Donohue, Elizabeth, Vincent Schiraldi, and Jason Ziedenberg. 1998. *School House Hype: School Shootings and Real Risks Kids Face in America.* New York: Justice Policy Institute.

Doob, Christopher Bates. 1999. *Racism: An American Cauldron.* 3d ed. New York: Longman.

Doppelt, Jack C., and Ellen Shearer. 1999. *Nonvoters: America's No-Shows.* Thousand Oaks, CA: Sage.

Dorai, Frances. 1998. *Insight Guide: Singapore.* Singapore: Insight Media, APA Publications.

Dore, Ronald P. 1976. *The Diploma Disease: Education, Qualification and Development.* Berkeley: University of California Press.

Doress, Irwin, and Jack Nusan Porter. 1977. *Kids in Cults: Why They Join. Why They Stay, Why They Leave.* Brookline, MA: Reconciliation Associates.

Dornbusch, Sanford M. "The Sociology of Adolescence." Pp. 233–259 in *Annual Review of Sociology, 1989,* edited by W. Richard Scott and Judith Blake. Palo Alto, CA: Annual Reviews.

Dotson, Floyd. 1991. "Community." p. 55 in *Encyclopedic Dictionary of Sociology.* 4th ed. Guilford, CT: Dushkin.

Dougherty, John, and David Holthouse. 1999. "Bordering on Exploitation." Accessed March 5 (http://www.phoenixnewtime.com/issies/1998-07-09/feature.html).

Dowd, James J. 1980. *Stratification among the Aged.* Monterey, CA: Brooks/Cole.

Downie, Andrew. 2000. "Brazilian Girls Turn to a Doll More Like Them." *Christian Science Monitor.* January 20. Accessed January 20 (http://www.csmonitor.com/durable/2000/01/20/fpls3-csm.shtml).

Doyle, James A. 1995. *The Male Experience.* 3d ed. Dubuque, IA: Brown & Benchmark.

———, and Michele A. Paludi. 1998. *Sex and Gender: The Human Experience.* 4th ed. New York: McGraw-Hill.

DPIC. 2000c. (See Death Penalty Information Center. 2000c).

Drucker, Peter F. 1999. "Beyond the Information Revolution." *Atlantic Monthly* 284 October:42–57.

Du Bois, W. E. B. 1909. *The Negro American Family.* Atlanta University. Reprinted 1970, Cambridge, MA: M.I.T. Press.

———. 1911. "The Girl Nobody Loved," *Social News* 2 (November):3.

Du, Hien Due. 1999. *The Vietnamese Americans.* Westport, CT: Greenwood Press.

Duberman, Lucille. 1976. *Social Inequality: Class and Caste in America.* Philadelphia: Lippincott.

Dugger, Celia W. 2001. "Relying on Hard and Soft Sells, India Pushes Sterilization." *New York Times,* June 22, Pp. A1, A10.

———. 1999. "Massacres of Low-Born Touch Off a Crisis in India." *New York Times,* March 15, p. A3.

Duke, Lynne. 1998. "Education Is Failing the Students." *Washington Post National Weekly Edition* 15 (June 26):16.

Dunbar-Ortiz, Roxanne. 1997. *Red Dirt: Growing Up Okie.* London: Verso.

Duneier, Mitchell. 1994a. "On the Job, but Behind the Scenes." *Chicago Tribune,* December 26, Pp. 1, 24.

———. 1994b. "Battling for Control." *Chicago Tribune,* December 28, Pp. 1, 8.

———. 1999. *Sidewalk.* New York: Farrar, Straus and Giroux.

Dunlap, Riley E. 1993. "From Environmental to Ecological Problems." Pp. 707–738 in *Introduction to Social Problems,* edited by Craig Calhoun and George Ritzer. New York: McGraw-Hill.

———, and William R. Catton, Jr. 1983. "What Environmental Sociologists Have in Common." *Sociological Inquiry* 53 (Spring):113–135.

Durand, Jorge, Emilio A. Parrado, and Douglas S. Massey. 1996. "Migradollars and Development: A Reconsideration of the Mexican Case." *International Migration Review* 30 (Summer):423–444.

Durkheim, Émile. [1912] 2001. *The Elementary Forms of Religious Life.* A new translation by Carol Cosman. New York: Oxford University Press.

———. [1893] 1933. *Division of Labor in Society.* Translated by George Simpson. Reprint, New York: Free Press.

———. [1897] 1951. *Suicide.* Translated by John A. Spaulding and George Simpson. Reprint, New York: Free Press.

———. [1845] 1964. *The Rules of Sociological Method.* Translated by Sarah A. Solovay and John H. Mueller. Reprint, New York: Free Press.

Durning, Alan B. 1993. "Supporting Indigenous Peoples." Pp. 80–100 in *State of the World,* edited by Lester R. Brown. New York: Norton.

Dynes, Russell R. 1978. "Interorganizational Relations in Communities under Stress." Pp. 50–64 in *Disasters: Theory and Research,* edited by E. L. Quarantelli. Beverly Hills, CA: Sage.

E

Ebaugh, Helen Rose Fuchs. 1988. *Becoming an Ex: The Process of Role Exit.* Chicago: University of Chicago Press.

Eberstadt, Nicholas. 2001. "The Population Implosion." *Foreign Policy* (March/April): 42–58.

Eckenwiler, Mark. 1995. "In the Eyes of the Law." *Internet World* (August):74, 76–77.

Eckholm, Erik. 1994. "While Congress Remains Silent, Health Care Transforms Itself." *New York Times,* December 18, Pp. 1, 34.

The Economist. 1994. "Parent Power." 331 (May 7):83.

———. 1995. Home Sweet Home." 336 (September 9):25–26, 29, 32.

———. 1996. "It's Normal to Be Queer." (January 6):68–70.

———. 1998. "Cruel and Ever More Unusual." 346 (February 14).

Education Commission of the States. 2001. *A Closer Look: State Policy Trends in Three Key Areas of the Bush Education Plan—Testing, Accountability and School Choice.* Accessed July 19 (http://www.ecs.org/clearinghouse/).

Education Week. 2000. "Who Should Teach? The States Decide." *Education Week Online.* 19 (No. 18):89. Available (www.edweek. org).

Edwards, Tamala M. 2001. "How Med Students Put Abortion Back in the Classroom." *Time* 157 (May 7): 59–60.

Efron, Sonni. 1997. "In Japan, Even Tots Must Make the Grade." *Los Angeles Times,* February 16, Pp. A1, A17.

———. 1998. Japanese in Quandary on Fertility." *Los Angeles Times,* July 27, Pp. A1, A6.

Egan, Timothy. 1998. "New Prosperity Brings New Conflict to Indian Country." *New York Times,* March 8, Pp. 1, 24.

Ehrenreich, Barbara. 2001. *Nickeled and Dimed: On (Not) Getting By in America.* New York: Metropolitan.

Ehrlich, Paul R. 1968. *The Population Bomb.* New York: Ballantine.

———, and Anne H. Ehrlich. 1990. *The Population Explosion.* New York: Simon and Schuster.

———, and Katherine Ellison. 2002. "A Looming Threat We Won't Face." *Los Angeles Times.* (January 20), p. M6.

Eisenberg, David M. et al. 1998. "Trends in Alternative Medicine Use in the United States, 1990–1997." *Journal of the American Medical Association* 280 (November 11): 1569–1636.

Eisler, Peter. 2000. "This Is Only a Test, but Lives Are at Stake." *USA Today,* June 30, Pp. 219–220.

Eitzen, D. Stanley, ed. 2001. *Sport in Contemporary Society: An Anthology.* 6th ed. New York: Worth.

Ekman, Paul, Wallace V. Friesen, and John Bear. 1984. "The International Language of Gestures." *Psychology Today* 18 (May): 64–69.

El Nasser, Haya. 1999. "Soaring Housing Costs Are Culprit in Suburban Poverty." *USA Today,* April 28, Pp. A1, A2.

———. 2001. "Minorities Reshape Suburbs." *USA Today,* July 9, p. 1A.

———, and Paul Overberg. 2001. "What You Don't Know about Sprawl." *USA Today,* February 22, Pp. 1A, 8A.

Elias, Marilyn. 1996. "Researchers Fight Child Consent Bill." *USA Today,* January 2, p. A1.

Ellingwood, Ken. 2001. "Results of Crackdown and Border Called Mixed." *Los Angeles Times,* August 4, p. B9.

Elliot, Helene. 1997. "Having an Olympic Team Is Their Miracle on Ice." *Los Angeles Times,* March 25, Sports Section, p. 5.

Ellis, Virginia, and Ken Ellingwood. 1998. "Welfare to Work: Are There Enough Jobs?" *Los Angeles Times,* February 8, Pp. A1, A30.

Ellison, Ralph. 1952. *Invisible Man.* New York: Random House.

Ellwood, David T., Rebecca M. Blank, Joseph Blasi, Douglas Kruse, William A. Niskanen, and Karen Lynn-Dyson. 2000. *A Working Nation: Workers, Work, and Government in the New Economy.* New York: Russell Sage Foundation.

Elmer-DeWitt, Philip. 1995. "Welcome to Cyberspace." *Time* 145 (Special Issue, Spring):4–11.

Ely, Robin J. 1995. "The Power of Demography: Women's Social Construction of Gender Identity at Work." *Academy of Management Journal* 38 (3): 589–634.

Emery, David. 1997. "The Kidney Snatchers." Accessed December 21, 1999 (http://urbanlegends.about.com/culture/urbanlegends/library/blkid.htm).

Engardio, Pete. 1999. "Activists Without Borders." *BusinessWeek,* October 4, Pp. 144–145, 148, 150.

Engels, Friedrich [1884] 1959. "The Origin of the Family, Private Property and the State." Pp. 392–394, excerpted in *Marx and Engels: Basic Writings on Politics and Philosophy,* edited by Lewis Feuer. Garden City, NY: Anchor.

England, Paula. 1999. "The Impact of Feminist Thought on Sociology." *Contemporary Sociology* 28 (May):263–268.

Enloe, Cynthia. 1990. *Bananas, Beaches, and Bases: Making Feminist Sense of International Politics.* Berkeley: University of California Press.

Entine, Jon, and Martha Nichols. 1996. "Blowing the Whistle on Meaningless 'Good Intentions.'" *Chicago Tribune,* June 20, Sec. 1, p. 21.

Entwistle, Doris R., Karl L. Alexander, Linda Steffel Olson. 1997. *Children, Schools and Inequality.* Boulder, CO: Westview Press.

Epstein, Cynthia Fuchs. 1999. "The Major Myth of the Women's Movement." *Dissent* (Fall):83–111.

Equal Employment Opportunity Commission. 2001. *Age Discrimination in Employment Act (ADEA) Changes FY 1992–FY 2000.* Accessed December 10 (http://www.eeoc.gov/stats/adea.html).

Ericson, Nels. 2001. "Substance Abuse: The Nation's Number One Health Problem." *OJJDP Fact Sheet* 17 (May):1–2.

Erikson, Kai. 1966. *Wayward Puritans: A Study in the Sociology of Deviance.* New York: Wiley.

———. 1986. "On Work and Alienation." *American Sociological Review* 51 (February):1–8.

———. 1994. *A New Species of Trouble: The Human Experience of Modern Disasters.* New York: Norton.

Etzioni, Amitai. 1964. *Modern Organization.* Englewood Cliffs, NJ: Prentice Hall.

———. 1985. "Shady Corporate Practices." *New York Times,* November 15, p. A35.

———. 1990. "Going Soft on Corporate Crime." *Washington Post,* April 1, p. C3.

———. 1996. "Why Fear Date Rape?" *USA Today,* May 20, p. 14A.

Evans, Peter. 1979. *Dependent Development.* Princeton, NJ: Princeton University Press.

Evans, Sara. 1980. *Personal Politics: The Roots of Women's Liberation in the Civil Rights Movement and the New Left.* New York: Vintage.

F

Facts on File Weekly News Report. 2001a. "Switzerland: Votes Solidly Reject EU Membership." Accessed March 2 (www.facts.com).

———. 2001b. "Great Britain: British Elections, 1997 and 2001." Accessed June 14 (www.facts.com).

Fager, Marty, Mike Bradley, Lonnie Danchik, and Tom Wodetski. 1971. *Unbecoming Men.* Washington, NJ: Times Change.

Fahs, Ivan J., Dan A. Lewis, C. James Carr, and Mark W. Field. 1997. "Homelessness in an Affluent Suburb: The Story of Wheaton, Illinois." Paper presented at the annual meeting of the Illinois Sociological Association, October, Rockford, IL.

Faludi, Susan. 1999. *Stiffed: The Betrayal of the American Man.* New York: William Morrow.

Farhi, Paul. 1995. "Selling Is as Selling Does!" *Washington Post,* April 30, p. H1.

———, and Megan Rosenfeld. 1998. "Exporting America." *Washington Post National Weekly Edition* 16 (November 30):6–7.

Farley, Maggie. 1998. "Indonesia's Chinese Fearful of Backlash." *Los Angeles Times,* January 31, Pp. A1, A8–A9.

Farley, Reynolds. 2001. *Identifying with Multiple Races: A Social Movement That Succeeded but Failed?* Ann Arbor: Population Studies Center, University of Michigan.

Farr, Grant M. 1999. *Modern Iran.* New York: McGraw-Hill.

Feagin, Joe R. 1983. *The Urban Real Estate Came: Playing Monopoly with Real Money.* Englewood Cliffs, NJ: Prentice Hall.

———. 1989. *Minority Group Issues in Higher Education: Learning from Qualitative Research.* Norman, OK: Center for Research on Minority Education, University of Oklahoma.

———, Harnán Vera, and Nikitah Imani. 1996. *The Agony of Education: Black Students at White Colleges and Universities.* New York: Routledge.

———. 2001. "Social Justice and Sociology: Agenda for the Twenty-first Century." *American Sociological Review* 66 (February):1–20.

Featherman, David L., and Robert M. Hauser. 1978. *Opportunity and Change.* New York: Aeodus.

Fein, Helen. 1995. "Gender and Genocide." Paper presented at the annual meeting of the American Sociological Association, Washington, DC.

Feinglass, Joe. 1987. "Next, the McDRG." *The Progressive* 51 (January):28.

Feketekuty, Geza. 2001. "Globalization—Why All the Fuss?" p. 191 in *2001 Britannica Book of the Year.* Chicago: Encyclopedia Britannica.

Felson, Marcus. 1998. *Crime and Everyday Life: Insights and Implications for Society.* 2d ed. Thousand Oaks, CA: Pine Forge Press.

Ferman, Louis A., Stuart Henry, and Michael Hoyman, ed. 1987. *The Informal Economy.* Newbury Park, CA: Sage. Published as September 1987 issue of *The Annals of the American Academy of Political and Social Science.*

Fernández, Sandy. 1996. "The Cyber Cops." *Ms.* 6 (May/June):22–23.

Fernea, Elizabeth. 1998. *In Search of Islamic Feminism: One Woman's Global Journey.* New York: Bantam Books.

Ferree, Myra Marx, and David A. Merrill. 2000. "Hot Movements, Cold Cognition: Thinking about Social Movements in Gendered Frames." *Contemporary Society* 29 (May): 454–462.

Ferrell, Tom. 1979 "More Choose to Live outside Marriage." *New York Times,* July 1, p. E7.

Feuer, Lewis S., ed. 1959. *Karl Marx and Friedrich Engels: Basic Writings on Politics and Philosophy.* Garden City, NY: Doubleday.

Fiala, Robert. 1992. "Postindustrial Society." Pp. 1512–1522 in *Encyclopedia of Sociology,* Vol. 3, edited by Edgar F. Borgatta and Marie L. Borgatta. New York: Macmillan.

Fields, Jason. 2001. "America's Families and Living Arrangements." *Current Population Reports,* Ser. Pp. 20–537. Washington, DC: Government Printing Office.

———, and Charles L. Clark. 1999. "Unbinding the Ties: Edit Effects of Marital Status on Same Gender Groups." Paper presented at the annual meeting of the American Sociological Association, August, Chicago.

Finder, Alan. 1995. "Despite Tough Laws, Sweatshops Flourish." *New York Times,* January 6, Pp. A1, B4.

Findlay, Steven. 1998. "85% of American Workers Using HMOs." *USA Today,* January 20, p. 3A.

Fine, Gary Alan. 1984. "Negotiated Orders and Organizational Cultures." Pp. 239–262 in *Annual Review of Sociology, 1984,* edited by Ralph Turner. Palo Alto, CA: Annual Reviews.

———. 1996. *Kitchens: The Culture of Restaurant Work.* Berkeley, CA: University of California Press.

———, and Patricia A. Turner. 2001. *Whispers on the Color Line: Rumor and Race in America.* Berkeley, CA: University of California Press.

Finkel, Steven E., and James B. Rule. 1987. "Relative Deprivation and Related Psychological Theories of Civil Violence: A Critical Review." *Research in Social Movements* 9:47–69.

Finkenauer, James O., and Patricia W. Gavin. 1999. *Scared Straight: The Panacea Phenomenon Revisited.* Prospect Heights, IL: Waveland Press.

Firestone, David. 1999. "School Prayer Is Revived as an Issue in Alabama." *New York Times,* July 15, p. A14.

Firestone, Shulamith. 1970. *The Dialectic of Sex: The Case for Feminist Revolution.* New York: Bantam.

Firtmat, Gustavo Perez. 1994. *Life on Hyphen: The Cuban-American Way.* Austin: University of Texas Press.

Fisher, Ian. 1999. "Selling Sudan's Slaves into Freedom." *New York Times,* April 25, p. A6.

Fitzgerald, Kathleen J., and Diane M. Rodgers. 2000. "Radical Social Movement Organization: A Theoretical Model." *The Sociological Quarterly* 41 (No. 4):573–592.

Flacks, Richard. 1971. *Youth and Social Change.* Chicago: Markham.

Flanders, Stephanie. 2001. "In the Shadow of AIDS, a World of Other Problems." *New York Times,* June 24, p. 3.

Flavin, Jeanne. 1998. "Razing the Wall: A Feminist Critique of Sentencing Theory, Research, and Policy." Pp. 145–164 in *Cutting the Edge,* edited by Jeffrey Ross. Westport, CT: Praeger.

Fletcher, Connie. 1995. "On the Line: Women Cops Speak Out." *Chicago Tribune Magazine,* February 19, Pp. 14–19.

Fletcher, Robert S. 1943. *History of Oberlin College to the Civil War.* Oberlin, OH: Oberlin College Press.

Flexner, Eleanor. 1972. *Century of Struggle: The Women's Rights Movement in the United States.* New York: Atheneum.

Flores, William V., and Riva Benmayor, ed. 1997. *Latino Cultural Citizenship: Claiming Identity, Space and Rights.* Boston: Beacon Press.

Fordham, Lynn Ashley. 2001. Paper presented at the annual meeting of Radiological Society of North America, Chicago.

Form, William. 1992. "Labor Movements and Unions," Vol. 3. Pp. 1054–1060 in *Encyclopedia of Sociology,* edited by Edgar F. Borgatta and Marie L. Borgatta. New York: Macmillan.

Fornos, Werner. 1997. *1997 World Population Overview.* Washington, DC: The Population Institute.

Forsythe, David P. 1990. "Human Rights in U.S. Foreign Policy: Retrospect and Prospect," *Political Science Quarterly* 105(3):435–454.

Fortune. 2001a. "Fortune 500: America's Largest Corporations." Accessed August 24 (www. Fortune.com).

———. 2001b. "Company Information: AOL Time Warner Inc." Accessed August 24 (www.Fortune.com).

Fox, Susannah. 2001. *Wired Seniors: A Fervent Few, Inspired by Family Ties.* Washington, DC: Pew Internet and American Life Project.

———, and Lee Rainie. 2001. *Time Online: Why Some People Use the Internet More Than Before and Why Some Use It Less.* Washington, DC: Pew Internet and American Life Project.

France, David. 2000. "Slavery's New Face." *Newsweek* 136 (December 18):61–65.

Franklin, John Hope, and Alfred A. Moss. 2000. *From Slavery to Freedom: A History of African Americans.* 8th ed. Upper Saddle River, NJ: Prentice Hall.

Fraser, Jill Andresley. 2001. *White Collar Sweatshop.* New York: Norton.

Freeman, Jo. 1973. "The Origins of the Women's Liberation Movement." *American Journal of Sociology* 78 (January):792–811.

———. 1975. *The Politics of Women's Liberation.* New York: McKay.

Freidson, Eliot. 1970. *Profession of Medicine.* New York: Dodd, Mead.

Freire, Paulo. 1970. *Pedagogy of the Oppressed.* New York: Herder and Herder.

French, Hillary. 2000. *Vanishing Borders: Protecting the Planet in the Age of Globalization.* New York: Norton.

French, Howard W. 2000a. "The Pretenders." *New York Times Magazine,* December 3, Pp. 86–88.

———. 2000b. "Women Win a Battle, But Job Bias Still Rules Japan." *New York Times,* February 26, p. A3.

———. 2001a. "Diploma at Hand, Japanese Women Find Glass Ceiling Reinforced with Iron." *New York Times,* January 1, p. A4.

———. 2001b. "Brooding Over Its Homelessness, Japan Sees a Broken System." *New York Times,* February 2, Pp. A1, A10.

Freudenheim, Milt. 1990. "Employers Balk at High Cost of High-Tech Medical Care." *New York Times,* April 29, Pp. 1, 16.

Frey, William H. 2001a. "Micro Melting Pots." *American Demographics,* June, Pp. 20–23.

———. 2001b. *Melting Pot Suburbs: A Census 2000 Study of Suburban Diversity.* Washington, DC: The Brookings Institution.

Fridlund, Alan. J., Paul Erkman, and Harriet Oster. 1987. "Facial Expressions of Emotion; Review of Literature 1970–1983." Pp. 143–224 in *Nonverbal Behavior and Communication,* 2d ed., edited by Aron W. Seigman and Stanley Feldstein. Hillsdale, NJ: Lawrence Erlbaum Associates.

Friedan, Betty. 1963. *The Feminine Mystique.* New York: Dell.

Friedland, Jonathon. 2000. "An American in Mexico Champions Midwifery as a Worthy Profession." *Wall Street Monitor,* February 15, Pp. A1, A12.

Friedrichs, David O. 1998. "New Directions in Critical Criminology and White Collar Crime." Pp. 77–91 in *Cutting the Edge,* edited by Jeffrey Ross. Westport, CT: Praeger.

Fries, Kenny. 1997. *Staring Back: The Disability Experience from the Inside Out.* New York: Penguin.

Friess, Steve. 2001. "Chinese Gays, Slowly Come Out into the Open." *USA Today,* March 9, p. 6A.

Fullerton, Howard N., Jr., 1997. "Labor Force 2006: Slowing Down and Changing Composition." *Monthly Labor Review* (November):23–38.

———. 1999. "Labor Force Projections to 2008: Steady Growth and Changing Composition." *Monthly Labor Review* (November):19–32.

Furstenberg, Frank, and Andrew Cherlin. 1991. *Divided Families: What Happens to Children When Parents Part.* Cambridge, MA: Harvard University Press.

G

Galant, Debra. 2000. "Finding a Substitute for Office Chitchat." *New York Times,* February 16, Sec. Retirement, p. 20.

Gale, Elaine. 1999. "A New Point of View." *Los Angeles Times,* January 11, Pp. B1, B3.

Gale Research Group. 2001. *Encyclopedia of Associations: National Organizations of the U.S.* Detroit: Gale Research Group.

Gallup. 2001. *Poll Topics and Trends: Race Relations.* Accessed January 28, 2002 (www.gallup.com/poll/topics/race.asp).

———. 2002a. *Americans Still Not Content with Abortion Laws.* January 22, 2002. Accessed January 28, 2002 (www.gallup.com).

Gamson, Joshua. 1989. "Silence, Death, and the Invisible Enemy: AIDS Activism and Social Movement 'Newness.'" *Social Problems* 36 (October):351–367.

———. 1998. *Freaks Talk Back: Tabloid Talk Shows and Sexual Nonconformity.* Chicago: University of Chicago Press.

Gans, Herbert J. 1991. *People, Plans, and Policies: Essays on Poverty, Racism, and Other National Urban Problems.* New York: Columbia University Press and Russell Sage Foundation.

———. 1995. *The War against the Poor: The Underclass and Antipoverty Policy.* New York: Basic Books.

Ganzeboom, Harry B. G., Ruud Luijkx, and Donald J. Treiman. 1989. "Intergenerational Class Mobility in Comparative Perspective." Pp. 3–84 in *Research in Social Stratification and Mobility,* edited by Arne L. Kalleberg. Greenwich, CT: JAI Press.

———, Donald J. Treiman, and Woult C. Ultee. 1991. "Comparative Intergenerational Stratification Research." Pp. 277–302 in *Annual Review of Sociology, 1991,* edited by W. Richard Scott. Palo Alto, CA: Annual Reviews.

Gardner, Carol Brooks. 1989. "Analyzing Gender in Public Places: Rethinking Goffman's Vision of Everyday Life." *American Sociologist* 20 (Spring):42–56.

———. 1990. "Safe Conduct: Women, Crime, and Self in Public Places." *Social Problems* 37 (August):311–328.

———. 1995. *Passing By: Gender and Public Harassment.* Berkeley: University of California Press.

Gardner, Gary, and Brian Halweil. 2000. *Underfed and Overfed: The Global Epidemic of Malnutrition.* Washington, DC: Worldwatch Institute.

Gardner, Howard. 2000. "The Testing Obsession." *Los Angeles Times,* December 31, Pp. M1, M6.

Gardner, Marilyn. 2001. "Media's Eye on Moms." *Christian Science Monitor,* May 30, Pp. 12–13.

Garfinkel, Harold. 1956. "Conditions of Successful Degradation Ceremonies." *American Journal of Sociology* 61 (March):420–424.

Garner, Roberta. 1996. *Contemporary Movements and Ideologies.* New York: McGraw-Hill.

———. 1999. "Virtual Social Movements." Presented at Zaldfest: A conference in honor of Mayer Zald. September 17, Ann Arbor, MI.

Garreau, Joel. 1991. *Edge City: Life on the New Frontier.* New York: Doubleday.

Garrison, Jessica. 2001. "Staying Home to Go to School." *Los Angeles Times,* May 8, p. B6.

Garza, Melita Marie. 1993. "The Cordi-Marian Annual Cotillion." *Chicago Tribune,* May 7, Sec. C, Pp. 1, 5.

Gates, Henry Louis, Jr. 1999. "One Internet, Two Nations." *New York Times,* October 31, p. A15.

Gauette, Nicole. 1998. "Rules for Raising Japanese Kids." *Christian Science Monitor,* October 14, Pp. B1, B6.

Gearty, Robert. 1996. "Beware of Pickpockets." *Chicago Daily News*, November 19, p. 5.

Gecas, Viktor. 1982. "The Self-Concept." Pp. 1–33 in *Annual Review of Sociology, 1982*, edited by Ralph H. Turner and James F. Short, Jr. Palo Alto, CA: Annual Reviews.

———. 1992. "Socialization." Pp. 1863–1872 in *Encyclopedia of Sociology*, Vol. 4, edited by Edgar F. Borgatta and Marie L. Borgatta. New York: Macmillan.

Geckler, Cheri. 1995. *Practice Perspectives and Medical Decision-Making in Medical Residents: Gender Differences—A Preliminary Report*. Wellesley, MA: Center for Research on Women.

Gelbspan, Ross. 2002. "Beyond Kyoto Lite." *The American Prospect*. (February 25), Pp. 26–27.

Gelles, Richard J., and Claire Pedrick Cornell. 1990. *Intimate Violence in Families*. 2d ed. Newbury Park, CA: Sage.

General Accounting Office. 2000. *Women's Health: NIH Has Increased Its Efforts to Include Women in Research*. Washington, DC: U.S. Government Printing Office.

———. 2001. *School Vouchers: Publicly Funded Programs in Cleveland and Milwaukee*. Washington, DC: U.S. Government Printing Office.

———. 2002. *A New Look Through the Glass Ceiling: Where Are the Women?* Washington, D.C.: General Accounting Office.

Gereffi, Bary, and Miguel Kovzeniewicz, ed. 1994. *Commodity Chains and Global Capitalism*. New York: Praegar.

Gerth, H. H., and C. Wright Mills. 1958. *From Max Weber: Essays in Sociology*. New York: Galaxy.

Gest, Ted. 1985. "Are White-Collar Crooks Getting Off Too Easy?" *U.S. News & World Report* 99 (July 1):43.

Geyh, Paul. 1998. "Feminism Fatale?" *Chicago Tribune*, July 26, Sec. 13, Pp. 1, 6.

Gibbs, Nancy. 1993. "Rx for Death." *Time*, May 31, Pp. 34–39.

———. 2001. "If You Want to Humble an Empire." *Time* (September, special issue).

Gill, Brian P., Michael Timpane, Karen E. Russ, and Dominic J. Brewer. 2001. *Rhetoric Versus Reality: What We Know and What We Need to Know About Vouchers and Charter Schools*. Santa Monica, CA: RAND.

Gillespie, Mark. 1999. "Poll Releases, April 6, 1999. U.S. Gun Ownership Continues Broad Decline." Accessed July 2, 2000 (http://www.gallup.com/poll/releases/pr990406.asp).

Giordano, Peggy C., Stephen A. Cernkovich, and Alfred DeMaris. 1993. "The Family and Peer Relations of Black Adolescents." *Journal of Marriage and Family* 55 (May): 277–287.

Giroux, Henry A. 1988. *Schooling and the Struggle for Public Life: Critical Pedagogy in the Modern Age*. Minneapolis: University of Minnesota Press.

GLAAD. 2001. *About GLAAD*. Accessed October 14 (www.glaad.org).

Gladwell, Malcolm. 2000. *The Tipping Point*. Boston: Little, Brown.

Glanton, Dahleen. 2001. "Sprawl Tests Atlanta's Limits." *New York Times*, August 7, Pp. 1, 16.

Glanz, James. 2001. "Darwin vs. Design: Evolutionists' New Battle." *New York Times*, April 8, Pp. 1, 32.

Glascock, Anthony P. 1990. "By Any Other Name, It Is Still Killing: A Comparison of the Treatment of the Elderly in American and Other Societies." Pp. 44–56 in *The Cultural Context of Aging: Worldwide Perspective*, edited by Jay Sokolovsky. New York: Bergen and Garvey.

Gleick, James. 1999. *Faster: The Acceleration of Just About Everything*. New York: Pantheon.

Global Alliance for Workers and Communities. 2001. *Workers' Voices: An Interim Report on Workers' Needs and Aspirations in Nine Nike Contract Factories in Indonesia*. Baltimore, MD: Global Alliance.

Global Reach. 2000. *Global Internet Statistics (by Language)*. September 30, 2000. Accessed November 7, 2000 (http://www.glreach.com/globstats/index.php3).

———. 2001. *Global Internet Statistics (by Language)*. Accessed October 14, 2001 (www.glreach.com).

Goering, Laura. 2001. "Mexico City Losing Gains in Air Quality." *Chicago Tribune*, July 5, p. 7.

Goffman, Erving. 1959. *The Presentation of Self in Everyday Life*. New York: Doubleday.

———. 1961. *Asylums: Essays on the Social Situation of Mental Patients and Other Inmates*. Garden City, NY: Doubleday.

———. 1963a. *Stigma: Notes on Management of Spoiled Identity*. Englewood Cliffs, NJ: Prentice Hall.

———. 1963b. *Behavior in Public Places*. New York: Free Press.

———. 1971. *Relations in Public*. New York: Basic Books.

———. 1979. *Gender Advertisements*. New York: Harper and Row.

Goffman, Erving. 1979. *Gender Advertisements*. Cambridge. MA: Harvard University Press.

Golden, Frederic. 1999. "Who's Afraid of Frankenfood?" *Time*, November 29, Pp. 49–50.

Goldman, Benjamin A., and Laura Fitton. 1994. *Toxic Wastes and Race Revisited: An Update of the 1987 Report on the Racial and Social Economic Characteristics of Communities with Hazardous Waste*. Washington, DC: Center for Policy Alternatives, United Church of Christ Commission for Racial Justice, and NAACP.

Goldman, Robert, and Stephen Papson. 1998. *Nike Culture: The Sign of the Swoosh*. London: Sage.

Goldstein, Andrew. 2001. "Setback for Vouchers." *Time* 156 (January 1):142.

Goldstein, Greg. 1998. "World Health Organization and Housing." Pp. 636–637 in *The Encyclopedia of Housing*, edited by Willem van Vliet. Thousand Oaks, CA: Sage.

Goldstein, Melvyn C., and Cynthia M. Beall. 1981. "Modernization and Aging in the Third and Fourth World: Views from the Rural Hinterland in Nepal." *Human Organization* 40 (Spring):48–55.

Gole, Nilofer. 1997. "Lifting the Veil—Reform vs. Tradition in Turkey—An Interview." *Manushi*, May 1.

Goleman, Daniel, 1991. "New Ways to Battle Bias: Fight Acts, Not Feelings." *New York Times*, July 16, Pp. C1, C8.

Gonnut, Jean Pierre. 2001. Interview. June 18, 2001.

Gonzales, John M. 1997. "Relearning a Lost Language." *Los Angeles Times*, May 26, p. A1.

Goode, Erica. 1999. "For Good Health, It Helps to Be Rich and Important." *New York Times*, June 1, Pp. 1, 9.

Goode, William J. 1959. "The Theoretical Importance of Love." *American Sociological Review* 24 (February):38–47.

Goodgame, Dan. 1993. "Welfare for the Well-Off." *Time* 141 (February 22):36–38.

Gordon, Jesse, and Knickerbocker. 2001. "The Sweat Behind the Shirt: The Labor History of a Gap Sweatshirt." *The Nation* 273 (September 3/10):14.

Gornick, Janet C. 2001. "Cancel the Funeral." *Dissent* (Summer):13–18.

———, and Marcia K. Meyers. 2001. "Support for Working Families: What the United States Can Learn from Europe." *American Prospect* (January):3–7.

Gornick, Vivian. 1979. "Introduction" to *Gender Advertisements*. Cambridge, MA: Harvard University Press.

Gottdiener, Mark, and Joe R. Feagin. 1988. "The Paradigm Shift in Urban Sociology." *Urban Affairs Quarterly* 24 (December):163–187.

———, and Ray Hutchison. 2000. *The New Urban Sociology*. 2d ed. New York: McGraw-Hill.

Gottfredson, Michael, and Travis Hirschi. 1990. *A General Theory of Crime*. Palo Alto, CA: Stanford University Press.

Gottschalk, Peter, Sara McLanahan, and Gary Sandefur. 1994. "The Dynamics and Intergenerational Transmission of Poverty and Welfare Participation." Pp. 85–108 in *Confronting Poverty: Prescriptions for Change*, edited by Sheldon H. Danziger, Gary D. Sandefur, and Daniel H. Weinburg. Cambridge, MA: Harvard University Press.

Gough, E. Kathleen. 1974. "Nayar: Central Kerala." Pp. 298–384 in *Matrilineal Kinship*, edited by David Schneider and E. Kathleen Gough. Berkeley: University of California Press.

Gouldner, Alvin. 1960. "The Norm of Reciprocity." *American Sociological Review* 25 (April):161–177.

———. 1970. *The Coming Crisis of Western Sociology*. New York: Basic Books.

Gove, Walter R., ed. 1980. *The Labelling of Deviance*, 2d ed. Beverly Hills, CA: Sage.

Gramsci, Antonio. 1929. *Selections from the Prison Notebooks*. Antonio Gramsci. Edited and translated by Quintin Hoare and Geoffrey Nowell Smith, eds. London: Lawrence and Wishort.

Greeley, Andrew M. 1989. "Protestant and Catholic: Is the Analogical Imagination Extinct?" *American Sociological Review* 54 (August):485–502.

———. 2001. *The Catholic Imagination*. Berkeley: University of California Press.

Green, Dan S., and Edwin D. Driver. 1978. "Introduction." Pp. 1–60 in *W. E. B. DuBois on Sociology and the Black Community*, edited by Dan S. Green and Edwin D. Driver. Chicago: University of Chicago Press.

Greene, Jay P. 1998. "A Meta-Analysis of the Effectiveness of Bilingual Education." Sponsored by the Toms River Policy Initiative. Accessed July 1 (http://data.Fas.harvard.edu/pepg/biling.htm).

Greenhouse, Linda. 1998. "High Court Ruling Says Harassment Includes Same Sex." *New York Times,* March 5, Pp. A1 , A17.

Greenhouse, Steven. 2000. "Report Faults Laws for Slowing Growth of Unions." *New York Times,* October 24, p. A14.

———. 2000. "Temp Workers at Microsoft Win Lawsuit." *New York Times,* December 13, p. C1.

———. 2001. "Problems Seen for Teenagers Who Hold Jobs." *New York Times,* January 29, Pp. A1, A22.

Greenman, Catherine. 2001. "Mapping Keeps NY Rescuers Safe." *Chicago Tribune,* October 8, Sec. 4, p. 2.

Greenwood, Ernest. 1957. "Attributes of a Profession." *Social Work* 2 (July):45–55.

Grieco, Elizabeth M., and Rachel C. Cassidy. 2001. "Overview of Race and Hispanic Origin." *Current Population Reports Series* CENBR/01–1. Washington, DC: U.S. Government Printing Office.

Grob, Gerald N. 1995. "The Paradox of Deinstitutionalization." *Society* 32 (July/August):51–59.

Grossman, David C. et al. 1997. "Effectiveness of a Violence Prevention Curriculum among Children in Elementary School." *Journal of the American Medical Association* 277 (May 28):1605–1617.

Groza, Victor, Daniela F. Ileana, and Ivor Irwin. 1999. *A Peacock or a Crow: Stories, Interviews, and Commentaries on Romanian Adoptions.* Euclid, OH: Williams Custom Publishing.

Gubrium, Jabe F., and James A. Holstein, eds. 2001. *Handbook of Interview Research: Context and Method.* Thousand Oaks, CA: Sage.

Guterman, Lila. 2000. "Why the 25-Year-Old Battle over Sociology Is More than Just 'An Academic Sideshow.'" *Chronicle of Higher Education,* July 7, Pp. A17–A18.

Gutiérrez, Gustavo. 1990. "Theology and the Social Sciences," in Paul E. Sigmund, *Liberation Theology at the Crossroads: Democracy or Revolution?* New York: Oxford University Press, Pp. 214–225.

Gwynne, S. C., and John E. Dickerson. 1997. "Lost in the E-Mail." *Time* 149 (April 21):88–90.

H

Haas, Michael, ed. 1999. *The Singapore Puzzle.* Westport, CT: Praeger.

Hacker, Andrew. 1964. "Power to Do What?" Pp. 134–146 in *The New Sociology,* edited by Irving Louis Horowitz. New York: Oxford University Press.

Hacker, Helen Mayer. 1951. "Women as a Minority Group." *Social Forces* 30 (October):60–69.

———. 1974. "Women as a Minority Group, Twenty Years Later." Pp. 124–134 in *Who Discriminates against Women?,* edited by Florence Denmark. Beverly Hills, CA: Sage.

Haines, Valerie A. 1988. "Is Spencer's Theory an Evolutionary Theory?" *American Journal of Sociology* 93 (March):1200–1223.

Hale, Ellen. 2001. "Many Britons Smile on Spread of Candid Cameras." *USA Today,* September 26, p. 9A.

Hall, Kay. 1999. "Work From Here." *Computer User* 18 (November):32.

Hall, Mimi. 1993. "Genetic-Sex-Testing a Medical Mine Field." *USA Today,* December 20, p. 6A.

Hall, Peter. 1977. *The World Cities.* London: Weidenfeld and Nicolson.

Hall, Robert H. 1982. "The Truth about Brown Lung." *Business and Society Review* 40 (Winter 1981–82):15–20.

Haller, Max, Wolfgang Konig, Peter Krause, and Karin Kurz. 1990. "Patterns of Career Mobility and Structural Positions in Advanced Capitalist Societies: A Comparison of Men in Austria, France, and the United States." *American Sociological Review* 50 (October):579–603.

Hallinan, Maureen T. 1997. "The Sociological Study of Social Change." *American Sociological Review* 62 (February):1–11.

Hani, Yoko. 1998. "Hot Pots Wired to Help the Elderly." *Japan Times Weekly International Edition,* April 13, p. 16.

Hank, Karsten. 2001. "Changes in Child Care Could Reduce Job Options for Eastern German Mothers." *Population Today* 29 (April):3, 6.

Harap, Louis. 1982. "Marxism and Religion: Social Functions of Religious Belief." *Jewish Currents* 36 (January):12–17, 32–35.

Harlow, Harry F. 1971. *Learning to Love.* New York: Ballantine.

Harmon, Amy. 1998. "The Law Where There Is No Land." *New York Times,* March 16, Pp. C1, C9.

Harrington, Michael. 1980. "The New Class and the Left." Pp. 123–138 in *The New Class,* edited by B. Bruce Briggs. Brunswick, NJ: Transaction.

Harris, Chauncy D., and Edward Ullman. 1945. "The Nature of Cities." *Annals of the American Academy of Political and Social Science* 242 (November):7–17.

Harris, Judith Rich. 1998. *The Nurture Assumption: Why Children Turn Out the Way They Do.* New York: Free Press.

Hart, Elva Tueviño. 1999. *Barefoot Heart: Stories of a Migrant Child.* Tempe, AZ: Bilingual Press.

Hartman, Chris, and Betsy Leondar-Wright. 2001. *Executive Excess 2001: Layoffs, Tax Rebates, The Gender Gap.* Boston: United for a Fair Economy.

———, and Jake Miller. 2001. *Bail Outs That Work For Everyone.* Boston: United for a Fair Economy.

Haskins, Ron, and Rebecca M. Blank. 2001. "Welfare Reform Reauthorization." *Poverty Research News* 5 (November/December):3–5.

Haub, Carl, and Diana Curnelius. 2001. *2001 World Population Data Sheet.* Washington, DC: Population Reference Bureau.

Hauser, Robert M., and David B. Grusky. 1988. "Cross-National Variation in Occupational Distributions, Relative Mobility Chances, and Intergenerational Shifts in Occupational Distributions." *American Sociological Review* 53 (October):723–741.

Haviland, William A. 1999. *Cultural Anthropology (Case Studies in Cultural Anthropology).* 9th ed. Ft. Worth: Harcourt Brace.

Hawkins, Darnell F., et al. 2000. "Race, Ethnicity, and Serious and Violent Juvenile Offending." *Juvenile Justice Bulletin,* June, p. 107.

Haynes, V. Dion. 2001. "Child-care Workers Seek Better Pay through Unions." *Chicago Tribune,* February 20, Pp. 1, 16.

Hayward, Mark D., Eileen M. Crimmins, Toni P. Miles, and Yu Yang. 2000. "The Significance of Socioeconomic Status in Explaining the Racial Gap in Chronic Health Conditions." *American Sociological Review* 65 (December):910–930.

Hayward, Mark D., William R. Grady, and Steven D. McLaughlin. 1987. "Changes in the Retirement Process." *Demography* 25 (August):371–386.

Health Canada. 1993. *Gender and Violence in the Mass Media.* Ottawa Canada: Health Canada.

Health Care Financing Administration. 2001. *National Health Care Expenditures Projections.* Accessed August 10 (http://www.hefa.gov/stats/NHE-proj/).

Hedley, R. Alan. 1992. "Industrialization in Less Developed Countries." Pp. 914–920 in *Encyclopedia of Sociology,* Vol. 2, edited by Edgar F. Borgatta and Marie L. Borgatta. New York: Macmillan.

Heguenbourg, Amy, and Jorge Arditi. 1999. "Fractured Resistances: The Debate over Assimilationism among Gays and Lesbians in the United States." *The Sociological Quarterly* 40 (No. 4):663–680.

Heikes, E. Joel. 1991. "When Men Are the Minority: The Case of Men in Nursing." *Sociological Quarterly* 32 (3):389–401.

Hellmich, Nanci. 2001. "TV's Reality: No Vast American Waistlines." *USA Today,* October 8, p. 7D.

Henly, Julia R. 1999. "Challenges to Finding and Keeping Jobs in the Low-Skilled Labor Market." *Poverty Research News* 3 (No. 1):3–5.

Henry J. Stimson Center. 2001. "Frequently Asked Questions: Likelihood of Terrorists Acquiring and Using Chemical or Biological Weapons." Accessed December 28, 2001 (www.stimson.org/cwc/acquse.htm#seek).

Henry, Mary E. 1989. "The Function of Schooling: Perspectives from Rural Australia." *Discourse* 9 (April): 1–21.

Henry, Tamara. 2000. "Scared at School." *USA Today,* April 11, Pp. D1, D2.

Herman, Andrew. 1999. *The "Better Angels" of Capitalism: Rhetoric, Narrative, and Moral Identity Among Men of the American Upper Class.* Boulder, CO: Westmer Press.

Herrmann, Andrew. 1994. "Survey Shows Increase in Hispanic Catholics." *Chicago Sun-Times,* March 10, p. 4.

Herrschaft, Daryl, and Kim I. Mills. 2001. *Issues and Legislation.* Accessed October 14 (www.hrc.org).

Hersch, Patricia. 1997. *A Tribe Apart: A Journey into the Heart of American Adolescence.* New York: Ballantine Books.

Hershey, Robert D., Jr. 1988. "Underground Economy Is Not Rising to the Bait." *New York Times,* January 24, p. E5.

Herskovits, Melville J. 1930. *The Anthropometry of the American Negro.* New York: Columbia University Press.

Hertz, Rosanna, and Nancy L. Marshall, eds. 2001. *Working Families: The Transformation of the American Home.* Berkeley: University of California Press.

Hesse-Biber, Sharlene, and Gregg Lee Carter. 2000. *Working Women in America: Split Dreams.* New York: Oxford University Press.

Hetherington, E. Mavis and John Kelly. 2001. *For Better or For Worse.* New York: Norton.

Hetzel, Lisa, and Annetta Smith. 2001. *The 65 Years and Over Population: 2000.* C2KBR/01–10. Washington, DC: U.S. Government Printing Office.

Hewlett, Sylvia Ann, and Cornel West. 1998. *The War Against Parents.* Boston: Houghton Mifflin.

Hillery, George A. 1955. "Definitions of Community: Areas of Agreement." *Rural Sociology* (2):111–123.

Himes, Vristine L. 2001. "Elderly Americans." *Population Bulletin* 56 (December).

Hirschi, Travis. 1969. *Causes of Delinquency.* Berkeley: University of California Press.

Hochschild, Arlie Russell. 1990. "The Second Shift: Employed Women Are Putting in Another Day of Work at Home." *Utne Reader* 38 (March/April):66–73.

———, with Anne Machung. 1989. *The Second Shift: Working Parents and the Revolution at Home.* New York: Viking Penguin.

Hodge, Robert W., and Peter H. Rossi. 1964. "Occupational Prestige in the United States, 1925–1963." *American Journal of Sociology* 70 (November):286–302.

Hodson, Randy, and Teresa A. Sullivan. 1995. *The Social Organization of Work.* 2d ed. Belmont, CA: Wadsworth.

Hoebel, E. Adamson. 1949. *Man in the Primitive World: An Introduction to Anthropology.* New York: McGraw-Hill.

Hoffman, Adonis. 1997. "Through an Accurate Prism." *Los Angeles Times,* August 8, p. M1.

Hoffman, Lois Wladis. 1985. "The Changing Genetics/Socialization Balance." *Journal of Social Issues* 41 (Spring):127–148.

Holden, Constance. 1980. "Identical Twins Reared Apart." *Science* 207 (March 21): 1323–1328.

———. 1987. "The Genetics of Personality." *Science* 257 (August 7):598–601.

Hollingshead, August B. 1975. *Elmtown's Youth and Elmtown Revisited.* New York: Wiley.

Holmes, Steven A. 1997. "Leaving the Suburbs for Rural Areas." *New York Times,* October 19, p. 34.

———. 1999. "Black Groups in Florida Split Over School Voucher Plan." *New York Times,* May 30, p. 15.

———. 2001. "The World According to AARP." *New York Times,* March 21, Pp. D1, D8.

Homans, George C. 1979. "Nature versus Nurture: A False Dichotomy." *Contemporary Sociology* 8 (May):345–348.

Hondagneu-Sotelo, Pierette. 2001. *Domestica: Immigrant Workers Cleaning and Caring in the Shadows of Affluence.* Berkeley: University of California Press.

Horgan, John. 1993. "Eugenics Revisited." *Scientific American* 268 (June): 122–128, 130–133.

Horn, Jack C., and Jeff Meer. 1987. "The Vintage Years." *Psychology Today* 21 (May):76–77, 80–84, 88–90.

Horowitz, Donald L. 2000. *Mob Rule: The Deadly Ethnic Riot.* Berkeley: University of California Press.

Horowitz, Helen Lefkowitz. 1987. *Campus Life.* Chicago: University of Chicago Press.

Horowitz, Irving Louis. 1983. *C. Wright Mills: An American Utopia.* New York: Free Press.

Horwitt, Sanford D. 1989. *Let Them Call Me Rebel: Saul Alinsky—His Life and Legacy.* New York: Knopf.

Hoschschild, Arlie Russell. 1997. *Time Bind: When Work Becomes Home and Home Becomes Work.* New York: Metropolitan Books, Holt.

Hosokawa, William K. 1969. *Nisei: The Quiet Americans.* New York: Morrow.

Hospice Foundation of America. 2002. *What Is Hospice?* Accessed January 2 (http://www. hospicefoundation.org/what_is/).

Houseman, John. 1972. *Run Through.* New York: Simon and Schuster.

Housing and Urban Development. 1999. *Stuart B. McKinney Homeless Programs.* Washington, DC: U.S. Government Printing Office.

———. 2001. *A Report on Worst Case Housing Needs in 1999: New Opportunity Amid Continuing Challenges.* Washington, DC: HUD.

Hout, Michael. 1984. "Occupational Mobility of Black Men: 1962 to 1973." *American Sociological Review* 49 (June):308–322.

———. 1988. "More Universalism, Less Structural Mobility: The American Occupational Structure in the 1980s." *American Journal of Sociology* 91 (May):1358–1400.

Howard, Judith A. 1999. "Border Crossings between Women's Studies and Sociology." *Contemporary Sociology* 28 (September):525–528.

Howard, Michael C. 1989. *Contemporary Cultural Anthropology.* 3d ed. Glenview, IL: Scott, Foresman.

Howard, Philip E., Lee Rainie, and Steve Jones. 2001. "Days and Nights on the Internet." *American Behavioral Scientist* 45 (November): 383–404.

Huang, Gary. 1988. "Daily Addressing Ritual: A Cross-Cultural Study." Presented at the annual meeting of the American Sociological Association, Atlanta.

Huber, Bettina J. 1985. *Employment Patterns in Sociology: Recent Trends and Future Prospects.* Washington, DC: American Sociological Association.

Huddy, Leonie, Joshua Billig, John Bracciodieta, Lois Hoeffler, Patrick J. Moynihan, and Patricia Pugliani. 1997. "The Effect of Interviewer Gender on the Survey Response." *Political Behavior* 19 (September):197–220.

Huff, Darrell. 1954. *How to Lie with Statistics.* New York: Norton.

Huffstutter, P. J., Tini Tran, and David Reyes. 1999. "Pirates of the High-Tech Age." *Los Angeles Times,* July 25, Pp. A1, A28–A29.

Hughes, Everett. 1945. "Dilemmas and Contradictions of Status." *American Journal of Sociology* 50 (March):353–359.

Human Rights Campaign. 2001. "Issues and Legislation." Accessed October 14. 2001 (www.hrc.org).

Hunt, Darnell. 1997. *Screening the Los Angeles "Riots": Race, Seeing, and Resistance.* New York: Cambridge University Press.

Hunter, Herbert, ed. 2000. *The Sociology of Oliver C. Cox: New Perspectives: Research in Race and Ethnic Relations,* vol. II. Stamford, CT: JAI Press.

Hunter, James Davison. 1991. *Culture Wars: The Struggle to Define America.* New York: Basic Books.

Hurh, Won Moo. 1994. *Korean Immigrants in America: A Structural Analysis of Ethnic Confinement and Adhesive Adaptation.* Rutherford, NJ: Fairleigh Dickinson University Press.

———. 1998. *The Korean Americans.* Westport, CT: Greenwood Press.

———, and Kwang Chung Kim. 1998. "The 'Success' Image of Asian Americans: Its Validity, and Its Practical and Theoretical Implications." *Ethnic and Racial Studies* 12 (October):512–538.

Hurley, Andrew. 2001. *Diners, Bowling Alleys and Trailer Parks: Chasing the American Dream in the Postwar Consumer Culture.* New York: Basic Books.

Hurn, Christopher J. 1985. *The Limits and Possibilities of Schooling,* 2d ed. Boston: Allyn and Bacon.

Hurst, Erik, Ming Ching Luoh, and Frank P. Stafford. 1996. "Wealth Dynamics of American Families, 1984–1994." Institute for Social Research, University of Michigan, Ann Arbor, MI. Unpublished paper.

Hymowitz, Carol, and Rachel Emma Silverman. 2001. "Can Work Place Stress Get Worse?" *Wall Street Monitor,* January 16, Pp. B1, B4.

I

Ibata, David. 2001. "Greener Pastures Devoured by Sprawl." *Chicago Tribune* (March 18), Pp. 1, 18.

Illinois Coalition Against the Death Penalty. 2000. "Basic Facts on the Death Penalty in Illinois." Accessed February 17, 2000 (http://www.keynet/nicadp/).

Immigration and Naturalization Service. 1999a. *Legal Immigration, Fiscal Year 1998.* Washington, DC: U.S. Government Printing Office.

———. 1999b. *1997 Statistical Yearbook of the Immigration and Naturalization Service.* Washington, DC: U.S. Government Printing Office.

Inglehart, Ronald, and Wayne E. Baker. 2000. "Modernization, Cultural Change, and the Persistence of Traditional Values." *American Sociological Review* 65 (February):19–51.

Ingraham, Chrys. 1999. *White Weddings: Romancing Heterosexuality in Popular Culture.* New York: Routledge.

Institute of International Education. 1998. "Foreign Students in U.S. Institutions 1997–1998." *Chronicle of Higher Education* 45 (December 11):A67.

———. 2001. *Open Doors on the Web.* Accessed December 13 (http://www.opendoorsweb.org).

International Crime Victim Survey. 2001. *Nationwide Surveys in the Industrialized Countries.* Accessed June 13 (http://ruijis.leidenuniv. nl/group/jfer/www/icvs/index.htm).

International Monetary Fund. 2000. *World Economic Outlook: Asset Prices and the Business Cycle.* Washington, DC: International Monetary Fund.

International Telework Association and Council. 2000. *Telecommuting (or Telework): Alive and Well or Fading Away?* Accessed April 17, 2001 (http://www. telecommute.org/about/tac/alive.shtm).

Inter-Parliamentary Union. 2001a. *Women—Key Players on the Political Stage.* Press release of IPU, 7 March, 2001.

———. 2001b. *Women in National Parliaments.* Accessed August 7 (www.ipu.org).

Irwin, Katherine. 2001. "Legitimating the First Tattoo: Moral Passage through Informal Interaction." *Symbolic Interaction* 24 (No. 1):49–73.

J

Jackson, Elton F., Charles R. Tittle, and Mary Jean Burke. 1986. "Offense-Specific Models of the Differential Association Process." *Social Problems* 33 (April):335–356.

Jackson, Philip W. 1968. *Life in Classrooms.* New York: Holt.

Jacobs, Andrew. 2001a. "A Nation Challenged: Neighbors, Town, Shed Its Anonymity to Confront the Bereaved." *New York Times.* (October 14).

———. 2001b. "A Suburb Pulls Together for Its Grieving Families." *New York Times.* (November 13), p. B1.

Jacobs, Charles A. 2001. "Slavery in the 21st Century." Pp. 310–311 in *Britannica Book of the Year 2001.* Chicago: Encyclopedia Britannica.

Jacobson, Jodi. 1993. "Closing the Gender Gap in Development." Pp. 61–79 in *State of the World,* edited by Lester R. Brown. New York: Norton.

Jaffee, David. 2001. *Organization Theory: Traditions and Change.* New York: McGraw-Hill.

Japan Times Staff. 1999. "80% Back Capital Punishment." *Japan Times International Edition* 14 (December 7):8.

Jasper, James M. 1997. *The Art of Moral Protest: Culture, Biography, and Creativity in Social Movements.* Chicago: University of Chicago Press.

Javna, John. 1986. *Cult TV.* New York: St. John's.

Jehl, Douglas. 1999. "The Internet's 'Open Sesame' Is Answered Warily." *New York Times,* March 18, p. A4.

Jencks, Christopher. 1994. *The Homeless.* Cambridge, MA: Harvard University Press.

Jenkins, Richard. 1991." Disability and Social Stratification." *British Journal of Sociology* 42 (December):557–580.

Jennings, M. Kent, and Richard G. Niemi. 1981. *Generations and Politics.* Princeton, NJ: Princeton University Press.

Jobtrak.com. 2000a. "Jobtrak.com's Poll Finds that Students and Recent Grads Only Plan to Stay with Their First Employer No Longer than Three Years." Press release January 6. Accessed June 29 (http://static. jobtrak.com/mediacenter/press_polls/poll_010600.html).

———. 2000b. "79% of College Students Find the Quality of an Employer's Website Important in Deciding Whether or Not to Apply for a Job." Accessed on June 29 (http://static.

jobtrak.com/mediacenter/press_polls/polls_061200.html).

Johnson, Anne M., Jane Wadsworth, Kaye Wellings, and Julie Field. 1994. *Sexual Attitudes and Lifestyles.* Oxford: Blackwell Scientific.

Johnson, Benton. 1975. *Functionalism in Modern Sociology: Understanding Talcott Parsons.* Morristown, NJ: General Learning.

Johnson, Jeffrey et al. 2002. Television Viewing and Aggressive Behavior During Adolescence and Adulthood. *Science* 295 (March 29): 2468–2471.

Johnson, Kenneth M. 1999. "The Rural Rebound." *Reports on America* 1 (September).

Johnson, Phylls, and Michael C. Keith. 2001. *Queer Awareness: The Story of Gay and Lesbian Broadcasting.* Carbondale, IL: Southern Illinois University.

Johnson, Richard A. 1985. *American Fads.* New York: Beech Tree.

Johnston, David Cay. 1994. "Ruling Backs Homosexuals on Asylum." *New York Times,* June 12, Pp. D1, D6.

———. 1996. "The Divine Write-Off." *New York Times,* January 12, Pp. D1, D6.

Jolin, Annette. 1994. "On the Backs of Working Prostitutes: Feminist Theory and Prostitution Policy." *Crime and Delinquency* 40 (No. 2):69–83.

Jones, Charisse. 1999. "Minority Farmers Say They've Been Cheated." *USA Today,* January 5, p. 9A.

Jones, James T., IV. 1988. "Harassment Is Too Often Part of the Job." *USA Today,* August 8, p. 5D.

Jones, Stephen R. G. 1992. "Was There a Hawthorne Effect?" *American Journal of Sociology* 98 (November):451–568.

Juhasz, Anne McCreary. 1989. "Black Adolescents' Significant Others." *Social Behavior and Personality* 17 (2):211–214.

K

Kagay, Michael R. 1996. "Experts Say Refinements Are Needed in the Polls." *New York Times,* December 15, p. 34.

Kaiser Family Foundation. 2001. *Few Parents Use V-Chip to Block TV Sex and Violence.* Menlo Park: Kaiser Family Foundation.

Kaiser, Rob. 2001. "Motorola Saga an Education for Harvard." *Chicago Tribune,* July 15, Pp. 1, 5.

Kalb, Claudia. 1999. "Our Quest to Be Perfect," *Newsweek* 131 (August 9):52–59.

Kalish, Richard A. 1985. *Death, Grief, and Caring Relationships.* 2d ed. Monterey, CA: Brooks/Cole.

Kalleberg, Arne L. 1988. "Comparative Perspectives on Work Structures and Inequality." Pp. 203–225 in *Annual Review of Sociology, 1988,* edited by W. Richard Scott and Judith Blake. Palo Alto, CA: Annual Reviews.

Kanellos, Nicholas. 1994. *The Hispanic Almanac: From Columbus to Corporate America.* Detroit: Visible Ink Press.

Kapferer, Jean-Noël. 1992. "How Rumors Are Born." *Society* 29 (July/August):53–60.

Kaplan, Esther. 1990. "A Queer Manifesto." *Village Voice,* August 14, p. 36.

Kasarda, John D. 1990. "The Jobs-Skills Mismatch." *New Perspectives Quarterly* 7 (Fall):34–37.

Katovich, Michael A. 1987. Correspondence. June 1.

Katz, Jonathan Ned. 1992. *Gay American History: Lesbians and Gay Men in the United States.* Rev. ed. New York: Meridian.

Katz, Michael. 1971. *Class, Bureaucracy, and the Schools: The Illusion of Educational Change in America.* New York: Praeger.

Kaufman, Leslie. 2000. "As Biggest Business, Wal-Mart Propels Changes Elsewhere." *New York Times* (October 27), Pp. A1, A24.

Kaufman, Phillip et al. 2001. *Indicators of School Crime and Safety: 2001.* Washington, DC: National Center for Education Statistics and Bureau of Justice Statistics.

Kearl, Michael C. 1989. *Endings: A Sociology of Death and Dying.* New York and Oxford: Oxford University Press.

Keating, Noah, and Brenda Munro. 1988. "Farm Women/Farm Work." *Sex Roles* 19 (August):155–168.

Kelley, Robin D. G. 1996. "Freedom Riders (the Sequel)." *The Nation* 262 (February 5):18–21.

Kelly, Katy, and Doug Levy. 1995. "HMOs Dogged by Issue of Cost vs. Care." *USA Today,* October 17, Pp. D1, D2.

Kelsoe, John R. et al. [12 authors]. 1989. "Re-evaluation of the Linkage Relationship between Chromosome LTP Loci and the Gene for Bipolar Affective Disorder in the Old Order Amish." *Nature* 342 (November 16): 238–243.

Kemper, Vicki, and Viveca Novak. 1991. "Health Care Reform: Don't Hold Your Breath." *Washington Post National Weekly Edition* 8 (October 28):28.

Kennickell, Arthur B., Martha Starr-McCluer, and Brian J. Surette. 2000. "Recent Changes in U.S. Family Finances: Results from the 1998 Survey of Consumer Finances." *Federal Reserve Bulletin* (January):1–29.

Kephart, William M., and William M. Zellner. 2001. *Extraordinary Groups: An Examination of Unconventional Lifestyles.* 7th ed. New York: Worth.

Kerbo, Harold R. 2000. *Social Stratification and Inequality: Class Conflict in Historical, Comparative, and Global Perspective.* New York: McGraw-Hill.

———, and John A. McKinstry. 1998. *Modern Japan.* Boston: McGraw-Hill.

Kilborn, Peter T. 2001. "Rural Towns Turn to Prisons to Reignite Their Economies." *New York Times,* August 1, Pp. A1, A11.

Kim, Kwang Chung. 1999. *Koreans in the Hood: Conflict with African Americans.* Baltimore: Johns Hopkins University Press.

Kimmel, Michael, and Michael A. Messner. 2001. *Man's Lives.* 5th ed. Needham Heights, MA: Allyn and Bacon.

Kincheloe, Joe L. 2002. *The Sign of the Burger: McDonald's and the Culture of Power.* Berkeley: University of California Press.

King, Leslie. 1998. "France Needs Children: Pronatalism, Nationalism, and Women's Equity." *Sociological Quarterly* 39 (Winter): 33–52.

———, and Madonna Harrington Meyer. 1997. "The Politics of Reproductive Benefits: U.S. Insurance Coverage of Contraceptive and Infertility Treatments." *Gender and Society* 11 (February):8–30.

King, Sharon A. 1999. "Mania for 'Pocket Monsters' Yields Billions for Nintendo." *New York Times,* April 26, Pp. A1, A18.

King, Ursula, ed. 1995. *Religion and Gender.* Oxford, England: Blackwell.

Kinkade, Patrick T., and Michael A. Katovich. 1997. "The Driver Adaptations and Identities in the Urban Worlds of Pizza Delivery Employees." *Journal of Contemporary Ethnography* 25 (January):421–448.

Kinsella, Kevin, and Victoria A. Velkoff. 2001. "An Aging World: 2001." *Current Population Reports,* Ser. 95, No. 01–1. Washington, DC: U.S. Government Printing Office.

Kinsey, Alfred C., Wardell B. Pomeroy, and Clyde E. Martin. 1948. *Sexual Behavior in the Human Male.* Philadelphia: Saunders.

———, ———, and Paul H. Gebhard. 1953. *Sexual Behavior in the Human Female.* Philadelphia: Saunders.

Kirk, Margaret 0. 1995. "The Temps in the Gray Flannel Suits." *New York Times,* December 17, p. F13.

Kitchener, Richard F. 1991. "Jean Piaget: The Unknown Sociologist." *British Journal of Sociology* 42 (September):421–442.

Klaus, Patsy A. 2000. *Crimes Against Persons Age 65 or Older, 1992–1997.* Washington, DC: U.S. Government Printing Office.

Klein, Naomi. 1999. *No Logo: Money, Marketing, and the Growing Anti-Corporate Movement.* New York: Picador (St. Martin's Press).

Kleinknecht, William. 1996. *The New Ethnic Mobs: The Changing Face of Organized Crime in America.* New York: Free Press.

Kleniewski, Nancy. 2002. *Cities, Change, and Conflict: A Political Economy of Urban Life.* 2d ed. Belmont, CA: Wadsworth.

Kluger, Jeffrey. "A Climate of Despair." *Time* (April 9):30–32, 34–36.

Knowles, James, Jere R. Behrman, Benjamin E. Dikono, and Keith McInnes. 1998. "Key Issues in the Financing of Viet Nam's Social Services." In *Financing of Social Services Project: Report to the Government of Viet Nam and the Asian Development Bank.* Bethseda, MD: Abt Associates.

Koenig, Frederick W. 1985. *Rumor in the Marketplace.* Dover, MA: Auburn House.

Kohn, Melvin L. 1970. "The Effects of Social Class on Parental Values and Practices." Pp. 45–68 in *The American Family: Dying or Developing,* edited by David Reiss and H. A. Hoffman. New York: Plenum.

Kolata, Gina. 1998. "Infertile Foreigners See Opportunity in U.S." *New York Times,* January 4, Pp. 1, 12.

———. 1999. *Clone: The Road to Dolly and the Path Beyond.* New York: William Morrow.

Komarovsky, Mirra. 1991. "Some Reflections on the Feminist Scholarship in Sociology." Pp. 1–25 in *Annual Review of Sociology,* edited by W. Richard Scott and Judith Blake. Palo Alto, CA: Annual Reviews.

Konieczny, May Ellen, and Mark Chaves. 2000. "Resources, Race, and Female-Headed Congregations in the United States." *Journal for the Scientific Study of Religion* 39 (September): 261–271.

Kopinak, Kathryn. 1995. "Gender as a Vehicle for the Subordination of Women Maquiladora Workers in Mexico." *Latin American Perspectives* 22 (Winter):30–48.

Koolhaas, Rem et al. 2001. *Mutations.* Barcelona, Spain: Actar.

Kozol, J. 1991. *Savage Inequalities.* New York: Crown.

Kretzmann, John P., and John L. McKnight. 1993. *Building Communities from the Inside Out: A Path Toward Finding and Mobilizing a Communities Assets.* Evanston, IL: Institute for Policy Research.

Kristof, Nicholas D. 1998. "As Asian Economies Shrink, Women Are Squeezed Out." *New York Times,* June 11, Pp. A1, A12.

Kübler-Ross, Elisabeth. 1969. *On Death and Dying.* New York: Macmillan.

Kunkel, Dale et al. 2001. *Sex on TV2.* Menlo Park, CA: Kaiser Family Foundation.

Kurtz, H., and S. Waxman. 2000. "Anti-Drug Shows Pay Off for TV." *San Jose Mercury News,* January 14, Pp. 1A, 24A.

Kurtz, Lester R., ed. 1999. *Encyclopedia of Violence, Place and Conflict.* San Diego, CA: Academic Press.

Kyodo News International. 1998a. "More Japanese Believe Divorce Is Acceptable." *Japan Times* 38 (January 12):B4.

L

L.A. Times Poll. 2000. "Abortion Poll." *Los Angeles Times,* June 18, p. A14.

La Ganga, Maria L. 1999. "Trying to Figure the Beginning of the End." *Los Angeles Times,* October 15, Pp. A1, A28, A29.

Labaree, David F. 1986. "Curriculum, Credentials, and the Middle Class: A Case Study of a Nineteenth Century High School." *Sociology of Education* 59 (January):42–57.

Ladner, Joyce. 1973. *The Death of White Sociology.* New York: Random Books.

Ladner, Matthew, and Maurice McTigne. 2001. *School Choice in New Zealand: Sixteen Years of Unprecedented Success.* Bentonville, AR: Children First America.

Lamb, David. 1997. "Viet Kieu: A Bridge Between Two Worlds." *Los Angeles Times,* November 4, Pp. A1, A8.

Landers, Robert K. 1988. "Why America Doesn't Vote." *Editorial Research Reports (Congressional Quarterly)* 8: Pt. 1, Pp. 82–95.

Landtman, Gunnar. 1968. *The Origin of Inequality of the Social Class.* New York: Greenwood (original edition 1938, Chicago: University of Chicago Press).

Lang, Eric. 1992. "Hawthorne Effect." Pp. 793–794 in *Encyclopedia of Sociology,* Vol. 2, edited by Edgar F. Borgatta and Marie L. Borgatta. New York: Macmillan.

Lappin, Todd. 1996. "Aux Armes, Netizens!" *The Nation* 262 (February 26): 6–7.

Larsen, Elena. 2000. *Wired Churches, Wired Temples: Taking Congregations and Missions into Cyberspace.* Washington, DC: Pew Internet and American Life Project.

Lasswell, Harold D. 1936. *Politics: Who Gets What, When, How.* New York: McGraw-Hill.

Lauer, Robert H. 1982. *Perspectives on Social Change.* 3d ed. Boston: Allyn and Bacon.

Laumann, Edward O., John H. Gagnon, and Robert T. Michael. 1994a. "A Political History of the National Sex Survey of Adults." *Family Planning Perspectives* 26 (February): 34–38.

———, ———, ———, and Stuart Michaels. 1994b. *The Social Organization of Sexuality: Sexual Practices in the United States.* Chicago: University of Chicago Press.

Lauritsen, John, and David Horstad. 1974. *The Early Homosexual Rights Movement (1864–1935).* New York: Times Change.

Lazarsfeld, Paul, Bernard Beretson, and H. Gaudet. 1948. *The People's Choice.* New York: Columbia University Press.

Lazarsfeld, Paul F., and Robert K. Merton. 1948. "Mass Communication, Popular Taste, and Organized Social Action." Pp. 95–118 in *The Communication of Ideas,* edited by Lymon Bryson. New York: Harper and Brothers.

Le Feber, Walter. 1999. *Michael Jordan and the New Global Capitalism.* New York: Norton.

Leacock, Eleanor Burke. 1969. *Teaching and Learning in City Schools.* New York: Basic Books.

Leavell, Hugh R., and E. Gurney Clark. 1965. *Preventive Medicine for the Doctor in His Community: An Epidemiologic Approach.* 3d ed. New York: McGraw-Hill.

Leavitt, Judith Walzer. 1996. *Typhoid Mary: Captive in the Public's Health.* Boston: Beacon.

Lee. Alfred McClung. 1983. *Terrorism in Northern Ireland.* Bayside, NY: General Hall.

Lee, Barrett A. 1992. "Homelessness." Pp. 843–847 in *Encyclopedia of Sociology,* Vol. 2, edited by Edgar F. Borgatta and Marie L. Borgatta. New York: Macmillan.

Lee, Heon Cheol. 1999. "Conflict Between Korean Merchants and Black Customers: A Structural Analysis." Pp. 113–130 in *Koreans in the Hood Conflict with African Americans,* edited by Kwang Chung Kim. Baltimore: Johns Hopkins University Press.

Lee, Jennifer A. 2001. "Tracking Sales and the Cashiers." *New York Times,* June 11, Pp. C1, C6.

Lee, Martha F. 1996. *The Nation of Islam: An American Millennium Movement.* Syracuse, NY: Syracuse University Press.

Lee, Taeku. 1998. "The Backdoor and the Backlash: Campaign Finance and the Politicization of Chinese-Americans." Research Roundtable Series, Harvard University, Cambridge, MA. Unpublished paper.

Lee, Tom. 2000. "The Gay Asian Male—Struggling to Find an Identity." *AsianWeek* 21 (June 22):15–17.

Lehne, Gregory K. 1995. "Homophobia among Men: Supporting and Defining the Male Role." Pp. 325–336 in *Men's Lives,* edited by Michael S. Kimmel and Michael S. Messner. Boston: Allyn and Bacon.

Lehnus, Donald J. 1977. *Who's On Time?* New York: Oceana Publications.

Leight, Kevin T., and Mary L. Fennell. 1997. "The Changing Organizational Context of Professional Work." Pp. 215–231 in *Annual Review of Sociology 1997,* edited by John Hagan. Palo Alto, CA: Annual Reviews.

Leinward, Donna. 2000. "20% Say They Used Drugs with Their Mom and Dad." *USA Today,* August 24, Pp. 1A, 2A.

Lemann, Nicholas. 1991. "The Other Underclass." *Atlantic Monthly* 268 (December):96–102, 104, 107–108, 110.

———. 1999. *The Big Test: The Secret History of the American Meritocracy.* New York: Farrar, Straus and Giroux.

Lemkow, Louis. 1987. "The Employed Unemployed: The Subterranean Economy in Spain." *Social Science and Medicine* 25 (2):111–113.

Lemonick, Michael D., and Alice Park Mankato. 2001. "The Nun Study." *Time* 157 (May 14):54–59, 62, 64.

Lengermann, Patricia Madoo, and Jill Niebrugge-Brantley. 1998. *The Women Founders: Sociology and Social Theory, 1830–1930.* Boston: McGraw-Hill.

Lenski, Gerhard. 1966. *Power and Privilege: A Theory of Social Stratification.* New York: McGraw-Hill.

———, Jean Lenski, and Patrick Nolan. 1995. *Human Societies: An Introduction to Macrosociology.* 7th ed. New York: McGraw-Hill.

Leo, John. 1987. "Exploring the Traits of Twins." *Time* 129 (January 12):63.

Leon, Sy. 1996. *None of the Above: Why Non-Voters Are America's Political Majority.* San Francisco: Fox and Wilkes.

Levin, Jack, and William C. Levin. 1980. *Ageism.* Belmont, CA: Wadsworth.

Levine, Felice. 2001. "Deja Vu All Over Again— The Tiahrt Amendment." *Footnotes* 29 (May/June).

Levinson, Arlene. 1984. "Laws for Live-In Lovers." *Ms.* 12 (July):101.

Levinson, Daniel J. 1978. *The Seasons of a Man's Life.* With Charlotte N. Darrow et al. New York: Knopf.

———. 1996. *The Season of a Woman's Life.* With Judy D. Levinson. New York: Knopf.

Levinson, David. 1996. *Religion: A Cross-Cultural Encyclopedia.* New York: Oxford University Press.

Levitt, Peggy. 2001. *The Transnational Villagers.* Chicago: University of California Press.

Lewin, Tamar. 1998a. "Report Finds Girls Lagging Behind Boys in Technology." *New York Times,* October 14, p. B8.

———. 1998b."Debate Centers on Definition of Harassment." *New York Times,* March 22, Pp. A1, A20.

———. 2000. "Differences Found in Care with Stepmothers." *New York Times,* August 17, p. A16.

———. 2001. "Anthrax Is Familiar Threat at Nation's Abortion Clinics." *New York Times,* November 7, p. B7.

Lewis, David Levering. 1994. *W. E. B. DuBois: Biography of a Race, 1868–1919.* New York: Holt.

———. 2000. *W. E. B. DuBois: The Fight for Equality and the American Century, 1919–1963.* New York: Holt.

Lewis Mumford Center. 2001. *Ethnic Diversity Grows, Neighborhood Integration Is at a Standstill.* Albany, NY: Lewis Mumford Center.

Liao, Youlian, Daniel L. McGee, Guichan Cao, and Richard S. Cooper. 2000. "Quality of the Last Year of Life of Older Adults: 1986–1993." *Journal of American Medical Association* 283 (January 26):512–518.

Lichter, S. Robert, Linda S. Lichter, and Daniel R. Amundson. 1999. *Merchandizing Mayhem: Violence in Popular Media, 1998–1999.* Washington, DC: CMPA.

Lieberman, David. 1997. "Conglomerates, News, and Children." Pp. 135–156 in *Conglomerates and the Media,* edited by Erik Barnouw et al. New York: New Press.

———. 1999. "On the Wrong Side of the Wires." *USA Today,* October 11, Pp. B1, B2.

Lieblich, Julia. 2001. "2700-Year-old Faith Faces Generation Gap." *Chicago Tribune,* July 5, p. 1.

Liebow, Elliot. 1993. *Tell Them Who I Am: The Lives of Homeless Women.* New York: Free Press.

Light, Ivan. 1999. "Comparing Incomes of Immigrants." *Contemporary Sociology* 28 (July):382–384.

Liker, Jeffrey K., Carol J. Hoddard, and Jennifer Karlin. 1999. "Perspectives on Technology and Work Organization." Pp. 575–596 in *Annual Review of Sociology 1999,* edited by Karen S. Cook and John Hagen. Palo Alto, CA: Annual Reviews.

Lillard, Margaret. 1998. "Olympics Put Spotlight on Women's Hockey." *Rocky Mountain News,* February 1, p. 8C.

Lin, Na, and Wen Xie. 1988. "Occupational Prestige in Urban China." *American Journal of Sociology* 93 (January):793–832.

Lin, Nan. 1999. "Social Networks and Status Attainment." Pp. 467–487 in *Annual Review of Sociology 1999,* edited by Karen S. Cook and John Hagen. Palo Alto, CA: Annual Reviews.

Lindner, Eileen, ed. 2000. *Yearbook of American and Canadian Churches 2000.* Nashville: Abingdon Press.

———, ed. 2001. *Yearbook of American and Canadian Churches 2001.* Nashville: Abingdon Press.

Lines, Patricia M. 1985. "A Briefing on Tuition Vouchers and Related Plans." *Footnotes* 22 (Spring):5–7.

Link, Bruce G. 1987. "Understanding Labeling Effects in the Area of Mental Disorders: An Assessment of the Effects of Expectations of Rejection." *American Sociological Review* 52 (February):96–112.

———, Frances T. Cullen, Elmer Struening, and Patrick E. Shrout. 1989. "A Modified Labeling Theory Approach to Mental Disorders." *American Sociological Review* 54 (June):400–423.

Linn, Susan, and Alvin F. Poussaint. 1999. "Watching Television: What Are Children Learning About Race and Ethnicity?" *Child Care Information Exchange* 128 (July):50–52.

Lipset, Seymour Martin. 1996. *American Exceptionalism: A Double-Edged Sword.* New York: Norton.

Lipson, Karen. 1994. "'Nell' Not Alone in the Wilds." *Los Angeles Times,* December 19, Pp. F1, F6.

Liska, Allen E., and Steven F. Messner. 1999. *Perspectives on Crime and Deviance.* 3d ed. Upper Saddle River, NJ: Prentice Hall.

Little, Kenneth. 1988. "The Role of Voluntary Associations in West African Urbanization." Pp. 211–230 in *Anthropology for the Nineties: Introductory Readings,* edited by Johnnetta B. Cole. New York: Free Press.

Lively, Kathryn J. 2001. "Occupational Claims to Professionalism: The Case of Paralegal Symbolic Interaction." 24 (No. 3):343–366.

Livernash, Robert, and Eric Rodenburg. 1998. "Population Change, Resources, and the Environment." *Population Bulletin* 53 (March).

Llanes, Jose. 1982. *Cuban Americans: Masters of Survival.* Cambridge, MA: Abt Books.

Lofland, John. 1981. "Collective Behavior: The Elementary Forms," Pp. 441–446 in *Social Psychology: Sociological Perspectives,* edited by Morris Rosenberg and Ralph Turner. New York: Basic Books.

———. 1985. *Protests: Studies of Collective Behavior and Social Movements.* Rutgers, NJ: Transaction.

Logan, John R. 2001. "From Many Shores: Asians in Census 2000." Accessed November 29, 2001 (http://mumford1.dyndns.org/cen2000/ Asianpop).

Lohr, Steve. 1994. "Data Highway Ignoring Poor, Study Charges." *New York Times,* May 24, Pp. A1, D3.

Lomborg, Bjorn. 2001. *The Skeptical Environmentalist: Measuring the Real State of the World.* Cambridge, England: Cambridge University Press.

Longworth, R. C. 1993. "UN's Relief Agendas Put Paperwork before People." *Chicago Tribune,* September 14, Pp. 1, 9.

Lorber, Judith. 1994. *Paradoxes of Gender.* New Haven, CT: Yale University Press.

Los Angeles Times. 1995. "Multicultural Medicine." October 21, p. B7.

Lowry, Brian, Elizabeth Jensen, and Greg Braxton. 1999. "Networks Decide Diversity Doesn't Pay." *Los Angeles Times,* July 20, p. A1.

Lukacs, Georg. 1923. *History and Class Consciousness.* London: Merlin.

Luker, Kristin. 1984. *Abortion and the Politics of Motherhood.* Berkeley: University of California Press.

———. 1996. *Dubious Conceptions: The Politics of Teenage Pregnancy.* Cambridge, MA: Harvard University Press.

———. 1999. "Is Academic Sociology Politically Obsolete?" *Contemporary Sociology* 28 (January):5–10.

Lum, Joann, and Peter Kwong. 1989. "Surviving in America: The Trials of a Chinese Immigrant Woman." *Village Voice* 34 (October 31):39–41.

Luster, Tom, Kelly Rhoades, and Bruce Haas. 1989. "The Relation between Parental Values and Parenting Behavior: A Test of the Kohn Hypothesis." *Journal of Marriage and the Family* 51 (February):139–147.

Lustig, Myron W., and Jolene Koester. 1999. *Intercultural Competence: Interpersonal Communication across Cultures.* 3d ed. New York: Longman.

Lutz, Catherine A., and Jane L. Collins. 1993. *Reading National Geographic.* Chicago: University of Chicago Press.

Lyall, Sarah. 2001. "Britain's Race Problem." *New York Times,* June 3, Sect. 4, Pp. 1–4.

Lyman, Rick. 2001. "Managers Say Reshuffling at AOL Plays to the Strengths." *New York Times,* December 6, p. C7.

Lyotard, Jean François. 1993. *The Postmodern Explained: Correspondence, 1982–1985.* Minneapolis: University of Minnesota Press.

M

MacFarquhar, Neil. 1999. "For First Time in War, E-Mail Plays a Vital Role." *New York Times,* March 29, p. A12.

Mack, Raymond W., and Calvin P. Bradford. 1979. *Transforming America: Patterns of Social Change.* 2d ed. New York: Random House.

MacLeod, Alexander. 2000. "UK Moving to Open All (E-)Mail." *The Christian Science Monitor,* May 5, Pp. 1, 9.

Magnier, Mark. 1999. "Equality Evolving in Japan." *Los Angeles Times,* August 30, Pp. A1, A12.

———. 2001. "Making a Killing in Japan." *Los Angeles Times,* January 12, Pp. A1, A10.

Maguire, Brendan. 1988. "The Applied Dimension of Radical Criminology: A Survey of Prominent Radical Criminologists." *Sociological Spectrum* 8 (2):133–151.

———. 2000. "Defining Deviancy Down: A Research Note Regarding Professional Wrestling." *Deviant Behavior* 2:551–565.

———, and Polly F. Radosh. 1999. *Introduction to Criminology.* Belmont, CA: Wadsworth/ Thomson Learning.

Mahbub ul Haq Human Development Centre. 2000. *Human Development in South Asia 2000.* Oxford, England: Oxford University Press for Mahbub ul Haq Human Development Centre.

Maine Times. 2001. Article on Wal-Mart's Plan to Build Near the Penja. January 4, 2001.

Maines, David R. 1977. "Social Organization and Social Structure in Symbolic Interactionist Thought." Pp. 235–259 in *Annual Review of Sociology, 1977,* edited by Alex Inkles. Palo Alto, CA: Annual Reviews.

———. 1982. "In Search of Mesostructure: Studies in the Negotiated Order." *Urban Life* 11 (July):267–279.

Malbin, Michael et al. 2002. New Interest Group Strategies-A Preview of Post McCain-Feingold Politics? Accessed May 7, 2002 at www.CFInst.org.

Malcolm, Andrew H. 1974. "The 'Shortage' of Bathroom Tissue: A Classic Study in Rumor." *New York Times,* February 3, p. 29.

Malcolm X, with Alex Haley. 1964. *The Autobiography of Malcolm X.* New York: Grove.

Malcomson, Scott L. 2000. *One Drop of Blood: The American Misadventure of Race.* New York: Farrar, Straus, and Giroux.

Malthus, Thomas Robert. 1798. *Essays on the Principle of Population.* New York: Augustus Kelly, Bookseller; reprinted in 1965.

———, Julian Huxley, and Frederick Osborn. [1824] 1960. *Three Essays on Population.* Reprint. New York: New American Library.

Manson, Donald A. 1986. *Tracking Offenders: White-Collar Crime.* Bureau of Justice Statistics Special Report. Washington, DC: U.S. Government Printing Office.

Marable, Manning. 2000. *How Capitalism Underdeveloped Black America.* Updated edition. Boston: South End Press.

Margolis, Eric, ed. 2001. *The Hidden Curriculum in Higher Education.* New York: Routledge.

Marklein, Mary Beth. 1996. "Telecommuters Gain Momentum." *USA Today,* June 18, p. 6E.

Markson, Elizabeth W. 1992. "Moral Dilemmas." *Society* 29 (July/August):4–6.

Marquis, Julie, and Dan Morain. 1999. "A Tortuous Path for the Mentally Ill." *Los Angeles Times,* November 21, Pp. A1, A22, A23.

Marshall, Victor W., and Judith A. Levy. 1990. "Aging and Dying." Pp. 245–260 in *Handbook of Aging and the Social Sciences,* edited by Robert H. Binstock and Linda K. George. San Diego: Academic Press.

Martelo, Emma Zapata. 1996. "Modernization, Adjustment, and Peasant Production." *Latin American Perspectives* 23 (Winter):118–130.

Martin, Philip, and Elizabeth Midgley. 1999. "Immigrants to the United States." *Population Bulletin* 54 (June):1–42.

———, and Jonas Widgren. 1996. "International Migration: A Global Challenge." *Population Bulletin* 51(April).

Martin, Susan E. 1994. "Outsider Within the Station House: The Impact of Race and Gender on Black Women Politics." *Social Problems* 41 (August):383–400.

Martineau, Harriet. 1896. "Introduction" to the translation of *Positive Philosophy* by Auguste Comte. London: Bell.

———. [1837] 1962. *Society in America.* Edited, abridged, with an introductory essay by Seymour Martin Lipset. Reprint. Garden City, NY: Doubleday.

Martinez, Elizabeth. 1993. "Going Gentle into That Good Night: Is a Rightful Death a Feminist Issue?" *Ms.* 4 (July/August):65–69.

Martinez, Valerie, Kay Thomas, and Frank R. Kenerer. 1994. "Who Chooses and Why: A Look at Five School Choice Plans." *Phi Delta Kappan* 75 (May):678–681.

Marx, Karl, and Friedrich Engels. [1847] 1955. *Selected Work in Two Volumes.* Reprint, Moscow: Foreign Languages Publishing House.

Masaki, Hisane. 1998. "Hashimoto Steps Down." *The Japan Times* 38 (July 20):1–5.

Mascia-Lees, Frances E., and Patricia Sharp, eds. 1992. *Tattoo, Torture, Mutilation, and Adornment: The Denaturalization of the Body in Culture and Text.* Albany: State University of New York Press.

Masland, Tom. 1992. "Slavery." *Newsweek* 119 (May 4):30–32, 37–39.

Mason, J. W. 1998. "The Buses Don't Stop Here Anymore." *American Prospect* 37 (March):56–62.

Massachusetts Department of Education. 2000. *Learning Support Service Progress: Safe Schools Program for Gay and Lesbian Students.* Accessed July 19, 2001 (http://www.doe.mass. edu/lss/program/ ssch.html).

Massey, Douglas S. 1998. "March of Folly: U.S. Immigration Policy After NAFTA." *The American Prospect* (March/April):22–23.

———. 1999. "International Migration at the Dawn of the Twenty-First Century: The Role of the State." *Population and Development Review* 28 (June):303–322.

———, and Nancy A. Denton. 1993. *American Apartheid: Segregation and the Making of the Underclass.* Cambridge, MA: Harvard University Press.

Matrix.Net. 2000. *State of the Internet, January 2000.* MMQ 701. Accessed October 14, 2001 (www.mids.org).

Matsushita, Yoshiko. 1999. "Japanese Kids Call for a Sympathetic Ear." *Christian Science Monitor,* January 20, p. 15.

Matthews, Jay. 1999. "A Home Run for Home Schooling." *Washington Post National Weekly Edition* 16 (March 29):34.

Mayer, Karl Ulrich, and Urs Schoepflin. 1989. "The State and the Life Course." Pp. 187–209 in *Annual Review of Sociology, 1989,* edited by W. Richard Scott and Judith Blake. Palo Alto, CA: Annual Reviews.

McChesney, Robert W. 1999. *Rich Media, Poor Democracy: Communication Politics in Dubious Times.* Urbana, IL: University of Illinois Press.

McCoy, Kevin, and Dennis Cauchon. 2001. "The Business Side of Terror." *USA Today,* October 16, Pp. 1B, 3B.

McCreary, D. 1994. "The Male Role and Avoiding Femininity." *Sex Roles* 31:517–531.

McDermott, Kevin. 1999. "Illinois Bill Would Repeal Law Requiring Listing of Campaign Donors on Internet." *St. Louis Post-Dispatch,* November 25, p. A1.

McDonald, Kim A. 1999. "Studies of Women's Health Produce a Wealth of Knowledge on the Biology of Gender Differences." *Chronicle of Higher Education* 45 (June 25):A19, A22.

McDowell, Edwin. 2001. "Indian Reservations Join the Tourist Circuit." *New York Times,* June 3, p. 3.

McFalls, Joseph A., Jr. 1998. "Population: A Lively Introduction." *Population Bulletin* 53 (September).

McFeely, William S. 2001. *Proximity to Death.* New York: Norton.

McGue, Matt, and Thomas J. Bouchard, Jr. 1998. "Genetic and Environmental Influence on Human Behavioral Differences." Pp. 1–24 in *Annual Review of Neurosciences.* Palo Alto, CA: Annual Reviews.

McGuire, Meredith B. 1997. *Religion: The Social Context.* 4th ed. Belmont, CA: Wadsworth.

McKinlay, John B., and Sonja M. McKinlay. 1977. "The Questionable Contribution of Medical Measures to the Decline of Mortality in the United States in the Twentieth Century." *Milbank Memorial Fund Quarterly* 55 (Summer):405–428.

McKinley, James C., Jr. 1999. "In Cuba's New Dual Economy, Have-Nots Far Exceed Haves." *New York Times,* February 11, Pp. A1, A6.

McKnight, John L., and John P. Kretzmann. 1996. *Mapping Community Capacity.* Evanston, IL: Institute for Policy Research.

McLane, Daisann. 1995. "The Cuban-American Princess." *New York Times Magazine,* February 26, Pp. 42–43.

McLaughlin, Abraham. 1998. "Tales of Journey from Death Row to Freedom." *Christian Science Monitor,* November 16, p. 2.

McLuhan, Marshall. 1964. *Understanding Media: The Extensions of Man.* New York: New American Library.

———, and Quentin Fiore. 1967. *The Medium Is the Message: An Inventory of Effects.* New York: Bantam Books.

McMahon, Colin. 1995. "Mexican Rebels' Struggle in Chiapas Is 'about the Future.'" *Chicago Tribune,* January 1, p. 6.

McPhail, Clark. 1991. *The Myth of the Madding Crowd.* New York: De Gruyter.

———. 1994. "The Dark Side of Purpose in Riots: Individual and Collective Violence." *Sociological Quarterly* 35 (January):i–xx.

———, and David Miller. 1973. "The Assembling Process: A Theoretical Empirical Examination." *American Sociological Review* 38 (December):721–735.

Mead, George H. 1934. In *Mind, Self and Society,* edited by Charles W. Morris. Chicago: University of Chicago Press.

———. 1964a. In *On Social Psychology,* edited by Anselm Strauss. Chicago: University of Chicago Press.

———. 1964b. "The Genesis of the Self and Social Control." Pp. 267–293 in *Selected Writings: George Herbert Mead,* edited by Andrew J. Reck. Indianapolis: Bobbs-Merrill.

Mead, Margaret. [1935] 2001. *Sex and Temperament in Three Primitive Societies.* New York: Perennial, HarperCollins.

Mechanic, David, and David Rochefort. 1996. "Comparative Medical Systems." Pp. 475–494 in *Annual Review of Sociology, 1996,* edited by John Hagan. Palo Alto, CA: Annual Reviews.

Mehren, Elizabeth. 1999. "Working 9 to 5 at Age 95." *USA Today,* May 5, Pp. A1, A21–A22.

Meier, Robert F., and Gilbert Geis. 1997. *Victimless Crime? Prostitution, Drugs, Homosexuality, Abortion.* Los Angeles: Roxbury.

Melia, Marilyn Kennedy. 2000. "Changing Times." *Chicago Tribune,* January 2, Sec. 17, Pp. 12–15.

Mendez, Jennifer Bickman. 1998. "Of Mops and Maids: Contradictions and Continuities in Bureaucratized Domestic Work." *Social Problems* 45 (February):114–135.

Merton, Robert K. 1968. *Social Theory and Social Structure.* New York Free Press.

———, and Alice S. Kitt. 1950. "Contributions to the Theory of Reference Group Behavior." Pp. 40–105 in *Continuities in Social Research: Studies in the Scope and Methods of the American Soldier,* edited by Robert K. Merton and Paul L. Lazarsfeld. New York: Free Press.

Messner, Michael A. 1997. *Politics of Masculinities: Men in Movements.* Thousand Oaks, CA: Sage.

Meyer, David S., and Nancy Whittier. 1994. "Social Movement Spillover." *Social Problems* 41 (May):277–298.

Meyers, Thomas J. 1992. "Factors Affecting the Decision to Leave the Old Order Amish." Presented at the annual meeting of the American Sociological Association, Pittsburgh.

Michels, Robert. 1915. *Political Parties.* Glencoe, IL: Free Press (reprinted 1949).

Migration News. 2001a. "Labor Unions." 8 (April). Accessed March 20 (http://migration.ucdavis.edu).

———. 2001b. "Mexico: Guest Workers." 8 (February). Accessed February 2 (http://migration.ucdavis.edu).

———. 2002a. "UK: Immigration, Race Relations." January 2002.

Milgram, Stanley. 1963. "Behavioral Study of Obedience." *Journal of Abnormal and Social Psychology* 67 (October):371–378.

———. 1975. *Obedience to Authority: An Experimental View.* New York: Harper and Row.

Miller, D. W. 2000. "Sociology, Not Engineering May Explain Our Vulnerability to Technological Disaster." *Chronicle of Higher Education* (October 15):A19–A20.

Miller, David L. 2000. *Introduction to Collective Behavior and Collective Action.* 2d ed. Prospect Heights, IL: Waveland Press.

———, and JoAnne DeRoven Darlington. 2002. *Fearing for the Safety of Others: Disasters and the Small World Problem.* Paper presented at Midwest Sociological Society, Milwaukee, WI.

———, and Richard T. Schaefer. 1993. "Feeding the Hungry: The National Food Bank System as a Non-Insurgent Social Movement." Presented at the annual meeting of the Midwest Sociological Society, Chicago.

Miller, G. Tyler, Jr. 1972. *Replenish the Earth: A Primer in Human Ecology.* Belmont, CA: Wadsworth.

Miller, George A., and Oleg I. Gubin. 2000. "The Structure of Russian Organizations." *Sociological Inquiry* 70 (Winter):74–87.

Miller, Jody. 2001. *One of the Guys: Girls, Gangs, and Gender.* New York: Oxford University Press.

Miller, Judith, Stephen Engelberg, and William J. Broad. 2001. *Germs: Biological Weapons and America's Secret War.* New York: Simon and Schuster.

Miller, Michael. 1998. "Abortion by the Numbers." *The Village Voice* 43 (January 27):58.

Miller, Reuben. 1988. "The Literature of Terrorism," *Terrorism* 11 (1):63–87.

Miller, Toby, Mitin Govil, John McMurria, and Richard Maxwell. 2001. *Global Hollywood.* Bloomington, IN: Indiana University Press.

Mills, C. Wright. [1959] 2000a. *The Sociological Imagination.* 40th Anniversary Edition: New Afterword by Todd Gitlin. New York: Oxford University Press.

———. [1956] 2000b. *The Power Elite.* A New Edition. Afterword by Alan Wolfe. New York: Oxford University Press.

Mills, Kim I., and Daryl Henschaft. 1999. *The State of the Workplace for Lesbian, Gay, Bisexual and Transgendered Americans 1999.* Washington, DC: Human Rights Campaign Foundation.

Mills, Robert J. 2001. "Health Insurance Coverage: 2000." *Current Population Reports,* Ser. P60, No. 215. Washington, DC: U.S. Government Printing Office.

Mindel, Charles, Robert W. Habenstein, and Roosevelt Wright, Jr. 1998. *Ethnic Families in America: Patterns and Variations.* 4th ed. Upper Saddle River, NJ: Prentice Hall.

Miner, Horace. 1956. "Body Ritual Among the Nacirema." *American Anthropologist* 58 (June):503–507.

Mingle, James R. 1987. *Focus on Minorities.* Denver: Education Commission of the States and the State Higher Education Executive Officers.

Mirapaul, Matthew. 2001. "How the Net is Documenting a Watershed Moment." *New York Times,* October 15, p. E2.

Mitchell, William J. 1999. *E-topia.* Cambridge, MA: MIT Press.

Mitofsky, Warren J. 1998. "The Polls-Review. Was 1996 a Worse Year for Polls than 1948?" *Public Opinion Quarterly* 62 (Summer):230–249.

Moeller, Susan D. 1999. *Compassion Fatigue.* London: Routledge.

Mogelonsky, Marcia. 1996. "The Rocky Road to Adulthood." *American Demographics* 18 (May):26–29, 32–35, 56.

Mollen, Milton. 1992. "*A Failure of Responsibility*": Report to Mayor David N. Dinkins on the December 28, 1991, Tragedy at City College of New York. New York: Office of the Deputy Mayor for Public Safety.

Monaghan, Peter. 1993. "Sociologist Jailed Because He 'Wouldn't Snitch' Ponders the Way Research Ought to Be Done." *Chronicle of Higher Education* 40 (September 1):A8, A9.

Money. 1987. "A Short History of Shortages." 16 (Fall, special issue):42.

Monmaney, Terence. 1995. "Ethnicities' Medical Views Vary, Study Says." *Los Angeles Times,* September 13, Pp. B1, B3.

Monteiro, Lois A. 1998. "Ill-Defined Illnesses and Medically Unexplained Symptoms Syndrome." *Footnotes* 26 (February):3, 6.

Montgomery, Marilyn J., and Gwendolyn T. Sorrell. 1997. "Differences in Love Attitudes Across Family Life Stages." *Family Relations* 46:55–61.

Moore, Joan, and Harry Pachan. 1985. *Hispanics in the United States.* Englewood Cliffs: Prentice Hall.

Moore, Thomas S. 1996. *The Disposable Work Force: Worker Displacement and Employment Instability in America.* New York: Aldine De Gruyter.

Moore, Wilbert E. 1967. *Order and Change: Essays in Comparative Sociology.* New York: Wiley.

———. 1968. "Occupational Socialization." Pp. 861–883 in *Handbook of Socialization Theory and Research,* edited by David A. Goslin. Chicago: Rand McNally.

Morehouse Research Institute and Institute for American Values. 1999. *Turning the Corner on Father Absence in Black America.* Atlanta: Morehouse Research Institute and Institute for American Values.

Morin, Richard. 2000a. "Point-and-Click Political Information." *Washington Post National Weekly Edition* 18 (December 11):34.

———. 2000b. "Will Traditional Polls Go the Way of the Dinosaur?" *Washington Post National Weekly Edition* 17 (May 15):34.

———. 2002. "A Record Low—and No One's Cheering." *Washington Post National Weekly Edition* 17 (January 14), p. 34.

Morland, John, Jr. 1996. "The Individual, the Society, or Both? A Comparison of Black, Latino, and White Beliefs about the Causes of Poverty." *Social Forces* 75 (December): 403–422.

Morris, Aldon. 2000. "Reflections on Social Movement Theory: Criticisms and Proposals." *Contemporary Sociology* 29 (May):445–454.

Morris, Bonnie Rothman. 1999. "You've Got Romance! Seeking Love on Line." *New York Times,* August 26, p. D1.

Morrison, Denton E. 1971. "Some Notes toward Theory on Relative Deprivation, Social Movements, and Social Change." *American Behavioral Scientist* 14 (May/June):675–690.

Morrow, John K. 1997. "Of Sheep Cloning and Cold Fusion." *Chicago Tribune,* March 7, p. 23.

Morse, Arthur D. 1967. *While Six Million Died: A Chronicle of American Apathy.* New York: Ace.

Morse, Jodie. 1999. "Cracking Down on the Homeless." *Time,* December 2000, Pp. 69–70.

Mosley, J., and E. Thomson. 1995. Pp. 148–165 in *Fatherhood: Contemporary Theory, Research and Social Policy,* edited by W. Marsiglo. Thousand Oaks, CA: Sage.

Moss, Phillip, and Chris Tilly. 2001. *Stories Employees Tell: Race, Skill, and Hiring in America.* New York: Russell Sage Foundation.

MOST. 2001. Home page of MOST. Accessed August 1 (http://www.mostonline.org).

Motorola. 2001. Interview with Human Resources, Harvard, IL. April 10.

Mullins, Marcy E. 2001. "Bioterrorism Impacts Few." *USA Today* (October 18) p. 16A.

Mumola, Christopher J. 2000. *Incarcerated Parents and Their Children.* Washington, DC: U.S. Government Printing Office.

Murdock, George P. 1945. "The Common Denominator of Cultures." Pp. 123–142 in *The Science of Man in the World Crisis,* edited by Ralph Linton. New York: Columbia University Press.

———. 1949. *Social Structure.* New York: Macmillan.

———. 1957. "World Ethnographic Sample." *American Anthropologist* 59 (August): 664–687.

Murphy, Caryle. 1993. "Putting Aside the Veil." *Washington Post National Weekly Edition* 10 (April 12–18):10–11.

Murphy, Dean E. 1997. "A Victim of Sweden's Pursuit of Perfection." *Los Angeles Times,* September 2, Pp. A1, A8.

———, and Clifford J. Levy. 2001. "The Evacuation That Kept a Horrible Toll from Climbing Higher." *New York Times,* September 21, p. B10.

Murray, Susan B. 2000. "Getting Paid in Smiles: The Gendering of Child Care Work." *Symbolic Interaction* 23 (No. 2):135–160.

Murray, Velma McBride, Amanda Willert, and Diane P. Stephens. 2001. "The Half-Full Glass: Resilient African American Single Mothers and Their Children." *Family Focus,* June, Pp. F4–F5.

N

Nader, Laura. 1986. "The Subordination of Women in Comparative Perspective." *Urban Anthropology* 15 (Fall/Winter): 377–397.

Naifeh, Mary. 1998. "Trap Door? Revolving Door? Or Both? Dynamics of Economic Well-Being, Poverty 1993–94." *Current Population Reports,* Ser. p. 70, No. 63. Washington, DC: U.S. Government Printing Office.

Nakane, Chie. 1970. *Japanese Society.* Berkeley: University of California Press.

Nakao, Keiko, and Judith Treas. 1990. *Computing 1989 Occupational Prestige Scores.* Chicago: NORC.

———, and ———. 1994. "Updating Occupational Prestige and Socioeconomic Scores: How the New Measures Measure Up." Pp. 1–72 in *Sociological Methodology,* edited by Peter V. Marsden. Oxford: Basil Blackwell.

Nash, Manning. 1962. "Race and the Ideology of Race." *Current Anthropology* 3 (June): 285–288.

Nass, Clifford, and Youngme Moon. 2000. "Machines and Mindlessness: Social Responses to Computers." *Journal of Social Issues* 56 (No. 1):81–103.

National Abortion and Reproductive Rights Action League Foundation. 2001. *Who Decides? A State-by-State Review of Abortion and Reproductive Rights.* 10th ed. Washington: NARAL Foundation.

National Advisory Commission on Criminal Justice. 1976. *Organized Crime.* Washington, DC: U.S. Government Printing Office.

National Alliance for Caregiving. 1997. *The NAC Comparative Analysis of Caregiver Date for Caregivers to the Elderly, 1987 and 1997.* Bethesda, MD: National Alliance for Caregiving.

National Alliance for the Mentally Ill. 2000. "What Is Mental Illness?" Accessed January 18 (http://www.nami.org/disorder/whatis. html).

National Alliance to End Homelessness. 2001. *Facts about Homelessness.* Accessed September 23 (www.naeh.org).

National Center for Education Statistics. 1996. *Education Indicators: An International Perspective.* Accessed July 19, 2001 (http://nces.ed.gov/pubs.ciip).

———. 2001. *Digest of Education Statistics 2000.* Washington, DC: U.S. Government Printing Office.

———. 1998. *Students' Report of School Crime: 1989 and 1995.* Washington, DC: U.S. Government Printing Office.

National Center for Health Statistics. 2001. *Fast Stats A to Z.* Accessed December 6 (http://www.cdc.gov/nchs/fastats).

National Center on Women and Family Law. 1996. *Status of Marital Rape Exemption Statutes in the United States.* New York: National Center on Women and Family Law.

National Homeschool Association. 1999. *Homeschooling Families: Ready for the Next Decade.* Accessed November 19, 2000 (http://www.n-h-a.org/decade.htm).

National Institute of Mental Health. 1999. *The Numbers Count: Mental Illness in America.* Washington, DC: U.S. Government Printing Office.

National Institute on Aging. 1999a. *Early Retirement in the United States.* Washington, DC: U.S. Government Printing Office.

———. 1999b. *The Declining Disability of Older Americans.* Washington, DC: U.S. Government Printing Office.

National Intelligence Council. 2000. *Global Trends 2015: A Dialogue About the Future with Nongovernment Experts.* Accessed January 2, 2001 (www.cia.gov).

National Law Center on Homelessness and Poverty. 1996. *Mean Sweeps: A Report on Anti-Homeless Laws, Litigation, and Alternatives in 50 United States Cities.* Washington, DC: National Law Center on Homelessness and Poverty.

National Marriage Project. 2001. *The State of Our Unions 2001.* Piscataway, NJ: The National Marriage Project.

National Organization for Men against Sexism. 2001. *Welcome: NOMAS.* Accessed June 16 (http://www.nomas.org).

National Right to Work Legal Defense Foundation. 2001a. *Right to Work States, 1999.* Accessed April 18, 2001 (http://www.nrtw.org/rtws.htm).

———. 2001b. *Issue Paper: Employees in Right to Work States.* Accessed April 18 (http://www.nrtw.org/a/rtwempl.htm).

National Telecommunications Information Administration. 1999. *Falling through the Net: Defining the Digital Divide.* Washington, DC: U.S. Government Printing Office.

National Vital Statistics Reports. 2000. "Births, Marriages, Divorces and Deaths: Provisional Data for October 1999." 48 (September 6).

———. 2001. "Births, Marriages, Divorces, and Deaths: Provisional Data for January–December 2000." 49 (August 22).

———. 2001b. "Births, Marriage, Divorce, and Deaths: Provision Data For April–June 2001." 50.

Navarro, Vicente. 1984. "Medical History as Justification Rather Than Explanation: A Critique of Starr's The Social Transformation of American Medicine." *International Journal of Health Services* 14 (4):511–528.

Nelson, Alondra, and Thuy Linh N. Tu with Alicia Headlam Hines, eds. 2001. *Technocolor: Race, Technology and Everyday Life.* New York: New York University Press.

Nelson, Jack. 1995. "The Internet, the Virtual Community, and Those with Disabilities." *Disability Studies Quarterly* 15 (Spring):15–20.

NetCoalition.com. 2001. Home Page. Accessed August 8 (www.netcoalition.com).

Neuborne, Ellen. 1996. "Vigilantes Stir Firms' Ire with Cyber-antics." *USA Today,* February 28, Pp. A1, A2.

New York Times. 1993. "Dutch May Broaden Euthanasia Guidelines." February 17, p. A3.

———. 1995a. "Reverse Discrimination of Whites Is Rare, Labor Study Reports." March 31, p. A23.

———. 1995b. "U.N. Rights Panel Declines to Censure China." March 9, p. A5.

———. 1998. "2 Gay Men Fight Town Hall for a Family Pool Pass Discount." July 14, p. B2.

———. 2001. "Sizing Up an Industry and AOL Time Warner's Place in It," December 6, p. C7.

Newburger, Eric C. 2001. "Home Computers and Internet Use in the United States: August 2000." *Current Population Reports,* Ser. p. 23, No. 207. Washington, DC: U.S. Government Printing Office.

Newman, William M. 1973. *American Pluralism: A Study of Minority Groups and Social Theory.* New York: Harper and Row.

Newsday. 1997. "Japan Sterilized 16,000 Women." September 18, p. A19.

NGLTF. 2001. "About National Gay and Lesbian Task Force." Accessed October 14, 2001 (www.ngltf.org).

Nibert, David. 2000. *Hitting the Lottery Jackpot: Government and the Taxing of Dreams.* New York: Monthly Review Press.

NICHD. 1998. *Early Childhood Care.* Accessed October 19, 2000 (http://www.nichd.nih.gov/publications/pubs/ early_child_care.htm).

Nie, Norman H. 1999. "Tracking Our Techno-Future." *American Demographics* (July):50–52.

———. 2001. "Sociability, Interpersonal Relations, and the Internet." *American Behavioral Scientist* 45 (November): 420–435.

———, and Lutz Erbring. 2000. "Study of the Social Consequences of the Internet." Accessible online (http://www.stanford.edu/group/sigss/). Palo Alto, CA: Stanford Institute for the Quantitative Study of Society.

Nielsen, Joyce McCarl, Glenda Walden, and Charlotte A. Kunkel. 2000. "Gendered Heteronormativity: Empirical Illustrations in Everyday Life." *Sociological Quarterly* 41(No. 2): 283–296.

Nixon, Howard L., II. 1979. *The Small Group*. Englewood Cliffs, NJ: Prentice Hall.

Nolan, Patrick, and Gerhard Lenski. 1999. *Human Societies: An Introduction to Macrosociology*. New York: McGraw-Hill.

NORC (National Opinion Research Center). 1994. *General Social Surveys 1972–1994*. Chicago: National Opinion Research Center.

Norman, Jim. 1996. "At Least 1 Pollster Was Right on Target." *USA Today*, November 7, p. 8A.

Novak, Tim, and Jon Schmid. 1999. "Lottery Picks Split by Race, Income." *Chicago Sun-Times*, June 22, Pp. 1, 24, 25.

Nun Study. 2001. *The Nun Study*. Accessed September 11 (www.nunstudy.org).

Nussbaum, Daniel. 1998. "Bad Air Days." *Los Angeles Times Magazine*, July 19, Pp. 20–21.

O

Oberschall, Anthony. 1973. *Social Conflict and Social Movements*. Englewood Cliffs, NJ: Prentice Hall.

The Observer (London). Human Rights Abuses by Country.

———. October 24, 1999. Accessed August 27, 2001 (www.guardian.co.uk).

O'Donnell, Mike. 1992. *A New Introduction to Sociology*. Walton-on-Thames, United Kingdom: Thomas Nelson and Sons.

Office of Justice Programs. 1999. "Transnational Organized Crime." *NCJRS Catalog* 49 (November/December):21.

Ogburn, William F. 1922. *Social Change with Respect to Culture and Original Nature*. New York: Huebsch (reprinted 1966, New York: Dell).

———, and Clark Tibbits. 1934. "The Family and Its Functions." Pp. 661–708 in *Recent Social Trends in the United States*, edited by Research Committee on Social Trends. New York: McGraw-Hill.

O'Hare, William P., and Brenda Curry White. 1992. "Is There a Rural Underclass?" *Population Today* 20 (March):6–8.

Okamoto, Dina G. and Lynn Smith-Lovin. 2001. "Changing the Subject: Gender, Status, and the Dynamics of Topic Change." *American Sociological Review* 66 (December):852–873.

Okano, Kaori, and Motonori Tsuchiya. 1999. *Education in Contemporary Japan: Inequality and Diversity*. Cambridge: Cambridge University Press.

Oliver, Melvin L., and Thomas M. Shapiro. 1995. *Black Wealth/White Wealth: New Perspectives On Racial Inequality*. New York: Routledge.

O'Neill, Brian, and Deborah Balk. 2001. "World Population Futures." *Population Bulletin* 56 (September).

O'Rand, Angele M. 1996. "The Precious and the Precocious: Understanding Cumulative Disadvantage and Cumulative Advantage Over the Life Course." *The Gerontologist* 36 (No. 2): 230–258.

Orfield, Gary, and Holly J. Liebowitz, eds. 2001. *Religion, Race, and Justice in a Changing American*. New York: The Twentieth Century Fund.

Orum, Anthony M. 1989. *Introduction to Political Sociology: The Social Anatomy of the Body Politic*. 3d ed. Englewood Cliffs, NJ: Prentice Hall.

———. 2001. *Introduction to Political Sociology*. 4th ed. Upper Saddle River, NJ: Prentice Hall.

Orwell, George. 1949. *1984*. New York: Harcourt Brace Jovanovich.

Osborne, Lawrence. 2001. "Regional Disturbance." *New York Times Magazine*, May 6, Pp. 98–99, 102.

Ouellette, Laurie. 1993. "The Information Lockout." *Utne Reader*, September/October, Pp. 25–26.

Owens, Lynn, and L. Kendall Palmer. 2000. *Public Betrayals and Private Portrayals: Activist Intention in Tension on the WWW*. Presented at the annual meeting of the American Sociological Association, Washington, DC.

P

Pagani, Steve. 1999. "End the 'Culture of Death,' Pope Tells America." Reuters Wire Service, January 23.

Page, Charles H. 1946. "Bureaucracy's Other Face." *Social Forces* 25 (October):89–94.

Paik, Haejung, and George Comstrock. 1994. "The Effects of Television Violence or Antisocial Behavior: A Meta-analysis." *Communication Research* 21:516–546.

Pamuk, E., D. Makui, K. Heck, C. Reuban, and K. Lochren. 1998. *Health, United States 1998 with Socioeconomic Status and Health Chartbook*. Hyattsville, MD: National Center for Health Statistics.

Parent's Television Council. 2001a. *What a Difference a Decade Makes*. Los Angeles: PTC.

——— 2001b. *The Sour Family Hour: 8 to 9 Goes from Bad to Worse*. Los Angeles: PTC.

Park, Robert E. 1916. "The City: Suggestions for the Investigation of Human Behavior in the Urban Environment." *American Journal of Sociology* 20 (March):577–612.

———. 1922. *The Immigrant Press and Its Control*. New York: Harper.

———. 1936. "Succession, an Ecological Concept." *American Sociological Review* 1 (April): 171–179.

Parker, Suzi. 1998. "Wedding Boom: More Rings, Tuxes, Bells, and Brides." *Christian Science Monitor*, July 20, Pp. 1, 14.

———. 2000. "The Vanishing Black Farmer." *Christian Science Monitor*. (July 13). Pp. 1, 3.

Parsons, Talcott. 1951. *The Social System*. New York: Free Press.

———. 1966. Societies: *Evolutionary and Comparative Perspectives*. Englewood Cliffs, NJ: Prentice Hall.

———. 1972. "Definitions of Health and Illness in the Light of American Values and Social Structure." Pp. 166–187 in *Patients, Physicians and Illness*, edited by Gartley Jaco. New York: Free Press.

———. 1975. "The Sick Role and the Role of the Physician Reconsidered." *Milbank Medical Fund Quarterly Health and Society* 53 (Summer): 257–278.

———, and Robert Bales. 1955. *Family: Socialization, and Interaction Process*. Glencoe, IL: Free Press.

Pate, Antony M., and Edwin E. Hamilton. 1992. "Formal and Informal Deterrents to Domestic Violence: The Dade County Spouse Assault

Experiment." *American Sociological Review* 57 (October):691–697.

Patterson, Orlando. 1998. "Affirmative Action." *Brookings Review* 16 (Spring):17–23.

Pattillo-McCoy, Mary. 1999. *Black Picket Fences: Privilege and Peril among the Black Middle Class*. Chicago: University of Chicago Press.

Patton, Carl V., ed. 1988. *Spontaneous Shelter: International Perspectives and Prospects*. Philadelphia: Temple University Press.

Paul, Pamela. 2001a. "Turning Up the Heat." *American Prospect* 23 (July):22–23.

———. 2001b. "The Death Penalty." *American Demographics* 23 (November):22–23.

Paulos, John Allen. 1988. *Innumeracy*. Harmondsworth, England: Penguin Books.

Paulson, Amanda. 2000. "Where the School Is Home." *Christian Science Monitor*, October 10, Pp. 18–21.

Pavalko, Ronald M., ed. 1972. *Sociological Perspectives on Occupations and Professions*. 2d ed. Itasca, IL: F. E. Peacock.

PBS. 2001. "Store Wars: When Wal-Mart Comes to Town." Accessed August 24, 2001 (www.pbs.org).

Pear, Robert. 1983. "$1.5 Billion Urged for U.S. Japanese Held in War." *New York Times*, June 17, Pp. A1, D16.

———. 1996. "Clinton Endorses the Most Radical of Welfare Trials." *New York Times*, May 19, Pp. 1, 20.

———. 1997a. "New Estimate Doubles Rate of H.I.V. Spread." *New York Times*, November 26, p. A6.

———. 1997b. "Now, the Archenemies Need Each Other." *New York Times*, June 22, Sec. 4, Pp. 1, 4.

Pearlstein, Steven. 2001. "Coming Soon (Maybe): Worldwide Recession." *Washington Post National Weekly Edition* 19 (November 12):18.

Pelton, Tom. 1994. "Hawthorne Works' Glory Now Just So Much Rubble." *Chicago Tribune*, April 18, Pp. 1, 6.

People. 2001. "Most Cover Appearances." April.

Perlman, Ilene. 2000. "Some Cover; Some Don't." *Christian Science Monitor*, August 11. Accessed August 14 (http://csmonitor.com).

Perlman, Janice E. 2001. *The Metamorphosis of Marginality: The Favelas of Rio de Janeiro: 1996–2001*. Paper presented at the annual meeting of the American Sociological Association, Anaheim, CA.

Perrow, Charles. 1999. *Normal Accidents: Living with High Risk Technologies*. Updated edition. New Brunswick, NJ: Rutgers University Press.

———. 1986. *Complex Organizations*. 3d ed. New York: Random House.

Perry, Suzanne. 1998a. "Human Rights Abuses Get Internet Spotlight." Reuters, February 4.

———. 1998b. "U.S. Data Companies Oppose Primary Laws." Reuters, March 19.

Peter, Laurence J., and Raymond Hull. 1969. *The Peter Principle*. New York: Morrow.

Petersen, William. 1979. *Malthus*. Cambridge, MA: Harvard University Press.

Peterson, Karen S. 2001. "Grandparents' Labor of Love." *USA Today*, August 6, p. D1.

Pew Charitable Trust. 2000. *Wired Churches, Wired Temples: Taking Congregations and Missions*. New York: The Pew Charitable Trust.

Pew Research Center for the People and the Press. 2001. "Youth Vote Influenced by Online Information." Accessed December 29, 2001 (www.people-press.org/online00rpt,htm).

PFLAG (Parents, Families, and Friends of Lesbians and Gays). 2001. *Frequently Asked Questions about PFLAG.* Accessed October 14 (www.pflag.org).

Phelan, Michael P., and Scott A. Hunt. 1998. "Prison Gang Members' Tattoos as Identity Work: The Visual Comments of Moral Careers." *Symbolic Interaction* 21 (No. 3):277–298.

Phillips, E. Barbara. 1996. *City Lights: Urban—Suburban Life in the Global Society.* New York: Oxford University Press.

Piaget, Jean. 1954. *The Construction of Reality in the Child.* Translated by Margaret Cook. New York: Basic Books.

Piller, Charles. 2000. "Cyber-Crime Loss at Firms Doubles to $10 Billion." *Los Angeles Times,* May 22, Pp. C1, C4.

———. 2001. "Terrorists Taking up Cyberspace." *Los Angeles Times,* February 8, Pp. A1, A14, A15.

Pinderhughes, Dianne. 1987. *Race and Ethnicity in Chicago Politics: A Reexamination of Pluralist Theory.* Urbana: University of Illinois Press.

Plant, Richard. 1986. *The Pink Triangle: The Nazi War against Homosexuals.* New York: Holt.

Platt, Leah. 2001. "Not Your Father's High School Club." *American Prospect* 12 (January 1):37–39.

Plomin, Robert. 1989. "Determinants of Behavior." *American Psychologist* 44 (February):105–111.

Polakovic, Gary. 2001. "Latinos, Poor Live Closer to Sources of Air Pollution." *Los Angeles Times* (October 18). Pp. B1, B12.

Pollak, Michael. 2000. "World's Dying Languages, Alive on the Web." *New York Times,* October 19, p. D13.

Pollack, William. 1998. *Real Boys: Rescuing Our Sons from the Myths of Boyhood.* New York: Holt.

Pomerance, Mary, ed. 2001. *Ladies and Gentlemen, Boys and Girls: Gender in Film at the End of the Twentieth Century.* Albany, NY: A State University of New York Press.

Pomfret, John. 2000. "A New Chinese Revolution." *Washington Post National Weekly Edition* (February 21):17–19.

———. 2001. "Where the Boys Are." *Washington Post National Weekly Edition* 18 (June 11):15.

———, and Philip P. Pan. 2001. "One Way to Stop a Nonviolent Group." *Washington Post National Weekly Edition* 18 (August 13):15.

Ponczek, Ed. 1998. "Are Hiring Practices Sensitive to Persons with Disabilities?" *Footnotes* 26 (No. 3):5.

Poniewozik. 2001. "What's Wrong with This Picture." *Time* 157 (May 28):80–81.

Population Reference Bureau. 1996. "Speaking Graphically." *Population Today* 24 (June/July):b.

———. 2000. "More Youths Take Alternative Route to Finish High School." *Population Today* 28 (January):7.

Powers, Mary G., and Joan J. Holmberg. 1978. "Occupational Status Scores: Changes Introduced by the Inclusion of Women." *Demography* 15 (May):183–204.

Prehn, John W. 1991. "Migration." Pp. 190–191 in *Encyclopedia of Sociology,* 4th ed. Guilford, CT: Dushkin.

Prentice, Eve-Ann. 2001. "No Go: Whites Not Welcome." *The Times* (London), April 20. Accessed June 3 (http://www. thetimes.co.uk).

Princeton Religion Research Center. 2000. "Nearly Half of Americans Describe Themselves as Evangelicals." *Emerging Trends* 22 (April):5.

———. 2001. "Born-Again Segment of Populace Trended Upward During 1990's." *Emerging Trends* 23 (April):1.

———. 2002. *Religion in America 2002.* Princeton, NJ: PRRC.

Prusher, Ilene R. 2001. "Well-ordered Homelessness: Life on Japan's Fringe." *Wall Street Journal,* May 14, Pp. 1, 8.

Pyle, Amy. 1998. "Opinions Vary on Studies That Back Bilingual Classes." *Los Angeles Times,* March 2, Pp. B1, B3.

Q

Quadagno, Jill. 2002. *Aging and the Life Course: An Introduction to Social Gerontology,* 2d ed. New York: McGraw-Hill.

Quarantelli, Enrico L. 1957. "The Behavior of Panic Participants." *Sociology and Social Research* 41 (January):187–194.

———. 1992. "Disaster Research." Pp. 492–498 in *Encyclopedia of Sociology,* Vol. 2, edited by Edgar F. Borgatta and Marie L. Borgatta. New York: Macmillan.

———, and James R. Hundley, Jr. 1975. "A Test of Some Propositions about Crowd Formation and Behavior." Pp. 538–554 in *Readings in Collective Behavior,* edited by Robert R. Evans. Chicago: Rand McNally.

Quinney, Richard. 1970. *The Social Reality of Crime.* Boston: Little, Brown.

———. 1974. *Criminal Justice in America.* Boston: Little, Brown.

———. 1979. *Criminology.* 2d ed. Boston: Little, Brown.

———. 1980. *Class, State and Crime.* 2d ed. New York: Longman.

R

Rainie, Lee. 2001. *The Commons of the Tragedy.* Washington, DC: Pew Internet and American Life Project.

———, and Andrew Kohut. 2000. *Tracking Online Life: How Women Use the Internet to Cultivate Relationships with Family and Friends.* Washington, DC: Pew Internet and American Life League.

———, and Dan Pakel. 2001. *More Online, Doing More.* Washington, DC: Pew Internet and American Life Project.

Ramet, Sabrina. 1991. *Social Currents in Eastern Europe: The Source and Meaning of the Great Transformation.* Durham, NC: Duke University Press.

Raybon, Patricia. 1989. "A Case for 'Severe Bias.'" *Newsweek* 114 (October 2):11.

Rayman-Read, Alyssa. 2001. "The Sound of Silence." *The American Prospect.* (Fall Special Supplement):A20–A24.

Read, Jen'nan Ghazal, and John P. Bartkowski. 1999. "To Veil or Not to Veil? A Case Study of Identity Negotiations Among Muslim Women in Austin, Texas." Presented at the annual

meeting of the American Sociological Association, August, Chicago.

Reddick, Randy, and Elliot King. 2000. *The Online Student: Making the Grade on the Internet.* Fort Worth: Harcourt Brace.

Redish, Martia H. 2001. *Money Talks: Speech, Economic Power, and the Values of Democracy.* New York: New York University Press.

Reese, William A., II, and Michael A. Katovich. 1989. "Untimely Acts: Extending the Interactionist Conception of Deviance." *Sociological Quarterly* 30 (2):159–184.

Regar, Tom. 2000. *Defending Animal Rights.* Urbana, IL: University of Illinois Press.

Reich, Robert B. 2001. "Working, but Not 'Employed.'" *New York Times,* January 9, p. H25.

Reinharz, Shulamit. 1992. *Feminist Methods in Social Research.* New York: Oxford University Press.

Religion Watch. 1995. "European Dissenting Movement Grows among Laity Theologians." 10 (October):6–7.

———. 2001. "Gay-Based MCC Funds Mainline Acceptance." 16 (April):2–3.

Remnick, David. 1998. "Bad Seeds." *New Yorker* 74 (July 20):28–33.

Rennison, Callie Marie. 2001. *Criminal Victimization 2000. Changes 1999–2000 with Trends 1993–2000.* Washington, DC: Bureau of Justice Statistics.

———, and Sarah Welchans. 2000. *Intimate Partner Violence.* Washington, DC: U.S. Government Printing Office.

Reskin, Barbara, and Irene Padavic. 1994. *Women and Men at Work.* Thousand Oaks, CA: Pine Forge Press.

Retsinas, Joan. 1988. "A Theoretical Reassessment of the Applicability of Kübler-Ross's Stages of Dying." *Death Studies* 12:207–216.

Rhodes, Eric Bryant. 2000. "Fatherhood Matters." *The American Prospect,* March 13, Pp. 48–52.

Richard, Amy O'Neill. 2000. *International Trafficking in Women to the United States: A Contemporary Manifestation of Slavery and Organized Crime.* Washington, DC: Center for the Study of Intelligence, CIA.

Richardson, James T., and Barend van Driel. 1997. "Journalists' Attitudes Toward New Religious Movements." *Review of Religious Research* 39 (December):116–136.

Richardson, Laurel, Verta Taylor, and Nancy Whittier, eds. 2001. *Feminist Frontiers.* 5th ed. New York: McGraw-Hill.

Richman, Joseph. 1992. "A Rational Approach to Rational Suicide." *Suicide and Life-Threatening Behavior* 22 (Spring):130–141.

Richtel, Matt. 2000. "www.layoffs.com." *New York Times,* June 22, Pp. C1, C12.

Rideout, Victoria J., Ulla G. Foehr, Donald E. Roberts, and Mollyann Brodie. 1999. *Kids & Media @ the New Millennium.* New York: Kaiser Family Foundation.

Ridgeway, Cecilia L., and Lynn Smith-Lovin. 1999. "The Gender System and Interaction." Pp. 191–216 in *The Annual Review of Sociology 1999,* edited by Karen Cook and John Hagan. Palo Alto, CA: Annual Review.

Riding, Alan. 1998. "Why 'Titanic' Conquered the World." *New York Times,* April 26, Sec. 2, Pp. 1, 28, 29.

Rifkin, Jeremy. 1995a. *The End of Work; The Decline of the Global Labor Force and the Dawn of the Post-Market Era.* New York: Tarcher/Putnam.

———. 1995b. "Afterwork." *Utne Reader* (May/June):52–62.

———. 1996. "Civil Society in the Information Age." *The Nation* 262 (February 26):11–12, 14–16.

———. 1998. *The Biotech Century: Harnessing the Gene and Remaking the World.* New York: Tarcher/Putnam.

Riley, John W., Jr. 1992. "Death and Dying." Pp. 413–418 in *Encyclopedia of Sociology*, Vol. 1, edited by Edgar F. Borgatta and Marie L. Borgatta. New York: Macmillan.

Riley, Matilda White, Robert L. Kahn, and Anne Foner. 1994a. *Age and Structural Lag.* New York: Wiley InterScience.

———, and ———, in association with Karin A. Mock. 1994b. "Introduction: The Mismatch between People and Structures." Pp. 1–36 in *Age and Structural Lag,* edited by Matilda White Riley, Robert L. Kahn, and Ann Foner. New York: Wiley InterScience.

Riley, Nancy E. 1996. China's 'Missing Girls:' Prospects and Policy." *Population Today,* February, Pp. 4–5.

Rimer, Sara. 1998. "As Centenarians Thrive, 'Old' Is Redefined." *New York Times,* June 22, Pp. A1, A14.

Riska, Elianne. 2001. *Medical Careers and Feminist Agendas: American, Scandinavian, and Russian Women Physicians.* Hawthorne, NY: Aldine de Gruyter.

Ritzer, George. 1977. *Working: Conflict and Change.* 2d ed. Englewood Cliffs, NJ: Prentice Hall.

———. 1995. *Modern Sociological Theory.* 4th ed. New York: McGraw-Hill.

———. 2000. *The McDonaldization of Society.* New Century Edition. Thousand Oaks, CA: Pine Forge Press.

Robberson, Tod. 1995. "The Mexican Miracle Unravels." *Washington Post National Weekly Edition,* January 6, p. 20.

Roberts, D. F. 1975. "The Dynamics of Racial Intermixture in the American Negro—Some Anthropological Considerations." *American Journal of Human Genetics* 7 (December): 361–367.

———, Lisa Henriksen, Peter G. Christenson, and Marcy Kelly. 1999. "Substance Abuse in Popular Movies and Music." Accessible online (http://www.whitehousedrugpolicy.gov/news/press/042899.html). Washington, DC: Office of Juvenile Justice.

———. C. Henricksen, and P. G. Christiansson. 1999. *Substance Use in Popular Movies and Music.* Washington, DC: U.S. Department of Health and Human Services, Substance Abuse and Mental Health Administration, and Office of National Drug Control Policy.

Roberts, Johnnie L. 2001. "All for One, One for AOL." *Newsweek,* January 1, Pp. 63–65.

Roberts, Keith A. 1995. *Religion in Sociological Perspective.* 3d ed. Belmont, CA: Wadsworth.

Roberts, Lynne D., and Malcolm R. Parks. 1999. "The Social Geography of Gender-Switching in Virtual Environments on the Internet." *Information, Communication and Society* 2 (Winter).

Roberts, Sam. 1994. "Hispanic Population Now Outnumbers Blacks in Four Major Cities as Demographics Shift." *New York Times,* October 9, p. 34.

Robertson, Roland. 1988. "The Sociological Significance of Culture: Some General Considerations." *Theory, Culture, and Society* 5 (February):3–23.

Robinson, James D., and Thomas Skill. 1993. "The Invisible Generation: Portrayals of the Elderly on Television." University of Dayton. Unpublished paper.

Robinson, Thomas N., Marta L. Wilde, Lisa C. Navracruz, K. Farish Haydel, and Ann Varady. 2001. "Effects of Reducing Children's Television and Video Game Use on Aggressive Behavior." *Archives of Pediatric Adolescent Medicine* 155 (January):17–23.

Rocks, David. 1999. "Burger Giant Does as Europeans Do." *Chicago Tribune,* January 6, Sec. 3, Pp. 1, 4.

Rodberg, Simon. 1999. "Woman and Man at Yale." *Culturefront Online.* Accessed September 9 (http://www.culturefront.org/culturefront/magazine/99/spring/ article.5.html).

Rodriguez, Clara E. 1997. *Latin Looks: Images of Latinas and Latinos in the U.S. Media.* Boulder, CO: Westmier.

Roeper, Richard. 1999. *Urban Legends.* Franklin Lakes, NJ: Career Press.

Roethlisberger, Fritz J., and W. J. Dickson. 1939. *Management and the Worker.* Cambridge, MA: Harvard University Press.

Romero, Mary. 1988. "Chicanas Modernize Domestic Service." *Qualitative Sociology* 11:319–334.

Romney, Lee. 1998. "Latinos Get Down to Business." *Los Angeles Times,* November 11, Pp. A1, A20.

Rose, Arnold. 1951. *The Roots of Prejudice.* Paris: UNESCO.

Rose, Peter I., Myron Glazer, and Penina Migdal Glazer. 1979. "In Controlled Environments: Four Cases of Intense Resocialization." Pp. 320–338 in *Socialization and the Life Cycle,* edited by Peter I. Rose. New York: St. Martin's.

Rosen, Laurel. 2001. "If U Cn Rd Ths Msg, U Cn B Txtin W/Millions in Europe and Asia." *Los Angeles Times,* July 3, p. A5.

Rosenbaum, Lynn. 1996. "Gynocentric Feminism: An Affirmation of Women's Values and Experiences Leading Us toward Radical Social Change." *SSSP Newsletter* 27 (1):4–7.

Rosenberg, Debra. 2001. "A Place of Their Own." *Newsweek* 137 (January 15):54–55.

Rosenberg, Douglas H. 1991. "Capitalism." Pp. 33–34 in *Encyclopedic Dictionary of Sociology,* 4th ed., edited by Dushkin Publishing Group. Guilford, CT: Dushkin.

Rosenblatt, Robert A. 2000. "AARP Struggles to Bridge Boomer Generation Gap." *Los Angeles Times,* May 16, Pp. A1, A10.

Rosenthal, Elisabeth. 2001. "College Entrance in China: 'No' to the Handicapped." *New York Times,* May 23, p. A3.

Rosenthal, Elizabeth. 1999a. "Women's Suicides Reveal Rural China's Bitter Roots." *New York Times,* January 24, Pp. A1, A8.

———. 1999b. "Web Sites Bloom in China, and Are Waded." *New York Times,* December 23, Pp. A1, A10.

———. 2000. "China Lists Controls to Restrict the Use of E-Mail and Web." *New York Times,* January 27, Pp. A1, A10.

Rosenthal, Robert, and Elisha Y. Babad. 1985. "Pygmalion in the Gymnasium." *Educational Leadership* 45 (September):36–39.

———, and Lenore Jacobson. 1968. *Pygmalion in the Classroom.* New York: Holt.

Rosier, Katherine Brown. 2000. *Mothering Inner-city Children: The Early School Years.* New Brunswick, NJ: Rutgers University Press.

Rosman, Abraham, and Paula G. Rubel. 1994. *The Tapestry of Culture: An Introduction to Cultural Anthropology.* 5th ed. Chapter 1, Map. p. 35. New York: McGraw-Hill.

Rosnow, Ralph L., and Gary L. Fine. 1976, *Rumor and Gossip: The Social Psychology of Hearsay.* New York: Elsevier.

Ross, John. 1996. "To Die in the Street: Mexico City's Homeless Population Booms as Economic Crisis Shakes Social Protections." *SSSP Newsletter* 27 (Summer):14–15.

Rossi, Alice S. 1968. "Transition to Parenthood." *Journal of Marriage and the Family* 30 (February):26–39.

———. 1964. "Gender and Parenthood." *American Sociological Review* 49 (February):1–19.

Rossi, Peter H. 1987. "No Good Applied Social Research Goes Unpunished." *Society* 25 (November/December): 73–79.

———. 1989. *Down and Out in America: The Origins of Homelessness.* Chicago: University of Chicago Press.

———. 1990. "The Politics of Homelessness." Presented at the annual meeting of the American Sociological Association, Washington, DC.

Rossides, Daniel W. 1997. *Social Stratification: The Interplay of Class, Race, and Gender.* 2d ed. Upper Saddle River, NJ: Prentice Hall.

Roszak, Theodore. 1969. *The Making of a Counterculture.* Garden City, NY: Doubleday.

Roxane Laboratories. 2000. "Daily Dosing of Available Antiretroviral Agents."

Roy, Donald F. 1959. "'Banana Time': Job Satisfaction and Informal Interaction." *Human Organization* 18 (Winter):158–168.

Rubin, Charles T. 1994. *The Green Crusade: A History of the Environmental Idea.* New Brunswick, NJ: Transaction Books.

Russo, Nancy Felipe. 1976. "The Motherhood Mandate." *Journal of Social Issues* 32:143–153.

Ryan, William. 1976. *Blaming the Victim.* Rev. ed. New York: Random House.

S

Sadker, Myra Pollack, and David Miller Sadker. 1985. "Sexism in the Schoolroom of the '80s." *Psychology Today* 19 (March): 54–57.

———, and ———. 2000. *Teachers, Schools, and Sociology.* 5th ed. New York: McGraw-Hill.

Safire, William. 1996. "Downsized." *New York Times Magazine,* May 26, Pp. 12, 14.

Sagarin, Edward, and Jose Sanchez. 1988. "Ideology and Deviance: The Case of the Debate over the Biological Factor." *Deviant Behavior* 9 (1):87–99.

Sale, Kirkpatrick. 1996. *Rebels against the Future: The Luddites and Their War on the Industrial Revolution* (with a new preface by the author). Reading, MA: Addison-Wesley.

———. 1997. "Ban Cloning? Not a Chance." *New York Times,* March 7, p. A17.

Salem, Richard, and Stanislaus Grabarek. 1986. "Sociology B.A.s in a Corporate Setting: How Can They Get There and of What Value Are They?" *Teaching Sociology* 14 (October):273–275.

Salinger, Adrienne. 1999. *Living Solo.* Kansas City, MO: Andrews McMeel.

Salins, Peter D. 1996. "How to Create a Real Housing Crisis." *New York Times,* October 26, p. 19.

Salkever, Alex. 1999. "Making Machines More Like Us." *Christian Science Monitor,* December 20, electronic edition.

Samuelson, Paul A., and William D. Nordhaus. 2001. *Economics.* 17th ed. New York: McGraw-Hill.

Samuelson, Robert J. 1996a. "Are Workers Disposable?" *Newsweek* 127, February 12, p. 47.

———. 1996b. "Fashionable Statements," *Washington Post National Weekly Edition* 13, March 18, p. 5.

Samuelson, Robert J. 2001. "The Specter of Global Aging." *Washington Post National Weekly Edition* 18 (March 11):27.

Sandberg, Jared. 1999. "Spinning a Web of Hate." *Newsweek* 134 (July 19):28–29.

Sassen, Saskia. 1999. *Guests and Aliens.* New York: The New Press.

Sassen, Saskia. 2001. *The Global City.* 2d ed. New Brunswick, NJ: Princeton University Press.

Saukko, Paula. 1999. "Fat Boys and Goody Girls." In Weighty Issues: Fatness and Thinness as Social Problems, edited by Jeffrey Sobal and Donna Mauer. New York: Aldine de Gruyter.

Savishinsky, Joel S. 2000. *Breaking the Watch: The Meaning of Retirement in America.* Ithaca, NY: Cornell University Press.

Sawyer, Tom. 2000. "Antiretroviral Drug Costs." Correspondence to author from Roxane Laboratories, Cincinnati, OH, January 19.

Sax, Linda J., Alexander W. Astin, William S. Korn, and Kathryn M. Mahoney. 2000. *The American Freshman National Norms for Fall 2000.* Los Angeles: Higher Education Research Institute, UCLA.

———. Jennifer A. Lindholm, Alexander W. Astin, William S. Korn, and Kathryn M. Mahomey. 2001. The American Freshman: National Norms for Fall 2001. Los Angeles: Higher Education Research Institute, UCLA.

Scarce, Rik. 1994. "(No) Trial (But) Tribulations: When Courts and Ethnography Conflict." *Journal of Contemporary Ethnography* 23 (July):123–149.

———. 1995. "Scholarly Ethics and Courtroom Antics: Where Researchers Stand in the Eyes of the Law." *American Sociologist* 26 (Spring):87–112.

Schachter, Jason. 2001. "Geographical Mobility: Population Characteristics." *Current Population Reports,* Ser. p. 20, No. 538. Washington, DC: U.S. Government Printing Office.

Schaefer, Peter. 1995. "Destroy Your Future." *Daily Northwestern,* November 3, p. 8.

Schaefer, Richard T. 1993. *Racial and Ethnic Groups.* 5th ed. New York: Harper Collins.

———. 1998a. "Differential Racial Mortality and the 1995 Chicago Heat Wave." Presentation at the annual meeting of the American Sociological Association, August, San Francisco.

———. 1998b. *Alumni Survey.* Chicago, IL: Department of Sociology, DePaul University.

———. 2002. *Racial and Ethnic Groups.* 8th Special Census ed. Upper Saddle River, NJ: Prentice Hall.

Schaefer, Sandy. 1996. "Peaceful Play." Presentation at the annual meeting of the Chicago Association for the Education of Young Children, Chicago.

Scheff, Thomas J. 1999. *Being Mentally Ill: A Sociological Theory.* 3d ed. New York: Aldine de Gruyter.

Schellenberg, Kathryn, ed. 1996. *Computers in Society.* 6th ed. Guilford, CT: Dushkin.

Schemo, Diana Jean. 2001. "In Covenant Marriage, Forging Ties that Bind." *New York Times,* November 10, p. A8.

Schiesel, Seth. 2001. "Vivendi: La Difference." *New York Times,* August 27, Pp. C1, C9.

Schlenker, Barry R., ed. 1985. *The Self and Social Life.* New York: McGraw-Hill.

Schleuning, Neala J. 1994. *Women, Community, and the Hormel Strike of 1985–1986.* Westport, CT: Greenwood.

Schmetzer, Uli. 1999. "Modern India Remains Shackled to Caste System." *Chicago Tribune,* December 25, p. 23.

Schmidt, William E. 1990. "New Vim and Vigor for the Y.M.C.A." *New York Times,* July 18, Pp. C1, C10.

Schnaiberg, Allan. 1994. *Environment and Society: The Enduring Conflict.* New York: St. Martin's.

Schnaiberg, Lynn. 1999. "Study Finds Home Schoolers Are Top Achievers on Tests." *Education Week* 18 (March 31):5.

Schrag, Peter. 2002. "Ashcroft's Hypocrisy." *The American Prospect,* January 14, Pp. 24–25.

Schulman, Andrew. 2001. *The Extent of Systematic Monitoring of Employee E-mail and Internet Users.* Denver, CO: Workplace Surveillance Project, Privacy Foundation.

Schur, Edwin M. 1965. *Crimes without Victims: Deviant Behavior and Public Policy.* Englewood Cliffs, NJ: Prentice Hall.

———. 1968. *Law and Society: A Sociological View.* New York: Random House.

———. 1985. "'Crimes without Victims': A 20 Year Reassessment." Paper presented at the annual meeting of the Society for the Study of Social Problems.

Schwab, William A. 1993. "Recent Empirical and Theoretical Developments in Sociological Human Ecology." Pp. 29–57 in *Urban Sociology in Transition,* edited by Ray Hutchison. Greenwich, CT: JAI Press.

Schwartz, Howard D., ed. 1987. *Dominant Issues in Medical Sociology.* 2d ed. New York: Random House.

Scioline, Elaine. 1993. "U.S. Rejects Notion That Human Rights Vary with Culture," *New York Times,* June 15, Pp. A1, A18.

Scott, Alan. 1990. *Ideology and the New Social Movements.* London: Unwin Hyman.

Scott, Ellen Kaye. 1993. "How to Stop the Rapists? A Question of Strategy in Two Rape Crisis Centers." *Social Problems* 40 (August):343–361.

Scott, Gregory. 2001. "Broken Windows behind Bars: Eradicating Prison Gangs through Ecological Hardening and Symbolic Cleansing." *Corrections Management Quarterly* 5 (Winter):23–36.

Second Harvest. 2001. *America's Second Harvest: Our Network.* Accessed April 10 (http://www.secondharvest.org/foodbanks.html).

Secretan, Thierry. 1995. *Going into Darkness: Fantastic Coffins from Africa.* London: Thames and Hudson.

Segall, Alexander. 1976. "The Sick Role Concept: Understanding Illness Behavior." *Journal of Health and Social Behavior* 17 (June): 163–170.

Segall, Rebecca. 1998. "Sikh and Ye Shall Find." *Village Voice* 43 (December 15):46–48, 53.

Segerstrāle, Ullica. 2000. *Defense of the Truth: The Battle for Science in the Sociobiology Debate and Beyond.* New York: Oxford University Press.

Seidman, Steven. 1994. "Heterosexism in America: Prejudice against Gay Men and Lesbians." Pp. 578–593 in *Introduction to Social Problems,* edited by Craig Calhoun and George Ritzer. New York: McGraw-Hill.

Seims, Sara. 2001. "Family Planning's Health Endangered." *Los Angeles Times,* August 26, p. M3.

Senior Action in a Gay Environment (SAGE). 1999. *One Family All Ages.* New York: SAGE.

Sernau, Scott. 2001. *Worlds Apart: Social Inequalities in a New Century.* Thousand Oaks, CA: Pine Forge Press.

Shapiro, Isaac. 2001. *The Latest IRS Data on After-Tax Income Trends.* Washington, DC: Center on Budget and Policy Priorities.

Shapiro, Joseph P. 1993. *No Pity: People with Disabilities Forging a New Civil Rights Movement.* New York: Times Books.

Sharma, Hari M., and Gerard C. Bodeker. 1998. "Alternative Medicine." Pp. 228–229 in *Britannica Book of the Year 1998.* Chicago: Encyclopaedia Britannica.

Shcherbak, Yuri M. 1996. "Ten Years of the Chernobyl Era." *Scientific American* 274 (April): 44–49.

Sheehy, Gail. 1999. *Understanding Men's Passages: Discovering the New Map of Men's Lives.* New York: Ballantine Books.

Shenon, Philip. 1995. "New Zealand Seeks Causes of Suicides by Young." *New York Times,* July 15, p. 3.

———. 1998. "Sailor Victorious in Gay Case on Internet Privacy." *New York Times,* June 12, Pp. A1, A14.

Sherman, Lawrence W., Patrick R. Gartin, and Michael D. Buerger. 1989. "Hot Spots of Predatory Crime: Routine Activities and the Criminology of Place." *Criminology* 27:27–56.

Sherrill, Robert. 1995. "The Madness of the Market." *The Nation* 260 (January 9–16):45–72.

Shibutani, Tamotshu. 1966. *Improvised News: A Sociological Study of Rumor.* Indianapolis: Bobbs-Merrill.

Shields, Rob, ed. 1996. *Cultures of Internet: Virtual Spaces, Real Histories, Living Bodies.* London: Sage.

Shinkai, Hiroguki, and Ugljea Zvekic. 1999. "Punishment." Pp. 89–120 in *Global Report on Crime and Justice,* edited by Graeme Newman. New York: Oxford University Press.

Shiver, Jube, Jr. 2000. "International Firms Gain Foothold in Washington." *Los Angeles Times,* March 12, Pp. A1, A21.

Shogren, Elizabeth. 1994. "Treatment against Their Will." *Los Angeles Times,* August 18, Pp. A1, A14–A15.

Short, Kathleen, Thesia Garner, David Johnson, and Patricia Doyle. 1999. "Experimental Poverty Measures: 1990 to 1997." *Current Population Reports,* Ser. p. 60, No. 205. Washington, DC: U.S. Government Printing Office.

Shupe, Anson D., and David G. Bromley. 1980. "Walking a Tightrope." *Qualitative Sociology* 2:8–21.

Sidiropoulos, Elizabeth et al. 1996. *South Africa Survey 1995/1996.* Johannesburg: South African Institute of Race Relations.

Sigelman, Lee, Timothy Bledsoe, Susan Welch, and Michael W. Combs. 1996. "Making Contact? Black-White Social Interaction in an Urban Setting." *American Journal of Sociology* 5 (March):1306–1332.

Silicon Valley Cultures Project. 2001. The Silicon Valley Cultures Project Website. Accessed January 19, 2002 (www.sjsu.edu/depts/anthrology/svcp).

Sills, David L. 1957. *The Volunteers: Means and Ends in a National Organization.* Glencoe, IL: Free Press.

———. 1968. "Voluntary Associations: Sociological Aspects." Pp. 362–379 in *International Encyclopedia of the Social Sciences,* Vol. 16, edited by D. L. Sills. New York: Macmillan.

Silver, Ira. 1996. "Role Transitions, Objects, and Identity." Symbolic Interaction 10 (1):1–20.

Simmel, Georg. 1950. *Sociology of Georg Simmel.* Translated by K. Wolff. Glencoe, IL: Free Press (originally written in 1902–1917).

Simmons, Ann M. 1998. "Where Fat Is a Mark of Beauty." *Los Angeles Times,* September 30, Pp. A1, A12.

———, and Robin Wright. 2000. "Gender Quota Puts Uganda in Role of Rights Pioneer." *Los Angeles Times,* February 23, p. A1.

Simmons, Tavia, and Grave O'Neill. 2001. *Households and Families: 2000.* Census Briefs C2KBR/01–8. Washington, DC: U.S. Government Printing Office.

Simon, Bernard. 2001. "Canada Warms to Wal-Mart." *New York Times* (November 1), Pp. B1, B3.

Simon, Joshua M. 1999. "Presidential Candidates Face Campaign Finance Issue." *Harvard Crimson,* July 2.

Simon, Stephanie. 2001. "Iowa Town Facing a Diversity Dilemma." *Los Angeles Times* (February 1), p. A5.

Simons, Marlise. 1996. "U.N. Court, for First Time, Defines Rape as War Crime," *New York Times,* June 28, Pp. A1, A10.

———. 1997. "Child Care Sacred as France Cuts Back the Welfare State." *New York Times,* December 31, Pp. A1, A6.

———. 2000. "Dutch Becoming First Nation to Legalize Assisted Suicide." *New York Times,* November 29, p. A3.

Simpson, Sally. 1993. "Corporate Crime." Pp. 236–256 in *Introduction to Social Problems,* edited by Craig Calhoun and George Ritzer. New York: McGraw-Hill.

Sjoberg, Gideon. 1960. *The Preindustrial City: Past and Present.* Glencoe, IL: Free Press.

Skolnick, Jerome H., and Elliot Currie, eds. 2000. *Crisis in American Institutions.* 11th ed. Needham Heights, MA: Allyn and Bacon.

Smart, Barry. 1990. "Modernity, Postmodernity, and the Present." Pp. 14–30 in *Theories of Modernity and Postmodernity,* edited by Bryan S. Turner. Newbury Park, CA: Sage.

Smart Growth. 2001. "About Smart Growth." Accessed August 24, 2001 (www.smartgrowth.org.).

Smeeding, Timothy, Lee Rainwater, and Gary Burtless. 2001. "United States Poverty in a Cross-National Context." *Focus* 21 (Spring):50–54.

Smelser, Neil. 1962. *Theory of Collective Behavior.* New York: Free Press.

———. 1963. *The Sociology of Economic Life.* Englewood Cliffs, NJ: Prentice Hall.

———. 1981. *Sociology.* Englewood Cliffs, NJ: Prentice Hall.

Smith, Christian. 1991. *The Emergence of Liberation Theology: Radical Religion and Social Movement Theory.* Chicago: University of Chicago Press.

Smith, Craig S. 2000. "Globalization Puts a Starbucks into the Forbidden City in Beijing." *New York Times,* November 25, Pp. B1, B2.

———. 2001. "Sect Clings to the Web in the Face of Beijing's Ban." *New York Times,* July 5, Pp. A1, A9.

Smith, Dan. 1999. *The State of the World Atlas.* 6th ed. London: Penguin Books.

Smith, David A. 1995. "The New Urban Sociology Meets the Old: Rereading Some Classical Human Ecology." *Urban Affairs Review* 20 (January):432–457.

Smith, David M. and Gary J. Gates. 2001. *Gay and Lesbian Families in the United States: Same-Sex Unmarried Partner Households.* Washington, D.C.: Human Rights Campaign.

Smith, Denise, and Hava Tillipman. 2000. "The Older Population in the United States." *Current Population Reports,* Ser. p. 20, No. 532. Washington, DC: U.S. Government Printing Office.

Smith, Greg. 1996. "Gender Advertisements Revisited: A Visual Sociology Classic." *Electronic Journal of Sociology* 2(1). Accessed August 10, 2001 (http://www. icaap. org/iuicode?100.2.1.1).

Smith, James F. 2000. "Changes in Population Create Opportunities for Mexico's Fox." *Los Angeles Times,* September 23, p. A2.

———. 2001. "Mexico's Forgotten Find Cause for New Hope." *Los Angeles Times,* February 23, Pp. A1, A12, A13.

Smith, Kristin. 2000. "Who's Minding the Kids? Child Care Arrangements." *Current Population Reports,* Ser. p. 70, No. 70. Washington, DC: U.S. Government Printing Office.

Smith, Michael Peter. 1988. *City, State, and Market.* New York: Basil Blackwell.

Smith, Patricia K. 1994. "Downward Mobility: Is It a Growing Problem?" *American Journal of Economics and Sociology* 53 (January):57–72.

Smith, Tom. 1999. *GSS News: Trendlets: An Inter-Racial Friendship.* Accessed December 17, 2001 (http://www.icpsr.uonich.edu/GSS/about/news/trends.htm).

———. 2001. *Estimating the Muslim Population in the United States.* New York: American Jewish Committee.

Smith, Tony. 2000. *Foreign Attachments: The Power of Ethnic Groups in the Making of American Foreign Policy.* Boston: Harvard University Press.

Smith, William L. 1999. *Families and Communities: An Examination of Nontraditional Lifestyles.* Thousand Oaks, CA: Sage.

Snell, Tracy L. 1997. *Capital Punishment 1996.* Washington, DC: U.S. Government Printing Office.

Snow, David A., Louis A. Zurcher, Jr., and Robert Peters. 1981. "Victory Celebrations as Theater: A Dramaturgical Approach to Crowd Behavior." *Symbolic Interaction* 4:21–42.

Snowdon, David. 2001. *Aging With Grace.* New York: Bantam.

Snyder, Thomas D. 1996. *Digest of Education Statistics 1996.* Washington, DC: U.S. Government Printing Office.

Sohoni, Neera Kuckreja. 1994. "Where Are the Girls?" *Ms.* 5 (July/August):96.

Sørensen, Annemette. 1994. "Women, Family and Class." Pp. 27–47 in *Annual Review of Sociology, 1994,* edited by Annemette Sørensen. Palo Alto, CA: Annual Reviews.

Soriano, Cesar G. 2001. "Latino TV Roles Shrank in 2000, Report Finds." *USA Today,* August 26, p. 3D.

Sorokin, Pitirim A. [1927] 1959. *Social and Cultural Mobility.* New York: Free Press.

South African Institute of Race Relations. 2001a. "The Future at your Fingertips." *Fast Facts* 2 (January):2.

South African Institute of Race Relations. 2001b. "South Africa Survey 2001/2002." Johannesburg: SA 1RR.

Southern Poverty Law Center. 2001. "Active Hate Groups in the United States in 2000." *Intelligence Report* (Spring):34–35.

Spalter-Roth, Roberta M., and Sunhwa Lee. 2000. "Gender in the Early Stages of the Sociological Career." *Research Brief* (American Sociological Association) 1(No. 2):1–11.

———, Jan Thomas, and Felice J. Levine. 2000. "New Doctorates in Sociology: Professions Inside and Outside the Academy." *Research Brief* (American Sociological Association) 1(No. 1):1–9.

Spear, Allan. 1967. *Black Chicago: The Making of a Negro Ghetto.* Chicago, IL: University of Chicago Press.

Specter, Michael. 1996a. "World, Wide, Web: 3 English Words." *New York Times,* April 14, Pp. E1, E5.

———. 1996b. "Russian Polls: Mostly Wrong, but the Only Game in Town," *New York Times,* May 15, Pp. A1, A6.

———. 1998. "Doctors Powerless as AIDS Rakes Africa." *New York Times,* August 6, Pp. A1, A7.

Spengler, Joseph J. 1978. *Facing Zero Population Growth: Reactions and Interpretations, Past and Present.* Durham, NC: Duke University Press.

Spielmann, Peter James. 1992. "11 Population Groups on 'Endangered' List," *Chicago Sun-Times,* November 23, p. 12.

Spitzer, Steven. 1975. "Toward a Marxian Theory of Deviance." *Social Problems* 22 (June):641–651.

Spradley, James H., and David W. McCurdy. 1980. *Anthropology: The Cultural Perspective.* 2d ed. New York: Wiley.

Squire, Peverill. 1988. "Why the 1936 Literary Digest Poll Failed." *Public Opinion Quarterly* 52 (Spring):125–133.

Squishinsky, Joel S. 2000. *Breaking the Watch: The Meaning of Retirement in America.* Ithaca, NY: Cornell University Press.

St. John, Eric. 1997. "A Prescription for Participation." *Black Issues in Higher Education* 14 (December 11):18–23.

Stack, Megan K. 2001. "E-Mail Capability Changes Lives of Sailors Far Away." *Los Angeles Times,* October 23, p. A3.

Staggenborg, Suzanne. 1988. "Consequences of Professionalization and Formalization." *American Sociological Review* 53 (August):585–606.

———. 1989a. "Stability and Innovation in the Women's Movement: A Comparison of Two Movement Organizations." *Social Problems* 36 (February):75–92.

———. 1989b. "Organizational and Environmental Influences on the Development of the Pro-Choice Movement," *Social Forces* 36 (September):204–240.

Stanley, Alessandra. 2001. "Battling the Skepticisms of a Global TV Audience." *New York Times,* November 1, p. B4.

Stark, Rodney, and William Sims Bainbridge. 1979. "Of Churches, Sects, and Cults: Preliminary Concepts for a Theory of Religious Movements." *Journal for the Scientific Study of Religion* 18 (June):117–131.

———. 1985. *The Future of Religion.* Berkeley: University of California Press.

———, and Laurence R. Iannaccone. 1992. "Sociology of Religion." Pp. 2029–2037 in *Encyclopedia of Sociology,* Vol. 4, edited by Edgar F. Borgatta and Marie L. Borgatta. New York: Macmillan.

Starr, Paul. 1982. *The Social Transformation of American Medicine.* New York: Basic Books.

Stavenhagen, Rodolfo. 1994. "The Indian Resurgence in Mexico." *Cultural Survival Quarterly,* Summer/Fall, Pp. 77–80.

Stedman, Nancy. 1998. "Learning to Put the Best Shoe Forward." *New York Times,* October 27.

Steffensmeier, Darrell, and Stephen Demuth. 2000. "Ethnicity and Sentencing Outcomes in U.S. Federal Courts: Who Is Punished More Harshly?" *American Sociological Review* 65 (October):705–729.

Steinberg, Jacques. 2000. "Test Scores Rise, Surprising Critics of Bilingual Ban." *New York Times,* August 20, Pp. 1, 16.

Steinhauer, Jennifer. 2000. "The New Landscape of AIDS." *New York Times,* June 25, Sect. 16, Pp. 1, 15.

Stenning, Derrick J. 1958. "Household Viability among the Pastoral Fulani." Pp. 92–119 in *The Developmental Cycle in Domestic Groups,* edited by John R. Goody. Cambridge, England: Cambridge University Press.

Stephen, Elizabeth Hervey. 1999. "Assisted Reproductive Technologies: Is the Price Too High?" *Population Today* (May):1–2.

Sternberg, Steve. 1999. "Virus Makes Families Pay Twice." *USA Today,* May 24, p. 6D.

Sterngold, James. 1992. "Japan Ends Fingerprinting of Many Non-Japanese," *New York Times,* May 21, p. A11.

Stevenson, David, and Barbara L. Schneider. 1999. *The Ambitious Generation: America's Teenagers, Motivated but Directionless.* New Haven: Yale University Press.

Stolberg, Sheryl. 1995. "Affirmative Action Gains Often Come at a High Cost." *Los Angeles Times,* March 29, Pp. A1, A13–A16.

———. 2000. "Alternative Care Gains a Foothold." *New York Times,* January 31, Pp. A1, A16.

Stone, Brad. 1999. "Get a Life?" *Newsweek* 133 (June 7):68–69.

Stoughton, Stephanie, and Leslie Walker. 1999. "The Merchants of Cyberspace." *Washington Post National Weekly Edition* 16 (February 15):18.

Strassman, W. Paul. 1998. "Third World Housing." Pp. 589–592 in *The Encyclopedia of Housing,* edited by Willem van Vliet. Thousand Oaks, CA: Sage.

Strauss, Anselm. 1977. *Negotiations: Varieties, Contexts, Processes, and Social Order.* San Francisco: Jossey Bass.

Strauss, Gary, and Del Jones. 2000. "Too-bright Spotlight Burns Female CEOs." *USA Today,* December 18, p. 3B.

Strom, Stephanie. 1999. "In Japan, From a Lifetime Job to No Job at All." *New York Times,* February 3, p. A1.

———. 2000. "Tradition of Equality Fading in New Japan." *New York Times* January 4, Pp. A1, A6.

Struck, Doug. 2001. "Life in the Shadows of Death." *International Herald Tribune,* May 4, Pp. 1, 2.

Strum, Charles. 1993. "Schools' Tracks and Democracy." *New York Times,* April 1, Pp. B1, B7.

Sugimoto, Yoshio. 1997. *An Introduction to Japanese Society.* Cambridge, England: Cambridge University Press.

Sumner, William G. 1906. *Folkways.* New York: Ginn.

Sutherland, Edwin H. 1937. *The Professional Thief.* Chicago: University of Chicago Press.

———. 1940. "White-Collar Criminality." *American Sociological Review* 5 (February): 1–11.

———. 1949. *White Collar Crime.* New York: Dryden.

———. 1983. *White Collar Crime: The Uncut Version.* New Haven, CT: Yale University Press.

———, and Donald R. Cressey. 1978. *Principles of Criminology.* 10th ed. Philadelphia: Lippincott.

Suttles, Gerald D. 1972. *The Social Construction of Communities.* Chicago: University of Chicago Press.

Swanson, Stevenson, and Jim Kirk. 1998. "Satellite Outage Felt by Millions." *Chicago Tribune,* May 21, Pp. 1, 26.

Sweet, Kimberly. 2001. "Sex Sells a Second Time." *Chicago Journal* 93 (April):12–13.

Szasz, Thomas S. 1971. "The Same Slave: An Historical Note on the Use of Medical Diagnosis as Justificatory Rhetoric." *American Journal of Psychotherapy* 25 (April):228–239.

———. 1974. *The Myth of Mental Illness* (rev. ed.). New York: Harper and Row.

T

Takezawa, Yasuko I. 1995. *Breaking the Silence: Redress and Japanese American Ethnicity.* Ithaca, NY: Cornell University Press.

Talbot, Margaret. 1998. "Attachment Theory: The Ultimate Experiment." *New York Times Magazine,* May 24, Pp. 4–30, 38, 46, 50, 54.

Tannen, Deborah. 1990. *You Just Don't Understand: Women and Men in Conversation.* New York: Ballantine.

———. 1994a. *Talking from 9 to 5.* New York: William Morris.

———. 1994b. *Gender and Discourse.* New York: Oxford University Press.

Tannock, Stuart. 2001. *Youth at Work: The Unionized Fast Food and Grocery Workplace.* Philadelphia: Temple University Press.

Tashman, Billy. 1992. "Hobson's Choices: Free-Market Education in Plan Vouches for Bush's Favorite Class." *Village Voice* 37 (January 21):educational supplement, Pp. 9, 14.

Taylor, Verta. 1995. "Watching for Vibes: Bringing Emotions into the Study of Feminist Organizations. Pp. 223–233 in *Feminist Organizations: Harvest of the New Women's Movement,* edited by Myra Marx Ferree and Patricia Yancy Martin. Philadelphia: Temple University Press.

Tedeschi, Bob. 2001. "E-Commerce Report." *New York Times,* September 17, p. C6.

Television Bureau of Advertisers. 2001. "TV Historical Data." Personal correspondence to author, July 13, 2001.

Telsch, Kathleen. 1991. "New Study of Older Workers Finds They Can Become Good Investments." *New York Times,* May 21, p. A16.

Terkel, Studs. 1974. *Working.* New York: Pantheon.

Terry, Sara. 2000. "Whose Family? The Revolt of the Child-Free." *Christian Science Monitor,* August 29, Pp. 1, 4.

Texeira, Erin. 2000. "Justice Is Not Color Blind, Studies Find." *Los Angeles Times,* May 22, Pp. B1, B8.

Theberge, Nancy. 1997. "'It's Part of the Game'—Physicality and the Production of Gender in Women's Hockey." *Gender and Society* 11 (February):69–87.

Therrien, Melissa, and Roberto R. Ramirez. 2001. "The Hispanic Population in the United States, March 2000." *Current Population Report,* Ser. p. 20, No. 535. Washington, DC: U.S. Government Printing Office.

Third International Mathematics and Science Study. 1998. *Mathematics and Science Achievement in the Final Year of Secondary School.* Boston: TIMSS International Study Center.

Third World Institute. 1999. *The World Guide 1999–2000.* Oxford, England: New Internationalist Publishers.

———. 2001. *The World Guide 2001–2002.* Oxford, England. New Internationalist Publishers.

Thomas, Gordon, and Max Morgan Witts. 1974. *Voyage of the Damned.* Greenwich, CT: Fawcett Crest.

Thomas, Jim. 1984. "Some Aspects of Negotiating Order: Loose Coupling and Mesostructure in Maximum Security Prisons." *Symbolic Interaction* 7 (Fall):213–231.

Thomas, Pattie, and Erica A. Owens. 2000. "Age Care!: The Business of Passing." Presented at the annual meeting of the American Sociological Association, Washington, DC.

Thomas, Robert McG., Jr. 1995. "Maggie Kuhn, 89, the Founder of the Gray Panthers, Is Dead." *New York Times,* April 23, p. 47.

Thomas, William I. 1923. *The Unadjusted Girl.* Boston: Little, Brown.

Thompson, Ginger. 2001. "Fallout of U.S. Recession Drifts South Into Mexico." *New York Times* (December 26), Pp. C1, C2.

———. 2001a. "Chasing Mexico's Dream into Squalor." *New York Times,* February 11, Pp. 1, 6.

———. 2001b. "Why Peace Eludes Mexico's Indians." *New York Times,* March 11, Sect. WK, p. 16.

Thomson, Elizabeth, and Ugo Colella. 1992. "Cohabitation and Marital Stability: Quality or Commitment?" *Journal of Marriage and the Family* 54 (May):259–267.

Thorne, Barrie. 1992. "Feminism and the Family: Two Decades of Thought." Pp. 3–30 in *Rethinking the Family,* edited by Thorne and Marilyn Yalom. Rev. ed. Boston: Northeastern University.

Thornton, Russell. 1987. *American Indians Holocaust and Survival: A Population History Since 1492.* Norman: University of Oklahoma Press.

Tierney, John. 1990. "Betting the Planet." *New York Times Magazine,* December 2, Pp. 52–53, 71, 74, 76, 78, 80–81.

Tierney, Kathleen. 1980. "Emergent Norm Theory as 'Theory': An Analysis and Critique of Turner's Formulation." Pp. 42–53 in *Collective Behavior: A Source Book,* edited by Meredith David Pugh. St. Paul, MN: West.

Tilly, Charles. 1993. *Popular Contention in Great Britain 1758–1834.* Cambridge, MA: Harvard University Press.

———. 1999. *Durable Inequality.* Berkeley: University of California Press.

Tobin, Joseph J., David T. H. Wu, and Dana H. Davidson. 1989. *Pre-School in Three Cultures: Japan, China and the United States.* New Haven, CT: Yale University Press.

Tolbert, Kathryn. 2000. "In Japan, Traveling Alone Begins at Age 6." *Washington Post National Weekly Edition* 17 (May 15):17.

Tonkinson, Robert. 1978. *The Mardudjara Aborigines.* New York: Holt.

Tönnies, Ferdinand. [1887] 1988. *Community and Society.* Rutgers, NJ: Transaction.

Touraine, Alain. 1974. *The Academic System in American Society.* New York: McGraw-Hill.

Trebay, Guy. 1990. "In Your Face." *Village Voice* 35 (August 14):14–39.

Treiman, Donald J. 1977. *Occupational Prestige in Comparative Perspective.* New York: Academic Press.

Trotter III, Robert T., and Juan Antonio Chavira. 1997. *Curanderismo: Mexican American Folk Healing.* Athens, GA: University of Georgia Press.

Tuchman, Gaye. 1992. "Feminist Theory." Pp. 695–704 in *Encyclopedia of Sociology,* vol. 2, edited by Edgar F. Borgatta and Marie L. Borgatta. New York: Macmillan.

Tucker, James. 1993. "Everyday Forms of Employee Resistance." *Sociological Forum* 8 (March):25–45.

Tumin, Melvin M. 1953. "Some Principles of Stratification: A Critical Analysis." *American Sociological Review* 18 (August):387–394.

———. 1985. *Social Stratification.* 2d ed. Englewood Cliffs, NJ: Prentice Hall.

Ture, Kwame, and Charles Hamilton. 1992. *Black Power: The Politics of Liberation.* Rev. ed. New York: Vintage Books.

Turkle, Sherry. 1995. *Life on the Screen: Identity in the Age of the Internet.* New York: Simon and Schuster.

———. 1999. "Looking Toward Cyberspace: Beyond Grounded Sociology." *Contemporary Sociology* 28 (November):643–654.

Turner, Bryan S., ed. 1990. *Theories of Modernity and Postmodernity.* Newbury Park, CA: Sage.

Turner, Craig. 1998. "U.N. Study Assails U.S. Executions as Biased." *Los Angeles Times,* March 4, p. A1.

Turner, J. H. 1985. *Herbert Spencer: A Renewed Application.* Beverly Hills, CA: Sage.

Turner, Ralph, and Lewis M. Killian. 1987. *Collective Behavior.* 3d ed. Englewood Cliffs, NJ: Prentice Hall.

Twaddle, Andrew. 1974. "The Concept of Health Status." *Social Science and Medicine* 8 (January):29–38.

Twombly, Jennifer, Sheila Crowley, Nancy Ferris, and Cushing N. Dolbeare. 2001. *Out of Reach 2001: American's Growing Wage-Rent Disparity.* Washington, D.C.: National Low Income Housing Coalition.

Tyler, Patrick E. 1995. "For China's Girls, Rural Schools Fail." *New York Times,* December 31, p. 5.

Tyler, William D. 1985. "The Organizational Structure of the School." Pp. 49–73 in *Annual Review of Sociology, 1985,* edited by Ralph H. Turner. Palo Alto, CA: Annual Reviews.

U

Uchitelle, Louis. 1996. "More Downsized Workers Are Returning as Rentals." *New York Times,* December 8, Pp. 1, 34.

———. 2001. "How to Define Poverty? Let Us Count the Ways." *New York Times,* May 26, Pp. A15, A17.

UNAIDS. 2001. *AIDS Epidemic Update: December 2001.* Geneva, Switzerland: World Health Organization.

United Nations Development Programme. 1995. *Human Development Report 1995.* New York: Oxford University Press.

———. 2000. *Poverty Report 2000: Overcoming Human Poverty.* Washington, DC: UNDP.

———. 2001. *Human Development Report 2001. Making New Technologies Work for Human Development.* New York: UNDP.

United Nations Human Rights Commission. 1997. "U.N. Human Rights Commission Acts on Texts." M2 PressWire, 4/9.

United Nations Population Division. 2001a. *World Marriage Patterns 2000.* Accessed August 2 (www.undp.org/popin/wdtrends/worldmarriagepatterns2000.pdf).

———. 1998. *World Abortion Policies.* New York: Department of Economic and Social Affairs, UNPD.

———. 2001b. *World Population Prospects, 2000 Revision.* New York: UNPD.

United Nations. 2000. *The World's Women 2000: Trends and Statistics.* New York: United Nations.

U.S. Committee for Refugees. 2001. *World Refugee Survey 2001.* Washington, DC: U.S. Committee for Refugees.

U.S. Conference of Mayors. 2001. *A Status Report on Hunger and Homelessness in America's Cities 2001.* Washington, D.C.: United States Conference of Mayors.

U.S. Department of State. 1997. *Bhutan County Report on Human Rights Practices for 1996.* Accessed July 15, 2001 (http://www.state.gov/www/global/human_rights/1996_hrp_report/bhutan.html).

U.S. English, Inc. 2001. *Official English: States with Official English Laws.* Accessed October 31, 2001 (http://www.us-english.org/inc/official/states.asp).

U.S. Surgeon General. 2001. *Youth Violence: A Report of the Surgeon General.* Washington, DC: U.S. Government Printing Office.

USA Today. 1998. "Did Tobacco Company Money Kill the Anti-smoking Bill?" June 22, p. 16A.

Utter, Jack. 1993. *American Indians: Answers to Today's Questions.* Lake Ann, MI: National Woodlands Publishing.

Uttley, Alison. 1993. "Who's Looking at You, Kid?" *Times Higher Education Supplement* 30 (April 30):48.

V

van den Berghe, Pierre. 1978. *Race and Racism: A Comparative Perspective.* 2d ed. New York: Wiley.

Van Slambrouck, Paul. 1998. "In California, Taking the Initiative—Online." *Christian Science Monitor,* November 13, Pp. 1, 11.

———. 1999a. "Netting a New Sense of Connection." *Christian Science Monitor,* May 4, Pp. 1, 4.

———. 1999b. "Newest Tool for Social Protest: The Internet." *Christian Science Monitor,* June 18, p. 3.

———. 1999c. "Netting a New Sense of Connection." *Christian Science Monitor,* June 18, p. 3.

van Vucht Tijssen, Lieteke. 1990. "Women between Modernity and Postmodernity." Pp. 147–163 in *Theories of Modernity and Postmodernity,* edited by Bryan S. Turner. London: Sage.

Vanneman, Reeve, and Lynn Weber Cannon. 1987. *The American Perception of Class.* Philadelphia: Temple University Press.

Vaughan, Diane. 1996. *The Challenger Launch Decision: Risky Technology, Culture, and Deviance at NASA.* Chicago: University of Chicago Press.

———. 1999. "The Dark Side of Organizations: Mistake, Misconduct, and Disaster." Pp. 271–305 in *Annual Review of Sociology,* edited by Karen J. Cook and John Hagan. Palo Alto: Annual Reviews.

Veblen, Thorstein. 1919. *The Vested Interests and the State of the Industrial Arts.* New York: Huebsch.

Vega, William A. 1995. "The Study of Latino Families: A Point of Departure." Pp. 3–17 in *Understanding Latino Families: Scholarship, Policy, and Practice,* edited by Ruth E. Zambrana. Thousand Oaks, CA: Sage.

Velkoff, Victoria A., and Valerie A. Lawson. 1998. "Gender of Aging." *International Brief,* Ser. IB, No. 98–3. Washington, DC: U.S. Government Printing Office.

Venkatesh, Sudhir Alladi. 2000. *American Project: The Rise and Fall of a Modern Ghetto.* Cambridge, MA: University of Chicago Press.

Ventura, Stephanie J., Joyce A. Martin, Sally C. Curtin, Fary Menacker, and Brady Hamilton. 2001a. "Births: Final Data for 1999." *National Vital Statistics Reports.* 49 (April 17).

———. 2001b. "Trends in Pregnancy Rates for the United States, 1976–1997: An Update." *National Vital Statistics Reports* 49 (June 6).

Ventura, Stephanie J., T. J. Mathews, and Bradley E. Hamilton. 2001c. "Birth to Teenagers in the United States, 1940–2000." *National Vital Statistics Reports* 49 (September 25).

Verhovek, Sam Howe. 1997. "Racial Tensions in Suit Slowing Drive for 'Environmental Justice,'" *New York Times,* September 7, Pp. 1, 16.

———. 2001. "U.S. Acts to Stop Assisted Suicides." *New York Times,* November 7, Pp. A1, A15.

Vernon, Glenn. 1962. *Sociology and Religion.* New York: McGraw-Hill.

Vernon, Jo Etta A. et al. [4 authors]. 1990. "Media Stereotyping: A Comparison of the Way Elderly Women and Men Are Portrayed on Prime-Time Television." *Journal of Women and Aging* 2 (4):55–68.

Vidaver, R. M. et al. 2000. "Women Subjects in NIH-funded Clinical Research Literature: Lack of Progress in Both Representation and Analysis by Sex. *Journal of Women's Health Gender-Based Medicine* 9 (June):495–504.

Vistica, Gregory. 2000. "One, Two, Three, Out." *Newsweek* 135 (March 20):57–58.

Vladimiroff, Christine. 1998. "Food for Thought." *Second Harvest Update* (Summer):2.

Vobejda, Barbara, and Judith Havenmann. 1997. "Experts Say Side Income Could Hamper Reforms." *Washington Post,* November 3, p. A1.

Voter News Service. 2000. "Breaking Down the Electorate." *Time* 156 (November 20):74.

W

Wacquant, Loïc J. D. 1993. "When Cities Run Riot." *UNESCO Courier,* February, Pp. 8–15.

Wages for Housework Campaign. 1999. *Wages for Housework Campaign.* Circular. Los Angeles.

Wagley, Charles, and Marvin Harris. 1958. *Minorities in the New World: Six Case Studies.* New York: Columbia University Press.

Waite, Linda. 2000. "The Family as a Social Organization: Key Ideas for the Twentieth Century." *Contemporary Sociology* 29 (May):463–469.

Waitzkin, Howard. 1986. *The Second Sickness: Contradictions of Capitalist Health Care.* Chicago: University of Chicago Press.

Waldinger, Roger, ed. 2001. *Strangers at the Gates: New Immigrants in Urban America.* Berkeley: University of California Press.

Walker, Samuel, Cassia Spohn, and Miriam De-Lone. 2000. *The Color of Justice: Race, Ethnicity, and Crime in America.* 2d ed. Belmont, CA: Wadsworth/Thomson.

Wallace, Ruth A., and Alison Wolf. 1980. *Contemporary Sociological Theory.* Englewood Cliffs, NJ: Prentice Hall.

Wallerstein, Immanuel. 1974. *The Modern World System.* New York: Academic Press.

———. 1979a. *Capitalist World Economy.* Cambridge, England: Cambridge University Press.

———. 1979b. *The End of the World As We Know It: Social Science for the Twenty-first Century.* Minneapolis: University of Minnesota Press.

———. 2000. *The Essential Wallerstein.* New York: The New Press.

Wallerstein, Judith S., Judith M. Lewis, and Sandra Blakeslee. 2000. *The Unexpected Legacy of Deviance.* New York: Hyperion.

Wallis, Claudia. 1987. "Is Mental Illness Inherited?" *Time* 129 (March 9):67.

Wal-Mart. 2001. "Wal-Mart News: Our Commitment to Communities." Accessed August 24, 2001 (www.walmartstores. com).

Wal-Mart Watch. 2000. "Riverside, California Swats Wal-Mart Away." Accessed August 24, 2001 (www.Walmartwatch.com).

Walsh, Mary Williams. 2001. "Reversing Decades-long Trend, Americans Retiring Later in Life." *New York Times,* November 16, Pp. A1, A13.

Warner, Michael. 1999. "The Trouble with Normal: Sex, Politics, and the Ethics of Queer Life." *New York Times*: The Free Press.

Washington Transcript Service. 1999. "Hillary Rodham Clinton Holds News Conference on Her New York Senatorial Bid." November 23.

Watts, Jerry G. 1990. "Pluralism Reconsidered." *Urban Affairs Quarterly* 25 (June):697–704.

Webb, Cynthia L. 2001. "The Workweek Gets Longer." *Washington Post National Weekly Edition,* September 10, p. 21.

Weber, Max. [1913–1922] 1947. *The Theory of Social and Economic Organization.* Translated by A. Henderson and T. Parsons. New York: Free Press.

———. [1904] 1949. *Methodology of the Social Sciences.* Translated by Edward A. Shils and Henry A. Finch. Glencoe, IL: Free Press.

———. [1904] 1958a. *The Protestant Ethic and the Spirit of Capitalism.* Translated by Talcott Parsons. New York: Scribner.

———. [1916] 1958b. *The Religion of India: The Sociology of Hinduism and Buddhism.* New York: Free Press.

———. [1921] 1964. *The Theory of Social and Economic Organization.* Translated by A. M. Hendersen and Talcott Parsons. New York: Free Press.

Wechsler, Henry et al. 2000. "College Binge Drinking in the 1990s: A Continuing Program." *Journal of American College Health* 48 (March):199–210.

Weeks, John R. 1999. Population: An Introduction to Concepts and Issues. 7th ed. Belmont, CA: Wadsworth.

———. 2002. *Population: An Introduction to Concepts and Issues.* 8th ed. Belmont, CA: Wadsworth.

Weigard, Bruce. 1992. *Off the Books: A Theory and Critique of the Underground Economy.* Dix Hills, NY: General Hall.

Weinstein, Deena. 1999. Knockin' The Rock: Defining Rock Music as a Social Problem. New York: McGraw-Hill/Primis.

———. 2000. Heavy Metal: *The Music and Its Culture.* Cambridge, MA: Da Capo.

———, and Michael A. Weinstein. 1999. "McDonaldization Enframed." Pp. 57–69 in *Resisting McDonaldization,* edited by Barry Smart. London: Sage.

Weinstein, Henry, Michael Finnegan, and Teresa Watanabe. 2001. "Racial Profiling Gains Support as Search Tactic." *Los Angeles Times,* September 24, Pp. A1, M9.

Wellman, Barry et al. [16 authors]. 1996. "Computer Networks as Social Networks: Collaborative Works Telework, and Virtual Community." Pp. 213–238 in *Annual Review of Sociology, 1996,* edited by John Hagan. Palo Alto, CA: Annual Reviews.

Wells-Barnett, Ida B. 1970. *Crusade for Justice: The Autobiography of Ida B. Wells.* Edited by Alfreda M. Duster. Chicago: University of Chicago Press.

Werum, Regina, and Bill Winders. 2001. "Who's 'In' and Who's 'Out': State Fragmentation and the Struggle over Gay Rights, 1974–1999." *Social Problems* 48 (August):386–410.

West, Candace, and Don H. Zimmerman. 1983. "Small Insults: A Study of Interruptions in Cross Sex Conversations between Unacquainted Persons." Pp. 86–111 in *Language, Gender, and Society,* edited by Barrie Thorne, Cheris Kramarae, and Nancy Henley. Rowley, MA: Newbury House.

———, and ———. 1987. "Doing Gender." *Gender and Society* 1 (June):125–151.

White, Jonathan R. 2002. *Terrorism: An Introduction.* Belmont, CA: Wadsworth.

Whyte, William Foote. 1981. *Street Corner Society: Social Structure of an Italian Slum.* 3d ed. Chicago: University of Chicago Press.

Wickman, Peter M. 1991. "Deviance." Pp. 85–87 in *Encyclopedic Dictionary of Sociology,* 4th ed., by Dushkin Publishing Group. Guilford, CT: Dushkin.

Wilford, John Noble. 1997. "New Clues Show Where People Made the Great Leap to Agriculture." *New York Times,* November 18, Pp. B9, B12.

Wilgoren, Jodi. 2001. "School Test Plan Comes Under Fire by State Officials." *New York Times,* July 17, Pp. A1, A16.

Wilkinson, Tracy. 1999. "Refugees Forming Bonds on Web." *Los Angeles Times,* July 31, p. A2.

Willet, Jeffrey G., and Mary Jo Deegan. 2000. "Liminality? and Disability: The Symbolic Rite of Passage of Individuals with Disabilities." Presented at the annual meeting of the American Sociological Association, Washington, DC.

Williams, Carol J. 1995. "Taking an Eager Step Back." *Los Angeles Times,* June 3, Pp. A1, A14.

Williams, Christine L. 1992. "The Glass Escalator: Hidden Advantages for Men in the 'Female' Professions." *Social Problems* 39 (3):253–267.

———. 1995. *Still a Man's World: Men Who Do Women's Work.* Berkeley: University of California Press.

Williams, J. Allen, Jr., Nicholas Batchuk, and David R. Johnson. 1973. "Voluntary Associations and Minority Status: A Comparative Analysis of Anglo, Black and Mexican Americans." *American Sociological Review* 38 (October):637–646.

Williams, Robin M., Jr. 1970. *American Society.* 3d ed. New York: Knopf.

———, with John P. Dean and Edward A. Suchman. 1964. *Strangers Next Door: Ethnic Relations in American Communities.* Englewood Cliffs, NJ: Prentice Hall.

Williams, Wendy M. 1998. "Do Parents Matter? Scholars Need to Explain What Research Really Shows." *Chronicle of Higher Education* 45 (December 11):B6–B7.

Wilmut, Ian et al. [5 authors]. 1997. "Viable Offering Derived from Fetal and Adult Mammalian Cells." *Nature* 385 (February 27):810–813.

Wilson, Edward O. 1975. *Sociobiology: The New Synthesis.* Cambridge, MA: Harvard University Press.

———. *On Human Nature.* Cambridge, MA: Harvard University Press.

———. 2000. *Sociobiology: The New Synthesis.* Cambridge, MA: Belknap Press, Harvard University Press.

Wilson, James R., and S. Roy Wilson. 2001. *Mass Media. Mass Culture: An Introduction.* 5th ed. New York: McGraw-Hill.

Wilson, John. 1973. *Introduction to Social Movements.* New York: Basic Books.

Wilson, Jolin J. 2000. *Children as Victims.* Washington, DC: U.S. Government Printing Office.

Wilson, Warner, Larry Dennis, and Allen P. Wadsworth, Jr. 1976. "Authoritarianism Left and Right." *Bulletin of the Psychonomic Society* 7 (March):271–274.

Wilson, William Julius. 1980. *The Declining Significance of Race: Blacks and Changing American Institutions.* 2d ed. Chicago: University of Chicago Press.

———. 1987. *The Truly Disadvantaged: The Inner City, the Underclass and Public Policy.* Chicago: University of Chicago Press.

———, ed. 1989. *The Ghetto Underclass: Social Science Perspectives.* Newbury Park, CA: Sage.

———. 1996. *When Work Disappears: The World of the New Urban Poor.* New York: Knopf.

———. 1999a. "Towards a Just and Livable City: The Issues of Race and Class." Address at the Social Science Centennial Conference, April 23. Chicago, IL: DePaul University.

———. 1999b. *The Bridge Over the Racial Divide: Rising Inequality and Coalition Politics.* Berkeley: University of California Press.

Winerip, Michael. 1998. "Schools for Sale." *New York Times Magazine,* July 14, Pp. 42–48, 80, 86, 88–89.

Winter, J. Alan. 1977. *Continuities in the Sociology of Religion.* New York: Harper and Row.

Wirth, Louis. 1928. *The Ghetto.* Chicago: University of Chicago Press.

———. 1938. "Urbanism as a Way of Life." *American Journal of Sociology* 44 (July):1–24.

Wolf, Charles, Jr. 2001. "China's Capitalists Join the Party." *New York Times,* August 13, p. A21.

Wolf, Naomi. 1992. *The Beauty Myth: How Images of Beauty Are Used Against Women.* New York: Anchor.

Wolf, Richard. 1996. "States Can Expect Challenges After Taking Over Welfare." *USA Today,* October 1, p. 8A.

Wolff, Edward N. 1999. "Recent Trends in the Distribution of Household Wealth Ownership." In *Back to Shared Prosperity: The Growing Inequality of Wealth and Income in America,* edited by Ray Marshall. New York: M. E. Sharpe.

———. 2002. *Top Heavy.* Updated ed. New York: New Press.

Wolinsky, Fredric P. 1980. *The Sociology of Health.* Boston: Little, Brown.

Wolraich et al. 1998. "Guidance for Effective Discipline." *Pediatrics* 101 (April):723–728.

Wood, Daniel B. 2000. "Minorities Hope TV Deals Don't Just Lead to 'Tokenism.'" *Christian Science Monitor,* January 19.

Wood, Julia T. 1994. *Gendered Lives: Communication, Gender and Culture.* Belmont, CA: Wadsworth.

Woodard, Colin. 1998. "When Rote Learning Fails against the Test of Global Economy." *Christian Science Monitor,* April 15, p. 7.

Wooden, Wayne. 1995. *Renegade Kids, Suburban Outlaws: From Youth Culture to Delinquency.* Belmont, CA: Wadsworth.

World Bank. 1995. *World Development Report 1994: Workers in an Integrating World.* New York: Oxford University Press.

———. 1997. *World Development Report 1997: The State in a Changing World.* New York: Oxford University Press.

———. 1999a. *World Development Report 1998/1999: Knowledge for Development.* New York: Oxford University Press.

———. 1999b. *World Development Indicators 1999.* New York: Oxford University Press.

———. 2000a. *World Development Report 1999/2000: Entering the 21st Century.* New York: Oxford University Press.

———. 2000b. *World Development Indicators 2000.* Washington, DC: World Bank.

———. 2000c. *World Development Report 2000/2001.* New York: Oxford University Press.

———. 2001a. *World Development Indicators 2001.* Washington, DC: The World Bank.

———. 2001b. *World Development Report 2002. Building Instructions for Markets.* New York: Oxford University Press.

World Desk Reference. 2001. *Vietnam.* Accessed July 19 (www.dk.com).

World Development Forum. 1990. "The Danger of Television." 8 (July 15):4.

World Health Organization (WHO) and UNICEF. 2000. *Global Water Supply and Sanitation Assessment 2000 Report.* Washington, DC: WHO and UNICEF.

World Resources Institute. 1998. *1998–1999 World Resources: A Guide to the Global Environment.* New York: Oxford University Press.

Wresch, William. 1996. *Disconnected: Haves and Have-Nots in the Information Age.* New Brunswick, NJ: Rutgers University Press.

Wright, Charles R. 1986. *Mass Communication: A Sociological Perspective.* 3d ed. New York: Random House.

Wright, Eric R., William P. Gronfein, and Timothy J. Owens. 2000. "Deinstitutionalization, Social Rejection, and the Self-Esteem of Former Mental Patients." *Journal of Health and Social Behavior* (March).

Wright, Erik Olin, David Hachen, Cynthia Costello, and Joy Sprague. 1982. "The American Class Structure." *American Sociological Review* 47 (December):709–726.

Wurman, Richard Saul. 1989. *Information Anxiety.* New York: Doubleday.

Wuthnow, Robert, and Marsha Witten. 1988. "New Directions in the Study of Culture." Pp. 49–67 in *Annual Review of Sociology, 1988,* edited by W. Richard Scott and Judith Blake. Palo Alto, CA: Annual Reviews.

Wynia, Matthew K. et al. 2000. "Physician Manipulation of Reimbursement Rules for Patients: Between a Rock and a Hard Place." *Journal of the American Medical Association* 286 (April 12):1858–1865.

Y

Yamagata, Hisashi, Kuang S. Yeh, Shelby Stewman, and Hiroko Dodge. 1997. "Sex Segregation and Glass Ceilings: A Comparative Statistics Model of Women's Career Opportunities in the Federal Government over a Quarter Century." *American Journal of Sociology* 103 (November):566–632.

Yap, Kioe Sheng. 1998. "Squatter Settlements." Pp. 554–556 in *The Encyclopedia of Housing,* edited by Willem van Vliet. Thousand Oaks, CA: Sage.

Yinger, J. Milton. 1970. *The Scientific Study of Religion.* New York: Macmillan.

———. 1974. "Religion, Sociology of." Pp. 604–613 in *Encyclopaedia Britannica,* Vol. 15. Chicago: Encyclopedia Britannica.

Young, Gay. 1993. "Gender Inequality and Industrial Development: The Household Connection." *Journal of Comparative Family Studies* 124 (Spring):3–20.

Z

Zald, Mayer N. 1970. *Organizational Change: The Political Economy of the YMCA.* Chicago: University of Chicago Press.

Zellner, William M. 1978. "Vehicular Suicide: In Search of Incidence." Western Illinois University, Macomb. Unpublished M.A. thesis.

———. 1995. *Counter Cultures: A Sociological Analysis.* New York: St. Martin's Press.

———. 2001. *Extraordinary Groups: An Examination of Unconventional Lifestyles.* 7th ed. New York: Worth.

———, and Marc Petowsky, eds. 1999. *Sects, Cults, and Spiritual Communities: A Sociological Analysis.* Westport, CT: Praeger.

Zhou, Xueguang, and Liren Hou. 1999. "Children of the Cultural Revolution: The State and the Life Course in the People's Republic of China." *American Sociological Review* 64 (February):32–36.

Zia, Helen. 1993. "Women of Color in Leadership." *Social Policy* 23 (Summer):51–55.

———. 2000. *Asian American Dreams: The Emergence of an American People.* New York: Farrar, Straus, and Giroux.

Zimbardo, Philip G. 1972. "Pathology of Imprisonment." *Society* 9 (April):4, 6, 8.

———. 1992. *Psychology and Life.* 13th ed. New York: HarperCollins.

———, Craig Haney, W. Curtis Banks, and David Jaffe. 1974. "The Psychology of Imprisonments: Privation, Power, and Pathology." In *Doing Unto Others: Joining, Molding, Conforming, Helping, and Loving,* edited by Zick Rubin. Englewood Cliffs, NJ: Prentice Hall.

Zimmer, Lynn. 1988. "Tokenism and Women in the Workplace," *Social Problems* 35 (February):64–77.

Zola, Irving K. 1972. "Medicine as an Institution of Social Control." *Sociological Review* 20 (November):487–504.

———. 1983. *Socio-Medical Inquiries.* Philadelphia: Temple University Press.

Zook, Matthew A. 1996. "The Unorganized Militia Network: Conspiracies, Computers, and Community." *Berkeley Planning Journal* 11:1–15.

Zuckerman, Laurence. 2001. "Divided, An Airline Stumbles." *New York Times,* March 14, Pp. C1, C6.

Zweigenhaft, Richard L., and G. William Domhoff. 1998. *Diversity in the Power Elite: Have Women and Minorities Reached the Top?* New Haven: Yale University Press.

Chapter 1

P. 4: Quotation from Katherine Irwin. 1999. "Getting a First Tattoo: Techniques of Legitimization and Social Change," dissertation, University of Colorado. Copyright 1999 by Katherine Irwin. Reprinted by permission.

P. 8: Table 1–1 from Gallup International. 1999. Survey results (February). Reprinted by permission of Gallup Poll News Service.

Chapter 2

P. 32: Quotation from Elijah Anderson. 1990. *Streetwise: Race, Class, and Change in an Urban Community*: 208, 220–221. Copyright 1990. Reprinted by permission of University of Chicago Press and the author.

P. 36: Cartoon © The New Yorker Collection 1980. James Stevenson from cartoonbank. com. All rights reserved.

P. 39: Cartoon DOONESBURY © 1989 G.B. Trudeau. Reprinted with permission of UNIVERSAL PRESS SYNDICATE. All rights reserved.

P. 49: Quotation and Figure 2–4 from Henry J. Kaiser Family Foundation, Executive Summary of Sex on TV 2. 2001:6. This information was reprinted with permission of the Henry J. Kaiser Family Foundation of Menlo Park, CA. The Kaiser Family Foundation is an independent health care philanthropy and is not associated with Kaiser Permanente or Kaiser Industries.

Chapter 3

P. 60: Quotation from Horace Miner. 1956. "Body Ritual Among the Nacirema," *American Anthropologist*, Vol. 58 No. 3. Reprinted by permission of the American Anthropological Association and the author from *American Anthropologist* 58(3). Not for sale or further reproduction.

P. 65: Fig. 3–1 "World Languages" from John L. Allen, *Student Atlas of World Geography*, 2/e, McGraw-Hill/Dushkin 2001. Copyright © 2001 by The McGraw-Hill Companies, Inc. Reprinted by permission of McGraw-Hill/Dushkin, a division of the McGraw-Hill Companies, Guilford, CT 06437

P. 69: Fig. 3–2 as reported in Astin et al. 1994; Sax et al. 2001. From UCLA Higher Education Research Institute. 2001. *The American Freshman: National Norms for Fall '01*. Reprinted by permission of UCLA Higher Education Research Institute.

P. 72: Fig. 3–3 illustration by Jim Willis. 1996. "The Argot of Pickpockets," *New York Daily News* (November 19): 5. © New York Daily News, LP. Reprinted by permission.

P. 72: Cartoon © 2003 by Sidney Harris. Used by permission.

P. 77: Fig. 3–4 from U. S. English website www.us-english.org Copyright, U.S. English, Inc.

Chapter 4

P. 84: Quotation from Mary Pattillo-McCoy. 1999. *Black Picket Fences: Privilege and Peril Among the Black Middle Class*: 100–02. Copyright 1999. Reprinted by permission of University of Chicago Press.

P. 87: Quotation from Constance Holden. 1980. "Identical Twins Reared Apart," *Science*, **207**: 1323–1328. Reprinted by permission from from Constance Holden, "Identical Twins Reared Apart," *Science*, **207**: 1323–1328, copyright 1980, American Association for the Advancement of Science.

P. 91: Quotation from Daniel Albas and Cheryl Albas. 1988. "Aces and Bombers: The Post-Exam Impression Management Strategies of Students." *Symbolic Interaction* 11 (Fall): 289–302. © 1988 by JAI Press. Reprinted by permission of University of CA Press and the authors. Reprinted from Symbolic Interaction. UC Press Journals, 2000 Center St., Suite 303, Berkeley, CA 94704–1223.

P. 91: Cartoon published in *Parade* Magazine, December 15, 1996, p. 11. © 2002. Reprinted courtesy of Bunny Hoest and *Parade* Magazine.

P. 98: Fig. 4–1 based on V. Rideout et al. 1999. Adapted from Kids and Media at the New Millennium, Kaiser Family Foundation, November 1999. In "Media Usage" figure, p. 8. This information was reprinted with permission of the Henry J. Kaiser Family Foundation of Menlo Park, CA. The Kaiser Family Foundation is an independent health care philanthropy and is not associated with Kaiser Permanente or Kaiser Industries.

P. 100: Fig. 4–2 from Commission on Behavioral and Social Sciences and Education. 1998. *Protecting Youth at Work*. Copyright 1998 by the National Academy of Sciences. Reprinted by permission of National Academy Press, Washington, DC.

Chapter 5

P. 108: Quotation from Philip G. Zimbardo. 1972. "Pathology of Imprisonment," *Society*, **9** (April): 4. Reprinted by permission of Transaction Publishers. Copyright © 1972 by Transaction Publishers.

P. 108: Quotation from Philip G. Zimbardo, C. Haney, W. C. Banks, and D. Jaffe. 1974. "The Psychology of Imprisonment: Privation, Power, and Pathology." In Z. Rubin (Ed.), *Doing Unto Others: Explorations in Social Behavior*: 61–73. Reprinted by permission of Philip G. Zimbardo, Stanford University.

P. 116: Cartoon by TOLES © The Buffalo News. Reprinted with permission of UNIVERSAL PRESS SYNDICATE. All rights reserved.

P. 121: Cartoon © The New Yorker Collection 1986 Dean Vietor from cartoonbank.com. All rights reserved.

P. 125: Fig. 5–2 from UNAIDS 2000:27 "AIDS epidemic update: December 2000." Reprinted with kind permission from UNAIDS.

P. 127: Fig. 5–3 developed by author in consultation with Roxane Laboratories, Columbus, OH.

Chapter 6

P. 134: Quotation from George Ritzer. 2000. *The McDonaldization of Society*, rev. ed new century edition.: 1–4, 10. Copyright © 1996. Reprinted by permission of Pine Forge Press, a division of Sage Publications.

P. 136: Cartoon © The New Yorker Collection 1979 Robert Weber from cartoonbank.com. All rights reserved.

P. 141: Cartoon © 2003 by Sidney Harris. Used by permission.

P. 146: Fig. 6–1 from James Allen Davis and Tom W. Smith. 2001. *General Social Surveys, 1972–2000*: 347. Published by the Roper Center, Storrs, CT. Reprinted by permission of National Opinion Research Center.

Chapter 7

P. 158: Quotation from David Demers, *Global Media: Menace or Messiah?* Cresskill, NJ: Hampton Press, 1999:3–6. Reprinted with the permission of Hampton Press.

P. 167: Cartoon by Jeff Stahler (United Feature Syndicate), reprinted by permission of Newspaper Enterprise Association, Inc.

P. 168: Fig. 7–2 from Anthony DePalma. 1999. "Rules to Protect a Culture Make for Confusion," *New York Times* (July 14): B1. Copyright © 1999 by The New York Times Co. Reprinted by permission.

P. 169: Table 7–2 data from Caro, "Who Are They?" and "Filmgoers," *Chicago Tribune* 2001:5,7. Copyright 2001 Chicago Tribune Company. All rights reserved. Used with permission.

P. 175: Table 7–3 from S. Robert Lichter, Linda S. Lichter, and Daniel R. Amundson. 1999. *Merchandising Mayhem: Violence in Popular Media 1998–1999.* Washington, DC: Center for Media and Public Affairs. Reprinted with permission from the publisher.

P. 176: Cartoon created by and used by permission of Kirk Anderson, St. Paul, MN.

Chapter 8

P. 182: Quotation from Robert F. Meier and Gilbert Geis. 1997. *Victimless Crime? Prostitution, Drugs, Homosexuality, Abortion:* 36–37. Published by and used by permission of Roxbury Publishing Co., Los Angeles.

P. 184: Fig. 8–1 from Henry Wechsler et al. 2002. "Trends in College Binge Drinking During a Period of Increased Prevention Efforts," *Journal of American College Health,* **50**(5): 203–217. Reprinted with permission of the Helen Dwight Reid Educational Foundation. Published by Heldref Publications, 1319 18th St. NW, Washington, DC 20036–1802. Copyright © 2002.

P. 190: Table 8–1 from William A. Reese II and Michael A. Katovich. 1989. "Untimely Acts: Extending the Interactionist Conception of Deviance," *Sociological Quarterly,* **30** (No. 2, Summer): 159–184. © 1989 by The Midwest Sociological Society; © 1989 by JAI Press. Reprinted by permission of University of California Press and the authors. Reprinted from The Sociological Quarterly. UC Press Journals, 2000 Center St., Suite 303, Berkeley, CA 94704–1223.

P. 191: Fig. 8-2 from P. J. Huffstutter. 1999. "Digital Pirates" in *Los Angeles Times* (July 25), p. A29 Copyright 1999 Los Angeles Times. Reprinted by permission.

P. 193: Table 8–2 from Robert K. Merton. 1968. *Social Theory and Social Structure:* p. 194 Copyright © 1967, 1968 by Robert K. Merton. Adapted by permission of The Free Press, a division of Simon & Schuster.

P. 193: Quotation from William J. Chambliss. 1972. Introduction to Harry King, *Box Man* (New York: Harper & Row). Reprinted by permission of the author.

P. 201: Cartoon © 2003 by Sidney Harris. Used by permission.

Chapter 9

P. 212: Quotation from Barbara Ehrenreich. 2001. *Nickel and Dimed: On (Not) Getting By in America:* 197–198. Copyright © 2001 by Barbara Ehrenreich. Reprinted by permission of Henry Holt & Company, LLC, for their imprint, Metropolitan Books; and by permission of International Creative Management, Inc.

P. 216: Fig. 9–1 from Adam Bryant. 1999. "American Pay Rattles Foreign Partners," *New York Times* (January 17): D1. Copyright © 1999 by The New York Times Co. Reprinted by permission.

P. 223: Fig. 9–2 Data on wealth from Edward N. Wolff. 1999. "Recent Trends in Wealth Ownership" for the conference volume *Benefits of Mechanisms for Spreading Asset Ownership in the U.S.* Published by Russell Sage Press. Reprinted by permission of the author.

P. 223: Fig. 9–3 from I. Shapiro. 2001. "The Latest IRS Data on After-Tax Income Trends" revised 2/26/01. Reprinted by permission of Center on Budget and Policy Priorities, Washington, DC.

P. 224: Cartoon by Frank Cammuso. The Post Standard, Syracuse, NY.

P. 225: Fig. 9–4 from Smeeding, Rainwater, and Buretless. *Focus: The Newsletter of the Institute for Research on Poverty,* Spring 2001, p. 51. Used by permission of Institute for Research on Poverty, Madison, WI.

P. 233: Cartoon by Ed Fischer © 1997 Rochester Post-Bulletin/Ed Fischer Syndicate/in *Best Editorial Cartoons,* June-July 1997, p. 25. Reprinted by permission of Ed Fischer, Rochester, MN.

Chapter 10

P. 240: Quotation from Robert Goldman and Stephen Papson. 1998. *Nike Culture: The Sign of the Swoosh:* 2, 6–8, 184. Reprinted by permission of Sage Publications Ltd. and the authors.

P. 242: Fig. 10–1 from Jesse Gordon & Knickerbocker in *The Nation* 273 (September 3/10, 2001), p. 14. Reprinted with permission.

P. 244: Fig. 10–2 adapted in part from Dan Smith. 1999. *The State of the World Atlas,* 6th ed.:14–15. Published by Penguin Books. Copyright Myriad Editions Limited. Used by permission of Myriad Editions. And adapted in part from Carl Haub and Diana Cornelius. 2001. *World Population Data Sheet 2001.* Reprinted by permission of Population Reference Bureau.

P. 247: Table 10–1 adapted in part from *Fortune.* 2001. "Fortune 500: America's Largest Corporations." Accessed August 24 (www.Fortune.com). Fortune Global 500. © 2001 Time Inc. All rights reserved. And

adapted in part from United Nations Development Programme. 2001. *United Nations Development Report 2001:*178–180. New York: Oxford University Press.

P. 248: Cartoon © 1994 Oliver Chin. Reprinted by permission of Oliver Chin, San Francisco.

P. 249: Fig. 10–3 adapted in part from United Nations Development Programme. 2001. *United Nations Development Report 2001:*182–184. New York: Oxford University Press.

P. 260: Fig. 10–5 adapted in part from *The Observer (London).* 1999 (October 24). Accessed August 27, 2001 (www.guardian.co.uk). Copyright © 1998 The Observer. Reprinted by permission. And adapted in part from Carl Haub and Diana Cornelius. 2001. *World Population Data Sheet 2001.* Population Reference Bureau.

Chapter 11

P. 268: Quotation from Helen Zia. 2001. *Asian American Dreams: The Emergence of an American People.* Copyright © 2000 by Helen Zia. Reprinted by permission of Farrar, Straus & Giroux, LLC.

P. 274: Fig. 11–2 from Southern Poverty Law Center. 2001. "Active Hate Groups in the United States," *2000 Intelligence Report* (Spring) pp. 34–35. Used by permission of Southern Poverty Law Center, Montgomery, AL.

P. 275: Fig. 11–2 from Anti-Defamation League. 2001. "Map of State Statutes" (www.adl.org/99hatecrime/map_statutes.html). Reprinted with permission of the Anti-Defamation League.

P. 284: Fig. 11–3 entitled "Melting Pots" in *American Demographics* 23 (June 2001): 20–21. This material first appeared in the June 2001 edition of American Demographics. It is reprinted with permission.

P. 285: Cartoon by Rob Rogers reprinted by permission of United Feature Syndicate, Inc.

P. 294: Fig. 11–6 from Philip Martin and Jonas Widgren. 1996. "Internal Migration: A Global Challenge." *Population Bulletin* **51** (April): 21, Fig. 3. Used by permission of Population Reference Bureau.

Chapter 12

P. 302: Quotation from Naomi Wolf. 1991. *The Beauty Myth:* 9–10, 12. From *The Beauty Myth* by Naomi Wolf, published by Chatto & Windus. Reprinted by permission of the Random House Group Ltd. and Abner Stein Literary Agency.

P. 305: Table 12–1 from Joyce McCarl Nielsen, Glenda Walden, and Charlotte A. Kunkel. 2000. "Gendered Heteronormativity: Empirical Illustrations in Everyday Life," *Sociological Quarterly* 41 (No. 2):287. © 2000 by the Midwest Sociological Society. Reprinted from *The Sociological Quarterly.* By permission of the authors and UC Press Journals, 2000 Center St., Suite 303, Berkeley, CA 94704-1223.

P. 309: Cartoon © 2003 by Sidney Harris. Used by permission.

P. 314: Cartoon reprinted by permission of Ed Stein, Denver, CO.

P. 316: Fig. 12–3 from James T. Bond, Ellen Galinsky, and Jennifer E. Swanberg. 1998. *The 1997 National Study of the Changing Workforce:* 40–41, 44–45. Copyright Families and Work Institute (www.familiesand work.org). Reprinted by permission.

P. 320: Fig. 12–4 from NARAL. 2001. *Who Decides?* 10th ed., January. Restrictions on Public Funding for Abortion. Used by permission of National Abortion and Reproductive Rights Action League (NARAL).

Chapter 13

P. 326: Quotation from Mitch Albom. 1997. *Tuesdays with Morrie: An Old Man, a Young Man, and Life's Greatest Lesson.* Copyright © 1997 by Mitch Albom. Used by permission of Doubleday, a division of Random House, Inc.; and Time Warner Books UK.

P. 334: Fig. 13–2 from AARP. 1998. "Baby Boomers Look Toward Retirement," press release June 1. Reprinted by permission of the American Association of Retired Persons.

Chapter 14

P. 348: Quotation from Cornel West and Sylvia Ann Hewlett. 1998. *The War Against Parents:* 21–22. Copyright © 1998 by Sylvia Ann Hewlett and Cornel West. Reprinted by permission of Cornel West/Watkins-Loomis Agency, Sylvia Ann Hewlett/Aaron Priest Literary Agency, and by Houghton Mifflin Company. All rights reserved.

P. 354: Quotation in box from Vanora Bennett. 1997. "Russia's Ugly Little Secret: Misogyny." *Los Angeles Times,* December 6, pp. A1, A11. Reprinted by permission of Los Angeles Times Syndicate.

P. 354: Cartoon published in *The Japan Times International,* March 1, 2000:20. Created and used by permission of Roger Dahl, The Japan Times.

P. 357: Quotation from Simon Rodberg. 1999. "Woman and Man at Yale," *Culturefront* **8:1** (Spring): 25. Reprinted from Culturefront, by permission of the New York Council for the Humanities.

P. 357: Quotation from Rebecca Segall. 1998. "Sikh and Ye Shall Find." *Village Voice* 43 (December 15): 48; 53. Used by permission of the author.

P. 363: Cartoon created and used by permission of Signe Wilkinson, Cartoonists & Writers Syndicate/cartoonweb.com.

P. 368: Quotation from Anthony DePalma. 1998. "Two Gay Men Fight Town Hall for a Family Pool Pass Discount," *New York Times* (July 14): B2. Copyright © 1998 The New York Times Co. Reprinted by permission.

Chapter 15

P. 378: Quotation from Vine Deloria, Jr. 1999. *For This Land: Writings on Religion in America:* 273–275, 281. Copyright © 1998. Reproduced by permission Routledge, Inc., part of the Taylor & Francis Group.

P. 388: Fig. 15–2 from Table 7 on p. 47 of Ronald Inglehart and Wayne Baker, "Modernization, Cultural Change, and the Persistence of Traditional Values," *American Sociological Review* 65 (February 2000): 19–51. Used by permission of American Sociological Association and the authors.

P. 392: Fig. 15–3 from Martin B. Bradley, Norman N. Greene, Jr., Dale E. Jones, Mac Lynn, and Lou McNeil. 1992. *Churches and Church Membership in the United States 1990.* Atlanta: Glenmary Research Center © Association of Statisticians of American Religious Bodies. Reprinted with permission.

Chapter 16

P. 402: Quotation from Jonathan Kozol. 1991. *Savage Inequalities: Children in America's Schools:* 85, 86, 87, 88. From *Savage Inequalities* by Jonathan Kozol, copyright © 1991 by Jonathan Kozol. Reprinted by permission of Crown Publishers, a division of Random House, Inc.

P. 405: Table 16–1 from Institute of International Education, "Opening Minds to the World," http://www.opendoorsweb.org Open Doors 2001 Report on International Educational Exchange, 2001, Hey-Kyung Koh, ed., New York, Institute of International Education. Used by permission.

P. 409: Cartoon created by and used by permission of Kirk Anderson, St. Paul, MN.

P. 418: Fig. 16–4 from Education Commission of the States. 2001. *A Closer Look: State Policy Trends in Three Key Areas of the Bush Education Plan—Testing , Accountability, and School Choice.* Reprinted by permission of Education Commission of the States.

P. 422: Fig. 16–6 from Children First CEO America 2001. Used by permission of Children First America, Bentonville, AR.

P. 423: Cartoon by Mike Ramirez, Copley News Service.

Chapter 17

P. 428: Quotation from Richard L. Zweigenhaft and G. William Domhoff. 1998. *Diversity in the Power Elite:* 3. 176–77, 192, 194. Copyright 1998. Reprinted by permission of Yale University Press.

P. 433: Table 17–1 from James Allen Davis and Tom W. Smith. 2001. *General Social Surveys, 1972–2000.* Published by the Roper Center, Storrs, CT. Reprinted by permission of National Opinion Research Center.

P. 436: Fig. 17–1 from Inter-Parliamentary Union. 2000. "Women in National Parliaments." Accessed January, 2000, at http://www.pu.org/wmn-e/world.htm. Used by permission of Inter-Parliamentary Union.

P. 439: Fig. 17–3 from Richard L. Zweigenhaft and G. William Domhoff. 2000. *Diversity in the Power Elite,* 4th edition: 96. Copyright 2000. Reprinted by permission of Yale University Press.

P. 442: Cartoon published in *USA Today* 3/20/01, p. 11A. © 2001 Steve Breen/ Copley News Service.

Chapter 18

P. 450: Quotation from Jeremy Rifkin. 1995a 6. *The End of Work:* 11–13. Copyright © 1995 by Jeremy Rifkin. Reprinted by permission of Putnam Berkley, a division of Penguin Putnam Inc.

P. 455: Fig. 18–1 from Menna Acharya. 2000. *Human Development in South Asia 2000: The Gender Question* (Mahbub ul Haq Human Development Centre), p. 54. Reprinted by permission of Oxford University Press, Karachi, Pakistan.

P. 463: Cartoon for *The New Republic,* published in *Washington Post* National Weekly Edition, February 26, 2000, p. 28. TOLES © The Buffalo News. Reprinted with permission of UNIVERSAL PRESS SYNDICATE. All rights reserved.

P. 464: Quotation from Sheryl Stolberg. 1995. "Affirmative Action Gains Often Come at a High Cost," *Los Angeles Times* (March 29): A14. Copyright 1995 Los Angeles Times. Reprinted by permission.

P. 466: Cartoon by Mike Peters in *Dayton Daily News.* © Tribune Media Services, Inc. Reprinted by permission.

Chapter 19

P. 472: Quotation from Lori Arviso Alvord, M.D. and Elizabeth Cohen Van Pelt. 1999. *The Scalpel and the Silver Bear:* 13–14. Copyright © 1999 by Lori Arviso Alvord and Elizabeth Cohen Van Pelt. Used by permission of Bantam Books, a division of Random House, Inc.

P. 476: Fig. 19–1 from John L. Allen. 2001. *Student Atlas of World Geography* (McGraw-Hill/Dushkin), Map. #24, p. 39. Copyright © 2001 by The McGraw-Hill Companies, Inc. Reprinted by permission of McGraw-Hill/Dushkin, a division of the McGraw-Hill Companies, Guilford, CT 06437.

P. 477: Fig. 19–2 from Carl Haub and Diana Cornelius. 2001. *World Population Data Sheet 2001*. Used by permission of Population Reference Bureau.

P. 486: Cartoon © 2003 by Sidney Harris. Used by permission.

P. 492: Cartoon by Jim Borgman. Reprinted with special permission of King Features Syndicate.

P. 493: Fig. 19–7 from World Bank 2001a:98–100. *World Development Indicators 2001*. Published by the World Bank. Used by permission.

Chapter 20

P. 500: Quotation from Mitchell Duneier. 2001. *Sidewalk*. Copyright © 1999 by Mitchell Duneier. Reprinted by permission of Farrar, Straus & Giroux, LLC.

P. 503: Table 20–1 based in part on Gideon Sjoberg. 1960. *The Preindustrial City: Past and Present* (Glencoe, IL: Free Press): 323–328. Copyright © 1960 by The Free Press. Adapted by permission of The Free Press, a division of Simon & Schuster. And based in part on E. Barbara Phillips. 1996. *City Lights: Urban-Suburban Life in the Global Society* (NY: Oxford University Press): 132–135. Copyright © 1981 by E. Barbara Phillips and Richard T. LeGates, 1996 by E. Babara Phillips. Used by permission of Oxford University Press, Inc.

P. 504: Table 20–2 United Nations data quoted in Brockerhoff. 2000. *An Urbanizing World*: 10. Used by permission of Population Reference Bureau.

P. 505: Fig. 20–1 based on data from Carl Haub and Diana Cornelius. 2001. *World Population Data Sheet 2001*. Used by permission of Population Reference Bureau.

P. 507: Cartoon by Henry Martin. © Tribune Media Services, Inc. All rights reserved. Reprinted by permission.

P. 507: Fig. 20–2 from Chauncy D. Harris and Edward Ullmann. 1945. "The Nature of Cities" in *Annals of the American Academy of Political & Social Science*, 242 (November): 13. Reprinted by permission of American Academy of Political & Social Science, Philadelphia.

P. 514: Fig. 20–3 from William H. Frey. June 2001. *Melting Pot Suburbs Study*: 7. Used by permission of Brookings Institution, Washington, DC.

P. 518: Cartoon published in *Japan Times International*, 7/16/99, p. 20. Created and used by permission of Roger Dahl, The Japan Times.

Chapter 21

P. 526: Quotation from Kai Erikson. 1994. *A New Species of Trouble: The Human Experience of Modern Disasters*: 11–12, 19. Copyright © 1994 by Kai Erikson. Used by permission of W. W. Norton Company, Inc.

P. 528: Fig. 21–1 from Carl Haub and Diana Cornelius. 2001. *World Population Data Sheet 2001*. Used by permission of Population Reference Bureau.

P. 531: Table 21–1 from United Nations Population Division. 2001. The World at Six Billion. Population Division of the Department of Economic and Social Affairs of the United Nations Secretariat (2002). The World at Six Billion. http://www.un.org/esa/population/publications/sixbillion/sixbillion.htm on February 2002. Used by permission.

P. 533: Cartoon used by permission of Signe Wilkinson/Philadelphia Daily News/Cartoonists and Writers Syndicate.

P. 539: Fig. 21–5 from Jeffrey Kluger. 2001. "A World of Offenders," *Time*, April 9: 30-31. © 2001 Time Inc., reprinted by permission.

Chapter 22

P. 550: Quotation from Richard Roeper. 1999. *Urban Legends*: 91-94. © 1999 Richard Roeper. Reprinted by permission of Career Press, Franklin, Lakes, NJ. All rights reserved.

P. 554: Gallaudet University. 1988. Leaflet in support of appointing a deaf president. Reprinted by permission of the publisher from John B. Christiansen and Sharon N. Barnartt, *Deaf President Now! The 1988 Revolution at Gallaudet University* (Washington D.C.: Gallaudet University Press, 1995) p. 22. Copyright 1995 by Gallaudet University.

Chapter 23

P. 574: Quotation from Debora L. Spar, *Ruling the Waves: Cycles of Discovery, Chaos, and Wealth from the Compass to the Internet*, 2001:327–329. Copyright © 2001 by Debora L. Spar, reprinted by permission of Harcourt, Inc.

P. 583: Fig 23–1 "Geographical Distribution of Internet Hosts, January 2000" from Matrix Information and Directory Services. 1998. Matrix Information and Directory Services, Inc. www.mids.org. Used by permission.

P. 587: Fig. 23–2 from www.glreach.com/globstats. Reprinted by permission of Euro-Marketing Associates.

P. 589: Cartoon © 1985 Carol * Simpson. Reprinted by permission of Carol * Simpson Productions.

P. 592: Cartoon © Mike Keefe, dePIXon Studios, Inc., Denver, CO.

Photo Credits

Name Index

Subject Index